EVIDENCE

EVIDENCE
Text, Problems, and Cases

Fifth Edition

RONALD J. ALLEN
John Henry Wigmore Professor of Law
Northwestern University School of Law

RICHARD B. KUHNS
Professor of Law
Washington University School of Law

ELEANOR SWIFT
Professor of Law
University of California at Berkeley School of Law

DAVID S. SCHWARTZ
Professor of Law
University of Wisconsin Law School

MICHAEL S. PARDO
Henry Upson Sims Professor of Law
University of Alabama School of Law

Wolters Kluwer
Law & Business

Published by Wolters Kluwer Law & Business in New York.

Wolters Kluwer Law & Business serves customers worldwide with CCH, Aspen Publishers, and Kluwer Law International products. (www.wolterskluwerlb.com)

Wolters Kluwer Law & Business
Attn: Order Department
PO Box 990
Frederick, MD 21705

Printed in the United States of America.

1 2 3 4 5 6 7 8 9 0

ISBN 978-0-7355-9640-5

Library of Congress Cataloging-in-Publication Data

Evidence : text, problems, and cases / Ronald J. Allen ... [et al.]. — 5th ed.
    p. cm.
  Includes bibliographical references and index.
  ISBN 978-0-7355-9640-5 (alk. paper)
  1. Evidence (Law)—United States.   I. Allen, Ronald J. (Ronald Jay), 1948-

KF8935.A83 2011
347.73'6—dc23
                                        2011039463

About Wolters Kluwer Law & Business

Wolters Kluwer Law & Business is a leading global provider of intelligent information and digital solutions for legal and business professionals in key specialty areas, and respected educational resources for professors and law students. Wolters Kluwer Law & Business connects legal and business professionals as well as those in the education market with timely, specialized authoritative content and information-enabled solutions to support success through productivity, accuracy and mobility.

Serving customers worldwide, Wolters Kluwer Law & Business products include those under the Aspen Publishers, CCH, Kluwer Law International, Loislaw, Best Case, ftwilliam.com and MediRegs family of products.

CCH products have been a trusted resource since 1913, and are highly regarded resources for legal, securities, antitrust and trade regulation, government contracting, banking, pension, payroll, employment and labor, and healthcare reimbursement and compliance professionals.

Aspen Publishers products provide essential information to attorneys, business professionals and law students. Written by preeminent authorities, the product line offers analytical and practical information in a range of specialty practice areas from securities law and intellectual property to mergers and acquisitions and pension/benefits. Aspen's trusted legal education resources provide professors and students with high-quality, up-to-date and effective resources for successful instruction and study in all areas of the law.

Kluwer Law International products provide the global business community with reliable international legal information in English. Legal practitioners, corporate counsel and business executives around the world rely on Kluwer Law journals, looseleafs, books, and electronic products for comprehensive information in many areas of international legal practice.

Loislaw is a comprehensive online legal research product providing legal content to law firm practitioners of various specializations. Loislaw provides attorneys with the ability to quickly and efficiently find the necessary legal information they need, when and where they need it, by facilitating access to primary law as well as state-specific law, records, forms and treatises.

Best Case Solutions is the leading bankruptcy software product to the bankruptcy industry. It provides software and workflow tools to flawlessly streamline petition preparation and the electronic filing process, while timely incorporating ever-changing court requirements.

ftwilliam.com offers employee benefits professionals the highest quality plan documents (retirement, welfare and non-qualified) and government forms (5500/PBGC, 1099 and IRS) software at highly competitive prices.

MediRegs products provide integrated health care compliance content and software solutions for professionals in healthcare, higher education and life sciences, including professionals in accounting, law and consulting.

Wolters Kluwer Law & Business, a division of Wolters Kluwer, is headquartered in New York. Wolters Kluwer is a market-leading global information services company focused on professionals.

SUMMARY
OF CONTENTS

Contents		*ix*
Preface		*xlv*
Acknowledgments		*xlix*
Introduction to the Study of Evidence		*li*
Special Notice on Citations		*liii*

Chapter One	The Case of People v. Johnson	1
Chapter Two	The Process of Proof: How Trials Are Structured	79
Chapter Three	Relevancy, Probative Value, and the Rule 403 Dangers	121
Chapter Four	Laying the Foundation for Proof	175
Chapter Five	The Character, Propensity, and Specific Acts Rules	235
Chapter Six	The Other Relevance Rules	327
Chapter Seven	The Impeachment and Rehabilitation of Witnesses	351
Chapter Eight	The Hearsay Rule	407
Chapter Nine	Lay Opinions and Expert Witnesses	631
Chapter Ten	The Process of Proof in Civil and Criminal Cases: Burdens of Proof, Judicial Summary and Comment, and Presumptions	717
Chapter Eleven	Judicial Notice	773
Chapter Twelve	Privileges	793

Table of Cases	919
Table of Authorities	931
Index	945

CONTENTS

Preface   xlv
Acknowledgments   xlix
Introduction to the Study of Evidence   li
Special Notice on Citations   liii

CHAPTER ONE

THE CASE OF PEOPLE v. JOHNSON

THE CASE OF PEOPLE v. JOHNSON   1

The People of the State of California v. James Johnson   2
    Notes and Questions   76

CHAPTER TWO

THE PROCESS OF PROOF: HOW TRIALS ARE STRUCTURED

THE PROCESS OF PROOF:
HOW TRIALS ARE STRUCTURED   79

A. THE ADVERSARY SYSTEM   80
B. THE ROLES OF THE TRIAL PARTICIPANTS   80
C. THE STRUCTURE OF THE TRIAL   82
    1. Pretrial Motions   82
    2. Jury Selection   82
    3. Preliminary Instructions   83
    4. Opening Statements   83
    5. Presentation of Evidence and the Burden of Production   84
        a. The Order of the Parties' Presentation of Cases   84
        b. The Burden of Production   85
    6. Post-evidence Matters   86

		7.	Closing Arguments	87
		8.	Jury Instructions and the Burden of Persuasion	88
		9.	Jury Deliberations and Verdict	88
		10.	Post-trial Motions	89
D.	EXAMINATION OF WITNESSES AND FRE 611			90
	1.	FRE 611		91
	2.	Interpretation and Illustration of FRE 611(a) and (b)		91
		a.	FRE 611(a): Breadth of the Court's Power	91
		b.	Direct Examination	92
		c.	FRE 611(b): The Scope of Cross-examination	92
		d.	Redirect and Recross-examination	93
	3.	Elaboration of FRE 611(a) and (b) and the Examination of Witnesses		93
		a.	Direct Examination	93
		b.	Cross-examination	94
			i. Strategy and Goals of Cross-examination	95
			ii. Cross-examination Technique	95
		c.	Direct Examination of "Adverse" and "Hostile" Witnesses	96
	4.	Interpretation and Illustration of FRE 611(c): Leading Questions		97
	5.	Elaboration of FRE 611(c) and Leading Questions		98
		a.	What Is a Leading Question?	98
		b.	Leading Questions: Tactical Considerations	99
E.	OBJECTIONS AND PRESERVATION OF ERROR FOR APPEAL: FRE 103			100
	1.	FRE 103		100
	2.	Interpretation and Illustration of FRE 103(a) and (d): Objections, Offers of Proof, and Preservation of Evidentiary Issues for Appeal		101
	3.	Elaboration of FRE 103(a)(1) and (2) and Objections		101
		a.	Two Types of Objections	101
		b.	Timing of Objections	103
		c.	Stating the Objection	105
		d.	Tactical Considerations	106
	4.	Elaboration of FRE 103(a) and (d): Preservation of Error for Appellate Review		106
		a.	Making the Record — in General	107
		b.	Making the Record for Appeal of Evidentiary Rulings	108
		c.	Standards of Appellate Review of Evidentiary Errors	108
F.	REFLECTIONS ON NATURAL REASONING AND THE ADVERSARY SYSTEM			109
	1.	The Adversary System Reconsidered		109
	2.	Why Have Rules of Evidence?		111
	3.	Natural Reasoning and the Trial Process		113

| | | 4. | The Behavior of Fact Finders | 116 |
| | | | Trial Objection Cheat Sheet | 118 |

CHAPTER THREE

RELEVANCY, PROBATIVE VALUE, AND THE RULE 403 DANGERS   121

A.	RELEVANCY — THE BASIC CONCEPT	121
	1. FRE 401 and 402	122
	2. Interpretation and Illustration of FRE 401 and 402	122
	a. Relevant Evidence Is Offered to Prove a Fact of Consequence (Materiality)	123
	b. Relevant Evidence Must Make a Fact of Consequence More or Less Probable	125
	i. FRE 401's Minimal Standard of "Any Tendency"	125
	ii. Inferential Reasoning Is Based on Generalizations from Knowledge and Experience	126
	iii. Relevancy Requires Reasonable Generalizations	126
	iv. Generalization Can Be the Subject of Proof	127
	v. Limits on Reasonable Generalizations	127
	vi. The Policy of FRE 401 Favors Admissibility	128
	c. Direct Versus Circumstantial Evidence	129
	d. Background Information	130
	e. Relevancy Is Not Sufficiency	131
	3. Elaboration of FRE 401 and 402	131
	Knapp v. State	131
	United States v. Stever	132
	Notes and Questions	134
	Key Points	135
	Problems	135
	4. Reflection on the Requirement of Relevancy	138
B.	PROBATIVE VALUE AND THE RULE 403 DANGERS	140
	1. FRE 403	140
	2. Interpretation and Illustration of FRE 403	141
	a. Probative Value	141
	i. Strength of the Underlying Inferences	142
	ii. Certainty of the Starting Point	142
	iii. Need	143
	Note	144
	b. Rule 403 Dangers	144
	i. Unfair Prejudice	144

		ii.	Confusion of the Issues	146
		iii.	Misleading the Jury	146
		iv.	Undue Delay, Waste of Time, and Needless Cumulative Evidence	147
	c.		Probative Value Substantially Outweighed by One of the FRE 403 Dangers	148
		i.	The Meaning of "Substantially Outweigh"	148
		ii.	The Effect of Limiting Instructions on the Balancing Process	149
			Notes and Questions	151
			Key Points	155
			Problems	155
3.			Elaboration of FRE 403: Appellate Review of Judicial Discretion Under FRE 403	157
			United States v. Hitt	159
			Notes and Questions	162
			Old Chief v. United States	162
			Notes and Questions	166
			Problems	168
4.			Reflection on Judicial Discretion to Admit and Exclude Evidence	168
C. REFLECTION ON THE BASIC CONCEPT OF RELEVANCY				169

CHAPTER FOUR

LAYING THE FOUNDATION FOR PROOF   175

A.	LAYING THE FOUNDATION FOR WITNESSES		175
	1.	FRE 601	176
	2.	Interpretation and Illustration of FRE 601	176
	3.	Elaboration of FRE 601: Challenging a Witness's Mental Competency	177
		Key Points	179
	4.	FRE 602	179
	5.	Interpretation and Illustration of FRE 602	179
		a. The Requirement of Personal Knowledge	179
		b. The Requirement of Evidence Sufficient to Support a Finding	180
		Key Point	181
		Problems	181
B.	THE AUTHENTICATION AND IDENTIFICATION OF EXHIBITS		182
	1.	FRE 901	182
	2.	Interpretation and Illustration of FRE 901	183
		a. What the Exhibit Is Claimed to Be	183
		b. The Requirement of Evidence Sufficient to Support a Finding	183

c.   FRE 901(b) Illustrates How to Produce Evidence Sufficient to
      Support a Finding   184
d.   Judicial Determinations of Sufficiency Under FRE 901(a)   185
e.   The Process of Laying the Foundation   186
3.   Elaboration of FRE 901: Real Evidence, Demonstrative and
      Computer-Generated Exhibits, Recordings and Written Documents   187
a.   Real Evidence   187
      i.   Identification Through a Readily Identifiable Characteristic   188
      ii.   Identification Through Chain of Custody   188
      iii. Unchanged Condition Established Through Chain of
            Custody   188
      iv.   Under FRE 901(a), the Complete Chain of Custody
            Is Not Always Required   189
            Key Points   191
            Problems   191
b.   Demonstrative Exhibits   192
      i.   Demonstrative Exhibits Must Assist the Trier of Fact   193
      ii.   Application of FRE 403 to Demonstrative Exhibits   193
c.   Demonstrations and Experiments in Court   193
d.   Recorded and Computer-Generated Reenactments,
      Animations, and Simulations of Events   194
            Key Points   195
            Problems   195
e.   Recordings   196
      i.   Satisfying the FRE 901 Foundation with a
            Percipient Witness   196
      ii.   "Silent Witness"-Satisfying the FRE 901 Foundation
            Without a Percipient Witness   197
      iii   Application of FRE 403 to Recordings   198
      iv   Voice Identification   199
            Key Points   199
            Problems   199
f.   Written Documents   201
      i.   Signature   201
      ii.   Contents and Other Circumstances   201
      iii. Ancient Documents   202
      iv.   Electronic Writings   203
            Key Point   204
            Problems   204
g.   FRE 901 Provides Flexibility in Application   206
4.   FRE 902   206
a.   FRE 902   206

		b.	Interpretation of FRE 902	207
			Key Point	209
			Problems	209
C.	THE BEST EVIDENCE RULE			210
	1.	FRE 1001, 1002, 1003, 1004, 1005, 1006, and 1007		210
	2.	Interpretation and Illustration of FRE 1001, 1002, 1003, 1004, 1005, 1006, and 1007		211
		a.	Summary of the Basic Principles of the Best Evidence Rule	211
			i. FRE 1002	211
			ii. FRE 1003	212
			iii. FRE 1004	212
			iv. FRE 1006	213
		b.	The Policies Underlying the Best Evidence Rule	214
			Seiler v. Lucasfilm, Ltd.	214
			Problem	216
	3.	Elaboration of FRE 1002 and 1006		216
		a.	When Is a Writing Offered to Prove Its Own Content Under FRE 1002?	216
			i. The Content of the Writing, Recording, or Photograph Is a Fact of Independent Legal Significance	217
			ii. The Writing, Recording, or Photograph Is Used to Prove an Event	217
			iii. Inscriptions on Objects Are Not Writings	218
			iv. Facts About the Writing Are Not Its "Content"	218
		b.	Types of Summaries and Rule 1006	218
			i. Voluminous Documents Underlying a Summary Must Be Admissible, But Need Not Be Admitted at Trial	218
			ii. Illustrative Aids	219
			iii. Analytic Summaries	219
			Key Points	220
			Problems	220
	4.	FRE 1008		221
	5.	Interpretation and Illustration of FRE 1008		221
			Key Points	223
			Problem	223
D.	JUDICIAL FACT-FINDING UNDER FRE 104			223
	1.	FRE 104		224
	2.	Interpretation and Illustration of FRE 104(a)		224
		a.	Questions of Admissibility Generally	224
		b.	Judicial Fact-finding Under FRE 104(a)	225

C. The Process of Decision Under FRE 104(a)   226
        Note   226
        Key Points   227
E. FRE 104, CONDITIONAL ADMISSIBILITY, AND THE
    PROBLEM OF CONDITIONAL RELEVANCY   227
    1. Interpretation and Illustration of FRE 104(b)   228
        a. Conditional Admissibility   228
        b. The Problem of Conditional Relevancy:
            The "Sufficiency" Standard of Proof in FRE 104(b)   229
    2. Elaboration of FRE 104(b): The Rule in Practice   229
        Notes and Questions   231
        Key Points   233
        Problems   233

CHAPTER FIVE

THE CHARACTER, PROPENSITY,
AND SPECIFIC ACTS RULES ·   235

A. THE RELEVANCE OF CHARACTER EVIDENCE TO
    PROVE CONDUCT ON A PARTICULAR OCCASION   235
B. GENERAL PROHIBITION ON USE OF CHARACTER
    AND "PAST SPECIFIC ACTS" EVIDENCE TO
    PROVE CONDUCT ON A PARTICULAR OCCASION   238
    1. FRE 404   238
    2. Interpretation and Illustration of FRE 404(a) and (b)   238
    3. Elaboration of the FRE 404(a) and 404(b) Character and
        Specific Acts Prohibitions   240
        a. The Rationale for Restricting Evidence of a
            Person's Character   240
            i.   Weakness of the Propensity Inference   240
            ii. Low Probative Value of the Evidence to
                 Prove Character   240
            iii. Diversion from Main Issues   241
            iv. "Bad Person" Prejudice   241
        b. Exceptions to the FRE 404(b) Prohibition Against the
            Use of Specific Acts   242
            Key Points   242
            Problems   243
C. THE ADMISSIBILITY OF SPECIFIC ACTS THAT ARE DEEMED
    RELEVANT WITHOUT A CHARACTER INFERENCE   244
    1. Interpretation and Illustration of FRE 404(b)(2)   244

2.   Elaboration of FRE 404(b)(2)   245
   a.   The Permissible Uses of Specific Acts Evidence   245
        i.   Evidence of Motive, Opportunity, Preparation, Plan,
              and the Like   246
        ii.   Evidence Showing Relevant States of Mind   246
        iii. Evidence Showing Identity   247
   b.   Preliminary Fact-finding with Respect to Whether the
        Person in Question Committed the Act   247
   c.   Probative Value and Prejudice Generally   248
        Key Points   249
        Problems   250
3.   Further Elaboration of FRE 404(b)(2)   251
   a.   The Problem of "Res Gestae"   252
   b.   The Problem of Specific Acts Evidence to Prove Intent or
        Knowledge   252
   c.   The Problem of Specific Acts Evidence to Prove
        Mental States That Are Not Disputed   253
        i.   The Argument for Exclusion   254
        ii.   The Impact of *Old Chief*   254
   d.   Past "Accidents" or "Coincidences" and the
        Anticoincidence Theory   255
   e.   Modus Operandi and the Character Inference   257
        Key Points   258
D. REFLECTION ON CHARACTER, PROPENSITY,
    AND SPECIFIC ACTS EVIDENCE   258
        United States v. Varoudakis   258
        Notes and Questions   265
        Problems   266
E. HABIT AND ROUTINE PRACTICE   267
1.   FRE 406   267
2.   Interpretation and Illustration of FRE 406   268
   a.   The Importance of Habit and Routine Practice Evidence   268
   b.   Methods of Proving Habit and Routine Practice   269
   c.   The Distinction Between Habit and Character   269
   d.   Judicial Fact-finding on the Question of Habit   270
3.   Elaboration of FRE 406   271
   a.   The Rationale for Permitting Habit and Routine
        Practice Evidence   271
   b.   The Strategy for Distinguishing Between
        Habit and Character   271
   c.   A Particular Application of the Character/Habit
        Distinction: Drinking "Habits"   272

		d.	Evidence of Custom or Routine Practice of an Organization	273
			Key Points	274
			Problems	275
F.	SIMILAR HAPPENINGS			276
	1.	No Specific Federal Rule for Similar Happenings		277
	2.	Similar Happenings, Character, and Habit Evidence Compared		278
	3.	The Approach to the Admissibility of Similar Happenings Evidence		279
	4.	The Application of FRE 403 to Similar Happenings Evidence in Practice		280
	5.	Similar Happenings Offered to Show an Institutional Policy or Practice		281
	6.	Evidence of Similar Nonhappenings		281
			Key Points	281
			Problems	282
G.	EXCEPTIONS TO THE PROHIBITION ON USE OF CHARACTER TO PROVE CONDUCT ON A PARTICULAR OCCASION			284
	1.	Interpretation and Illustration of FRE 404(a)(2), (3)		284
		a.	FRE 404(a)(2)(A) and (B): A Criminal Defendant's Right to Open the Door to Character Evidence	285
		b.	FRE 404(a)(2)(A) and (B): The Prosecution's Right to Respond to a Defendant's Character Evidence	285
		c.	FRE 404(a)(2)(C): The Prosecution's Right to Use Character Evidence to Respond to Defense Attacks on the Victim's Conduct	286
		d.	The FRE 404(a)(2) Requirement of Pertinence	286
		e.	FRE 404(a)(3): The Character of Witnesses	287
	3.	Elaboration of the FRE 404(a)(2) Exceptions		287
		a.	The Relevance of Character Evidence in People v. Johnson	287
		b.	The Rationale for the FRE 404(a)(2) Exceptions	290
		c.	Evidence of Character in Civil Actions	290
			Key Points	291
	4.	Interpretation and Illustration of FRE 404(b) and 405(a): How Character Is Proven When the FRE 404(a)(2) and (3) Exceptions Apply		291
			Problems	292
	5.	Elaboration of the Permissible Methods of Proving a Person's Character to Show Action in Accordance with Character		293

a. The Prohibition Against the Use of Specific Acts 293
b. The Probative Value of Opinion and Reputation
Evidence to Prove Character 294
c. Reputation Evidence Versus Opinion Evidence 295
Key Points 296
d. The Cross-examination of Character Witnesses 296
i. The Relevance of the Specific Acts Inquiries 296
ii. The Prejudicial Impact of Specific Acts Questions 297
iii. The Relationship Between the Character Trait
and the Specific Acts Inquiries 297
iv. The Character Witness's Likely Knowledge
of the Specific Act 297
v. The Cross-examiner's Reasonable Belief That
the Act Occurred 298
vi. Acts, Arrests, and Convictions 299
vii. The Form of the Questions on Cross-examination 299
e. Limitations on the Use of Character Evidence
in Practice 300
i. The Inherent Weakness of Good Character
Evidence 300
ii. The Potential Unfairness of FRE 405 300
Key Points 301
Problems 301
H. EVIDENCE OF A PERSON'S CHARACTER WHEN
CHARACTER IS AN ESSENTIAL ELEMENT OF A
CLAIM OR DEFENSE 302
1. Interpretation and Illustration of FRE 405(b) 303
2. Elaboration of FRE 405(b) 303
a. In General 303
b. Reputation Versus Character in Defamation Cases 304
Key Point 305
Problems 305
I. EVIDENCE OF SEXUAL ASSAULT AND
CHILD MOLESTATION 306
1. FRE 413-415 307
2. Interpretation and Illustration of FRE 413-415 307
a. The Relationship Between FRE 413-415 and Other
Rules of Evidence 307
i. FRE 413-415 and FRE 404 307
ii. FRE 413-415 and FRE 403 308
iii. FRE 413-415 and Other Rules of Evidence 308
b. FRE 413-415 and Preliminary Fact-finding 309

	c.	The Broad Definition of "Offense of Sexual Assault"	309
	d.	The Meaning of "Without Consent" in FRE 413(d)(2) and (3)	309
3.		Elaboration of FRE 413-415	310
	a.	The Application of FRE 403 to Previously Inadmissible Character Evidence	310
	b.	The Underlying Rationale for Rules 413-415	311
		i. Unfair Prejudice	311
		ii. Probative Value and Recidivism	312
		iii. A Contextual Assessment of Probative Value	312
	c.	The Significance of FRE 413-415 to Federal Litigation	313
		Key Points	314
		Problems	314

J. EVIDENCE OF AN ALLEGED VICTIM'S PAST SEXUAL BEHAVIOR OR DISPOSITION IN SEX OFFENSE CASES — 315

1.		FRE 412	316
2.		Interpretation and Illustration of FRE 412	316
	a.	The Relevance of an Alleged Victim's Sexual Behavior or Disposition to Prove Conduct	317
	b.	The Underlying Propensity Theory	317
	c.	The Scope of FRE 412	318
		i. The Meaning of "Other Sexual Behavior" and "Sexual Predisposition"	318
		ii. The Applicability of FRE 412 When the Issue Is the Victim's Behavior on a Particular Occasion	318
		iii. The Applicability of FRE 412 in Other Contexts	319
		iv. Hostile Work Environment Cases	319
		v. The Admissibility of "Other Sexual Behavior" and "Sexual Predisposition" Evidence in Civil Cases	320
		vi. The Admissibility of "Other Sexual Behavior" and "Sexual Predisposition" Evidence in Criminal Cases	320
		vii. The Notice Requirement	321
3.		Elaboration of FRE 412	321
	a.	The Rationale for a Rule Excluding Evidence of Prior Sexual Behavior and Sexual Predisposition	321
	b.	Two Approaches to the Exclusion of Other Sexual Behavior and Sexual Predisposition Evidence	322
	c.	Rape Shield Rules and the Defendant's Right to Testify	323
	d.	FRE 412 and Discovery in Civil Cases	323
		Key Points	324
		Problems	324

CHAPTER SIX

THE OTHER RELEVANCE RULES

THE OTHER RELEVANCE RULES   327

A. INADMISSIBLE TO PROVE "NEGLIGENCE," "CULPABLE
    CONDUCT," OR "LIABILITY"   327
    1. FRE 407   328
    2. Interpretation and Illustration of FRE 407   328
        a. The Exclusionary Mandate   328
            i.   The Inference of Negligence or Culpable Conduct   328
            ii.   Activities That May Be Subsequent
                  Remedial Measures   328
            iii. There Is No Intent or Motive Requirement   330
            iv.   The Effectiveness of the Remedial Action   330
            v.   The Timing of the Remedial Action   330
        b. Permissible Uses of Subsequent-Remedial-Measure
            Evidence   331
        c. The "If Disputed" Requirement   331
        d. The Relationship Between FRE 407 and FRE 403   331
    3. Elaboration of FRE 407   332
        a. The Rationales for FRE 407   332
            i.   Low Probative Value   332
            ii.   Countervailing FRE 403 Factors   332
            iii. Not Discouraging Desirable Conduct   333
            iv.   Not Punishing Desirable Conduct   333
        b. Subsequent Remedial Measures by Third Persons   333
            Key Points   334
            Problems   334
    3. FRE 408   335
    4. Interpretation and Illustration of FRE 408   335
        a. The Exclusionary Mandate; Permissible Uses; FRE 403   335
        b. Conduct or Statements Made During Negotiations   336
        c. The "Disputed Claim" Requirement   337
        d. The Applicability of FRE 408 to Criminal Cases   337
        e. A Party's Own Offer of Compromise   338
        f. Compromises and Offers of Compromises by Third Persons   338
    5. FRE 409   339
    6. Interpretation and Illustration of FRE 409   339
        a. The Exclusionary Mandate   339
        b. The Admissibility of Statements Made in Conjunction
            with Medical and Similar Payments   339
        c. FRE 409 Permits Evidence of Payment for Purposes
            Other Than to Show Liability   339

		d.	What Constitutes a "Similar" Expense?	340
	7.	FRE 411		340
	8.	Interpretation and Illustration of FRE 411		340
		a.	The Exclusionary Mandate	340
		b.	The Permissible Uses of Evidence of Liability Insurance	341
			Key Points	341
			Problems	341
B.	REFLECTION RULES 407-409, 411			344
C.	WITHDRAWN GUILTY PLEAS, PLEAS OF NO CONTEST, AND STATEMENTS MADE DURING PLEA DISCUSSIONS			344
	1.	FRE 410		344
	2.	Interpretation and Illustration of FRE 410		345
		a.	Withdrawn Guilty Pleas	345
		b.	Pleas of No Contest	345
		c.	Statements Made in Conjunction with the Process of Making and Negotiating Pleas	345
		d.	The Scope of FRE 410(a)(4)	346
		e.	The FRE 410(b) Exceptions	347
		f.	Waiver of FRE 410's Exclusionary Mandate	347
			Key Points	348
			Problems	348

CHAPTER SEVEN

THE IMPEACHMENT AND
REHABILITATION OF WITNESSES   351

A.	BASIC CONCEPTS			351
	1.	Impeachment: The Inferential Process		351
		a.	The Testimonial Inferences	351
		b.	Types of Impeachment Evidence	353
		c.	Impeachment Evidence Versus Substantive Evidence	354
	2.	Extrinsic Evidence and Impeachment		355
	3.	Bolstering Credibility		356
B.	IMPEACHMENT AND REHABILITATION WITH CHARACTER EVIDENCE			357
	1.	FRE 608		357
	2.	Interpretation and Illustration of FRE 608(a)		358
		a.	Reputation and Opinion Evidence to Prove Character for Untruthfulness	358
		b.	The FRE 608(a)(2) Limitation on Evidence of Good Character for Truthfulness	358

		Key Points	359
		Problems	360
3.		Interpretation and Illustration of FRE 608(b)	360
	a.	The Prohibition Against the Use of Extrinsic Evidence	361
	b.	The Limited Scope of Permissible Inquiry	361
	c.	No Fifth Amendment Waiver	361
4.		Elaboration of FRE 608(b)(1): Questioning Witnesses About Their Own Specific Acts	361
	a.	The Rationale for the Prohibition Against Extrinsic Evidence	361
	b.	The Scope of Permissible Questions to Prove Character for Untruthfulness	362
		i. The Meaning of Untruthfulness	362
		ii. Questions About Arrests, Charges, and Administrative or Judicial Findings	363
	c.	Questions About Specific Acts and FRE 403	363
	d.	Good-Faith Requirement; Practical Considerations	364
	e.	Specific Acts Showing Good Character for Truthfulness	365
	f.	"Cross-Examination"	365
5.		Elaboration of FRE 608(b)(2): Questioning Character Witnesses Regarding Specific Acts of the Witnesses They Testify About	366
		Key Points	366
		Problems	367
6.		FRE 609	370
7.		Interpretation and Illustration of FRE 609(a) and (b)	370
	a.	The Two FRE 609(a)(1) Balancing Tests	371
		i. Probative Value	371
		ii. Unfair Prejudice	371
		iii. The Reverse FRE 403 Balancing Test for Criminal Defendants	372
		iv. The FRE 403 Balancing Test for Other Witnesses	372
		v. The Factual Circumstances of the Crime	372
	b.	The Automatic Admissibility of FRE 609(a)(2) "Dishonest Act or False Statement" Convictions	373
		i. The Rule	373
		ii. The Meaning of "Dishonest Act or False Statement"	373
		iii. The Significance of the Underlying Details of the Crime	374
	c.	The FRE 609(b) Reverse Balancing Test	374
8.		Elaboration of FRE 609(a)	375
	a.	The Rationale for Permitting Impeachment with FRE 609(a)(1) Convictions	375

      b.   Prior Convictions and Prejudice   376

      c.   Extrinsic Evidence   376

      d.   The Factual Details of the Conviction   376

      e.   The Relationship Between FRE 609(a) and FRE 608(b)   377

      f.   Hearsay   377

      g.   Practical Considerations   378

          Key Points   380

          Problems   380

C.   IMPEACHMENT AND REHABILITATION WITH
A WITNESS'S PRIOR STATEMENTS   382

   1.   FRE 613   383

   2.   Interpretation and Illustration of FRE 613   383

      a.   FRE 613(a)   384

      b.   FRE 613(b)   384

   3.   Elaboration of Impeachment with Prior Inconsistent Statements   385

      a.   FRE 613(b)'s Departure from the Common Law   385

      b.   Extrinsic Evidence in Practice: Practical Considerations   385

      c.   Probative Value and FRE 403 Concerns   386

         i.   The Risk of Improper "Substantive" Use   386

        ii.   Loss of Memory and Inconsistency   387

        iii.   Inconsistent Statements About Collateral Matters   387

           Key Points   388

           Problems   388

   4.   The Impeachment of Experts with Statements in Treatises   389

   5.   Prior Consistent Statements   389

      a.   Admissibility for Truth Pursuant to FRE 801(d)(1)(B)   389

      b.   Admissibility to Rehabilitate Pursuant to FRE 401- 403?   389

         i.   Putting Inconsistent Statements in Context Following
Impeachment with Prior Inconsistent Statement   390

        ii.   Rehabilitation with Consistent Statements in
Other Contexts   390

      c.   Extrinsic Evidence   391

          Key Points   391

          Problems   391

D.   OTHER IMPEACHMENT TECHNIQUES   393

   1.   Bias   394

      a.   Relevance   394

      b.   Extrinsic Evidence   395

      c.   Possible FRE 403 Limitations on Extrinsic Evidence of Bias   395

      d.   Bias Versus Character   395

          Key Points   396

          Problems   396

		2.	Mental or Sensory Incapacity	398
			a. Relevance	398
			b. Extrinsic Evidence	398
			c. Mental Incapacity as a Bar to Testimony	399
			Keys Points	399
			Problems	399
		3.	Contradiction	400
			a. Relevance	400
			b. Extrinsic Evidence	401
			c. The "No Extrinsic Evidence to Impeach on a Collateral Matter" Doctrine	401
			i. What Is Not Collateral Generally	401
			ii. Evidence That Is Directly Relevant to the Issues in Litigation	402
			iii. Evidence That Impeaches a Witness Apart from Contradiction	402
			iv. Evidence That Logically Undermines a Witness's Story	402
			v. A Test for "Collateralness"	402
			Key Points	403
			Problems	403
E.	REFLECTION ON THE IMPEACHMENT PROCESS			404

CHAPTER EIGHT

THE HEARSAY RULE

				407
A.	THE GENERAL RULE OF EXCLUSION AND THE DEFINITION OF HEARSAY			407
	1.	FRE 801 and 802		408
	2.	Interpretation and Illustration of FRE 801 and 802		408
		a.	The Relevancy of Sally's Testimony Depends on Generalizations About Sally's Testimonial Qualities	409
		b.	The Relevancy of Sally's Hearsay Statement Also Depends on Generalizations About Sally's Testimonial Qualities	411
		c.	Hearsay Policy Differentiates Between Witnesses and Hearsay Declarants	412
			Key Points	415
			Problems	415
	3.	Elaboration of FRE 801 and 802: Implications of the General Rule of Exclusion		416
		a.	Identifying What a Hearsay Statement Is Offered to Prove	416

  b.   Testimony by Witnesses About Their Own
       Out-of-Court Statements May Still Be Hearsay   417
  c.   Hearsay, Lay Opinions, and the Firsthand
       Knowledge Rule   418
  d.   Multiple Hearsay   418
       Key Points   419
       Problems   419
4.   Interpretation and Illustration of FRE 801(c): Nonhearsay
     Statements with No Hearsay Dangers   419
  a.   Nonhearsay Uses   420
       i.   Effect on the Listener   421
       ii.   Legally Operative Facts   422
       iii. Identifying Nonhearsay Uses   423
  b.   Statements Relevant for Both Nonhearsay and Hearsay Uses   424
       Key Point   424
       Problems   424
5.   Interpretation and Illustration of FRE 801(a)(2):
     Nonverbal Conduct   426
  a.   The Relevancy of Nonverbal Conduct to Prove Belief   426
  b.   Application of FRE 801(a)(2)   427
       i.   Assertive Conduct   427
       ii.   Nonassertive Conduct   428
       iii. FRE 801(a)(2)'s Intent Test   428
6.   Elaboration of FRE 801(a)(2): Justification for the
     Distinction Between Assertive and Nonassertive Conduct   429
  a.   Absence of Hearsay Danger   429
  b.   Necessity   430
  c.   Should Nonassertive Conduct Be Excluded from the
       Definition of Hearsay?   430
       i.   The Difficulty of Applying the Intent Test   430
       ii.   The Danger of Ambiguity   431
       iii. Is the Admission of Nonassertive Conduct Good Policy?   431
  d.   Disguised Assertions   431
       Key Points   432
       Problems   433
7.   Utterances Relevant for the Truth of the Declarant's
     Unstated Beliefs   434
  a.   The Relevancy of Unstated Beliefs   435
  b.   Application of FRE 801(a)(1) and (c)   436
       i.   The Literal Approach   437
       ii.   The Common Law Approach   437
       iii. FRE 801(a)-(c) Rejects the Common Law Approach   438

8.	Elaboration of FRE 801: Courts Reject the Liberal Approach and Apply an "Intent" Test		438
	a.	The Judicially Created Intent Test	439
	b.	The Difficulties of Applying an Intent Test	439
	c.	Some Courts Still Adhere to the Common Law Approach	441
		Key Points	442
		Notes and Questions	442
		Problems	443
9.	Reflection on the Definition of Hearsay: Should FRE 801 Be Revised?		444

B. A GENERAL APPROACH TO THE ADMISSION OF HEARSAY UNDER THE EXEMPTIONS AND EXCEPTIONS — 445

1.	Justification for the Exemptions and Exceptions	445
2.	The Categorical Approach	446
3.	The Process of Admission	446
4.	The Foundational Requirements	446
5.	Multiple Exemptions and Exceptions May Apply	447
6.	The Confrontation Clause	448

C. HEARSAY EXEMPTIONS — 448

1.	FRE 801(d)(1) and (2)		448
2.	Interpretation and Illustration of FRE 801(d)(1): The Testifying Declarant Must Be "Subject to Cross-examination About the Prior Statement"		449
	a.	Preliminary Fact-finding	449
		i. The Declarant Is Testifying at Trial	449
		ii. Examination Concerning the Statement	450
		iii. Denial of, or Inability to Remember, the Prior Statement	450
		iv. Inability to Remember the Underlying Events	450
		v. Personal Knowledge Is Required	452
	b.	Other Justifications for the FRE 801(d)(1) Exemptions	452
3.	Interpretation and Illustration of FRE 801(d)(1)(A): Prior Inconsistent Statements		452
	a.	Preliminary Fact-finding	452
		i. Inconsistency	452
		ii. Inconsistency Due to Evasion	453
		iii. Under Penalty of Perjury and at a Trial, Hearing, or Other Proceeding	453
	b.	Justification for the FRE 801(d)(1)(A) Limitations	453
	c.	Prior Inconsistent Statements Not Within FRE 801(d)(1)(A)	454
4.	Interpretation and Illustration of FRE 801(d)(1)(B): Prior Consistent Statements		454

	a.	Preliminary Fact-finding	454
		i. An Express or Implied Charge of Recent Fabrication or Improper Influence or Motive	454
		ii. To "Rebut" the Charge	455
	b.	Justification for the FRE 801(d)(1)(B) Limitation	456
	c.	Prior Consistent Statements Not Within FRE 801(d)(1)(B)	456
5.		Interpretation and Illustration of FRE 801(d)(1)(C): Prior Statements of Identification	456
	a.	Preliminary Fact-finding	456
		i. The Statement Identifies a Person as Someone the Declarant Perceived Earlier	457
		ii. Identifies a Person	458
	b.	Justifications for the Admissibility of Prior Statements of Identification	458
	c.	Constitutional Concerns	459
		Key Points	459
		Problems	459
6.		Interpretation and Illustration of FRE 801(d)(2): Party Admissions in General	462
7.		Interpretation and Illustration of FRE 801(d)(2)(A): A Party's Own Statements	463
	a.	Preliminary Fact-finding	463
	b.	Individual and Representative Capacity	464
	c.	Admissions, Personal Knowledge, and Lay Opinions	465
8.		Elaboration of FRE 801(d)(2)(A): Justifications for the Admissibility of Party Admissions	465
	a.	The Opportunity to Explain	466
	b.	Fifth Amendment Concerns	466
	c.	Responsibility for One's Own Statements and Fairness	466
9.		Further Elaboration of FRE 801(d)(2)(A)	467
	a.	Preliminary Fact-finding on the Identity of the Declarant	467
	b.	Admissibility of Party Admissions in Multiparty Cases: The *Bruton* Problem	468
10.		Interpretation and Illustration of FRE 801(d)(2)(B): Adoptive Admissions	469
	a.	Preliminary Fact-finding	469
	b.	Justification for the Admissibility of Adoptive Admissions	469
	c.	Adoption by Silence	470
11.		Interpretation and Illustration of FRE 801(d)(2)(C) and (D): Admissions by Agents, Servants, and Employees	471
	a.	Preliminary Fact-finding	471
		i. Statements by Attorneys	471

	ii.	Other Specifically Authorized Statements	472
	iii.	Statements Made During the Relationship That Concern a Matter Within the Scope of an Agent's Employment	472
b.		Justification for the Admissibility of Statements Under FRE 801(d)(2)(C) and (D): Necessity, Fairness, and Reliability	473
c.		Personal Knowledge and Lay Opinions	474
d.		Admissions by Government Employees	474

12. Interpretation and Illustration of FRE 801(d)(2)(E): Co-conspirators' Admissions — 475
   a. Preliminary Fact-finding — 475
      i. Proof of Co-membership — 476
      ii. During the Course of the Conspiracy — 476
      iii. In Furtherance of the Conspiracy — 477
   b. Justification for the Admissibility of Co-conspirators' Admissions — 477

13. Elaboration of FRE 801(d)(2)(E): Applying FRE 104 to the Co-conspirator Exemption — 477
   a. Bourjaily v. United States — 478
   b. The Amendment to FRE 801(3)(2): The Requirement of Additional Evidence — 478
   c. Process for Admission of a Co-conspirator's Statement — 479
      Key Points — 480
      Problems — 480

D. HEARSAY EXCEPTIONS NOT REQUIRING THE UNAVAILABILITY OF THE DECLARANT — 483
  1. FRE 803 — 484
  2. Interpretation and Illustration of FRE 803(1): Present Sense Impressions — 486
   a. Preliminary Fact-finding — 486
   b. Justification for the Admissibility of Present Sense Impressions — 487
  3. Interpretation and Illustration of FRE 803(2): Excited Utterances — 487
   a. Preliminary Fact-finding — 487
   b. Justification for the Admissibility of Excited Utterances — 488
  4. Elaboration of FRE 803(1) and (2): Effects of the Categorical Approach — 489
   a. The Categories Determine Admissibility — 489
   b. The Categorical Terms Require Judicial Interpretation — 490
      i. Time Lapse Between Event and Statement — 490

		ii.	Content of the Statement	491
	c.		Use of the Statement Itself in Preliminary Fact-finding	492
	d.		Proof of Personal Knowledge	493
			Key Points	493
			Problems	494
5.			Interpretation and Illustration of FRE 803(3): State-of-Mind Declarations	496
	a.		Preliminary Fact-finding	496
	b.		Justification for the State-of-Mind Exception	497
	c.		State-of-Mind Utterances Are Classified as Either Direct or Circumstantial	498
6.			Elaboration of FRE 803(3): Relevant Uses of State-of- Mind Evidence	498
	a.		Future and Past State of Mind of the Declarant	498
	b.		Future Conduct of the Declarant	499
	c.		Evidence of State of Mind Used to Prove Past Facts	500
	d.		The *Hillmon* Case	500
		i.	Walters's Future Conduct	501
		ii.	Hillmon's Future Conduct	501
		iii.	Recent Interpretations of *Hillmon*	502
			Key Points	503
			Problems	503
			Note	505
7.			Interpretation and Illustration of FRE 803(4): Statement for Medical Diagnosis or Treatment	505
	a.		Preliminary Fact-finding	506
	b.		Justification for the Admissibility of Statements for Medical Purposes	506
	c.		Statements About the Cause or External Source Must Be "Pertinent"	507
	d.		Requiring Proof of Medical Purpose	508
	e.		Statements Made for Diagnostic Evaluations for Litigation	508
8.			Elaboration of FRE 803(4): Patient's Statements as the Basis for Expert Opinion	509
			Key Points	509
			Problems	510
9.			Interpretation and Illustration of FRE 803(5): Past Recollection Recorded	510
	a.		Preliminary Fact-finding	511
		i.	The Contents of the Statement	511
		ii.	The Declarant Must Be a Witness with Failed Memory	511

		iii.	Made with Personal Knowledge and Fresh Memory	511
		iv.	The Record Reflects the Witness's Knowledge Accurately	512
		v.	The Record May Only Be Read to the Jury	513
	b.	Justification of the Admissibility of Past Recollection Recorded	513
10.	Elaboration of FRE 803(5)	513
	a.	Past Recollection Recorded Can Be Created by Multiple Declarants	513
	b.	Multiple Hearsay Requires a Hearsay Exception or Exemption for Each Level	514
	c.	Present Recollection Refreshed	515
	d.	The Impact of FRE 612 on Refreshing Recollection	516
		Key Points	517
		Problems	517
11.	Interpretation and Illustration of FRE 803(6): Business Records	518
	a.	Preliminary Fact-finding	518
		i.	The Broad Scope of 803(6)(B)	519
		ii.	Personal Knowledge and Near Contemporaneity Are Required	519
		iii.	Made Pursuant to a "Business Duty"	520
		iv.	Custodian or Other Qualified Witness	521
	b.	Justification for the Admissibility of Records of Regularly Conducted Activities	522
12.	Elaboration of FRE 803(6)	522
	a.	Exclusion for Untrustworthiness	523
		i.	Burden of Persuasion	523
		ii.	Circumstances Indicating Lack of Trustworthiness	523
	b.	Opinions and Diagnoses	524
	c.	Records Containing Multiple Levels of Hearsay	525
		i.	Sources of Information with No Business Duty	525
		ii.	Use of Multiple Exceptions and Exemptions	526
	d.	Computer Documents and Electronic Data	527
		Key Points	528
		Problems	528
13.	Interpretation and Illustration of FRE 803(8): Public Records and Reports	531
	a.	Preliminary Fact-finding	531
		i.	Activities of the Office	531
		ii.	Matters Reported Pursuant to a Legal Duty, Excluding Matters Observed by Law-Enforcement Personnel in Criminal Cases	532

		iii.	Factual Finds in Investigative Reports	532
		iv.	Exclusion for Lack of Trustworthiness	533
	b.		Justification for the Admissibility of Public Records	534
14.			Elaboration of FRE 803(8)(B): The Meaning of "Law Enforcement Personnel"	534
	a.		The Meaning of Law Enforcement Personnel	534
		i.	Prosecutorial Function	535
		ii.	Routine and Regular Activities	535
	b.		The Relationship Between FRE 803(8)(A)(ii) and (iii), and Other Exceptions	536
15.			Elaboration of FRE 803(8)(C): The Problem of Multiple Hearsay Sources Within Investigative Reports	537
	a.		Is the Report Itself Admissible?	537
	b.		Are Otherwise Inadmissible Hearsay Sources Admissible?	538
	c.		Administrative Findings	538
16.			Other Exceptions for Records Under FRE 803	539
			Key Points	539
			Problems	540
17.			Interpretation and Illustration of FRE 803(22): Judgment of Previous Conviction	541
	a.		Preliminary Fact-finding	541
	b.		Justification for the Admissibility of Criminal Judgment	542
	c.		The Admission of Misdemeanor Convictions for Impeachment	542
E.			HEARSAY EXCEPTIONS REQUIRING THE UNAVAILABILITY OF THE DECLARANT	543
1.			FRE 804	543
2.			Interpretation and Illustration of FRE 804(a): Grounds for a Finding of Unavailability	544
	a.		Preliminary Fact-finding	544
	b.		Preference for Former Testimony or Deposition	545
	c.		Reasonable Means to Procure Attendance	545
	d.		Unavailability Caused by the Proponent	546
	3.		Interpretation and Illustration of FRE 804(b)(1): Former Testimony	547
	a.		Preliminary Fact-finding	547
		i.	"Trial, Hearing or Lawful Deposition"	547
		ii.	Opportunity to Develop by Same Party or a Predecessor in Interest	548
		iii.	Opportunity and Similar Motive	548
		iv.	No Opportunity	549
		v.	No Requirement of "Offered on Same Issue"	549

     b.   Justification for the Admissibility of Former Testimony   549

4.   Elaboration of FRE 804(b)(1)   550
     a.   The Opportunity to Develop Testimony   550
     b.   Identity of Parties   550
     c.   Former Testimony Offered Against a Party
         Who Was Not a Party to the Original Action   551
         i.   In a Civil Case, the Party in the Former
            Proceeding May Also Be a Predecessor in Interest   551
         ii. What Is a Predecessor in Interest?   552
     d.   Lack of Similar Motive Due to Difference in
         Procedural Context   552
     e.   Method of Introducing Former Testimony   553
     f.   Objections to the Contents of the Former Testimony   554
         Key Points   554
         Problems   554

5.   Interpretation and Illustration of FRE 804(b)(2):
    Dying Declarations   555
     a.   Preliminary Fact-finding   555
     b.   Justification for the Admissibility of Dying Declarations   556
         Key Point   557

6.   Interpretation and Illustration of FRE 804(b)(3):
    Declarations Against Interest   557
     a.   Preliminary Fact-finding   558
         i.   Content Against Interest   558
         ii. Ascertaining the Declarant's Knowledge   559
         iii. Distinct from Party Admission   559
     b.   Justification for the Admissibility of Declarations
         Against Interest   559

7.   Elaboration of FRE 804(b)(3)   559
     a.   Doubts About the Underlying Rationale for the Exception   559
         i.   Mixed Motive Statements   560
         ii. Statements Made with No Motive to Lie   560
     b.   Requirement of Corroboration for Statements Against
         Penal Interest Offered to Exculpate the Accused   560
     c.   Statement That Inculpate Accomplices   561
     d.   The Corroboration Requirement as Applied to
         Inculpatory Statements   562
         Key Points   562

8.   Interpretation and Illustration of FRE 804(b)(4):
    Statements of Personal or Family History   563
     a.   Preliminary Fact-finding   563

i.	Personal Knowledge of One's Own Personal and Family History	563
ii.	Statements of Relations and Intimate Associates	563
iii.	Concerning Personal History	563
b.	Justification for the Admissibility of Statements of Personal or Family History	564
	Key Points	564
	Problems	564

9. Interpretation and Illustration of FRE 804(b)(6): Forfeiture by Wrongdoing — 566
   a. Preliminary Fact-finding — 567
      i. The Declarant Was a Witness or a Potential Witness Against a Party — 567
      ii. The Party Engaged in Wrongdoing That Did Procure the Unavailability of the Declarant — 567
      iii. Intent to Procure the Declarant's Unavailability as a Witness — 568
      iv. Content of Declarant's Statement — 568
   b. Justification for the Admissibility of Forfeiture by Wrongdoing Statements — 569
   c. Acquiescence in Wrongdoing — 569
   d. Application of FRE 403 — 570
   e. Is an FRE 104(c) Hearing Required? — 570
      Key Points — 571
      Problems — 571

F. THE RESIDUAL EXCEPTION — 572
   1. FRE 807 — 572
   2. Interpretation and Illustration of FRE 807 — 572
      a. Preliminary Fact-finding — 572
      b. Circumstantial Guarantees of Trustworthiness — 573
         i. Reliability of Testimonial Qualities — 573
         ii. Independent Corroboration — 574
      c. Equivalency — 575
      d. Near Miss — 575
      e. Offered to Prove a Material Fact — 575
      f. More Probative on the Point Than Other Reasonably Available Evidence — 575
      g. Serve the General Purposes of the Rules and Interests of Justice — 576
      h. Notice — 576
   3. Elaboration of FRE 807: How Much Hearsay Is Admitted Under the Residual Exception? — 577

		Key Points	578
		Problems	578
G.		HEARSAY AND THE CONFRONTATION CLAUSE	579
	1.	Ohio v. Roberts	580
		a. Firmly Rooted Hearsay Exceptions	581
		b. Not Firmly Rooted Exceptions Require "Particularized Guarantees of Trustworthiness"	581
	2.	Crawford v. Washington	581
		Crawford v. Washington	581
		Key Points	592
		Problems	593
		Notes	593
	3.	The Definition of Testimonial Statements After Crawford v. Washington: Statements Made During Questioning by Poilice	594
		a. The "Primary Purpose" Test: Davis v. Washington	595
		Davis v. Washington, Hammon v. Indiana	595
		Key Points	602
		Problem	603
		Notes and Questions	603
		b. The Primary Purpose Test: Michigan v. Bryant	604
		Problems	608
		Notes and Questions	609
		c. Medical Interviews and Examinations	610
	4.	The Definition of Testimonial Statements After Crawford v. Washington: Government Forensic Reports	611
		a. Melendez-Diaz v. Massachusetts	611
		Notes	615
		b. Bullcoming v. New Mexico	615
		Problem	616
		Notes	617
	5.	Nontestimonial Statements After Crawford	619
	6.	Testimonial Statements That Satisfy the Confrontation Right	619
		a. The Declarant Testifies	619
		b. Unavailability and Prior Opportunity for Cross-examination	620
		i. Unavailability	620
		ii. Prior Opportunity for Cross-examination	620
	7.	Exceptions to the Requirement of Confrontation	621
		a. Dying Declarations	621
		b. "Forfeiture-by-Wrongdoing"	621
		i. The Majority Opinion in Giles	622
		ii. The Concurring Opinion of Justices Souter and Ginsburg	623

iii.   The Dissenting Opinion in *Giles*   623
       Notes and Questions   624
H.   REFLECTION ON THE HEARSAY RULE   625
     1.   The Traditional Goals of Hearsay Policy   625
     2.   The Reliability Theory Does Not Work   625
     3.   A Rule of Discretion   626
     4.   Abolition   627
     5.   Reformulating Hearsay Policy   627
          a.   Is There a Need for a Hearsay Rule in Modern
               Civil Litigation?   627
          b.   Regulation Premised on the Excesses of the
               Adversary System   628
          c.   Notice-based Admission in Civil Cases: Reliance
               on the Adversary System   628
          d.   Why Hearsay Should Be Treated Differently in
               Criminal Cases   629
          e.   Conclusion   629

CHAPTER NINE

LAY OPINIONS AND EXPERT WITNESSES   631

A.   LAY OPINIONS   633
     1.   FRE 701   633
     2.   Interpretation and Illustration of FRE 701   633
          a.   Fact Versus Opinion   634
          b.   Rationally Based on the Perception of the Witness   635
          c.   Helpful to Clearly Understanding the Witness's
               Testimony or to Determining a Fact in Issue   636
          d.   Not Based on Scientific, Technical, or Other
               Specialized Knowledge Within the Scope of Rule 702   638
     3.   Elaboration of FRE 701: Trial Court Discretion   640
          Key Points   642
          Problems   642
B.   EXPERT WITNESSES   646
          Samuel Gross, Expert Evidence   647
          Carol Krafka et al., Judge and Attorney Experiences,
          Practices, and Concerns Regarding Expert Testimony
          in Federal Civil Trials   648
     1.   FRE 702   649
     2.   Interpretation and Illustration of FRE 702   650
          a.   Scientific, Technical, or Other Specialized Knowledge 650

		b.	Help the Trier of Fact	650
		c.	A Witness Qualified as an Expert	651
		d.	FRE 403 and Litigation Incentives	652
		e.	Summary Witnesses	653
	3.	Elaboration of "Scientific Evidence" Under FRE 702: *Frye* and *Daubert*		653
		a.	From *Frye* to *Daubert*	653
			Daubert v. Merrell Dow Pharmaceuticals, Inc.	655
			Notes and Questions	663
	4.	Elaboration of Technical or Other Specialized Knowledge Under *Kumho Tire*		668
			Kumho Tire Company, Ltd. v. Carmichael	668
			Note	672
			Key Points	672
			Problems	673
	5.	Reflection on Scientific Evidence and the *Daubert* Case		677
	6.	FRE 705		682
	7.	Interpretation and Illustration of FRE 705		683
	8.	FRE 703		684
	9.	Interpretation and Illustration of FRE 703		684
	10.	Elaboration of FRE 703: Opinions Based on Otherwise Inadmissible Evidence		686
			Key Points	691
			Problems	691
C.	OPINIONS ON AN ULTIMATE ISSUE			693
	1.	FRE 704		693
	2.	Interpretation and Illustration of FRE 704(a)		693
	3.	Interpretation and Illustration of FRE 704(b)		695
			Key Point	697
			Problems	697
D.	COURT APPOINTED EXPERTS			699
	1.	FRE 706		699
	2.	Interpretation and Illustration of FRE 706		699
E.	RECENT CONTROVERSIES IN FORENSIC SCIENCE AND VARIETIES OF SCIENTIFIC EVIDENCE AND EXPERT TESTIMONY			701
	1.	Problems in Forensic Science		701
	2.	Some Specific Controversies		706
		a.	Recent Debates in DNA Testing	706
		b.	Psychological and Behavioral Sciences	706
		c.	Toxic Tort Causation	707
		d.	Traditional Law Enforcement Investigative Tools	709

			i.	Handwriting Identification	710
			ii.	Fingerprint Identification	711
			iii.	Compositional Analysis of Bullet Lead	714
				Question	715

CHAPTER TEN

THE PROCESS OF PROOF IN CIVIL AND CRIMINAL CASES: BURDENS OF PROOF, JUDICIAL SUMMARY AND COMMENT, AND PRESUMPTIONS

717

A.	THE PROCESS OF PROOF IN CIVIL CASES	718
1.	The Burdens of Proof in Civil Cases	718
	a. The Burden of Production	718
	i. The Role of and Rationale for Production Burdens	718
	ii. The Relationship Between Production Burdens and Persuasion Burdens	719
	iii. The Relationship Between the Burden of Production and the Burden of Persuasion Illustrated	719
	iv. Procedural Mechanisms for Enforcing Burdens of Production	721
	v. The Allocation of Burdens of Production	722
	Key Points	722
	b. The Burden of Persuasion	722
	i. Burdens of Persuasion Are Decision Rules That Manage Uncertainty	722
	ii. The Premises Underlying the Preponderance Rule	723
	iii. Higher Burdens of Persuasion	724
	iv. The Meaning of "Preponderance of the Evidence" in Practice	725
	v. The Relative Nature of the Burden of Persuasion	725
	vi. The Allocation of the Burden of Persuasion	726
	Schechter v. Klanfer	726
	Notes and Questions	728
	Key Points	730
2.	Judicial Summary and Comment in Civil Cases	730
	a. The Advantages and Disadvantages of Permitting Summary and Content	731
	b. The Criteria for Evaluating Judicial Summary and Content	732
	c. Standardized Comments	733

d. The Relationship Between Comments on the Evidence
and the Burden of Persuasion   733
Key Points   733
Notes and Questions   734
3. Presumptions in Civil Cases   734
a. Irrebuttable or Conclusive Presumptions   735
Key Points   736
Problems   736
b. Mandatory Rebuttable Presumptions   737
i. Mandatory Rebuttable Presumptions That Shift a
Burden of Production   737
Notes and Questions   738
Key Points   738
ii. Mandatory Rebuttable Presumptions That Shift the
Burden of Persuasion   739
Notes and Questions   740
Key Points   740
iii. Decision-making with Respect to the Facts
Giving Rise to Mandatory Presumptions   740
Key Point   740
Problems   741
c. Permissive or "Weak" Presumptions   741
Key Points   742
d. The Complexity of Presumptions   742
Notes and Questions   742
e. The Federal Rules Approach to Presumptions   746
i. The "Federal Statute" Exception   746
ii. The Relationship Between FRE 301 Presumptions
and Other Means of Allocating Burdens of Proof   747
Key Points   747
B. THE PROCESS OF PROOF IN CRIMINAL CASES   747
1. The Burdens of Proof in Criminal Cases   748
a. The Burden of Persuasion: *In re Winship*'s Mandate
of Proof Beyond a Reasonable Doubt   748
Notes and Questions   749
Key Point   751
b. The Scope of *Winship*: Explicit Shifts in the Burden of
Persuasion and Other Matters   751
i. The *Mullaney* Decision   751
ii. The *Patterson* Decision   752
iii. The Functional Equivalence of *Mullaney* and *Patterson* 754
iv. *Mullaney*'s Departure from *Winship*   754

		v.	Evaluating *Mullaney* and *Patterson:* The Theory	
			That the Greater Includes the Lesser	754
		vi.	Giving Content to *Winship:* Tests for Assessing the	
			Validity of Affirmative Defenses	755
			(1) The Elements Test	755
			(2) The Political Compromise Test	756
			(3) The Proportionality Test	756
			(4) Justice Powell's Two-Part Test	757
		vii.	Affirmative Defenses After *Patterson*	757
			Martin v. Ohio	758
			Notes and Questions on *Martin*	760
			Key Points	761
			Notes and Questions on the Application of *Winship*	
			in Other Contexts	762
	c.	The Burden of Production in Criminal Cases		764
		Notes and Questions		765
		Key Points		765
2.	Judicial Summary and Comment on the Evidence in Criminal Cases			766
	Notes and Questions			766
3.	Presumptions in Criminal Cases: The Impact of *Winship*			767
	Notes and Questions			769
	Key Points			769
	Problems			770

CHAPTER ELEVEN

JUDICIAL NOTICE   773

A.	JUDICIAL NOTICE OF ADJUDICATIVE FACTS			773
	1.	FRE 201		773
	2.	Interpretation and Illustration of FRE 201(a) and (b)		774
		a.	Types of Adjudicative Facts That Are Frequently Noticed	774
		b.	The Scope of FRE 201(a): What Are Adjudicative Facts?	774
		c.	The Scope of FRE 201(b): The Required State of	
			Knowledge of Adjudicative Facts That May Be	
			Judicially Noticed	775
	3.	Elaboration of FRE 201(a) and (b)		776
		a.	Further Illustration of 201(b) Standards	776
			In re Thirtyacre	776
		Notes and Questions		777
		b.	Sources of Information Under FRE 201	777
	4.	Interpretation and Illustration of FRE 201(c) and (e)		778

5.   Interpretation and Illustration of FRE 201(d) and (f)   778
      a.   Judicial Notice of Adjudicative Facts in Civil Cases:
            Mini Directed Verdicts   778
      b.   Judicial Notice of Adjudicative Facts in Criminal Cases:
            Judicial Comments   779
      c.   Timing of Judicial Notice   779
            i.   Judicial Notice to Preserve Civil Verdicts   779
            ii.   Judicial Notice to Preserve Criminal Verdicts   780
                  Key Points   780
                  Notes and Questions   780
                  Problems   781
B. JUDICIAL NOTICE AS PART OF JUDICIAL DECISION-MAKING   782
    1.   Judicial Cognizance of Common Knowledge
          Without Formal Judicial Notice   783
          a.   The Jury's General Background Knowledge   783
          b.   Judges' Own Background Knowledge   784
                In re Marriage of Tresnak   784
                Notes and Questions   786
    2.   Judicial Cognizance of Legislative Facts   786
          Notes and Questions   788
    3.   Judicial Notice of Substantive Law   788
          Key Point   788
          Problems   789

CHAPTER TWELVE

PRIVILEGES   793

A. THE LAW OF PRIVILEGE   793
    1.   A General Introduction   793
    2.   The Unique Operation of Privilege Rules   794
    3.   Historical Background and Current Status of Privilege Rules 796
B. GENERAL STRUCTURE OF PRIVILEGES   798
    1.   Holder of the Privilege   798
    2.   Invocation   798
    3.   Scope and Limits   801
    4.   Waiver   801
    5.   Exceptions   802
    6.   Drawing Adverse Inferences from Invoking a Privilege   802
    7.   Constitutional Limitations on Privilege   803
C. THE ATTORNEY-CLIENT PRIVILEGE   804
    1.   Elements of the Privilege   804
          a.   Communications with a Lawyer or Representative
                of a Lawyer   805

	b.	Communications for the Purpose of Legal Service	807
	c.	The Scope of Confidential Communications Included in Privilege	808
	d.	Limitations on Waiver of the Privilege	808
	e.	Interpretation of the New Rule	810
		i. Purpose of FRE 502	810
		ii. Limitation to FRE 502	811
	f.	Aspects of the New Rule	811
		i. Scope of the Waiver Under FRE 502(a) and Subject Matter Waiver	811
		ii. When Does a Inadvertent Disclosure Waive Protection Under FRE 502(b)?	811
		iii. If Disclosure Is Made in a State Proceeding, the More Protective Law Will Apply Under FRE 502(c)	812
		iv. Controlling Effect of a Court Order Under FRE 502(d)	812
		v. Controlling Effect of a Party Agreement Under FRE 502(e)	813
		vi. Controlling Effect of FRE 502	813
	g.	Additional Concerns Raised by FRE 502	813
		i. The Rule Does Not Eliminate the Need to Review Documents Prior to Disclosure	813
		ii. The Constitutionality of the Rule's Application to State Court Proceedings	814
		iii. The Rule May Not Significantly Reduce the Cost of Discovery	814
		iv. The Rule May Jeopardize the Attorney-Client Privilege	815
		Key Points	815
		Notes and Questions	815
		Problems	816
		Note on the Attorney-Client Privilege, the Work-Product Doctrine, and the Ethical Duty of Confidentiality	818
		Notes and Questions	820
		Problems	821
2.	The Corporate Client		822
		Upjohn Co. v. United States	823
		Key Points	831
		Notes and Questions	831
		Problems	833
3.	The Government Client		834
4.	Exceptions to the Privilege		836
	a.	Breach of Duty by a Lawyer or Client	836
	b.	Document Attested by a Lawyer	836
	c.	Identity of Client, Fee Information, and Related Matters	836

		d.	Communication in Furtherance of a Crime or Fraud	837
			Problems	838
	5.		Reflection on the Attorney-Client Privilege	839
			Ronald J. Allen et al., A Positive Theory of the Attorney-Client Privilege and the Work Product Doctrine	840
			Notes and Questions	854
D.	THE MARITAL PRIVILEGES			856
	1.		The Marital Communication Privilege	857
		a.	Elements of the Privilege and Its Justifications	857
		b.	Holder	857
		c.	Scope of the Privilege	857
			i. Valid Marriage	857
			ii. Confidentiality	859
			iii. What Is a "Communication"?	859
		d.	Exceptions	860
			Problems	861
	2.		The Marital Testimonial Privilege	862
		a.	Elements of the Privilege and Its Justifications	862
			Trammel v. United States	862
			Notes and Questions	867
		b.	Exceptions	868
			Key Points	869
			Problems	870
E.	THE PHYSICIAN-PATIENT AND PSYCHOTHERAPIST- PATIENT PRIVILEGES			870
	1.		The Physician-Patient Privilege	871
	2.		The Psychotherapist-Patient Privilege	872
		a.	Jaffee v. Redmond	872
			Jaffee v. Redmond	872
			Notes and Questions	883
		b.	Scope of the Privilege After Jaffee	884
			i. Who Is a Psychotherapist?	884
			ii. Communications	885
			iii. Waiver	885
		c.	Exceptions to the Privilege	886
			i. Constitutional Limits	886
			ii. Compelled Disclosures	887
			iii. Dangerous Patient	888
			iv. Crime-Fraud Exception	889
			Key Points	889
			Problems	889

F.	THE CLERGY-COMMUNICANT PRIVILEGE		890
	1.	The Privilege and Its Justifications	891
	2.	Scope of the Privilege	891
		a. Definition of Clergy	892
		b. Nature of the Communication	893
		c. Expectation of Confidentiality	893
		d. Exceptions	894
		Key Points	895
		Problems	895
G.	OTHER PRIVILEGES		896
	1.	Other Professional-Client Relationships	896
	2.	Parent-Child Privilege	897
	3.	Communications Made in Settlement Negotiations	899
	4.	Privileges Protecting Outside Sources of Information	901
		a. Government Informant's Privilege	901
		b. Journalist's Privilege	902
		c. Scholar's (Academic Researcher's) Privilege	903
	5.	Peer Review Privilege	904
	6.	Self-evaluative Privilege	906
	7.	Government Privileges—Executive Privilege	907
		a. State Secrets Privilege	907
		b. Presidential Communications Privilege	909
		c. Official Information (Deliberative Process) Privilege	912
	8.	Miscellaneous Privileges	915
		Problems	916

Table of Cases	*919*
Table of Authorities	*931*
Index	*945*

PREFACE

In this fifth edition of our book, we maintain our focus on the study of evidence law through the text of the Federal Rules of Evidence and the ideas and principles that underlie them. The book presents the rules in a systematic format that is used consistently throughout. This format provides students with the text of the rules, the basic interpretation and illustration of the rules' terms, an elaboration of principles and policies used to explain and interpret the rules, illustrations from recent case law, and a set of problems that calls for the application of each significant rule in its most basic as well as its most challenging contexts.

The most significant change in this edition is the restyling of the Federal Rules of Evidence themselves. The restyling of the rules, a project of the U.S. Judicial Conference, has been in the works for several years. As of this writing, they are under consideration by the Congress of the United States and are scheduled to become effective on December 1, 2011. We have incorporated these restyled Rules throughout the book. The purpose of the restyling project has been to clarify the text of each rule, not to change any rule's substantive content or application. Some changes in wording have been made (some consistently throughout the rules), and some rules have been re-organized into subparts and subsections for the purpose of clarity. The lettering and numbering of these subparts largely conform to the lettering and numbering of the original rules, but not always. In the book, we have noted when changes in wording may require special attention.

The second major change is, understandably, the addition of significant new material on the Confrontation Clause. Two principal Supreme Court opinions are included—*Crawford v. Washington* and *Davis v. Washington*. The other four cases decided by the Court since 2006 are excerpted and analyzed through Notes and Questions. Throughout this section, problems have been added that test the application of the evolving confrontation doctrine.

The casebook text has been edited throughout, adding new excerpts from judicial opinions, updating the case citations that illustrate application of the rules, and adding new problems. We have sought throughout to present each set of problems in ascending order of difficulty—easy, medium, and difficult. This edition still includes ongoing "saga" problems that build, in successive chapters, on each developing "saga" fact pattern. These unique problems demonstrate how the rules of evidence actually apply to individual items of evidence in "layers" as students' knowledge of those rules increases.

We have not been content to present a mass of doctrines and cases. We have endeavored instead to show, through discursive text and problems, the relationship between the theories underlying the rules and the rules themselves. This emphasis on the underlying theories reflects our view that the study of any field of law should not consist primarily of ingesting enormous amounts of doctrinal "stew." Rather, the pursuit should be gaining an understanding of the conditions that give rise to the forms of regulation of decision making that are contained in the rules of evidence.

From its inception, another factor has heavily influenced this book. We believe that the field of evidence is in large measure a coherent whole rather than an amalgam of virtually unrelated parts. Unlike traditional works on evidence, we present an analytic theme in our text that attempts to show the underlying relationships between the various common law categories of evidence. This theme is relevancy and the assumptions about decision making that inhere in a system of proof based on relevancy. With this theme we explore all of the major Federal Rules of Evidence, requiring students to develop a systematic approach to the admission of evidence that begins with the relationship of evidentiary facts to the essential elements of the case. Only with such a beginning can the exclusionary principles, and judicial interpretation and application of them, be understood.

We also emphasize the process by which facts are established in court, and the roles played by each of the participants in the courtroom. Chapter One begins with the study of a transcript from a real case. This introduces students to the process of analyzing evidence in terms of the essential elements of a legal dispute, as well as experiencing what is at stake in even run-of-the-mill trials. We believe that the transcript serves as an effective introduction to much of the course to follow. Although accurate fact finding is the dominant goal of trial, the rules of evidence also regulate with other goals in mind, such as efficiency, fairness and incentives to out-of-court behavior. Beginning with the transcript, which we return to throughout the text, highlights these matters. We have also generated a series of problems on the transcript so that student investment in reading it pays off with a deeper understanding of the context within which isolated evidence issues arise and are resolved.

Chapter Two, The Process of Proof, provides additional background information on trial process and strategy that brings the evidence course alive. It describes how trials are structured, how witnesses are examined, and it begins our exploration of the relationship between inferential reasoning as used by the fact finder and the process of presenting proof at trial.

Chapter Three examines the single most important concept in the study of evidence—relevancy—and introduces students to the trial judge's "discretion" to exclude even relevant, and probative, evidence. Some judicial opinions, including the U.S. Supreme Court's majority opinion in Old *Chief v. United States*, give students a more concrete understanding of how the context of the whole "case" can influence the judge's exercise of discretion. Chapter Four contains the rules that establish the required "foundation" for many different types of evidence, including FRE 104 and the problem of conditional relevance. Chapter Five focuses on the character and propensity rules. We start by introducing the primary rule of exclusion, the policies that justify exclusion, and the policing of the borderline between forbidden "character" and permitted "non-character" uses of specific acts. We then turn to instances in which character is a permissible topic of proof. Chapter Six contains the remaining relevancy rules.

Chapter Seven presents the doctrines of impeaching and rehabilitating witnesses, prior to the study of the hearsay rule. The attention paid to examining witnesses, we believe, paves the way for Chapter Eight's treatment of hearsay. Chapter Eight contains revised text on the problem of "implied assertions" that we think streamlines presentation without sacrificing complexity. Chapter Nine, which focuses on the rules governing lay and expert witness opinion testimony, includes principal Supreme Court cases, the amendments to the Federal Rules, effective in 2000, and excerpts from the National Academy of Science Report in 2009 largely critiquing the current state of the forensic sciences. Chapter Ten has reorganized the presentation of the burdens of proof and presumptions by focusing separately on civil and criminal law. Chapter Eleven has streamlined the study of judicial notice; and the book concludes, as before, with an examination of rules of privilege in Chapter Twelve, including material on the new Federal Rule 502 concerning waiver of the attorney-client privilege.

Despite the substantial amount of text, this book is not a treatise on the law of evidence. We have not attempted to cover "everything." Rather, we have put together materials that we believe will contribute to the effective teaching of the law of evidence. Our selection of materials has been driven by one criterion alone. We have selected materials that in our judgment are the most effective pedagogical tools.

Also in this edition, we are joined by a new co-author, Professor Michael S. Pardo of the University of Alabama School of Law. Professor Richard Kuhns, who with Professor Ron Allen originally conceived this book and contributed so much to every new edition, has retired from co-authorship. We are indebted to many individuals who have assisted us in various ways in creating this fifth edition. Professor Allen would particularly like to thank Lindsey Sullivan and John Riordan for extraordinary research assistance. Professor Swift is very grateful to Micah Sucherman, Sarah Pauly, Maryam Sharifi, Micah Moon, Eddy Park and Pat Byrnes for their research assistance and enthusiasm for the law of evidence. Professor Pardo would like to thank Will Morris for his excellent research assistance.

Ronald J. Allen
Eleanor Swift
David S. Schwartz
Michael S. Pardo

November 2011

ACKNOWLEDGMENTS

The authors gratefully acknowledge permission to reprint excerpts from the following:

Allen, Ronald J., The Evolution of the Hearsay Rule to a Rule of Admission, 76 Minn. L. Rev. 797 (1992). Reprinted with permission.

Allen, Ronald J. et al., A Positive Theory of the Attorney-Client Privilege and the Work Product Doctrine, 19 J. Legal Stud. 359 (1990). Reprinted with permission.

Blakely, Newell H., Article IV: Relevancy and Its Limits, 30 Hous. L. Rev. 281 (1993). Reprinted with permission.

Chayes, Abram, The Role of the Judge in Public Law Litigation, 89 Harv. L. Rev. 1281 (1976). Reprinted with permission.

Gross, Samuel R., Expert Evidence, 1991 Wis. L. Rev. 1113 (1991). Copyright © 1991 by The Board of Regents of the University of Wisconsin System. Reprinted by permission of the Wisconsin Law Review.

Krafka, Carol et al., Judge and Attorney Experiences, Practices, and Concerns Regarding Expert Testimony in Federal Civil Trials. Federal Judicial Center (2002).

Kuhns, Richard B., The Propensity to Misunderstand the Character of Specific Acts Evidence, 66 Iowa L. Rev. 777 (1981). Reprinted with permission.

McCormick, Charles Tilford et al., McCormick on Evidence (Kenneth S. Broun ed., 6th ed. 2006). Reprinted with permission of the West Group.

Park, Roger C., A Subject Matter Approach to Hearsay Reform, 86 Mich. L. Rev. 51 (1987). Reprinted with permission.

Pennington, Nancy, and Reid Hastie, Juror Decision-Making Models: The Generalization Gap, 89 Psychol. Bull. 246 (1981). Reprinted with permission.

Seigel, Michael L., Rationalizing Hearsay: A Proposal for a Best Evidence Hearsay Rule, 72 B.U. L. Rev. 893 (1992). Reprinted with permission. Copyright © 1992 by Boston University Law Review, Boston University. Forum of original publication. Boston University bears no responsibility for any errors which have occurred in reprinting, translation, or editing.

INTRODUCTION
TO THE STUDY
OF EVIDENCE

Evidence law is, in one sense, one of the most practical courses that you will take in law school. It is the study of rules in action, rules that are interpreted and applied in the often heated context of adversarial litigation over matters of life and death, personal rights (and obligations), property rights, human relationships, and even such matters as the structure of government and the meaning of the Constitution. As you read the text, the judicial opinions, and the problems in this book, you will be analyzing and evaluating the impact that evidence law has on the litigants and the outcomes of their cases. One of the most significant manifestations of evidence law is the rules of evidence. We concentrate in this book on the Federal Rules of Evidence. The Federal Rules were adopted by Congress in 1975, and since then close to 40 states have revised their rules of evidence, in many instances adopting the Federal Rules virtually verbatim. When you first read the Federal Rules of Evidence you many think them to be cold and sterile doctrines written in abstract conceptual terms, but you will soon find them imbued with the human drama of the courtroom. Behind the masks of the law there are real people who are called on to testify concerning matter of great personal and social import, as well as parties whose cases rest on that testimony.

The study of evidence, however, is not just the study of the rules of evidence. It is the study of the vast complex of ideas, principles, customs, and values underlying the process of litigation. The rules of evidence give form and content to this process — they determine the admissibility of evidence, define the roles of all the participants at trial (judge, jury, advocates, and witnesses), and structure the relationships among these various actors. They reflect our society's views on many issues, among them: (1) the appropriate means of resolving disputes; (2) the nature of knowledge, what it means to "know" something, and how knowledge is transmitted to others; (3) the dynamics of small group decision-making, and the confidence that we invest in the common person to reach wise and informed judgments that affect the lives of fellow citizens; (4) moral and ethical concerns, such as how difficult it should be for the prosecution to obtain a conviction in a criminal case, or whether certain individuals (spouses, children, friends) should have a privilege not to testify against those close to them; and (5) the relationship between the ideal of justice and the value of efficiency. The rules of evidence rest on and are a crystallization of these various, often conflicting, views. To understand the rules requires an understanding of the compromises they make between competing beliefs and interests; thus, to study the rules one must engage with the foundation of beliefs that underlies them.

The study of evidence will serve any lawyer well, no matter what specialization that person pursues. Obviously litigators must know and understand the rules of evidence in order to use them effectively. Do not overlook that while litigation is virtually always the worst-case scenario of any legal transaction, competent lawyers must always be prepared for it no matter what the nature of the relevant legal enterprise happens to be. If a contractual relationship fails or a merger is not consummated and litigation results, what will matter is how well the parties will be able to defend their respective positions. That will be determined in significant measure by the application of the rules of evidence in the trial itself, and by their implications throughout pretrial procedures, including negotiations leading to settlement.

To use the rules effectively, one must understand their meaning, source, and purpose. To do so requires that one see the rules in relationship to the assumptions, values, and concerns that give rise to them. Even if—indeed, especially if—one intends to become a litigator, it will not do to be content with a cursory grasp of the language of the various rules. One must be in a position to work with the rules, and to argue for one's position from the perspective of the purposes that underlie the relevant provisions.

For those who do not intend to become litigators, and who are reasonably sure that their legal transactions will never collapse into disputes, it is essential to see the rules as summaries of underlying social, philosophical, and moral beliefs and to look carefully at those beliefs. For such individuals, the value of the inquiry lies not in some future utility but instead in its enlightenment of our shared vision of how disputes should be resolved in a civilized society. With that enlightenment may come—indeed, we hope *will* come—disagreement. You may not like all that you see; and if you do not, you will be in a better position to work for change through the legislative and rule-making processes.

We attempt in these materials to facilitate an inquiry into the meaning and use of the rules of evidence as well as all that underlies them. At times we focus extensively—in fact, almost exclusively—on the rules themselves, while at other times we deal quite explicitly with the assumptions and values from which the rules are derived. On completion of this inquiry, you should have a thorough understanding of the rules of evidence, as well as considerable appreciation for the concerns that give rise to them.

SPECIAL NOTICE ON CITATIONS

In general, some citations and footnotes have been omitted from quoted material without indication. Footnotes are numbered consecutively in each chapter; that is, the original footnote numbers in quoted material have not been retained. Footnotes in quoted material that are written by the casebook authors are marked "—EDS." In addition, throughout the text we quote from the Federal Rules of Evidence and from the Federal Rules' legislative history without giving specific citations. The Federal Rules quoted in the text are the restyled Rules approved by the U.S. Supreme Court and transmitted to the Congress, presumably to become effective on December 1, 2011. The restyled Rules are available at http://www.supremecourt.gov/orders/courtorders/frev11.pdf.

The Notes of the advisory committee appointed by the Supreme Court to draft the rules remain applicable to the restyled Rules. The Advisory Committee Notes are set forth at 56 F.R.D. 183. The judiciary committees of both the House of Representatives and the Senate held hearings on the Federal Rules. The report of the House Committee is H.R. Rep. No. 650, 93d Cong., 1 Sess. (1973), appearing at 1974 U.S.C.C.A.N. 7075; and the report of the Senate is S. Rep. No. 1277, 93d Cong., 2d Sess. (1974), appearing at 1974 U.S.C.C.A.N. 7051. The Conference Committee report is H.R. Rep. No. 1597, 93d Cong., 2d Sess. (1974), and appears at 1974 U.S.C.C.A.N. 7098.

We have deleted *cert. denied* references throughout the book.

EVIDENCE

CHAPTER ONE

THE CASE OF PEOPLE v. JOHNSON

We start with an edited transcript of a real trial, People v. Johnson.[1] A trial transcript is a good place to start for a number of reasons. Most of you have not experienced litigation, and the transcript allows you to study a complete trial, to get a sense of its structure and dynamic, that is, a sense of how it is put together and how it unfolds. The transcript introduces you to the principal stages of trial process so that you can begin to appreciate the organization of a case, who is doing what to whom, and why. The transcript also introduces you to the Federal Rules of Evidence[2] and gives an overview of much that is to follow in succeeding chapters. We hope that you will get a sense of the rules of evidence in action, and an awareness of the distinction between the rules in real life and their theoretical justifications.

Another reason we begin with a transcript is to increase your understanding of the human element at work in the law of evidence. The *Johnson* case involves serious issues of real people in a dangerous environment with a lot at stake. The case concerns criminal charges of battery brought against an inmate at a California state prison. But Pelican Bay is not just any prison; rather, it was designed as a high-tech "state of the art" facility to house the state's most violence-prone inmates. The Security Housing Unit (SHU) at Pelican Bay was designed for control of prison gang members, not for rehabilitation. A class action lawsuit brought under the federal civil rights act alleged that the isolation conditions in the SHU amounted to cruel and unusual punishment. Prisoners housed in the general population areas of the prison also complained of the use of excessive force by guards and the denial of basic medical attention and access to legal counsel. In January of 1995, U.S. District Court Judge Thelton Henderson found that Pelican Bay staff routinely used unwarranted violence on inmates (based on 105 pages of documented violent incidents including assaults, beatings, and naked cagings in inclement weather, and an unusually high number of lethal shootings). He also found that Pelican Bay operated a medical and mental health care program that

---

1. The names of all the participants have been changed to provide some anonymity to the parties involved. In addition, we have added footnotes, made very minor editorial changes, and eliminated essentially repetitious testimony.

2. The *Johnson* case was tried in California state court and was governed by the California Evidence Code. The California Code, enacted in 1965, was extremely influential in the drafting of the Federal Rules of Evidence seven years later and there are only a few substantive differences between the Code and the Rules. We refer to the applicable Federal Rules in the footnotes to the transcript.

was significantly deficient. The judge ordered prison officials to stop housing mentally ill inmates in the SHU, but refused to hold that incarceration there constituted cruel and unusual punishment for all prisoners. Judge Henderson's opinion is reported as Madrid v. Gomez, 889 F. Supp. 1146 (N.D. Cal. 1995).

As you begin reading the transcript, remember that much has already occurred in the *Johnson* case. The parties have selected a jury and have participated in a preliminary hearing, mutual discovery, and motions in limine. These pretrial events shape issues of proof, as you will see. In addition, they shape the understanding of the participants: Judges are informed, and perhaps influenced, by what they learn in the pretrial stage; jurors are educated in the voir dire process; and the lawyers learn more about the respective strengths and weaknesses of their own case and that of their opponent. Indeed, this last point cannot be overemphasized. The single most important variable in success at litigation is preparation. If you take away one "rule" of evidence from this course, let it be "prepare, prepare, prepare." As you read the transcript, try to get an insight into how well these lawyers prepared.

THE PEOPLE OF THE STATE OF CALIFORNIA v. JAMES JOHNSON

Superior Court, Del Norte County, California
DATE: Monday, July 27, 1992, 1:45 p.m.

1   **Appearances**

For the People: William Cummings, II, Esq., District Attorney
For the Defendant: Mark Deemer, Esq., Attorney at Law
THE COURT: In the People versus Johnson let the record reflect that all
5   jurors, counsel and the defendant are present. I am going to read to you
now the charge that has been filed against the defendant, again reminding you that the information is not evidence but is charged as follows:[3]
"Superior Court of Del Norte, State of California. The People of the State of California, plaintiff, versus James Johnson, C-66125, defendant, No. 92-190-X. Information.
10   "The District Attorney of the County of Del Norte, State of California, hereby charges James Johnson (C-66125) with having committed, in the County of Del Norte, the crime of:
"Count 1. Battery on a correctional officer, in violation of Section 4501.5
15   of the Penal Code, a felony.
"On or about March 28, 1992, the defendant did willfully and unlawfully being a person confined in a State Prison of this state, commit a battery

---

3. The role of the judge includes informing the jury of the substantive law that will govern the jury's verdict. In California, an information is the pleading filed in Superior Court for the prosecution of a felony. Is there any reason why the judge read the information to the jury rather than simply reading the Code section that the defendant allegedly violated? Is there any reason why the judge did not try to translate the legalese into English?

1 upon the person of any individual who is not himself a person confined therein to wit, Officer Huston.

"Count 2. Battery on correctional officer, in violation of Section 4501.5 of the Penal Code, a felony.

5 "On or about March 28th 1992, the defendant did willfully and unlawfully being a person confined in a State Prison of this state, commit a battery upon the person of any individual who is not himself a person confined therein to wit, Officer Van Berg.

"Dated June 23rd, 1992, William Cummings, II, District Attorney.

10 Signed Wm. Cummings for Richard Davis Deputy District Attorney."[4]

MR. DEEMER: At this time there is a motion to exclude witnesses. I see two are in the courtroom.

THE COURT: All persons who are present as witnesses in the matter will have to remain outside the courtroom and not discuss their testimony with any

15 other witnesses until the hearing is concluded.[5] Counsel are responsible for enforcing this order as to their own witnesses.

Now, before we get under way with the evidence there are also a few other things. One is an instruction that I will read to you that will cover how you are to handle certain things that may come up during the course of the

20 trial. Because you must determine the facts in this case solely from the evidence, you must be guided by the following principles.[6] One, you must not consider as evidence any statement or arguments of counsel, meaning the attorneys, except that if counsel agree or stipulate to any fact you must regard such fact as being conclusively proved.

25 Second, you must not consider as evidence any off the record evidence that was rejected or any evidence that is stricken out by me.

Third, as to any question to which an objection is sustained, you must not speculate as to what the answer might have been or as to the reason for the objection.

30 And fourth, since a question is not evidence you must not suspect that any insinuation suggested by a question is true. In other words, you can consider the questions only as they supply meaning to the answer. Because, for instance, an answer of "yes" or an answer of "no" doesn't mean anything unless you know what the question was. But the question is not evidence. Only the evidence

35 that comes from the witness is evidence. So nothing that is said in a question should be assumed by you to be true or considered by you to be fact.

It may also happen during the course of the trial, in fact it has happened a couple times already, that you have seen we'll have what are called bench conferences, and this is where the attorneys come up here to the bench and

---

4.   Substantive law provides the essential elements that the prosecution will have to prove to obtain a conviction. What are the essential elements of the crimes with which defendant Johnson is charged? *Battery* is not defined in the information but an instruction on the elements of a battery is given at page 64 infra. In a civil case, the essential elements of the plaintiff's case are derived from the common or statutory law that governs the dispute.

5.   FRE 615 permits the court to exclude witnesses from the courtroom while another witness is testifying to safeguard against the possibility of "contaminating" a witness. The objective is to preclude a witness from altering or modifying testimony to explain or dovetail with the testimony of another witness.

6.   When you have finished reading the instructions, consider how well they communicate the salient aspects of the role that the jurors are about to undertake. Note in particular that the judge provides very little illumination concerning the legal standards relevant to this trial. Why do you suppose that is?

1   we discuss matters out of your hearing. The reason for this is from time to time
things come up in the course of the trial. Sometimes it has to do with objections to the admissibility of evidence. Sometimes it has to do with motions
the attorneys are making before the court or other matters that should be
5   heard out of the presence of the jury. If it is going to be something lengthy
we'll probably give you a recess and have you step out of the court room. But
if it is something very brief, to save the time of doing that, we come up here
to the bench and we try and speak in tones of voice that are low enough and
for that very reason you should try not to overhear what we are saying. If it
10   would help you, certainly feel free to converse among yourselves as long as it
is not about the case. If you would like to stand up in place and stretch and
generally make yourself comfortable, feel free to do that and we can get back
to you shortly if that happens.[7]

If there is anyone in the jury that feels they need a recess for any reason,
15   please do not hesitate or feel embarrassed. If you need to use the rest room
or whatever it is, I would rather take care of it, just take a few minutes and
break the proceedings and have you take care of it and then you won't be
distracted and thinking about something else when you are listening to the
evidence when we are here in court.

20   Also, if any of you would like to take notes you may do so. Usually it's not
necessary. I expect in this case where it's going to be a fairly short trial lasting
a couple days or so that you will probably be able to hold most everything in
your memory. We do have the court reporter taking everything down on a
word for word basis. So during your deliberations if you need to know exactly
25   what some witness said that will be available to you and that testimony can
be read back to you by the reporter. A few juries like to take notes and you
may if you wish.

The one caution is you should be very careful that your note taking does
not interfere with your ability to closely watch and observe the witnesses as
30   they give their testimony because it oftentimes happens in trials and it may
happen in this trial that one witness will testify to something and another will
testify to exactly the opposite. Just in the words that they are saying you may
not be able to figure out which one you believe. It may be necessary for you
to rely upon such things as facial expression or tone of voice or what we call
35   body language, the general things that we use in our day to day life when we
decide whether we believe what somebody is telling us or we don't. Don't let
your note taking interfere with closely watching and scrutinizing and observing the witnesses as they testify.

Also, you should not on your own undertake any investigation of this
40   matter.[8] You should not try to interview any witnesses, not try to visit the
scene where anything may have happened. You should not consult any ref-

---

7.   A "bench conference" or a "sidebar" may be initiated by either side or by the judge when a point
of contention or procedure arises that requires resolution for the smooth functioning of the proceeding.
Most bench conferences are on the record — that is, they are recorded by the court reporter — but they
occur outside the jury's hearing, in order to keep the jury from overhearing what is discussed. Longer hearings on the admissibility of evidence may also be held without the jury present. See FRE 104.

8.   Why shouldn't jurors learn more about the specific facts of the case by conducting their own
inquiry? Jurors bring their own background knowledge and general experience with them, and they use
this knowledge to interpret the testimony they hear. Wouldn't it be useful for them to read up on subjects
that are pertinent to the dispute as well?

erence works and you should not try to perform any experiments. And that is because the evidence in this case, strictly the evidence that comes from the witnesses, is all that should be considered in deciding what your verdict should be in this case. So do not try to gather evidence of facts or information from any other source except from the witnesses.

I have already mentioned to you that you should be very careful not to — when you encounter the attorneys or other people involved in this case during the recesses be very careful not to fall into conversation with them.[9] We mentioned that before lunch.

One final thing and that is that you should not consider as evidence the fact that the defendant is here in physical custody of officers. You should not take into consideration as evidence either for him or against him whether he is confined in physical restraints or the clothing that he is wearing or that there may be additional security here in the courtroom. Those are not facts that should be considered in any way as showing whether the defendant is guilty or not guilty. Disregard those matters and decide the case strictly on the evidence.

All right. The final thing before we get under way with the evidence is that the attorneys have the opportunity to make opening statements to the jury and these are very brief outlines the attorneys could give you if they wish showing what they expect the evidence in the case is going to prove. Sometimes it happens, of course, that the evidence comes out differently from what they expect. The witness may remember something differently from what one or the other of the attorneys may think the witness is going to testify to. But generally speaking the attorneys can give a fair outline of what's going to happen in the case and what they expect the issues are going to be. But, of course, if there is any difference between what they say the evidence is going to be and what it actually is, of course you follow the evidence.

Since the prosecution has the burden of proof and presents evidence first, the prosecutor makes the first opening statement. When he is finished defense counsel has a choice. He can either make his opening statement at that time or if he prefers he can wait until the prosecution presents their evidence and then make his opening statement. Mr. Cummings?[10]

MR. CUMMINGS: Thank you, Your Honor.[11] Ladies and gentlemen, we are about to get under way and the purpose of my opening statement is basically to give you some idea of where I believe our witnesses are going to take us

9.   Why should jurors not discuss the case with anyone else, including other jurors? Jurors are undergoing a learning process. Does learning occur most effectively when the learner sits passively, as this instruction directs these jurors to do? What are possible risks of discussion that offset its value in an educational process? Why is the court imposing this type of decision-making process on the jury?

10.   What aspect of the jury's role did the judge focus on in the instructions? Do the instructions prepare the jury for its decision-making role? Has the judge adequately informed the jury about the role of the court or the adversaries?

11.   The primary purposes of an opening statement are to state the facts that the advocate expects to produce at trial; to present these facts within the framework of a story or theme that is persuasive and that will be the basis for closing argument; and to personalize the client. Argument about what inferences should be drawn from the evidence is made in the closing arguments, not here. The opening statement is also used to introduce the jury to weaknesses in the case. Jury surveys have shown that opening statements are very important in jury decision-making, and that jurors often vote consistently with views they form during the opening. See the discussion in Chapter Two, Section F. Reflections on Natural Reasoning and the Adversary System.

in testimony. Witnesses are the people who testify from the witness stand, nowhere else. In other words, as the judge told you, what the attorneys have to say is not evidence, and you notice neither side here have raised their hands to tell the truth and nothing but the truth. So your testimony comes from the witness stand.

As the prosecutor in the case I expect to call three, probably four witnesses. I may call more. I have an option of putting on rebuttal witnesses if I want to. You will see that if it happens. Eye witnesses are going to start out with Officer Huston who has worked at Pelican Bay State Prison who is what we call a percipient witness, which means he saw, he was present when the incident happened in 1992 at one of the branches at Pelican Bay State Prison. They call it B Facility. And I will have testimony about what B Facility means and what type of people are housed in B Facility.

The defendant, Mr. Johnson, was in his cell with his cell mate, a person by the name of Butler and that for whatever reason they refused to give up some trays, food trays. That on that date, March the 28th, 1992, Butler and inmate Johnson were in their cell. They had been fed in their cell, and, as I indicated before, for unknown reasons they weren't going to give up their trays.

At that point in time several officers were summoned to go over to the cell and try to talk to them to give up their trays. And it's a mainline production, meaning they have to feed, get back the trays, and they have a lot of people to take care of. Officer Huston will testify that basically there was a couple trays inside the cell and that he and other officers went into his cell along with some other people and talked to them about giving up the trays.

Officer Huston will tell you — and I would suspect Officer Van Berg will tell you basically the same story — that Mr. Johnson had possession of the trays, he was holding on to them, and that in the door of the cell, the actual cell door, there was a little food port door. You can slide one tray at a time through there. And you can't slide two through and you can't slide one with a lot of garbage piled on top, just enough to slide one tray back and forth.

For whatever reason, inmate Johnson, the defendant in this case, was standing in the cell with the trays in his hand and he had had some discussion with the officers about a package. He wanted some package. And he was not going to relinquish those two trays. So basically what happened in the case, as Officers Huston and Van Berg and Walker will testify, is that a sergeant sent some of them over to discuss the matter with inmate Johnson and to try to persuade them basically verbally to give up the tray, "we have got to get on our route, our day's business."

He asked at that point in time to see a sergeant. And the officers will testify that what they told Johnson at that point in time was, "We'll get you a sergeant; we'll have a sergeant drop by and talk to you, but we can't do it right now. We have got our work to do. We have got to finish up what we are doing."

At that point Johnson was going to give up the trays. He was not verbally abusive. He was not physically — didn't appear to be physically dangerous at that point. He was just standing there with his trays. So the officer — and he wasn't too far back from the cell door. So one of the officers, the Officer Smith, signaled to the gentleman who controls — the sectional officer who

1 controls the doors electronically or hydraulically but they are controlled from a different location — go ahead and open up the cell door.

So the cell door was opened a substantial distance, wide enough for somebody to charge out. And behind the door you have Johnson hanging on
5 to the two trays piled with garbage. And basically at that point with Walker in front, Van Berg, Smith was there and Huston was there, their testimony is going to be that Johnson dropped the trays, kind of lowered his head a little bit and charged Officer Walker who was kind of at the head of this line where he can get the job done.

10 At that point in time the officers met him. The approximate location was the doorway to the cell. Stopped him at the door as he tried to approach them rapidly. He was swinging his fists, clenched right fist, that the officers basically pushed him back into the cell. The cells are not that large. Got him on top of a table and subdued him. One officer had handcuffs on one side of
15 him and Mr. Johnson still was swinging, being combative. He was still trying to injure people and they were trying to subdue him. So four or five officers at this point, trying to subdue him and get him cuffed up, handcuffed.

During the course of that melee two officers were injured. One ended up with a broken bone — I think it was a bone chip in his thumb — and was off work
20 a period of time, suffered some injuries. Another officer went down to Sutter Coast Hospital with a shin injury, received a small laceration on his shin.

These are the two counts of battery that I am going to ask you to consider. The people will put on a final witness, probably an officer by the name of Henderson who will testify about a 969B package. It's a package of docu-
25 ments from the prison certified to verify that that person was lawfully in custody at Pelican Bay State Prison at the time. I do have to prove that he was in custody at the time. And it basically establishes the fact that he was in our prison system as well, which is another element that I have to prove.

I would expect at this point in time that would be my case in chief.
30 Depending on how and what the defense puts on, I may call rebuttal witnesses, probably officers or actually two lieutenants, Foster and Kurtz. I will call those two as rebuttal. Thank you.

MR. DEEMER: Reserve.[12]

THE COURT: First witness.

35 MR. CUMMINGS: Officer Huston I believe is outside.

THE COURT: Raise your right hand.

GEORGE HUSTON

called as a witness by the People, after having been sworn to tell the truth, the
40 whole truth and nothing but the truth, was examined and testified as follows:

THE CLERK: Be seated and state your name and address for the record.

THE WITNESS: George Huston, Pelican Bay State Prison.

---

12.   Defense counsel is reserving his right to make his opening statement following the presentation of the state's case. Should he have delayed, or should he have made his statement right now? Most defense attorneys make their opening statement right after the plaintiff or prosecution in order to challenge that version of the case and to make sure that the jury hears both sides. Otherwise, there is a risk that the jury is already convinced by the time the defense begins.

1   *Direct Examination*

Q: *BY MR. CUMMINGS:* Thank you, Your Honor. Sir, what's your occupation?[13]
A: Correctional officer.
5 Q: How long have you been a correctional officer?
A: Six years.
Q: Where are you currently employed?
A: Pelican Bay State Prison.
Q: How long have you worked at Pelican Bay?
10 A: Since November '89.
Q: Was that basically the opening date for the prison?
A: Yes.
Q: So you are part of the original team that started out at the institution?
A: Yes, sir.
15 Q: Sir, were you working in the capacity of a correctional officer on March the 28th, 1992?
A: Yes.
Q: Did you have occasion to come into contact with an inmate by the name of Johnson seated at the other end of this table?
20 A: Yes.
Q: Do you recognize him today?
A: Yes, I do.
Q: What facility was he housed in, do you know?
A: Facility B.
25 Q: What is the significance of Facility B?
A: It's a general population.
Q: As opposed to what, sir?
A: Security Housing Unit.
Q: Is there a transition of inmates from one facility like SHU, Security Housing
30   Unit, to, say, general population?
A: Yes.
MR. DEEMER: Objection. I don't see the relevance.
THE COURT: Sustained.
Q. BY MR. CUMMINGS: Officer, what type of people — what type of inmates
35   are typically housed in Facility B?
MR. DEEMER: Again, objection. I don't see the relevance.
THE COURT: Approach the bench.

(The following bench conference was had outside the presence of the jury.[14])

---

13.   As you read the prosecutor's direct examinations, make a note of what testimony you think tends to establish the essential elements of the prosecution's case against the defendant. For example, at what point does Officer Huston provide testimony to show that the defendant's alleged battery was committed against a person not confined in State Prison?

14.   Here, the bench conference was recorded by the court reporter. If the conference were held off the record, the lawyers must remember to summarize what occurred for the record when the trial goes back on the record. Failure to "perfect the record" may result in an inability to appeal any asserted error in the trial judge's ruling.

1   *THE COURT:*   Where is the relevance?

MR. CUMMINGS: The relevance is the fact that Facility B is a transition facility from Security Housing Unit to General Population and there are more incidents of violence and reported violence in general at Facility B than there

5   is in the General Population. Conversely there is less out of SHU.

MR. DEEMER: Less what?

MR. CUMMINGS: Less reported violence and there is actually less in SHU than there is in Facility B. Facility B is a transition facility where they take people who have been in SHU and kind of mainline them back into the way

10   of General Population.

THE COURT: How does that help the jury?

MR. CUMMINGS: I think where you have an allegation of battery against the officers I think it's important that they understand that the facility which this person was housed is a facility where — it's a facility where people go, they

15   are in transition. I am not going to say in transition from what to what. The fact of the matter is that you have already given these preliminary rulings that you are going to allow Mr. Deemer to go into some issues of "Do you know Officer Walker's propensity" or "Do you know his reputation for violence among other inmates?"[15] I think when you have that kind of testimony com-

20   ing out, I think it is relevant on the issue that in Facility B we have people who are in fact more prone to violence and have proven to be more prone to violence and are in fact in transition trying to get back into the general mainstream of General Population.

THE COURT: I will allow you to establish that this is a maximum security

25   section, but I think the implication that the jury is likely to get from this testimony if you are allowed to go forward with it is in fact he has just been in trial for something coming out of SHU. I don't think you should be allowed to do that because it gets into impermissible character evidence.[16] So if you want to describe physically what Facility B is and if you want to describe what

30   precautions are taken in Facility B, you can do that. But you can't go into what he may have done in prison unless it becomes otherwise relevant. At this point I don't think it is relevant so I am going to sustain the objection.

(The following proceedings were had in open court.)

Q. BY MR. CUMMINGS: Officer Huston, would you tell me physically how Facility B is set up? Are they single-celled, are they double-celled cells?

---

15.   If an advocate knows that an evidentiary problem is likely to arise at trial, the advocate can attempt to get a pretrial resolution of that issue. Motions to suppress illegally obtained evidence are examples of this. A more general procedure involves filing a motion in limine. Motions in limine (meaning at the threshold) can be used to get pretrial rulings on virtually any evidentiary question. Here, the defense has obtained a ruling from the judge that he will admit reputation evidence about one of the officers. Whether raising an evidentiary objection in a motion in limine is sufficient to preserve that objection for appeal is discussed in Chapter Two.

16.   Why is the judge going to admit reputation evidence with respect to Officer Walker, but not character evidence with respect to the defendant? The answer to this question requires analysis of why character evidence is relevant. The testimony regarding Walker's reputation for violence would be relevant to show defendant's state of mind of fear of Walker, whereas the testimony about the defendant's violent character would be relevant to show that he acted in conformity with his character and was the aggressor. As you will see in Chapter Five, infra, under FRE 404 character evidence is normally not admitted to show that a person committed an act in conformity with that character. This is one example of the general principle that relevancy is a necessary but not a sufficient condition for admissibility.

1 A: They are double-celled cells.
   Q: Are they arranged in what sort of a format?
   A: One hundred twenty-eight inmates available per housing unit, eight housing units.
5 Q: This is still a Level IV maximum security prison setting; is that correct?
   A: Yes.
   Q: Sir, do you work or were you working on March the 28th, 1992, in B Facility?
   A: Yes, I was.
10 Q: What was your position or what did you do in B Facility?[17]
   A: Yard officer.
   Q: What's a yard officer?
   A: Yard officer maintains safety and security on the yard, General Population inmates. And in that first response, emergency response.
15 Q: When you say "first response," what do you mean by "first response"?
   A: In an emergency I am designated to respond anywhere in the facility.
   Q: So if there was an incident in B Facility, it would be expected that you would respond; is that correct?[18]
   A: Yes.
20 Q: Are you aware of an incident involving inmate Johnson on March 28th of this year?
   A: It wasn't really an incident.
   Q: What was it?
   A: It was a simple denial of a breakfast tray. When an inmate gets fed in the
25   morning they are supposed to — after breakfast they gave up their breakfast trays and silverware. Floor officer on that day said that inmate Johnson and his cellie, cell mate Butler, were holding their breakfast trays.
   Q: And at some point in time somebody summoned you; is that correct?
   A: Yes.
30 Q: Who was that, do you know
   A: I don't remember on the day. There was several of us and we were told to go over and see if we could get the breakfast trays.
   Q: What did you expect to do that day, did you know?
   A: Go over and simply, "Give us the trays."
35 Q: Talk to them first?
   A: Yeah.
   Q: Is that what you did?
   A: I didn't myself. The officer that ordered him to give up the trays is the one that ordered — gave him the direct order.
40 Q: Which officer ordered him to give up the trays?
   A: Officer Smith.

---

17.   Notice the form of the prosecutor's questions to Officer Huston concerning his work at B Facility and the incident involving the defendant. The prosecutor is using "who, what, where, when, why, and how" questions. A direct examination usually takes the form of short, nonsuggestive questions that, when asked and answered in sequence, tell the witness's story efficiently.

18.   The prosecutor here, and three questions later, is using a common form of "leading question" that explicitly suggests the answer that the advocate is looking for. The tag "isn't that correct" or "isn't it true that" permits only a yes or no answer. Thus, the information that the jury hears is really supplied by the lawyer's question; the witness's response simply confirms or denies it.

1　Q: Was the order to give up the trays once or more than once if you know?

　　A: More than twice.

　　Q: Could you see from where you were at inmate Johnson inside his cell?

　　A: Yes.

5　Q: Physically tell us how he appeared at the time that he was ordered to give up and relinquish those two trays.

　　A: Quiet. Did not say anything except he asked to see the sergeant.

　　Q: Did he indicate why he wanted to see a sergeant?

　　A: No.

10　Q: Did he have anything in his hands as you remember?

　　A: Not at that immediate moment. After the food port was opened, he picked up his trays and acted like he was going to give us the trays.

　　Q: You indicated the food port. Where is the food port located?

　　A: In the middle of the door about waist high.

15　Q: Can you describe it for us?

　　A: It's approximately probably a four-to-five-inch opening. Has a door on it, probably twelve inches wide.

　　Q: It's a hinged door?

　　A: Yes.

20　Q: And that door opens and shuts?

　　A: Yes, and it is locked when it's not used.

　　Q: It is locked when it's not used?

　　A: When it's not used.

　　Q: Normally a person can pass how many trays through a food port opening?

　　A: One.

25　Q: How many trays did inmate Johnson have in his hands?

　　A: He had two trays with disposable garbage on the top of them.

　　Q: Would those two trays with the garbage on top pass through the food port door?

　　A: No.

30　Q: How would a person normally pass the trays through, just slide them through?

　　A: Yes. Officer would unlock the food port and it's got another lock. When you pull down on it and at that time they pass the food tray through and the officer grabs it and takes it.

35　Q: At some point in time it became clear to you that inmate Johnson was not going to slide the trays through the food port door.

　　A: No. When he picked up the trays and brought them to the food port it was not subtle, I guess. He didn't say anything, he was calm, walked up to the door and held the tray.

40　Q: At that point in time did somebody order the door be opened?

　　A: Yes. Officer Smith.

　　Q: And is that an appropriate method to get back the trays?

　　A: Yes.

　　MR. DEEMER:　Excuse me. A, lack of qualifications; B, lack of foundation;

45　　and, C, it's leading.[19]

19.　The objection's references to lack of qualifications and foundation amount to the same thing. Does this witness possess the knowledge to answer the question adequately? Essentially the witness is

1 *THE COURT:*   Are you asking for an expert opinion, Mr. Cummings?
   Q. BY MR. CUMMINGS: Officer Huston, you stated that you have worked as
      a correctional officer at Pelican Bay for six years?
   A: Yes.
5 Q: And during those six years, did you receive special education and training for
      your job?
   A: Yes.
   Q: What was that?
   A: There are training manuals, and training courses for correctional officers on-
10   site and throughout the state that we attend.
   Q: And does this training include the handling of specific problems that inmates
      sometimes cause?
   A: Yes it does.
   Q: And based on this training, do you have an opinion on the proper means to
15   handle situations like inmate Johnson's, that is, on whether it is appropriate
      to open the cell door? Just tell us whether you have an opinion.
   A: Yes I do.
   MR. CUMMINGS: I would offer Officer Huston's opinion now based on his
      special experiences and training at Pelican Bay.
20 *THE COURT:* You may answer.
   Q. BY MR. CUMMINGS: Is opening the cell door an appropriate way to get
      back the food trays?
   A: Yes, on the General Population side it is. If the inmates are General Population
      inmates so they are out of their cells a lot of the time and if they are, what
25   we say, programmed and everything else and they seem calm and everything
      else, well, we — yeah, we get the trays that way, especially when they have
      more than two trays or have two trays with garbage on the top.
   Q: I am going to draw a distinction here between the Secured Housing Unit, the
      SHU inmates, and the General Population inmates. Inmate Johnson was at
30   that point a General Population inmate?
   A: Yes, he was.
   Q: And if this incident had occurred on the Secured Housing Unit side, the other
      section of the prison, would the doors have been opened in this fashion?
   A: Absolutely not.
35 Q: So the procedure is different from your experience whether a person is in
      General Population or is in the Secured Housing Unit?
   A: Yes, it is.
   Q: For inmate Johnson, housing in General Population, this was an appropriate
      way to retrieve the trays, if necessary?
40 A: Yeah.
   Q: Was the door opened?
   A: Yes, the door was opened.
   Q: What happened when the door opened?

---

being asked to offer an opinion concerning the proper operation of the prison system. To do so, he should
be qualified as an expert, who is a specially qualified person empowered under the Rules of Evidence to
offer testimony because of special competence. See FRE 702. Opinions by nonexperts are admissible in
somewhat limited, but very important, circumstances. See FRE 701.

1 A: Inmate Johnson — when the door was opened up inmate Johnson immediately instantly dropped the food trays. He was standing just inside the door, up next to the door. Dropped the food trays immediately and bowed his head, brought up his fists and just tried to come through the door and hit
5   Officer Walker in the chest.

 Q: Where did Officer Walker make contact or where did Johnson make contact with Walker?

 A: In the door. In the doorway after the door was opened. Officer Walker was on the outside of the cell.

10 Q: Do you recall the other officers who were present?

 A: The other officers that I knew that were present were Officer Smith and Officer Walker and Officer Van Berg.

 Q: Were there other officers there that you don't recall by name?

 A: Yes, Officer White was there, but I didn't find that out until after the
15   incident.

 Q: When officers are retrieving food items, trays, et cetera, in General Population are they wearing protective gear?

 A: No.

 Q: What happened when Johnson charged the officers and made contact with
20   Walker?

 A: Officer Walker immediately grabbed him and pushed him inside the cell and inmate Johnson fell back up against the desk area, which is approximately three feet inside the cell.

 Q: What was inmate Johnson doing at that time?

25 A: Combative.

 MR. DEEMER: One moment, Your Honor. I am going to object to that term. It's conclusionary.[20]

 THE COURT: Overruled.

 Q. BY MR. CUMMINGS: Describe for me what you mean by "combative"?

30 A: Swinging his arms, not complying with orders, using his strength.

 Q: What sort of orders were being given to Johnson at that time?

 A: To cuff up.

 Q: What's cuff up?

 A: Handcuff.

35 Q: Standard procedure?

 A: Yes.

 Q: Was there a cell mate in the same cell?

 A: Yes.

 Q: Do you recall his name?

40 A: Inmate Butler.

 Q: What did inmate Butler do, if anything?

 A: Inmate Butler was immediately told to get down by Officer Smith in the cell.

 Q: What does "get down" mean?

---

20. The objection that a question calls for a conclusion is just another way to say that it calls for an opinion. Here the opinion would be a lay opinion, not an expert opinion. But is "combative" a fact or an opinion? What is the difference? Even though the objection is overruled, note how the prosecutor develops the record by having the witness explain what "combative" means.

1 A: "Get down" means hit the floor in a prone position.

    Q: Did he comply?

    A: Yes, he did comply immediately.

    Q: And he was secured, too?

5 A: Yes, Officer Smith restrained him.

    Q: Why was inmate Johnson and inmate Butler secured, handcuffed? What's the purpose?

    A: Because if they are combative or not complying with orders; disciplinary reasons, you know.

10 Q: Officer safety reasons?

    A: Yes, officer safety and security.

    Q: Inmate Butler basically did exactly what he was told to do?

    A: Yes, he did.

    Q: Was there kind of a wrestling or a pushing or a shoving or some sort of an

15   altercation inside the cell?

    A: Yes. Inmate Johnson was not complying. He was swinging, he was kicking, he was using his strength against us. In fact, after we got him pushed up against the desk area, we couldn't get him handcuffed in the cell. So we brought him out of the cell, put him in the prone position outside the cell.

20   He was in the prone position. He wouldn't give up his hands for restraint. I finally got one handcuff on the right wrist. Several orders — he wouldn't give up his left one. He kept it underneath him. When I did get it out from underneath him, he brought — and husbanding his strength he wouldn't let me have his wrists. It took me a little while to get him restrained and in the

25   left handcuff. He was resisting it.

    Q: Using both his hands and his feet?

    A: Both hands and feet.

    Q: Was he saying anything during this period of time?

    A: No.

30 Q: Sir, were you injured in that altercation?

    A: Yes, I was.

    Q: Describe your injuries for us.

    MR. DEEMER: Excuse me. May we approach the Bench at this time?

(The following proceedings were had at the bench, outside the hearing of the jury.)

35 MR. DEEMER: My understanding is that the witness is going to testify that he received a gash and yet he also testifies at the preliminary hearing — and I assume his testimony isn't going to change today — that he doesn't know how he received the injury. So I think this testimony at this point becomes irrelevant.

40 MR. CUMMINGS: I think that's an awkward summary. What he is going to testify to is he received the injuries as a result of this melee. He cannot testify that inmate Johnson slugged him, kicked him or directly caused it. But for the melee he certainly would not have been injured in that fashion. Obviously this witness can testify to what he observed on his own body. He doesn't have

45   to be a doctor or a nurse or anything else to testify what injuries he personally received on his own body, and that's all I am looking for, and whether or not he went to the hospital or went home or returned to work.

1   *THE COURT*:   I would possibly preclude you or limit you in some fashion if
      you attempted to call a doctor.
    MR. CUMMINGS: I have no intention of it.
    THE COURT: He can testify to his own knowledge what he observed on his
5   own body. I am not going to preclude him from that.

(The following proceedings were had in open court.)

    Q. BY MR. CUMMINGS: Officer Huston, where were you injured?
    A: My left shin had a one-inch gash.
    Q: Did you ever seek medical attention for that?
10   A: Yes, they did a triage and then I was sent to Sutter Coast Hospital.
    Q: And you were treated at Sutter Coast?
    A: Yes.
    Q: How long did this whole thing take — or how little time did it take?
    A: Everything happened real fast. I couldn't give you a time on it. Everything was
15   instantaneous from the time the food trays were dropped and Mr. Johnson trying
     to get through the door and I really couldn't give you — several — probably several
     seconds. When the adrenaline is flowing you have no idea how long it is.
    Q: Sir, when you are working as a yard officer as you were that day, do you carry
     a side-handled baton?
20   A: Yes, I do.
    Q: In this incident involving inmate Johnson did you have to — or did you have
     time to remove your side-handled baton?
    A: I did not. At that time I had no time to.
    Q: I take it, then, you were not expecting trouble when the door was being
25   opened.
    A: Absolutely not.
    Q: You were taken by surprise?
    A: Yes, I was.
    MR. CUMMINGS: Thank you sir. Nothing further.
30

Cross-examination

    Q. BY MR. DEEMER: Officer Huston, who at that point unlocked the food
     port?
    A: Officer Smith.
    Q: And then was anything done with the food port prior to the door being
35   opened?
    A: You mean was there anything — it was opened prior to the door being —
    Q: But was it then closed again?
    A: I could not say whether it was or not.
    Q: Now, did any of the other officers at the time you were all at the door — and
40   I take it there is eight or ten officers at the door; is that correct?
    A: I have no idea if there was eight or ten. I am saying there was the four that I
     know of.
    Q: But there were more than four. There were some other officers —
    A: I understand that there was, but I didn't have any identification and know
     who the officers are and how many others.

 1 Q: Hey, I am not trying to trip you. All I am trying to figure out is there were four
          officers there that you know including yourself?
     A: Yes.
     Q: And there were some officers you didn't know?
 5   A: Yes.
     Q: You don't remember what the total number of the other officers were?
     A: No.
     Q: Could it have been as many as eight or ten?
     A: I guess maybe, yes.
10   Q: Now, did any of the officers just prior to the time the cell door was opened
          put on some gloves?
     A: I have no idea. I didn't put any on my myself, no.
     Q: Do you recall any officers putting on — pulling out the side-handled batons,
          PRC 24 or something like that?
15   A: No, I don't recall that.
     Q: Now, when the door was opened — first of all, there is absolutely nothing
          aggressive about the defendant up until the time the door is opened; is that
          correct?
     A: No, there wasn't anything aggressive about him until he dropped the
20   trays.
     Q: Okay. And when the door is opened Walker is standing in front of him?
     A: Yes.
     Q: And at that point the defendant is standing there and he has got two trays in
          his hands and he just drops the trays like that; is that correct?
25   A: Instantly.
     Q: And brought his hands up toward his head?
     A: He brought them up, yeah.
     Q: How were they shaped when he brought them up towards his head?
     A: In a clenched fist.
30   Q: And at that point you observed Walker push him?
     A: I, at that point — he had struck Walker in the chest.
     Q: With what?
     A: With his fist.
     Q: And then Walker pushed him back?
35   A: And Walker pushed him back into the cell.
     Q: And then the melee ensues?
     A: Yes.
     Q: Now, you search inmates' cells frequently, don't you?
     A: In my job once in a while I do.
40   Q: And when you search an inmate's cell, whether he is in General Population
          or in SHU, the first thing you do is get the inmate out of the cell; is that
          correct?
     MR. CUMMINGS: Objection. Relevance.
     THE COURT: Overruled. You may answer.
45   THE WITNESS: If you are going to search the cell, yes, you bring the inmate
          out and — out of the cell.
     Q. BY MR. DEEMER: In your training except when you are forming some sort
          of what they call a cell extraction team, you are never supposed to be in the

1   same room like a closed room, like a cell or a sally port or something like that
      with an inmate, are you?[21]

A: Not in a cell with an inmate. In a sally port, yeah, you are in with the General
      Population inmates.

5 Q: Let's stick with a cell. The reason you don't go into a cell with an inmate is
      because you are afraid something might happen; is that correct?

A: It's safety and security.

Q: So wouldn't the normal procedure of removing these trays have been to order
      the inmates to the cell port to cuff up and remove them from the cell?

10 A: It depends on the circumstances.

Q: All right. How long have you known Officer Walker?

A: Approximately one and a half years.

Q: You weren't at Folsom with him?

A: No.

15 Q: If something is to be removed forcibly from an inmate or an inmate is to be forc-
      ibly moved, isn't the normal way to do it by means of a cell extraction team?

A: If he is to be forcibly removed from his cell?

Q: Either something is to be forcibly removed from him or he is to be forcibly
      moved from the cell. In either instance — and he is in the cell. Isn't the cell

20   extraction team normally the way to do that?

A: If he fails to comply with cuffing up and stuff like that, yes, it could be done.

Q: Prior to opening the cell door you never asked the inmate to cuff up, did
      you?

A: No, not that I — not myself, no.

25 Q: Now, when you opened the door — or excuse me. When the door was
      opened, did you expect that the trays were going to be handed out to you?

A: Yes. Yes, I did think he was going to give the trays to the officer.

Q: Now, in connection with this case did you prepare some sort of a report?

A: Yes, I did a 115, CDC 115 report.

30 Q: And that's a rules violation report?

A: That's a rules violation report.

Q: And that's basically what is done for disciplinary purposes; is that correct?

A: Yes.

Q: Do you have a copy of that with you?

35 A: Yeah, yes, I do.

Q: Could you look at that? Have you got it there?

A: Yes.

Q: On the CDC 115 — and I am asking you to go down one, two, three lines,
      the sentence that begins "The inmates were given repeated orders." Would

40   you read that to yourself?

A: "The inmates were given — "

Q: Just read it to yourself. You don't have to read it to the jury.

A: Yes.

Q: All right. And in that report basically you state that Officer Smith instructed

45   the control booth officer, quote, "to open the door to the cell in order for staff
      to enter and retrieve the trays." Is that correct?

---

21.   What is an extraction team? A sally port? Again, is the lawyer attending to the jury?

1 A: What line are you reading there?
   Q: One, two, three, four, five, six lines down. I think that is the fifth line down. "Officer Smith instructed the control booth officer," quote, "to open the door." Do you see that there?
5 A: Yes.
   Q: So Smith instructed — what you thought at least at that point in time was that staff was going to enter and retrieve the trays; is that correct?
   A: Well, when you say "enter," if I am handing my hand through the door I am entering the cell.
10 Q: But earlier you testified that he was going to hand — you expected the trays to be handed out; is that correct?
   A: Yes, hand them right at the door, yes.
   Q: Now, on the next line down you indicate that Johnson rushed toward Correctional Officer Walker; is that correct?
15 A: Yes.
   Q: Attempting to strike him with clenched fists; is that correct?
   A: Yes.
   Q: Doesn't say any place in there that he actually struck him with a clenched fist, does it?
20 A: What line are we reading here? Yes.
   Q: It doesn't say that, does it?
   A: No.
   Q: And it doesn't say anything in your report about an open food port, does it?
   A: No.
25 Q: It doesn't say anything in your report about who opened the food port, does it?
   A: No.
   Q: Sir, do you remember testifying at the preliminary hearing?
   A: Yes, I do.
   Q: Is it correct to state — you have had an opportunity to review your prelimi-
30   nary hearing transcript, haven't you?
   A: Yes, I did read it.
   Q: By the way, did you discuss your testimony with some of the other officers?
   A: No.
   Q: And is it correct that based on your testimony from the preliminary hearing
35   transcript you don't know how you received the gash in your leg?
   A: No, I don't.
   Q: And, sir, in connection with injuries that you received on the job you get some sort of Workers' Comp; is that correct?
   MR. CUMMINGS: Objection. Relevance.[22]
40 MR. DEEMER: Want me to make my offer of proof in front of the jury or the bench?
   THE COURT: Overruled. You may answer.
   THE WITNESS: Yes. Yes, I do get workmen's compensation.

---

22.   Relevance refers to whether an item of evidence tends to prove the proposition it is offered to prove, and whether that proposition is of significance — is material — to the litigation. Here, the objection is that Workers' Compensation payments have no significance — are not "material" — to the litigation. Relevancy is examined in Chapter Three.

1   *Q. BY MR. DEEMER:*   And officers get a different level of Workers' Comp if
       they are injured by an inmate as opposed to some sort of accidental injury;
       isn't that correct?

     A: Yes.

5   *Q:*   If you are injured by an inmate you get three-quarters of your base pay as
       Workers' Comp. If you just happened to have an ordinary injury on the job
       it's one-half; is that correct?

     A: No. If it's an assaultive by an inmate the first three days I get back on sick
       time. So in other words, if I am out on sick time because of an injury from
10   an inmate, well, then I don't lose those three days' sick time. It's taken off my
       books and it's covered. Doesn't come off my books.

     Q: But if you have been injured on an ordinary type accident, that would come
       off your books?

     A: Yes, the first three days would be on-site injury. The first three days I would
15   lose, okay, and then would be picked up by workmen's comp.

     Q: And there is also a difference in the Workers' Comp rate, too; isn't there?

     MR. CUMMINGS: Same objection. Relevance.

     THE COURT: Overruled.

     THE WITNESS: It's two-thirds pay whether it is one injury or not, whether it's
20   a staff injury from an inmate or —

     MR. DEEMER: No further questions.

Redirect Examination[23]

     Q. BY MR. CUMMINGS: If a person is in General Population is it to the best
       of your knowledge appropriate for food trays to be retrieved in the fashion
25   that they were retrieved in this case? In other words, open up the door a
       little bit.

     A: Yes.

     Q: There was nothing wrong with that?

     A: No. I had a housing unit for a year and a half down there with General
30   Population inmates. They are programmed inmates.

     Q: Tell us what "programmed" means.

     A: Program is they go to work, they are — disciplinaries are very few, they are
       usually not staff assaultive. I don't know how to say this. They are calm
       inmates. They are programmed to prison life.

35   *Q:*   Now, that is very different from somebody who is in another portion of the
       institution that is, a SHU, Security Housing Unit, inmate; is that correct?

     A: Oh, yes, it's a lot different in Security Housing Unit.

     Q: If hypothetically this same incident happened on the Secured Housing Unit
       side of Pelican Bay, which is not where it occurred, if it happened over there
40   would it be appropriate for the correctional officers to order a door opened
       to retrieve the tray?

     A: No.

     Q: Why not?

---

23.   The two parties in this case constantly seesawed back and forth with redirect and recross-
examinations, trying to have the last word. This is quite boring for the jury, and usually develops no new
information. Much of this repetitive testimony has been edited out of this transcript.

1 A: Because they are assaultive to inmates or staff. They are highly disciplinary.
   Q: Is it safe to say that if they are in the other side, the Secured Housing Unit
        side, you are basically expecting trouble all the time?
   A: Yes.
5 Q: Are you expecting less trouble or hopefully none at all when they are in the
        General Population side?
   A: Yes, hopefully, yes.
   Q: What would you have done if inmate Johnson had been in the Secured
        Housing Unit? What would have been appropriate then?
10 A: I would have a vest on. I would have a partner with me before I went to the
        cell. When I picked up the breakfast tray I would open the food port. There
        would only be one inmate up to the food port and he would pass the tray in
        and I would not be standing in front of the food port.
   Q: You take additional precautions?
15 A: Oh, yes.
   Q: It's embarrassing to even ask you this, but are you in any way financially ben-
        efitted by getting injured on the job?
   A: Heavens, no. I have got a scar to prove it, and I don't like my scar.
   Q: That scar came out of this incident?
20 A: Yes, it did.
   MR. CUMMINGS: Thank you sir. Nothing further.
   MR. DEEMER: Nothing.
   THE COURT: Thank you. You are excused. You can either leave or stay, as you
        wish. Next witness.
25 MR. CUMMINGS: Officer Van Berg.
   THE COURT: Come up to the front, please, and raise your right hand.

RICHARD VAN BERG

called as a witness by the People, after having been sworn to tell the truth, the
whole truth and nothing but the truth, was examined and testified as follows:

30 THE CLERK: Be seated in the witness chair and state your name and business
        address for the record.
   THE WITNESS: Richard Van Berg.

Direct Examination

   Q. BY MR. CUMMINGS: Your business address is fine. Pelican Bay State
35   Prison?
   A: Right.
   Q: Officer, what's your occupation?
   A: Correctional officer.
   Q: How long have you been so employed?
40 A: Six years.
   Q: Where are you currently stationed?
   A: Pardon?
   Q: What's your current assignment at the prison?

1   A: B Facilities at Pelican Bay.
    Q: How long have you been at Pelican Bay?
    A: Two and a half years.
    Q: You were there when the institution opened?
5   A: Yes.
    Q: Sir, were you working as a correctional officer on March the 28th, 1992?
    A: Yes, I was.
    Q: Did you have occasion on that day to come into contact with an inmate by
        the name of Johnson?
10 A: Yes, I did.
    Q: Same individual seated at the end of counsel table?
    A: Yes, it is.
    Q: Do you recall where he was?
    A: He was inside of his cell.
15 Q: Was there a cell mate?
    A: Yes, there was.
    Q: Do you recall his name?
    A: Not offhand.
    Q: What is your routine assignment in B Facility?
20 A: I am a search and escort officer.
    Q: Would you tell us what a search and escort officer does?
    A: Searches cells, escorts inmates, delivers 115 rules violations, assists the pro-
        gram sergeant. He has a variety of duties.
    Q: Were you involved in attempting to retrieve some trays from inmate Johnson
25   on that date?
    A: Yes, I was.
    Q: Were you assigned to that or was that your normal duty for that day? Did
        someone tell you to assist?
    A: I was ordered to go to A block and assist in receiving the trays.
30 Q: Had you had any prior contact with inmate Johnson?
    A: No.
    Q: Do you know inmate Johnson at all?
    A: No.
    Q: What other officers were in front of inmate Johnson's cell when you got
35   there?
    A: The only two that I recall were Officer Smith and Walker.
    Q: Were there other officers besides those two and you don't recall the names?
    A: Yes.
    Q: Did you hear Officer Smith make any orders or any commands of inmate
40   Johnson?
    A: Yes.
    Q: What did he order him to do?
    A: He ordered him to return the food trays to him through the food port on
        several occasions.
45 Q: I take it two or more?
    A: Yes.
    Q: Could you observe what inmate Johnson was doing from your position?
    A: From what I could see he was just standing at the door holding his food
        trays.

1   Q: Door was closed at that point?
    A: Yes.
    Q: I am referring to the full cell door now, not the food port door.
    A: Right. The food port was open.
5   Q: Do you recall if the food port door was open?
    A: Yes.
    Q: Did you have a pretty good view of the person behind that door?
    A: Fairly well, yeah.
    Q: You can tell whether or not they are swinging their arms or they look like
10   they might be combative, I take it.
    A: Yes.
    Q: Did it appear to you that inmate Johnson was going to be combative?
    A: No, he was just standing there holding those two trays and had once asked to
        speak to a sergeant.
15 Q: And did you hear anybody reply what would happen as far as getting a ser-
        geant to see him?
    A: He was told that he could see a sergeant but first he had to return the food
        trays.
    Q: Did he say anything?
20 A: No.
    Q: Did he take one of the trays off the other tray and slide it on through the food
        door as ordered?
    A: No.
    Q: He just stood there with the two trays in his hand?
25 A: Yes.
    Q: At some point in time did Officer Smith order the door be opened?
    A: Yes.
    Q: Was the door open?
    A: Yes, it was.
30 Q: Was it open wide enough so that inmate Johnson could charge through if he
        wanted to?
    A: Yes.
    Q: Were you expecting that to happen?
    A: No.
35 Q: Did inmate Johnson — was he verbally assaultive or verbally threatening at all?
    A: No.
    Q: Was he physically assaultive? Did he appear to be physically dangerous at
        all?
    A: No, not at that point.
    Q: When the cell door opened what happened?
40 A: Inmate Johnson just dropped the food trays and rushed, you know, one sud-
        den step towards the door.
    Q: Did he do anything with his hands?
    A: I seen one hand come out through the cell door. I believe it was his right hand
        and it was in a clenched fist. Officer Walker was standing right up against the
45   door so when it opened he was attempting to assault Officer Walker.
    Q: Let me make this clear. Did inmate Johnson make forward motions towards
        Correctional Officer Walker?
    A: Yes.

1 Q: Or did Officer Walker make motions towards Johnson?
    A: No, inmate Johnson stepped towards Officer Walker.
    Q: So he moved forward?
    A: Yes.
5 Q: Did he appear to be attempting to fight or strike Walker?
    A: Yes
    MR. DEEMER: One moment. That's leading.
    THE COURT: Overruled. You may answer.
    Q. BY MR. CUMMINGS: Did you see inmate Johnson strike Officer Walker?
10 MR. DEEMER: Same objection.
    THE COURT: Overruled. You may answer.
    THE WITNESS: Actual body contact, no.
    Q. BY MR. CUMMINGS: Is that because from your position you couldn't see it?
    A: Yes.
15 Q: What did you see Officer Walker do when inmate Johnson moved toward
       him?
    A: The two just came together, Officer Walker had ahold of inmate Johnson
       and they were going back inside the cell.
    Q: Is that appropriate? Is that what a correctional officer should do in that situa-
20   tion is take command of him?
    A: Yes.
    Q: At some point in time did you come in contact with the other officers' hands
       on inmate Johnson?
    A: Yes.
25 Q: Was that inside the cell or outside the cell?
    A: That was outside the cell.
    Q: And why did you get involved at that point?
    A: I assisted Officers Walker and I believe Huston in trying to get inmate
       Johnson's arm behind him so we could place it in handcuffs.
30 Q: And at that point in time was inmate Johnson being combative?
    A: Yes.
    Q: Was he being resistive?
    A: Yes, absolutely.
    Q: Was he complying with the orders that were being given him at that point?
35 A: No.
    Q: Were you injured, sir?
    A: Yes, I was.
    Q: Where?
    A: My left thumb.
40 Q: How?
    A: I'm not sure how it happened.
    Q: In the course of that altercation you were injured, I take it.
    A: Yes.
    Q: Did you seek medical attention?
45 A: Yes, I did.
    Q: Where did you go?
    A: Sutter Coast Hospital.
    Q: Did they tell you that something had happened to your hand?
    A: Yes, I had a bone chip.

1   Q: One of the bones in your hand was chipped?
    A: Yes, sir.[24]
    MR. CUMMINGS: Thank you sir. Nothing further.

Cross-examination

5   Q. BY MR. DEEMER: I have been watching you around the court. Those cow-
         boy boots aren't state issue, are they?
    A: No.
    Q: Sir, you wrote a report in this matter, didn't you?
    A: Yes, I did.
10 Q: You have a copy of that report with you, don't you?
    A: Not with me, no.
    MR. DEEMER: If I could approach the witness, Your Honor.
    THE COURT: Yes.
    Q. BY MR. DEEMER: You will have to pardon my underlining, but I would
15   like to show you your report and see if it refreshes your recollection at all.[25]
    MR. CUMMINGS: I don't believe there has been a question posed that indi-
         cates he does not recall.
    MR. DEEMER: I would just appreciate it if he would review it.
    THE WITNESS: Yes, I'm done with that.
20 Q. BY MR. DEEMER: There is nothing in that report that gives any indication
         about a food port being opened, is there?
    A: No.
    Q: How high up is the food port from the floor?
    A: I'm going to guess probably three and a half feet.
25 Q: And the food port is up high enough so that, for example, if you want to move
         an inmate or have an inmate cuff up that he can basically back up to the food
         port and stick his hands sort of like that; is that correct?
    A: Yes.
    Q: And so basically the food port is probably just a little bit lower than waist high
30   for most people?
    A: Yeah, probably pretty close to waist high.
    Q: Now, who opened the food port?
    A: Officer Smith, I believe.
    Q: And how did he open the food port?
35 A: Take your key and take the padlock off the food port and then open it up.
    Q: And again your report doesn't make any mention about the defendant
         being — requested to pass food trays through the food port, was there?
    A: No.

---

24.   Does Officer Van Berg have personal knowledge of the bone chip in his thumb? He does have
knowledge of what the hospital told him about his injury, but if he testified "They told me I had a bone
chip," it would be hearsay under FRE 801 and would be inadmissible unless it fit within an exception
under FRE 803 or 804.

25.   Is the report admitted into evidence? Should it be? Normally an advocate can "refresh the
memory" of a witness in any fashion that the judge will allow. If one party uses a document to refresh a
witness's memory, the opposing party will be permitted to inspect it, examine the witness on it, and in
many cases admit it into evidence. See FRE 612.

1 Q: Now, as a practical matter while the defendant is standing in front of the door with these — he is standing with two trays in his hand; is that correct?

A: Yes.

Q: If the port is open the trays could just be slid right through; isn't that

5   correct?

A: One at a time, yes.

Q: And of course also if the doors — if the food tray door is open somebody could just reach in and grab a tray fairly easily, is that correct, if somebody handed it to them?

10 A: If it was pushed out to you. I wouldn't advise anybody sticking their hands though there.

Q: Would it be fair to state that most of the inmates are afraid of Officer Walker?[26]

A: That what?

15 Q: That the inmates are afraid of Officer Walker?

A: No.

Q: And you don't know how you sustained the injury that you sustained?

A: No.

MR. DEEMER: No further questions.

20 MR. CUMMINGS: Officer Walker.

BRANDON WALKER

called as a witness by the People, after having been sworn to tell the truth, the whole truth and nothing but the truth, was examined and testified as follows:

THE CLERK: Be seated in the witness box and state your name and business

25   address for the record, and could you also spell your name, please?

THE WITNESS: Brandon Walker and I am at Pelican Bay State Prison.

Direct Examination

Q. BY MR. CUMMINGS: Thank you. Sir, what's your occupation?

A: Correctional officer.

30 Q: How long have you been a correctional officer?

A: Just over five years.

Q: What prison are you currently assigned to?

A: Pelican Bay State Prison.

Q: How long have you been at Pelican Bay?

35 A: Since April of '91.

Q: Where did you come from, what institution?

A: Folsom.

Q: Sir, were you a correctional officer on duty on March the 28th, 1992?

A: Yes, I was.

40 Q: Did you have occasion on that date to come into contact with inmate Johnson?

---

26.   How would the witness know this? What objections can be made to this question? Why was none made?

1   A: Yes.
    Q: Do you recognize inmate Johnson today?
    A: Yes, I do, sir. He is sitting over next to Mr. Deemer.
    Q: Before March the 28th, 1992, the day of this incident, did you know inmate
5   Johnson?
    A: No, I did not.
    Q: Had you had any prior contact to your knowledge with inmate Johnson at
         Pelican Bay?
    A: Not to my knowledge.
10 Q: What about at Folsom?
    A: Not to my knowledge.
    Q: What's your assignment at Pelican Bay or what was your assignment on
         March the 28th?
    A: B Facility, 7 block, floor.
15 Q: What's a floor officer do?
    A: We do just cell searches. We have to take inmates to R and R for packages or
         for picture ID, we take them there. Basically it's an escort position.
    Q: Is feeding part of your normal duties?
    A: Oh, yes, sir.
20 Q: Actually takes up quite a bit of time?
    A: Well, for cell feeding it takes about an hour to feed both buildings. And then
         if we are feeding in the dining room it takes anywhere from an hour and a
         half to two hours.
    Q: When you say you worked normally 7 Block, is that the same block that
25   inmate Johnson is on?
    A: No, sir.
    Q: I believe he is in 8 Block; is that correct?
    A: That is correct.
    Q: Were you sent to inmate Johnson's cell that day?
30 A: Yes, I was.
    Q: Who sent you?
    A: Sergeant Kurtz.
    Q: What were you told?
    A: I was told that he had two food trays that he would not give up and we were
35   to go and relinquish those trays.
    Q: How did you expect to do that, do you know?
    A: Well, ideally it would have been to open the food port and have him hand us
         the trays.
    Q: When you arrived on March the 28th, what other officers were present out-
40   side Johnson's cell?
    A: My partner. He came. The two yard officers, Smith and Huston, they came.
         And Officer Van Berg. So there were five of us.
    Q: Do you know whether any of those officers normally work 8 Block or were
         they all sent?
45 A: They were all sent from the yard.
    Q: When you arrived did you make — did you order inmate Johnson to give up
         the trays?
    A: No.

1   Q: Did you hear somebody else do it?
    A: Yes.
    Q: Who?
    A: Officer Smith.
5   Q: How many times, roughly?
    A: Three or four. He had been sitting on his bed and then when he started tell-
         ing him to give up the trays then he stood up and stood at the door. So three,
         four times maybe.
    Q: Was inmate Johnson saying anything to any of the officers at that time?
10 A: No, he indicated that he had a 602, which is an appeal form that the inmate
         fills out for a sergeant, and then he was requesting to see a sergeant at that
         time.
    Q: Did you hear anybody respond to his request to see a sergeant?
    A: Yes, Officer Smith did.
15 Q: What did he say?
    A: He said that he would be permitted to see the sergeant but that we needed to
         have the food trays at that time.
    Q: Why couldn't you just stop the whole operation and get him a sergeant right
         away?
20 A: Because sergeants on the yard have got other duties and if we were to set
         precedents in calling a sergeant over every time there was a small problem,
         then sergeant — we wouldn't be able to operate with just one sergeant in the
         yard.
    Q: Somebody ordered the door to be opened?
25 A: Yes.
    Q: Who?
    A: Smith.
    Q: And when Officer Smith ordered the door be opened, you were the first one
         who would normally have contact with whoever was behind it?
30 A: Right, because of my position where the door was opening. As the door
         opened I was number one.
    Q: What were you expecting to happen?
    A: I was expecting to get the trays and then to leave.
    Q: I take it you had your own job to do that day?
35 A: Yes.
    Q: Did you carry on that day a side-handled baton?
    A: Every day, yes.
    Q: In this incident did you pull your side-handled baton?
    A: No, I did not.
40 Q: Did you use your side-handled baton in any fashion?
    A: No, sir.
    Q: If you are expecting trouble, officer, do you normally pull out your side-
         handled baton if you are anticipating it?
    A: If I am anticipating it, yes.
45 Q: Were you anticipating trouble on this day in this incident?
    A: No, I was not based on — he was not showing any signs of any kind of tension
         or anger or anything. He was merely standing with two trays with trash all
         over them.

1   Q: That's what I want to go into next. Was he being verbally abusive to
         anybody?
    A: Not at all.
    Q: Did he give you indications from his body language that he was going to be
5   aggressive or going to be violent?
    A: None.
    Q: The door opened up. What happened next?
    A: He dropped the food trays.
    Q: Then what happened?
10 A: Then he lunged towards me.
    Q: Did he make contact with you?
    A: Yes, he did.
    Q: What part of his anatomy struck what part of your anatomy?
    A: He attempted to strike me in the facial area with his fists, but as soon as he
15   lunged towards me and basically, you know, grabbed my body, then I was
         able to turn him back around and push him back into the cell trying to put
         him on the floor.
    Q: Is that what you are trained to do?
    A: Yes.
20 Q: Is that what you are supposed to do to take control of the situation?
    A: Yes.
    Q: And when you got your hands on him did he go backwards or what
         happened?
    A: No. We were kind of almost kind of like dancing. We were kind of wrestling
25   standing up and trying to get him to go to the floor and the whole time he
         was still trying to punch me. You know, he was punching me in the side.
    Q: You two were basically face to face real close together?
    A: Right, holding on to one another.
    Q: And you are doing your best to hold on to him and he is attempting to strike
30   you?
    A: Yes.
    Q: And he is striking you?
    A: Yes, he is. And kicking.
    Q: And kicking? Were there other officers behind you?
35 A: Yes, there was.
    Q: Did several of them go into the cell also?
    A: Yes.
    Q: At some point in time did you actually end up on the ground?
    A: Yes, I did.
40 Q: Did somebody get a handcuff on him?
    A: Before he left the cell he had handcuffs.
    Q: One or both, do you remember?
    A: He had both.
    Q: Before he left the cell?
45 A: Uh-huh.
    Q: Was he resisting being handcuffed?
    A: Ever since — ever since he lunged towards me. See, when we are assaulted
         out there it's our job to, you know, communicate as much as possible telling

1   him what we want them to do. And in this case we were all telling him to get
    down and his cellie was possibly a problem. So one of the officers went in
    and told him to stay back and he resisted the whole time.

    Q: When you say "he," you are referring to Johnson.
5   A: Inmate Johnson, yes.
    Q: Were you injured to the point of having to receive any outside medical
         treatment?
    A: No, I was not.
    MR. CUMMINGS: Thank you sir. Nothing further.

10   *Cross-examination*

    Q. BY MR. DEEMER: Sir, you prepared a report in this matter, did you not?
    A: Yes, I did, sir.
    Q: And you got it with you?
    A: Yes.
15 Q: And you got an opportunity to review it today, haven't you?
    A: Yes.
    Q: That report doesn't mention anything about food ports, does it?
    A: Well, or cell ports.
    Q: I am talking about your report, the one you signed.
20 A: Yes, sir, I am looking at that right now. No, it does not indicate.
    Q: And when the door gets open you say the defendant dropped the trays; is that
         correct?
    A: Yes, yes, he did.
    Q: About how far from the door is he when the trays dropped?
25 A: An inch. Well, the trays — we have to count for the distance that composes
         the trays was about maybe twelve inches plus a couple more. He was within
         a foot and a half.
    Q: And the door opens and the trays drop; is that correct?
    A: That is correct.
30 Q: Do you recall seeing his head drop?
    A: No, I don't recall that.
    Q: Do you recall what he did with his head?
    A: No, I don't.
    Q: You say Johnson's hands come up; is that correct?
35 A: I'm sorry?
    Q: Johnson's hands come up?
    A: His hands come up simultaneously as he is lunging toward me, yes.
    Q: And how far out the door does he get?
    A: Just about — he wasn't all the way out of the door.
40 Q: You came here from Folsom; is that correct?
    A: That is correct.
    Q: And regardless of what your beliefs are about what your behavior patterns
         are, isn't it fair to state that inmates are generally afraid of you?
    MR. CUMMINGS: Objection. Lack of foundation.
45 THE COURT: Overruled. You may answer.

1 *THE WITNESS*:   I don't know the fact that an inmate is afraid of me. Why
       would they be afraid of me?[27]
   Q. BY MR. DEEMER: Well, I will put it this way. Are you aware of the fact that
       inmates are afraid of you because you tend to be, say, a little bit more physi-
5   cal with them than they think you should be?
   A: No, I don't think that's accurate.
   MR. DEEMER: I have no further questions.

Redirect Examination

   Q. BY MR. CUMMINGS: Sir, why did you transfer from Folsom to Pelican
10   Bay?
   A: The area.
   Q: I take it it was your choice?
   A: Oh, yes.
   Q: Do you know what a 602 is?
15 *A*:   Oh, yes.
   Q: What is it?
   A: It's an inmate appeal form.
   Q: Is that where the inmate typically could write down grievances regarding an
       officer?
20 *A*:   Sure.
   Q: When an inmate grieves an officer on a 602 that's an actual document,
       correct?
   A: Yes, it is.
   Q: Are you made aware of that?
25 *A*:   I am supposedly. If it pertains to me, yes.
   Q: And by CDC policies are you required to respond to that?
   A: Within five days.
   Q: To an actual written response?
   A: Yes.
30 *Q*:   To your knowledge had you had any other contact with Johnson anywhere in
       the CDC system or outside the CDC system before March 28th of this year?
   A: Prior to the day that he refused to give up his food tray, I don't think I have
       ever met the man.
   MR. CUMMINGS: Thank you. Nothing further.
35

Recross-examination

   Q. BY MR. DEEMER: Emotionally exciting though, isn't it?
   MR. CUMMINGS: Objection. Relevance.
   THE COURT: Overruled. You may answer.
   Q. BY MR. DEEMER: It's emotionally exciting, though, isn't it, when you are
40   involved in an altercation?
   A: Well, is a victim emotionally excited?
   Q: Well, it's emotionally exciting when you win, isn't it?
   MR. CUMMINGS: Object as being argumentative.

---

27.   How would he know the answer to that question? Why was this allowed?

1   *THE COURT*:   Sustained as argumentative.

    Q. BY MR. DEEMER: When you get into one of these altercations with an inmate is it fair to say your adrenaline gets pumped up pretty good?

    A: Oh, absolutely. And then understand this, it's not my desire to go and get

5   into a physical altercation because not only is that not my job, but I could get hurt. And so when I am asked by the department to go and do something that is going to require possibly physically taking something away or restraining them, I have possibilities of getting hurt and that's not what my intentions are.

10 Q: When you go to — when you went to the door you are not dressed the way you are now, are you?

    A: Oh, no.

    Q: You got a jumpsuit on of some sort. Let me rephrase it. Some sort of utility type fatigues on; is that correct?

15 A: I might have. If we are not on lock-down then I am not entitled to wear the jumpsuit-type clothing.

    Q: Do you recall whether you had a jumpsuit-type clothing on or fatigue clothing?

    A: I was not wearing fatigues, no.

20 Q: What were you wearing that particular day?

    A: I don't recall.

    Q: But regardless of what you are wearing when you go in there, your name tag or some sort of a name thing is on.

    A: Absolutely.

25 Q: Your shirt?

    A: That's part of the uniform, yes.

    Q: And those cell doors, they got little holes in them, don't they?

    A: Yes.

    Q: When you stand up close to the cell door you can look outside and you can

30   see what's there?

    A: I'm sure I wouldn't have to stand even right up to the cell door. You can probably see me if I was standing in the day room with my name.

    MR. DEEMER: No further questions.

(Court was adjourned at 4:05 P.M., to be resumed at 9:00 A.M., Tuesday, the 28th
35 day of July, 1992.)

    Crescent City, California
    Tuesday, July 28, 1992, 9:00 A.M.

    THE COURT: The record will reflect that all jurors, counsel and defendant are present. You may call your next witness.

40 *MR. CUMMINGS*:   Officer Smith.

Stephen Smith

called as a witness by the People, after having been sworn to tell the truth, the whole truth and nothing but the truth, was examined and testified as follows:

1 *THE CLERK:*   Please be seated and state your name and business address for the record.

THE WITNESS: Stephen Smith, Pelican State Prison.

Direct Examination

5 *Q. BY MR. CUMMINGS:*   Sir, what's your profession?

A: Correctional officer.

Q: How long have you been a correctional officer?

A: Eight years.

Q: What institutions have you worked at?

10 A: I worked at the Idaho State Prison for two years, San Quentin for three and a half years, and I have been in Pelican Bay for approximately three years.

Q: Are you part of the start-up team up here?

A: Yes, sir.

Q: Sir, were you a correctional officer employed in that capacity on March the 15 28th, 1992?

A: Yes, sir, I was.

Q: And did you have occasion to come into contact with inmate Johnson and actually Johnson's cell mate Butler on that date?

A: Yes, I did.

20 Q: Under what circumstances?

A: I was — I'm a yard officer. I was out on a yard and my supervisor asked me, wanted me to go over to A block and pick up a tray. Apparently Mr. Johnson didn't want to give up his food tray that morning out of his cell. So I went over to pick up the tray.

25 Q: And where was inmate Johnson in the cell when you first saw him?

A: He was sitting on the end of the bunk, the lower bunk.

Q: Where were the trays if you remember?

A: The trays were approximately less than a foot inside the door sitting on the floor next to the wall.

30 Q: How many were there?

A: There was two trays with a pile of garbage on them.

Q: Would those trays pass through the food port door if they wanted to?

A: If you took the tray, took the garbage off and everything one at a time they would.

35 Q: If you were going to pass it through the food port door would you have to pass it lengthwise or could you pass them crosswise?

A: Lengthwise.

Q: So I take it the food port door is somewhat narrow.

A: I really can't tell you the exact width of it. I have never measured one, but it 40 would be difficult to put a tray through sideways.

Q: What exactly did you order inmate Johnson to do?

A: Well, if I may, I didn't order him at first. What I did is I walked up. He was sitting on the end of the bunk. He had a piece of paper in his hand. As I arrived at his cell I said, "How are you doing? What's up? Are you having a bad day?" 45 Mr. Johnson at that time stood up. He said, "I need to see a sergeant, man." I said, "Well, you can see a sergeant later on. Right now I am here to pick up those trays. Sergeant asked me to get them."

1   At that time he walked over towards the door. He had some paperwork in
his hand, a 602, a green piece of paper. Started to come towards the door and
he never spoke again. He reached down, picked up the trays, both trays with
a pile of garbage. He had them both in his hand like in this manner. He had

5   the piece of paper underneath holding all of that in his hands. He walked
over to the door. And it's a normal procedure — as I walked up to the door I
had already opened up the port —

Q: The food port door?
A: Yes, sir. I had opened that up. It's a little slot about this wide, that high. I

10   already opened that up as I arrived and he stood there in front of the door.
He never spoke again, not another word.

Q: Did you ask him anything else?
A: Yes, I asked him at that time, "Can I have the trays?" He stood there looking
at me.

15   Q: No response?
A: No response, just stood there looking. I asked him a second time, "Are you
going to give me the trays?"

Q: Let me show you this photograph that has been marked Exhibit 1 for identification. Can you tell me what that is a photograph of?

20   A: It's the port door.
Q: Do you mean the food port door like the one in inmate Johnson's cell
door?

A: Yes.
Q: How do you know?

25   A: It looks just like the food port doors in all the cells in B facility.
Q: Is it a fair and accurate picture of the food port door?
A: Yes.

MR. CUMMINGS: I move the admission of People's Exhibit 1.[28]

MR. DEEMER: This photograph may be misleading, Your Honor, because it

30   does not show the width of the cell door. It does not show how wide the food
port door is, to any scale.

MR. CUMMINGS: There has already been testimony that the port door is
twelve inches wide, wide enough for the tray. The jury knows this, so the
photograph is not misleading.

35   THE COURT: I'll admit it in this situation since there has been testimony about
its width already. Exhibit 1 is received in evidence.

Q. BY MR. CUMMINGS: Now, Officer, if the door to this food port is open,
and you are standing in front of it, you can pass your trays through here just
by sticking them through?

---

28.   Generally speaking, to have an exhibit admitted into evidence the attorney must first have
the exhibit marked for identification by the court reporter. By marking an exhibit for identification and
then by referring to the identification number or letter when the exhibit is used, the attorney can ensure
that the record accurately reflects which exhibit is being discussed. The attorney must then introduce
the necessary foundational testimony to show that the exhibit is what the attorney claims it to be. Then
the proponent offers the exhibit into evidence ("Your Honor, we now offer Exhibit 1 into evidence"),
and makes sure that the trial court rules on its admissibility. The requirement of authentication is a prerequisite to the admissibility of evidence, and thus it is for the judge to decide whether the conditions of
admissibility have been satisfied under the terms of FRE 901(a). Authentication of all kinds of exhibits is
discussed in Chapter Four.

1   A: One at a time. It was obvious that he had such a load in his hands that he
         could not pass them through the port.
    Q: Did it appear to you that inmate Johnson was acting aggressively towards the
         correctional officers?
5   A: Well, when we first arrived no, sir. He had a very docile attitude. He was not
         aggressive. That's why we went with the procedure we did. There was no vul-
         garities, which is the normal — you usually get, "Well, I want to see so and so;
         you are not doing this and that." There was no argumentativeness out of him
         at all. When I explained to him, "You will see the sergeant after you give me
10   the trays, I will tell the sergeant to come and talk to you," he got up, walked
         over in a very docile manner.
    Q: If an inmate had been acting violently, verbally abusive, kicking, spitting,
         screaming, would it then be appropriate to have the door opened?
    A: No.
15 Q: What is the difference?
    A: Well, if the inmate is violent, we just can't open the door up and have him
         attack us. So if he is already in his cell, we are not going to open the door up
         just to get, you know, a bunch of trouble.
    Q: Do you know why inmate Johnson wanted to see a sergeant?
20 A: I found out later. I didn't know then. But apparently he had a 602, something
         about some property. He wanted his property right now or something and I
         don't work the unit so I wasn't involved in that. I found out later.
    MR. DEEMER: Objection. Hearsay and not the best evidence. If there is going
         to be testimony about the 602 report it should be admitted on its own.
25 MR. CUMMINGS: The exact contents are not important here, Your Honor.
         He had a complaint. That's all we're testifying to.
    THE COURT: Testimony about the complaint in general is permitted. Detail
         about the contents is not important.
    Q. BY MR. CUMMINGS: So, tell us in general what a 602 is.
30 A: A 602 is an appeal process that the convicts use if there is a discrepancy, any
         type of discrepancy. They can utilize it if they don't get enough toothpaste,
         if they think they want some toothpaste. If an officer is disrespectful they can
         utilize a 602, which is an appeal process. We have four different levels on that.
         It will come to you directly, which is an informal level, which you respond
35   directly to that convict. If he has a complaint against me, I file or I give him
         a written answer on that. It is processed through the department. We have a
         system where it is logged in a log and then once — if he is not satisfied with
         my response, he sends it on up the line. There are four separate levels.
    Q: So there is a whole appeal process for inmates to air their grievances?
40 A: Yes, sir.
    Q: Is the point of that to cut down on friction between correctional officer staff?
    A: Absolutely. That is the main purpose of the 602 process is to alleviate any
         problems at a lower level.
    MR. CUMMINGS: Thank you. Nothing further.

45   *Cross-examination*

    Q. BY MR. DEEMER: Sir, is it fair to state that some inmates at least have a cer-
         tain fear of officers' use of force and violence, whether or not that is justified?

 1 A: I'm sure they probably feel that way.
    Q: And is it also fair to state that if an officer starts into a cell with the presence
          of other officers that it would be reasonable for an inmate to assume that
          some sort of force and violence is going to be imposed upon him?
 5 MR. CUMMINGS: Objection. Lack of foundation.[29]
    THE COURT: Overruled. You may answer.
    THE WITNESS: I don't think so. We are on a GP.
    Q. BY MR. DEEMER: You are what?
    A: It's a General Population and many times we go in the cells with the inmates
10   there.
    Q: But basically the more officers — talking of the type of situation we are talk-
          ing about here. The more officers that are outside the door, the more likely
          it is for an inmate to believe that because of his refusal when that door is
          opened, what is going to happen?
15 A: Whenever we have a problem we always send over a lot of officers. That is
          not an unusual thing. And we do not open the door up and rush in there and
          do anything. In the three years that I have worked B Facility, I have never cell
          extracted anyone on second watch, not one time.
    MR. DEEMER: One moment. No further questions.
20 MR. CUMMINGS: Nothing.
    THE COURT: Thank you. You are excused. You can leave or stay as you wish.
          Next witness.
    MR. CUMMINGS: Yes. Ruth Taylor.
    THE COURT: Come up to the front and raise your right hand.

25   RUTH TAYLOR

    called as a witness by the People, after having been sworn to tell the truth, the
    whole truth and nothing but the truth, was examined and testified as follows:

    THE CLERK: Be seated in the witness chair and state your name and business
          address for the record and could you spell your name for us, please.
30 THE WITNESS: Sure. My name is Ruth Taylor and my business address is
          Pelican Bay State Prison.
    THE COURT: You may examine.

                                    Direct Examination

    Q. BY MR. CUMMINGS: Thank you, Your Honor. Miss Taylor, what's your
35   occupation?
    A: I am a correctional case records specialist.
    Q: Tell us what your job basically entails.
    A: Analyzing commitments, calculating release dates, normally case work for
          the inmates.
40 Q: Keeping track of how many days they gain or they lose and when they are
          due out?

___

29.   Under FRE 701, a lay witness's opinion must be rationally based on personal knowledge.
Could Officer Smith know what is reasonable for inmates to assume? As it turns out, he does have personal
knowledge on which to base his opinion and defense counsel probably regrets asking this question.

1   A: Yes, sir.
     Q: Do you have with you today the C File — and I will ask you in a minute what
           a C File is. But do you have the C File of inmate Johnson?
     A: Yes, I do.
5   Q: What is a C File?
     A: It's a collection of all of his records during the period that he was incarcerated
           with the Department of Corrections under that CDC number. It is main-
           tained by the Department of Corrections and contains all original records,
           except medical records, pertaining to that inmate's incarceration, including
10   information on sentencing, classification actions, disciplinary hearings and
           grievances, and parole. Information related to an inmate's movement in and
           out of the prison system is summarized on a sheet attached to the cover of
           the file.
     Q: I am going — do you know what a 969B package is?
15   A: Yes, I do. It is a collection of certified copies of documents from the C file,
           including abstracts of judgments and the chronological case history.
     Q: This has been marked People's Exhibit No. 2 for identification and would
           ask you to identify that if you could, please.

     (Exhibit 2 was marked.)

20   A: Yes.
     Q: Does it show abstracts, court abstracts?
     A: Yes, it does.
     Q: What is an abstract?
     A: That is the document the courts provide committing an individual to the
25   Department of Corrections.
     Q: Are those true copies, certified to be true copies of the ones in the original C
           File?
     A: Yes, they are.
     Q: And to the best of your knowledge are they identical to the ones in the C
30   File?
     A: Yes, they are.
     MR. CUMMINGS: Thank you, ma'am. Move People's 2 in.
     MR. DEEMER: Objection, yes, sir, to pages — well, considering the cover let-
           ter page 1, would be pages 2 and 3, the chronological listings, in view of the
35   fact there is great varieties of inadmissible hearsay.
     THE COURT: Any reason why those pages should not be included?
     MR. CUMMINGS: It will be stipulated that in any case he is a state inmate.
     MR. DEEMER: We'll stipulate he is an inmate.
     THE COURT: Both sides are stipulating the defendant was a state inmate on the
40   date of this alleged offense, which would have been March 28th, 1992?[30]

---

     30.   Parties can stipulate that certain facts are not subject to dispute for purposes of deciding their
case. Such an agreement relieves the party with the burden of proof from having to submit evidence on
the stipulated fact. And the opponent may be willing to stipulate to facts that are uncontrovertible or that
might require evidentiary proof that is even more harmful or embarrassing to their own case. Because
stipulations eliminate the need for proof, their enforcement can be justified on grounds of efficiency.
     There is recent authority that a court can require the prosecution in a criminal case to accept a
stipulation offered by the defendant, and thus to forego proof of the stipulated fact, when that proof is not

1 *MR. CUMMINGS:*   With that stipulation I will withdraw Exhibit 2.

THE COURT: Ladies and gentlemen, you should regard the fact that the defendant was confined as an inmate in the state prison on March 28th, 1992 as being conclusively true because of the stipulation without any further proof
5   as to that fact.

MR. CUMMINGS: Thank you. Nothing further.

MR. DEEMER: I have no questions.

THE COURT: You are excused. You may leave or stay as you wish.

MR. CUMMINGS: No further witnesses, Your Honor.

10 *THE COURT:*   People rest?

MR. CUMMINGS: I am resting.[31]

(The following proceedings were had outside the presence of the jury.)

THE COURT: Let the record reflect that the jury has left the court room. We still have left the attorneys and defendant.

15 *MR. DEEMER:*   Motion to dismiss at this time.[32] The information charge is battery on Huston and a battery on Van Berg. Battery is described as the unlawful application of force upon the person of another. Van Berg does not know how he got injured. Huston does not know how he got injured. There is no testimony — no testimony from anybody that any of these injuries were
20   inflicted by the defendant. There is no testimony about any of his feet coming in contact. There is no testimony about what he had on in the way of shoes. There is no testimony of his fists coming in contact. And frankly I never felt there was enough evidence to even bring this case past the preliminary hearing stage. Judge Schott did.

25   But we are at trial now and there is simply not enough evidence before the jury from which the jury can conclude beyond a reasonable doubt that a battery has been committed upon these officers. They could have scraped themselves going through a door. Anything could have happened. And there is absolutely no evidence whatsoever of the defendant striking either Officer
30   Van Berg or Officer Huston, and I don't think you can submit this case to the jury at the present time. You are just asking them to totally speculate as to what took place.

MR. CUMMINGS: Sometimes I wonder whether Mr. Deemer and I actually sat through the same trial and heard the same evidence. I find it somewhat
35   amazing when he says there is no evidence of any direct striking. There is no evidence and that is true of any direct striking. No one can testify truthfully

---

probative of any other fact or issue in the case. But a party may not be required to forego proof when this would impair the presentation of the party's case or would be relevant to other issues. The effect of stipulations on the application of FRE 403 is discussed in Chapter Three.

31.   The prosecution has now completed its case. The court will entertain various motions from defense counsel; after that the defense will present whatever case it chooses to. Before reading the remainder of the transcript, think about how the prosecution has proved its case and about what you might do were you defense counsel.

32.   At the close of the prosecution's case, the defense may move for judgment of acquittal based on the insufficiency of the evidence to sustain a conviction. The test in California, which is fairly standard, is whether there is "substantial evidence" — that is, evidence that is reasonable, credible, and of solid value — such that a reasonable trier of fact could find the defendant "guilty beyond a reasonable doubt" on each element of the offense. People v. Johnson, 26 Cal. 3d 557, 606 P.2d 738 (1980). The same test is applied by an appellate court deciding an appeal that alleges insufficiency of the evidence.

1   that this right blow caused injury to my left hand or et cetera. However, what
      the testimony is very clear on and is clear from multiple witnesses is that
      the fracas continued, resistance continued. He was kicking. Multiple officers
      testified he was kicking. Multiple officers testified he was swinging over and
5   over again with a clenched fist.
          A couple of officers viewed it a little differently. One saw him duck down
      as to put his head down. A couple officers did not see it that way. It's just the
      perception of different officers perceiving the same incident slightly differ-
      ent, an honest recitation of what the facts were.
10   You have a person who is obviously of a stocky build, of a firm stature,
      and he is for some reason hell-bound that he is going to go ahead and do
      what he can to make his point for whatever reasons. Drops those trays and
      moves forward at a rapid motion. Multiple officers testified in an aggressive
      fashion. Defense attorney would have you believe that Walker walks in and
15   subdues him. That's not what the testimony was.
          Walker's testimony was that "he was on top of me pushing me back for
      a while; I was on top of him pushing him back for a while." He even said
      it was "kind of like dancing" at one point and basically the whole time the
      order is to "get down," none of which are being complied with. I mean what
20   standard are we going to put on correctional officers in a prison? Are we
      going to say, "Unless you can come in and say this person kicked me in my
      left thumb and because of that I know I was injured"? These officers know
      they were injured because inmate Johnson caused a nothing incident to
      grow into a significant injury with two injuries, both of which required some
25   hospital treatment. Submit it.
THE COURT: The motion is denied. I agree that the case is weak, particularly
      with the two counts that are charged. Had there been a charge of an assault
      against Officer Walker it would be almost a slam dunk.[33] There is plenty of
      evidence to suggest to the jury that count. But that was not charged. As to the
30   two who were charged I think the jury can draw the inference because there
      was ample testimony of the defendant striking and kicking in the course
      of this struggle. They could draw the inference that it was kicks or blows
      from the defendant causing injury to Officers Huston and Van Berg. So the
      motion is denied.[34]
35 MR. CUMMINGS: Your Honor, People have a motion at this time basically to
      amend and conform the information to the facts as they were deduced dur-
      ing the trial. That would be Count 3, Penal Code Section 4501.5, the victim
      being Walker.
    MR. DEEMER: Your Honor, I think it's a little bit late for that motion. Number
40   one, the district attorney has rested. Prior to that he might have made the
      motion. Secondly, the real problem is there really isn't any testimony to sup-
      port that allegation in the 995. Motions to attend — Mr. Cummings did the
      preliminary hearing in this matter and he is the one that did the charging,

---

33.   So why wasn't the defendant charged with assault on Walker?
34.   Consider the prosecution and defense theories of what evidence is necessary to sustain a
conviction for the crime of battery. Wouldn't there likely be case law on this point that should be helpful
to the court? Why didn't either lawyer refer to any? When you read the judge's final charge to the jury,
notice whether the court gives the jury any instructions that are helpful in answering the question "what
is a battery."

1   and I think that if that's the way he feels at this point in time, that — I mean
       he has simply charged — there is just no way that he should be allowed to
       add Count 3 at this point in time or to amend it.
       THE COURT: Well, there is no showing of why that could not have been done
5   in a timely fashion. Apparently the facts were out front in the beginning, at
          least at the time of the hearing. So the motion to amend is denied. Anything
          further before we hear the defense case?
       MR. CUMMINGS: No, Your Honor.
       MR. DEEMER: No, Your Honor.
10   THE COURT: Return the jury to the courtroom, please.

       (The jury was returned to the courtroom.)

       THE COURT: The jury has returned to the courtroom. Both attorneys and
          defendant are present. It is the defense case, Mr. Deemer.
       MR. DEEMER: Thank you. Ladies and gentlemen of the jury, it's my oppor-
15   tunity at this time to outline to you basically where I expect the defense case
          is going to go. And again, you never know what witnesses are going to testify
          to sometimes so I may end up being surprised. But essentially what I believe
          took place is this.[35] Is that the defendant was notified that a package had
          arrived — that he was aware of the fact somehow or other that a package had
20   been sent to him by his family. A substantial period of time goes by.
             The first thing that happens is that apparently the wrong Johnson is
          taken down to get the package. To get the package the inmates in General
          Population have to go to what they call R and R, which I understand stands
          for release and receiving or receiving and release or something of that sort. I
25   wonder if there is some sort of analogy with R and R in the service.
             So apparently around the 12th of March the wrong Johnson goes down
          to R and R to get the package. The next day — and probably most of you
          remember this; it was the 13th of March — the electricity goes off and there
          was some delays. Now, the officer that's in charge of doing the R and R rou-
30   tine and escorting inmates out to get the package had to go on vacation. So
          he leaves a note in the sergeant's office or in the office in this unit, which the
          defendant watches this note written and gets stuck up on one of those little
          post-em slips to go down and get the package.
             This officer goes on vacation and this drags on and drags on. The defen-
35   dant says "I want to see a lieutenant or a sergeant I can get my package." That
          never happens. Finally on the 28th he withholds the tray, which I agree is
          disobedient. He is asked to give up the tray.
             Now, essentially everything that you have heard up until the time that
          the defendant drops the trays is consistent with the defendant's recollection
40   except one or two things. Number one, the defendant does not recall the tray
          slot being opened and is standing there waiting for the tray slot to be opened
          in order to slide the trays through the slot.
             The second thing is that he has this recollection of Officer Walker plac-
          ing gloves on just before the doors open. And the third thing is that the

       35.   It is actually improper for a lawyer to express a belief as to what happened. Why might that be
    so? Why, in any event, did the state not object at this point?

1   defendant has been incarcerated as you have heard since around 1983 or '85
         and he knows Officer Walker, knows who Officer Walker is. Officer Walker
         came up here from Folsom and he knows what Walker's reputation is. At
         least among the inmates Officer Walker has a reputation for pounding on
5   inmates.

         So there he is standing with the trays in his hand. Walker is on the other
         side. He can obviously identify him because it says Walker on the name tag.
         And the door opens and instead of the tray slot opening, the door opens and
         he figures he is going to get pounded. He drops the trays, drops his head,
10   puts his hands up over his head, and as the officers testified, the melee
         ensues.

         The defense testified that to his knowledge he never, ever came in con-
         tact with Officer Huston or Officer Van Berg, which is really curious because
         so far they have — and I doubt that it will come back to this, but neither of
15   them testify as to any contact by them between them and the defendant in
         terms of force. And the only officer he comes in contact with is this Officer
         Walker until after he is escorted out of the cell, at which place some addi-
         tional incidents take place. But it wasn't any of the officers that got battered
         at that time.

20   There are two other inmate, possibly three other inmate witnesses. One
         of them is the defendant's cell mate, whose recollection of the incident is
         somewhat different from the officers and who I believe in essence is going
         to testify that Officer Walker came in, just piled through the door and the
         defendant ended up getting beaten. The other inmate is an inmate who is
25   in an adjacent cell who could see the crowd of what they believed is eight or
         ten officers outside the door and see this incident take place. There is — one
         of these two inmates, I'm not sure which, was with the defendant I believe
         at some point in time prior to this incident and observed Walker engaging
         in some, shall we call it, aggressive conduct towards another inmate outside
30   a kitchen area and then some comments made by either Walker or Walker
         and Van Berg afterwards. And which goes to basically what he thinks is going
         to happen when the door opened.

         Now, what I got to have you understand is this, is that I'm not trying
         to establish that Walker is a bad guy or is an aggressive officer in this case.
35   The key thing is this, if you have reason to believe that you are going to be
         assaulted you can do something to defend yourself. And in essence I believe
         what the testimony is going to show is that the defendant had this belief that
         when this door opens he drops — I mean he is standing there totally not
         aggressive, dropped the trays, okay, ducks his head and does the most normal
40   thing that all of us would do under those circumstances, puts his hands over
         his head to avoid getting beat.[36]...

GEORGE BUTLER

called as a witness by the Defendant, after having been sworn to tell the truth, the
whole truth and nothing but the truth, was examined and testified as follows:

36.   What do you think of the style and effectiveness of this opening statement? Has defense counsel personalized his client? Has he effectively summarized the facts concerning the defense of self-defense
and presented them as a memorable story or theme?

1 *THE CLERK:* Could you state your name for the record, please.
     THE WITNESS: George Butler.

Direct Examination

    Q. BY MR. DEEMER: Mr. Butler, you are an inmate out at Pelican Bay,
5   right?
    A: Yes.
    Q: And the jury is going to know this anyhow. You are out there because you are
      convicted of a felony of some sort?[37]
    A: Yes.
10 Q: What kind of felonies have you been convicted of?
    A: Robbery.
    Q: Anything else?
    A: Battery.
    Q: And do you know Mr. Johnson?
15 A: Yes.
    Q: How do you know him?
    A: He was my cell mate.
    Q: How long was he your cell mate?
    A: Three months.
20 Q: And where was he your cell mate?
    A: In Pelican Bay B Facility, 8 Block.
    Q: And do you remember an incident taking place with him on or about, say,
      towards the end of March sometime?
    A: Yes.
25 Q: Where did that incident take place?
    A: In his cell.
    Q: Do you recall — I take it you got fed in the cell that day; is that correct?
    A: Yes.
    Q: Why were you fed in the cell?
30 A: Because we was on institutional lock-down.
    Q: Institutional lock-down?
    A: Yes.
    Q: What's that mean?
    A: They was having problems out off the main facilities and for institutional
35   security reasons they felt the best to feed us in our cells.
    Q: And did you get fed in your cells that morning?
    A: Yes.
    Q: Did somebody come around to pick up the trays?
    A: Yes.
40 Q: Do you know whether or not the trays were turned over?
    A: Yes.

---

37.   FRE 609 provides that felony convictions may be admitted to impeach the character for truthfulness of any testifying witness. Why would inmate Butler's commission of the crimes of robbery and battery have anything to do with his truthfulness on the witness stand at this trial? The defense could make a motion in limine seeking a ruling that Butler's convictions should not be admissible under Rule 609. If this is not successful, the defense will often bring out the convictions on direct examination — as was done here — to minimize the impact on the jury.

1   Q: They were or weren't?
    A: No.
    Q: And do you know why the trays weren't turned over?
    A: Yes.
5   Q: Can you tell the court why — or the jury why?
    A: Because we had a problem. We was having a problem with the cell in which
        my cell mate felt the need to talk to the sergeant, you know, a higher, you
        know, correctional officer other than a floor officer.
    Q: What was that problem?
10 A: My cell mate had a package up in R and R. They continuously played around
        with him and wouldn't give him his package and which is a known proce-
        dure is go to the higher person in the chain of command. And he continu-
        ously asks the floor officer can he speak to a sergeant, which the floor officer
        continually denied and ignored him.
15 Q: How long had this problem been going on about a package?
    A: About 30 days.
    Q: Would you tell the jury what R and R is?
    A: It's receiving and release. It's where if you get mail packages it comes to there
        and they got to inspect and everything. They will call you up there when
20   your property is ready to come get it.
    Q: And do you know — do you know how Johnson got notified there was a pack-
        age of some sort?
    A: Yes. In the beginning of the month they told him that he had a package up
        there, but they want to send it back home because that they didn't have a
25   proper form on the top of the box. So they told him to send the address and
        everything back to R and R. But about 20 days later he filled the 602 — that's
        a document that you form when you have a grievance with the correctional
        facility. And they wrote him back and said that they would talk to him about
        it. And they told him his package has been sitting up there for like 20, 30
30   days, and they say they would give it to him and he continuously asked the
        correctional officers about it and they just ignored him.
    Q: How often are you allowed to get packages?
    MR. CUMMINGS: Objection. Relevance.
    THE COURT: Overruled.
35 THE WITNESS: I believe every 90 days, 90 days to six months, I believe.
    Q. BY MR. DEEMER: Ninety days to six months?
    A: Yes.
    Q: What kind of packages? These packages come from your family?
    A: Yes.
40 A: What do they send you?
    A: Shoes, sweat suits and thermals, you know, little food to eat.
    Q: Little what?
    A: Food, little cookies and chips, Kool-Aid.
    Q: And on the day this incident took place was it an officer that you asked to be
45   taken back out initially?
    A: Yes.
    Q: What was the next thing that happened?
    A: He asked us to get our trays up. And my cell mate said, "I would like to speak
        to a sergeant." And the officer said, "Give us the trays." The officer didn't say,

1   "Well, I will go get a sergeant." He said, "Give me the trays." And then my
    cellie said, "I want to talk to a sergeant." And the officer just closed the door
    to the cell and say, "You guys will be sorry for this," and walked off.

Q: Then did some other officers appear?

5 A: Yeah, about 20 minutes later we sitting in the cell and about like — it was
    about seven to twelve officers walked inside the building with their gloves
    and everything on, you know, and came to the door and said, "Give us the
    trays." And my cellie, he walked up to the door, they cracked the door open
    and ran up in there.

10 Q: How many times do you recall when the officers were there at the front of the
    door, how many times do you recall somebody asking for the tray to be given?

    A: They only said it one time.

    Q: Do you recall whether the cell port was open or closed at that time?

    A: The door to the cell?

15 Q: The port.

    A: It was closed.

    Q: Did you ever see the cell port open?

    A: No.

    Q: And when the door was open what happened?

20 A: They rushed in. They just rushed in.

    Q: What did your cellie do?

    A: He was like — they had him held — like three or four held him. They rushed
    me and pushed me to the back of the wall and told me to get down.

    Q: Did you see what happened after that?

25 A: No. Then they picked me up and they said, "Let's take him out." They had
    him handcuffed and they was grabbing him by his arms and they said — I
    think he had a cut or something on the side. They said, "This must be a
    weapon." And the MTA was laughing about it. In the sally port they was
    banging him up against the wall, and he pushed my head against the wall

30 and took us to the — outside in front of the program office.

    Q: All right. Where was Johnson cuffed up to the best of your recollection?

    A: In the cell.

    Q: Now, do you know Officer Walker?

    A: Excuse me?

35 Q: Do you know who Officer Walker is?

    A: No. I believe he is a tall officer. I don't really —

    Q: And when you saw — have you ever — excuse me. When you saw the number
    of officers you saw outside the door, what did you think was going to happen?

    MR. CUMMINGS: Objection. Relevance. Calls for speculation.

40 THE COURT: Overruled. You can answer.

    THE WITNESS: I knew they was going to rush up in there.

    Q. BY MR. DEEMER: That was what was in your mind?

    A: Yes.

    MR. DEEMER: No further questions.

45   *Cross-examination*

    Q. BY MR. CUMMINGS: Mr. Butler, how long had you lived with your cell
    mate, Mr. Johnson?

 1 A: I think about three months.
    Q: Are you pretty good friends with him?
    A: Yeah, he was all right.
    Q: Do you know whether or not Mr. Johnson has any gang affiliation?
 5 A: No.
    MR. DEEMER: Objection. That's irrelevant. Highly prejudicial.
    THE COURT: The no answer will stand. However, it's not relevant.
    Q. BY MR. CUMMINGS: Sir, do you have any gang affiliation?
    A: Yes.
10 Q: What is it?
    A: I'm a Crip.
    MR. DEEMER: Well, again there is some case law just came down. Counsel
        knows that is clearly not admittable under these circumstances.
    MR. CUMMINGS: I will do it here or I will do it at the side bar.
15 THE COURT: Approach the bench.

    (The following proceedings were had outside the presence of the jury.)

    MR. CUMMINGS: I believe Lieutenant Stokes is the one who can testify to
        the fact that he has knowledge, I find out today, that Mr. Johnson is also a
        Crip. That is also typical to put fellow gang members of the same gang in
20   the same cells.
    THE COURT: How is he going to confess that he is a Crip?
    MR. CUMMINGS: Through intelligence gathering techniques. I'm not sure
        exactly how.
    MR. DEEMER: You haven't provided me with any discovery on this.
25 MR. CUMMINGS: I just found out today.
    THE COURT: Intelligence gathering techniques other than hearsay?[38]
    MR. CUMMINGS: Well, certainly if he asked the person and he admitted it, it
        would be an admission. I would have an exception to the hearsay.[39]
    MR. DEEMER: But the problem is that whether or not they are gang mem-
30   bers at this stage of the proceedings is really totally irrelevant and highly
        prejudicial.
    MR. CUMMINGS: No, it is not. It is not irrelevant because what a gang expert
        is I believe Lieutenant Stokes will testify that gang members testify in a fash-
        ion that is helpful to other gang members and that's also been common
35   knowledge of the jury.[40] And probably don't even need an expert for that.
    MR. DEEMER: First of all, if you were to ask my client if he were a gang mem-
        ber he would simply deny it. Secondly, if you were a gang member based
        on what other gang members — based on what I know about and they had
        confidential information sufficient to establish that — based on what I know

---

    38.   Lieutenant Stokes does not appear to have firsthand knowledge that inmate Johnson is a gang
member, as would be required by FRE 602. Therefore, he would be relating hearsay if he stated that his
"intelligence sources" had told him that Johnson was a Crip.
    39.   As you will see in Chapter Eight, statements made by parties, in this case by inmate Johnson,
are exempted from the general prohibition against hearsay under FRE 801. Thus if Johnson himself told
Stokes that he was a Crip, Stokes could testify about this statement to the jury.
    40.   Do you think the behavior of gang members is well known to the public? Why would it be well
known to this particular jury?

1   about the handling of these matters, it wouldn't be a General Population. He
would be in SHU.

MR. CUMMINGS: Pure speculation.

MR. DEEMER: It's not speculation because that is their policy and I mean —

5   MR. CUMMINGS: This gentleman has an admitted gang affiliation and he is
in GP.

THE COURT: If you can show that this defendant has admitted to some officer
that he is a member of the same gang as this witness, you might be able to make
it, other than by hearsay. But certainly if it's going to be the usual way that they

10   determine they are gang members just by confidential informants, they can make
administrative decisions based on that, but that's not admissible in court. So you
have established this defendant is a member of the gang and the defendant is —

MR. DEEMER: If he proposes to go with somebody else — other than an admission, if it is based on some sort of confidential arrangement —

15   MR. CUMMINGS: That has already been ruled on. I am clear on the rule.

THE COURT: All right.

(The following proceedings were had in open court.)

Q. BY MR. CUMMINGS: Mr. Butler, you already indicated that you have been
or at least you are a member of the Crips; is that correct?

20   A: Yes.

Q: What is the Crips?

A: An organization in Los Angeles.

Q: What kind of organization?

A: A neighborhood protecting organization.

25   Q: Is "a gang" a fair term to apply to that or not?

A: No, that's not a fair term.

Q: Sir, when you were in your cell — do you recall what day this happened by
the way?

A: Saturday. It happened on Saturday.

30   Q: Do you know what month?

A: It was May or March the 28th.

Q: March the 28th is the date. And on March the 28th when this incident
started to happen where were you in your cell?

A: I was sitting at the desk.

35   Q: An officer earlier testified that you were sitting either — I think you testified you were sitting either at the desk or on a bunk. Does that sound
possible?

A: Yes, 'cause I was at the desk.

Q: So the officer would have been truthful about that; is that correct?

40   A: Yes.

Q: The officer, one of the officers also testified that when the incident actually
started that you stood up for a short period of time; is that correct?

A: Yes.

Q: So the officer would have been truthful about that; is that correct?

45   A: Yes.

Q: The officer, one of the officers testified that you were given a command the
same way that you said you had been to get down and the officer testified that
you complied fully. Is that what you did, exactly what you were told?

1 A: Yes.

Q: Is that accurate?

A: Yes.

Q: So the officer is being truthful about that; is that correct?

5 A: Yes.

Q: The officer testified the way they are trained in their procedures require them to basically secure you or handcuff you until the incident is over and then release you. Is that what happened?

A: To me, yes.

10 Q: To you, correct?

A: Yes.

Q: So the officer was truthful in that line of questioning; is that correct?

A: Yes.

Q: You indicated that you heard your cell mate request a package; is that

15   correct?

A: He requested to talk to the sergeant.

Q: About a package.

A: Yes.

Q: And what was the response of the officers at that point?

20 A: When they came to the door they had the gloves and everything on. They came up, they said "give us the trays." And my cellie says, "Can I talk to a sergeant" "Give us the trays." I bent and my cellie bent over to the doors. And there was no talking until they rushed in there hollering "get down, get down."

25 Q: Did your cell mate at some point in time drop the trays in his hands?

A: He didn't have time to touch them. When he bent over, the door opened up.

Q: Did he have the trays in his hand?

A: I don't believe so.

30 Q: Is that because you were in the back of the cell and couldn't see everything?

A: No, I was standing — the reason why I was standing up is because when they say "give us the trays" I was going to attempt to give them the trays. He was in front. So when he bent over I stood and that's when the door opened up.

Q: Did you see your cell mate raise either one of his two arms?

35 A: No.

Q: Did you see your cell mate make a fist?

A: No.

Q: Did you see your cell mate swing at any of the officers?

A: No.

40 Q: Sir, from the position that you were in inside the cell did your roommate, your friend, Mr. Johnson, did he kind of duck his head down?

A: He bent over to grab the trays, of course.

Q: You are saying he did not have his trays in his hands; is that correct?

A: That's correct.

45 Q: How many trays were on the floor in front of him?

A: Two.

Q: Was there some garbage piled up on top of them?

A: No, food.

Q: Food or whatever. Was there a mound of something on top of them?

1 A: No.
   Q: Can you put two food trays through the food port door in the cell door at the
        same time?
   A: Yes.
5 Q: You don't have to feed them out one at a time?
   A: No.
   Q: And if there is some garbage piled on top, some paperwork, wrappers, what-
        ever, some disposable garbage on top, can you feed them through that food
        port door?
10 A: Yes, you would have to compact it down a little bit.
   MR. CUMMINGS: Thank you sir. Nothing further.
   MR. DEEMER: No questions.
   THE COURT: You are excused. Thank you. Next witness.
   MR. DEEMER: Call inmate Green.

15   MICHAEL GREEN

called as a witness by the Defendant, after having been sworn to tell the truth, the
whole truth and nothing but the truth, was examined and testified as follows:

THE CLERK: Would you state your name for the record and spell it, please.
THE WITNESS: Michael Green.

20   *Direct Examination*

Q. BY MR. DEEMER: Mr. Green you are an inmate at Pelican Bay; is that
     correct?
A: Yes.
Q: And you are in there because you have been convicted of a felony. The jury
25   is going to know this anyhow so go ahead and tell them what the felony is.
A: Murder.
Q: Any others?
A: (No audible response.)
Q: And do you know Johnson, Mr. Johnson?
30 A: Yes.
Q: Did you know him around the end of March 1992?
A: Yes.
Q: Do you recall an incident taking place either — well, excuse me. Where did
     you live in relationship to where he lived?
35 A: In the next cell.
Q: Do you recall an incident taking place in connection with attempting to get
     a food tray from him sometime?
A: Yes.
Q: Do you recall what date that was?
40 A: No.
Q: Do you recall what time of day it was?
A: The morning.
Q: Do you have any recollection of what day of the week it was?

1   A: No.
    Q: First of all, do you recall how many officers you could see outside his cell?
    A: About eight.
    Q: And what did you observe those officers do?
5   MR. CUMMINGS: Objection. Vague as to time.
    Q. BY MR. DEEMER: Well, when you first observed the officers, what did you observe the officers do?
    A: Come to Johnson's cell.
    Q: In front of the cell, yes.
10 A: They was talking to him.
    Q: Do you recall what they said?
    A: No, I was in the vent.
    Q: You were what?
    A: I was listening in the vent.
15 Q: What did you hear?
    A: They had asked him to give him the tray.
    Q: And did he say anything?
    A: Yeah, he was going to give them the tray.
    Q: Then how were the officers that were outside — did you take a look to see
20   how they were dressed?
    A: They was in —
    Q: What were they wearing?
    A: Police uniforms.
    Q: After he said something about giving the tray, then what happened?
25 A: One of the police, they didn't care. They just went to get it anyway.
    Q: Now, do you know who Officer Walker is?
    A: Yeah, I know him.
    Q: Did you see him there that day?
    A: Yeah, I seen him.
30 Q: How long have you known him?
    A: Just since he has been over there.
    Q: In where, Pelican Bay?
    A: Yeah, since I have been in Pelican Bay.
    Q: Did you ever know him at Folsom?
35 A: I never been to Folsom.
    Q: Do you have a fear of Officer Walker?
    A: Yeah.
    Q: Why is that?
    A: Because I hear he is, you know, a bad cop.[41]
40 Q: When you say he is a "bad cop," you mean what?
    A: That he is no good, he sets inmates up and, you know, he don't go by the policy of Pelican Bay.
    Q: I am having a hard time understanding.

---

41.   In questioning inmate Green, is defense counsel seeking to prove that Officer Walker is, in truth, a "bad cop" who roughs up inmates? Or, is he seeking to prove that Walker has a bad reputation and that, whether true or not, this reputation causes inmates to fear him? The first purpose would be to prove that Walker was aggressive and acted consistently with his character, inadmissible under FRE 404. The second would be reputation evidence used to prove effect on Johnson's state of mind. Keep this distinction in mind as you read the testimony of inmate Johnson, and of Lieutenant Stokes later in the transcript.

1   A: He doesn't go by the policy of Pelican Bay.

      Q: All right. And do you know — have you ever seen him rough anybody up?

      A: No.

      Q: What about Officer Van Berg, do you know him?

5   A: Yeah.

      Q: Do you know what his reputation is amongst the inmates?

      A: Same thing.

      Q: And do you recall any discussion between officers and inmate Johnson with respect to a sergeant?

10   A: Yeah, he had asked — he had been trying to see the sergeant for his package prior to the events several days and on that day and before all the doors came, but they kept denying him.

      Q: Then after the officers went into the cell, when they came back out again did you see anything?

15   A: Yeah, they had him handcuffed, pulling his hair. They had him bent over, pulling his — how they grab his hands.

      Q: Did they move him past your cell or in some other direction?

      A: Just go straight out.

      MR. DEEMER: No further questions.

20   *Cross-examination*

      Q. BY MR. CUMMINGS: Mr. Green, you indicated that you have previously been convicted of a murder; is that true?

      A: Yeah.

      Q: First or second degree?

25   A: First.

      Q: You said that was your only felony conviction?

      A: Yeah, it is.

      Q: Did you go to trial or did you plead?

      A: I went to trial.

30   Q: At the same time you went to trial were you charged with Count 2, an assault with a deadly weapon on the person, use of a firearm.

      A: That's all in with the murder.

      Q: But you were convicted of that, too, weren't you?

      A: Yeah, everything.

35   Q: Were you convicted also of burglary at first degree?

      A: Yeah.

      Q: All at the same time?

      A: It's all during the same offense.

      Q: What's your term you are serving, sir?

40   A: Life sentence.

      Q: You indicated that you — let me go back a little bit. You indicated that you did hear the officers asking for trays; is that correct?

      A: Yes.

      Q: And how many times did they ask?

45   A: I can't remember.

      Q: Once, twice, three, four times?

1 A: I don't remember.
   Q: Was it more than once?
   A: I don't remember.
   Q: How good of a position are you in to hear when you got your ear up to that
5   vent?
   A: All I got to do is jump up on the sink and put my ear to the vent and I can
       hear what goes on in the next cell.
   Q: Pretty darn well?
   A: Pretty darn well.
10 Q: You indicated that you personally expressed some concern, some fear regard-
       ing Officer Walker; is that true?
   A: Uh-huh.
   Q: What are you basing it on?
   A: What am I basing it on?
15 Q: Yeah. You testified that you never saw him rough anybody up; is that
       correct?
   A: Right.
   Q: So this is stuff —
   A: But I had an experience with police that do that sort of thing.
20 Q: But you are not talking about Officer Walker, are you?
   A: No.
   Q: You are talking about some other policemen.
   A: Yeah.
   Q: You basically have a fear or a concern with a lot of cops, a lot of policemen
25   about getting roughed up, don't you?
   A: With anybody?
   Q: I think the answer to that probably is how would you answer that? Do you?
   A: I mean if I hear you use unprofessional cop, of course.
   Q: Are you personally scared, concerned for your own safety around probably
30   most cops?
   A: No, not most cops.
   Q: Around a certain percentage of them?
   A: Just the ones I know don't go by the procedure.
   Q: And had you ever been roughed up by Officer Van Berg?
35 A: No, but I seen him in action.
   Q: Do you know what Van Berg looks like?
   A: No, I know what he looks like.
   Q: Tall, short?
   A: Short.
40 MR. CUMMINGS: Thank you, sir. Nothing further.

Redirect Examination

   Q. BY MR. DEEMER: But it is common knowledge amongst black inmates
       that Officer Walker as — you people that Officer Walker is prone to beat on
       you; is that correct?
45 A: Uh-huh.
   MR. DEEMER: No further questions.

1   *MR. CUMMINGS*:   Nothing.
     THE COURT: Anything further of this witness?
     MR. DEEMER: No, sir.
     THE COURT: You may step down. The next witness.
5   *MR. DEEMER*:   Call the defendant.

JAMES JOHNSON

called as a witness by the Defendant, after having been sworn to tell the truth, the whole truth and nothing but the truth, was examined and testified as follows:

     THE CLERK: Please state your full name for the record.
10   *THE WITNESS*:   James Johnson.

Direct Examination

     Q. BY MR. DEEMER: Mr. Johnson, you are an inmate at Pelican Bay State
         Prison?
     A: Yes, sir.
15   Q: Are you — or obviously you are there because you have been convicted of a
         felony.
     A: Rape.
     Q: How many times?
     A: Once.
20   *MR. CUMMINGS*:   Say that again.
     THE DEFENDANT: Once.
     Q. BY MR. DEEMER: And back sometime in February or March was there a
         problem concerning a package of some sort?
     A: Yes, there was.
25   Q: And would you explain to the jury what that problem was?
     A: Well, February my family and them send me a package. The package — I
         didn't know that the package was there in the institution until the institution
         sent me a little form and let me know that they had the package. But they say
         the package was improper to issue to me because the fact that the package
30   didn't have a form on top of the package. So they wouldn't let me have the
         package. But instead the officer that was working down there, I wrote a 602
         out to the officer and he wrote me back and let me know I could come down
         there and we can settle the difference over the package. He stated this to the
         officer that was working on floor to bring me out. But instead of bringing me
35   down there they brought this other Johnson down there in my place because
         they didn't see fit to use the numbers which we go by, C numbers, D num-
         bers and things like that in prison.
             Now, by them not doing that and just going by the last name there was a
         mistake made. So they sent the wrong guy down there. When I come back I
40   talked to the floor officer and floor officer let me know that my package was
         down there and he would make an effort to get me down there on time. That
         was on Friday. But on occasion they get me down there they couldn't get me
         down there because there was so much going on. Friday he wrote out a note

1   and he stuck it on the window. I am right there in the office with him. He
     stuck it on the window and he stated on the note for the next officer to come
     on to take me down on R and R.

          I am asking all the officers that's in the building that know about the note
5   that he left in there, let me go down and get my package. Now, they tell me,
     "We can't let you go down there now; we got the lights went out on us; we
     can't let you go down there. So we try next Friday." And that next Friday
     continued on and continued on and continued on until so many Fridays.

          Now, I started asking the floor officer to see a sergeant. They wouldn't let
10   me see a sergeant, too. I asked them over and over again to let me see a ser-
     geant and the sergeant never come see me. So I found out that my package
     had been setting down there 27 days after that. You know what I'm saying?
     So now nobody is making no efforts to let me get my property. You know
     what I'm saying?

15   So what I do is at that Friday they had an incident in the building, build-
     ing eight. They had an incident where another convict cut another convict
     with a razor. That put us on lock-down. We can't go nowhere. We can't do
     nothing. No moving or nothing.

          So now that Saturday before that incident happened I asked them about
20   a sergeant and he told me no. So that Saturday came along. I asked the floor
     officer that morning about seeing the sergeant. He said no. I took the trays
     and I hold the trays.

MR. CUMMINGS: Objection, Your Honor, at this point. No question
     pending.

25 Q. BY MR. DEEMER: So Saturday morning you held the trays, right?
     A: Uh-huh.
     Q: What time do you guys get fed?
     A: We got fed around seven.
     Q: And does somebody come around to get the trays?
30   A: Yeah.
     Q: Who comes around to get the trays?
     A: Floor officer.
     Q: When you are being fed how does he get the trays?
     A: He come by and you can unlock the tray slot to receive trays.
35   Q: And what did you tell him when he unlocked the tray slot?
     A: I told him I would like to see a sergeant. He said, "No, you ain't seeing no
          sergeants." So I say, "I am going to hold these trays until I see a sergeant."
     Q: Then what did he do with the tray slot?
     A: He locked the tray slot back and he said I was in trouble and he walked to
40   the next cell and picked up their trays and walked out the block. Then when
          he came back about 20 minutes, 30 minutes later, he came back with at least
          12 officers. When they come in the building, Walker is in front of all the
          officers.
     Q: When they come up, where is Walker standing? Do they come up to the cell
45   door?
     A: Yeah.
     Q: Who was in the lead?
     A: Walker.

1   Q: Do you know him?
    A: Yes, I do.
    Q: How long have you known him?
    A: I been knowing him ever since Folsom.
5   Q: Did you ever have contact with him there?
    A: I had contact with him and I know of other inmates that had contact with
         him, too.
    Q: And does that — did that cause some sort of apprehension to you?
    A: Yes, it does.
10 Q: Could you explain to the jury what apprehension your prior association and
         knowledge of Walker caused in you?
    A: The officer as he claimed to be is not — he is not a good officer at all. He give
         you this one side of him. He will give you this one side of him and then the
         next time you see him is another side that came out in him and he is violent.
15   He is a violent officer.[42]
    Q: What did you think would happen to you when Walker showed up?
    A: I thought — what I thought was going to happen did happen. When he
         opened up that door and ran in on him, he assaulted me.
    Q: Did the officers come up to the door of the cell?
20 A: Walker was the only officer. It wasn't no Smith, there wasn't no Huston. It
         wasn't no Van Berg. It wasn't none of them guys. Walker was the only guy
         that came and ordered — they say Smith ordered the officer open up the
         door. Smith did not order officer to open up the door. It was Walker that
         ordered them to open up the door.
25 Q: Did anybody talk to you — before they opened the cell door did anybody talk
         to you about giving up the trays?
    A: Walker asked me — he asked me and my cellie — we both in the cell. He
         says, "Are you going to give up the trays?" I gets up off my bed and go and
         pick up the trays. As soon as I get ready to pick up the trays, the door come
30   open and Walker run in on me.
    Q: Was the cell port open at any time?
    A: No.
    Q: What do you do when Walker comes in on you?
    A: There wasn't nothing I could do but cover myself up because I already knew
35   what was coming.
    Q: What happened?
    A: Walker come up in there socking me with the gloves that he had on.
    Q: And how long did that go on?
    A: That went on for about a good two seconds.
40 Q: Then what happened?
    A: Then all the rest of the officers came in, they come in the cell, and they
         was all like grabbing me over this way, grabbing me over that way. And then
         when they did get me on the ground and gets me handcuffed, it wasn't I was
         resisting the officer. I wasn't resisting no officer at all.
45 MR. CUMMINGS: Objection.
    Q. BY MR. DEEMER: At some point they got you on the ground?

---

42.   Again, consider what the defense is seeking to prove: that Officer Walker is in fact a violent
officer, or that inmate Johnson has reason to believe that he is, and therefore fears him?

1 A: Yes.
   Q: They described you as resisting.
   A: No, wasn't no resisting.
   Q: What happened?
5 A: Once Walker ran into the cell on me and have me on the table, me off the table, put me on the floor, and handcuffed me right away. It can't be no more than three seconds for them to do all that.
   Q: Then what happened?
   A: They took me out the building. Van Berg had my hair behind like this, pull-
10   ing my hair. Took me out the section, took me right there on the side of the section right where the entrance is to coming into the building, and Van Berg took my head and smashed it into the wall.
   Q: Did he say anything?
   A: He said he been wanting to do that for a long time.
15 Q: Did he use any expression which you might think is impolite in front of a jury? Do you remember that?
   A: (No audible response.)
   Q: It's all right if you don't. Did you ever have any contact with Officer Huston.
20 A: I never had no contact with Officer Huston.
   Q: Other than Mr. Van Berg grabbing you by the head —
   A: I never had no contact with Officer Van Berg.
   Q: Did you ever kick Officer Van Berg?
   A: No, I never touched him. I never touched Officer Huston neither.
25 Q: You indicate that you had some other — you say you have known Walker for a long time.
   A: Yeah.
   Q: How long had you known him at Folsom?
   A: It's New Folsom. He was there up until the time he came here, which was
30   two years ago. And when he was there he had the same type of attitude that he got here.
   Q: While he has been up here have you ever observed him, either he or Van Berg — have you ever observed him lay hands on an inmate?
   A: Yes, I have.
35 Q: Where did that take place?
   A: In the kitchen.
   Q: What happened then?
   A: He snatched a Hispanic guy up off the seat, took him out the kitchen, drug him by the hair out of the kitchen in the front by the sally port and jumped
40   on the guy.
   Q: Then when they came back do you recall a statement being made?
   A: Yes, Van Berg said that the guy that he did like that had assaulted the staff, and it wasn't like that.
   Q: Did that — how did that make you feel?
45 A: At the time I looked at it like this: If they did him like that, who would be next? You know what I'm saying? And he showed — it shows in the action that anybody could have been next, you know? That's not no frequent thing. It's not nothing that a person — a person has to be taught to treat somebody

1   like that. And it had to have been in all this time to do this. This is not no
       "I'm going to do this today and tomorrow I am not going to do it." This is an
       everyday occasion when they can do this.
   Q: Did this cause you to fear Officer Walker?
5 A: Yes, it did.
   Q: Are there other inmates, for example, besides yourself and inmate Green
       who is here that have expressed to you their fear of Mr. Walker?
   A: There is plenty of guys that I ran across that have the same feeling.
   Q: Is that fear more in connection with — is that by black inmates or is that all
10   inmates?
   A: It's about all inmates, not just black inmates.
   MR. DEEMER: No further questions.

Cross-examination

   Q. BY MR. CUMMINGS: Mr. Johnson, you indicated that you had been con-
15   victed, what, one time before of rape?
   A: Yes.
   Q: It sounds like you took real personal offense at the way Officer Walker treated
       you; is that true?
   A: No, it wasn't the way he treated me.
20 Q: What was it?
   A: The things I knew about him.
   Q: So it wasn't what he did, it's what you thought he was going to do.
   A: It wasn't what I thought — it wasn't what I was thinking he was going to do. It's
       what I knew he was going to do. Once I seen him in the front of the line, I knew.
25 Q: In other words, Officer Walker didn't have to do anything. As you just said,
       when you saw him in the front of that line in your mind you were sure to
       yourself, I'm positive of that, you knew what was coming.
   A: Yes.
   Q: Now, given that state of mind, sir, your state of mind, you were going to pro-
30   tect yourself?
   A: No, I was not going to protect myself.
   Q: Why not?
   A: There wasn't no need to protect myself.
   Q: There wasn't any need?
35 A: No, there was no need to protect myself.
   Q: Let me see if I got this straight. You are positive in your own mind that
       Walker, who you fear is at the head of the line, you see it doors go closed and
       you know what's going to happen, don't you?
   A: Yes.
40 Q: And you are not scared?
   A: I'm not going to put up no defense towards him.
   Q: So you didn't act in self-defense.
   A: I didn't act at all.[43]

___

   43.   Given this testimony, what story of the incident, from the defendant's point of view, should
defense counsel argue to the jury? This testimony contradicts the officers' testimony that they saw the
defendant raise his fist against Officer Walker. Would the raising of the fist be justified under the theory

1 Q: Do you respect the rights of other people?
   A: Yes, I do.
   Q: And you want them to respect your rights, too?
   A: Yes, I do.
5 Q: You had indicated earlier that you were convicted one time of rape, Sir?
   A: Yes, I was.
   Q: Were you paroled out of the Department of Corrections?
   A: Yes.
   Q: Sometime in '84?
10 A: August 31st, '84.
   Q: That's exactly the right date, August 31st, 1984. And went home for a
        while?
   A: Yes.
   Q: Did you end up back in the criminal system?
15 A: Yes.
   Q: And was that as a result of a 1985 conviction again out of Long Beach, Count
        2, you were convicted of a rape by force or fear?
   A: Yes.
   Q: Also convicted of a burglary first degree?
20 A: Yes.
   Q: Sentenced to 23 years state prison?
   A: Yes.
   Q: Sir, do you have any gang affiliations?
   A: No.
25 Q: Your testimony was that at the head of that cell door that Officer Walker was
        there and you knew him.
   A: Yeah.
   Q: And at least you knew of him.
   A: Yes.
30 Q: Smith wasn't there?
   A: Smith was there, Smith was there, but Smith was not like Smith say he was
        on the side of the door. Smith was way behind. He was way behind Walker.
        Walker is the only one in front of this door. Walker is the only one. Ain't
        no — I can't even imagine at that time that this happened that any other
35   officers could have been in front of Walker. It wasn't no other officer in front
        of Walker. It was only Walker in front of the cell.
   Q: Now, the officers testified almost unanimously — and you heard them — that
        actually it was unanimously that you were acting aggressive once the cell
        door opened and you dropped the trays.
40 A: No, I was not acting aggressively at all with no officers, period.
   Q: Sir, have you ever acted aggressively?
   A: What do you mean?
   Q: Are you an aggressive person?
   A: I think everybody have aggression in them.
45 Q: And I know you said for the defense attorney you weren't resisting, but tell us
        what you were doing.

---

of self-defense — a use of force reasonably necessary to prevent an injury that the defendant reasonably
believes to be imminent?

1 A: I wasn't doing — it wasn't too much that I could do, period.

Q: Officer Walker testified that he was the first one through, made contact with you — or actually you made contact with him close to the door. True or not true?

5 A: That's not true.

Q: Where did contact get made?

A: Contact got made when that door came open and Walker ran up in that cell on me. That's where contact got made, the only contact.

Q: Multiple officers testified that they saw a clenched fist, probably your right fist, come swinging at the front officer. True or not true?

10

A: Not true.

Q: Officers are lying about that?

A: Officers are lying about that.

Q: Officers testified they saw you kicking. True or not true?

15 A: Not true.

Q: Officers lying about that?

A: Officers are lying about that.

Q: All of them?

A: All of them.

20 Q: Officers testified that you were difficult to handcuff. True or not true?

A: Not true.

Q: Officers are lying about that, too?

A: Yes, sir.

Q: Officers testified that you ended up going from inside the cell to the outside

25   of the cell so that they could finish up what they had to do, which was get you cuffed up and secured.

A: I was handcuffed on the outside of the cell, yes. That's where they brought me out of the cell to the outside of the cell.

Q: And you got handcuffed.

30 A: Yes.

Q: So the officers were telling the truth about that?

A: They had to get me handcuffed.

Q: How well do you know Officer Walker?

A: I know him — I know him quite — I think I know him well enough.

35 Q: How many times did you come in contact?

A: I come in contact with Officer Walker this time here and a time when he was in New Folsom.

Q: So one time three years ago or more and one time up here?

A: Yes.

40 Q: Two times three years apart?

A: Yes. But I see him do other things besides how many times I know him.

MR. CUMMINGS: Nothing further.

THE WITNESS: Him and Van Berg, too.

Redirect Examination

Q. BY MR. DEEMER: Are you right-handed or left-handed?[44]

---

44.   Why is this question asked? More importantly, pay attention to whether any further reference is made to the answer.

1   A: I am left-handed.
    MR. DEEMER: No further questions.
    MR. CUMMINGS: Nothing.

    (There was a lunch recess taken from 12:00 P.M. to 1:38 P.M. of the same day.)

5   THE COURT: The district attorney is now present and, Mr. Deemer, you have
        indicated you do not intend then to call any further witnesses?
    MR. DEEMER: No, sir.
    THE COURT: Defense rests. Prosecution, any rebuttal evidence?
    MR. CUMMINGS: Yes, Your Honor. Lieutenant Stokes.
10 MR. DEEMER: Your Honor, while he is calling Lieutenant Stokes, could we
        have an offer of proof at the bench?
    THE COURT: Yes, approach the bench.

    (The following proceedings were had outside the presence of the jury.)

    MR. CUMMINGS: I intend to call Stokes and ask him whether or not he is
15   aware of the professional reputation of Correction Officer Walker.
    MR. DEEMER: The only thing you can ask him is whether or not — what his
        reputation is among the inmates. What his reputation is among the staff, I
        don't think is very relevant.
    THE COURT: I am going to overrule the objection because although the
20   inmates and the staff are not precisely the same, they are a part of the com-
        munity within the prison and are in communication with one another on
        a constant basis. So reputation is something that is back and forth and it is
        the kind of thing that would be known. And it's a question that goes solely to
        reputation and not to prior incidents in the officers' personnel file. I think
25   the whole Pitchess issue is side stepped anyway, so you can ask strictly about
        reputation.
    MR. CUMMINGS: Reputation both among the inmates and among the cor-
        rectional staff?
    THE COURT: Yes, if he knows. Of course, foundation first.
30 MR. CUMMINGS: I just want to make it clear in the record that we are at the
        rebuttal stage at this point.
    THE COURT: Right, the defense has rested.[45]
    MR. CUMMINGS: Exactly.

    (The following proceedings were had in open court.)

35   ROBERT STOKES

    called as a witness by the People, after having been sworn to tell the truth, the
    whole truth and nothing but the truth, was examined and testified as follows:

---

45.   Rebuttal evidence is put on by the prosecution after the defense has rested. It is restricted to evidence made necessary by defendant's case — such as response to new evidence or to new grounds of innocence — and should not include what the prosecutor should have proved in the case-in-chief.

1   *Rebuttal Examination*

> *Q. BY MR. CUMMINGS:*   Thank you, Your Honor. Lieutenant, we know that
> you are currently employed as a lieutenant and you were employed as a lieu-
> tenant, a correctional lieutenant, on March the 28th, 1992, when you were
5 at Pelican Bay State Prison, correct?
> A: Yes, sir.
> Q: What were your duties on the 28th of March this year?
> A: I was the watch commander, second watch, six o'clock in the morning until
> two o'clock in the afternoon.
10 Q: Lieutenant, as a watch commander are you responsible for any specific busi-
> ness within the prison or as a whole on that shift?
> A: I am basically in charge of the overall security of the prison. And as the
> watch commander I coordinate any problems that one facility would have
> that would need assistance from another facility.
15 Q: Are you directly responsible for B Facility when you are on duty?
> A: No, sir, I am not.
> Q: Do you have occasion to work with or direct the work of different correc-
> tional officers?
> A: Yes, sir, I have.
20 Q: Sir, do you know the reputation among the inmates of certain correctional
> officers?
> A: Yes, I do.
> Q: Where does that information come from?
> A: That comes —
25 Q: How is it you would know that?
> A: Specifically, sir, are we talking about the staff, specific staff in B Facility?
> Q: Yes, specific staff. Do you have occasion in your job capacity to know what
> the reputation is of certain staff members among the inmates?
> A: Yes, sir, I would. Mainly through the appeal process.
30 Q: Would you explain that?
> A: The appeal process is a way of airing grievances by the inmates. It is generally
> recorded on a CDC 602.
> *MR. DEEMER:*   Excuse me, Your Honor. If this is the basis of his knowledge,
> I don't think that he ought to be allowed to testify to that. Moreover, that is
35 just hearsay statements of the inmates.
> *THE COURT:*   Approach the bench, counsel.

(The following proceedings were had outside the presence of the jury.)

> *THE COURT:*   Well, I'm not going to permit Bob go into specific instances to
> prove conduct on a particular occasion. But I will allow him to go as far as
40 he has, i.e., to show that that's generally how he keeps his finger on the pulse
> of what's going on in there. But that point we are going to have to get to the
> bottom-line question of what reputation is, if there is one.
> *MR. CUMMINGS:*   That's fine. This is being preliminary and foundational.
> That's all.
45 *THE COURT:*   I will note for the record that since I handle several hundred
> habeas corpus issues a year and almost all of that have to go through the

1   602 process before they go to court and usually the 602s are attached, I read
     hundreds of 602s myself and I am aware that they give a pretty good over-
     view of what's — what the scuttlebutt is inside the prison. So it seems to me
     that this is an appropriate place for his source of knowledge, but not specific
5   instances, as to reputation generally.
     MR. CUMMINGS: That's fine.

(The following proceedings were had in the presence of the jury.)

Q. BY MR. CUMMINGS: Sir, in your capacity as a lieutenant in Pelican Bay
     State Prison have you had occasion to determine what you believe is the
10   reputation of Officer Walker among the inmates?
A: Yes, sir, I have.
Q: What would your opinion be as to what his reputation is among the
     inmates?
A: Among — his reputation among inmates and of staff — and as he worked for
15   me for 13 months — is he is an excellent officer; he is very fair and he is very
     understanding and he runs a very smooth block.[46]
Q: And what are you basing this on?
A: My 13 months of supervision of B Facility.
Q: And when you were supervising B Facility was Officer Walker one of the
20   officers in your command?
A: Yes, sir, he was.
Q: And that was for a period of 13 months?
A: Approximately 11 months for Officer Walker. He left for two months and
     then came back.
25   MR. CUMMINGS: Thank you, sir. Nothing further.

Cross-examination

Q. BY MR. DEEMER: When was the last time you discussed Officer Walker's
     reputation amongst inmates?
A: I'm sorry.
30   Q: Have you ever discussed Officer Walker's reputation with inmates?
A: No, sir, I have not.
Q: All right. And as a practical matter as a lieutenant you really don't have that
     much contact with inmates, do you?
A: Not as much as you do as a sergeant over an officer.
35   Q: And basically what you are really familiar with is reputation amongst the
     other correctional officers. Would that be fair to say?
A: No, I am familiar with his manner of doing his job for that time that he
     worked for me.
Q: Are you aware of the fact that at least one lieutenant out there has refused to
40   have Officer Walker on his or her watch because of problems?
A: I'm not familiar with that, no, sir.
Q: Do you know Lieutenant Rodriguez?

    46.   Is it possible that this testimony about Officer Walker's reputation among inmates can be based
solely on the 602 forms? Do the 602 forms contain such positive assertions about officers?

1   A: I know of Lieutenant Rodriguez, yes.

     Q: Does she have something to do with B Facility?

     A: I believe she works the evening watch from two o'clock in the afternoon till ten o'clock at night.

5   Q: And you are aware of the fact that she has refused to work on the watch with Officer Walker?

     A: I am not aware of it, no, sir.

     Q: No further questions.

     MR. CUMMINGS: Nothing further.

10   THE COURT: May he be excused?

     MR. DEEMER: Yes.

     MR. CUMMINGS: Yes.

     THE COURT: You can leave or stay as you wish. Any further evidence, prosecution?

15   MR. CUMMINGS: No, People would rest. People have rested.

     THE COURT: Defense?

     MR. DEEMER: I have one witness but she is not going to be able to be here, Your Honor, so I have no choice but to rest at this time.

     THE COURT: Both sides rest then?

20   MR. CUMMINGS: Yes.

     THE COURT: What remains, ladies and gentlemen, is to put their jury instructions in their final form. That could not be done until this point, although there has been some done to this point already. I am going to give you a recess for that purpose.

25   (The following proceedings were had in the presence of the jury.)

     THE COURT: Let the record reflect that all jurors, counsel, and defendant are present. Ladies and gentlemen of the jury, you have heard all the evidence and now it is my duty to instruct you on the law that applies to this case.

30   The law requires that I read the instructions to you, and you will have these instructions in written form in the jury room to refer to during your deliberations.

     You must base your decision on the facts and the law. You have two duties to perform. First, you must determine the facts from the evidence received in the trial and not from any other source. A fact is something proved directly or

35   circumstantially by the evidence or by stipulation. A stipulation is an agreement between attorneys regarding the facts. Second, you must apply the law that I state to you, to the facts, as you determine them, and in this way arrive at your verdict and any finding you are instructed to include in your verdict.

     You must accept and follow the law as I state it to you, whether or not

40   you agree with the law. If anything concerning the law said by the attorneys in their arguments or at any other time during the trial conflicts with my instructions on the law, you must follow my instructions.

     You must not be influenced by pity for a defendant or by prejudice against him. You must not be biased against the defendant because he has been arrested

45   for these offenses, charged with a crime, or brought to trial. None of these circumstances is evidence of guilt and you must not infer or assume from any or all of them that he is more likely to be guilty than innocent. You must not

1 be influenced by mere sentiment, conjecture, sympathy, passion, prejudice, public opinion, or public feeling. Both the People and the defendant have a right to expect that you will conscientiously consider and weigh the evidence, apply the law, and reach a just verdict regardless of the consequences.[47]

5 Statements made by the attorneys during the trial are not evidence, although if the attorneys have stipulated or agreed to a fact, you must regard that fact as conclusively proved.

If an objection was sustained to a question do not guess what the answer might have been and do not speculate as to the reason for the objection.

10 Do not assume to be true any insinuation suggested by a question asked a witness. A question is not evidence and may be considered only as it enables you to understand the answer.

Do not consider for any purpose any offer of evidence that was rejected, or any evidence that was stricken by the court; treat it as though you had 15 never heard it.[48]

Evidence consists of testimony of witnesses, writings, material objects, or anything presented to the senses and offered to prove the existence or non-existence of a fact.

Evidence is either direct or circumstantial. Direct evidence is evidence 20 that directly proves a fact, without the necessity of an inference. It is evidence which by itself, if found to be true, establishes that fact.

Circumstantial evidence is evidence that, if found to be true, proves a fact from which an inference of the existence of another fact may be drawn.

An inference is a deduction of fact that may logically and reasonably be 25 drawn from another fact or group of facts established by the evidence.

It is not necessary that facts be proved by direct evidence. They may be proved also by circumstantial evidence or by a combination of direct evidence and circumstantial evidence. Both direct evidence and circumstantial evidence are acceptable as a means of proof. Neither is entitled to any 30 greater weight than the other.

However, a finding of guilt as to any crime may not be based on circumstantial evidence unless the proved circumstances are not only (1) consistent with the theory that the defendant is guilty of the crime, but (2) cannot be reconciled with any other rational conclusion. If the circumstantial evidence permits 35 two reasonable interpretations, one of which points to the defendant's guilt and the other to his innocence, you must adopt that interpretation that points to the defendant's innocence, and reject that interpretation that points to guilt.

Further, each fact which is essential to complete a set of circumstances necessary to establish the defendant's guilt must be proved beyond a reason-40 able doubt. In other words, before an inference essential to establish guilt may be found to have been proved beyond a reasonable doubt, each fact or circumstance upon which such inference necessarily rests must be proved beyond a reasonable doubt.[49]

---

47.   Why does the judge give this instruction? Does it describe the normal way an individual absorbs information? If not, why is an artificial decision-making process being urged upon the jury?

48.   Such instructions are common in the course of a trial. Do you think jurors are influenced by rejected or stricken evidence, a judge's instruction notwithstanding?

49.   What, exactly, might this instruction mean? See the discussion of "circumstantial evidence" in Chapter Three.

1   Every person who testifies under oath is a witness. You are the sole judges of the believability of a witness and the weight to be given the testimony of each witness.

In determining the believability of a witness you may consider anything
5   that has a tendency in reason to prove or disprove the truthfulness of the testimony of the witness, including but not limited to any of the[50] following:

The extent of the opportunity or the ability of the witness to see or hear or otherwise become aware of any matter about which the witness has testified;

10   The ability of the witness to remember or to communicate any matter about which the witness has testified; The character and quality of that testimony;

The demeanor and manner of the witness while testifying; The existence or nonexistence of a bias, interest, or other motive;

15   Evidence of the existence or nonexistence of any fact testified to by the witness;

The attitude of the witness toward this action or toward the giving of testimony;

A statement previously made by the witness that is consistent or incon-
20   sistent with the testimony of the witness or the witness's prior conviction of a felony.

Discrepancies in the witness's testimony or between his or her testimony and that of others, if there were any, do not necessarily mean that the witness should be discredited. Failure of recollection is a common experience; and
25   innocent misrecollection is not uncommon. It is a fact, also, that two persons witnessing an incident or a transaction often will see or hear it differently. Whether a discrepancy pertains to a fact of importance or only to a trivial detail should be considered in weighing its significance.

A witness who is willfully false in one material part of his or her testimony
30   is to be distrusted in others. You may reject the whole testimony of a witness who willfully has testified falsely as to a material point, unless, from all the evidence, you believe the probability of truth favors his or her testimony in other particulars.

You are not bound to decide an issue of fact in accordance with the testi-
35   mony of a number of witnesses, which does not convince you, as against the testimony of a lesser number or other evidence, which appeals to your mind with more convincing force.

You may not disregard the testimony of the greater number of witnesses merely from caprice, whim, or prejudice, or from a desire to favor one side
40   against the other. You must not decide an issue by the simple process of counting the number of witnesses who have testified on the opposing side. The final test is not in the relative number of witnesses, but in the convincing force of the evidence.

The fact that a witness has been convicted of a felony, if such be a fact, may
45   be considered by you only for the purpose of determining the believability

---

50.   This instruction tracks the language of Cal. Evid. Code §780, which lists permissible topics of impeachment. You will study the Federal Rules governing cross-examination and impeachment in Chapter Seven.

1   of that witness. The fact of such a conviction does not necessarily destroy or impair a witness's believability. It is one of the circumstances that you may take into consideration in weighing the testimony of such a witness.

A defendant in a criminal action is presumed to be innocent until the
5   contrary is proved, and in case of a reasonable doubt whether his guilt is satisfactorily shown, he is entitled to a verdict of not guilty. This presumption places upon the People the burden of proving him guilty beyond a reasonable doubt.

Reasonable doubt is defined as follows. It is not a mere possible doubt
10 because everything relating to human affairs and depending on moral evidence is open to some possible or imaginary doubt. It is that state of the case, which after the entire comparison and consideration of all the evidence, leaves the mind of the jurors in that condition that they cannot say that they feel an abiding conviction or a moral certainty of the truth of the charge.[51]

15 In the crimes charged in the information there must exist a union or joint operation of act or conduct and general criminal intent. To constitute general criminal intent it is not necessary that there should exist an intent to violate the law. When a person intentionally does that which the law declares to be a crime, he is acting with general criminal intent, even though he may
20 not know that his act or conduct is unlawful.

Any person who, while confined in a state prison, commits a battery upon a person who is not themselves confined in a state prison, is guilty of a felony.

Every person who willfully and unlawfully uses any force or violence
25 upon the person of another is guilty of battery.

As used in the foregoing instruction, the words "force" and "violence" are synonymous and mean any unlawful application of physical force against the person of another, even though it causes no pain or bodily harm or leaves no mark and even though only the feelings of such person are injured by the
30 act. The slightest unlawful touching, if done in an insolent, rude, or angry manner, is sufficient.

It is not necessary that the touching be done in an actual anger or with actual malice; it is sufficient if it was unwarranted and unjustifiable.

The touching essential to a battery may be a touching of the person, of
35 the person's clothing, or of something attached to or closely connected with the person.

It is lawful for a person who is being assaulted to defend himself from attack if, as a reasonable person, he has grounds for believing and does believe that bodily injury is about to be inflicted upon him. In doing so
40 such person may use all force and means which he believes to be reasonably necessary and which would appear to a reasonable person in the same or similar circumstances to be necessary to prevent the injury which appears to be imminent.[52]

I have not intended by anything I have said or done, or by any ques-
45 tions that I have asked, or by any ruling I may have made, to intimate or

---

51.   Does either advocate make use of this reasonable-doubt instruction in closing argument?
52.   Does either advocate make use of this self-defense instruction in closing argument? Which party has the burden of proof on this issue? Does the judge ever make this clear?

1   suggest what you should find to be the facts, or that I believe or disbelieve
     any witness.

         The People and the defendant are entitled to the individual opinion of
     each juror. Each of you must consider the evidence for the purpose of reach-
5   ing a verdict if you can do so. Each of you must decide the case for yourself,
     but should do so only after discussing the evidence and instructions with the
     other jurors.

         Do not hesitate to change an opinion if you are convinced it is wrong.
     However, do not decide any question in a particular way because a majority
10   of the jurors, or any of them, favor such a decision.

         Do not decide any issue in this case by chance, such as the drawing of lots
     or by any other chance determination.

         The attitude and conduct of jurors at all times are very important. It
     is rarely helpful for a juror at the beginning of deliberations to express an
15   emphatic opinion on the case or to announce a determination to stand for
     a certain verdict. When one does that at the outset, a sense of pride may be
     aroused, and one may hesitate to change a position even if shown it is wrong.
     Remember that you are not partisans or advocates in this matter. You are
     impartial judges of the facts.

20   In your deliberations do not discuss or consider the subject of penalty or
     punishment. That subject must not in any way affect your verdict.

         At this time the attorneys will give their closing summations, and like the
     opening summations they are not evidence. They are a chance for the attor-
     neys to sum up for you what they claim the evidence has shown.[53] In doing
25   that I assume they will discuss both the testimony that you have heard and
     also some of the instructions I have read to you. Of course, if you notice any
     difference between what they tell you the evidence is and what the instruc-
     tions were, you must decide what the evidence is and follow my instructions
     that I have given to you.

30   Since the prosecution has the burden of proof the prosecutor makes the
     first closing summation followed by defense counsel, and then in order that
     each side will have an opportunity to reply to the other, the prosecutor is
     allowed a rebuttal argument.

     MR. CUMMINGS: Thank you, Your Honor. Ladies and gentlemen, this is my
35   opportunity to sum up what I believe the evidence has been, which is just
     what the judge explained to you. If anything you hear from me differs from
     what your own recollection was, from what your recollection of what the
     witnesses swore to tell you the truth about on the witness stand, you should
     go by your own recollection and you should go by your own notes. Neither
40   counsel is trying intentionally to mislead you, and sometimes when we are

---

53.   Closing argument is the final opportunity for the advocates to speak directly to the jury about
the case. Many closing arguments contain summations of the evidence, meaning a recitation of the
key witnesses and key testimony. But where the case is not long and complicated, and where not many
witnesses have testified, the jury may not need much help keeping things straight. Summing up the evidence should be contrasted, then, with arguing the evidence, where the advocate seeks to persuade the
jury about contested facts and about why his or her client is entitled to prevail. Such arguments should
be simple enough to be clearly understood, and sound enough to withstand the jury's scrutiny. As you
read the closing arguments of the prosecution and the defense, consider whether these two standards
have been met.

explaining our case we are thinking a witness or two ahead and sometimes we don't get exactly all the details right.

I told you in the beginning that I expected the case to be predominantly Pelican Bay State Prison officers. It was. I told you that it was going to involve two batteries. In reality it involved three batteries. I will explain that in a little bit. It involves the credibility of numerous officers. This was a scenario which I believe the very first officer, Officer Huston, almost wanted to sum up as a great big nothing originally because that's really what it was, something that the inmate himself had some control over.

Inmates for whatever reason do things that you and I do not understand and we are never going to understand because we don't think that way and we are not in that environment. But for some reason inmate Johnson chose to draw the line that day over some package that he claimed that he wasn't getting, may or may not be true. Maybe it's 100 percent true for all I know. Entirely possible. However, in any case, as the officer explained to you in court and to Mr. Johnson in his cell, that wasn't the way to go about it.

Pelican Bay State Prison and the State of California cannot stop all things and run in and get this man, a sergeant, at that point in time and run and get his parcel for him. It's just not possible. They deal with a mainline system or a mainline production and it really is. You are feeding a tremendous number of inmates, got to get trays back, you have got to go on to the next one, you have got another job assignment. That's what these officers had to do.

What is interesting is that it appears that the major thrust of the evidence in this case is not, although the defendant denies doing it, is not so much that it didn't happen — he certainly acknowledges that it happened — but it was all their fault. Of course, it is never their fault. It is always somebody else's fault. But what we really have here and what the defense would like to paint the picture of is that Walker, Officer Walker, is on trial.[54] See, Officer Walker ought to be sitting over there where inmate Johnson is because what they are really trying to do is prosecute Officer Walker, and I urge you and the law urges you to stay focused on who is on trial. The person on trial in this case is inmate Johnson. There is no other. It is inmate Johnson that caused the fracas. It is inmate Johnson that drew the line. It is inmate Johnson who decided for whatever reason something was going to give that day and something did give and of course it had nothing to do with him.

So the People put on witnesses like Officer Huston, who when I asked him about "Would you describe for us what happened on March the 28th, 1992 as that incident," his response was something like "I mean, it wasn't really even an incident originally," and it wasn't an incident. It escalated into an incident and it is a serious matter where two officers were injured.

In this situation it is important to remember that basically none of the officers that were actually there came in and testified in court were assigned to Mr. Johnson's care. They were rovers.

They were yard officers. They were other block officers who were called by the sergeant and went to go and basically talk this guy out of his trays, do

54.   Here the prosecutor seems to be challenging the defense theory of the case, that Officer Walker was the first aggressor. This puts the defense on the defensive, as you will see.

1   what was necessary to talk him out of his trays, get the trays back and get on
     with their own assignments, and that's exactly what they tried to do.

         Classic situation where three officers tell you what they see and what they
     feel is exactly what happened, and I'm sure you all noticed there were some
5   differences between Officer Huston's version, Officer Van Berg's version and
     Officer Walker's version. Those are the three primary ones that ended up in
     the cell at least in one point in time and there were three different versions
     to a slight degree.[55]

         One person has the inmate holding two trays. Don't be confused. It is
10   not important whether he is holding two trays in two separate hands or two
     trays in one hand. That's not important. What is important is that the officers
     are telling you the truth because the three stories do not come out exactly
     the same. These three officers or these four officers or these five officers did
     not get together and decide, "Okay, folks, this is what happened," because
15   obviously you are not going to have some small discrepancies, and one of the
     instructions in the jury instruction package that the judge just read to you
     and that you will see back in the jury room is that people who see and hear
     an event often see and hear it differently and report it differently. That does
     not mean they are not being truthful. Be more suspicious of the people that
20   take the stand and tell you five people in a row exactly what happened almost
     verbatim. Common sense tells you there is probably something wrong.

         In this case they relayed that basically the officer that did most of the talk-
     ing was Smith. Smith came in and told you what he said. He explained that
     he made a demand that basically started out as a request. It escalated into
25   a demand or an order to return the trays, get the trays back. He made com-
     ments like, "Are you having a bad day today, guy?" and stuff to that effect,
     something to try to spark the guy to just give up the trays. They have got their
     job to do. These are not correctional officers who are dealing with Johnson
     on a regular basis. There is no vendetta here. The only one who alleges any
30   sort of vendetta is Johnson.

         You heard Officer Walker say, "I don't know inmate Johnson." I don't
     recall any officer that was there that had any prior dealings with this particu-
     lar inmate. Now, that doesn't mean that this inmate was necessarily lying to
     you when he says, "There is some sort of history here between Walker and
35   myself." He may very well believe that for reasons you and I cannot under-
     stand. But in his mind he may be telling the truth in his own mind. That
     happens unfortunately quite often.

         So basically the way the story seemed to shake out remarkably consis-
     tently in his point of view was the person, inmate Johnson, gets up in the
40   cell. He is holding them in front of him, he is roughly a little bit behind, foot,
     foot and a half, whatever, behind the door. Smith again signals to the control
     booth officer to open the door.

         As soon as the door is opened wide enough for a person to get through if
     he wanted to, trays are dropped instantly, denied by the defendant, but the
45   officers were all pretty consistent. And immediately — and some officers saw

---

55.   The prosecutor is able to summarize the testimony of several officers by emphasizing the consistency in their stories. Arguing the facts involves more than reciting testimony; it requires choosing those
facts and inferences that together create the story that should win the case.

1 him duck his head, some officers didn't, and you would have to understand
that they all had a different perspective. That's common sense. They all had
a different perspective from where they were.

The ones closer are going to see a little bit better than the ones behind.
5 One officer had to go off to the side and look through what is the equivalent of a window so he could see whether or not Johnson had any weapons
because he is concerned for the officers. He actually left and went off to one
side.

So you had a person who has just dropped the trays, who was not showing
10 any sign of aggression before. He is not being violent and everybody agrees
on this, no sign of aggression. If they were trying to make Johnson out to be
a bad guy, they would make him out to be violent, they would make him out
to be verbally abusive, they would make him out to be throwing a fit, acting out some frustration or some anger. And they were all consistent in that
15 there was no hint that this guy was going to go off and unfortunately these
people do go off at times. Folks do blow up in prisons and that happened in
this case.

So he drops his trays and the officers were not exactly the same as to
what they saw, but it was remarkably similar to what the threat was. They
20 saw inmate Johnson making a forward motion coming at the officer in front,
Walker. Walker happened to be in front. He of course was going to be the
one that came in contact with him first. It's the only logical conclusion.

Walker basically does what he is trained to do, wrestles with the guy for a
while. He even says it is even like dancing a little bit, but basically gets him
25 back into the cell, and the whole time he is saying, "Get down, get down,
knock it off, stop the aggression," and that's for everybody's safety, including
the inmates. Butler, the defendant's roommate, cell mate in his cell, does
exactly what he is told and he basically complies with all instructions. He gets
cuffed up for a few minutes while they secure the situation and it's all over.

30 Is that what happens with this gentleman? No, it is not. He continues
to fight. Every officer was consistent to the extent that the aggression continued, the fighting continued, kicking and fists were going. And then the
officer, I believe it was Van Berg who was trying to handcuff him, said, "I
couldn't get the second cuff on him." So they did what they had to do. They
35 got him cuffed up. Perfectly reasonable, perfectly responsible to do when
you are operating in a maximum-level prison. You are not operating out of
the streets of Crescent City. You are not operating at Del Norte High School.
You are operating in a maximum-security prison.

Every officer had a little bit different version, but every officer also had
40 a little bit different role and a little bit different perspective as to where they
were.

I started out by saying that this is a credibility issue and you should think
of it as a credibility issue and think about, as the judge explained to you in
the instructions, who has a motive in this case. Let's say a motive to lie. You
45 can consider that. Who has a motive to be less than truthful with you?[56] Four

---

56.   How persuasive do you find the arguments that follow concerning the motives of the officers
and the inmates to lie? What could the defense argue in response? Which group do you think had the
most compelling reason to lie about the incident?

correctional officers who come in here and swore to tell you the whole truth and they got their law enforcement career on the line. If they were caught lying they would lose their jobs. I am sure their whole usefulness to the California correction system goes right out the window.

Or the defendant? You heard the defendant is serving 20-plus years or about. Some of his witnesses, one of which is serving life for murder in the first degree who has nothing to lose with a few lies. Not a thing. We can't do anything to him and he knows that. And everybody basically admitted to one degree or another that they are friends. One of the inmates admitted that he was a Crip. The defendant denied any Crip affiliation but they were room-mates together. There is some degree of friendship among the whole group of them. I think that's fairly obvious.

It is fair to look at who has the motive to tell you the truth, who has got the motive to lie in that case. There is no motive on the part of the correc-tional officers, but coming here and telling you basically what happened as best they can recall. In this case one of the elements the People do have to prove — and I do have to prove that he was a state prisoner at the time of the incident. It's a small thing, but it has been proven. That was stipulated to. It just means that both defense attorney and I agreed he was a state prisoner at the time the judge accepted the stipulation, and that is a fact that has been proven at this point in time. No further documentary evidence or anything else need be given.

The verdict forms in this case are basically three separate pieces of paper. The first one is going to have Count 1 on it and it's going to say was guilty and it will name — it will say battery and it will name Officer Huston being the victim of that battery. Officer Huston was the first gentleman who testified, who testified that as a result of this fracas, had it not been for this fracas with this fight, he would not have gotten a gash. He got a gash in his shin, went to Sutter Coast and got medical treatment. That's an injury. That's more than a battery, okay? But certainly qualifies as a battery. But that's Count 1. I am asking you to return a verdict of guilty on Count 1.

A separate piece of paper has Count 2. Again it's a battery and it's a battery of, in this case, Officer Van Berg. Officer Van Berg was the second officer that testified. As a result of this fracas he cannot tell you exactly what blow but that's not what their attention is focused on. Their attention is focused on quieting people down and breaking it up. As a direct result of this fracas and this fight he ended up with a bone chip knocked on his hand, basically a fracture of one of the bones in his hand, and ended up going to Sutter Coast and was treated medically for it. Those are two batteries.

Let's talk a little bit about how simple the section is, the section of the law is. Penal Code section 4501.5, which is the battery section, it says, "Any person who while confined in a state prison," we have stipulated to that, he is confined in the state prison, "commits a battery on a person who is not themselves confined in a state prison," that would be staff, correctional offi-cers, civilian workers, "is guilty of a felony," period. It's one sentence. It's not a big complicated law. "Any person who while confined in the state prison commits a battery upon a person who is not themselves confined in a state prison is guilty of a felony."

1   I told you earlier I would define battery for you, too, while I am at it. Battery has a one-sentence definition. "Every person who willfully and unlawfully uses any force or violence upon the person of another is guilty of a battery," period. That's it.[57]

5   I told you earlier there was a third battery in the case and legally there is a third battery in the case and I am not asking you to return a verdict of guilty on that. It is not before you for your consideration. But a battery does not require injuries. Legally speaking you don't have to have people actually injured.

10   The relevant portion of that instruction says the slightest unlawful touching, if done in an insolent, rude or angry manner is sufficient for a battery. So no injury need result. So you really could have another battery which was not charged as far as the victim being Officer Walker because he was attacked basically when the person charged the front door. That was not
15   charged. Thank you, ladies and gentlemen.

MR. DEEMER: I don't mean to sound like I am running away. When I opened that door to get something I remember one time many years ago when I was a deputy district attorney down in Compton with an attorney there who had problems and one day after going to trial he said, "Your Honor," he says, "I
20   am going out to get the witness, going to solve my case and prove my client innocent," and he walked out the door. We all sat around and sat around and nothing happened. Sat around and nothing happened and finally they sent the bailiff out to get him. He had completely forgotten about the trial and he was sitting in his office talking to clients.[58]

25   Mr. Cummings always makes a lot of fun about my chart and I admit I use it on a regular basis. I am supposed to stop waving my hands so I wave the stick instead. This is basically kind of a circumstantial evidence case and I know that there is a lot of direct testimony about what people observed, but unfortunately one of the things you have to do when you evaluate that
30   testimony is to decide do people see what they really say they saw. That is, you have to evaluate some circumstances that go around that testimony because there is a lot of things that cause people to perceive — that may cause Johnson to perceive things one way and the officers to perceive things a different way.[59]

35   What you got to do with this is figure out what's going on in this guy's mind, what's he doing. And one of the things — basically three rules which you are going to get in the jury instructions. First of all, the circumstances have to be consistent with the theory. Not only consistent with the theory of defense guilt, but it can't be reconciled with any other rational conclusion.
40   Each fact necessary to the set of circumstances has to be proved beyond a reasonable doubt.

And of course the other thing which I also keep on the back of this — I only billed the court once for this by the way — is the presumption of

---

57.   Advocates often refer to the instructions during closing argument, particularly those that define critical legal terms. Here, the prosecutor reads the definition of battery, but makes no argument that the facts proved against the defendant satisfy the definition.

58.   Jury attention is at its peak during the first minutes of argument. Does defense counsel accomplish anything with this opening gambit?

59.   Does defense counsel argue from the facts how inmate Johnson *did* perceive things?

1   innocence. You got to remember that burden is on the district attorney, not on me. I don't have any burden. James Johnson doesn't have any burden. And if there is a reasonable doubt as to whether James is guilty or not, you got a moral obligation and a legal obligation to come back with a not-guilty

5   verdict. You got to remember that. That's very important.

So when you look at that — and part of this I will sort of backtrack over Mr. Cummings's argument. You look at that and you talk about, first of all, the motive to be truthful. All right. These officers don't have a motive to be untruthful. Well, you know, there is something I found really interesting is

10   that when they got Lieutenant Stokes on the stand about how we really stress making sure these officers write down every last important detail. What's the important detail that wasn't in any of the reports by their own admission? There isn't anybody that mentions anything about the cell port in the reports but the witnesses were asked about it. Not a one. Not even Lieutenant

15   Stokes.

All right. I think Lieutenant Stokes made it clear, his testimony made it clear that these reports start out at the lower level and get passed on up to the upper level, and I think it's highly unlikely that he, in the kind of environment you are dealing with out there, that you are not going to get a certain

20   amount of cover your derriere. And this isn't because they are trying to protect themselves against the inmates.

I think what you are dealing with is a suggestion where they are kind of — they got to make it look good and I think that's a normal course of events, make it look good to the higher-ups, that the lower-downs are doing

25   the job right. In other words, the farther up the paperwork goes, you want to make sure there is no criticism that is going to float back down to the bottom. So there is a motive and there is a motive to ignore things.[60]

When I look at the circumstances in this case, the first thing that struck me is that the three officers all — and demeanor of a witness is something

30   you can look at. The three officers that testified about the assaultive behavior all give the appearance — I'm sorry, I don't know how to express it — of being — give the appearance of being cowboys. There is just something about their manner, their dress, their boots, everything. They are cowboys. And I suspect that they run that institution pretty much the same way. That's

35   the first thing that bothers me.[61]

The second thing, a significant item is the cell port. The third thing is the defendant — by the way, the comment was made that the defendant's motive is, "Well, I don't want to accept responsibility; it is always somebody else's fault." And again I think that same issue goes with the

40   report-writing issue. I mean, I dare say that any of you that get in an auto accident and write a report to your insurance company are going to try to diminish your fault somewhat. There is very few of us that come around and say, "Yeah, I made a left turn in front of the guy and smacked him and that's it."

---

60.   Was this an effective argument about the officers' motive to be untruthful about the incident? Did it respond to the prosecutor's argument about motive?

61.   Does defense counsel weave in the other facts that might support the defendant's story that the officers were the first aggressors?

1   The officers have the same motive. They want to make sure it's somebody else's fault and that's inevitable. That affects their appreciation — excuse me, their perception. But you go and you look at the circumstances and Johnson obviously wanted something done about his seeing a sergeant. He listened to
5   a great number of people, "Well, the sergeant can't see everybody," although this problem seems to have been one that had been floating around since the first part of the month. And Mr. Cummings says Johnson chose to draw the line. I agree. He drew the line, "I want something done; I want to see a sergeant."
10   And it's obvious from the testimony that if he just kept on drawing the line at some point in time he would have seen a sergeant. That doesn't mean Johnson made a choice to go out and start battering the officer or officers.[62] When you look at the circumstances surrounding this whole situation, Johnson is calm, he is not abusive, and all the testimony is, depending on
15   who perceived it correctly — and there is obviously some different perceptions — he is standing there. When the door opens he doesn't throw the tray at the officers. He just drops it.[63]
     And the general testimony is that his head drops down and I gather whatever was going on with his fists, whether it was pushing towards the officer or
20   whatever, there was no — I guess there is even some discrepancy amongst the officers' testimony as to whether there was, quote, an assault or an attempt to assault the officer — or Officer Walker.[64] But, you know, I am accused of putting Officer Walker on trial and I apologize. But, you know, you are dealing with somebody that's in a maximum-level prison, level four, and I'm
25   not concerned with really whether Walker is a bad guy or not as I told you originally. You know, there is a lot of testimony around here brought in by the prosecution about Walker as a great officer, he is wonderful. I expect CDC staff to stick with each other on those kind of issues. You notice none of them go down the inmate population and say, "Hey, have you guys had
30   problems with Walker," or, "What's your opinion about Walker in terms of how he uses force and violence?"
     I think what's significant is that this inmate is terrified of him and at least two other inmates seem to think that — or one other inmate, rather, says, "You know, I have seen him engage in this kind of conduct before." You are
35   kind of totally at the mercy of those cops out there. It's not like being out in the street.
     So he is standing here and he is waiting for the cell port door to be opened. Now, possibly the cell port door was open.[65] I suspect the cell port door was closed. But even if it is open you notice nobody ever says, "Pass the food tray
40   through the cell port." It's, "Give us the food tray, give us the food tray."

---

62.   This appears to be a response to the prosecutor's theme that inmate Johnson chose to have this aggressive encounter with the officers. Defense counsel does present some of the facts that tell the story from Johnson's point of view. Notice, however, that on a few key points, he does not forcefully argue the truth of Johnson's own testimony.
63.   The defendant testified that he bent over to pick up the trays.
64.   Defense counsel does not mention that the defendant testified that he was lefthanded, whereas Officers Van Berg and Smith testified that it was Johnson's right fist that was thrust through the cell door at Walker.
65.   The defendant testified that the food port door was closed.

You know, if this cell port is, say, basically at waist high or a little below — some say it's a little below, it's twelve inches wide, six inches high and four inches deep — I can understand how in his perception even if the officers are right about the cell port door being open — and I question that — I can understand from his perception how standing there he would be aware of the cell port door opening.

What happened? The cell door opens and here is Walker. What goes through his mind? "I am going to get the you know what beat out of me." He drops the trays, ducks and the melee ensues. I really think that's an honest interpretation of what happen. And it's obvious that in any kind of a confrontation like that the officers are going to see and believe in the fact that they are going to assume that an assault has taken place and obviously the inmate is the one that's going to get blamed.[66]

I think what really happens is the officers may well have perceived this as a battery, but what happens is Mr. Johnson figures, "I am going to get the you know what kicked out of me," he drops the trays and down he goes. Now, regardless of how you see that initial confrontation, Mr. Cummings is right. The issue involving a battery against Walker ain't on trial here today. The issue that's on trial is was there a battery against Van Berg and was there a battery against Huston.

You know what? If you sit back and think about the testimony I will bet your recollection is the same as mine. There wasn't one bit of testimony about this defendant striking any other officer. In fact, none of the officers — neither of those two officers testified the defendant struck him. They didn't testify that way at the preliminary hearing. They didn't testify here that way.

I assume with all these other officers, "Oh, yeah, I saw him strike Van Berg," or, "I saw him strike somebody else with his foot" or something of this sort. None of — nobody has testified about the defendant striking anybody other than Walker and that issue isn't on trial here. Huston and Van Berg both stated — and I'm going to just paraphrase their testimony to my notes — but I believe that there was a question to the effect of, you know, on Officer Huston's part, "Do you know how you received the gash specifically?" "No." And on Van Berg's part, "Do you know how you got hurt?" "No."

I don't know if they banged their legs on the cell door. I don't know if they banged their legs when Van Berg was banging my client's head against the wall, if he banged his thumb by accident at the same time. I don't know what happened. And you don't know what happened. The problem is that you can't speculate as to what happened because without that evidence that's presented before you in some way, shape or form that my client kicked them or hit them or did something like that, the DA doesn't have a case. And there is absolutely not one bit of evidence before the court as to Van Berg and as to Huston and I think you need to go look at that and go into that jury room and come back with a verdict of not guilty.

---

66. Could everybody be telling the truth? Perhaps the defendant did drop the trays, duck his head from fear, and even raise his fist to protect himself, but perhaps his behavior was interpreted as aggressive by the equally fearful officers. Wouldn't this be an appropriate point in the argument for the defense counsel to remind the jury of the self-defense instruction, and to argue that it applies? Or even to relate this self-defense theory to the reasonable doubt instruction?

1   This case has absolutely no business wasting your time and your money.
This is not — the defendant is entitled to a not-guilty verdict. There is absolutely no contact where the defendant is exercising force. There is lots of
force being exercised on the defendant. But there is absolutely not one shred

5   of evidence that the defendant exercised any force against Huston or Van
Berg.[67] Thank you.

MR. CUMMINGS: I would suspect Mr. Deemer has been watching the
Olympics on TV the last couple of nights and he has watched how some
of the referees score those boxing matches where one makes contact, okay,

10   that's a point. That one didn't score, this one did score. Ladies and gentlemen, this whole argument regarding that not one bit of evidence did either
one of these officers actually testify that a blow struck them causing that
injury and the DA doesn't have a case is nonsense. It's ridiculous.

There is nothing in the law that requires any officer to come in here or

15   anybody to tell you or anybody else that "It was his third right jab that caught
my thumb that jammed it against the floor that caused the injury." It's ridiculous. Think about it logically.

What the law is trying to prevent and punish is the acts and the resulting
injury. Because you have officers who are honest enough to come up here

20   and say, "We can't tell you exactly what blow it was, I can't tell you exactly
even when it happened because professionally what we are trying to do is
subdue a person, get him down, get him quiet, get him cuffed. We are trying
to do it fast for everybody's safety, officer safety, safety of this gentleman, safety
of his roommate, cell mate, everybody involved," and that's what they are sup-

25   posed to be doing. That's what the State of California pays them to do.

So this idea that because they cannot truthfully tell you exactly what blow
caused the injury the People don't have a case is not true. Legally it's just a
fiction, a lie. It seems like Mr. Deemer and the defense is — what they are
really trying to say is that Walker had it in for — at least this guy believed

30   that Walker had it in for him. Remember the testimony from the defendant
himself. Had two prior contacts. Walker recalls none but then again he probably deals with thousands of people, or has in his career. It's had two prior
contacts with him, one at Folsom and one here. Based upon that and some
other perceptions that he has from other people he is scared to death of an

35   officer that he doesn't have regular contact with, scared to death.

Ladies and gentlemen, that type of an argument, if that were legally sufficient for a self-defense argument, which is what he is really saying, he is
really saying that it was perfectly appropriate for Johnson in this case to do
what he did. Now, the defense is trying to minimize, of course, what he

40   did. The defense would have you believe, "Well, you know, he was covering up his head so of course he had to drop the trays; and because he didn't
throw the trays at the officer, which is one thing he could have done, then it
couldn't really be an assault."

That's ridiculous. He chose to drop the trays, maybe duck, maybe not

45   duck. The evidence is 50/50 on that. But in any case it was real clear about

---

67.   Shouldn't the judge's instructions cover the question whether evidence of direct touching is
required for battery? Do they? It is the advocate's responsibility to request instructions on issues of law that
are raised by the facts. Then the advocate can read those instructions to the jury during closing.

1   right fist coming up clenched and moving forward, him being the aggressor.
     I even asked one officer is there any way — it's almost embarrassing asking
     these questions. But is there any way that you could have mistaken him for
     bowing down, the forward motion. He said no. Did he act aggressively? Was
5   he acting violently? At that point he was. That's all that mattered.[68]
         Because Johnson initiated that and the officers responded in a profes-
     sional and appropriate fashion and because of that two of them were injured
     and that's all we are asking you to return a verdict on are those two counts.
     Nothing more. It is real important that people realize that the burden is
10   on the People and I do have to prove my case and I have to prove my case
     beyond a reasonable doubt and just that, beyond a reasonable doubt.
         As the law says, it is not a mere possible doubt, because everything is
     open to some doubt. In other words, you can have some doubt and you can
     still convict Mr. Johnson of Counts 1, Counts 2. You can have some doubt.
15   I could not and I cannot and no prosecutor can ever prove their case beyond
     any shadow of a doubt. This is not *Perry Mason*. Nor can we do it beyond
     any possible doubt. I can't do it. I don't believe anybody can because we are
     dealing with human fears and human people and you are always going to
     have different perceptions. Always do.
20   It's just gut level feelings, folks. Beyond a reasonable doubt, four cor-
     rectional officers come in here and tell you what happened on March the
     28th, 1992, to the point where you believe beyond a reasonable doubt that
     what they say happened really did happen; and if you can do that, you can
     find Mr. Johnson guilty of Count 1, guilty of Count 2. Thank you very
25   much.
     THE COURT: You shall now retire and select one of your number to act as
     foreperson. He or she will preside over your deliberations. In order to reach
     verdicts all twelve jurors must agree to the decision, to the findings you
     have been instructed to include in your verdict. As soon as all of you have
30   agreed upon a verdict so that when polled each may state truthfully that the
     verdict expresses his or her decision, dated and signed by your foreperson
     and then return with them to this courtroom. Return any unsigned verdict
     forms.
         Count 1 has to do with Officer Huston. Count 2 is identical except it
35   applies to the allegation concerning Officer Van Berg. It is either guilty or
     not guilty, date and sign the verdict form.

(The bailiff was sworn.). . .

(At 6:37 P.M. court was reconvened.)

THE COURT: Let the record reflect the defendant and both attorneys and the
40   jury are present in court. Mr. Baker, has the jury reached a verdict?
     MR. BAKER: Yes, sir.

---

68.   The theory of a self-defense claim is that the defendant has the right to respond with reasonable force when he has reasonable fear of bodily injury. Thus, inmate Johnson's aggressive move, if it
occurred, could be viewed as a reasonable response to the aggression he feared from the assembled group
of officers. Is this ever explained to the jury?

1   *THE COURT*:   Hand the verdict to the bailiff, please.
    THE CLERK: "Superior Court of the State of California, County of Del Norte,
         People of the State of California versus James Johnson. We the jury impan-
         eled in the above-entitled matter find the defendant, James Johnson, guilty
5   of battery on a correctional officer in violation of Section 4501.5 of the Penal
         Code, Officer Huston, Count 1.

         We the jury empaneled in the above-entitled matter find the defendant,
    James Johnson, guilty on Count 2, battery on correctional officer in viola-
    tion of Section 4501.5 of the Penal Code, Officer Van Berg.

NOTES AND QUESTIONS

1. Defendant Johnson appealed his conviction to the District Court of Appeals
in California. The appellate court stated that "[t]he only real dispute in appellant's
case was who provoked the incident." Was this the way the case was presented to
the jury in the closing arguments? Did the defense attorney even make an argument that the correctional officers started the melee? Consider the evidence in the
case that would sustain such an argument, or the related argument that the various
combatants misinterpreted each other's conduct to be aggressive. Think about the
stories you could tell to the jury that would raise a reasonable doubt about Johnson's
guilt.

2. Would evidence of other incidents at Pelican Bay have affected the outcome
in *Johnson*? Here is an excerpt from Judge Henderson's opinion in the Pelican Bay class
action, Madrid v. Gomez, 889 F. Supp. 1146, 1162, 1199-1200 (N.D. Cal. 1995):

> ...Castillo refused to return his food tray in protest against a correctional officer who
> had called him and other inmates derogatory names. After leaving the tray near the front
> of the cell, Castillo retreated to the back and covered himself with his mattress for protec-
> tion, in anticipation of a cell extraction. . . . Castillo, who is small in stature, made no
> verbal threats or aggressive gestures. . . .
>
> To accomplish [his] removal, two rounds from a 38 millimeter gas gun were fired
> into the cell. A taser gun was also fired, striking Castillo in the chest and stomach.
> Then, without attempting to retrieve the tray, . . . some number of officers entered the
> cell. . . . Castillo testified that one of the officers then hit him on the top of the head
> with the butt of the gas gun, knocking him unconscious. When he regained conscious-
> ness, he was on the floor with his face down. An officer was stepping on his hands and
> hitting him on the calves with a baton. . . . When he regained consciousness again, he
> was dragged out of the cell face down; his head was bleeding, and a piece of his scalp
> had been detached or peeled back. . . . [H]e was taken to the infirmary and then the
> hospital. . . .

On the basis of this and other incidents, Judge Henderson concluded:

> We agree that the extent to which force is misused at Pelican Bay, combined with the fla-
> grant and pervasive failures in defendants' systems for controlling the use of force...reveal
> an affirmative management strategy.... All together, [the evidence] paints a picture of a
> prison that all too often uses force, not only in good faith efforts to restore and maintain
> order, but also for the very purpose of inflicting punishment and pain.

Why do you think the defense lawyer in *Johnson* did not put the "management strategy" of Pelican Bay on trial? If the lawyer had tried, would the judge have permitted it? How many incidents would have to be tried in such a case? How would the prosecution have responded? How long would the *Johnson* case have taken to try if other incidents were explored at trial?

CHAPTER TWO

THE PROCESS OF PROOF: HOW TRIALS ARE STRUCTURED

As you begin your study of the law of evidence, it can be useful to put yourself in the role of the trial lawyer trying to present a case persuasively to the jury. This necessarily requires you to imagine at the same time how the trial process appears to the jurors. It is a bewildering mixture of the familiar and the unfamiliar. To begin with, most litigated events involve conventional human affairs. Although the prison setting in the *Johnson* case is outside the personal experience of most people, the crucial question for decision is simply how a fight came about, which reduces, as is typical, to the question of whom to believe—here, the inmate or the guards. Although the issues that typify litigation are usually within general experience, the decision-making methodology differs radically from the manner in which an ordinary citizen makes day-to-day decisions. The trial setting is unusual, perhaps on occasion mystifying, and often intimidating for jurors. Indeed, a theme running through the trial process that you may have already detected is the insulation of the jury from much of what happens during trial. Although, historically, juries were allowed to decide issues of law as well as fact—even as late as the end of the nineteenth century in the United States—the modern jury decides only factual issues. Therefore, virtually all legal discussion—including the proper substantive and procedural law to be applied to the case, and whether evidence should be admitted or excluded—occurs outside the hearing or presence of the jury. Relatively brief legal discussions in the midst of trial may be conducted in a sidebar conference, in which the lawyers and judge talk in low voices so as not to be heard by the jurors. Longer discussions are held either in the judge's chambers, or, if in the courtroom, at times when jurors are not present.

This theme of jury insulation also runs through the evidence course, because, to a large degree, the rules of evidence focus directly on the question of what evidence the jury will be allowed to hear. The policy implications of most evidence rules are therefore based on someone's answer to the question: What is the effect on the accurate resolution of disputes of allowing a jury to consider this type of information?

A.   THE ADVERSARY SYSTEM

The rules structuring litigation, including the rules of evidence, are derived from, and implement, the dominant theory of dispute resolution in this country, known as the adversary system. Adverse parties each present a self-serving version of the truth to a presumably disinterested fact finder, judge or jury, which hears the evidence the parties present and decides in a disinterested fashion what actually happened, and thus what verdict is appropriate. The adversarial process, in turn, is derived from a conception of the appropriate role of government in the resolution of disputes between private individuals and between the state and an individual. The government has the obligation to provide a fair and disinterested forum for the impartial resolution of disputes; and for the most part that is all the government has an obligation, or a right, to do. Even in criminal cases, the courts stand apart from the prosecution, treating the representatives of the sovereign as though they were representing a private party. The parties are responsible for investigating the case, preparing the case for trial, and in large measure controlling the presentation of evidence at trial. In this country, many believe that adversarial investigation and presentation of evidence is more likely to yield a verdict consistent with the truth than is a process more dominated by a tribunal.

This conception of the role of the government in the resolution of disputes is not universally shared. In the "inquisitorial" systems of many Western European countries disputes are not "private" matters to the extent that they are in the United States, and the adjudicative tribunal often involves itself actively in investigation, and controls the trial process much more than the litigants do. Those who favor continental systems are inclined to the view that control by a disinterested tribunal will lead to less abuse and manipulation of the evidence, thus increasing the chances that judgments consistent with the truth will emerge. For a discussion of these and related matters, see Mirjan Damaska, The Faces of Justice and State Authority (1986); Mirjan Damaska, Evidentiary Barriers to Conviction and Two Models of Criminal Procedure, 121 U. Pa. L. Rev. 506 (1973); John Langbein, The German Advantage in Civil Procedure, 52 U. Chi. L. Rev. 823 (1985); Ronald J. Allen, Stefan Köck, Kurt Riechenberg, and D. Toby Rosen, The German Advantage in Civil Procedure: A Plea for More Details and Fewer Generalities in Comparative Scholarship, 82 Nw. U. L. Rev. 705 (1988); Mirjan Damsaka, Evidence Law Adrift (1997).

B.   THE ROLES OF THE TRIAL PARTICIPANTS

Although probably quite familiar to you from fictional and real-life courtroom dramas, the well-defined roles of participants in a trial are worth briefly reviewing: *Witnesses* are people with knowledge of out-of-court events who are called on to reveal that knowledge in court, under oath, in front of the judge, jury, and litigants.

The jury (meaning each of its members) uses its senses to perceive information in the courtroom and its reasoning capacity to evaluate and make inferences about that information in order to reach a conclusion about which version of disputed events is (closer to?) the truth. Jurors are expected to come to conclusions about disputed facts in the case without bringing to bear any outside or firsthand knowledge of their own: Typically, they know nothing about the case beforehand, and (as in the *Johnson* case, page 4, supra) are instructed by the judge not to investigate the facts on their own. However, jurors are not expected to disregard their own generalized background knowledge and experience, and indeed it is assumed that they will use their knowledge and experience in reasoning and making inferences about the evidence before them. As is typical, the jury instructions in the *Johnson* case did not give the jury any guidance about what its reasoning process should be, other than to define "inference" and "circumstantial evidence," and to rule out certain "irrational" factors: emotions, the number of witnesses on a side, chance, or the drawing of lots. Pages 62-63, supra.

The advocates provide information to the jury through the use of witnesses, documents, and other exhibits.[1] Because the jury is passive, the role of the advocates is to investigate, interview, select, prepare, and present the sources of information that the advocates think will most advance their respective cases. This competitive process is at the heart of the adversary system of proof and it results in the presentation of competing and contradictory versions of events. The advocates also argue inferences and conclusions to the jury, but the jury is instructed that attorneys' statements are not evidence.

The judge controls the trial process by setting limits, primarily pursuant to the rules of evidence, on the advocates' proof in the interests of rationality of results, fairness between the parties, social and moral values, and efficiency. The judge has power to make all the trial participants conform to their roles in courtroom behavior and decorum. In addition, the judge may call witnesses and may question witnesses whether called by the court or not. See FRE 611 and 614. But the judge is not supposed to control the content or the overall presentation of the advocates' cases. Thus, a standard jury instruction states that neither side had to produce all witnesses who might have knowledge of the facts, or present all objects or documents that might be mentioned. Throughout this course you should ask whether the judge should have the power to keep knowledge about the disputed facts from the jury.

A note on bench trials: The rules of evidence have been created and shaped over time with the jury in mind as the fact finder. However, many trials are held without a jury. While the parties in most criminal cases and many civil claims for damages have a constitutional right to trial by jury, the parties sometimes waive that right and agree to a try the case to the judge without a jury. In addition, many civil cases—primarily, those seeking so-called equitable relief, such as injunctions—are tried before a judge without a jury. In such "bench trials," the judge acts not only as the decision maker on points of law and admission or exclusion of evidence, but also as the sole fact finder, weighing the evidence. A similar situation is presented by "evidentiary hearings": pretrial proceedings (such as a preliminary hearing in a criminal case) in which witnesses are called to testify. The rules of evidence typically apply in bench trials and evidentiary hearings, but because no jury is present, the application of the rules may be relaxed somewhat. The theory is that a judge, due to experience and professional training, can disregard inadmissible evidence far more easily and effectively than a jury. Therefore, erroneous admission or exclusion of evidence is thought to be less problematic; and the judge can couch findings in such a way as to claim that the decision would not be affected by a particular doubtful evidentiary ruling.

---

1. The judge in *Johnson* instructed the jury that "[e]vidence consists of testimony of witnesses, writings, material objects, or anything presented to the senses and offered to prove the existence or non-existence of a fact." Page 62, supra.

C.   *THE STRUCTURE OF THE TRIAL*

1.   Pretrial Motions

Trials usually begin with "motions *in limine*" (pronounced "in **lim**-in-ay," meaning "at the threshold"). These are motions made by the parties to obtain rulings on anticipated evidentiary problems. Parties anticipating the introduction of problematic evidence by their adversaries make motions in limine to *exclude* that evidence, though motions in limine can be used to get a pretrial ruling on any evidentiary question. Motions in limine are often made in writing, with short supporting briefs, and argued outside the presence of the jury.

Tactical considerations will typically drive counsels' decisions on whether to file motions in limine. For example, a criminal defendant, such as Johnson, may want to testify only if the jury will not learn of his prior criminal convictions. In order to make an informed decision about whether to testify, the defendant could file a motion in limine asking that the prior convictions be excluded from evidence. This would eliminate uncertainty as to whether the defendant's prior felonies will come before the jury. If no motion in limine were made, defense counsel would have to wait until the prosecutor were to ask, while cross-examining the defendant, "Isn't it a fact, Mr. Johnson, that you were convicted of rape in 1981?" and then object. Even if the objection were sustained, the jury, having heard the question, might nevertheless believe the prosecutor had a good-faith basis for asserting that the defendant had such a conviction. But if defense counsel were to have made a successful motion in limine, the prosecutor would be instructed ahead of time by the judge not to ask such a question at all.

2.   Jury Selection

Following motions *in limine*, the jury selection process begins. Jury selection varies both in the process for selection and the number of jurors empanelled, depending on the type of case and the jurisdiction; anywhere from six to 12 jurors may be required. In federal court, 12 jurors sit in criminal trials and six in civil trials.

The jury selection process is founded on the belief that trials are more likely to result in an accurate verdict—assigning liability or blame only where warranted by the facts—by having cognitively competent, disinterested jurors. Consequently, the process allows parties to object to potential jurors who are incompetent, who have a financial or emotional interest in the case, or who cannot put aside any preconceptions about the case they may have in order to decide it based on the evidence produced at trial.

The primary means of selecting a jury is by questioning the jury "venire"— the group from whom the jury panel will be chosen—in order to uncover any ground for dismissing them. The questioning process, called "voir dire,"[2] may be

---

2.   "Voir" is pronounced "vwahr" and "dire" is usually pronounced "deer," although the prevailing pronunciation in the South is "dire" (as in "dire straits"). The term *voir dire* applies not only to jurors in jury selection, but also to trial witnesses, when the latter are asked questions outside the presence of the jury in order to determine whether some aspect of their testimony will be admitted into evidence in front of the jury.

conducted by the trial judge, the lawyers, or by means of a written questionnaire, or by a combination of any of the three. (The most common practice in federal court is for the judge to do the questioning, with the lawyers' participation limited to suggesting questions to ask.) Questions may be directed to individual jurors, or to the venire as a whole. The judge can dismiss potential jurors "for cause" (such as some type of bias for or against one of the parties) or practical reasons (such as inability to serve for the length of the trial). The lawyers can request dismissal for cause, or may make so-called peremptory challenges. Because the lawyers are not required to give reasons for exercising peremptory challenges, they may be used, as a practical matter, for any reason at all, or no reason beyond a hunch or a whim. The only constraints on peremptory challenges are that each side is given only a limited number, and that they may not be used merely because of the race or sex of the potential juror. See Batson v. Kentucky, 476 U.S. 79 (1986) (race); J.E.B. v. Alabama ex rel. T.B., 511 U.S. 127 (1994) (sex).

Properly conducted, voir dire is a sensible way to begin a trial designed to elicit a rational verdict. Even if people are generally rational, competent actors, from time to time some are also unable to put aside interests and biases that may infect their decisions (as is true of judges as well, who are disqualified for similar reasons). Investing some time and effort in removing such people from the trial makes eminent good sense. Like much of the trial process, the laudable social goal is achieved through taking advantage of the self-interest of the parties, whose respective desires to wind up with the most favorable jury possible will, it is hoped, cancel out and result in a reasonably fair-minded panel of jurors.

3.   Preliminary Instructions

Once the jury is empanelled and sworn, the judge will typically issue some preliminary jury instructions. Again, practice varies from court to court, and judge to judge: These instructions may be nothing more than admonitions not to talk about the case prior to jury deliberations; or may include certain generic guidelines about considering the evidence or credibility of witnesses; or, less typically, may even include instructions about the substantive law governing the case. In *Johnson*, the court read the jury a series of generic instructions as well as the "information," the written criminal pleading setting forth the charge, which stated the statutory elements of the alleged crime.

4.   Opening Statements

Now, the lawyers take turns introducing their respective cases to the jury, in the order in which they will present evidence: The plaintiff (civil) or prosecution (criminal) proceeds first, then the defendant. An opening statement is neither evidence nor argument, but is supposed to be a compact narrative of what the lawyer believes in good faith the evidence will show. The "official" purpose is to provide the jury with a coherent overview of the case to make it easier for the jurors to assimilate the testimony they will soon hear, testimony that may necessarily tell the story in a fragmented, nonchronological fashion.

Argument is not allowed in an opening statement, and can result in an objection being sustained. Generally speaking, conclusions or inferences derived from the evidence, contentions about legal rules, and comments about witness credibility are considered "argument." For example, pointing out weaknesses in your adversary's case would clearly constitute objectionable argument. However, the line between a factual statement and an argument is not always clear, much like the distinction between factual news reporting and editorializing, and is equally hard to draw. A great deal falls into a gray area between "evidence" and "argument." Consider the facts of People v. Johnson: To say in an opening statement that "the defendant violently attacked Officer Walker" is closer to "argument" than is "the defendant punched Officer Walker with his fists," yet both could be considered statements of evidence. How much leeway the lawyers get depends heavily upon the discretion of the trial judge. A good practical method to assess the evidence/argument distinction is to ask whether a witness could say it on the stand—if so, then it is probably evidence.

Notwithstanding the rule against argument, the lawyers are advocates, and they will present the facts in the light most favorable to their cases. A well-presented opening statement can, without editorializing, offer a compelling argument for one side, and many trial advocates contend that juries begin to make up their minds on hearing the opening statements. (There is empirical research to support this view.)

Trial lawyers often describe the opening statement as the lawyer's "covenant with the jury." The representations about what "the evidence will show" are best viewed as promises, because the jury may resent or mistrust the lawyer whose claims in the opening statement are not backed up by evidence admitted during trial. This means that it is risky in the opening statement to stress evidence whose admissibility is in doubt.

5.   Presentation of Evidence and the Burden of Production

The evidence-presentation phase is obviously the core of the trial. The manner in which the parties introduce evidence is discussed below. (See infra, Section D.) This section deals with the order in which the parties present their cases and with the key, related issue of the burden of production.

a.   *The Order of the Parties' Presentation of Cases*

After opening statements, the plaintiff/prosecution presents its case-in-chief. This means calling a series of witnesses to the stand. Primarily through the direct examination of these witnesses,[3] the plaintiff/prosecution must present evidence sufficient to prove—that is, sufficient to support a finding by the jury to establish—each element of its cause of action (or of the crime charged). In the *Johnson* case, for example, the charge of battery (one of several charges against Johnson) required the prosecution to prove: (1) willful and unlawful (2) use of force or violence (3) upon the person of another.

After the plaintiff or prosecution "rests" its case, and any motion to dismiss is heard (and denied), defendant's case begins. Like the plaintiff, the defendant conducts direct examinations of witnesses, but the thrust of the defense case is to cast

---

3.   Two important devices make it unnecessary, in many instances, to prove facts through testimony or other evidence at trial: These are known as "stipulation" (facts agreed by the parties) and "judicial notice" (see Fed. R. Evid. 201, discussed in Chapter Eleven, infra).

doubt on the plaintiff's evidence and to present evidence sufficient to prove each element of any affirmative defenses.

When the defense rests its case, the plaintiff/prosecution has an opportunity to call witnesses in a so-called rebuttal case. (The term *case-in-chief* is used to distinguish the plaintiff's main case from its rebuttal case.) The presentation of rebuttal evidence proceeds in the same way as in the case-in-chief, except that the scope of rebuttal evidence is limited. Rebuttal evidence must respond to either (a) matters raised as part of defendant's affirmative defenses; or (b) attacks during the defense case on the credibility of the plaintiff/prosecution's evidence. Normally, a plaintiff or prosecutor will not be allowed to repeat evidence presented in its case-in-chief, or to present evidence that should have been part of its case-in-chief. A defendant may be entitled to a "sur-rebuttal" (a rebuttal to the rebuttal), but this is unusual. The rebuttal case is necessarily much shorter than the case-in-chief.

b. The Burden of Production

The "burden of production" (discussed in detail in Chapter Ten) means producing enough evidence so that a "reasonable" fact finder can make a finding for the plaintiff or prosecution on each element of the civil claim or criminal charge. The "fact finder," again, is the jury in jury trials (or the judge in bench trials). The "finding" involved is a finding of the facts necessary to establish those elements of the claim or charge, and it must meet the applicable "burden of persuasion"—"beyond a reasonable doubt" in criminal cases, and "more likely than not" (also known as "a preponderance of the evidence") in civil cases.

Thus, the plaintiff meets its burden of production in civil cases with evidence sufficient for a reasonable jury to find that the facts establishing each element of the plaintiff's claim are more likely than not true. In a tort case, for instance, the plaintiff has to present evidence sufficient for jury findings on duty, breach, causation, and damages. In a criminal case, the prosecution meets its burden of production if it offers enough admissible evidence so that a reasonable jury can find that each element of the crime charged has been established "beyond a reasonable doubt." In the *Johnson* case, for example, this meant producing evidence sufficient for the jury to find beyond a reasonable doubt that, among other things, Johnson "touched" Huston or Van Berg in the manner described in the jury instructions.

(Note: In civil cases, defendants have the burden of production on their affirmative defenses. In criminal cases, however, the prosecution has the burden of production to *negate* any defenses, such as "self defense" in the *Johnson* case.)

A failure by the plaintiff or prosecutor to meet the burden of production on each element of a claim can result in a judgment as a matter of law for the defense on that claim. Motions for judgment as a matter of law can be made at several different points in the litigation process. In civil cases, motions for summary judgment (before trial), nonsuit/directed verdict/dismissal (after plaintiff's case-in-chief), directed verdict (after close of evidence) or JNOV (after verdict) all argue that the moving party wins the case on facts that are not genuinely disputed. (In federal civil cases, such motions made during or after trial are now all called motions for judgment as a matter of law. See Fed. R. Civ. P. 50.) In criminal cases, only the defendant can move for judgment as a matter of law, and may do so after the prosecution's case-in-chief, after close of evidence or after the verdict.

There is a basic similarity between all these motions seeking judgment as a matter of law on a factual record: In each, the court is supposed to refrain from usurping the jury's role. This means that the judge should not resolve conflicts in the evidence or questions of witness credibility. Moreover, if the party with the burden of production has produced enough evidence to support a finding by a reasonable jury, the court should not issue judgment based on the judge's own view of how the jury should decide the case. Put another way, the judge has to make all inferences in favor of the party opposing judgment as a matter of law.

The verbal formulae for judgment as a matter of law may sound different in summary judgment as compared to a post verdict motion, and in civil as compared to criminal cases, but they are all essentially the same: whether there is evidence sufficient for a reasonable jury to find for the prosecutor or plaintiff (or civil defendant on an affirmative defense). A defense counsel in a civil case might argue:

> Your Honor, plaintiff's evidence is not sufficient to support a finding by a reasonable jury that its version of the facts is more likely than not true. Some of the necessary facts are just plain missing, and on others, the evidence is based on inferences that are just too weak. Plaintiff's case should not get to the jury; judgment should be granted as a matter of law.

For criminal cases, substitute "prosecution" for "plaintiff" and "beyond a reasonable doubt" for "more likely than not."

The burden of production, and the resultant prospect of losing a judgment as a matter of law, has important implications for the order in which a party will present its evidence. While evidence that arises during the defendant's case can ultimately be relied upon by the plaintiff or prosecution as proof of such elements, it is extremely unwise for a plaintiff or prosecutor to do so, because the defense can make its motion for judgment as a matter of law at the end of the plaintiff's (or prosecutor's) case-in-chief, without putting on any of its own witnesses. The defense in People v. Johnson, did just that, arguing that there was insufficient testimony to show that the alleged battery victims, Huston and Van Berg, were ever actually touched by the defendant Johnson.

6.   Post-evidence Matters

After the close of evidence, the court may take up certain legal matters with the lawyers outside the presence of the jury. The defendant may make a motion for "directed verdict" on the ground that "no reasonable jury" could find for the plaintiff because the evidence, as a matter of law, fails to establish one or more elements of the plaintiff's claims; or that the plaintiff has not raised sufficient evidence to dispute an affirmative defense. Similarly, the plaintiff could move for judgment as a matter of law on the ground that the defendant has not raised sufficient evidence to dispute its claims. (The prosecution cannot move for a directed verdict of guilt, because that would be deemed a violation of the criminal defendant's Sixth Amendment right to jury trial.)

At this stage the parties also argue over jury instructions. Most courts require the litigants to submit proposed jury instructions. These are to assist the court, which has the ultimate responsibility to decide how the jury will be instructed; indeed, the trial court can come up with its own instructions, and need not adopt what is proposed by the parties. Many of the instructions are standard (and may be contained in books or manuals of "pattern" jury instructions). The parties typically agree quickly upon generic instructions of the sort given in every case—an instruction on the burden of persuasion, for example. Arguments usually arise over how to instruct the jury on substantive law, particularly in areas where the law is developing or unsettled. If a party disagrees with an instruction the court decides to give, it may object and argue instructional error as a basis for appeal. For that reason, some trial judges, hoping to reduce grounds for appeal, may try to pressure or cajole the parties to agree on compromise instructions on controversial points.

In order to avoid keeping the jury waiting while the final jury instructions are physically typed up, the court may hold the jury instruction conference before the close of evidence; however, most judges like to wait until the evidence phase is near an end, because some important jury instruction questions will depend upon what evidence was actually presented. Once these legal issues are resolved, the jury is called back to the courtroom for one last phase of presentations—closing argument and jury instructions.

7. Closing Arguments

Unlike opening statements, in which argument and discussion of the law are prohibited, closing argument permits both. In closing argument, the lawyers "argue" the facts. Significantly, they may only discuss facts based on evidence admitted at trial. "Arguing the facts" is not merely summarizing the evidence; rather, lawyers in closing argument should analyze the evidence, identifying and arguing for the inferences and conclusions they believe should be drawn from it. A critical feature of closing argument should be to explain to the jury the chain of inferences that connect the evidentiary facts heard by the jury with the facts of consequence in the case. If you found the closing argument of defense counsel Deemer in the *Johnson* trial to have been unsatisfactory, an important reason for this may be that he failed to establish this inferential chain as to much of his key evidence. Throughout this book, we use diagrams to illustrate this chain of inferences, which you will see is necessary not only to argue the significance of evidence to a jury, but also to determine the application of such rules as relevance and hearsay.

An effective closing presents a coherent story of the events that proves one's case, while trying to show how the most likely interpretation of every point of conflict or ambiguity in the evidence supports that story. The lawyers should stress evidence corroborating key points of their cases as well as evidence that undermines the credibility of witnesses whose testimony contradicts key points.

Finally, it is also important to weave key jury instructions into the closing argument: In this way, the lawyers can show the jury how they believe the evidence maps onto the controlling substantive law—how they have proved the elements of their case and how the other side has failed to cast doubt on the proof or to prove its own case. This aspect of the closing links the facts of consequence with the essential elements required by the substantive law, a point that we illustrate diagrammatically throughout this book.

Courts vary in their practice of whether closing argument goes before or after jury instructions. The important point is that disagreement over jury instructions has been resolved before closing argument. That way, even if closing argument goes before the jury is actually instructed, the lawyers can refer to the jury instructions in their closing.

8.   Jury Instructions and the Burden of Persuasion

Because jury instructions are a fertile source of "error" for the losing litigant to raise on appeal, most trial judges instruct the jury by simply reading word-for-word the written set of instructions. While extemporizing or ad-libbing might keep the jury's attention better than a droning verbatim recitation, trial judges typically opt for the prudent (if dull) approach of sticking to the script. (An exception to this might be the type of boilerplate instructions and admonitions given to the jury before opening statements.) Jury instructions can be quite lengthy and complex, and difficult if not impossible to remember on one hearing. Thus, courts in many jurisdictions provide the jury with a written copy of the instructions to take into the jury room for their deliberations; strangely, however, many courts do not allow that, and at most will offer only verbal repetition of instructions if it occurs to the jurors to request it.

An important concept explained to the jury in every case in the form of a jury instruction (and usually by the lawyers in closing argument as well) is the burden of persuasion. Earlier, we explained the burden of production as requiring a party to produce evidence sufficient to support a finding on a particular issue. The burden of persuasion specifies the degree of certainty that the jury must have in order to make a finding on a particular issue. This concept is further explained in Chapter Ten. In civil cases, the jury must find by a preponderance of the evidence that the plaintiff's claims are true. A preponderance of the evidence means greater than a 50 percent probability, or "more likely than not." In criminal cases, the burden of persuasion is guilt "beyond a reasonable doubt."

9.   Jury Deliberations and Verdict

After closing arguments and jury instructions, the jurors go into the jury room for their deliberation. Jurors are allowed to have all the exhibits—the documents and objects admitted into evidence—with them in the jury room. They can also request to have portions of testimony read back to them (and are usually instructed that they can do this). Such "read-backs" involve bringing the jurors back into the courtroom, with the lawyers present, to hear the court-reporter reading the testimony from the stenographic notes (typically in a monotone). Some courts allow jurors to take notes during trial, and to bring their notes with them into deliberations. While jurors may ask questions about the facts or the law during deliberations (by having the bailiff bring out a note to the judge), the answers are often very uninformative. Unless the parties agree on a response, the judge will be loath to create grounds for appeal with an informative but arguably erroneous response to a question.

Again, depending on the type of case, the jury verdict may or may not have to be unanimous. While unanimity is required in federal criminal cases, many jurisdictions permit nonunanimous verdicts in civil and even some criminal cases. Federal civil verdicts must be unanimous unless the parties agree otherwise. Fed. R. Civ. P. 48.

In criminal cases, a verdict takes the form of a decision—guilty or not guilty—on each crime charged. Civil verdicts present more possibilities. In some trials, the jury is asked only for a general verdict—"we find for the plaintiff," plus an amount of money damages, where that is the issue, or "we find for the defendant." In many cases, particularly where the legal issue has a more complex structure, the court may use a "special verdict" form or "jury interrogatories." Under these latter practices, the jury is asked for its answers to a series of questions from which a judgment can be derived. These questions might ask for separate jury findings on each element of a claim or a defense. Given that the burden of proof is on the plaintiff to prove each element of its case, a special verdict form or jury interrogatories may work to the defendant's advantage, because a "wrong" answer to any one of several questions may result in a defense judgment. On the other hand, if a general verdict is used in a legally complex case, the jury may not have followed the correct path to its final verdict. Such mistakes in the jury's reasoning process are not considered proper grounds for an appeal. Indeed, the evidence rules in most jurisdictions prohibit any inquiry into the jury's mental processes or deliberations. See, e.g., FRE 606(b). Once the jury has rendered its final verdict, and announced it in court, the jury is dismissed.

Some trials are "bifurcated" or even "trifurcated"—conducted in two or three separate phases, each one with its own set of jury instructions and closing arguments, and its own separate verdict. Examples of this are civil cases involving punitive damages and criminal cases involving the death penalty. In both these examples, the logically prior issue is liability or guilt—is the defendant liable at all?—whereas the issue of penalty, which may be based (at least in part) on other bad conduct separate from the tort or crime alleged in the case, calls for evidence irrelevant to liability or guilt but that might sway the jury against the defendant. These kinds of cases are thus "bifurcated" into a "liability" or "guilt" phase—whether the defendant committed the tort or crime—and a "penalty" phase. The penalty phase is not even reached if the jury returns a defense verdict in the liability phase.

10. Post-trial Motions

Once the jury has rendered its verdict and been dismissed, the jury trial proper is over. Significantly, the "verdict" is not the same as the "judgment" in a case. A verdict is the jury's ultimate decision. A judgment is a judicial act that concludes a case. After a jury trial, the trial judge eventually enters a judgment on a jury verdict. The judgment, usually a short document of a page or two signed by the trial judge, may do nothing more than restate the jury's verdict. In some cases, however, the judgment may include further issues that are not decided by a jury—such as injunctive relief, for example. It is the judgment, rather than the verdict itself, which has such legal effects as res judicata and that is subject to appellate review. Also, the judgment may differ from the jury verdict if, for example, the court grants a post-trial motion reversing the verdict.

Post-trial motions form an important aftermath of the trial. They do not occur right away, but within periods of a few weeks (set by statute or court rule) after the jury's verdict, but before the entry of judgment in the case. There are two types of post-trial motions: motion for judgment notwithstanding the verdict, and motion for new trial. The party that loses the case (or loses at least one ultimate issue) can bring either of these motions, and typically brings both together. In essence, a post-trial motion is an "appeal" from a jury verdict, only it is made to the trial judge rather than to an appellate court. And, indeed, an appeal from a jury verdict to a court of appeal requires that these motions have been made; technically, appellate review of a jury trial is actually review of a trial court decision denying a motion for new trial or for judgment notwithstanding the verdict.

A motion for judgment notwithstanding the verdict (also known by its Latin equivalent, "judgment *non obstante veredicto*," or "JNOV" for short) seeks judgment as a matter of law, on the ground that (again, considering the evidence in the light most favorable to the nonmoving party), the court can say that no reasonable jury could have reached this particular verdict. If the motion is granted, the court reverses the jury verdict and enters a directly contrary judgment: A defense verdict is overruled and judgment entered for the plaintiff, or vice versa.

A judgment notwithstanding the verdict allows the court, in effect, to delay the type of decision put to it in a directed verdict motion. A court might be inclined to direct a verdict in favor of the defendant, for example, due to the apparent insufficiency of the plaintiff's evidence. By deferring its ruling on this question until after the jury renders its verdict, however, the court allows the jury the opportunity to find against the plaintiff and thereby possibly avoids the need itself to make an outcome-dispositive ruling that would be subject to appellate review. In federal court, a motion for judgment notwithstanding the verdict can only be made if the moving party had previously moved for a directed verdict. (Fed. R. Civ. P. 50(b).)

The parties can move for a new trial on any of several grounds: erroneous jury instructions, excessiveness or inadequacy of a jury's damage award, irregularities in the trial or the jury deliberations, or—most significant for our purposes—erroneous admission or exclusion of evidence. These new trial motions argue that significant errors undermined the trial, which, therefore, must be done over.

The losing party can also move for a new trial on the ground that the verdict is "against the weight of the evidence." This is a lower standard than that required to get a judgment as a matter of law. Put another way, while a JNOV argues, in essence that the nonmoving party has failed to meet its burden of production, a new trial motion typically argues that the nonmoving party failed to meet its burden of persuasion. In contrast to motions for judgment as a matter of law, the trial judge gets to weigh conflicting evidence and assess witness credibility in considering whether to grant a new trial. Again, granting a new trial motion results in trying the case over, rather than determining the outcome of the case.

D.   *EXAMINATION OF WITNESSES AND FRE 611*

The questioning (or "examination") of witnesses, and the witnesses' answers—their testimony—form the core of the trial, as seen above. Most evidence in most trials takes the form of testimony. Of course, documents, photographs, demonstrative and other tangible objects are introduced into evidence. However, as we will see in this course, the rules of evidence require presentation of testimony about documentary or tangible evidence to establish its admissibility and often to explain its significance. (Documentary and tangible evidence requires a witness to provide foundation testimony unless the parties agree to forgo the formalities.) Therefore, witness testimony is generally the most crucial form of evidence.

The examination of witnesses in the evidence-presentation phases of the trial follows a pattern of taking turns. The party calling the witness conducts a direct examination. The opposing party cross-examines, with cross-examination being limited in scope to matters raised on direct examination. The party calling the witness may respond to points made on cross by conducting a redirect examination. Recross and further redirect examinations can be permitted.

The rules for presenting testimony, including the order of examinations, are not set out in the rules of evidence or any procedural code. Rather, they arise from an unwritten tradition of trial practice that has developed over the years. The only provision of the Federal Rules dealing directly with witness examinations is FRE 611, which seems to take largely for granted the established modes of presenting direct and cross-examinations, specifying only a few limitations and otherwise granting the trial judge broad discretion over "the mode and order" of examining witnesses.

1.   FRE 611

RULE 611.   MODE AND ORDER OF EXAMINING WITNESSES AND PRESENTING EVIDENCE

(a) *Control by the Court; Purposes.* The court should exercise reasonable control over the mode and order of examining witnesses and presenting evidence so as to:
   (1) make those procedures effective for determining the truth;
   (2) avoid wasting time; and
   (3) protect witnesses from harassment or undue embarrassment.

(b) *Scope of Cross-Examination.* Cross-examination should not go beyond the subject matter of the direct examination and matters affecting the witness's credibility. The court may allow inquiry into additional matters as if on direct examination.

(c) *Leading Questions.* Leading questions should not be used on direct examination except as necessary to develop the witness's testimony. Ordinarily, the court should allow leading questions:
   (1) on cross-examination; and
   (2) when a party calls a hostile witness, an adverse party, or a witness identified with an adverse party.

2.   Interpretation and Illustration of FRE 611(a) and (b)

a.   FRE 611(a): Breadth of the Court's Power

FRE 611(a) recognizes in broad terms the sweeping authority of the judge to control the examination of witnesses during the trial. Indeed, even the two express provisions purporting to limit the scope of cross-examination (subsection (b)) and the use of leading questions (subsection (c)) may be overridden in the discretion of the trial judge to serve the purposes outlined in Rule 611(a). This principle is reflected by the words "should" in Rule 611(b) and (c) and the Advisory Committee Note to FRE 611(a), which states:

Spelling out detailed rules to govern the mode and order of interrogating witnesses and presenting evidence is neither desirable nor feasible. The ultimate responsibility for the effective working of the adversary system rests with the judge. The rules set forth the objectives which he should seek to attain.

Thus, the following discussion of FRE 611 and witness examination is best under-stood not as a summary of binding rules, but rather as a description of the common trial practice that judges tend to follow out of long-standing tradition.

b.   Direct Examination

Trials are usually won or lost on the strength of a party's case-in-chief rather than the weaknesses in the opponent's case. Direct examination—the questioning of wit-nesses you call in your case-in-chief—is the most straightforward and effective way to prove your case. Indeed, each party must plan to meet its burden of production with evidence developed through direct examination. It is simply not feasible—or strate-gically sound—to depend on eliciting needed evidence through cross-examination. Therefore, direct examination is extremely important, and probably the dominant feature of success at trial.

FRE 611 says nothing affirmatively about direct examination, but simply assumes that direct examination will be conducted. As we discuss below, FRE 611(b) states that direct examination should set a limit on the scope of cross-examination and in 611(c) provides that, with limited exceptions, leading questions should not be used on direct examination.

c.   FRE 611(b): The Scope of Cross-examination

Cross-examination is one of the defining features of the adversary system. "For two centuries, common law judges and lawyers have regarded the opportunity of cross-examination as an essential safeguard of the accuracy and completeness of testi-mony. They have insisted that the opportunity is a right, not a mere privilege."[4] Direct examination generally reflects some degree of cooperation between the examiner and the witness, and therefore raises the danger that the witness will be permitted, if not encouraged, to present a self-serving version of events. Cross-examination is an effec-tive way to test the witness's credibility and show that there may be another side to the story. It also provides some of the more exciting moments in a trial.

FRE 611(b) establishes, as a guideline, that two general areas of inquiry are per-missible for cross-examination. First, it is permissible to explore matters about which the witness has testified on direct examination. For example, in the *Johnson* case defense counsel's cross-examination of the correctional officers explored details of the altercation about which the witnesses testified on direct examination.

Second, it is always permissible to ask questions that may impeach the credibility of the witness even though there may have been no reference to these matters on

---

4.   John W. Strong, et al., McCormick on Evidence 34 (5th ed. 1999). Wigmore suggested that the "abuses and puerilities often found associated with cross-examination" were outweighed by its value. "It may be that in more than one sense it takes the place in our system which torture occupied in the medi-aeval system. . . . Nevertheless, it is beyond any doubt the greatest legal engine ever invented for the dis-covery of truth." 2 John Henry Wigmore, A Treatise on the System of Evidence in Trials at Common Law 1697 (1904). The latter phrase is oft-repeated. See, e.g., California v. Green, 399 U.S. 149, 158 (1970).

direct examination. For example, the prosecutor in the *Johnson* case cross-examined Johnson's cell mate, George Butler, about Johnson's and Butler's gang affiliations even though this subject was not part of the direct examination (pages 44, 56, supra). The purpose of these questions, as the sidebar conference makes clear, was to undermine Butler's credibility by showing his bias or prejudice in favor of Johnson. Similarly, in the *Johnson* case it was appropriate for the prosecutor to ask defense witnesses about prior convictions not mentioned on direct examination because proof of prior convictions is one of the traditional ways to impeach a witness's character for truthfulness.

The same principle applies to the rehabilitation of witnesses on cross-examination. Thus, if a direct examiner impeaches a hostile witness, it would be appropriate to rehabilitate the witness on cross-examination with questions about matters relating to credibility that were not covered on direct examination.

Unless the court exercises its discretion pursuant to the last sentence of FRE 611(b), it is improper to explore on cross-examination subjects that were not mentioned on direct examination and that do not affect the credibility of a witness. Consider, for example, the testimony in the *Johnson* case of Ruth Taylor, the records specialist (page 35, supra). Her direct examination testimony was limited to questions about Johnson's criminal record. Thus, even if Taylor had been an eyewitness to the jail cell incident, it would have been inappropriate, in the absence of special permission from the court, to question her about the incident on cross-examination. If the defendant wanted to explore the matter with Taylor, the proper course of action would be to call her as a witness during the presentation of the defense.

d.   *Redirect and Recross-examination*

The direct examiner may conduct a redirect examination when cross-examination has been completed. The scope of redirect is limited to matters that were raised in cross-examination; this means that the direct examiner is usually not permitted to prove an essential element of the case that was overlooked, although judges vary widely in how strictly they will enforce this limitation.

Recross and further redirect examinations are sometimes allowed. Each such successive examination is smaller in scope since it is limited to responding to the immediately preceding redirect or recross-examination. Although the party calling the witness is theoretically entitled to the "last word," judges will not let this process go on ad nauseam. Such seesawing back and forth with redirect and recross, trying to have the last word, can irritate the judge and jury, and usually develops no new information. (This occurred frequently in the *Johnson* trial, but has been edited out of the transcript in Chapter One.)

3.   Elaboration of FRE 611(a) and (b) and the Examination of Witnesses

a.   *Direct Examination*

On direct examination, the goal is to let the witness provide pieces of narrative, in his or her own words, that build an overall "story" to the jury. It is important to help your witness appear as credible as possible, since the witness will be supporting your case. Furthermore, most of the evidence you will introduce at trial comes in through direct examination. Although you can also introduce evidence through cross-examination, the danger in relying on cross-examination (by definition, the questioning of witnesses called by your opponent) to introduce key evidence is that you have no control over what witnesses your opponent will call; if your opponent elects not to call a witness you were counting on to introduce some vital testimony, document, or other evidence, you may find you have failed to prove some essential element of your case.

Conducting an effective direct examination can be more challenging than you might think. Generally speaking, the witness will describe one or more incidents or factual occurrences, things the witness did or perceived. Your role as questioner is generally that of a skilled, sympathetic interviewer. Imagine that you know someone who has a very interesting story to tell, and that you would like someone else to hear the story. Although you could tell the story in your own words, you believe it would be much more effective coming from the person who had the experience firsthand. The witness should be allowed to testify in a narrative format, with the lawyer's questions keeping the story moving forward, keeping the witness from digressing, and helping to vary the pace so the witness's story does not become boring.

Questions for the most part should be open-ended: "What happened next?" "What did you see?" "Why did you do that?" Witnesses should be allowed to explain their actions. One way to remind a witness to concentrate on communicating with the jury is occasionally to begin a question with an admonition: "Tell the jury . . ." As the direct examiner, you also have to pace the testimony by asking several short questions and answers followed by a question with a longer narrative answer, followed by short questions again. Consider the kind of narrative that occurs when a lawyer fails to pace the testimony with questions, such as when defendant Johnson spoke at the outset of his direct examination. Was this an effective presentation of Johnson's story? Should witnesses be allowed to testify in that manner?

As a general rule, a witness you call in your case will be cooperative enough to meet with you in advance. (There is an important exception to this. See "c. Direct Examination of 'Adverse' and 'Hostile' Witnesses," below.) This means that you can and should "prepare" the witness by giving some idea of the subject matter you plan to cover. Many attorneys rehearse the direct examination, asking the planned questions and giving tips about how to answer them. The idea of this is not to put words in the witness's mouth but to help the witness tell the story effectively and avoid pitfalls that would unduly damage credibility. Preparing the witness, while essential, also poses an additional challenge. Having rehearsed the direct testimony with a cooperative witness and become thoroughly familiar with it, you must nevertheless appear to have a genuine interest in the questions being asked and to ensure as much as possible that the witness is not merely reciting a rehearsed text, but sincerely communicating to the jury.

b.   Cross-examination

FRE 611(b) embodies the "American" or "restrictive" rule of cross-examination, in contrast to the wide-open rule of cross-examination, used in the English trial system, which permits the opposing party to question witnesses about anything that is relevant to the case. The primary advantage of the American rule is that it allows the parties to control the development of their cases. For example, the plaintiff may wish to introduce a document into evidence early on in the trial and may need to call the defendant or somebody closely associated with the defendant to authenticate the document. Even if the witness has knowledge of other aspects of the case, the plaintiff, for reasons of strategy, may not want to go into those matters at this time or with this witness. If the plaintiff limits the direct examination to the question of authentication, application of the restrictive cross-examination rule will prevent the defendant on cross-examination from exploring the witness's knowledge about other aspects of the case.

The primary advantage of the English rule is that it avoids the necessity of determining what the scope of direct examination was. While the English rule also avoids the necessity of recalling witnesses who may have testimony to give regarding several issues in a case, FRE 611(b) reserves for the trial judge the discretion to accomplish the same efficiency by permitting questions about matters that are beyond the scope of direct examination, in which case the examination shall be conducted "as if on direct examination." This means, in effect, that the witness has become the cross-examiner's witness and that, therefore, "leading questions should not be used . . . except as may be necessary to develop the witness' testimony." FRE 611(c).

i.   **Strategy and Goals of Cross-examination.**   An important strategic goal for you as a cross-examiner is to take advantage of the subtle opportunity to argue your case. Whole lines of questioning can develop themes that you can emphasize by repetition and then argue to the jury in closing. Leading questions, which can be asked on cross-examination, also provide an opportunity to make assertions that emphasize the inferences or interpretations you want the jury to draw from the evidence.

A second goal of cross-examination is to fill in gaps in your evidence or obtain favorable admissions. Sometimes an adverse witness is the only witness who can provide admissible testimony needed to establish an element of your claim or defense, or to tell part of the story you want to convey to the jury. In many instances, you may have to call such a witness yourself as an "adverse witness." In addition to filling in gaps, some witnesses called by your opponent may make (voluntarily or otherwise) admissions favorable to your side. Helpful testimony can be particularly strong when it comes from the mouth of the adversary or his witnesses.

Finally, you can use cross-examination questions to control damage by minimizing the effect of adverse testimony by one or both of two means. Without discrediting the witness, you can try to show how the witness's version of the facts is consistent with, or at least not inconsistent with, your theory of the case. Or you can discredit the witness by attacking his or her credibility, either on specific points or overall. Typically, a witness will not have been called by your opponent to testify unless that testimony helps the opponent's case. (If it does not, you may not need to bother with cross-examination.) There are several techniques for discrediting, or attacking the credibility of, a witness. These techniques, known collectively as "impeachment," are discussed in Chapter Seven.

ii.   **Cross-examination Technique.**   The manner of conducting cross-examination is perhaps most easily understood by contrasting it with direct examination. Because direct examination seeks to develop the story through the witness's own words and to bolster the witness's credibility, the direct examiner wants the jury to focus on the witness. Factual information arising out of the testimony should therefore come from what the witness says, not the questioner. Questions should be shorter than the answers; and should generally be open-ended. The question "why" is often effective on direct.

On cross-examination, by contrast, the lawyer wants to provide (in effect) most of the information the jury hears, while attempting to limit what the witness actually says by asking leading questions. This usually means making an assertion of fact to which the witness can fully respond by simply agreeing with a "yes" or "no" answer. Skilled cross-examiners try to formulate precise, narrow questions that don't call for explanation, keeping open-ended questions to a minimum. In particular, "how" and "why" questions are generally avoided like the plague: Such questions are an open-ended invitation to the witness to give a self-serving explanation of the facts and argue inferences adverse to your case. After a "why"-type question, you may be standing there while the witness goes on at length and you have no basis to shut the witness off.

An old saw about cross-examination is not to ask "one question too many." This usually means that you shouldn't ask the witness to agree to a conclusion or inference that constitutes the point you will make in closing argument, even if you feel that the conclusion follows logically from a series of propositions that the witness has agreed to. The witness will invariably disagree and attempt to give a self-serving explanation, arguing his or her own case. It can be difficult to know when you have reached the stopping point where the next question is the "one too many." If words like "thus" and "therefore" seem to be part of the question, that is a red flag not to ask it.

c.   Direct Examination of "Adverse" and "Hostile" Witnesses

FRE 611(c) sets forth two circumstances in which a direct examination may be conducted in the manner of a cross-examination, using leading questions and following the tactics of cross-examination: the direct examination of "adverse" and "hostile" witnesses.

"Adverse witness" is a term used in common legal parlance to refer to "an adverse party, or a witness identified with an adverse party" within the meaning of FRE 611(c). This concept includes not only the adverse party, but also his/her/its agents, employees, and people who, through legal or other ties, are strongly identified with the adverse party. It is not uncommon to call such an adverse witness in your case-in-chief. You would typically call an adverse witness where some item of evidence necessary to prove your case is uniquely within the knowledge of the adverse witness; or where there is reason to believe that the adverse witness will be so disliked or disbelieved by the jury that his testimony will necessarily help rather than hurt your case. An example would be calling the alleged sexual harasser to the stand to show the jury what a bad guy he is, with the goal of thereby supporting the plaintiff's credibility. If an adverse witness is necessary or strategically helpful to your case, you may not want to run the risk of waiting to cross-examine this witness. Your adversary may not call this witness; or may do so but keep the direct examination so circumscribed that you will not be able to cover the subjects you want on cross-examination. (See FRE 611(b), limiting scope of cross-examination.)

When questioning an adverse witness on direct examination, you are allowed to use leading questions and, as a tactical matter, should use all the techniques of cross-examination. Although using cross-examination techniques, you do not have a limitation on the scope of questioning as you do on an actual cross-examination. When you are finished, your adversary has the right to do a "friendly cross-examination," during which leading questions will normally be prohibited, as though that were a direct examination. See Advisory Committee Notes to FRE 611(c) (the word "Ordinarily" in "Ordinarily leading questions should be permitted on cross-examination" is designed to encourage judges to prohibit leading questions on "friendly cross-examination").

A "hostile witness" is one who is presumed friendly or neutral when called to the stand (i.e., a non-adverse witness), but who, during questioning, demonstrates an attitude sufficiently hostile to the questioner to raise an inference of opposition to the examiner's client or identification with the adverse party. The examining attorney then asks the court to declare the witness "hostile." If the court does so, the examiner can proceed with leading questions, and may want to use the other cross-examination techniques as well.

In addition to asking leading questions, the party calling an adverse or hostile witness may also impeach that witness — attack the witness's credibility using the techniques and rules discussed in Chapter Seven. According to FRE 607, "the credibility of a witness may be attacked by any party, including the party calling the witness." Indeed, the rule suggests that a party may impeach a witness on direct examination even if the witness is not formally adverse or hostile. FRE 607 abolishes the common law "voucher rule," according to which a party who called a witness was held to vouch for the credibility of that witnesses. See 3A John Henry Wigmore, Evidence §896, at 658-660 (James Chadbourne rev. 1970). Despite the unqualified language in FRE 607, some courts have held that it is impermissible to impeach one's own witness if the impeachment is a subterfuge to get otherwise inadmissible evidence before the jury. The admissibility of evidence for impeachment purposes, when that evidence is inadmissible as "substantive evidence," is discussed in Chapter Seven.

4.   Interpretation and Illustration of FRE 611(c): Leading Questions

Leading questions are questions that suggest the answer the examiner is seeking. A classic example of a leading question takes the form of a statement with a brief interrogative tag at the beginning or end, such as "You saw defendant Johnson lunge out of his cell with his fist, didn't you?" FRE 611(c) confirms — again, in the form of a guideline to the trial judge — the common practice that leading questions are normally prohibited on direct, but allowed on cross-examination. This rule thus accounts for the most obvious difference between the mode of conducting direct and cross-examination. ("Redirect" is treated the same as direct examination, and recross the same as cross-examination for purposes of the leading question rule.) The assumption underlying FRE 611(c) is that a witness is likely to be friendly or at least cooperative with the party calling the witness, and will not be equally cooperative with the cross-examiner. This presumed bias against the cross-examiner may make leading questions essential in order to get at the truth. If counsel were not permitted to ask a very specific "Isn't it true that . . .?" question that calls for a yes or no answer, it might be impossible adequately to explore the details and nuances of the witness's knowledge and testimonial qualities. Conversely, because of the witness's presumed willingness to cooperate with the direct examiner, there is thought to be a risk that the suggestiveness in leading questions on direct examination may cause the witness to distort the truth in the direct examiner's favor.

5.   Elaboration of FRE 611(c) and Leading Questions

a.   *What Is a Leading Question?*

A leading question is best defined as one that suggests the answer the questioner wants the witness to give. This definition is probably overbroad; on some level, many if not most questions asked on direct suggest in some way what the questioner wants the witness to say. If they didn't, there would be no way to direct the witness's attention to the type of information the examiner is seeking. Therefore, many, perhaps most, questions that fit this definition will ultimately be allowed, because the judge (or opposing counsel) believes them to be nonleading or else to be "borderline" or close calls that do not merit the trouble of making or sustaining an objection. Ultimately, the "test" of a leading question may often come down to a matter of degree—how suggestive is the question?—that is heavily dependent on context. You have to develop an intuitive feel for when these "borderline" questions are leading or nonleading.

A common misconception is that questions calling for "yes or no" answers are leading; in actuality, some in that form are, some aren't. For example, "Do you live in Chicago?" is not leading.

Leading questions are often phrased as an assertion of fact, ending either with a tone of voice implying a question mark at the end, or with an actual verbal tag asking the witness to agree.

You were at home the night of the murder, isn't that correct [. . . isn't that true?. . .
   right? . . . weren't you?]?
Weren't you at home the night of the murder?
You were at home the night of the murder?
Isn't it a fact that you were at home the night of the murder?

In this form, the questions are clearly leading. But questions can be leading without taking this form. It is the suggestion of the desired answer that makes a question leading. A typical leading question occurs when the questioner suggests a fact to a witness who seems to have overlooked it. Consider the following piece of direct examination of Officer Huston from the *Johnson* trial (page 14, supra).

Q: Why was inmate Johnson and inmate Butler secured, handcuffed? What's the
    purpose?
A: Because if they are combative or not complying with orders; disciplinary reasons,
    you know?
Q: Officer safety reasons?
A: Yes, officer safety and security.

The prosecutor wanted the witness to give "safety" as the reason for handcuffing the inmates, but the witness said "discipline" instead. Imagine that defense counsel had made a timely objection after "Q: Officer safety reasons?" and that the objection was sustained (as it should be). The problem with the question is its leading form, not that the answer will put inadmissible matter before the jury. (This will be further explained when we deal with the subject of "objections.") Here, the prosecutor can then simply rephrase the question.

Q. BY MR. CUMMINGS: Okay, Officer Huston, was "officer safety" a further reason to handcuff the inmates?
MR. DEEMER: Objection. That's still leading.
THE COURT: Sustained.

This question is phrased more like a normal question than a statement, but it is really no different from the first time it was asked: It still suggests the desired answer.

Q. BY MR. CUMMINGS: [Huge sigh.] Did you have any reasons other than disciplinary reasons for handcuffing the inmates?

This question may be borderline. It could technically be construed as leading because, in the present context, the question suggests that Huston should say "yes." Whether a question unduly suggests the desired answer may often depend on context. But the judge would in all likelihood overrule a "leading" objection at this point; also the jury will start to think that the objecting lawyer did not want the information to come out.

A: Yes.
Q: What other reason or reasons?
A: Officer safety.

To be sure, the "leading" objection did not keep the witness from supplementing his answer in the manner suggested by the questioner—an attentive witness would know what he's supposed to say from the first phrasing of the leading question. However, the objections may serve to make the point to the jury that the ultimate answer was the "lawyer's answer" more than the witness's, and—who knows?—the questioner might have moved on without getting the answer after the first objection was sustained.

b.   Leading Questions: Tactical Considerations

In practice, there will be considerable variation in how much leading you can "get away with" in direct examination. If the opposing counsel does not object, the court is unlikely to stop you on its own initiative. Even if objections are made, the trial judge has virtually unreviewable discretion to allow leading questions. In the *Johnson* case, the prosecutor got away with numerous leading questions that were truly objectionable because the defense counsel didn't bother to object (perhaps because he was discouraged that the judge overruled his "leading" objection when he made one). See, e.g., pages 10, 19-20, 23, supra.

There is a down side, however, to asking a lot of leading questions. Because the focus on direct examination should be on the witness, rather than on the examiner, leading questions can backfire as a direct examination technique. A witness who delivers key testimony in response to leading questions on direct examination will give the impression of saying whatever the lawyer wants, and can lose credibility. And of course, conducting a direct examination in this way makes the examiner vulnerable to objection: "Your Honor, counsel is testifying rather than the witness." On the other hand, if the witness is weak, equivocal, or otherwise has difficulties getting his testimony out in his own words, it may on balance be better to lead than not—if you can get away with it.

E.   OBJECTIONS AND PRESERVATION OF ERROR FOR APPEAL: FRE 103

The substantive rules of evidence revolve most clearly around two features of the trial process that remain to be considered: trial objections, and "making a record" that preserves evidentiary issues for appellate review. These two subjects are closely intertwined. Evidentiary rulings admitting evidence over objection will virtually never be the basis of appellate reversal without a clear, direct, and correct objection in the trial record. If evidence is excluded, the losing side must make sure that the substance of the evidence, and the theory of its admissibility, are apparent from the record in order to preserve the issue for appeal. FRE 103(a)(2). It is the job of the advocates to create a record that adequately reflects the objection, any response to it, and the judge's ruling. This is called "perfecting the record" and "preserving the issue for appeal." In this section we will first discuss the principles and mechanics of objections, and then turn to appellate review of the trial record.

1.   FRE 103

RULE 103.   RULINGS ON EVIDENCE

(a) *Preserving a Claim of Error.* A party may claim error in a ruling to admit or exclude evidence only if the error affects a substantial right of the party and:

(1) if the ruling admits evidence, a party, on the record:

(A) timely objects or moves to strike; and

(B) states the specific ground, unless it was apparent from the context; or

(2) if the ruling excludes evidence, a party informs the court of its substance by an offer of proof, unless the substance was apparent from the context.

(b) *Not Needing to Renew an Objection or Offer of Proof.* Once the court rules definitively on the record—either before or at trial—a party need not renew an objection or offer of proof to preserve a claim of error for appeal.

(c) *Court's Statement About the Ruling; Directing an Offer of Proof.* The court may make any statement about the character or form of the evidence, the objection made, and the ruling. The court may direct that an offer of proof be made in question-and-answer form.

(d) *Preventing the Jury from Hearing Inadmissible Evidence.* To the extent practicable, the court must conduct a jury trial so that inadmissible evidence is not suggested to the jury by any means.

(e) *Taking Notice of Plain Error.* A court may take notice of a plain error affecting a substantial right, even if the claim of error was not properly preserved.

2. Interpretation and Illustration of FRE 103(a) and (d): Objections, Offers of Proof, and Preservation of Evidentiary Issues for Appeal

An objection is the means by which a lawyer can interrupt the trial to oppose the introduction of evidence. Although objections are most frequently made to questions or answers during a witness's testimony, objections can be made to any type of evidence: real evidence, demonstrative evidence, or testimony. The purpose of an objection is twofold: (1) if the objection is sustained, to increase your chances of winning the trial by excluding harmful evidence from consideration by the trier of fact; (2) if the objection is overruled, to preserve for appeal your argument that the evidence should have been excluded, pursuant to FRE 103(a)(1).

When an objection is made, one of three things will usually happen. The court will "sustain" (agree with) the objection, "overrule" (disagree with) the objection, or ask counsel for further elaboration or argument, usually outside the hearing of the jury, such as at the sidebar. If the judge rules on the objection right away, the losing lawyer may feel it necessary to try to make further argument before the trial proceeds any further, and may ask to approach the bench to argue the point. Trial lawyers typically request such sidebar conferences when the judge's ruling will admit significantly prejudicial evidence, or will deprive the party of an opportunity to present evidence at the right moment in the trial.

Moreover, where an objection has been sustained, it may be necessary for the lawyer offering the evidence to approach the bench to make an offer of proof. FRE 103(a) (2) provides that in order to preserve an appeal of an erroneous ruling excluding evidence (an incorrectly sustained objection), the party must "[make] the substance of the evidence . . . known to the court" unless the substance "was apparent from the context in which the questions were asked." This procedure of advising the court of the substance of the excluded evidence is called an "offer of proof." Id. An offer of proof can take the form of a statement on the record by counsel summarizing what the excluded evidence would show (e.g., "Your Honor, the witness would testify that Officer Smith told him that the prison was on lockdown because Officer Walker had beaten an inmate.").

FRE 103(a) provides that an evidentiary ruling will be a ground for reversal on appeal only if two conditions are met. The error must "affect a substantial right" of a party, meaning that the ruling made some difference in the outcome of the trial. Second, the party must have made a timely objection and, where the ruling excludes evidence, an "offer of proof" alerting the court to the substance of the excluded evidence. Failure to object will probably mean that the judge's ruling, or the adversary's behavior, cannot be grounds for reversal. There is an exception to this general rule. "Plain" error, referred to in FRE 103(d), means an error so serious, and so obvious, that it can be grounds for reversal even though no objection was made to it during trial. The trial judge should have noticed it, and it is highly probable that it affected the outcome. This doctrine was originally developed in criminal cases to protect defendants from the errors of appointed counsel. Under FRE 103(d) it applies in civil cases as well.

3. Elaboration of FRE 103(a)(1) and (2) and Objections

a. Two Types of Objections

There are two basic types of objections: an objection to the improper form of a question, and an objection to the admissibility of the answer.

An objection to admissibility of the answer is intended to exclude inadmissible evidence. Such objections are made when it appears that the question, even if properly phrased, calls for evidence barred by exclusionary rules of evidence or whose relevance or foundation has not been established. Most of the substantive law of evidence that you will study in this course concerns these questions of admissibility, and the grounds for ruling on the objections are for the most part found in the rules of evidence.

An objection to the form of the question is intended to regulate the mode of questioning and the behavior of the examiner. In contrast to objections going to admissibility, objections as to form are governed by traditional trial practice and the trial judge's inherent, discretionary authority rather than formal evidence rules.[5] Examples of objections to the form of the question include "leading," "argumentative," see pages 10, 23, 30-31, supra, or "calls for a narrative response." Other examples of objections to the form of the question include "compound," "vague," "ambiguous," "mischaracterizes the testimony." (See "Trial Objection Cheat Sheet," page 118, infra.)

Questions objectionable as to form may be sustained even though the evidence they seek is ultimately admissible. Consider the beginning of Officer Van Berg's direct examination in People v. Johnson (page 20, supra):

Q: Did you have occasion on that day [March 28] to come into contact with an inmate by the name of Johnson?
A: Yes, I did.
Q: Same individual seated at the end of counsel table?
A: Yes.

The last question is leading, and would have been objectionable had the defendant's identity as the perpetrator been in dispute. It would be the form of the question that is objectionable, not the answer. The same information could be obtained through a proper nonleading question:

Q: Do you see that person in the courtroom today?
A: Yes.
Q: Where?
A: Seated next to the defense counsel.

A common mistake of inexperienced attorneys is to move on to the next question after an objection to the form of the question—such as "leading"—has been sustained.

Questions can violate more than one rule relating to form, and it is appropriate to mention multiple grounds for the objection.

Q: Did you see the defendant first lunge at Officer Walker and then eventually strike Officer Huston?

---

5. An arguable "source" of authority to rule on objections as to form is FRE 611(a), which directs the trial judge to "exercise reasonable control over the mode and order of interrogating witnesses and presenting evidence[.]" Courts rarely cite FRE 611(a) for these or other purposes, however. In fact the rule adds little, if anything, to what is explicit or implicit in other rules. For example, FRE 403 provides authority to exclude cumulative evidence, and FRE 102 admonishes courts to construe the rules "to secure fairness in administration, elimination of unjustifiable expense and delay, and promotion of growth and development of the law of evidence to the end that the truth may be ascertained and proceedings justly determined."

DEFENSE COUNSEL: Objection: leading, compound.
THE COURT: Sustained.

In addition to its leading form, the question is also compound because it asks the witness to describe two logically separable facts of importance to the case. The objections can also be made one after the other, if the first one is overruled.

DEFENSE COUNSEL: Objection, compound.
THE COURT: Overruled.
DEFENSE COUNSEL: Leading.
THE COURT: Sustained.

It is also possible, of course, that a question can be framed in an objectionable form and seek arguably inadmissible matter. Consider the discussion of "Facility B" during the Huston direct examination in *Johnson*. Suppose the prosecutor, Cummings, had introduced this subject with the question:

Q: Isn't Facility B a transition facility for violent inmates coming out of SHU, before they are placed in general population?

This question is not only leading (an objection to form), but it also calls for arguably inadmissible character evidence to the effect that defendant Johnson is a violent person because he was housed in Facility B. This example also illustrates how a timely objection will not always be adequate to prevent the jury from hearing inadmissible matter—here, it was embedded in the prosecutor's leading question.

b.   Timing of Objections

Making timely objections is probably the most difficult trial skill to learn. In a very short time—often no longer than the second or two before the witness answers the question—you have to determine whether the question is objectionable, on what basis, whether tactically the objection is worth making, and then actually say "objection," typically while getting to your feet. This is challenging to do. But failing to make a timely objection can result in a failure of both goals of objecting at all. A failure to object—and even an untimely objection—fails to keep the evidence from the jury, and normally waives the evidentiary error on appeal. There is a narrow exception to this so-called contemporaneous-objection rule: Under FRE 103(d), an appellate court may correct "plain error" in spite of the absence of a contemporaneous objection. The plain error exception is used "sparingly," and only to correct "particularly egregious errors" that would result in a miscarriage of justice if not corrected. United States v. Young, 470 U.S. 1, 15 (1985).

A timely objection to the form of the question must be made before the question is answered. This point is easy to understand. In *Johnson*, the defense counsel was consistently late in objecting to the prosecutor's questions (see, e.g., page 23):

Q: Did he appear to you to be attempting to fight or strike Walker or any of the officers?
A: Yes.
MR. DEEMER: One moment. That's leading.

If the answer is given before the objection, judges will often allow the answer to stand, and will either overrule the objection or simply say, "the witness already answered" or "the answer stands." But there is also an expectation that the witness should not jump the gun with his answer. If the witness answers an objectionable question after the objecting lawyer has already started speaking or before the judge rules, the judge may strike the answer and caution the witness not to answer questions while objections are being made or ruled on.

A timely objection to the inadmissibility of an answer must be made as soon as the inadmissibility becomes apparent. This can be tricky. Typically, it will be apparent that a question is likely to call for an objectionable response: "Did they tell you that something had happened to your hand?" sounds like it calls for inadmissible hearsay, for example. Or suppose a supervising correctional officer were to testify that he sent the correctional officers to Johnson's cell to retrieve the trays, but that he did not go himself. If such a witness were asked whether Johnson hit or kicked Huston or Van Berg, the question would clearly call for speculation or lack the foundational requirement of firsthand knowledge. Where a clear potential for an inadmissible answer inheres in the question, the objection should be made before the answer is given. However, in contrast to objections to the form of the question, where the judge is unlikely to strike the answer, if you did not object fast enough to an inadmissible answer, you might still object belatedly and ask the judge to strike the answer.

Sometimes, the objectionable matter cannot be anticipated from the question. "Tell us what happened next" is generally an unobjectionable question, but the witness could say all kinds of things that are not admissible testimony. Consider, for example the lengthy narrative defendant Johnson gave in response to defense counsel's question "Would you explain to the jury what that problem [concerning the package] was?" The lengthy answer that followed contained some arguably objectionable hearsay and irrelevant matter. It is fair game to cut the witness off with an objection and motion to strike as soon as the objectionable character of the answer becomes clear; most judges will be more lenient about striking inadmissible portions of an answer in this situation, even if you did not jump in at the first possible moment. For example:

Q: Tell us what happened next.
A: Well, the Sergeant told me we were on lockdown because —
COUNSEL: Objection. Hearsay. Move to strike.
THE COURT: Sustained. The answer is stricken.

When inadmissible matter has gotten in front of the jury and you failed to object (presumably because you couldn't anticipate the objectionable matter from the question) the proper response is a motion to strike the offending testimony, and perhaps a request for the judge to admonish the jury to disregard it.

Q: Tell us what happened next.
A: Well, the Sergeant told me we were on lockdown because another inmate had gotten beat up by Officer Walker.
COUNSEL: [Snapping belatedly to attention.] I move to strike the last answer. It's inadmissible hearsay.
THE COURT: The last answer is stricken. The jury will disregard it.

c.   Stating the Objection

An objection is not preserved for appeal unless "a timely objection or motion to strike appears of record, stating the specific ground for the objection." FRE 103(a)(1).

In practice, you will encounter and even make both specific and general objections. A general objection is an expression of an objection without stating the grounds. Where the basis for the objection seems obvious, the lawyer may say nothing more than "objection"—or the judge may rule on it without waiting for the lawyer to specify the grounds. You may hear similarly "general" objections using some boiler-plate phrase that does not specify the ground, such as "Objection to the form of the question," or one that is merely vague and conclusory, such as "irrelevant, incompe-tent, and immaterial." It may not hurt your case if you make a general objection that is sustained, because your goal of keeping the evidence out is accomplished, and you have no basis to appeal your own successful objection. If a general objection is over-ruled, however, it is likely to be deemed to waive the issue on appeal for failure to state the ground. Therefore, it is better practice to specify your grounds in the objection.

It is vital to state the correct basis for the objection. The judge is required to rule only on the stated ground of the objection. If you state an invalid basis for an other-wise proper objection, your objection could be overruled even if it could have been sustained on another ground. Judges do not usually cue an attorney as to the correct objection, or make the correct objection on their own. More likely, the judge will simply overrule an incorrect objection.

Specific objections need only communicate the basic reason for the objection. "Objection, hearsay" should probably be sufficient to preserve the point for appeal; it is not necessary to spell out your theory as to how the only relevant use of the out-of-court statement is for the hearsay purpose of proving the truth of the matter asserted. Indeed, most judges frown upon so-called speaking objections—making arguments in the course of stating an objection—and may even specifically warn the lawyers at the start of the trial to refrain from doing so. The general rule of decorum, then, is to state the ground for an objection as succinctly as possible; and if extended argument is needed, the objecting lawyer is expected to request a sidebar conference.

As you can see from the "Trial Objection Cheat Sheet," which follows on pages 118-119, there are certain commonly used words or phrases to make certain routine objections. But these are not magic words; anything that gets the point across suc-cinctly will do. "Objection, calls for inadmissible character evidence" and "Objection, Rule 404" probably would both suffice to make the same point. In addition, laundry lists of common or boilerplate objections should not obscure the fact that an objec-tion can be based on any rule or principle that would exclude the evidence. Some of these principles may not be adequately expressed in the common boilerplate terms.

Some experienced trial practitioners suggest trying to put objections into plain language rather than using legal buzz-words. Since the objection tends to signal the jury that you want to keep them from hearing something, that impression may only be reinforced when the objection is stated in legalese. Thus, it may be preferable to say "Objection—this witness has no way of knowing who wrote the document" rather than to say "Objection—lack of foundation." On the other hand, using plain language could run afoul of a judge's warning against "speaking objections." In addition, there may be occasions when you want to obscure your reasons from the jury. You have to use your judgment.

If offending matter has already been stated by the witness, the proper procedure is to make a motion to strike. You need to specify both the grounds for the motion (which are the same kinds of points as grounds for objections) and the portion of testimony you contend should be stricken. "I move to strike the witness's answer in its entirety. It's hearsay." or "Motion to strike as nonresponsive. I move to strike the witness's answer after the word 'yes.'" Having testimony stricken is, of course, a much less effective remedy than preventing it from coming into the record before the jury. As the old saying goes, "you can't unring a bell." However, it should be done to preserve the issue for appeal. Moreover, the remedy can have a practical consequence if the jury asks for a "read-back" of the trial transcript during jury deliberations: Stricken portions of testimony are omitted from the read-back.

d.   Tactical Considerations

Many objectionable questions are asked with impunity because the opposing counsel decides an objection is not worth making. Again, an objection signals to the jurors that counsel wants to keep them from hearing some information. This could create an impression of having something to hide, and this downside of objecting has to be weighed against the damage to one's case if the evidence comes in. Other downsides to objecting can include irritating the judge or jury, or (if the objection is made during your opponent's cross-examination of your witness) possibly confusing the witness. Objections to the form of a question may simply cue your adversary to phrase a clearer, more effective question. Moreover, an objection can often underscore the damaging aspects of an objectionable question, and wisdom may on these occasions dictate silence in the hope that the jury will miss the point. Finally, objectionable questions sometimes will be helpful to your case either because the specific answer will be helpful or because the question will "open the door" to helpful testimony that might not otherwise be admissible.

On the other hand, there are tactical advantages to making objections. Jurors will expect the lawyers to make some objections, which gives you some leeway to do so without reaching an irritation threshold. Moreover, by sitting mute while your witness is being flogged with seemingly unfair questions, you may send a signal that you are being lazy, inattentive, or indifferent to your case. Finally, objections—particularly if sustained—can disrupt the rhythm or flow of your opponent's examination or leave your opponent stumped as to how to ask a proper question to get in some important piece of evidence.

Of course, these tactical considerations in favor of objections—particularly those regarding disruption of one's adversary's questioning—do not justify making objections in bad faith. To be sure, some trial attorneys will cross the line and make objections purely to rattle the opposing counsel; but one hopes that bad karma will be visited upon them. You should have a good-faith, arguable basis for any objection you make.

4.   Elaboration of FRE 103(a) and (d): Preservation of Error for Appellate Review

The appellate court reviewing the defendant's conviction in People v. Johnson ruled that the prosecutor committed prosecutorial misconduct by referring to Johnson's alleged gang membership when questioning inmates Butler and Johnson, and in closing argument to the jury. (See pages 44-45, 56, and 69, supra). The court held this to be misconduct because no evidence was ever produced that gave the prosecutor reasonable grounds for believing that Johnson was in fact a gang member. The court held the error was harmless, however, because

> the passing mention of gangs was a peripheral matter in appellant's case. The jury knew that the defense witnesses were inmates in a maximum security prison [and that] appellant was a rapist, Butler a robber, and Green a murderer. In these circumstances, it is not reasonably probable that the jury's assessment of credibility would have been materially different if gangs had never been mentioned.

How are such issues concerning erroneous admission (or exclusion) of evidence raised and preserved for appellate review?

a.   Making the Record—in General

When a judgment is rendered based on a jury or bench trial, any appeal is most likely to focus on the evidence "in the record." Appellate questions of substantive law will look at whether sufficient evidence supports the legally defined elements of the claims or defenses. Evidentiary questions will consider whether the appellant's rights were unduly harmed by excluding evidence that should have been admitted or admitting evidence that should have been excluded. Such determinations can't be made without, typically, a review of "the record" of the trial.

The phrase "the record" often is meant as a broad reference to the trial court's file on the case. It contains all the court papers filed by the parties' lawyers, transcripts of any trial or evidentiary hearing held by the court, and any evidence submitted in a trial, hearing, or motion. The trial "record" is a subset of the court's file, including the trial transcripts and exhibits. The key point is that the record serves as the universe of facts and trial court rulings within which an appellate court must operate in making its rulings on appeal. Appellate courts are not allowed to "go outside the record" by considering facts or legal arguments that have not been presented to the trial court.

At trial, therefore, it is vitally important for counsel to be attentive to the record to ensure that it is complete, both in terms of evidence and legal arguments and rulings. "Making the record" very often means nothing more or less than having what is said recorded (typically stenographically) and ultimately transcribed by the court reporter so that it becomes part of the official trial transcript. Sometimes, the judge, either inadvertently or by design, will conduct some important moments of legal argument or ruling during the trial without the court reporter present—an argument in chambers or a sidebar conference, for example, might go unrecorded, and therefore be "off the record." In such cases, it is the responsibility of the lawyer to put the matter "on the record"—that is, to summarize what occurred when the court reporter is back on duty and making the verbatim record. Otherwise the matter occurring off the record could be effectively insulated from appellate review. For example, the sidebar conference involving whether to admit evidence about "Facility B" in *Johnson* happened to be held on the record. Had it not been, an appellate court would have been no more able to review the issues raised in that discussion than you would have been as a reader of the transcript.

Likewise, lawyers have to be conscious of the record becoming garbled or confusing. There are a number of mistakes that inexperienced trial lawyers occasionally make that can be avoided by paying careful attention to what is occurring at trial. Think about the following issues: (a) overlapping—if a trial is being conducted with a court reporter, which is still typical today, the reporter cannot accurately record what happens when more than a single person talks at once. In such a circumstance, the careful attorney will be sure to go back and explain "for the record" what transpired; (b) spelling—names often cause problems because quite different spellings are often pronounced similarly (e.g., White, Whyte, Wite, Wyatt); (c) figures—when an attorney says "thirty-one-o-four," does this mean 3104, 31.04, 30,104, or what? Make sure it is clear; (d) gestures—make sure gestures are explained ("let the record show that the witness pointed at the defendant").

b.   Making the Record for Appeal of Evidentiary Rulings

For purposes of appeal of evidentiary rulings, "making the record" means complying with FRE 103. The appealing party must have made ("on the record") a specific objection or an offer of proof, depending on whether the disputed item of evidence was admitted or excluded. See FRE 103(a)(1) and (2). This requirement of FRE 103(a) is a mainstay of the adversary system. The judge is not responsible for running an error-free trial. Rather, the burden is on the parties to protect their own interests through timely arguments aimed at redressing errors that significantly affect their interests. The advocates must therefore take the initiative to object to their opponents' improper use of evidence or other inappropriate courtroom behaviors. In addition, the advocates must make known the grounds for their objections, and the opponent is always given the opportunity to respond. Only then is the judge required to, and is in a better informed position to, make a ruling that affects the conduct of the trial. This requirement raises the stakes of the lawyer's tactical decisions as to when or when not to object.

Motions in limine and FRE 103 interact in important ways. Formerly in many federal courts (and still in several state court systems), if a motion in limine to exclude evidence was denied, the advocate was required to renew the objection to the evidence at trial in order to preserve the issue for appeal. Effective December 1, 2000, however, FRE 103(a) was amended to provide that any "definitive ruling on the record admitting or excluding evidence, either at or before trial" is now sufficient "to preserve a claim of error for appeal." This amendment was specifically intended to apply to "so-called *in limine* rulings." Advisory Committee Notes to FRE 103.

c.   Standards of Appellate Review of Evidentiary Errors

Analytically, appellate courts proceed through two steps in considering whether a trial judgment should be reversed for an erroneous evidentiary ruling. The first analytical step asks "was there error?" Most, but not all, trial court decisions about whether to admit or exclude evidence are reviewed on appeal under an "abuse of discretion" standard. This means the appellate court will not "substitute its judgment" for that of the trial court—that is, the appellate court will not redecide the issue as though it were the original decision maker. (The latter kind of appellate review is called "independent" or "de novo" review. De novo review is applied to trial court rulings deemed "questions of law," such as whether the court selected the correct legal rule or interpreted it properly. This is discussed further in Chapter 3, Section B.3.) Under the abuse of discretion standard, to find error at all, the appellate court has to conclude that the trial court's decision was not merely wrong, but something close to an unreasonable decision.

Second, if there was error, was the error "harmless"? FRE 103(a) states that an appeal based on an erroneous ruling admitting or excluding evidence at trial cannot win a reversal unless the error affects a "substantial right" of the party. "Substantial right" has been construed by courts in most circumstances as invoking the "harmless error" standard. An error is harmless if it did not affect the outcome of the trial. Would the jury have reached the same result had the erroneously admitted evidence been excluded (or had the erroneously excluded evidence been admitted)? If so, the error is harmless. California Evidence Code §353, interpreted in the appeal of the *Johnson* case, similarly requires that the error resulted in a "miscarriage of justice." Both FRE 103 and the California Code thus require the appellate court to answer the same question—how likely is it that the error actually affected the outcome?

What degree of certainty must there be in evaluating the hypothetical state of affairs (the outcome of the trial had the error not been made)? Here, there is some variation among different courts. For example, the U.S. Court of Appeals for the Ninth Circuit formulated the "harmless error" standard as requiring the appellate court to affirm the trial court if the evidentiary error "more probably than not was harmless," or if there was a "fair assurance" that the error was harmless (e.g., United States v. Hitt, 981 F.2d 422 (9th Cir. 1992)). The Third Circuit phrased the standard differently: The trial court will be affirmed only if it is "highly probable" that the evidentiary error did not affect substantial rights (e.g., McQueeney v. Wilmington Trust Co., 779 F.2d 916 (3d Cir. 1985)). The California standard applied in the People v. Johnson appeal holds that a judgment should be reversed only if it is "reasonably probable" that the error affected the outcome.

The foregoing has assumed what might be thought of as "garden variety"—that is to say, nonconstitutional—error. Some erroneous evidentiary rulings are held to violate constitutional rights—for example, erroneous admission of hearsay might violate a criminal defendant's Sixth Amendment right to confront opposing witnesses. Where constitutional error occurs, the trial court judgment will be affirmed only if the error was "harmless beyond a reasonable doubt."

F.   REFLECTIONS ON NATURAL REASONING AND THE ADVERSARY SYSTEM

1.   The Adversary System Reconsidered

In the United States, the adversary system remains the dominant theory of litigation. The concept that disputes are for the most part private matters controlled by private individuals before relatively passive judges does not seem under serious reconsideration on a broad scale. Perhaps it should be, however, for at least two reasons.

The first is that the adversary system is based on the assumption that each party will be effectively represented, which means among other things that the parties will have the resources necessary to fund the litigation. This assumption is often false and can lead to poor presentation of one side or the other (or both) of a dispute. Such wealth disparity can in turn lead to the dramatic effect of litigants with resources being systematically and on occasion decisively favored over their impecunious adversaries.

The second reason for reconsidering our commitment to the adversarial system is the possibility that the nature of cases being litigated is changing from the bipolar assumptions of the traditional model, which involves two private litigants disputing an essentially private matter, to a "public law model" that looks much different. Consider the following:

> The characteristic features of the public law model are very different from those of the traditional model. The party structure is sprawling and amorphous, subject to change over the course of the litigation. The traditional adversary relationship is suffused and intermixed with negotiating and mediating processes at every point. The judge is the dominant figure in organizing and guiding the case, and he draws for support not only on the parties and their counsel, but on a wide range of outsiders—masters, experts, and oversight personnel. Most important, the trial judge has increasingly become the creator and manager of complex forms of ongoing relief, which have widespread effects on persons not before the court and require the judge's continuing involvement in administration and implementation. School desegregation, employment discrimination, and prisoners' or inmates' rights cases come readily to mind as avatars of this new form of litigation. But it would be mistaken to suppose that it is confined to these areas. Antitrust, securities fraud and other aspects of the conduct of corporate business, bankruptcy and reorganizations, union governance, consumer fraud, housing discrimination, electoral reapportionment, environmental management—cases in all these fields display in varying degrees the features of public law litigation. . . .
>
> [As a consequence of this changing model of litigation] [t]he courts . . . continue to rely primarily on the litigants to produce and develop factual materials, but a number of factors make it impossible to leave the organization of the trial exclusively in their hands. With the diffusion of the party structure, fact issues are no longer sharply drawn in a confrontation between two adversaries, one asserting the affirmative and the other the negative. The litigation is often extraordinarily complex and extended in time, with a continuous and intricate interplay between factual and legal elements. It is hardly feasible and, absent a jury, unnecessary to set aside a contiguous block of time for a "trial stage" at which all significant factual issues will be presented. The scope of the fact investigation and the sheer volume of factual material that can be exhumed by the discovery process pose enormous problems of organization and assimilation. All these factors thrust the trial judge into an active role in shaping, organizing and facilitating the litigation. We may not yet have reached the investigative judge of the continental systems, but we have left the passive arbiter of the traditional model a long way behind. [Abram Chayes, The Role of the Judge in Public Law Litigation, 89 Harv. L. Rev. 1281, 1282-1283, 1284, 1297-1298, 1302 (1976).]

These two matters, wealth disparity and the changing nature of litigation, cast some doubt on the foundations of the adversarial system of litigation, although they are by no means dispositive arguments against it. As you proceed with your studies, consider on the one hand whether full-blown adversarial litigation within the rules of evidence is too complex and burdensome for simple, straightforward cases involving at least one party with relatively scarce resources, and on the other hand whether the adversarial process and strict rules of evidence are too rigid and crude to deal with complex modern litigation. Think also of what possible alternatives there might be.

Yet another issue to consider emerges from the *Johnson* transcript. The rules of evidence are not rigidly adhered to at every turn in a trial; in many specific instances, they are either largely ignored or applied for the most part with a large dose of lenient discretion. On the other hand, at a few crucial places in the trial the rules of evidence seem to matter a great deal and lead to pointed arguments. In the *Johnson* trial, for example, this occurred where character evidence is disallowed in order to preclude inference of action in conformity therewith. See pages 8-9, supra. Why is that? Is that a healthy or a troubling sign? How typical do you think the transcript is in this respect?

As you will also see, each year more and more cases involve expert testimony of various kinds, which means that one or both of the litigants think that the case can be tried fairly only by employing specialized knowledge that is beyond the common knowledge and experience of the layperson. As your studies progress, ask how well the legal system takes advantage of the knowledge and expertise of other disciplines. For that matter, how well does it take advantage of the knowledge of the common citizen? That question leads to the next issue.

2.   Why Have Rules of Evidence?

To resolve disputes about past events, we have to make judgments about what actually happened. This means finding facts, which in turn requires evidence of those facts. The law of evidence structures the process of proof at trial, but it does so with an interesting constraint. In many instances the individuals deciding the facts will be laypersons chosen at large from the community to serve on juries. They are amateurs at legal fact-finding. Jurors are not, however, amateurs at fact-finding in general. Every competent member of society from an early age begins to collect and perfect methods of fact-finding that facilitate navigating the environment, and most of us do so with remarkable efficiency. In large measure, the law relies on these natural reasoning processes that its fact finders (juror or judge) possess. Indeed, the law could rely on them exclusively. It could permit the parties to present whatever evidence they like, the fact finders to make whatever investigation they like, and let the natural reasoning process of the fact finders lead them to whatever decision they believe to be appropriate. This would be a system of free proof rather than one constrained by a complex law of evidence.

Obviously, the legal system has not adopted a system of free proof, or else the previous sentence would have ended your course on evidence. It instead regulates the process of proof in various ways for various reasons. Some of these ways and their underlying reasons are perfectly understandable and uncontroversial. Others are more problematic. Consider the following justifications for regulating the proof process and reflect on how persuasive they are:

(1) *Efficiency.* Litigants pay only a small fraction of the cost of maintaining the judicial system. Judicial resources are provided free of charge to litigants, and they constitute a large subsidy to litigation. The litigants have virtually no incentive to preserve judicial resources; indeed they have every incentive to squander them in an effort to win their cases. A system of free proof allowing the litigants to do more or

less what they liked would lead to a substantial wasting of judicial resources. Further, a rich litigant could simply wear down a more impecunious opponent through the endless presentation of trivia. For both reasons, trials are structured by judges to keep irrelevant, redundant, and unimportant issues out of the process in order to maximize the value of the resources available to decide disputes and in order to advance the likelihood that truth will determine outcomes. See FRE 403.

(2) *Policy.* Various policies extraneous to the system of litigation itself are affected by litigation. Consider two general examples. First, compelling witnesses to testify about certain kinds of communications they have had can have a destructive effect on human relationships, both professional and personal. Maintaining the privacy of these relationships are equally or more important than accurate adjudication, and thus litigation is structured to protect them through the provision of various privileges—such as attorney-client, psychotherapist-patient, or husband-wife—that exempt certain individuals from testifying in certain circumstances. See Article V of the Federal Rules of Evidence.

The second general example of extraneous policy considerations has to do with encouraging kinds of socially useful activity other those arising out of confidential communications. Suppose an accident occurs at a bridge, and the owner of the bridge does some repair to the bridge that reduces the probability of a similar accident occurring. The act of repair may indicate that the bridge was dangerous and thus be evidence of negligence on the owner's part. Admitting evidence of the act of repair at trial to prove negligence will create disincentives for future bridge owners to repair their bridges. In order to encourage the reduction of social risk, after-the-fact repairs are excluded at trial. See FRE 407. There are many similar examples. See FRE 408-410.

(3) *Accuracy.* Another argument for regulating the proof process is to help jurors avoid reaching erroneous results. One reason for the hearsay rule (Article 8 of the Federal Rules) is the belief that jurors cannot accurately appraise hearsay evidence. FRE 403 allows judges to keep "unfairly prejudicial" evidence from the jury, on the ground that admitting it risks leading jurors away from rationality. This argument, paradoxically, calls into question the very institution of jury decision-making. The argument is in essence that the proof process must be controlled in order to keep distracting, prejudicial, and difficult-to-appraise material away from the jury, because such material will lead the jurors to substitute emotion or caprice for rationality, thus increasing the risk of wrong results. Consider in the next section how the trial process both accommodates and attempts to modify how the law assumes jurors will reason and behave.

(4) *Fairness.* Rules regulating admission and exclusion of evidence can also be justified for their tendency to promote fairness to the parties. One aspect of fairness relates to the system's goal of achieving factually accurate results. Rule 403, which allows the trial judge to exclude evidence that may cause "unfair prejudice" to the objecting party, is an obvious example of such a fairness-based rule. Rules restricting evidence of a party's "character" or his conduct before or after the relevant events in the case (see FRE 404) are designed, in part, to prevent juries from punishing parties for matters other than their specifically alleged wrongdoing. Another value related to fairness is that the system regards participants as fully autonomous individuals whose choices control many aspects of the proceedings, such as the responsibility to prepare and present their own case and to object to improper evidence from the opponent (see FRE 103). Finally, burdening the proponent with the obligation of presenting its own

evidence with a foundation that aids the jury's decision-making (authenticating exhibits under FRE 901 and presenting original documents under FRE 1002) can be seen as preventing the proponent from overwhelming the opponent with unfair evidentiary burdens.

3.   Natural Reasoning and the Trial Process

As we previously indicated, the trial must look somewhat strange from the point of view of the jurors. Jurors typically sit passively through disjointed presentations of evidence, although there are now some experiments being done with allowing jurors to ask questions during the presentation of evidence that suggest jury questions may promote juror understanding of the facts and issues, and alleviate doubts about the trial evidence. Steven D. Penrod and Larry Heuer, Tweaking Commonsense: Assessing Aids to Jury Decision Making, 3 Psychol. Pub. Poly. & L. 259 (1997); see also Franklin Strier, The Road to Reform: Judges on Juries and Attorneys, 30 Loy. L.A. L. Rev. 1249 (1997). Particularly because of the passivity of jurors, the judge's initial instructions to the jury and the parties' opening statements are crucial—they are the only sources of information that will create a context for the jury. Only after the close of the evidence does the judge typically give full instructions on the law, as occurred in *Johnson*. Often the instructions are not clear, although the ones in *Johnson* are for the most part fairly clear. Consider, though, the instruction on reasonable doubt, on page 69, supra:

> Reasonable doubt is defined as follows. It is not a mere possible doubt because everything relating to human affairs and depending on moral evidence is open to some possible or imaginary doubt. It is that state of the case, which after the entire comparison and consideration of all the evidence, leaves the mind of the jurors in that condition that they cannot say that they feel an abiding conviction or a moral certainty of the truth of the charge.

How helpful is that? Can it be made any clearer? This instruction is somewhat vague because the idea lying behind it is s omewhat vague. In many cases, however, the instructions are vague because they are filled with incomprehensible legalese that simply leaves the jury baffled. The lack of helpfulness of many jury instructions, and the resultant lack of comprehension of them, is scandalous in a system dedicated to both lay decision makers and rationality. Again, though, can you think of any reason why such a scandal continues to persist? Jury instructions are not just the means by which jurors are controlled by trial judges. They are also one of the important means by which appellate judges control trial judges. Jury instructions embody the substantive law that the trial judge applies to the trial, and appellate courts review jury instructions nondeferentially. Moreover, in contrast to evidentiary errors, instructional errors are almost never deemed "harmless" by appellate courts. What might be the implications of that point? In any event, you should ask yourself whether this ordering of events makes sense, and whether the jury should be better informed by the trial judge at an earlier time in the process.

Professor Phoebe Ellsworth has spent considerable time studying the deliberative process of jurors. Her work confirms prior work and anecdotal experience that, notwithstanding the difficulties, juries are quite good at fact-finding. Her work also confirms earlier findings that jurors are less adept at dealing with the legal issues in cases. She recently summarized her findings in a way that vividly captures the difficulty of being a juror:

> There is no reason to believe that the jurors' misunderstanding of the law is a function of their mental capacities. It seems more plausible that the system is set up to promote misunderstanding. Factors blockading the serious jury trying to perform its task include: the convoluted, technical language; the dry and abstract presentation of the law following the vivid, concrete, and often lengthy presentation of evidence; the requirements that jurors interpret the evidence before they know what the verdict choices are; the fact that juries usually do not get copies of the instructions to take with them into the jury room; the lack of training in the law for jurors as part of their jury duty; the general failure to discover and correct jurors' preconceptions about the law; the failure to inform jurors that they are allowed to ask for help with the instructions; and the fact that those who do ask for help are often disappointed by a simple repetition of the incomprehensible paragraph. [Phoebe Ellsworth, Are 12 Heads Better Than 1?, 38 Law Quadrangle Notes 56, 64 (1995).]

The jurors' task involves finding facts and applying the law to those facts. We say we want the hallmark of trials to be rational deliberation, which includes accurate fact-finding and an adequate understanding of the law, yet the structure of trials is somewhat, perhaps significantly, at odds with effective learning on the part of jurors. Why might that be so? How would power shift at trials if they were structured otherwise? Is much of what you have seen designed to keep control of a trial in the hands of the lawyers? The trial judge? Is that sensible?

We have so far concentrated on the manner in which jurors learn about the litigated events. After the presentation of evidence and closing argument of counsel, juries retire to deliberate and reach a verdict. The law's reach extends to this aspect of the process as well. Because certainty is never possible to achieve at trial, jurors are instructed as to the proper decision rule to apply in the face of the inevitable uncertainty with which they will have to grapple. This comes in the form of an instruction on burdens of persuasion. In civil cases, the normal burden of persuasion is proof by a preponderance of the evidence; in criminal cases it is proof beyond reasonable doubt. Jurors are told that the relevant burden of persuasion is to be applied to "every element" of the cause of action. These matters are discussed in detail in Chapter Eleven.

Coupling the burden of persuasion to "every element" seems unproblematic on its face, but there is a problem lurking in the shadows. This coupling recommends an unnatural decision-making process to jurors. If followed literally, jurors would be obligated to analyze the various combinations and permutations of elements, applying the appropriate burden of persuasion as they go. There are two difficulties. First, this procedure would quickly get impossibly complicated; second, people do not typically reason about conventional, everyday affairs in this fashion. The chart below shows how complicated and unconventional the recommended decision-making process is. Compiled by Professors Nancy Pennington and Reed Hastie, the chart on the following page displays the jury instructions for a relatively simple homicide case involving a defense of self-defense.

Had you come across something like this chart in a book on chemical analysis or medical diagnosis, it perhaps would not have appeared strange; but as a protocol for juror decision-making, it appears completely out of place. The chart, and the instructions it implements, implies that the focus at trial is on the discrete issues

JUROR DECISIONMAKING
Decision Alternatives and Attributes: Murder Case

Decision alternative	Attribute				Decision rule
	1. Identity	*2. Mental state*	*3. Circumstances*	*4. Actions*	
Not guilty	Not the right person	NA	NA	No Killing	1 or 4
Self-defense (not guilty)	Right person	(a) Fear of life (b) Fear of great bodily harm	Under immediate attack	(a) Killing (b) Exhaust escape (c) In defense (d) Reasonable retaliation	1 and (2a or 2b) and 3 and 4a and (4b and 4c and 4d)
Manslaughter	Right person	(a) Heat of sudden passion (b) Diminished capacity	(a) Great provocation (b) Threat to life not immediate	(a) Did not exhaust escape (b) Became the attacker (c) Used excessive force	1 and (2a or 2b) and (3a and 3b) and (4a and 4b and 4c)
Second degree murder	Right person	Intent to inflict injury likely to result in death	Insufficient provocation	(a), (b), (c) Like manslaughter (d) Use deadly weapon (e) Deliberate, cruel act	1 and (2 or [3 and 4d] and 4e) and (4a or 4b or 4c)
First degree murder	Right person	(a) Intent to kill (b) Purpose formed (motive)	(a) Insufficient provocation (b) Interval between plan and killing	(a), (b), (c) Like manslaughter (d) Formed plan to kill (e) Killed in accordance with plan	1 and (2a and 2b) and (3a and 3b) and (4a or 4b or 4c) and 4d and 4e

Note: NA=not applicable

Source: Nancy Pennington and Reed Hastie, Juror Decision-Making Models: The Generalization Gap, 89 Psychol. Bull. 246, 251 (1981).

identified as "elements"; but as we have already commented, the jurors are not fully informed of those elements until just prior to retiring to deliberate. In the *Johnson* case, for example, battery was not defined until the court's closing instructions. The focus at trial is thus not on whether some formal element is true or false; it is on competing versions of reality—in the *Johnson* case, who started the fight and why? Even the lawyers in *Johnson* more or less ignore the elements in their closing arguments, focusing again on the two competing versions of reality. To be sure, the competing versions of reality involve differing elements. And once the jury has settled on "what happened," it must consult the judge's instructions to determine who wins, which is precisely the finding that emerges from the empirical work of Nancy Pennington and Reed Hastie.

That the process of deliberation involves mediating among the conflicting versions of what happened rather than a minute parsing of the individual elements of the causes of action is supported by another consideration. Any decision-making methodology to which a chart like the one above could be applied would have to involve issues with relatively clear answers. Chemical analysis provides a good example.

Litmus paper turns blue or red when immersed in an acid or an alkaline solution; a solvent does or does not dissolve a substance. Trials rarely involve questions that can be answered so unequivocally. At the end of the day, the jury in the *Johnson* case will have to decide who started the fight and why, but in doing so the jurors will have to sift through a lot of ambiguous and conflicting testimony.

That the intellectual task at trial involves organizing the proffered evidence in light of competing versions of the plausible is unavoidable, given the structure of trials. Cases possess ambiguity because of the need to organize large amounts of data (evidentiary complexity), to resolve conflicting and inconsistent testimony (evidentiary tension), and to fill in intermediate premises unsupported by evidence presented at trial (evidentiary gap). The presentation of information at trial quite obviously must be incomplete in the typical case (neither Officer Huston nor Officer Van Berg could say how they received their injuries) and often inconsistent information will be presented (eyewitness testimony about Officer Walker's conduct differed considerably). Witnesses testify only to what they have observed, and rarely will one witness observe everything relevant to any particular litigated issue.

Even in a case with a single witness, what is observed must be richer than what is related, if for no other reason than that memory decays with time. In addition, rhetorical skills invariably are less developed than observational skills. Consider a simple example—a case involving assault where part of the proof is testimony that the defendant made "threatening" gestures toward the plaintiff. Testimony characterizing seemingly simple gestures is often a summary of richly textured human acts that may be observed with ease but related only with difficulty, which is precisely why lay opinions such as this are often allowed. To understand such testimony, the juror must reconstruct this richly textured event. And of course in doing so, the juror may have to account for testimony to the effect that the gesture was not made in a threatening way. As case complexity increases, it is implausible that a juror merely continues to add data to the data banks rather than organizing and simplifying the data, which after all is how individuals apparently cope with the complexity of everyday life. One remembers a trip to the store yesterday rather than walking to the garage, opening the door, entering the garage, opening the car door, searching for the proper key, identifying the ignition, and so on.

There is another interesting aspect of jury decision-making that is highlighted by the chart. The chart suggests an orderly, deductive approach to decision-making: Lay out the assumptions and deduce the correct results. At some point, jurors will indeed "deduce" their verdict in such a fashion, but probably only after all the hard work is done. The hard work involves figuring out what happened. In that effort, deduction, the law's prize tool in virtually all other areas, takes a back seat to induction. Consider again the closing arguments in the *Johnson* case. Neither side attempted to lay out a formal proof of guilt or innocence; instead, they used the testimony to stitch together a story that, they hoped, would seem plausible to the jurors, given their (the jurors') general knowledge and experience.

4.   The Behavior of Fact Finders

The advocates at trial attempt to persuade the fact finder by advancing plausible accounts of what happened, but what seems "plausible" to a person is determined by the sum of that person's knowledge and experience rather than by the outcome of formal logical manipulations. That this is so is evident from your own experience. Reflect for a moment on how you appraise the things that you see. You look for patterns in them, searching for common threads, especially ones that tie what you are observing to what you have previously observed, although always holding yourself open to the twin possibilities that something is unique in the event under observation or that you made a mistake previously in what you came to believe. You engage in various kinds of analogical reasoning, some involving cause and effect, some filling in unobserved aspects of what you are observing by reference to what you have come to believe is commonly associated with what you presently are viewing; you rely on generalizations formed out of prior experience, and so on. These are the tools that humans use to understand, navigate, and manipulate their environment, and not surprisingly they are the tools that jurors use to resolve the disputes of historical fact before them. At the end of the day, when a consensus has emerged out of bringing the combined experience of the jurors to bear on the evidence presented at trial, the jurors look to the verdict options to determine who wins and loses. And probably on occasion when they do so and see the implications of their positions, they reconsider. To this extent there is a relationship between the largely (but not exclusively) inductive processes that drive evidence comprehension and deliberation and the virtually exclusively deductive process that drives verdict selection.

The instructions on elements, in short, merely provide the verdict options. By contrast, few instructions are given on how to reason or deliberate, because jurors, as competent members of their community, are assumed to know how to do both, an assumption that is surely correct. Judges do typically give one instruction about jury reasoning, the one given in the *Johnson* case—"use your common sense." If more elaborate instructions are necessary, the argument becomes one for deciding cases in some other way.

One last point. At the beginning of the *Johnson* transcript, the judge instructed the jury on what "evidence" is. Think about the nature of "evidence": What exactly, is it? Before reading these pages, you most likely would have thought it a dumb question—"evidence," obviously, is the testimony and exhibits at trial. Is that now so obvious? The testimony and exhibits at trial are meaningless until interpreted by a human observer—judge or juror. Moreover, the interpretation given to any piece of evidence cannot be determined in advance, for it is a function of the background and experience of the fact finder. If "evidence" is what is presented at trial, how can it be that one fact finder thinks the "evidence" proves guilt and another innocence? Does everyone in this class agree that defendant Johnson was guilty of a battery, or do some believe he should have been acquitted? The point we want you to think about, though, is the dynamic nature of trials and "evidence." There is a relational aspect to "evidence"; it (the evidence) is what some human being thinks it is, and what that person thinks it is cannot be determined in advance by a set of rules. If it could, fact-finding perhaps could make the transformation from being largely inductive to largely deductive; but if it could, jurors (and judges) would become superfluous. Another way of looking at this is that historical fact-finding requires judgment in addition to logic—not in contrast to logic, but in addition to it.

The necessary reliance on judgment is one of the distinguishing features of peculiarly human institutions, which the law of evidence surely is for all of its pretense to analytical rigor. These are matters we would encourage you to reflect on as you proceed throughout the course. Nor are they just matters of academic interest. You are about to turn the page to begin your study of the concept of relevancy. Right at the heart of that concept lie many of the issues we have been addressing here.

TRIAL OBJECTION CHEAT SHEET

Note: this list of objections is not intended to be exhaustive. A comma separating objections suggests interchangeable phrasing; a semicolon suggests different but closely related objections.

OBJECTIONS TO THE FORM OF THE QUESTION:

Argumentative	Question contends that the witness must agree with a disputable inference, is framed as if it were closing argument to the jury, or seeks to pick a fight with the witness or embarrass the witness. This objection is often made (and sustained) inappropriately to questions that are proper, vigorous cross-examination, as in "Objection, Your Honor, tough question!"
Asked and answered	Question has previously been asked of the same witness by the same examiner. (Does not apply to question asked by the opposing counsel.) Technically, there is nothing wrong with repeating questions, but judges may sustain this objection if they feel testimony is cumulative, or the examination is too lengthy or out of control.
Assumes facts not in evidence	Question is phrased so that to answer it, the witness would have to adopt, by implication, an asserted fact that is in dispute but that has not been proved.
Calls for narrative	Question asks the witness to describe events very broadly or generally. Technically, there is nothing wrong with a "narrative" answer, and many questions can only be phrased in open-ended fashion to avoid leading; rather the danger is that the question will permit the witness to ramble and possibly interject inadmissible evidence. The objection might also be phrased as "too general."
Compound	Question asks the witness to testify about more than one separate fact.
Leading	Question suggests the desired answer to the witness; improper during direct examination of friendly or neutral witnesses, but okay on cross-examination or direct examination of adverse or hostile witnesses.
Misstates the evidence; mischaracterizes the testimony	Premise of the question distorts the evidence that has been presented, or misquotes the witness's testimony.
Unintelligible; vague; ambiguous; confusing	Question is not sufficiently clear to be answered. "Unintelligible" means garbled; "vague" means not sufficiently specific; "ambiguous" means susceptible of two or more different interpretations.

OBJECTIONS TO ADMISSIBILITY OF THE ANSWER (OR PROFFERED EXHIBIT):

Hearsay	Answer to question would call for (or evidentiary item contains) a statement other than one made by the witness while testifying at trial, offered to prove the truth of the matter asserted.
Irrelevant	Answer has no probative value relating to any fact of consequence to the case.
Lack of foundation	Insufficient factual basis has been established to show that the witness has requisite knowledge (personal sensory perception or experience, expert opinion, lay opinion, knowledge of character) to give admissible testimony; or to show that exhibit is what its proponent claims.
Lack of authenticity	Insufficient factual basis to show that exhibit is what its proponent claims.
Calls for speculation, speculative	Answer to question calls for the witness to speculate or guess about matters beyond witness's factual knowledge; this is a form of "foundation" objection.
Calls for opinion; calls for conclusion	Answer would violate the rule limiting lay (nonexpert) opinion to those opinions and inferences that are based on the witness's perception of an event and are helpful to the jury in understanding the facts.
Inadmissible character evidence	Violates FRE 404.
More prejudicial/ misleading/etc. than probative, Rule 403	Probative value substantially outweighed by one or more of the Rule 403 dangers.
Cumulative	Answer would repeat earlier testimony. This is not technically improper, but comes within judge's discretion under Rule 403. This objection is often stated as "Asked and answered."
Nonresponsive	Witness has given an "evasive" answer that does not fairly meet the substance of the question.
Beyond the scope of the question	Answer has exceeded the scope of the question (i.e., the witness has "volunteered" information that was not asked for); this assumes the answer has been given, and is therefore a basis for a motion to strike.
Beyond the scope of direct/cross-/redirect/etc. examination	Question seeks testimony that is not responsive to immediately preceding examination. Testimony is supposed to respond to matters raised in the immediately preceding examination (i.e., cross responds to direct, redirect responds to cross, recross responds to redirect, etc.).
Not the best evidence	Answer would violate the best evidence rule, which requires use of original writing, recording, or photograph to prove its contents.

CHAPTER THREE

RELEVANCY, PROBATIVE VALUE, AND THE RULE 403 DANGERS

A. *RELEVANCY—THE BASIC CONCEPT*

Relevancy is the foundational principle for all modern systems of evidence law. Only *relevant* evidence helps the jury achieve rational outcomes, meaning outcomes based on the jurors' use of their reasoning capacity. The basic tenets of this principle were spelled out more than a century ago by James Bradley Thayer, upon whose creative shoulders Wigmore erected his Treatise on Evidence in Trials at Common Law:

> Observe ... one or two fundamental conceptions. There is a principle—not so much a rule of evidence as a presupposition involved in the very conception of a rational system of evidence, as contrasted with the old formal and mechanical systems[1]—which forbids receiving anything irrelevant, not logically probative. How are we to know what these forbidden things are? Not by any rule of law. The law furnishes no test of relevancy. For this, it tacitly refers to logic and general experience—assuming that the principles of reasoning are known to its judges and ministers, just as a vast multitude of other things are assumed as already sufficiently known to them.
>
> There is another precept which should be laid down as preliminary, in stating the law of evidence; namely, that unless excluded by some rule or principle or law, all that is logically probative is admissible. This general admissibility, however, of what is logically probative is not, like the former principle, a necessary presupposition in a rational system of evidence; there are many exceptions to it. Yet, in order to [have] a clear conception of the law, it is important to notice this also as being a fundamental proposition. In an historical

---

1. [Continental legal systems had a formal system of required proof. For example, a conviction for a serious crime could only be had upon the presentation of two eyewitnesses or a confession. Circumstantial evidence would not do. But strong circumstantial evidence constituted a "half-proof" that legitimated the use of torture in order to extract a confession, and so on. For discussions, see John Langbein, Torture and the Law of Proof: Europe and England in the Ancien Régime (1977); L. Jonathan Cohen, Freedom of Proof, in Facts in Law (William L. Twining, ed., 1983); Mirjan Damaska, The Death of Legal Torture, 87 Yale L.J. 860 (1978).—EDS.]

sense it has not been the fundamental thing, to which different exclusions were exceptions. What has taken place, in fact, is the shutting out by the judges of one and another thing from time to time; and so, gradually, the recognition of this exclusion under a rule. These rules of exclusion have had their exceptions; and so the law has come into the shape of a set of primary rules of exclusion; and then a set of exceptions to these rules....

In stating thus our two large, fundamental conceptions, we must not fall into the error of supposing that relevancy, logical connection, real or supposed, is the only test of admissibility; for so we should drop out of sight the chief part of the law of evidence. When we have said (1) that, without any exception, nothing which is not, or is not supposed to be, logically relevant is admissible; and (2) that, subject to many exceptions and qualifications, whatever is logically relevant is admissible; it is obvious that, in reality, there are tests of admissibility other than logical relevancy. Some things are rejected as being of too slight a significance, or as having too conjectural and remote a connection; others, as being dangerous, in their effect on the jury, and likely to be misused or overestimated by that body; others, as being impolitic, or unsafe on public grounds; others, on the bare ground of precedent. It is this sort of thing, as I said before—the rejection on one or another practical ground, of what is really probative—which is the characteristic thing in the law of evidence; stamping it as the child of the jury system. [James Bradley Thayer, A Preliminary Treatise on Evidence at the Common Law 264-266 (1898).]

The discussion of relevancy under the Federal Rules of Evidence that follows is the foundation for your study of evidence law in this casebook. It provides you with analytic tools to develop, articulate, and defend your own theories of why evidence is relevant in any factual dispute. You may not often observe these tools at work in courtroom arguments about relevance—trials move too quickly to permit the full-blown analysis that we present below. But this analysis is fundamental to the understanding of relevancy that you must have as the proponent, opponent, or judge of the admissibility of evidentiary facts. And you will soon see that the application of all rules of evidence flows from the initial question: Why is the evidentiary fact relevant?

1.   FRE 401 and 402

RULE 401.   TEST FOR RELEVANT EVIDENCE

Evidence is relevant if: (a) it has any tendency to make a fact more or less probable than it would be without the evidence; and (b) the fact is of consequence in determining the action.

RULE 402.   GENERAL ADMISSIBILITY OF RELEVANT EVIDENCE

Relevant evidence is admissible unless any of the following provides otherwise:

- the United States Constitution;
- a federal statute;
- these rules; or
- other rules prescribed by the Supreme Court.

Irrelevant evidence is not admissible.

2.   Interpretation and Illustration of FRE 401 and 402

If a proper objection is made, judges will exclude all evidence that is *not relevant*, under FRE 401 and 402. In deciding whether an item of evidence is relevant under FRE 401, a judge must consider two issues: (1) Is the item offered to prove a fact that "is of consequence" to the case? (2) Could a reasonable jury think that the item has a tendency to make that fact of consequence more (or less) probable? The common law perceived these two issues as two separate concepts—*materiality* (meaning the connection to a fact of consequence in the case) and *relevancy* (meaning that the connection was logically probative). While the term *materiality* is not used in the Federal Rules (the Advisory Committee Note to FRE 401 rejects the term as "loosely used and ambiguous"), it is still common parlance among judges and trial lawyers and you should be familiar with it.

a.   Relevant Evidence Is Offered to Prove a Fact of Consequence (Materiality)

In general, a proposition of fact is "of consequence" (i.e., material) in a legal dispute if it matters to the legal resolution of that dispute; that is, if it can be connected through inferential reasoning to one of the essential legal elements of the substantive law that governs the case. This relationship can be illustrated with a simple diagram:

Diagram 3-1

$$EF \longrightarrow FOC \longrightarrow EE$$

The arrow drawn from the EF (the evidentiary fact offered into evidence) to the FOC (the fact of consequence the EF is offered to prove) represents an inference that the jury can make. The EF is evidence presented to the jury in the courtroom; the FOC is a proposition of fact that is not presented but that the jury can decide to believe, on the basis of drawing an inference; the FOC connects to the EE (essential element) again through an inference.

Consider this example:

Diagram 3-2

If an eyewitness testifies that she saw the defendant holding a smoking gun over the victim, this is an evidentiary fact offered into evidence. From this testimony, the jury may make the inference that defendant did in fact shoot the victim. This is a fact of consequence, because from it the jury may infer the identity of the person who caused the victim's death, which is an essential element in the law of homicide.

The substantive law determines the essential elements in every case. In the *Johnson* case, for example, the essential elements of the crime with which Johnson was charged were (1) the unlawful use of force or violence (2) by a person incarcerated in state prison (3) against a person not incarcerated. The prosecution presented testimony from several eyewitnesses that Johnson was kicking and struggling with the correctional officers both inside and outside his cell. This testimony was relevant to prove that Johnson used force and violence, as required by the first essential element listed above. Now consider the defense attorney's question to inmate Butler concerning the frequency with which prisoners at Pelican Bay are allowed to receive packages from home (page 42, line 32, supra). Does this information tend to prove a fact of consequence in the *Johnson* case? Can you identify any connection between it and one of the essential elements? If you cannot, then the information may be irrelevant—"immaterial," in common law parlance—and would be excluded under FRE 401 and 402.

The relevance of some evidentiary facts requires that several inferences be made prior to reaching a readily identifiable fact of consequence to the litigation. For example, the prosecution offered testimony that Officer Huston suffered a gash on his left shin (page 15, line 8, supra). The following diagram shows how this testimony can be used to prove that Johnson used force and violence against Huston, as required by the first and third essential elements in the Johnson case:

Diagram 3-3

EF	→	IF	→	FOC	→	EE
Huston testifies that he had a gash on his shin after the struggle		Huston did have a gash on his shin after the struggle		Johnson's struggling caused the gash		Johnson used force and violence against Huston

The first inference to the IF (inferred fact) is that Huston's testimony is true—he did have the gash *after* the struggle with Johnson. From this inferred fact, the fact of consequence can be identified.

Sometimes even longer chains of reasoning are required. For example, inmate Butler testified that the correctional officers were wearing their gloves when they approached Johnson's cell (page 42, line 6, supra). This evidentiary fact connects to the defense theory that the guards started the fight with Johnson. Wearing gloves generates the inference that a guard is prepared to have contact with an inmate, not just to collect a food tray; and if a guard is prepared to have contact, he intends to fight; and if he intends to fight, then he starts the fight; and if the guards start the fight, then Johnson's use of force and violence may be self-defense and not unlawful. This chain of inferences is shown in Diagram 3-4.

Diagram 3-4

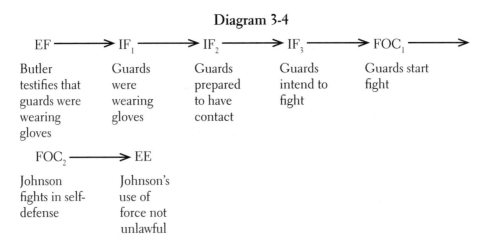

EF	→	IF_1	→	IF_2	→	IF_3	→	FOC_1	→
Butler testifies that guards were wearing gloves		Guards were wearing gloves		Guards prepared to have contact		Guards intend to fight		Guards start fight	

FOC_2	→	EE
Johnson fights in self-defense		Johnson's use of force not unlawful

Each arrow represents an inference in the chain starting from the evidentiary fact, leading to a series of inferred facts, which connect to what can easily be identified as facts of consequence, which then connect to an essential element in the case. Notice that more than one fact of consequence is identified in this diagram. There is no principle of evidence law that requires that only one inference in a chain of reasoning be "correctly" identified as the fact that is of consequence to the dispute. An FOC is simply an inference along the chain of reasoning that is more closely related to the EE, and therefore can be more easily identified as being "of consequence" to the dispute. Whether the chain of reasoning is long or short, what is important to remember is that the facts of consequence in a case cannot be determined without knowing the essential elements of the substantive law that governs the dispute. Black v. M & W Gear Co., 269 F.3d 1220, 1236 (10th Cir. 2001) (plaintiff's husband killed in a rollover of his tractor lawnmower manufactured by defendant; husband's alcohol consumption irrelevant because contributory negligence is not a defense in a product liability case).

b.   Relevant Evidence Must Make a Fact of Consequence More or Less Probable

Once the proponent identifies the fact of consequence, the proponent must also be prepared to show why, stated in the terms of FRE 401, the evidence offered makes the fact of consequence *more or less probable*.

i.   FRE 401's Minimal Standard of "Any Tendency."   FRE 401 defines relevant evidence as having "any tendency" to make the existence of a fact of consequence more or less probable. This is a minimal test of logically probable inferences from the offered item to a fact of consequence. For example, in determining the relevance of inmate Butler's testimony in the *Johnson* case that the guards wore gloves, it need only be the case that "guards who wear gloves are somewhat more likely to have anticipated contact with inmates than if they were not wearing gloves." In general, the judge will find the offered fact relevant if a reasonable jury could think that it makes a fact of consequence somewhat more or less likely than it would be were the evidence not known. Professor Vaughn Ball analyzes the results of this comparison in the following way:

> If and only if the probability ... is the same with and without the evidence, the evidence is irrelevant.... If these probabilities are different, the evidence is relevant. It seems to be recognized on all sides that the *size* of the change is of no importance in determining relevancy.... [T]here are no degrees of relevancy. It seems everywhere conceded that the term *relevant* refers to the distinction between some probative force and no probative force ... between some change in probability and no change. [Vaughn C. Ball, The Myth of Conditional Relevancy, 14 Ga. L. Rev. 435, 446 (1980).]

But in a specific instance, how does the proponent of evidence articulate why it makes a fact of consequence more or less probable? And if the opponent objects, how does the judge decide whether FRE 401 is satisfied? The answer to these questions requires an understanding that reasoning from an evidentiary fact to a fact of consequence requires the use of generalized knowledge and experience.

ii.   Inferential Reasoning Is Based on Generalizations from Knowledge and Experience.   Inferential reasoning requires generalized knowledge and experience, as well as the various intellectual tools discussed on pages 116-118 of Chapter Two, to make the rational connections from evidence to facts of consequence as illustrated in the diagrams above. We all have a well-developed body of generalized knowledge that we use in our inferential reasoning, as described by Professors David A. Binder and Paul Bergman:

> All of us ... have accumulated vast storehouses of commonly-held notions about how people and objects generally behave in our society. From this storehouse one formulates a generalization about typical behavior. The generalization, in turn, becomes the premise which enables me to link specific evidence with an element one hopes to prove. [David A. Binder and Paul Bergman, Fact Investigation 85 (1984).]

The Advisory Committee Note to FRE 402 calls these generalizations "principles evolved by experience or science, applied logically to the situation at hand." As the excerpt from Thayer points out, there are virtually no legal rules governing this test of relevancy; rather, the test is one of "logic and general experience."

To test whether a specific evidentiary fact is logically probative of a specific fact of consequence, the judge examines the generalizations underlying each inference in the proponent's proposed chain of reasoning. For example, the inferential leap from "the guards wore gloves" to "the guards were prepared to fight" requires a generalization about the behavior of prison guards. Such a generalization might be articulated as follows: "Guards probably don't wear gloves to pick up food trays, but they would be likely to wear gloves when they prepare to come into contact with inmates." What do you think of this generalization? Does it support the necessary inference? Does it make the inferred fact more probable? Because such generalizations are only rough estimates of human behavior (and other kinds of occurrences), they cannot "prove" that an inference is true. Nevertheless, they do operate as part of a type of syllogistic reasoning: from major premise (the generalization) and minor premise (the evidentiary fact) to the conclusion (the inference to be drawn). This form of reasoning, based on generalizations from knowledge and experience, can also be diagrammed:

Diagram 3-5

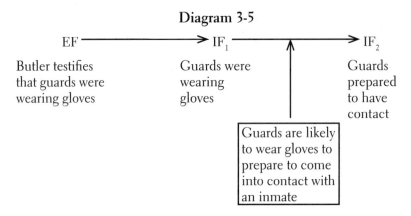

iii.   Relevancy Requires Reasonable Generalizations.   Judges will admit evidence as making a fact of consequence more or less probable when there are *reasonable* generalizations based on common knowledge and experience that will support each inference in the chain of reasoning. Phrased another way, the test of relevancy is "whether a reasonable person might believe the probability of the truth of the consequential fact to be different if that person knew of the proffered evidence." 2 Jack B. Weinstein and Margaret A. Berger, Weinstein's Federal Evidence §401.04[2] (b) (Joseph M. McLaughlin, ed., Matthew Bender 2d ed. 2001). The judge thus evaluates the reasonableness of the underlying generalizations from the perspective of the reasonable juror. From the perspective of the litigants, both proponent and opponent, articulating the underlying generalizations for the judge is essential to any debate over their reasonableness.

    iv. Generalizations Can Be the Subject of Proof. What if the opponent objects that a generalization necessary to an item's relevance is either unknown to the jury or unreasonable, and the judge also has the same doubts? In such a case, the judge can require the proponent of the evidentiary fact to produce evidentiary support for the generalization itself. In the *Johnson* case, for example, the judge might ask: "How would the jury know that guards wear gloves to prepare for contact with inmates?" The judge could require the defense to produce testimony about glove-wearing practices in Facility B at Pelican Bay. This would turn the underlying generalization into an evidentiary fact in the chain of reasoning:

Diagram 3-6

$EF_1 \longrightarrow IF_1 \qquad + \qquad EF_2 \longrightarrow IF_2$

| Butler testifies guards were wearing gloves | Guards were wearing gloves | | A witness testifies that guards wear gloves in Facility B when they expect to have physical contact with an inmate | Guards prepared to have contact |

A proponent will have to present proof of an underlying generalization if the judge requires it. Of course, the proponent may also offer such proof simply to persuade the jury that the generalization has particularly strong probative force.

    v. Limits on Reasonable Generalizations. There are many types of generalized knowledge, all of which may be involved in factual adjudication:

> Generalizations range over a broad spectrum. At one end are scientific laws ... well-founded scientific opinions ... and widely shared conclusions based upon common experience (for instance, everyone knows that a driver must stop at a red light). In the middle are commonly held, but unproven or unprovable beliefs (for instance, fleeing the scene of a crime is evidence of a guilty conscience). At the other end are biases or prejudices that may be strongly held irrespective of available data ... and less strongly held but still operative beliefs (for instance, men's fixed designs are probably carried out). [Terence Anderson and William Twining, Analysis of Evidence 68 (1991).]

Judges do not require objective proof of most generalizations that sound reasonable, due to the lack of empirical knowledge about most of human behavior. Nevertheless, there are at least two obvious limits implicit in the "reasonable juror" test: The necessary generalizations cannot be known to the judge to be false ("people can see through brick walls")[2] and they cannot be pure speculation ("people with red hair seem to be more aggressive than people with black hair").[3] A relevance theory based on such generalizations should be rejected. Some generalizations express invidious stereotypes based on factors such as gender, race, ethnicity, religion, age, and sexual preference. Once articulated, many such generalizations probably fall within the "false" or "guesswork" categories of unacceptability, or lack any connection to the individual case. Jinro America Inc. v. Secure Investments, Inc., 2001 U.S. App. LEXIS 25987, at *37 (9th Cir. 2001) (majority held syllogism "(a) Korean businesses generally are corrupt; (b) Jinro is a Korean business; (c) therefore, Jinro is corrupt" to be impermissible under FRE 403; concurrence held that generalizations about Korean businesses were irrelevant to prove Jinro's conduct). Of course, stereotypes and biases may also surface during confidential jury deliberations if the background facts necessary to trigger them are available. Some of these problematic stereotypes have been identified and addressed in the Federal Rules. For example, FRE 610 prohibits evidence of religious beliefs or opinions on the question of credibility, and FRE 412 limits the use of evidence of a victim's sexual behavior or predisposition in cases involving allegations of sexual misconduct. It is also assumed that a diverse jury will express a range of views during deliberation and will correct for such stereotypes.

vi. The Policy of FRE 401 Favors Admissibility.   What if the judge rejects a proponent's generalization, based on the judge's own idiosyncratic view of the world? For example, a judge might think: "I just don't believe that guards wear gloves in anticipation of contact with inmates. I think that guards wear gloves to keep their hands clean." Excluding evidence that the guards wore gloves, based on the judge's personal views and beliefs of how the world works, or of how people behave, would distort the flow of information to the jury.

This raises the question of how certain the trial judge has to be that the evidentiary fact has the minimal relevant connection to the case. FRE 401 does not contain a specific standard of proof, unlike FRE 104, which you will read about later. The absence of a specifically higher standard, plus the policies underlying the minimal test of relevancy established in FRE 401, persuade us that the judge should find evidence to be relevant if the judge believes there is any probability that the relevant connection exists. Thus, even if there are alternative explanations of the glove-wearing practices of guards at Pelican Bay, if the proponent's underlying generalizations are reasonable, the evidence is relevant.

By so strongly favoring admissibility, FRE 401 reduces idiosyncratic exclusions of evidence. As stated in the Weinstein and Berger treatise, implicit in the Federal Rules is the concept that the relevance of evidence is determined by whether the

---

2.   Conversations in the cockpit of an airliner just before crashing were not relevant to the mental state and psychic damages of the passengers because the passengers could not hear the conversations. Pregeant v. Pan Am. World Airways, Inc., 762 F.2d 1245, 1249 (5th Cir. 1985) (error harmless).

3.   Testimony by an expert that it was "possible" but "not probable" that the defendant's Nike sneaker was the source of an inculpatory footprint was excluded as "lacking probative value" under Rule 401. United States v. Ferreira, 821 F.2d 1, 5 (1st Cir. 1987). Whether this ruling was rightly decided under FRE 401 would depend on the nature of the generalization that the expert relied on to find a "possibility."

evidence *could influence a reasonable juror or reasonable jury*, rather than whether the evidence does or would influence the trial judge. The minimal test of relevancy serves one of the most important goals of the Federal Rules of Evidence: to promote rational decision-making by promoting the jury's access to relevant evidence. For a synopsis of the philosophical, academic, and legal debates underlying "the strong federal policy favoring admissibility of, and reliance on, all helpful information . . . ," you should read District Judge Jack B. Weinstein's opinion in United States v. Shonubi, 895 F. Supp. 460, 492 (E.D.N.Y. 1995), 103 F.3d 1085 (2d Cir. 1997) (sentence vacated).

c.   Direct Versus Circumstantial Evidence

The common law distinguished between two types of relevant evidence: direct and circumstantial. Direct evidence typically is defined as evidence that, if believed, establishes an essential element without any additional intervening inferences. For example, if the correctional officers had testified in the *Johnson* case that they saw Johnson kick Officers Huston and Van Berg, this testimony, if believed, would have been direct evidence that Johnson committed a battery. And the testimony of an eyewitness identifying a bank robber, if believed, would be direct evidence of the element of identity. In both examples, the fact of consequence is itself identical, or essentially identical, to the essential element, the difference being the legal terminology in which the essential element is phrased.

In most cases, however, the connection between an evidentiary fact and an essential element is not so immediate and may require many intervening inferences. This type of evidence is known as *circumstantial*. Suppose a witness testifies that immediately after a bank was robbed, he saw the defendant (charged with the bank robbery) running a block away from the bank. This would be viewed as circumstantial evidence of the defendant's guilt on the ground that the testimony does not directly establish the essential element of identity. Additional inferences are necessary to explain the defendant's conduct in such a way as to connect the defendant to the robbery—he was attempting to flee to avoid being caught after he had committed the crime. And because there are numerous other explanations for the defendant's running, an inference of identity does not automatically follow.

Analytically, there is no difference between direct and circumstantial evidence because both require the jury to use inferential reasoning. Direct evidence establishes an essential element only if the jury believes the eyewitness, and this requires inferential reasoning about the eyewitness's ability to observe the event correctly, to remember it, and to describe it honestly and accurately. These standard issues of credibility must be resolved by the fact finder in order to evaluate any testimonial evidence, and they are the kinds of issues about which people use natural reasoning constantly in their everyday life. Generally speaking, then, what distinguishes circumstantial from direct evidence is the length of the inferential chain.

It is important to note that the labels "direct" and "circumstantial" do not reflect the evidence's probative force. Circumstantial evidence can often be more reliable than direct evidence. A fingerprint or blood spot found on a murder weapon, identified as the defendant's by fingerprint analysis or DNA testing, are examples of circumstantial evidence that can be very accurate, and are probably more reliable than many eyewitnesses, as will be discussed in Chapter Nine.

We would venture to say that *all* litigated cases rely on at least some circumstantial evidence, and many essential elements (intent, for example) are typically proved only in this way. Nevertheless, some jurisdictions still distinguish between circumstantial and direct evidence in instructing the jury as was done in the *Johnson* case — that each fact in a chain of circumstantial evidence necessary to proof of guilt must be proved beyond a reasonable doubt (page 62, line 38, supra). This instruction cannot possibly be applied to every intermediate inferred fact in a chain of reasoning, and giving such an instruction is very confusing to the jury. The ultimate inference of guilt in a criminal case will typically depend on a number of intermediate inferred facts, each proved by a number of individual items of evidence. Only rarely will any one such fact, of itself, be *necessary* to proof of guilt. As stated by the High Court of Australia:

> [I]t may sometimes be necessary or desirable to identify those intermediate facts which constitute indispensable links in a chain of reasoning towards an inference of guilt. Not every possible intermediate conclusion of fact will be of that character. If it is appropriate to identify an intermediate fact as indispensable it may well be appropriate to tell the jury that that fact must be found beyond reasonable doubt before the ultimate inference can be drawn. But where ... the evidence consists of strands in a cable rather than links in a chain, it will not be appropriate to give such a warning. It should not be given in any event where it would be unnecessary or confusing to do so. It will generally be sufficient to tell the jury that the guilt of the accused must be established beyond reasonable doubt and, where it is helpful to do so, to tell them that they must entertain such a doubt where any other inference consistent with innocence is reasonably open on the evidence....
>
> [T]he prosecution bears the burden of proving all the elements of the crime beyond reasonable doubt. That means that the essential ingredients of each element must be so proved. It does not mean that every fact — every piece of evidence — relied upon to prove an element by inference must itself be proved beyond reasonable doubt....Indeed, the probative force of a mass of evidence may be cumulative, making it pointless to consider the degree of probability of each item of evidence separately. [51 A. Crim. R. 181, 184-185 (1990).]

d.   *Background Information*

In most cases, judges admit some testimony that may not seem to have any obvious connection to any fact of consequence in the case. Reasonable background information about the witness who is testifying is "always admissible ... it allows the jury to make better informed judgments about the credibility of a witness and the reliability of that witness' observations." United States v. McVeigh, 153 F.3d 1166, 1201 (10th Cir. 1998). And when witnesses describe actions or events, they are often allowed to describe them in some detail, simply to help the jury relate to and understand what it did not and cannot see for itself. Inmate Butler's explanation of how inmates receive packages from home, referred to on page 124, supra, is an example of such detail. The Latin phrase *res gestae* — meaning "things done" — is often used to justify the admission of broader context to an important incident. Parties also use many kinds of exhibits that in and of themselves do not tend to prove any fact of consequence but that are nonetheless part of, or illustrate, the story to which the jury is listening.

The Advisory Committee Note to FRE 401 explicitly approves of the admission of this kind of contextual evidence, despite its lack of immediate consequence to the case:

> Evidence which is essentially background in nature can scarcely be said to involve disputed matter, yet it is universally offered and admitted as an aid to understanding.

Charts, photographs, views of real estate, murder weapons, and many other items of evidence fall in this category.

e.   Relevancy Is Not Sufficiency

The question of admissibility under FRE 401 is separate from the question whether an item of evidence is sufficient proof of an essential element to justify sending a case to the jury. The question of admissibility goes to logical effect, and "any tendency" under FRE 401 requires only a minimum level of logical effect. The question of sufficiency refers to the burden of production discussed in Chapter Two at pages 85-86; that is, whether a reasonable person could be persuaded by the evidence to the level demanded by the applicable burden of persuasion. Both burdens will be discussed further in Chapter Ten. Typically, a party's case will require many items of evidence to meet the burden of producing evidence sufficient to support a verdict. As the Advisory Committee Note to FRE 401 states, quoting McCormick's treatise, "A brick is not a wall."

Moreover, most items of evidence will not trigger just one inference or just one underlying explanatory generalization. Evidence typically can be interpreted in several different ways, thus triggering competing and often contradictory inferences. For example, several competing explanations have probably already occurred to you as to why the guards were wearing gloves (if they were) in the *Johnson* case. These competing explanations may be made the subject of proof by the opponent, and may be argued to the jury during closing argument. It is usually for the jury, in its ultimate deliberations, to choose among them. To be admitted under FRE 401, an item of evidence is tested from the perspective of its proponent. The evidence needs only to make a fact of consequence *somewhat more or less likely than it would be were the evidence not known.*

3.   Elaboration of FRE 401 and 402

Two judicial opinions, rendered over 100 years apart, illustrate the low threshold of probative connection required by the concept of relevance, both at common law and under the Federal Rules.

KNAPP v. STATE[4]
168 Ind. 153, 79 N.E. 1076 (1907)

The appellant appeals from a judgment in the above-entitled cause, under which he stands convicted of murder in the first degree. Error is assigned on the overruling of a motion for new trial.

Appellant, as a witness in his own behalf, offered testimony tending to show a killing in self-defense. He afterwards testified, presumably for the purpose of showing that he

---

4.   [For an interesting discussion of the *Knapp* case and the appropriate manner of analyzing the questions it raises, see Richard D. Friedman, Route Analysis of Credibility and Hearsay, 96 Yale L.J. 667, 679 (1987).—Eds.]

had reason to fear the deceased, that before the killing he had heard that the deceased, who was the marshal of Hagerstown, had clubbed and seriously injured an old man in arresting him, and that he died a short time afterwards. On appellant being asked, on cross-examination, who told him this, he answered: "Some people around Hagerstown there. I can't say as to who it was now." The state was permitted, on rebuttal, to prove by a physician, over the objection and exception of the defense, that the old man died of senility and alcoholism, and that there were no bruises or marks on his person. Counsel for appellant contend that it was error to admit this testimony; that the question was as to whether he had, in fact, heard the story, and not as to its truth or falsity. While it is laid down in the books that there must be an open and visible connection between the fact under inquiry and the evidence by which it is sought to be established, yet the connection thus required is in the logical processes only, for to require an actual connection between the two facts would be to exclude all presumptive evidence. Within settled rules, the competency of testimony depends largely upon its tendency to persuade the judgment. As said by Wharton: "Relevancy is that which conduces to the proof of a pertinent hypothesis." 1 Wharton, Ev. §20. In Stevenson v. Stuart, 11 Pa. 307, it was said: "The competency of a collateral fact to be used as the basis of legitimate argument is not to be determined by the conclusiveness of the inferences it may afford in reference to the litigated fact. It is enough if these may tend in a slight degree to elucidate the inquiry, or to assist, though remotely, to a determination probably founded in truth."

We are of opinion that the testimony referred to was competent. While appellant's counsel are correct in their assertion that the question was whether appellant had heard a story to the effect that the deceased had offered serious violence to the old man, yet it does not follow that the testimony complained of did not tend to negative the claim of appellant as to what he had heard. One of the first principles of human nature is the impulse to speak the truth. "This principle," says Dr. Reid, whom Professor Greenleaf quotes at length in his work on Evidence (volume 1 §7n), "has a powerful operation, even in the greatest of liars; for where they lie once they speak truth 100 times." Truth speaking preponderating, it follows that to show that there was no basis in fact for the statement appellant claims to have heard had a tendency to make it less probable that his testimony on this point was true. Indeed, since this court has not, in cases where self-defense is asserted as a justification for homicide, confined the evidence concerning the deceased to character evidence, we do not perceive how, without the possibility of a gross perversion of right, the state could be denied the opportunity to meet in the manner indicated the evidence of the defendant as to what he had heard, where he, cunningly perhaps, denies that he can remember who gave him the information. The fact proved by the state tended to discredit appellant, since it showed that somewhere between the fact and the testimony there was a person who was not a truth speaker, and, appellant being unable to point to his informant, it must at least be said that the testimony complained of had a tendency to render his claim as to what he had heard less probable. . . .

Judgment affirmed.

UNITED STATES v. STEVER

603 F.3d 747 (9th Cir. 2010)

[Defendant Stever appealed his conviction on one count of conspiracy to manufacture 1,000 or more marijuana plants and one count of manufacture of marijuana in violation of 21 U.S.C. §841. Stever sought to defend on the ground that the marijuana growing operation found on an isolated corner of his mother's 400-acre property was the work of one of the Mexican drug trafficking organizations (DTOs) that had recently infiltrated Eastern Oregon. Stever sought discovery from the government of materials related to the operations of DTOs in Eastern Oregon, and made proffers of proof at trial for the following purposes: (1) to rebut the inference that the owners of the property must have been involved in the marijuana operation, because Mexican DTOs have grown marijuana by trespassing on large tracts of public and private land in Eastern Oregon without the knowledge of the owners; (2) to buttress the inference that this particular marijuana operation was the work of a Mexican DTO by demonstrating that operations run by Mexican DTOs have several distinctive characteristics in common with this operation; and (3) to show that Mexican DTOs are secretive and familial and so are unlikely to have involved a local Caucasian in their operations.

The government argued that those inferences were not relevant to Stever's guilt or innocence. The district court agreed. The court refused to compel discovery and rejected Stever's proffers of proof, repeatedly insisting that evidence about who else was responsible for the marijuana operation was not relevant to assessing the likelihood that Stever was involved. On appeal, the Court of Appeals rejected both of the district court's rulings on the basis of the following analysis of relevance.]

The district court's conclusion was illogical. Evidence is relevant if it has "*any* tendency to make the existence of any fact that is of consequence to the determination of the action more probable or less probable than it would be without the evidence." Fed. R. Evid. 401 (emphasis added). The requested evidence, if it existed, tended to show that a Mexican DTO planted the marijuana. It also tended to make it more probable that Stever was not involved, as there would then be an alternative explanation for the grow that would not entail the consent, much less the participation, of any of the Stevers.

The Government makes several arguments in support of the district court's ruling. First, the Government argues that evidence must relate to a *particular* Mexican DTO to be probative of Stever's innocence. This argument fails. Evidence that makes it more likely that a Mexican DTO—any Mexican DTO—was responsible for this operation makes it less likely that Stever was.

Next, the Government argues that a showing that this grow was the work of a Mexican DTO would not tend to exonerate Stever, because Stever could have conspired with the DTO. Although such cooperation is certainly possible, Stever correctly argues that his guilt is *less likely* with Mexican DTO involvement than without it, both because without such involvement a jury would naturally assume that someone with legitimate authority over the land was at least in part responsible, and because he proffered evidence of the exclusivity of Mexican DTO operations....

Finally, the Government argues that the evidence would invite the jury to engage in impermissible speculation about Mexican DTOs and their "correlat[ion] with the Stever property grow." But the district court is not free to dismiss logically relevant evidence as speculative: "[I]f the evidence [that someone else committed the crime] is in truth calculated to cause the jury to doubt, the court should not attempt to decide for the jury that this doubt is purely speculative and fantastic but should afford the accused every opportunity to create that doubt." United States v. Vallejo, 237 F.3d 1008, 1023 (9th Cir. 2001) (quoting John Henry Wigmore, *Evidence in Trials at Common Law* §139 (1983)) (alterations in original). The jury will still be instructed to decide whether a doubt created by the evidence is a reasonable one and, if it is not, to convict. Viewed in that light, the danger the Government invokes is only the danger that the jury will not follow the instructions given, a risk which we may not entertain in light of "the crucial assumption underlying our constitutional system of trial by jury that jurors carefully follow instructions." [Citation omitted.]

Moreover, as the Government conceded, the case against Stever was circumstantial. Prosecutors asked the jury to infer that Stever was involved in the operation based primarily on its location on his property and his various interactions with Pulido [one of his employees], who *was* linked to the operation by physical evidence. Stever sought to counter the circumstantial inferences that the Government asked the jury to draw with evidence of other, logically relevant circumstances from which obverse inferences to those sought by the Government could be drawn. The district court's conclusion that the discovery was not relevant was thus based on a misapplication of the principles of logical relevance, and the denial of Stever's motion to compel therefore an abuse of discretion.

[Judgment reversed on the ground that Stever was denied his Sixth Amendment right to make a defense, an error that was not harmless.]

NOTES AND QUESTIONS

1. Although the court in *Knapp* does not state the essential elements of the case under the substantive law, you can probably deduce those elements yourself from the *Johnson* case. What are they? How do the evidentiary facts testified to by the physician connect to a fact of consequence in the case? Can you draw a diagram of this connection? Are the tests of relevance stated in the court's opinion similar, if not identical, to FRE 401 and 402?

2. The court articulates the chain of reasoning that it relies on to establish the relevance of the physician's testimony. It requires a generalization about the truthtelling propensities of people. Is this generalization reasonable? Why does the court think so? Do you?

3. Notice the emphasis that the court gives to the defendant's inability to remember who told him about the incident involving the old man. What is the court's point? Consider this point again after reading Section B, infra on FRE 403.

4. Stever's discovery request for government reports, training materials, and other documents relating to Mexican DTOs in Eastern Oregon was made pursuant to Fed. R. Crim. P. 16(a)(1)(E)(i), which provides that the government must disclose all "documents ... within the government's possession, custody or control ... [that are] material to preparing the defense." The government never denied that it possessed such materials; it simply considered them irrelevant and refused to make anything available to Stever.

5. Read the *Stever* opinion a second time. It discusses and applies what it calls the "principles of logical relevance." It illustrates the importance of the careful articulation of relevance theories; points out the low threshold of probative connection under the "any tendency" standard of FRE 401; states the appropriate means for judicial control of jury speculation; and emphasizes the importance of presenting the jury with competing inferences in a circumstantial evidence case.

6. The classic articles that have forged the concept of logical relevancy adopted by the Federal Rules of Evidence and described in this chapter are George F. James,

Relevancy, Probability and the Law, 29 Cal. L. Rev. 689 (1941); Herman C. Trautman, Logical or Legal Relevancy—A Conflict in Theory, 5 Vand. L. Rev. 385 (1952). See also 2 Jack B. Weinstein and Margaret A. Berger, Weinstein's Federal Evidence §401 (Joseph M. McLaughlin ed., Matthew Bender 2d ed. 2001); 1A Wigmore on Evidence §37 (Peter Tillers rev. 1983).

The approach of the Federal Rules is typically contrasted with that of Wigmore, who argued that the law distinguished between "logical" and "legal" relevancy. 1 John Henry Wigmore, Evidence in Trials at Common Law §28, at 409-410 (3d ed. 1940): "[L]egal relevancy denotes ... something more than a minimum of probative value." It is not altogether clear what this means. Presumably, Wigmore was attempting to distinguish between evidence that had some very slight probative value and that which had considerably more persuasive force. The concept of "legal relevancy" does not appear in the Federal Rules, but it is a term that is still used by some practicing lawyers and judges. For our purposes, relevancy refers only to the minimal threshold test of FRE 401. But FRE 401 taken in combination with FRE 403, to be discussed in Section B, infra, may provide outcomes consistent with Wigmore's approach. If an item of evidence has only a barely perceptible logical effect, it is also likely either to be misleading or to lead to delay and waste of time, thus being excludable under FRE 403.

KEY POINTS

1. FRE 402 requires that evidence must be relevant to be admitted at trial, and that all relevant evidence is admissible unless otherwise provided.

2. FRE 401 requires that to be relevant, an evidentiary fact must connect by a process of inferential reasoning to a "fact of consequence" in the case. The essential elements of the substantive law that governs the case determine what facts are "of consequence."

3. FRE 401 requires that to be relevant, an evidentiary fact must make a fact of consequence "more or less probable." The judge decides this issue under the "any tendency" standard by examining the necessary inferences and the reasonableness of the generalizations underlying them.

PROBLEMS

3.1. Consider the following items of evidence from the *Johnson* case. Are they relevant under FRE 401? State the argument for the proponent of the evidence: What fact of consequence (and essential element) is the item offered to prove? Why does the item make this fact more or less probable? Then make the opponent's argument.

(a) The prosecution asked Officer Huston, "What type of inmates are typically housed in Facility B?" (Page 8, line 34, supra.) Why would this information be relevant?

(b) Several correctional officers testified that the reports that they wrote following the incident did not state that they opened the food port door before the cell door was opened electronically.

(c) The prosecution asked inmate Butler whether he was a gang member and whether defendant Johnson was a gang member. Butler answered that he

himself was a Crip and that he did not know if Johnson had any gang affiliation. (Page 44, lines 4-11, supra.)

3.2. At 2:00 P.M. in the afternoon of September 15, 2010, Denise Driver stopped
her school bus at its regular stop on Cedar Street. Several young school children
between the ages of 8 and 12 left the bus and stood on the gravel shoulder along
the side of Cedar Street. As the bus started forward, it hit one of the children, Paul
Pedroso, age 10. Paul has been hospitalized since the accident.

Paul's parents have sued Driver and Driver's employer, the San Ramon School
District, for negligence on Paul's behalf. They allege that Driver failed to keep a proper
lookout and veered off the roadway onto the gravel shoulder where Paul was standing
quietly, waiting for the bus to pass. Driver and the school district allege that Driver kept
a proper lookout; that Paul was not standing quietly but was playing tag with several
other children along the side of the road; and that when Paul ran out into the roadway
unexpectedly, Driver had no opportunity to stop in time to avoid hitting him.

At trial in the case of Pedroso v. Driver, Denise Driver testifies in her own defense.
Assume that she is a competent witness. During the direct examination of the driver,
the following questions and answers occur.

1   Q: Are you still employed as a bus driver?
2   A: No, I quit after the accident.
3   Q: Why?
4   A: It is just like trying to haul a truck load of diamonds. (Voice breaks)
5   Every one of those kids were precious and I just did not have the
6   heart to go back.
7   Q: Would you like a glass of water?
8   A: No, I am okay.

During cross-examination of the driver by the plaintiffs' attorney, the following
occurred:

9   Q: Isn't it true that you received a speeding ticket for driving the school bus
10   with the children in it, at 70 miles per hour in a 45 m.p.h. speed zone just
11   a month before 11 the accident in this case occurred?
12   A: Yes.

As attorney for the defendant, what is your theory of relevance for the testimony
at lines 4-6?

As attorney for the plaintiff, what is your theory of relevance for the question and
answer in lines 9-12? For each item, state the connection between the EF and the EE.

3.3. In the case of United States v. Ray, Bernard Ray, the Chief Executive Officer
of Rundown Corp., is charged with the federal crime of trading on inside information. The prosecution must prove that Ray intended to profit from the purchase or
sale of securities by using "inside" information—information confidential within
Rundown and not yet known to the public. Specifically, the prosecution alleges that
Ray sold 100,000 shares of Rundown stock on March 16, 2010 that Ray made this
sale based on his knowledge of "inside" information that Rundown was facing disastrous losses during the upcoming second quarter (April to June) of 2010; and that Ray
intended to profit from this sale. In fact, Rundown Corp. did suffer disastrous financial

losses between April and June of 2010, causing the company to file for bankruptcy in December of 2010.

These losses had been projected by Rundown Corp.'s outside auditing firm in early March of 2010. The chief outside auditor Arthur Andrews sent a confidential memorandum stating these loss projections to the office of June Jacobs, the Chief Financial Officer of Rundown, that was delivered to Jacobs on the morning of March 14. Later in the afternoon of March 14, chief auditor Andrews also sent an e-mail to Jacobs advising her to inform Ray about these projections. Ray claims that he was not informed about the projected losses until March 18, just before the weekly meeting of Rundown's Executive Committee. If called as a witness, Jacobs will assert her Fifth Amendment privilege to refuse to testify about these events. The government has a copy of the March 14 e-mail from Andrews to Jacobs that it wants to enter into evidence to prove that Ray knew about the projected losses before March 16.

Is the e-mail relevant under the standard of FRE 401? Why?

3.4. In the case of State v. Blair, on September 14, 2010, Norma Waits, a 35-year-old woman, was brutally attacked in her apartment. There were no signs of forced entry. Norma's housekeeper found Norma unconscious the next morning and then called 911.

Norma was a successful and beloved singer for the local Opera Company. After an extensive investigation, police arrested Jimmy Blair, a 45-year-old prominent entertainment lawyer, and charged him with aggravated assault and battery and attempted murder. Norma does not remember the attack and cannot identify the attacker.

Jimmy and Norma had been dating since 2007. Their relationship began when they met at a fundraising gala for the Opera. Norma's friends reported that Jimmy was charming and supportive. None of them had suspected any trouble, though they did note that Norma had become more isolated in the two years preceding the attack. Norma's best friend stated that she had been unable to see much of Norma in 2010, despite repeated attempts to arrange activities. Additionally, Norma's career had begun to falter, and she took an extensive leave from the Opera, citing unspecified health problems. As the prosecution builds its case against Jimmy, many items of potentially admissible evidence are considered. For the following items, decide whether you think each item is relevant under FRE 401 and 402 and why. Identify the fact of consequence that the item might make more or less probable, and the generalizations needed to support any inferences. Is other evidence needed to determine relevance?

(a)   A friend of Norma's says that a month before the attack, Norma told the friend that she planned to tell Jimmy that she was going to break up with him and leave the Bay Area soon. Norma also said that she was afraid Jimmy would be furious.

(b)   A police witness would testify that on the morning after the attack, police found a suitcase in Norma's apartment half-packed with her belongings. The police also found a plane ticket for a flight to Los Angeles on that day with Norma's name on it. The ticket was torn in half.

(c)   Exhibits include photographs of Norma showing severe bruising on parts of her body that would normally be covered by clothing. The photos are date stamped July 25, 2009. A police witness will testify that she found these photographs in a locked drawer in Norma's apartment, which she opened with a key found among Norma's personal effects.

3.5. During the course of a professional United States Soccer League game, a player for the Blazers, Bob Broadback, was injured by a blow struck by Tony Trapp, a player for the opposing Tomcats. The injury occurred immediately after the Blazers had scored and appeared likely to win the game. Just before the score, Broadback and Trapp had run into each other and both had fallen onto the field. As Broadback was getting up, Trapp struck a blow with his forearm to the back of Broadback's head and neck. Broadback suffered a serious neck injury.

Broadback files a personal injury lawsuit against Trapp for battery. Broadback must prove that Trapp's blow caused his injury. If Broadback also proves that Trapp struck him "with the specific intent to cause grievous injury," then Broadback can claim punitive damages. In his deposition, Trapp has testified that his contact with Broadback was a mere "slap," that "stuff like that happens all the time during games," and that Broadback must have been injured when they ran into each other on the field.

(a)   At trial, Broadback offers a recorded excerpt from the televised filming of the soccer game that shows the sequence of events leading up to and including the blow by Trapp to Broadback's neck. The recording also shows an Official Referee immediately ejecting Trapp from the game. Trapp objects on grounds of relevance. What ruling and why?

(b)   Broadback also offers a copy of Article V, Section A, Subsection (3) of the Official Rules Governing the Conduct of Play (Rules) of the United States Soccer League, which reads as follows:

All players are prohibited from striking another player on the head, face or neck with the hand, wrist, forearm, elbow or clasped hands.

Is this Rule relevant? To prove what?

4. Reflection on the Requirement of Relevancy

The Federal Rules of Evidence have as their central goal the factually accurate resolution of disputes that are brought to federal court. This is not to say that other values do not affect the Rules, as explicitly stated in FRE 102, or that the search for truth does not accommodate other values. It is to say, however, that the dominant policy expressed in the Rules, in the Advisory Committee Notes, in judicial interpretations, and professional and academic commentary is the pursuit of factually accurate outcomes.

This policy rests on a belief that disinterested fact finders, such as jurors, have the capacity to reconstruct prior events by using their powers of reasoning—by drawing inferences from evidence presented to them in the courtroom, based on their own generalized knowledge and experience. To the extent that the evidence presented is accurate and complete and the jury's generalizations are accurate, this reasoning process can yield accurate outcomes. The accuracy of this reasoning process is advanced in no small measure by the requirement of relevancy discussed above.

The trial system, in short, pursues the search for truth from the perspective of a correspondence theory of knowledge. It assumes that things happen and that what happens is knowable by human beings. The system also assumes that accurate knowledge is produced through human reasoning—that persons (witnesses) can coherently communicate information about happenings to disinterested third parties (jurors) who then will draw accurate inferences based on that information. You can see that the role of witnesses and the role of the jury described on pages 80-81, supra, are grounded in these assumptions.

Suppose, though, that you are convinced that there is a reality and that you can know it. Are you as convinced that your fellow human beings can know it, or do you have doubts about the rationality of the human species? Even if you are a disinterested observer of events, is anyone else? How often have you seen a person's perceptions of an event determined by ideology or wishful thinking? Consider the videotape of the Los Angeles police arrest of and use of force against Rodney King. Viewers' perceptions of that event could apparently differ dramatically. If that is not an uncommon occurrence, what are its implications for the social reconstruction of reality that occurs at trial based on the testimony of witnesses whose perception may be affected by factors that are not rational?

Moreover, how much faith do you have in disinterested third parties such as jurors drawing the appropriate inferences about what happened based on the evidentiary facts described to them by witnesses? How different was student opinion in your class about the credibility of witnesses in the transcript of the *Johnson* case in Chapter One? Do people use a uniform body of generalized knowledge and experience to evaluate such data? Or are you more impressed with the remarkable divergence of opinion that constantly seems to follow from the presentation of information to a group of individuals? Again, does that increase or decrease your faith in the rationality of the trial process?

Empirical research has also been done on the intellectual strategies that people use—alone and in groups—to come to conclusions about disputed facts. The landmark works in this field that may have the most compelling applications to jury decision-making are Michael J. Saks and Robert F. Kidd, Human Information Processing and Adjudication: Trial by Heuristics, 15 Law & Socy. Rev. 123 (1980-1981), and Amos Tversky and Daniel Kahneman, Judgment Under Uncertainty: Heuristics and Biases, 185 Science 1124 (1974). Recent work on the "narrative theory" of jury decision-making includes Nancy Pennington and Reid Hastie, A Cognitive Theory of Juror Decision Making: The Story Model, 13 Cardozo L. Rev. 519 (1991) and Dan Simon, A Third View of the Black Box: Cognitive Coherence in Legal Decision Making, 71 U. Chi. L. Rev. 511 (2004). The following offer good overviews of the empirical literature on juries: Vidmar and Hans, American Juries: The Verdict (2007); Shari Diamond, Beyond Fantasy and Nightmare: A Portrait of the Jury, 54 Buff. L. Rev. 717 (2006). This literature offers practitioners the opportunity to understand jurors' decision-making strategies, and it offers law reformers the opportunity to improve the procedures and evidentiary policies underlying our system of trial.

Questions about the validity of the assumption of jury rationality are of great importance. The outcomes of jury fact-finding are always uncertain. There is no methodology and no objective point of view within the system of trials to test whether the jury has correctly decided the ultimate facts.[5] To the extent that one has doubts about

---

5.   The results of DNA testing may come as close to "objective certainty" as our system can provide. Numerous persons convicted of rape or murder have been freed from incarceration on the basis of subsequent DNA testing (not available at the time of trial) of body samples, such as hair and semen, found on the victim. The testing virtually excludes the defendant as the source of the samples. In one such case, however, the prosecutor remains convinced that the released convict was guilty: "It really doesn't change my opinion that much. . . . The case was a circumstantial-evidence case. There was a myriad of [sic] circumstances that pointed in his direction." *New York Times*, August 23, 2001.

jury rationality, one should have serious reservations about continuing our current system of trial. On the other hand, to the extent one has greater faith in our capacity to understand and communicate our knowledge about the world in a rational manner, then one may feel somewhat more sanguine about the model of jury reasoning. And whatever degree of skepticism you possess, you must also consider what alternatives there are to our reliance on this model.

Additional critical perspectives on the assumptions and policies that underlie the Federal Rules of Evidence can be found in Kenneth W. Graham Jr., There'll Always Be an England: The Instrumental Ideology of Evidence, 85 Mich. L. Rev. 1204, 1219-1220, 1227-1234 (1987); Rosemary C. Hunter, Gender in Evidence, Masculine Norms vs. Feminist Reforms, 19 Harv. Women's L.J. 127 (1996); Kit Kinports, Evidence Engendered, 1991 U. Ill. L. Rev. 413; Michael L. Seigel, A Pragmatic Critique of Modern Evidence Scholarship, 88 Nw. U. L. Rev. 995, 998 (1994); Frederick Schauer, On the Supposed Jury Dependence of Evidence Law, 155 U. Pa. L. Rev. 165 (2006); Todd E. Pettys, The Emotional Juror, 76 Fordham L. Rev. 1609 (2007).

B. PROBATIVE VALUE AND THE RULE 403 DANGERS

FRE 403 affords the trial court authority to exclude evidence that is admittedly relevant under Rules 401 and 402, but that the judge believes might distract the jury from its role of rational decision-making. This authority also existed under the common law, referred to as *judicial discretion*. As you read FRE 403, you will see that the rule provides guides for the exercise of the court's discretionary power to exclude. The judge is not free to choose between admission and exclusion unrestrained by fixed principles. Rather, the judge has some flexibility in choice of outcome, but is restrained by standards articulated in the rule. Rule 403 does not allow a trial judge "to remove relevant evidence from the jury's universe solely because he finds the evidence unpersuasive; the ultimate arbiter of the persuasiveness of the proof must be the factfinder, not the lawgiver." Blake v. Pellegrino, 329 F.3d 43, 47 (1st Cir. 2003). Remember that the judge's power to exclude under FRE 403 means that the advocates cannot present all the relevant evidence they would like to offer to the jury, and the jury will not see and hear admittedly relevant information.

1. FRE 403

RULE 403.   EXCLUDING RELEVANT EVIDENCE FOR PREJUDICE, CONFUSION, WASTE OF TIME, OR OTHER REASONS

The court may exclude relevant evidence if its probative value is substantially outweighed by a danger of one or more of the following: unfair prejudice, confusing the issues, misleading the jury, undue delay, wasting time, or needlessly presenting cumulative evidence.

2.   Interpretation and Illustration of FRE 403

When the opponent objects to the admission of evidence on any of the grounds stated in the rule, the judge must carefully evaluate the probative value of the offered item, estimate the "Rule 403 danger" that it poses, and then apply the terms of the balancing test that the rule sets forth. Relevant evidence is to be excluded only if its probative value is *substantially* outweighed by one of the rule's articulated dangers. The rule itself and its Advisory Committee Note give judges little guidance in interpreting the meaning of its terms. How is the judge to measure probative value? What is the difference between "confusion of the issues," "misleading the jury," and "unfair prejudice"? We will develop the meaning of these terms in some detail. We believe that careful analysis of the Rule 403 dangers can have a critical impact on the trial judge's ruling.

Consider an example of evidence raising Rule 403 dangers. James Johnson, the defendant, testified in the *Johnson* case that he observed Officer Walker attack another inmate, allegedly for no good reason: "He snatched a Hispanic guy up off the seat, took him out the kitchen, drug him by the hair out of the kitchen in the front by the sally port and jumped on the guy" (page 54, lines 32-43, supra). This testimony was offered to show that Johnson had good reason to fear Officer Walker when Walker came to his cell door. This testimony about Officer Walker's conduct on another occasion could also cause the jury to think about Walker, not about Johnson's state of mind. The jury could think that Walker is a bad person and hold this against the government; also, the jury could think that Walker has a propensity for violence and therefore would have attacked Johnson. As we explain at page 145, infra, these are the two ways in which this evidence might be unfairly prejudicial to the government's case. Thus, Johnson's testimony might be objected to by the prosecution under FRE 403,[6] and the judge must weigh the probative value of the evidence against these risks of unfair prejudice.

a.   Probative Value

To decide the merits of a Rule 403 objection, the judge must first analyze the persuasive effect that the item of evidence will be likely to have on the jury's thinking about the fact of consequence it is offered to prove. This is its *probative value*. Remember that evidence is relevant if it has "any" tendency to make the fact of consequence more or less probable; probative value measures the strength of the effect on the probabilities, even if only in general terms like "highly," "somewhat," or "minimally" probative. Defendant Johnson's testimony as to Officer Walker's conduct is clearly relevant to show that Johnson had reason to fear Walker, but what is its probative value? In United States v. Buchanan, 964 F. Supp. 533, 537 (D. Mass. 1997), the district court posed the issue as follows:

> In evaluating probative value I am obliged to consider first "how strong a tendency" the proffered evidence has to prove the issue of consequence in the litigation,... and second, the proponent's need for the evidence.

---

6.   California Evidence Code §352, on which FRE 403 is based, contains essentially the same balancing test:

The court in its discretion may exclude evidence if its probative value is substantially outweighed by the probability that its admission will (a) necessitate undue consumption of time or (b) create substantial danger of undue prejudice, of confusing the issues, or of misleading the jury.

i.   Strength of the Underlying Inferences.   Most courts and commentators agree that the primary measure of probative value is the strength of the inferences that connect the evidentiary fact to the fact of consequence and then to an essential element in the case. This strength depends on the rough probabilities of the generalizations underlying those inferences. If, as Johnson said, he saw Officer Walker beat up another inmate with no provocation, then a generalization underlying the inference that Johnson feared Walker could be articulated as follows:

Diagram 3-7

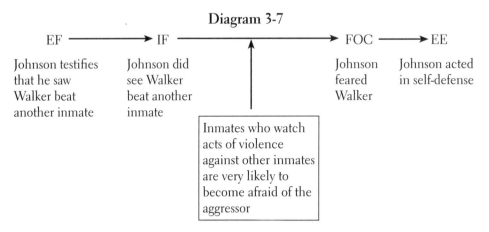

The judge's rough estimate of the probability expressed in this generalization—here, the frequency with which inmates do become afraid, estimated as "very likely"—is the major component of the judge's estimate of the probative value of Johnson's testimony. There is no single "correct" way to articulate this generalization, and there is no precise or accurate way to estimate its degree of frequency. Human behavior rarely can be reliably predicted. Moreover, details of the offered evidence would affect how the generalization is framed, such as was the beating extremely violent? Would it cause extreme or only mild fear in the minds of other inmates? Additional evidentiary facts can also increase or decrease the probative value of the offered item. Were such beatings frequent or unusual? Was there already "bad blood" between Johnson and Walker, or between the Hispanic inmate and Walker? Some of these facts could be the subject of further testimony from Johnson, or from additional witnesses as well. The fact finder, if the evidence is admitted, will then make inferences from these facts, based on its own background knowledge and experience. You can see that the judge's estimate is just that—a rough attempt to place a value on an inference that a reasonable jury could make and that cannot be quantified with precision.

ii.   Certainty of the Starting Point.   The certainty of the evidentiary fact that is the starting point of the inferential chain can also affect probative value. For example, what if Johnson testified that he "thought" it was Officer Walker who beat the other inmate but he "wasn't sure"? If witnesses admit that they are themselves uncertain about what facts they actually perceived, or if a document contains ambiguous language, the evidentiary fact presented is less certain. Judges may lower their estimate of the probative value that they attribute to the evidence for purposes of FRE 403. United States v. Rodriguez-Cabrera, 35 F. Supp. 2d 181, 184 (D.P.R. 1998) (meaning of defendant's nod so ambiguous that prejudice substantially outweighs probative value). However, a judge's doubts about a witness's truthfulness do not lower the certainty of the starting point of that witness's testimony. For example, should defendant Johnson be believed when he said he saw Officer Walker attack another inmate? Doubts about Johnson's credibility could reduce the probative value of the facts he testifies about. But courts *do not count the witness's credibility* when estimating probative value. 22 Charles Alan Wright and Arthur R. Miller, Federal Practice and Procedure §5214 at 265-266; United States v. Wallace, 124 Fed. Appx. 164, 167 (4th Cir. 2005) ("the credibility of a witness has *nothing to do with* whether or not his testimony is probative with respect to the fact which it seeks to prove."). The prevailing view is that evaluating the credibility of witnesses is a matter uniquely within the competence of the jury, and that the judge's role is to estimate the probative value of testimony *if believed*. If judges were to use their discretionary power under FRE 403 to exclude the testimony of witnesses they do not believe, then the jury's principal fact-finding function would be vastly diminished.

iii. **Need**. The Advisory Committee Note to FRE 403 mentions two other factors that a judge may take into account in applying the rule's balancing test. First, the Note advises that judges should balance "the probative value of and *need* for the evidence against the harm likely to result from its admission" (emphasis added). Then, the Note closes with the statement that the "availability of other means of proof" may also be weighed in the decision to exclude evidence on grounds of unfair prejudice. No explanation of these terms is given, nor is the judge advised how to take these factors into account. Case law reveals that there are many ways in which judges do take need into account. The centrality of the point to be proved with the proffered evidence, the degree to which this point is disputed by the opponent, and the strength of the evidence in proving the point, can demonstrate a party's need for evidence. United States v. DeLaurentis, 83 F. Supp. 2d 455, 467-468 (D.N.J. 2000) (evidence that defendant engaged in a prior criminal scheme with government's star witness was necessary to rehabilitate that witness's credibility after defendant's attack, and was particularly probative of the witness's truthfulness).

Need for a particular item of evidence because there is no alternative means of proving a fact of consequence can also affect the FRE 403 decision. Courts have held that such need for evidence "should be weighed along with its probative value to determine whether it should be admitted under Rule 403 [but] need ... does not make the evidence more likely to prove that which it is offered to prove." United States v. Stout, 509 F.3d 796, 800 (6th Cir. 2007). Thus, if unfair prejudice substantially outweighs the probative value of an item, the court may still exclude the item despite lack of other means of proof.

Alternatively, if there is already substantial evidence on the same point, there is less need for an additional item. Frank v. County of Hudson, 924 F. Supp. 620, 626 (D.N.J. 1996) (evidence of unrelated child sexual abuse by a defendant in a sexual harassment and discrimination case was excluded, although admissible under FRE 413-415, because four plaintiffs making similar accusations of defendant's workplace harassment "reduces the relative weight" of the proffered child abuse evidence); United States v. Bell, 516 F.3d 432, 445 (6th Cir. 2008) (quantity of illegal drugs possessed, along with drug scales, a cutting board and other drug paraphernalia, substantially reduced government's need for past drug distribution convictions to prove defendant's "intent" to distribute).

You can see that this fine-tuning of the Rule 403 factors requires that the judge be familiar with evidence that is already admitted and that is expected to be admitted at trial. The judge may also need to inquire about what other evidence is available to the parties. In United States v. Gonsalves, 668 F.2d 73, 75 (1st Cir. 1982), evidence of defendant's threat leveled against an eyewitness who would testify against him was admissible as showing consciousness of guilt despite the risk of unfair prejudice. The government's eyewitness identification evidence against defendant was strong, and defendant's alibi evidence was equally strong; the appellate court affirmed in part because the government had no other means to corroborate its eyewitnesses and its need was "substantial." If the judge is not able to make this contextual judgment at the time a Rule 403 objection is made, the judge can defer decision until later in the trial when more evidentiary context has been provided, using the technique of conditional admissibility that will be discussed in Chapter Four, Section E, infra.

NOTE

Some commentators believe that the length of the inferential chain of reasoning reduces the probative value of an item of evidence. They reason that the more inferences that are necessary to make this connection, the more opportunity a jury has for making an error in its inferential reasoning process. (A doctrine related to this perceived risk, still persistent in some jurisdictions, is that an "inference upon an inference" is not allowable.) *We do not agree with this general proposition.* A higher number of inferential steps in a chain of reasoning does not automatically reduce probative value. Indeed, DNA evidence, for example, requires complicated chains of reasoning and can yield a high probability. While it is true that some chains of reasoning are longer and some are shorter, the important point is that some are stronger in the sense of being more convincing, while some are weaker in the sense of being not very persuasive. At issue is the strength of the connection between the evidentiary fact and the final inference rather than the number of steps that must be taken to get to that final conclusion. This is a function primarily of the strength of the generalizations underlying each step.

b.   Rule 403 Dangers

The second step in resolving a Rule 403 objection is for the judge to estimate the danger that the item of evidence poses to the jury's rational decision-making process and to the judicial system's interest in efficient decision-making. FRE 403 identifies major sources of risk of error in the jury's reasoning process. Evidence that is unfairly prejudicial or confusing or that will mislead the jury can be excluded. In addition, if the production of evidence causes undue delay, is a waste of time, or is needlessly cumulative, it may be excluded as well. Whatever the kind of danger, the judge will attempt to make a realistic estimate of the danger posed. This will include the *nature of the danger, the likelihood that the jury will be negatively affected, and the probable degree of the harmful effect.* And if a single item of evidence raises more than one of these probative dangers, this may significantly increase the probable degree of harm.

i.   **Unfair Prejudice.**   The term *unfair prejudice* refers to the danger that evidence might suggest an improper basis upon which the jury could decide the case. Evidence is *not* unfairly prejudicial simply because it is detrimental to a party's case.

If all evidence adverse to a defendant was subject to exclusion under F.R.E. Rule 403, then no government evidence would ever be deemed admissible. The test ... is not whether the evidence is detrimental, but whether it is so unfairly prejudicial as to substantially outweigh its probative value. [United States v. Weinstock, 153 F.3d 272, 278 (6th Cir. 1998).]

Case law has established that there are two principal risks of unfair prejudice within the scope of FRE 403. The first risk is that evidence about a party can trigger a response that has nothing to do with its logical connection to a fact of consequence. This response can turn the jury against that party (or in favor of that party) and improperly influence the jury's decision-making. The Advisory Committee Note to FRE 403 suggests that this improper reaction is "commonly, though not necessarily, an emotional one." Wigmore describes the danger as occurring when evidence would "be likely to stimulate an excessive emotion or to awaken a fixed prejudice ... and thus dominate the mind of the tribunal and prevent a rational determination of the truth." John Henry Wigmore, Code of Evidence 355 (3d ed. 1942).

For example, recall the testimony of defendant James Johnson concerning Officer Walker's attack on another inmate, discussed on page 141, supra. Walker's attack might trigger a response of anger or disgust that prejudices the jury against Walker. There is a risk that this prejudice could influence the outcome in the *Johnson* case in an unfair way, such as the jury viewing a verdict in favor of Johnson as a punishment of Walker. If a Rule 403 objection is made, the trial judge would have to estimate this danger of unfair prejudice by identifying the nature of the danger and its likely effect. United States v. Bell, 516 F.3d 432, 445 (6th Cir. 2008) ("evidence of Bell's prior crimes painted a picture of Bell as a repeat drug offender, greatly increasing the chance that the jury would punish him not for his involvement in the offense at issue, but rather because he appeared to be a 'bad guy'"). Evidence that could generate undue sympathy for a party can also be excluded as unfairly prejudicial. Lewis v. City of Chicago Police Dept., 590 F.3d 427, 440 (7th Cir. 2009) (evidence that plaintiff suffered a broken neck when accidentally hit on the head during a forced house entry was excluded as highly inflammatory in the context of her employment claim of retaliation).

The second principal risk of unfair prejudice is if evidence admitted for a proper purpose could also be used by the jury in a manner that violates a rule of evidence law. For example, Officer Walker's attack on the other inmate triggers the permissible inference that defendant Johnson feared Walker. It also triggers an impermissible inference about Officer Walker's propensity to use violence against inmates in general, and thus to use violence against Johnson. This is impermissible under FRE 404(b), which prohibits the use of prior specific acts, such as Walker's attack, to prove action in conformity with character, as we will see in Chapter Five. The risk that the jury will use Johnson's testimony for this improper purpose qualifies as a danger of unfair prejudice under FRE 403. Johnson's testimony thus has a proper relevant use—to prove that he feared Walker—as well as an improper use—to prove Walker's violent character. If the prosecution objects to Johnson's testimony, FRE 403 requires the judge to balance the testimony's permissible probative value against the danger that it will be used improperly. In Smith v. City of Oakland, 538 F. Supp. 2d 1217 (N.D. Cal. 2008), plaintiff sued two Oakland police officers for violating his constitutional rights by planting a semi-automatic rifle in his residence in order to frame him. The officers sought to cross-examine Smith about his being a candidate for "three-strikes" penalty in California if he possessed the rifle, thus giving him a powerful motive to lie. The court ruled under FRE 403:

> Mr. Smith already possessed a strong motive to lie ... because his parole was subject to revocation for illegal possession of the gun. Moreover, any probative value to the three strikes evidence was substantially outweighed by the danger of unfair prejudice. Strikes are given for serious felonies only, and thus there was a significant risk that the jury would infer that Mr. Smith was a violent offender and improperly consider the evidence as character evidence.

    ii. Confusion of the Issues. Evidence confuses the issues when it focuses the jury's attention too closely on a factual issue that is not central to the outcome of the case. Such issues are termed *collateral*, which usually means that their connection to the essential elements is trivial and may be based on complicated or attenuated theories of relevance. Typically, then, proof of collateral issues will require the use of multiple witnesses or will consume considerable time in court. If the jury gets involved and interested in deciding a collateral issue, it will spend less of its attention on the important questions. It is not that these collateral issues are irrelevant; rather, they are too distracting and tend to *confuse the issues*. For example, evidence of several other incidents of violence against inmates at Pelican Bay, offered by the defense to show that defendant Johnson was justified in being fearful of prison guards, would require testimony from several witnesses, and might be hotly disputed by the prosecution. The jury might confuse the issues and focus its attention on whether those other incidents occurred, instead of on whether Johnson committed the alleged acts of battery. Halvorsen v. Baird, 146 F.3d 680 (9th Cir. 1998) (evidence from six witnesses that each had been involuntarily detained in a detoxification center when they were not drunk was not permitted to bolster plaintiff's case that he had been treated similarly; risk of confusing jury by involving it in a dispute over whether these six individuals were drunk or not).

    Another risk of confusion in the *Johnson* case would be that the evidence of additional violent incidents might cause the jury to focus on an issue that is not a question that the jury is being asked to decide in the lawsuit—such as the prison's policy toward inmates at Pelican Bay. In contrast, in United States v. Crosby, 75 F.3d 1343, 1348 (9th Cir. 1996), the court held that the trial court erred in excluding as "confusing" evidence that the victim's own husband may have committed the assault for which the defendant was on trial. This evidence was not confusing, the appellate court said, because it "added no new issues to the case, as it dovetailed neatly with defendant's theory that someone else had committed the crime."

    iii. Misleading the Jury. Courts often refer to evidence as both "confusing and misleading" and make no effort to distinguish between the two dangers. The danger of being *misleading*, however, usually involves a risk that an item of evidence will cause the jury to draw a *mistaken* inference. In Jones v. Ford Motor Co., 320 F. Supp. 440 (E.D. Va. 2004), plaintiff alleged that a defect in the design of the Ford cruise control system caused her automobile to accelerate suddenly, resulting in her personal injuries. To prove that Ford was on notice of the defective condition, the plaintiff offered government reports from Canada and Japan about sudden acceleration problems with cruise control systems in General Motors cars. The district court excluded these reports under Rule 403 as potentially misleading, since the cruise control systems in Ford cars were not functionally similar and the jury could mistakenly equate them to the General Motors systems. Facts taken out of context or presented in a falsely suggestive manner can also trigger this danger.

Courts are usually not persuaded by the argument that a jury will be misled into giving evidence more weight than it deserves. Juries are assumed to possess reliable generalized knowledge and experience that allows them to evaluate most aspects of human affairs that are presented at trial. Occasionally, however, the risk of overvaluation can rise to the level of "misleading" the jury. For example, videotaped reenactments of accidents or other events have been called misleading because jurors may treat them as documentations of the actual event. Many courts reject a criminal defendant's lie detector evidence on the grounds that the jury may over-value polygraph results as an indicator of truthfulness because of their scientific nature. United States v. Call, 129 F.3d 1402, 1406 (10th Cir. 1997). But a court should not exclude such testimony simply on the theory that scientific techniques by their very nature overwhelm the jury. United States v. West, 962 F.2d 1243, 1248 (7th Cir. 1992) (error to exclude psychiatrist's testimony on the ground that it would mislead the jury with confusing psychiatric terminology—"there was nothing more technical or confusing about [the doctor's] testimony here than the psychiatric testimony in most cases"); In re Paoli R.R. Yard PCB Litigation, 35 F.3d 717, 746 (3d Cir. 1994) ("[t]here must be something about the particular scientific technique such as its posture of mythic infallibility that makes it especially overwhelming").

The use of complex statistics and probabilistic evidence, such as DNA identification evidence, epidemiological studies in toxic tort cases and employer hiring practices in discrimination cases, is also challenging for the jury. Even experts do not agree about the proper calculation and interpretation of the probability of a DNA match in "cold hit" cases, where the match is the only evidence connecting a defendant to the charged crime. David H. Kaye, Rounding Up the Usual Suspects: A Legal and Logical Analysis of DNA Trawling Cases, 87 N.C. L. Rev. 425 (2009). Even where the probability data is empirically valid, there is still a risk that the translation of statistical probability into "real numbers" that the jury can understand may mislead or confuse the jury: "The apparent precision of statistical evidence often stands in marked contrast to the uncertainties of other testimony.... The danger is that such evidence will overshadow equally probative but admittedly unscientific and anecdotal nonstatistical evidence." The Evolving Role of Statistical Assessments as Evidence in the Courts 150 (Report of the Panel on Statistical Assessments as Evidence in the Courts) (Stephen E. Fienberg, ed., 1989). "The danger ... is that statistics on the frequency with which certain blood type combinations occur in a population will be understood by the jury to be a quantification of the likelihood that the defendant, who shares that unique combination of blood characteristics, is guilty." State v. Joon Kyu Kim, 398 N.W.2d 544, 548 (Minn. 1987).

Despite the risk of over-persuasion, the probative value of, and the need for, this kind of evidence is very high. State statutes provide for the use of blood testing and probability estimates in paternity cases, and many courts have approved the admission of probability testimony about DNA testing when it is properly presented and challenged. Other commentators believe that jurors tend to prefer anecdotal evidence and will ignore statistical evidence when it conflicts. Research on this juror response to statistical versus anecdotal evidence is not yet decisive.

iv. Undue Delay, Waste of Time, and Needless Cumulative Evidence. Each of these dangers illustrates a different aspect of the same underlying problem: The introduction of evidence always absorbs court time, incurs expense by the opposing parties and by the state-run judicial system, and expends the attention of the jury. The dangers of delay and waste of time are easily quantifiable. For example, if a continuance is required for production of evidence or to transport the jury to view the scene of the crime, the trial will be delayed. And if a trial judge has imposed strict time limits on the length of trials, requests for extension of time to present rebuttal evidence are decided under the FRE 403 balancing test: "As a general rule, evidence may not be excluded solely to avoid delay.... Under Rule 403, the court should consider the probative value of the proffered evidence and balance it against the harm of delay." General Signal Corp. v. MCI Telecommunications Corp., 66 F.3d 1500, 1509-1510 (9th Cir. 1995). Courts have held that evidence may waste the jury's time if offered to prove stipulated, collateral, or background facts. And research does show that "the longer a trial goes, the more the jury forgets and the less accurate the decision becomes." Securities and Exchange Commission v. Koenig, 557 F.3d 736, 739 (7th Cir. 2009).

The danger underlying *needless presentation of cumulative evidence* is less quantifiable. It includes the expenditure of trial time on repetitive testimony, plus the risk of losing the attention of the jury. During the *Johnson* trial, Officer Smith described for the prosecution what happened between Officer Walker and defendant Johnson when Johnson's cell door was opened. Officers Huston, Van Berg, and Walker had already testified about this occurrence. Thus, the defense might have objected, in the terms of FRE 403, that Officer Smith's testimony was a needless presentation of cumulative evidence and should be excluded. Here the judge must assess the degree to which the testimony actually is repetitive. Obrey v. Johnson, 400 F.3d 691 (9th Cir. 2005) (in an action alleging a pattern of discriminatory promotion practices, testimony from three witnesses who would have testified to their own experiences of discrimination was not cumulative or repetitive as it tended to support the pattern or practice theory). Also, there may be reasons why repetition is needed—such as the centrality of the fact of consequence being proved, the degree to which that fact is in dispute, and the probative value of the corroboration itself. It is unlikely that Officer Smith's testimony would be considered "needless" in the Johnson case, since Johnson's behavior was the central focus of the dispute and each side offered several witnesses to the events. Coles v. Jenkins, 1998 WL 964506 (W.D. Va. 1998) (court denied motion in limine to prevent defendant's use of three experts to testify regarding the dangerousness of a state highway, since each expert had a slightly different area of expertise).

c.   Probative Value Substantially Outweighed by One of the FRE 403 Dangers

The final step is for the trial judge to weigh the probative value of the offered item of evidence against the danger that this item poses under FRE 403. FRE 403 offers no criteria by which these concepts are to be calibrated. How does one determine when a danger *substantially outweighs* probative value?

i.   The Meaning of "Substantially Outweigh."   There does not appear to be a scale—a common measure—with which to compare probative value versus the degree of risk that Rule 403 dangers pose to the jury's reasoning process. If that is so, *a fortiori* there is no means of calibrating which weighs more. There is no "quantum effect on rationality" that can be assigned to an item of evidence. One way that judges might think about the balancing test is to predict an overall effect of an item of evidence on the jury: What is the likelihood that the "bad" aspect of the evidence will seriously dominate the mind of the jury, overwhelming the "good" aspect? If the likelihood seems high, admission of such evidence may lead to "bad" fact-finding as the incremental "badness" of the evidence exerts itself, and exclusion under FRE 403 would be justified.

We might ask, however, why evidence should ever be admitted if its "bad" aspect appears to dominate over the "good" to even a small degree? Would not such evidence always taint the jury's fact-finding? The rule's requirement that probative value be outweighed "substantially" appears to require that some risks of negative impact be tolerated. This is sensible because the judge's ability to predict such effects is so imprecise.

Another way to think about the requirement of substantiality is that it measures the judge's confidence level: Evidence should be excluded only when the judge is quite confident that the prejudicial aspects of the evidence outweigh its probative value. The requirement can be thought of, in other words, as providing a burden of proof to be applied under FRE 403 to the admission of evidence. The burden in FRE 403 favors wrongful decisions to admit evidence over wrongful decisions to exclude it. This is in keeping with the strong belief of the drafters of the Federal Rules of Evidence that the underlying principles of the rules—truth and justice—will best be furthered when more rather than less evidence is deemed admissible.

In practice, how do judges conduct the balancing test of FRE 403? One commentator suggests the following table to show how Rule 403 would properly operate:

Probative value of offered relevant evidence	Negative effect of Rule 403 listed factor	Whether trial court may exclude evidence
High	High, Mid, or Low	No
Mid	High	No (Perhaps Yes)*
	Mid or Low	No
Low	High	Yes
	Mid	No (Perhaps Yes)*
	Low	No

 *If probative value were near the bottom of the "mid" range and the negative effect extremely high, or if probative value were extremely low and the negative effect near the top of the "mid" range, Rule 403 might allow exclusion.

[Newell Blakely, Article IV: Relevancy and Its Limits, 30 U. Hous. L. Rev. 281, 317 (1993).]

ii.   The Effect of Limiting Instructions on the Balancing Process.   The balancing of probative value versus a Rule 403 danger is also affected by FRE 105, which provides as follows:

> When evidence which is admissible as to one party or for one purpose but not admissible as to another party or for another purpose is admitted, the court, upon request, shall restrict the evidence to its proper scope and instruct the jury accordingly.

The Advisory Committee Note to FRE 403 states that "[i]n reaching a decision whether to exclude on grounds of unfair prejudice, consideration should be given to the probable effectiveness or lack of effectiveness of a limiting instruction."

This means that when an item of evidence has a proper relevant use to prove a fact of consequence but also creates the risk of an improper use—an impermissible inference or an unfairly prejudicial effect—the judge may give a limiting instruction that directs the jury to consider the evidence only for its proper use. In the example from the *Johnson* case, Johnson's testimony about Officer Walker's attack on another inmate could have been accompanied by a limiting instruction—that the jury was to consider this testimony only for its effect on Johnson's state of mind, and for no other purpose. If the judge believes that the jury will probably follow such an instruction, the judge may find that the risk of unfair prejudice is lowered and will admit the item. Other instructions can be given that could reduce the confusing or misleading risks of admitted evidence. The judge's belief that the jury can and will follow limiting instructions could decrease the judge's estimation of the risk of Rule 403 dangers.

It is not clear, however, that the jury can or will follow such an instruction. Social science researchers have attempted to investigate this issue. The findings from many empirical studies are summarized in Lieberman and Arndt, Understanding the Limits of Limiting Instructions, 6 Psychol. Pub. Poly. & L. 677 (2000). Some of this research has concluded that the giving of an instruction may serve to emphasize the inadmissible evidence or improper inference, which may be more damaging than simply letting the matter go unnoticed. Other studies show that jurors follow limiting instructions selectively, and should be more likely to follow them when the judge offers an explanation as to why jurors should ignore certain uses of the evidence. The most common explanation for the failure of jurors to follow limiting instructions is that jurors react negatively to limits on their ability to perform "free behaviors"—especially when they are instructed to ignore uses of evidence that appear to them highly relevant. However, a recent study found that limiting instructions given *prior to* exposure to gruesome crime photos produced a pro-defense bias in survey responses. The authors hypothesize that pre-exposure instructions "function as a forewarning about the potential for bias and allow for attempts to avoid or correct bias" whereas limiting instructions given at the close of trial arrive after evidence has been encoded and perhaps judged, "when jurors are impotent to remove the influence of emotions that have infused processing." Cush and Delahunty, The Influence of Limiting Instructions on Processing and Judgments of Emotionally Evocative Evidence, 13 Psych., Psychol. & Law 110, 120 (2006). Overall, the effectiveness of limiting instructions may be hindered by the jury's lack of understanding of the policy behind a rule of exclusion and the jury's lack of comprehension of the instruction itself. See Peter Meijes Tiersma, Reforming the Language of Jury Instructions, 22 Hofstra L. Rev. 37 (1993). Lieberman and Arndt propose a number of strategies for mitigating the problem of ineffectiveness, including judicial instructions that "soft sell" the limits on the jury and emphasize issues of procedural fairness. 6 Psychol. Pub. Poly. & L. at 704-705 (2000).

As a general rule, however, courts assume that instructions do effectively exclude improper evidence from the jury's consideration. The U.S. Supreme Court has offered the following rationale:

> The rule that juries are presumed to follow their instructions is a pragmatic one, rooted less in the absolute certitude that the presumption is true than in the belief that it represents a

reasonable, practical accommodation of the interests of the state and the defendant in the criminal justice process. [Richardson v. Marsh, 481 U.S. 200, 211 (1987).]

And an experienced trial judge supports the giving of limiting instructions:

> While the videos might be used by the jury improperly, a limiting instruction to the jury, here given repeatedly, specifying the purpose for which they can use the videos is sufficient to ensure that there will be no unfair prejudice to the defendant....
>
>   There is always some danger that the jury will ignore the court's instructions about the limited way in which evidence should be considered. Juries in the product liability cases tried in this court have been responsible. The "runaway jury" concern is not substantiated. [Gonzalez v. Digital Equipment Corp., 8 F. Supp. 2d 194, 198 (E.D.N.Y. 1998) (Weinstein, J.).]

   Judicial reliance on the use of limiting instructions to resolve FRE 403 problems will be demonstrated throughout this book. United States v. Candelaria-Silva, 162 F.3d 698 (1st Cir. 1998) (evidence of defendant's flight admitted as evidence of guilt of the crime charged; danger that jury would give it undue weight was cured by court's instruction that flight may not always reflect feelings of guilt, that many innocent people flee, and that flight alone is insufficient to sustain a conviction). In some circumstances, however, courts recognize that limiting instructions are not a "sure-fire panacea for the prejudice resulting from the needless admission of [prejudicial] evidence." United States v. Haywood, 280 F.3d 715, 724 (6th Cir. 2002). In United States v. Garcia-Rosa, 876 F.2d 209, 222 (1st Cir. 1989), the court held that the prejudicial effect of the evidence was so severe that it could not "be remedied merely through a limiting instruction ... [and] [i]f limiting instructions could remedy all such errors, the government would easily be able to circumvent Rule ... 403." And in Stockman v. Oakland Dental Center, 480 F.3d 791, 804 (6th Cir. 2007), the limiting instruction was not given until the jury charge, "making it all the more difficult to un-ring the bell ... [and] opened Defendants' case to the full brunt of the injury."

   Are limiting instructions the best resolution to Rule 403 problems? Some commentators urge that rather than reforming limiting instructions, they should be abolished, and that this will require trial judges to weigh probative value versus risk of unfair prejudice more carefully in making FRE 403 decisions.

NOTES AND QUESTIONS

   1. Numerous cases in federal court apply Rule 403 to the prosecution's use of photographs, videotapes and other demonstrative evidence to portray the graphic effects of violent crime and accidents. The inflammatory nature of such exhibits calls for careful analysis of their probative value and limitations on their use.

   In United States v. Yahweh, 792 F. Supp. 104 (S.D. Fla. 1992), the district judge admitted gruesome autopsy photographs from "arguably the most violent case ever tried in a federal court." The defendant objected to the use of these photographs, particularly in enlarged format, under FRE 403. To determine probative value, the judge carefully reviewed the relevance of each of the photographs and noted that the enlarged size was necessary to furnish the detail that corroborated witnesses' description of events prior to death. The judge required the medical examiners to select those photographs that illustrated their testimony and to explain the need for each photograph on the basis of content and size. In addition, the judge found that the display of the enlarged photographs enabled all jurors simultaneously to follow the witnesses' testimony. The judge also brought his own background knowledge and experience out into the open:

> For twenty years, this court has stood by the jury box to observe as witnesses testified in front of the jury box concerning exhibits being published to the jury there. In this court's view, the larger 30" × 40" pictures were the right size to illustrate and clarify the witness' testimony; in fact, even the 16" × 20" size was inadequately small by comparison. [Id. at 108.]

On the issue of unfair prejudice, the judge determined that the blown-up photos did not distort the nature of the wounds, acknowledged the grisly nature of the pictures, and ordered that the most offensive ones be reduced in size to 16" × 20" for use in jury deliberations. The photographs were not, in the judge's opinion, flagrantly or deliberately gruesome depictions of the crime. The judge also "carefully observed the jurors and their reactions to the photos.... [T]he jurors showed no signs of being disturbed by the exhibits." Id. at 168. Finally, the judge commented on the nature of unfair prejudice cognizable under FRE 403:

> Relevant evidence is inherently prejudicial; but it is only unfair prejudice, substantially outweighing probative value, which permits exclusion of relevant matter under Rule 403. Unless trials are to be conducted on scenarios, on unreal facts tailored and sanitized for the occasion, the application of Rule 403 must be cautious and sparing.... It is not designed to permit the court to "even out" the weight of evidence, to mitigate a crime.... [Id. at 106.]

2. Appellate courts are also likely to defer to the conscientious efforts of trial judges to limit the amount and impact of potentially prejudicial evidence. In a case involving the leaking of confidential government information about ongoing criminal investigations for purposes of "short-selling" in the securities market, testimony was given that some of the leaked information concerned one of the defendant's possible involvement in the attacks on September 11, 2001. That defendant objected under FRE 403. The appellate court held:

> The record thus demonstrates that, far from abusing its discretion, the district court engaged in precisely the sort of "conscientious assessment" that our precedents require.... It carefully weighed the probative value of the 9/11-related evidence the Government wished to offer, excluded that evidence that was more potentially prejudicial than probative (such as references to Al Qaeda), issued limiting instructions to the jury on several occasions [to the effect that the defendant was not involved in terrorism or the events of 9/11], and continued to keep tight control over the introduction of such evidence even after [a different] defendant's testimony explicitly addressed the topic of 9/11. [United States v. Royer, 549 F.3d 886, 903 (2d Cir. 2008.]

3. In capital punishment cases, statements from victims and victims' families about the effect of the defendant's conduct are admitted in the sentencing phase of trial, after guilt has been determined. But in the prosecution of Timothy McVeigh for the 1998 bombing of the federal building in Oklahoma City, statements from

victims about the horrific injuries they and others suffered were admitted during the guilt phase of trial. The appellate court acknowledged that "[t]he description of the destruction and carnage following the explosion is the most emotionally powerful of the evidence presented during the guilt phase." United States v. McVeigh, 153 F.3d 1166, 1202-1203 (10th Cir. 1998). Proof of how the crime occurred was, however, held to be probative of the elements of the crimes charged—use of a weapon of mass destruction and a malicious intent to kill. Id. Testimony concerning long-term effects of the bombing, however, such as loss of jobs, attendance at funerals, and the lasting emotional trauma of severe injury, were found to be "not particularly relevant" to the guilt phase and to have emotional content. Any error in the admission of such testimony was, however, held to be harmless. Id. at 1203-1204.

4. There are many cases involving various ways in which parties, and sometimes their lawyers, attempt to destroy, alter, or suppress evidence that is adverse to their position in a lawsuit. Instances of such "spoliation" take many forms—subornation of perjury, threats to and intimidation of witnesses, solicitation of murder of a witness, and alteration or destruction of documents. Evidence of spoliation conduct is generally admissible against the spoliator—giving rise to an inference that evidence was unfavorable to the spoliator's position or to an inference of the party's general consciousness of guilt or liability. See generally Kathleen Kedigh, Spoliation: To the Careless Go the Spoils, 67 U. Mo. (K.C.) L. Rev. 597 (1999) (describing the standards of proof of spoliation and the other remedies available, including discovery sanctions, exclusion of the spoliator's evidence, and a separate tort claim against the spoliator).

For our purposes, evidence of spoliation offered at trial raises recurring questions of relevance and of unfair prejudice under Rule 403. In a civil case involving circumstantial proof that the plaintiff attempted to suborn favorable perjured testimony from a witness, the Third Circuit stated the relevance theory as follows, citing analysis from Wigmore's treatise, existing case law and the text of FRE 401 itself:

> One who believes his own case to be weak is more likely to suborn perjury than one who thinks he has a strong case, and a party knows better than anyone else the truth about his own case. Thus, subornation of perjury by a party is strong evidence that the party's case is weak. Admittedly the conclusion is not inescapable: Parties may be mistaken about the merits or force of their own cases. But evidence need not lead inescapably towards a single conclusion to be relevant.... The evidence of subornation here does cast into doubt the merits of [plaintiff's] claim, even if it does not extinguish them. [McQueeney v. Wilmington Trust Co., 779 F.2d 916, 921 (3d Cir. 1985).]

Spoliation behavior is usually illegal and may involve threats of violence or worse. Thus, evidence of such behavior raises a risk of unfair prejudice, in the sense of generating an emotional response against the party as a "bad person," under Rule 403. The court in McQueeney reversed the trial court's decision to exclude evidence of the plaintiff's alleged attempt to suborn perjury with the following analysis of its probative value and potential for unfair prejudice:

> Intuition and the unanimity of the commentators and numerous courts that have considered it suggest not only that subornation of perjury is relevant but that it is powerful evidence indeed.... The court did not articulate any reasons for its finding of prejudice, and this does not appear to us to be the kind of evidence with obvious or overwhelming potential for unfair prejudice. In the absence of a showing of particularized danger of

unfair prejudice, the evidence must be admitted. Were we to rule otherwise, evidence could be excluded on an unfounded fear of prejudice and we would effectively preclude all evidence of subornation of perjury. [Id. at 922-923.]

Consider whether in *McQueeney* the Third Circuit has, in effect, created a precedential ruling of law on the strong probative value and general lack of unfair prejudicial effect of spoliation evidence. We return to the topic of appellate rulings on Rule 403 questions on pages 157-159, infra.

5. The doctrine of curative admissibility permits a party to introduce normally inadmissible evidence in order to respond to specific evidence that the opponent has introduced previously. It is related to FRE 403 in that this evidence is *needed* to respond effectively to the opponent's prior submission. The broadest statement of the curative admissibility doctrine is as follows:

> The rule of "opening the door," or "curative admissibility," gives the trial court discretion to permit a party to introduce otherwise inadmissible evidence on an issue (a) when the opposing party has introduced inadmissible evidence on the same issue, and (b) when it is needed to rebut a false impression that may have resulted from the opposing party's evidence.... When a defendant offers an innocent explanation he "opens the door" to questioning into the truth of his testimony, and the government is entitled to attack his credibility on cross-examination. A defendant has no right to avoid cross-examination into the truth of his direct examination, even as to matters not related to the merits of the charges against him. [United States v. Elfgeeh, 515 F.3d 100, 128 (2d Cir. 2008).]

As you can see, the doctrine permits the court to waive an opponent's evidentiary objections in order to prevent the opponent from gaining an unfair advantage.

In *Elfgeeh*, defendants were charged with operating an illegal money-transmitting business. There was evidence that some of the funds, transmitted by defendants from New York to Yemen, were being paid to groups involved in "tribal wars, blood feuds and violence" within Yemen. The trial court ruled this evidence inadmissible under FRE 403 but held that if the defendants themselves testified that they merely transmitted money to help Yemeni immigrants send money home to their family and friends, "it would open the door to allow the government to attempt to show that the [defendants] sent money instead for bellicose purposes." Id. at 128. When the defendants made three separate statements that their money transmittals were to families of their clients, the government was allowed to ask a defendant "whether he knew that the money he sent was being used to buy arms and ammunition and was allowed to submit documentary evidence obliquely referring to such use ... in order to attack [the defendant's] credibility." Id.

Most, but not all, jurisdictions recognize some version of the curative admissibility doctrine, although there is no Federal Rule of Evidence dealing with the subject. Byrd v. Maricopa County Sheriff's Dept., 565 F.3d 1205 (9th Cir. 2009) (plaintiff's videotape initially excluded under FRE 403 later admitted under doctrine of curative admissibility after defense counsel mentioned the tape and suggested it had been edited or destroyed); Henderson v. George Washington University, 449 F.3d 127, 139 (4th Cir. 2006) (in a malpractice case, plaintiff's evidence of a report of a similar procedure on another patient excluded under FRE 403 as confusing to the jury, but admitted under the curative admissibility doctrine when the defense relied on the exclusion of the report in cross-examining the plaintiff's expert, using the court's ruling "not only to shield themselves from potentially damaging evidence, but also ... as a sword to slice through the foundation" of plaintiff's case).

KEY POINTS

1. An objection made under FRE 403 to an item of evidence requires the trial judge to determine whether admission of the evidence creates any Rule 403 danger to the jury's decision-making process and, if so, whether this danger will substantially outweigh the probative value of the evidence.

2. Probative value means the degree to which the evidence will alter the probabilities of a fact of consequence and an essential element in the case. This is determined primarily by the judge's estimate of the strength of the generalizations connecting the evidence to the disputed issue and by the proponent's need for the evidence.

3. The judge estimates the risk of harm from evidence that bears a Rule 403 danger by predicting the nature of the jury's reaction to the evidence, the degree of that reaction, and the likelihood that the harmful reaction will occur.

4. Because FRE 403's balancing test requires the danger to *substantially* outweigh the probative value, even a very significant risk of danger may not result in exclusion if there are no alternative or less dangerous means of proving the fact of consequence. The court will also use a limiting instruction to reduce the danger in order to admit the evidence.

PROBLEMS

3.6. Return to Problem 3.1, State v. Johnson, at page 135. Does the question posed to Officer Huston in (a) present any of the Rule 403 dangers? How would you rule on an FRE 403 objection?

3.7. Return to Problem 3.2, Pedroso v. Driver, at page 136. Does evidence of Driver's testimony in (a) present any of the Rule 403 dangers? How would you rule on an FRE 403 objection?

3.8. In Problem 3.2, what if the plaintiffs request that the jury be taken to the scene of the accident in order to view Cedar Street and the gravel shoulder? What arguments could be made in support of and in opposition to this request under FRE 401 and 403?

3.9. Return to Problem 3.3, United States v. Ray, at page 136. The prosecution offers the following evidence:

(a)   In October 2005, Ray sold 25,000 shares of Rundown stock one week before a major and abrupt fall in Rundown's share price.

(b)   In May 2007, Ray purchased 30,000 shares of Rundown 30 days before the company announced the profitable acquisition of a competitor, an event which caused the stock price to rise by 25 percent.

Will the defense prevail if it objects to this evidence under FRE 403?

3.10. Ross was arrested by the FBI on charges of using counterfeit checks to purchase used cars from individual sellers. He made the following statements while being booked at the FBI field office, after he had been given the *Miranda* warnings:

(a) "I'm hoping that federal prison is better than state prison ... and that they sell protein supplements like they do in state prison."
(b) "I want to hurry up and get to Milan (a federal prison) so I can start lifting weights."

The prosecution wants to offer these statements against Ross at his trial through the testimony of an FBI agent who overheard them. What would be the theory of relevance? If Ross objects under FRE 403, how should the court rule? Note that the statements could be admitted against Ross as "party admissions" under the hearsay rule, FRE 801(d)(2)(A).

3.11. K and G were indicted for arson in the burning of a diner that they owned in Great Neck, New York. The report of the Fire Marshal's Office concludes that the diner fire had been intentionally set. The prosecution will prove that K and G owned two diners; that their diner in Westbury, Connecticut, operated at a profit; and that the diner in Great Neck sustained serious losses for several years. The prosecutor wants to introduce the following evidence: the fact that K and G had not paid property taxes on the Great Neck diner for several years; the fact that tax liens had been recorded against the diner; testimony from a cook at the Westbury diner that K and G asked him whether he knew anyone who would be willing to "start a fire." Are these items admissible? Are they sufficient to send the case to the jury? What if K and G testify that they were about to make a profitable sale of the Great Neck diner?

3.12. Douglas is being prosecuted for burglary. The prosecutor offers W_1 to testify that Douglas usually wore a black "New York Yankees" cap and jacket and W_2, an expert on gangs, to testify that in Douglas's neighborhood such black clothing is likely to signify membership in a gang. The prosecutor argues that this is relevant circumstantial evidence that Douglas committed the burglary, since gang members are more likely to commit burglaries than people who are not members of gangs.

The defense attorney objects under Rules 401 and 403 to the testimony of W_1 and W_2 and argues that if the objection is overruled, the defense will have to call W_3, another gang expert, to testify that wearing the cap and jacket does not show gang membership and that gang members are no more likely to commit burglary than anyone else. Defense counsel would also call W_4, Douglas's brother, to testify that Douglas is an avid Yankees fan. What arguments can be made for and against admission of the testimony of W_1 and W_2?

3.13. Carl Smith was arrested at Washington National Airport when the X-ray machine disclosed a suspicious metallic object in the paper bag he was carrying. This object was a loaded Beretta pistol wrapped in red cloth and a pair of pants. Smith was charged with attempting to board an aircraft with a concealed weapon. Smith claimed that the pistol was planted in his shopping bag by someone else at the airport and that he did not intend to board an airplane because he had no ticket and no luggage.

To support its claim that Smith was in knowing possession of the gun, the prosecution offered evidence of Smith's Jamaican citizenship, his possession of $450 in cash, and the presence of marijuana residue in his pants pocket. These facts, it claimed, showed that Smith met the "drug courier" profile, an informally compiled abstract of characteristics thought typical of persons carrying illicit drugs, used to argue reasonable suspicion in support of drug trafficking stops; further, it argued, drug couriers frequently carry guns for protection. Should the district court admit this evidence and permit an FBI agent to testify as an expert about the drug courier profile and its relevance to the crime charged?

3.14. Cynthia Richards allegedly slipped and fell on a Halloween costume in the "seasonal" area of a Kmart store. She claims that Kmart was negligent in failing to adequately maintain its store by not locating and picking up the costume before the accident. Kmart denies negligence, contending that its policy and practices of maintaining the store were reasonable.

During discovery, a Kmart supervisor testified that the store had no particular schedule for patrolling the store for cleanup, but that all employees were trained to pick up clutter promptly and that this policy is stated in the Handbook given to all employees. Ken Ceasar, a Kmart customer service employee on duty the night of Richards's fall, testified that he was in charge of watching the whole floor, that he had no knowledge that the costume was in the aisle, that he always walked the aisles and picked up items that were not supposed to be on the floor "as soon as he discovered them." Ceasar also stated that he had no particular memory of his own actions on the night in question.

Kmart has filed a motion in limine to exclude a videotape made secretly in the store by an investigator for Richards. The videotape was made one year after the incident, during Halloween season. It is a genuine video, and has not been altered or edited in any way. It shows merchandise on two unidentified store aisles that had fallen to the floor, and it shows Mr. Ceasar ignoring the merchandise and stepping on it, rather than promptly removing it. Prepare arguments for Kmart and for Richards on this motion in limine.

3.15. Denise McCallum is charged with armed robbery for holding up a convenience store at gunpoint. The police found a .38 caliber, "snub-nosed" revolver in a trash can a block away from the convenience store, and the store clerk told police that the robber's gun "looked just like that one." Consider arguments for and against an FRE 403 objection to the admission of the following evidence offered by the prosecutor at trial:

(a)   Testimony of McCallum's roommate that two months before the robbery, she saw a snub-nosed .38 caliber revolver in McCallum's bedroom. Official statistics report that there are known to be at least 25,000 such handguns in the possession of individuals in the city.

(b)   Evidence that McCallum was unemployed for six months before the robbery.

3.   Elaboration of FRE 403: Appellate Review of Judicial Discretion Under FRE 403

Application of FRE 403 calls for the exercise of judicial discretion, meaning that the judge applies criteria and standards that are not mechanical but require the use of *judgment*. The trial court makes judgments that estimate the probability of inferences; that evaluate the nature, likelihood, and degree of dangers to jury decision-making;

and that compare probative value to those dangers. On appeal, these judgments are reviewed under the abuse of discretion standard, which is a very deferential standard of appellate review. It means that appellate courts will tolerate trial court decisions that the appellate judges would not have made themselves. Reversal is justified only when the trial court "abuses" its discretion:

> Had any one of us been in a position to exercise the discretion committed to a trial judge ... we would have no hesitancy in stating that the decision would have been otherwise; but as appellate judges we cannot find that the action of the district judge was so unreasonable and so arbitrary as to amount to a prejudicial abuse of the discretion necessary to repose in trial judges during the conduct of a trial. [Napolitano v. Compania Sud Americana De Vapores, 421 F.2d 382, 384 (2d Cir. 1970).]

There are many reasons why appellate courts defer to the trial courts' judgments under FRE 403. Here are some of them:

(1) *Complexity and Uncertainty.* The Rule 403 balancing test requires complex fact-based judgments unique to each case. Judgments about probative value and the Rule 403 dangers are at best, as we have just discussed above, rough estimates and predictions of effect on the jury's decision-making. The estimates that are made in one case may have little bearing in the next. The ultimate standard of "substantially outweighs" also requires balancing where there is no calibration for the weighing process, and the standard is such that precision is not called for. What is "substantial" can vary greatly among judges: "[T]he district court is engaged in a 'comparison of intangibles' and is thus 'afforded a special degree of deference.'" Estate of Moreland v. Dieter, 395 F.3d 747, 755 (7th Cir. 2005).

(2) *Competence.* The trial judge has more experience than appellate judges with making judgments of this kind. The trial judge is also closer to the evidence in the particular case, meaning that the judge has watched its presentation in the context of the entire trial and has observed its effect on the particular jury: "Only in an extreme case are appellate judges competent to second-guess the judgment of the person on the spot, the trial judge." Id.

(3) *Tolerance for Outcomes That Appear Inconsistent.* Under an abuse of discretion standard of review, appellate courts will affirm trial court outcomes that may appear to be inconsistent, even in cases that appear to be similar to the appellate court. That is what it means for the appellate court to "defer" to the trial court's judgment, even when it (or another trial court) might have decided the Rule 403 question differently. Largely because of the factors of competence, complexity, and uncertainty, appellate courts may not be able to know whether outcomes actually are inconsistent, and probably could not create sufficiently detailed precedent necessary to achieve uniform and consistent outcomes among trial courts. The contextual facts of Rule 403 decisions affect the weighing process too greatly.[7] The abuse of discretion standard of review is an acknowledgment of the limits of the knowledge of an outside reviewer.

---

7. In countering the prosecution's argument that one of its prior opinions conclusively established how a Rule 403 balancing should come out, the Ninth Circuit replied:

> [The prior opinion] doesn't help the government because it did not purport to set a minimum level for probative value under Rule 403. Nor could it, as probative value must be weighed against offsetting factors, such as delay, which differ in every case. Moreover, probative value itself can only be determined in light of the evidence and arguments of a particular case. [United States v. Crosby, 75 F.3d 1343, 1348 (9th Cir. 1996).]

Most appellate decisions affirm district courts' FRE 403 decisions, whether they admit or exclude the disputed evidence. The standard of review for abuse of discretion is often defined somewhat differently by the Circuit Courts of Appeal. Here is a clear statement of the applicable principles: "Under this standard, we will leave rulings about admissibility of evidence undisturbed unless we are 'left with the definite and firm conviction that the [district] court ... committed a clear error of judgment in the conclusion it reached upon a weighing of the relevant factors or where it improperly applies the law or uses an erroneous legal standard.'" United States v. Lucas, 357 F.3d 599, 608 (6th Cir. 2004). Thus, there are some errors in applying Rule 403 that appellate courts will hold to be errors of law, such as not giving the terms of the rule their legally correct meaning, Blake v. Pellegrino, 329 F.3d 43, 45 (1st Cir. 2003) ("When ... the admission or exclusion of evidence involves a question of law, such as the proper interpretation of a provision contained in the Federal Rules ... , we afford de novo review"), or violating a criminal defendant's constitutional right to put on witnesses in his defense, United States v. Turning Bear, 357 F.3d 730, 734 (8th Cir. 2004) (improper exclusion of opinion testimony about a witness's credibility under Rule 403 held to violate the defendant's Fifth and Sixth Amendment rights to present witnesses in his defense).

Some balancing decisions are held to be abuses of discretion when the results are "clear errors of judgment," plainly against the logic and effect of the facts in the case. McQueeney v. Wilmington Trust Co., 779 F.2d 916 (3d Cir. 1985) (discussed at page 154, supra). And appellate courts also try to ensure that district courts will engage in the full consideration of all the Rule 403 factors. See, e.g., Securities and Exchange Commission v. Peters, 978 F.2d 1162, 1172 (10th Cir. 1992) (failure to consider adequately the possibility of a limiting instruction, contrary to suggestion in the Advisory Committee Note to FRE 403, is considered to be significant in finding abuse of discretion); United States v. McCallum, 584 F.3d 471, 477 (2d Cir. 2009) (the district court gave no explanation for its conclusion under FRE 403; the appellate court held that "[w]ithout the benefit of its reasoning we are in no position to assume that the court appreciated the seriousness of the risk that introducing the convictions would undermine the fairness of the trial.").

Sometimes appellate review of FRE 403 decisions does create precedent for district courts to follow. Consider the *McQueeney* case discussed in Note 4 at pages 153-154, supra. The two appellate opinions presented below will give you practice in evaluating probative value and FRE 403 dangers yourself, and in applying the rule's balancing test. You should ask yourself why the appellate court found an abuse of discretion, and whether its decision will have precedential effect.

UNITED STATES v. HITT

981 F.2d 422 (9th Cir. 1992)

KOZINSKI, Circuit Judge.

Dale Lee Hitt was convicted of possessing an unregistered machine gun in violation of 26 U.S.C. §5861(d). The government alleged he had altered a semiautomatic rifle so it would discharge more than one shot per trigger pull—the defining characteristic of a machine gun. 26 U.S.C. §5845(b). The rifle had indeed been modified in a way consistent with the government's theory, though Hitt's lawyer suggested it had been modified by its previous owner. Some internal parts usable for machine guns (but not themselves illegal) were found in a gun case in Hitt's room, but Hitt's lawyer suggested they too might have come from the rifle's previous owner.

The key question, though, was whether the rifle would in fact rapid-fire. The government and Hitt each had their own experts test-fire it: In the government's test, the rifle did fire more than one shot per trigger pull, but when Hitt's expert (witnessed by two police officers) tested it, it didn't. Hitt's expert suggested the gun may have fired automatically in the government's test because of a malfunction, perhaps because the internal parts were dirty, worn or defective. In response, the government introduced a photograph of the rifle which, it argued, showed the rifle was neither dirty, worn nor defective.

Unfortunately, the photograph showed nothing of the gun's interior. All the jury could see was the outside, and not very well at that, as the gun occupied only a small part of the 4" × 6" photograph. The rest was taken up by about a dozen other weapons—nine other guns, including three that looked like assault rifles, and several knives—all belonging to Hitt's housemate. Hitt objected to admission of the photograph under Fed. R. Evid. 403, but the district court overruled his objection.

I

A. Under Fed. R. Evid. 402, "[a]ll relevant evidence is admissible," except as otherwise provided. We let jurors see and hear even marginally relevant evidence, because we trust them to weigh the evidence appropriately. Nonetheless, when the probative value of the evidence is "substantially outweighed by the danger of unfair prejudice...or misleading the jury," Fed. R. Evid. 403, the evidence must be kept out.

B. The photograph's probative value was exceedingly small. The defense theory was that the gun fired as an automatic because the *internal* parts were dirty, worn or defective. The prosecution understood this too: When the prosecutor cross-examined the defendant's expert, he asked whether there was "exceptional dirt *in*" the rifle, and whether there were "worn or dirty parts *in* that machine."

But the gun's external appearance reveals nothing at all about its internal state. Firearms are designed so the internal parts suffer most of the strain from the discharge. Wear, dirt and defects that affect the internal mechanism generally have no effect on the firearm's appearance; it's not uncommon for a gun that looks clean and in working order to misfire because of dirt or defects inside. Here there was absolutely no indication that the type of wear, dirt or defect Hitt's expert was talking about could be seen by inspecting the outside of the gun.

Moreover, even if the rifle's inside condition were somehow related to its outside appearance, it's virtually impossible to tell whether the gun is clean or dirty from the photograph, in which the rifle is seen from several feet away. The photograph might well have been excludible under Rule 402 as totally irrelevant, had a Rule 402 objection been made.

C. At the same time, the photograph was fraught with the twin dangers of unfairly prejudicing the defendant and misleading the jury. It showed a dozen nasty-looking weapons, which the jury must have assumed belonged to Hitt. The photograph looked like it was taken at Hitt's residence: The guns were laid out in an obviously residential room; the jury knew Hitt was arrested at home, the photograph was talked about in the same breath as two others identified at trial as having been taken in Hitt's bedroom. Moreover, there was no one else the jury could have suspected of owning the guns. Hitt's roommate, who in fact owned all the other weapons, wasn't even mentioned during Hitt's trial. Inferring that all the weapons were Hitt's wasn't just a plausible inference; it was the only plausible inference.

Once the jury was misled into thinking all the weapons were Hitt's, they might well have concluded Hitt was the sort of person who'd illegally own a machine gun, or was so dangerous he should be locked up regardless of whether or not he committed this offense. Rightly or wrongly, many people view weapons, especially guns, with fear and distrust. Like evidence of homosexuality, see, e.g., United States v. Gillespie, 852 F.2d 475, 478 (9th Cir. 1988); Cohn v. Papke, 655 F.2d 191, 194 (9th Cir. 1981), or of past crimes, see, e.g., United States v. Bland, 908 F.2d 471, 473 (9th Cir. 1990), photographs of firearms often have a visceral impact that far exceeds their probative value. See, e.g., United States v. Green, 648 F.2d 587, 595 (9th Cir. 1981) (per curiam). The prejudice is even greater when the picture is not of one gun but of many.

But the photograph could do more than arouse irrational fears and prejudices. It could also lead the jury to draw some perfectly logical—though mistaken—inferences. Hitt's main defense was that he had the bad luck of owning a rifle that was defective or dirty, or perhaps had been modified by its previous owner. A jury that thought Hitt owned almost a dozen guns could very reasonably have viewed this argument with skepticism. The jurors could have inferred that a gun enthusiast like Hitt would be able to tell if the gun had been modified by someone else, or be able to make the modifications himself. Or they could have thought that someone that interested in guns would naturally keep them clean and in good working order. Of course, the jury shouldn't have drawn these inferences, because none of the other guns were Hitt's. Yet the inferences were entirely plausible once the jury concluded Hitt owned the whole arsenal.

D. The district judge has wide latitude in making Rule 403 decisions. But this latitude isn't unlimited. Where the evidence is of very slight (if any) probative value, it's an abuse of discretion to admit it if there's even a modest likelihood of unfair prejudice or a small risk of misleading the jury.

The evidence here was not only highly prejudicial and at most marginally probative—it was also misleading. It's bad enough for the jury to be unduly swayed by something a defendant did; it's totally unacceptable for it to be prejudiced by something he seems to have done but in fact did not. Admitting the photograph, with nothing at all to keep the jury from being misled—no limiting instruction, no redaction—violated Rule 403.

II

Having determined there was error, we must next decide whether it was harmless. There is a conflict in our circuit about the standard of review for harmless error. Some cases require that we affirm only if we can say with "fair assurance" that the error was harmless. This standard seems to have the Supreme Court's blessing. See Kotteakos v. United States, 328 U.S. 750, 764-65, 90 L. Ed. 1557, 66 S. Ct. 1239 (1946). Other Ninth Circuit cases compel affirmation if it is "more probable than not" that the error was harmless. See, e.g., United States v. Lui, 941 F.2d 844, 848 (9th Cir. 1991)....[8]

---

8. This isn't just wordplay: A 55% likelihood that the error was harmless qualifies as "more probable than not," but it's hardly a "fair assurance" of harmlessness. Kotteakos defines "fair assurance" as absence of a "grave doubt," 328 U.S. at 765, and a 45% chance that the defendant would have been acquitted but for the error certainly seems like a "grave doubt." While we obviously don't deal in such precise probabilities, "more probable than not" and "fair assurance" can, in some cases, lead to conflicting results.

We needn't resolve this conflict here, though, because the error wasn't harmless under either standard. This was a close case: An expert on one side claimed the gun fired more than one shot per trigger pull; an expert on the other (corroborated by two police officers) said it didn't. The photograph may well have made the difference between acquittal and conviction. We can't say it was more probable than not that Hitt would have been convicted without the photograph. A *fortiori*, then, we can't say with "fair assurance" that he would have been convicted without it.

NOTES AND QUESTIONS

1. Judge Kozinski's opinion in *Hitt* relies on two empirical generalizations to estimate probative value and the danger of unfair prejudice. What are they? How does Judge Kozinski know they are valid? Were they the subject of proof at trial? Is there any justification offered for them?

2. Did the prosecution need to use the photograph in *Hitt* to rebut the suggestion that the interior of Hitt's rifle was dirty or worn? Was there alternative, less prejudicial evidence available? For example, where was the rifle itself? Who has the obligation to raise the issue of minimizing the misleading impact of the photograph?

3. Judge Kozinski also stated a general rule for conducting the balancing test under FRE 403: "Where the evidence is of very slight (if any) probative value, it's an abuse of discretion to admit it if there's even a modest likelihood of unfair prejudice or a small risk of misleading the jury." How does this language fit within the table reproduced on page 149, supra? Does it contradict the FRE 403 requirement that the danger "substantially" outweigh the probative value?

OLD CHIEF v. UNITED STATES
519 U.S. 172 (1997)

SOUTER, Justice.

[Petitioner Johnny Lynn Old Chief was arrested in 1993 after a fracas involving at least one gunshot. He was charged with assault with a dangerous weapon, using a firearm in relation to a crime of violence, and with violation of 18 U.S.C. §922(g)(1), which makes it unlawful for anyone "who has been convicted in any court of a crime punishable by imprisonment for a term exceeding one year" to "possess in or affecting commerce, any firearm."[9] In the indictment, Old Chief was charged with having been convicted of an earlier assault causing serious bodily injury. Before trial, he requested that the trial court order the government not to mention any detail regarding the prior conviction except to state that defendant had been convicted of a crime punishable by imprisonment exceeding one year. This was treated as an offer to stipulate and agree that the jury could be instructed that he had been convicted of such a crime as required under §922(g)(1). Old Chief contended that Rule 403 rendered the name and nature of his prior offense unfairly prejudicial, since the jury

---

9.   "[A] crime punishable by imprisonment for a term exceeding one year" is defined to exclude "any Federal or State offenses pertaining to antitrust violations, unfair trade practices, restraints of trade, or other similar offenses relating to the regulation of business practices" and "any State offense classified . . . as a misdemeanor and punishable by a term of imprisonment of two years or less." 18 U.S.C. §921(a)(20).

was likely to generalize his earlier bad act into bad character, and to use his character as increasing the probability that he did the bad act with which he was now charged. The government refused to join in any stipulation and insisted on its right to prove its case its own way. The district court agreed, ruling that if the government did not want to stipulate, it did not have to. At trial, the government introduced a document regarding Old Chief's prior conviction that showed that on December 18, 1988, he did knowingly and unlawfully assault Rory Dean Fenner, said assault resulting in serious bodily injury" for which Old Chief was sentenced to five years' imprisonment.

Justice Souter's opinion noted that the jury's potential use of this prior conviction for a propensity inference would violate FRE 404(b), and thus the admission of Old Chief's specific prior conviction raised a risk of unfair prejudice that must be analyzed under Rule 403.]

As for the analytical method to be used in Rule 403 balancing, two basic possibilities present themselves. An item of evidence might be viewed as an island, with estimates of its own probative value and unfairly prejudicial risk the sole reference points in deciding whether the danger substantially outweighs the value and whether the evidence ought to be excluded. Or the question of admissibility might be seen as inviting further comparisons to take account of the full evidentiary context of the case as the court understands it when the ruling must be made. This second approach would start out like the first but be ready to go further. On objection, the court would decide whether a particular item of evidence raised a danger of unfair prejudice. If it did, the judge would go on to evaluate the degrees of probative value and unfair prejudice not only for the item in question but for any actually available substitutes as well. If an alternative were found to have substantially the same or greater probative value but a lower danger of unfair prejudice, sound judicial discretion would discount the value of the item first offered and exclude it if its discounted probative value were substantially outweighed by unfairly prejudicial risk. As we will explain later on, the judge would have to make these calculations with an appreciation of the offering party's need for evidentiary richness and narrative integrity in presenting a case, and the mere fact that two pieces of evidence might go to the same point would not, of course, necessarily mean that only one of them might come in. It would only mean that a judge applying Rule 403 could reasonably apply some discount to the probative value of an item of evidence when faced with less risky alternative proof going to the same point. Even under this second approach, as we explain below, a defendant's Rule 403 objection offering to concede a point generally cannot prevail over the Government's choice to offer evidence showing guilt and all the circumstances surrounding the offense.[10] . . .

The first understanding of the Rule is open to a very telling objection. That reading would leave the party offering evidence with the option to structure a trial in whatever way would produce the maximum unfair prejudice consistent with relevance. He could choose the available alternative carrying the greatest threat of improper influence, despite the availability of less prejudicial but equally probative evidence. The worst he would have to fear would be a ruling sustaining a Rule 403 objection, and if that occurred, he could simply fall back to offering substitute evidence. This would be a strange rule. It would be very odd for the law of evidence to recognize the danger

---

10. While our discussion has been general because of the general wording of Rule 403, our holding is limited to cases involving proof of felon status. On appellate review of a Rule 403 decision, a defendant must establish abuse of discretion, a standard that is not satisfied by a mere showing of some alternative means of proof that the prosecution in its broad discretion chose not to rely upon.

of unfair prejudice only to confer such a degree of autonomy on the party subject to temptation, and the Rules of Evidence are not so odd.

Rather, a reading of the companions to Rule 403, and of the commentaries that went with them to Congress, makes it clear that what counts as the Rule 403 "probative value" of an item of evidence, as distinct from its Rule 401 "relevance," may be calculated by comparing evidentiary alternatives. The Committee Notes to Rule 401 explicitly say that a party's concession is pertinent to the court's discretion to exclude evidence on the point conceded.

... The Notes to Rule 403 then take up the point by stating that when a court considers "whether to exclude on grounds of unfair prejudice," the "availability of other means of proof may ... be an appropriate factor."...

Old Chief's proffered admission would, in fact, have been not merely relevant but seemingly conclusive evidence of the element. The statutory language in which the prior-conviction requirement is couched shows no congressional concern with the specific name or nature of the prior offense beyond what is necessary to place it within the broad category of qualifying felonies, and Old Chief clearly meant to admit that his felony did qualify, by stipulating "that the Government has proven one of the essential elements of the offense." App. 7. As a consequence, although the name of the prior offense may have been technically relevant, it addressed no detail in the definition of the prior-conviction element that would not have been covered by the stipulation or admission. Logic, then, seems to side with Old Chief....

There is, however, one more question to be considered before deciding whether Old Chief's offer was to supply evidentiary value at least equivalent to what the Government's own evidence carried. In arguing that the stipulation or admission would not have carried equivalent value, the Government invokes the familiar, standard rule that the prosecution is entitled to prove its case by evidence of its own choice, or, more exactly, that a criminal defendant may not stipulate or admit his way out of the full evidentiary force of the case as the Government chooses to present it.

This is unquestionably true as a general matter. The "fair and legitimate weight" of conventional evidence showing individual thoughts and acts amounting to a crime reflects the fact that making a case with testimony and tangible things not only satisfies the formal definition of an offense, but tells a colorful story with descriptive richness. Unlike an abstract premise, whose force depends on going precisely to a particular step in a course of reasoning, a piece of evidence may address any number of separate elements, striking hard just because it shows so much at once; the account of a shooting that establishes capacity and causation may tell just as much about the triggerman's motive and intent. Evidence thus has force beyond any linear scheme or reasoning, and as its pieces come together a narrative gains momentum, with power not only to support conclusions but to sustain the willingness of jurors to draw the inferences, whatever they may be, necessary to reach an honest verdict. This persuasive power of the concrete and particular is often essential to the capacity of jurors to satisfy the obligations that the law places on them. Jury duty is usually unsought and sometimes resisted, and it may be as difficult for one juror suddenly to face the findings that can send another human being in prison, as it is for another to hold out conscientiously for acquittal. When a juror's duty does seem hard, the evidentiary account of what a defendant has thought and done can accomplish what no set of abstract statements ever could, not just to prove a fact but to establish its human significance, and so to implicate the law's moral underpinnings and a juror's obligation to sit in judgment. Thus, the prosecution may fairly seek to place its evidence before the jurors, as much to tell a story of guiltiness as to support an inference of guilt, to convince the jurors that a guilty verdict would be morally reasonable as much as to point to the discrete elements of a defendant's legal fault.

But there is something even more to the prosecution's interest in resisting efforts to replace the evidence of its choice with admissions and stipulations, for beyond the power of conventional evidence to support allegations and give life to the moral underpinnings of law's claims, there lies the need for evidence in all its particularity to satisfy the jurors' expectations about what proper proof should be. Some such demands they bring with them to the courthouse, assuming, for example, that a charge of using a firearm to commit an offense will be proven by introducing a gun in evidence. A prosecutor who fails to produce one, or some good reason for his failure, has something to be concerned about. "If [jurors'] expectations are not satisfied, triers of fact may penalize the party who disappoints them by drawing a negative inference against that party." Saltzburg, A Special Aspect of Relevance: Countering Negative Inferences Associated with the Absence of Evidence, 66 Calif. L. Rev. 1011, 1019 (1978) (footnotes omitted). Expectations may also arise in jurors' minds simply from the experience of a trial itself. The use of witnesses to describe a train of events naturally related can raise the prospect of learning about every ingredient of that natural sequence the same way. If suddenly the prosecution presents some occurrence in the series differently, as by announcing a stipulation or admission, the effect may be like saying, "never mind what's behind the door," and jurors may well wonder what they are being kept from knowing. A party seemingly responsible for cloaking something has reason for apprehension, and the prosecution with its burden of proof may prudently demur at a defense request to interrupt the flow of evidence telling the story in the usual way. . . .

In sum, the accepted rule that the prosecution is entitled to prove its case free from any defendant's option to stipulate the evidence away rests on good sense. A syllogism is not a story, and a naked proposition in a courtroom may be no match for the robust evidence that would be used to prove it. People who hear a story interrupted by gaps of abstraction may be puzzled at the missing chapters, and jurors asked to rest a momentous decision on the story's truth can feel put upon at being asked to take responsibility knowing that more could be said than they have heard. A convincing tale can be told with economy, but when economy becomes a break in the natural sequence of narrative evidence, an assurance that the missing link is really there is never more than second best.

This recognition that the prosecution with its burden of persuasion needs evidentiary depth to tell a continuous story has, however, virtually no application when the point at issue is a defendant's legal status, dependent on some judgment rendered wholly independently of the concrete events of later criminal behavior charged against him. As in this case, the choice of evidence for such an element is usually not between eventful narrative and abstract proposition, but between propositions of slightly varying abstraction, either a record saying that conviction for some crime occurred at a certain time or a statement for admitting the same thing without naming the particular offense. The issue of substituting one statement for the other normally arises only when the record of conviction would not be admissible for any purpose beyond proving status, so that excluding it would not deprive the prosecution of evidence with multiple utility; if, indeed, there were a justification for receiving evidence of the nature of prior acts on some issue other than status (i.e., to prove "motive, opportunity, intent, preparation, plan, knowledge, identity, or absence of mistake or accident," Fed

Rule Evid. 404(b)), Rule 404(b) guarantees the opportunity to seek its admission. Nor can it be argued that the events behind the prior conviction are proper nourishment for the jurors' sense of obligation to vindicate the public interest. The issue is not whether concrete details of the prior crime should come to the jurors' attention but whether the name or general character of that crime is to be disclosed. Congress, however, has made it plain that distinctions among generic felonies do not count for this purpose; the fact of the qualifying conviction is alone what matters under the statute.... The most the jury needs to know is that the conviction admitted by the defendant falls within the class of crimes that Congress thought should bar a convict from possessing a gun, and this point may be made readily in a defendant's admission and underscored in the court's jury instructions. Finally, the most obvious reason that the general presumption that the prosecution may choose its evidence is so remote from application here is that proof of the defendant's status goes to an element entirely outside the natural sequence of what the defendant is charged with thinking and doing to commit the current offense. Proving status without telling exactly why that status was imposed leaves no gap in the story of a defendant's subsequent criminality, and its demonstration by stipulation or admission neither displaces a chapter from a continuous sequence of conventional evidence nor comes across as an officious substitution, to confuse or offend or provoke reproach.

Given these peculiarities of the element of felony-convict status and of admissions and the like when used to prove it, there is no cognizable difference between the evidentiary significance of an admission and of the legitimately probative component of the official record the prosecution would prefer to place in evidence. For purposes of the Rule 403 weighing of the probative against the prejudicial, the functions of the competing evidence are distinguishable only by the risk inherent in the one and wholly absent from the other. In this case, as in any other in which the prior conviction is for an offense likely to support conviction on some improper ground, the only reasonable conclusion was that the risk of unfair prejudice did substantially outweigh the discounted probative value of the record of conviction, and it was an abuse of discretion to admit the record when an admission was available. What we have said shows why this will be the general rule when proof of convict status is at issue, just as the prosecutor's choice will generally survive a Rule 403 analysis when a defendant seeks to force the substitution of an admission for evidence creating a coherent narrative of his thoughts and actions in perpetrating the offense for which he is being tried.

The judgment is reversed, and the case is remanded to the Ninth Circuit for further proceedings consistent with this opinion.

NOTES AND QUESTIONS

1. Justice Souter's discussion of the "evidentiary richness" and "narrative integrity" components of probative value reflect the theory of jury reasoning that we noted in Chapter Two on page 115—that jurors focus at trial on competing versions of reality, not on whether a formal element of law is true or false. Considerable research indicates that juries evaluate evidence within the framework of a story, or narrative account, of the events central to the case. Jurors start to construct a story at the start of trial, and then accept or reject evidence in relation to the narratives that are available to them as the trial continues. At the end of this process, jurors will usually accept one story as the "best" account of "what happened" and match it to the verdict definitions

in the instructions. This "story model" of jury decision-making is founded on empirical work of social scientists. A classic work is Nancy Pennington and Reid Hastie, A Cognitive Theory of Juror Decision Making: The Story Model, 13 Cardozo L. Rev. 519 (1991). Evidentiary richness and narrative integrity can be seen as contributing to the quality of an advocate's story.

Use of these factors in making and reviewing decisions under FRE 403 would not seem to be limited to §922(g)(1) cases. For example, in United States v. Vallejo, 237 F.3d 1008 (9th Cir. 2001), defendant Vallejo was charged with illegal importation of marijuana in a car he was driving from Mexico to the United States. Vallejo claimed that he did not know that the packages of marijuana were hidden inside the vehicle. The Ninth Circuit held that it was error for the district court to exclude Vallejo's evidence of the identity of the person who he claimed had hidden the drugs in the car, intending to smuggle them into the United States himself. The court made the point that the need to satisfy juror expectations added to the probative value of this evidence. The court wrote: "Vallejo ... was not allowed to provide an answer for the jurors' question: 'If defendant did not know there were drugs in the car and did not place them there himself, who did?'" Id. at 1023.

2. Justice Souter's opinion holds that the trial court should have "discounted" the probative value of the proffered evidence of Old Chief's actual felony conviction because other evidence—the stipulation as to his status as a felon—was of equal probative force and was substantially less prejudicial. What does "discount" mean? Is this another way of stating that the prosecution did not "need" to prove the actual conviction, and that the lack of need should be dispositive in the balancing under FRE 403 under these circumstances?

3. Despite the Old Chief opinion, some prosecutors continue to offer evidence of the nature of a defendant's prior felony in cases filed under 18 U.S.C. §922(g)(1), and some district courts continued to admit such evidence over a defense offer to stipulate to the defendant's status as a felon. Appellate courts have found error when the prior felony would generate the risk of unfair prejudice but in many cases found the error to be harmless due to the "overwhelming evidence" of the defendant's unlawful possession of a firearm. See, e.g., United States v. Harris, 130 F.3d 829, 830 (8th Cir. 1998) ("When evidence of a defendant's guilt is overwhelming, the Old Chief violation is harmless."); Comment, The Undoing of Old Chief: Harmless Error and Felon-in-Possession-of-Firearms Cases, 48 Kan. L. Rev. 431, 457 (2000), suggests that the "effect-on-the-verdict" standard of harmless error replace the "weight of the evidence" standard, requiring "the judge to consider the proceedings in their entirety to determine whether the error had a substantial effect on the jury's decision."

4. Also following Old Chief, parties have offered a wide variety of stipulations to avoid the admission of evidence that bears the danger of unfair prejudice. In the majority of cases, trial courts have rejected such stipulations and appellate courts have refused to extend Old Chief beyond its holding on the issue of "status" §922(g)(1). See, e.g., United States v. Hall, 152 F.3d 381, 401 (5th Cir. 1998) (defendant's offer to stipulate to the identity of a murder victim and the cause of death did not render irrelevant photographs of victim's body in a decomposed state after defendant had buried it); United States v. Crowder, 141 F.3d 1202 (D.C. Cir. 1998) (defendant's offer to stipulate to intent element in crime of possession of drugs with intent to distribute does not render government's evidence of a similar crime inadmissible to prove intent); United States v. Hammoud, 381 F.3d 316, 342 (4th Cir. 2004) (not error to show the jury excerpts from tapes found in his home; defendant's stipulation that the tapes were

produced by a terrorist organization did not relieve the government from its burden of proving that defendant *knew* that the organization engaged in terrorist activity; tapes showed speeches by organization leaders advocating violence). But see United States v. Merino-Balderrama, 146 F.3d 758 (9th Cir. 1998) (in a prosecution for possession of child pornography videos, the trial court allowed the jury to watch the videos; defendant had offered to stipulate to their pornographic content but denied ever watching them and thus denied the requisite element of *knowing* what the videos were. The appellate court held this was error because the videos were highly prejudicial, the box covers of the videos were equally probative on the issue of knowledge since they depicted child pornography, and defendant admitted he had seen the covers).

PROBLEMS

3.16. Plaintiff Jones filed an action against her employer for racial harassment and discriminatory discharge under Title VII of the Civil Rights Act amounting to "an objectively hostile and abusive work environment." As part of her proof, plaintiff offered her union representative to testify that when the representative confronted one of Jones's supervisors, Bill, with her complaints about her treatment, Bill said: "If the dumb n***** doesn't like it she can sign out."

At trial, the judge excluded the union representative's testimony under Rule 403, stating on the record that it was "so prejudicial and so inflammatory" that it had to be excluded, even though it was of "heavy" relevance. Later the court also acknowledged "it is what is normally called a 'smoking gun' kind of statement" but it was a "very, very exacerbating kind of evidence," and that it was "very prejudicial," and that the decision was "close."

Jones lost at trial and appeals the judgment, asserting, among other things, that exclusion of Bill's statement was error. Should the appellate court find that error was committed? On what grounds?

3.17. D is charged with knowingly transmitting two images of child pornography through interstate commerce via his computer. He denies making any such transmission and claims that many other people use his computer. To prevent the jury from viewing the two images, the defendant offers to stipulate that the two images are child pornography in that they "contain visual depictions of minors under the age of eighteen, engaging in sexually explicit conduct." Should the trial judge accept this stipulation or permit the jury to see the images? If the images are shown, consider what limiting instruction the court should give.

4.   Reflection on Judicial Discretion to Admit and Exclude Evidence

The exercise of judicial discretion required by FRE 403 allows the trial court considerable freedom to admit or exclude evidence. As we have stated above, appellate courts treat lower court Rule 403 decisions with great deference, and appellate findings of abuse of discretion are infrequent. As you study the major rules of exclusion in this casebook, you will see that these rules—the character rule, the other relevance rules, the hearsay rule, the best evidence rule and the rules of privilege—do not grant such explicit discretion to the trial court. Rather, these exclusionary rules, and their exceptions, are so-called bright-line rules. Some of these, such as the rule prohibiting the use of extrinsic evidence to prove specific acts that impeach a witness's truthfulness, are truly "bright line." Others control the admission/exclusion decision with doctrinal definitions and categories.

The categorical rules operate in two ways. The hearsay rule, for example, establishes categories that require judicial fact-finding; the character rule establishes categories of permissible uses of specific acts that require the trial judge to identify particular noncharacter theories of relevance. Under both types of categorical rules, the trial judge's task is to determine whether the proffered item of evidence fits within a doctrinal category. This decision of whether the item "fits" usually is determinative of admission or exclusion. Thus, discretion—the estimation and balancing of probative value and dangers to jury decision-making—is not exercised under these categorical rules. This is not because the categorical terms are applied mechanically; they require very careful thinking by the trial judge. But it is a different kind of thinking, and it can be treated less deferentially by appellate courts if they treat the application of the categorical term as a question of law.

As you study these major exclusionary rules, you should consider the justifications for their bright-line or categorical nature as opposed to the discretionary standards of Rule 403. Think in terms of how best the exclusionary policy of the rule can be enforced; which type of rule best serves the goals of accurate outcomes, fairness to the parties, and an efficient judicial system; and which type of rule judges are most competent to decide and to review. You will also see that there are some fairly recent trends in judicial application of the major exclusionary rules that erode their bright-line nature. Trial courts are making estimates of probative value and using this factor to decide whether admission under the categorical rule is justified. Appellate court deference to this non-rule-based exercise of discretion in admission/exclusion decisions, combined with the harmless error doctrine, leaves these decisions unreviewed.

More will be said about these categorical rules, and their erosion through the introduction of discretionary thinking, in Chapters Five and Eight, infra.

C.   REFLECTION ON THE BASIC CONCEPT OF RELEVANCY

The essence of the Federal Rules' approach to relevancy is that evidence is relevant if it has the capacity to influence a disinterested person on a fact of consequence. What the infinitive *to influence* means in this context is somewhat vague, though. We know when we have a sense of being "convinced" or "persuaded" or of being placed in "doubt" by an argument or by evidence. But must an analysis of the influence of evidence stop at such an ephemeral point? Some have argued that it must. See, e.g., Henry M. Hart, Jr. and John T. McNaughton, Evidence and Inference in the Law, 87 Daedalus 40, 44 (Fall 1958):

> The adjudicative facts of interest to the law, being historical facts, will rarely be triable by the experimental methods of the natural sciences.... For the most part the law must

settle disputed questions of adjudicative fact by reliance upon the ambiguous implications of non-fungible "traces"—traces on human brains and on pieces of paper and
traces in the form of unique arrangements of physical objects.

Perhaps Hart and McNaughton are correct that the law must be satisfied with
evidence in the form of "traces on human brains." But must the implications of these
traces be ambiguous? There has been great interest recently in efforts to articulate in
a more rigorous fashion what it means for evidence to have persuasive force. These
efforts have centered primarily on the implications of a theorem of mathematics
known as Bayes' Theorem, which provides a rigorous method for combining a person's assessment of the probability of an event with new evidence concerning that
event to arrive at a new assessment of the probability of the event. For what follows we
are indebted to Professor Richard Lempert's work on Bayes' Theorem, which can be
found in Richard Lempert, Modeling Relevance, 75 Mich. L. Rev. 1021 (1977). That
work was heavily influenced by Professor John Kaplan's article, Decision Theory and
the Factfinding Process, 20 Stan. L. Rev. 1065 (1968), which in turn was heavily influenced by Vaughn C. Ball, The Moment of Truth: Probability Theory and Standards
of Proof, 14 Vand. L. Rev. 807 (1961). Some commentators have proposed alternatives
to Bayes' Theorem, see Jonathan L. Cohen, The Probable and the Provable (1977),
while others have critiqued its application to jury reasoning, among them William L.
Twining and Alex Stein, Evidence and Proof, The International Library of Essays in
Law and Legal Theory (1992); Ronald J. Allen, Rationality, Algorithms, and Juridical
Proof: A Preliminary Analysis, 1 Intl. J. of Evidence and Proof 253 (1997); Ronald
J. Allen and Michael S. Pardo, The Problematic Value of Mathematical Models of
Evidence, 36 J. Legal Studies. 107 (2007); Craig R. Callen, Notes on a Grand Illusion:
Some Limits on the Use of Bayesian Theory in Evidence Law, 57 Ind. L.J. 1 (1982);
David Kaye, Naked Statistical Evidence, 89 Yale L.J. 601 (1980); Nancy Pennington
and Reid Hastie, A Cognitive Theory of Juror Decision Making: The Story Model, 13
Cardozo L. Rev. 519 (1991).

English mathematician Thomas Bayes (1702-1761) demonstrated that the following formula is derivable from the axioms of conventional probability. In the formula,

O_G	=	odds of guilt or liability
$O_{G/E}$	=	odds of guilt or liability given the new evidence (E)
$P_{E/G}$	=	probability of obtaining the evidence in question if the person is guilty or liable
$P_{E/not\ G}$	=	probability of obtaining the evidence in question if the individual is not guilty or liable

The formula is:

$$O_{G/E} = \frac{P_{E/G}}{P_{E/notG}} \times O_G$$

This formula expresses that the odds of guilt or liability after evidence is received are
determined by the relationship between the probability of obtaining the evidence
if the person is guilty or liable and the probability of obtaining the evidence if the
person is not guilty or liable. In other words, to go from a prior assessment of the odds
of liability to an assessment in light of the new evidence requires that the prior assessment be modified by the likelihood that the evidence would have been presented

at trial if the person is liable as compared to the likelihood that it would have been presented if the person is not liable.

Do not let the discussion of probability theory obscure an important insight here. What makes evidence "relevant" is its capacity to influence the fact finder. That, in turn, is a function of the probability of receiving the evidence if the person is liable as compared to the probability of receiving the evidence if the person is not liable. Take a simple example. Suppose that in a burglary case, the prosecution wished to introduce evidence that the defendant does not like the Chicago Bears. If the defendant is guilty, the probability of receiving this evidence is a function of the proportion of burglars who are Chicago Bears fans, which we shall assume is .95 (at least in Chicago). The probability of receiving the evidence if the defendant is not guilty is a function of the proportion of nonburglars who are Chicago Bears fans, and there is no reason to think that proportion would differ from the proportion of burglars who are fans of the Bears. Thus, the ratio of these probabilities (.95/.95) is 1.0, and 1.0 multiplied by the prior odds of guilt will result in no change in those odds. Therefore, this evidence is irrelevant because it has no impact on the assessment of the odds of guilt.

We do not suggest that this way of viewing relevance has any value other than perhaps explaining how some rational people may evaluate evidence. Even as an explanatory effort, however, it has serious limitations. The formula requires that the decision maker have a preliminary assessment of the odds of guilt or liability *before* the receipt of an item of evidence that is subjected to Bayesian analysis, and it is unclear what that should be in our system of trials (especially criminal trials). Davis v. State, 476 N.E.2d 127, 138 (2d Dist. Ct. App. Ind. 1985) (in applying Bayes' Theorem, expert witnesses, who testified to the probabilities of parentage derived from blood test evidence, properly employed a neutral prior probability (50/50) instead of a prior probability variable based upon circumstantial, nontest evidence of the defendants' parentage). In addition, the probabilities associated with most evidence will virtually always defy quantification. More troublesome still, Bayes' Theorem requires that the decision maker evaluate each bit of evidence as it is introduced, rather than permitting the decision maker to hear all the evidence and deliberate on all of it at the conclusion of the trial process. At trial, by contrast, jurors are explicitly told not to form any conclusions until all the evidence is in. The reason for this is the belief that once opinions are formed they are hard to change. Individuals will rationalize new evidence they hear to make it consistent with their preconceptions. To the extent this is true, the party first producing evidence would have a great advantage at trial, since presumably that evidence will tend to establish that party's case. And, while it may be correct that if the likelihood ratio is 1 after the correct questions about the probabilities of obtaining evidence are asked, it is not clear that correct answers to those questions can be obtained in litigation. Care must be taken in thinking about relevancy and Bayes' Theorem.

Consider evidence that a defendant (charged with bank robbery) was running from the scene of the bank robbery that took place close to a train station. Fleeing might mean that the defendant robbed the bank and is trying to escape. It also might mean that she is trying to catch a train. Assume that it could be established as an empirically valid proposition that 70 percent of the people running from the crime are running because of guilt. The probability of obtaining the evidence of running if the defendant is guilty is .7; the probability of obtaining the evidence if defendant is innocent is .3. So far, the prosecution would be able to show the relevance of the evidence of running. Now suppose that defendant establishes that 70 percent of the people near a train station who are running are doing so to catch a train. Now, is the probability of obtaining the evidence of running if defendant is innocent also .7? If so, is the likelihood ratio under Bayes' Theorem 1? The trouble with relying on this ratio in litigation is that these are not the only two explanations of people running that will occur to the jury, and these other explanations could change the ratio. Many other evidentiary facts in the case, such as how fast or slow the defendant is running, or what she is wearing, will also affect the probabilities of each explanation of what the running means. And, of course, there are very few statements about the probabilities of human behavior that can be established with such precision. In most cases, the likelihood ratio cannot be established definitively and the judge will admit the evidence, leaving it up to the jury to interpret or explain it.

Bayes' Theorem, in short, is an interesting way of thinking about the idea of relevance, even if it is not completely compatible with the trial process. It also provides a useful way to think about the grounds of exclusion under the Federal Rules. Unfair prejudice, confusion, or misleading of the jury exists whenever the jury forms a likelihood ratio that is quite different from what the "true" likelihood ratio is. This can occur whenever the jury misevaluates either component of the ratio for whatever reason.

There is another way to think about the grounds for exclusion that also involves some simple mathematics and that permits taking into account a fact finder's preferences. "Unfair prejudice" describes the situation where the preferences of the fact finder are affected for reasons essentially unrelated to the persuasive power of the evidence to establish facts of consequence in the case. Assume that the defendant in the burglary case has been arrested for other offenses in the past and assume further that a prior record has no empirical relationship with the probability that a person has committed a subsequent crime. Suppose evidence of the prior record is admitted at trial. One effect of that evidence may be to reduce the fact finder's concern with accuracy. Given that the defendant has had previous brushes with the law, the fact finder may then think that even if the defendant did not commit the crime charged she undoubtedly committed others, and consequently it would do no great wrong to convict her even if she is innocent of this particular charge. Given the defendant's background, in other words, the "disutility" (i.e., cost) of a wrongful conviction is not what it would be with a person who has never been in trouble with the law.

A fact finder's appraisal of the disutility of one type of error as compared to another can be articulated algebraically. We are indebted to John Kaplan, Decision Theory and the Factfinding Process, 20 Stan. L. Rev. 1065 (1968) for much of what follows. In the formula,

D_g	=	the disutility of acquitting a guilty person or returning a wrongful verdict for a defendant in a civil case
D_i	=	the disutility of convicting an innocent person or of returning a wrongful verdict for a plaintiff in a civil case
P	=	the probability necessary to return a verdict of guilty or liability in a civil case

A rational decision maker presumably decides issues in such a way as to minimize the disutilities associated with the decision. When the relevant facts are known, that is a simple matter, but in the context of trials the facts are not known with certainty. Therefore, a way must be found to take account of that uncertainty. This can be done through the concept of "expected disutility," which is the disutility associated with a decision multiplied by the probability that the decision is factually accurate. Suppose that there is a disutility of 10 (whatever the units of "disutility" may be) associated with convicting an innocent person and a disutility of 1 associated with acquitting a guilty person. How should a decision maker decide when faced with imperfect knowledge? The formula below provides some guidance:

$$P > \frac{1}{1 + \frac{D_g}{D_i}}$$

Plug the figures suggested above into the formula. If $D_g = 1$ and $D_i = 10$, then:

$$P > \frac{1}{1 + \frac{1}{10}} = .91$$

In a criminal case, then, if it is 10 times worse to convict an innocent person than to acquit a guilty person, a jury should vote for conviction only when guilt has been established to a probability of at least .91. Compare this to civil cases. The normal view in civil cases is that the disutility of a wrongful verdict for a defendant is equal to that of a wrongful verdict for a plaintiff. Thus, $D_g = D_i$ and the formula reduces to $P > .5$, which is the normal burden of proof in civil cases.

Suppose that in a certain case there is no disutility in convicting an innocent man. Suppose that a heinous crime has outraged a community and someone—it really does not matter much who—must be punished in order to expiate the anger and fear of the citizens. In such a case, as the value of D_i nears zero, the denominator of the fraction becomes a very large number. Therefore, in order to convict there need only be a probability $P > 1/$ [a very large number], which equals a very *small* probability. Anyone will do, in short, so long as someone is sacrificed to the community's needs.

Now consider the other side of the coin, where it is the sense of a community that a person has already been punished enough for her digressions. For example, consider the case of the president of a small-town bank who has embezzled funds and been caught. The person has lost her job and has been disgraced publicly. When brought to trial, the jurors may feel that no more punishment is due. In the formula, Dg (the disutility of acquitting a guilty person) falls to zero. Consequently, the denominator of the fraction approaches 1, and thus the probability needed to convict, P, becomes 1.0. This cannot occur, and the individual is acquitted.

Obviously, these examples and this way of thinking about preferences and prejudice only roughly mirror what occurs in the real world, yet they provide some insights into the decision-making process. The effective advocate will not only provide a compelling factual story, but in addition will, to the extent permitted (and much greater latitude will be given in criminal cases), attempt to demonstrate why the costs of a verdict for that advocate's adversary are too high. To the extent a party is able to do this, the scales have been tilted in that party's favor.

Whether or not this discussion has been enlightening about the reality of the trial process, it is at least instructive about one meaning of the word *prejudice* in FRE 403. "Prejudicial" information is that which would tend to make the fact finder balance the disutilities of wrongful decisions inconsistently with the requirements of law. In other words, it would be prejudicial in a civil case to provide information that would tend to influence the jury to think it five times worse to return a wrongful plaintiff's verdict than a wrongful defendant's verdict. Similarly, because in criminal cases the law requires proof beyond a reasonable doubt, it would be prejudicial to admit evidence that would cause the fact finder in a criminal case to think it equally bad to acquit a guilty person as to convict an innocent person.

Note, however, that while this discussion may be enlightening about prejudice, it says very little about when prejudice "substantially outweighs" probative value, which is the standard under FRE 403, and we have little to add to our previous discussion of that issue. To briefly reiterate, there are three variables: the nature of the inappropriate effect (an effect that cannot be logically justified); the strength of the judge's conviction that the evidence will have that inappropriate effect on the jury; and the magnitude of the illogical or harmful effect. A judge will not know for certain that a jury will be inappropriately influenced by evidence; the judge can only appraise the likelihood that the evidence will have that effect. Moreover, it seems reasonable to think that some evidence will be more powerful than other evidence in its harmful impact on the jury. We suggest that "substantiality" is some mix of these two variables. The trial judge could be convinced beyond a reasonable doubt that the evidence would have a serious harmful effect. Alternatively, the judge could conclude that there is some small possibility that the evidence would have some slight improper effect, thus moving the jury away from an accurate outcome. For most judges, "substantiality" probably lies somewhere between these two extremes.

CHAPTER FOUR

LAYING THE FOUNDATION FOR PROOF

There is a universal principle of evidence law that no evidence is admissible until it is first shown to be what its proponent claims that it is. This universal requirement is sometimes called *laying the foundation* for proof. Remember that in the *Johnson* case the judge instructed the jury that "[e]vidence consists of testimony of witnesses, writings, material objects, or anything presented to the senses and offered to prove the existence or non-existence of a fact" (page 62, line 14, supra). In this chapter, you will study the rules that establish what foundation is required to secure the admission into evidence for these various types. Section A discusses the necessary foundation for introducing testimony from witnesses (FRE 601-606). Section B presents the various foundational requirements for exhibits, including real, demonstrative, documentary, and electronic evidence (FRE 901 and 902). Section C concerns the cluster of rules commonly known as "the best evidence rule" (FRE 1001-1008). Sections D and E focus on FRE 104, the rule allocating fact-finding on preliminary foundational questions between judge and jury.

The foundational requirements differ for each type of evidence, but in all cases the proponent must present foundational facts that are adequate under the rules presented in this chapter. Failure to do so may give rise to an objection from the opponent and then to exclusion by the court. Thus, the effect of these foundational requirements is to give the judge additional control—beyond FRE 401, 402, and 403—over what evidence the advocates may present to the jury and to increase the information available to the jury for its decision-making process. Satisfaction of the foundational requirements does not guarantee admission either. Other exclusionary rules, to be studied in subsequent chapters, may still apply.

A.   *LAYING THE FOUNDATION FOR WITNESSES*

Witnesses are produced at trial to present information to the trier of fact. Our system of proof assumes that the trier, through the process of inferential reasoning described in Chapter Three, can evaluate the credibility of witnesses and can reconstruct events based on the information they present in court. The foundational requirements for witnesses are set forth in FRE 601 (competency), FRE 602 (personal knowledge), FRE 603 (oath or affirmation to testify truthfully), and FRE 605 and 606 (incompetency of judge and jurors to testify in the case before them). These rules, in effect, define what a "witness" is. The Advisory Committee Notes to each of these rules contain useful discussion of the principles underlying each foundational requirement. The rules regulating the admission of lay and expert opinion testimony of witnesses are contained in Article VII of the Federal Rules and will be discussed in Chapter Nine.

1.   FRE 601

RULE 601.   COMPETENCY TO TESTIFY IN GENERAL

Every person is competent to be a witness unless these rules provide otherwise. But in a civil case, state law governs the witness's competency regarding a claim or defense for which state law supplies the rule of decision.

2.   Interpretation and Illustration of FRE 601

FRE 601 states a bold general assumption: that every person is competent to testify as a witness. The boldness of this assumption is best understood against the historical background of the strict regulations imposed at common law, and later in most states by statute. These were rules of competency that kept certain categories of persons off the witness stand entirely. Spouses were incompetent to testify for or against a spouse. Persons interested in the suit, including parties, could not testify. Atheists were categorically held to be incompetent, as were felons, young children, and the mentally ill. All of these categories were, as you can see, aimed at persons who judges and legislators thought were not trustworthy. It was assumed that they either possessed a motive for coloring the facts in favor of their interest, or suffered defects of character, youth, or mental capacity that created risks of untrustworthiness. In addition, the opponent could challenge a witness on grounds of individual incompetence. The party presenting the witness would then have to demonstrate that the witness did possess what are commonly called the four testimonial qualities—the ability to observe events, to remember them, to relate them accurately, and to understand the duty to tell the truth.

The first sentence of FRE 601 abolishes all categorical grounds of incompetence, subject only to the limit that where state law furnishes the rule of decision in federal court, a state-created category of incompetency will be applied. FRE 605 and 606 do prohibit the presiding trial judge and members of the sitting jury from testifying in the case at issue. These prohibitions are established not because of doubts about the trustworthiness of such witnesses, but because of the procedural complications and the potentially unfair prejudicial effect such testimony would be likely to have on the (other) jurors.

In general, however, the Advisory Committee Note to FRE 601 makes clear that, apart from the judge and the jury, people who witnessed relevant events cannot be prevented from testifying solely because of their status or their interest in the case. Note, however, that the fact of a witness's status (a felony conviction or a spousal or familial relationship to a party) or a witness's interest in the outcome of a case might still affect that witness's truthfulness. Thus, such facts are relevant, and are usually admissible, to impeach the credibility of the testifying witness, as you will see in Chapter Seven. The Federal Rules of Evidence permit the jury to decide whether such status or interest affects a witness's credibility, whereas the categorical incompetencies of statutes and the common law would have withheld that witness from the jury entirely.

3.   Elaboration of FRE 601: Challenging a Witness's Mental Competency

The Advisory Committee Note to FRE 601 states that "[n]o mental or moral qualifications for testifying as a witness are specified." FRE 603, which you should read, abolishes the moral qualification of taking a religious oath in favor of acknowledgment of the secular obligation to testify truthfully. Thus, it is correct to say that there are no moral, and certainly no religious, qualifications to be a witness. But can it be correct that "every person" is competent to testify, no matter what that person's physical or mental condition? Is there no longer any authority under FRE 601 for a federal judge to decide that an individual witness's testimonial abilities are so impaired—either temporarily or permanently—that the witness should not testify? For example, in the *Johnson* case, the defense considered calling another inmate, Grant, to testify about a prior incident involving Officer Walker. Grant had recently been found mentally incompetent to stand trial because he was unable to understand the nature of the proceedings against him or to aid in his own defense. Because of this mental condition, the defense conceded that Grant "rambled all over the place" and had a very short attention span. The court held as follows:

> Well, competent to stand trial and competent to take an oath are not the same. And if anything I would say standing trial involved a good many more considerations. If Grant appears to be reasonably rational as the questioning proceeds, he can testify. If his testimony comes out as gibberish, of course, we can terminate the testimony. [Transcript, People v. Johnson.]

The court in *Johnson* had power under Cal. Evid. Code §701 to disqualify a witness "incapable of expressing himself concerning the matter so as to be understood ... or ... incapable of understanding the duty of a witness to tell the truth."

Since the authority to disqualify is not mentioned in FRE 601, the federal circuit courts of appeal have taken two primary approaches to challenges to the competency of a witness like Grant. In United States v. Ramirez, 871 F.2d 582, 584 (6th Cir. 1989), the court held that FRE 601 could not be used to evaluate the ability of persons to testify:

> The authority of the court to control the admissibility of the testimony of persons so impaired in some manner that they cannot give meaningful testimony is to be found outside of Rule 601. For example, the judge always has the authority under Rule 403 to balance the probative value of testimony against its prejudicial effect. Similarly, under Rule 603, the inability of a witness to take or comprehend an oath or affirmation will allow the judge to exclude that person's testimony. An argument can also be constructed that a person might be impaired to the point that he would not be able to satisfy the "personal knowledge" requirement of Rule 602.

Other courts have asserted that, under FRE 601 itself, the trial court retains the authority it had under common law to disqualify a witness as incompetent if he lacks the capacity to recall or does not understand the duty to testify truthfully. See, e.g., United States v. Cassidy, 48 Fed. Appx. 428 (4th Cir. 2002). Under either view, the trial court may need to hold a hearing on the competency issue at which the witness in question would be placed under oath and examined out of the presence of the jury. Other testimony, such as that from treating physicians, could also be taken. Hometown Folks, LLC v. S&B Wilson, Inc., 2007 U.S. Dist. LEXIS 77605, at *6-7 (E.D. Tenn. 2007) ("Dr. Owens stated that he did not think [the witness] would be able to say 'I don't know' if he truly didn't know the answer to a question ... because [he] does not have the capacity to determine whether he knows the answer or not."). The judge has ample authority to hold such a hearing under FRE 104(c) and would decide the preliminary question of incompetence under FRE 104(a) by a preponderance of the evidence. In Section D of this chapter, we will discuss this fact-finding process in greater detail.

Appellate courts seldom overturn a trial court's finding that a witness is competent to testify, emphasizing that most disabling factors should be treated as matters affecting credibility for the jury to resolve, not as matters of competence. For example, in United States v. Cassidy, supra, the appellate court stated the following:

> At various times during his testimony, the witness spoke very slowly and nodded and chuckled inappropriately to the jury. The court excused the jury and instructed the witness to stop acting in this manner. During voir dire examination the behavior of the witness became even more bizarre. He had trouble recalling certain events, contradicted himself repeatedly, and seemed to be disoriented. At one point he could not tell the court for several minutes what day of the week it was .... The court decided to deny the motion to strike ... [and] noted that the erratic behavior of the witness would weigh heavily against his credibility in the eyes of the jury.... The district court did not clearly abuse its discretion in admitting the testimony.... Where there is doubt, we will respect the district court's finding that sufficient credibility existed to permit the jury to 'hear the testimony for what it is worth." [48 Fed. Appx. at 445.]

Also, appellate courts may reverse the trial court's exclusion of the testimony of a witness who had been found insane and incompetent to stand trial if there is evidence in the record that the witness had sufficient memory, understood the oath, and could communicate what he saw. United States v. Lightly, 677 F.2d 1027, 1028 (4th Cir. 1982).

Child witnesses can raise troublesome issues of competence with regard to their ability to remember events and to relate them accurately and truthfully. A federal statute establishes a presumption of competency for children who are victims of crimes of abuse and who have witnessed crimes against others. 18 U.S.C. §3509(c). A competency examination may be held only if compelling reasons exist and only upon motion by the opposing party and an offer of proof of incompetency. United States v. Walker, 261 F. Supp. 2d 1154, 1155 (D.N.D. 2003) (defendant's request for a competency hearing on his claim that the child witness was "merely repeating a well-drilled narration of the alleged incident without understanding it" rejected under the statute as supported by no evidence or offer of proof of any coaching.) Such examination is conducted primarily by the court away from the jury, with attorneys but not parties present. The questions focus on the child's "ability to understand and answer simple questions." 18 U.S.C. §3509(c)(8) (1996). In United States v. Allen J., 127 F.3d 1292,

1296 (10th Cir. 1997), the court held that the child witness's failure to respond to the trial judge's questions, her wrong answers to some of counsel's questions, and her nonsensical answers to others raised questions of credibility, not competence. Courts are particularly protective of child witnesses when defendants request independent psychological testing. Such judicial power should be "exercised sparingly"; no court "has held the refusal to order a witness to undergo a psychiatric examination [to be] a violation of the defendant's constitutional rights"; and the court "must consider the infringement on a witness's privacy, the opportunity for harassment, and the possibility that an examination will hamper law enforcement by deterring witnesses from coming forward." United States v. Morris, 2009 U.S. Dist. LEXIS 8572, at *11-17 (E.D. Tenn. 2009).

KEY POINTS

1. FRE 601 establishes that all persons are competent to testify. In most cases, facts that bear on competency are treated as affecting the weight of the witness's testimony but do not disqualify the witness.

2. Particular challenges to the competency of individual witnesses may be resolved as a matter of the trial court's Rule 601 authority, or under FRE 602, FRE 603, and FRE 403.

4.   FRE 602

RULE 602.   NEED FOR PERSONAL KNOWLEDGE

A witness may testify to a matter only if evidence is introduced sufficient to support a finding that the witness has personal knowledge of the matter. Evidence to prove personal knowledge may consist of the witness's own testimony. This rule does not apply to a witness's expert testimony under Rule 703.

5.   Interpretation and Illustration of FRE 602

FRE 602 mandates that before a witness may testify about a matter, the witness must be shown to have personal knowledge of that matter by evidence "sufficient to support a finding." The requirement that witnesses must "know" the matters about which they testify as a result of their own sensory perception is essential to our system of proof: Witnesses perceive real world events and describe these events to the jury, and the jury perceives the witnesses and evaluates whether or not to rely on them.

a.   The Requirement of Personal Knowledge

The most common kind of personal knowledge is visual perception, making the witness an eyewitness or *percipient witness* who was present at an event or occurrence. For example, the prosecutor in the *Johnson* case referred to the correctional officers as percipient witnesses because they were present at the incident and perceived it (page 6, line 10, supra). However, knowledge can be based on any of the senses. Inmate Green, for example, testified to what he heard at the vent between his cell and defendant Johnson's (page 48, line 14, supra). FRE 701, the rule regulating the admission of opinion testimony from lay witnesses, also contains a personal knowledge requirement. If a witness's testimony is *not* based on personal knowledge, then it is probably based either on speculation or on what someone else has said to the witness, which makes it disguised hearsay, as will be discussed in Chapter Eight.

b.   The Requirement of Evidence Sufficient to Support a Finding

As FRE 602 makes explicit, the proponent of a witness must produce evidentiary facts that the judge finds are "sufficient to support a finding" of personal knowledge; that is, a jury could *reasonably find* that it is more probable than not that the witness has personal knowledge. Note that this is the same standard applied to preliminary questions of fact under FRE 104(b) and under FRE 901 as well, as you will see in Sections E and B of this chapter. Under all of these evidence rules, in both civil and criminal cases, the trial court screens the proponent's evidence by applying the same "sufficiency" standard of proof. If a "sufficient" showing of personal knowledge is still disputed by the opponent, then final resolution of the question is given to the jury as part of its decision-making role.

To satisfy the sufficiency standard, usually all the proponent needs to do is to ask whether the witness did in fact see or hear the matters that are about to be described to the jury. FRE 602 provides that the witness's own testimony—"I saw that"—will suffice. Additional corroboration that the witness did in fact perceive the matter is admissible, but would not be necessary to satisfy the sufficiency standard. A jury could reasonably believe the witness's testimony, and the judge may not evaluate credibility. The Supreme Court articulated this standard in the context of a discussion of FRE 104(b):

> In determining whether the Government has introduced sufficient evidence to meet Rule 104(b), the trial court *neither weighs credibility nor makes a finding* that the Government has proved the conditional fact by a preponderance of the evidence. The court simply examines all the evidence in the case and decides whether the jury *could reasonably find* the conditional fact ... by a preponderance of the evidence. [Huddleston v. United States, 485 U.S. 681, 690 (1988) (emphasis added).]

And commentators have described the "sufficiency" standard similarly:

> The concept of sufficiency does not concern the question whether the trier actually will make such a finding, that is, [it does not concern] ordinary questions of credibility or the persuasive effect that evidence will actually have on the mind of the particular jury or judge as trier of fact. It does not ordinarily matter, therefore, that the testimony of the fact may be contradicted or impeached....
>
> Sufficiency is not primarily concerned with credibility nor with the choice among competing permissible inferences; ... all conflicts in the evidence are resolved against the party who challenges the sufficiency of the evidence, including conflicts and contradictions within a witness's or a party's own testimony.... The proponent is entitled to the most favorable of competing rational inferences and to have inferences drawn from

the most favorable findings. [Fleming James Jr., Geoffrey Hazard Jr. and John Leubsdorf, Civil Procedure §7.19 at 436, 441 (5th ed. 2001).]

In civil cases, motions for summary judgment are often decided on the basis of affidavits, which must state facts on personal knowledge. Fed. R. Civ. P. 56(e). If the foundation for the affiant's knowledge is not set forth in the affidavit with some particularity, it may not be sufficient to raise a genuine issue of material fact. Sheppard v. Union Pac. R.R. Co., 2005 U.S. Dist. LEXIS 1987 (E.D. Mo. 2005).

KEY POINT

FRE 602 requires that all witnesses (other than experts testifying to their opinions) must have personal knowledge of the matters about which they testify. The proponent of a witness must present evidence sufficient to support a finding of the witness's personal knowledge, typically by having the witness testify that the witness saw, heard, or otherwise perceived those matters.

PROBLEMS

4.1. Review the testimony by Officers Huston and Van Berg in the *Johnson* case concerning the injuries they claimed they received in the struggle with Johnson (pages 14 and 23, supra.) Did the officers speak from personal knowledge? Would you object to any of their testimony if you were the defense? Could you lay a proper foundation under Rule 602 if you were the prosecutor?

4.2. You are the lawyer for the plaintiffs in Problem 3.2 at page 136. What questions would you ask to lay the foundation for the following witnesses?

(a) An elderly retired neighbor who lives near the bus stop where Paul was injured and who says he can offer eyewitness testimony that Paul was standing on the gravel shoulder when he was hit.

(b) A coworker of Denise Driver who, you suspect, could testify that after the accident Driver said to her, "I shouldn't have been in such a hurry."

(c) Another of Driver's coworkers who could testify that, from chatting with other bus drivers, she believes that Driver feels guilty about the accident. Should this testimony be admitted?

4.3. The plaintiff's deceased husband suffered from asbestos-related diseases as a result of his occupational exposure to asbestos. At issue is whether the decedent was exposed to products manufactured by defendant OCF. In his deposition, the decedent identified an OCF product as an asbestos material with which he knew he had worked. But he also testified that his memory was adversely affected by the morphine he was taking: "It throws me out of gear. It's killing my brain. I'm screwed up. Sometimes my memory goes to heck, sometimes it doesn't." OCF claims that the deposition shows that the decedent was confused, inconsistent, and not certain about his knowledge of the OCF product. Do you think the court should strike the decedent's deposition testimony pursuant to FRE 601 or FRE 602?

B.   *THE AUTHENTICATION AND IDENTIFICATION OF EXHIBITS*

In addition to witnesses, information is conveyed to the jury through the use of exhibits. The term *exhibits* encompasses a wide array of items — real and demonstrative evidence; written documents of all kinds; audio, video, and photographic recordings; and electronic and digital data compilations. The foundational requirement for exhibits is set forth explicitly in FRE 901.

1.   FRE 901

RULE 901.   AUTHENTICATING OR IDENTIFYING EVIDENCE

(a) *In General.* To satisfy the requirement of authenticating or identifying an item of evidence, the proponent must produce evidence sufficient to support a finding that the item is what the proponent claims it is.

(b) *Examples.* The following are examples only — not a complete list — of evidence that satisfies the requirement:

(1) *Testimony of a Witness with Knowledge.* Testimony that an item is what it is claimed to be.

(2) *Nonexpert Opinion About Handwriting.* A nonexpert's opinion that handwriting is genuine, based on a familiarity with it that was not acquired for the current litigation.

(3) *Comparison by an Expert Witness or the Trier of Fact.* A comparison with an authenticated specimen by an expert witness or the trier of fact.

(4) *Distinctive Characteristics and the Like.* The appearance, contents, substance, internal patterns, or other distinctive characteristics of the item, taken together with all the circumstances.

(5) *Opinion About a Voice.* An opinion identifying a person's voice — whether heard firsthand or through mechanical or electronic transmission or recording — based on hearing the voice at any time under circumstances that connect it with the alleged speaker.

(6) *Evidence About a Telephone Conversation.* For a telephone conversation, evidence that a call was made to the number assigned at the time to:

(A) a particular person, if circumstances, including self-identification, show that the person answering was the one called; or

(B) a particular business, if the call was made to a business and the call related to business reasonably transacted over the telephone.

(7) *Evidence About Public Records.* Evidence that:

(A) a document was recorded or filed in a public office as authorized by law; or

(B) a purported public record or statement is from the office where items of this kind are kept.

(8) *Evidence About Ancient Documents or Data Compilations.* For a document or data compilation, evidence that it:

(A) is in a condition that creates no suspicion about its authenticity;

(B) was in a place where, if authentic, it would likely be; and

(C) is at least 20 years old when offered.

(9) *Evidence About a Process or System.* Evidence describing a process or system and showing that it produces an accurate result.

(10) *Methods Provided by a Statute or Rule.* Any method of authentication or identification allowed by a federal statute or a rule prescribed by the Supreme Court.

2.   Interpretation and Illustration of FRE 901

There are two parts to FRE 901. FRE 901(a) establishes the basic foundation and the evidentiary standard that the proponent of an exhibit must satisfy. FRE 901(b) sets forth examples of the kinds of foundation facts that the drafters of the Federal Rules decided should satisfy that standard.

FRE 901(a) requires the proponent of an exhibit to do two things: (1) state what the proponent *claims* the exhibit to be; and (2) produce evidence "sufficient to support a finding" that it is what the proponent claims. While it is difficult to grasp these concepts in the abstract, some general comments about the application of FRE 901 will serve as a framework for specific examples and problems discussed below.

a.   *What the Exhibit Is Claimed to Be*

As you learned in Chapter Three, the proponent of any item of evidence must have in mind a theory as to why that item is relevant to prove facts that are of consequence in a case. For exhibits, relevance requires the proponent of an exhibit to articulate some connection between the exhibit and the parties or the litigated events in the case. This *connection* is typically what the proponent *claims* the exhibit to be for purposes of FRE 901(a). This *connection* is what courts require the proponent to prove in order to identify or authenticate the exhibit. The Rule 901 foundation, therefore, follows from the articulation of why tangible objects, photos, recordings, or written documents are relevant.

Consider as an example a rental agreement between Harry, a landlord, and Jane, a tenant. Jane has filed suit against the landlord for failure to make promised improvements and offers the rental agreement as an exhibit. The rental agreement states that the owner of the property must make specific improvements. Harry, the defendant, claims that no written agreement was ever signed, that Jane has a month-to-month tenancy, and that there is no obligation to make improvements. Jane therefore seeks to introduce the rental agreement into evidence to prove that the defendant does have this obligation. On this theory of relevance, Jane *claims* that the exhibit is an agreement *signed by the defendant landlord*.

Jane may also have to prove other facts to establish that the written agreement is relevant to her case—for example, that it covers *the time period* during which repairs should have been made. Typically, courts treat the authentication burden as a narrow one that does not include *all facts* necessary to relevance, but only those that establish the basic connection to the parties or events. The Advisory Committee Note to Rule 901(a) illustrates this point: "[A] telephone conversation may be irrelevant because on an unrelated topic or because the speaker is not identified. The latter aspect is the one here involved."

b.   *The Requirement of Evidence Sufficient to Support a Finding*

Under FRE 901(a), Jane would need to produce evidence sufficient to support a finding that the rental agreement is what she claims it to be—the agreement signed by Harry, the defendant landlord. Imagine if the attorney for Jane simply handed the rental agreement to the jury. How would the jury know what it is? The attorney cannot just tell the jury what it is (you know from the instructions to the jury in the *Johnson* case that what an attorney says to the jury is not evidence). Of course, the jury might infer simply from looking at the document that it was signed by the defendant if the name on the document is the same as the defendant's. But what if the name was a very common one? Or just initials? The jury would not be able to make this inference with a very high degree of certainty. United States v. Skipper, 74 F.3d 608, 612 (5th Cir. 1996) (mere similarity in name between a criminal defendant and the person named in the record of a prior conviction alone does not satisfy the identification requirement of Rule 901). So while the signed document on its own might satisfy FRE 401 (having some tendency to show that the defendant signed the document), FRE 901(a) requires more. It requires the proponent to satisfy a higher standard of probability—*evidence sufficient to support a finding*—that it was the defendant landlord who actually signed the document. How can this be done?

c.   *FRE 901(b) Illustrates How to Produce Evidence Sufficient to Support a Finding*

FRE 901(b) now comes into play. It sets forth various options for satisfying the FRE 901(a) requirement. Jane's foundational evidence might come from the testimony of someone who saw the landlord sign the agreement—a person with personal knowledge under FRE 901(b)(1); or, circumstantial evidence can be offered, such as the testimony of someone who can recognize the landlord's signature (FRE 901(b)(2)); or, a comparison between the landlord's signature on another document and on the rental agreement itself (FRE 901(b)(3)). Whatever method is used, the added requirement of satisfying FRE 901 affects the parties, the jury, and the judge. Jane, the party proponent, has the added burden of locating the proper witness and presenting that witness at trial. The jury will get the added benefit of learning additional foundation facts in order to make its decision about the connection of the rental agreement to the tenant's case. For example, if Jane is able to satisfy FRE 901(b)(1), the jury could draw the inferences shown in Diagram 4-1:

Diagram 4-1

EF$_1$	+	EF$_2$ $\longrightarrow$	FOC $\longrightarrow$	EE
Rental agreement with landlord's name hand-written on it		Witness testifies, "I saw landlord sign the agreement"	Agreement was signed by the landlord	Landlord has promised to make improvements

The judge will have the added power to exclude the tenant's exhibit if the FRE 901(a) requirement is not satisfied. You can see the utility of the FRE 901(b) examples. If the proponent's foundation falls squarely within one, the trial judge will routinely decide that the FRE 901(a) burden is satisfied. But often the evidence is more ambiguous.

For example, what if Jane testifies that she mailed the agreement to Harry's business address and received the agreement by return mail with a signature added? This foundation calls for the application of FRE 901(b)(4), since the contents of the document (the name) and the circumstances (mailing it to Harry and receiving it by return mail) indicate that the landlord signed it. But would Jane's testimony satisfy the FRE 901(a) standard of "evidence sufficient to support a finding"?

d.   Judicial Determinations of Sufficiency Under FRE 901(a)

As stated in the previous discussions of FRE 602, pages 180-181, supra, evidence "sufficient to support a finding" means evidence upon which the judge thinks a jury *could* reasonably find a fact to be more likely true than not. The judge will not assess credibility in making this determination. Thus, in the hypothetical just discussed, the judge will assume that Jane's testimony about mailing the rental agreement is true. The judge's determination of "sufficiency" will depend primarily on the judge's assessment of the strength of the generalizations underlying the inference that it was the defendant who signed the agreement and sent it back to the tenant by return mail. The judge's task of making this rough estimate of underlying probabilities involves the same thought process as estimating probative value under FRE 403. How likely is it that landlords will receive rental agreements that have been mailed to them, will sign them, and will return them by mail immediately? *Could* a jury reasonably believe that it is more likely than not? Additional evidence—such as that Harry opens all of his own mail—would increase the probability that Harry did sign it.

As will be discussed on page 231 of this chapter, when the judge applies a "sufficiency" standard to screen preliminary questions of fact, the opponent can present contradictory evidence to the court. Harry could still testify that he did not sign the agreement, that the signature is not genuine, or that he was out of town on the day the agreement was received and mailed. All of this evidence would be heard by the judge, perhaps outside the presence of the jury pursuant to FRE 104(c). Courts have consistently held that the sufficiency standard "'does not erect a particularly high hurdle'. . . . Indeed, 'the proponent of the evidence is not required to rule out all possibilities inconsistent with authenticity, or to prove beyond any doubt that the evidence is what it purports to be.' Rather, a court may find proper authentication merely upon a showing that 'a reasonable juror could find in favor of authenticity or identification.'" CA, Inc. v. Simple, Inc., 2009 U.S. Dist. LEXIS 25242, at *49 (E.D.N.Y.) (citations omitted). If the court decides the preliminary question of fact in Jane's favor, the judge will find that FRE 901(a) has been satisfied and will admit the rental agreement into evidence.

Admission of the agreement does not end the matter, however. Harry can then submit all of his conflicting evidence to the jury, and the court may instruct the jury that it must decide the question whether Harry signed the agreement as part of its ultimate deliberations in the case. "[T]he jury ultimately resolves whether evidence admitted for its consideration is that which the proponent claims." Lorraine v. Markel Am. Ins. Co., 241 F.R.D. 534, 539 (D. Md. 2007). After all, if the signature is not Harry's, he has probably made no promise to make improvements. If the judge concludes that no jury could *reasonably* find that Harry signed the rental agreement, Jane has not fulfilled the FRE 901(a) burden. The judge will then exclude the agreement from the jury's deliberations. United States v. Schultz, 917 F. Supp. 1320, 1339 (N.D. Iowa 1996) (documents from defendant's alleged gambling operations held inadmissible under Rule 901(a) because sufficiency standard not met; no government witness testified that the documents were actually seized from a specific location controlled by defendant; rather, testimony was only that the documents were "consistent with" the types of documents seized there). In Jane's case, exclusion of the rental agreement might mean that she loses her case against Harry.

e.   The Process of Laying the Foundation

An exhibit is typically received into evidence after being given a number or letter designation to show which party submitted the exhibit and its sequence in the trial. In most trials, the mechanics of marking and numbering exhibits occurs before the trial itself, outside the presence of the jury, by agreement between the parties. An exhibit will be numbered "for identification" only, prior to its admission into evidence. At trial, the proponent shows the exhibit first to the opposing attorney and then to the witness who is going to testify about it. The proponent then questions the witness about the exhibit, presumably eliciting foundational facts sufficient to satisfy the FRE 901(a) requirements.

In the tenant's case against the landlord, for example, the tenant might produce a witness for purposes of proving the requisite foundation.[1]

Q: Please tell the jury your name and occupation.
A: My name is Joseph Jones and I am not employed.
Q: Do you know the defendant Harry Hunt in this case?
A: Yes, he is my uncle.
Q: Did you previously work in the defendant's office?
A: Yes, I worked there two summers ago.
Q: I am handing you a piece of paper marked plaintiff's Exhibit 7 for identification. Do you recognize it?
A: Yes
Q: What is it?
A: It is a rental agreement from my uncle's office.
Q: How do you know that?
A: It is printed with his business logo, and it states that it is a rental agreement between himself and Jane Smith, Tenant.
Q: Do you recall seeing this particular agreement before?
A: Yes.
Q: Could you tell us how you remember it?
A: It was the first day I was working for my uncle two years ago. He asked me to deliver some rental agreements to his tenants after he signed them. He had a stack of them. This one was on top.
Q: What happened next?
A: He signed the whole stack of them, and then gave them to me to deliver. As I said, this one was on top and I took it to the apartment at the address shown here. I really liked the apartment, which is why I remember it.

---

1.   An extremely helpful text which contains numerous examples of foundational testimony is Edward J. Imwinkelried, Evidentiary Foundations (7th ed. 2008).

Q: So to the best of your recollection, you saw the defendant sign Exhibit 7 two years ago?

A: Right.

Q: Your Honor, I now offer plaintiff's Exhibit 7 into evidence.

After the foundation is laid, the proponent asks the judge to admit the exhibit "into evidence." The opponent may object, either because the foundation is not adequate under FRE 901(a) or on grounds of some other exclusionary rule, such as hearsay or FRE 403. The judge will rule on the objection, or the parties may present further testimony from the testifying witness or from other witnesses first. If other witnesses are necessary, the judge may conditionally admit the exhibit *subject to* additional evidence being produced, using the technique of conditional admission to be discussed in Section E, infra. If the judge overrules the objection and admits the exhibit, it retains its number and is recorded by the court clerk as an official part of the record. It may then be inspected by the jury. Exhibits remain in the custody of the clerk during trial; they are taken into the jury room during deliberations and are part of the record on appeal.

3. Elaboration of FRE 901: Real Evidence, Demonstrative and Computer-Generated Exhibits, Recordings and Written Documents

The foundational requirements established by FRE 901 are described in the rule's title as requirements of "authentication" or "identification." These are not doctrinal terms that have a single, well-defined meaning. "Identification" usually refers to *who* authored a writing, *what* is pictured in a photograph, or *whose* voice was heard speaking; "authentication" usually refers to the *genuineness* of *what* the exhibit is in connection to the specific facts of the case. Also, two of the FRE 901(b) illustrations add an element of accuracy—the requirement of FRE 901(b)(2) that nonexpert familiarity with handwriting be acquired apart from the litigation, and the requirement of FRE 901(b)(9) that the process that produced the exhibit is accurate. The standard of FRE 901(a) is flexible, and the FRE 901(b) examples are not exhaustive. The starting point is always to ask: Why is this exhibit relevant? What does the proponent claim it to be, based on its connection to the parties or to the litigated events in this case? The kinds of foundations that have traditionally satisfied Rule 901 are discussed below and serve as examples and analogies for the authentication of exhibits of all types.

a. Real Evidence

Real evidence refers to tangible items that played some role in the litigated event and from which the jury may draw inferences. Examples are the weapons used in a crime or a home appliance that is alleged to be defective. The item's connection to the specific events in dispute makes it relevant, and that connection is "what the proponent claims" for purposes of satisfying FRE 901.

Thus, the foundation for real evidence typically consists of a witness who can identify the item's physical involvement in the case. Consider a murder trial where the prosecution wishes to introduce a knife under the relevance theory that it is the murder weapon. Not just any knife will do. Under FRE 901(a), the prosecution must claim that this knife has a connection to the specific events or parties in the case. A typical claim would be either that the knife was found at the crime scene or that it belongs to the defendant.

Suppose that several months have elapsed between the finding of the knife at the crime scene and its introduction as an exhibit at trial. How does the witness who found the knife, and who is called on to identify the knife in court, know that it is the one he found?

i.   **Identification Through a Readily Identifiable Characteristic.**   One typical method of identification is that the witness may recognize the knife—typically because it has a readily identifiable characteristic. The witness's personal knowledge satisfies FRE 901(b)(1). The identifier could be a unique design or initials on the handle, as shown in Diagram 4-2:

Diagram 4-2

EF$_1$	+	EF$_2$ $\longrightarrow$	FOC
A knife marked as Exhibit A has the initials "KRS" on its handle		Police officer testifies, "I can identify the knife marked Exhibit A as the knife I found at the crime scene because I recognize the initials 'KRS' on the handle"	The knife marked Exhibit A was found at the crime scene

Or the identifier could be a label, a number, or a tag affixed to the knife when it was discovered. In United States v. Abreu, 952 F.2d 1458, 1467-1468 (1st Cir. 1992), a drug agent testified that he recognized a shotgun as the one he seized at defendant's apartment by identifying the evidence tag placed on the gun at the time of seizure and by his signature on the tag. This would satisfy FRE 901(b)(4). Sometimes a fingerprint on a weapon is used as the identifying characteristic. In *Abreu*, a palmprint was also found on the shotgun. The foundation for identifying the print as defendant's was incomplete under FRE 901(b)(3) because there was no testimony that the inked palmprint specimen used for comparison was the defendant's.

ii.   **Identification Through Chain of Custody.**   Chain of custody is the second typical method of identification, most often used when an exhibit is generic and has no readily identifiable characteristic. For example, the links in the chain of custody of the knife would consist of the people who handled the knife between the time of its discovery at the crime scene and its appearance in the courtroom. A complete chain of custody under FRE 901(b)(4) would require the testimony of *all* such people plus testimony to show that the exhibit was stored in a secure place when it was not being handled.

iii.   **Unchanged Condition Established Through Chain of Custody.**   The chain of custody can also establish that the item was not tampered with and has been in the same condition as when it was discovered. This showing may be required if the condition of the item is as important as its identity. For example, the knife found at the crime scene might have fingerprints on it, or a substance seized from a defendant might be an illegal drug. The complete chain of custody would show that these conditions existed when the items were found, when they were tested, and perhaps even when they were presented in court. If the knife is tested for fingerprints — or if a chemical test is conducted on drugs seized from a defendant — the laboratory technician becomes part of the chain of custody. There needs to be evidence that the knife or the drug that reached the laboratory was the same knife or drug found at the crime scene or seized from the defendant, and that it had not been tampered with since. A complete chain of custody can be quite burdensome to prove, as shown in Jeter v. Commonwealth, 607 S.E. 734, 737-740 (Va. App. 2005). Testimony from the detective who seized the substance from defendant established that he immediately sealed the suspected cocaine in a "clear plastic baggie," then at the station placed it in a lock-sealed envelope, sealed the envelope with evidence tape, and marked the envelope with the date, his initials, and his identification number; gave the envelope to an authorized agent of the Division of Forensic Sciences (DFS), who gave it to a security officer at DFS, who gave the envelope to the laboratory analyst. The envelope was in the analyst's "continuous care and control" while he was performing the analytical tests on the suspected cocaine. And, after performing the analyses, the analyst resealed the envelope with evidence tape and marked the envelope with his initials, the date, and the lab number. Both the analyst and the detective identified the envelope at trial. This established every "vital link" in the chain of possession, thereby demonstrating with "reasonable certainty" that the evidence had not been altered, substituted, or contaminated.

   iv.   Under FRE 901(a), the Complete Chain of Custody Is Not Always Required.   Cases decided under FRE 901(a) make it clear that the complete chain of custody need not always be proved to satisfy the sufficiency standard. Even where gaps exist in the chain of custody of substances that require testing, courts have held that a jury *could* reasonably find that the exhibit in question was adequately identified and still in an unchanged condition. For example, in United States v. Shaw, 920 F.2d 1225, 1229 (5th Cir. 1991), amphetamine seized from the defendant's motel room was properly admitted despite such gaps. The evidence custodian could not recall who delivered the drug to the Department of Public Safety (DPS) for analysis or whether it was placed in the DPS night deposit box, and access to the drug was available to numerous DPS chemists. "A break in the chain of custody will not necessarily lead to the exclusion of the evidence .... Rather, 'the ultimate question is whether the authentication testimony is sufficiently complete so as to convince the court that [a reasonable jury could not find it more probable] that the original item had been exchanged with another or otherwise tampered with.'" United States v. Grant, 967 F.2d 81, 82 (2d Cir. 1992). In making this decision, courts routinely give the government the benefit of a *presumption* that evidence has been handled properly. United States v. Glawson, 322 Fed. Appx. 957 (11th Cir. 2009) (absent evidence to the contrary, the trial judge may assume that a police officer would not tamper with exhibits). Thus, a claim of tampering must be supported by specific evidence to contest the government's proof of chain of custody. If the court admits a disputed item of real evidence under FRE 901(b), at trial the opponent may again contest the identity of the exhibit or its possible changed condition and try to persuade the jury that it has no relevance or probative value in the case.

In *United States v. Ladd*, 885 F.2d 954, 956-957 (1st Cir. 1989), blood and urine samples were drawn from the body of the deceased to determine the presence of cocaine and heroin. The samples were sent to the State Laboratory and to a private laboratory (CSL) for analysis. At the State Lab, the procedures were sloppy enough to cause some concern about authenticity:

> [T]estimony supported a finding that the samples of Massey's bodily fluids, once delivered, were stored in a loosely-tied bag in a refrigerator in the laboratory; that the bag (if not the individual jars) was numbered and labelled; that the samples were removed for internal testing and eventually replaced; that the laboratory's procedures were followed on these occasions; and that the tested samples comprised Massey's blood and urine, respectively. This evidence, we think, was sufficient to sanction admissibility of the State Lab's reports.
>
> To be sure, defense counsel's attack on the laboratory's protocol, and on the storage and handling of the specimens, was robust. He showed that access was easy and cross-checking minimal. He probed skillfully at weaknesses in the safeguards employed, casting doubt on the samples' security and on the effectiveness of the state's preventatives. Fundamentally, however, this cross-examination went to the weight of the evidence, not to its admissibility.
>
> In the last analysis, the prosecution's chain-of-custody evidence must be adequate—not infallible. Here, some links in the chain were rusty, but none were missing. Without question, the defense succeeded in showing a certain sloppiness, regrettable in a forensic laboratory. Yet the net effect of any such disarray on the authenticity of the evidence depended on what inferences a reasonable factfinder might choose to draw from it. Where, as in this case, a trier chooses among plausible (albeit competing) inferences, appellate courts should not intrude....

In the private lab, however, a defect in the identification of the samples required exclusion:

> The tests conducted by the private laboratory, CSL, do not fare nearly as well. When a blood sample is received by the State Lab, it is assigned an identification number. Massey's blood sample was numbered T87-1938-BBO. When the decision was made to forward the sanguineous specimen to CSL for more critical testing, a messenger called for it. According to CSL's records, the sample it received was numbered T87-1936-BBO. The last-digit discrepancy ("1938" versus "1936") was never explained. It was later struck over—the "6" altered to look like an "8"—but the record is silent as to when, where, how or why this emendation occurred. The record is likewise inscrutable as to the identity of the reviser.
>
> Perhaps most puzzling, the prosecution made almost no effort to clear up the discrepancy. It chose not to present the testimony of the State Lab staffer who released the sample, the courier, or the CSL staffer who logged it in. Similarly, the prosecution offered no evidence to show whether the allegedly miswritten number (T87-1936-BBO) was assigned to some other specimen still in house, or to account for that designation. In short, there was no competent proof to indicate that the sample extracted from Massey's corpse was the one which CSL tested. An important step in the custodial pavane was omitted.
>
> The conclusion is, we think, inescapable. As to CSL's findings, the linkage was not merely rusty—it had parted. Due to the missing link, the CSL test results should not have been admitted into evidence.

Once an item of real evidence has been authenticated, it is still potentially subject to the judge's discretion to exclude pursuant to FRE 403. However, it is customary for judges to treat real evidence as being highly probative and thus of considerable assistance to the jury, sometimes with little analysis of what the jury would learn for purposes of deciding a fact of consequence in the case. Thus, the admission of even gruesome objects has been upheld if they played a part in the litigated events.

KEY POINTS

1. Real evidence is a tangible exhibit that played some role in the events that are in dispute at trial.

2. Real evidence is usually identified pursuant to FRE 901(b)(1) by testimony from a witness who recognizes the exhibit because of its readily identifiable characteristic, or by testimony concerning its chain of custody pursuant to FRE 901(b)(4). FRE 901(a) requires the judge to decide whether the proffered testimony is evidence sufficient to support a finding of the exhibit's identity. For some real evidence such as drugs or blood samples, it is also necessary to establish the exhibit's unchanged condition.

3. Real evidence may be subject to exclusion under FRE 403.

PROBLEMS

4.4. Darren is charged with possessing an unregistered sawed-off shotgun in violation of federal law. "Possession" is defined as the control of, or ability to control, the weapon. At trial, a federal agent testifies as follows: "I conducted a lawful search of the home of Rhonda Adams; I found Darren asleep in the master bedroom; I searched the master bedroom and found a black attaché case under the bed in which Darren was sleeping; I opened the case, and it contained a sawed-off shotgun." Now the prosecution wants to offer a sawed-off shotgun into evidence as Exhibit 2. The prosecutor claims that Exhibit 2 is the gun found in the black attaché case in the room where Darren was sleeping. First, the agent will identify Exhibit 2 as being a Korean-made Shinn A Sipja 12-gauge shotgun with a sawed-off barrel and cutback stock. What additional questions would the prosecution ask the agent to satisfy FRE 901(a)? Try to use both the readily identifiable characteristic and the chain of custody methods of identifying real evidence.

4.5. Home run king Barry Bonds testified under oath to a grand jury charged with investigating the distribution of illegal anabolic steroids by the BALCO laboratory. Bonds denied knowingly using such steroids. Bonds was then charged with 10 counts of making false statements to the grand jury. Federal agents executed a search warrant on BALCO and searched its premises. The government found samples of urine that tested positive for the presence of illegal anabolic steroids. The government claims that these are samples of Bonds' urine. It contends that Bonds's urine samples were obtained by his trainer, Greg Anderson, and then taken by Anderson to BALCO employee James Valente. Valente delivered the samples to Quest Diagnostics, which sent the samples and test results back to BALCO. The test results do not identify Bonds as the source of the urine. Quest can identify the tested urine samples as coming from Valente. Valente will testify that each time Anderson gave him the urine samples, Anderson said something to the effect of "this is from Bonds." Greg Anderson refuses to testify and has been jailed for contempt of court. Have the urine samples been adequately identified as coming from Bonds?

4.6. Jim Zeal and Stephani Goldstein were in a sailboat, the *Rastafari*, when it was stopped and boarded by the U.S. Coast Guard on the high seas, some 300 nautical miles southeast of Miami, Florida. The boarding officers searched the vessel and discovered a large quantity of a green leafy substance. Subsequently, Zeal and Goldstein were charged with conspiracy to import marijuana into the United States.

(a) At trial nine months later, the prosecution offers into evidence 11 nautical charts with navigational markings on them indicating a planned route between Kingston, Jamaica, which the government offers to show was a standard port of call for drug runners, and Miami. The prosecution asserts that the Coast Guard had seized the charts from the boat and that they are relevant to prove the conspiracy of illegal importation. To establish the authenticity of the charts, the prosecution calls Coast Guard Ensign Smythe, who testifies that he recognizes the charts as the ones he seized from the boat, and then deposited in the safe aboard the Coast Guard cutter, because of drawings of Bob Marley on each one. Is this testimony sufficient under FRE 901(b)(1)?

(b) The prosecutor also wants to establish that the leafy green substance found on board the *Rastafari* is marijuana. The prosecutor plans to show Exhibit C, a bag containing a leafy green substance, to a government chemist who testifies that, based on her in-court inspection, the substance in the bag is marijuana. But first, the prosecution offers Ensign Smythe to testify that he seized a bag of a leafy green substance from the ship and placed it in the Coast Guard safe along with the charts, and that while Exhibit C "could be" that bag, he does not know whether it is. Does this testimony satisfy FRE 901? What if FBI Agent Owens testifies that he found both the bag and the charts in the same box in the FBI evidence room and brought them to the courthouse. Would that be sufficient?

b.   Demonstrative Exhibits

Demonstrative exhibits reproduce or depict persons, objects (such as items of real evidence that are not brought into court) or scenes that are connected to the litigated events in the case. Examples are models, diagrams, drawings, or photographs. These exhibits are offered to illustrate or explain the testimony of witnesses, including experts, and to present or summarize significant portions of complex and voluminous documents. They can be referred to by counsel during opening and closing arguments. In theory at least, demonstrative exhibits do not have independent probative value on the substantive issues in a case. They are relevant and admitted into evidence because they assist the jury in understanding testimonial, documentary, and real evidence. Visual aids that are termed *illustrative* are not exhibits and are not admitted into evidence, as discussed at page 219, infra.

Demonstrative exhibits are authenticated by testimony from the witness whose testimony they illustrate. This witness has knowledge of the nature of the exhibit's content and the connection of that content to the case. For example, the prosecution might offer a photograph of the knife in Diagram 4-2 that was allegedly found at the crime scene. A witness who saw the real knife (or whatever was the subject of the demonstrative evidence) might testify, "I recognize the knife in the photograph because of the initials 'KRS' on the handle. This is a photograph of the knife I found at the crime scene." If a drawing, or a model, of the knife were proffered, the witness would testify in a similar manner.

i. Demonstrative Exhibits Must Assist the Trier of Fact. The proponent must also be prepared to show that the exhibit is a "fair," or "accurate," or "true" depiction of what the proponent claims that it portrays. Although this additional requirement is not part of the literal FRE 901 burden, courts enforce it to make sure a demonstrative exhibit will *assist* the trier of fact by increasing its understanding of the relevant events. This normally will be assumed with real evidence. It would be highly unusual, for example, for a trial court to exclude from evidence a murder weapon on the ground that the jury does not need to observe the weapon for purposes of its deliberations, even if such a conclusion might be correct.

Photos, drawings, diagrams, or models can be described as "fair and accurate" depictions of what they represent by the person who made them or by a person who saw the real thing. In the *Johnson* case, Officer Smith testified to the foundation for Exhibit 1, a photograph of a food port door in Facility B (page 33, lines 18-27, supra). He affirmed that Exhibit 1 was a "fair and accurate picture" of the door. Notice that Smith could say this even though he did not take the photograph himself. United States v. Lawson, 494 F.3d 1046, 1052 (D.C. Cir. 2007) ("A photograph may be authenticated if a witness with knowledge of the scene testifies that it accurately depicts the scene it purports to represent"); United States v. Gonzalez, 279 Fed. Appx. 806, 810 (11th Cir. 2008) (photo of defendant, standing among what appeared to be marijuana plants, identified by a witness who had no knowledge of photographer or date of photograph). Claims that a demonstrative exhibit is misleading or prejudicial would be decided under FRE 403.

ii. Application of FRE 403 to Demonstrative Exhibits. Some demonstrative exhibits are generally admitted as a matter of course, such as photographs of the scene of a crime or accident. But sometimes their admission raises Rule 403 dangers such as unfair prejudice and risk of misleading the jury. Photographs of gruesome and even ghastly injuries at a crime scene or autopsy may generate the danger of unfair prejudice; complex charts and graphs may present a danger of misleading the jury; and even photographs may be misleading (and have lower probative value) if they portray a scene in a different condition than when the relevant incident occurred. The judge decides the FRE 403 objection in typical fashion, by estimating the exhibit's probative value and weighing that against the pertinent danger. Recall the district court's decision admitting autopsy photographs in United States v. Yahweh, described on pages 151-152, supra.

c. Demonstrations and Experiments in Court

Sometimes a witness's testimony about an out-of-court event can be aided by a demonstration or experiment in court. Both are tested for relevancy under FRE 401 and FRE 403 because of their potential for misleading or confusing the jury. The proponent of the demonstration must lay a proper foundation establishing the similarity of circumstances and conditions between the out-of-court event and the in-court presentation. The conditions need not be identical, but they must be sufficiently similar to provide a fair comparison. In United States v. Gaskell, 985 F.2d 1056, 1060-1061 (11th Cir. 1993), a demonstration by an expert witness as to the amount of force needed to cause a seven-month-old infant's fatal injuries was held inadmissible. Shaking the rubber doll was not substantially similar due to stiffness of the doll's neck, differences in the weight of head, and absence of testimony concerning the number of oscillations required to produce the infant's injuries. Andrews v. State, 811 A.2d 282, 296 (Md. 2002) (error for the trial court to treat the differences between the infant and the doll as affecting the weight of opinion rather than the admissibility of the demonstration).

d.   Recorded and Computer-Generated Reenactments, Animations, and Simulations of Events

A variety of filmed recordings and computer-generated evidence can be used in trials to portray out-of-court events for the jury, typically in personal injury and criminal cases. *Reenactments and re-creations of events* are recordings that use human models, live persons, and/or real objects and instrumentalities; *animations* typically consist of computer-generated drawings that depict people or objects in motion. Both are used simply to illustrate both events and conclusions that witnesses have already testified to, and they are subject to the same requirement of being "fair and accurate" representations as a single drawing. They must accurately reflect the testimony and the physical evidence and the reasonable inferences that the testifying expert has drawn from them. For such exhibits, the computer is "no more or less than a drafting device." State v. Tollardo, 77 P.3d 1023, 1028 (N.M. Ct. App. 2003). Re-creations of the circumstances of an accident must also meet the requirements of "substantial similarity" applied in in-court demonstrations and experiments. Burchfield v. CSX Transportation, Inc., 636 F.3d 1330, 1336-1337 (11th Cir. 2011) (video showing experiments with the braking system of a railcar excluded because foundation failed to satisfy burden of similarity of circumstances and conditions of plaintiff's accident). If experiments present more abstract and general "scientific" principles, this showing of similar conditions is not required. Id. at 1334.

A different form of computer-generated evidence, called *simulations*, are created when the expert uses a computer to develop the opinion. They are produced by inputting information into a computer program that determines how an event "must have happened" and then provides a visual image of that conclusion. A simulation adds information beyond the testimony of percipient witnesses, both in terms of the data inputs into the computer and the programming that analyzes and then graphically portrays the output. State v. Tollardo, supra (a simulation is a "computer-generated exhibit created when information is fed into a computer that is programmed to analyze the data and draw a conclusion from it"). The most complete foundation for simulated accident reconstruction will involve the authenticity and sufficiency of the input data, and under FRE 901(b)(9), the reliability of the underlying technical or scientific principles, the accuracy of the computer's operating system, and the accuracy of the mathematical formulae programmed into the computer.[2] Extensive

---

2.   Gregory P. Joseph, A Simplified Approach to Computer-Generated Evidence and Animations, 43 N.Y.L. Sch. L. Rev. 875 (1999-2000) contains checklists for most types of and uses for simulations.

pretrial discovery is typically required to permit the opponent to challenge the exhibit effectively and to cross-examine the witnesses presenting it.

Of course, the use of recorded reenactments and both forms of computer-generated evidence are subject to objection under FRE 403. The principal risks are that the presentation inevitably simplifies the real-world events and that much data pertinent to accident reconstruction are supplied by outside sources who are unknown to the jury. Cautionary instructions are typically given concerning the limited purpose of an animation, the limited facts it is based on, and the jury's role in ultimately deciding those facts. Hinkle v. City of Clarksburg, 81 F.3d 416, 425 (4th Cir. 1996) (approving a limiting instruction that states: "This animation is not meant to be a recreation of the events, but rather it consists of a computer picture to help you understand [the expert's] opinion . . . the video is not meant to be an exact recreation of what happened during the shooting, but rather it represents [the expert's] evaluation of the evidence presented"). Nevertheless, there is concern among courts that jurors will be misled or overly influenced by such animated exhibits. In Racz v. R. T. Merryman Trucking, Inc., 1994 WL 124857, at *5 (E.D. Pa. 1994), the court excluded the defendant's computer-generated reconstruction of an accident made by an accident reconstruction expert. The reconstruction was based on that expert's evaluation of testimony about the accident:

> Because the expert's conclusion would be graphically depicted in a moving and animated form, the viewing of the computer simulation might more readily lead the jury to accept the data and premises underlying the defendant's expert's opinion, and, therefore, to give more weight to such opinion than it might if the jury were forced to evaluate the expert's conclusions in the light of the testimony of all of the witnesses, as generally occurs in such cases.

In contrast, some commentators view animations as a superior form of communication for the trier of fact. They condense information into a single package, are more understandable than charts or oral testimony, and are retained longer in memory. Edward J. Imwinkelried, Evidentiary Foundations, §4.09[4][a] (7th ed. 2008).

KEY POINTS

1. Demonstrative exhibits reproduce the likeness of some tangible object, person, or scene and are helpful to the jury's understanding of other testimonial, documentary, or real evidence. More complex forms of demonstrative exhibits include in-court demonstrations and experiments and out-of-court reenactments, animations, and simulations.

2. Demonstrative exhibits are usually identified pursuant to FRE 901(b)(1) by testimony from a witness as to what their contents are, the witness's basis for being able to identify them, and the witness's opinion that they are a fair and accurate reproduction.

3. Demonstrative evidence may be subject to exclusion under FRE 403.

PROBLEMS

4.7. In the *Hitt* case, page 159 supra, how did the prosecution authenticate the photograph that included Hitt's rifle? Who do you think the foundation witness was?

4.8. In the *Johnson* case, if the prosecutor asked Officer Huston to look at a model of the food port door that was constructed before the trial, what questions would the prosecutor ask to lay the foundation to admit the model into evidence as an exhibit? Suppose that the prosecutor wants to show that two food trays cannot fit through the model food port door. What other exhibits would be needed for this demonstration? What questions would the prosecutor ask to lay the foundation for the demonstration? What other considerations should enter into the judge's decision whether to admit the model or permit the demonstration?

4.9. Return to Problem 3.5 on page 138. Should the court permit the plaintiff, Broadback, to demonstrate to the jury the force of Trapp's blow to his neck? How might he do this?

e.   Recordings

Audio, video, and photographic recordings of events that occurred outside the courtroom are a cross between demonstrative evidence and eyewitness testimony. Although they may be offered together with the testimony of a witness who perceived the events, the recordings themselves are an independent record of them, imprinted not in human memory but on tape or film or some other medium by mechanical, electronic, or other processes. The recording reveals what the equipment "saw" or "heard," perhaps with less risk of human fallibility than an eyewitness. Consider, for example, if the fight in the *Johnson* case had been recorded by an automatic video camera. Even though there were many eyewitnesses to the melee, the film record would be an independent version of the event that could be used as substantive evidence (just as was the famous video of the use of force by Los Angeles police against Rodney King). Indeed, wouldn't the "memory" of the video recording be more reliable than either the guards' or the inmates' versions? Such a recording, if properly authenticated, would be admissible as substantive proof as to what out-of-court events occurred.

i.   Satisfying the FRE 901 Foundation with a Percipient Witness.
When a camera or other device records what a witness is also seeing, that "percipient witness" can authenticate the recording. The foundation is similar to that for demonstrative evidence under FRE 901(b)(1). The witness would identify the events in the recording, state the basis for the witness's ability to identify the events, and affirm that the recording is a "fair," or "accurate," or "true" record of the events perceived. For example, a government informant who participated in taped conversations could authenticate both the recording and the transcripts of the tape by testifying that they were correct to the best of his knowledge. United States v. Wright, 932 F.2d 868, 880 (10th Cir. 1991). This is indeed a very simple foundation! At common law, courts took a much stricter attitude to ensure the accuracy of tape and film recordings, requiring proof of the equipment operator's qualifications, the working condition of the equipment, and the absence of material alterations, typically through a complete chain of custody of the recording itself from the time it was made until presentation in the courtroom. The following commentary explains why courts now permit a simplified foundation:

> First, there are now electronic techniques for determining whether a tape has been altered .... Secondly and more importantly, the courts have gone back to fundamentals and [have] begun to treat the question of a tape recording's authenticity as a simple

question ... under Federal Rule 104(b) .... Has the proponent presented sufficient evidence to support a rational finding of fact that the tape recording is authentic? Given that test, many modern courts are no longer insisting on the traditional, strict foundation .... If a witness testifies that he or she heard a conversation and that the tape accurately reproduces the conversation, there is a permissive inference of the tape's genuineness. [Edward J. Imwinkelried, Evidentiary Foundations, §4.06[1] (7th ed. 2008).][3]

ii. "Silent Witness"—Satisfying the FRE 901 Foundation Without a Percipient Witness.   Sometimes a recording device records what no human witness has seen or heard, or what no human can see—like the X-ray taken of Officer Van Berg's broken thumb chip. When a recording thus functions as a "silent witness," a percipient witness does not exist and cannot testify to the simplified foundation. Instead, "recordings made by ... equipment that operate[s] automatically ... may satisfy the requirements of the [FRE] ... so long as a witness testifies to the type of equipment or camera used, its general reliability, the quality of the recorded product, the process by which it was focused, or the general reliability of the entire system." United States v. Stephens, 202 F. Supp. 2d 1361, 1368 (N.D. Ga. 2002). For example, in United States v. Pageau, 526 F. Supp. 1221, 1224 (N.D.N.Y. 1981), a sound and video recording of an assault by prison guards on an inmate was admitted based on a foundation as to the accuracy of the recording process, despite lack of testimony from any percipient witness that it was a fair and accurate representation of the events. By now, of course, courts trust the science that underlies most recording processes and do not require proof of the basic scientific theories. United States v. Harris, 55 M.J. 433, 438 (CAAF 2001) ("Any doubt as to the general reliability of the video cassette recording technology has gone the way of the BETA tape."). But the operation of a particular automatic camera or a hospital's X-ray taken of a particular patient does require some foundational testimony to satisfy FRE 901(b)(9)—evidence that the process or system produced an accurate result. In *Harris*, no witness described the accuracy of the particular video camera. Instead, evidence of the time and date on the film itself was sufficient to show that the camera was working properly. Id. at 439.

Courts do differ, however, in the degree to which they require the complete foundation set forth above. Courts can read FRE 901(a) narrowly to require proof only of the identity of what was recorded and perhaps a minimal chain of custody to prove the continued integrity of the recording but not the recording's accuracy. In an opinion where the crux of the case against the defendant was 32 audio and videotapes, for example, the court declined to require the strict traditional foundation for each tape. It found sufficient the operator's testimony that the taping equipment was "routinely checked" to make sure it was working properly, and that after recording the tapes, he turned them over either to an FBI agent or to a state police officer. The FBI agent then described the chain of custody of the tapes. United States v. Sivils, 960 F.2d 587, 597 (6th Cir. 1992). "Computer technology makes alteration of photographs a *possibility*. . . . [T]he Government need only show by direct or circumstantial evidence a '*reasonable probability*' that the evidence is authentic." United States v. Harris, supra, at 440.

3.   Some federal circuits have raised the burden in criminal cases and have held that the prosecution must provide "clear and convincing evidence" that a tape recording is a "true, accurate, and authentic recording of a conversation, at a given time, between the parties involved." United States v. Welch, 945 F.2d 1378, 1383 (7th Cir. 1991). Accord, United States v. Morrison, 153 F.3d 34, 56 (2d Cir. 1998).

This trend is consistent with one of the major thrusts of the Federal Rules, which was to liberalize the admission of evidence. Courts acknowledge this trend: "Unprecedented technological advances over the last twenty years have dramatically increased the ease with which electronic recordings may be altered to suit the proponent's objectives. Yet, these same advances have also greatly improved our ability to detect and expose such electronic tampering." United States v. Stephens, 202 F. Supp. 2d at 1369. Even so, some cases call for a more complete and specific foundation when there is no percipient witness available to authenticate recordings. In *Stephens*, the prosecution presented the testimony of three police agents who had outfitted a confidential informant (later deceased) with four different surveillance devices. Two different recorders were used to produce audio recordings of face-to-face drug transactions between the informant and the defendant. A vehicular bullet camera, attached to the informant's car, produced a video recording of the encounters. In addition, at least one agent had the informant and the defendant under observation during all of their meetings. The *Stephens* court opined: "[T]he government has presented the most careful and comprehensive foundational authentication evidence that this jurist has ever seen." Id. at 1369.

Recordings can also be authenticated by their content alone. In Gonzalez v. Digital Equip. Corp., 8 F. Supp. 2d 194, 197 (E.D.N.Y. 1998), videos created by IBM and Apple to demonstrate product safety features and solutions to problems arising from computer keyboard usage were authenticated as to their source pursuant to FRE 901(b)(4) by their internal labels, the manner of their production, and the information that they contained.

iii. Application of FRE 403 to Recordings.   Sometimes the admission of recordings can raise dangers under FRE 403. Video recordings that portray gruesome events such as personal injuries, autopsies of crime victims, or the details of tort or crime sites, are frequently objected to as unfairly prejudicial. Because of the immediacy of their visual impact, they have added capacity to generate emotional responses and may arouse the jury's hostility or sympathy for one side, thus influencing the outcome in an unfair way. Hall v. Brannan, 670 S.E.2d 87, 94 (Ga. 2008) (video recording in police cruiser of murder of the officer, defendant fleeing, and victim's dying breaths held admissible, although deeply disturbing). Such evidence can also be misleading if its contents do not correspond closely enough to the actual conditions and context of the events that are at issue at trial if it is edited or recorded from a particular perspective. A related probative danger is confusion of the issues, which could occur if the jury's attention is distracted by the dramatic power of a recording from a careful evaluation of the issues in dispute. United States v. Guthrie, 557 F.3d 243 (6th Cir. 2009) (defendant objected that video of police pursuit by numerous officers with lights and sirens blazing portrayed him as a dangerous criminal; court held that video actually depicted the charged crime of carjacking in progress).

In each case, the trial court will weigh these dangers against the probative value of the recording pursuant to the balancing test of FRE 403, and the appellate court will reverse only for abuse of discretion. Government of the Virgin Islands v. Albert, 241 F.3d 344, 350 (3d Cir. 2001) (gruesome 45-minute video of crime victim shown to jury; thoughtful concurring opinion stated "to hold that admitting this evidence was not an abuse of the trial judge's discretion is equivalent to ruling that admitting unduly inflammatory evidence can never be cause for reversal; if this evidence was not unduly inflammatory, then nothing is.").

iv. **Voice Identification.**   When a recording of a conversation is offered into evidence, it is usually relevant because of the identity of one or more of the speakers. To establish that identity, the proponent typically relies on FRE 901(b)(5), which permits the use of opinion testimony from a witness "based on hearing the voice at any time under circumstances that connect it with the alleged speaker." This burden has been held to require only minimal familiarity: "Any person may identify a speaker's voice if he has heard the voice at any time." United States v. Stillis, 2006 U.S. Dist. LEXIS 41949, at *6 (E.D. Pa. 2006).

KEY POINTS

1. Recordings of events may be authenticated pursuant to FRE 901 if a percipient witness can testify that the recording is a fair and accurate record of the real-world event.

2. If the recording functions as a "silent witness" because there is *no* percipient witness to the event, FRE 901 may require proof of the recording process and of the chain of custody of the recording itself.

3. Recordings may be subject to exclusion under FRE 403.

PROBLEMS

4.10. Return to Problem 3.5 on page 138. How would Broadback's attorney lay the proper foundation for item (a), the recorded excerpt from the televised filming of the soccer game? Might defendant Trapp make any other objections?

4.11. During his trial on federal charges of drug sales, the defendant challenges the authenticity of Exhibit 8, a tape recording offered against him, claiming that the tape was altered to incriminate him. X, a confidential informant employed by the federal Drug Enforcement Administration (DEA), testified that he recorded four conversations, during which drug sales were made, that he had with the defendant between July 17 and July 19, 2004; that he used a microrecording device to make these recordings; that Exhibit 8 is the microcassette upon which the conversations were recorded; that he turned the cassette and recorder over to his DEA contact without altering the tape in any way; that he has not seen the cassette and recorder since; and that he recognizes his own voice and the voice of the defendant. Is this testimony sufficient to establish the authenticity of Exhibit 8 under either the percipient witness or "silent witness" foundation? Why?

4.12. John Packer was convicted of the crime of conspiring to collect debts by extortionate threats of violence. Key evidence at trial included FBI tape recordings of telephone calls made to the victim of the threats. In these calls, threats were made by a man calling himself Tony G. The recordings were authenticated through the testimony of an FBI agent who was unable to identify the voice of the person calling himself Tony G. Later in the trial, the recordings were connected to Packer through the testimony of two State Troopers. State Trooper A identified the "Tony G voice" as that of Packer, based upon hearing Packer speak when Trooper A was present at his arrest a year previously. State Trooper B also identified the voice as that of Packer. Trooper B had known Packer since childhood. On cross-examination, Trooper B admitted that he was asked by the FBI "to identify the voice of Packer" rather than being asked merely to identify the voice. Does the testimony of Troopers A and B satisfy FRE 901?

4.13. Robert Grant is charged with two counts of selling crack cocaine. The evidence against him is based on the testimony of DEA Agent Mary Gray, who was working undercover. An informant, now deceased, told Agent Gray that she could get crack from "Bobby" but did not tell her "Bobby's" last name. Agent Gray can testify as follows: (1) in August 2010 she met with the person introduced to her as "Bobby" and the informant; (2) Bobby sold her 30 grams of crack cocaine for $2,000; (3) Bobby gave her his pager number; (4) later in August she paged Bobby and asked to buy more crack cocaine; (5) Bobby met her the next day and sold her 50 grams of crack for $3,000. These two sales are the basis for charges against Bobby.

However, at Bobby's trial in 2011, Agent Gray cannot positively identify the defendant Robert Grant as "Bobby." No lineup identification was ever made. There is some evidence linking Grant to the pager number used by "Bobby," but there is also evidence that many other people had access to this pager.

The government plans to offer Gray to testify that in November 2010 she paged Bobby, he called back, she recognized his voice, she then recorded their telephone conversation during which Bobby agreed to sell her one kilo of crack cocaine, and that Exhibit 10 is the recording she made, which is a true and accurate recording of her conversation with Bobby. This sale never actually took place. Why is Exhibit 10 relevant? What is it claimed to be? Has it been authenticated? What does it prove about the defendant's guilt?

The government then offers DEA Agent Randy Jones, who processed Robert Grant at the federal lock-up after Grant's arrest in April 2011. Jones will testify that he recognizes the voice of "Bobby" on the tape as Robert Grant's voice. Is the tape now admissible to prove that "Bobby" is Robert Grant?

4.14. Able, Bold, and Curry (the protesters) participated in an anti-war protest in Freedom National Historic Park on July 4, 2010. The protest started peacefully but got out of control, and Park Rangers moved in to restore order. The three protesters were arrested and found guilty of "refusing to obey the lawful order of a Park Ranger."

At the trial, a Park Ranger, Officer Miller, testified that he made a two-hour videotape of the entire protest with a hand-held video camera. He further testified that he was familiar with the camera that he used; that it had operated correctly on the day in question; and that following the protest, he removed the videocassette from the camera and labeled it with his name and the date and gave it to the video technician at the Park Ranger office. However, the tape that the government produced at trial was only 15 minutes long. This tape, admitted as Exhibit 5, was not in the cassette that had been labeled by Officer Miller. There was no witness who could testify as to how it was created or about what happened to Miller's video after it was delivered to the Park Ranger technician. Miller testified, "I picked up this tape at the Park Ranger station before bringing it to court" and "to the best of my recollection, this tape shows pretty much what I saw at the last 15 minutes of the protest on July 4th."

The video portrays rowdy scenes of a protest in Freedom Park. In these scenes, Able, Bold, and Curry can be seen throwing garbage at park statues. Many other demonstrators are wearing "death" masks. The Park Rangers can be heard ordering groups of demonstrators to "back off," to "disperse," and finally to "lie down on the ground," and Able, Bold, and Curry are visible in the video. They remained standing both during and after the giving of these orders.

Assume all proper objections were made under the FRE that we have studied so far. Did the trial judge commit error in admitting the video into evidence?

f. Written Documents

Typically, a written document is relevant because its contents are connected to the litigated events of a case by the identity of its author or by knowledge of its organizational source. This connection is proved by evidence authenticating the writing pursuant to FRE 901, typically by proof of the identity of the author or of its organizational source. The law of evidence, however, does not treat the signature or recital of authorship on the face of a document, without more, as sufficient proof of authenticity. FRE 901(b) includes several illustrations of how to lay a foundation that is sufficient to authenticate a written document.

i. Signature. Proof of the genuineness of a signature is sufficient to identify the author of a writing. Observation of the act of signing a document, as exemplified by the testimony of the landlord's nephew in our hypothetical case between the tenant and the landlord (page 186, supra), will satisfy FRE 901(b)(1). Identification of a signature based on familiarity with handwriting will satisfy FRE 901(b)(2), and under FRE 901(b)(3) either the jury or an expert may compare the signature on the exhibit itself with a specimen that has been authenticated pursuant to FRE 901. United States v. Saddey, 393 F.3d 669 (6th Cir. 2005) (under FRE 901(b)(3) a lay person can identify and compare signatures). For example, in N.L.R.B. v. General Wood Preserving Co., 905 F.2d 803, 810 (4th Cir. 1990), 17 signatures were authenticated by employees who identified them as their own; six others were authenticated by witnesses who had observed the six named employees sign the documents; and five others were authenticated by comparing them with specimens bearing authenticated signatures. In United States v. Hamama, 2010 U.S. Dist. LEXIS 64956 (E.D. Mich. 2010), documents were authenticated as belonging to the Iraqi Intelligence Service (IIS) by an expert witness who recognized the distinctive swirls and marks, used in Iraq as signatures, belonging to specific IIS officers.

ii. Contents and Other Circumstances. FRE 901(b)(4) is an extremely broad and flexible standard that permits proof of authorship or source through many types of evidence. For example, the author of an anonymous letter may be identified by a document's contents, United States v. Thompson, 449 F.3d 267, 274 (1st Cir. 2006) (contents of letter precisely fit Thompson's circumstances and predicament in May 2004, facts known peculiarly to him), and return address (Thompson's address). The circumstances in which documents are found are also pertinent. United States v. Gonzalez-Maldonado, 115 F.3d 9, 20 (1st Cir. 1997) (notebook found in a person's briefcase in that person's room, along with an identification card, is sufficiently authenticated as belonging to that person by such circumstantial evidence); and documents produced by the alleged source in pretrial discovery are properly authenticated. But such circumstances are not always adequate. United States v. Jackson, 636 F.3d 687 (5th Cir. 2011) (testimony of DEA officer insufficient to authenticate alleged drug ledgers handed over by known drug trafficker due to lack of information as to who prepared the ledgers and what they recorded).

Records of a business or other institution can be authenticated as to their source under FRE 901(b)(4) through proof of matching letterhead, comparison with matching forms, testimony about the routine practices of the institution in generating such records, and through testimony of a custodian about how the business's filing or data retrieval system operates and that the document was retrieved from a certain file or in a certain way. In United States v. Hamama, 2010 U.S. Dist. LEXIS, at *7-8, IIS documents were identified as authentic by a former IIS officer based on their routing information, their use of standardized forms, and their consistency with how the IIS collected and recorded information about its intelligence sources. If a computerized data retrieval process or system is used, further testimony may be required to satisfy the requirement of FRE 901(b)(9) that the computerized process must produce an accurate result. United States v. Whitaker, 127 F.3d 595, 601 (7th Cir. 1997) (computer records were authenticated as used by defendant to keep track of drug transactions by the testimony of an FBI agent describing how he retrieved them from defendant's computer by installing Microsoft Money on the computer and printing out the documents).

FRE 901(b)(7) provides for the authentication of certain types of public records or reports. Proof that they "are from the public office where items of this nature are kept" can be provided by testimony from the custodian, such as Ruth Taylor in the *Johnson* case, or by a certificate of authenticity from the public office. Or, a witness may simply testify that the record is from the appropriate public office. United States v. Farrah, 2007 U.S. App. LEXIS 19310 (4th Cir. 2007) (INS record custodian had knowledge of document kept by the INS and testified that the documents in the Farrahs' file are what the government claims).

iii.   Ancient Documents.   If a writing is more than 20 years old and is in a place where it would likely be if it were authentic, two of the requirements for admitting the document as "genuine" pursuant to FRE 901(b)(8) will be satisfied. In Threadgill v. Armstrong World Industries, Inc., 928 F.2d 1366, 1376 (3d Cir. 1991), correspondence dating from the 1930s that showed corporate knowledge of the dangers of asbestos had first been stored in a company vault, then moved to a personal office in 1969, and finally returned to the corporation's Director of Environmental Affairs in 1974. The court held that the manner of retaining the documents was what might have been expected. United States v. Portrait of Wally, 663 F. Supp. 232, 255 (S.D.N.Y 2009) (unsigned, undated typed letter found in a Biedermeier bureau owned by alleged writer of the letter, in her London home, along with other papers belonging to her, 20 years after her death, held authentic under FRE 901(b)(8)).

The third requirement of this rule—that the document be in such condition as to create no suspicion concerning its authenticity—has been interpreted narrowly by some courts dealing with German documents generated during World War II that implicate current U.S. citizens in Nazi war crimes. That is, suspicions that go to the accuracy of the contents of the document, or to its completeness, do not count. The only issue that the proponent must address is whether the documents are the type of document they are claimed to be, typically by their storage location and by the expert testimony of historians who specialize in Nazi-era German history and Nazi policies and practices. "[W]hether the contents of the document [an identity card] correctly identify the defendant goes to its weight and is a matter for the trier of fact." United States v. Demjanjuk, 367 F.3d 623, 631 (6th Cir. 2004). These German documents, like many ancient documents, are admitted to prove the truth of the matters they record; thus, they are hearsay. An extremely broad "ancient documents" exception to the rule excluding hearsay, FRE 803(16), provides for the admission of a "document in existence twenty years or more the authenticity of which is established."

 iv. **Electronic Writings**.   Due to the enormous growth in electronic commerce in recent years, the recording, communication, and preservation of digital information pervades our society. Understandably, then, electronic writings (also known as "e-evidence") are increasingly used in both civil and criminal litigation. Most common are computer-generated data files, e-mails and Internet postings. The authentication of such electronic writings can be hotly contested when authorship is in dispute. There are no subsections of FRE 901(b) that address these new electronic technologies specifically, but FRE 901 provides flexibility in applying its standard of sufficiency. Courts have developed analogies to traditional writings in admitting e-mails, chat group discussions, Web postings, and many other forms of e-evidence.

 Like traditional writings, e-mails (and more recently text messages) may be authenticated in many ways. For example, courts have recognized that e-mails may be authenticated by lay witness testimony, expert testimony, comparison with an authenticated exemplar, or by the e-mail's distinctive characteristics. Lorraine v. Markel Am. Ins. Co., 241 F.R.D. 534, 555 (D. Md. 2007); Mark D. Robins, Evidence at the Electronic Frontier: Introducing E-Mail at Trial in Commercial Litigation, 29 Rutgers Computer & Tech. L.J. 219, 228 (2003) ("Other factors that courts frequently consider in authenticating writings and other items will similarly apply to e-mail messages."). The electronic signature may not be sufficient to establish authorship, however, because of the risk of manipulation of e-mail headers. Additional data such as the address that an e-mail bears, the use of the "reply" function to generate the address of the original sender, the content of the information included in the e-mail, and other circumstances can suffice. United States v. Siddiqui, 235 F.3d 1318, 1322 (11th Cir. 2000). E-mails containing defendant's name and e-mail address in the headers, and obtained in hard copy form from defendant's apartment, are admissible to show that defendant received them and was a co-conspirator. United States v. Vaghari, 2009 U.S. Dist. LEXIS 64793, at *27 (E.D. Pa.).

 Authorship of identity-protected postings on chat groups can be determined by content and circumstances. United States v. Simpson, 152 F.3d 1241 (10th Cir. 1998) (Simpson had contended that the government had to prove his authorship of the postings by handwriting, writing style, or voice as required by FRE 901(b)(2)-(5); court held that content such as self-identification, and circumstances such as finding copies of postings near Simpson's computer, sufficed.)

 Courts are skeptical about attributing the content of documents obtained from a website to the organization or individual who maintains the site. "Anyone can put anything on the Internet ... the Court holds no illusions that hackers can[not] adulterate the content on any web-site from any location at any time." St. Clair v. Johnny's Oyster & Shrimp, Inc., 76 F. Supp. 2d 773, 775 (S.D. Tex. 1999). Web postings, therefore, require proof of the process by which they were generated. In re Homestore. Com, Securities Litigation, 347 F. Supp. 2d 769, 782-783 (C.D. Cal. 2004) ("To be authenticated, some statement or affidavit from someone with knowledge is required; for example, Homestore's web master or someone else with personal knowledge would be sufficient."). Information retrieved from government websites, however, has been treated as self-authenticating, subject to proof that the webpage does exist at the governmental web location through the URL and the titles of the pages. Williams v. Long, 585 F. Supp. 2d 679 (D. Md. 2008).

Finally, courts have also adopted a skeptical attitude toward unsupported claims of alteration or tampering with regard to e-evidence. In CA, Inc. v. Simple, Inc., 2009 U.S. Dist. LEXIS 25242, at *55-56 (E.D.N.Y.), plaintiff CA proffered an archive CD that allegedly reconstructed a website as it existed in 1998, in order to prove that defendant's patent for a "windowed content manifestation environment" was invalid because it was anticipated by the 1998 site. The components of the archive CD were authenticated by the testimony of Meininger, whose website it was and who put the archive CD together, and by the "metadata" time stamps, which provided the date and time each file in the archive CD had been created orginally. Defendant Simple proffered no evidence that the archive CD or its time stamps had been tampered with:

> Instead, Simple merely alludes to the notion that "you never can tell what's going on with, you know, young folks."... The mere theoretical possibility that the archive CD could have been altered does not make it inadmissible, rather the possibility of tampering may only be considered when weighing the archive CD's corroborative value.... Simple has put forward nothing more than bare assertions that the archive CD could have been altered. . . . [T]he Court finds [it] ... highly corroborative of Meininger's oral testimony.

KEY POINTS

1. Written documents are usually identified pursuant to FRE 901 by testimony that identifies the author or the source of the document, typically using the signature, the contents, the location of the document, or other circumstances.

2. Writings created by new electronic technologies are identified and authenticated by analogies to Rule 901(b) illustrations.

PROBLEMS

4.15. Return to Problem 3.4, State v. Blair, at page 137. Police found a postcard in Norma's apartment postmarked September 12, 2010. In handwriting it says "See you at 9:00 P.M. on the 14th." It is signed "Jimmy." The government claims that Jimmy Blair wrote this postcard. Why is it relevant? What options are there to authenticate it?

4.16. Return to Problem 3.5 on page 138. How would Broadback's attorney lay the foundation for item (b), the excerpt from the Official Rules of the Soccer League?

4.17. Return to Problem 3.2, Pedroso v. Driver, at page 136. Driver testifies that she received a letter in the mail from the School Board, which she identifies as Exhibit A, urging her to return to work. Driver's attorney offers Exhibit A into evidence. Plaintiffs object for lack of authentication. How should Driver's attorney respond? What result?

Exhibit A

San Ramon School Board
2001 Main Street
San Ramon, CA 94901

Dear Ms. Driver,

The San Ramon School Board urges you to return to your work as a school bus driver as soon as you feel able to do so. You have always been a safe driver, and the tragic accident of a month ago does not change our high opinion of you.

/S/ Jean Smith
President, San Ramon School Board

4.18. Kleenit Kleaning Company is suing Travellers Insurance Company for coverage of the costs of cleaning up a toxic waste site Kleenit created between 1967-1970. Unfortunately, the alleged policy of insurance is lost. To establish that payments were made from 1967-1970 from Kleenit to Travellers, Kleenit proffers expense ledgers for those years that show such payments. The ledgers, found in Kleenit's offices, are handwritten, at times illegible, with some notations that are indecipherable. A former Kleenit employee would testify that an outside accountant, Mr. Nash, would have prepared the ledgers in connection with Kleenit's year-end accounting, and that Nash kept the ledgers in his own office until he retired, at which time he transferred the documents to Kleenit's office. Nash is deceased. Are the ledgers admissible under FRE 901? Consider all options.

4.19. Return to Problem 3.3, United States v. Ray, at page 136. For each item of evidence or alleged fact below, identify the various possibilities for laying a proper foundation under FRE 901. Note that there may be more than one approach for each item of evidence. Also, think about this from the standpoint of investigating the case: What evidence would you want to gather before trial in order to introduce the evidence at trial. Once at trial, what different witnesses could you call, and what questions would you ask?

(a)   Exhibit 1: A copy of Andrews' confidential written memo to Rundown CFO June Jacobs dated March 14, 2009.
(b)   Exhibit 2: A copy of Chief Auditor Andrews' e-mail to Jacobs, also dated March 14, 2009.
(c)   Ray's sale of 100,000 shares on March 16, 2009.

4.20. Plaintiff Burch, an African-American woman, has filed suit against her former employer, a Fifth Avenue New York Department Store, for discrimination against her in the terms and conditions of her employment. Plaintiff alleges that African-American employees of the Fifth Avenue Store are compelled, as a condition of their employment, to either retain the hair color they were born with or color their hair only dark brown or black to conform with the color of their skin, while non-African-American employees sport hair highlights and colors other than their "natural" hair color without being threatened with termination. During her testimony at trial, Burch proffers a photograph that she states that she found and downloaded from Facebook, and that shows a white employee of the Fifth Avenue Store, Elaine, with bright red hair that is not her natural color. Is this testimony sufficient to authenticate the photograph? Would additional information be necessary to secure its admission into evidence?

g.   FRE 901 Provides Flexibility in Application

You can see from these FRE 901(b) illustrations that what it means to identify or authenticate particular types of evidence varies widely. There is no one "correct" foundation that must be satisfied in each case, or for each particular type. Courts apply the standard of Rule 901(a) flexibly and do not always require that a particular subsection of Rule 901(b) be satisfied. The treatises on evidence law are full of fascinating case law examples of the kinds of foundations that have been laid to authenticate exhibits—particularly those that are susceptible to tampering and change of condition. Over time, courts do tend to distill the elements of an adequate foundation into criteria that they apply routinely. But in drafting the ultimate criterion of FRE 901(a) so loosely—that a matter is what the proponent claims it to be—the drafters of the Federal Rules have permitted flexibility in the application of the authentication requirement. Remember, however, that the starting point of your analysis of the requisite foundation should always be relevancy.

4.   FRE 902

a.   FRE 902

RULE 902.   EVIDENCE THAT IS SELF-AUTHENTICATING

The following items of evidence are self-authenticating; they require no extrinsic evidence of authenticity in order to be admitted:

(1) *Domestic Public Documents That Are Signed and Sealed.* A document that bears:

(A) a seal purporting to be that of the United States; any state, district, commonwealth, territory, or insular possession of the United States; the former Panama Canal Zone; the Trust Territory of the Pacific Islands; a political subdivision of any of these entities; or a department, agency, or officer of any entity named above; and

(B) a signature purporting to be an execution or attestation.

(2) *Domestic Public Documents That Are Not Sealed but Are Signed and Certified.* A document that bears no seal if:

(A) it bears the signature of an officer or employee of an entity named in Rule 902(1)(A); and

(B) another public officer who has a seal and official duties within that same entity certifies under seal—or its equivalent—that the signer has the official capacity and that the signature is genuine.

(3) *Foreign Public Documents.* A document that purports to be signed or attested by a person who is authorized by a foreign country's law to do so. The document must be accompanied by a final certification that certifies the genuineness of the signature and official position of the signer or attester—or of any foreign official whose certificate of genuineness

relates to the signature or attestation or is in a chain of certificates of genuineness relating to the signature or attestation. The certification may be made by a secretary of a United States embassy or legation; by a consul general, vice consul, or consular agent of the United States; or by a diplomatic or consular official of the foreign country assigned or accredited to the United States. If all parties have been given a reasonable opportunity to investigate the document's authenticity and accuracy, the court may, for good cause, either:

(A) order that it be treated as presumptively authentic without final certification; or

(B) allow it to be evidenced by an attested summary with or without final certification.

(4) *Certified Copies of Public Records.* A copy of an official record—or a copy of a document that was recorded or filed in a public office as authorized by law—if the copy is certified as correct by:

(A) the custodian or another person authorized to make the certification; or

(B) a certificate that complies with Rule 902(1), (2), or (3), a federal statute, or a rule prescribed by the Supreme Court.

(5) *Official Publications.* A book, pamphlet, or other publication purporting to be issued by a public authority.

(6) *Newspapers and Periodicals.* Printed material purporting to be a newspaper or periodical.

(7) *Trade Inscriptions and the Like.* An inscription, sign, tag, or label purporting to have been affixed in the course of business and indicating origin, ownership, or control.

(8) *Acknowledged Documents.* A document accompanied by a certificate of acknowledgment that is lawfully executed by a notary public or another officer who is authorized to take acknowledgments.

(9) *Commercial Paper and Related Documents.* Commercial paper, a signature on it, and related documents, to the extent allowed by general commercial law.

(10) *Presumptions Under a Federal Statute.* A signature, document, or anything else that a federal statute declares to be presumptively or prima facie genuine or authentic.

(11) *Certified Domestic Records of a Regularly Conducted Activity.* The original or a copy of a domestic record that meets the requirements of Rule 803(6)(A)-(C), as shown by a certification of the custodian or another qualified person that complies with a federal statute or a rule prescribed by the Supreme Court. Before the trial or hearing, the proponent must give an adverse party reasonable written notice of the intent to offer the record—and must make the record and certification available for inspection—so that the party has a fair opportunity to challenge them.

(12) *Certified Foreign Records of a Regularly Conducted Activity.* In a civil case, the original or a copy of a foreign record that meets the requirements of Rule 902(11), modified as follows: the certification, rather than complying with a federal statute or Supreme Court rule, must be signed in a manner that, if falsely made, would subject the maker to a criminal penalty in the country where the certification is signed. The proponent must also meet the notice requirements of Rule 902(11).

b. Interpretation of FRE 902

FRE 902 defines those documents that, on the basis of their appearance or self-evident content alone, are so likely to be authentic that the proponent need produce no extrinsic evidence to prove it.

Certain kinds of public documents and public records have been produced by a formal process that triggers a generalization that the document itself, and the signatures on it, are very likely to be genuine. The formalities, such as a seal or a statement of certification as required by FRE 902(1)-(4) and (8), indicate that someone has paid attention to genuineness. Self-authentication under FRE 902(1) requires that the document bear the official seal, not a copy of it. United States v. Hampton, 464 F.3d 687, 689 (7th Cir. 2006) ("The rationale of Rule 902(1), according to the Committee Notes, is that a seal is difficult to forge. But that is not true of a copy of a seal . . . "). For similar reasons, notarization of a signature is not sufficient under FRE 902(3); a final certification is required. A passport has been held to be a public document, which must be accompanied by official certifications to be self-authenticating under FRE 902(2) or (3). United States v. Pluta, 176 F.3d 43, 49 (2d Cir. 1999). Depositions, court records, public reports, notices, assessments, and payment of federal tax liens may all be self-authenticated under FRE 902(4) if accompanied by the proper certification. The 969B package, offered into the *Johnson* case as Exhibit 2, contained certified copies of the original documents in Johnson's C File (page 36, line 15, supra). It was thus probably a self-authenticating public record under the California equivalent to FRE 902(4). A public authority's printed publications, handbooks, manuals, regulations, and documents published on a website are self-authenticating under FRE 902(5) without a certification.

Other kinds of writings, just from looking at them, trigger a generalization that they are genuine because they are very difficult to forge. For example, it may more reliably be inferred that the writings defined in FRE 902(5)-(7) and (9) are from the source they appear to be from. Specht v. Google, Inc., 758 F. Supp. 2d 570 (N.D. Ill. 2010) (a news story from Forbes.com is not automatically self-authenticating as a periodical; printing a serial publication involves work and expense that make forgery unlikely while web printouts do not carry the same degree of authenticity). However, this justification for the rule has been weakened: "[M]odern technological developments [computers, scanners, publishing software, and internet access] make it easier to produce ... a counterfeit." Wright and Gold, Federal Practice and Procedure: Evidence §7140 (2000). Pursuant to FRE 902(7), trade inscriptions and the like — "Macintosh Portable" on computers, "Product of Malaysia" inscriptions — are usually treated as establishing the authenticity of the item to which they are affixed, as well as their own genuineness. There is split authority as to whether writings such as an owner's manual, or electronic writings such as e-mail messages, that bear a company's trademark should also be considered self-authenticating. Whitted v. General Motors Corp, 245 F.3d 1200 (7th Cir. 1995) (trade inscription on cover of owner's manual does not authenticate the contents of the manual).

FRE 902(11) and (12) became effective in December 2000 and are referred to in FRE 803(6), discussed at page 521, infra. They are intended to simplify the authentication of business records and to substitute a written declaration for the production at trial of a custodian or other live witness. It has been held that the author of the certification does not need personal knowledge of the contents of the specific business records, but must have knowledge of how the records were created and maintained. In re Enron Creditors Recovery Corp., 376 B.R. 442, 456-458 (Bankr. S.D.N.Y. 2007). One unanswered question is whether the written declaration must include detailed information to support each factor of FRE 803(6) — that, for example, the record was made "as a regular practice" — or whether the declaration can simply recite that conclusion. Most reported cases refer to verbatim recitation of the required factors. Neighbors Law Firm, P.C. v. Highland Capital Mgmt., L.P., 2010 WL 3767140 (E.D.N.C.) (the court found no authority for plaintiffs' assertion that the declaration is insufficient because it does not provide specific details of the applicable maintenance and retention policy). However, the court in Rambus, Inc v. Infineon

Techs. Ag, 348 F. Supp. 2d 698 (E.D. Va. 2004) found that the specific facts stated in the declarations were insufficient to satisfy the requirements of FRE 803(6). Notice of a party's intent to use Rules 902(11) and (12), together with the records themselves, must be provided to the opponent for verification and potential challenge. If only conclusory statements are made in written declarations, then the burden falls on the opponent to take discovery on the underlying specific facts.

As stated in the Advisory Committee Note to FRE 902, admission of a document pursuant to Rule 902 is not dispositive of authenticity. The opponent can offer proof that the document is a phony or bears a forged signature. Self-authentication also does not resolve questions as to the source or accuracy of information that is reported in self-authenticated documents. United States v. Bisbee, 245 F.3d 1001, 1007 (8th Cir. 2001) (evidence tending to contradict the facts reported in certified documents does not render the documents inadmissible). Objections can also still be made that inadmissible hearsay statements or expert opinions are included in, for example, newspapers or periodicals.

KEY POINT

FRE 902 provides that some written documents can be authenticated by their appearance alone, without the testimony of a foundation witness. The opponent may still dispute the authenticity of these "self-authenticating" documents.

PROBLEMS

4.21. To prove that two persons are not U.S. citizens and have been illegally smuggled into the United States, the government offers their alleged passports from Poland. To authenticate the documents, an INS supervisory inspector, with extensive experience in conducting inspections to exclude persons from the United States, testifies that he recognizes the passports as genuine Polish passports. When asked the basis for his opinion, he states: "They're identified as such right on the document." Sufficient?

In the same case, the INS inspector offers Volume Two of the INS Handbook of Regulations, which, on its title page, states that it is issued by the Department of Homeland Security and bears a facsimile of the official seal of the Department. When asked how he recognizes the exhibit as the genuine volume he answers "Look at the title page." Sufficient? What is the difference between the passports and Volume Two?

4.22. In defending a personal injury suit filed by an employee injured while operating a milling machine, the employer sought to prove the year of manufacture of its machine. It did so by offering the serial number of its machine plus Exhibit C, an excerpt from the "Serial Number Reference Book for Metalworking Machinery—11th Edition," published by the "Machinery Dealers National Association." The excerpt includes the cover, the title page, and pages 114-115; the latter contains a list of what appear to be serial numbers for Bridgeport milling machines for each year from 1950 to 1977. The employer asserts that this excerpt is self-authenticating under FRE 902(6) as a periodical because it is published and updated by the Association every five years. What result?

C.   THE BEST EVIDENCE RULE

The best evidence rule—really a cluster of rules—imposes additional foundational requirements on the proponent of writings, recordings, and photographs. The theory of the rule is simple: When a writing, recording, or photograph is offered to prove its content, the chances are good that the original will be more trustworthy than a copy. Therefore, the best evidence rule creates a requirement for the production of originals. The requirement may be excused, and other "secondary" evidence of the contents may be admitted if the absence of the original is explained or justified.

1.   FRE 1001, 1002, 1003, 1004, 1005, 1006, and 1007

RULE 1001   DEFINITIONS THAT APPLY TO THIS ARTICLE

In this article:

(a) A "writing" consists of letters, words, numbers, or their equivalent set down in any form.

(b) A "recording" consists of letters, words, numbers, or their equivalent recorded in any manner.

(c) A "photograph" means a photographic image or its equivalent stored in any form.

(d) An "original" of a writing or recording means the writing or recording itself or any counterpart intended to have the same effect by the person who executed or issued it. For electronically stored information, "original" means any printout—or other output readable by sight—if it accurately reflects the information. An "original" of a photograph includes the negative or a print from it.

(e) A "duplicate" means a counterpart produced by a mechanical, photographic, chemical, electronic, or other equivalent process or technique that accurately reproduces the original.

RULE 1002.   REQUIREMENT OF THE ORIGINAL

An original writing, recording, or photograph is required in order to prove its content unless these rules or a federal statute provides otherwise.

RULE 1003.   ADMISSIBILITY OF DUPLICATES

A duplicate is admissible to the same extent as the original unless a genuine question is raised about the original's authenticity or the circumstances make it unfair to admit the duplicate.

RULE 1004.   ADMISSIBILITY OF OTHER EVIDENCE OF CONTENT

An original is not required and other evidence of the content of a writing, recording, or photograph is admissible if:

(a) all the originals are lost or destroyed, and not by the proponent acting in bad faith;

(b) an original cannot be obtained by any available judicial process;

(c) the party against whom the original would be offered had control of the original; was at that time put on notice, by pleadings or otherwise, that the original would be a subject of proof at the trial or hearing; and fails to produce it at the trial or hearing; or

(d) the writing, recording, or photograph is not closely related to a controlling issue.

RULE 1005.   COPIES OF PUBLIC RECORDS TO PROVE CONTENT

The proponent may use a copy to prove the content of an official record—or of a document that was recorded or filed in a public office as authorized by law—if these conditions are met: the record or document is otherwise admissible; and the copy is certified as correct in accordance with Rule 902(4) or is testified to be correct by a witness who has compared it with the original. If no such copy can be obtained by reasonable diligence, then the proponent may use other evidence to prove the content.

RULE 1006.   SUMMARIES TO PROVE CONTENT

The proponent may use a summary, chart, or calculation to prove the content of voluminous writings, recordings, or photographs that cannot be conveniently examined in court. The proponent must make the originals or duplicates available for examination or copying, or both, by other parties at a reasonable time or place. And the court may order the proponent to produce them in court.

RULE 1007.   TESTIMONY OR STATEMENT OF A PARTY TO PROVE CONTENT

The proponent may prove the content of a writing, recording, or photograph by the testimony, deposition, or written statement of the party against whom the evidence is offered. The proponent need not account for the original.

2.   Interpretation and Illustration of FRE 1001, 1002, 1003, 1004, 1005, 1006, and 1007

a.   Summary of the Basic Principles of the Best Evidence Rule

i.   FRE 1002.   FRE 1002 provides the basic principle of the best evidence rule: An original is required when a proponent seeks to prove the content of a writing, recording, or photograph. Each is defined very broadly under FRE 1001(a), (b), and (c) to include any form of writing, any form of recording, and any form of storage.[4] However, the scope of FRE 1002 does not extend beyond proving the content of writings, recordings, and photographs. There is *no* explicitly articulated "best evidence principle" enacted in the Federal Rules that requires the proponent to offer the best evidence of *whatever* it is that he or she wishes to prove. Generally speaking, a party may prove its case by any admissible evidence, regardless of whether anything "better" (i.e., more persuasive or reliable) is available. Of course, the advocate may be motivated to use the most highly probative evidence in order to persuade the jury, but evidence law gives the judge little control over the advocate's choice.

What constitutes an *original* that will satisfy FRE 1002 is also defined broadly by FRE 1001(d): any "counterpart intended to have the same effect by the person who executed or issued it," such as carbon or photocopies when a document is executed in

---

4.   The original FRE 1001 listed specific types of writings and recordings and included "or other form of data compilation." It can be assumed that the restyled Rule includes all of these types and all other forms of writings and recordings known or as yet unknown. The original Rule also listed specific types of photographic images included within the definition of photograph. It can be assumed that the restyled Rule includes all of these types as well as all equivalents and forms of storage known or as yet unknown.

quadruplicate; any negative or print of a photograph; and any printout or other output of electronically stored data if shown to reflect the data accurately.[5] The key issue in applying Rule 1002 is the determination of when the "content" of these kinds of items is being proved, discussed at pages 216-218, infra.

    ii.   FRE 1003.   FRE 1003 provides that duplicates may be furnished instead of an original in most circumstances. FRE 1001(e) broadly defines *duplicate* to include photocopies, which are commonly used. CD versions of audio recordings originally made on a digital memory chip can be admitted as duplicates. Enhanced copies of recordings also qualify as duplicates. In United States v. Seifert, 351 F. Supp. 2d 926, 928 (D. Minn. 2005), the court admitted a digitally enhanced copy of a surveillance videotape as a duplicate pursuant to FRE 1001(4) (now FRE 1001(e)), finding that the copy was a "fair and accurate depiction of the original .... The enhancements more readily reveal, but remain true to, the recorded events." The technician testified to all of the steps used to enhance the image, including changing the tape from analog to digital, correcting the images to real time, enlarging the objects of interest to fill the screen, and adjusting brightness and contrast. Concerns about whether a recording is of such poor quality that it cannot be understood by the jury are determined under Rule 403, once the recording has been authenticated.

    FRE 1003 provides that a duplicate may not be used if the opponent presents evidence that disputes the authenticity of the original, or if other aspects of the original or duplicate—incompleteness, erasures, defects—make it unfair for the proponent to use the duplicate. In Ruberto v. Commissioner, 774 F.2d 61 (2d Cir. 1985), for example, photocopies of cancelled checks were excluded as duplicates because the copies of the backs of the checks, where the endorsement would be visible, could not be matched to the copies of the fronts of the checks. But in United States v. Sinclair, 74 F.3d 753, 760-761 (7th Cir. 1996), the court upheld admission of photocopies of the defendant's allegedly false expense account reports submitted to his employer, although the copies did not reproduce the reverse side of the originals. The court found that the omitted portions would not have affected the usefulness of the copies since all they would have shown were itemizations of less than $200 out of thousands of dollars of claimed expenses.

    iii.   FRE 1004.   FRE 1004 provides the standard catalog of common law exceptions that justify or explain why a proponent should not be required to produce an original. Loss or destruction of the original, pursuant to FRE 1004(a), may be proved by testimony from a person with knowledge, or by circumstantial evidence that the proponent has made a reasonable, diligent, and unsuccessful search for the original. The proponent need not explain with absolute certainty what happened to the original, but has the burden to prove that its loss or destruction was not in bad faith.[6] Negligent destruction of documents has been held insufficient to establish bad faith. Cross v. United States, 149 F.3d 1190 (10th Cir. 1998) (the purposeful destruction or withholding of original documents and the fabrication of secondary evidence will support a finding of bad faith under FRE 1004).

---

    5.   Consistent with case law, the restyled rule makes explicit that an "original" can be generated from all forms of electronically stored information, not just computers.
    6.   The restyled rule now seems to allocate this burden to the proponent explicitly. The drafting of the original rule was less clear but case law has held consistently that the proponent must prove that the loss or destruction was not by the proponent acting in bad faith.

If originals are not lost but are in the possession of others, the court may require the proponent to show that they cannot be obtained by the proponent's reasonable, diligent, and unsuccessful use of judicial process or other inquiry pursuant to FRE 1004(b). United States v. Crisp, 190 F.R.D. 546, 553 (E.D. Cal. 1999) (government's mere allegation that taxpayers did not produce business records that were returned to them held to be insufficient). If the original is in the possession of the opponent, then, pursuant to the requirements of FRE 1004(c), secondary evidence of its content may be offered if the opponent was on notice that the original[7] would be the subject of proof but failed to produce it at trial. If the opponent has described the content of a writing in testimony, deposition, or in a written admission, FRE 1007 permits the use of this description against that party to prove such content, without accounting for the absence of the original.

It is important to note that Rule 1004 permits the proponent to use any "other evidence" of the content of the original. No preference is given to any particular type of secondary evidence once the original is not available. A common form of secondary evidence is the oral testimony of a witness who once perceived the original and claims to remember it. United States v. Shores, 93 Fed. Appx. 868 (6th Cir. 2004) (police testimony describing photograph in defendant's bedroom admissible under FRE 1004(3) (now 1004(c)) because photograph was still in defendant's possession). All types of copies are also equally acceptable. For example, in United States v. Ross, 33 F.2d 1507 (11th Cir. 1994), transcripts of tape recorded telephone conversations in Spain were admissible as secondary evidence where the recordings had been destroyed in a routine procedure by Spanish police. Official records are an exception to this principle of equal acceptability. FRE 1005 establishes a priority for proof of such official records: A certified copy or a copy that a witness can testify is correct is preferred over other types of secondary evidence. Only if such copies cannot be obtained with "reasonable diligence" may other evidence of contents be given.

iv. FRE 1006. FRE 1006 permits the proponent of voluminous writings, recordings, and photographs to present the contents of these items in the form of a summary, chart, or calculation. These voluminous materials must themselves be shown to be admissible. Peat, Inc. v. Vanguard Research, Inc., 378 F.3d 1154, 1160 (11th Cir. 2004) ("Rule 1006 is not a back-door vehicle for the introduction of evidence which is otherwise inadmissible."). The trial judge has substantial discretion to decide whether the underlying originals are too voluminous to be conveniently examined in court. United States v. Hart, 2009 WL 2552347 (W.D. Ky.) (summary of relevant portions of chat logs admitted when presenting entirety of each chat log would encompass days' worth of material, some of it irrelevant).

The proponent is obligated to produce the originals in time to permit the opponent to examine and copy them, obviously to check the summary for any errors or inconsistencies, and for purposes of cross-examination. Courts are strict in enforcing this requirement. United States v. Modena, 302 F.3d 626, 633 (6th Cir. 2002) (willingness to provide underlying documents, if requested prior to trial, is inadequate; opponent has absolute right to production of underlying material, and party seeking to use summary must state when and where material may be reviewed even absent a

---

7. The original rule required notice that the "content" would be the subject of proof. The restyled rule's change to the "original" appears to be more specific.

discovery request). If the originals are no longer available, Rule 1006 would not apply, but a summary might be admissible under FRE 1004 as secondary evidence.

b.   The Policies Underlying the Best Evidence Rule

The following opinion of the Ninth Circuit Court of Appeals concerns a party's attempt to offer secondary evidence of detailed drawings when that party's good-faith loss of the originals had not been proved. The opinion discusses the policies that justify requiring production of originals in general, as well as when nonproduction is not excused.

SEILER v. LUCASFILM, LTD.
808 F.2d 1316 (9th Cir. 1986), cert. denied, 484 U.S. 826 (1987)

FARRIS, Circuit Judge.

Lee Seiler, a graphic artist and creator of science fiction creatures, alleged copyright infringement by George Lucas and others who created and produced the science fiction movie *The Empire Strikes Back*. Seiler claimed that creatures known as "Imperial Walkers" which appeared in *The Empire Strikes Back* infringed Seiler's copyright on his own creatures called "Garthian Striders." *The Empire Strikes Back* appeared in 1980; Seiler did not obtain his copyright until 1981....

FACTS

Seiler contends that he created and published in 1976 and 1977 [drawings of] science fiction creatures called Garthian Striders. In 1980, George Lucas released *The Empire Strikes Back*, a motion picture that contains a battle sequence depicting giant machines called Imperial Walkers. In 1981 Seiler obtained a copyright on his Striders, depositing with the Copyright Office "reconstructions" of the originals as they had appeared in 1976 and 1977.

Seiler contends that Lucas' Walkers were copied from Seiler's Striders which were allegedly published in 1976 and 1977. Lucas responds that Seiler did not obtain his copyright until one year after the release of *The Empire Strikes Back* and that Seiler can produce no documents that antedate *The Empire Strikes Back*.

Because Seiler proposed to exhibit his Striders in a blow-up comparison to Lucas' Walkers at opening statement, the district judge held an evidentiary hearing on the admissibility of the "reconstructions" of Seiler's Striders. Applying the "best evidence rule," Fed. R. Evid. 1001-1008, the district court found at the end of a seven-day hearing that Seiler lost or destroyed the originals in bad faith under Rule 1004(1) and that consequently no secondary evidence, such as the post-*Empire Strikes Back* reconstructions, was admissible. In its opinion the court found specifically that Seiler testified falsely, purposefully destroyed or withheld in bad faith the originals, and fabricated and misrepresented the nature of his reconstructions. The district court granted summary judgment to Lucas after the evidentiary hearing.

On appeal, Seiler contends (1) that the best evidence rule does not apply to his works, [and] (2) that if the best evidence rule does apply, Rule 1008 requires a jury determination of the existence and authenticity of his originals....[8]

DISCUSSION

1. APPLICATION OF THE BEST EVIDENCE RULE

... We hold that Seiler's drawings were "writings" within the meaning of Rule 1001(1); they consist not of "letters, words, or numbers" but of "their equivalent." To hold otherwise would frustrate the policies underlying the rule and introduce undesirable inconsistencies into the application of the rule. . . .

In the days before liberal rules of discovery and modern techniques of electronic copying, the rule guarded against incomplete or fraudulent proof. By requiring the possessor of the original to produce it, the rule prevented the introduction of altered copies and the withholding of originals. The purpose of the rule was thus long thought to be one of fraud prevention, but Wigmore pointed out that the rule operated even in cases where fraud was not at issue, such as where secondary evidence is not admitted even though its proponent acts in utmost good faith. Wigmore also noted that if prevention of fraud were the foundation of the rule, it should apply to objects as well as writings, which it does not. . . .

The modern justification for the rule has expanded from prevention of fraud to a recognition that writings occupy a central position in the law. When the contents of a writing are at issue, oral testimony as to the terms of the writing is subject to a greater risk of error than oral testimony as to events or other situations. The human memory is not often capable of reciting the precise terms of a writing, and when the terms are in dispute only the writing itself, or a true copy, provides reliable evidence. To summarize . . . the importance of the precise terms of writings in the world of legal relations, the fallibility of the human memory as reliable evidence of the terms, and the hazards of inaccurate or incomplete duplication are the concerns addressed by the best evidence rule. . . .

. . . The contents of Seiler's work are at issue. There can be no proof of "substantial similarity" and thus of copyright infringement unless Seiler's works are juxtaposed with Lucas' and their contents compared. Since the contents are material and must be proved, Seiler must either produce the original or show that it is unavailable through no fault of his own. Rule 1004(1). This he could not do.

The facts of this case implicate the very concerns that justify the best evidence rule. Seiler alleges infringement by *The Empire Strikes Back*, but he can produce no documentary evidence of any originals existing before the release of the movie. His secondary evidence does not consist of true copies or exact duplicates but of "reconstructions" made after *The Empire Strikes Back*. In short, Seiler claims that the movie infringed his originals, yet he has no proof of those originals.

The dangers of fraud in this situation are clear. The rule would ensure that proof of the infringement claim consists of the works alleged to be infringed. Otherwise, "reconstructions" which might have no resemblance to the purported original would suffice as proof for infringement of the original. Furthermore, application of the rule

---

8.   [The Court's decision on the Rule 1008 issue is discussed at pages 222-223, infra.—Eds.]

here defers to the rule's special concern for the contents of writings. Seiler's claim depends on the content of the originals, and the rule would exclude reconstituted proof of the originals' content. Under the circumstances here, no "reconstruction" can substitute for the original.

Seiler argues that the best evidence rule does not apply to his work, in that it is artwork rather than "writings, recordings, or photographs." He contends that the rule both historically and currently embraces only words or numbers. Neither party has cited us to cases which discuss the applicability of the rule to drawings.

To recognize Seiler's works as writings does not, as Seiler argues, run counter to the rule's preoccupation with the centrality of the written word in the world of legal relations. Just as a contract objectively manifests the subjective intent of the makers, so Seiler's drawings are objective manifestations of the creative mind. The copyright laws give legal protection to the objective manifestations of an artist's ideas, just as the law of contract protects through its multifarious principles the meeting of minds evidenced in the contract. Comparing Seiler's drawings with Lucas' drawings is no different in principle than evaluating a contract and the intent behind it. Seiler's "reconstructions" are "writings" that affect legal relations; their copyrightability attests to that.

A creative literary work, which is artwork, and a photograph whose contents are sought to be proved, as in copyright, defamation, or invasion of privacy, are both covered by the best evidence rule. We would be inconsistent to apply the rule to artwork which is literary or photographic but not to artwork of other forms. Furthermore, blueprints, engineering drawings, architectural designs may all lack words or numbers yet still be capable of copyright and susceptible to fraudulent alteration. In short, Seiler's argument would have us restrict the definitions of Rule 1001(1) to "words" and "numbers" but ignore "or their equivalent." We will not do so in the circumstances of this case.

Our holding is also supported by the policy served by the best evidence rule in protecting against faulty memory. Seiler's reconstructions were made four to seven years after the alleged originals; his memory as to specifications and dimensions may have dimmed significantly. Furthermore, reconstructions made after the release of *The Empire Strikes Back* may be tainted, even if unintentionally, by exposure to the movie. Our holding guards against these problems.

PROBLEM

4.23. What if Seiler had not published drawings but had built models of Garthian Striders in 1976 and 1977, and had obtained a copyright based on a reconstruction of those models in 1981? Would the result be different? Do the policies of the best evidence rule apply equally to models?

3.   Elaboration of FRE 1002 and 1006

a.   *When Is a Writing Offered to Prove Its Own Content Under FRE 1002?*

The best evidence rule requires an original only when the proponent is offering a writing, recording, or photograph as relevant *to prove its own content*. When the precise terms of the writing are at issue, accuracy is important and the original would be required. This happens in two principal ways.

i. The Content of the Writing, Recording, or Photograph Is a Fact of Independent Legal Significance.   The content of a writing, recording, or photograph may be a fact of independent legal significance in the case under the applicable substantive law. For example, writings may themselves constitute a crime or tort. In an obscenity prosecution, the content of an allegedly obscene film must be proved as an essential element of the case. United States v. Levine, 546 F.2d 658 (5th Cir. 1977). Similarly, in a libel suit, the allegedly libelous writing is offered to prove that its own contents are libelous. When there are disputes over terms of written agreements (such as contracts, wills, and trusts), and either the substantive law requires the agreement to be proved by the writing or the party chooses to rely on the writing to prove the terms, the best evidence rule applies. For example, in our landlord-tenant hypothetical on page 183, supra, the tenant, Jane, would have had to produce the original written rental agreement in order to prove the landlord's obligation to make improvements. In still other cases, the contents of a document are at issue because they prove notice. Tracinda Corp. v. DaimlerChrysler AG, 2005 U.S. Dist. LEXIS 5096 (D. Del.) (contents of newspaper article at issue when used to prove defendants were aware of the matters reported).

In all of these examples, the writings and recordings are "nonhearsay" statements, relevant as legally operative facts or for their effect on the listener (or viewer), as will be discussed on pages 422-423 of Chapter Eight, infra. As such, their exact content must be proved and Rule 1002 applies.

ii. The Writing, Recording, or Photograph Is Used to Prove an Event. Writings and recordings can provide a record of the happening of many different kinds of events—a business ledger, for example, records what items the salesperson sold and what price was paid. What people have said, for example in testimony they gave at trial, may also be viewed as an event that might be recorded by a stenographer or by a tape recording. When the proponent uses a percipient witness to prove that an event happened, there is no requirement that the proponent produce a recorded version of that event instead. The witness's testimony is being used to prove the *event*, not the *content of a record*. "The fact that a video recording may at times be in fact the 'best' evidence of what occurred does not render first-hand testimony of the event incompetent." Jackim v. Sam's E., Inc., 378 Fed. Appx. 556, 565-566 (6th Cir. 2010). In United States v. Howard, 953 F.2d 610 (11th Cir. 1992), a federal agent could testify about a conversation that he overhead, even though it was also tape recorded. The testimony was offered to prove the contents of the conversation, not the contents of the tape recording.

However, the proponent may *choose* to use a writing, recording, or photograph to prove that an event occurred. For example, in the *Johnson* case, the fight in Johnson's cell was the out-of-court event at issue. It may be proved, as it was in the trial, by oral testimony. But if the prosecutor chooses to use a writing (such as Officer Walker's report) or a recording (such as a videotape) to prove what happened, he would be using the writing or the recording to prove its contents and the original would be required. As you will see in Chapter Eight, if writing is offered to prove that an event happened, it will probably be treated as hearsay and a hearsay exception must be found.

Courts have held that when expert testimony quotes from records to show the basis for the expert's opinion, the records are not being offered to prove their content. Lang v. Cullen, 725 F. Supp. 2d 925, 954 (C.D. Cal. 2010). And when testimony concerning the search of a data base is offered to prove the *absence* of a particular document, in order to prove the *nonhappening* of an event, this testimony is held not to constitute proof of the records' contents. United States v. Lee, 2011 WL 1832545 (W.D.N.Y.).

iii.   Inscriptions on Objects Are Not Writings.   Inscriptions on objects—"chattels" as they are called at common law—are usually not treated as "writings" under FRE 1002, and the best evidence rule does not apply. United States v. Yasmin, 868 F.2d 130 (5th Cir. 1989) ("an object bearing a mark is both a chattel *and* a writing"). Courts have discretion to treat such objects as a writing depending on the need for the exact inscription, the simplicity or complexity of the inscription, and the ease or difficulty of production. United States v. Duffy, 454 F.2d 809 (5th Cir. 1972) (admission of shirt with laundry mark D-U-F found in stolen car did not violate rule where inscription was simple and evidence not critical).

iv.   Facts About the Writing Are Not Its "Content."   In some cases, a writing may be referred to, but it is the fact that the writing exists, and not the precise terms of its content, that the proponent is trying to prove. In these cases, FRE 1002 does not apply. As an example, bank robberies come within the jurisdiction of the federal courts if the bank deposits are insured by the Federal Deposit Insurance Corporation (FDIC). Testimony of a witness that the deposits "are insured" has been held sufficient; production of the original insurance policy is not required. United States v. Sliker, 751 F.2d 477, 483 (2d Cir. 1984) (the proof required is the fact of insurance, not the content of the insurance policy). Testimony *about* a writing, or about an event that happens to be recorded in a writing, can be difficult to distinguish from testimony about the content of a writing. Uncertainty often is resolved by treating a document's contents as "collateral" to the proceeding, and thus excused from the requirement that an original be produced under FRE 1004(e). Jackson v. Crews, 873 F.2d 1105 (8th Cir. 1989) (defendant not using testimony about printed flyer to prove its contents; but if he had been, contents were collateral).

b.   Types of Summaries and Rule 1006

i.   Voluminous Documents Underlying a Summary Must Be Admissible, But Need Not Be Admitted at Trial.   A summary of voluminous documents admitted pursuant to FRE 1006 is itself evidence and obviates the need to introduce the original material into evidence. Therefore, courts have held that when a summary or chart is offered as a Rule 1006 exhibit, the proponent must establish that the documents underlying it are admissible in evidence. United States v. Bray, 139 F.3d 1104, 1109 (6th Cir. 1998) (a chart or summary based on inadmissible hearsay, or on documents that are irrelevant, unfairly prejudicial, or nonauthenticated, would not be admitted). In United States v. Samaniego, 187 F.3d 1222, 1223-1226 (10th Cir. 1999), the Circuit court held that the district court had made an error of law by not requiring the government to prove that the telephone records underlying the proffered summary were admissible as business records under FRE 803(6). The government had to lay the required foundation or forgo the use of the summary. Note that the summary itself is prepared for trial and need not conform to the business record requirements of Rule 803(6), but its mode of preparation must be the subject of testimony. Badgett v. Rent-Way, Inc., 350 F. Supp. 2d 642 (W.D. Pa. 2004).

It is not required, however, that the underlying voluminous materials are *actually* admitted at trial because the rule provides that the summary may substitute for those materials:

> [G]iven Rule 1006's provision that the underlying documents need not themselves be in evidence, however, it is plain that a summary admitted under Rule 1006 is itself the evidence that the trier of fact should consider.... Once a Rule 1006 summary is admitted, it may go to the jury room, like any other exhibit. [United States v. Bray, 139 F.3d at 1109.]

ii. Illustrative Aids.   To be distinguished from Rule 1006 summaries are summaries and charts that are used simply as "illustrative" or "pedagogical" aids to summarize and display the testimony of a witness or documentary evidence that has already been admitted at trial. Id. at 1111-1112 (describing pedagogic devices, or illustrative aids such as chalkboard outlines, flip charts, or drawings). Such devices are not within the terms of FRE 1006. In re Viagra Products Liab. Litig., 658 F. Supp. 2d 950, 967 (D. Minn. 2009) (excluding an expert witness's "chronology" because it "does not summarize 700,000 documents, but instead chooses a few documents among many to highlight. . . . [T]here is no evidence that the jury could not be presented with these same documents and draw from them the relevant regulatory history of Viagra"). The use of such aids, and the foundation for their accuracy, is controlled by the trial judge pursuant to FRE 611(a) and FRE 403. There is authority that these aids should not be admitted into evidence as exhibits and should not be taken into the jury room. United States v. Buck, 324 F.3d 786 (5th Cir. 2003). Many courts endorse the use of illustrative aids as a trial management technique "so long as an appropriate limiting instruction informs the jury that the chart itself is not evidence but is only an aid in evaluating the evidence." United States v. DeBoer, 966 F.2d 1066, 1069 (6th Cir. 1992).

iii. Analytic Summaries.   A third type of summary or chart combines the characteristics of a Rule 1006 exhibit and a Rule 611(a) illustrative aid. That is, these summaries are not merely illustrative because they contain an analysis, made by the person who created the summary, of data that has already been admitted into evidence. The accuracy of such analytic summaries should be screened by the court. United States v. Taylor, 210 F.3d 311, 315 (5th Cir. 2000) (reversible error to admit an "organizational chart" of a drug conspiracy that did not accurately reflect the underlying testimony). And an analytic summary may not reflect assumptions, inferences, or projections about the evidence without accompanying expert testimony. Eichorn v. AT&T Corp., 484 F.3d 644 (3d Cir. 2007). Circuit courts are split on whether this type of summary should be admitted into evidence as an exhibit under Rule 1006, in addition to the underlying data. Either way, the jury is instructed that the summary is not independent evidence of its subject matter, that it is only as valid and reliable as the underlying evidence it summarizes, and should be disregarded if the jury finds it inaccurate. United States v. Armstrong, 619 F.3d 380 (5th Cir. 2010).

KEY POINTS

1. FRE 1002 requires the proponent of a writing, recording, or photograph to produce the original item when the proponent is trying to prove the content of the item. This requirement applies when the content of the item has independent legal significance or when the item is the record of an event and the proponent has chosen it as the means of proving the event.

2. FRE 1003 permits the proponent to produce a duplicate instead of the original in most circumstances.

3. FRE 1004 permits the proponent to produce secondary evidence of the original if the absence of the original can be explained or justified. No particular type of secondary evidence is preferred. Only FRE 1005 states a preference for certified or compared copies of public records.

4. FRE 1006 permits the use of summaries of voluminous writings, recordings, and photographs without the admission of the originals into evidence. The originals or duplicates must, however, be available to the opponent. A summary admitted under Rule 1006 is itself substantive evidence.

PROBLEMS

4.24. Return to Problem 4.19, United States v. Ray, at page 205. Does FRE 1002 apply to the government's offer of Exhibits 1 and 2? Why? Do Exhibits 1 and 2 satisfy FRE 1002? Could the government prove Ray's stock sale on March 16, 2009, by calling Ray's stock broker as a witness and asking her whether she sold Ray's 100,000 shares of Rundown stock at his direction March 16th? Would this violate FRE 1002?

4.25. Defendant Smith was convicted of the crime of being a felon in possession of a firearm under 18 U.S.C. §922(g). One element of this crime is that the firearm had traveled in interstate commerce. To prove this element, the district court admitted the testimony of Agent Andrews of the Bureau of Alcohol, Tobacco, Firearms and Explosives (ATF). The Agent testified that "based on [his] training and experience," he was able to determine that "Smith's Talon Industries Model T200 pistol was manufactured in Montana." On cross-examination, the Agent acknowledged that he had never been to the factory in Montana, nor had he talked to any of the employees at that factory, but that he had consulted an ATF computerized database that had been compiled "over many, many years as agents have done this practice and had communication with various firearms manufacturers from around the world." Defendant Smith has appealed on the ground that Smith's testimony was inadmissible in violation of FRE 1002. What result?

4.26. Workman, a dentist, was indicted for his participation in a scheme to conceal his income and assets from the Internal Revenue Service. In 1991, before the indictment was issued, Workman was interviewed by Donna Jackson, a lawyer representing Workman's wife in their divorce proceedings. The conversation, in which Workman made statements about concealing assets, was tape recorded. Ms. Jackson also took notes. Ms. Jackson's secretary, who was not present at the interview, typed a transcription of the conversation based on the tape recording. Assume that the tape, the notes, the transcript, Jackson, and her secretary are still available. What are the several ways in which the prosecution could present the content of the 1991 conversation at Workman's trial? Would any of the best evidence rules apply?

The prosecution now learns that Ms. Jackson erased the tape in the ordinary course of business, lost her notes, and does not remember the contents of the conversation. Can the transcript be admitted into evidence?

4.27. In a wrongful death case alleging that the defendant driver was intoxicated when his car crossed a median strip in a divided highway, causing a head-on collision with the plaintiff's intestate, the plaintiff offers testimony from the state police officer who was first on the scene of the accident. The officer would testify that when he approached the defendant's car, he saw several empty bottles of Budweiser beer on the front seat. Must the plaintiff produce the original labels and bottles?

4.28. Return to Problem 4.6 at page 192. To prove that Jim Zeal and Stephani Goldstein were conspiring to import marijuana from outside of the United States, the prosecution offers the testimony of Ensign Chandler who also boarded the *Rastafari*. Chandler will testify that he discovered a global positioning system (GPS) in the boat; that a GPS device uses global positioning satellites to track and record the location of any device and therefore the location of an object, such as the boat, to which the device is attached; and that the backtrack feature on the GPS graphed the *Rastafari's* journey from Kingston, Jamaica, to the point at which it was seized by the Coast Guard. Chandler will have to admit that he did not seize the GPS or obtain any record of the data he observed as a display on its screen. The defendants object on the grounds that Chandler's testimony violates the best evidence rule. What result?

4.29. In a libel suit, the plaintiff alleges that the defendant sent a typewritten letter to plaintiff's employer with defendant's signature on it, stating that plaintiff was a liar and thief. The plaintiff offers a black and white photocopy of the letter into evidence, properly authenticated by the employer's assistant who made the photocopy from the original letter as soon as it was received. The defendant claims that the signature is not his and objects pursuant to FRE 1002 and 1003 that the copy is inadequate for handwriting analysis of the signature since he always used a special colored ink. What result? What if the assistant testifies that he made a thorough search for the original that proved fruitless? Would this make the copy admissible? Or could the plaintiff testify as to the contents of the letter and forget about the photocopy?

4.   FRE 1008

RULE 1008.   FUNCTIONS OF THE COURT AND JURY

Ordinarily, the court determines whether the proponent has fulfilled the factual conditions for admitting other evidence of the content of a writing, recording, or photograph under Rule 1004 or 1005. But in a jury trial, the jury determines—in accordance with Rule 104(b)—any issue about whether:
(a) an asserted writing, recording, or photograph ever existed;
(b) another one produced at the trial or hearing is the original; or
(c) other evidence of content accurately reflects the content.

5.   Interpretation and Illustration of FRE 1008

FRE 1008 makes a specific allocation of fact finding between judge and jury in the application of the best evidence rules. The judge's general authority to make the preliminary determinations that are necessary to apply all of the rules of evidence is established in FRE 104. We discuss this general authority under Rule 104 in detail, in Section D, infra. Reading Section D will aid in understanding Rule 1008.

As the first sentence of Rule 1008 indicates, preliminary facts necessary to the application of FRE 1001-1007 are questions for the judge to decide under Rule 104(a) *unless* FRE 1008(a), (b) or (c) applies. Here are some of the preliminary issues that may arise under these rules:[9]

(1) whether an offered writing, recording or photograph is an "original" under Rule 1001(d);

(2) whether a given writing, recording or photograph qualifies as a duplicate and is thus presumptively admissible under Rules 1001(e) and 1003;

(3) whether a genuine question is raised as to the authenticity of the original for purposes of Rule 1003;

(4) whether an original is lost or destroyed, and whether a diligent search has been conducted for the original under Rule 1004(a);

(5) whether the proponent lost or destroyed evidence in bad faith;

(6) whether an original can be obtained by any available judicial process under Rule 1004(b); and

(7) whether an adverse party has possession or control over the original and, if so, whether proper notice was given to that party under Rule 1004(c).

If these questions of fact are disputed, the judge is to decide them pursuant to FRE 104(a), by a preponderance of the evidence, as we discuss in Section D, infra.

However, the second sentence of Rule 1008 provides that three specific factual questions are for the trier of fact to determine "in accordance with Rule 104(b)." This means that the judge should not decide the question by a preponderance of the evidence, but should determine only whether there is sufficient evidence to support a jury finding on the matter. See page 229, infra. If there is, the question should be given to the jury to decide. The Advisory Committee Note to Rule 1008 explains that these are questions that "go beyond the mere administration of the rule preferring the original and into the merits of the controversy." In Tinley v. Poly-Triplex Technologies, Inc., 2009 WL 812150 (D. Colo. 2009), the court denied summary judgment in a dispute over the existence of a contract that was central to the outcome of the case. The existence of the contract was supported by little more than the parties' own conflicting testimony, and the witnesses' credibility was properly for a jury to decide.

In the opinion in Seiler v. Lucasfilm, Ltd., supra, the appellate court held that the district court had correctly concluded that the best evidence rule did apply to Seiler's drawings. Therefore, Seiler had to produce his original drawings unless excused pursuant to FRE 1004(a). The district judge had decided under FRE 1004(a) and FRE 104(a) that Seiler had destroyed all originals of his drawings in bad faith, obviously taking Seiler's credibility into account. This ruling meant that Seiler's nonproduction of his original drawings was not excused, and therefore no secondary evidence of their contents (his reconstructions) could be admitted. Seiler, however, contended that the judge was required to give to the jury the question under FRE 1008(c) whether "other evidence of contents" (his reconstructions) correctly reflected the contents of his original drawings, and thus had to admit his reconstructions. The appellate

---

9. This list is based on a similar list set forth in Stephen Saltzburg, Michael M. Martin, and Daniel J. Capra, 3 Federal Rules of Evidence Manual 2096-2097 (7th ed. 1998).

court held, however, that the Rule 1008(c) did not come into play unless the district court had decided the Rule 1004(a) issue in Seiler's favor. If the district judge had decided that Seiler's loss of his original drawings was in good faith, the judge would not then be permitted to refuse admission to Seiler's reproductions because the court did not believe that the reconstructions genuinely reflected Seiler's originals. It would be for the jury to resolve this issue under FRE 1008(c). In a similar case, Lowry's Reports, Inc. v. Legg Mason, Inc., 271 F. Supp. 2d 737, 756 (N.D. Md. 2003), the court acknowledged that the jury, not the court, "determines whether the original existed and whether other evidence accurately reflects its terms .... Nevertheless, the court must first determine whether there is sufficient evidence of good-faith loss or destruction...."

KEY POINTS

1. FRE 1008 provides that most preliminary questions of fact under the best evidence rules are for the judge to decide pursuant to FRE 104(a), and the judge will admit or exclude the offered evidence accordingly.

2. If the opponent properly raises an issue as to the existence of or the true content of the original, then that question of fact must go to the jury under FRE 104(b), and the judge must admit the evidence to permit the jury to decide it.

PROBLEM

4.30. Flanagan sues Zeppelin Electric Products, Inc., alleging that an oral agreement was made whereby Flanagan would remove gravel from Zeppelin's lot for consideration of $65 per hour. Flanagan and his crew toiled away until the gravel was completely removed. Zeppelin refused to pay Flanagan's bill, disputing the actual number of hours worked. At trial Flanagan offers into evidence a summary of data that he says he transcribed each week from tally sheets recorded at the worksite, indicating the number of hours worked by each employee. He claims that the tally sheets were discarded or lost. Defense counsel objects on the ground that the summary violates the best evidence rule and claims that the so-called tally sheets probably never existed. What result under FRE 1004, 1006, and 1008? What fact questions would the judge instruct the jury to decide?

D.   JUDICIAL FACT-FINDING UNDER FRE 104

FRE 104 establishes the power of the judge to decide preliminary questions concerning the admissibility of evidence and the process by which these questions are to be decided. It is an important rule, and you will want to reread this section as you encounter it throughout the course. We discuss it here because you have now become familiar with several rules of evidence that illustrate the different kinds of decisions that judges make under Rule 104. In particular, we focus here on judicial fact-finding pursuant to Rule 104(a).

1.   FRE 104

RULE 104.   PRELIMINARY QUESTIONS

(a) *In General.* The court must decide any preliminary question about whether a witness is qualified, a privilege exists, or evidence is admissible. In so deciding, the court is not bound by evidence rules, except those on privilege.

(b) *Relevance That Depends on a Fact.* When the relevance of evidence depends on whether a fact exists, proof must be introduced sufficient to support a finding that the fact does exist. The court may admit the proposed evidence on the condition that the proof be introduced later.

(c) *Conducting a Hearing So That the Jury Cannot Hear It.* The court must conduct any hearing on a preliminary question so that the jury cannot hear it if:

(1) the hearing involves the admissibility of a confession;

(2) a defendant in a criminal case is a witness and so requests; or

(3) justice so requires.

(d) *Cross-Examining a Defendant in a Criminal Case.* By testifying on a preliminary question, a defendant in a criminal case does not become subject to cross-examination on other issues in the case.

(e) *Evidence Relevant to Weight and Credibility.* This rule does not limit a party's right to introduce before the jury evidence that is relevant to the weight or credibility of other evidence.

2.   Interpretation and Illustration of FRE 104(a)

a.   *Questions of Admissibility Generally*

The trial judge's decision to admit or exclude an item of evidence always requires the judge to answer one or more preliminary questions necessary to the application of the rules of evidence. There are at least three kinds of preliminary questions: questions of law, questions of fact, and questions that require the exercise of discretion. FRE 104(a) provides that, in general, all of these preliminary questions are to be decided by the court.

For example, application of the best evidence rules discussed in Section C required the trial court in the *Seiler* case to determine whether Seiler had lost or destroyed his original drawings in bad faith. This required the court to find the facts about Seiler's conduct and then to apply the legal standard of "bad faith" to those facts. As another example, FRE 403 presents several questions of law for a court, such as what is the meaning of the term *unfair prejudice*; that is, what dangers to jury reasoning does that term include? Rule 403 also requires judicial discretion: estimating the probative value of an item of evidence; evaluating the degree of danger to jury reasoning; and determining whether the danger "substantially" predominates over probative value.

As you study the Federal Rules of Evidence throughout this course, you should be able to identify, usually from the text of the rules themselves, whether the judge is deciding questions of law or fact, or is exercising discretion, in applying each rule. This is not an abstract exercise. As an advocate, you must be prepared to make your offers of proof and arguments to help the judge perform each kind of decision-making task.

b.   Judicial Fact-finding Under FRE 104(a)

The application of many evidence rules requires determination of preliminary questions of fact that are for the judge to decide pursuant to Rule 104(a). Under the best evidence rules, if a party asserts that *a testator's original will existed but was destroyed in a fire*, that is a question of fact that must be decided in order to determine, under FRE 1004(a), whether nonproduction of the original is excused. Another example that may be familiar to you is the evidence rule that creates a "privilege" for communications between attorney and client, meaning that such communications are not admissible at trial. Application of the privilege, in order to secure exclusion of the communication, requires determination of the preliminary fact question that the communication was *made during the attorney-client relationship.*

FRE 104(a) states the general principle that preliminary questions of fact shall be determined by the court, but it does not contain an explicit standard of proof. The Supreme Court has held that judges are to decide preliminary questions of fact under FRE 104(a) "by a preponderance of the evidence" *in both civil and criminal cases.* Bourjaily v. United States, 483 U.S. 171, 175 (1987).

> Evidence is placed before the jury when it satisfies the technical requirements of the evidentiary Rules, which embody certain legal and policy determinations. The [admissibility] inquiry . . . is not whether the proponent of the evidence wins or loses his case on the merits, but whether the evidentiary Rules have been satisfied. Thus, the evidentiary standard is unrelated to the burden of proof on the substantive issues, be it a criminal case . . . or a civil case. . . . The preponderance standard ensures that before admitting evidence, the court will have found it more likely than not that [the facts that are necessary to] the technical issues and policy concerns addressed by the Federal Rules of Evidence have been afforded the consideration. [Id.]

Thus, Rule 104(a) imposes a persuasion burden on preliminary fact questions. Typically, the proponent, the party asserting that application of an evidence rule permits admission of an item, must bear this burden. The proponent must produce evidence that actually persuades the judge that the preliminary fact is more probable than not. If it is the opponent who is using an evidence rule to exclude an item—such as the application of the attorney-client privilege—the opponent then bears the burden of satisfying the application of the exclusionary rule.

The persuasion burden under Rule 104(a) means that the judge must be persuaded that it is more likely than not that the preliminary fact is true—in our examples, that the testator's original will was destroyed by fire, or that the client's attorney-client communication was made during the relationship. In making this decision, the judge is the fact finder and takes the credibility of witnesses into account. And, by the terms of Rule 104(a), the judge is not bound by the rules of evidence, except for privileges. This means that the judge may take otherwise inadmissible evidence, such as hearsay, into account. As we shall see in Chapter Eight, this also means that the judge may take the contents of the proffered item itself into account, even though it has not yet been admitted. If the judge is not persuaded on the preliminary question of fact, the judge will not apply the rule in favor of the party seeking application of the rule; in our two examples, the judge would not admit secondary evidence because nonproduction of the original will would not be excused; and the judge would not exclude the attorney-client communication.

c.   *The Process of Decision Under FRE 104(a)*

There are well-accepted procedures that govern judicial decisions of preliminary fact questions under FRE 104(a), although the rule does not state many specifics. When the parties are in dispute over a preliminary question of fact, both sides may present evidence to the judge on the factual issue. This may take place in front of the jury or outside the presence of the jury to protect it from hearing inadmissible evidence. Rule 104(c) leaves the question whether to hold such a hearing to the discretion of the judge, except with regard to the voluntariness of a confession.

The jury is not instructed to re-decide the preliminary question. Nor is the jury ever told what preliminary facts the judge has found. In United States v. Tracy, 12 F.3d 1186 (2d Cir. 1993), for example, the court held that the trial judge erred in telling the jury that, since the fact of conspiracy had been proved to his satisfaction, the statements of alleged co-conspirators were admissible under an exception to the hearsay rule. When the judge is persuaded about a Rule 104(a) preliminary fact and admits an offered item, the opponent may still challenge the admitted item's weight and credibility, and may introduce evidence that reduces its probative value, as provided by FRE 104(e). Such evidence may also challenge the existence of the preliminary fact, but the jury is not instructed to redecide the preliminary question.

You can see that decision-making on preliminary questions necessary to the admission of evidence could absorb a great deal of trial time and energy. Even if the jury is excluded from FRE 104(c) hearings, the jury's time is wasted. There are two principal devices for resolving these issues before trial. In civil cases, many judges require that disputes over the admissibility of evidence be resolved through pretrial discovery and agreements reached at pretrial conferences. In both civil and criminal cases, motions in limine can be filed to seek determinations of admissibility and exclusion of particular evidence before trial. But sometimes preliminary issues catch both parties and the judge by surprise, and considerable trial time can be spent deciding them.

NOTE

The classic treatment of the policies underlying the division of authority between judge and jury on most preliminary questions is John M. Maguire and Charles S. Epstein, Preliminary Questions of Fact in Determining the Admissibility of Evidence, 40 Harv. L. Rev. 392 (1927). These authors conclude that authority over preliminary questions is justifiably allocated to judges, as FRE 104(a) does, for several reasons: (1) to reduce the complexity of jury trials (by not having to instruct juries on preliminary fact questions); (2) to expedite the trial process by eliminating these questions from trial; (3) to increase the predictability of the outcomes of admissibility decisions (because judges will decide preliminary questions and make admissibility decisions at the same time); (4) to preserve issues in a clear and coherent fashion for appeal (because rulings by judges under FRE 104(a) are on the record and can be appealed); and (5) to promote the substantive concerns underlying the various exclusionary policies of the rules of evidence (by giving to the judge *rather than to the jury* the authority to decide whether exclusionary policies apply). While each of these reasons makes some sense, the most powerful justification is that *preliminary questions of fact connected to the policies* of evidence law should be decided by the court. When evidence is excluded by the character or hearsay rules because it may reduce the rationality of jury decision-making, there is a persuasive reason to give the exclusion decision to the judge exclusively. If the FRE 104(b) sufficiency standard were employed, "the legal policy underlying the hearsay rule would be furthered incompletely, if at all." State v. Carlson, 808 P.2d 1002, 1009 (Or. 1991).

Additional readings on preliminary fact-finding in general and the policies underlying Rule 104 and its application are Norman M. Garland and Jay A. Schmitz, Of Judges and Juries: A Proposed Revision of Federal Rule of Evidence 104, 23 U.C. Davis L. Rev. 77 (1989); John Kaplan, Of Mabrus and Zorgs—An Essay in Honor of David Louisell, 66 Cal. L. Rev. 987 (1978); Stephen A. Saltzburg, Standards of Proof and Preliminary Questions of Fact, 27 Stan. L. Rev. 271 (1975).

KEY POINTS

1. Most preliminary questions of fact raised by the application of the rules of evidence to decide the admissibility of an offered item are for the judge to decide pursuant to FRE 104(a).

2. Both parties may present evidence on FRE 104(a) preliminary questions of fact, and the judge must be persuaded by a preponderance of the evidence by the party asserting the application of the rule.

3. In deciding preliminary questions pursuant to FRE 104(a), the judge may consider evidence that would not be admissible under the rules of evidence, but may not consider privileged evidence.

4. After the judge decides the preliminary question under FRE 104(a), the judge either admits or excludes the item. The judge does not inform the jury about the decision on the preliminary question.

5. The opponent may attempt to reduce the item's probative value, if the item of evidence is admitted, with evidence that the preliminary fact is not true, but the jury does not redecide the preliminary question.

E.   FRE 104, CONDITIONAL ADMISSIBILITY, AND THE PROBLEM OF CONDITIONAL RELEVANCY

Determining the relevancy of an offered item of evidence pursuant to FRE 401 and 402 sometimes raises a question about one or more related issues of fact. For example, in the *Johnson* case on page 44, line 6, defense counsel objected that the testimony of Johnson's cellmate, Butler, that Butler himself belonged to a gang, the Crips, was not relevant. There was a related issue of fact that was missing—whether defendant Johnson was also a member of the Crips. Without some evidence that Johnson also belonged to the same gang, Butler's testimony about his own gang membership would not be relevant to prove that Butler had a specific motive to lie to help Johnson, his fellow gang member.

Most offered items of evidence require additional contextual facts to link them to the dispute. And all items of evidence require the use of generalized propositions of fact that support the inferences necessary to reach a fact of consequence. These generalizations could be made a matter of proof if the judge is skeptical about whether they are reasonable. For example, generalized knowledge about the guards' glove-wearing practices in Facility B might have been necessary to establish the relevance of inmate Butler's offered testimony that the guards were wearing gloves on page 43, line 6.

1.   Interpretation and Illustration of FRE 104(b)

FRE 104(b) speaks to this issue of related facts being necessary to relevancy in two ways:

> *Relevance That Depends on a Fact.* When the relevance of evidence depends on whether a fact exists, proof must be introduced sufficient to support a finding that the fact does exist. The court may admit the proposed evidence on the condition that the proof be introduced later.

First, Rule 104(b) explicitly approves the "conditional admissibility" of offered items when additional facts or generalizations are necessary to establish their relevance. Second, the rule appears to establish the "sufficiency" standard of proof for the determination of those additional facts or generalizations. We shall discuss both meanings of the rule.

a.   Conditional Admissibility

The missing fact of Johnson's membership in the Crips was supposed to be the subject of additional testimony from Lieutenant Stokes. If needed, the guards' glove-wearing practices could have been the subject of testimony from a Pelican Bay guard. But this additional testimony could not be given until inmate Butler, who was testifying about the *offered items* (that he was a Crip and that the guards were wearing gloves) left the witness stand. So how could the judge obtain the evidence necessary to determine whether the offered items were relevant while Butler was still testifying?

This problem can be resolved by *conditional admissibility*, a process by which an item of evidence can be admitted provisionally, subject to the proponent's later production of additional evidence. The judge did admit inmate Butler's offered testimony of his own gang membership "conditioned upon" Lieutenant Stokes's testimony about Johnson's gang membership. FRE 104(b) explicitly permits this practice. If the necessary evidence is not subsequently produced, the judge should strike the conditionally admitted item from the record and instruct the jury not to consider it. In fact, Butler's testimony that he was a Crip should have been struck from the record because the prosecution offered no evidence that defendant Johnson was also a Crip. However, the defense never requested that this testimony be struck.

Of course, the opponent to the offered item may be convinced that the proponent actually has no evidence of the additional fact and could be concerned that the jury will not later disregard the item that has been admitted "conditionally" despite the judge's instruction to do so. The opponent can state this concern to the trial judge and ask the judge to require the proponent to produce the necessary evidence before any admissibility decision is made. Normally, however, the judge will let each party present the evidence in the order in which each sees fit.

There are other situations in which evidence is admitted "conditioned upon" the proponent offering additional proof. For example, when judges balance probative value versus a danger under FRE 403, the full probative value of the evidence, its full measure of danger, or the proponent's need for it, may not be apparent until additional evidence is taken in the case. Here, the court's ability to admit the offered item conditioned upon subsequent proof that enhances its probative value or reduces its Rule 403 danger is extremely useful.

The device of conditional admissibility thus includes admitting an item of evidence provisionally and controlling the order of proof if necessary. If the proponent of the conditionally admitted item fails to provide the necessary required proof of the additional fact, the item of evidence should be excluded and the jury instructed to disregard that item. United States v. Anderson, 933 F.2d 1261 (5th Cir. 1991) (reversal of arson conviction required when trial court failed to exclude evidence of four previous fires that had been admitted conditionally; the government failed to prove necessary the facts that the four previous fires were arson and that defendant was involved).

b.   The Problem of Conditional Relevancy: The "Sufficiency" Standard of Proof in FRE 104(b)

The text of FRE 104(b) also seems to require proof of the additional facts that are necessary to relevance by "evidence sufficient to support a finding." This appears to be a higher standard than the "any tendency" standard stated in FRE 401. And so, this language has led to the identification of a special evidence doctrine that suggests there is a *special class of identifiable cases of "conditional relevance"* where the relevance of an offered item of evidence depends on the existence of some other fact. For this class of cases, the other fact then has to be proved under the "sufficiency" standard. However, as we have stated above, *most* offered items require additional facts to link them to the case at hand, and *all* offered items of course require generalizations to support their relevance. Thus, the question arises as to whether Rule 104(b) should be applied by courts to a *special class* of disputes about relevance.

This result would seem to contravene both the letter and the spirit of minimal relevance standard of Rule 401. Remember, relevance does not mean sufficiency; "any tendency" does not mean "could reasonably be more probable than not." FRE 104(b), however, would appear to require the judge to apply the higher threshold of sufficiency. If no "conditional relevance" issue is raised by the parties, the court would typically treat the relevance of offered items of evidence as a Rule 401 question. If the issue is raised by an opponent's objection, a fact necessary to relevance may become a 104(b) question if the objecting lawyer persuades the judge that Rule 104(b) applies and the judge thinks that the necessary fact is sufficiently important and disputed.

2.   Elaboration of FRE 104(b): The Rule in Practice

In actual practice, however, there are very few reported cases in which preliminary questions of fact are identified and formally decided under FRE 104(b). The reported federal cases raise questions of *notice*, e.g., United States v. Ansaldi, 372 F.3d 118, 130-131 (2d Cir. 2004) (admissibility of an FDA paper on the effects of a date-rape drug depended on evidence sufficient to support a finding that defendant was aware of the contents of the paper) and the *basis for lay or expert opinion testimony*, e.g., United States v. Peays, 2010 U.S. Dist. LEXIS 112947, at *7 (W.D. Pa.) (in pros-ecution of defendant for gun possession, evidence of defendant's cocaine possession necessary pursuant to FRE 104(b) to admit expert testimony from Officer Warfield characterizing guns as "tools of the trade" for drug traffickers). Under the Supreme Court opinion in Huddelston v. United States, 485 U.S. 681 (1988), the sufficiency standard of FRE 104(b) applies to the determination whether a specific act was com-mitted, and by whom, pursuant to FRE 404(b), as discussed on page 247 of Chapter Five, infra.

In Gierlinger v. Gleason, 1995 U.S. Dist. LEXIS 14723, at *7-11 (W.D.N.Y.), the District Court made use of both aspects of FRE 104(b) discussed above. Gierlinger filed suit against Gleason, her Troop Commander in the New York State Police (NYSP) for sex discrimination and retaliatory discharge under 42 U.S.C. §1983. Her Complaint alleged discriminatory conduct against her at the NYSP Academy and the Wellsville Station, as well as within her Troop. Prior to trial, the court considered whether Gleason could be held responsible for the acts of others:

> Gierlinger must prove either (1) Gleason's personal involvement in the alleged acts and/or conditions that amounted to violations of Gierlinger's rights or (2) Gleason's actual knowledge of and acquiescence in the acts and/or conditions that allegedly deprived Gierlinger of her rights. Before any of the enumerated evidence [of conduct at the Academy or Wellsville Station] is relevant and receivable, a proper foundation needs to be laid to establish that Gleason had notice or knowledge of such event, conversation, circumstance, document etc.
>
> *FRE 104(b)* specifically deals with the matter at hand: . . .The relevancy (and there-fore, admissibility) of the listed items depends upon the notice to or knowledge on the part of Gleason of those items. Notice or knowledge can be shown in many ways; either can be shown directly through proof of conversations or documentation, or can be inferred from the notoriety of or widespread and common knowledge regarding an event or condition.
>
> In a case of this type, much of the evidence is very susceptible to emotional responses and reactions by the lay persons who will comprise the jury. . . . Therefore, in order to assist the trial jury in the accurate and effective ascertainment of the truth and to avoid needless consumption of the time of and expense to this Court and the parties and their attorneys, this Court deems it appropriate to require an order, or sequence, of proof.
>
> This Court will require that competent proof be introduced showing that Gleason was personally involved in or had knowledge of a particular event etc. ... whether listed above or otherwise ... as a condition precedent to the admissibility of any evidence thereof. Such proof must be such that a reasonable jury could find that Gleason had such involvement or knowledge, prior to his recommending Gierlinger's termination. [Citing Huddleston v. United States, 485 U.S. 681, 689-690 (1987) (under FRE 104(b) the judge decides "whether the jury could reasonably find the conditional fact . . . by a preponderance of the evidence").]
>
> If such proper evidentiary foundation is provided, such evidence of Gleason's involve-ment or knowledge will be allowed to be presented to the jury. The final determination of Gleason's involvement or knowledge will be made by the jury based upon its deter-mination of the credibility of the witnesses and in light of the pertinent law as explained to them by this Court.

Therefore, without such proper foundation, Gierlinger's testimony about her experiences at the Academy is not admissible; however, her testimony ... will not be ruled inadmissible on relevancy grounds if this Court contemporarily receives assurances from Gierlinger's attorney that he will adduce particular evidence on the basis of which reasonable jurors could infer that Gleason was involved in or knew of such events and/ or Gierlinger's complaints concerning the same prior to his recommendation that Gierlinger's NYSP career be ended—and if such evidence is later adduced.

As illustrated in *Gierlinger*, typically the proponent must present evidence or make an offer of proof as to how the "sufficiency" standard will be satisfied, the same as for FRE 602 and FRE 901. Judges may permit both sides to present evidence and may hold a hearing outside the presence of the jury pursuant to Rule 104(c). All of the evidence for and against the question must be admissible into evidence. In screening the sufficiency of this evidence, the judge may not take witnesses' credibility into account, as discussed on page 180, supra. If the judge finds that there is evidence sufficient to support a finding of the preliminary fact, then the judge will admit the offered item and may instruct the jury that the jury itself first must decide the preliminary question, and must decide it favorably, before using the offered item of evidence in its decision-making. The opponent may contest the preliminary question at trial and argue to the jury that the offered item is irrelevant because the preliminary question is not established.

NOTES AND QUESTIONS

1. Could the results in *Ansaldi*, *Peays*, and *Gierlinger* be accomplished through the use of FRE 403? In each case, the risk of unfair prejudice to the defendant from the offered items seems high if the predicate "conditional facts" were not correct. Could a court require the proponent to increase the probative value of the predicate facts by introducing more evidence to support them, or else risk exclusion of the proffered items?

2. Prior to the Federal Rules of Evidence, judges usually assumed the authority to decide all preliminary questions of fact themselves, pursuant to the preponderance of the evidence standard or even a higher "clear and convincing" standard of proof for some questions. The lower standard of FRE 104(b) protects, at least to some degree, the authority of the jury over fact-finding. If preliminary questions raised by FRE 602 (personal knowledge) and FRE 901 (authentication and identification) were to be decided by the judge under the preponderance standard of FRE 104(a), "the functioning of the jury as a trier of fact would be greatly restricted and in some cases virtually destroyed. These are appropriate questions for juries." Advisory Committee Notes to FRE 104. This policy is consistent with the overarching goal of the Federal Rules: to promote rational decision making through the admission of relevant evidence.

3. Commentators are generally critical of FRE 104(b) insofar as it will result in exclusion of evidence that would be admitted under the lower standard of FRE 401 and that the jury would find useful. Vaughn C. Ball, The Myth of Conditional Relevancy, 14 Ga. L. Rev. 435, 445-454 (1980); Ronald J. Allen, The Myth of Conditional Relevancy, 25 Loyola L.A. L. Rev. 871 (1992); Dale A. Nance, Conditional Relevance Reinterpreted, 70 B.U. L. Rev. 447, 459-462 (1990); Richard Friedman, Conditional Probative Value: Neoclassicism Without Myth, 93 Mich. L. Rev. 439, 449 (1994). But

see David S. Schwartz, A Foundation Theory of Evidence, 100 Geo. L. Rev. 95 (2011) (defending FRE 104(b) and arguing critics are mistaken).

In addition, in even the simplest trials, "much evidence makes sense only in conjunction with other evidence, and at almost every step of the way it would be plausible, in an arid and coldly logical sense, to say that the proof at hand can only make a difference if some other point is proved or accepted on the basis of common experience in the world. Yet stopping a trial to entertain such arguments, decide which point should be proved first, obtain a commitment to prove some other point, assess the sufficiency of proof, and even instruct the jury, would confound trials, confuse everyone, and hamstring lawyers and judges." Christopher B. Mueller and Laird C. Kirkpatrick, Evidence §1.13 (2d ed. 1999).

4. FRE 104(b) could be amended as follows to retain the technique of conditional admissibility—admitting evidence "subject to" additional proof of factual propositions or generalizations that will make it relevant—without deviating from the relevancy standard of FRE 401:

> (b) Relevancy. The court shall admit evidence over a relevancy objection upon, or subject to, a finding that the evidence could rationally influence a reasonable person's assessment of any fact that is of consequence to the determination of the action. [Ronald J. Allen, The Myth of Conditional Relevancy, 25 Loyola L.A. L. Rev. 871, 883-884 (1992).]

A similar revision of FRE 104(b) could focus on "probative value conditional on further evidence"—where an evidentiary fact's probative value is not sufficient to overcome an FRE 403 objection, for example, the court should admit the offered evidence subject to the introduction of additional evidence that increases probative value sufficiently. Friedman, 93 Mich. L. Rev. at 472.

5. In his article A Foundation Theory of Evidence, cited above, Professor Schwartz argues that the criticisms of the concept of conditional relevance under FRE 104(b) are mistaken, and that no amendments to FRE 104(b) are warranted. According to Schwartz, FRE 104(b) simply states a generalized version of a foundation requirement. While this requirement applies to all evidence, a potential conditional relevance objection arises only in the exceptional case where a fact needed to connect an item of evidence to the offering party's theory of the case is missing and cannot be filled in by a background "generalization" from the jury's common knowledge. According to Schwartz, conditional relevance critics misperceive FRE 104(b)'s function as an ordinary foundation requirement when they characterize it as a heightened relevance threshold. The fears that trials will be hamstrung by FRE 104(b) jury findings are greatly exaggerated, because the jury "finding" in the rule is hypothetical, simply supplying the threshold used by the judge to screen evidence if a conditional relevance objection is made.

In a similar vein, it has been argued that FRE 104(b) is a valuable tool that "reflects the [jury's] need to refrain from considering information when the benefits of doing so do not justify the costs that would result." Craig Callen, Rationality and Relevancy: Conditional Relevancy and Constrained Resources, 2003 Mich. St. L. Rev. 1243, 1248. More specifically, Professor Callen contends that Rule 104(b) "limits parties' ability to offer evidence that might not warrant the jury's efforts to evaluate it" by requiring evidence sufficient to support a finding on preliminary conditions of fact "when that evidence (i) significantly lowers the cost of evaluating the proffered evidence or adds to its benefits and (ii) would be likely to be available if the inference that the proffering party wishes to prove were true." Id. at 1301. Would this standard be satisfied by the required proof of "notice or knowledge" in *Gierlinger*?

KEY POINTS

1. If a "factual condition" necessary to establish the relevance of an offered item of evidence is in serious dispute, FRE 104(b) provides that the court may admit the offered item "conditional upon" later proof of the necessary fact.

2. The FRE 104(b) standard is higher than the FRE 401 "any tendency" standard. In some cases, courts require the proponent to satisfy the higher standard of "evidence sufficient to support a finding" in proving a "condition of fact" deemed necessary to the relevance of an offered item of evidence.

3. Both parties may present evidence on FRE 104(b) "factual condition" questions, and the judge must determine whether there is evidence sufficient to support a finding that the preliminary fact is true. In making this decision, the judge may consider only evidence that would be admissible to the jury.

4. After the judge determines the sufficiency of the evidence on the preliminary question under FRE 104(b), as under FRE 602 and 901, the judge either admits or excludes the offered item. The judge does not inform the jury about his or her determination of sufficiency.

5. The opponent may present evidence relevant to disprove the preliminary fact to the jury. The jury will decide the preliminary fact as part of its ultimate decision-making. The judge may instruct the jury that it must decide the preliminary fact question before it can consider the offered item of evidence to which it pertains.

PROBLEMS

4.31. Return to Problem 4.19, United States v. Ray, at page 205. Exhibits 1 and 2 have been admitted into evidence. Exhibit 3 is a photocopy of Exhibit 1. It bears original handwritten initials "BR" on the upper left corner. Government investigators have obtained the following information from interviewing Beth Barker:

> I have been employed as Bernard Ray's executive secretary since 2000. I follow the following practice in handling Mr. Ray's mail, including hand delivered documents. Each work day I place incoming mail and other delivered documents in the "in" box on Mr. Ray's desk at around 10 A.M., around 1:30 P.M. and around 4:00 P.M. At 8:30 A.M. each morning, I take all of the documents in Mr. Ray's "out" box, check to make sure that Mr. Ray has initialed them, and then place them in Mr. Ray's files. Mr. Ray always reads and initials his mail and other documents and puts them in his "out" box. In response to a request from federal investigators, on September 1 of 2010 I found Exhibit 3 in Mr. Ray's files in a folder labeled "Correspondence–Andrews." I recognize the initials "BR" as Mr. Ray's handwriting.

The prosecution offers Exhibit 3 into evidence to prove that Ray read Exhibit 3, bearing Bernard Ray's initials on it, prior to his sale of stock on March 16, 2009. Is there a "conditional relevance" objection to admitting the memo? Is there an argument that the existence of the memo, without more, is sufficient to meet this conditional relevance objection? Would the testimony of Barker be sufficient to meet this conditional relevance objection? What should the trial court do?

4.32. Return to Problem 4.13 on page 200. Would the doctrine of conditional admissibility apply to the government's proof? How? Was a "factual condition" proved under FRE 104(b)? Which fact?

4.33. Plaintiff seeks to prove that defendant Asbestos, Inc. (AI), a manufacturer of asbestos fireproofing material, knew or should have known of the dangers of asbestos before selling its product to Plaintiff, and that AI was therefore liable to Plaintiff for failure to warn. AI sold the asbestos material to Plaintiff in September of 1970. Plaintiff's only evidence that AI had knowledge of the danger of such material is an undated five-page document warning of the dangers of asbestos, found in the bottom of a file drawer belonging to an AI official, in a stack of unrelated and undated papers. The drawer was labeled "1969-1972." Should the document be admitted into evidence against AI?

4.34. Defendant Cox is charged with the murder of David Lee. Cox's close friend Hamley was in jail at the time of Lee's murder, charged with molesting Lee's child. In fact, four days before Lee's murder, Hamley was charged at a court hearing with three additional felonies based on David Lee's testimony. The court refused to reduce Hamley's bond despite testimony from Hamley's mother. Cox was not present at that hearing, although he spent almost every day at the Hamley house during this time. At Cox's murder trial, the state offers a deputy prosecutor to testify about what happened at the Hamley court hearing, on the theory that Cox murdered Lee as an act of retaliation against Lee because Hamley was still imprisoned. Cox objects to this testimony on the ground that the state has not proved beyond a reasonable doubt that Cox knew what happened at the court hearing. What should the trial court do?

CHAPTER FIVE

THE CHARACTER, PROPENSITY, AND SPECIFIC ACTS RULES

The law of evidence would be very simple if it were the case that "all relevant evidence is admissible," but FRE 402 goes on to say *"except* as otherwise provided ... by these rules." The exceptions and qualifications to the general rule admitting relevant evidence are the focus of many of the Federal Rules of Evidence. FRE 403, as you have seen, allows the trial judge to exclude relevant evidence on a discretionary, case-by-case basis. In contrast, FRE 404-415 establish certain categorical exclusions of otherwise relevant evidence. In this chapter, we will focus on the most important of these rules: the exclusion of otherwise relevant character evidence and of so-called past specific acts. FRE 404-406 and 412-415.

As we begin our examination of these rules, you should keep in mind that the exclusionary provisions may not be a complete bar to the admissibility of a particular piece of evidence. Rather, they prohibit the proponent from offering the evidence only in a particular context or for a particular purpose. For example, FRE 404(b) limits the use of specific acts to prove character but authorizes their use for other purposes, such as to prove motive or intent. Thus, in order to apply the rules properly, you must ask the question that should always be your first question: What is the proponent of the evidence trying to prove? In other words, what is the proponent's theory of relevance? Only after you answer this question will you be able to apply the rules.

A. THE RELEVANCE OF CHARACTER EVIDENCE TO PROVE CONDUCT ON A PARTICULAR OCCASION

Imagine a simple tort case in which a pedestrian is hit by a car and injured. The plaintiff pedestrian claims that he was walking in a clearly marked crosswalk when the defendant driver negligently drove his SUV into him. The defendant claims that the plaintiff was contributorily negligent because he darted out into the middle of the street and was not in the crosswalk. What sort of evidence would the attorneys want to put before the jury to corroborate the testimony of their clients?

Suppose counsel for the plaintiff has the following evidence —

(1)   Witness 1, who has seen the defendant drive on many occasions, to testify that the defendant is a careless driver who often fails to stop for pedestrians in crosswalks;

(2)   Witness 2, a public records custodian, together with Exhibits A through E, public records establishing that the defendant has had several car accidents and traffic infractions in the past;

(3)   Witness 3, a shopkeeper whose storefront overlooks the crosswalk, to testify that he sees the plaintiff cross the street nearly every day, and that he invariably uses the crosswalk

— and the defendant offers

(4)   Witness 4, a friend of the defendant, to testify that the defendant has remade himself into a very safe driver in the past two years.

All of this evidence meets the basic test of relevance under FRE 401, tending to make a fact of consequence (was the driver negligent? was the pedestrian contributorily negligent?) more likely or less likely. While this evidence may not be compelling by itself, you can see that a rational jury could find it useful to consider. As a matter of common sense, it is easy to see how each item of evidence is logically connected to the issues that the parties have to prove in the case. Yet, for reasons that will be explained in this chapter, only the testimony of Witness 3 is likely to be admitted; the rest should be excluded as improper character evidence under FRE 404.

A few definitions will be helpful in analyzing the material presented in this chapter.

1. *Propensity* means a tendency of a person or thing to behave in a certain way. A common thread in this chapter is the "propensity inference" — an argument that evidence about propensity is relevant to show how a person or thing behaved or operated on a specific occasion that is the subject of the litigation. All four of the examples of evidence in the Pedestrian v. Driver hypothetical are of this nature.

2. *Character* (FRE 404) is a type of propensity, probably the most common and familiar. Neither the Federal Rules nor their common law counterparts, however, define the terms *character* or *character trait*. This absence of a definition can occasionally raise difficulties. For a working definition, *character* in evidence law is a tendency of a person to act a certain way, and evidence of a person's character is relevant — but, as we shall see, generally inadmissible — to show that he committed a particular act consistent with his character trait on a specific occasion that is the subject of the litigation. As will be seen, evidence that the defendant is a "negligent" or "careless" driver is character evidence.

3. *Past specific acts*, also known as "other crimes, wrongs or acts" (FRE 404(b)) are instances of a person's past conduct that are not the subject of *this case*. That is, they are not the conduct giving rise to alleged civil or criminal liability in the litigation before the court — they may be in the future, they may have been in the past, but not *now*. Yet such past specific acts may nevertheless be *relevant* to the current case. In the Pedestrian v. Driver hypothetical, the driver's past accidents and traffic infractions are examples of "past specific acts" or "other ... acts." Defendant Driver should not be held liable in this case for any traffic mishaps other than hitting Plaintiff Pedestrian.

Yet those infractions and accidents other than hitting Plaintiff Pedestrian are relevant to the case, because they give rise to an inference that Driver may have driven negligently on the occasion in question when he collided with Plaintiff Pedestrian. Similarly, the many specific (although perhaps countless) times Pedestrian walked in the crosswalk prior to the accident are not themselves the subject of the litigation. What matters is whether Pedestrian walked inside the crosswalk when he was hit by Driver. But the prior instances may give rise to an inference that he stayed inside the crosswalk on the occasion in question.

4. *Habit* (FRE 406) refers to a propensity that the law of evidence distinguishes from character. While character evidence is generally excluded, evidence of habit is admissible. Generally speaking, propensities toward conduct that is more consistent, routine, and repetitive tend to be categorized as "habit," while conduct that is less so tends to be called "character." It might also be said that "habits" tend to be somewhat more morally neutral while behavior that is more morally loaded tends to be categorized as "character." The testimony of Witness 3 in the above hypothetical, that Pedestrian invariably walks within the lines of the crosswalk, would probably be admitted as habit evidence.

In preparing a case for trial, it is natural for litigants to search out evidence of character and past specific acts. In terms of sheer volume, most evidence introduced in trials (civil or criminal) is circumstantial evidence, and evidence of character and past specific acts is a very commonplace, easily found, and intuitive form of circumstantial evidence. The personalities of all of us are often conceived of as a set of "character traits," and our lives are a constant stream of actions. Who we are and what we do are closely intertwined. In a typical litigated case, where it is disputed whether a (civil or criminal) defendant acted in a certain way, what could be more natural than to look at the kind of person the defendant is, and what he has done before, in order to determine whether he committed the acts alleged in the litigation? If a person is charged with fraud, it would be useful to know whether he is "honest." If he is alleged to have committed an assault, it seems relevant to know whether he is "violent." The "character" inference is a commonsense form of reasoning which holds that a person with a dishonest character is more likely than an honest person to have committed the fraud in question; or that a violent person is more likely than a nonviolent one to initiate a physical assault. (See Diagram 5-1, infra.) Thus, use of character evidence is tempting for litigants.

It is crucial to see how past specific acts fit into the character inference. How do we know what someone's character is? How do we know whether a person is "careless" or "dishonest" or "violent"? And how would we prove that in court, in the absence of a rule restricting such proof? Perhaps the most intuitive answer is to look at the person's conduct. As summed up by the adage "handsome is as handsome does," character traits are ultimately generalizations drawn from specific instances of conduct. Thus, "past specific acts" are the intuitively obvious source of character evidence and in practice are often relevant to prove character, which in turn is relevant as circumstantial evidence of how a person may have acted on a particular (disputed) occasion. This chain of reasoning is illustrated in Diagram 5-2, infra. As commonsense and intuitive as this chain of reasoning may be, it is precisely what the Federal Rules *prohibit*. As we will see, while evidence of character may *sometimes* be used to prove or disprove conduct on a specific occasion, FRE 404(b) does not allow past specific acts to prove *character* in order to prove, in turn, conduct on a specific occasion.

B.   GENERAL PROHIBITION ON USE OF CHARACTER AND "PAST SPECIFIC ACTS" EVIDENCE TO PROVE CONDUCT ON A PARTICULAR OCCASION

1.   FRE 404

RULE 404.   CHARACTER EVIDENCE; CRIMES OR OTHER ACTS

(a) *Character Evidence.*

(1) *Prohibited Uses.* Evidence of a person's character or character trait is not admissible to prove that on a particular occasion the person acted in accordance with the character or trait.

(2) *Exceptions for a Defendant or Victim in a Criminal Case.* The following exceptions apply in a criminal case:

(A) a defendant may offer evidence of the defendant's pertinent trait, and if the evidence is admitted, the prosecutor may offer evidence to rebut it;

(B) subject to the limitations in Rule 412, a defendant may offer evidence of an alleged victim's pertinent trait, and if the evidence is admitted, the prosecutor may:

(i) offer evidence to rebut it; and

(ii) offer evidence of the defendant's same trait; and

(C) in a homicide case, the prosecutor may offer evidence of the alleged victim's trait of peacefulness to rebut evidence that the victim was the first aggressor.

(3) *Exceptions for a Witness.* Evidence of a witness's character may be admitted under Rules 607, 608, and 609.

(b) Crimes, Wrongs, or Other Acts.

(1) *Prohibited Uses.* Evidence of a crime, wrong, or other act is not admissible to prove a person's character in order to show that on a particular occasion the person acted in accordance with the character.

(2) *Permitted Uses; Notice in a Criminal Case.* This evidence may be admissible for another purpose, such as proving motive, opportunity, intent, preparation, plan, knowledge, identity, absence of mistake, or lack of accident. On request by a defendant in a criminal case, the prosecutor must:

(A) provide reasonable notice of the general nature of any such evidence that the prosecutor intends to offer at trial; and

(B) do so before trial — or during trial if the court, for good cause, excuses lack of pretrial notice.

2.   Interpretation and Illustration of FRE 404(a) and (b)

Our initial focus is on two parts of FRE 404:

(a) *Character Evidence.*

(1) *Prohibited Uses.* Evidence of a person's character or character trait is not admissible to prove that on a particular occasion the person acted in accordance with the character or trait . . . .

(b) *Crimes, Wrongs, or Other Acts.*

(1) *Prohibited Uses.* Evidence of a crime, wrong, or other act is not admissible to prove a person's character in order to show that on a particular occasion the person acted in accordance with the character.

The text of FRE 404(a) begins by prohibiting the use of evidence of a person's character to prove action in accordance with that character trait on a particular occasion. This general prohibition, which is substantially a restatement of the common law, provides the backdrop against which the more specific and detailed rules admitting and excluding various forms of character evidence must be understood. The basic prohibitions of FRE 404(a) and 404(b) (putting aside, for the moment, the qualifications and exceptions stated in the rule) are broad and straightforward. Under FRE 404(a), evidence of character is not permitted to show action on a particular occasion. This bars the basic inference shown in Diagram 5-1:

Diagram 5-1

EF	IF	FOC
Evidence of a person's character trait (e.g., "careless driving")	The person in fact has that character trait (defendant is a careless driver)	Action in accordance with that character on a specific occasion (e.g., negligence in colliding with plaintiff)

FRE 404(b) elaborates further on this principle by making clear that past specific acts cannot be admitted to show that a person had a certain character trait and acted in accordance with it on a particular occasion. This inference, too, relies on the prohibited character inference. As a matter of logic, evidence of past conduct similar to the acts that allegedly give rise to liability — for instance, evidence of past driving infractions and accidents to show that it is more likely that the driver was negligent in the incident in question — is usually relevant precisely because we make the character inference. Driver's past driving conduct shows him to be a certain type of driver, the kind who is more likely to do that type of thing — negligent driving — on further occasions. FRE 404(b) thus prohibits the chain of inferences shown in Diagram 5-2:

Diagram 5-2

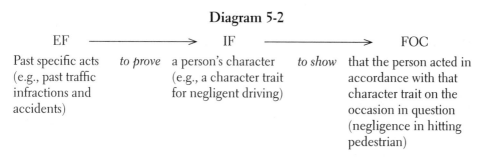

EF		IF		FOC
Past specific acts (e.g., past traffic infractions and accidents)	*to prove*	a person's character (e.g., a character trait for negligent driving)	*to show*	that the person acted in accordance with that character trait on the occasion in question (negligence in hitting pedestrian)

(Note: The words "prove" and "show" in FRE 404 are used interchangeably.) FRE 404(b)'s prohibition of a particular mode of proving character to show action in conformity with that character trait may seem unnecessary given the general prohibition in FRE 404(a). But there are two good reasons for spelling it out. First, there are limited exceptions set out in FRE 404(a)(2) in which character evidence may be offered to prove conduct on a specific occasion. FRE 404(b) makes clear that even when these exceptions apply, the means of proving character cannot include past specific acts.

Second, as suggested above, past specific acts are a common and intuitively obvious form of evidence that litigants are naturally inclined to look for. Absent the express prohibition in FRE 404(b), it might not be sufficiently clear to courts and litigants that specific acts evidence is in many instances relevant only because it proves character in order to show actions in accordance with character, i.e., that the relevance of this evidence depends on the prohibited character inference. FRE 404(b) stands as a reminder that past specific acts evidence is objectionable on this ground. (Whether and in what circumstances these objections will ultimately be sustained remains to be seen, infra.)

3.   Elaboration of the FRE 404(a) and 404(b) Character and Specific Acts Prohibitions

a.   *The Rationale for Restricting Evidence of a Person's Character*

There are good reasons for restricting the use of character evidence to show a person's action in accordance with that character:

i.   Weakness of the Propensity Inference.   First, the probative value of character evidence to show action in accordance with character will seldom, if ever, be very great. A person who is generally honest will at least occasionally be less than fully honest; a person whom we may fairly describe as having a violent character will on many occasions react to adverse situations in a peaceful manner. Moreover, on the occasion giving rise to the litigation, there may have been particular stresses on the individual or some other unusual circumstances that increased the likelihood of acting "out of character."

In the *Johnson* case, for example, evidence of Walker's reputation for violence is relevant to show that he was violent at the time of the alleged jail cell altercation. Yet the evidence does not suggest that Walker was violent in a majority of his encounters with inmates. If that were the case, it is unlikely that he would have retained his job. Rather, the defendant's evidence suggests only that Walker happened to be violent somewhat more often than the other correctional officers. Alternatively, consider the prosecution's evidence about Walker's *good* character. Walker may have been a generally peaceful person, but the stress of the incident with Johnson could have caused Walker to act "out of character." Even if one fully credits the defense evidence and discounts the prosecution evidence (or vice versa), the evidence tells the fact finder very little about the likelihood that Walker behaved violently at the one specific time that is the focus of the litigation. In short, the inference in Diagram 5-1 from a general character trait like violence, peacefulness, honesty, or dishonesty (IF) to action in conformity with that character trait on a specific occasion (FOC) is likely to be quite weak. For discussions of empirical evidence suggesting the low probative value of character evidence, see David P. Leonard, The Use of Character to Prove Conduct: Rationality and Catharsis in Evidence Law, 58 U. Colo. L. Rev. 1, 26-31 (1987); Miguel A. Mendez, Essay: The Law of Evidence and the Search for Stable Personality, 45 Emory L.J. 221 (1996).

ii.   Low Probative Value of the Evidence to Prove Character.   Furthermore, the inference from the evidence offered (e.g., the testimony about Walker's reputation for violence) to what a person's character actually is (EF to IF) may itself be weak. As will be seen below, when character evidence is permitted, it must take the form of the witness's opinion about a person's character or that person's character "reputation" in the community. Such evidence often comes across as too vague and general to be convincing. How convinced were you by the inmates' testimony about Walker's reputation for violence in the *Johnson* case?

Evidence of past specific acts — for instance, specific instances in which Walker beat an inmate, if such evidence existed — may be much more powerful than general opinions, but even that evidence may not be very probative of a person's character. While a person's character is undoubtedly reflected in his conduct, how much conduct do we need to observe before we can make reliable "character" judgments? Would two instances of Walker assaulting inmates suffice to prove that he had a "character" to be violent toward inmates? What if those incidents were "out of character" for him?

iii. **Diversion from Main Issues.**   If the character evidence is disputed, there is a risk of digressing into a "minitrial" on character and diverting the fact finder's attention from the main issues in the case. In *Johnson*, for example, there was conflicting testimony about Walker's reputation for violence or nonviolence. Moreover, the risk of confusion of issues would be heightened if character was to be proven by past specific acts. If, for instance, the defense in *Johnson* wanted to introduce evidence that Walker had previously assaulted two inmates, we can easily see the potential for minitrials on those incidents. Were those prior assaults similar in relevant respects to Johnson's situation? Did Walker provoke the assault or simply defend himself? How many facts are disputed about the prior assaults, and how many witnesses are there to those events?

iv. **"Bad Person" Prejudice.**   Character evidence may also be unfairly prejudicial, particularly if it is evidence of the character of a party to the lawsuit. Inherent in the concept of character — or at least in the attributes that most people and most courts think of as character — is a moral quality or sense of rightness or wrongness. Consider, for example, the meaning of the words we use to describe what we refer to as character traits, e.g., *honesty, dishonesty, peacefulness,* and *violence.* Evidence that a litigant possesses one of these traits may arouse an emotional response and dispose the jury to decide in favor of that person if it is a positive character trait or against the person if it is a negative one.

This danger is intensified when a negative character inference might be drawn from past specific acts. Consider, for example, a murder case in which the prosecutor offers evidence that the defendant has committed an unrelated murder on a prior occasion. One way that this evidence is relevant is to show that the defendant has a generally violent character — and more specifically, a character trait to commit murder — and thus may have committed the murder on the occasion in question. At the same time, the prejudicial impact of the evidence may be substantial. The jury is likely to have little sympathy for a one-time murderer even if it has a reasonable doubt about the defendant's guilt on the current charge. The jurors may also make unfounded assumptions about the likelihood that someone who has committed murder in the past will do so again. The risk is probably especially great that a jury, on hearing about a criminal defendant's bad character, may be willing to ignore a reasonable doubt and convict a person who may not (in the jurors' view) have been sufficiently punished in the past and who may commit crimes in the future. But as Justice Cardozo famously said, "the law has set its face against the endeavor to fasten guilt upon [a criminal defendant] by proof of character or experience predisposing to an act of crime." People v. Zackowitz, 254 N.Y. 192, 172 N.E. 466 (1930).

As you can see from the foregoing points, character evidence raises classic FRE 403 issues, in which probative value must be weighed against FRE 403 dangers of consumption of time, confusion of issues and unfair prejudice. FRE 404 can be understood as reflecting a judgment that the FRE 403 dangers inherent in character evidence will so often substantially outweigh the probative value that it makes sense to exclude it as a general rule rather than to permit case-by-case decisions on whether to admit it. And while character evidence admissible under the FRE 404(a) exceptions can be proven by opinion or reputation testimony, it cannot be proven by past specific acts. Although specific acts may be slightly more probative of character than vague, general reputation or opinion evidence, the FRE 403-type dangers of minitrials and unfair prejudice are probably much greater. Therefore, you can see the reason underlying 404(b)'s categorical prohibition of specific acts to prove character to prove conduct on a particular occasion.

b.   Exceptions to the FRE 404(b) Prohibition Against the Use of Specific Acts

Despite the unqualified nature of the prohibition against specific acts evidence in FRE 404(b), there are limited instances in which it is permissible to use evidence of a person's specific acts to prove that person's character to show action in accordance with character. FRE 608(b) and 609, which we will consider in Chapter Seven, explicitly authorize the use of specific acts for this purpose. The revised Federal Rules dealing with the admissibility of sexual misconduct evidence, FRE 413-415, also contemplate the use of specific acts to prove character to show action in accordance with character.

There are also a number of purposes for which specific acts are admissible because they are not offered pursuant to the prohibited chain of inferential reasoning set out in Diagram 5-2. (See Sections C and H, infra.)

KEY POINTS

1. Evidence of a person's character is relevant to show the person's action in accordance with character on a particular occasion.

2. The Federal Rules prohibit the use of character evidence to show action in accordance with character except in the situations set forth in FRE 404(a) (discussed in Section G, infra).

3. The Federal Rules do not define "character" or "character trait." Typically, character traits are qualities or aspects of a person that tend to be reflected in occasional, rather than routine, conduct and tend to have moral overtones (e.g., honesty or dishonesty) and, therefore, inherent prejudice.

4. Past specific acts, or instances of conduct other than the ones that form the subject matter of the litigation, are often relevant to prove character in order to show action in accordance with that character trait on a specific occasion. However, they are excluded from evidence for this purpose by FRE 404(b).

PROBLEMS

5.1. Return to Problem 3.3, United States v. Ray, at page 136. The prosecution offers evidence that (a) in October 2005, Ray sold 25,000 shares of Rundown stock one week before a major and abrupt fall in Rundown's share price; and (b) in May 2007, Ray purchased 30,000 shares of Rundown 30 days before the company announced the profitable acquisition of a competitor, an event that caused the stock price to rise by 25 percent. For what purposes is this evidence relevant? Is it objectionable?

5.2. Return to Problem 3.4, State v. Blair, at page 137. The prosecution offers the following evidence. For what purposes is this evidence relevant? Is it objectionable?

(a)   That in 2008, Blair pleaded guilty to a charge of simple assault after making an unprovoked attack with his fists on a man in a bar.

(b)   Testimony from Blair's then-girlfriend that on two occasions in 2005 she called 911 because Blair had beaten her. She received medical treatment on both occasions, though she did not press charges against Blair.

(c)   That Blair was arrested for battering Norma in September 2008. Norma received medical treatment for her injuries, but no charges were filed against Blair.

5.3. Return to the case of United States v. Hitt, at page 159. Recall that the prosecution offered a photograph of the defendant's rifle surrounded by several guns that were not his. Suppose that the guns did in fact belong to Hitt. With that assumption, what arguments could be made for the relevance of the photograph? Can any objection be made under FRE 404(b)? Can you think of any additional arguments in support of an FRE 403 objection?

5.4. Return to Problem 3.2, Pedroso v. Driver, at page 136. The plaintiff offers the following evidence. For what purposes is this evidence relevant? Is it objectionable?

(a)   Testimony of the transportation supervisor for the entire school district that defendant Driver "is the best and most safety conscious driver in the district."

(b)   Testimony from the same witness that Driver "had a spotless driving record prior to this incident."

(c)   Testimony from Driver's neighbor that Driver had been depressed for weeks prior to the incident and that "half a dozen" empty liquor bottles could be seen in Driver's trash each week.

(d)   Driver's admission that she had been speeding while driving her bus route prior to the incident.

5.5. Joseph Zachary has been convicted of first degree murder for the premeditated killing of Marty Coppola. According to the evidence presented to the jury, Zachary got into a heated argument with Coppola at a bar. He went back to his apartment where he retrieved a 9 mm pistol, returned to the bar and shot Coppola. To prove premeditation, the prosecution argued that Zachary returned to the bar intending to kill Coppola. The defense argued for first degree manslaughter based on (1) Zachary's testimony that he did not intend to use the gun on Coppola and (2) corroborated testimony that Zachary pulled the gun only after Coppola tried to punch him in the face. The prosecution, over defense counsel's objection, introduced evidence that Zachary also owned a .38 caliber magnum revolver and a .45 caliber pistol in addition to the murder weapon. No evidence was offered about how or why Zachary chose the 9 mm pistol. In admitting the evidence of the other guns, the trial judge agreed with the prosecutor's argument that the evidence "shows the defendant had a murderous propensity."

Assuming that all arguments have been properly preserved for appeal, what arguments should the defense make to the appellate court that the evidence concerning the other guns should have been excluded from the trial? How should the prosecutor respond?

C.   THE ADMISSIBILITY OF SPECIFIC ACTS THAT ARE DEEMED RELEVANT WITHOUT A CHARACTER INFERENCE

The basic provision of Rule 404(a) prohibits a certain kind of propensity inference — specifically, a "character" inference, one that asks the fact finder to infer that a person acted a certain way on the occasion in question because it was his "character" to act that way. The basic provision of FRE 404(b) emphasizes this prohibition with respect to evidence of past specific acts. But nothing in these rules prohibits the use of past specific acts that are relevant for some purpose other than to prove character to prove, in turn, conduct on a particular occasion. In other words, past specific acts that are relevant without making the full character inference illustrated in Diagram 5-2, supra, are not excluded by FRE 404(b)(1).

Because, as seen above, past specific acts are an important and common type of evidence, the drafters of the rules did not leave this point about their admissibility for non-character purposes to implication, but chose instead to spell it out in FRE 404(b)(2). There are a variety of labels for the type of evidence considered here: specific acts evidence, prior bad acts, bad conduct evidence, uncharged misconduct, and so forth. We tend to use the term *past specific acts*. Regardless of the terminology, the issues are the same.

1.   Interpretation and Illustration of FRE 404(b)(2)

FRE 404(b)(2) provides:

> (2) *Permitted Uses; Notice in a Criminal Case.* This evidence [of a crime, wrong or other act] may be admissible for another purpose, such as proving motive, opportunity, intent, preparation, plan, knowledge, identity, absence of mistake, or lack of accident. On request by a defendant in a criminal case, the prosecutor must:
>
> (A) provide reasonable notice of the general nature of any such evidence that the prosecutor intends to offer at trial; and
>
> (B) do so before trial — or during trial if the court, for good cause, excuses lack of pretrial notice.

We have seen that, pursuant to FRE 404(b)(1), a person's specific acts are not admissible to prove the person's character in order to show action in accordance with character. Specific acts may be admissible, however, pursuant to FRE 404(b)(2) to prove a fact of consequence that is not called "character" or a "character trait." While specific acts offered for some noncharacter purpose are often prior bad acts of a criminal defendant offered by the prosecution, nothing in the rules of evidence limits the noncharacter use of specific acts to acts that are somehow "bad" or to acts of a criminal defendant.

In order to admit evidence pursuant to FRE 404(b)(2), the proponent must satisfy three requirements. First, the proponent must articulate some noncharacter purpose for which the specific acts evidence is relevant. Second, the proponent must introduce evidence that the person who allegedly committed the act in fact did commit the act. Third, the proponent must be prepared to respond to a likely FRE 403 objection to the evidence.

Assume, for example, a case in which the defendant is charged with shooting a police officer, and the prosecution wants to introduce evidence that the defendant robbed a bank shortly before the shooting. The prosecution would first have to articulate a noncharacter purpose for introducing evidence of the defendant's involvement in the bank robbery. In this case, the prosecution would maintain that the bank robbery evidence is offered, not to show that the defendant more likely shot the police officer in accordance with a general character for dishonesty or lawlessness, but rather to establish a motive for the shooting: Because the defendant had recently robbed a bank, the defendant had a particular fear of capture and, therefore, a motive for shooting the police officer. Second, the prosecution would have to have evidence — perhaps, for example, a videotape of the robbery or eyewitness testimony — sufficient to support a finding that the defendant was indeed the bank robber. (Note: This aspect of the 404(b)(2) proof procedure is an example of a "fact condition" under FRE 104(b), subject to the "evidence sufficient to support a finding" standard. See Chapter Four, Section E.) Finally, the prosecution would have to be prepared to respond to an objection that the probative value of the bank robbery evidence (to prove that the defendant had a motive for the shooting and, therefore, that the defendant did shoot the officer) is substantially outweighed by the FRE 403 exclusionary factors.

If the proponent of the evidence is the prosecutor, there is a fourth requirement — that the prosecution respond to a criminal defendant's demand for notice. According to the Advisory Committee Note on this notice requirement (added by a 1991 amendment), its purpose is "to reduce surprise and promote early resolution on the issue of admissibility." The rule states no absolute time limits and no particular form that the request and response must take.

2. Elaboration of FRE 404(b)(2)

a. The Permissible Uses of Specific Acts Evidence

FRE 404(b) prohibits the use of specific acts evidence only when offered to prove character to prove conduct in accordance on a specific occasion. Any relevant purpose of specific acts evidence that falls outside that chain of inferences (described in Diagram 5-2) falls outside the prohibition of FRE 404(b) and is potentially admissible. Technically, it should have been unnecessary to set out any permissible noncharacter purposes in FRE 404, but FRE 404(b)(2) happens to list the traditional purposes for which the common law permitted the use of specific acts. However, the phrase "such as" in FRE 404(b) expressly makes clear that the list is not exhaustive. To secure admission pursuant to the second sentence of FRE 404(b), it is not necessary to identify one of the listed purposes. It is sufficient for the proponent of specific acts evidence to convince the court that the evidence is offered for some purpose other than proving a person's character to prove conduct in accordance with character on a specific occasion.

Recall that the "past specific acts" we are discussing are acts that appear to be unrelated to the litigated events, although in many cases they might themselves have been the basis for civil or criminal liability. The eight examples listed in FRE 404(b) (2) — motive, opportunity, intent, preparation, plan, knowledge, identity, or absence of mistake or accident — can be grouped into three broad and overlapping categories that might be of help you to discern patterns in the kinds of specific acts evidence deemed to avoid the FRE 404(b)(1) exclusion.

i.   Evidence of Motive, Opportunity, Preparation, Plan, and the Like. Sometimes the events giving rise to civil or criminal liability are an inextricable part of a larger story involving other actions by a party. These other actions are in turn relevant to an essential element, tending to prove who did the act or what the act was. The prosecution in a homicide case might want to present evidence that the defendant stole a gun in a burglary a week before the homicide to explain how he came into possession of the gun used in the crime — an example of *opportunity* or *preparation*. In the same homicide case, the prosecution might offer evidence that the defendant was involved with the victim in a drug deal that went bad, in order to establish the defendant's *motive* to kill the victim. Or, under a different set of facts, a homicide might be part of a broader *plan* or scheme to further a drug-dealing conspiracy — if the victim were a potential witness against the conspirators, or a competing drug dealer — in which case the prosecution might offer specific acts evidence in the form of evidence of the (uncharged) drug dealing conspiracy.

"Motive," "opportunity," "preparation," and "plan," are all terms that capture the idea of essential aspects of the story of the case, such that the story can only be fully understood if the other actions are presented to the jury. As we saw in the *Old Chief* case, litigants have an acknowledged strong interest in presenting evidence that tells the jury a story that is coherent and has "narrative integrity" — that doesn't leave the jury wondering "how" and "why." In addition, these kinds of facts are relevant in other ways, typically as circumstantial evidence tending to show *identity* — who committed the crime or conduct that is the subject of the litigation — or the fact that the crime or conduct occurred, where those facts are in dispute.

It could be said that the examples given above are not properly considered "past specific acts" at all, in the sense we that have been using the term. Why not? Because, at least in some cases, they arguably are indeed part of a single, cohesive chain of events giving rise to liability. Even if this is so, they nevertheless are frequently lumped into the "past specific acts" category to the extent that they theoretically could have been the subject of additional civil claims or criminal charges.

ii.   Evidence Showing Relevant States of Mind.   States of mind are at issue in many litigated cases: Mental states may be an element of the criminal charge or the civil claim, and the defendant can put his state of mind at issue by asserting mistake, accident, or lack of knowledge. In such cases, past specific acts can be admissible for the noncharacter purpose of proving *knowledge, intent* or *absence of mistake or accident*. The same evidence that showed "preparation" or "motive" in the homicide example above, may also be relevant to show an intent to kill or the kind of premeditation that must typically be shown in a murder case. Past specific acts might also show the requisite knowledge. For instance, in a prosecution for conspiracy to distribute narcotics, the prosecution might offer a prior conviction for dealing cocaine to show the defendant's knowledge that the substance he transported was in fact cocaine.

This last example also illustrates what is meant by *absence of mistake or accident*. Past specific acts may be relevant to rebut a defendant's assertion that he is not liable or guilty because he was mistaken about crucial facts or that the conduct was unintentional. In the cocaine dealing example, if the defendant claims he did not know the white powder was cocaine, his past conviction for dealing powder cocaine would be relevant to undermine that claim. Past specific acts are also occasionally offered to rebut a claim of "accident" under the so-called doctrine of chances. For instance, in a case where an alleged arsonist charged with burning down his business to collect insurance proceeds claims that the fire was an accident, the prosecution might introduce evidence of prior purported accidents in which the same defendant lost other businesses in fires and collected insurance proceeds. The theory is that such accidents are unlikely to recur with the same person so frequently, implying that intentional conduct must be involved.

iii.   Evidence Showing Identity.

In cases where the defense theory is that the wrongful conduct was perpetrated by some other known or unknown person, past specific acts can be relevant as circumstantial evidence that the defendant is indeed the perpetrator. To be sure, "other conduct" offered for any of the other noncharacter purposes above is ultimately relevant to "identify" the defendant as the culprit. *Identity* is probably listed separately as a way of including the "modus operandi" theory: Where other conduct is so distinctive and nearly identical in its attributes or methods to the litigated conduct as to suggest by itself that the same perpetrator did the past and present acts, it can be admitted as showing identity.

b.   *Preliminary Fact-finding with Respect to Whether the Person in Question Committed the Act*

The probative value of specific acts evidence for any of the noncharacter purposes covered by FRE 404(b) depends in part on the strength of the proof that the person committed the act and, if culpability is important to the relevance of the evidence, that the person did so culpably. What standard should the trial judge use in determining whether to admit the specific acts evidence? In Huddleston v. United States, 485 U.S. 681 (1988), the Supreme Court resolved a conflict in the federal circuits by holding that the question of the person's culpable involvement was one of conditional relevance governed by FRE 104(b). Thus, under the Federal Rules, the proponent of the evidence can satisfy the preliminary fact requirement by introducing "evidence sufficient to support a finding" by a preponderance of the evidence that the person was culpably involved in the act. This standard of proof is relatively low, as we discussed at pages 184-185, supra.

Despite *Huddleston*, some state courts continue to apply an FRE 104(a)-type standard in assessing a person's involvement in prior acts. In these states, as a condition of admissibility, the proponent of the evidence must *persuade the trial judge* that (a) the person allegedly responsible for the act did in fact commit the act and (b) the person did so culpably (if culpability in the commission of the act is important to its relevance, as it usually is). Although both West Virginia and Colorado have evidence rules that are identical to FRE 104(a) and (b), both states' courts have held that the question of the defendant's culpable involvement in a prior bad act was one for the court to determine by a preponderance of the evidence pursuant to FRE 104(a). State v. McGinnis, 455 S.E.2d 516 (W. Va. 1995); People v. Garner, 806 P.2d 366 (Colo. 1991). Cf. Harrell v. State, 884 S.W.2d 154, 160-161 (Tex. Crim. App. 1994) (other crimes evidence admissible only if court finds pursuant to Tex. R. Crim. Evid. 104(b) evidence sufficient to support a finding *beyond a reasonable doubt* that person was culpably involved in the act).

The principal reason for using the higher FRE 104(a) preliminary fact standard would be to protect criminal defendants from the unfair prejudice that inheres in the admission of a defendant's bad acts. As you read the remaining materials in this section, consider whether it is appropriate to adjust preliminary fact rules to deal with unfair prejudice or whether it is preferable to deal with unfair prejudice by relying exclusively on a rule like FRE 403, which specifically sets forth a balancing test for assessing probative value and unfair prejudice.

c.   *Probative Value and Prejudice Generally*

Finding a relevant "noncharacter" purpose for specific acts evidence under FRE 404(b)(2) and satisfying the preliminary fact standard does not mean that the evidence is automatically admissible. The term "may" in FRE 404(b) makes it clear that admissibility is subject to compliance with the other rules of evidence, the most important of which in the context of specific acts evidence is FRE 403. Past specific acts evidence offered under FRE 404(b)(2) nearly always raises a potential FRE 403 objection. This is because in virtually every (perhaps every) instance in which past specific acts are offered for one of the FRE 404(b)(2) purposes, there will still be the risk that the jury will consider the past conduct for the impermissible purpose of proving character to prove conduct in accordance with character on a specific occasion. Thus, for example, if the prosecutor in a homicide case offers evidence of the defendant's burglary-theft of a gun to show preparation and opportunity, the jury may nevertheless use the evidence to determine that the defendant has a character to commit crimes and is therefore more likely to have committed the homicide — or is just a bad person who should be punished on that basis. In other words, past specific acts evidence that fits within FRE 404(b)(2) is likely to be relevant for two purposes — one admissible, the other not. Thus, a classic FRE 403 objection is presented, based on the argument that the prejudice flowing from the impermissible purpose substantially outweighs the probative value of the permissible purpose.

Factors for the court to consider in making the FRE 403 balancing decision include

(1)   how probative the noncharacter purpose is of some contested issue in the case;

(2)   how probative the specific act is to prove the noncharacter purpose (e.g., whether there is a sufficiently close temporal proximity between the specific act and the crime charged; whether there is a "substantial similarity" between the past act and the crime charged, see United States v. Haywood, 280 F.3d 715 (6th Cir. 2002));

(3)   how probative the evidence is to establish that the act occurred (e.g., whether there is a dispute about the nature of the act or the defendant's involvement in it);

(4)   how much of a risk of unfair prejudice would result from introduction of the evidence (e.g., how heinous is the specific act); and

(5)   how effective a limiting instruction is likely to be in reducing the risk of unfair prejudice.

In sum, when the prosecution offers specific acts evidence against a criminal defendant, there inevitably will be the risk of "bad person" prejudice: Jurors may be willing to ignore a reasonable doubt because they regard the defendant as a bad person who perhaps has not been sufficiently punished for prior misdeeds and who may commit similar bad acts in the future. In addition, there is a risk that the jury may use the act in an improper character-propensity sense as evidence that the defendant committed the crime charged. Keep in mind, though, that FRE 403 is a rule favoring admissibility (probative value must be "substantially outweighed" by the countervailing factors) and that there is a long tradition of admitting prejudicial specific acts evidence for noncharacter purposes. On the basis of our anecdotal impressions and review of reported cases (admittedly unscientific data, since reported cases may not be representative of the many unreported day-to-day decisions by trial courts), it appears that in practice, FRE 403 is seldom a barrier to the admissibility of specific acts evidence.

KEY POINTS

1. FRE 404(b) prohibits the use of specific acts *only* to prove character to show action in accordance with character.

2. Admissibility of specific acts for noncharacter purposes requires the proponent to do three things: (a) convince the judge that there is a legitimate noncharacter purpose for the evidence; (b) satisfy the preliminary fact standard with respect to the culpable involvement of the person who allegedly committed the act; and (c) respond to an FRE 403 objection.

3. The list of purposes in FRE 404(b) for which specific acts evidence may be admissible is not exhaustive. Specific acts evidence may be admissible for *any* noncharacter purpose.

4. Under the Federal Rules, the question of whether a person was culpably involved in the specific acts is an FRE 104(b) preliminary fact question. The proponent can satisfy the standard by offering evidence sufficient to support a finding by a preponderance of the evidence that the person was culpably involved in the act.

5. FRE 403 may sometimes require exclusion of specific acts evidence offered for noncharacter purposes.

PROBLEMS

5.6. Consider whether the specific acts evidence should be admissible in the following cases:

(a)   Jill's home was burglarized, and there was no evidence of a forced entry. In the case against the defendant, the prosecution offers evidence that a week before the burglary, the defendant stole Jill's purse containing her key ring.

(b)   The defendant is charged with growing marijuana. She claims that her friends are responsible and that she thought the plants were weeds. The prosecution offers eyewitness testimony from a neighbor that he had seen the defendant harvest marijuana on her property the year previously.

(c)   The defendant is charged with killing X, who was about to testify as an eyewitness in a major drug conspiracy trial. The prosecution offers evidence of the defendant's participation in the conspiracy.

5.7. Jerry Kozinski is being tried for burglary of an office building. A "Z" was found spray-painted on the front door of the burglarized building the same morning the burglary was discovered. The prosecution offers the following evidence. Is it admissible?

(a)   Evidence that Kozinski had pleaded guilty to a residential burglary two years ago in which a "Z" was found spray painted on the front door of the burglarized house.

(b)   Records from Blockbuster Video showing that Kozinski had rented "The Mark of Zorro" (in which the protagonist leaves behind a letter "Z" at the scenes of his exploits) eight times in the past three years.

5.8. Return to Problem 5.4, Pedroso v. Driver, at page 000. Reconsider each of the offered items of evidence in light of FRE 404(b)(2). Is the admissibility of any of this evidence affected in light of the additional rule?

5.9. Return to Problem 3.3, United States v. Ray, at page 000. The prosecution offers evidence that (a) in October 2005, Ray sold 25,000 shares of Rundown stock one week before a major and abrupt fall in Rundown's share price; and (b) in May 2007, Ray purchased 30,000 shares of Rundown 30 days before the company announced the profitable acquisition of a competitor, an event which caused the stock price to rise by 25 percent. Assume that the defense counsel's earlier FRE 403 objection to this evidence (see Problem 3.9, at page 155) has been overruled. Can the defense object to this evidence under FRE 404? Does that objection suggest any additional arguments for an FRE 403 objection? How should the prosecutor respond?

5.10. Return to Problem 3.4, State v. Blair, at page 000. The prosecution offers the following evidence. What arguments can be made for and against admission?

(a)   That in 2008, Blair pleaded guilty to a charge of simple assault after making an unprovoked attack with his fists on a man in a bar.

(b)   Testimony from Blair's ex-girlfriend that he had beaten her on two occasions in 2005. She received medical treatment on both occasions, though she did not press charges against Blair.

(c)   That Blair was arrested for battering Norma in September 2008. Norma received medical treatment for her injuries, but no charges were filed against Blair.

5.11 Return to Problem 3.5 on page 138. A retired player on the Tomcats team who has played with Trapp for the past 10 years would testify hat Trapp often has extreme outbursts of rage when the Tomcats are losing. He also would testify that when that happens, he has seen Trapp hit players from the opposing team on several occasions.

5.12. Greg Simpson is charged with armed robbery and burglary. According to the testimony of Fred Able, a knife-wielding man wearing jeans, a T-shirt, and a ski mask broke into his home by coming through an unlocked window. The intruder, who had a slight limp and appeared to be over six feet tall, demanded Able's money and threatened to kill him if he called the police. The prosecution offers the testimony of Pam Wellington that one week before the incident at Able's house, a man who she identifies as Simpson came to her door, said his car had broken down, and asked to use the telephone. He was wearing jeans and a T-shirt. Before Wellington could respond, Simpson pushed his way into the house, pulled out a knife and demanded Wellington's money and jewelry. As Wellington began to comply, her dog attacked Simpson and bit him in the leg. Simpson fled through the front door. Simpson is six feet tall. Both crimes occurred at approximately 11:00 A.M. in the same neighborhood. Simpson objects to Wellington's testimony on the grounds that the evidence (a) is impermissible character evidence, (b) should be excluded because of FRE 403, and (c) should be excluded because he was acquitted of burglary and attempted robbery in the Wellington incident. How should the court rule?

5.13. Garvin is charged with illegal possession of a firearm, which was discovered in a Cadillac parked outside Garvin's house. Garvin frequently used the Cadillac, which belonged to his aunt. The prosecution wishes to introduce evidence that Garvin had previously been arrested for robbery, that the police were at his house to execute a warrant to search for proceeds of robbery, that they discovered the key to the Cadillac during the search, and that Garvin's aunt then identified herself as the owner of the Cadillac and consented to its search. How much of this evidence should be admissible? For what purpose?

3.   Further Elaboration of FRE 404(b)(2)

Our description of three categories of specific acts evidence admissible under FRE 404(b)(2) — essential parts of a larger story (motive, opportunity, preparation, plan), states of mind (knowledge, intent, absence of mistake, lack of accident), and identity (including modus operandi) — was not intended to suggest that any past specific act that can be shoehorned into one of these descriptors should be deemed admissible. On the contrary, we believe that lax application of the 404(b)(2) categories poses a real risk of undermining the policies behind the basic 404(b) prohibition of past specific acts to prove character to prove conduct on a particular occasion. In the sections that follow, we consider specific applications of FRE 404(b)(2) that may well be in some tension with the prohibitory language of FRE 404(b)(1).

a.   The Problem of "Res Gestae"

While evidence of past acts to show "motive" or "opportunity" might supply elements that fill out the story of the case, they are also independently relevant: For example, a person with a motive is more likely to have done the act in question than someone with no motive. However, parties sometimes argue for admission of evidence that is not technically relevant on the ground that it purportedly involves the "same transaction" as the conduct at issue in the case, or helps to "complete the story" of the case. Such evidence is often called *res gestae*, a Latinism that may give the argument to admit such evidence more weight than it deserves. For example, it is all too easy for a prosecutor to argue that prior criminal acts of a defendant are part of the "larger narrative" the prosecution wants to tell. Consider People v. Zackowitz, 254. N.Y. 192, 172 N.E. 466 (1930), which forms the basis of Problem 5.5 at page 243, supra. The prosecution did in fact argue that the past acts evidence was relevant background narrative (using the term *res gestae*). But why was that particular part of the narrative at all helpful, let alone necessary to understanding the "story" of the crime? Judge Cardozo, writing for the court, plainly believed it was not.

Courts have taken different views on how carefully to limit marginally relevant or irrelevant past acts evidence that is offered only to "complete the story." Compare United States v. Bowie, 232 F.3d 923, 929 (D.C. Cir. 2000) ("there is no general 'complete the story' or 'explain the circumstances' exception to Rule 404(b) in this Circuit") with United States v. Brooks, 670 F.2d 625, 628-629 (5th Cir. 1982) (admitting evidence that marijuana was found in defendant's car as "arising out of the same transaction or series of transactions as the charged offense" of possession of cocaine with intent to distribute). In our view, courts should not admit such evidence unless it is necessary to a coherent and intelligible description of the conduct giving rise to civil or criminal liability.

b.   The Problem of Specific Acts Evidence to Prove Intent or Knowledge

FRE 404(b) identifies "intent" and "knowledge" as two of the permissible noncharacter uses of past specific acts evidence. "Intent" and "knowledge" are two ways of describing the kinds of mental states that permeate our laws. Acts that may be deemed nonculpable under an "innocent" state of mind might give rise to civil or criminal liability with a "guilty" state of mind. The presence of "knowledge" or "intent" may convert an accident or innocent mistake into a crime or tort. (Consider Holmes's famous quip, "even a dog knows the difference between being tripped over and being kicked.")

Some courts have formulated the admissibility of past specific acts evidence to prove such states of mind this way: "Where a defendant claims that his conduct has an innocent explanation, prior act evidence is generally admissible to prove that the defendant acted with the state of mind necessary to commit the offense charged." United States v. Zackson, 12 F.3d 1178, 1182 (2d Cir. 1993). In *Zackson*, for example, the prosecution introduced evidence that the defendant had previously participated in a marijuana-selling conspiracy to rebut his contention that he did not willingly participate in a cocaine-dealing conspiracy.

How does the prior marijuana selling prove intent without making a character inference? The relevance of the prior marijuana conspiracy is to prove that the defendant has a propensity to engage intentionally in drug-selling activities, offered to show that he so intended on the occasion of the charged cocaine conspiracy. It appears to us that this use of past specific acts requires the very type of character inference prohibited by FRE 404(b)(1).

Perhaps one could view "intent" as something other than "conduct," so that the use of past specific acts to prove *intent* on a particular occasion is different from the prohibited use of past specific acts to prove *conduct* on a particular occasion. Or perhaps the law of evidence could be seen as making an "intent exception" to the prohibition of specific acts to prove character to prove conduct on a specific occasion as a pragmatic concession to the need for circumstantial evidence to prove states of mind. Whatever the justification, many courts and commentators seem willing to gloss over the difficulty that use of past specific acts to prove intent violates the prohibition in FRE 404(b)(1).

Finally, consider this question: Are "knowledge" and "intent" different? They might be distinguished this way: "Knowledge" is an understanding of the nature of the elements of an act, while "intent" is the conscious purpose to do that act. But in application, such a distinction may be overly subtle or even a moot point. Many legal rules lump "intent" and "knowledge" together. The federal Controlled Substances Act, for instance, defines numerous drug crimes in terms of acts that are done "knowingly *or* intentionally." 21 U.S.C. §§841, 846 (emphasis added). Nevertheless there may be instances in the context of past specific acts evidence where this distinction could matter. Perhaps knowledge may be something that, once acquired, is usually retained indefinitely, so that proving that someone knew something in the past proves that he knew it on a subsequent occasion without a character inference. In contrast, intentions are subject to change and vary with circumstances. There is no reason to infer that someone who intentionally to kicked a dog a year ago kicked a different dog yesterday rather than, as claimed, accidentally tripped over it — unless one infers a character trait for kicking dogs.

c.   The Problem of Specific Acts Evidence to Prove Mental States That Are Not Disputed

The danger of allowing past specific acts to prove character to prove mental states is particularly troubling in the following scenario. Suppose the defendant is charged with the sale of heroin. Prosecution witnesses will include the alleged purchaser and individuals who can identify the substance as contraband and establish a chain of custody. The defense will be that the police arrested the wrong person and that the defendant had nothing to do with the heroin transaction to which the prosecution's evidence relates. The prosecution offers evidence that the defendant knowingly sold heroin two years ago on the ground that this prior sale is evidence of the defendant's knowledge, which is one of the elements of the offense. The defendant objects: "knowledge of what"? The prosecution responds: "knowledge of what heroin is and knowledge of what a heroin sale is." The defendant then objects that the evidence should be excluded according to FRE 403. In support of the objection, the defendant offers (a) to stipulate that whoever sold the heroin did so with the requisite knowledge and (b) to accept a jury instruction explaining the stipulation to the jury.

i.   The Argument for Exclusion.   As we pointed out in our initial discussion of FRE 403 the need for evidence is one of the factors to consider in making the FRE 403 determination. Even without the stipulation and jury instruction, there may be little need for the prior act evidence in the heroin sale case as long as the defendant does nothing to suggest lack of knowledge. It seems likely that the jury would infer knowledge from the facts of possession and sale and from the failure to deny knowledge. Thus, even if one believes there is a strong inferential link between the prior knowing sale and present knowledge, the evidence, in context, appears to have low probative value. (Do you think the prosecutors would consider dropping the drug sale case if they did not have evidence of previous drug selling?) The stipulation and jury instruction further decrease the need for the evidence.

Against this low probative value, one must assess the FRE 403 risk of unfair prejudice. If the evidence were admitted, there is the risk that the jury would consider it in two improper ways: First, the jury might infer that because the defendant sold heroin once before, the defendant is the kind of person who has a character trait for selling heroin and, therefore, probably sold it on this occasion. This particular chain of inferences, however, is clearly prohibited by FRE 404(b)(1). Second, there is the risk of "bad person" prejudice: The jurors may be willing to forgo a reasonable doubt in order to convict and remove from the streets someone who is involved with drugs. The lack of need for the evidence coupled with the possibility of misuse of the evidence by the jurors creates a strong argument to exclude the prior heroin sale evidence on FRE 403 grounds.

Early leading cases on this issue held that the past specific act evidence should be excluded where the defendant offered to stipulate. See United States v. Colon, 880 F.2d 650, 660 (2d Cir. 1989); United States v. Jenkins, 7 F.3d 803, 806-807 (8th Cir. 1993); United States v. Crowder, 87 F.3d 1405, 1410 (D.C. Cir. 1996), *vacated and remanded*, 519 U.S. 1087 (1997), *reversed on remand*, 141 F.3d 1202 (D.C. Cir. 1998) (en banc).

ii.   The Impact of *Old Chief*.   Recall that in Old Chief v. United States, page 162, supra, the Supreme Court acknowledged that the FRE 403 balancing process must include the "assessment of evidentiary alternatives." The Court then held that the defendant's stipulation precluded the prosecution from introducing evidence of the defendant's prior conviction when the conviction was relevant only to show the defendant's legal status as a former felon. At the same time, the Court observed that the probative value of evidence includes its "descriptive richness," its contribution to the "narrative integrity" of a party's case, and its ability to convince a jury of what is "morally reasonable." With respect to FRE 404(b) issues, the Court stated in dictum:

> The issue of substituting one statement [i.e., the stipulation] for the other [i.e., the evidentiary proof] normally arises only when the record of conviction would not be admissible for any purpose beyond proving status, so that excluding it would not deprive the prosecution of evidence with multiple utility; if, indeed, there were a justification for receiving evidence of the nature of prior acts on some issue other than status (i.e., to prove "motive, opportunity, intent, preparation, plan, knowledge, identity, or absence of mistake or accident," Fed. Rule Evid. 404(b)), Rule 404(b) guarantees *the opportunity to seek* admission. [519 U.S. at 190 (emphasis added).]

What impact should *Old Chief* have on our sale-of-heroin hypothetical? Superficially, *Old Chief* seems to state two general rules about when prosecutors are free to decline defense stipulations that would eliminate prosecution evidence: a general rule that prosecutors may decline such stipulations, and a narrow exception in the circumstances of a defendant's "status." Yet the central focus of *Old Chief* is less about "stipulations" than about the FRE 403 balancing process. In the above drug-dealing hypothetical, there seems to be no greater need to prove intent than to prove a defendant's status as a felon: Because it is not disputed, intent is reduced to something of a technicality and is not part of the narrative of the prosecution's case. It seems clear to us that under the FRE 403 balancing process, the past acts of drug dealing to prove (undisputed) intent should usually be excluded.

In fact, most courts have taken the opposite view, holding that *Old Chief* generally supports the admissibility of such evidence. United States v. Bilderbeck, 163 F.3d 971, 977-978 (6th Cir. 1999); United States v. Williams, 238 F.3d 871, 876 (7th Cir. 2001). At least two courts of appeals have held that *Old Chief* overrules or at least greatly restricts prior circuit precedent allowing defendants to rely on stipulations to avoid the prejudicial impact of prior crimes offered to show intent or knowledge. United States v. Hill, 249 F.3d 707 (8th Cir. 2001); United States v. Crowder, 141 F.3d 1202 (D.C. Cir. 1998) (en banc). We view these cases as mistakenly decided, to the extent that they seem to construe *Old Chief* as a sort of restriction on the need for a careful FRE 403 balancing in situations where defendants offer to stipulate to a technical issue to preclude prejudicial past acts evidence.

d. Past "Accidents" or "Coincidences" and the Anticoincidence Theory

What does FRE 404(b) have to say in cases where the defendant disputes intent — by claiming mistake or accident — and the prosecution (or plaintiff) wants to offer evidence of prior similar purported "accidents"? Another application of FRE 404(b)(2) that carries the potential for misuse is the so-called *anticoincidence theory of relevance*, also known as "the doctrine of chances." Used to refute a defense of "mistake or accident," the anticoincidence theory is based on the generalization that if the specific acts are sufficiently numerous and similar to the crime charged, "coincidence" or "randomness" is unlikely to explain their occurrence. Instead, it is more likely that there is some unifying causal explanation — for example, a single person's intentional, repetitive action — for the occurrence of such numerous and similar events. As one court colorfully put it, "The man who wins the lottery once is envied; the one who wins it twice is investigated." United States v. York, 933 F.2d 1343, 1350 (7th Cir. 1991); see United States v. Beechum, 555 F.2d 487, 495 (5th Cir. 1977), *vacated on other grounds*, 582 F.2d 898 (5th Cir. 1978) (en banc) ("doctrine of chances is the idea that '[t]he prior commission of similar acts reduces the possibility that a conceded act of disputed intent was performed with innocent intent'"); Mark Cammack, Using the Doctrine of Chances to Prove Actus Reus in Child Abuse and Acquaintance Rape: People v. Ewoldt Reconsidered, 29 U.C. Davis L. Rev. 355 (1996); Edward J. Imwinkelried, The Use of Evidence of an Accused's Uncharged Misconduct to Prove Mens Rea: The Doctrines That Threaten to Engulf the Character Evidence Prohibition, 130 Mil. L. Rev. 41, 54-75 (1990).

Consider the following hypothetical: Adam White is charged with aggravated battery on his three-year-old son, Jeremy, who suffered a facial bruise and a broken left arm. White claims that the injuries occurred when Jeremy accidentally fell down a flight of stairs. The prosecution offers to prove that on three prior occasions when Jeremy was in the custody of his father he suffered broken bones, and that on two occasions White brought Jeremy's younger sister, Ruth, to the hospital emergency room with severe head injuries.

Defense counsel objects that the past specific acts are offered to prove that White has a character trait for physically abusing his children and is therefore barred under FRE 404(b). The prosecutor responds that the evidence is offered for the noncharacter purpose of proving "absence of mistake or accident" pursuant to FRE 404(b)(2) under the anticoincidence theory. Defense counsel then objects that there is not evidence sufficient to support a finding, as required under *Huddleston* and FRE 104(b), that any of the prior incidents are (as the prosecution claims) intentional batteries by White rather than accidents or batteries committed by someone else.

Viewing each incident in isolation, the defense argument seems to have merit: There is not evidence sufficient to support a finding of the defendant's culpable involvement with respect to any single incident. But how likely is it that mere coincidental occurrence of similar "accidents" can explain all of the injuries? Instead, it may be rational to infer that intentional acts account for at least some of the injuries. Moreover, the defendant is the only identifiable person present at the time the incidents occurred. Thus, it seems reasonable to believe — perhaps even highly probable — that the defendant was culpably involved in one or more of the incidents, even though we do not know which one(s). Is the evidence sufficient to support a finding by a reasonable trier of fact under FRE 104(b) that the defendant was probably culpably involved in one or more of the past incidents as well as the present one? However that question is answered, it seems appropriate in this type of situation to focus attention for preliminary fact-finding on the acts in the aggregate rather than on each individual incident viewed separately.

Finally, defense counsel could object under FRE 403 that, even if there is evidence sufficient to support a finding that the *prior* acts were intentionally committed by White, that is insufficiently probative that the *current* incident was nonaccidental to overcome the FRE 403 dangers of undue prejudice and confusion of issues.

As you can see, the doctrine of chances allows past specific acts to prove intent where there may not be evidence sufficient to support a finding that any single past specific act was itself intentional. To be relevant, "anticoincidence" evidence has to support the inferences both that at least some of the past "accidents" were not in fact accidents and that the number of past nonaccidents suffices to refute the defense of accident on the occasion giving rise to the current claim or charge.

This reasoning process poses an obvious danger of creating a significant "doctrine of chances" loophole in FRE 404(b)'s specific acts prohibition. First, as Professor Imwinkelried has pointed out, one can always conceptualize the inference from specific act to character to action in accordance with character in terms of the doctrine of chances. Imwinkelried, supra, at 54-67. For example, evidence of a murder defendant's prior violent acts — which would be objectionable as evidence of the defendant's violent character to show action in accordance with that character — can be portrayed as "doctrine of chances" evidence. The prosecutor could focus on the objective improbability that the prior acts and the act in question would have occurred randomly and suggest that, therefore, the defendant must be culpably responsible for them as well as the act that is the subject of the current prosecution.

A second, closely related problem: How do we know when we have enough past purported "accidents" to refute the current claim of accident or coincidence?

Prosecutors have often argued — sometimes successfully — that one prior incident is enough. Compare United States v. York, 933 F.2d 1343, 1350 (7th Cir. 1991) (upholding admission of evidence of prior unsolved murder of defendant's wife to rebut claim that death of defendant's business partner was accidental) with Wynn v. State, 718 A.2d 588 (Md. 1998) (reversing admission of prior incident of allegedly knowing possession of stolen goods offered to rebut defense that current possession of stolen goods was not knowing). But if one or two or even a few prior incidents are deemed enough to satisfy the anticoincidence theory — at least for occurrences more commonplace than winning the lottery — much of FRE 404(b)'s basic prohibition could be eroded, at least in cases where a party claims mistake or accident.

On closer examination, the doctrine of chances looks a lot like a version of the character inference prohibited by FRE 404(b)(1). If it is justified, it is in cases where the statistical inference is strong enough to make the evidence more probative than garden-variety evidence of past specific acts. The question is: "How frequently does a typical, innocent person suffer this type of loss?...Once the inquiry focuses on relative frequency, it is evident that sometimes even just one uncharged incident will be admissible to trigger the doctrine of chances." Imwinkelreid, supra, at 53-54; see also Westfield Ins. Co. v. Harris, 134 F.3d 608, 615 (4th Cir. 1998) (evidence that defendant made at least seven prior fire insurance claims probative of whether fire in question was deliberately set or an accident).

A final concern is this: Are unaided intuitions of jurors sufficient to make what is arguably a complex statistical inference? You have undoubtedly encountered instances in which statisticians have estimated the likelihood that a certain eventuality "could have occurred by chance." Indeed, in criminal cases, forensic evidence is often expressed in terms of statistical probabilities. An argument could be made that, in many — if not all — cases, courts should require expert statistical evidence to establish how many incidents are sufficient to trigger the doctrine of chances.

e.   Modus Operandi and the Character Inference

A "modus operandi" is a pattern of behavior sufficiently distinctive or idiosyncratic to support the inference that the same person who committed the prior act must also have committed the one in question in the current case. It is thus relevant where the defendant denies committing the act in the case before the court. Because a high degree of distinctiveness and similarity is required to establish modus operandi, the doctrine will necessarily apply only in limited circumstances. See United States v. Thomas, 321 F.3d 627, 635 (7th Cir. 2003).

Courts have traditionally accepted past specific acts evidence under a "modus operandi" theory under FRE 404(b) and its common law analogues for the noncharacter purpose of proving "identity." Yet, as suggested above in the case of "intent," it is difficult to see how modus operandi evidence is relevant to prove identity without making a character inference. The proponent asks the fact finder to infer that the defendant has a propensity to act in a certain distinctive way, as shown by past instances, and therefore acted in that way on the occasion in question. The only justification to treat modus operandi evidence differently from other character evidence is that, because of the high standard of uniqueness and similarity of the behavior, it is more probative than generic character evidence.

KEY POINTS

1. FRE 404(b)(2) permits use of past specific acts to prove "intent" even though, arguably, the relevance of such evidence depends on making the same sort of character inference usually prohibited by FRE 404(b)(1).

2. Where "intent" or "knowledge" is an element of the criminal charge or civil claim but is not disputed by the defendant, the use of past specific acts to prove intent should arguably be excluded under FRE 403. However, at least in drug prosecutions, most courts have held that *Old Chief* usually supports admission of such evidence.

3. The "doctrine of chances" allows admission of prior incidents as to which the defendant denies culpable involvement in order to rebut a defense of "mistake or accident" under the "anticoincidence" theory — the argument that it is extremely unlikely that the past and current incidents could have occurred randomly without the defendant's intentional involvement.

D.   REFLECTION ON CHARACTER, PROPENSITY, AND SPECIFIC ACTS EVIDENCE

UNITED STATES v. VAROUDAKIS
233 F.3d 113 (1st Cir. 2000)

LIPEZ, Circuit Judge. . . . The government alleged that defendant George Varoudakis, charged with arson and conspiracy to commit arson in violation of 18 U.S.C. §844(i) and 18 U.S.C. §371, hired an acquaintance to burn down his failing restaurant, Destinations, in order to collect insurance proceeds. Following his conviction, Varoudakis argues on appeal that the district court abused its discretion by admitting evidence of a prior bad act, namely, testimony by Varoudakis's long-time girlfriend and co-conspirator in the Destinations arson, Cheryl Britt, that she saw Varoudakis set fire to his leased car sixteen months before the Destinations fire. We agree with Varoudakis that the evidence should have been excluded under Rule 403, and that the error was not harmless. Accordingly, we vacate the judgment.

I.

In 1991, George Varoudakis opened a restaurant and night club called Destinations at One Congress Street in Boston. The establishment's general manager was Cheryl Britt, Varoudakis's girlfriend since the mid-1980s. Initially, Destinations succeeded financially, but business declined about a year after it opened. Varoudakis paid his suppliers cash on delivery and owed his workers back wages. His landlord claimed $600,000 in back rent and damages, and began eviction proceedings in December 1994.

In late 1994, after several years of carrying insurance that was inadequate under the terms of his lease, Varoudakis increased the contents insurance coverage for Destinations to $500,000 and bought business interruption insurance for $100,000.

Cheryl Britt testified that Varoudakis told her he increased the insurance so he could burn the restaurant and collect the insurance proceeds.

Britt testified that several weeks before the April 1995 fire, Varoudakis told her to stop paying Destinations's bills. As a result, Britt did not pay the February 1995 insurance bill. On March 27, 1995, the insurance policy was cancelled. At trial, Varoudakis relied on the cancellation to contest the government's theory that he burned Destinations to collect insurance. Britt, however, testified that Varoudakis did not know the insurance was cancelled.

Also sometime in March, Varoudakis began moving sound and lighting equipment from Destinations to a property he owned in Everett. Several employees worked long hours loading the equipment into trucks on the days and nights leading up to the fire. According to Britt and others, the removal included a drop-safe, tables, kitchen equipment, liquor, and paperwork. More than $100,000 worth of equipment was removed.

Britt and her sister, Diane Casey, testified that at the end of March 1995, Varoudakis hired Casey's boyfriend, Nick Adams, to torch Destinations. Britt said that Varoudakis told her to pay Adams $2,000 when the job was completed.

Destinations burned on April 4, 1995. Investigators determined that arson caused the fire. Varoudakis did not dispute this finding at trial.

Cheryl Britt initially denied to investigators that Varoudakis had hired Adams to set the fire. After she learned that Varoudakis had accused Casey and Adams, and after investigators told her she could be indicted, she implicated Varoudakis. In the course of these discussions with investigators in October 1995, Britt was promised immunity. However, she lied about her involvement in the fire and her relationship with Varoudakis to investigators and in two grand jury appearances. The government did not revoke her immunity. At Varoudakis's trial, Britt was one of the government's main witnesses.

[A]fter a thirteen-day trial, a jury convicted Varoudakis of both arson and conspiracy to commit arson. . . .

II.

At trial, the court allowed Cheryl Britt to testify that in December 1993 she saw Varoudakis set fire to a Cadillac he had leased. Britt said that Varoudakis parked the car on a piece of property he owned in Everett and that he left in another car to buy gasoline, with her as a passenger. When he returned, he threw newspapers into the back of the Cadillac, poured gasoline over them, and ignited the newspapers. Britt said Varoudakis told her that he torched the car because the lease had expired and he owed excess mileage charges, and that he expected insurance to cover the loss. On cross-examination of Britt, Varoudakis offered the car lease agreement to impeach Britt's testimony that the lease had expired. The agreement showed that the lease had 23 months remaining. Following Britt's testimony, Officer Richard Gamby of the Everett Police Department testified that he investigated the burning of a Cadillac in December 1993 that matched Britt's description.

Varoudakis argues that the car fire evidence should not have been admitted under Rule 404(b) because its sole purpose was to demonstrate criminal propensity, or that the evidence should not have been admitted under Rule 403 because its probative value was substantially outweighed by its unfairly prejudicial effect. The government responds that the car fire evidence was properly admitted, or, if not, that its admission was harmless error.

We review the district court's determination that the prior bad act evidence was admissible under 404(b) and 403 for an abuse of discretion.

A.   STANDARD FOR ADMISSION UNDER FEDERAL RULE OF EVIDENCE 404(b)

Rule 404(b) provides that evidence of a defendant's prior bad acts may not be admitted to prove his criminal character or propensity to commit crimes of the sort for which he is on trial. To admit evidence of prior bad acts, a trial court must find that the evidence passes two tests. First, the evidence must have "special relevance" to an issue in the case such as intent or knowledge, and must not include "bad character or propensity as a necessary link in the inferential chain." Second, under Rule 403, evidence that is specially relevant may still be excluded if its probative value is substantially outweighed by the danger of unfair prejudice.

As the text of Rule 404(b) indicates, prior bad act evidence may be specially relevant if, for example, it goes to the defendant's intent, knowledge, plan, absence of mistake, or identity. Additionally, prior bad acts may be admitted in conspiracy cases under 404(b) if they "explain the background, formation, and development of the illegal relationship." We have focused on two factors to determine the probative value of prior bad act evidence: "the remoteness in time of the other act and the degree of resemblance to the crime charged."

B.   APPLYING RULE 404(b)

1.   The Court's Ruling

Immediately before the opening statements of counsel, in response to a motion in limine filed by the defendant to exclude the car fire evidence, the court ruled that Britt's testimony about the car fire would be admissible to show Varoudakis's "plan, knowledge, and intent" in relation to whether he "knowingly participated in a common scheme to defraud." In support of this rationale, the court cited the government's allegations that Varoudakis committed both the car fire and the Destinations arson "for a financial motive" and with "one of the same conspirators [Britt]."

The court cited United States v. Gonzalez-Sanchez, 825 F.2d 572 (1st Cir.), cert. denied, 484 U.S. 989 (1987), as authority for its ruling. In *Gonzalez-Sanchez*, the defendants, who were gang members, were convicted of an October 1981 arson. The trial court admitted prior bad act evidence primarily concerning two other recent fires. Like the arson charged, both fires had also destroyed businesses owned by the defendants and insured by the same insurance company. These fires occurred just two months and six months before the October 1981 fire. In upholding the court's decision to admit the evidence, we said: "The issue at trial was not just whether [defendant] Latorre committed arson. The broader issue was whether Latorre knowingly participated in a common scheme to defraud." Id. at 581.

There are important differences between the facts supporting a common scheme rationale in *Gonzalez-Sanchez* and this case. Unlike the recurring fires in *Gonzalez-Sanchez* — three arsons of business properties in six months — Britt's testimony does not suggest a plan connecting the car fire to the Destinations fire. In United States v. Lynn, 856 F.2d 430 (1st Cir. 1988), we held that evidence of a prior conviction for marijuana was not admissible to show a common plan or scheme connected to the defendant's instant prosecution for marijuana distribution because there was no evidence that the previous offense "leads in a progression" to the second. Id. at 435. Similarly here, no evidence suggests that "a continuing or connected scheme" linked the car fire and the Destinations fire. Id. . . .

Finally, the court said that the car fire was specially relevant to Varoudakis's motive to commit the Destinations fire because, in both instances, he allegedly committed arson to alleviate a financial burden by collecting insurance proceeds. Unlike knowledge and intent, motive is not an element of the crime that the government must prove. For that reason, proof of motive must be offered to show some other element, for example, that the crime was committed, the identity of the accused, or the accused's requisite mental state.

When prior bad act evidence is offered to prove a motive for the crime, "courts must be on guard to prevent the motive label from being used to smuggle forbidden evidence of propensity to the jury." That is the problem here. As proof of motive, the car fire testimony is offered as circumstantial evidence that Varoudakis committed the Destinations fire. It involves an inference of propensity as "a necessary link in the inferential chain." *Frankhauser*, 80 F.3d at 648. Put most simply, the government argues that Varoudakis's commission of the car fire arson in response to financial stress makes it more likely that he committed the restaurant arson in response to financial stress. Contrast this forbidden inference with the permissible inference to be drawn in a case in which the prior bad act — say, a botched robbery by the defendant that was frustrated by the ineptitude of his cohort — provided the motive for the defendant's subsequent assault on his cohort. There the prior bad act would provide circumstantial evidence of the commission of the assault without the involvement of any propensity inference.

In a case that also involved arson of a restaurant owned by the defendant, the Eleventh Circuit excluded evidence that the defendant, in a separate incident, threatened to "burn out" a tenant after she did not pay a full month's rent. See United States v. Utter, 97 F.3d 509, 514 (11th Cir. 1996). As in this case, the government argued that the tenant's testimony would show "how the defendant reacts to financial stress." Id. The court rejected this rationale, stating: "This is the type of character and propensity evidence prohibited by Rule 404(b)." Id. See also *Lynn*, 856 F.2d at 436. For the same reason, we find error in the district court's financial motive rationale.

2.   *The Britt-Varoudakis Relationship*

There is, however, a proper rationale for admitting the car fire evidence under 404(b) that differs subtly, but importantly, from the district court's rationale that Britt was a co-conspirator in both fires. The government urges on appeal that the car fire evidence was properly admitted because it demonstrates the background and formation of the conspiratorial relationship between Varoudakis and Britt during the planning for and commission of the Destinations fire.

In United States v. Escobar-De Jesus, 187 F.3d 148, 169 (1st Cir. 1999), we said that prior bad act evidence is admissible "to help the jury understand the basis for the co-conspirators' relationship of mutual trust."

Cheryl Britt's relationship with George Varoudakis was similarly material to the conspiracy case against him. Britt testified to the key facts that Varoudakis hired Nick Adams to torch Destinations and that he believed he still had insurance when the arson took place. Britt's testimony also refuted Varoudakis's alibi, and his claim that he removed the sound system and other equipment for a legitimate purpose.

Britt knew these things because Varoudakis trusted her. Her testimony that he allowed her to watch him torch his Cadillac demonstrated that trust. It also demonstrated Varoudakis's willingness to involve her in some way in his illegal acts. Like the prior bad act evidence admitted in *Escobar-De Jesus*, Britt's car fire testimony helped explain the nature of their relationship.

The defense argues that the prior bad act evidence should not be admissible to show the background and formation of Britt's relationship with Varoudakis because Varoudakis did not dispute that he and Britt were long-time intimates. At first blush, this argument seems plausible. However, we have held that evidence of prior bad acts may be probative even when it is relevant to an issue that the defendant does not contest. . . . [T]he fact that the defendant does not contest the issue for which the prior bad act evidence is offered does not, "by itself, remove those issues from the case."

We conclude, therefore, that the car fire evidence is specially relevant under Rule 404(b) to Varoudakis's relationship with Britt because it shows that he trusted her so much that he was willing to commit a crime in her presence. . . .

C.   *Rule 403*

Prior bad act evidence that surmounts the bar of Rule 404(b) may still be inadmissible under Rule 403. This rule requires the trial court to exclude the evidence if its probative value is substantially outweighed by "the danger of unfair prejudice." Fed. R. Evid. 403. Otherwise relevant evidence may also be excluded if its probative value is substantially outweighed by "confusion of the issues, or misleading [of] the jury, or by considerations of undue delay, waste of time, or needless presentation of cumulative evidence."

The district court's determination on this issue merits great deference on appeal. Nonetheless, we find that in this case the district court erred in finding that the car fire evidence was admissible under Rule 403.

Under Rule 403's weighing test, "it is only unfair prejudice which must be avoided." We stress "unfair" because "by design, all evidence is meant to be prejudicial." Id. Usually, courts use the term "unfair prejudice" for evidence that invites the jury to render a verdict on an improper emotional basis. For example, we have upheld the exclusion of prior bad act evidence in part because it was "undeniably explosive," *Gilbert*, 229 F.3d at 26. We are also cautious when the prior act is a "shocking or heinous crime likely to inflame the jury."

As the district court noted, the car fire evidence is not particularly shocking. There is little danger that it swayed the jury toward a conviction on an emotional basis. But Rule 403 also protects defendants from unfair prejudice resulting from criminal propensity evidence. As the Supreme Court has stated, improper grounds under Rule 403 "certainly include . . . generalizing a defendant's earlier bad act into bad character and taking that as raising the odds that he did the later bad act now charged." Old Chief v. United States, 519 U.S. 172, 180 (1997).

To be sure, all prior bad act evidence involves some potential for an improper propensity inference. That is why, under Rule 404(b), the possibility that a jury may infer something negative about a defendant's character or propensity to commit crime does not make the evidence inadmissible unless *no* permissible inference may also be drawn. Under Rule 403, however, that risk of an improper criminal propensity inference should be considered in light of the totality of the circumstances, including the government's need for the evidence given other available testimony, to prove the issue identified pursuant to the 404(b) special relevance analysis. See *Old Chief*, 519 U.S. at 184 ("what counts as the Rule 403 'probative value' of an item of evidence, as distinct from its Rule 401 'relevance,' may be calculated by comparing evidentiary alternatives").

Here is the crux of our analysis. "The prejudice to an opponent can be said to be 'unfair' when the proponent of the evidence could prove the fact by other, non-prejudicial evidence." Wright & Graham, supra, §5214. Doubts about the probative value of prior bad acts evidence are thus "compounded" when prosecutors have other evidence available, "rendering negligible their need to show intent by the prior bad acts."

There is clearly a tension between Rules 404(b) and 403. The more similar the prior bad act evidence is to the charged crime, the more likely it is to be deemed relevant under 404(b). Yet the more the prior bad act resembles the crime, the more likely it is that the jury will infer that a defendant who committed the prior bad act would be likely to commit the crime charged. This is precisely the kind of inference that Rule 403 guards against.

D. Applying Rule 403

The government primarily used the car fire evidence to cast Varoudakis as an arsonist. In its opening statement, the government said the following: "Now, the Defendant knew very well how to plan an arson because this wasn't the first arson he had planned." Although Rule 404(b) permits the admission of prior bad acts evidence as proof of plan, we have already concluded that no common plan or scheme linked the car fire and the Destinations fire. In reality, this opening statement underscored Varoudakis's criminal propensity to burn Destinations because of the car fire. In questioning Britt about the car fire, the government did not stress the development of her relationship with Varoudakis, a proper rationale for admission under 404(b). Instead, Britt's testimony focused on the facts of the car fire and Varoudakis's statement to her that he burned the car to collect insurance coverage.

Moreover, as in *Gilbert*, the probative value of the car fire evidence was minimal. The government did not need the car fire to demonstrate the close nature of Varoudakis's relationship with Britt. Britt testified that she and Varoudakis began a romantic relationship in about 1985, and that they lived together for six years, beginning in about 1989, in an apartment that Varoudakis helped Britt purchase. Britt said Varoudakis bought her jewelry and furniture and took her on expensive vacations.

The government also did not need the car fire evidence to prove Varoudakis's knowledge or intent relating to the Destinations arson. Varoudakis denied setting the fire at all, rather than arguing that he burned Destinations unknowingly or unintentionally. There was no evidence suggesting that Varoudakis was an innocent "tool" of others in the arson conspiracy like the defendant in *Gonzalez-Sanchez*, 825 F.2d at 581. The absence of a dispute on these issues weighs against admitting the evidence under 403. See *Gilbert*, 229 F.3d at 24 (citing as a factor weighing in favor of exclusion that "four of the five issues adduced by the government in support of admitting the [prior bad act] evidence do not appear to be much in dispute in this case.").

Britt's testimony revealed that the government did not need the car fire evidence to establish Britt's close relationship with Varoudakis, the only legitimate purpose of the evidence under 404(b). The absence of any other special relevance under 404(b), including those cited by the court and the government, was also discernible at this juncture. The propensity danger of the evidence was unmistakable. Thus the probative value of the car fire evidence was substantially outweighed by the danger of unfair prejudice at the time the district court admitted it. That ruling was erroneous.

We add two further observations. First, given the nature of appellate review, with its restrictions to the cold record, we rarely reverse a district court's judgment about the admissibility of prior bad act evidence pursuant to the weighing analysis of Rule 403. Indeed, as we have said repeatedly, "only in exceptional circumstances will we reverse the exercise of a district court's informed discretion vis a vis the relative weighing of probative value and unfairly prejudicial effect." We reiterate our commitment to that principle. Here, however, we have the exceptional case that requires us to intervene.

Second, although we do not reach the conclusion that we must intervene on the basis of hindsight, we do reach it with advantages unavailable to the district court.

By contrast, the prosecution does have these advantages of context and time. Before trial, the prosecution generally knows the totality of its case and how the prior bad act evidence fits into it. The prosecution also has the time to analyze rigorously whether the exceptions to Rule 404(b),[1] and the limitations of Rule 403, apply to the facts. The failure to engage in that analysis leads to the needless complications we find in this case and others. . . . United States v. Simon, 842 F.2d 552, 556 (1st Cir. 1988) (Torruella, J., concurring) ("Almost any excuse or far-fetched theory is made to fit within [Rule 404(b)'s] truly exceptional language.").

In oft-quoted language, Justice Jackson explained why our rules of evidence are so wary of propensity evidence:

> The State may not show defendant's prior trouble with the law, specific criminal acts, or ill name among his neighbors, even though such facts might logically be persuasive that he is by propensity a probable perpetrator of the crime. The inquiry is not rejected because character is irrelevant; on the contrary, it is said to weigh too much with the jury and to so overpersuade them as to prejudge one with a bad general record and deny him a fair opportunity to defend against a particular charge. [Michelson v. United States, 335 U.S. 469, 475-76 (1948) (footnotes omitted) (quoted approvingly in Old Chief, 519 U.S. at 181)].

Despite the fairness implications of the prosecution's use of prior bad act evidence, the prosecution too often pushes the limits of admissibility of this evidence, knowing its propensity power and gambling that the time constraints on the trial court, the court's broad discretion, the elasticity of Rule 404(b), and the harmless error rule of the appellate court, will save it from the consequences of overreaching. That is not always a good gamble.

[The judgment was vacated after the court further found that the error at trial was not harmless.]

---

1. Because of its many exceptions to the general statement that prior bad act evidence should not be admitted, Rule 404(b) is sometimes understood as one of inclusion, and sometimes as one of exclusion. Whatever the proper formulation, the exceptions must not swallow the rule.

NOTES AND QUESTIONS

1. *Varoudakis* essentially replicates the three-step analytical process described in Section C.1 for offering past specific acts evidence. The prosecution articulated a claimed noncharacter purpose (several in fact) for which the evidence of the car-arson was relevant. The parties litigated a factual dispute over whether in fact the car fire was an arson to recover insurance proceeds. And finally, an FRE 403 objection was considered, since the danger of unfair prejudice due to the jury's drawing the impermissible character inference is present, despite the apparent existence of valid noncharacter purposes.

2. See if you can answer the following questions about FRE 404 and the *Varoudakis* case:

(a)   The defendant disputed the prosecution's claim that the car fire was in fact an arson to recover insurance proceeds. Conflicting evidence on that point was presented to the jury. If the question of whether the past specific act occurred at all (or occurred in the relevant way asserted by the offering party) is disputed, why would the jury be permitted to hear that evidence? Under what rule?

(b)   Apparently, the prosecution offered other instances of past specific acts of defendant Varoudakis that were not objected to (or at least not discussed by the court as raising difficulties). These included his decision to stop paying the restaurant's bills and his landlord's claim of $600,000 in unpaid rent and unspecified "damages." Suppose the defense had objected to this evidence as inadmissible under FRE 404(a) and (b)(1) because it was offered to show his generally bad character as a deadbeat and an irresponsible tenant. How should the court have ruled on such an objection?

(c)   Why wasn't the alleged car-arson admissible to show Varoudakis's "knowledge, plan, intent or motive" as argued by the prosecution? Did the court of appeals get that issue right?

(d)   Nevertheless, the appellate court held that the car-arson evidence overcame an FRE 404(b)(2) objection. On what theory? Does that theory fall within any of the categories in 404(b)(2)? If not, does that mean the court made a mistake?

(e)   What ultimately is the basis for excluding the evidence?

(f)   The court seemed concerned about what the prosecution said about the car-arson evidence in its opening statement and closing argument. How did that factor into the court's analysis? A standard principle of trials is that "statements and arguments of counsel are not evidence." Shouldn't a reviewing court look only at the evidentiary record, and not at counsel's statements and arguments, in determining the FRE 403 and 404 issues raised in this case?

3. It is unusual for courts to be openly critical of attorneys, as the *Varoudakis* court was in the last few paragraphs of the opinion. What was the court getting at?

4. Courts and commentators frequently refer to the prohibition against use of specific acts evidence in FRE 404(b)(1) as a prohibition against the use of "propensity evidence" or a prohibition against making "propensity inferences" or using specific acts for "propensity purposes." Almost all of the permissible uses of specific acts

evidence, however, also require the fact finder to make propensity inferences that are very similar to the propensity inference that FRE 404(b)(1) prohibits. Thus, despite the common association of the term *propensity* with FRE 404(b)(1), the concept of "propensity" is not helpful in determining what FRE 404(b) prohibits and what it permits.

FRE 404(b) does not use the term *propensity* to distinguish between the prohibited and permissible uses of specific acts evidence. Rather, FRE 404(b) uses the term *character*. The Federal Rules, however, do not attempt to define *character*. According to Professor Richard Kuhns, "All character evidence offered to show action in conformity with character is propensity evidence, but not all propensity evidence is character evidence. The question, therefore, necessarily arises whether one can give some additional independent content to the term character or character trait." Richard B. Kuhns, The Propensity to Misunderstand the Character of Specific Acts Evidence, 66 Iowa L. Rev. 777, 794-796 (1981). Professor Kuhns argues that the term *character* is used by courts "when the evidence has an indirect bearing on an issue and, therefore, a relatively low probative value." Yet, in many instances, permissible uses of specific acts evidence, such as identity, intent, or modus operandi, rely on a propensity inference that is difficult to distinguish from character.

PROBLEMS

5.14. Felix Unger is charged with arson for allegedly intentionally setting fire to a business he owns, the Odd Cuppa Joe Diner, in order to collect on insurance proceeds. Unger contends that the fire, which destroyed the diner, was an accident. The prosecution offers the following evidence. Is it admissible?

(a) Evidence that two other businesses owned by Unger burned down, one 20 years ago and one 10 years ago, and that he claimed the fires were accidental. In each instance, he collected insurance proceeds.

(b) Evidence that Unger pleaded guilty to arson in connection with the fire 10 years ago.

5.15. Patty Wurst is being tried for bank robbery. She asserts the defense of duress based on the contention that her codefendants, members of a religious cult, kidnapped her and threatened to kill her if she did not participate in the robbery. In rebuttal, the prosecution offers evidence that Wurst had robbed a convenience store a year before her alleged kidnapping. Is the evidence admissible?

5.16. Return to Problem 5.5 at page 243. Assume that the trial court admitted evidence of the other guns, not to show Zachary's "murderous prosperity," but to "complete the story of the crime." Based on all that you have read, how should Zachary's appeal be argued by the defense and prosecution? How should the appeal be decided?

5.17. (a) In her trial for possession of one kilogram of cocaine with intent to sell, Ann has pleaded not guilty. The prosecution offers the testimony by a police officer that three weeks prior to the charged crime, Ann sold cocaine to Brenda. The defense objects, and the following colloquy takes place at the side bar:

DEFENSE: It's improper character evidence, Your Honor.
PROSECUTOR: No, it's admissible on the issue of intent.

DEFENSE: We haven't put intent in issue here, Your Honor, so at best the testimony is premature. And there wasn't even a conviction, so it can't get in.

What should be the ruling of the trial court on these arguments, and why?

(b) During the defense case-in-chief, Ann testifies that she didn't know that the one kilogram of material found in the trunk of her car was cocaine. On cross-examination, the prosecutor asks, "Isn't it true, Ann, that you were involved in drugs 11 years ago, which led to a conviction for selling heroin?" Ann's truthful answer would be "Yes." The defense again invokes the rule against character evidence, but the prosecutor claims, "It goes to knowledge, intent, and plan, Your Honor." What should be the ruling of the trial court on this argument, and why?

5.18. Martha Woods is charged with the murder of her eight-month-old preadoptive foster son, Paul. Paul was placed with Ms. Woods when he was five months old. Up to that time he had been a normal, healthy baby. On five occasions during the first month that he was with Ms. Woods, Paul suffered instances of gasping for breath and turning blue from lack of oxygen. On the first four occasions, he responded to mouth-to-mouth resuscitation. On the last occasion he went into a coma and died a week later.

On each occasion Paul was in Ms. Woods's custody and only she had access to him. On each occasion Paul was taken to the hospital, and on the first four occasions he was released after several days in apparently good health. A pathologist testified as an expert witness for the prosecution that Paul's death was not an accident. The witness said he was 75 percent certain that Paul's death was homicide caused by smothering, and he attributed the 25 percent doubt to the possibility of some disease currently unknown to medical science.

The government offers to prove Ms. Woods has had custody of or access to nine children who suffered a minimum of 20 episodes of cyanosis (a blue coloring due to lack of oxygen). Three of the children were her own; two were adopted; two were relatives; and two were children of friends. Seven of the nine children died.

Should the evidence be admitted?

E.   HABIT AND ROUTINE PRACTICE

Although the Federal Rules, like the common law, severely limit the circumstances in which a party may introduce character evidence to show action in accordance with character, both the Federal Rules and the common law permit the use of evidence of a person's habit to show action in accordance with that habit on a particular occasion. Similarly, they both permit evidence of business custom or the routine practice of an organization to show action in accordance with that custom or practice.

1.   FRE 406

RULE 406.   HABIT; ROUTINE PRACTICE

Evidence of a person's habit or an organization's routine practice may be admitted to prove that on a particular occasion the person or organization acted in accordance with the habit or routine practice. The court may admit this evidence regardless of whether it is corroborated or whether there was an eyewitness.

2.   Interpretation and Illustration of FRE 406

Most of the Federal Rules address the issue of exclusion or admissibility; FRE 406, which announces that a certain category of evidence is admissible, seems technically unnecessary: Since FRE 402 makes all relevant evidence admissible unless it is subject to an exclusionary rule, and since nothing in the Federal Rules excludes evidence of "habit" (as distinct from "character"), there is no reason to suppose that relevant habit evidence would not be admissible.[2] Nonetheless, FRE 406 serves two important functions.

First, FRE 406 places no special restrictions on admitting habit evidence. Although most jurisdictions today do not limit the use of habit and routine practice evidence, many older cases — including some federal cases — required eyewitnesses or other corroboration to admit the evidence. FRE 406 makes clear that these former restrictions no longer apply.

Second, FRE 406 provides a useful clarification that habit evidence is not subject to the strictures of FRE 404-405 even though habit evidence closely resembles character evidence in its form and logic. Like traits of "character," "habits" are tendencies or propensities of persons to behave in certain predictable ways. Like character evidence, the relevance of habit evidence depends on what we have called a "propensity inference" — the inference that a person is more likely to have acted in a certain way on a particular occasion if it was his propensity (character or habit) to act in such a way.

Organizations may also have behavioral propensities, but, as will be explained later in this section, FRE 406 implies that inadmissible character traits are understood by evidence law to be traits of individual persons, rather than collective groups of persons.

a.   The Importance of Habit and Routine Practice Evidence

Habit or routine practice evidence can be very useful circumstantial proof of action on a particular occasion. For example, to show that Alex was in the crosswalk of an intersection when he was hit by the defendant's car, Alex may introduce evidence of his habit for using the crosswalk at that intersection. To establish this habit Helen may testify, "I have seen Alex cross the street at this intersection hundreds of times, and every time he used the crosswalk."

Moreover, evidence of routine practice of an organization may sometimes be the only way to prove action on a particular occasion. Consider, for example, how an

---

2.   Prior to the restyling, FRE 406 provided that evidence of habit or organizational routine is "*relevant* to prove that the conduct of the person or organization on a particular occasion was in conformity with the habit or routine practice." FRE 406 (2010) (emphasis added). The relevance of such evidence is even more obvious than its admissibility. Clearly, FRE 406 was always intended to distinguish this type of "propensity" evidence from character evidence barred by FRE 404, and the replacement of the word "relevant" with "may be admitted" in the restyled rule should not change the rule in substance.

insurance company could prove that it had sent out a cancellation notice. It seems unlikely that any employee would have a specific memory of mailing the notice in question. The insurance company, however, will probably be able to rely on its routine practice to prove that the notice was sent: The company could introduce a copy of the cancellation notice along with the following testimony of one of the company employees: "This copy came from our filing cabinet. It is the routine practice of the company to put such copies in the file only when originals are prepared, signed, and placed in the outgoing mail box. Every day at 3:00 P.M., a designated employee takes mail from our outgoing mailbox and deposits it with the U.S. mail." The sorts of organizations to which FRE 406 applies must be cohesive enterprises rather than loose associations. See United States v. Rangel-Arreola, 991 F.2d 1519, 1523 (10th Cir. 1993).

b.   Methods of Proving Habit and Routine Practice

FRE 406 does not deal with the types of evidence that a proponent may use to prove habit or routine practice in order to prove conduct on a particular occasion, but that would be unnecessary. The FRE 404(b) prohibition on specific acts evidence to prove "character" does not apply to the use of specific acts to prove "habit," which by definition is distinct from character. Typically, proponents use evidence of the type described in the foregoing illustrations: The habit witness is likely either to mention a number of specific acts or to offer a summary or "opinion" based on a large number of observations that are not individually described. If the court characterizes the summary as opinion testimony rather than specific act testimony, that characterization should cause no problem as long as the opinion meets the helpfulness and firsthand knowledge requirements of FRE 701, the lay opinion rule. A routine practice witness may describe specific instances or, as in the illustration, describe generally what the practice is.

Although reputation evidence is one of the traditional methods of proving a character trait, a proponent should not be able to use reputation evidence to prove habit or routine practice. Reputation evidence offered for this purpose would be hearsay, and while there is a hearsay exception for reputation evidence offered to prove character, FRE 803(21), there is no exception for reputation evidence offered to prove habit or routine practice.

c.   The Distinction Between Habit and Character

Federal Rules 404-406 restrict the use of character evidence but not habit evidence to show conduct on a particular occasion, and as suggested above, habit evidence closely resembles character evidence and relies on the same kind of "propensity" inference in order to be relevant. Thus, the classification of a person's propensity as "habit" rather than "character" is frequently dispositive of its admissibility.

The Federal Rules define neither "character" nor "habit." However, both common usage and the case law suggest that the term *habit* refers to a propensity that is much more specific and routine than a character trait. For example, getting up every morning at 6:00 A.M. is an activity that as a matter of common usage we would refer to as a habit, whereas being violent (which typically is not something that occurs in a regularized, routine manner) is something we would call a character trait. Similarly, as we suggested, a court would probably regard testimony about Alex's crossing the same intersection in the crosswalk as habit evidence. Charmley v. Lewis, 302 Or. 324, 729 P.2d 567 (1986). Courts, however, would consider testimony that Alex acted carefully and cautiously *in general* as evidence of a character trait. Should evidence that a person "regularly stayed within crosswalks when crossing the street" be regarded as character evidence or habit evidence? Cf. Kovacs v. Chesapeake & Ohio Ry., 134 Mich. App. 514, 351 N.W.2d 581 (1984) (testimony that person approached railroad crossings in prudent, careful manner admissible as evidence of habit).

Although courts rely almost exclusively on the extent to which activity is specific and routine in deciding whether to call it habit evidence, there is another factor that tends to distinguish habit from character. As the preceding crosswalk and 6:00 A.M. rising examples suggest, activity that we think of as constituting a habit tends to be morally neutral, at least compared to character traits, which have a more salient moral connotation: being violent is bad; being careful is good.

The same factors that distinguish habit from character — regularity, specificity, and moral neutrality — inhere in what the common law referred to as business custom and what FRE 406 refers to as "routine practice of an organization." Indeed, according to the Advisory Committee Note to FRE 406, this phrase refers to "behavior on the part of a group" that is "equivalent" to the behavior of an individual that we characterize as habit.

d.   *Judicial Fact-finding on the Question of Habit*

The immediately preceding discussion has dealt with whether a particular activity is a habit or a character trait. A closely related but distinct issue, which can arise both with proffered habit evidence and with proffered routine practice evidence, is whether the evidence establishes the existence of the habit or routine practice in the particular case. Reconsider, for example, the illustration in which Helen offered to testify about Alex's habit of using the crosswalk at a particular intersection. The first question that one must ask is whether the activity is the type that can qualify as a habit rather than a character trait. In other words, is crossing a particular intersection in the crosswalk, if sufficiently regularized, a habit as opposed to a character trait? Assuming that the answer is affirmative, one must then consider whether the witness's testimony can establish that Alex's activity is sufficiently regularized to be his habit. If Helen had seen Alex cross the intersection many times, always using the crosswalk, the answer to this second question would also be affirmative. On the other hand, if Helen offered to testify (1) that Alex used the crosswalk only 60 percent of the time or (2) that she had seen Alex cross at the intersection only three times, a court would exclude the evidence on the ground that it does not show Alex's habit. In the first alternative, Alex's activity is not sufficiently regularized or routine; in the second alternative, Helen's knowledge of Alex's activity is insufficient to determine whether the activity is regularized and routine. Consider what the result should be if Helen offered to testify that on all of the hundreds of times she had seen Alex use the crosswalk she was crossing the street with him. Should this evidence be admissible to prove Alex's habit to show that he was using the crosswalk on the occasion in question, when he was alone?

In situations in which it is arguably a close question (1) whether the type of activity could fit within the habit or routine practice category or (2) whether in the particular case the evidence is sufficient to establish the habit or routine practice, courts tend to exercise fairly tight control over the admissibility of the evidence. Courts rarely articulate the precise bases for their conclusions, however. Consider, for example, a situation in which a court has excluded proffered habit evidence on the ground that the witness has not observed the activity enough times to establish whether the habit in fact exists. The court may have decided by a preponderance of the evidence pursuant to FRE 104(a) that the evidence did not establish a habit. Alternatively, the court, applying FRE 403, may have concluded that the relatively low probative value of the evidence (in light of the few instances to which the witness could testify) did not warrant taking the time to litigate the matter. It may not be clear which of these theories the court relied on. Indeed, the court may not specifically have considered these two theoretically distinct justifications for its exclusionary decision.

3. Elaboration of FRE 406

a. The Rationale for Permitting Habit and Routine Practice Evidence

The factors that tend to distinguish habit and routine practice from character — the relatively more routine and specific nature of the activity and the absence of moral connotation — suggest the rationales for permitting evidence of the former and severely restricting evidence of the latter. First, because of the regularized, specific nature of habit and routine practice evidence, it is likely to be much more probative of action on a particular occasion than is character evidence. In other words, the generalization that people have a propensity to act in accordance with their habits is likely to be true more of the time than the generalization that people act in accordance with their character traits. Second, to the extent that habit or routine practice evidence is morally neutral, it does not have the potential for prejudice that inheres in character evidence. Gamerdinger v. Schaefer, 603 N.W.2d 590, 594 (Iowa 1999). In addition, given the difficulty of recalling a specific instance of routine, repetitive behavior, habit, or routine practice may be the only evidence available for an individual, or particularly an organization to prove a particular instance of conduct.

b. The Strategy for Distinguishing Between Habit and Character

Legal authority distinguishing habit from character is less clear than one would like. The Advisory Committee Note to FRE 406 is vague, if not inconsistent, on this point. The Note begins by quoting McCormick's Handbook on the Law of Evidence that habit is "more specific" than character and is defined as a "person's regular practice of meeting a particular kind of situation with a specific type of conduct, such as the habit of going down a particular stairway two stairs at a time, ... or of alighting from railway cars while they are moving." But the Note follows this only slightly helpful definition by citing language from a case suggesting that habit means activities of "invariable regularity that are perhaps not 'volitional.'" Advisory Committee Note to FRE 406 (quoting Levin v. United States, 338 F.2d 265 (D.C. Cir. 1964)).

While the *Levin* definition seems unduly narrow, the McCormick passage does not tell us much about any qualitative difference between character and habit; nor does it provide us with much of a basis for labeling activity that falls between the fairly extreme examples of generality and specificity. For example, what about evidence that a person (a) is a careful driver, (b) always or usually stops at stop signs, (c) always or usually stops at a particular stop sign? The case law indicates that the first and probably the second pieces of evidence would be character evidence and that the last piece of evidence would be habit evidence. Jones v. Southern Pacific Railroad Co., 962 F.2d 447, 448 (5th Cir. 1992) (nine various safety violations over 29-year period not evidence of habit); Weil v. Seltzer, 873 F.2d 1453 (D.C. Cir. 1989) (passing off steroids as antihistamines not habit; habit is something that occurs with "invariable regularity"); Simplex Inc. v. Diversified Energy Systems, Inc., 847 F.2d 1290 (7th Cir. 1988) (supplier's conduct in making late deliveries on other contracts not a habit); Charmley v. Lewis, 302 Or. 324, 729 P.2d 567 (1986) (frequently crossing same intersection within unmarked crosswalk is habit evidence). These results, however, are by no means obvious from McCormick's description. For an excellent discussion of the difficulties in distinguishing between character and habit, see 1A John Henry Wigmore, Evidence in Trials at Common Law 1624-1630 (Peter Tillers rev. 1983).

Given the difficulty in articulating *a priori* criteria for distinguishing between habit and character, the advocate who wishes to convince a judge that evidence should fall into one category or the other should follow a twofold strategy. First, of course, it will be important to look at the existing case law and to draw analogies to and distinctions from situations in which courts have designated evidence as habit or character. Second, one should try to relate the desired classification to the evidentiary justifications for having different rules for habit evidence and character evidence in the first place. For example, if the specificity of the conduct, the consistency of the behavior, and its contextual similarity to the conduct at issue suggest relatively high probative value, argue that these specific factors warrant placing the evidence in the habit category. Similarly, to the extent that there is a risk of unfair prejudice, argue that risk of prejudice is one of the hallmarks of character evidence and that the evidence in question therefore should fall in the character category. Focusing on probative value and prejudice has the benefit of promoting rational evidentiary decision-making, though to be sure, this focus will not always provide easy answers to the question whether one is dealing with habit or character. The reality seems to be that the distinction between habit and character is a difference of degree rather than a clear categorical distinction.

c.   *A Particular Application of the Character/Habit Distinction: Drinking "Habits"*

The occasional difficulties in distinguishing character from habit are well illustrated by the special, but frequently recurring, situation of evidence of a person's alcohol consumption practices offered as circumstantial evidence of intoxication on a specific occasion. Consider a case in which the defendant is charged with vehicular homicide following a hit-and-run accident on a Friday evening and the prosecution wants to establish that the defendant was drunk at the time of the accident. Assume that the prosecutor is prepared to introduce eyewitness testimony about the defendant's propensity to drink and drive. Regardless of whether one regards a drinking problem as an illness, presenting such evidence to the jury is likely to be prejudicial in the sense that jurors may tend to ignore a reasonable doubt because of their lack of sympathy for a person who drinks and drives. Thus, in this respect, for evidentiary purposes a tendency to drink too much — or at least a tendency to drink too much and then drive — is like a character trait. On the other hand, if the evidence of drinking were quite specific — for example, drinking six or seven shots of whiskey between 5:00 P.M. and 6:00 P.M. every Friday after work for the last 50 Fridays — the activity is as regular and routine as much of the evidence that gets the label *habit*.

Ultimately, admissibility of the prosecution's evidence in our vehicular homicide prosecution will turn on comparing the precise nature of the evidence with the existing case law. As the Advisory Committee's Note to FRE 406 points out, "evidence of intemperate 'habits' is generally excluded when offered as proof of drunkenness in accident cases." A number of courts, however, admit evidence of a person's drinking propensities that tend to be specific and routine. Loughan v. Firestone Tire & Rubber Co., 749 F.2d 1519, 1522-1523 (11th Cir. 1985) ("uniform pattern of behavior" over six years that included drinking on job, usually drinking in early morning hours, and carrying beer cooler in truck); State v. Kately, 270 N.J. Super. 356, 637 A.2d 214 (1993) (admitting testimony that defendant had been drinking in field across from defendant's home every night each week for about a year, that defendant would consume from one to two six-packs of beer, and that defendant was drunk four or five nights a week).

d.   Evidence of Custom or Routine Practice of an Organization

Do organizations have character traits? An argument can be made that, as far as the law of evidence is concerned, they do not: The character evidence prohibitions set out in FRE 404 apply to evidence of the character of "a person." While corporations and other organizations may be treated as a "person" for certain legal issues, FRE 406 distinguishes between the conduct of "a person" and that of "an organization." Reading FRE 404 and 406 together, and giving the same terms the same meaning, thus suggests that "a person" in FRE 404 does not include organizations.

If a court assumes that organizations do not have character traits, then there is no risk of slipping across the "line" that theoretically distinguishes habit from character, and these courts may not look to precisely the same criteria for proving the custom or practice of an organization as they do for proving the habit of an individual. While courts may insist upon a showing that an organizational practice is routine and repetitive, they might not insist that the conduct be morally neutral or even so commonly repeated as to happen on a daily basis. See Vining ex rel. Vining v. Enterprise Financial Group, 148 F.3d 1206 (10th Cir. 1998) (applying FRE 406 to admit routine practice evidence of abusive pattern of insurance policy rescissions); United States ex rel. Koch v. Koch Industries, 1999 U.S. Dist. LEXIS 16632 (N.D. Okla. Sept. 28, 1999) (applying FRE 406 to admit routine practice evidence of company-wide, management-directed scheme to mismeasure the volume of oil it produced on virtually all leases).

As with habit, an objection can be made to evidence of the custom or routine practice of an organization on the ground that the proffered specific acts of the organization are insufficient to establish the custom or practice, or that the witness offering an opinion of the organizational practice lacks sufficient firsthand knowledge of the claimed practice. In addition, the opponent can object to organizational practice evidence under FRE 403 by arguing that, for example, past bad acts of the organization have low probative value for proving a routine practice, but high prejudicial effect. However, in one important respect, the objections to organizational practice evidence may differ from the objections that can be made to individual habit evidence. The opponent can object to evidence offered to show the habit of a person by arguing that the propensity is in fact not a habit, but rather a character trait. In contrast, there may be no "character" objection to evidence of organizational practice. Note, however, that even where past specific acts of an organization may be deemed insufficiently routine to fit within FRE 406, the evidence may still be deemed admissible as "past similar happenings," discussed in Section F, infra.

The kinds of organizations contemplated in FRE 406 are made up of human beings, and in many cases, the custom or practice of the organization will necessarily be shown by evidence of specific acts of individuals who work for or otherwise constitute the organization. Likewise, when FRE 406 speaks of using "routine practice" to prove the "conduct of . . . [an] organization on a particular occasion," the rule glosses over the reality that organizations act through their individual agents or employees. This reality should occasionally raise the red flag of an objectionable character inference if the proponent of the evidence is trying to use purported organizational practice to prove the conduct of an individual.

In a comparatively straightforward case of routine organizational practice, consider again the problem of an insurance company proving it sent out a cancellation notice based on an inference from its routine practice of mailing such notices. The inference from the routine practice is that the notice "was sent by the company." Clearly, some unidentified person or persons did the sending, but the law of evidence seems to gloss over this on the theory that the identity of the employee(s) who did the sending is not so important, and the conduct is legally attributable to the organization anyway.

A somewhat more problematic example might arise where the routine practice of the organization involves misconduct. Numerous instances of police brutality or employment discrimination might be offered to show a "pattern and practice" of such misconduct as circumstantial evidence that the plaintiff suffered such a wrong on a particular occasion. If the numbers are sufficient to establish the "routine practice" of the organization, it should be permissible for the jury to infer conduct on a particular occasion so long as the proponent seeks to prove the organization's conduct, as opposed to the conduct of a particular person. It is unclear whether such evidence is more appropriately admitted as "routine practice" under FRE 406, see *Vining*, supra, or instead as evidence of "similar happenings" governed by FRE 401-403. See Sprint/ United Management Co. v. Mendelsohn, 552 U.S. 379 (2008) (analyzing alleged company-wide pattern of discriminatory acts under FRE 403). The distinction is probably academic, however.

KEY POINTS

1. FRE 406 places no specific limitations on the use of habit or routine practice evidence to show action on a particular occasion.

2. The admissibility of habit or routine practice evidence is likely to turn on the resolution of two closely related but distinct questions: Is the activity in question a habit (or routine practice), or is it a character trait? Is the evidence in the particular case sufficient to establish the existence of the habit or routine practice?

PROBLEMS

5.19. Return to Problem 3.2 at page 136, supra. Leaving aside any problem of hearsay, is Driver's Exhibit A admissible to show her habit of good driving?

5.20. Consider the following two offers of evidence:

(a) Defendant Lefty Frizzell is charged with shoplifting some tools from Deuce Hardware. At trial, he testifies that he bought the items but was not given a sales receipt. In rebuttal, the prosecution offers testimony of the store manager that it was the standard practice of the cashiers to give sales receipts for every purchase. Is the testimony admissible over the defense's objection that this is inadmissible character evidence?

(b) Defendant Harry Lately is being sued for negligence for speeding through a yellow light and colliding with the plaintiff's car on Lately's way to work. The plaintiff offers the testimony of Lately's supervisor that Lately was "frequently late to work and always seemed to be in a rush." Is the testimony admissible over the defense's objection that this is inadmissible character evidence?

5.21. Return to Problem 3.3, United States v. Ray, at page 136. The prosecution offers Beth Barker as a witness. On direct examination, Barker is prepared to testify:

> I have been employed as Bernard Ray's executive secretary since 2003. I followed the following practice in handling Mr. Ray's mail, including hand delivered documents and intra-office memos. I would place incoming mail and other delivered documents in the "in" box on Mr. Ray's desk three times each day, at around 10 A.M., around 1:30 P.M. and around 4:00 P.M. At 8:30 A.M. each morning, I take all of the documents in Mr. Ray's "out" box, check to make sure that Mr. Ray has initialed them, and then place them in Mr. Ray's files. Mr. Ray always reads and initials his mail and other documents and puts them in his "out" box. In response to a request from federal investigators, on September 1, 2011, I found Exhibit 3 in Mr. Ray's files. Exhibit 3 is a March 14, 2010 memo from auditor Arthur Andrews to Rundown CFO June Jacobs. It has Mr. Ray's initials in the top left corner.

Any objections? What additional questions might the prosecution have to ask in order to secure admission of this testimony?

5.22. You are preparing to prosecute Petro R. for aggravated manslaughter involving a fatal hit-and-run accident. There is no dispute that Mr. R. was driving his car on a Sunday evening and that he hit another car that was waiting to make a turn, killing the driver. Your theory of the case is that Mr. R. was drunk at the time of the accident and that his intoxication supports the aggravated manslaughter charge, which requires "extreme indifference to human life." Mr. R. was never tested for drunkenness because he had left the scene.

You have a witness, Bernie Zurella, the bartender, who is prepared to testify as follows:

> For the past five years Mr. R. has come into the bar virtually every weekend; usually both Saturday and Sunday nights. He always stays about an hour, drinks vodka steadily,

becomes loud and noisy, and leaves. I really cannot remember whether he was actually at the club on the night of the accident.

Will you be able to use this testimony?

5.23. The plaintiff has sued the defendant manufacturer for injuries sustained when a can of refrigerant exploded. The plaintiff claims that the explosion was caused by a defect in the product, and the manufacturer claims that the explosion resulted from the plaintiff's use of a heating coil to heat the refrigerant before pouring it, contrary to the instructions on the can. Should the court admit the manufacturer's evidence that it was the plaintiff's habit to use an immersion heating coil to heat cans of refrigerant? What additional information, if any, would you want to know to decide the admissibility issue?

5.24. How should the court rule in the following cases?

(a) A bank teller seeks to withdraw a guilty plea to theft on the ground that it was involuntary. To prove that the teller entered the plea with full awareness of his rights and the consequences of the guilty plea, the state offers to prove the trial judge's habit of providing defendants with this information before accepting a plea. The proffered evidence consists of the judge's testimony about her own practices and three transcripts from unrelated cases in which the judge informed defendants of their rights and the consequences of a guilty plea.

(b) In a medical malpractice suit against a drug manufacturer, the defendant claims that it is not liable because its sales representative fully informed the treating doctor of the dangers associated with the drug. The defendant offers the testimony of the sales representative that he had a habit of discussing the dangers of the drug in question with physicians, that the discussion included information about a particular study detailing the dangers, and that the presentations to physicians would "go virtually the same way with every physician."

(c) In a medical malpractice suit against a doctor, the plaintiff alleges that she was not adequately informed about the risks of the surgery she underwent. To establish the doctor's practice of not providing adequate information for an informed consent, the plaintiff offers the testimony of three other patients of the defendant. They will all testify that they had the same procedure as the plaintiff and that the information they received about the surgery was virtually identical to the information the plaintiff claims to have received. Should this evidence be admissible? Would your answer change if there were only two such witnesses? Seven witnesses? Ten?

F. SIMILAR HAPPENINGS

In thinking about "past specific acts" or occurrences other than those giving rise to the civil claim or criminal charge, there remains one further category aside from those covered by FRE 404, 405, and 406. This category is typically referred to as "similar happenings," and it entails prior conduct by persons or occurrences involving inanimate objects that are offered for some purpose other than to prove character, habit, or routine practice. Evidence of similar happenings (or nonhappenings) falls into three broad categories:

> **(1) Organizational propensity offered to prove conduct on a specific occasion.** Past similar conduct of, or occurrences within, an organization, offered to show that the organization has a "propensity" toward certain acts or occurrences to prove the organization's conduct (strictly speaking, the conduct of one or more agents or employees of the organization) on a specific occasion. Organizational "propensity" is some factor attributable to the organization, rather than to chance (typically a formal or informal policy), that would tend to cause the acts or occurrences. (An argument could be made that this type of evidence falls within, or at least overlaps with, FRE 406.)

Examples include evidence of numerous instances of race discrimination against others to show a company-wide practice offered as circumstantial proof that the company discriminated against the plaintiff; evidence of other contracts between the plaintiff and the defendant offered to prove the terms of the current contract between the plaintiff and the defendant; evidence of prior safety violations of a company to raise an inference of negligent behavior on the occasion giving rise to the plaintiff's injury; past fraudulent transactions by a company to show fraud against the plaintiff on a particular occasion.

> **(2) Organizational liability based on policy, practice or notice.** Past similar conduct of, or occurrences within, an organization, offered to establish an element of liability, such as "notice" or "pattern or practice" liability, or to establish a standard of care.

Examples include prior safety violations of a company to show that the company "knew or should have known" about potentially tortious conditions; repeated acts of police misconduct to show an institutional "policy, pattern or practice," the latter being an element of municipal liability for torts of employees; evidence of a routine custom of vehicle safety inspections to show a standard of care that was breached in a case where no safety inspection was made prior to the accident in question.

> **(3) Characteristics of objects.** Past similar behavior or operation of, or occurrences involving, an inanimate object.

Examples include evidence that an instrumentality has caused other similar injuries in the past (e.g., that people have injured themselves falling on the same set of stairs, or that an allegedly defective product or machine has malfunctioned in the past); or evidence that similar objects have had other characteristics similar to an object at issue in the case (such as evidence that similar real properties have a value comparable to the value claimed in a property dispute).

1. No Specific Federal Rule for Similar Happenings

There is no specific Federal Rule dealing with similar happenings. Indeed, you might wonder why it is even considered a particular category of evidence at all.

Yet courts and commentators do, in fact, usually treat evidence of similar happenings or nonhappenings as a distinct category of evidence, see, e.g., 1 McCormick on Evidence §196-200 at 691-710 (John W. Strong, ed., 5th ed. 1999), probably for two reasons. First, similar happenings evidence bears close resemblance to the kinds of "past specific acts" evidence that is strictly regulated by FRE 404-406. Second, the reasoning process that makes "similar happenings" evidence relevant often relies on a propensity inference similar to that involved in character evidence. Thus, the same kinds of recurring FRE 403 dangers that undoubtedly underlie FRE 404 may arguably exist for similar happenings. Perhaps for this reason, many older cases reflect a fairly strict judicial control — as a matter of case law applying FRE 403 and its common law analogues — over similar happenings evidence. Modern cases have liberalized admission of similar happenings evidence and tend to treat it as a classic instance of FRE 403. The bottom line is that similar happenings evidence is governed only by FRE 401-403.

2.   Similar Happenings, Character, and Habit Evidence Compared

If you take another look at the examples of the three categories of similar happenings evidence, you can see some obvious points of comparison with the kinds of "propensity" evidence we have studied so far in this chapter. Category (1) resembles character evidence prohibited by FRE 404(b), in that past similar happenings are being offered to show organizational propensity to prove the conduct of the organization on a specific occasion. The reason FRE 404(b) does not apply is that the propensity in question is not that of a person, but a thing. Even though most organizations consist of groups of people, so long as the propensity is being attributed to an organization, courts will usually not consider it to be "character" evidence. Similarly, category (3) evidence is offered to show the propensity of a thing (like a machine or a piece of property). This too falls outside the scope of FRE 404 since character (as that term is understood by most courts) is an attribute of individual people, not inanimate objects.

Category (1) of similar happenings evidence probably overlaps with routine practice evidence under FRE 406, which allows proof of the routine practice of an organization in order to prove conduct on a specific occasion. But there will undoubtedly be instances in which a court will find evidence of organizational behavior to be insufficiently routine or morally neutral to qualify as FRE 406 evidence. For instance, a company may often defraud customers, but perhaps not so often as to make it a "routine." Again, such evidence is analogous to evidence of an organization's "character," but the law of evidence recognizes character traits only of individual persons. Therefore, specific acts to prove the (quasi) "character" of an organization to prove the organization's conduct on a specific occasion comes within the "similar happenings" rather than the "character" rubric. Ultimately, it is somewhat academic whether such evidence is deemed to fall within FRE 406 or the "similar happenings" category: either way, the admission or exclusion is likely to depend on an application of FRE 403 factors. See Sprint/United Management Co. v. Mendelsohn, 552 U.S. 379 (2008) (rejecting per se rule against admitting evidence of discriminatory acts by supervisors other than the alleged perpetrator in the particular case, and analyzing such evidence under FRE 403).

Category (2) resembles evidence covered by FRE 405(b): The past similar happenings are offered to prove something other than conduct of the organization on a particular occasion. The organization's "propensity" — its pattern or practice, for instance — is a fact of consequence or essential element by itself.

Where the proponent offers evidence of an "institutional propensity," the opponent of the evidence should be alert to the possibility that the evidence is really a disguised effort to prove the character of an individual. The use of past specific acts to show organizational propensity makes sense if the acts tend to show a causal mechanism by which some factor intrinsic to the organization — a formal or informal policy, for example — supports the inference that the individual acts or occurrences are not based on random factors. (The relevance of such similar acts evidence may be, in effect, a kind of "doctrine of chances" theory raising similar dangers of misuse.)

If, as is often the case, the purported "similar happenings" are really the actions of a person offered to show how that person behaved on a particular occasion, the admissibility of the proffered evidence will necessarily involve a consideration of FRE 404-406. Consider a product liability case in which the plaintiff sustained injuries after a can of refrigerant exploded. The defendant claims the can exploded because, contrary to the instructions on the can, the plaintiff used an immersion heating coil to heat the refrigerant. To substantiate this claim, the defendant offers evidence that on other occasions the plaintiff used a heating coil to heat cans of refrigerant. If the court regards the evidence as showing the plaintiff's character trait for carelessness, it is inadmissible under FRE 404. On the other hand, (1) if the court finds that the evidence falls within some noncharacter FRE 404(b) purpose or (2) if the court regards the evidence as sufficient to establish a habit, the evidence is potentially admissible. Either way, however, what on the surface appears to have been a past similar happening involving the can of refrigerant turns out to be a question of individual human behavior.

3. The Approach to the Admissibility of Similar Happenings Evidence

Don't be too caught up in the notion of "similarity" with all similar happenings evidence. Assuming the proponent of similar happenings evidence offers witnesses with firsthand knowledge of these events, the only rules that a judge will probably have to consider are FRE 401-403. Since no rule makes similarity a special condition of admissibility, it is not an FRE 104 preliminary fact for the judge to consider. Rather, the judge's task is to determine only whether the evidence is relevant and if so whether the probative value is substantially outweighed by the countervailing FRE 403 factors. As with any evidence, the probative value of similar happenings evidence depends on the purpose for which the evidence is offered. The probative value may or may not depend heavily on similarity of the proffered happenings. For example, in a civil rights suit alleging municipal liability based on a "pattern and practice" of excessive force by police, it may be that the only relevant "similarity" of the incidents is that they were all committed by members of the defendant's police force. On the other hand, in a product liability case, courts may require a showing of similarity of past injury incidents to establish that the other users all used the product as directed and thereby eliminate possible causes of injury other than product defect.

Similarity in this category of evidence really refers to the presence or absence of extraneous factors that will make the past happenings more or less probative for the case at hand. This probative value is balanced against the FRE 403 dangers: waste of time, confusion of issues, and unfair prejudice caused by risk of improper inferences. Although FRE 403 is the governing rule, many courts considering "similar happenings" evidence render decisions without making explicit reference to FRE 403 and instead discuss admissibility in terms of the similarity of the prior incidents. See First Security Bank v. Union Pac. R. Co., 152 F.3d 877 (8th Cir. 1998).

4.   The Application of FRE 403 to Similar Happenings Evidence in Practice

Since the FRE 403 balancing test favors admissibility, one's initial instinct may be that courts should be liberal in admitting similar happenings evidence when the only barrier to admissibility is FRE 403. The case law is consistent with this instinct when similar happenings evidence is offered to show *notice* of a possible defect (e.g., prior fuel tank explosions offered to show defendant had notice of dangerous placement of fuel tank). Four Corners Helicopters, Inc. v. Turbomeca, 979 F.2d 1434 (10th Cir. 1992). When the issue is notice, the probative value of the evidence depends primarily on whether the defendant was or should have been aware of the other incidents and not on how similar they are to the incident that gave rise to the litigation. But see First Security Bank v. Union Pac. R. Co., 152 F.3d 877 (8th Cir. 1998) (substantial similarity required even when evidence offered to show notice).

By contrast, when the probative value of the evidence depends on the degree of similarity among the happenings, courts are likely to require a high degree of similarity as a condition of admissibility. Most federal courts speak of a requirement of "substantial similarity." First Security Bank v. Union Pac. R. Co., supra; Wheeler v. John Deere Co., 862 F.2d 1404, 1407 (10th Cir. 1988). For example, if the plaintiff offers incidents of uncontrollable skidding by cars with Acme tires to prove Acme tires caused the plaintiff's car to skid uncontrollably, the evidence is not likely to be admissible unless the plaintiff can introduce evidence of similarity in the type of road, weather conditions, and other factors that tend to eliminate alternative causal explanations for the skidding incidents. Brooks v. Chrysler Corp., 786 F.2d 1191 (D.C. Cir. 1986) (excluding other automobile accidents because of insufficient showing of substantial similarity). Perhaps one can justify this careful screening by courts on the ground that the probative value of similar incidents standing alone is sufficiently low that it is substantially outweighed by the FRE 403 efficiency and confusion factors.

In making the FRE 403 determination, one should look not merely at the time that it will take initially to introduce the evidence but also at the total time that it will take to deal with the evidence. Once the proponent introduces the evidence, the other party is likely to feel compelled to respond with evidence suggesting that the events did not occur at all or that there are not relevant similarities among the events — a process that may be quite time consuming. Thus, unless the proponent is prepared to demonstrate at the outset that the evidence has more than minimal probative value, an FRE 403 decision to exclude similar happenings evidence may often be warranted.

5.   Similar Happenings Offered to Show an Institutional Policy or Practice

One of the most important uses of similar happenings is to show an institutional policy or practice. For example, in a prisoners' class action challenging the practices of violence at Pelican Bay Prison, the setting that gave rise to the *Johnson* case in Chapter One, the plaintiffs relied on testimony and records describing numerous incidents of excessive force against inmates to establish their claim that state prison officials were aware of the problem at Pelican Bay and, in fact, "implicitly sanctioned the misuse of force and acted with knowing willingness that harm occur." Madrid v. Gomez, 889 F. Supp. 1146, 1199-1200 (N.D. Cal. 1995). See also Austin v. Hopper, 15 F. Supp. 2d 1210 (M.D. Ala. 1998). In that lawsuit, the institutional practice was itself the focal point of the suit: Liability followed directly from the establishment by the plaintiffs of the institutional practice, without having to draw further inferences about conduct on a specific occasion.

In civil rights cases brought by individuals against a municipal police force for police brutality, evidence of other incidents of excessive force is legally necessary in order for plaintiffs to win a judgment against a city, county, or other "municipality": "[A] plaintiff must prove a specific pattern of conduct or series of incidents violative of constitutional rights in order to sustain the existence of a municipal policy or custom." Sherrod v. Berry, 827 F.2d 195, 206 (7th Cir. 1987); see Monell v. New York City Dept. of Social Servs., 436 U.S. 658 (1978).

6.   Evidence of Similar Nonhappenings

"Similar happenings" evidence is also understood to include evidence of nonhappenings offered to prove lack of notice or that an event did not occur or did not occur in the manner or for the reason alleged (e.g., evidence of the absence of people falling down a staircase to rebut the plaintiff's claim that the staircase was dangerous). See generally Annot., Admissibility, in Negligence Action, of Absence of Other Accidents or Injuries, 10 A.L.R.5th 371 (1993). In this type of case a court is likely to require evidence that the conditions were similar during the time of the nonhappenings. In addition, the court is likely to require a significant number of nonhappenings. Whereas evidence that two or three people fell down a staircase may be quite probative to show that the staircase was dangerous, evidence that two or three people managed to use the staircase without falling is not very probative of the proposition that the staircase is safe. Those two or three people may fortuitously have avoided the dangerous spot. Evidence that several hundred people used the staircase without falling under conditions similar to the conditions that existed when the plaintiff fell, however, is quite probative of the proposition that the staircase was not dangerous at the time of the plaintiff's fall.

KEY POINTS

1. Evidence of similar happenings or nonhappenings is offered to show such matters as (a) the behavioral propensity of an organization or an object, (analogous

to the "character" of a person) to show the behavior of the organization (or its agents or employees) on a specific occasion, (b) the institutional policy of an organization where that is a fact of consequence or essential element, or (c) the behavior or characteristics of an inanimate object.

2. There is no specific Federal Rule governing the use of similar happenings. As a practical matter in most cases the controlling rules are likely to be FRE 401-403.

3. Because similar happenings evidence involves either no propensity inference at all, or else a propensity inference about organizations or things rather than individual persons, it is not considered to be evidence of "character" or "habit" and is therefore not governed by FRE 404-406.

4. Except when similar happenings evidence is offered to show notice, courts tend to require a showing of similarity as a condition of admissibility.

PROBLEMS

5.25. Henry purchased Acme Household Cleanser and used it for the first time to clean his kitchen. He suffered severe burns where the cleanser came into contact with his skin. Henry sues Acme Corp., the manufacturer, for strict product liability, alleging $50,000 in damages. Henry offers testimony that during the five years before the incident seven people were severely burned by Acme Household Cleanser and that four of these instances were reported to Acme. Should any of this evidence be admissible?

5.26. Paul Preston has sued National Motor Corporation (NMC) for personal injuries arising out of an auto accident in which his "Bounder" sports utility vehicle rolled over while making a tight turn on a highway entrance ramp. Preston claims that a design defect in the Bounder makes it prone to rollover accidents. Preston offers evidence showing 50 incidents of rollovers by Bounders on entrance or exit ramps while traveling at or below the speed limit. On what basis could the defense object? Should the evidence be admitted?

5.27. The plaintiff William Lane has brought a damages action against the Los Angeles Police Department for violating his civil rights by using a potentially lethal "chokehold" in making arrests under circumstances where deadly force is not warranted. Lane offers evidence of 20 incidents in which the chokehold was applied to persons other than himself. Lawyers for the LAPD argue that the evidence is inadmissible character evidence to prove that Lane was choked on a specific occasion and that the other incidents are too dissimilar from one another to be probative and too sporadic to constitute a routine practice under FRE 406. Lane argues that the evidence is offered to prove that the LAPD had a "custom, policy, pattern or practice" of unwarranted use of the chokehold. Should the evidence be admitted?

5.28. Layla Calhoun's estate has brought a wrongful death action against the R&D Railroad. Calhoun was killed instantly when her car collided with a train at a railroad crossing. The crossing is a busy one with more than 10 trains passing by every day. Calhoun was traveling east and the train was traveling north. The crossing had warning signs and lights but no crossing gates. The plaintiff's expert, a traffic engineer, will testify that the crossing was abnormally dangerous, primarily because of the absence of a crossing gate. The plaintiff would like to introduce the following evidence:

(a) a report about the crossing prepared by the traffic engineer for litigation in a different case eight years ago; the report reaches essentially the same conclusion that the engineer is going to testify to now;
(b) evidence of five other accidents occurring at the same intersection;
(c) the opinion of a former head of the National Transportation Safety Board that the defendant has "corporate indifference" to safety issues.

How much of this evidence should be admissible? For what purpose(s)? With respect to the evidence in (b), what additional information may be important to your answer? For example, should it matter whether the accidents occurred at the same time of day or whether the trains and the automobiles were coming from the same direction as the train and automobile involved in this suit?

5.29. Fred Johnson is suing Farming Partners for breach of an oral contract for the sale of tomatoes grown by Johnson. Johnson claims that the contract was for the sale of tomatoes outright at a quoted price. Farming Partners claims that the agreement was for it to take the tomatoes on consignment. To establish Farming Partners' routine business practice, Johnson offers the testimony of two other tomato farmers that they entered into oral contracts with Farming Partners for the sale of tomatoes, that the contracts were for outright sales, and that Farming Partners breached the contracts by maintaining the position that they had accepted the tomatoes only on a consignment basis. Is this evidence admissible?

5.30. Peter French has brought a sex discrimination suit against his former employer, Acme Mortgage Co. French had worked as a loan originator, whose job it was to procure applications for mortgage loans. He claims that Jane Brown, a loan processor, engaged in sexually provocative behavior and that she refused to process the loan applications he secured unless he would have sex with her. French has a document, purportedly signed by his and Brown's supervisor recommending that French be fired. The document says, "French has complained to me about Brown's sexual harassment. The situation has become intolerable. I know French's complaints are true, but in the current market it's easier to replace an originator than a processor. I recommend we fire French." Shortly after the date on the document, French was fired.

Acme claims never to have seen the document prior to the litigation. Moreover, Acme personnel will testify that they were unaware of any sexual harassment complaints about Brown and that French was fired for inadequate job performance.

Acme wishes to introduce into evidence:

(a) a written contract between French and a former employer, Don Wilson, that contains terms extremely favorable to French along with the testimony of Wilson that his signature is a forgery, that there was no such agreement, that he saw the document for the first time after French had brought a breach of contract suit against him, and that French ultimately lost the law suit;
(b) evidence that French was unsuccessful in two suits against other former employers.

How much of this evidence should be admissible?

5.31. Ed Naples has brought an action against Acme Lawn Tool Company for breach of an oral employment contract. Acme fired Naples six months after he had been hired as Vice President for Sales. Naples claims the contract was for a fixed term of one year; Acme claims that it was an "at will" contract. Acme offers the testimony of several members of the Acme Board of Directors that all officers of the company are employed on an at-will basis. Should this evidence be admitted? What, if any, additional information would be helpful to your decision?

5.32. Pamela King has sued the Whoopie Amusement Park for personal injuries she sustained riding on Whoopie's roller coaster. According to Pamela's testimony, "A tree limb hit me in the face when I was riding on the roller coaster." The force of the blow broke her glasses and pieces of the lens were lodged in her eye. As part of its defense Whoopie offers the testimony of the amusement park manager (a) that during the entire summer up to the time of the plaintiff's injury nobody had complained about low-hanging branches along the path of the roller coaster and (b) that on the day the plaintiff was injured over 1,000 other persons rode the roller coaster without incident. For what purposes is the defendant's evidence relevant? Should it be admitted?

5.33. Return to Problem 3.2 at page 136. Should Driver be permitted to testify on direct examination that she has never had a driving accident?

G. EXCEPTIONS TO THE PROHIBITION ON USE OF CHARACTER TO PROVE CONDUCT ON A PARTICULAR OCCASION

1.   Interpretation and Illustration of FRE 404(a)(2), (3)

There are four exceptions to FRE 404(a)'s prohibition on character evidence to prove conduct on a specific occasion. These are set out in FRE 404(a)(2) and (3). FRE 404(a) provides:

(a) *Character Evidence*.

(1) *Prohibited Uses*. Evidence of a person's character or character trait is not admissible to prove that on a particular occasion the person acted in accordance with the character or trait.

(2) *Exceptions for a Defendant or Victim in a Criminal Case*. The following exceptions apply in a criminal case:

(A) a defendant may offer evidence of the defendant's pertinent trait, and if the evidence is admitted, the prosecutor may offer evidence to rebut it;

(B) subject to the limitations in Rule 412, a defendant may offer evidence of an alleged victim's pertinent trait, and if the evidence is admitted, the prosecutor may:

(i) offer evidence to rebut it; and

(ii) offer evidence of the defendant's same trait; and

(C) in a homicide case, the prosecutor may offer evidence of the alleged victim's trait of peacefulness to rebut evidence that the victim was the first aggressor.

(3) *Exceptions for a Witness*. Evidence of a witness's character may be admitted under Rules 607, 608, and 609.

a.   FRE 404(a)(2)(A) and (B): A Criminal Defendant's Right to Open the Door to Character Evidence

A criminal defendant is free to introduce evidence of the defendant's own "pertinent trait" of character (FRE 404(a)(2)(A)) or of the victim's character (FRE 404(a)(2)(B)). This is often called "opening the door" to the character issue. For example, in the *Johnson* case the defendant could have introduced evidence of his own peaceful character for the purpose of showing action in accordance with that character trait at the time of the altercation with the prison guards (i.e., for the purpose of showing that he was behaving peacefully and was not the aggressor). FRE 404(a)(2)(A). Similarly, Johnson could have introduced evidence that one or more of the prison guards who were victims had a violent character in order to suggest that they were the aggressors in the incident. FRE 404(a)(2)(B). In fact, Johnson did introduce evidence of prison guard Walker's character for violence (see, e.g., pages 48, 52-53). As we discuss in subsection 3, infra, however, it is not clear that Johnson introduced the evidence to suggest that Walker was the first aggressor.

b.   FRE 404(a)(2)(A) and (B): The Prosecution's Right to Respond to a Defendant's Character Evidence

When a defendant elects to open the character evidence door, the prosecution in its rebuttal case may introduce character evidence to rebut the defendant's evidence. For example, if an assault defendant introduces evidence of the defendant's own good character for peacefulness, the prosecution can respond with evidence that the defendant has a character trait for violence in order to show that the defendant was the aggressor. FRE 404(a)(2)(A). Similarly, if an assault defendant introduces evidence of the victim's character for violence in order to suggest that the victim was the aggressor, the prosecution may respond with evidence of the victim's character for peacefulness. FRE 404(a)(2)(B)(i). In the *Johnson* case, some of the prosecution's rebuttal focused on Officer Walker's good character (page 60, supra). One thing the prosecution may have been attempting to do was to prove Walker's good character so that the jury could infer that Walker did not act improperly at the time of the altercation with Johnson.

Note that when defendants open the door to a victim's bad character, they also open the door to their own bad character. FRE 404(a)(2). Thus, in the preceding hypothetical where the assault defendant introduced evidence of the victim's character for violence, the prosecutor could respond not only with evidence of the victim's character for peacefulness, FRE 404(a)(2)(B)(i), but also with evidence of the defendant's character for violence, (B)(ii).

Whenever the prosecution is rebutting the defendant's character evidence, the prosecution's evidence must be about the same character trait addressed by the defendant's evidence. This limitation is implicit in the term *rebut*, and FRE 404(a)(2)(B)(ii) makes the limitation explicit when the prosecution responds to evidence of the victim's bad character with evidence of the defendant's "same" bad character. Thus, in the foregoing hypotheticals, the prosecutor could not respond to the defendant's evidence about the victim's violence or the defendant's peacefulness with evidence of the victim's honesty or the defendant's dishonesty. This prosecution evidence would not *rebut* the defendant's evidence because a person can be both violent and honest or peaceful and dishonest.

c.   *FRE 404(a)(2)(C): The Prosecution's Right to Use Character Evidence to Respond to Defense Attacks on a Homocide Victim's Conduct*

FRE 404(a)(2)(C) also provides that the prosecution may introduce evidence of a homicide victim's character for peacefulness, if the defendant has suggested that the victim was the first aggressor. Assume, for example, that Johnson had killed Officer Walker and was being prosecuted for homicide. Assume further that Johnson or other defense witnesses testified that Walker was the first aggressor and that Johnson had acted in self-defense. This defense testimony is not character evidence. The defendant is not trying to show Walker's general character for violence. Rather, the defendant is offering evidence of specific actions of Walker that constitute an element of the self-defense claim. The prosecutor, however, can respond to this testimony with evidence of Walker's good character for peacefulness. This character evidence is admissible because Johnson introduced evidence that Walker had been the first aggressor; it is not dependent upon Johnson's opening the door to his own or Walker's character. However, since *Johnson* was not actually a homicide case, the prosecution could not open the door to Walker's peaceful character to show action in accordance with character.

Even if *Johnson* had been a homicide case, the prosecution could not have opened the door to defendant Johnson's character for violence. The prosecution can never introduce evidence of the defendant's character unless the defendant has first introduced character evidence. The possibility that the prosecution might improperly open the door to Johnson's character was the focus of a sidebar early on in the *Johnson* case. When the prosecution sought, over objection, to inquire into the nature of the facility where the defendant was housed, the court indicated that the prosecution witnesses could describe Facility B but could not directly state that the inmates in that facility tended to be violent (pages 8-9, supra). If the jurors heard such testimony about the inmates, they might infer that Johnson, one of the inmates, was a violent person and therefore probably had acted violently at the time of the alleged attack on the guards.

d.   *The FRE 404(a)(2) Requirement of Pertinence*

According to FRE 404(a)(2)(A) and (B) the defendant's and the prosecution's character evidence must tend to establish a "pertinent" character trait. For example, in the *Johnson* case it would have been permissible for the defendant to introduce evidence of his own character for peacefulness or evidence of a prison guard victim's character for violence to show that the guard, not Johnson, was the aggressor. Similarly, it would be permissible for a defendant charged with perjury to introduce evidence of the defendant's character for honesty to show that the defendant did not intentionally lie on the particular occasion in question. In the *Johnson* case, however, it would not have been permissible for the defendant to have introduced evidence of a prison guard's character for dishonesty to show that the guard was the aggressor; and it would not be permissible to introduce evidence of a perjury defendant's character for peacefulness to show that the defendant did not commit the perjury.

e.   FRE 404(a)(3): The Character of Witnesses

FRE 404(a)(3) is a cross-reference to the rules that permit the impeachment and rehabilitation of witnesses with evidence of their character for truthfulness. The relevance of any witness's testimony depends upon the assumption that the witness is testifying truthfully. Thus, parties are permitted to introduce evidence that either undermines or supports a witness's truthfulness. One way to do this is to show the witness's character for truthfulness. From evidence that a witness has a bad (or good) character for truthfulness, one can infer that the witness is acting in accordance with that character trait by being untruthful (or truthful) on the witness stand. We will consider the rules that govern evidence of a witness's character for truthfulness in Chapter Seven. For now, it is sufficient for you to know that FRE 404(a)(3) is a cross-reference to those rules.

3.   Elaboration of the FRE 404(a)(2) Exceptions

a.   The Relevance of Character Evidence in People v. Johnson

The evidence of Walker's character in the *Johnson* case is relevant for two distinct purposes. Diagrams 5-3 and 5-4 illustrate these two purposes.

As Diagram 5-3 indicates, reputation evidence of Walker's character is relevant to show that Walker acted in accordance with that character on March 28, 1992 (i.e., to show that he may have been the aggressor against Johnson). The evidence, however, may not be admissible for this purpose under FRE 404(a)(2), which permits the defendant to open the door to a pertinent character trait of "the victim of the crime." Although Walker was one of the correctional officers present at the scene, the defendant was charged with battery against only Officers Huston and Van Berg (pages 2-3, supra). Thus, in a formal sense, Walker was not the victim of any crime. What arguments can you make that the evidence of Walker's character should nonetheless be admissible to prove that Walker was the first aggressor?

Diagram 5-4 illustrates an alternative theory of relevance. Because the reputation evidence of Walker's violent character was introduced in conjunction with evidence that the defendant knew of the reputation, the evidence is relevant to a claim of self-defense. One element of self-defense is that any aggressive action by a defendant must be the result of a reasonable fear of bodily harm. Johnson's awareness of Walker's reputation for violence suggests the reasonableness of Johnson's actions. Similarly, the prosecution testimony that Walker was not known among the inmates as a violent person is evidence from which one may infer that Johnson had no reason to fear Walker.

This second theory of relevance does not involve using character evidence to show action in accordance with character. Therefore, it is not within the scope of FRE 404; rather, admissibility of the evidence for this purpose depends solely on the application of the basic relevance concepts embodied in FRE 401-403. The fact of consequence is what Johnson was thinking when Johnson acted, not whether Walker

Diagram 5-3

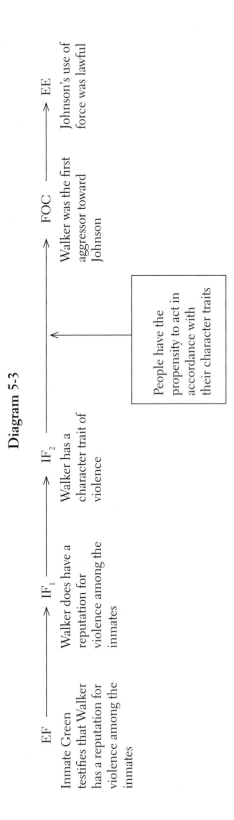

EF ⟶ IF₁ ⟶ IF₂ ⟶ FOC ⟶ EE

Inmate Green testifies that Walker has a reputation for violence among the inmates

Walker does have a reputation for violence among the inmates

Walker has a character trait of violence

Walker was the first aggressor toward Johnson

Johnson's use of force was lawful

People have the propensity to act in accordance with their character traits

Diagram 5-4

$EF_1 \longrightarrow IF_1$

Inmate Green testifies
that Walker has a
reputation for violence
among the inmates

Walker does have a
reputation for violence
among the inmates

+

$EF_2 \longrightarrow FOC \longrightarrow EE$

Johnson knew of
Walker's reputation
for violence

Johnson feared Walker's
use of force against him

Johnson's use of
force was

acted in accordance with Walker's character. Indeed, for the purpose of showing what Johnson was thinking, it does not matter whether Walker really was a violent or peaceful person. What is important is whether the defendant had a reasonable (even if incorrect) belief that Walker was violent.

We suggest that you reread pages 40, 52-53, 55-57, and 71-73, supra, in Chapter One. Did the judge and the attorneys adequately distinguish these two theories of relevance?

b.   The Rationale for the FRE 404(a)(2) Exceptions

As we have seen, there are substantial concerns justifying the FRE 404(a)(1) prohibition against the use of character evidence to show a person's action in accordance with character. One might ask why, then, there are any exceptions to the FRE 404(a)(1) general rule of exclusion. First, as we suggested in subsection B.3.a, above, the problem of unfair prejudice is likely to be greatest with respect to evidence of a criminal defendant's bad character. This type of evidence, however, will never be admissible unless the defendant chooses to open the door to the character evidence inquiry. Second, despite the low probative value of character evidence to show action on a particular occasion and despite the risk of unfair prejudice to the prosecution (e.g., the jury may be willing to acquit a guilty defendant who assaulted a person with a bad character), a criminal defendant should not have to face the consequences of conviction without having had every opportunity to establish a reasonable doubt. Proof of the defendant's good character or the victim's bad character may establish such a doubt.

Third, any risk of unfair prejudice to the defendant from evidence of a victim's good character seems relatively remote. The concern here is that jurors, on hearing of the victim's good character, would be willing to convict a defendant about whose guilt they had a reasonable doubt but who they believe nonetheless may have committed a crime against a good person. Moreover, the defendant has the right to keep the victim-character evidence door closed except in homicide cases where the defendant claims that the victim was the first aggressor. In these relatively rare instances, the defendant and the victim may have been the only persons present at the time of the killing. The unavailability of the victim to contradict the defendant's evidence arguably justifies allowing the prosecution to resort to character evidence to establish its case.

c.   Evidence of Character in Civil Actions

FRE 404(a)(3) allows impeachment and rehabilitation of witnesses based on their character for truthfulness pursuant to FRE 607-609, which applies to both criminal and civil actions. Otherwise, there are no exceptions in civil cases to 404(a)(1)'s prohibition on character evidence to prove action on a particular occasion. FRE 404(a)(2) expressly applies only to criminal cases, and thus overrules a small handful of earlier decisions that had allowed defendants to open the door to character in civil actions based on culpable conduct proscribed by the criminal law (e.g., a civil assault and battery case). Some states may still allow such limited use of character evidence in some civil cases.

KEY POINTS

1. The Federal Rules allow a criminal defendant to open the door to the use of character evidence to show action in accordance with character in the situations set forth in FRE 404(a)(2):

(a)   a criminal defendant may open the door to a pertinent trait of the defendant's own good character, in which case the prosecution may then offer evidence to rebut that same character trait;

(b)   a criminal defendant may open the door to a pertinent trait of the victim's bad character, in which case the prosecution may then offer evidence to rebut that same character trait of the victim and to prove the same pertinent trait of the defendant's bad character;

(c)   in a homicide case the prosecution may open the door to the victim's character for peacefulness in order to rebut the defendant's claim that the victim was the first aggressor.

2. Any party may introduce character evidence for impeachment and rehabilitation purposes to the extent allowed by FRE 607-609.

3. When the use of character evidence is permissible, the character evidence must relate to a pertinent character trait.

4. Except in the context of impeaching and rehabilitating witnesses, FRE 404 prohibits the use of character to show action in accordance with character in civil cases.

4.   Interpretation and Illustration of FRE 404(b) and 405(a): How Character Is Proven When the FRE 404(a)(2) and (3) Exceptions Apply

When character evidence is admissible under one of the FRE 404(a)(2) or (3) exceptions, in what form can the evidence be offered? Rules 404(b)(1) and 405(a) govern this question. FRE 404(b)(1) provides:

> Evidence of a crime, wrong, or other act is not admissible to prove a person's character in order to show that on a particular occasion the person acted in accordance with the character....

RULE 405.   METHODS OF PROVING CHARACTER

(a) *By Reputation or Opinion.* When evidence of a person's character or character trait is admissible, it may be proved by testimony about the person's reputation or by testimony in the form of an opinion. On cross-examination of the character witness, the court may allow an inquiry into relevant specific instances of the person's conduct.

There are three possible ways one might try to prove character in the absence of the above rules. First, a witness might offer specific instances of conduct of the person whose character is in question. One's character, after all, is known to others by how one behaves. Second, a witness could offer to testify that in the witness's opinion the person in question has the particular character trait. Finally, a witness could offer to testify that the person has a reputation in the community for having the kind of character trait that is relevant to the litigation. An individual's reputation is what people say about the individual, and when reputation evidence is offered to prove character, it is the truth of the reputation that is important. Thus, reputation evidence is hearsay — evidence of what people out of court say about the individual offered to prove the truth of what they say. FRE 803(21) provides an exception to the hearsay rule for evidence of reputation offered to show an individual's character.

FRE 404(b)'s prohibition on the use of specific acts to prove a person's character for the purpose of showing action in accordance with that character trait expressly applies to the FRE 404(a) exceptions. Therefore, even where character evidence is admissible under FRE 404(a)(1) or (2), it may not be proven by past specific acts. For example, during the prosecution's rebuttal in the *Johnson* case, the trial judge made it clear that Lieutenant Stokes could not testify about specific acts for the purpose of proving Walker's good character (page 58, supra).

FRE 405(a) provides that reputation evidence and opinion evidence are permissible means of proving character *whenever* a party offers admissible character evidence to show action in accordance with that character. Assume, for example, that in the *Johnson* case, Walker was properly considered a victim (which technically he was not, because no charge was based on the alleged assault on him). Assume further that the defense and the prosecution were interested in proving Walker's character for violence or peacefulness for the purpose of showing whether he was the first aggressor. See Diagram 5-3 at page 288, supra. The following evidence could be used for this purpose: Inmate Green, a defense witness, testified on direct examination that Walker had a reputation for being a "bad cop" (page 48, supra); on redirect examination Green testified that Walker was known among the inmates — that is, had a reputation among the inmates — for violence; and during the prosecution's rebuttal case, Lieutenant Stokes testified Walker had the reputation as a good correctional officer (page 60, supra). Pursuant to FRE 405(a) it also would have been permissible for these witnesses to offer their opinions about Walker's violence or peacefulness.

For ease of reference, we will refer to witnesses who give reputation or opinion testimony about a person's character pursuant to FRE 405(a) as "character witnesses." The last sentence of FRE 405(a) permits the opposing party to ask character witnesses specific acts questions on cross-examination. We deal with this part of the rule in subsection 5.e, infra.

PROBLEMS

5.34. In the *Johnson* case, assume that one of the charges was assaulting Officer Walker. For what purposes, if any, should the following evidence be admissible?

(a) Officer Huston's testimony for the prosecution that on several previous occasions Johnson had assaulted other prisoners and prison guards;

(b) Inmate Green's testimony for the defense that Officer Walker has a reputation for violence;

(c) Officer Walker's testimony for the prosecution in rebuttal that Johnson has a reputation for violence.

5.35. The defendant has been charged with perjury before a federal grand jury. As part of its case-in-chief the prosecutor offers the following evidence:

(a) W_1's testimony that he knows of at least five occasions on which the defendant has lied.
(b) W_2's testimony that the defendant has a reputation in the community for dishonesty.

As part of the defense, the defendant offers the following evidence:

(c) W_3's testimony that the defendant has a reputation in the community for honesty. Which pieces of evidence are objectionable?

5.36. Mayer is charged with assault with a deadly weapon and claims self-defense. In his defense, Mayer offers testimony that (a) two weeks before the alleged assault the victim had threatened him with a knife, (b) the victim had a reputation for carrying weapons, and (c) on the morning of the trial the victim threatened to kill Mayer's sister. For what purposes is this evidence relevant? Is it admissible?

5.37. Clarence Hill is being prosecuted for the attempted murder of Ted Ellsworth in a jurisdiction that views mere words as potentially adequate provocation, which would be a defense to the attempted murder charge.

Clarence and several eyewitnesses testify as follows: They and Ted Ellsworth were all in a local tavern, and Hill and Ellsworth were at opposite ends of the bar. Ellsworth taunted Hill with racial slurs and derogatory references to Hill's wife. Hill became enraged and shot Ellsworth.

The prosecutor is convinced that these witnesses are lying and wants to introduce the testimony of Ruth Watson that Ellsworth has a reputation in the community for peacefulness, compassion, and absence of racial prejudice. Ellsworth is not available to testify. Is Ruth Watson's testimony admissible?

5.38. On the night of October 7, Elton Haywood called the police to report a prowler in his backyard and then went outside with a shotgun to search for the prowler. When the police arrived, they mistook Haywood for the prowler, and despite — or perhaps because of — Haywood's loud, persistent protestations, they handcuffed him. Eventually the police took Haywood to the Dry-U-Out Detoxification Facility, where he spent the night locked in a cell with a urine-soaked floor. Haywood has filed a civil rights and false imprisonment suit against the facility and several of its employees. Although Haywood has had a drinking problem in the past, he claims that he had had nothing to drink on the night of the incident and that he was wrongfully detained. The defendants offer expert opinion testimony that Haywood is an alcoholic and that a common characteristic of alcoholics is to deny that they have been drinking when they plainly have. Is the evidence admissible?

5. Elaboration of the Permissible Methods of Proving a Person's Character to Show Action in Accordance with Character

a. The Prohibition Against the Use of Specific Acts

The FRE 404(b)(1) prohibition against the use of specific acts to prove character to show action in accordance with character may seem counterintuitive. The people that we know — or that we think we know — the best are likely to be people that we know by their deeds. Thus, it would seem that specific acts evidence would often be the most probative form of character evidence. Nonetheless, as discussed above, there are substantial FRE 403-type countervailing concerns that justify excluding specific acts to prove character to show action in accordance with character. These include: bad person prejudice stemming from evidence of prior *bad* acts; confusion of issues and undue consumption of time if there are factual disputes surrounding the alleged prior conduct; and the relatively low probative value of the character inference generally.

As discussed above, there are limited instances in which it is permissible to use evidence of a person's specific acts to prove that person's character to show action in accordance with character. FRE 608(b) and 609 contemplate use of specific acts to prove the character of a witness for truthfulness or untruthfulness, and FRE 413-415 contemplate the use of specific acts to prove character to show action in accordance with character in certain cases of sexual misconduct.

b.   *The Probative Value of Opinion and Reputation Evidence to Prove Character*

The probative value of opinion or reputation evidence to prove a person's character will depend in part on how long, how well, and in what contexts the witness has known (opinion) or has known about (reputation) the person whose character the evidence is offered to prove. The common law (which did not permit opinion evidence at all in most jurisdictions) required that a reputation witness testify to the person's reputation in the community. In theory, this focus on the community as a whole was designed to ensure that evidence be fairly reflective of the views about the person in question. As a practical matter today, however, there will not be many instances in which an individual has a reputation throughout the entire community in which the person lives. Indeed, in our complex, urbanized society, it is not clear what the entire community would be. Courts wisely recognize this fact and permit reputation testimony to be based on what a witness has heard in some relevant community — perhaps the neighborhood where the person lives or the place where the person works. Consider, for example, the *Johnson* case, where defense counsel objected on relevance grounds to evidence of Walker's good reputation among the prison staff. According to the defense, the evidence should have been limited to Walker's reputation among the inmates, but the judge disagreed:

> I am going to overrule the objection because although the inmates and the staff are not precisely the same, they are a part of the community within the prison and are in communication with one another on a constant basis. So reputation is something that is back and forth and it is the kind of thing that would be known. [Page 58, supra.]

Even if there is no difficulty in defining the relevant community, there may be a question whether the witness knows or knows about the individual well enough to testify in the form of opinion or reputation. The Federal Rules do not deal specifically with the foundation requirement for character witnesses. FRE 403, however, provides latitude for trial judges to exclude testimony that is marginally probative because the witness does not have much of a basis for knowing or knowing about the person in question. United States v. Watson, 669 F.2d 1274 (11th Cir. 1982) (not error to exclude testimony of character witness who knew individual for brief period of time, which did not coincide with relevant events at trial).

Character witnesses are likely to be friendly, cooperative witnesses on direct examination. Thus, if the witness in fact has a sufficient basis for offering character evidence, there should seldom be any difficulty in eliciting the appropriate foundational information and in getting responses in the form of reputation or opinion testimony to questions about pertinent character traits. Michelson v. United States, 335 U.S. 469, 471 (1948), where a bribery defendant opened the door to his own character, provides a good, albeit somewhat sparse, example of a direct examination of a character witness:

Q: Do you know the defendant Michelson?
A: Yes.
Q: How long do you know Mr. Michelson?
A: About 30 years.
Q: Do you know other people that know him?
A: Yes.
Q: Have you had occasion to discuss his reputation for honesty and truthfulness and for being a law-abiding citizen?
A: It is very good.
Q: Have you talked to others?
A: Yes.
Q: And what is his reputation?
A: Very good.

For an elaboration of the common law foundation requirements for reputation and opinion testimony, see Mason Ladd, Techniques and Theory of Character Testimony, 24 Iowa L. Rev. 498 (1939).

c. Reputation Evidence Versus Opinion Evidence

Opinions are generalizations from more specific facts, and an opinion about a person's character will naturally be a generalization based on the witness's perception of that person's behavior. In situations other than character testimony, when a witness testifies in the form of opinion, it is permissible — indeed, desirable — to inquire into the underlying basis for the opinion on both direct and cross-examination. Because of this standard practice, the use of opinion evidence to prove character creates the possibility that the opinion witness could testify about various specific acts that provide the basis for the opinion. The common law's reluctance to permit litigation over specific acts is precisely the reason that the majority common law rule prohibited opinion testimony, along with specific acts testimony, to prove character to show action in accordance with character.

Nonetheless, witnesses who are called to testify about an individual's character are likely to have rather strong personal feelings about the individual who is the subject of their testimony. If they testify in terms of reputation, the real gist of what they are thinking and of what motivates their testimony may well be their *opinion* about the defendant's character. Recognizing this possibility, the drafters of the Federal Rules took the position that these character witnesses should be permitted to offer their opinions directly. Thus, FRE 405(a) permits both reputation and opinion testimony in all instances in which character evidence is admissible. At the same time, however, the Advisory Committee Note to FRE 405 makes it clear that the use of opinion testimony to prove character to show action in accordance with character should "be confined to the nature and extent of observation and acquaintance upon which the opinion is based." Opinion testimony should not be allowed to evolve into testimony about specific acts on which the opinion may be based.

KEY POINTS

1. FRE 404(b) prohibits the use of specific acts to prove a defendant's character for the purpose of showing action in accordance with character, except in the limited situations governed by FRE 413-415, FRE 608(b), and FRE 609, which we will consider later.

2. FRE 405(a) permits the proponent to offer both reputation and opinion testimony in the limited situations in which FRE 404(a) allows the use of character evidence to show a person's action in accordance with character.

3. If a character witness offers opinion testimony, it is not permissible to explore on direct examination the specific acts that may be the basis for the witness's opinion.

d.   The Cross-examination of Character Witnesses

Although a character witness cannot testify about specific acts on direct examination, the cross-examiner is allowed to question the character witness about specific acts relevant to character, pursuant to the last sentence of FRE 405(a). Assume, for example, that John Smith is charged with murder and that as part of the defense Mary Martin testifies, pursuant to FRE 404(a)(1), that John has a good reputation in the community for peacefulness. The prosecutor, when cross-examining Mary, can ask about various violent acts that John supposedly committed.

i.   The Relevance of the Specific Acts Inquiries.   The permissible relevant purpose for asking specific acts questions in the preceding example is *not* to prove John's character for violence. Indeed, FRE 404(b) prohibits questions about specific acts to prove John's character. Rather, the permissible relevant purpose of the prosecutor's questions is to test Mary's credibility as a reputation witness: If she denies having heard of the acts of violence, one can infer that she does not have a very good sense of what John's reputation is; and if she has heard of the acts, one may doubt the truth of her testimony (or question her conception of what a reputation for peacefulness means). United States v. Adair, 951 F.2d 316, 319 (11th Cir. 1992); United States v. Alvarez, 860 F.2d 801, 826-827 (7th Cir. 1988).

Because the specific act questions are admissible only to impeach the character witness and not to prove the character of the person who is the subject of the testimony, the party calling the character witness is entitled to a limiting instruction pursuant to FRE 105. For example, in our John and Mary hypothetical, the judge might say, "Ladies and gentlemen of the jury, I instruct you that the questions the prosecutor asked Ms. Martin about various acts of violence allegedly engaged in by Mr. Smith were asked for the sole purpose of assessing Ms. Martin's knowledge of Mr. Smith's reputation. You must not consider them as evidence of Mr. Smith's character."

   ii. The Prejudicial Impact of Specific Acts Questions.   To the extent that jurors are unwilling or unable to follow a limiting instruction regarding specific acts questions posed pursuant to FRE 405(a), there is a two-fold risk of prejudice. In the preceding hypothetical, for example, the jurors may infer from the questions to Mary about John's violent acts that John is a violent person and may have acted in accordance with that violent character trait by murdering the victim of the charged crime, as the prosecution has alleged. This use of the evidence would violate FRE 404(b), thereby raising the FRE 403 danger of unfair prejudice in the sense that the jury may use the evidence in a logically relevant but legally impermissible manner. In addition, the jurors may be willing to ignore a reasonable doubt if they regard John as a bad, dangerous person. This possibility raises the FRE 403 danger of unfair prejudice in the sense that the jurors may base their decision on an emotional and legally improper ground.

   The most prejudicial specific acts questions, as the preceding hypothetical demonstrates, are those that relate directly to the character trait about which the character witness testified. These questions, however, are also likely to be the most probative for the legitimate purpose of testing a character witness's knowledge of the defendant's character for peacefulness. Since FRE 405(a) specifically authorizes these questions, and since high prejudice is likely always to be a concomitant of high probative value with FRE 405(a) specific acts questions, courts regularly permit the cross-examiner to ask character witnesses questions that are in fact extremely prejudicial.

   iii.   The Relationship Between the Character Trait and the Specific Acts Inquiries.   Specific act inquiries made pursuant to FRE 405(a) must be "relevant" to the character trait about which the character witness testified on direct examination. One aspect of this relevance requirement is that the specific acts must relate to the character trait in question. For example, in our hypothetical involving Mary's testimony about John's reputation for peacefulness, it would be appropriate to ask Mary about John's specific acts of violence but not about acts of dishonesty. United States v. Westerbrook, 896 F.2d 330, 335 (8th Cir. 1990) (character witness testified as to defendant's honesty; improper to ask character witness about defendant's conviction for possessing controlled substance).

   One might argue that, in a minimal FRE 401 sense, any bad act is relevant to a bad character trait, and any good act is relevant to a good character trait. Moreover, since the purpose of the inquiry is to test the character witness's knowledge of the principal witness's character, the key to relevance arguably should be the likely notoriety of the act rather than its relationship to the character trait about which the witness testified. Nonetheless, courts are likely to require that FRE 405(a) specific acts questions to character witnesses relate to the character trait about which the witness has testified — a result that one can probably justify under FRE 403, if not FRE 401.

   iv.   The Character Witness's Likely Knowledge of the Specific Act.   A second restriction on the use of specific acts evidence to impeach a character witness is also a matter of relevance — or at least probative value for the purpose of FRE 403 balancing.

The questions should be limited to acts about which the witness is likely to have known or to have heard. United States v. Alvarez, 860 F.2d 801, 827 (7th Cir. 1989). For example, if Mary on direct examination testified that she had known John well for five years and was familiar with his reputation during that time, it may not be reasonable to expect that she would have heard about an isolated act of violence that occurred 15 years ago. Even if she had heard about the act, it may not be reasonable to expect a single 15-year-old act of violence to affect her view of John's reputation for peacefulness during the past five years. But see Alvarez, supra (trial court did not abuse its discretion by permitting inquiry about specific act occurring 10 years before character witness giving reputation testimony knew the defendant). Cf. Michelson v. United States, 335 U.S. 469 (1948) (where two character witnesses testified to knowing defendant 30 years and a third character witness testified to knowing defendant half that long, not error to allow questions about matters that occurred 20 and 27 years ago).

Assessing whether a character witness is likely to have heard of any particular act will involve consideration of several factors. For example, in our Mary and John hypothetical, how well and how long has Mary known or known about John? Is John's act likely to have been the subject of discussion because of the nature of the act? Is John the kind of person whose activities are likely to be known to people situated similarly to Mary? Questions that are only marginally probative for legitimate impeachment purposes may be excluded because of their low probative value and high degree of unfair prejudice.

v.   The Cross-examiner's Reasonable Belief That the Act Occurred.   A third limitation on the use of specific acts questions (not specifically mentioned in FRE 405(a)) relates to the cross-examiner's belief that the specific acts occurred. If the prosecutor had no knowledge about whether John, in our hypothetical, had committed any violent acts, it should be permissible to ask Mary in a nonsuggestive manner, "Do you know of any violent acts that John has committed?" However, any but the most general inquiry about specific acts is likely to suggest to the jury that the cross-examiner believes that the act occurred. When such an implication inheres in the question, the cross-examiner must have a reasonable basis for believing that the act occurred. United States v. Adair, 951 F.2d 316, 319 (11th Cir. 1992); United States v Alvarez, supra.

Some courts have suggested that the better practice is to require the cross-examiner to demonstrate the factual basis to the judge, outside the presence of the jury, before asking the questions. United States v. Reese, 568 F.2d 1246 (6th Cir. 1977). In Alvarez, supra, the court followed this practice, and the prosecutor responded with an affidavit from an FBI officer stating that defendant had confessed to the act in question.

In discussing this limitation on the cross-examination of character witnesses, the Supreme Court in Michelson v. United States, supra, noted that as a matter of logical relevance the requirement should be that the cross-examiner of the reputation witness have a reasonable belief that there were *rumors about the act*, regardless of whether it in fact occurred. Nonetheless, the Court approved the existing rule requiring the cross-examiner to demonstrate to the judge the reasonable basis for believing that the *act in fact occurred*:

> But before this relevant and proper inquiry [here, a question to the defendant's character witness about the defendant's arrest] can be made, counsel must demonstrate privately to

the court an irrelevant and possibly unprovable fact — the reality of the arrest. From this permissible inquiry about reports of arrest, the jury is pretty certain to infer that defendant had in fact been arrested and to draw its own conclusions as to character from that fact. The [requirement of a reasonable basis] thus limits legally relevant inquiries to those based on legally irrelevant facts in order that the legally irrelevant conclusion which the jury probably will draw from the relevant questions will not be based on unsupported or untrue innuendo. It illustrates Judge Hand's suggestion that the system may work best when explained least. Yet, despite its theoretical paradoxes and deficiencies, we approve the procedure as calculated in practice to hold the inquiry within decent bounds. [335 U.S. at 481 n.18.]

vi.   Acts, Arrests, and Convictions.   Like *Michelson*, decisions under the Federal Rules permit prosecutors to ask defense character witnesses not only about defendants' prior *acts* but also about their prior *arrests*. United States v. Wellons, 32 F.3d 117 (4th Cir. 1994); United States v. Jordan, 722 F.2d 353, 358 (7th Cir. 1983). An arrest, however, is "conduct" by the police, not the defendant.

As a matter of logical relevance, asking about the arrest rather than the conduct leading to it is not inappropriate. The purpose of the question is to test what the character witness knows or has heard about the defendant, and in some instances there may have been as much or more publicity about the arrest than the underlying acts. On the other hand, if there is reason to believe that the defendant did not engage in the conduct leading to the arrest, the question may be particularly prejudicial. There is always the risk that the jury may use a specific act question improperly to infer that the defendant has a bad character. If the defendant has engaged in the conduct suggested by the question, the jury at least gets an accurate assessment of the kind of person the defendant is. Evidence of the defendant's arrests creates not only this risk but also the risk that the jury will regard the arrest, perhaps incorrectly, as evidence that the defendant actually engaged in the illegal activity. Nonetheless, inquiry about arrests may be appropriate. United States v. Grady, 665 F.2d 831, 834-835 (8th Cir. 1981) (permitting inquiry about arrests on charges that were later dismissed).

Sometimes specific act questions to a defendant's character witness refer to the defendant's prior convictions. United States v. Collins, 779 F.2d 1520 (11th Cir. 1986). Like an arrest, a defendant's prior conviction is logically relevant — without regard to the truth of the underlying facts — to test the character witness's awareness of the defendant's background or reputation. Permitting questions about convictions, however, may be even more prejudicial than permitting questions about arrests. While there may be little likelihood that the defendant did not commit the acts leading to a conviction, the very certainty of those facts, as validated by the conviction, may make it especially difficult for the jury to disregard the improper inference that the defendant is a bad person.

vii.   The Form of the Questions on Cross-examination.   The common law, which in most jurisdictions permitted a criminal defendant to use only reputation evidence when opening the door to character, was quite exacting about the proper form of specific acts questions on cross-examination. Since the direct examination testimony was limited to what the witness had *heard* people say about the defendant, asking on cross-examination whether the witness *knew* about some bad act was objectionable. The proper form for the specific acts questions on cross-examination was, "Have you heard ... ?" not "Did you know ... ?" By contrast, if the jurisdiction happened to permit opinion testimony on direct examination, a witness offering an opinion about the defendant's character presumably would be basing that opinion in whole or in part on personal knowledge. Thus, it would be proper to ask on cross-examination whether the opinion witness knew about specific acts.

If there were ever sound reasons for insisting on the proper form of cross-examination questions about specific acts, those reasons have been seriously eroded by the allowance of opinion as well as reputation testimony on direct examination. The Advisory Committee Note to FRE 405 asserts that the distinctions in the form of the cross-examination questions "are of slight if any practical significance" and that the second sentence of FRE 405(a) "eliminates them as a factor in formulating questions." United States v. Scholl, 166 F.3d 964, 974 (9th Cir. 1999) (no merit to argument that "Did you know … ?" rather than "Have you heard … ?" was improper in cross-examining character witness).

e.   Limitations on the Use of Character Evidence in Practice

i.   The Inherent Weakness of Good Character Evidence.   The most common use of character evidence to show action in accordance with character pursuant to FRE 404(a)(1) and (2) is a criminal defendant's opening the door with evidence of the defendant's own *good* character. Nonetheless, for reasons that are probably apparent, the occasions on which criminal defendants elect to open the door to the character evidence inquiry are relatively rare. In most cases, reputation and opinion evidence about a defendant's good character is not likely to be highly persuasive. The ban on using specific acts to prove character means that the opinion or reputation witness cannot provide persuasive or illustrative examples to support the opinion or reputation testimony. As a result, that testimony will necessarily take the form of (often bland) generalities. In sharp contrast, the cross-examiner of such character witnesses can go into specific bad acts under FRE 405(b). Depending on what the prior bad acts look like, they are potentially very persuasive and effective in undermining the positive character testimony.

Consider, then, who is likely to benefit from a rule that permits criminal defendants to open the door to character evidence. Or to put the issue somewhat differently, consider what kinds of people you would like to be able to call as character witnesses if you were a criminal defendant. To the extent that criminal defendants may benefit from the use of character evidence, is the benefit likely to be derived from the content of the character testimony or from the character (and/or reputation) of the character witnesses? If the character of the character witnesses is likely to make the biggest difference, is it desirable to have a rule that, in effect, benefits people primarily because of whom they know?

ii.   The Potential Unfairness of FRE 405.   We have already noted that courts may exclude on FRE 401-403 grounds questions about acts that do not relate to the character trait in issue and that are sufficiently remote from the time frame about which the character witness testified. As we pointed out above, however, FRE 403 is not often applied to exclude Rule 405 specific acts questions. As a result, FRE 405 appears to give a significant unfair advantage to the cross-examiner. For example, in our preceding murder hypothetical, the defendant, John, is limited to the use of relatively bland reputation or opinion evidence of his peaceful character. The prosecutor, by contrast, can ask Mary, the character witness, about all sorts of violent acts in which

John may have engaged. Granted, in theory the purpose of the prosecutor's questions is not to prove the defendant's character but only to impeach the credibility of the character witnesses. And granted, the defendant is entitled to a limiting instruction from the judge. How likely is it, though, that the jury will be able to confine its consideration of the violent acts to the theoretically legitimate impeachment purpose?

Is it sufficient to answer that the process is not unfair because the defendant has the choice initially to decide whether to open the door to character evidence? If you are defense counsel and if you feel compelled to call character witnesses, what can you do to blunt the effect of the prosecutor's cross-examination of your character witnesses?

KEY POINTS

1. Whenever a character witness testifies in the form of reputation or opinion about a person's character, FRE 405(a) permits the opposing party to ask the witness on cross-examination about specific acts committed by the person who is the subject of the character testimony. Courts also permit questions about the person's arrests or convictions.

2. The specific acts (or arrests or convictions) must relate to the character trait about which the witness has testified.

3. The purpose of the specific acts question is to impeach the testimony of the character witness, not to show the character of the person about whom the witness has testified.

PROBLEMS

5.39. Return to Problem 5.35 at page 293, where the defendant has been charged with committing perjury before a federal grand jury. Assume that there is no objection to W_3's testimony that the defendant has a reputation in the community for honesty.

On cross-examination of W_3 the prosecutor asks:

(a) "Did you know that the defendant was convicted of perjury five years ago?"
(b) "Did you know that last year the defendant was arrested and charged with obtaining money by false pretenses?"
(c) "Have you heard that the defendant was investigated for filing a false income tax return ten years ago?"
(d) "Have you heard that the defendant was convicted of assault last year?"

In rebuttal, the prosecution offers the following evidence:

(e) W_4's testimony that in her opinion the defendant is a very dishonest person.
(f) W_4's testimony that this opinion is based on her having observed the defendant lie and cheat on several previous occasions.

Which pieces of evidence are objectionable?

5.40. Dick Davis is charged with the murder of Ralph Green and claims self-defense. After the prosecution has presented its case, Davis offers the following evidence:

(a) W_1 to testify that he and Davis are Elks, that he knows Davis well from weekly meetings, and that Davis has an excellent reputation for honesty among the Elks.
(b) W_2 to testify that Ralph Green has a reputation in the community for violence.
(c) W_3 to testify that two years ago Ralph Green was convicted of aggravated assault, a felony.
(d) W_4 to testify that she told the defendant of three different times that she had seen the victim make unprovoked attacks on other people.

In rebuttal, the prosecution offers the following evidence:

(e) W_5 to testify that Ralph Green has a reputation in the community for peacefulness.
(f) W_6 to testify that Davis has a reputation in the community for violence.

Which evidence is objectionable?

5.41. Return to Problem 3.3, United States v. Ray, at page 136. Is the following evidence admissible? Might the answer change depending on the order in which the evidence is offered?

(a) For the prosecution: Testimony from a partner in the brokerage firm that handled Bernard Ray's stock transactions: "Bernard Ray is an unusually shrewd and well-informed investor. He personally directs each and every trade of shares in his account."
(b) For the defense: Testimony from June Jacobs, Rundown's CFO: "Bernard Ray, although a great salesman and inspirational leader to the company, is extremely unsophisticated about finance and securities markets. He delegated all financial matters to others in both the running of the company and in decision-making regarding his personal investments."
(c) For the defense: Five instances since the year 2005 in which major trades of securities (other than Rundown stock) were made at the discretion of one of Bernard Ray's brokers.
(d) For the prosecution: Evidence that Ray has a PhD in economics.

H. EVIDENCE OF A PERSON'S CHARACTER WHEN CHARACTER IS AN ESSENTIAL ELEMENT OF A CLAIM OR DEFENSE

Consider an action in which Martha sues George for libel because George has circulated a leaflet claiming that Martha was dishonest. An element of Martha's claim is that the allegedly libelous statement is false. Since the statement that Martha is dishonest is a statement about her character, Martha's actual character for dishonesty is an essential element of her claim.

Nothing in FRE 404 or in any other Federal Rule specifically prohibits or restricts the use of character evidence when character *is an essential element of a claim or a defense*. FRE 405, however, addresses the type of character evidence that one can use in this type of situation.

1.   Interpretation and Illustration of FRE 405(b)

RULE 405.   METHODS OF PROVING CHARACTER

(b) *By Specific Instances of Conduct.* When a person's character or character trait is an essential element of a charge, claim, or defense, the character or trait may also be proved by relevant specific instances of the person's conduct.

Occasionally, the substantive law makes a person's character an essential element of a claim or a defense, as the element of falsity (or in some jurisdictions, the defense of truth) does in a defamation action when an allegedly defamatory statement is a statement about a person's character. For example, the fitness or character of a person is a factor to consider in deciding whether to award child custody to that person. A claim that a hospital was negligent in hiring a careless physician makes the physician's carelessness — that is, character for lack of care — an element that the plaintiff must establish in order to recover. Similarly, a negligent entrustment claim that the defendant was negligent in permitting a careless, unqualified employee to drive the plaintiff's vehicle makes the employee's character for lack of care an element that the plaintiff must prove in order to prevail. In wrongful death cases, the plaintiff's damages may depend in part on the character of the decedent, thereby making the decedent's character an essential element of proof.

FRE 405(b), in conjunction with FRE 405(a), makes it clear that all three forms of character evidence — reputation, opinion, and specific acts — are potentially admissible when character is an essential element of a claim or defense. For example, in our libel hypothetical in which George wants to establish the truth of the statement that Martha is a dishonest person, George could call witnesses to testify (1) that Martha had a reputation for dishonesty in the community, (2) that in the witnesses' opinion Martha was dishonest, and (3) that Martha had engaged in specifically described dishonest acts.

The only limitation on the use of any of these types of evidence to prove character when character is an essential element of a claim or defense is FRE 403. In particular with respect to specific acts, courts should balance the probative value of the acts in proving the character trait at issue against (1) the risk that the evidence may engender an emotional response from the jury and (2) the time and effort it would take to litigate the details of what the person may or may not have done.

2.   Elaboration of FRE 405(b)

a.   In general

When the substantive law makes the character of a person an essential element of a claim or a defense, the party with the initial burden of producing evidence will have to introduce character evidence in order to avoid a directed verdict. By contrast, when character evidence is offered to show action in accordance with character, it is, as the Advisory Committee notes, "circumstantial" evidence of a person's conduct, and it is *never essential* that character evidence be offered for this purpose. Consider, for example, a prosecution for a crime involving "dishonest" acts — such as embezzlement or perjury — where the defense offers evidence of the defendant's good character for honesty. The substantive criminal law does not make the defendant's character for dishonesty or honesty an element of the crime or any defense; the defendant may be guilty or innocent of the charged embezzlement or perjury regardless of whether the defendant happens to be a generally dishonest or a generally honest person. Evidence of the defendant's character for honesty, however, is relevant in that it generates one possible, though not essential, inference that the defendant did not act dishonestly by embezzling or committing perjury.

It may be worth noting that FRE 405(b)'s express permission of the use of past specific acts to prove character when character is an essential element is not inconsistent with, or an exception to, the specific acts prohibition in FRE 404(b). Again, FRE 404 prohibits using character evidence *only* to prove conduct in accordance with that character trait on a specific occasion. Note how, here, character is not being offered to show that someone acted a certain way on a particular occasion. Proof of character in the foregoing examples is an end in itself — it is proof of the essential element or fact of consequence — rather than circumstantial proof of some further conduct. Looked at another way, the use of character in FRE 405(b) does not fall within the chain of inferences described in Diagrams 5-1 and 5-2 at page 239, supra, and does not fall within the specific acts prohibition of 404(b) at all. So even if 405(b) did not expressly mention that specific acts are permitted — indeed, even if it had not been written at all — it would still be the case that character as an essential element would be subject to proof by any relevant means. FRE 405(b) is thus another "reminder" to courts (like FRE 404(b)(2) and FRE 406) not to apply the character and specific acts prohibitions beyond their confined boundaries.

b.   *Reputation Versus Character in Defamation Cases*

In our discussion of FRE 404(a), we noted that evidence of a person's reputation is one way to prove a person's character. It is important to keep in mind, particularly in the context of defamation actions, the difference between "character" and "reputation." *Character* is an integral part of a person. *Reputation*, by contrast, is what people say about a person. In defamation actions, a plaintiff's reputation — regardless of whether it happens to coincide with the plaintiff's actual character — is always relevant, because the substantive law makes injury to reputation the basis for assessing damages. Consider, for example, the previous hypothetical in which George circulated a pamphlet stating that Martha was dishonest. Her damages, if she prevails on the substantive claim, will be based on how much George's statement damaged her reputation, not on what kind of a person she is or was. Character becomes an essential element in a defamation action, as we illustrated previously with the George and Martha example, only if (1) the defendant claims that the allegedly defamatory statement is true and (2) the statement is one about the plaintiff's character.

The interesting question, not addressed in the Federal Rules, is whether one should be able to use specific acts to prove a character trait for the purpose of establishing reputation. On the one hand, evidence of character is certainly relevant to prove reputation: If we know, for example, that a person is honest, it is more likely (than if we knew nothing about the person's character) that the person has a reputation for honesty. On the other hand, the same considerations that militate against using specific acts to prove character to infer action in accordance with character also exist when specific acts are offered to prove character for the purpose of inferring what a person's reputation is. There may be time-consuming distracting litigation about a variety of specific acts, and proof of the specific acts may be extremely prejudicial.

KEY POINT

When character is an essential element of a claim or a defense, FRE 405(b) permits proof of character with specific acts evidence. (In addition, it is always permissible to prove character with reputation or opinion evidence pursuant to FRE 405(a).)

PROBLEMS

5.42. Paul Vincent has sued Office Barn for injuries he sustained from being physically abused by store security guard Arnold Stallone, who mistakenly believed Vincent had been shoplifting. The claim is negligent supervision and/or hiring, and the plaintiff must prove (1) that Stallone had a propensity for violence and (2) that Office Barn knew or should have known of the propensity and was therefore negligent in hiring him as a security guard and in failing to supervise him adequately. Vincent offers the following testimony. Is it admissible?

(a) W_1 to testify that he has known Stallone for 10 years, and in his opinion, Stallone is a violent person.
(b) W_2 to testify that Stallone beat him up with no provocation in a bar one year before Stallone began working at Office Barn.
(c) W_3 to testify that Stallone had been arrested four times, and convicted twice, for assault prior to working for Office Barn.

Office Barn offers the following testimony. Is it admissible?

(d) W_4 to testify that she has lived in the same neighborhood as Stallone for five years and that he has a reputation as a peaceful person.

5.43. Return to Problem 3.2 at page 136. Is the evidence of Driver's speeding ticket likely to be admissible? For what purpose(s)?

5.44. Paul Plant, a candidate for public office, has sued Diane Daniels for defamation for circulating a pamphlet stating that Paul is a violent person with a bad temper and that on May 23 Paul stole a pistol from a local sporting goods store. Paul testifies that both statements are untrue.

(a) Paul calls Edgar James, who offers to testify that since the publication of the pamphlet Paul has had a reputation in the community for violence and for dishonesty.

(b) Diane calls Zelda Young, who offers to testify that she observed Paul engaged in a fistfight at a local tavern last year.

(c) Diane calls Florence Newman, who offers to testify that before the alleged defamation Paul had a reputation in the community for being violent and for being dishonest.

(d) Diane calls Winston Hampton, who offers to testify that on two occasions last year when he was with Paul, Paul stole merchandise from a local department store.

Assuming that proper objections are made, which pieces of evidence should be admissible?

5.45. The defendant is charged with the sale of heroin. He claims that he was entrapped by the entreaties of the purchaser, a supposed friend who was in fact an undercover narcotics officer. According to the substantive law, the defense of entrapment is not available if the defendant was predisposed to commit the crime. To show predisposition the prosecution offers evidence (a) that the defendant has the reputation in the community as a drug dealer and (b) that on five specific occasions the defendant has sold drugs to schoolchildren. Should the defendant's objections to these pieces of evidence be sustained?

I. EVIDENCE OF SEXUAL ASSAULT AND CHILD MOLESTATION

As part of the Violent Crime Control and Enforcement Act of 1994, Congress enacted three rules, FRE 413-415, that relate to the admissibility of sexual misconduct evidence in cases involving charges of sexual assault and child molestation. The obvious purpose of the rules is to make sexual misconduct evidence more freely admissible. In our discussion of these rules, the terms *sexual assault* and *sexual misconduct* include both sexual assault and child molestation.

Evidence commentators have been particularly critical of FRE 413-415, which were enacted directly by Congress and not subject to the typical rule-making process. Charles Alan Wright and Kenneth W. Graham Jr., Federal Practice and Procedure §5411-5417B (Supp. 2001); Edward J. Imwinkelried, A Small Contribution to the Debate over the Proposed Legislation Abolishing the Character Evidence Prohibition in Sex Offense Prosecutions, 44 Syracuse L. Rev. 1125 (1993); Perspectives on the Proposed Federal Rules of Evidence 413-415, 22 Ford. Urban L.J. 265 (1995).

Because most criminal sexual assault cases arise in state courts, a significant potential impact of FRE 413-415 is as a model for state evidence codes. Approximately three-quarters of the states have evidence rules based on the Federal Rules. States, however, have not rushed to adopt these new rules. But see Ariz. R. Evid. 404(c); Cal. Evid. Code §1108 (West 1995); Mo. Ann. Stat. §566.025 (Vernon Supp. 2001).

1.   FRE 413-415

RULE 413.   SIMILAR CRIMES IN SEXUAL-ASSAULT CASES

(a) *Permitted Uses.* In a criminal case in which a defendant is accused of a sexual assault, the court may admit evidence that the defendant committed any other sexual assault. The evidence may be considered on any matter to which it is relevant.

(b) *Disclosure to the Defendant.* If the prosecutor intends to offer this evidence, the prosecutor must disclose it to the defendant, including witnesses' statements or a summary of the expected testimony. The prosecutor must do so at least 15 days before trial or at a later time that the court allows for good cause.

(c) *Effect on Other Rules.* This rule does not limit the admission or consideration of evidence under any other rule.

(d) *Definition of "Sexual Assault."* In this rule and Rule 415, "sexual assault" means a crime under federal law or under state law (as "state" is defined in 18 U.S.C. § 513) involving: (1) any conduct prohibited by 18 U.S.C. chapter 109A; (2) contact, without consent, between any part of the defendant's body — or an object — and another person's genitals or anus; (3) contact, without consent, between the defendant's genitals or anus and any part of another person's body; (4) deriving sexual pleasure or gratification from inflicting death, bodily injury, or physical pain on another person; or (5) an attempt or conspiracy to engage in conduct described in subparagraphs (1)-(4).

RULE 414.   SIMILAR CRIMES IN CHILD MOLESTATION CASES

[This rule is similar in structure and content to FRE 413, but it applies to offenses of child molestation rather than sexual assault. Section (d) defines "child" as "a person below the age of fourteen" and removes the "without consent" phrase that occurs in subdivisions (2) and (3) of FRE 413.]

RULE 415.   SIMILAR ACTS IN CIVIL CASES CONCERNING SEXUAL ASSAULT OR CHILD MOLESTATION

[This rule makes FRE 413 and FRE 414, including the notice requirement, applicable to civil cases in which a claim is based on a party's alleged sexual assault or child molestation.]

2.   Interpretation and Illustration of FRE 413-415

a.   *The Relationship Between FRE 413-415 and Other Rules of Evidence*

i.   FRE 413-415 and FRE 404.   The purpose of FRE 413-415 is to liberalize the admissibility of character evidence in sexual assault and child molestation cases, by removing the two primary objections that would otherwise be available under FRE 404. First, the prosecution is permitted to open the door to use of character evidence in such cases, a right otherwise reserved to criminal defendants under FRE 404(a). Second, the prosecution may offer past specific acts of sexual assault or child molestation as evidence that the defendant committed the current offense, notwithstanding the FRE 404(b) ban on past specific acts to prove character to show action in accordance on a particular occasion. United States v. Enjady, 134 F.3d 1427, 1431 (10th Cir. 1998) (Congress intended "to lower the obstacles to admissibility of propensity evidence in a defined class of cases"). This liberalization of the pre-existing rules is consistent with the language of FRE 413-415: sexual assault evidence *"is admissible* and may be considered for its bearing on *any matter* to which it is relevant" (emphasis added). In addition, this understanding of FRE 413-415 is suggested by their legislative history (David J. Karp, Evidence of Propensity and Probability in Sex Offense Cases and Other Cases, 70 Chi. Kent L. Rev. 15, 15 n.* (1995); Dale A. Nance, Forward: Do We Really Want to Know the Defendant?, 70 Chi.-Kent L. Rev., 3, 8 (1994)) and by the Justice Department, which lobbied for the enactment of the rules (Karp, supra at 19).

Consider, for example, a case in which the defendant is charged with attempted rape and the prosecution offers to prove that on two occasions within the past five years the defendant had sexually assaulted two women. Assume that the two women were unrelated to the victim of the attempted rape and that there were no unusual similar features among the three incidents. Are the two prior incidents relevant to identify the defendant as the perpetrator of the crime charged? Perhaps, but only because the evidence shows a general tendency to engage in sexual assaults. That sounds like a description of character evidence. If so, then the evidence, before the adoption of FRE 413, would have been inadmissible pursuant to both FRE 404(a) and FRE 404(b)(1). FRE 413 removes the FRE 404 impediments to the admissibility of relevant sexual assault evidence.

ii.   FRE 413-415 and FRE 403.   When FRE 413-415 were first enacted, there was some concern that these rules made no explicit reference to existing exclusionary rules and no indication of the extent to which judges may have discretion to exclude sexual misconduct evidence under FRE 403.[3] However, every appellate case dealing with this issue has concluded that sexual misconduct evidence is subject to FRE 403 balancing. United States v. Guardia, 135 F.2d 1326 (10th Cir. 1998). In fact, some of these cases have suggested that if FRE 403 were not available to exclude prejudicial evidence of sexual misconduct, admitting such evidence would violate a defendant's due process right to a fair trial. United States v. Castillo, 140 F.3d 874 (10th Cir. 1998) (FRE 414); United States v. Enjady, 134 F.3d 1427 (10th Cir. 1998) (FRE 413). Thus, in the attempted rape hypothetical, the defendant could argue that the prior sexual assaults should be excluded on FRE 403 grounds.

iii.   FRE 413-415 and Other Rules of Evidence.   Can the FRE 413-415 language that prior sexual assault evidence is admissible be construed as an exception to other exclusionary rules of evidence, such as the hearsay rule? The argument strikes us as unsound. "Congressional proponents of the legislation creating Rule 413 intended that 'the general standards of the rules of evidence will continue to apply, including

---

3. Typically, when the Federal Rules address the potential admissibility of evidence, they use the term "may." See, e.g., FRE 404(b) (specific acts evidence "may, however, be admissible for other purposes"). *May* indicates that admissibility is subject to other exclusionary provisions, including a court's power to exclude probative evidence pursuant to FRE 403. By contrast, FRE 413-415 state that sexual misconduct evidence "is admissible," thereby giving rise to the argument — wrong, in our view, and properly rejected by the courts — that judges may have less discretion to exclude or that exclusionary rules may not be applicable to such evidence. It is worth noting that, in the one instance where the drafters of the Federal Rules clearly intended for admissibility to be mandatory, the rule states that the evidence *"shall be* admitted." FRE 609(a)(2) (emphasis added), discussed in Chapter Seven.

the restriction on hearsay evidence and the court's authority under rule 403 to exclude evidence whose probative value is substantially outweighed by its prejudicial effect.'" 2 Weinstein's Federal Evidence 413-411 (2d ed. 2005). In light of the uniform view that FRE 403 can be invoked to exclude sexual assault evidence, it seems likely that courts will conclude that other established rules — for example, the hearsay rule — are also applicable to evidence offered pursuant to FRE 413-415. Thus, in the attempted rape hypothetical, it is unlikely that a court would permit the prior sexual assaults to be proven by out-of-court hearsay statements that would not otherwise be admissible.

b.   FRE 413-415 and Preliminary Fact-finding

As is the case with specific acts evidence admissible pursuant to FRE 404(b)(2), there is no requirement that the sexual assault resulted in a conviction or even a criminal charge. If there is a question about the nature of the defendant's involvement in an alleged sexual assault, a court should resolve this issue in the same manner that it resolves the issue when there is a question about a defendant's culpable involvement in other types of specific acts. Under the Federal Rules, as a result of the Supreme Court's decision in *Huddleston*, discussed at page 247, supra, there must be "evidence sufficient to support a finding" (FRE 104(b)) that the defendant was culpably involved in the act. United States v. Mann, 193 F.3d 1172 (10th Cir. 1999). For example, in the preceding rape hypothetical, assume that the defendant offers the testimony of a friend who provides the defendant with an alibi for the times of the noncharged sexual assaults; assume further that the prosecution's proof of those specific acts consists of the alleged victims' testimony and that there is a history of personal animosity between the alleged victims and the defendant. Even though the judge may disbelieve the alleged victims, there is sufficient "evidence to support a finding" under FRE 104(b) that the assaults occurred, because the judge is not permitted to take credibility into account. Thus, the prosecution would have satisfied the preliminary fact requirement.

c.   The Broad Definition of "Offense of Sexual Assault"

The definition of what constitutes an "offense of sexual assault" is potentially very broad. Any acts having the characteristics described in §§(d)(2) through (d)(5) are apparently included as long as some state has enacted a criminal statute that embraces that conduct. Assume, for example, in our rape hypothetical that the prosecution seeks to introduce evidence that the defendant has engaged in consensual sexual activity that involves pain or injury. If any state happens to encompass that sexual activity within its criminal law, the prosecution's evidence arguably falls within the scope of the rule as admissible even if the activity is not a federal crime or a crime in the state where the defendant is being prosecuted.

d.   The Meaning of "Without Consent" in FRE 413(d)(2) and (3)

Nothing in FRE 413 indicates whether the term *consent* in section (d) means legal or actual consent. Consider a situation in which a defendant is charged with the rape and the victim is an adult. Prior sexual contact with other adults against their will (i.e., without *actual* consent) is without question a type of sexual assault that falls within the scope of FRE 413. What about prior sexual contact with a minor that was with the minor's actual consent but not legal consent because of the minor's age? Should this type of evidence be admissible? Should it matter whether the defendant was aware of the minor's age?

3.   Elaboration of FRE 413-415

a.   *The Application of FRE 403 to Previously Inadmissible Character Evidence*

The clear intent of FRE 413-415 is to make previously inadmissible evidence admissible. How, if at all, is a judge to take into account this mandate for more liberal admissibility in making the FRE 403 determination with respect to a particular piece of evidence?

Perhaps not surprisingly, the cases take a variety of approaches to this issue. At one extreme is Frank v. County of Hudson, 924 F. Supp. 620 (D.N.J. 1996), where the court stated, "Child sexual abuse deservedly carries a unique stigma in our society; such highly prejudicial evidence should therefore carry a very high degree of probative value if it is to be admitted." Id. at 626-627. The analysis in *Frank* suggests that FRE 403 is likely to require exclusion of sexual misconduct evidence not falling within one of the traditional noncharacter purposes for admitting specific acts evidence. That may or may not be desirable as a matter of policy. As a matter of law, it is wrong because it makes FRE 413-415 a nullity.

At the other extreme, some courts have been willing to admit evidence of very old, seemingly isolated, and sometimes dissimilar instances of sexual misconduct. For example, in United States v. Meacham, 115 F.3d 1488 (10th Cir. 1997), where the defendant was charged with transporting a minor in interstate commerce with the intent that she engage in sexual activity, the court held that it was proper to admit two similar incidents of child molestation that occurred over 30 years earlier. There was no evidence of more recent incidents with third persons to indicate a continuing pattern of conduct. See also United States v. Gabe, 237 F.3d 954 (8th Cir. 2001) (20-year-old incident of child molestation admissible); United States v. Eagle, 137 F.3d 1011 (8th Cir. 1998) (upholding admission of evidence of prior statutory rape of defendant's current common law wife in prosecution for child molestation); United States v. Larson, 112 F.3d 600 (2d Cir. 1997) (16- to 20-year-old similar incidents of child molestation admissible; 21- to 23-year-old similar incidents excluded). For two cases in which the court of appeals first held that the admission of specific acts evidence pursuant to FRE 404(b) was prejudicial error and then later held that the same evidence was properly admissible pursuant to FRE 414, see United States v. Sumner, 204 F.3d 1182 (8th Cir. 2000), and United States v. LeCompte, 131 F.3d 767 (8th Cir. 1997).

Despite — or perhaps because of — the variety of approaches to FRE 403, the results in particular cases may sometimes have more to do with the nature of the case than with what the court articulates about the relationship between FRE 403 and FRE 413-415. Although in the past courts have been divided on the admissibility of sexual assault evidence in child molestation cases, David P. Bryden and Roger

C. Park, "Other Crimes" Evidence in Sex Offense Cases, 78 Minn. L. Rev. 529, 531 n.12 (1992), the trend seems to be strongly in favor of admitting such evidence under FRE 414. United States v. Gabe and United States v. LeCompte, supra; Christina E. Wells and Erin Elliott Motley, Reinforcing the Myth of the Crazed Rapist: A Feminist Critique of Recent Rape Legislation, 81 B.U. L. Rev. 127, 177-178 (2001). In rape cases, on the other hand, courts traditionally appear to have been less willing to admit prior sexual assault evidence in acquaintance rape cases than in stranger rape cases, see Bryden and Park, supra at 531 n.11, and this tendency may be continuing. Both in acquaintance rape cases (FRE 413) and in sexual harassment actions involving acquaintances (FRE 415), courts have seemed particularly sensitive to unfair prejudice concerns and have not been reluctant to exclude sexual misconduct evidence. United States v. Acevedo, 117 F.3d 1429 (table of unpublished decisions), No. 96-2149, 1997 U.S. App. LEXIS 17578 (10th Cir. July 14, 1997); Cleveland v. KFC Natl. Mgmt. Co., 948 F. Supp. 62 (N.D. Ga. 1996). For a discussion of these and other similar cases, see Wells and Motley, supra; Jane Harris Aiken, Sexual Character Evidence in Civil Actions: Refining the Propensity Rule, 1997 Wis. L. Rev. 1221.

The apparent willingness to exclude sexual assault evidence in cases involving alleged sexual misconduct by an acquaintance may be undermining one of the objectives of FRE 413 and FRE 415. Bryden and Park, supra at 576-582, note that in acquaintance rape cases in which defendants claim consent, there may be a relatively greater need for sexual assault evidence. There is not as likely to be physical evidence to establish that a rape occurred. Thus, the defendant's prior sexual misconduct may be particularly important in resolving the inevitable credibility conflict between the defendant and alleged victim. Karen Andrews, The Admissibility of Other-Crimes Evidence in Acquaintance-Rape Prosecutions, 17 S. Ill. U. L.J. 341 (1993); Sara Beale, Prior Similar Acts in Prosecutions for Rape and Child Sex Abuse, 4 Crim. L.F. 307 (1993).

b.   The Underlying Rationale for Rules 413-415

Regardless of how much or how little FRE 413-415 in practice have liberalized the use of sexual misconduct evidence, their underlying premises must be (1) that sexual misconduct evidence has relatively high probative value to show action on a particular occasion and (2) that the probative value of this type of evidence is not likely to be outweighed by its prejudicial impact. Both of these propositions may be true, but neither is free from doubt. Because of the controversy surrounding FRE 413-415, we include references here to some of the legal and social science literature that has examined these two basic propositions.

i.   Unfair Prejudice. The prejudicial impact of any specific acts evidence — that is, the extent to which it may make the jury willing to ignore a reasonable doubt and convict a bad, perhaps dangerous person — is a function of how bad or dangerous the specific acts are in the minds of the fact finder. We suspect many of you and many jurors share the view that child molestation and sexual assault are among the most serious and heinous crimes. To the extent that this assessment is correct, the only justification for creating an exception to the prohibition against the prosecution's opening the door to proof of the defendant's character and doing so even with specific acts evidence is the relatively high probative value of such evidence.

ii. Probative Value and Recidivism.   The already liberal admissibility of sexual misconduct evidence in some jurisdictions suggests that at least some courts regard sexual assault evidence as more probative than other types of character evidence. Moreover, some — perhaps many — of you may believe intuitively that prior sexual misconduct evidence is particularly probative propensity evidence. The important empirical question is whether this intuition is in fact true with respect to sexual miscon-duct against third persons. Repeated abuse of the same person — particularly a spouse or son or daughter — may be quite common. Evidence of repeated sexual violence against the same person, however, is likely to be considered noncharacter evidence and, therefore, potentially admissible in any event pursuant to FRE 404(b)(2).

Studies of recidivism indicate that the recidivism rate for sexual offenders is not consistently higher than for other serious crime offenders. Roger Park, however, has argued that the important recidivism factor should be how often sex offenders commit other sex crimes in comparison to how often other offenders commit crimes similar to the ones of which they were convicted. Roger C. Park, Character at the Crossroads, 49 Hast. L.J. 717, 756-754 (1998). By this standard, the propensity of rapists to be recidivists is relatively high. Id. at 762. Moreover, sex crimes are known to be underre-ported, and recidivism statistics rely on arrest and conviction rates. A. Nicholas Groth, Robert E. Longo, and J. Bradley McFadin, Undetected Recidivism among Rapists and Child Molesters, 28 Crime & Delinquency 450 (1982). Forty-five percent of all rapes in the United States are never reported, and studies show that only 5 to 10 percent of acquaintance rape cases are reported. Karen Andrews, The Admissibility of Other-Crimes Evidence in Acquaintance-Rape Prosecutions, 17 S. Ill. U. L.J. 341, 342-343 (1993). Moreover, there is evidence that police do not pursue an arrest if they do not believe the victim. Gary D. LaFree, Rape and Criminal Justice: The Social Construction of Sexual Assault 59-60, 66-69, 207-226 (1989); Julie Horney and Cassia Spohn, Rape Law Reform and Instrumental Change in Six Urban Jurisdictions, 25 Law and Soc. Rev. 117 (1991).

iii.   A Contextual Assessment of Probative Value.   Consider the likely impact of one's political and social values in assessing the probative value of sexual assault evi-dence. If one regards sexual assaults as largely analogous to all other violent crimes, then there is no reason for character evidence rules to differ across those crimes. The generally low probative value of character evidence to show action in accordance with character and the potential for unfair prejudice to criminal defendants would militate against using the action-in-accordance with character inference in all cases.

On the other hand, if one considers sexual assaults as one manifestation of a male-dominated social structure that tends to discriminate against and oppress women — espe-cially women of color and poor women — in a variety of ways, it is reasonable to expect that prosecutors, judges, and fact finders may approach sexual assault cases with some of the biases that inhere in that societal oppression. Special rules of admissibility to compensate for those biases may be appropriate. Bryden and Park, supra at 583.

Legal literature suggests that this type of discriminatory bias does exist. Empirical research based on Uniform Crime Reports and real and mock jury trials reveals that men are more likely to rape women of color and poor women, but are less likely to be convicted when they do so. If the perpetrators are convicted, they serve less jail time when these women are their victims. One explanation is that judges and juries are more likely to see these women as sexually available and therefore not capable of being assaulted. Gary D. LaFree, Rape and Criminal Justice: The Social Construction of Sexual Assault 219-220 (1989); G. Chezia Carraway, Violence Against Women of Color, 43 Stan. L. Rev. 1301 (1991); Kimberle Crenshaw, Mapping the Margins: Intersectionality, Identity Politics, and Violence Against Women of Color, 43 Stan. L. Rev. 1241 (1991); Dorothy E. Roberts, Rape, Violence, and Women's Autonomy, 69 Chi.-Kent L. Rev. 359 (1993). In addition, traditional and still currently powerful stereotypes blame the woman for acquaintance rape or even deny that the activity is rape when the woman is seen as contributing to her predicament. Lois Pineau, Date Rape: A Feminist Analysis, 8 Law and Philosophy 217 (1989). See also Andrews, supra; David P. Bryden and Sonja Lengnick, Rape in the Criminal Justice System, 87 J. Crim. L. & Criminology 1194 (1997); Karen M. Kramer, Note, Rule by Myth: The Social and Legal Dynamics Governing Alcohol-Related Acquaintance Rapes, 47 Stan. L. Rev. 115 (1994). These attitudes make jurors willing to discount, if not disbelieve, victims' stories, and since there often will be no evidence of physical injury in an acquaintance rape situation, the victim's credibility will usually be critical to a successful prosecution. To the extent that jurors share these stereotypical attitudes the likelihood of a conviction is small; and if juries are unlikely to convict, prosecutors are unlikely to bring cases. Admitting evidence of a defendant's prior sexual assaults may challenge the jurors' stereotypes and in turn make prosecutors more willing to pursue acquaintance rape cases. Allowing evidence of a defendant's prior sexual assault record also may increase convictions in cases where poor women and women of color are the victims.

Perhaps this bias and stereotyping explains the pre-FRE 413-415 state of the law. As we noted there, many courts have tended to be relatively liberal in admitting evidence of a defendant's prior sexual conduct in child molestation cases and in cases involving sexual assaults by strangers. This same liberal view of admissibility, however, has not extended to cases involving sexual assault by an acquaintance. We can think of no basis for believing that a sexual assault defendant's prior sexual conduct is likely to be less probative in acquaintance assault situations than in stranger assault situations.

Some feminists have argued that FRE 413-415 merely re-enforce societal stereotypes of rapists as vicious predators and revive the idea that women who make accusations of rape need to have a corroborating witness (in these cases, women who have been prior victims). Aviva Orenstein, No Bad Men!: A Feminist Analysis of Character Evidence in Rape Trials, 49 Hastings L.J. 663 (1998); Wells and Motley, supra. Does this analysis change your views about the desirability of FRE 413-415?

c.   *The Significance of FRE 413-415 to Federal Litigation*

The controversy surrounding the adoption of FRE 413-415 focused almost exclusively on the role of FRE 413 and FRE 414 in criminal prosecutions. As we noted at the outset of Section E, however, sexual assault and child molestation are predominantly state crimes. Thus, although most of the limited number of FRE 413-415 cases to date are criminal cases, there will probably be relatively few opportunities for federal courts to apply FRE 413 and FRE 414. By contrast, FRE 415 — the civil case counterpart to FRE 413 and FRE 414 — may become the primary vehicle for giving content to the federal sexual misconduct rules. 23 Wright and Graham, supra at §5411B (Supp. 2001). For example, plaintiffs with sexual harassment claims (including fedcral civil rights suits) based on unlawful sexual touching may seek to introduce evidence of the defendants' prior sexual misconduct pursuant to FRE 415. Cleveland v. KFC Natl. Mgmt. Co., 948 F. Supp. 62 (N.D. Ga. 1996); Jane Harris Aiken, Sexual Character Evidence in Civil Actions, 1997 Wis. L. Rev. 1221.

KEY POINTS

1. FRE 413-415 permit the use of specific acts to prove a person's character or propensity for engaging in sexual assault to prove action on a particular occasion.

2. Evidence potentially admissible under FRE 413-415 may be excluded pursuant to FRE 403.

PROBLEMS

5.46. Defendant has been charged with "intentionally having sexual contact with a minor with the intent to become sexually aroused or gratified." During its case in chief the prosecution introduced evidence that the defendant lured a three-year-old girl into his home, fondled her, and gave her a piece of candy. Defendant testified in his own behalf and denied the incident. On rebuttal, the prosecution offers the testimony of a 12-year-old girl that, a week before the alleged incident with the three-year-old girl, the defendant offered the witness $20 if she would come into his home and expose herself. Should the evidence be admitted?

5.47. Alex Abrams is charged with attempted sexual assault and battery. Brenda Bailey, the alleged victim, testifies that she was at a bar where she met a man whom she identifies as the defendant Abrams; that he followed her to her car as she left the bar after midnight; that he grabbed her from behind, pinned her to the ground, and attempted to assault her sexually; and that her screams brought other patrons from the bar and her assailant ran away. Abrams testifies that Bailey has misidentified him; that it was a dark night; and that he had been at the bar earlier but left before midnight and was at home when the alleged attack occurred.

The prosecution seeks to admit the following evidence: testimony from two women that seven years ago and five years ago, respectively, they were sexually assaulted by Abrams after he followed them out of a bar. Should this evidence be admitted prior to the adoption of FRE 413-415? After their adoption?

Would the result be different if the sexual assaults were more recent? If they had occurred during the daytime at the women's homes?

5.48. Carl Corbin is charged with rape. Doris Davis, the alleged victim, testifies that she met Corbin in a bar; that they talked for a while and she agreed to accompany him to another bar for drinks and dancing; that after spending a few hours at this second bar she accepted his offer of a ride back to her car; that along the way he stopped at a park and said he wanted to have sex with her; that she said no and told him she was afraid she would get pregnant; and that he forcibly raped her. Corbin testifies that Davis consented to have sexual relations with him after a fun evening.

The prosecution seeks to admit the following evidence: testimony from a woman that she had dated Corbin for a brief period of time three years ago; that he wanted to have sexual relations with her; that she told him no but he then forced her to have sex; and that she never reported the incident to anyone. Should this evidence be admitted prior to the adoption of FRE 413-415? After their adoption?

Would the result be different if the woman would testify that she met Corbin in a bar; that after a few drinks and dancing he offered to drive her home; that he stopped at the same park where he had stopped with Davis; and that he forced her have sex after she said no?

5.49. Agatha Lewis has brought an action for damages against Brian Bellows, who, she alleges, transmitted AIDS to her. Agatha establishes with blood test evidence that she did not have the AIDS virus 18 months ago, that she now has the virus, and that Brian has the virus. Agatha testifies that she is not an intravenous drug user, that she has not had a blood transfusion, and that the only person with whom she has had intimate sexual contact subsequent to the negative AIDS test is Brian. She further testifies that she met Brian at a party; that they went to his apartment after the party and had sexual intercourse; that she had sexual intercourse with him two or three additional times in the next two weeks; and that she had no further contact with him. In his defense, Brian admits that he met Agatha at a party. He claims that he gave her a ride to her apartment after the party and that he did not on that night or on any other occasion have sexual intercourse with Agatha. In rebuttal Agatha offers the testimony of three women that during the past year they met Brian at parties and had brief sexual affairs with him. Should this evidence be admitted prior to the adoption of FRE 413-415? After their adoption?

5.50. Steve Sanders, a 21-year-old college junior, is charged with the rape of Betty Brown, a classmate. According to the prosecution, the rape occurred during their first (and only) date. Sanders admits having had intercourse, but he claims that Brown consented. The prosecution offers the following pieces of evidence:

(a)   the testimony of Ann Williams, a 16-year-old high school student, that she recently had consensual sexual intercourse with Sanders;
(b)   the testimony of Ellie Wilson, another student, that on her first date with Sanders he was extremely aggressive and ripped some of her clothing before she could stop him;
(c)   a wallet belonging to Mary Miller that was seized from Sanders's room and Mary Miller's testimony that one month ago a masked man raped her in the laundry room of the dormitory and stole her wallet (Sanders claims that he found the wallet on a street corner the night before it was seized from his room, and that he was studying in the library at the time of the rape).

How should the court rule prior to the adoption of FRE 413-415? After their adoption?

J.   EVIDENCE OF AN ALLEGED VICTIM'S PAST SEXUAL BEHAVIOR OR DISPOSITION IN SEX OFFENSE CASES

Until fairly recently, many courts were quite liberal in permitting rape and other sex crime defendants to introduce evidence of the alleged victim's sexual history when the defendant claimed that the victim had consented. The most common form of prior sexual history evidence was reputation testimony, but a number of jurisdictions also permitted specific acts evidence. Starting in the 1970s, states began to enact "rape shield" legislation to curb the admissibility of some of this evidence. FRE 412, which was most recently amended in 1994, was also the product of specific legislative action. Congress added FRE 412 to the Federal Rules in 1978. For a discussion of the background and legislative history of Rule 412, see 23 Charles Alan Wright and Kenneth W. Graham Jr., Federal Practice and Procedure §5381 at 483-491 (1980), §5381.1 at 190-199 (Supp. 2001).

1. FRE 412

RULE 412. SEX-OFFENSE CASES: THE VICTIM'S SEXUAL BEHAVIOR OR PREDISPOSITION

(a) *Prohibited Uses.* The following evidence is not admissible in a civil or criminal proceeding involving alleged sexual misconduct: (1) evidence offered to prove that a victim engaged in other sexual behavior; or (2) evidence offered to prove a victim's sexual predisposition.

(b) *Exceptions.*

(1) *Criminal Cases.* The court may admit the following evidence in a criminal case:

(A) evidence of specific instances of a victim's sexual behavior, if offered to prove that someone other than the defendant was the source of semen, injury, or other physical evidence;

(B) evidence of specific instances of a victim's sexual behavior with respect to the person accused of the sexual misconduct, if offered by the defendant to prove consent or if offered by the prosecutor; and

(C) evidence whose exclusion would violate the defendant's constitutional rights.

(2) *Civil Cases.* In a civil case, the court may admit evidence offered to prove a victim's sexual behavior or sexual predisposition if its probative value substantially outweighs the danger of harm to any victim and of unfair prejudice to any party. The court may admit evidence of a victim's reputation only if the victim has placed it in controversy.

(c) Procedure to Determine Admissibility.

(1) *Motion.* If a party intends to offer evidence under Rule 412(b), the party must:

(A) file a motion that specifically describes the evidence and states the purpose for which it is to be offered;

(B) do so at least 14 days before trial unless the court, for good cause, sets a different time;

(C) serve the motion on all parties; and

(D) notify the victim or, when appropriate, the victim's guardian or representative.

(2) *Hearing.* Before admitting evidence under this rule, the court must conduct an in camera hearing and give the victim and parties a right to attend and be heard. Unless the court orders otherwise, the motion, related materials, and the record of the hearing must be and remain sealed.

(d) Definition of "Victim." In this rule, "victim" includes an alleged victim.

2. Interpretation and Illustration of FRE 412

FRE 412 has a twofold rationale. First, the combination of relatively low probative value and significant countervailing FRE 403 concerns warrants, at least in criminal cases, a flat rule of exclusion rather than individual case-by-case balancing to determine admissibility. Second, independent of FRE 403 concerns, substantive policy considerations justify the exclusion of relevant evidence. Thus, FRE 412 excludes some evidence of an alleged sexual assault victim's sexual conduct in order to protect the alleged victim from harassment and embarrassment and to avoid deterring such a person from testifying about the sexual assault.

a.   The Relevance of an Alleged Victim's Sexual Behavior or Disposition to Prove Conduct

Some people adamantly maintain that evidence of a sexual assault victim's prior sexual history is irrelevant to the issue of consent. FRE 412 (b)(1)(B), however, explicitly permits proof of sexual behavior between the defendant and the alleged victim to prove the victim's consent. Moreover, there is no explicit limitation on the use of prior sexual conduct to prove consent in civil cases. Is such conduct relevant under the minimal test of FRE 401? Consider an alleged victim whose only prior consensual intercourse was in the context of a marriage relationship. What generalizations can you frame that say something about the likelihood that such a victim consented or did not consent to sexual intercourse with a stranger? With an acquaintance? If the defendant's defense of consent is based on evidence that is arguably ambiguous as to whether the victim consented, is evidence of the alleged victim's prior consensual sexual conduct with third persons probative of consent? Again, can you think of a generalization that permits one to make the inference from the evidentiary fact (prior sexual conduct) to the fact of consequence (consent)? We suggest that in both examples the relevance of the evidence depends on being able to frame generalizations about the alleged victim's propensities regarding sexual conduct.

b.   The Underlying Propensity Theory

The concept of relevance with which we have been dealing explicitly and implicitly throughout the course rests on the premise that individuals have propensities to behave in particular ways and that we can arrive at reasonable conclusions about historical facts by taking these propensities into account. For example, at the most basic level, when a person says that event X occurred, we regard the person's statement as relevant, at least in a minimal FRE 401 sense, to establish that X occurred because we assume, on the basis of our common experience, that individuals generally have a propensity to tell the truth. Similarly, a premise underlying the character evidence rules is that individuals have propensities to behave in characteristic ways and that if we know something about the individuals' conduct on some occasions, we can make reasonable — although sometimes admittedly quite weak — inferences about their conduct on other occasions. Given this pervasive reliance on the premise that we can infer something about an individual's conduct on some occasions if we know how the individual behaved on other occasions, and given the very low FRE 401 threshold requirement for "relevance," courts have not been willing to reject all evidence of an alleged victim's prior sexual behavior as irrelevant to the issue of consent.

Indeed, before rape shield legislation such as FRE 412, the rape defendant's right to introduce reputation evidence about the victim's prior sexual conduct was regarded as an application of the general principle, codified in FRE 404(a)(2), that a defendant can introduce reputation (and under FRE 405(a), opinion) testimony to prove the victim's character to show action in accordance with that character trait by the victim. In other words, just as a homicide defendant claiming self-defense could introduce evidence of the victim's reputation for violence to suggest that the victim was the first aggressor, it was regarded as appropriate for the rape defendant claiming consent to introduce evidence of the victim's reputation for promiscuity or lack of chastity to suggest that the victim consented to the intercourse.

The theoretical justification for introducing evidence of specific instances of the victim's consensual sexual intercourse was more varied. Some courts claimed that the evidence was admissible to show the victim's "intent." Other courts admitted the evidence to "impeach" the credibility of the rape victim without bothering to explain what relationship existed between consensual sexual intercourse and general truth-telling. Still other courts frankly admitted that the specific acts evidence was being used in a propensity sense or that it was being used to show character. These latter courts took the position that there was an exception to the propensity-character rule for evidence of prior sexual conduct, an exception that one might analogize to the use of a criminal defendant's prior sexual misconduct in sexual assault prosecutions.

c.   The Scope of FRE 412

FRE 412 excludes most evidence of an alleged victim's prior sexual behavior and sexual predisposition, even when it is relevant under the above-described propensity theory. We will deal with the reasons for this rejection of past practice in the next section. Here we want to focus on the actual application of FRE 412.

i.   The Meaning of "Other Sexual Behavior" and "Sexual Predisposition." The exclusionary provisions in FRE 412(a) come into play only with respect to evidence of "other sexual behavior" and "sexual predisposition." The rule does not define either of these phrases, but the Advisory Committee's Note provides some examples. *Sexual behavior* "connotes all activities that involve actual physical conduct ... or that imply sexual intercourse or conduct" — for example, "use of contraceptives," "birth of an illegitimate child," or "venereal disease." It also includes "activities of the mind, such as fantasies or dreams." *Sexual predisposition* includes "evidence that does not directly refer to sexual activities or thoughts but that the proponent believes may have a sexual connotation for the factfinder" — for example, evidence "relating to the alleged victim's mode of dress, speech, or lifestyle."

ii.   The Applicability of FRE 412 When the Issue Is the Victim's Behavior on a Particular Occasion. If a defendant offers evidence for the purpose of showing the alleged victim's sexual conduct on a particular occasion, the theory of relevance presumably will be that the evidence shows something about the sexual predisposition (i.e., propensity) of the individual and that from this predisposition one can infer how the victim behaved on a particular occasion. Thus, all evidence (whether in the form of reputation, opinion, or specific act) offered to show conduct on a particular occasion would be evidence of "sexual predisposition." If evidence of dressing in a provocative manner, telling lewd jokes, or soliciting sex were offered for this purpose, it would not be necessary to determine whether the evidence constituted "other sexual behavior." Such evidence, when offered to show the alleged victim's sexual conduct on a particular occasion, either is evidence of "sexual predisposition" or is irrelevant.

Such character evidence offered by a criminal defendant falls within the terms of FRE 404(a)(2) — opening the door to a "pertinent" character trait of the victim. However, as the Advisory Committee has explained, the pending amendment to FRE 404(a)(2) makes clear that character evidence relating to the victim's sexual predisposition offered to show conduct on a particular occasion "is governed by the more stringent provisions of Rule 412."

iii. The Applicability of FRE 412 in Other Contexts.

The definitions of "other sexual behavior" and "sexual predisposition" become important when evidence of an alleged victim's prior activity is offered for some purpose other than to show sexual conduct on a particular occasion. Assume, for example, that a defendant is charged with rape and claims that the alleged victim has falsely accused him. To suggest a motive for the false accusation the defendant offers to testify that he had threatened to reveal to the alleged victim's spouse that the alleged victim had a secret job as a nude dancer and had solicited sex from him.

Do these activities constitute "sexual behavior"? Perhaps the answer is yes with respect to soliciting sex, for the Advisory Committee's Note indicates that sexual behavior includes "activities of the mind, such as fantasies or dreams." Nude dancing, on the other hand, seems to fall more readily into the Advisory Committee's description of "sexual predisposition" — activity that "may have a sexual connotation for the fact finder ... [such as] mode of dress ... or lifestyle." It is not clear, however, that evidence is governed by FRE 412 merely because it may suggest a sexual predisposition to the fact finder. If the activity in question is not "sexual behavior," it falls within the scope of FRE 412 only if it is "offered to prove any alleged victim's sexual predisposition." Does the language "To prove ... sexual predisposition" apply only to evidence offered to show action in accordance with that predisposition, or does it apply to evidence that may suggest to the fact finder a sexual predisposition but that is offered for some other purpose? In our hypothetical, the defendant would argue that the evidence of nude dancing (and soliciting sex, if that activity is not "sexual behavior") is being offered to prove the alleged victim's motive for lying, not her sexual predisposition.

If nude dancing and soliciting sex fall within the FRE 412(a) general exclusionary rule for "other sexual behavior" or "sexual predisposition," the evidence is inadmissible unless it falls within one of the FRE 412(b) exceptions. If these activities do not fall within either of the prohibited categories of evidence, the only limits on the admissibility of the evidence are FRE 401-403.

iv. Hostile Work Environment Cases.

There is at least one line of cases holding that FRE 412 applies to evidence suggesting a sexual predisposition even when the evidence is offered to prove something other than the alleged victim's action in accordance with the predisposition. In sex discrimination suits based on a hostile work environment, defendants frequently claim that the plaintiffs welcomed or created the environment that they claim is discriminatory. To establish this defense they have offered to show that the plaintiffs have behaved provocatively, used vulgar, sex-charged language, and engaged in other behavior that is similar to the activity about which they are complaining. Courts have held that FRE 412 applies to this evidence. Socks-Brunot v. Hirschvogel Inc., 184 F.R.D. 113 (S.D. Ohio 1999); Sheffield

v. Hilltop Sand & Gravel Co., 895 F. Supp. 105, 108-109 (E.D. Va. 1995). According to *Socks-Brunot*:

> Evidence tending to prove both prior sexual conduct of the plaintiff and workplace conversations of the plaintiff is covered by Rule 412. Generally, evidence admissible for one purpose but inadmissible for another may be heard by a jury, pursuant to Federal Rule of Evidence 105. The general rule is inapplicable with regard to evidence covered by Rule 412. [184 F.R.D. at 119.]

But cf. Morales-Evans v. Administrative Office of the Courts, 102 F. Supp. 2d 577, 581 n.7 (D.N.J. 2000) (evidence of prior sexual relationship with supervisor considered only "to provide context" for supervisor's allegedly inappropriate remark; "not ... considered as evidence of sexual predisposition or behavior ...; therefore this consideration does not run afoul of Rule 412.").

v.   The Admissibility of "Other Sexual Behavior" and "Sexual Predisposition" Evidence in Civil Cases.   In hostile work environment and other civil cases the balancing test in FRE 412(b)(2) governs admissibility of evidence of an alleged victim's sexual behavior and predisposition. *This test differs from the FRE 403 balancing test in two respects.* First, it is a reverse FRE 403 test. In contrast to FRE 403, which favors admissibility, FRE 412(b)(2), by requiring that the probative value must substantially outweigh countervailing factors, favors exclusion. Wolak v. Spucci, 217 F.3d 157, 163 (2d Cir. 2000).

Second, one should probably interpret "unfair prejudice" in FRE 403 as referring only to prejudice against a party to the litigation. The Advisory Committee Note to FRE 403 states that "'[u]nfair prejudice' ... means an undue tendency to suggest decision on an improper basis, commonly, though not necessarily, an emotional one." By contrast, FRE 412(b)(2) specifically refers to prejudice against a party *and* harm to the alleged victim. Consider, for example, an alleged rape victim's civil suit against a defendant who claims that the plaintiff consented to the intercourse. If the defendant offers evidence of prior consensual intercourse with the plaintiff, the court must weigh the probative value of this evidence against both the risk that the evidence may make the jury unfavorably disposed toward the plaintiff (FRE 403-type prejudice) and the harm to the victim (e.g., embarrassment, invasion of privacy) from the presentation of evidence about the victim's prior sexual activity.

vi. The Admissibility of "Other Sexual Behavior" and "Sexual Predisposition" Evidence in Criminal Cases.   For criminal cases FRE 412(b)(1) delineates only three exceptions to the general rule of exclusion. The first two exceptions are quite narrow: evidence of (a) the victim's sexual behavior with third persons to suggest that they may be the source of semen or injury and (b) the victim's sexual behavior with the defendant to suggest consent. As a result, these exceptions may not encompass all of the situations in which, in fairness, a court should permit a criminal defendant to introduce evidence of an alleged victim's sexual behavior or predisposition. The rule acknowledges this possibility by providing in the third exception for admission in those cases in which "exclusion ... would violate the constitutional rights of the defendant." This language is a reference (1) to the due process doctrine that a criminal defendant has the constitutional right to present a defense and (2) to the Sixth Amendment confrontation clause right to confront and cross-examine witnesses. While these rights do not allow criminal defendants to present evidence and cross-examine witnesses in complete disregard of the rules of evidence, the Supreme Court has held that rules of evidence cannot unduly restrict these rights. There was, of course, no need to include the third exception in the rule. The Constitution is the supreme law of the land. If the defendant has a constitutional right to introduce the evidence, no nonconstitutional rule can justify exclusion.

If the defendant's evidence falls within one of the first two exceptions, it is not automatically admissible. Rather, the evidence must be "otherwise admissible under these rules." Consider, for example, a rape case in which the defendant claims that the alleged victim consented to the sexual intercourse. To prove consent, the defendant offers to testify that on one occasion three years ago he had consensual sex with the victim. This evidence falls within the FRE 412(b)(1)(B) exception, but the court retains discretion to exclude the evidence on FRE 403 grounds.

vii.   The Notice Requirement.   The notice and hearing requirement in FRE 412(c) is more demanding than any other notice requirement in the Federal Rules. Cf. FRE 404(b), FRE 413-415. Any notice requirement has the potential for increasing the thoughtfulness of the decision-making process simply because it gives the parties time to prepare their arguments. A stringent notice requirement may have the additional impact of deterring litigants from pressing weak claims.

3.   Elaboration of FRE 412

a.   *The Rationale for a Rule Excluding Evidence of Prior Sexual Behavior and Sexual Predisposition*

There are substantial reasons to be concerned about the liberal admissibility of an alleged sexual assault victim's sexual history. The ability to introduce evidence of the victim's sexual history gives the defendant the opportunity to try to make the victim and the victim's character the focal point of the litigation. The prospect of a degrading and humiliating examination by defense counsel may discourage many victims from cooperating with prosecutors, or even reporting sexual assaults in the first place. One cannot, however, attribute the humiliation and degradation of rape victims solely — or perhaps even primarily — to liberal rules of admissibility for prior sexual conduct. Disbelief of, disrespect for, and insensitivity toward rape victims has existed throughout the criminal justice system. Susan Brownmiller, Against Our Will: Men, Women and Rape 408-420 (1976); Colleen A. Ward, Attitudes Toward Rape: Feminist and Social Psychological Perspectives (1995); Morrison Torrey, When Will We Be Believed? Rape Myths and the Idea of a Fair Trial in Rape Prosecutions, 24 U.C. Davis L. Rev. 1013 (1991).

In cases that are tried, there may be disputes about whether the victim in fact engaged in any of the conduct that the defendant wishes to attribute to the victim. In addition, there are the risks that the jury may overestimate the probative value of the prior sexual history evidence on the question of consent or be prejudiced against the victim because of the sexual conduct. There is evidence that juries may too readily acquit defendants because they disbelieve a female victim or believe that "she got what she deserved." Harry Kalven and Hans Zeisel, The American Jury 249-254

(1966); David P. Bryden and Sonja Lengnick, Rape in the Criminal Justice System, 87 J. Crim. L. and Criminology 1194 (1997); Aviva Orenstein, No Bad Men!: A Feminist Analysis of Character Evidence in Rape Trials, 49 Hastings L.J. 663 (1998); Beverly J. Ross, Does Diversity in Legal Scholarship Make a Difference?: A Look at the Laws of Rape, 100 Dick. L. Rev. 795 (1966); Torrey, supra. Because of prevailing racism, class biases, and sexual stereotypes, this phenomenon is particularly likely to occur when the victim is a woman of color or a poor woman or when she was acquainted with the man who raped her. Gary D. LaFree, Rape and Criminal Justice: The Social Construction of Sexual Assault 219-220; G. Chezia Carraway, Violence Against Women of Color, 43 Stan. L. Rev. 1301 (1991); Kimberle Crenshaw, Mapping the Margins: Intersectionality, Identity Politics, and Violence Against Women of Color, 43 Stan. L. Rev. 1241 (1993); Lois Pineau, Date Rape: A Feminist Analysis, 8 Law & Philosophy 217 (1989); Dorothy E. Roberts, Rape, Violence, and Women's Autonomy, 69 Chi.-Kent L. Rev. 359 (1993).

Finally, there is the problem that prior sexual history will frequently be of no more than marginal relevance to the question of whether the victim consented on the occasion in question. Indeed, as we noted earlier, one of the principal reasons that the rules of evidence severely restrict the use of character to show action in accordance with character is that the strength of the inference from character to action on a particular occasion is almost invariably weak. We can think of no reason to believe that the inference from prior consensual intercourse — especially if the activity is with third persons — to consent with the defendant is a particularly strong propensity inference.

In theory, FRE 403 and its common law counterparts might have been adequate devices for taking into account these concerns that warrant caution in the use of evidence of a rape victim's prior sexual conduct. However, the policy of protecting a rape victim from humiliation is not, strictly speaking, the sort of concern that readily fits among the FRE 403 dangers. Moreover, in practice, many individuals perceived — correctly, we believe — that courts were often too willing to admit marginally probative, highly prejudicial evidence of the victim's prior sexual activity in rape and other sexual assault prosecutions. The response to this perception has been the adoption of "rape shield" rules or statutes such as FRE 412 that specifically address and limit the situations in which evidence of a victim's prior sexual conduct may be admitted.

Since rape shield provisions are now common, it is difficult to assess how liberal judges would have been in admitting evidence of victims' past sexual behavior and sexual predisposition in the absence of such rules. Some might argue that recent increased public awareness and concern with sexual assault crimes, e.g., the enactment of FRE 413-415, make rape shield provisions less necessary today than when they were first enacted. Others firmly believe, as we suggested earlier, that attitudes stereotyping women as sexual objects and as provoking sexual contact in innocent situations will find their way into the jury box. From this perspective, rape shield provisions continue to be vitally important both as devices for contributing to accurate fact-finding and as symbolic affirmations of the independence and individuality of women.

b.   Two Approaches to the Exclusion of Other Sexual Behavior and Sexual Predisposition Evidence

FRE 412 presents an interesting example of two quite different approaches to the problem of regulating the admissibility of sexual behavior and sexual predisposition evidence. In civil cases, where there is no established doctrine of constitutionally required evidence, Congress chose to rely exclusively on a balancing test that favors exclusion. By contrast, in criminal cases, where the constitutionally required evidence doctrine provides what is in effect a safety valve for an overly strict exclusionary rule, Congress created only two specific, very narrow exceptions to a general rule of exclusion.

Do you think it is desirable to have an evidentiary rule that tends to force courts to resolve issues of admissibility in terms of constitutional law? In any event, are the criteria for determining whether evidence is constitutionally required likely to be applied consistently from case to case?

Particularly in light of your analysis and discussion of the following problems, consider whether it would be preferable to have a general balancing test for both criminal and civil cases. If your answer is no, are there any additional exceptions that you would add to FRE 412(b)(2)?

c.   Rape Shield Rules and the Defendant's Right to Testify

When a criminal defendant seeks to testify about a rape victim's prior sexual conduct, there may be a conflict between the jurisdiction's rape shield rule and the constitutional right to testify, a right closely related to the due process and confrontation clause rights that we have been discussing. The Seventh Circuit dealt with such a situation in Stephens v. Miller, 13 F.3d 998 (7th Cir. 1994) (en banc), a case that generated seven opinions. We urge you to read *Stephens* and to consider (1) whether the court resolved the constitutional issue properly and (2) what implications *Stephens* may have for the questions we raised at the end of subsection c, supra.

d.   FRE 412 and Discovery in Civil Cases

The prohibition in FRE 412 raises recurring issues in certain civil cases, particularly sexual harassment cases, about the scope of pretrial discovery into, for example, the sexual behavior or predisposition of a plaintiff alleging sexual harassment. It is a black-letter principle of civil procedure that the scope of discovery is broader than the scope of evidentiary admissibility at trial. The Federal Rules of Civil Procedure require parties to respond fully to discovery requests that are "reasonably calculated to lead to the discovery of admissible evidence." Fed. R. Civ. P. 26. The prospect of compelled disclosure of private or embarrassing information in discovery raises many of the same problems — deterring plaintiffs from filing meritorious claims or witnesses from coming forward — addressed by FRE 412, but FRE 412 deals expressly only with admission of evidence at trial, not disclosure in pretrial discovery. For a compelling instance of invasive discovery into female plaintiffs' sexual histories in a sexual harassment case, see Jenson v. Eveleth Taconite Co., 130 F.3d 1287 (8th Cir. 1997); Clara Bingham and Laura Leedy Gansler, Class Action: The Story of Lois Jenson and the Landmark Case That Changed Sexual Harassment Law (2002).

Courts have held, in the context of objections to discovery requests or motions for protective orders, that discovery requests into a plaintiff's sexual behavior are governed by Fed. R. Civ. P. 26(c). However, because that provision expressly incorporates the ultimate admissibility of evidence as a benchmark, it is clear that FRE 412 should be taken into account in deciding discovery motions on these issues. See Sanchez v. Zabihi, 166 F.R.D. 500, 510-502 (D.N.M. 1996). Indeed, the Advisory Committee Note to proposed FRE 412 states that "in order not to undermine the rationale of Rule 412, however, courts should enter appropriate orders pursuant to Fed. R. Civ. P. 26(c) to protect the victim against unwarranted inquiries and to ensure confidentiality. Courts should presumptively issue protective orders barring discovery unless the party seeking discovery makes a showing that the evidence sought to be discovered would be relevant[.]" Arguably, the party seeking discovery should also show that the evidence would not be barred by FRE 412.

KEY POINTS

1. FRE 412 severely limits the extent to which a party can introduce evidence of an alleged victim's sexual predisposition or sexual behavior in both criminal and civil cases.

2. FRE 412(a) and (b)(1) prohibit a criminal defendant from introducing such evidence unless it is (1) specific instances of sexual behavior with a third person offered to show the source of semen, injury, or other physical evidence; (2) specific instances of sexual behavior with the defendant offered to show consent; or (3) constitutionally required evidence.

3. In civil cases, evidence of an alleged victim's sexual predisposition or behavior is admissible only if it satisfies the FRE 412(b)(2) reverse FRE 403 balancing test that takes into account both prejudice to a party and harm to the alleged victim.

PROBLEMS

5.51. Return to Problem 5.48 at page 314. To prove that Davis in fact consented to sexual intercourse, the defense seeks to admit the following evidence:

(a)   testimony from Corbin that he and Davis had consensual sexual relations on several prior occasions;

(b)   testimony from three men that they had met Davis at bars and had consensual sex with her;

(c)   testimony that Davis has a reputation in the community for promiscuity;

(d)   testimony from Sue Smith, a friend of Corbin, that at the first bar on the night in question Davis told Smith that she was attracted to Corbin and would like to have sexual relations with him.

Should this evidence be admitted prior to the adoption of FRE 412? After its adoption, assuming the defense has complied with the procedural requirements of FRE 412(c)?

5.52. In Problem 5.51, assume that Corbin claims that he did not have the requisite mental state for rape because he reasonably (although perhaps mistakenly) believed that Davis had consented to sexual intercourse. Should any of the evidence be admissible to support his claim prior to the adoption of FRE 412? After its adoption?

5.53. The defendant, a successful banker with no known history of sexual misconduct, is accused of sexually assaulting the teenage daughter of his next door neighbor. He claims that she is falsely accusing him because he threatened to reveal to her parents that she and the defendant's son were having a sexual affair. FRE 412 is applicable. Should the court sustain the prosecution's objection to the defendant's evidence about the alleged victim's sexual affair?

5.54. Dawkins, age 23, has been charged with forcibly raping M.M., a 15-year-old girl. Dawkins claims that he believed M.M. was 18 and that she consented. M.M. will testify about the rape. The medical evidence is inconclusive on the question of whether there had been forcible rape. The prosecution wants to offer evidence that two years ago Dawkins forcibly raped his 12-year-old niece and claimed that she had consented. Dawkins wants to offer evidence that last year M.M. charged Craig Wilson with rape. Assume, alternately, (a) that Wilson is unavailable to testify, (b) that, if permitted, Wilson will testify and deny the rape, and (c) that, if permitted, Wilson and other witnesses will present compelling evidence that the rape charge against Wilson was false. FRE 412-414 are applicable. How should the court rule?

5.55. Frances Meyer, a police officer, has brought sex discrimination hostile work environment action against the police chief, the mayor, and the town of Pleasantville. Her claim includes allegations that pornographic magazines and wall posters were continually on display at the police station despite her objections; that the police chief would regularly relate in her presence the plots of pornographic movies; that he pinched her buttocks; that he continually told her she was "really missing something" by not having sex with him; and that he used lewd language in her presence. The defense is based on the theory that Meyer welcomed or encouraged this type of behavior. For this purpose the defense offers evidence that Meyer herself told lewd jokes at the police station; that she regularly watched pornographic movies at home; that she was having a very public affair with a married man; that she would talk at the police station about her sexual fantasies; and that on several occasions she had gone to a strip club. FRE 412 is applicable. Should some or all of the defense evidence be admissible?

5.56. Bryan, a 25-year-old superstar basketball player, is charged with felony sexual assault on a 19-year-old woman, Mary, who worked at the front desk in a resort hotel where Bryan was staying. Bryan admits having sex with Mary in his hotel room but asserts it was consensual. Mary asserts that Bryan forced her to have sexual relations and that she said "no" several times. There are no other witnesses to these events.

Mary received a medical examination approximately 15 hours after the encounter with Bryan. The exam revealed some internal injuries that the prosecution claims are consistent with the use of force during sexual relations, although the report of a prosecution expert states that the injuries could also be consistent with consensual sex. Bryan's T-shirt was found to have a small stain of Mary's blood on it. Are the following items of evidence admissible?

(1)   In its case in chief, the prosecution offers the testimony of three women as follows: W_1 says that 10 years ago, she and Bryan were "making out" when he tore her blouse off and fondled her; W_2 says that in college she and Bryan were dating and having consensual sex but that several times he was very aggressive and intimidated her into having sexual relations when she didn't want to; W_3 says that she met Bryan in a hotel a year ago, flirted with him, and then went to his hotel room where he forced her to have sex.

(2)   The defense will ask several witnesses about Mary's sexual activities in the three days before her hospital examination. Their answers will reveal several sexual encounters, possibly including one (based on DNA evidence) after the events with Bryan and before Mary's hospital exam.

(3)   For the defense, hospital records showing that Mary was treated for an intentional overdose of a prescribed antidepressant medication one month before the encounter with Bryan, which the defense claims was an "attention-seeking" suicide attempt. (The court would first have to hold that Mary waived her right to keep her medical records private.)

CHAPTER SIX

THE OTHER RELEVANCE RULES

In Chapter Five we noted that the Federal Rules — like the common law — have a variety of rules, sometimes referred to as "relevance rules," which exclude relevant evidence. In Chapter Five we discussed the relevance rules regulating character evidence. Our focus in this chapter will be on relevance rules that make evidence inadmissible to prove fault or liability, but that permit such evidence for other purposes. FRE 407-409, 411. What unites these rules is that they exclude relevant evidence, in part, to encourage various types of out-of-court conduct and to serve policy goals external to the goal of accurate fact-finding at trial. We conclude the chapter with a discussion of FRE 410, which makes inadmissible certain evidence relating to guilty pleas.

A. INADMISSIBLE TO PROVE "NEGLIGENCE," "CULPABLE CONDUCT," OR "LIABILITY"

The Federal Rules preclude evidence of subsequent remedial measures (FRE 407), compromises and offers of compromise (FRE 408), payment of medical and other similar expenses (FRE 409), and liability insurance (FRE 411) to prove fault or liability. These rules do not exclude evidence altogether. Rather, they prohibit the proponent from offering the evidence to prove liability or fault. For example, FRE 408, which prohibits offer-of-compromise evidence for this purpose, acknowledges that offers of compromise may be admissible for other purposes, such as showing the bias of a witness. Thus, as with the character evidence rules we examined in Chapter Five — and as you will see with the impeachment and hearsay rules we examine in Chapters Seven and Eight — your analysis of admissibility must always begin with the question of relevance: *What* is the proponent of the evidence trying to prove; *what* is the proponent's theory of relevance? Only after you answer these questions will you be able to apply a relevance rule.

If the answer to the relevance inquiry is that there is both a permissible and an impermissible purpose for which the proponent may wish to offer the evidence, admissibility of the evidence will depend on the application of FRE 403: Is the probative value of the evidence for the permissible purpose substantially outweighed by the risk that the jury may consider the evidence for the impermissible purpose? If the answer is no (i.e., if the answer is that the evidence is admissible), the party against whom the evidence is admitted will be entitled to a limiting instruction pursuant to FRE 105.

1. FRE 407

FRE 407.   SUBSEQUENT REMEDIAL MEASURES

When measures are taken that would have made an earlier injury or harm less likely to occur, evidence of the subsequent measures is not admissible to prove:

- negligence;
- culpable conduct;
- a defect in a product or its design; or
- a need for a warning or instruction.

But the court may admit this evidence for another purpose, such as impeachment or — if disputed — proving ownership, control, or the feasibility of precautionary measures.

2.   Interpretation and Illustration of FRE 407

a.   *The Exclusionary Mandate*

i. The Inference of Negligence or Culpable Conduct.   When a person alters a condition or object that caused an injury and the change could make future injury less likely, one possible inference to draw from the remedial action is that the person who made the alteration believed that the object or condition before the alteration posed an unreasonable risk of injury. If we know that the person responsible for the object or condition has this belief, it is more likely that the object or condition did create an unreasonable risk of injury than if we knew nothing about the person's belief. Indeed, pursuant to this theory of relevance, when a party to an action takes subsequent remedial action, it is equivalent to a recognition of fault. Diagram 6-1 illustrates this reasoning.

In addition to negligence and culpable conduct, FRE 407's exclusionary mandate extends to subsequent remedial measures offered to prove product defects and the need for a warning or instruction.

ii.   Activities That May Be Subsequent Remedial Measures.   A subsequent remedial measure is any action that a person takes after an event that reduces the likelihood of an event's reoccurrence. It may include, for example, an employer's change in its promotion policy, Hamilton v. New York, 627 F.3d 50, 53 (2d Cir. 2010) (evidence employer changed promotion policy to involve more individuals to "help prevent unsuccessful candidates from feeling as if they were unfairly passed over" excluded as a subsequent remedial measure in employment-discrimination case); sending a memorandum to employees urging them to observe safety regulations, First Security Bank v. Union Pac. R. Co., 152 F.3d 877 (8th Cir. 1998) (admonishing employees about location of rail cars in relation to crossing); altering the design of a product, Flaminio v. Honda Motor Co. 733 F.2d 463 (7th Cir. 1984) (motorcycle design); repairing or

Diagram 6-1

EF ──────────→ IF₁ ──────────→ IF₂ ──────────→ FOC ──────────→ EE

EF	IF₁	IF₂	FOC	EE
Eyewitness testifies that, after an accident in which a toy rifle discharged, the manufacturer designed a safety catch for the toy	Manufacturer did design a safety catch for a toy rifle after an accident	Manufacturer believed that the toy rifle created an unreasonable risk of injury without the safety catch	The toy rifle did create an unreasonable risk of injury without the safety catch	The manufacturer was negligent in producing the toy rifle without the safety catch

altering the condition of property, Knight v. Otis Elevator Co., 596 F.2d 84 (3d Cir. 1979) (placing "guards" around elevator buttons); disciplining or firing an individual whose alleged negligence was responsible for an accident, Specht v. Jensen, 863 F.2d 700 (10th Cir. 1988) (disciplining police officers for violation of Fourth Amendment); Hull v. Chevron U.S.A., Inc. 812 F.2d 584 (10th Cir. 1987) (firing forklift operator following accident); sending a recall notice, Chase v. General Motors Corp., 856 F.2d 17 (4th Cir. 1988) (recall of cars manufactured before design change); changing rules or regulations, Ford v. Schmidt, 577 F.2d 408 (7th Cir. 1978) (change in prison regulations); or posting warning signs, In re Joint Asbestos Litigation, 995 F.2d 343 (2d Cir. 1993) (posting warning sign on asbestos product).

iii.   There Is No Intent or Motive Requirement.   FRE 407 applies to measures that would have made earlier injuries less likely had the measures been implemented before the injuries. The inferences prohibited by FRE 407 — from subsequent action to negligence, culpable conduct, defect, or the need for a warning — depend on beliefs by those engaging in subsequent actions that prior conditions were unreasonably dangerous. In other words, without these beliefs, the evidence is irrelevant for proving the prohibited purposes. David P. Leonard, The New Wigmore §2.2 (2002) ("Relevancy is assumed on the basis that the evidence constitutes a recognition of fault by the party whose conduct is in question."). In applying FRE 407's exclusionary mandate, however, there is no additional requirement that the subsequent actions were done with the intent or motive to prevent future injuries or to make conditions safer. See Chlopek v. Federal Ins. Co., 499 F.3d 692, 700 (7th Cir. 2007) (rejecting argument that a change in a warning was not "remedial" because it was not prompted by safety concerns: "motive for making the change is irrelevant.").

iv.   The Effectiveness of the Remedial Action.   Courts rarely focus on how effective a remedial measure would have been in making earlier injury or harm less likely. For example, courts readily accept that firing an employee can be a subsequent remedial measure within the meaning of FRE 407 without examining whether the action is likely to reduce the chance of future accidents. There is, however, precedent for the proposition that FRE 407 does not apply to investigations that are not "remedial" but only "initial steps toward ascertaining whether any remedial measures are called for." Fasanaro v. Mooney Aircraft Corp., 687 F. Supp. 482, 487 (N.D. Cal. 1988). Compare Rocky Mountain Helicopters, Inc. v. Bell Helicopters, 805 F.2d 907, 918 (10th Cir. 1986) (investigative reports not subsequent remedial measures) with Maddox v. Los Angeles, 792 F.2d 1408, 1417 (9th Cir. 1986) ("investigation and measures taken were remedial measures").

v.   The Timing of the Remedial Action.   For evidence of a remedial measure to be inadmissible under FRE 407, it must occur after "an earlier injury or harm." The purpose of this language, according to the Advisory Committee Note, is to make it clear that "the rule applies only to changes made after the occurrence that produced the damages giving rise to the action." Thus, if the defendant changed a product design after the plaintiff was injured, FRE 407 would apply to prevent the plaintiff from introducing evidence of the design change to show defect. On the other hand, if the defendant took the remedial action subsequent to the injuries of several other people but prior to the plaintiff's injury, FRE 407 would not preclude admissibility of the design change. Trull v. Volkswagon, Inc., 187 F.3d 88 (1st Cir. 1999).

b.   Permissible Uses of Subsequent-Remedial-Measure Evidence

FRE 407 makes it clear that subsequent-remedial-measure evidence may be admissible for other purposes. As with FRE 404(b), the list of permissible purposes in FRE 407 is not exclusive. Subject to FRE 403 and other exclusionary rules, subsequent-remedial-measure evidence may be admissible for *any* purpose other than to show negligence, culpable conduct, defect, or the need for a warning or instruction.

The purposes listed in the second sentence of FRE 407 are the permissible purposes for which subsequent-remedial-measure evidence is most likely to be relevant. For example, the fact that the defendant repaired a staircase suggests that the defendant was the owner of the building containing the staircase or that the defendant, rather than somebody else, had control over the staircase and was responsible for keeping it in good order. Cf. Lee v. E.I. Dupont, 249 F.3d 362 (5th Cir. 2001) (subsequent design change to scaffold admissible against defendant to show that defendant rather than plaintiff's employer was responsible for maintaining the scaffold). If a defendant testifies that the staircase was in good condition at the time of the accident, the fact that the defendant had repaired or authorized the repair of the staircase is relevant to impeach the defendant's credibility: Making or authorizing the repair seems inconsistent with the witness's testimony that the staircase was safe at the time of the accident. Cf. Anderson v. Malloy, 700 F.2d 1208 (8th Cir. 1983) (in rape victim's negligence action against motel operator, defendant testified that safety chains and peep holes on doors would only provide false sense of security and that everything necessary for security had been done; plaintiff permitted to show subsequent installation of safety chains and peep holes both to show feasibility and to impeach defendant). Finally, as we suggested previously, taking subsequent remedial action rebuts a defendant's claim that it was not feasible to maintain the staircase in a safer condition. Cf. Dixon v. International Harvester Co., 754 F.2d 573 (10th Cir. 1985) (defendant claimed additional protective metal on logging vehicle not feasible because it would impair vision; evidence of subsequent installation of protective metal on similar vehicles admissible).

c.   The "If Disputed" Requirement

Even if the "if disputed" phrase did not appear in FRE 407, FRE 403 should be a basis for excluding evidence of a subsequent remedial measure offered to prove an issue that is not disputed. By the terms of the rule, the "if disputed" phrase does not apply to evidence offered for impeachment. There is no need for it to do so. Impeachment evidence is evidence offered to undermine the credibility of a witness, and every witness's credibility is regarded as a matter that can be disputed. See FRE 611(b). Prior to the 2011 restyling amendments to the FRE, the "if disputed" requirement was phrased as "if controverted," and therefore prior judicial opinions applying FRE 407 will use the "if controverted" language.

d.   The Relationship Between FRE 407 and FRE 403

When a party offers subsequent-remedial-measure evidence for a legitimate, disputed purpose, the question of admissibility in theory should turn on the applicability of FRE 403: Is the probative value of the evidence for the legitimate purpose (e.g., feasibility) substantially outweighed by the possibility that the jurors may use the evidence for the impermissible purpose of inferring negligence or other culpable conduct? In fact, if subsequent-remedial-measure evidence is relevant to prove some contested issue other than negligence, culpable conduct, defect, or need for a warning, the result almost invariably is that the evidence is admissible. Christopher B. Mueller and Laird C. Kirkpatrick, Federal Evidence §130 (2d ed. 1994). If so, the party against whom the evidence is admitted is entitled to a limiting instruction.

Courts, however, do sometimes rely on FRE 403 to exclude evidence that does not fit within FRE 407's language but that may raise similar policy concerns. See, e.g., Bogosian v. Mercedes Benz, Inc., 104 F.3d 472 (1st Cir 1997) (excluding evidence of modifications made to a product after purchase by plaintiff, but before injury, because jurors may overestimate probative value).

3.   Elaboration of FRE 407

a.   *The Rationales for FRE 407*

There are four rationales for FRE 407. These rationales also apply to other rules — FRE 408 (offers of compromise), 409 (medical expenses), and 411 (liability insurance) — that exclude evidence to prove negligence, liability, or culpable conduct. We discuss these other rules later in this chapter.

   i.   Low Probative Value.   First, the evidence may have relatively low probative value for the prohibited purposes. Although a defendant may have engaged in subsequent measures to remedy prior negligence, culpability, defect, or the need for a warning, the defendant may have engaged in the same conduct for a variety of other reasons. For example, a defendant may take subsequent remedial action to make a product safer out of an abundance of caution even though there was no negligence or design defect at the time of an injury. (Indeed, the injury or harm at issue may have revealed information for making conditions safer, which the defendant could not have reasonably foreseen beforehand.) The defendant may also undertake subsequent changes for reasons unrelated to improving safety. Similarly, a party may offer to compromise a claim (FRE 408) in order to avoid litigation costs, not because the party is at fault.

   ii.   Countervailing FRE 403 Factors.   Second, countervailing FRE 403 considerations may warrant exclusion. These considerations include a concern that admission of the evidence to prove negligence or fault may tend to mislead the jury. Jurors may reasonably expect that the evidence they hear has a bearing on what they are supposed to decide. Thus, if they hear evidence that in fact has low probative value, they may be misled into thinking that the evidence is more probative than it really is. Moreover, jurors may overestimate the probative value of the evidence because of "hindsight bias." Jurors who learn that a defendant responded to an accident or injury by making changes may overestimate how likely the defendant should reasonably have foreseen the accident or injury ahead of time. See Dan M. Kahan, The

Economics — Conventional, Behavioral, and Political — of "Subsequent Remedial Measures" Evidence, 110 Colum. L. Rev. 1616 (2010).

Although jurors may overestimate the probative value of evidence of subsequent remedial measures (and this overvaluation may contribute to erroneous decisions), keep in mind that depriving jurors of relevant and probative remedial evidence may also contribute to erroneous decisions.

iii.   Not Discouraging Desirable Conduct.   Third, the rules excluding evidence to prove liability or fault traditionally have been justified on the ground that we do not want to discourage individuals from engaging in socially desirable conduct such as making conditions and products safer. In this respect, these rules are similar to some rules of privilege. We exclude evidence of confidential communications between lawyers and clients in part because we do not want to discourage clients from being candid when they consult lawyers for legal advice. Similarly, we exclude evidence of subsequent remedial measures, offers of compromise (FRE 408), payment of medical expenses (FRE 409), and maintaining liability insurance (FRE 411) to prove fault, in part because we do not want to discourage individuals from engaging in these types of socially desirable conduct.

Consider whether this justification provides a sufficient basis for excluding relevant evidence. To what extent do you think individuals take into account — or even know — the rules of evidence in making decisions about subsequent remedial measures, offers of compromise, or payments of medical expenses? (The answer may depend to a substantial extent on whether the individual has sought the advice of counsel before engaging in the activity.)

iv.   Not Punishing Desirable Conduct.   A fourth rationale for these rules is that — regardless of low probative value, misleading the jury, or deterring socially desirable conduct — we do not want to punish or disadvantage individuals for doing good things. This rationale is most frequently associated with the exclusionary rule for payment of medical expenses, sometimes referred to as the "good Samaritan" rule. We suggest, however, that the rationale is equally applicable to — and perhaps more compelling than the deterrence rationale for — the limitations on the use of remedial measures, offers to compromise, and insurance.

b.   Subsequent Remedial Measures by Third Persons

Courts frequently admit evidence of remedial measures taken by persons other than the party against whom the evidence is offered. See Diehl v. Blaw-Knox, 360 F.3d 426, 430 (3d Cir. 2004) (following plaintiff's injury, employer modified piece of road-widening equipment that injured plaintiff; evidence of modification admissible against manufacturer of equipment); Mehojah v. Drummond, 56 F.3d 1213 (10th Cir. 1995) (suit against ranch by couple whose automobile struck cattle on highway; FRE 407 not applicable to subsequent installation of fence by owner of land leased to ranch); Pau v. Yosemite Park & Curry Co., 928 F.2d 880 (9th Cir. 1991) (suit against bike rental company following fatal accident on National Park trail; evidence that Park Service posted sign prohibiting bikes following the accident not precluded by FRE 407); but see In re Air Crash Disaster, 86 F.3d 498 (6th Cir. 1996).

KEY POINTS

1. FRE 407 makes evidence of subsequent remedial measures inadmissible to prove negligence, culpable conduct, defect, or need for a warning or instruction.

2. FRE 407's exclusionary mandate applies only to remedial action taken after the event that is the subject of the litigation.

3. Subject to FRE 403, subsequent-remedial-measure evidence may be admissible for other purposes, the most likely of which are those listed in FRE 407: to show ownership, control, feasibility, or to impeach the credibility of a witness. The evidence should be admissible for these other purposes only if they are disputed issues in the case.

PROBLEMS

6.1. Return to Problem 3.2 at page 136. Assume that six months ago the San Ramon School District adopted a policy requiring all of its bus drivers to take a special driver education course each year. Will the plaintiff be able to admit evidence of this policy adoption?

6.2. Return to Problem 3.14 at page 157. The plaintiff, Cynthia Richards, offers evidence that shortly after the accident the Kmart supervisor who testified during discovery required store employees to walk the aisles every 15 minutes to look for clutter on the floor. Can you articulate a theory of relevance for this evidence? For the theory of relevance you have identified, should the evidence be excluded under FRE 407?

Would your answers change if the supervisor testifies at trial: "At the time of Ms. Richards's accident our store was very safe; no policy of patrolling the store was necessary because our employees always picked up clutter in the aisles immediately"? Again try to articulate a theory of relevance for this evidence and explain whether it should be excluded under FRE 407.

6.3. Lisa Evans is suing the Jones Manufacturing Co. for the wrongful death of her husband, Edward. Edward suffered injuries that resulted in his death when a coworker turned on an industrial baling machine, manufactured by the defendant, when Edward was inside the hopper attempting to clear a jam. Lisa wishes to introduce evidence that after Edward's death

(a) Jones Manufacturing Co. fired the individual responsible for designing safety features on the baler; and

(b) Edward's employer, Loman Industries, modified the baler by installing an access door to the hopper and by making the baler inoperable when the access doors were open.

Jones objects that both items of evidence should be excluded under FRE 407. Should Jones's objections be sustained?

6.4. Eugene Wright is suing the Loop Ladder Co. for personal injuries that he received when a ladder on which he had been standing fell to the ground with him on it. Eugene claims that a plastic tip on the ladder was too weak and that it broke, causing the ladder to fall. The defendant claims that the plastic tip broke from the impact of the fall or at some later time. An expert witness testifies for the defendant that the tip was adequate for its purpose. Plaintiff offers evidence that shortly after his accident, the Loop Ladder Company substituted a strengthened plastic cap on all of its ladders. Should this evidence be excluded under FRE 407? Would it make any difference in your analysis if the expert were a Loop employee who had authorized the change in the plastic tip?

6.5. Return to Problem 5.25 at page 282. Consider the admissibility of the following evidence against Acme:

(a) testimony that following the incident involving Henry, Acme hired outside consultants to prepare a report on the safety of its cleanser;
(b) the consultants' post-accident report analyzing the toxicity of the cleanser;
(c) testimony that following the report Acme reduced the toxicity of its cleanser formula.

Would any of your answers change if an Acme executive had testified, "There is nothing safer than Acme Cleanser"?

3. FRE 408

RULE 408. COMPROMISE OFFERS AND NEGOTIATIONS

(a) *Prohibited Uses.* Evidence of the following is not admissible — on behalf of any party — either to prove or disprove the validity or amount of a disputed claim or to impeach by a prior inconsistent statement or a contradiction:

(1) furnishing, promising, or offering — or accepting, promising to accept, or offering to accept — a valuable consideration in compromising or attempting to compromise the claim; and

(2) conduct or a statement made during compromise negotiations about the claim — except when offered in a criminal case and when the negotiations related to a claim by a public office in the exercise of its regulatory, investigative, or enforcement authority.

(b) *Exceptions.* The court may admit this evidence for another purpose, such as proving a witness's bias or prejudice, negating a contention of undue delay, or proving an effort to obstruct a criminal investigation or prosecution.

4. Interpretation and Illustration of FRE 408

a. *The Exclusionary Mandate; Permissible Uses; FRE 403*

One plausible inference to draw from offers of compromise is that the offerors — like people who take subsequent remedial action — believe they were at fault in the incident giving rise to a claim against them. If they have this belief, one can then make the further inference that they were in fact at fault. In short, one way in which compromising or offering to compromise a claim is relevant is as a tacit recognition of fault or liability.

As is the case with subsequent-remedial-measure evidence, there are other possible explanations for wanting to compromise a claim. For example, some individuals who adamantly believe they are not at fault may be willing to settle a claim because the potential litigation costs are significantly greater than the amount of settlement.

The FRE 408 mandate excluding compromise evidence to prove the validity or amount of a claim and the list of permissible uses for compromise evidence are the equivalent of the two sentences in FRE 407. To encourage settlements, FRE 408 excludes evidence of compromises and of offers to compromise on the questions of liability for or the amount of claims. At the same time, the rule makes it clear that such evidence may be admissible for other purposes. The list of other purposes, which is not exclusive, includes the purposes for which offers of compromise are most likely to be relevant. For example, to show the bias of a witness who testifies for the plaintiff, the defendant may want to establish that the witness had previously settled a similar claim with the defendant for less than the witness had wanted, see Croskey v. BMW of North America, Inc., 532 F.3d 511, 519 (6th Cir. 2008), or that the witness's claim against the plaintiff includes a provision for the plaintiff to pay to the witness a portion of any judgment obtained against the defendant, see Brocklesby v. United States, 767 F.2d 1288 (9th Cir. 1985). A municipality's settlement of a police brutality action may be admissible to show that the municipality knew of and condoned the officer's conduct. Spell v. McDaniel, 824 F.2d 1380 (4th Cir. 1987). Proof of negotiations and offers to compromise may indicate that a party was acting in good faith to resolve a claim and thus rebut a charge of undue delay, Californian & Hawaiian Sugar Co. v. Kansas City Terminal Warehouse Co., 602 F. Supp. 183 (W.D. Mo. 1985), or was acting in bad faith, Athey v. Farmers Ins. Exch., 234 F.3d 357 (8th Cir. 2000) (compromise negotiations admissible to show bad faith in negotiating); Bankcard Am., Inc. v. Universal Bancard Sys., Inc., 203 F.3d 477, 484 (7th Cir. 2000) ("It would be an abuse of Rule 408 to allow one party during compromise negotiations to lead his opponent to believe he will not enforce applicable time limitations and then object when the opponent attempts to prove the waiver of time limitations"). Offers of compromise during an income tax audit may be admissible to show the taxpayer's knowledge and to rebut a claim of good faith in a tax evasion prosecution. United States v. Hauert, 40 F.3d 197 (7th Cir. 1994). Compromise evidence may also be admissible to prove "absence of mistake" or that an event was not an "isolated incident." See Orr v. Albuquerque, 531 F.3d 1210, 1219 (10th Cir. 2008) (compromise evidence admissible to prove that "Ms. Vigil's treatment of Officers Orr and Paiz was not a random accident, as defendants claim, but part of a larger and deliberate pattern of treating pregnant women differently from other employees.").

FRE 408 also prohibits using compromise evidence to impeach a witness "by a prior inconsistent statement or a contradiction." Such uses of compromise evidence, according to the Advisory Committee, "would tend to swallow the exclusionary rule and would impair the public policy of promoting settlements."

Unlike FRE 407, FRE 408(b) does not contain "if disputed" language in specifying permissible uses. Nonetheless, in order to have sufficient probative value to overcome an FRE 403 objection, the purpose for which the evidence is offered should be a disputed issue in the case.

b.   Conduct or Statements Made During Negotiations

FRE 408 excludes not only compromises and offers of compromise but also — at least in civil actions — conduct or statements made during compromise negotiations. (We discuss FRE 408 and criminal prosecutions in subsection d.) This is a significant departure from the common law rule, which excluded only statements of offer and acceptance. Consider, for example, a situation in which Amy and John are involved in an automobile accident. Amy threatens to sue, asserting that John was at fault and must pay for the damage to Amy's car. John offers one of the following responses:

(1)   "Let's settle this matter ourselves so we don't have to pay fat fees to lawyers. I'll give you $500 and we'll call everything even."

(2)   "There's no need to deal with lawyers, who'll demand a fat fee. This was my fault. I'll give you $500 and we'll call everything even."

Assume that Amy rejects the settlement offer and sues John. Both the common law and FRE 408 would preclude use of the offers of compromise against John to prove liability. The common law, but not FRE 408, would permit Amy to use John's acknowledgment of fault in the second statement to prove liability.

c.   The "Disputed Claim" Requirement

Offers of compromise and statements of fault are inadmissible pursuant to FRE 408 only if made during compromise negotiations over a disputed claim. If there is no disputed claim or if the statement of fault occurs outside the context of compromise negotiations, the statement of fault will be admissible. For example, in the preceding hypothetical if John made the offer and statement of fault before Amy made any claim, the statement would be admissible. Big O Tire Dealers, Inc. v. Goodyear Tire & Rubber Co., 561 F.2d 1365, 1372-1373 (10th Cir. 1977) (statements admissible as "business communications"; "discussions had not crystallized to the point of threatened litigation"). If John conceded full liability and was not attempting to reach a compromise, his statements also would be admissible. Perzinski v. Chevron Chem. Co., 503 F.2d 654 (7th Cir. 1974) (salesperson's statement that company would "take care of" plaintiff admissible).

In applying FRE 408, the trial judge must usually decide some preliminary questions of fact. What type of information is likely to be important to the preliminary question whether there is a disputed claim and a legitimate attempt to compromise that claim? Reconsider whether John's initial two statements, which we characterized as having been made after Amy threatened to sue, would be admissible under the following circumstances:

(a)   There had been no threat to sue.
(b)   The threat had been a spontaneous outburst at the time of the accident.
(c)   The possible suit had been mentioned in the context of a polite but restrained conversation between Amy and John about various options available to them.
(d)   The value of Amy's claim did not exceed $500. (Does it matter whether John or a reasonable person would probably have been aware of this fact?)

To what extent are the foregoing factors relevant to the judge's decision whether Amy and John were engaged in compromise negotiations over a disputed claim?

The answer to the foregoing question, of course, depends in part on how courts interpret "a disputed claim," and the courts of appeals provide varying answers. For example, compare Blu-J, Inc. v. Kemper C.P.A. Group, 916 F.2d 637, 642 (11th Cir. 1990) (FRE 408 exclusionary rule applies to "statements or conduct . . . intended to be part of the negotiations toward compromise") with Big O Tire Dealers v. Goodyear Tire & Rubber Co., supra at 1373 (FRE 408 exclusionary rule applies only after discussions "crystalize to the point of threatening litigation").

d.   The Applicability of FRE 408 to Criminal Cases

If a person admits some wrongdoing in the course of negotiations to settle a civil claim, may the prosecution use the statement against the wrongdoer in a subsequent criminal prosecution? FRE 408 prohibits the use of compromises and offers and acceptances in criminal prosecutions, but it creates a limited exception to the general prohibition against the use of *conduct or a statement made during compromise negotiations*. The exception — that is, the right to use in criminal prosecutions conduct and statements made during civil compromise negotiations — exists when "negotiations related to a claim by a public office in the exercise of its regulatory, investigative, or enforcement authority." To illustrate a factual scenario that fits the scope of this exception, the Advisory Committee cited United States v. Prewitt, 34 F.3d 436, 439 (7th Cir. 1994). *Prewitt* was a mail fraud prosecution in which the court upheld the admissibility of statements of fault made during the compromise of a civil securities enforcement action. According to the Advisory Committee, "Where an individual makes a statement in the presence of government agents, its subsequent admission in a criminal case should not be unexpected."

e.   A Party's Own Offer of Compromise

In Pierce v. F.R. Tripler & Co., 955 F.2d 820, 828 (2d Cir. 1992), the court held that FRE 408 applies to a party's effort to introduce its own offer of compromise. *Pierce* was an age discrimination suit in which the defendant, to show mitigation of damages, sought to introduce its offer of a job to the plaintiff. Although the purpose of the offer was to contest the amount of a claim, the defendant had argued that the policies underlying FRE 408 were inapplicable when a party sought to introduce evidence of its own offer of compromise. The "on behalf of any party" language in FRE 408 was intended to codify the result in *Pierce*. The Advisory Committee offered two reasons for the amendment. First, the offeror's revealing its own offer could "reveal the fact that the adversary entered into settlement negotiations," which would undermine the policy of FRE 408. Second, "proof of statements and offers made in settlement would often have to be made through the testimony of attorneys, leading to the risks and costs of disqualification."

f.   Compromises and Offers of Compromises by Third Persons

Consider a case in which the plaintiff sues the defendant, a restaurant, for food poisoning. The plaintiff claims that the restaurant was responsible for mishandling the food. The defendant seeks to introduce evidence that it had made a claim against its food supplier for $300,000, and that the supplier had settled the claim for $250,000. The defendant argues that the settlement evidence is an admission by the supplier that the supplier provided the restaurant with adulterated food, and that the adulteration — not the defendant's alleged mishandling of the food — was responsible for the food poisoning.

Just as we suggested that evidence of a third person's subsequent remedial measure does not implicate the policies underlying FRE 407 (see page 333, supra), evidence of a third person's offer of compromise does not implicate the policies underlying FRE 408. The negotiations and settlement have nothing to do with the party against whom the evidence is offered, and it will be adequate protection for the third person to exclude the evidence if and when the third person becomes a party. Courts, however, have taken different approaches for compromise evidence involving distinct claims and third parties. Compare Towerridge, Inc. v. T.A.O., Inc., 11 F.3d 758, 770 (10th Cir. 1997) ("Rule 408 does not require the exclusion of evidence regarding the settlement of a claim different from the one litigated") with C&E Serv., Inc. v. Ashland,

Inc., 539 F. Supp. 2d 316, 320 (D.D.C. 2008) ("The very policy of Rule 408 would be defeated if it did not operate to preclude the admissibility of settlement negotiations in a case involving another party or another claim.").

5.   FRE 409

RULE 409.   OFFERS TO PAY MEDICAL AND SIMILAR EXPENSES

Evidence of furnishing, promising to pay, or offering to pay medical, hospital, or similar expenses resulting from an injury is not admissible to prove liability for the injury.

6.   Interpretation and Illustration of FRE 409

a.   *The Exclusionary Mandate*

Just as evidence of a subsequent repair or an offer to compromise may be relevant as a recognition of fault, paying or offering to pay another person's medical expenses may be relevant for similar reasons: The payments may imply that those paying believe they are legally responsible for the injuries.

For reasons similar to Rules 407 and 408, FRE 409 excludes such evidence to prove liability. For example, if a driver hits a pedestrian and offers to pay the pedestrian's medical expenses, neither the offer nor the payment is admissible to prove the driver's liability. Similarly, if an insurance company pays a person's medical expenses before any trial or settlement, evidence of the payment is not subsequently admissible to prove the insurance company's liability. See Galarnyk v. Hostmart Mgmt., 55 Fed. Appx. 763 (7th Cir. 2003) (plaintiff "fell in the bathroom of [a motel], converting gravitational energy to kinetic energy with such effectiveness that he punched a hole in the wall"; offers by defendant and defendant's insurance carrier to pay medical expenses not admissible to show liability).

b.   *The Admissibility of Statements Made in Conjunction with Medical and Similar Payments*

In one significant respect FRE 409 differs from FRE 408: Statements made in conjunction with the payments — including statements of fault — are *not* excluded. According to the Advisory Committee:

> This difference in treatment arises from fundamental differences in nature. Communication is essential if compromises are to be effected, and consequently broad protection of statements is needed. This is not so in cases of payments [governed by FRE 409], where factual statements may be expected to be incidental in nature.

c.   *FRE 409 Permits Evidence of Payment for Purposes Other Than to Show Liability*

Although FRE 409 does not include an illustrative list of possible permissible uses for evidence of medical and similar payments, this evidence — like FRE 407, 408, and 411 — may be admissible for any relevant purpose other than to prove liability.

See, e.g., Savoie v. Otto Candies, Inc., 692 F.2d 363 (5th Cir. 1982) (maintenance payments to prove status as seaman).

d.   What Constitutes a "Similar" Expense?

FRE 409 is rarely invoked, perhaps because there are not enough good Samaritans among us. If there were, an issue that would undoubtedly arise in applying FRE 409 is what constitutes "similar expenses." For example, should evidence of paying to have an automobile repaired or paying subsistence income while an individual is recuperating from injury be excluded? See Great Coastal Express, Inc. v. Atlanta Mut. Cos., 790 So. 2d 966 (Ala. Civ. App. 2000) (state equivalent of FRE 409 not a bar to evidence that defendant paid for some of clean up following fuel leak; evidence admissible to infer defendant's negligence).

7.   FRE 411

RULE 411.   LIABILITY INSURANCE

Evidence that a person was or was not insured against liability is not admissible to prove whether the person acted negligently or otherwise wrongfully. But the court may admit this evidence for another purpose, such as proving a witness's bias or prejudice or proving agency, ownership, or control.

8.   Interpretation and Illustration of FRE 411

a.   The Exclusionary Mandate

This rule is similar in purpose, structure, and application to FRE 407-409. With respect to liability insurance, however, the probative value of the forbidden inference is particularly weak: The underlying premise of the forbidden inference is that people with liability insurance are likely to be less careful than people without insurance, who will be individually responsible for the injuries they cause. Moreover, liability insurance is so pervasive that it is doubtful that individuals take into account the rules of evidence in deciding whether to obtain or to forgo obtaining liability insurance.

If evidence of liability insurance were admissible on the question of fault, there would be a substantial risk of unfair prejudice. Jurors might be inclined to impose damages because of insurance or to forgo or minimize damages out of sympathy for the uninsured. On the other hand, given the pervasiveness of liability insurance, if an uninsured party is not able to present evidence of absence of insurance, there is a risk that the jury may assume the party is insured and impose damages on the basis of this incorrect assumption. Moreover, empirical studies of jurors indicate that, despite instructions to the contrary, jurors frequently discuss and make assumptions about insurance. See, e.g., Shari Seidman Diamond and Neil Vidmar, Jury Ruminations on Forbidden Topics, 87 Va. L. Rev. 1857, 1876 (2001) (in a study of 40 tort cases, jurors discussed insurance in 85 percent of the cases). If jurors will rely on their beliefs about insurance in their deliberations (even when they are instructed not to), would a rule that provides the jury with accurate information about insurance in the case be better than the current rule?

b. The Permissible Uses of Evidence of Liability Insurance

Like FRE 407-409, FRE 411 excludes evidence of liability insurance only to prove negligence or wrongful conduct. The second sentence of FRE 411 lists the most common permissible uses of evidence of liability insurance. Like the lists of permissible purposes in FRE 407 and FRE 408, the FRE 411 list is not exclusive. When there is a permissible purpose, the admissibility of the evidence should depend on the application of FRE 403, and FRE 403 should require at a minimum that the issue for which the evidence is offered is disputed.

Liability insurance offered for some legitimate, disputed purpose is usually admitted. Morton v. Zidell Explorations, Inc., 695 F.2d 347 (9th Cir. 1982) (proof of purchasing insurance to rebut claim that contract not in effect); Hunziker v. Scheidemantle, 543 F.2d 489 (3d Cir. 1976) (proof of insurance covering alleged agent to prove agency); Newell v. Harold Shaffer Leasing Co., 489 F.2d 103 (5th Cir. 1974) (maintaining insurance introduced to show ownership or control). If, as is frequently the case, an insurance investigator testifies about the results of an investigation, evidence that the investigator represents a company that insures one of the parties will probably be admissible both as part of the general background information about the witness and as an indication of the possible bias of the witness. Conde v. Starlight I, Inc., 103 F.3d 210 (1st Cir. 1997); see also Cook v. Rockwell Intl. Corp., 580 F. Supp. 2d 1071, 1155 (D. Colo. 2006) (evidence of indemnification obligations to defendants admissible to prove bias or prejudice of witnesses affiliated with indemnitor).

KEY POINTS

1. Under FRE 408, 409, and 411, evidence of compromises, offers of compromise, payment or offers to pay medical and similar expenses, and liability insurance is not admissible to prove liability.

2. Subject to FRE 403, such evidence may be admissible for other purposes. The permissible purposes listed in FRE 408 and FRE 411, like the permissible purposes listed in FRE 407, are the most common purposes for which evidence governed by those rules is likely to be admissible, but the lists are not exclusive.

3. When evidence is offered for a theoretically legitimate permissible purpose, FRE 403 should require exclusion if the issue is not a disputed one.

PROBLEMS

6.6. Return to Problem 3.2 at page 136.

(a) Paul's mother offers to testify that shortly after the accident she received a note from Driver with $200. The note, which the plaintiff would like to introduce into evidence, says: "I'm so sorry about Paul's accident. I'm not a rich person but I hope this will help with some of the expenses."

(b) Plaintiff wishes to introduce evidence that after the law suit was filed, the school district offered to settle the suit for $25,000.

(c) In cross-examining the school district's accident reconstruction expert, plaintiff wishes to show that the witness has a professional relationship with the School District's liability insurance carrier.

Should any of this evidence be admitted?

6.7. Dave Defendant, while sitting in Evidence class, was preoccupied with his plans for the semester break. His hot coffee spilled on Paula Plaintiff, who was sitting next to him. Paula suffered a serious burn in the area where the coffee spilled. She sued Dave for negligence and Espresso-to-Go, where Dave purchased the coffee, for a defectively designed take-out cup, alleging $50,000 in damages. Paula offers to testify as follows on direct examination:

Q: Paula, what happened immediately after the spill?
A: Dave said he would pay for my ruined clothes.
Q: Did you ever talk to Dave about the case again?
A: Yes. After I filed this suit, Dave saw me in the hall one day and said he was sorry I had been hurt because he had been so clumsy and that he'd like to talk more but he was late for class. Then the next day he said he didn't think my case was worth $50,000, but that he'd like to pay all my bills and give me money for a "bar trip" after graduation.

What objections should defense counsel make to this testimony?

6.8. Assume that Paula settles with Dave and proceeds to trial against Espresso-to-Go.

(a) Paula calls Dave to testify about the incident and to describe the severity of Paula's burns. Are the following questions by defense counsel on cross-examination objectionable: "Isn't it true that you were sued by Paula for your own negligence? And isn't it true that you and Paula reached a compromise of that claim for a mere $500? And isn't it true that Paula really dropped the suit against you in exchange for your testimony here today?"

(b) Can Paula introduce evidence of Espresso-to-Go's substantial liability insurance policy? Would your answer change if, at trial, the owner of Espresso-to-Go had mentioned during testimony (1) that its products were so low risk that the company did not carry much insurance or (2) that he could not afford to lose the lawsuit because he needed everything to care for his ailing mother?

6.9. Paul Preston has sued Daniel Dripps for damages for assault and battery after Dripps attacked Preston at their daughters' hockey game. In a mediation session to discuss settlement, Preston's lawyer says that Preston would settle for payment of his medical expenses plus $5,000 if Dripps would admit he was wrong and apologize. Dripps says, "Well, I am sorry — I was in the wrong." He counter-offers to offer an apology and pay the medical expenses and no more. Preston says he doubts Dripps's sincerity about the apology. To demonstrate Dripps's sincerity, Dripps's attorney shows Preston's attorney an entry from Dripps's diary the day of the fight saying that he was at fault and was sorry. Negotiations break down over the $5,000. The day after the mediation, Preston's counsel sends out a document request demanding production of the diary, which the plaintiff had not known about prior to the mediation. Eventually, the case goes to trial. Is the following evidence offered by Preston admissible?

(1) Dripps's statement at the mediation that he was sorry and is in the wrong;
(2) Dripps's willingness to cover Preston's medical expenses;
(3) The entry from Dripps's diary admitting fault;
(4) Evidence that Dripps's homeowners' insurance company denied coverage for the alleged assault and battery on the ground that the policy did not cover intentional wrongful acts. (Preston argues that it shows that the insurance company found Dripps to have acted wrongfully and intentionally.)

Would any of your answers be different if this were a criminal prosecution of Dripps for battery?

6.10. Pam Palmer has sued Dick Davis for injuries she received in an automobile accident involving her car and the cars of Davis and Walter Williams. According to the plaintiff's complaint she was headed west on a two-lane road when Davis, who was heading east, crossed the road into her lane of traffic and hit her. Davis claims that he had been taking necessary evasive action in an unsuccessful effort to avoid hitting another car that had suddenly pulled in front of him from a side street. The driver of the third car was Walter Williams.

Williams has testified for the plaintiff that Davis was responsible for the accident. According to Williams, he had been traveling east at a normal rate of speed when Davis, who was speeding, suddenly approached from the rear. In an unsuccessful effort to avoid hitting Williams, Davis veered to the left, clipping the rear end of Williams's car and hitting the plaintiff's car as well.

Davis offers to show that he had filed suit against Williams for damage to his automobile and that Williams had paid Davis $500 to settle the suit, in which Davis had asked for $2,000. Should this evidence be admitted over plaintiff's objection?

6.11. Roland Nast has filed an age discrimination suit against the Jones Hardware Co. for failing to promote him to a manager position and giving the job instead to a much younger employee.

(a) Although Nast had a reputation for being a bit hotheaded and argumentative, Jim Jones, president of Jones Hardware, maintained during settlement negotiations that Nast's attitude and personality had nothing to do with his not getting the manager job. Instead, according to Jones, the problem was Nast's tardiness record. At trial, however, Jones testified that Nast's attitude and personality were primary factors in the decision not to promote him to a manager position. Can Nast introduce Jones's settlement negotiation statements?

(b) To rebut the claim of discrimination, Jones Hardware offers evidence that after Nast filed his complaint Jones Hardware offered Nast a position at a different branch store. This newly offered position had the same salary as the manager salary. Should the evidence be admitted?

B.   REFLECTION ON RULES 407-409, 411

Consider whether it makes sense for the Federal Rules to retain the exclusionary mandates set forth in FRE 407-409 and FRE 411. Commentators have pointed out, particularly with respect to FRE 407, that it is common for proponents to be able to articulate some alternative, permissible reason for admitting the evidence. See, e.g., David. P. Leonard, Selected Rules of Limited Admissibility, The New Wigmore §2.8 (2002). To the extent that one can readily find some alternative permissible theory for the use of evidence that is subject to these rules, one can with good reason question the desirability of the rules in their present form: If courts tend to resolve the FRE 403 balance between the permissible and impermissible use in favor of admissibility (which is usually the case), and if one doubts the efficacy of limiting instructions, the rules in fact would seem not to be serving their designed purposes very well. Alternatively, if the FRE 403 balance were usually to come out in favor of exclusion, the rules would be stated in a deceptively (and thus perhaps undesirably) narrow manner: Despite the limited nature of the express exclusionary mandates, FRE 403 concerns could make the mandates quite broad.

Regardless of whether most decisions involving FRE 407-409 and FRE 411 result in admission or exclusion of the evidence, it may be that judges are simply applying the FRE 403 balancing test wisely on a case-by-case basis. Or perhaps the inherent difficulty of balancing and the breadth of judicial discretion lead to arbitrary and inconsistent results from case to case. Unfortunately, we do not have enough reliable information to assess the need for these rules. Consider, for example, FRE 407's limitation on evidence of subsequent remedial measures. The rule depends on assumptions regarding how the presence or absence of the rule affects or would affect behavior — i.e., that the rule encourages people to make conditions safer and that its absence would deter such behavior — but we do not have reliable information about whether the rule actually produces or would produce these effects. (For further discussion of the empirical assumptions underlying FRE 407 and the limited information available regarding these assumptions, see Kahan, supra.)

Perhaps answers will emerge as we gain more experience and sophistication in studying the operation of the rules of evidence in practice. In the meantime, however, these potential problems should not be ignored. The task of the rule drafters should be to devise the best possible rules in light of the best available information (based on logic, empiricism, and intuition) as to how various alternative formulations of the rules are likely to work in practice.

C.   WITHDRAWN GUILTY PLEAS, PLEAS OF NO CONTEST, AND STATEMENTS MADE DURING PLEA DISCUSSIONS

1.   FRE 410

RULE 410.   PLEAS, PLEA DISCUSSIONS, AND RELATED STATEMENTS

(a) *Prohibited Uses*. In a civil or criminal case, evidence of the following is not admissible against the defendant who made the plea or participated in the plea discussions:

(1) a guilty plea that was later withdrawn;

(2) a nolo contendere plea;

(3) a statement made during a proceeding on either of those pleas under Federal Rule of Criminal Procedure 11 or a comparable state procedure; or

(4) a statement made during plea discussions with an attorney for the prosecuting authority if the discussions did not result in a guilty plea or they resulted in a later-withdrawn guilty plea.

(b) *Exceptions.* The court may admit a statement described in Rule 410(a)(3) or (4):

(1) in any proceeding in which another statement made during the same plea or plea discussions has been introduced, if in fairness the statements ought to be considered together; or

(2) in a criminal proceeding for perjury or false statement, if the defendant made the statement under oath, on the record, and with counsel present.

2.   Interpretation and Illustration of FRE 410

a.   Withdrawn Guilty Pleas

Once a defendant has pleaded guilty, the defendant may withdraw the plea only with the permission of the court. The standards for permitting withdrawal of a plea typically are not articulated with any degree of specificity, but there must be "cause" or some good reason to permit the withdrawal. A court is likely to permit withdrawal of a plea if there is reason to believe that the plea is inaccurate because the defendant is innocent or if it appears that the defendant's rights were violated in the process of procuring the plea. To the extent that the concern is with the violation of the defendant's rights, exclusion may be necessary in order to make the remedy for the violation meaningful. If the prosecutor could respond to a withdrawn plea by using that plea against the defendant in a subsequent proceeding, the value of withdrawal as a remedy would often be substantially undermined. To the extent that the concern is with the reliability of a plea, the fact that a judge has already determined that the plea is unreliable casts doubt on the plea's probative value.

b.   Pleas of No Contest

Only some jurisdictions permit pleas of no contest, and where they are permitted the court usually must approve the pleas. Pleas of no contest are by their nature compromises. They constitute acquiescence to a criminal conviction without an admission of guilt or a determination of guilt after an adjudicatory trial. Their compromise nature makes uncertain their probative value to prove that the person committed the acts charged. Moreover, use of no-contest pleas for this purpose may undermine the initial value of the plea as a device to encourage settlement. Olsen v. Correiro, 189 F.3d 52 (1st Cir. 1999).

c.   Statements Made in Conjunction with the Process of Making and Negotiating Pleas

Federal Rule of Criminal Procedure 11, to which FRE 410(a)(3) refers, governs plea bargaining and the judicial acceptance or rejection of guilty pleas. By specifically excluding (a) statements made in Rule 11 plea bargaining proceedings and (b) statements made in the course of plea bargaining with prosecutors, FRE 410(a)(3) and (4) operate in the criminal negotiating process as the counterpart to FRE 408's prohibition against using evidence of attempts to settle or compromise civil claims.

As a matter of general principle, and perhaps even as a matter of practical reality, one may question the soundness of such a rule. An offer to plead guilty, at least if the plea is to a relatively serious charge, may have more probative value than the offer to settle — even for a substantial amount of money — a civil claim. Moreover, the offers to plead guilty that are excluded by FRE 410 usually occur in the context of plea negotiations, and there are several reasons why settling or compromising criminal charges may be regarded as undesirable and, therefore, something to be deterred. First, the possibility of pleading guilty to a charge that is substantially less severe than the crime initially charged may have the undesirable effect of pressuring an innocent individual to plead guilty in order to avoid the risk of possible conviction on the more serious charge. Second, the possibility of a plea to a lesser charge may have the arguably undesirable effect of undermining a legislatively dictated mandatory sentence for the crime initially charged or of limiting the range of the judge's sentencing discretion. Finally, a consequence of encouraging or even condoning plea bargaining is the possibility of unfairness or at least the appearance of unfairness from what are or seem to be inconsistent and arbitrary plea bargaining decisions from case to case by prosecutors. This, in turn, may lead to cynicism about or disrespect for the criminal law and perhaps undermine the force of criminal prohibitions and sanctions as general deterrents.

Despite these concerns, the Supreme Court has acknowledged that plea bargaining is an acceptable method for disposing of criminal cases, Santobello v. New York, 404 U.S. 257 (1971), and the reality is that plea bargaining is pervasive in the criminal justice system. Depending on the jurisdiction, anywhere from 70 percent to 95 percent of all criminal charges are disposed of by guilty pleas, and many of these pleas are the result of plea negotiations. Moreover, the criminal justice system does not have the resources to process the current and ever increasing volume of cases without heavy reliance on guilty pleas. Thus, as a practical matter, plea bargaining is a fact of life. In light of this reality, it may be at least as important to encourage guilty pleas as it is to encourage settlement of civil cases. Just as excluding statements made in conjunction with offers to settle civil suits may facilitate the negotiating process, excluding statements made during plea negotiations may facilitate obtaining guilty pleas.

d.   The Scope of FRE 410(a)(4)

There are two important limitations on the scope of the rule excluding statements covered by FRE 410(a)(4). First, the statements must be made "in the course of plea discussions." For example, if a defendant is merely seeking leniency in the charging decision without suggesting any possibility of pleading guilty, a court may conclude that the conversation is not a plea discussion. Similarly, seeking dismissal of charges against third persons may be outside the scope of plea negotiations, United States v. Doe, 655 F.2d 920 (9th Cir. 1980), as are statements made following the completion of plea negotiations, United States v. Perry, 643 F.2d 38 (2d Cir. 1981). Second, the defendant's statements must be made "to an attorney for the prosecuting authority."

For example, statements to police officers, who have no formal authority to plea bargain in any event, do not fall within the FRE 410(a)(4) exclusion. United States v. Stern, 313 F. Supp. 2d 155, 167-168 (S.D.N.Y. 2003); United States v. Brumley, 217 F.3d 905 (7th Cir. 1997). Statements made to police officers as part of the plea negotiation, however, may be covered by the rule if the police are acting as agents of the prosecutor. United States v. Millard, 139 F.3d 1200 (8th Cir. 1998).

Even if the statements are made to a prosecuting attorney, they may not be protected. There is a split of authority on the question of whether proffer sessions that explore possible cooperation with the government but that do not include discussions of a guilty plea fall within the FRE 410 exclusionary mandate. Compare United States v. Morgan, 91 F.3d 1193, 1195-1196 (8th Cir. 1996) (statements not protected) with United States v. Frank, 173 F.R.D. 59, 69 (W.D.N.Y. 1997) (statements protected). See United States v. Stein, 2005 U.S. Dist. LEXIS 11141 (E.D. Pa.) (collecting cases).

There is substantial precedent for approaching the question whether FRE 410 is applicable from the perspective of the defendant. Statements will not be admissible if the defendant (or the defendant's attorney speaking as an agent) had a subjective belief that plea negotiations with a prosecuting authority were taking place and if that belief was objectively reasonable. United States v. Olsen, 450 F.3d 635 (7th Cir. 2006); United States v. Sayakhom, 186 F.3d 928 (9th Cir. 1999); United States v. Bridges, 46 F. Supp. 2d 462 (E.D. Va. 1999) (collecting cases).

e.   The FRE 410(b) Exceptions

The two enumerated exceptions to in FRE 410(b) will rarely be of consequence. The first exception merely acknowledges the rule of completeness encompassed in FRE 106. For example, if a defendant introduces part of a statement made in conjunction with plea negotiations, the prosecution can introduce other statements that provide a context or explanation for the statement introduced by the defendant. The second exception in effect permits the prosecution to bring perjury charges against a defendant who lies under oath during plea negotiations. Perjury prosecutions are relatively rare, however; and in any event, plea negotiations are seldom under oath.

f.   Waiver of FRE 410's Exclusionary Mandate

In United States v. Mezzanatto, 513 U.S. 196 (1995), the Supreme Court held that a defendant may waive the FRE 410(a)(4) exclusionary mandate with regard to the impeachment use of statements made in the process of plea negotiations. In Mezzanatto, the prosecutor, at the outset of plea discussions with the defendant and his counsel, insisted on the right to be able to use Mezzanatto's statements against him for impeachment purposes in the event of a trial. Mezzanatto agreed to this waiver, and during the plea discussions he made some incriminating statements. The prosecutor, however, terminated the plea negotiations at least in part because of some false statements that Mezzanatto had made. The case proceeded to trial. Mezzanatto testified, and over his objection the prosecution introduced into evidence some of Mezzanatto's plea bargain statements to impeach his testimony. In his opinion for the

Court, Justice Thomas rejected the defendant's claims that waiver was inconsistent with the purpose of FRE 410 and that the possibility of waiver provided potential for prosecutorial overreaching.

In dictum Justice Thomas suggested that the waiver would be valid even if it were not limited to the impeachment use of the statements. Only Chief Justice Rehnquist and Justice Scalia expressed agreement with this dictum. Nonetheless, several federal circuits have extended *Mezzanatto* by upholding waivers that allow prosecutors to use FRE 410 evidence substantively to rebut any contrary evidence offered by the defendant, United States v. Hardwick, 544 F.3d 565 (3d Cir. 2008); United States v. Velez, 354 F.3d 190, 196 (2d Cir. 2004); United States v. Rebbe, 314 F.3d 402 (9th Cir. 2002); United States v. Krilich, 159 F.3d 1020 (7th Cir. 1998), or even substantively in their cases-in-chief. United States v. Mitchell, 633 F.3d 997 (10th Cir. 2011); United States v. Sylvester, 583 F.3d 285 (5th Cir. 2009); United States v. Young, 223 F.3d 905 (8th Cir. 2000); United States v. Burch, 156 F.3d 1315 (D.C. Cir. 1998). Consider the potential impact of the Court's decision. It seems likely that at least some defendants will be unwilling to enter into plea negotiations if prosecutors demand waivers. Of course, prosecutors could choose to forgo the demand in some or all of those cases. If a demand for waiver becomes the standard prosecutorial policy, however, there may well be a net decrease in the number of defendants willing to enter into plea negotiations. On the other hand, perhaps the opportunity to obtain waivers will make prosecutors more willing than they were previously to enter into plea negotiations.

KEY POINTS

1. FRE 410(a)(1) and (2) provide that a defendant's withdrawn guilty pleas and pleas of nolo contendere are not admissible against the defendant.

2. FRE 410(a)(3) provides that a defendant's statements made during a judicial plea-acceptance proceeding are not admissible against the defendant if the guilty plea was withdrawn or was a plea of no contest.

3. FRE 410(a)(4) provides that a defendant's statements made during plea discussions are not admissible against the defendant. According to the language of FRE 410(a)(4), statements qualify for exclusion only if they are made (a) to a prosecuting attorney, (b) during plea discussions, and (c) the discussion failed to result in a guilty plea or it resulted in a plea that was later withdrawn.

4. In determining whether the "plea discussions" and "attorney for the prosecuting authority" requirements are satisfied, courts consider the matter from the defendant's perspective. The statements will be excluded if the defendants have a subjective belief that they are engaging in plea discussions with a prosecuting attorney and if that belief is objectively reasonable.

5. Defendants may waive the right not to have plea bargaining statements used against them, at least for impeachment purposes.

PROBLEMS

6.12. Attorney Yvonne Gruber heard a rumor that her client, Dawn Carson, was about to be indicted for income tax evasion. On behalf of Carson, Gruber spoke with an assistant U.S. Attorney about the possibility of a plea bargain. In response to a question, Gruber acknowledged that her client would be willing to plead guilty to a relatively minor charge. There were no further discussions, and Carson was eventually indicted for income tax evasion. Can the prosecution use Gruber's statement about Carson's willingness to plead guilty? Would your answer be different if Gruber had contacted the IRS and had the conversation with an IRS agent?

6.13. In the course of plea negotiations with an assistant U.S. Attorney, Tom Mason, after acknowledging that he sold heroin on three specific occasions, entered into a cooperation agreement. According to the agreement, Mason would not be prosecuted if he helped the police develop evidence against his supplier. Mason reneged on the agreement and is now being prosecuted for sale of heroin. During its case in chief the prosecution offers Mason's statement about selling heroin. Should Mason's objection be sustained? Does you answer depend upon whether the cooperation agreement contained a waiver of Mason's FRE 410 rights?

6.14. Return to Problem 3.2 at page 136. Assume that Driver was charged with reckless driving, a misdemeanor, as a result of the accident with Paul. Driver is grief stricken and has no interest in fighting the charge. Moreover, she is worried that if she seriously contests the ticket and is found guilty, the penalty may be stiffer than if she pleads guilty. If Driver pleads guilty, however, the plea can be used against her in a civil suit. The jurisdiction does not permit nolo pleas. What advice can you give her?

CHAPTER SEVEN

THE IMPEACHMENT AND REHABILITATION OF WITNESSES

Our concern in this chapter is with the theory and methods of impeaching and rehabilitating the credibility of witnesses. Some trials and much courtroom drama turn on the question of credibility. The rules of evidence considered here establish the framework within which the opposing parties may present evidence of witnesses' credibility to the jury. Many of the issues and techniques discussed in this chapter will also apply to impeaching and rehabilitating the credibility of hearsay declarants (i.e., those who make statements out of court that are admitted as evidence at trial). See FRE 806. We discuss the impeachment of hearsay declarants in Chapter Eight.

A. BASIC CONCEPTS

1. Impeachment: The Inferential Process

a. The Testimonial Inferences

The strength and accuracy of any witness's testimony depends upon certain testimonial abilities: A witness must be able to observe events, to remember them, and to relate them honestly and accurately. The jury must make inferences about these abilities — the ability to be honest, to narrate accurately, to perceive, and to remember — in order to credit the truth of what a witness says. For example, when a witness testifies, "The defendant's car ran the red light," the jury, in crediting this testimony, must infer that (1) the witness is communicating that the defendant was driving a car that did not stop at a red light; (2) the witness believes this assertion; (3) the witness's belief is based on the witness's accurate perception of what happened; and (4) the witness accurately remembers what happened.

Diagram 7-1

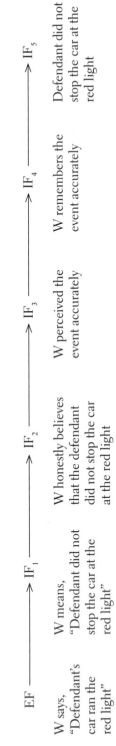

EF ——————→ IF$_1$ ——————→ IF$_2$ ——————→ IF$_3$ ——————→ IF$_4$ ——————→ IF$_5$

W says, "Defendant's car ran the red light"

W means, "Defendant did not stop the car at the red light"

W honestly believes that the defendant did not stop the car at the red light

W perceived the event accurately

W remembers the event accurately

Defendant did not stop the car at the red light

Diagram 7-1 illustrates these inferences. If any of the inferences in the diagram is false, the evidence is not relevant to prove that the defendant did not stop at the red light. To help ensure that they are not false, the law requires witnesses to testify from firsthand knowledge (FRE 602) and to affirm that they will testify truthfully (FRE 603). For several reasons, however, the law does not generally require the proponent of evidence to make any other special showing regarding the accuracy of these inferences as a condition of admissibility. First, although there are obvious exceptions, our common experience tells us that people tend to be honest and accurate in most situations. (Consider the chaos in which we would live if the foregoing statement were not generally true.) Second, typically witnesses will testify to general background information about their residences and occupations, which will provide some minimal personal information for the jury to consider in assessing the strength of the inferences. Third, in the Anglo-American legal system, the task of assessing the accuracy of these inferences traditionally has been one for the jury rather than the judge. Finally, opposing counsel will have the opportunity to try to raise doubts about the strength of these inferences.

b. Types of Impeachment Evidence

Impeachment is the process of trying to raise doubts about the inferences illustrated in Diagram 7-1. It is, in other words, an attempt to show that a witness may have inadvertently narrated the events incorrectly, lied, misperceived the events about which the witness testified, or forgotten some or all of what happened. To the extent that the fact finder believes the impeaching evidence, the fact finder should conclude that what the witness said is less likely to be accurate than if there had been no impeaching evidence.

If the witness has offered an opinion or conclusion about some matter, there is a further impeachment concern. Consider, for example, a witness's testimony that the defendant was drunk. Even if the witness is sincere, is using the term *drunk* in a commonly understood sense, correctly perceived the events, and recalls them accurately, the witness may have misevaluated the defendant's symptoms and used erroneous generalizations for either of two reasons. First, the witness may not be a very good judge of drunkenness. For example, the witness may have associated loud, boisterous talk with drunkenness without realizing that the defendant always speaks in a loud, boisterous manner. Second, the defendant's symptoms, although indicative of drunkenness, may in fact have had some other source. The impeaching party may suggest both of these possibilities to the fact finder, and the fact finder may then tend to disregard the witness's opinion.

There are a variety of ways to impeach a witness:

(1) Evidence that a witness has a character trait for untruthfulness suggests that the witness may be untruthful on the witness stand.
(2) Showing that the witness has a bias or interest in the case suggests a motive for being untruthful.
(3) Attacks on other testimonial qualities such as the witness's narrative or perceptive abilities may also undermine a witness's credibility. Such attacks may focus on general abilities (e.g., color blindness) or on the specific exer-

cise of those abilities on the occasion relevant to the case (e.g., witness not wearing glasses at time event observed).

(4) Proof of a witness's inconsistent statements suggests that the fact finder should be skeptical about the accuracy of the witness's testimony.

(5) Testimony from other sources that contradicts the witness may reduce the witness's believability.

c.   Impeachment Evidence Versus Substantive Evidence

Evidence offered to impeach the credibility of a witness — like all other evidence that is admitted — must be relevant to prove or disprove some fact that is of consequence to the litigation. If it were not, the impeachment evidence would be inadmissible pursuant to FRE 402. The difference between evidence offered for "impeachment" purposes and evidence offered for "substantive" purposes is in the relevance theory that leads to a fact of consequence.

The evidentiary facts discussed in this chapter relate to essential elements of a case because they may influence the jury's evaluation of witnesses. Sometimes evidence that impeaches the credibility of witnesses will also be relevant and admissible as substantive evidence of an essential element. When this is the case, there is no need to consider whether the evidence is admissible to impeach a witness because the evidence will already be admitted for its substantive purpose (i.e., as evidence that makes a fact of consequence more or less probable independent of its effect on the credibility of a witness). In other words, evidence must be analyzed for its impeachment purpose only when it is inadmissible for a substantive purpose, which will often be the case. Here are three examples to illustrate these points:

(1) In the case of a bank robbery, the teller who handed money over to the robber may testify that the defendant was not the robber. Other witnesses, customers in the bank, may identify the defendant as the robber. A police officer may establish that the teller is the sister of the defendant. The testimony of the customers contradicts — and therefore implicitly impeaches — the credibility of the teller (and vice versa), but each witness's testimony is also independently admissible on the substantive question of the robber's identity. The testimony of the police officer is not independently admissible for a substantive purpose; its only relevance is to impeach the credibility of the teller by showing bias.

(2) In the running-the-red-light hypothetical, the defendant wishes to impeach the plaintiff's witness with the witness's prior inconsistent statement, not made under oath, that the light was green when the defendant entered the intersection. Because of the hearsay rule, the prior statement is inadmissible as substantive evidence that the light was green. FRE 801(d)(1)(A). The defendant, however, may use the prior inconsistent statement, without regard to its truth, to infer that the witness's direct examination testimony is not accurate. Knowing that the witness has made inconsistent statements about the same subject, regardless of which statement is true, casts some doubt on the witness's credibility. On one of the two occasions the witness may have been lying; at the very least, the inconsistency shows that the witness is not particularly careful about narrating the events of the accident.

(3) Della Dean is charged with perjury and testifies in her own defense. To impeach the truthfulness of Della's testimony, the prosecution offers evidence that Della was convicted of perjury two years ago. It would be impermissible under FRE 404 to introduce evidence of past perjury to prove that Della committed perjury on the occasion charged in the current indictment. Because Della has testified as a witness, however, it will be permissible to introduce her prior conviction in order to impeach her character for truthfulness. FRE 609(a). The inferential process is as follows: Because Della has committed perjury, she is a generally untruthful person, who may be lying on the witness stand.

Evidence admitted for the purpose of impeaching the credibility of a witness will sometimes not be admissible for a substantive purpose — either because it would be irrelevant, as in the first hypothetical, or because some exclusionary rule (e.g., the hearsay rule or FRE 404(b)) would prohibit its substantive use, as in the latter two hypotheticals. When evidence is not admissible for a substantive purpose, you must also evaluate whether it may be admitted for an impeachment purpose.

When evidence is admissible only to impeach the credibility of a witness, the limited admissibility has three significant consequences. First, the proponent of the evidence cannot rely on that evidence as substantive evidence to satisfy a burden of production in response to a motion for summary judgment or judgment as a matter of law. Second, the proponent cannot rely on the evidence as substantive proof of disputed facts during closing argument. Third, whenever the evidence is relevant but inadmissible for a substantive purpose, the party against whom the evidence is offered can make an FRE 403 objection and, if the evidence is admitted, is entitled to a limiting instruction. Consider, for example, the hypothetical in which the defendant introduced evidence that a plaintiff's witness had made an inconsistent statement about whether the defendant ran the red light:

- The defendant could not rely on the substance of the inconsistent statement to support the production burden on the question of contributory negligence.
- If the case went to the jury, the defendant could argue that the inconsistency suggested the witness was mistaken or lying about the color of the light, but the defendant could not argue that the statement was a truthful assertion that the light was green for the defendant.
- The plaintiff would be entitled to an instruction that the jury could use the statement only to assess the witness's credibility, not as substantive evidence of the color of the light.

Do you think jurors are likely to be able to understand or follow a limiting instruction? If not, would it be desirable either (1) to exclude the evidence altogether on FRE 403 grounds or (2) to forgo the limiting instruction? See Section E, infra.

2. Extrinsic Evidence and Impeachment

One can impeach a witness (1) by examining (usually cross-examining) the witness and (2) by introducing extrinsic evidence. *Extrinsic evidence* means any evidence other than that developed through direct or cross-examination of the witness. It may be an exhibit, such as a record of a prior conviction, or the testimony of another witness that impeaches the first witness by showing, for example, bias or an inconsistent statement that the first witness denied making.

As we discuss various impeachment techniques, we will consider the extent to which courts are likely to permit extrinsic evidence.

3.   *Bolstering Credibility*

FRE 608(a) prohibits introducing reputation or opinion evidence of a witness's good character for truthfulness unless the witness's character for truthfulness has been attacked. This prohibition is a specific application of the general common law rule that prevented a party from bolstering a witness's credibility until after there had been an attempt to impeach the witness's credibility. For example, if X testified for the plaintiff that the defendant's car ran through a red light and if there had been no effort to impeach X's credibility, the plaintiff could not introduce evidence of X's character for truthfulness or X's prior consistent statements. The Federal Rules contain no *general* prohibition against bolstering a witness's credibility prior to any impeachment. Nonetheless, federal courts will sometimes assert this general prohibition. See, e.g., United States v. Bolick, 917 F.2d 135, 137-140 (4th Cir. 1990) (referring to a general ban on preimpeachment bolstering: "We are among the courts to adhere to that time-honored principle."). When a party attempts to introduce preimpeachment bolstering evidence not specifically excluded by FRE 608(a), however, admissibility under the Federal Rules should turn on an application of FRE 403. In most cases of attempted preimpeachment bolstering, a reasoned application of FRE 403 will probably bring about the same exclusionary result as the common law rule. In the absence of impeachment, jurors are not likely to disbelieve a witness. In such a case, the independent bolstering evidence will have little independent probative value, and, therefore, it is not worth the court's time to hear the evidence. In situations in which the FRE balancing favors admission, however, the proponent of the evidence should argue that FRE 608(a)(2) applies only to reputation or opinion evidence relating to truthfulness, that the Federal Rules have not adopted the *general* common law anti-bolstering rule, and that admissibility of bolstering evidence (other than reputation or opinion evidence) should be governed by FRE 401-403.

Although most reported cases dealing with preimpeachment bolstering involve attempts to show that a witness is being truthful, sincerity is only one of several testimonial qualities. As we discussed in subsection 1 at pages 351-353, supra, the value of a witness's testimony depends not only on the witness's sincerity but also on the witness's perceptions, memory, and ability to narrate events accurately. As with bolstering evidence regarding sincerity, the admissibility of evidence regarding these other testimonial qualities should also turn on FRE 403.

A common situation in which parties attempt to offer preimpeachment bolstering evidence is by introducing a witness's prior consistent statements. See United States v. Wells, 623 F.3d 332, 345 (6th Cir. 2010) ("By prematurely calling attention to prior consistent statements in the opening statement, a prosecutor creates the chance of mistrial and an issue for appeal."). We discuss the use of prior consistent statements in Section C below.

B.   IMPEACHMENT AND REHABILITATION WITH CHARACTER EVIDENCE

In Chapter Five we considered evidentiary restrictions on the substantive use of character evidence. We noted that one of the FRE 404(a) exceptions to the general prohibition against using character evidence to show action in conformity with character was the use of character evidence for impeachment and rehabilitation. FRE 404(a)(3). It is to this subject that we now turn. We are concerned here with using evidence of a witness's character for truthfulness to infer action in conformity with that character trait on a particular occasion (i.e., to infer that the witness is either lying or telling the truth on the witness stand). FRE 608 refers to a witness's "character for truthfulness or untruthfulness." Unless the context suggests a contrary meaning, our use of the term *truthfulness* includes both truthfulness and untruthfulness.

The rules governing impeachment and rehabilitation with character evidence, as well as the rules governing other forms of impeachment and rehabilitation evidence, apply to *all* witnesses and to *all* kinds of cases. With some minor exceptions that we will discuss in due course, it makes no difference whether the witness happens to be a party. A party may use character evidence to impeach a witness in civil as well as criminal trials, and criminal defendants do not have the option to keep the door closed to inquiries about any witness's character for truthfulness.

Because the rules governing the use of character evidence for impeachment purposes (FRE 404(a)(3), 608, and 609) are different from the rules governing character evidence for substantive purposes (FRE 404(a)(1) and (2), 404(b), and 405) and because both sets of rules are intricate, the general subject of character evidence may seem confusing. The best way to eliminate the confusion is to focus initially on what should always be the first question: How is the evidence relevant? Once you answer this question, it should be relatively easy to apply the proper rules.

1.   FRE 608

RULE 608.   A WITNESS'S CHARACTER FOR TRUTHFULNESS OR UNTRUTHFULNESS

(a) *Reputation or Opinion Evidence.* A witness's credibility may be attacked or supported by testimony about the witness's reputation for having a character for truthfulness or untruthfulness, or by testimony in the form of an opinion about that character. But evidence of truthful character is admissible only after the witness's character for truthfulness has been attacked.

(b) *Specific Instances of Conduct.* Except for a criminal conviction under Rule 609, extrinsic evidence is not admissible to prove specific instances of a witness's conduct in order to attack or support the witness's character for truthfulness. But the court may, on cross-examination, allow them to be inquired into if they are probative of the character for truthfulness or untruthfulness of:

(1) the witness; or

(2) another witness whose character the witness being cross-examined has testified about.

By testifying on another matter, a witness does not waive any privilege against self-incrimination for testimony that relates only to the witness's character for truthfulness.

(Our initial discussion focuses on FRE 608(a). We discuss the remainder of the rule later in this section.)

2.   Interpretation and Illustration of FRE 608(a)

a.   *Reputation and Opinion Evidence to Prove Character for Untruthfulness*

One method to impeach a witness is with reputation or opinion evidence offered to prove the witness's character for untruthfulness in order to suggest that the witness is lying on the witness stand. For example, in the *Johnson* case the defendant could have called witnesses to testify that Officer Huston (or any other prosecution witness) had a reputation for being untruthful. FRE 608(a) permits both reputation and opinion evidence of character for untruthfulness. The process of eliciting reputation or opinion testimony from a character witness pursuant to FRE 608(a) is identical to the process described in Chapter Five, where we dealt with the use of reputation and opinion evidence for substantive purposes. For a review of the foundation requirement and a discussion of why opinion witnesses should not be permitted to set forth the factual bases for their opinions, see pages 295-296, supra. FRE 608(a) limits the use of reputation or opinion evidence to "character for truthfulness or untruthfulness." This limitation repudiates the position of a few jurisdictions, which have permitted parties to impeach witnesses with evidence of general bad character or bad moral character. According to the Advisory Committee Note:

> In accordance with the bulk of judicial authority, the inquiry is strictly limited to character for veracity, rather than allowing evidence as to character generally. The result is to sharpen relevancy, to reduce surprise, waste of time, and confusion, and to make the lot of the witness somewhat less unattractive.

After a witness's character for truthfulness has been attacked, the opposing party may then rehabilitate the witness by introducing evidence regarding the witness's good character for truthfulness. Just as the impeaching evidence is offered to suggest the witness is lying on the witness stand, the rehabilitation evidence is offered to suggest the witness is being sincere on the witness stand.

b.   *The FRE 608(a) Limitation on Evidence of Good Character for Truthfulness*

According to FRE 608(a) reputation or opinion testimony regarding a witness's good character for truthfulness is not admissible until the witness's character has been "attacked." It is not entirely clear, though, what kind of impeachment constitutes an attack on character for truthfulness. Courts traditionally have regarded impeachment by showing prior convictions, FRE 609, or bad acts that did not result in convictions, FRE 608(b), as an attack on a witness's character. Thus, rehabilitation with reputation or opinion evidence would be appropriate. For example, since the prosecution in the *Johnson* case impeached the credibility of both inmate Michael Green and the defendant with evidence of prior convictions (page 49, lines 21, 35; page 55, line 14, supra), it would have been permissible for the defendant to call witnesses who would offer their opinions that Green and Johnson were truthful individuals. On the other hand, courts have declared that some prior acts are not relevant to attack a witness's character for truthfulness. See United States v. Holden, 557 F.3d 698, 702 (6th Cir. 2009) ("As a general matter, prior drug use is not relevant to a witness's character for truthfulness.").

Although proof of bias may suggest that a witness is not testifying truthfully, courts generally regard proof of a witness's bias as not being an attack on the witness's *character* for truthfulness. United States v. Figueroa, 548 F.3d 222 (5th Cir. 2008) (cross-examining witness about swastika tattoos relevant to bias toward defendant not character for untruthfulness). For example, in the *Johnson* case, if the prosecution could have established that Johnson and his cellmate belonged to the same gang (page 18, line 37, supra), this evidence would show the cellmate's possible bias but not the cellmate's bad character for truthfulness. Similarly, proof in a civil case that a witness for the plaintiff had recently gone through an acrimonious, contested divorce with the defendant suggests that the witness may be biased against the defendant but not that the witness is a generally untruthful person. Thus, FRE 608(a) would not permit Johnson or the defendant in the civil action to rehabilitate the impeached witness by offering opinion or reputation evidence of that witness's good character for truthfulness. Depending on the circumstances of the case, however, some evidence of bias may also constitute an attack on the witness's character, thus permitting FRE 608(a) rehabilitation evidence. See, e.g., United States v. Medical Therapy Sciences, Inc., 583 F.2d 36, 41 (2d Cir. 1978) (evidence of corrupt conduct by a witness that indicates bias, such as embezzling money, may also constitute an attack on witness's character for truthfulness). The key inquiry is whether the evidence of bias also suggests that the witness has a character for untruthfulness.

Sometimes there will be disagreement about how to categorize the impeaching evidence. For example, recall in the *Johnson* case that defense counsel on cross-examination of Officer Huston suggested Huston's alleged injury in the altercation with Johnson was fabricated because of the workers' compensation rules (page 18, line 37, supra). This inquiry suggests a particular bias or motive to lie. Does it also impugn Huston's character for truthfulness, so that the prosecution could have responded with FRE 608(a) character witnesses to testify about Huston's reputation for truthfulness? See if you can articulate a difference between character and bias that justifies different treatment under FRE 608(a).

KEY POINTS

1. FRE 608(a) permits a party to impeach the credibility of a witness by offering extrinsic evidence in the form of opinion or reputation testimony about the witness's character for untruthfulness. The evidence must focus on untruthfulness, not general moral character.

2. FRE 608(a) permits reputation or opinion evidence offered to prove a witness's good character for truthfulness only after the opposing party has attacked the witness's character for truthfulness.

PROBLEMS

7.1. Darby is being prosecuted for the armed robbery of a liquor store proprietor. During the presentation of the prosecution's case the proprietor made a positive identification of Darby as the robber. As part of the defense, Darby calls Sue Williams to testify that the proprietor has a reputation in the community for lying. Is the evidence admissible?

7.2. In the same case, another defense witness offers to testify that the proprietor has a reputation in the community for not remembering faces and for misidentifying people. Is the evidence admissible? Would your answer be different if the witness offered to testify that on the basis of her experience with the proprietor she is of the view that the proprietor has difficulty remembering faces and often misidentifies people?

7.3. Harper was arrested for sale of cocaine and accepted the government's offer to cooperate in obtaining evidence against his supplier. Harper identified Ellsworth as the supplier, and Ellsworth was eventually charged with sale of cocaine. At Ellsworth's trial, Agent Fowler, who was in charged of the investigation, testified that Harper had delivered what was in fact cocaine to him, and Harper testified that he had obtained the cocaine from Ellsworth. During the cross-examination of Harper, defense counsel elicited information about Harper's cooperation with the police. During the cross-examination of Agent Fowler, defense counsel elicited that Harper had three independent sources for cocaine. On redirect of Agent Fowler, the prosecutor asks:

(a)   Do you believe Mr. Harper received the cocaine involved in this case from a source other than the defendant, Ellsworth?
(b)   In your opinion is Mr. Harper's testimony in this case truthful?
(c)   In your opinion is Mr. Harper a truthful person?

How should the court rule on Ellsworth's objections to these questions? Would any of your answers be different if defense counsel had referred to Harper as a liar in the opening statement? If defense counsel had elicited from Harper on cross-examination that two years ago he was convicted of embezzlement?

7.4. Dan Dickson is charged with perjury and testifies in his own behalf. The prosecutor's cross-examination fails to shake Dickson's story or cast doubt on his credibility. Dickson then offers the testimony of Willa Wilson that Dickson has a good reputation in the community for truthfulness. Is Wilson's testimony admissible?

3.   Interpretation and Illustration of FRE 608(b)

FRE 608(b) provides:

(b) *Specific Instances of Conduct.* Except for a criminal conviction under Rule 609, extrinsic evidence is not admissible to prove specific instances of a witness's conduct in order to attack or support the witness's character for truthfulness. But the court may, on cross-examination, allow them to be inquired into if they are probative of the character for truthfulness or untruthfulness of:
(1) the witness; or
(2) another witness whose character the witness being cross-examined has testified about.
By testifying on another matter, a witness does not waive any privilege against self-incrimination for testimony that relates only to the witness's character for truthfulness.

a.   The Prohibition Against the Use of Extrinsic Evidence

FRE 608(b) prohibits the use of extrinsic evidence of a witness's specific acts to *support or attack* the witness's character for truthfulness. FRE 608(b) and a majority of states, however, do permit inquiry into (1) a witness's own acts during the examination of that witness, and (2) the acts of "another witness whose character the witness being cross-examined has testified about." The prohibition against the use of extrinsic evidence means that the examiner is bound by the answer of the witness; the impeaching party cannot introduce extrinsic evidence to contradict the witness. For example, in the *Johnson* case, defense counsel could have asked Officer Huston if he lied on his job application form. If Huston denied lying, however, defense counsel could not prove the lie by introducing the job application form, which would be extrinsic evidence, and then proving with other extrinsic evidence that the information contained on the form was false. Similarly, if another witness had testified that Huston had a good reputation for truthfulness, then that witness could be asked on cross-examination whether he knew Huston had lied on the job application form. However, defense counsel could not prove the lie with extrinsic evidence.

b.   The Limited Scope of Permissible Inquiry

FRE 608(b) is consistent with FRE 608(a) in that the specific acts must relate to character for truthfulness. See, e.g., United States v. Holden, supra (witness's prior marijuana use is not relevant impeachment evidence under 608(b)). This rule is considerably narrower than the rules in some state jurisdictions, which permit inquiry into acts relevant to prove a generally bad moral character. The result in these latter jurisdictions is that almost any bad act is relevant; and if the act is relevant, courts have almost invariably permitted the inquiry.

c.   No Fifth Amendment Waiver

Because of the centrality of cross-examination to our adversary system, the giving of testimony by a witness is regarded as a waiver or forfeiture of the witness's Fifth Amendment right against self-incrimination, at least with respect to the subject matter of the witness's direct examination testimony. The last sentence of FRE 608(b) makes it clear that testifying is not a waiver of the privilege with respect to questions that are permissible only to undermine the witness's credibility. Consider, for example, our hypothetical question about whether Officer Huston had lied on his job application form. If making false statements on the form were a crime, Officer Huston could rely on the Fifth Amendment to refuse to answer.

4.   Elaboration of FRE 608(b)(1): Questioning Witnesses About Their Own Specific Acts

a.   The Rationale for the Prohibition Against Extrinsic Evidence

Not permitting the examiner to challenge the witness's answer with extrinsic evidence of bad character for truthfulness may sometimes appear unfair. For example, in our hypothetical in which Officer Huston denies that he lied on his job application form, assume that defense counsel is prepared to authenticate the job application form and to call 10 witnesses who will testify that the facts stated in the application are false. What could be better impeaching evidence than this extrinsic proof that the witness had lied not only on the job application form but also on the witness stand?

Perhaps the answer is that there could not be a more relevant or more effective impeachment. The effectiveness of the impeachment, however, depends on the certainty with which the impeaching party can establish the lie. It may be, for example, that the job application form is a forgery, that the statements on the job application are reasonably subject to more than one interpretation, or that the witnesses who would testify that Officer Huston lied on the application are themselves dishonest. If the impeaching party is allowed to introduce the extrinsic evidence, the party whose witness was impeached should have an opportunity to counter that evidence. And if that opportunity exists, a substantial amount of time and energy could be devoted to litigating the truth or falsity of facts whose only value is to impeach the credibility of a witness. Moreover, there would be the potential for this type of minitrial with every witness. Thus, while it may be true that catching the witness in a lie on the stand would be extremely effective impeachment, FRE 608(b), out of concern with the time and distraction that could result from litigating collateral matters, prohibits the impeaching party from introducing extrinsic evidence to prove the lie.

Consider the adequacy of this justification for the absolute ban on extrinsic evidence. Some extrinsic evidence may be very probative of untruthfulness and bear few dangers of a protracted minitrial. Some commentators believe that it would be preferable to rely exclusively on FRE 403 and to make admissibility decisions on a case-by-case basis. Kevin C. McMunigal and Calvin William Sharpe, Reforming Extrinsic Impeachment, 33 Conn. L. Rev. 363 (2001). What would be the advantages and disadvantages of a more discretionary rule?

b.   The Scope of Permissible Questions to Prove Character for Untruthfulness

   i.   **The Meaning of Untruthfulness.**   Although the Advisory Committee Note to FRE 608(b) makes it clear that the terms *truthfulness* and *untruthfulness* are intended to limit the types of specific acts about which one may inquire, there is not uniform agreement about the scope of the limitation. At the extremes, courts tend to find that perjury or other instances of making false statements suggest untruthfulness, United States v. Velarde, 485 F.3d 553 (10th Cir. 2007) (prior false accusations by witness); United States v. Jensen, 41 F.3d 946 (5th Cir. 1994) (submission of false tax return and false loan documents to obtain loan); see also United States v. Torres, 569 F.3d 1277 (10th Cir. 2009) (prosecution witness's prior breach of agreement with DEA relevant under FRE 608(b)), and that acts of violence (e.g., murder, destruction of property) or drug crimes do not suggest untruthfulness, United States v. Geston, 299 F.3d 1130, 1137 (9th Cir. 2002) (violent conduct while under influence of alcohol not probative of untruthfulness); United States v. Wilson, 344 F.2d 1208 (10th Cir. 2001) (drug crimes not probative of truth or untruth). There is, however, a gray area where courts sometimes reach seemingly inconsistent results. Compare, e.g., United States v. Wilson, 985 F.2d 348, 352 (7th Cir. 1993) (bribery probative of untruthfulness) with United States v. Rosa, 891 F.2d 1063, 1069 (3d Cir. 1989) (bribery "not the kind of conduct which bears on truthfulness or untruthfulness").

ii.   Questions about Arrests, Charges, and Administrative or Judicial Findings.

Sometimes an impeaching party will have evidence that a witness was arrested or charged with some offense relating to untruthfulness or that an administrative or judicial body has found that a witness behaved in a manner indicating untruthfulness. For example, the witness may have been arrested for or charged with falsifying loan documents; the witness may have been disbarred for deceitful conduct; or a judge in an earlier proceeding may have implicitly or explicitly found that the witness had lied. In these situations FRE 608(b) permits the impeaching party to ask about the underlying conduct — whether the witness in fact falsified documents, engaged in deceitful conduct, or lied in an earlier proceeding. But what about asking whether the witness was *arrested* or *charged* with falsifying documents, whether the witness was *disbarred* for the deceitful conduct, or whether a *judge found* that the witness had lied?

A witness's arrest or a factual finding about the witness is not a specific instance of the *witness's* conduct. Rather, as we pointed out in Chapter Five at page 299, supra, an arrest or a finding is activity engaged in by the arresting officer or the fact finder. Moreover, as we point out in Chapter Eight at pages 431-432, infra, this type of evidence is hearsay. The witness is not being asked directly whether the witness engaged in the conduct. Instead, the witness is being asked whether somebody else — the arresting officer (or person who authorized the arrest) or the fact finder — *said* that the witness engaged in the conduct. And, of course, that statement of the police officer or the fact finder is relevant to impeach the witness only if one believes the truth of what the officer or fact finder said. For this reason, some courts have limited FRE 608(b) questioning to the witness's conduct in these instances. See, e.g., United States v. Holt, 486 F.3d 997 (7th Cir. 2007) (not abuse of discretion for trial court to allow cross-examination of police officer about his conduct but to exclude questioning about whether the officer was suspended for the conduct); United States v. Davis, 183 F.3d 231, 257 n.12 (3d Cir. 1999) ("the government cannot make reference to [the defendant's] . . . suspension or that Internal Affairs found he lied . . . . The government needs to limit its cross-examination to the facts underlying those events."). Other courts, however, have permitted these questions. See, e.g., United States v. Whitmore, 359 F.3d 609 (D.C. Cir. 2004) (judge's finding that witness had lied); United States v. Scott, 74 F.3d 175,177 (9th Cir. 1996) (question about prior arrest).

c.   Questions About Specific Acts and FRE 403

FRE 608(b) states that courts "may" allow questions about specific acts when they are probative of character for truthfulness. Even when specific acts are probative of character for truthfulness, courts may exercise their discretion and exclude such questions because of FRE 403 concerns. First, in some instances the witness's conduct, even if relevant for untruthfulness, may have low probative value. Compare Ad-Vantage Telephone Directory Consultants, Inc. v. GTE Directories Corp, 37 F.3d 1460 (11th Cir. 1994) (accountant's 1969 sanction for ethical violation inadmissible on FRE 403 grounds because of remoteness in time) with United States v. Munoz, 233 F.3d 1117, 1135 (9th Cir. 2000) (14- to 16-year-old incident not too remote). Second, if the witness acknowledges an act of untruthfulness, there is a risk of unfair prejudice.

See United States v. Bunchan, 580 F.3d 66 (1st Cir. 2009) ("The district court's determination that the nature of sexual assault charges was not sufficiently probative of [the witness's] character for truthfulness to outweigh the serious danger of prejudicing the jury against him was well within its discretion."). This risk is particularly great if the witness happens to be a party: The jury may be willing to decide against the party because the jury regards the witness as a bad person. United States v. DeGeratto, 876 F.2d 576, 582-583 (7th Cir. 1989) (emphasizing prejudicial nature of cross-examination about defendant's involvement in prostitution without discussing how such evidence was probative of truthfulness). Third, if there are numerous inquiries about the specific acts of truthfulness, there are likely to be concerns with time-consumption and confusion of the issues. Fourth, even if the witness honestly denies having committed a dishonest act, there is a risk that the jury may be more swayed by the suggestiveness of the question than by the answer. United States v. Dring, 930 F.2d 687, 692 (9th Cir. 1991) (quoting McCormick on Evidence for proposition that a "'slashing cross-examination may carry strong accusations of misconduct and bad character, which the witness's denial will not remove from the jury's mind'"). Finally, if the witness is a party and if the question relates to conduct similar to the conduct that is the subject of the litigation, there is a risk that the jury will consider the evidence, contrary to the dictate of FRE 404(b), as evidence that the defendant engaged in the conduct that is the subject of the litigation. United States v. Pintar, 630 F.2d 1270, 1285-1286 (8th Cir. 1980) (prosecution unduly emphasized illegal kickbacks that were not part of the charge and not admissible pursuant to FRE 404(b) in cross-examination of defendant).

Despite the FRE 403 grounds for objecting to FRE 608(b) questions, courts typically are quite liberal in permitting inquiry about specific acts to prove character for impeachment purposes. According to the Advisory Committee, "Effective cross-examination demands that some allowance be made for going into matters of this kind." See also David P. Leonard, Appellate Review of Evidentiary Rulings, 70 N.C. L. Rev. 1155 (1992), a particularly thoughtful analysis of the role of appellate courts in reviewing trial judges' FRE 608(b) decisions.

d.   Good-Faith Requirement; Practical Considerations

Because of the suggestiveness that is likely to inhere in a question about a specific act relating to truthfulness, courts have held that the examiner must have a good-faith basis for believing that the act occurred. United States v. DeGeratto, 876 F.3d 576, 584 (7th Cir. 1989). Such a requirement is probably satisfied, for example, by knowledge that the witness had been arrested for the activity that is the subject of the question or by hearsay information obtained during the investigation of the case. See United States v. Whitmore, 359 F.3d 609 (D.C. Cir. 2004) (record from state Motor Vehicle Administration provided reasonable basis to ask witness about suspended driver's license, even though record was hearsay).

A litigant who suspects that the opponent may ask a question without a factual basis for the inquiry should request a hearing on that issue outside the presence of the jury. Similarly, if a litigant suspects that the opponent may ask about some act falling outside the truthfulness limitation in FRE 608(b), the litigant should consider filing a motion in limine seeking a ruling on the issue. Unless the litigant knows that the opponent is aware of the potential impeaching evidence, however, filing such a motion may have the undesirable effect of alerting the opponent to the evidence.

An additional practical consideration in criminal cases concerns the constitutional obligation of prosecutors under Brady v. Maryland, 373 U.S. 83 (1963), to turn over evidence favorable to the defense. Federal appellate circuits have acknowledged recently that this obligation extends to evidence that the defense may use to impeach government witnesses under FRE 608(b). United States v. Torres, 569 F.3d 1277 (10th Cir. 2009) (abuse of discretion by trial court in failing to find *Brady* violation when prosecutor failed to disclose government witness, a confidential informant, had previously breached an agreement with the government and had been involved in unrelated criminal conduct); see also United States v. Price, 566 F.3d 900 (9th Cir. 2009); United States v. Johnson, 519 F.3d 478 (D.C. Cir. 2008); United States v. Velarde, 485 F.3d 553 (10th Cir. 2007).

e. *Specific Acts Showing Good Character for Truthfulness*

The primary focus of the case law and the literature dealing with FRE 608(b) (1) is on questions relating to untruthfulness. Nonetheless, FRE 608(b) specifically permits questions that are probative of *"truthfulness or untruthfulness"* (emphasis added), and there is precedent for permitting litigants to question witnesses about good acts that tend to show the witness's own truthful character. Unlike FRE 608(a), FRE 608(b) does not provide that evidence showing a truthful character is permissible only after the opposing party has attacked the witness's character. Nonetheless, as we suggested earlier, courts may rely on FRE 403 to prohibit preimpeachment efforts to bolster a witness's credibility. The likely reason courts and commentators devote little attention to FRE 608(b)(1) good acts is that such evidence is obviously self-serving and, therefore, seldom worth objecting to or even attempting to introduce.

The first sentence of FRE 608(b), which prohibits extrinsic evidence, applies to specific acts relating to both truthfulness and untruthfulness. United States v. Melia, 691 F.2d 672, 674-675 (4th Cir. 1982) (improper to rehabilitate witness with extrinsic evidence that witness helped to solve various crimes). A witness responding to questions that put the witness in a favorable light, however, is likely to be cooperative. Thus, there is virtually no risk that an examiner inquiring about good acts will receive an unfavorable answer.

f. *"Cross-Examination"*

FRE 608(b) states that the court may allow specific instances to be inquired into "on cross-examination." For two reasons, however, the term *cross-examination* should not be interpreted literally. First, FRE 607 permits parties to impeach the credibility of their own witnesses. Therefore, a party who calls a witness, and attempts to impeach that witness, may ask 608(b) questions on direct examination. Second, FRE 608(b) refers to specific instances relating to character for truthfulness and untruthfulness. A party inquiring into specific acts under FRE 608(b) will not have an interest in asking both types of questions. One party will typically ask 608(b) questions relating to untruthfulness on cross-examination, and then the opposing party may attempt to rehabilitate the witness by inquiring into specific acts relating to truthfulness on redirect examination.

5.   Elaboration of FRE 608(b)(2): Questioning Character Witnesses Regarding Specific Acts of the Witnesses They Testify About

FRE 608(b)(2) addresses an issue we have considered previously: the cross-examination of reputation or opinion witnesses to test their knowledge of the reputation or the basis for the opinion about which they testify.

Once a character witness has given reputation or opinion testimony pursuant to FRE 608(a), the opposing party — in addition to impeaching the character witness with questions about the character witness's own acts of untruthfulness (FRE 608(b)(1)) — may impeach the character witness in the same manner in which a party may impeach character witnesses who give reputation or opinion testimony pursuant to FRE 404(a)(1) and (2): The impeaching party may ask the character witness if the character witness is aware of relevant specific acts committed by the person whose character was the subject of the witness's testimony. For example, if, as we hypothesized earlier about the *Johnson* case, the defense had called witnesses to testify that in their opinion Johnson was a truthful person, it would have been appropriate to ask these witnesses on cross-examination both about their own acts of untruthfulness (FRE 608(b)(1)) and about their knowledge of acts of dishonesty in which Johnson had engaged (FRE 608(b)(2)). It would not have been appropriate, however, to ask them if they knew about Johnson's previous rapes. As FRE 608(b) makes clear, the specific acts must relate to the character trait about which the FRE 608(a) character witness testified — truthfulness — and rapes are not (very) probative of truthfulness.

This FRE 608(b)(2) impeachment process is identical to the process for impeaching character witnesses that we described in Chapter Five. In effect, FRE 608(b)(2) is a specific, somewhat awkwardly worded application to FRE 608(a) character witnesses of the general principle set forth in the second sentence of FRE 405(a): "On cross-examination [of a character witness who offers reputation or opinion testimony], the court may allow an inquiry into relevant specific instances of the person's conduct." As is the case in the context of relying on FRE 405(a) to impeach FRE 404(a) character witnesses, (1) the cross-examiner must have a good-faith basis for asking the questions, United States v. Reese, 568 F.2d 1246, 1249 (6th Cir. 1977), and (2) the legitimate purpose of the inquiry is to impeach the credibility of the character witness, *not* to prove the character of the principal witness, about whom the question is asked. Indeed, using the character witness's testimony about the principal witness's specific act to prove the principal witness's truthfulness would violate the FRE 608(b) prohibition against using extrinsic evidence to prove the principal witness's character.

KEY POINTS

1. FRE 608(b)(1) permits the impeachment and rehabilitation of witnesses with questions about the witnesses' own specific acts that show character for truthfulness. The examiner is bound by the witness's answer to such questions and may not introduce extrinsic evidence to challenge the answer.

2. FRE 608(b)(1) specific-acts questions must relate to character for truthfulness, and they are subject to exclusion on FRE 403 grounds.

3. When an FRE 608(a) character witness offers opinion or reputation testimony about another witness's character for truthfulness, FRE 608(b)(2) permits the

opposing party to ask the character witness about specific acts probative of truthfulness that the other witness may have committed. The purpose of the questions is to test the basis for the character witness's reputation or opinion testimony.

PROBLEMS

7.5. Defendant is on trial for a burglary, which took place at 10:00 P.M. in a house at 1251 Hazel Street. Defendant has bright red hair. The defense calls Jones to testify, and Jones testifies as follows: "On the night of the burglary, I was walking out of the Century Pub around 10:00 P.M. The Pub is across the street from 1251 Hazel Street. I saw a man with black hair running out of the house at 1251 Hazel Street."

In order to impeach Jones, may the prosecution:

(a)   call another witness, Smith, to testify that Jones has a bad reputation for truthfulness in their neighborhood?

(b)   ask Jones whether he lied on a job application a year ago when he denied ever having been convicted of a crime? Suppose the prosecution has a copy of both the job application and a record of Jones's conviction for armed robbery four years ago. If Jones denies lying on the job application, may the prosecution respond by admitting an authenticated copy of the job application? An authenticated record of the conviction?

7.6. Defendant is charged with the sale of heroin. Two alleged purchasers and the arresting officer will be prosecution witnesses. There is evidence that one alleged purchaser in recent years has threatened and intimidated individuals who could offer incriminating evidence against him for his own drug trafficking activity and that the other alleged purchaser lied under oath in a civil action 13 years ago. The arresting officer, according to the defendant, stole $1,400 from the defendant at the time of the arrest. The officer denies the charge. The government has filed a motion in limine asking the court to preclude the defendant from asking about these incidents during cross-examination of the witnesses. How should the court rule?

7.7. Sam Browning is charged with murder. He plans to testify in his own behalf and to call Walt Williams to testify that Browning has a good reputation for peacefulness. The prosecutor has a good-faith basis for believing that three years ago Browning was involved in a bribery scheme; that he beat his wife (although no charges have ever been filed); and that last year Williams filed a false income tax return.

(a)   Can the prosecutor ask Browning about the bribery incident? The beating?

(b)   Can the prosecutor ask Williams if he has heard that Browning was involved in a bribery scheme three years ago? That Browning beat his wife three years ago?

(c)   Can the prosecutor ask Williams if he intentionally filed a false income tax return last year?

7.8. Ed Duke is being prosecuted for murdering Harry Howe, owner of Harry's Hash House. Harry was found dead on the floor of his Hash House and the till was open and empty. At trial Fred Finley testifies for the prosecution that the day before the murder Ed Duke said he was going to get Harry.

(a)   On cross-examination of Finley, defense counsel asks Finley whether he has ever been arrested for possession of marijuana.

(b)   Alex Adams offers to testify that several years ago he was an altar boy at the local church, that Finley was a chorister, and that several times Alex saw Finley steal church property such as cups and other religious objects.

(c)   Jane Jackson, a neighbor of Finley's parents, offers to testify that she has known Finley for Finley's entire life and that in her opinion he is untruthful.

(d)   In rebuttal, the prosecution calls Mark Mayer, who offers to testify that he lives in the same neighborhood as Fred Finley and that he knows Finley's reputation in the neighborhood for truth and veracity is good.

(e)   On cross-examination of Mayer, defense counsel asks if Mayer has heard that Finley was convicted of perjury two years ago.

Should objections to any of this evidence be sustained?

7.9. Davenport, a former police officer, is charged with obstructing justice by revealing the name of an undercover informant to the subject of an investigation. The prosecution has developed the following information about Davenport:

(a)   Prior to the criminal charge, the police department had fired Davenport after an administrative hearing, which resulted in findings that Davenport had committed a number of offenses including the alleged obstruction of justice.

(b)   Three years ago Davenport was suspended by the police department for 30 days for misappropriating departmental gasoline. Davenport took the gasoline for personal use and signed another officer's name in the gas log.

(c)   Two years ago Davenport was found to have taken a subway pass from a young man and ripped it up. Davenport denied taking the pass, but another officer found the pass, and Internal Affairs determined that Davenport had been lying.

(d)   Last year Alma Jones complained to the police department about Davenport's conduct when he arrested her for speeding. She claims that he was verbally abusive, that he threw her on the hood of the car and put a gun to her head, and that he offered to give her only a warning if she would have sex with him.

Assume Davenport will testify in his defense and deny the obstruction charge. To what extent and how can the prosecution use the above information in cross-examining Davenport? Please prepare specific questions for the prosecutor to ask.

7.10. Williams is charged with being a convicted felon in possession of a firearm. The only evidence of his possession was the testimony of Detective David Martin. Martin testified that while giving chase, he saw Williams throw a black object. After arresting Williams, Martin returned to the area and found a gun that showed signs of being thrown against a wall. Williams claims that he had no gun and that it was planted by Martin.

Can Williams cross-examine Martin about (a) a Superior Court judge's finding that Martin lied on the stand during a trial, (b) Martin's driver's license being suspended for driving while intoxicated and the fact that Martin never reported the information to his superiors, and (c) Martin's failure to comply with a court order to pay child support?

Consider whether the court should permit Williams to call the following witnesses:

(a)   Johnny Caravella to testify about a news story he wrote five years ago that identified Detective Martin as the subject of many police harassment complaints in the neighborhood. The sources for the story were unnamed people who lived in Martin's neighborhood.

(b)   Defense attorney Alice Weaver to testify that Martin has a reputation in the "court community" for being untruthful. Weaver's testimony is based on the opinions of three other defense lawyers she knows and her own experience with cases in which Martin has been a witness.

(c)   Chris Brown, an acquaintance of Martin, to testify that Martin wrongfully arrested him for drug possession, that a friend's belongings went missing when Martin arrested the friend, and that in his (Brown's) opinion Martin is very dishonest. Until six years ago Brown lived in Martin's neighborhood and saw Martin almost daily. Brown continues to see Martin regularly when he returns to the neighborhood to visit his mother.

7.11. The defendant is being tried for sexually molesting his seven-year-old stepdaughter. The stepdaughter is one of the prosecution witnesses. Consider whether any of the following evidence should be admissible:

(a)   After the prosecution has presented its case, the defendant calls several witnesses to testify that the stepdaughter is manipulative and often lies.

(b)   During the cross-examination of one of these witnesses, the prosecution asks whether the witness is aware of the fact that the stepdaughter recently admitted breaking an expensive antique even though she could easily have blamed her brother for the incident.

(c)   During cross-examination of the defendant, the prosecutor inquires about whether the defendant molested his former wife's daughter. (The prosecutor knows that there was a complaint filed against the defendant with respect to that incident, that the charges were dropped, and that the defendant was divorced shortly thereafter.)

(d)   During cross-examination of the defendant, the prosecutor also inquires about whether the defendant misrepresented his college class standing in campaign speeches made three years ago during an unsuccessful campaign for a legislative seat.

(e)   As part of its rebuttal, the prosecution calls a clinical psychologist who had examined the stepdaughter. The psychologist offers to testify that (i) she never had trouble with the stepdaughter saying things that were untrue and (ii) psychological research shows that less than 1 percent of child sexual abuse claims are false.

7.12. Doris Delorme has been charged with possession of heroin with intent to sell. The heroin was discovered in a small private airplane in which Doris and Wally Winter, an alleged co-conspirator, were riding. Wally initially testified that Doris was part of their conspiracy and that Doris knew the heroin was on the airplane. The prosecutor then offered to elicit from Wally that he had pleaded guilty pursuant to a plea agreement that included a commitment to testify truthfully against Doris and, if requested, to take lie detector tests. What objection can Doris make to this evidence? What objection could Doris make if the prosecutor offered the evidence only after Doris had established that she had just obtained a divorce from Wally's brother and that Wally was convicted of perjury three years ago?

6.   FRE 609

RULE 609.   IMPEACHMENT BY EVIDENCE OF A CRIMINAL CONVICTION

(a) *In General.* The following rules apply to attacking a witness's character for truthfulness by evidence of a criminal conviction:

(1) for a crime that, in the convicting jurisdiction, was punishable by death or by imprisonment for more than one year, the evidence:

(A) must be admitted, subject to Rule 403, in a civil case or in a criminal case in which the witness is not a defendant; and

(B) must be admitted in a criminal case in which the witness is a defendant, if the probative value of the evidence outweighs its prejudicial effect to that defendant; and

(2) for any crime regardless of the punishment, the evidence must be admitted if the court can readily determine that establishing the elements of the crime required proving — or the witness's admitting — a dishonest act or false statement.

(b) *Limit on Using the Evidence After 10 Years.* This subdivision (b) applies if more than 10 years have passed since the witness's conviction or release from confinement for it, whichever is later. Evidence of the conviction is admissible only if:

(1) its probative value, supported by specific facts and circumstances, substantially outweighs its prejudicial effect; and

(2) the proponent gives an adverse party reasonable written notice of the intent to use it so that the party has a fair opportunity to contest its use.

[Section (c) restricts the use of convictions that have been the subject of pardon or annulment; section (d) restricts the use of juvenile adjudications; and section (e) provides that the pendency of an appeal does not make evidence of a conviction inadmissible.]

7.   Interpretation and Illustration of FRE 609(a) and (b)

FRE 609(a) permits impeachment with two types of convictions: (1) convictions for serious crimes (i.e., those punishable by imprisonment for more than one year, which is the federal definition of a felony), and (2) convictions, regardless of potential punishment, for crimes involving a dishonest act or false statement. The theory of relevance underlying the use of both types of prior convictions is similar to the theory of relevance underlying inquiries about specific instances of conduct pursuant to FRE 608(b)(1): The witness's specific acts that are the basis for the conviction show a general character trait or disposition for untruthfulness from which one can infer that the witness may not be telling the truth on the witness stand. The limitations of FRE 609 do not apply when prior convictions are offered for a relevant purpose other than to prove the witness's character for truthfulness, such as to show contradiction or bias. United States v. Gilmore, 553 F.3d 266, 272 (3d Cir. 2009) (defendant's prior drug convictions admissible to contradict his testimony that he never sold drugs); United States v. Allen, 540 F.3d 821, 824 (8th Cir. 2008) (witness's prior conviction for misdemeanor domestic battery admissible to show witness was prohibited from possessing a firearm and, therefore, had a self-interested motive in denying knowledge or possession of a firearm in a car in which he and defendant were arrested).

An essential feature of FRE 609 is that, unlike FRE 608(b), it contains no prohibition against the use of extrinsic evidence. Thus, if a witness denies a conviction, it is permissible to establish the conviction with extrinsic evidence — for example, with a record of the conviction.

a.   The Two FRE 609(a)(1) Balancing Tests

If a conviction falls within FRE 609(a)(1) — that is, if it is a felony that is *not* a crime involving a dishonest act or false statement (e.g., if it is murder) — its admissibility to impeach a witness is subject to a balancing test. The balancing test for all witnesses *except* criminal defendants is FRE 403. For criminal defendants who are witnesses, FRE 609(a)(1) mandates a reverse-FRE 403 test: The probative value must outweigh the prejudice to the defendant. Whereas FRE 403, by requiring that the probative value must be substantially outweighed by the countervailing factors, favors admissibility, and in effect puts the burden on the party arguing for exclusion to justify that result, the reverse FRE 403 test in FRE 609 favors exclusion and in effect puts the burden on the prosecution to justify admissibility.

Consider, for example, a situation in which a witness has been released from imprisonment for murder six years ago. In deciding whether to admit evidence of the murder conviction to impeach the witness, the judge must first assess the probative value of the conviction. Then the judge must assess the prejudicial impact of the evidence and apply the appropriate balancing test. All of the issues that you studied in Chapter Three concerning the application of FRE 403 apply to the trial judge's decision.

   i.   Probative Value.   The evidentiary fact that the conviction is offered to prove is the truthfulness of the witness at the time of the witness's testimony. Thus, the probative value assessment should include consideration of (1) the age of the conviction, (2) how probative murder is to show bad moral character or general disposition for law-breaking, which in turn shows a disposition for untruthfulness, and (3) the witness's intervening behavior. Six years may seem like a long time, and murder may not seem very probative of untruthfulness. On the other hand, six years is only slightly more than half of the time period prescribed in FRE 609(b), and in the absence of mitigating circumstances relating to the murder, it may be reasonable to infer that a person who is willing to commit such a serious crime has little regard for the law, including the requirement to testify truthfully. Moreover, a crime that in isolation may not seem very probative of truthfulness may be more probative if it is part of a continuing pattern of untruthfulness. Thus, conduct reflecting on truthfulness during the time between release from imprisonment and giving testimony should be an important part of the probative value determination. United States v. Gilbert, 668 F.2d 94, 97 (2d Cir. 1981) (conviction admissible; age of conviction and subsequent history did not suggest abandonment of earlier ways).

   ii.   Unfair Prejudice.   Against the probative value assessment the judge must balance the potential for unfair prejudice. Here there are two primary concerns: First, to what extent will the jury consider the witness to be a bad person and, therefore, be disposed against the witness? For example, if the witness is the defendant, there is a risk that jury may ignore the reasonable doubt standard because it regards the defendant as a bad or dangerous person. Even if the witness is not a party, there is a risk that prejudice against the witness may spill over and affect the jury's attitude about the party who called the witness.

Second, to what extent is there a risk that the jury may use the conviction not only in its proper propensity sense to prove that the witness may be untruthful on the witness stand but also in an improper propensity sense? For example, if the witness is a defendant charged with a crime of violence, there is a risk that the jury, in violation of the prohibition in the first sentence of FRE 404(b), may use the murder conviction as evidence of the defendant's character for violence, for the purpose of inferring that the defendant behaved violently in committing the crime charged. This risk is particularly high when the witness is the defendant and the prior crime is similar in nature to the one at issue in the current trial.

iii.   The Reverse FRE 403 Balancing Test for Criminal Defendants.

The probative value of the murder conviction to prove untruthfulness remains the same regardless of whether the witness is a party to the action. The prejudice, however, is likely to be greatest when the witness is a criminal defendant. Even if the jury regards a nonparty witness as a bad person, it seems less likely that the jury would respond by thinking ill of and, as a result, punishing the party who called the witness. And the risk that a jury may utilize a prior conviction in an improper propensity sense exists only if some conduct of the witness is the subject of the current litigation. That, of course, will always be the case with criminal defendants who testify on their own behalf.

Because the risk of prejudice to criminal defendants is particularly high and because the probative value versus prejudice balancing process is inherently imprecise, FRE 609(a)(1) employs a reverse FRE 403 balancing test for witnesses who are criminal defendants. As a result, it is somewhat more likely, at least in theory, that the murder conviction — and other FRE 609(a)(1) convictions — will be admissible against witnesses who are not criminal defendants than against criminal defendants.

iv.   The FRE 403 Balancing Test for Other Witnesses.

FRE 609(a) does not give civil parties who are witnesses the benefit of the reverse FRE 403 balancing test. Rather, FRE 609(a) treats them in the same manner as it treats nonparty witnesses. Their prior convictions will be admissible unless the probative impeachment value of the convictions is substantially outweighed by the FRE 403 countervailing factors.

The subject matter of civil litigation often does not involve the same type of morally culpable conduct that is typically the subject of criminal prosecutions. As a result, the risk of prejudice from using prior convictions for impermissible propensity purposes may be less in civil cases generally than in criminal prosecutions. Moreover, civil litigants as a class are not as likely to have prior convictions as are criminal defendants. On the other hand, some civil claims — for example, fraud or sexual assault — involve allegations of criminal conduct; and as we suggested in subsection iii, supra, the risk of bad person prejudice is likely to be greater with party witnesses than with nonparty witnesses. Do you think civil party witnesses should receive the same reverse balancing test that criminal defendants receive?

v.   The Factual Circumstances of the Crime.

When courts balance the probative value of a conviction against its unfair prejudice and other countervailing factors, they frequently discuss the issue in only general terms — such as the type, the punishment, the date, and the number of convictions — because this is the information that will be presented to the jury. United States v. Howell, 285 F.3d 1263 (10th Cir. 2002). We discuss the factual details that may be presented below in subsection 8.d. Courts also inquire into the facts underlying a conviction when determining whether a conviction involves a "dishonest act or false statement" for purposes of FRE 609(a)(2). We discuss this issue below in subsection 7.b.

b.   The Automatic Admissibility of FRE 609(a)(2) "Dishonest Act or False Statement" Convictions

i.   The Rule.   "Dishonest act or false statement" convictions, as the language of FRE 609(a)(2) makes clear, are automatically admissible without regard to balancing and without regard to the seriousness of the crime. In short, if the conviction is for a crime involving a dishonest act or false statement, it is unnecessary to consider what the potential penalty for the crime is or any potential prejudicial impact of the conviction. As long as the conviction falls within the time limitation set forth in FRE 609(b), a court has no discretion to exclude it. For example, if a witness had been convicted of a misdemeanor offense of making a false statement on some type of application form, the impeaching party could admit the conviction to impeach the witness even if the conviction were nine years old and thus arguably not very probative of the witness's truth-telling on the witness stand now, nine years later. Even if the witness were a criminal defendant charged with the identical crime the evidence would be admissible.

ii.   The Meaning of "Dishonest Act or False Statement."   Because of the automatic admissibility for crimes involving dishonest acts or false statements, the contours of this category of crimes are extremely important. To the extent that one equates "dishonest act" with "illegal," all crimes are crimes involving a dishonest act. Clearly, however, the term *dishonest* in FRE 609(a)(2) should not be interpreted that broadly, for limitations in FRE 609(a)(1) would then be meaningless.

Prior to the 2011 restyling amendments, FRE 609(a)(2) referred to crimes involving "dishonesty or false statement," and the Advisory Committee Note to FRE 609 equates "dishonesty or false statement" with the common law classification *crimen falsi*. The Senate Judiciary Committee Report and the Conference Report on the Federal Rules contain the following identical elaboration:

> [It means] crimes such as perjury or subornation of perjury, false statement, criminal fraud, embezzlement or false pretenses, or any other offense, in the nature of *crimen falsi* the commission of which involves some element of untruthfulness, deceit or falsification bearing on the accused's propensity to testify truthfully.

Federal courts have interpreted "dishonesty or false statement" relatively narrowly. United States v. Osazuwa, 564 F.3d 1169, 1175 (9th Cir. 2009) ("It is undisputed that bank fraud is an act of dishonesty"); United States v. Harper, 527 F.3d 396, 408 (5th Cir. 2008) ("theft by check convictions fall under Rule 609(a)(2)"); United States v. Morrow, 977 F.2d 222 (6th Cir. 1992) (counterfeiting is crime of "dishonesty or false statement"); Wagner v. Firestone Tire & Rubber Co., 890 F.2d 652 (3d Cir. 1989) (forgery is crime of "dishonesty or false statement"); Walker v. Horn, 385 F.3d 321,

334 (3d Cir. 2004) (robbery is not crime of dishonesty or false statement); United States v. Mejia-Alarcon, 995 F.2d 982 (10th Cir. 1993) (conviction for unauthorized use of food stamps not within FRE 609(a)(2)); United States v. Karmer, 923 F.2d 1557 (11th Cir. 1991) (misdemeanor theft not usually within FRE 609(a)(2)). There are gray areas, however, and the case law is not entirely consistent. Compare, e.g., United States v. Wilson, 985 F.2d 348 (7th Cir. 1993) (failure to file income tax return is crime of "dishonesty or false statement") with Cree v. Hatcher, 969 F.2d 34 (3d Cir. 1993), (failure to file income tax return not within FRE 609(a)(2)). See generally Stuart P. Green, Deceit and Classification of Crimes: Federal Rule of Evidence 609(a)(2) and the Origins of Crimen Falsi, 90 J. Crim. L. & Criminology 1087 (2000).

   iii.   The Significance of the Underlying Details of the Crime.   FRE 609(a)(2) provides that a conviction falls within its scope when "the court can readily determine that establishing the elements of the crime required proving — or the witness's admitting — a dishonest act or false statement." In the absence of the witness's admission, the Advisory Committee provides examples of what may satisfy the "readily apparent" requirement:

> Where the deceitful nature of the crime is not apparent from the statute and the face of the judgment — as, for example, where the conviction simply records a finding of guilt for a statutory offense that does not reference deceit expressly — a proponent may offer information such as *an indictment, a statement of admitted facts, or jury instructions to show that the factfinder had to find, or the defendant had to admit, an act of dishonesty or false statement in order for the witness to have been convicted.* (Emphasis added.)

In United States v. Jefferson, 623 F.3d 227, 234-235 (5th Cir. 2010), for example, the court concluded that a prior conviction for obstruction of justice involved a dishonest act or false statement, and thus qualified under FRE 609(a)(2), because the indictment in that case alleged that the witness attempted to persuade another to lie to federal law enforcement authorities. See also United States v. Collier, 527 F.3d 695, 699 (8th Cir. 2008) (conviction for credit card fraud within 609(a)(2) because offense included "intent to defraud" as a statutory element).

c.   The FRE 609(b) Reverse Balancing Test

   All prior convictions falling within the scope of FRE 609(a) — including dishonest act and false statement convictions — are subject to a reverse FRE 403 balancing test in FRE 609(b) if they fall outside the 10-year time period specified in that subsection. The 10-year time period runs from the date of conviction or release from imprisonment, whichever is later. See United States v. Rogers, 542 F.3d 197, 201 (7th Cir. 2008) ("confinement" for purposes of FRE 609(b) "does not include periods of probation or parole" — "The clock starts at the witness's release from any physical confinement."). Thus, for example, a 12-year-old perjury conviction for which the witness served a three-year sentence would be automatically admissible despite the age of the conviction. If the witness had been imprisoned for only one year, however, FRE 609(b) would apply, and the conviction would be admissible only if its probative value substantially outweighed its prejudice — a test that, by virtue of the term *substantially,* is even more stringent than the reverse FRE 403 test in FRE 609(a).

Indeed, although courts have not developed specific standards to distinguish FRE 609(b) balancing from FRE 609(a) balancing, they have indicated that FRE 609(b) convictions should rarely be admissible. United States v. Bensimon, 172 F.3d 1121, 1126-1127 (9th Cir. 1999).

8.   Elaboration of FRE 609(a)

a.   *The Rationale for Permitting Impeachment with FRE 609(a)(1) Convictions*

FRE 609(a) — like the rules in most states — permits a trial judge to balance probative value and prejudice in deciding whether to admit evidence of felonies, regardless of whether the underlying conduct could reasonably be described as having a bearing on the witness's character for truthfulness. The rule is thus far broader than FRE 608(b).

The common law origin of the prior conviction impeachment device probably accounts in part for its breadth and its uniform acceptance:

> At common law a person's conviction of treason, any felony, or a misdemeanor involving dishonesty (*crimen falsi*), or the obstruction of justice, rendered the convict completely incompetent as a witness. These were said to be "infamous" crimes. Thanks to statutes or rules virtually universal in the common law world, this primitive absolutism has been abandoned. The disqualification for conviction of crime has been repealed, and by specific provision or by decision it has been reduced to a mere ground for impeaching credibility. [1 McCormick on Evidence § 42, at 184-85 (Kenneth S. Broun ed., 6th ed., 2006).]

In addition, the rule is justified by the belief that prior convictions, even if they are based on activity that does not relate very directly to truthfulness, may be especially relevant to the question of the witness's general credibility. Neither courts nor commentators, however, attempt to justify the assumption that convictions for acts only remotely related to truthfulness (e.g., aggravated assaults) may be especially probative of truthfulness on the witness stand. But see Campbell v. Greer, 831 F.2d 700 (7th Cir. 1987) ("The proposition that felons perjure themselves more often than other, similarly situated witnesses . . . is one of many important empirical assertions about law that have never been tested, and may be false."); Schmude v. Tricam Indus., Inc., 556 F.3d 624, 628 (7th Cir. 2009) (asserting that the assumption that convicted felons are more likely to lie on the witness stand is "underinclusive, since many people who have committed a felony have not been caught.").

Consider to what extent the following explanation justifies FRE 609: A person of generally bad moral character is more likely to lie than a person of generally good moral character. Indeed, compelling proof of bad moral character may be particularly probative of untruthfulness. All of us, however, from time to time engage in "bad" acts that tend to suggest bad moral character; and since few, if any, of us are likely to consider ourselves to be of bad moral character, it must follow that a single bad act — or even a series of bad acts — is not necessarily very probative of general moral character. Thus, in the absence of a conviction, most jurisdictions prohibit inquiry into these acts unless they are likely to have more than very marginal value to the question whether the witness is lying — that is, unless they relate fairly directly to that issue by suggesting a character trait of untruthfulness as opposed to general bad moral character. On the other hand, because the criminal law tends to proscribe only the most reprehensible activity, convictions — especially when they are for serious crimes — are likely to be particularly probative of bad moral character and, therefore, untruthfulness.

b.   Prior Convictions and Prejudice

Most prior convictions admissible under FRE 609(a) are likely to be more preju- dicial than most nonconviction bad act evidence admissible under FRE 608(b). This is so because the substantive law tends to criminalize the most reprehensible behav- ior; because police and prosecutors tend to focus their limited resources on the most serious offenders; and because the fact of conviction represents the community's judg- ment of moral condemnation. As a result, there is a relatively high risk that juries may be predisposed against witnesses who are shown to have prior convictions. Whenever the witness is a party or somebody closely associated with the party, jurors' attitudes about the witness may improperly affect their decision.

In assessing probative value and prejudice pursuant to FRE 609(a)(1) and FRE 609(b), it is important to keep in mind the significance of the similarity between the prior conviction evidence and the current criminal charge. When the witness is a criminal defendant (or some other person whose alleged actions are the basis for the current litigation), similarity between the current criminal allegations and the facts underlying the impeachment evidence enhances the *prejudice*, not the proba- tive value, of the prior conviction. The only permissible inference to draw from the conviction is that the witness is an untruthful person and therefore may be lying on the witness stand.

c.   Extrinsic Evidence

Convictions are the result of a plea or a fact finder's beyond-a-reasonable-doubt finding of guilt. They provide highly probative evidence that the underlying bad acts occurred, and the fact of a conviction can be easily established with a public record. Thus, the concern with time-consuming litigation about collateral matters that argu- ably justifies the FRE 608(b) prohibition against extrinsic evidence, see pages 361- 362, supra, does not apply to convictions offered pursuant to FRE 609, which may be proven with extrinsic evidence. In practice, however, there is seldom any need for such extrinsic evidence. Because a party can so easily establish a conviction, it is unlikely that a witness will deny the conviction in the first place. Indeed, as we discuss at page 379, infra, if a prior conviction will be admissible to impeach a witness, the party calling the witness may have the witness acknowledge the conviction on direct examination.

d.   The Factual Details of the Conviction

Just as courts have an interest in avoiding lengthy inquiry into alleged bad acts that have not resulted in convictions, courts also have an interest in not spending a great deal of time exploring the facts underlying a witness's conviction. Moreover, eliciting the factual details underlying a conviction is likely to increase its prejudicial impact. Thus, courts typically will permit the impeaching party to mention the name of the crime, when and where it occurred, what sentence was imposed, and nothing more. United States v. Lopez-Medina, 596 F.3d 716, 738 (10th Cir. 2010) ("Ordinarily it is improper for the prosecution to examine into the details of the crime . . . . The cross-examination should be confined to the essential facts of conviction, nature of crime, and the punishment."); United States v. Osazuwa, supra ("Absent exceptional circumstances, evidence of a prior conviction for impeachment purposes may not include collateral details and circumstances attendant upon the conviction."); United States v. Commanche, 577 F.3d 1261 (10th Cir. 2009) (abuse of discretion for trial court to allow detail that defendant's prior two felony convictions involved sharp objects when defendant was on trial for allegedly stabbing two men); United States v. Pandozzi, 887 F.2d 1526, 1534-1535 (1st Cir. 1989) (impeachment with sexual assault conviction; proper to elicit that crime was sexual assault and to prohibit reference to fact that victim was a child). The details of a conviction that may be admitted will depend on an application FRE 403. See United States v. Lopez-Medina, supra ("A district court must conduct a Rule 403 balancing test before determining [whether to admit or exclude evidence] other than the fact and date of such convictions."). Further details regarding a crime may be admissible if, for example, the witness tries to explain away or minimize the seriousness of the crime. United States v. Amachia, 825 F.2d 177 (8th Cir. 1987); see also United States v. Commanche, supra (witness does not "open the door" to details about the conviction merely by answering questions about it).

e.   The Relationship Between FRE 609(a) and FRE 608(b)

To what extent may parties rely on FRE 608(b) to admit additional details or specific acts related to criminal convictions that may be admitted under FRE 609? Recognizing the potential for FRE 608(b) to undermine limitations on the details of criminal conduct that may be presented under FRE 609, several federal appellate courts have clarified recently that FRE 608(b) may not be used to admit specific acts related to criminal convictions. FRE 608(b) applies only to specific acts that did not result in a criminal conviction; FRE 609 governs impeachment with criminal convictions and any underlying conduct. United States v. Osazuwa, 564 F.3d 1169 (9th Cir. 2009) ("Echoing the observations of the Fifth, Eighth, and Tenth Circuits, we hold that Rule 608(b) permits impeachment only by specific acts that have not resulted in a criminal conviction. Evidence relating to impeachment by way of criminal conviction is treated exclusively under Rule 609"); United States v. Lightfoot, 483 F.3d 876 (8th Cir. 2007); United States v. Parker, 133 F.3d 322 (5th Cir. 1998); Mason v. Texaco, Inc., 948 F.2d 1546 (10th Cir. 1991).

f.   Hearsay

Regardless of whether the prior conviction is elicited from the witness or proved extrinsically with the record of conviction, the evidence is hearsay. The theory underlying FRE 609 is that the witness committed the acts that constitute the elements of the crime for which the witness was convicted and that proof of these acts suggests something important about the witness's credibility. In other words, the conviction is a manifestation of the jury's or the judge's assertion in an earlier proceeding that the witness committed the acts essential for the conviction, and it is the truth of this assertion that is critical to the relevance of the evidence. To the extent one doubts the reliability of this assertion, one should also doubt the probative value of the evidence for its impeaching purpose. For a recent argument that problems regarding the reliability of convictions and guilty pleas fall disproportionately on racial minorities, and that FRE 609 exacerbates these problems by generating evidence for further convictions, see Montré D. Carodine, "The Mis-Characterization of the Negro": A Race Critique of the Prior Conviction Impeachment Rule, 84 Ind. L.J. 521, 526 (2009) ("Rules such as Rule 609 keep Blacks ensnared in the criminal justice system, perpetuating the criminalization of a staggering percentage of the Black population.").

The Federal Rules, as well as a number of other jurisdictions, have a judgments exception to the hearsay rule. Typically, however, the judgments exception is narrower than the rule authorizing impeachment with prior convictions. For example, FRE 803(22) extends the judgments exception only to convictions for crimes punishable by imprisonment for more than one year, whereas FRE 609(a)(2) authorizes the use of "dishonest act or false statement" convictions regardless of the potential penalty. If courts have even noticed this conflict between FRE 609(a) and FRE 803(22), they have not been bothered by it. Courts considering the admissibility of misdemeanor convictions for impeachment under FRE 609(a)(2) have relied on that rule, which deals specifically with that issue, and have ignored the limitations in the more general FRE 803(22).

g.   Practical Considerations

Frequently parties will file motions in limine seeking an advance ruling on whether prior convictions will be admissible against them. In deciding whether or not to testify in their criminal trials, defendants will want to know ahead of time whether their prior convictions will be admissible to impeach them. The admissibility determination may affect a defendant's trial strategy in two important ways. First, defendants who learn their prior convictions will be admissible for impeachment purposes may choose not to testify in order to prevent the jury from learning about the convictions. There is some empirical evidence suggesting that the admission of a criminal defendant's prior convictions contributes to the likelihood of a guilty verdict. Harry Kalven Jr. and Hans Zeisel, The American Jury 159-160 (1966); Anthony N. Doob and Hershi M. Kirshenbaum, Some Empirical Evidence on the Effect of Sec. 12 of the Canada Evidence Act Upon the Accused, 15 Crim. L.Q. 88, 91-95 (1972-1973). However, other evidence suggests that the prejudicial impact of prior convictions may not be as strong as is commonly asserted or assumed. See Ronald J. Allen and Larry Laudan, The Devastating Impact of Prior Crimes Evidence and Other Myths of the Criminal Justice Process, 101 J. Crim. L. & Criminology 493 (2011) (discussing a recent study of over 350 state court criminal trials in which the acquittal rates for defendants with prior convictions was similar for defendants who had their convictions admitted at trial and for those who did not have their convictions admitted: 20.3 percent versus 23.9 percent).

Second, when a defendant chooses to testify and the defendant's prior convictions will be admissible, it will often be tactically important for the defendant to mention admissible prior convictions on direct examination. If the jury learns of the convictions for the first time on cross-examination, there is the risk that the jury will be prejudiced against the defendant for not "coming clean" on direct examination. The direct examiner, however, obviously has no interest in calling to the jury's attention convictions that would not otherwise be admissible.

In the *Johnson* case, defense counsel brought out on direct examination the prior convictions of the defendant, his cellmate, Butler, and inmate Green. Unfortunately, however, the direct examination was not complete with respect to Green's prior convictions. Thus, the prosecution was still able to benefit from the implication that the witness was not fully forthcoming on direct examination (page 49, lines 21-40, supra).

Judges will frequently rule on motions in limine regarding the admissibility of convictions before a defendant has to decide whether to testify. There is apparently no obligation to make such a ruling, however. In Luce v. United States, 469 U.S. 38 (1984), the Supreme Court held that a defendant who chose not to testify after the trial judge refused to rule on his motion in limine could not seek reversal on the ground that the convictions should not have been admissible. To preserve that claim, the Court held, the defendant must testify.

The *Luce* Court relied primarily on two factors. First, there was a concern that with a contrary holding defendants who had no genuine interest in testifying might file motions in limine in the hope of creating reversible error in the event that the court ruled the convictions to be admissible. Second, Luce made his motion before trial and did not accompany it with any indication of how he planned to impeach prosecution witnesses or what the testimony of defense witnesses (including himself) would be. In this context, the Supreme Court quite reasonably took the position that the trial judge may not have had enough information to engage in the balancing process required by FRE 609.

Consider what should happen if the defendant receives an unfavorable ruling on a motion in limine before testifying. Can the defendant acknowledge the conviction on direct examination in order to remove any inference of hiding unfavorable information and at the same time preserve the admissibility issue for appeal? Despite the fact that this situation does not implicate the two concerns that were central to *Luce*, the Supreme Court in Ohler v. United States, 529 U.S. 753 (2000), held 5 to 4 that a defendant who acknowledges prior convictions on direct examination after a ruling that they will be admissible pursuant to FRE 609 cannot claim on appeal that the admissibility decision was erroneous. See also United States v. McConnel, 464 F.3d 1152, 1162 (10th Cir. 2006) (extending *Ohler*'s waiver rule to impeachment evidence under FRE 608(b)). For a case refusing to follow *Ohler* and reaching the opposite result, see State v. Daly, 623 N.W.2d 799 (Iowa 2001). Which decision do you think is better — *Ohler* or *Daly*?

Even after *Ohler* and *Luce*, a defendant who contemplates the possibility of testifying should probably pursue a motion in limine to exclude prior convictions. If the judge rules on the motion, the defendant at least will have a better sense of the consequences of testifying.

For defense counsel who pursue such motions, there are several important considerations. First, and most important, while there may be legitimate tactical reasons for withholding some information from the court and the prosecution, a defense counsel who is serious about wanting a ruling on the motion should provide the trial court with as much information as possible to make the decision. For example, the defense should indicate what the impeachment of prosecution witnesses is likely to entail, what the defense testimony will probably be, and why the defendant's testimony is important for a fair trial. Providing the judge with this information removes one of the principal concerns expressed by *Luce*.

Second, if the court does not grant the motion before trial, defense counsel should renew the motion at the close of the prosecution case and, if necessary, again immediately before the defendant will have to decide whether to take the stand. At each renewal of the motion defense counsel should refine the argument for exclusion of the convictions in light of the evidence that has been presented and the anticipated evidence. At some point along the way it is likely that the court will have sufficient information to make a reasoned FRE 609 ruling. And if the judge has all of the relevant information, there is no reason why the judge should not rule on the motion. Indeed, in this type of situation the defendant might argue that — particularly in light of the *Luce* and *Ohler* — it is an abuse of discretion and an unreasonable burden on the defendant's right to testify for the judge to refuse to make the ruling.

Third, if the trial judge is reluctant to make a definitive FRE 609 balancing decision without knowing what the evidence in the case actually is, defense counsel should seek a conditional ruling: For example, as long as the evidence presented by the defendant is limited to the representations accompanying this motion, the defendant's prior convictions are not admissible.

KEY POINTS

1. FRE 609(a)(2) provides that convictions involving dishonest acts or false statements falling within the 10-year time limit described in FRE 609(b) are automatically admissible to impeach all witnesses (including criminal defendants) without regard to penalty or balancing.

2. FRE 609(a)(1) provides that other convictions falling within the 10-year time limit are admissible only if they are punishable by more than a year's imprisonment and if they satisfy the appropriate balancing test.

3. The balancing test for all witnesses except criminal defendants is FRE 403 (admissible unless probative value substantially outweighed by countervailing factors); the balancing test for criminal defendants who are witnesses is a reverse FRE 403 test (probative value must outweigh the prejudicial impact on defendant).

4. The 10-year time limitation in FRE 609(b) runs from the date of conviction or the date of release from imprisonment, whichever is more recent.

5. In federal courts, a defendant who acknowledges prior convictions on direct examination following an in limine ruling that the convictions will be admissible cannot challenge the in limine ruling on appeal. State courts are split on this issue.

PROBLEMS

7.13. Return to Problem 7.5 at page 367. During cross-examination, may the prosecution ask Jones whether he has ever been convicted of armed robbery? If Jones answers, "No," may the prosecution respond by admitting an authenticated record of Jones's conviction from four years ago?

7.14. Return to Problem 3.5 at page 138. Suppose Trapp testifies consistently with his deposition. Broadback's attorney has an authenticated record of Trapp's felony conviction for illegally possessing methamphetamine. The attorney also has an authenticated copy of a recent application for a life insurance policy in which Broadback denied ever using illegal drugs. During cross-examination, may Broadback's attorney:

(a)   ask Trapp whether he was convicted for possessing methamphetamine? If Trapp denies the conviction, may Broadback's attorney introduce the record of conviction?

(b)   ask Trapp whether he lied on his life insurance application? If he denies doing so, may the attorney introduce the application and the record of conviction?

7.15. Ellen Jamison is being prosecuted for perjury, and she testifies in her own defense. Eight years ago Ellen was convicted of perjury, and last year she was convicted of felonious assault against her husband. Can the prosecutor introduce evidence of these convictions?

7.16. James Burton is being prosecuted for illegal weapons possession. The weapon, a pistol, was found during a legal search of the house where James was living. The house is owned by James's mother, Teresa, and she has testified that the pistol belonged to a former boarder. Fifteen years ago Teresa was convicted of making a false statement under oath and third degree larceny. The convictions were the result of her having made false statements on an application for food stamps. Can the prosecutor introduce evidence of these convictions?

7.17. In the *Johnson* trial, which occurred in 1992, the following convictions were used to impeach the credibility of defense witnesses:

(a)   robbery and battery (years not specified) by George Butler, the defendant's cellmate;

(b)   first degree murder, assault with a deadly weapon, and first degree burglary (years not specified) by Michael Green, another inmate;

(c)   rape (paroled in 1984) and first degree burglary (1985) by the defendant, Johnson.

Which of these convictions would be most likely and least likely to be admitted pursuant to FRE 609?

7.18. Mary Davenport is charged with possession of cocaine discovered during a legal search of the vehicle she was driving. In her defense she establishes that she had borrowed the car from a friend, and she testifies she had no idea that the cocaine was present. On cross-examination can the prosecution introduce evidence that nine years ago she was convicted of attempted possession of a controlled substance? Would your answer be different if, on direct examination, Mary not only denied knowledge of the cocaine in the car but also testified, "With the education my father gave me not to get involved in drugs, I never did"? Why?

7.19. Tom Jackson has filed a federal civil rights against Larry Oster, a prison guard, for injuries sustained in what Jackson claims was an unprovoked assault. Jackson is currently in prison for life with no possibility of parole as a result of his conviction eight years ago for aiding and abetting his brother in the murder of a police officer. Jackson has filed a motion in limine asking the court to exclude any reference to the conviction. Oster has filed a motion in limine asking the court to rule that for impeachment purposes the defendant can introduce evidence that the conviction was for murdering a police officer and that Jackson is serving a life sentence without possibility of parole. How should the court rule?

7.20. Houghton has been charged with bank robbery, using a firearm during the robbery, and possession of a firearm after having been convicted of a felony. Houghton was convicted of murder 15 years ago and paroled three years ago. He is willing to stipulate that he has been "convicted of a felony," and he plans to testify that he was not the robber. In a motion in limine he asks the court to exclude any evidence of or reference to the prior conviction except for the stipulation. How should the court rule?

7.21. Dawn Drabble is charged with robbery. In cross-examining a prosecution witness, Dawn wishes to show that the witness was convicted of felonious assault eight years ago. Later, Dawn testifies in her own defense, and the prosecution offers to show that she was convicted of felonious assault eight years ago. Are the convictions admissible?

7.22. Alex Dean is being prosecuted for murder. He has testified that he was with a friend at the time of the alleged killing. On cross-examination the prosecutor asked Alex if he had falsely stated that he had no criminal record on a job application filed with the Acme Parts Co. three years ago. Alex responded that he had applied for a job with Acme and that he had not lied on the job application form. The prosecutor now offers into evidence (1) Alex's job application form in which he responded "No" to the question whether he had ever been convicted of a crime and (2) a public record of Alex's conviction for armed robbery seven years ago. Alex has objected to the admissibility of both documents. What result?

7.23. Jane and Ed Farley are charged with embezzlement, and they both plan to testify. Dan Evans will testify for them as a character witness. Jane Farley was convicted of filing a false income tax return 15 years ago, and Ed Farley was convicted of felonious theft five years ago. Dan Evans was convicted of misdemeanor battery two years ago. Pursuant to FRE 608(b) the prosecutor plans to ask the following questions on cross-examination:

(a) To Jane Farley: Isn't it true that you filed a false income tax return 15 years ago?

(b) To Ed Farley: Isn't it true that five years ago you made false representations to induce individuals to invest in a get-rich-quick scheme? (As the prosecutor knows, this was the underlying basis for theft charge.)

(c) To Dan Evans: Isn't it true that two years ago you pretended to be a friend to Joe Newhouse and lured him to a deserted building where you knew he would be beaten? (As the prosecutor knows, this was the basis for the battery charge; Evans was convicted as an aider and abettor.)

Are any of these questions objectionable?

C.   IMPEACHMENT AND REHABILITATION WITH A WITNESS'S PRIOR STATEMENTS

A witness's prior statement — that is, a statement made at another time and place prior to the witness's current testimony — falls within the core definition of hearsay, and thus may be inadmissible, if the statement is offered to prove its truth. FRE 801(a)-(c); FRE 802. Sometimes a witness's prior statement will be admissible for its truth because it falls within an exception to the hearsay rule or an explicit exemption from the definition of hearsay. FRE 801(d), 803-804, 807. If a witness's prior statement is admissible for its truth, there is no need to consider whether it may *also* be admissible for the nonhearsay purpose of impeaching or rehabilitating the witness. We discuss hearsay in Chapter Eight. Our focus here is on the nonhearsay use of prior inconsistent and consistent statements that are not independently admissible for their truth.

When a witness's prior inconsistent statements are offered to impeach the witness, the relevance of this evidence derives not from its truth but from its inconsistency with the witness's trial testimony. Proof of an inconsistency, regardless of which statement is true, suggests that the witness may have lied in making one of the statements or that the witness for some other reason — for example, faulty memory or lack of interest in the subject matter — has on one occasion not reported accurately what happened. Such proof allows the impeaching party to argue to the jury that the witness is not reliable. The admissibility of a prior inconsistent statement for an impeaching purpose is governed by FRE 401-403, that is, whether it is relevant for an impeaching purpose, its probative value for this purpose, and whether its probative value is substantially outweighed by FRE 403 concerns. In addition, FRE 613 establishes the process for admitting prior inconsistent statements that are relevant and admissible under FRE 403.

A witness's prior consistent statements may also be relevant for the nonhearsay purpose of rehabilitating a witness's testimony. The theory of relevance is similar to that for prior inconsistent statements. Proof that a witness has made statements consistent with the witness's current testimony suggests, apart from the truth of the prior statements, that the witness is careful and thoughtful in speaking about the matter to which the statements relate. Thus, except to the extent that there is reason to believe the witness is deliberately telling consistent lies, knowing about the consistency gives us more reason to credit and rely on the witness's testimony than we would have without evidence of the consistency.

1.   FRE 613

RULE 613.   WITNESS'S PRIOR STATEMENT

(a) *Showing or Disclosing the Statement During Examination.* When examining a witness about the witness's prior statement, a party need not show it or disclose its contents to the witness. But the party must, on request, show it or disclose its content to an adverse party's attorney.

(b) *Extrinsic Evidence of a Prior Inconsistent Statement.* Extrinsic evidence of a witness's prior inconsistent statement is admissible only if the witness is given an opportunity to explain or deny the statement and an adverse party is given an opportunity to examine the witness about it, or if justice so requires. This subdivision (b) does not apply to an opposing party's statement under Rule 801(d)(2).

2.   Interpretation and Illustration of FRE 613

FRE 613 establishes the process by which an examiner may introduce evidence of a witness's prior inconsistent statement for the purpose of impeaching the witness's credibility. Typically, the examiner will confront the witness with a prior inconsistent statement during cross-examination.

a.   FRE 613(a)

FRE 613(a) makes it clear that the examiner need not disclose the contents of a prior inconsistent statement to the witness before asking whether the witness made the statement. This provision formally abolishes the rule derived from the Queen Caroline's Case, 2 Br. & B. 284, 129 Eng. Rep. 976 (1820), which required, at least with respect to written statements, that the witness be shown the statement prior to any questioning about the statement. The rationale for the rule of the *Queen's Case* stems from a concern that the witness may honestly have forgotten what is or appears to be an inconsistent statement. If such a witness were not shown the statement prior to questioning, a clever cross-examiner might be able to get the witness to deny having made the statement, thereby giving the false impression that the witness was a liar. On the other hand, showing the statement to the witness before questioning gives the dishonest witness the opportunity to concoct a false story that minimizes the impact of the inconsistency. For this reason many commentators have criticized the *Queen's Case* rule, which the Advisory Committee Note to FRE 613(a) characterizes as a "useless impediment to cross-examination."

FRE 613(a) provides that opposing counsel has the right, upon request, to learn of the statement. According to the Advisory Committee Note, this provision "is designed to protect against unwarranted insinuations that a statement has been made when the fact is to the contrary." Assume, for example, that defense counsel had reason to believe that one of plaintiff's eyewitnesses to an automobile accident had made a statement inconsistent with the witness's trial testimony about who was at fault. Counsel could interrogate the witness about whether the witness had ever made such a statement without first revealing its contents to the witness. Upon request, however, defense counsel would have to reveal the inconsistent statement to plaintiff's counsel.

b.   FRE 613(b)

FRE 613(b) also acknowledges that extrinsic evidence of inconsistent statements may be admissible, but it provides that in most instances there is a twofold condition for the admissibility of extrinsic evidence. The witness must have an opportunity to explain the statement, and the opposing party must have an opportunity to explore the inconsistency with the witness. To fulfill these requirements the party offering the prior inconsistent statement must generally do so when the witness is still testifying or must make sure that the witness is available for recall. United States v. Moore, 149 F.3d 773, 781-782 (8th Cir. 1998).

Requiring that the witness have the opportunity to explain the statement gives the fact finder a reasonable basis for evaluating the alleged inconsistency. For example, the witness may have a plausible explanation for why an apparently inconsistent statement is not in fact inconsistent, or the witness may deny having made the statement, in which case the fact finder will have to assess the relative weight of the extrinsic evidence and the witness's denial.

The "if justice so requires" exception exists because there may be situations in which it is not possible to give the witness an opportunity to explain the apparent inconsistency. Consider, for example, a situation in which the impeaching party becomes aware of the prior inconsistent statement only after the witness has been dismissed and is no longer available. In such a case it may further the search for truth to permit extrinsic evidence of the inconsistent statement without any opportunity for the witness's explanation rather than to exclude the impeaching evidence altogether.

The final sentence of FRE 613(b) provides another exception to the usual requirement that the witness have an opportunity to explain or deny the statement: The requirement is inapplicable to inconsistent statements by a party falling within FRE 801(d)(2). That rule provides that a party's prior statements may be admissible for their truth regardless of whether the party testifies. Thus, there is no need to restrict admissibility under FRE 613 when the party happens to be a witness.

3.   Elaboration of Impeachment with Prior Inconsistent Statements

a.   *FRE 613(b)'s Departure from the Common Law*

The common law imposed a rigorous foundation requirement as a condition for introducing extrinsic evidence of an inconsistent statement. The impeaching party could not introduce extrinsic evidence of a witness's statement without first indicating the precise time and place of the statement and the person to whom it was made and then asking the witness whether the witness had made the statement. The drafters of the Federal Rules made clear their intent to have a more flexible foundation requirement. According to the Advisory Committee Note to FRE 613(b):

> The traditional insistence that the attention of the witness be directed to the statement on cross-examination is relaxed in favor of simply providing the witness an opportunity to explain and the opposite party an opportunity to examine on the statement, with no specification of any particular time or sequence.

As a result of this liberalization of the common law foundation requirement, it is possible that an impeaching party may introduce extrinsic evidence of an inconsistent statement without ever having mentioned the statement to the witness. Consider, for example, a situation in which the witness suggests on direct examination that the defendant was speeding. Now suppose that the opposing counsel has information that the witness had said the defendant was not speeding. Under FRE 613, opposing counsel on cross-examination may do nothing more than get the witness to reconfirm the direct examination testimony. Then, later in the trial during the presentation of the defense case, counsel may attempt to introduce extrinsic evidence of the inconsistent statement. As long as the witness has not been dismissed and is subject to recall (or perhaps as long as witness is available and can be called anew by the opposing party), extrinsic evidence of the statement may be admissible.

b.   *Extrinsic Evidence in Practice: Practical Considerations*

Some trial judges have prohibited litigants from introducing extrinsic evidence of prior inconsistent statements that they made no effort to explore with the witness on cross-examination, and appellate courts have upheld these decisions on the ground that the trial judges were appropriately exercising discretion to control manner and order of proof. FRE 611(a). United States v. Sutton, 41 F.3d 1257, 1260 (8th Cir. 1994). As a result, the impeaching party in these cases lost the opportunity to show the inconsistent statement. To avoid this situation, unless counsel feels that there is a compelling tactical reason not to do so, the safe course of action is to lay the traditional common law foundation and to confront the witness with the inconsistent statement on cross-examination. (Indeed, many cross-examiners regularly use the elements of that foundation as part of their impeachment technique.) If the impeaching party lays the common law foundation and the witness denies making the inconsistent statement, the door should be open to proof of the statement with extrinsic evidence. If the party admits the statement, it is less clear whether extrinsic evidence of the statement will be admissible. Some courts take the position that the witness's acknowledgment of the statement removes any need for the extrinsic evidence, while other courts permit extrinsic evidence. The appropriate course of action, in our view, is not to have a flat rule of inadmissibility or admissibility but rather to view the issue as one governed by FRE 401-403.

c.   *Probative Value and FRE 403 Concerns*

Since everyone occasionally makes inconsistent statements, proof of an apparently trivial inconsistency does little, if anything, to impeach a witness's credibility. If the inconsistency relates to the subject matter of the lawsuit, however, it provides a reason to be wary generally of the witness's testimony. The inconsistency, regardless of which statement is true, suggests either that the witness is willing intentionally to lie about the subject matter of the litigation or at least that the witness has been careless and inaccurate in reporting information important to the resolution of the litigation.

i.   The Risk of Improper "Substantive" Use.   When an inconsistent statement relates to an issue in the lawsuit, there is, of course, the possibility that the jury will consider the statement not merely for its impeachment value but also for its truth. The risk of improper use is a danger of unfair prejudice within the scope of FRE 403. This risk of unfair prejudice, however, will seldom, if ever, be a basis for exclusion of the evidence. Inconsistent statements about the issues in the lawsuit are likely to be more probative for impeachment purposes than inconsistent statements about unrelated matters. Thus, the most prejudicial inconsistent statements are also the most probative for their impeachment value. As you know, the FRE 403 balancing test favors admissibility. Thus, the FRE 403 unfair prejudice argument is not likely to succeed unless the objecting party can show some way in which the statement at issue is likely to be uniquely prejudicial in comparison to other inconsistent statements. For a rare example of a case holding that prior inconsistent statements should have been excluded because their impeachment value was outweighed by the risk that the jury would use the statements for their truth, see United States v. Logan, 121 F.3d 1172 (8th Cir. 1997). Cf. United States v. Young, 248 F.3d 260, 268 (4th Cir. 2001) (probative value of witness's ambiguous responses to questions (e.g., "uhm-hmm") outweighed by risk that jury would consider truth of matters asserted in questions).

ii.   Loss of Memory and Inconsistency.   There is at least one type of situation in which an FRE 403 unfair prejudice argument should have a reasonable chance of succeeding. If a witness who testifies to a lack of memory about an event has made a prior statement about the event, some courts view the claimed current loss of memory and the prior statement as inconsistent with each other. When it is reasonable to regard the loss of memory as feigned and, therefore, tantamount to a denial of the earlier statement, the characterization of the statements as inconsistent is reasonable. To the extent that the claimed loss of current memory seems plausible, however, there is no inconsistency between the witness's testimony and the prior statement. United States v. DeSimone, 488 F.3d 561, 572 (1st Cir. 2007) (not abuse of discretion to find no inconsistency between prior statement and trial testimony because it was "not implausible" that the witness did not recall a conversation that took place five years before trial). Thus, the prior statement has relatively low probative value for its legitimate impeachment use, but there is no reduction in the likelihood that the jury will consider the prior statement for its truth.

iii.   Inconsistent Statements About Collateral Matters.   Sometimes a witness's alleged inconsistent statement will be about a collateral matter — a matter that is wholly unrelated to the issues in the case. If an inconsistent statement is about a collateral matter, its probative value may be so low that on at least some occasions the FRE 403 efficiency concerns should require its exclusion. Consider, for example, a situation in which George sees an automobile accident as he is leaving a movie theater. A month later, in an interview with an insurance investigator, George states that he had been going to the theater every night the week of the accident because there was a Bogart festival. He further relates that he had seen *Casablanca* on the night of the accident. (Which Bogart movie George saw may be technically irrelevant to the issues in the case, but it is not unusual for a witness to include such details as part of a narrative of events.) At the trial George's testimony is consistent with his earlier statement in every respect except that he says he had seen *Key Largo* on the night of the accident. Assume that there is no dispute about what night the accident occurred and that it was the night that *Key Largo* was shown. Assume further that everyone concedes that there was not an accident on the night *Casablanca* was shown. Despite the facts that the inconsistency is collateral to the issues in the case and that it seems plausible that a person might have conflicting memories about which of two Bogart movies was showing on a particular night during the Bogart festival, one might want to permit the impeaching party to examine George about the inconsistency. The very low probative value of the evidence, however, may not warrant the consumption of time required to call an additional witness to offer extrinsic evidence of the inconsistency. Indeed, this is the result mandated by a common law rule that prohibited extrinsic evidence of an inconsistent statement about a collateral matter. Moreover, some federal courts have specifically adopted this rule. United States v. Grooms, 978 F.2d 425 (8th Cir. 1992); United States v. Tarantino, 846 F.2d 1384, 1409-1410 (D.C. Cir. 1998) (reciting the FRE 403 discretionary balancing test as authority).

Despite the cases approving the "collateralness" doctrine, the admissibility of extrinsic evidence of inconsistent statements under the Federal Rules should not turn on whether the statements are collateral in some common law sense. Rather, the important question for admissibility should be whether the probative value of the inconsistent statement for its impeachment value is substantially outweighed by countervailing FRE 403 factors. See United States v. Higa, 55 F.3d 448, 452 (9th

Cir. 1995) (court has discretion to admit prior inconsistent statements on collateral matters).

KEY POINTS

1. Prior inconsistent statements may be admissible for the nonhearsay purpose of impeaching the credibility of a witness.

2. FRE 613(b) provides that normally a party may not introduce extrinsic evidence of a prior inconsistent statement unless the witness has an opportunity to explain or deny the statement and opposing counsel has an opportunity to question the witness about the statement.

3. Although FRE 613(b) liberalizes the common law foundation requirement for extrinsic evidence of inconsistent statements, some federal courts prohibit extrinsic evidence if the impeaching party does not call the statement to the witness's attention.

PROBLEMS

7.24. Return to Problem 7.5 at page 367. May the prosecution introduce testimony from a police officer who investigated the burglary that, when he first spoke with Jones the night of burglary, Jones said that he saw someone running from the house at 1251 Hazel Street but that it was dark and he could not see who it was?

7.25. Return to Problem 3.2 at page 136. Assume that Jake O'Leary, an eyewitness, testifies for the defense that Driver did not veer off the roadway onto the gravel shoulder. Plaintiffs' counsel has a written statement from Pam Peters, Jake's former girlfriend, that the evening after the accident Jake said, "That bus driver should have been more careful." Can plaintiffs' attorney ask O'Leary about the statement on cross-examination? If the question is permitted and Jake denies having made the statement, can plaintiff's attorney call Pam to testify that Jake made the statement?

7.26. Ed Macy is charged with felonious assault. He claims not to have been the assailant and will present an alibi defense. During his incarceration prior to trial, Macy's cell mate told him that Wally Wilder had confessed to committing the assault. At trial, Macy calls Wilder as a defense witness, and Wilder denies any involvement in the assault. Can Macy (a) ask Wilder about Wilder's alleged confession to the cell mate or (b) call the cellmate to testify about Wilder's alleged confession?

7.27. Danny Dickson has been charged with murdering a fellow prison inmate. Three inmates testified for the prosecution that Danny committed the murder, and none of them was cross-examined. Later in the trial Danny offered the testimony of two other inmates to the effect that the prosecution witnesses had told them that Danny had not committed the murder. The prosecution objects to this evidence. What result?

7.28. Return again to Problem 3.2 at page 136. Plaintiffs' counsel has located Wanda White, another school bus driver, who had dinner with Driver shortly after the accident. According to White, Driver said that she was going to quit her job because she hated "having to deal with those little brats every day." Can plaintiff's attorney call White to testify to this statement? Does your answer depend upon (a) whether Driver testifies as set forth at page 136, line 4? (b) whether plaintiff's counsel first asks Driver about the statement on cross-examination?

7.29. Review the direct and cross-examination of Officer Huston in the *Johnson* case (page 8, line 2, supra). What was the relevance of defense counsel's questions on cross-examination about whether the incident report prepared by Officer Huston made any reference to an open food port? Would that inquiry be appropriate under the Federal Rules? Would it be appropriate under the Federal Rules to introduce the incident report to show that it contained nothing about the food port?

4.   The Impeachment of Experts with Statements in Treatises

FRE 803(18) contains a relatively broad hearsay exception for learned treatises. The Advisory Committee acknowledged that in part the rationale for this hearsay exception is that it "avoids the unreality of admitting evidence for the purpose of impeachment only, with an instruction to the jury not to consider it otherwise." The hearsay exception, however, does more than merely eliminate the need for a limiting instruction. FRE 803(18) does not require that any particular expert relies on or acknowledges the treatise as authoritative, nor does it require that the statements in the treatise be inconsistent with any expert's testimony. Thus, as other portions of the Advisory Committee Note make clear, the purpose of the exception is to permit affirmative use of statements in learned treatises apart from whatever impeachment value they may have.

5.   Prior Consistent Statements

As we noted at pages 382-383, supra, prior consistent statements may be relevant for two distinct purposes: to prove the truth of their contents, in which case they implicate hearsay concerns, and to rehabilitate or bolster a witness's credibility by demonstrating that the witness has spoken consistently about a matter.

a.   Admissibility for Truth Pursuant to FRE 801(d)(1)(B)

FRE 801(d)(1)(B) exempts from the definition of hearsay a witness's statement that is "consistent with the declarant's testimony and is offered to rebut an express or implied charge that the declarant recently fabricated it or acted from a recent improper influence or motive in so testifying." As we discuss in Chapter Eight at pages 454-456, infra, this rule makes admissible for their truth prior consistent statements that previously were admissible only for the nonhearsay purpose of showing consistency; and as we also discuss there, the Supreme Court in Tome v. United States, 513 U.S. 150 (1995), has interpreted FRE 801(d)(1)(B) narrowly: Only prior consistent statements made prior to the time that a motive to fabricate or an improper influence arose fall within the scope of the rule. Thus, there are many prior consistent statements that cannot be admitted under this hearsay exemption.

b.   Admissibility to Rehabilitate Pursuant to FRE 401-403?

Neither the Federal Rules nor *Tome* explicitly addresses the question whether prior consistent statements that do not satisfy the *Tome*-FRE 801(d)(1)(B) criteria may

nonetheless be admissible, not for their truth but for the *nonhearsay* purpose of rehabilitating a witness. If the answer is yes, the party against whom the evidence is admitted would be entitled to a limiting instruction.

**i.   Putting Inconsistent Statements in Context Following Impeachment
with Prior Inconsistent Statement.**   When a witness has been impeached with prior
inconsistent statements, the uniform view is that contemporaneous prior consistent
statements not satisfying the criteria of FRE 801(d)(1)(B) may be admissible to clarify
or explain the alleged inconsistency. For example, in United States v. Denton, 246
F.3d 784 (6th Cir. 2001), after the defendant impeached a prosecution witness with
specific portions of a prior statement that he claimed were inconsistent with the witness's testimony, the prosecutor was permitted to show portions of the prior statement
that were consistent with the testimony. This view is consistent with both the principle of completeness in FRE 106 and the FRE 613(b) requirement that a witness
have an opportunity to explain or deny an inconsistent statement. See also United
States v. Wells, 623 F.3d 332 (6th Cir. 2010) (prior consistent statements of prosecution witnesses admissible during direct examination when defense counsel suggested
improper motive and recent fabrication during opening statement).

ii.   Rehabilitation with Consistent Statements in Other Contexts.   In other
contexts courts are divided on the question of whether FRE 801(d)(1)(B) regulates
the use of prior consistent statements offered to rehabilitate witnesses. According to
one view, FRE 801(d)(1)(B) governs the use of prior consistent statements for both
hearsay and rehabilitation purposes; if the statement is not admissible for its truth, it is
not admissible to rehabilitate. United States v. Miller, 874 F.2d 1255, 1273 (9th Cir.
1989); United States v. Quinto, 582 F.2d 224 (2d Cir. 1978). This view holds that the
primary objective of FRE 801(d)(1)(B) is to eliminate the need for a limiting instruction when prior consistent statements are admissible. To state the matter somewhat
differently, the objective is to make all consistent statements admissible for their truth.
Thus, there will never be an occasion to admit a prior consistent statement and tell
the jury it may not consider the statement for its truth.
     The contrary view is that FRE 801(d)(1)(B) is nothing more than a hearsay
exemption. United States v. Ellis, 121 F.3d 908 (4th Cir. 1997). Since there is no rule
restricting the use of prior consistent statements for nonhearsay purposes, the admissibility of prior consistent statements to rehabilitate should be governed by FRE 401-
403. Thus, there may be times when it is appropriate to introduce — with a limiting
instruction, if requested — a prior consistent statement that does not fall within the
scope of FRE 801(d)(1)(B).
     Here are three examples of consistent statements that are relevant to rehabilitate
a witness on nonhearsay theories of relevance and that would not be admissible for
their truth pursuant to FRE 801(d)(1)(B):

(1) Plaintiff brings an action for negligence as a result of having been exposed to
a potentially fatal chemical. Plaintiff's key witness, a former employee of the defendant, testifies that she caused the exposure. Assume that the defendant establishes that
the witness had been fired immediately after the incident, thereby giving the witness a
motive to fabricate testimony damaging to the defendant. Assume further that the witness's son was exposed to the chemical at the same time and that the witness made a
prior consistent statement two weeks after the firing while admitting the son, who had

just developed symptoms of the exposure, to the hospital. Here, one might reasonably conclude that prior consistent statement made after the motive to fabricate arose rehabilitates the witness because the motive to be truthful about the son's exposure outweighs the motive to fabricate.

(2) If a witness denies making a prior inconsistent statement or denies that it was inconsistent, proof of a prior statement consistent with the witness's trial testimony suggests that the alleged prior inconsistent statement may not have been made or that in context it may not have been as inconsistent as the impeaching party claims it is.

(3) When a party has attacked a witness's character for truthfulness, proof of a prior consistent statement may suggest that the witness's testimony is not behavior in conformity with the supposed dishonest character trait (or it may suggest that the witness is being consistently dishonest).

Do you think the prior consistent statements in the foregoing examples should be admissible? If so, should they be admissible for their truth or only for the limited purpose of rehabilitating the witness?

c.   *Extrinsic Evidence*

If a prior consistent statement is admissible, there is no specific prohibition against or limitation on proof of the statement by extrinsic evidence. Typically, however, a party will be eliciting the statement from the witness who made it, and the witness is likely to be friendly to the examiner. Thus, there will seldom be any need for extrinsic evidence.

KEY POINTS

1. Prior consistent statements offered to rebut an express or implied charge of recent fabrication or improper influence are admissible for their truth pursuant to FRE 801(d)(1)(B) as long as the statements were made before the motive to fabricate arose.

2. Prior consistent statements made in conjunction with allegedly inconsistent statements are admissible to put allegedly inconsistent statements in context even if the consistent statements do not satisfy FRE 801(d)(1)(B).

3. In other contexts, there is a split of authority on the question whether the Federal Rules permit the nonhearsay rehabilitation use of prior consistent statements not falling within FRE 801(d)(1)(B).

PROBLEMS

7.30. Return to Problem 3.2 at page 136. Assume the following occurred on direct examination of Driver after the direct examination set forth at page 136:

Q: Did you drive the bus onto the gravel shoulder?
A: No.
Q: In the days following the accident did you discuss it with anyone?
A: Yes, with my friend Wanda.
Q: And what did you talk about.

A: I told her that I'd been very careful, that I hadn't driven the bus onto the gravel shoulder, and that I felt so sad for those dear little children that I thought I was going to have to quit my job.

Is any of this evidence objectionable? Would your answer be different if this were redirect and if evidence of the "little brats" statement (see Problem 7.28 at page 388) had been elicited on cross-examination? In answering this last question, does it matter whether the discussion with Wanda referred to in Problem 7.28 and the discussion with Wanda referred to here were (a) part of the same conversation or (b) conversations occurring on different days?

7.31. Pam Peters has brought an action for personal injuries against the Ace Department Store for injuries that she claims to have sustained when she fell on some ice in the parking lot on January 23. Peters first consulted an attorney in March, and the suit was filed in April. The trial is taking place the following December. On direct examination Peters testified about the accident, the severe bruises that she suffered, and the continuing backaches and headaches that she has had continually from the day of the injury. During cross-examination defense counsel elicited the fact that Peters did not mention the fall or her alleged injuries when she visited her doctor for a routine checkup on March 1. Later in the trial the defendant offered the testimony of two women who have monthly bridge games with Peters to the effect that Peters said nothing about the fall or any injuries at their bridge games on January 30 and on February 28. Plaintiff objects to the admissibility of this evidence.

In rebuttal, the plaintiff offers the testimony of Ed Peters, Pam Peters's husband, that she told him about the accident on January 23 and that she has frequently mentioned headaches and backaches — at least two or three times a week ever since January 23. The defendant has objected to Ed Peters's testimony.

Should either plaintiff's or the defendant's objection be sustained?

7.32. Return to Problem 3.3 at page 136. On direct examination, Beth Barker testifies for the prosecution that she definitely remembers placing the March 14, 2010, auditor's memo in Ray's "in box" on the afternoon of March 14 and removing it the next day from his "out box," and that Ray's initials were on the memo.

(a)   Consider the following cross-examination of Ms. Barker:

Q: Ms. Barker, on July 10, 2011, you made a statement in my office that was recorded by my assistant, did you not?
A: Yes.
Q: And at that session in my office I asked you some questions about a March 14, 2010, auditor's memo, did I not?
A: Yes.
Q: Isn't it true that I asked you the following questions and you gave the following answers: [reading from the transcript prepared by the assistant]

Q: Ms. Barker, of all the memos you deal with, do you specifically recall the March 14 memorandum from Rundown's auditors?
A: No, I can't say that I recall that specific memo.

Should the prosecutor's objection to defense counsel's reading from the transcript be sustained?

(b) Defense counsel next offers into evidence Exhibit B, an authenticated written statement of Beth Barker dated December 19, 2009, which states (in pertinent part):

I, Beth Barker, declare
    I have removed hundreds of documents from Bernard Ray's "in box" in the years I worked as his secretary.
    I do not have a specific recollection of the March 14, 2010, auditor's memo.
    I declare under penalty of perjury that the foregoing is true and correct to the best of my knowledge.

[signed] Beth Barker

Should the prosecutor's objection to the admission of Exhibit B be sustained?

(c) On cross-examination, defense counsel asks Barker the following:

Q: Ms. Barker, on August 12, 2011, were you arrested for embezzling $250 from a petty cash fund while you were employed at Rundown?
A: Yes.
Q: And when did the alleged embezzlement occur?
A: I don't remember?
Q: Was it before August 1st?
A: I don't remember.
Q: Ms. Barker, isn't it a fact that you made up this story about seeing the signed memo in Bernard Ray's mail box in order to get a deal with the prosecutor on your embezzlement charge?
A: No, that's not true.
DEFENSE COUNSEL: I have no further questions.

On redirect, the prosecutor offers into evidence an authenticated written statement of Beth Barker dated June, 30, 2011, stating that "I recall removing the March 14, 2010, auditor's memo from Mr. Ray's "out box" on March 15, 2010. It had Mr. Ray's initials on it, and I filed it." There is a dispute as to whether the alleged embezzlement occurred before or after June 30.

Should the June 30 statement be admitted over defense counsel's objection?

D.   OTHER IMPEACHMENT TECHNIQUES

Recall that at the outset of the impeachment discussion we described impeachment as the process of attempting to raise doubts about the testimonial abilities of witnesses — that is, to show that the witness is lying, careless with words, imperceptive, or forgetful. The Federal Rules specifically address only two permissible methods for raising these doubts: attacking a witness's character and showing a witness's prior inconsistent statement. The process of impeachment, however, is not so limited. The common law permitted the impeachment of witnesses with evidence of unorthodox religious beliefs, bias, mental or sensory incapacity, and contradiction.

FRE 610 prohibits relying on the content of a witness's religious beliefs to assess credibility: "Evidence of a witness's religious beliefs or opinions is not admissible to attack or support the witness's credibility." For impeachment techniques that the Federal Rules do not specifically address, FRE 401-403 determine the admissibility of evidence.

1.   Bias

a.   Relevance

Courts and commentators frequently attach the label "bias" to what Wigmore identified as three methods of showing a witness's "emotional incapacity." According to Wigmore:

> Three different *kinds of emotion* constituting untrustworthy partiality may be broadly distinguished — bias, interest, and corruption: *Bias*, in common acceptance, covers all varieties of hostility or prejudice against the opponent *personally* or of favor to the proponent personally. [E.g., intimate family relationship with one of the parties.] *Interest* signifies the specific inclination which is apt to be produced by the relation between the witness and the *cause at issue* in the litigation. [E.g., the expectation of favorable treatment from the prosecutor or sentencing judge in return for the testimony.] *Corruption* is here to be understood as the *conscious false intent* which is inferrible from giving or taking a bribe or from expressions of a general unscrupulousness for the case at hand. [E.g., an attempt to bribe another witness or the receipt of money for *testimony*.] The kinds of evidence available are two:
>
> [1]   the *circumstances of the witness' situation*, making it "a priori" probable that he has some partiality of emotion for one party's cause;
> [2]   the *conduct of the witness* himself, indicating the presence of such partiality, the inference here being from the expression of the feeling to the feeling itself.
>
> [3A John Henry Wigmore, Evidence §947, at 782 (James Chadbourn rev. 1970) (emphasis original).]

Proof of any of these types of bias can be particularly effective in discrediting a witness because it is highly probative of insincerity. Compare, for example, the likely impact of a prior inconsistent statement or an FRE 608(b) bad act with proof of a witness's close relationship with or expected favorable treatment from one of the parties. All of us make inconsistent statements at least occasionally, and having a bad character for truthfulness may mean nothing more than that the person is untruthful a bit more often than most people. Neither of these forms of impeachment suggests any particular reason to believe that the witness is being untruthful on the particular occasion of the witness's current testimony. By contrast, the types of bias described by Wigmore suggest a specific, concrete motive for fabricating testimony or at least being less than fully candid.

b. Extrinsic Evidence

In United States v. Abel, 469 U.S. 45 (1984), the Supreme Court upheld the proof of bias with extrinsic evidence under the Federal Rules. The evidence in *Abel* consisted of testimony from a prosecution witness that a defense witness and the defendant were both members of the same secret prison gang that required its members to commit perjury, theft, and murder on each member's behalf. Which type of bias, under Wigmore's analysis, does this suggest? Remember that the prosecution in the *Johnson* case tried to prove that defendant Johnson and his cell mate, Butler, belonged to the same gang outside of prison.

c. Possible FRE 403 Limitations on Extrinsic Evidence of Bias

Despite *Abel*, the right to introduce extrinsic evidence of bias is not automatic under the Federal Rules. Typically, evidence of bias is highly probative, but if the witness fully admits the bias or if the evidence in fact suggests little about the witness's possible bias, a court should probably sustain an FRE 403 objection to extrinsic evidence. United States v. Adams, 799 F.2d 665, 671 (11th Cir. 1986) (extrinsic evidence of bias excluded because bias adequately shown through cross-examination). Evidence of bias may also raise the FRE 403 issue of unfair prejudice. Consider, for example, United States v. Abel, supra:

> Respondent argues that even if the evidence of membership in the prison gang were relevant to show [witness Mills's] bias, the District Court erred in permitting a full description of the gang and its odious tenets . . . .
>
> Respondent specifically contends that the District Court should not have permitted Ehle's precise description of the gang as a lying and murderous group. Respondent suggests that the District Court should have cut off the testimony after the prosecutor had elicited that Mills knew respondent and both may have belonged to an organization together. This argument ignores the fact that the type of organization in which a witness and a party share membership may be relevant to show bias . . . . The attributes of the Aryan Brotherhood — a secret prison sect sworn to perjury and self-protection — bore directly not only on the fact of bias but also on the source and strength of Mills' bias. The tenets of this group showed that Mills had a powerful motive to slant his testimony towards respondent, or even commit perjury outright.
>
> A district court is accorded a wide discretion in determining the admissibility of evidence under the Federal Rules. Assessing the probative value of common membership in any particular group, and weighing any factors counseling against admissibility is a matter first for the district court's sound judgment under Rules 401 and 403 . . . . [469 U.S. at 53-54.]

Some courts also consider whether the witness was given an opportunity to explain or deny the evidence of bias in determining whether extrinsic evidence ought to be admitted. United States v. Betts, 16 F.3d 748, 764 (7th Cir. 1994).

d. Bias Versus Character

A troublesome issue that sometimes arises — particularly with the type of evidence that Wigmore refers to as "corruption" — is whether the evidence should fit within the "bias" category or the "character" category. For example, is proof that the witness attempted to bribe another witness evidence of corruption-bias, or is it evidence of character, or both? Is the evidence of gang membership in *Abel* character evidence or evidence of bias or both? The issue is important because extrinsic evidence of the witness's conduct is admissible to prove bias but not to prove character under FRE 608(b).

The issue is difficult to resolve in part because the term *character* is not defined. Similarly, the contours of *corruption*, which the Advisory Committee's Note to FRE 608 equates with "character" and distinguishes from "bias" and "interest," are not clear. Moreover, it is not clear to what extent one should regard the concepts of character and bias as mutually exclusive or as potentially overlapping. In *Abel* the Court noted that the evidence of gang membership may show a bad character for truthfulness as well as bias. The Court suggested but did not decide that the FRE 608(b) prohibition against extrinsic evidence to prove character should not apply when the evidence is relevant and otherwise admissible to show bias.

To the extent that it is reasonable to infer from the corrupt act that the witness has some particular concern about or interest in the outcome of the present litigation, the evidence has relatively high probative value on the question of whether the witness's testimony is tainted because of this interest. Thus, it seems appropriate to attach the bias label to the evidence in order to permit exploration of the matter with extrinsic evidence. On the other hand, if the *only* reasonable inference to draw from the corrupt act is that the individual has a general lack of integrity or disregard for the truth, the probative value of the evidence to suggest untruthfulness on one specific occasion on the witness stand is relatively low. This evidence should receive the "character" label in order to prevent the possibility of time-consuming and distracting exploration of the matter with extrinsic evidence. In short, as Wigmore observed, "The only distinction that is here legitimate is between conduct indicating a corrupt moral character in general and conduct indicating a specific corrupt intention for the case at hand." 3A John Henry Wigmore, Evidence §963, at 808-810 (James Chadbourn rev. 1970).

KEY POINTS

1. Showing a witness's bias is relevant to impeach the witness's credibility, because the bias suggests a particular reason or motive for the witness to lie or at least be less than completely candid.

2. There is no Federal Rule of Evidence dealing with bias. FRE 401-403 govern admissibility of evidence of bias.

3. Extrinsic evidence of bias is admissible, subject to FRE 403.

PROBLEMS

7.33. Return to Problem 3.2 at page 136. Assume that plaintiff called Nancy Patterson, an accident reconstruction expert, who testified that in her opinion the bus veered on the roadway and was on the gravel shoulder when it hit Paul. Defense counsel has learned that Patterson is receiving a $5,000 fee, that she has testified 10 times on behalf of plaintiffs and only once on behalf of defendants, and that her husband's sister is married to Paul's uncle. Plaintiff's counsel has filed a motion in limine requesting that the court not permit any mention of these matters on the grounds that they are irrelevant and prejudicial. The motion is accompanied by affidavits from Patterson and other accident reconstruction experts stating that a $5,000 fee is in the low to normal range for the work that she has done and an affidavit from Patterson stating that she has not seen or heard from her husband's sister in over five years.

How should the court rule on the motion?

If the court denies the motion, can plaintiffs' counsel call other experts to testify that the fee is in the low to normal range?

7.34. Joan Dominick is being prosecuted for selling and conspiring to sell controlled substances. According to the prosecution's case, the conspiracy has lasted for a number of years and has involved three closely knit families. Joan acknowledges that some members of her family were involved in the conspiracy, and she admits being acquainted with the other alleged co-conspirators. However, she claims that she was not involved in any illegal activity. The principal witness against Joan is Sean Matthews, an acknowledged member of the conspiracy, who has pleaded guilty and entered into a cooperation agreement with the government. According to Sean, Joan supplied him with large quantities of drugs on a number of occasions. On cross-examination, Joan wants to inquire about (a) the extent of Sean's involvement in the conspiracy, (b) his plea, and his cooperation agreement, (c) an occasion five years ago when she rejected his sexual advances and he became angry, and (d) a 10-year-old drug scam in which Sean lost $30,000 and claimed (incorrectly, according to Joan) that Joan was responsible for defrauding him. How much of this inquiry should the court permit?

7.35. Stella Starlet is a rising movie star, rock singer, and television personality. She has sued Frances Fisher, her former manager and agent, for fraud and breach of contract. Stella's services were in great demand, and according to the complaint Fisher would negotiate contracts only with individuals willing to pay a substantial sum, above the negotiated contract amount, in cash directly to Frances. One of Stella's key witnesses is Ken Olsen, a former employee of Fisher. Olsen testified in detail about Fisher's demanding and receiving sums to book Stella that were never accounted for. The following cross-examination of Olsen took place without objection:

Q: Do you know Stella Starlet personally?
A: Yes.
Q: You're quite fond of her, aren't you?
A: Well, I like her and respect her.
Q: You feel indebted to her, don't you?
A: Indebted? No.
Q: Isn't it true that in the two months prior to this trial she has taken you to dinner at expensive restaurants on at least seven occasions?
A: No, she has never done that.
Q: And isn't it true that last month she bought you diamond cuff links and a new set of expensive golf clubs?
A: No.
Q: Two weeks ago when you were having lunch with your friend Tom Thompson at the River Edge Cafe, didn't you tell Thompson that Stella had taken you to dinner seven times in the last two months and that she had bought you diamond cuff links and new golf clubs?
A: No.

As part of its defense, the defendant calls Tom Thompson to testify that two weeks ago at the River Edge Cafe, Ken Olsen was bragging that he had had dinner with Stella Starlet on seven occasions in the last two months and that she recently bought him diamond cuff links and new golf clubs. Should this evidence be admitted over plaintiff's objection?

7.36. Joyce Addison has filed a racial discrimination in employment suit against State University, which recently fired her. On cross-examination of Joyce can the university ask about allegations of racial discrimination that she made against two previous university employers?

2.   Mental or Sensory Incapacity

a.   Relevance

Any sensory or mental deficiency that inhibits a witness's ability to perceive events accurately at the time they occur or to remember and to narrate accurately what happened at the time of trial is relevant to cast doubt on the witness's credibility. Thus, for example, it is relevant to prove that a witness suffers from faulty memory; some form of mental illness that contributes to a witness's inability to distinguish fact from fantasy; intoxication at the time of the event to which the testimony relates or while on the witness stand; or color blindness if accuracy with respect to color is important. Indeed, any fact relating to the witness's general testimonial capacities for narration, perception, and memory or about the exercise of these capacities on the occasion in question is relevant to impeach the witness. Subject to a court's discretion to control the mode of cross-examination (FRE 611(a)) and to FRE 403, it is permissible to inquire about these matters during the examination of the witness whose sensory or mental condition is at issue. United States v. Robinson, 583 F.3d 1265 (10th Cir. 2009) (reversible error to exclude evidence about prosecution witness's mental health, prescription medication use, and auditory hallucinations); United States v. Pryce, 938 F.2d 1343, 1345 (D.C. Cir. 1991) (prejudicial error to limit questions about witness's hallucinations to the time frame of the events about which witness testified); United States v. DiPaola, 804 F.2d 225, 229-230 (2d Cir. 1986) (permissible to exclude questions about witness's drinking problem in the absence of any showing that witness was under the influence at the time of the events or when giving testimony); Roberts v. Hollocher, 664 F.2d 200, 203 (8th Cir. 1981) (questions about Roberts's drug use permissible because they were "relevant to Roberts' physical state at the time of the alleged incidents and to his ability to accurately recall those incidents").

b.   Extrinsic Evidence

In addition to making inquiry on cross-examination, parties may introduce extrinsic evidence of a witness's mental or sensory incapacity. Courts traditionally have regarded such evidence as showing something different from a moral incapacity or character trait. Thus, the restrictions on the proof of character are not applicable. As a result, for example, courts have permitted extrinsic evidence of such matters as strange, seemingly irrational acts of a witness, expert testimony from a psychiatrist about a witness's mental capacity, and courtroom experiments to demonstrate a witness's poor memory or eyesight.

It is appropriate to decide on a case-by-case basis how extensive a cross-examination to permit and how much, if any, extrinsic evidence to introduce about a witness's sensory or mental incapacity. The Federal Rules take this approach. In the absence of any exclusionary rule, admissibility decisions should turn on the application of FRE 401-403 and, if expert testimony is offered, FRE 702-706.

c.   Mental Incapacity as a Bar to Testimony

In considering an individual's mental incapacity it is important not to confuse mental incapacity as a subject matter for impeachment with mental incapacity as a complete bar to testimony. Early in the development of the common law, courts barred individuals regarded as mentally deranged or defective from testifying. As we discussed in Chapter Four, FRE 601 now presumes that every person is competent to be a witness, including a person with mental illness. If an individual's mental condition prevents the individual from understanding the oath or the obligation to testify truthfully, however, that would be a legitimate reason for refusing to let the individual testify.

KEY POINTS

1. Courts regard a witness's sensory or mental incapacity as something different from a character trait. Thus, impeachment on these grounds is not limited by FRE 404 or FRE 608. Indeed, there is no Federal Rule dealing specifically with this form of impeachment.

2. FRE 401-403 and, if expert testimony is involved, FRE 702-706 govern proof of a witness's sensory or mental incapacity.

PROBLEMS

7.37. Al Drummond has been charged with possession and sale of cocaine. The key government witness is Jimmy Jones, an informant and, according to the government, a former co-conspirator in drug trafficking with Drummond. Jones had already pleaded guilty and been sentenced for his involvement in the drug incident for which Drummond is on trial. On cross-examination of Jones, defense counsel (with a factual basis for each question) asks:

(a)   "Isn't it true that you are a heroin addict?"
(b)   "Isn't it true that you are under the influence of heroin right now on the witness stand?"
(c)   "Isn't it true that last week you sold two ounces of heroin to James Edwards?"

Are any of these questions objectionable? If objections are not made or are overruled, can the defendant later introduce extrinsic evidence to prove that Jones is an addict? Was under the influence of heroin on the witness stand? Sold heroin last week to James Edwards?

The defense calls as a witness Dr. Helen James, who is qualified as an expert on mental disorders. She offers to testify that she recently diagnosed Jimmy Jones as suffering from AKSS syndrome, a severe mental disorder. Should plaintiff's objection to this evidence be sustained?

7.38. Return to Problem 5.38 at page 293. If the court rules that the evidence is not admissible substantively, may the defendant nonetheless introduce the expert testimony to impeach Haywood's credibility?

3.   Contradiction

a.   Relevance

The last traditional method of impeaching a witness's credibility is by means of contradiction — that is, introducing evidence that contradicts something the witness has said. For example, if the witness said that she was wearing a yellow dress when she saw the automobile accident, it would contradict her testimony to establish that she was wearing a blue dress on that occasion; and if one can establish that a witness is incorrect about one thing, it is arguably appropriate to infer that the witness may be wrong about other things, including perhaps the substantively important aspects of the witness's testimony.

As Wigmore observed:

> The peculiar feature of [the] probative fact of error on a particular point [i.e., contradiction] is its *deficiency with respect to definiteness* and its *wide range with respect to possible significance*. Looking back over the various [impeachment devices] already considered, it will be seen that the evidence in those classes of cases was aimed clearly and specifically at a particular defect; it showed either that or nothing. Former perjury would indicate probably a deficient sense of moral duty to speak truth; relationship to the party, a probable inclination to distort the facts, consciously or unconsciously . . . .
>
> [Evidence of contradiction] is not offered as definitely showing any specific defect of any of these kinds, and yet it may justify an inference of the existence of any one or more of them. We know simply that an erroneous statement has been made on one point, and we infer that the witness is capable of making an erroneous statement on other points. We are not asked, and we do not attempt to specify, the particular defect which was the source of the proved error and which might therefore be the source of another error. The source might be a mental defect as to powers of observation or recollection; it might be a lack of veracity character; it might be bias or corruption . . . . The inference is only that since, for this proved error, there was *some unspecified defect* which became a source of error, the same defect may equally exist as the source of some other error, otherwise not apparent. [3A John Henry Wigmore, Evidence §1000, at 957-958 (James Chadbourn rev. 1970) (emphasis original).]

All of us, of course, from time to time make erroneous statements that can be contradicted. Thus, at least in the absence of showing many contradictions by the same witness, see id. §1000, at 958, proof of contradictions about matters unrelated to the issues being litigated — for example, that the witness in the preceding example was wearing a blue dress instead of a yellow dress — are often of only marginal probative value to impeach the witness's credibility.

b. Extrinsic Evidence

FRE 401-403 govern the admissibility of evidence of contradiction, and as is the case with evidence of sensory or mental defects, courts applying FRE 403 may permit cross-examination but exclude extrinsic evidence to prove the contradiction if the contradiction appears to have little probative value to impeach the witness. For example, in our blue dress hypothetical, a court may permit some cross-examination about the color of the witness's dress, but if the witness does not admit being wrong about the color of her dress, the court may not permit the impeaching party to establish the contradiction with extrinsic evidence by calling other witnesses to testify that the dress was in fact blue. The color of the witness's dress is not relevant to any issue in the case; and although it is not uncommon for witnesses to include irrelevant details in their testimony, contradicting such matters is typically not very probative of how reliable the witness's testimony is on relevant, disputed facts. Thus, under FRE 403, it will seldom if ever be worth the time and risk of confusing the jury to prove these contradictions with extrinsic evidence. As we observed earlier, all of us occasionally make statements that are subject to contradiction, and as the Wigmore excerpt points out it is seldom clear precisely what testimonial deficiency a contradiction shows.

c. The "No Extrinsic Evidence to Impeach on a Collateral Matter" Doctrine

At common law the admissibility of extrinsic evidence to contradict a witness was governed by the general principle that one may not introduce extrinsic evidence to impeach on a collateral matter. This is the same principle that we mentioned earlier in discussing extrinsic evidence of prior inconsistent statements, at pages 387-388, supra. For example, in the blue dress hypothetical, the collateralness doctrine would require exclusion of extrinsic evidence contradicting the witness's testimony that she had been wearing a yellow dress and also extrinsic evidence of a prior inconsistent statement in which she stated that she had been wearing a blue dress at the time of the accident. The color of the dress is collateral in that it has no bearing on an issue in the case.

We offer an examination of the collateralness doctrine here for two reasons. First, although the Federal Rules do not mention the collateralness doctrine, some federal courts have adopted and apply it both in the contradiction context, United States v. Catalan-Roman, 585 F.3d 453, 469 (1st Cir. 2009), and in the inconsistent statement context, United States v. Grooms, 978 F.2d 425 (8th Cir. 1992). Second, mastering the collateralness doctrine requires focusing on the inferential process involved in the use of evidence that contracts a witness, and this focus is critical to a reasoned, persuasive argument about admissibility in FRE 403 terms.

i. What Is Not Collateral Generally. Whether extrinsic evidence is collateral and therefore inadmissible pursuant to the collateralness doctrine is not always intuitively obvious. Three types of facts are *not* collateral:

(1) facts relevant to the substantive issues in the case;
(2) facts relevant, apart from the contradiction, to impeach the credibility of a witness, if extrinsic evidence is generally admissible for the noncontradiction impeachment purpose; and

(3)   facts recited by the witness that, if untrue, logically undermine the witness's story.

See 1 McCormick on Evidence § 49, at 232-38 (Kenneth S. Broun ed., 6th ed., 2006).

ii.   Evidence That Is Directly Relevant to the Issues in Litigation.   Evidence that is directly relevant to substantive issues can be introduced for its substantive value apart from any impeachment value that it may have. In effect, the impeachment value of the evidence is secondary. As we stated earlier, if evidence is independently admissible, there is no need to consider whether it is also admissible for impeachment purposes.

iii.   Evidence That Impeaches a Witness Apart from Contradiction.   The collateralness doctrine should not prohibit the use of extrinsic evidence that both contradicts the witness and also impeaches credibility in some other way, as long as it is clear that extrinsic evidence would be admissible for that independent impeachment purpose (e.g., to prove bias or a prior conviction). On the other hand, if a specific impeachment rule prohibits extrinsic evidence as FRE 608(b) does, it would undermine that prohibition to admit extrinsic evidence on the theory that the evidence contradicts the witness. Consider for example, the impact of a contrary rule with respect to FRE 608(b). In every case in which the witness denied committing a bad act, the proponent of the extrinsic evidence could argue that extrinsic evidence of the bad act was being offered not to prove character for untruthfulness but to show a contradiction. If that argument were accepted, the prohibition against extrinsic evidence in FRE 608(b) would become meaningless.

iv.   Evidence That Logically Undermines a Witness's Story.   Contradictions that logically undermine the witness's story are also considered noncollateral. To illustrate this third category, consider a personal injury action in which Sadie testifies for the plaintiff and explains that she happened to see the accident as she was walking home from the grocery store where she had gone to purchase milk for her children. Proof that Sadie bought beer instead of milk would contradict her story, but such proof would not logically undermine her testimony. What she bought is collateral. Thus, on cross-examination counsel could question Sadie about what she bought, but the counsel would have to accept her answers; extrinsic evidence would be inadmissible. On the other hand, evidence that Sadie had not been in the area of the grocery store at all suggests that she may not have seen the critical events to which she testified. Just as there would be no general prohibition against extrinsic evidence that Sadie was almost blind, there should be no prohibition against the use of extrinsic evidence suggesting that Sadie might not physically have been in a position to observe what she claimed to have seen. In short, proof that Sadie had not been near the grocery store on the day of the accident tends logically to undermine her story about the accident. Thus, it should not be regarded as collateral, and extrinsic evidence of her absence from the store should be admissible.

v.   A Test for "Collateralness."   There is a commonly stated test for collateralness that, if properly understood and applied, is consistent with all we have said so far: Could the fact have been proven with extrinsic evidence for any purpose except to show a (mere) contradiction? If the answer is yes, if, in other words, there is some relevant, permissible use for extrinsic evidence above and beyond its value as showing a mere contradiction, it is not collateral. On the other hand, if the only permissible purpose for offering the evidence is to prove a contradiction, the extrinsic evidence is collateral. Thus, for example, in our preceding illustrations it would not be collateral to prove by extrinsic evidence (a) a prior conviction that the witness denied, (b) facts constituting bias that the witness denied, (c) substantively relevant events that the witness denied, or (d) Sadie's absence from the grocery store. It would be collateral to prove (a) that the witness was wearing a blue dress instead of a yellow dress, (b) that the witness falsely denied committing a dishonest act, or (c) that Sadie bought beer.

KEY POINTS

1. Proving a contradiction is relevant to cast doubt on the credibility of a witness. FRE 401 and 403 govern the admissibility of evidence for this purpose.

2. Rather than invoking FRE 401-403, some federal courts rely on the common law prohibition against the use of extrinsic evidence to impeach on a collateral matter to exclude extrinsic evidence that contradicts a witness on a collateral matter. Extrinsic evidence is collateral if the fact that the evidence establishes cannot be proven with extrinsic evidence for any purpose other than to show the contradiction.

3. In most cases proper application of FRE 403 would probably lead to the same result as the common law prohibition against extrinsic evidence to contradict on a collateral matter.

PROBLEMS

7.39. Return to Problem 7.5 at page 367. For the following evidence, may the prosecution (1) question Jones about it during cross-examination, and (2) introduce extrinsic evidence if he denies it:

(a)   that Jones had ten beers at the Pub;
(b)   that the woman he was speaking with at the Pub was wearing a red dress;
(c)   that Jones left the Pub at 11:00 P.M.?

7.40. Dan Duncan is charged with possession of cocaine with intent to distribute. After the prosecution has completed its case, Duncan testifies that he works with disabled children and would not smuggle drugs for a million dollars; and he portrays himself as an anti-drug counselor who teaches kids to stay away from drugs. In its rebuttal case, can the prosecution offer witnesses to testify that (a) Duncan has been arrested for possessing cocaine and (b) Duncan sold them cocaine?

7.41. Return to Problem 3.2 at page 136. Assume that Eddie Keller, a 13-year-old who had been on the bus with Paul, testifies for the plaintiff that Driver veered onto the gravel shoulder and hit Paul. Plaintiff's counsel then asks Eddie what happened next and he replies, "I don't know. I was scared. I went straight home and stayed in my room until supper." Defense counsel has learned from Jim Tobin, one of Eddie's classmates, that Eddie did not go straight home. Instead, he went to the local playground where he found Jim and beat him up in order to settle an argument that had developed earlier in the day. Can defense counsel ask Eddie about the incident with Jim? If there is no objection and Eddie denies the incident, can defense counsel call Jim to testify that Eddie beat him up?

7.42. See Problem 7.41. After beating up Jim, Eddie went to the corner drug store, where he was caught trying to steal comic books and candy. Can defense counsel ask Eddie about this incident? If there is no objection and Eddie denies the attempted theft, can defense counsel call Mark Manning, the druggist, to testify about what happened?

7.43. Defendant is charged with a liquor store robbery that occurred Sunday shortly after noon. To establish an alibi, W_1 testifies for Defendant as follows: "On Sunday morning at 12:15 P.M., as I was walking out of church, I observed Defendant across the street." (Other testimony establishes that the church and the liquor store are at opposite ends of the city.) W_2 offers to testify for the prosecution that on Sunday morning at about 12:15 P.M. he saw W_1 walking out of an all-night bar. Defendant objects to this evidence on the ground that its admission would violate (a) FRE 608(b)'s prohibition against extrinsic evidence of specific instances of conduct, (b) the general prohibition against the use of extrinsic evidence to impeach on a collateral matter, and (c) FRE 403. How should the court rule?

7.44. Daniels is charged with selling cocaine to an undercover police officer. Daniels testified on direct examination that he did not sell the drugs. He further testified that at the time of the alleged sale he had been playing dice with several other people, one of whom periodically left the game and returned with cash. Daniels suggested that the companion was the seller and that the undercover officer identified the wrong person. On cross-examination, the prosecutor asked if Daniels had actually seen the companion sell the cocaine. Daniels responded negatively. The prosecutor then asked Daniels if he was familiar with cocaine, and Daniels responded that he had never seen cocaine.

The prosecutor knows that Daniels tested positively for cocaine use three times in the last two years. Can the prosecutor inquire about these matters on cross-examination or introduce extrinsic evidence of the tests?

E.   REFLECTION ON THE IMPEACHMENT PROCESS

In our initial discussion of the difference in the inferential process between using evidence for impeachment purposes and using evidence for substantive purposes, we used two examples of situations in which evidence is relevant for both substantive and impeachment purposes but potentially admissible only for the latter purpose. See pages 354-355, supra. One involved a witness's inconsistent statement not under oath about the color of a traffic light at the time of an automobile accident. On direct examination the witness testified that the light was red. The inconsistent statement was that the light was green. The other example involved a prior conviction for perjury by a defendant-witness who was charged with perjury. In both examples the permissible impeachment use of the evidence involves an inferential chain of reasoning that arrives at an essential element in the case by a route that is more circuitous than the chain of reasoning required to make the evidence relevant for its prohibited substantive purpose: This circuitous route requires the fact finder to make an inference that what the witness says is not reliable.

The Inconsistent Statement Case. Because of the hearsay rule the witness's inconsistent statement is not admissible as a direct assertion that can be relied on to prove that the light was green. The statement is admissible, however, because its inconsistency suggests fabrication or lack of care in making the statement that the light was red. Thus, the witness may have been unreliable in claiming that light was red. And, if it was not red, it must have been some other color — green, or perhaps yellow.

The Perjury Case. Because of FRE 404(b) the witness-defendant's prior perjury conviction is not admissible as evidence of the defendant's character for untruthfulness to prove directly that the defendant lied at the time of the alleged perjury. The conviction is admissible, however, to suggest that the defendant is an untruthful person who may be lying on the witness stand. Thus, the defendant may have been unreliable in denying the alleged perjury. This leaves as the alternative the proposition that the defendant committed the perjury as charged.

What justifies permitting the jury to take the circuitous route but not the direct route to the same conclusion? Even if there is a reasonable answer to the preceding question, do you believe that trial judges are capable of instructing juries on the distinction and that jurors are capable of comprehending and acting on the instruction?

If the distinction between the impeachment use and the substantive use of a prior inconsistent statement or a prior perjury conviction is not one that judges and juries are likely to be able to appreciate and understand, there is a fundamental problem with our current approach to "impeachment" evidence. Moreover, it is a problem that, at least in practice, is not adequately addressed by the balancing process of FRE 403: In the overwhelming number of cases in which there is more than very marginal impeachment value to evidence that is inadmissible substantively, it will be admitted with limiting instructions. For example, in the perjury hypothetical, the defendant is entitled to an instruction that the prior perjury conviction is admissible only to impeach the credibility of the defendant as a witness and that it is not proper to infer that because the defendant committed perjury once before it is more likely that the defendant committed perjury on the occasion in question. If we are serious about the "substantive" prohibitions, we should not be so ready to admit for impeachment purposes evidence that in theory is inadmissible for substantive purposes; or if we want to admit evidence for impeachment purposes that theoretically is not admissible substantively, we need to rethink the desirability of the substantive prohibitions.

One possibility would be to retain the current distinctions between impeachment and substantive uses of evidence only for the purpose of deciding whether or at what point evidence will be admissible. In other words, specific acts would still be inadmissible as part of a prosecutor's case-in-chief to prove character to show action in conformity with character, and unsworn prior statements would initially be inadmissible for their truth. However, if this type of evidence gains enough added relevance from its impeachment value that it should be admissible for that purpose, it should be admissible for whatever probative value it has for any matter of consequence in the litigation. The primary benefit of this proposal is that it would eliminate often confusing and difficult-to-follow limiting instructions.

CHAPTER EIGHT

THE HEARSAY RULE

The general rule excluding hearsay is one of the hallmarks of the Anglo-American law of evidence. It establishes as a general proposition that when statements are made by people outside of court, those statements are not admissible when offered to prove the truth of the matters asserted therein. But recall the excerpt from Thayer's Treatise quoted in Chapter Three: "[T]he law has come into the shape of a set of primary rules of exclusion; and then a set of exceptions to these rules. . . ." James Bradley Thayer, A Preliminary Treatise on Evidence at Common Law 26 (1898). The hearsay rule illustrates this principle. FRE 802 is the primary rule of exclusion. It is, however, subject to 29 exceptions and 8 exemptions pursuant to which many kinds of hearsay statements are admitted.

We will examine the exemptions in Section C and the exceptions in Sections D, E, and F of this chapter. Initially, however, it is important to understand what hearsay is, how it is defined, and what justifies its exclusion from the fact-finding process of trial. Remember that the classification of evidence as hearsay or not hearsay is not necessarily determinative of admissibility. Evidence of an out-of-court statement that is not hearsay may be inadmissible for some other reason (e.g., privilege), and evidence that is hearsay may be admissible under one of the exemptions or exceptions. Your desire ultimately to admit or exclude a particular out-of-court statement should not influence your initial analysis of whether that statement falls within the definition of the exclusionary rule.

A. THE GENERAL RULE OF EXCLUSION AND THE DEFINITION OF HEARSAY

Exclusion of hearsay requires a test that judges apply to individual items of evidence. Under FRE 801(c), hearsay is a statement offered "to prove the truth of the matter asserted." This brief definition of hearsay is deceptively simple. Its application will require an understanding of the reasons for the hearsay prohibition — reasons that are captured only imperfectly in any brief doctrinal definition.

1.   FRE 801 and 802

RULE 801.   DEFINITIONS THAT APPLY TO THIS ARTICLE; EXCLUSIONS FROM HEARSAY

(a) *Statement.* "Statement" means a person's oral assertion, written assertion, or non-verbal conduct, if the person intended it as an assertion.

(b) *Declarant.* "Declarant" means the person who made the statement.

(c) *Hearsay.* "Hearsay" means a statement that

(1) declarant does not make while testifying at the current trial or hearing; and

(2) a party offers in evidence to prove the truth of the matter asserted in the statement.

(d) *Statements That Are Not Hearsay.* A statement that meets the following conditions is not hearsay:

(1) *A Declarant-Witness's Prior Statement.* The declarant testifies and is subject to cross-examination about a prior statement, and the statement:

(A) is inconsistent with the declarant's testimony and was given under penalty of perjury at a trial, hearing, or other proceeding or in a deposition;

(B) is consistent with the declarant's testimony and is offered to rebut an express or implied charge that the declarant recently fabricated it or acted from a recent improper influence or motive in so testifying; or

(C) identifies a person as someone the declarant perceived earlier.

(2) *An Opposing Party's Statement.* The statement is offered against an opposing party and:

(A) was made by the party in an individual or representative capacity;

(B) is one the party manifested that it adopted or believed to be true;

(C) was made by a person whom the party authorized to make a statement on the subject;

(D) was made by the party's agent or employee on a matter within the scope of that relationship and while it existed; or

(E) was made by the party's co-conspirator during and in furtherance of the conspiracy.

The statement must be considered but does not by itself establish the declarant's authority under (C); the existence or scope of the relationship under (D); or the existence of the conspiracy or participation in it under (E).

RULE 802.   THE RULE AGAINST HEARSAY

Hearsay is not admissible unless any of the following provides otherwise:
- a federal statute;
- these rules; or
- other rules prescribed by the Supreme Court.

(Our initial discussion focuses on FRE 801(a)-(c) and 802. We discuss FRE 801(d) in Section C.)

2.   Interpretation and Illustration of FRE 801 and 802

To appreciate the significance of the general rule of exclusion, consider that a friend of yours, Sally, tells you that she saw a gray SUV run through a red light and hit a pedestrian. Would you believe Sally? Would you rely on her information? If you know that Sally is a trustworthy person, and that she usually is a careful observer of things and has a good memory, you would probably have little reason to doubt what she says. You would view Sally as a reliable source of information about the accident. We learn many useful things about people, events and conditions from what others tell us.

Sally's knowledge about the accident would be particularly useful in a lawsuit brought by the pedestrian against the driver of the SUV. Sally herself could be called as a *witness*. In response to a question about what she saw, she would testify, "On June 1, I observed the gray SUV run a red light and hit a pedestrian." Or, if Sally made this same statement to her friend George after the accident, George could then be called as a witness and could testify about what Sally told him: "On June 2, Sally told me that on June 1 she had seen a gray SUV run a red light and hit a pedestrian." Sally's own testimony would be welcome in any courtroom in America. But George's testimony would be excluded by the hearsay rule. Why? Apply the terms of FRE 801(a)-(c): George's testimony describes (1) a *statement* (an "oral assertion"); (2) the statement is made by a *declarant* (Sally is "the person who made the statement"); (3) the statement was *not* made by Sally *while testifying at the current trial or hearing*; and (4) the statement is being offered by the pedestrian *to prove the truth of the matter asserted by the declarant* (that the gray SUV ran the red light). Thus, Sally's statement is *hearsay* and George's testimony about that statement would be inadmissible under FRE 802.

Notice that the term *hearsay* applies to Sally's statement because when she made it she was an out-of-court declarant; the hearsay rule operates to exclude evidence of that statement no matter how it is presented in court — through testimony such as George's, through a letter Sally wrote to George, through a tape recording of Sally speaking to George, or even if Sally testified about her own out-of-court statement. And, by the way, there is no traditionally recognized hearsay exception that would admit Sally's out-of-court statement.

a. The Relevancy of Sally's Testimony Depends on Generalizations About Sally's Testimonial Qualities

Why should Sally's statement of belief about the gray SUV be admitted if Sally says it in court as a witness, but be excluded if George reports her statement to the jury? The answer to this question, which involves an explication of hearsay policy, begins with relevancy. Under FRE 401, Sally's testimony as a witness is offered to prove that it is more likely that the SUV did run the red light and hit a pedestrian. We know from our study of impeachment in Chapter Seven that inferences about Sally's narration, sincerity, perception, and memory are necessary to connect her statements to the fact of consequence. These inferences about Sally's four testimonial qualities, and the generalizations that underlie them, are shown in Diagram 8-1. The final inference — from the accuracy of Sally's belief to the conclusion about the event itself — is an inference that does not rest on a generalization about one of Sally's testimonial qualities. Rather, it expresses the assumption underlying the model of rational fact-finding, that people's beliefs about the world can and do correspond to reality.

It is possible that, contrary to the generalizations articulated in Diagram 8-1, Sally did not speak accurately and honestly, or did not perceive accurately or remember

Diagram 8-1

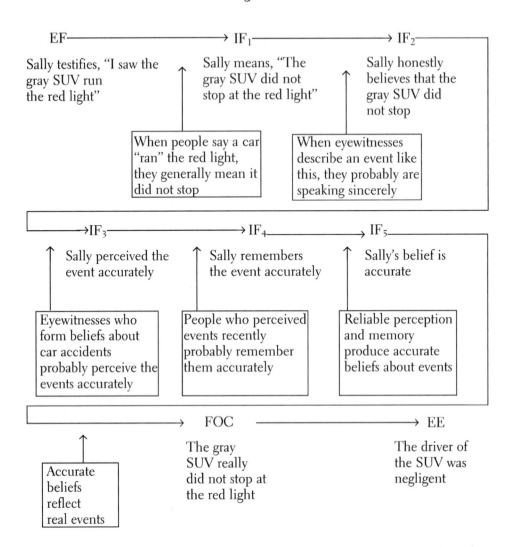

accurately the event involving the SUV. If this is so, then relying on her belief about this event generates risks of error. We refer to these risks as *testimonial dangers*, or *hearsay dangers* when an out-of-court statement is being considered.

If Sally has mistakenly used the wrong words (a *narration* danger), then the SUV that she saw may be green, not gray. A narration problem may exist if speakers mistakenly use incorrect words or carelessly omit a critical word. An *ambiguity* danger exists if it is unclear from the context what the speaker is intending to assert. For example, if a person says, "Jon had a great catch," is the reference to fishing or baseball? The answer may be clear from the context within which the statement is made, but ambiguity problems arise when the hearer or reader misinterprets what the speaker is thinking and communicating. Thus, even when Sally is sincere, narration and ambiguity dangers mean that an inference from her words to what she means to say — IF₁ in the Diagram 8-1 — may be incorrect.

If Sally is trying to deceive the listener (a *sincerity* danger), her words will misrepresent what she really believes. If Sally is lying, then the inference from Sally's words to her belief about the SUV that we (or the jury) as listeners attribute to Sally — IF_2 in the Diagram — will not correspond to what she actually knows about the accident.

Inferences about Sally's perception and memory affect the congruity between what Sally honestly believes she saw and what actually happened. To prove that the SUV did fail to stop at the red light, Sally's belief about what happened must be accurate — Sally must have observed the incident accurately (a *perception* danger). Perception as used here includes impressions received from any of the senses. The identification of an odor or the hearing of a person's speech would present perception issues. A memory problem arises if Sally has forgotten details about the event she perceived; for example, that the gray car was a truck not a SUV (a *memory* danger). If there are perception or memory problems with Sally's statement, then the inferences of perception (IF_3) or memory (IF_4) will be incorrect and the ultimate inference that Sally's belief accurately reflects what the SUV did (the FOC) will also be incorrect.

To summarize: We cannot know with absolute certainty whether Sally is lying or using the wrong words or misperceived or has forgotten what happened. Each of these risks can affect the relevance of Sally's eyewitness testimony. We assume, on the basis of our common experience, that people generally tend to be truthful and accurate in their statements. Thus, Sally's statement that the gray SUV ran the red light would be relevant to the pedestrian's lawsuit and we leave it to the jury to evaluate her testimonial qualities.

b.   The Relevancy of Sally's Hearsay Statement Also Depends on Generalizations About Sally's Testimonial Qualities

The very same inferences about Sally's testimonial qualities are necessary if Sally's statement is presented to the jury as hearsay. This can be illustrated with the example of George testifying about Sally's out-of-court statement to the jury. The inferential chain of reasoning shown in Diagram 8-2, an abbreviated version of Diagram 8-1, would be necessary to the relevancy of George's testimony.

Diagram 8-2

EF $\longrightarrow$	Four testimonial $\longrightarrow$	IF_1
George testifies that Sally told him, "I saw a gray SUV run the red light"	inferences regarding George's narration, sincerity, perception, and memory	George's belief about what Sally said is accurate
$\hookrightarrow IF_2 \longrightarrow$	Four testimonial $\longrightarrow$	IF_3
"Sally really did say, "I saw a gray SUV run the red light"	inferences regarding Sally's narration, sincerity, perception, and memory	Sally's belief about the gray SUV is accurate
$\hookrightarrow$ FOC $\longrightarrow$	EE	
A gray SUV really did not stop at the red light	The driver of the SUV was negligent	

As you can see, inferences about Sally's testimonial qualities are the same in form and in basic content as they were in Diagram 8-1. Essentially, then, the content of the jury's inferential reasoning process about the probative value of what Sally says about the SUV is the same whether she testifies or not. Moreover, the same potential risks of error arise from her four testimonial qualities, risks that are termed *hearsay dangers*.

The relevance of hearsay has also been illustrated with a "testimonial triangle,"[1] which collapses the four inferences into two legs of a triangle:

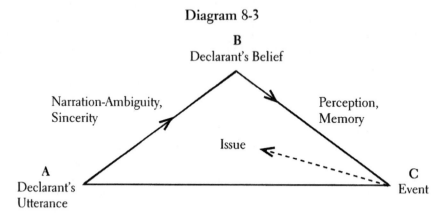

Diagram 8-3

The triangle starts with the declarant's words — spoken or written outside of court — which are usually presented to the jury through testimony or an exhibit. The left leg of the triangle from A to B represents the inference from the declarant's words to the declarant's state of mind of "belief," an inference that requires reliance on the declarant's sincerity and narrative ability. The right leg from B to C represents the inference from the declarant's state of mind of belief to the existence of an event that caused that belief. This inference requires reliance on the declarant's perception and memory, and on our general assumption that accurate beliefs correspond to real events. Thus, the relevance of Sally's statement requires both legs of the testimonial triangle, and requires that we make the inferences about all four of Sally's testimonial qualities. Once again, this is the same structure of inferential reasoning that the jury would make if Sally were presented to testify as a witness. Why then does the hearsay rule differentiate so sharply between Sally's statement as a witness and her statement as a hearsay declarant?

c.   Hearsay Policy Differentiates Between Witnesses and Hearsay Declarants

The most common answer to this question focuses on three factors that differentiate witnesses (like Sally speaking in court) from hearsay declarants (like Sally speaking

---

1.   The testimonial triangle concept was first popularized for the academic legal community by Professor Laurence Tribe in his article Triangulating Hearsay, 87 Harv. L. Rev. 957 (1974) and in Richard O. Lempert and Stephen A. Saltzburg, A Modern Approach to Evidence (1977). For a much earlier version of the triangle, see Charles Kay Ogden and Ivor Armstrong Richards, The Meaning of Meaning 10-12 (1927).

out of court). First, the witness in the courtroom is always under oath, thereby theoretically minimizing the likelihood of insincerity, whereas a declarant's out-of-court statement may or may not be made under oath. Moreover, the solemnity and formality of the court proceedings may cause the witness to be particularly careful about properly narrating the event.

Second, the jury is able to observe the demeanor of the in-court witness. Observing how the witness responds and reacts to questions, particularly on cross-examination, may give the jurors a somewhat better sense of the witness's sincerity, narrative ability, perception, and memory than they would get from having the content of the statement related to them by some third person. While demeanor evidence is often criticized as an ineffective indicator of outright insincerity, its use in evaluating other aspects of witness and party behavior has been noted. The opportunity for the trier of fact to assess the credibility of witnesses in person is a principal reason for the deference that appellate courts afford to factual findings at the trial level. See, e.g., Olin Guy Wellborn III, Demeanor, 76 Cornell L. Rev. 1075, 1077 (1991).

Third, and most important, the in-court witness is subject to cross-examination, which the opponent may use to elicit facts from the witness that are relevant to all four of the witness's testimonial qualities. We have seen in Chapter Seven how the topics of impeachment can all be addressed through cross-examination of a witness. The witness's answers, and the behavior of the witness in responding to questions, may clarify ambiguity, reveal mistakes in narration, reveal weaknesses in perception or memory, and provide information about the witness's character for truthfulness, the witness's bias, or the witness's motive to misrepresent the facts of the case. In addition, fear of cross-examination may motivate witnesses to be truthful and accurate in their testimony.

Without cross-examination, it is feared, hearsay statements may bear more testimonial dangers that are not exposed to the jury and hence may be *less reliable* than in-court testimony. Some witnesses, of course, may beat the system and lie quite persuasively. But to recognize that possibility is to recognize only that our adjudicatory system is not perfect. It is a truism, and many trial lawyers believe, that in the context of our adversary system, cross-examination is "beyond any doubt the greatest legal engine ever invented for the discovery of truth." 5 John Henry Wigmore, Evidence in Trials at Common Law 32 (James Chadbourn ed. 1974).

The problem with hearsay is succinctly stated by the District of Columbia Circuit:

> The problem with hearsay is that it deprives the defendant of the opportunity to cross-examine the person who uttered the statement at issue. Here, the government presented allegations of prior drug dealing, and the defendant was unable to cross-examine the person who made them. At the time of the testimony, that person — the less-than-reputable convict, Thomas Rose — was sitting in a federal correctional institution. Meanwhile in court, telling Rose's story, was the clean-cut FBI agent, Neil Darnell. Thus, Evans had no opportunity to "test[] the recollection and sift[] the conscience" of his accuser . . . Cross-examination may be the "greatest legal engine ever invented for the discovery of truth," . . . but it is not of much use if there is no one to whom it can be applied. [United States v. Evans, 216 F.3d 80, 84 (D.C. Cir. 2000).]

However, even though cross-examination of a hearsay declarant is usually not possible, it is not the only way to expose potential hearsay dangers. A hearsay declarant's inconsistent statements, bias against one of the parties, or untruthful character may be shown through the testimony of other witnesses or exhibits. FRE 806 explicitly permits impeachment of hearsay declarants: "When a hearsay statement . . . has been admitted in evidence, the declarant's credibility may be attacked . . . by any evidence that would be admissible for those purposes if the declarant had testified as witness." Furthermore, cross-examination may not always contribute to accurate fact-finding. Cross-examination leads to the exposure of a witness's deliberate falsehood much less frequently in real life than in courtroom dramas. It may yield only the jury's intuitive sense about a witness's general credibility. But some witnesses may appear to be less than reliable, when in fact they are only shy or nervous or scared. Stereotypes can also affect the jury's perception of who is, or is not, a reliable witness.

Nevertheless, it is certainly more difficult and burdensome for the opponent to obtain and present impeaching facts about hearsay declarants. Cross-examination of a live witness does operate as an efficient means of providing relevant information about a witness's testimonial qualities to the jury. And the *Evans* case above also shows that a proponent could use hearsay as a strategic choice to keep a less-than-convincing declarant off the witness stand. For all these reasons, the opponent's lack of ability to cross-examine a hearsay declarant is the primary reason for excluding hearsay evidence.

Hearsay policy may be summarized as follows: A witness's oath, demeanor, and cross-examination are thought to reduce testimonial dangers and to make in-court testimony *more reliable*. Cross-examination also increases the likelihood that testimonial dangers — sincerity, narration-ambiguity, perception, or memory problems — will be exposed and evaluated by the jury. And it generates information that helps the jury decide whether to rely on a witness's statement. Therefore, because of these differences between a witness's in-court testimony and declarant's out-of-court statement, hearsay is viewed as less reliable and more difficult for the jury to evaluate. It is excluded in the interest of increasing the accuracy of jury decision-making. And we remind you that whenever the relevance of an out-of-court statement requires inferences about all four testimonial qualities of the declarant, or the complete trip around the triangle, then hearsay policy is implicated.

It is not an argument for excluding hearsay that the witness who reports a hearsay statement to the jury while on the stand (like George) may be lying, or be mistaken, about what the hearsay declarant (like Sally) said. All testimony bears risks of misperception, faulty memory, and fabrication. A witness who reports hearsay is no different. We rely on oath, the formalities of the courtroom, demeanor, and cross-examination to help the jury evaluate the testimonial qualities of all witnesses (including George).

Hearsay policy could operate as a rule of preference. If a hearsay declarant like Sally is *available* to testify as a witness, it may be preferable to have her testify at the trial. But what if the hearsay declarant is not available to testify? Sally may be ill or out of the country. If we still want to exclude her hearsay statement, we are not talking about a rule of preference but about whether the jury will hear Sally's information at all. If Sally is unavailable, how critical is it to provide the opportunity for the opponent to cross-examine her? Should we exclude relevant evidence for the sake of whatever benefit cross-examination might have brought?

It is still much too soon for you to be formulating any definitive judgments about these issues. But you should keep them in mind as you continue to study the definition of hearsay.

KEY POINTS

1. Hearsay is a person's statement (a) that is made at a time other than while the person is testifying at the hearing in which the statement is offered and (b) that is offered to prove the truth of the matter asserted in the statement.

2. A hearsay statement may be oral or it may be written.

3. Hearsay policy is to exclude hearsay because there is no oath, no observation of demeanor, and no opportunity to cross-examine the hearsay declarant to determine if there are sincerity, narration-ambiguity, perception, or memory problems (the testimonial or hearsay dangers).

4. If an out-of-court statement is offered to prove the sincere belief of the declarant in the matter asserted, and then to prove the accuracy of that belief about an event, then all four testimonial qualities of the declarant are involved in the relevancy of the statement and hearsay policy is implicated.

PROBLEMS

8.1. Return to Problem 3.2, Pedroso v. Driver, at page 136. If the defendant denies (on line 00) that she received a speeding ticket, the plaintiffs will offer the ticket itself into evidence. How can the ticket be authenticated? Defendants will object that it is hearsay. Is it?

8.2. Return to Problem 3.3, United States v. Ray, at page 136. June Jacobs' assistant would testify for the prosecution that on the afternoon of March 14, 2010, Jacobs told the assistant that she had just gotten some bad news and that she was going to Ray's office to tell him. Would this testimony be hearsay? What if Jacobs sent a text message to the outside auditor Andrews: "Just told CEO about loss projections." Hearsay? What if Jacobs testified under oath to a grand jury that on March 14, 2010 she told Ray about the loss projections?

8.3. Return to Problem 3.4, State v. Blair, at page 137. The prosecutor seeks to admit the following out-of-court statements by Norma. Who would testify to present this evidence? Are the statements hearsay? Do you think they should be excluded?

(a) A friend of Norma's says that a month before the attack, Norma told the friend, "Last week I told Jimmy that I was going to break up with him and leave the Bay Area soon. Jimmy was furious."

(b) In 2008, Norma's mother visited her apartment. Norma was upset and crying. Norma said to her mother that Jimmy had lost his temper and hit her earlier that day, and that when she tried to leave her apartment, he threw a vase at her. The mother saw the shattered vase on the floor.

(c) Inside the locked drawer in which police found photographs of Norma showing severe bruising and date-stamped July 25, 2009, a handwritten diary was also found. On the page dated July 21, 2009, it stated: "Jimmy beat me after an argument."

3.   Elaboration of FRE 801 and 802: Implications of the General Rule of Exclusion

a.   *Identifying What a Hearsay Statement Is Offered to Prove*

The truth-of-the-matter-asserted test of FRE 801(c) requires the identification of the "matter" that an out-of-court statement is offered to prove. Looking at the testimonial triangle in Diagram 8-3 on page 412, supra, the event at point C — that the SUV failed to stop at the red light — is the fact of consequence that, for purposes of FRE 801(c), the declarant's utterance is offered to prove. This fact must then be connected to an essential element in a lawsuit. The line running from point C to "Issue" represents any further inferences that may be necessary to reach the essential element in the case. In this hypothetical, the only remaining inferential task after reaching point C is to decide whether failing to stop at the red light violated the requisite standard of care and therefore satisfies the essential element of negligence.

In many cases, however, after reaching point C, several additional inferences will be necessary for the utterance to be relevant to an essential element in the case. For example, George might testify that Sally said to him, "I had the green light and was just about to cross Main Street when I saw the gray SUV coming toward me down Main Street. It passed in front of me and hit a pedestrian who was also crossing Main Street with the green light." For this evidence to be relevant, the complete trip around the testimonial triangle is necessary to prove that Sally's statements — that she and the pedestrian had the green light — are true. Then, further inferences can be made: first, that if Sally and the pedestrian did have the green light, the red light must have been showing for oncoming traffic on Main Street; second, that the SUV therefore had the red light; third, that the SUV therefore failed to stop at this red light as illustrated in Diagram 8-4.

Are Sally's out-of-court statements to George hearsay? Clearly, they are *statements* made by a *declarant not while testifying at the trial*. Applying FRE 801(c), are they *offered to prove the truth of the matter asserted*? You might answer "no," because

Diagram 8-4

it seems that her statements are offered to prove that the driver of the SUV failed to stop at the red light and Sally's statement did not assert this. But this is not a correct analysis. The truth-of-the-matter-asserted test should be applied to the last inference that depends on Sally's testimonial qualities. This is FOC_1 — that Sally did have the green light. Sally's statement *is* being offered to prove the truth of this assertion. Only if FOC_1 is true can the conclusion about the driver being negligent be drawn. The truth of FOC_1 rests on generalizations about all four of Sally's testimonial qualities; thus hearsay policy is implicated. The further inferences that connect Sally's statements to the essential element in the case *do not relate to her beliefs and do not require any further reliance on her narrative ability, sincerity, perception, or memory.* Thus, they do not implicate hearsay policy. Do not be misled into applying FRE 801(c) to the final conclusions — that the light for the SUV was red, that the SUV failed to stop at the red light, or that the SUV driver was negligent. Sally's statements are hearsay. They are offered to prove the truth of the matters "asserted in the statement," as FRE 801(c) defines hearsay.

This same analysis must be made each time you apply the truth-of-the-matter-asserted test of FRE 801(c). If an inference that the matters contained in the declarant's assertions are true is required for relevance, then the assertions are "offered to prove" those matters, even if those matters are just a necessary step in the chain of reasoning that continues to some further conclusion.

b.   Testimony by Witnesses About Their Own Out-of-Court Statements May Still Be Hearsay

FRE 801(b) defines a "declarant" as a person who made a statement. This term generally is used to refer to people when they made statements *outside of court*, and we have used it that way in the preceding sections. When people make statements to the jury in court, under oath, and subject to cross-examination, they are, obviously, functioning as witnesses. When witnesses testify in court about statements that they themselves made *not while testifying in the current trial or hearing*, those statements are defined as hearsay by FRE 801(c). For example, in the case of the gray SUV, suppose that Sally testifies as a witness that "right after the accident, I remember telling George that the gray SUV ran the red light." Sally is testifying about her own hearsay statement. In this circumstance the hearsay declarant (Sally) is in fact in the courtroom and can be cross-examined. Some commentators have therefore argued that if witnesses report their own out-of-court statements, their evidence should not be regarded as hearsay. See, e.g., Edmund M. Morgan, Hearsay Dangers and the Application of the Hearsay Concept, 62 Harv. L. Rev. 177, 192-193 (1957). Others disagree, contending that cross-examination is less valuable when it is conducted long after the statement was made. And, if a witness's prior statements were not hearsay, witnesses could refer to and rely on their own prior *prepared* statements in their testimony. This is undesirable since the witness was not subject to cross-examination or to the scrutiny of the jury when preparing those statements. The various positions in the debate over the hearsay status of prior statements of witnesses are described in the Advisory Committee Note to FRE 801(d)(1). Under FRE 801(c), prior statements of witnesses are defined as hearsay unless specifically exempted. See FRE 801(d)(1), which we will examine in Section C infra.

c.   *Hearsay, Lay Opinions, and the Firsthand Knowledge Rule*

You have previously encountered the lay opinion rule (FRE 701) and the first-hand knowledge rule (FRE 602) in Chapter Four. Here we address briefly the relationship between those rules and the hearsay rule.

Consider a situation in which Ellen, a bystander, is prepared to testify in the suit between the pedestrian and the driver of the gray SUV. Ellen might testify that "The gray SUV ignored the red light and hit the pedestrian in the crosswalk." There are three possible bases for Ellen's belief: First, she may have observed the entire incident; second, Sally may have told her what happened; or third, on the basis of her observation of the position of the car and the pedestrian after the accident, she could have concluded that the defendant's SUV must have run the red light. If the second variation were true, Ellen would in effect be relating a hearsay statement. She has no firsthand knowledge of the event herself. In the third variation, Ellen's testimony that the defendant ignored the red light would be a lay opinion, based on her firsthand knowledge of the position of the car and the person who was hit. If she testified about the facts she did observe, instead of just stating her conclusion, the jury might be just as capable as she is to draw the appropriate inference.

If the opponent is unsure about the basis for Ellen's testimony, the initial objection can always be "lack of firsthand knowledge." The objecting attorney should immediately ask the judge to permit inquiry, outside the presence of the jury, into the basis for Ellen's testimony. The opponent should ask, "How do you know that the defendant ignored a red light?" If this inquiry reveals that Ellen is in fact relating hearsay ("Sally told me what happened"), the objecting attorney can then change the objection to hearsay. If the inquiry reveals that Ellen is expressing an opinion that is not based on her observation of the accident itself, then the objection would be lack of firsthand knowledge or a lay opinion objection. What is important, as a practical matter, is for the attorney to make some objection that will get the judge's attention and permit inquiry, preferably without the jury listening, into the basis for the witness's knowledge. Once the basis of knowledge is established, it should be relatively easy for the parties to address the question of why the evidence should or should not be admissible.

d.   *Multiple Hearsay*

On some occasions evidence will contain multiple hearsay. Consider, for example, the pedestrian's attempt to prove that the gray SUV went through a red light by offering a properly authenticated police report that states "George reports that 'Sally told me that the gray SUV ran the red light.'" Here we have multiple hearsay. We care about the sincerity, narration, perception, and memory of the police officer who wrote the report, as well as both Sally and George, and none of them is on the witness stand subject to cross-examination when making their statements.

If the plaintiff called George as a witness to testify from memory about what Sally said, we would have single hearsay. If the plaintiff called the police officer as a witness to testify about what George said, we would still have double hearsay. Sally is still a declarant because her statement continues to be offered for its truth. In addition, George is a declarant as well. In multiple hearsay situations, the evidence will be inadmissible unless there is a hearsay exception or exemption for each layer of hearsay. FRE 805 provides that "[h]earsay within hearsay is not excluded by the rule against hearsay if each part of the combined statements conforms with an exception to the rule."

KEY POINTS

1. If a statement made outside of court is offered to prove the truth of what it asserts, it is defined as hearsay even though the declarant is the witness who is testifying about the statement.

2. A hearsay objection is appropriate after determining that a witness does not have firsthand knowledge of the events testified to, but is relying on what others have said.

3. Some hearsay statements include additional hearsay within them. In such cases of multiple hearsay, each hearsay component must be admissible through an exception or exemption.

PROBLEMS

8.4. Return to Problem 3.5, Broadback v. Trapp, on page 138. During his own testimony, plaintiff Broadback testifies as follows:

(a) "I told the ambulance driver that I felt tremendous pain after my collision with Trapp."
   The ambulance driver then testifies that one of Broadback's teammates spoke to her on the way to the hospital:
(b) "The teammate told me that 'Trapp has always had it in for Broadback.'"
(c) "The teammate also said that he heard Trapp say 'I did this on purpose.'"

Are any of these statements objectionable as hearsay?

8.5. John and Mary Smith had a son, Brent, who was born on August 20, 1976. John and Mary were killed in a plane crash, and their son, if he survived them, was entitled to inherit their entire estates. In a probate proceeding in December 2000, an individual offers to testify as follows to establish his right to inherit the assets of John and Mary Smith: "My name is Brent Smith. I was born on August 20, 1976. I am 24 years old. I am the son of John and Mary Smith." Is any of this testimony objectionable as hearsay?

4. Interpretation and Illustration of FRE 801(c): Nonhearsay Statements with No Hearsay Dangers

Not all out-of-court statements are hearsay. A critical aspect of the definition of hearsay is that, under the proponent's relevance theory, the statements are offered to prove the *truth* of the matters they assert. Many out-of-court statements are not offered for this relevance theory; they are offered for a *nonhearsay* use.

a. Nonhearsay Uses

In our hypothetical concerning the gray SUV and the pedestrian, consider the following testimony of Sally about an event she witnessed: "In the morning, just before the accident, when I was getting gasoline at the service station, I heard Mike, a mechanic, say to the defendant who was driving a gray SUV, 'Your brakes are in bad shape. It would be dangerous for you to drive that SUV.'" Is Mike's statement hearsay? It is a statement made by a declarant who is not testifying at trial, but is it offered for the relevance theory of proving the truth of the matter Mike is asserting? The proponent of Sally's testimony, the plaintiff, might well argue as follows:

> Your Honor, we are not offering this evidence to prove the truth of the matter asserted by the mechanic — that the brakes were in fact bad. Rather, we are offering the evidence to prove only that the mechanic spoke those words. This is relevant to show that the defendant had notice of the dangerous condition of his brakes before he got into his car and drove through the red light. One of the things that we must prove in order to prove one of our claims of negligence is that the defendant either knew or should have known about the dangerous condition of his brakes. This out-of-court statement is relevant to show that he did have such knowledge.

On this theory of relevance, evidence of Mike's statement is not hearsay. Sally's testimony tends to prove that Mike's statement was made, and Mike's statement is relevant for what is called the "nonhearsay" use of "notice." It tends to prove that the driver heard these words and knew his brakes were bad, a fact of consequence in the case. In terms of FRE 801(c), the proponent is not offering Mike's statement to prove that the matters asserted are true. In terms of the inferential process in Diagram 8-1, the proponent is not offering Mike's statement to prove that Mike's beliefs about the condition of the brakes are accurate in order to prove that the brakes were bad. Indeed, it is not being offered to prove anything about the Mike's belief. This can be illustrated with the following testimonial triangle:

The line from the declarant's utterance at point A to the Issue represents the inference required to use Mike's statement to prove the fact of consequence — that the driver of the SUV had notice that his brakes were bad. The relevance of the evidence does *not* depend on making the inference from A to B or from B to C. Relevancy does

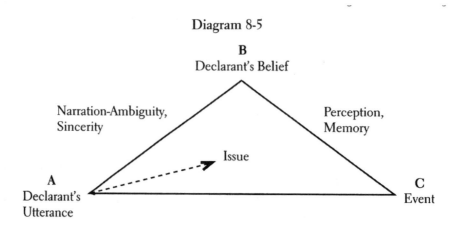

Diagram 8-5

B
Declarant's Belief

Narration-Ambiguity,   Perception,
Sincerity   Memory

Issue

A   C
Declarant's   Event
Utterance

not depend on what belief was in Mike's mind, or on whether that belief was accurate and corresponded to some event in the real world. Stated another way, relevance does not depend on Mike's memory, perception, sincerity, or narration. Therefore, hearsay policy is not implicated. There is no need to be concerned about the lack of oath, demeanor, and cross-examination of Mike.

   i. Effect on the Listener. In sum, the proponent of Mike's statement is offering it for the relevant nonhearsay use of showing its *effect on the listener*. Given the warning, the driver of the SUV had notice and therefore had the opportunity to respond. How the warning affected him — his conduct in responding to it — is relevant to whether he breached a requisite duty of care, which is an essential element of a negligence case. None of the inferences required for relevance depends on Mike's testimonial qualities, as shown in Diagram 8-6.

Diagram 8-6

EF →	IF$_1$ →	FOC$_1$
Sally testifies that she heard Mike tell the driver of a gray SUV, "Your brakes are in bad shape"	Mike did say to the driver of a gray SUV, "Your brakes are in bad shape"	The driver heard Mike's statement

FOC$_2$ →	FOC$_3$ →	EE
The driver disregarded the statement and continued to drive the gray SUV	The driver failed to stop at the red light because the SUV's brakes failed	The driver was negligent in failing to exercise reasonable care after being warned

Of course, we do care about whether Mike spoke any words at all (is Sally lying?), whether Sally heard the words correctly, and whether, at the time she testifies, Sally remembers accurately what was said. But Sally is a witness, making her statement in court, under oath, and can be cross-examined on all these points. The proponent's theory of relevance — that the driver was *unreasonable* in disregarding Mike's warning — depends on Mike's *apparent* sincerity, not on Mike's *actual* sincerity. It also requires that the driver hear Mike's statement — thus, that Mike's words were spoken loudly enough for the driver to hear. Anybody who heard the warning — Sally, Mike himself, a bystander — can testify about the loudness of the warning and the apparent sincerity with which it was given. In his own defense, the driver of the SUV may claim that it was reasonable for him to disregard what the mechanic said because Mike was always joking about brakes. But that is a defense, and does not alter the nonhearsay status of Sally's testimony for the plaintiff as to what she heard Mike say.

   Out-of-court statements offered to prove their *effect on the listener* are relevant in many different kinds of cases. Liability under the substantive law of torts and crimes often turns on the reasonableness of a listener's response to *warnings, notices, instructions, and threats.* In a civil rights action for an unwarranted shooting by police officers, brought against the officers and their supervisors, prior complaints charging abuse by one of the officers were not hearsay because they were offered to show the failure of the supervisors to respond to the prior complaints. Gutierrez-Rodriguez v. Cartagena, 882 F.2d 553, 575 (1st Cir. 1989). The effect of a statement can also be to create a specific state of mind, such as *knowledge, duress, good faith, provocation, or reasonable apprehension of bodily harm.* This state of mind may be an essential element in a civil or a criminal case. For example, whether a police officer acted with "probable cause" in making an arrest may be determined by what the officer was told the arrested person was doing. Reports of "homosexual violence" among prison inmates to prison officials are relevant to prove the officials' "deliberate indifference" — the state of mind required in a civil rights suit. Roland v. Johnson, 933 F.2d 1009 (6th Cir. 1991). In a case involving the issue of bad-faith denial of insurance coverage, appraisal reports were not offered to show the amount of loss actually suffered, but instead to show what information the insurance company had when it denied the claim. Talmage v. Harris, 486 F.3d 968, 975 (7th Cir. 2007). Finally, statements made to a listener can provide *motive* for conduct, and thus are relevant to explain the listener's subsequent behavior.

   ii.   Legally Operative Facts.   Another relevant nonhearsay use for an out-of-court statement is when the statement is itself a *legally operative fact.* For example, suppose Paul says to Sarah outside of court, "I offer to sell you my five-year old horse for $500." To prove the age of the horse, Paul's statement to Sarah is hearsay. In an action to establish that there was an offer for the sale of the horse, Sarah — or Paul or anyone else who heard the words — could testify to what Paul said. Under the substantive law of contracts, the words are themselves the event to be proved — the offer. McNaboe v. NVF Co., 2000 U.S. Dist. LEXIS 4418, at *39 (D. Del. 2000) ("The words the offerors . . . uttered in making the offer are admissibile as nonhearsay as they are utterances to which the law attaches duties and liabilities."). Anyone who heard Paul's statement can testify that it was made, just as any eyewitness to an automobile accident could testify to the event that the gray SUV ran a red light. In the words of the Seventh Circuit:

> [This kind of utterance echos] the linguist's distinction between performative and illocutionary utterances. The latter narrate, describe, or otherwise convey information, and so are judged by their truth value (information is useful only if true — indeed is *information* only if it is true); the former — illustrated by a promise, offer, or demand-commit the speaker to a course of action. Performative utterances are not within the scope of the hearsay rule, because they do not make any truth claims. [United States v. Montana, 199 F.3d 947, 949 (7th Cir. 1999).]

   Such utterances do not make truth claims because none of the inferences required for relevance depend on Paul's testimonial qualities. No memory or perception danger exists because Paul is not relating some fact that he has observed. Moreover, under the objective theory of contracts, there is no sincerity or narration-ambiguity danger, for we do not have to make any inference that Paul is sincere. The proponent's theory of relevance is that Paul said the words in an *apparent* manner such that the offeree might reasonably be expected to take it seriously; this would be a valid offer. And whether the words were spoken in an *apparently* serious manner is something about which anyone who heard the words can testify and be fully cross-examined. Paul's subjective intent or understanding may be relevant to the issue of mutual mistake, which Paul may raise as a defense. But mistake only becomes an issue once there has been an offer and an acceptance. Thus, to prove the offer, Paul's statement is nonhearsay. Its relevance can be illustrated on the testimonial triangle as the line from A to the Issue: From the fact that Paul spoke the words, we infer an essential element in a contract case.

Many different kinds of statements are *legally operative facts* because principles of substantive law give them independent legal significance. For example, in litigation over whether a group insurance policy is excluded from ERISA coverage, the policy itself is admissible as nonhearsay, "excluded from the definition of hearsay . . . because it is a legally operative document that defines the rights and liabilities of the parties." Stuart v. Unum Life Ins. Co., 217 F.3d 1145, 1153 (9th Cir. 2000). Some statements are acts done with words that, under the substantive law, give rise to civil obligations or consequences — acknowledging debts, words of defamation or slander. And some words are criminal acts — perjury, extortionate threats, offers to sell drugs, statements forming a conspiracy. For example, a statement soliciting a bribe was held to be a legally operative fact, "important for the mere fact that the words were said and not for the truth of the matter." Transportes Aereos Pegaso v. Bell Helicopter Textron, Inc., 623 F. Supp. 2d 518, 530 (D. Del. 2009). Sometimes verbal statements have immediate legal significance when they also accompany nonverbal acts. If information about the context within which such statements were made is necessary, it can be supplied by anyone who was there. Cross-examination of the declarant is not necessary to supply it.

iii.   Identifying Nonhearsay Uses.   A proponent's stock response to a hearsay objection in court is "not offered for its truth, Your Honor." That response will not satisfy a thoughtful judge or a well-trained opponent. The proponent should be able to articulate the nonhearsay theory of relevance; for example, that the statement is offered to prove an effect on the listener (regardless of its truth) and that this effect on the listener is a fact of consequence in the case. The proponent should also be able to explain *why* exclusion of the statement is not appropriate; that is, why hearsay policy is *not* implicated. The critical point is that the evidence is relevant without reliance on the declarant's testimonial qualities.

Some texts and study aids provide a laundry list of nonhearsay uses for out-of-court statements. Such lists typically include the two nonhearsay uses already identified — statements relevant for their effect on the listener and statements that are legally operative facts (also called "verbal acts"). The lists also include *prior inconsistent statements* offered to impeach witnesses, as discussed in Chapter Seven at pages 382-388, supra, and statements offered as *circumstantial evidence of the declarant's state of mind*. A leading treatise, Christopher B. Mueller and Laird C. Kirkpatrick, Evidence §8.20-21 at 829-834 (2d ed. 1999), also includes words that operate as identifying characteristics of an object (a license plate, a trade insignia) and words that have a performative aspect that dominates the assertive aspect (the ability to speak French, or to speak at all). These written or spoken words generate logical factual inferences that have nothing to do with their "truth" value; thus they might be called *"logically operative facts."* While these lists may help you to identify some common nonhearsay uses for out-of-court statements, the key to understanding nonhearsay is to focus on the inferences necessary to the relevance of the out-of-court statement. The list is no substitute for the analysis that underlies it.

b.   *Statements Relevant for Both Nonhearsay and Hearsay Uses*

Sally's testimony about what Mike the mechanic said to the driver of the gray SUV could also be relevant to prove that the brakes on the Honda were in fact bad. If offered for this purpose, the evidence is clearly hearsay. Relevance would depend on the mechanic's sincerity, narration, perception, and memory. It would be excluded if no hearsay exception applies.

When a particular piece of evidence is admissible for one purpose (to prove notice) but inadmissible for another (to prove the brakes were bad), the question of admissibility is one of discretionary balancing for the trial judge under FRE 403. The risk of unfair prejudice is that the jury, even after being given limiting instructions, will use the evidence for its improper hearsay purpose (here, to prove bad brakes). Is the probative value of the evidence for the admissible purpose (here, notice) substantially outweighed by the danger of unfair prejudice? We have seen in the discussion of FRE 403 in Chapter Three that need for the evidence can alter the balancing when there are alternative means to prove notice. If there are not, the need for evidence of Mike's warning will be very high. And in many cases, other evidence to prove the truth that the SUV's brakes were bad will already have been admitted. This diminishes the risk of unfair prejudice. The Rule 403 decision is made within these contextual facts of the specific case.

KEY POINT

When an out-of-court statement is offered to prove its effect on the listener, or some legally operative fact, or some other matter where relevance does not depend on inferences about the accuracy of declarant's belief about an event, the statement is not hearsay. It is not offered for the truth of the matter it asserts.

PROBLEMS

As you examine the following problems, consider why the out-of-court statements are relevant and whether they are hearsay or nonhearsay. We have discussed three ways of articulating the hearsay test, and you should try to apply each one. Ignore the possibility that the statement may fall within a hearsay exception and focus solely on the question of whether the evidence is hearsay.

8.6. The Federal Election Commission (FEC) has brought an enforcement action against the Christian Coalition for violating federal campaign finance laws during congressional elections in 2000, 2002, and 2004. Federal law prohibits corporations and labor unions from using their general treasury funds to make direct contributions to candidates; but they can make expenditures related to federal elections so long as these expenditures are for communications that do not expressly advocate the election or defeat of a clearly identified candidate. The Christian Coalition is a corporation and in 2002 it paid for its Executive Director to speak at a conference in Montana. In this videotaped speech, the Executive Director said that Montana's Democratic Congressman Pat Williams "is one of your top targets in the entire nation," and, "We're going to see Pat Williams sent bags-packing back to Montana in

November of this year." The FEC asserts that this violates federal law. The Christian Coalition objects that the videotape of the speech is hearsay. What result?

8.7. Lucy Rawlins is suing Lagoon Resort in the State of Hawaii for injuries she allegedly suffered during a scuba diving trip organized by the Resort. Resort's defense is that Rawlins signed a valid form that releases it from liability for the claim Rawlins has alleged against it. The general manager of Lagoon Resort testifies that he is responsible for explaining the release to guests, obtaining signatures, and filing and storing these records. He claims that Exhibit A is the Liability Release Form signed by Rawlins. Rawlins does not contest that she signed Exhibit A but objects that it is hearsay. What result?

8.8. In a libel suit, Plaintiff alleges that the defendant sent a signed, typewritten letter to Plaintiff's employer stating that plaintiff was a liar and thief. Plaintiff offers an authenticated photocopy of the letter into evidence. Defendant objects that the letter is hearsay. What result? Defendant then calls a coworker of Plaintiff who will testify that Plaintiff lied on the job and stole from the company. Plaintiff objects that this testimony is hearsay. What result? Coworker also testifies that "For years Plaintiff has had a reputation in the company for lying and stealing on the job." Is this testimony hearsay? Is it inadmissible character evidence?

8.9. Return to Problem 3.3, United States v. Ray, at page 136. To prove that Ray was responsible for the sale of his 100,000 shares of Rundown stock, the prosecution offers the letter signed by Ray to his broker directing the broker to make the sale. Hearsay? To prove that Ray gave this order on March 16, 2010, the prosecution points to the handwritten date of "March 16, 2010" on the letter. Hearsay?

8.10. In a prosecution of Joe Jamal for bank robbery, FBI Agent Guerrero testifies that a confidential FBI informant identified Jamal as a suspect. Defense counsel objects that the testimony is hearsay, offered to prove the truth of the matter asserted. The government claims that the testimony is offered to explain the Agent's investigatory procedures and to show why he developed a photo identification display for witnesses that included Jamal's photograph. What ruling?

8.11. In a racketeering prosecution pursuant to the RICO statutes, a witness for the prosecution appears visibly nervous, speaks haltingly, and changes his testimony several times, but finally does identify one of the defendants as the person who paid him to deposit cash in phony bank accounts, a violation of RICO. At the close of the witness's testimony, the prosecutor asks whether the defendants have threatened him. The witness responds that two of the defendants called him at his home a week before the trial and made threats on his life if he testified. Hearsay?

8.12. Joseph Blackstone, a professor of economics at a leading business school, is charged with insider trading in violation of 18 U.S.C. §78. Blackstone was a director of NF, a small natural foods company that was purchased by the Kellogg Company in February of 2011. Just prior to the purchase, several of Blackstone's family and friends purchased large amounts of stock in NF and made a significant profit when Kellogg purchased the company. Blackstone is charged with tipping all of these individuals with inside information about the impending Kellogg purchase. Blackstone denies communicating any tips about the purchase and states that all of the individuals could have learned of the purchase through "leaks" in the industry and in the press. At trial, Blackstone offers the following testimony of Voss, one of his friends: "In January of 2011, I heard that a Yahoo message board contained a rumor about the Kellogg purchase." Should the court exclude this testimony as hearsay?

8.13. Sondra Evers is suing Jones's Deli for personal injuries sustained when she slipped and fell on a pool of spilled ketchup near the food takeout counter. Sondra claims that the ketchup had been on the floor long enough for Jones's employees to have known about it. Sondra calls Bertha Barlow, who offers to testify as follows: "About half an hour before Ms. Evers had her accident, I was walking past the takeout counter when I overheard someone exclaim loudly, 'There's ketchup on the floor!'" Should this testimony be excluded as hearsay? What if Bertha also testifies that she saw a Jones's Deli clerk near the takeout counter when she heard the statement?

8.14. Return to Problem 3.2, Pedroso v. Driver, at page 136. Max testifies for defendants that he always rode the same school bus with Paul Pedroso and Paul's friend Tom, and that Paul and Tom used to play tag after getting off the bus together. Max testifies that on the day of the accident, he heard Tom say "Paul, you're *it*" as the two boys left the bus. Plaintiffs object to this testimony as hearsay. What result?

8.15. Brian Andronico is charged with conspiracy to distribute counterfeit currency. An undercover agent, Pamela Mertz, testified that she made purchases of counterfeit money from a man driving a car with the license plate "ICE 2000." The prosecution can prove that the license plate "ICE 2000" is registered to Andronico. The defendant objects on grounds of authentication, best evidence, and hearsay. Should Mertz's testimony be admitted?

8.16. To prove consciousness as a basis for pain and suffering after an accident, plaintiff offers a witness to testify as follows: "Within 30 seconds of the accident I was at the plaintiff's side. She was lying on the ground, and I shouted to a passerby, 'Get help; she's unconscious.' At that moment the plaintiff said, 'I'm not unconscious.'" Is the evidence hearsay?

5.   Interpretation and Illustration of FRE 801(a)(2): Nonverbal Conduct

a.   *The Relevancy of Nonverbal Conduct to Prove Belief*

Thus far all of our examples of hearsay have involved oral or written utterances, but in some instances hearsay is completely nonverbal. Consider, for example, the following testimony offered by a police officer in a battery prosecution: "When I arrived at the bar that was the scene of the fight, I asked who threw the first punch. One of the women who was present pointed at Jim Harris, the defendant, who was wearing a red shirt." This testimony is relevant to prove the woman's belief, as shown by her nonverbal conduct, that Harris threw the first punch. Consider Diagram 8-7 on page 427.

This theory of relevance depends on inferences about the testimonial qualities of the police officer, who is a witness, and of the woman. The inference from the woman's conduct (IF_1) to her belief (IF_3) (from A to B on the testimonial triangle) and the inference from her belief to the occurrence of the event at issue (FOC) (from B to C on the testimonial triangle) show that all of the hearsay dangers are present. The woman may have been falsely representing her belief to get Jim Harris in trouble (a sincerity risk); the arm movement may have been an involuntary tic that was not based on any belief about Jim (an ambiguity risk); the woman may not have seen clearly who threw the first punch (a perception risk); and she may have forgotten who threw the first punch by the time the officer asked (a memory risk). Indeed, in terms

Diagram 8-7

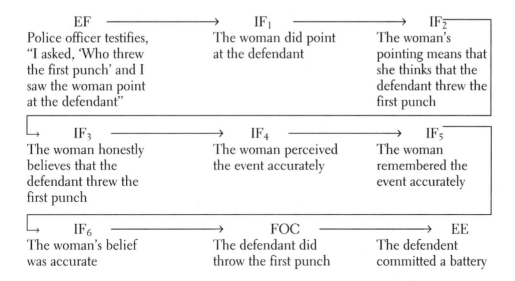

of the inferential process involved in using this evidence to prove that Harris threw the first punch, there is no pertinent difference between the intentional pointing and a verbal response that identifies Harris (e.g., "It was Jim Harris" or "It was the man in the red shirt").

Remember that often conduct is just conduct, offered to prove that an act was done, without regard to the actor's belief. In a medical malpractice case, the defendant physician testified that while treating his patient's snake bite, he placed a telephone call to a toxicology specialist. Since the content of that call was not disclosed, this testimony revealed only the doctor's intent to place the call and was not hearsay. Field v. Anderson, 2006 WL 3043431 (W.D. Ky.).

b. Application of FRE 801(a)

FRE 801(a) defines a "statement" as "a person's oral assertion, written assertion. or *nonverbal conduct, if the person intended it as an assertion.*" (Emphasis added.) Applying this definition to our hypothetical raises a preliminary question of fact: Did the woman intend her nonverbal conduct (pointing) to be an assertion of her belief that Jim threw the first punch? What facts would you contend are relevant to the question of her intent? If the woman did so intend, her act of pointing, commonly called *assertive conduct*, will be found to be a "statement" and will be excluded as hearsay. If she did not so intend, her act is commonly called *nonassertive conduct*, and it may be admitted because it is not a "statement" and therefore not hearsay.

i. Assertive Conduct. Sometimes conduct is intentionally used by the actor as a substitute for words. That is, the actor wants to communicate a belief and uses conduct to do so. By raising your hand in class, for example, you communicate "I want to speak." Or by shaking your head from side to side when asked a question, you communicate that your answer is "no." Both of these actions would usually be *intended by the actor to be assertions* of what the actor is thinking. If they are so intended, then in the words of the Advisory Committee Note, such conduct "is clearly the equivalent of words, assertive in nature, and [is] to be regarded as a statement." The act of pointing, mentioned in the Note, would typically be found to be assertive conduct, intended as the equivalent of words, and thus would be hearsay.

   ii.   Nonassertive Conduct.   Sometimes conduct is not intended by the actor as an assertion. In our hypothetical about the fight in the bar, what if the woman did not point at Jim Harris but instead carefully maneuvered Jim to the back door of the bar and gave him a push out the door. If the police officer saw her do this and arrested Jim Harris, would the officer's testimony as to what the woman did be relevant in the battery prosecution? Would it be hearsay? It can be inferred from her conduct that the woman believed Jim started the fight, that her belief was accurate, and that Jim did in fact start the fight. Thus, her conduct is relevant. But unlike the act of pointing, the act of carefully pushing Jim out of the back door may not be intended by the woman to assert her belief in Jim's guilt. She may be trying to protect Jim, and the last thing she wants is for the police officer to arrest him. If she does not intend to communicate her belief, then her conduct is nonassertive and, under the definition of FRE 801(a), would not be a "statement" and therefore would not be hearsay.
   However, you can see that the relevance of the woman's conduct, even if it is nonassertive, depends on inferences about all of her testimonial qualities. If any of these inferences is false, the woman's conduct is not relevant to prove Jim started the fight. For example, the woman may actually think Jim did not start the fight but wants the police to think he did (a sincerity risk); or she may want him to leave the bar for other reasons, such as that he has illegal drugs in his possession (an ambiguity risk). There are also potential perception and memory dangers: the woman may have confused Jim with another man wearing a red shirt who actually threw the first punch, or she may have forgotten what she actually saw. These are the same risks we have previously identified with regard to the woman pointing at Jim; and if the woman shouted "Jim Harris" in response to the officer's question, the same risks would be present.

   iii.   FRE 801(a)'s Intent Test.   FRE 801(a) creates a doctrinal test for determining whether any particular item of nonverbal conduct evidence is or is not hearsay. Nonverbal conduct intended as an assertion, is hearsay; nonverbal conduct not intended as an assertion is not hearsay. This test thus involves a preliminary question of fact: Was the actor's nonverbal conduct intended as an assertion? This preliminary question will be decided on the basis of the *nature of the conduct* and the *circumstances surrounding it* as presented by both parties. There will be some close cases, and there may be situations in which conduct that is normally nonassertive is in fact intended to be assertive. For example, if the woman pushing Jim Harris out the back door made a lot of noise and called attention to her conduct, these contextual facts could generate the inference that she was intending to communicate her belief in Jim's guilt to the police officer.
   FRE 104 governs the preliminary fact-finding that is necessary to the judge's application of FRE 801(a)'s intent test. Should the question of "intent" be governed by FRE 104(a) or (b)? As you know from Chapter Four, preliminary questions of fact are for the judge under FRE 104(a), unless they are necessary to the relevance of the offered evidence. In the hypotheticals that we have just discussed, the woman's intent to use

her conduct to assert Jim's guilt is not necessary to the relevance of that conduct. The relevance of her conduct does depend on *her belief* about who started the fight; but that she *intends to assert that belief* is not an inference that is necessary to relevance. Instead, it is a test imposed by hearsay policy, as we discuss below, Thus, under FRE 104(a), the judge must be persuaded by a preponderance of the evidence on the question of intent. The Advisory Committee Note to FRE 801 states that "the rule is so worded as to place the burden upon the party claiming that the intention existed; ambiguous and doubtful cases will be resolved against him and in favor of admissibility." To what language in FRE 801 do you think the Advisory Committee is referring?

6.   Elaboration of FRE 801(a): Justification for the Distinction Between Assertive and Nonassertive Conduct

Since the relevance of both the woman pointing and the woman pushing Jim out the back door depends on the accuracy of her belief and requires a complete trip around the testimonial triangle, both kinds of conduct implicate hearsay policy. Yet only the assertive conduct of the woman pointing is defined as hearsay; the nonassertive conduct of pushing Jim is not hearsay under FRE 801(a)'s definition. Why?

a.   *Absence of Hearsay Danger*

The Advisory Committee's Note to FRE 801(a) suggests that nonassertive conduct should not be defined as hearsay because of the probable absence of any sincerity danger. If an actor has a belief about a disputed fact — that Jim Harris threw the first punch — but is not intending to assert or to communicate that belief, then the actor cannot be "lying" about it. It is the view of the Advisory Committee that a person can be insincere — can tell a lie — only if the person is intending to communicate a particular fact that would be the subject of the lie. Without the intent to assert that fact, there is no opportunity to fabricate it. Is this a common sense generalization? Do you agree with it? Is the absence of sincerity risk a sufficient reason to admit the woman's pushing Jim as not hearsay?

Surprisingly and unaccountably, the Advisory Committee Note to FRE 801(a) asserts that the testimonial qualities other than sincerity also do not present a high risk: "Admittedly [nonassertive conduct] is untested with respect to the perception, memory, and narration (or their equivalents) of the actor, but the *Advisory Committee is of the view that these dangers are minimal in the absence of an intent to assert . . .* " (emphasis added). On what empirical data does the Advisory Committee base this conclusion? There seems to be nothing inherent in nonassertive conduct that tends to reduce or eliminate the other hearsay dangers. Can you think of anything about the woman's conduct in pushing Jim out the back door that reduces the danger of ambiguity (she was worried about illegal drugs) or perception (she confused Jim with another man in a red shirt)? The Note indicates that the actor's motivation to be accurate and the need to rely on the actor's own conduct can reduce the degree of perception and memory dangers. But these factors are not built into FRE 801(a), and the woman's conduct in pushing Jim could be admitted as not hearsay without any reduction in the perception or memory danger involved.

Thus, you should ask yourself whether the probable absence of just one hearsay danger (sincerity) is sufficient justification for removing nonassertive conduct from the definition of hearsay altogether. When we study the hearsay exceptions, we will see that the probable absence of one or more of the hearsay dangers is a principal justification for many of them.

b.   Necessity

In general, excluding relevant evidence because of some hearsay dangers may be too great a price to pay when it is very burdensome or perhaps even impossible to obtain other, "better" evidence on the same point. Thus, "necessity" is a reason for many of the exceptions to the hearsay rule. The concern about nonassertive conduct is that it is so pervasive and so often relied on as a matter of course in our everyday lives that we would be giving up too much relevant evidence by classifying such conduct as hearsay. For example, if we look out the window and see people wearing heavy overcoats, we assume it is cold outside; if a northbound vehicle proceeds through an intersection with a traffic light, we assume the driver thinks that the light is green for that vehicle; if we see people on the street begin to put up their umbrellas, we assume they believe it has begun to rain; if a shopkeeper repairs a loose board in the thresh-old to a shop after someone has tripped on it, we assume the shopkeeper thinks the loose board was dangerous. In these situations, the individual actors have beliefs about events or conditions that motivate their conduct; but they are probably not *intending to assert* the belief that it is cold, that the light is green, that it is raining, or that the loose board is dangerous.[2] Their conduct would not be defined as hearsay under FRE 801(a).

Another variation of the necessity argument for treating nonassertive conduct as not hearsay is that attorneys are not immediately sensitive to the hearsay characteristics of such evidence. If a rule treating nonassertive conduct as hearsay would be only sporadically applied, the rule arguably ought not to exist at all.

c.   Should Nonassertive Conduct Be Excluded from the Definition of Hearsay?

Whether the foregoing reasons are sufficient to exclude nonassertive conduct from the hearsay prohibition has long been the subject of academic debate.

i.   The Difficulty of Applying the Intent Test.   One concern relates to the task of classifying conduct as assertive or nonassertive. The judicial task of determining under FRE 801(a) whether conduct is intended as an assertion is not easy, and inevitably entails the risk that the wrong decision will be made, either because the actor has cleverly disguised an assertion (e.g., the woman is trying to communicate that Jim

---

2.   In Chapter Six, page 328, supra, we noted that subsequent remedial measures might be relevant to prove the belief of the actor that the situation remedied was dangerous. Now you can see why such conduct is unlikely to be classified as hearsay — it is unlikely that such actors are intending by their conduct to assert "dangerousness." But do not forget that the relevance of remedial measures to prove liability or fault still requires a complete trip around the testimonial triangle.

is guilty by pushing him out the door when she knows he is not), because insufficient evidence of intent is available, or because the court misapplies the concept of intent to assert. Even if judges reach the correct result most of the time, considerable time and effort is spent arguing and deciding the question of intent.

   ii.   **The Danger of Ambiguity.**   A second, and perhaps more substantial, concern is that significant hearsay dangers are still attached to such conduct. The lack of intent to assert inevitably increases the ambiguity danger. Conduct can be the product of many different beliefs, and the fact finder may attribute a belief to the actor that the actor does not in fact hold. We have seen that the woman may have other reasons for pushing Jim out the back door. Similarly, a driver going through the intersection is unlikely to be intending to assert that the light is green but it may also be wrong to infer that the driver believes that the light is green. The driver may know that the light is red but because of some emergency the driver feels compelled to ignore the red light. A substantial ambiguity problem means the conduct has low probative value to prove the specific belief for which it is offered. At some point the conduct may be so ambiguous, and the probative value so low, that a court could rely on FRE 403 to exclude the evidence. Moreover, the driver of the car may be color-blind, or distracted, and may not have perceived the color of the stop light. As noted previously, there is nothing about all nonassertive conduct that tends to minimize perception or memory problems.

   iii.   **Is the Admission of Nonassertive Conduct Good Policy?**   Remember that the principal impact of the rule excluding hearsay is to require the presentation of witnesses, subject to oath, demeanor, and cross-examination. If the woman's pointing is assertive conduct, the proponent *must produce that woman as a witness* (unless her conduct falls within a hearsay exception or exemption). If her conduct is nonassertive, she *need not be called as a witness*. However, cross-examination of the woman might uncover some risk of her insincerity. And, it might provide specific information about her belief that would obviously reduce the ambiguity risk. Furthermore, it is generally thought that cross-examination is most effective in exposing perception and memory problems, neither of which is minimized by the fact that out-of-court conduct is nonassertive. This might argue for defining nonassertive conduct as hearsay, which would require the proponent to bring the actor to court to testify and to be cross-examined. There is a middle ground between defining all nonassertive conduct as hearsay, thus excluding it wholesale, and FRE 801(a)'s position of allowing it to be admitted wholesale. It would be possible to define hearsay as including all conduct relevant to prove belief; then to create a hearsay exception for nonassertive conduct; and to condition the applicability of that exception on the unavailability of the actor. Or the exception could be conditioned on a case-by-case showing of the kind of motivation or reliance by the actor that minimizes perception and memory dangers. Do you think such alternatives would be preferable to the Federal Rules' approach?

d.   *Disguised Assertions*

   Sometimes evidence that appears to be nonassertive conduct is in fact relevant only because of underlying assertive behavior of particular persons. The easiest example is when a judgment of conviction for a crime is used to prove that the defendant did do the illegal act. The conviction is relevant because it is evidence that 12 jurors voted, or one judge decided, that the defendant did do the act. Such conduct clearly is *intended to assert the belief in guilt*. Because the jury's vote may not appear on the face of the judgment of conviction itself, it is what we call a *disguised* assertion. Convictions are uniformly classified as hearsay. Once again, locating the hidden declarant (the jury) who is making a disguised assertion (the verdict of guilt) depends on your identification of the inference of belief that is necessary for the relevance of the offered item of evidence.

Now consider evidence that Greta was arrested (not convicted) for robbery. Is the arrest hearsay, if used to prove that Greta actually committed the illegal act? The answer depends on whether the arrest is assertive or nonassertive conduct of the hidden declarants, the officers who arrested Greta. There are several ways to analyze this problem. The officers may have been making the arrest because they observed Greta in the act and thus they believed that she did commit the robbery. If so, we think it is appropriate to regard their conduct in arresting her as their intended assertion of that belief. Alternatively, the officers may have been executing a warrant or acting in response to a victim's accusation. They have no firsthand knowledge of Greta's behavior and may not be intending to assert their own belief about her criminal activity. But the officers are making the arrest only because another hidden declarant — the individual who made an accusation or the officer who signed the affidavit for the warrant — did make an intended assertion of belief that Greta robbed the bank. The apparently nonassertive arrest is occurring only because of, and is relevant only because of, this disguised assertion of belief in Greta's guilt, the fact that the evidence is being offered to prove. The evidence, therefore, should be regarded as hearsay.

Consider also testimony that John's driver's license was revoked, which is offered to prove that John engaged in unsafe driving. It may well be that the hidden declarant, the person who generated the paperwork that officially revoked John's license, was acting in a bureaucratic manner and was not intending to assert anything about how John drove. Nonetheless, the revocation is occurring only because somebody — presumably the judge who found John guilty of a traffic offense — asserted that John had engaged in some illegal driving activity.

Our characterization of the arrest and revocation evidence as assertive is either a minority position or a refinement that most discussions of nonassertive activity do not bother to make. McCormick classifies the revocation evidence as nonassertive. See Charles T. McCormick, The Borderland of Hearsay, 39 Yale L.J. 489, 491 (1930). See also Ted Finman, Implied Assertions as Hearsay: Some Criticisms of the Uniform Rules of Evidence, 14 Stan. L. Rev. 682, 683 n.4 (1962) (citing conduct that leads to the institutionalization of a patient as nonassertive). Morgan, on the other hand, characterizes the institutionalization evidence and the revocation evidence as assertive. Edmund M. Morgan, Hearsay Dangers and the Application of the Hearsay Concept, 62 Harv. L. Rev. 177, 190 (1948). What do you think?

KEY POINTS

1. Evidence of nonverbal conduct is sometimes offered to prove the accuracy of the beliefs of the actor about events. If the actor is intending to communicate that belief through conduct, then the evidence is defined as hearsay. The actor's testimonial

qualities of sincerity, perception, and memory are involved in the relevancy of the conduct.

2. If the actor is not intending to communicate belief, then the evidence is defined as not hearsay and is admitted to prove the truth of that belief, even though the actor's testimonial qualities of perception and memory are still involved.

3. The question of the actor's intent is a preliminary question of fact for the judge to decide pursuant to FRE 104(a). The burden to persuade the judge on the question of intent is on the opponent who is objecting to the admission of the actor's conduct as hearsay.

PROBLEMS

8.17. Ed Stephens is being prosecuted for bank robbery. Eyewitnesses claim that the robber wore a loud Hawaiian shirt. The prosecution offers the following testimony of Officer Emily James:

> The day after the robbery, I was following leads on various possible suspects. I went to the Stephens's home, and found only Mrs. Stephens there. I asked her if she would give me the shirt that her husband wore the previous day. She handed me a Hawaiian shirt, which is marked as Exhibit A. I also watched her as she entered the bedroom and I saw her conceal a leather bag under the bed. After she gave me the shirt, I conducted a search for the leather bag and found that it was full of money, which is marked as Exhibit B.

Defense counsel has objected to this entire testimony, and to Exhibits A and B on grounds of hearsay. What result?

8.18. Ralph Benson and Jerry Jackson owned a small yacht that they kept docked on Leech Lake, Minnesota. On the morning of June 15, Ralph, his wife, and two children set off across the lake in the yacht. A storm suddenly arose on the lake, and nobody has seen the Benson family or the yacht since that morning. Jackson sued the company that insured the yacht against damage or loss due to bad weather. The insurance company relies on a clause in the policy that permits recovery only if the yacht was navigable at the time of the loss. To prove that the yacht was navigable, Jerry Jackson offers to testify, "On the morning of June 15, I observed Ralph Benson carefully look around the yacht, place his wife and children on board, and set off across the lake." Counsel for the insurance company objects to this testimony on the ground that it is hearsay.

8.19. Return to Problem 8.13 at page 426, supra, Sondra Evers's case against Jones's Deli.

(a)   Plaintiff Evers offers a videotape prepared at the request of her attorney showing her activities at her home, as relevant to prove the serious effect of the fall on her physical condition.

(b)   For the defendant, Karen Larson would testify: I am the manager of Jones's Deli and I was at the store from 8:00 A.M. until 5:30 P.M. on the day Ms. Evers fell. On that day I received no complaints about any spilled ketchup on the floor. Is this testimony relevant? What additional facts might the proponent need to present? Should the testimony be excluded on grounds of hearsay?

8.20. Ben Jacobsen, a 50-year-old former railroad firefighter, is charged with homicide for fatally shooting a man who had been sleeping in a box car in an infrequently used area of the switching yard. The crime occurred at approximately 11:00 A.M. on Tuesday, July 23. Jacobsen claims that he is not guilty and suggests that two teenage boys committed the crime. He calls to the stand Harry Winters, a railroad employee, who offers to testify as follows: "Shortly after 11:00 A.M. on Tuesday, July 23, I observed two teenage boys near the box car. They were running away from it." Is this evidence hearsay?

8.21. Plaintiff is suing a police officer for false arrest. The officer arrested Plaintiff for driving while under the influence of intoxicating liquor. At trial, Plaintiff submits properly authenticated proof that she had been acquitted by a jury of the charge in question. Hearsay?

8.22. Return to Problem 8.10 at page 425, supra. What if Agent Guerrero had not testified as to the specific contents of the confidential informant's statement but did testify that "in the course of my investigation leading to defendant Jamal's arrest, I had contact with a confidential informant." Hearsay?

8.23. To prove that Darcey had been using drugs, testimony of one of Darcey's friends is offered: "Last December 31, I visited Darcey at the State Drug Rehabilitation Center, where he is a patient." Hearsay?

8.24. In the prosecution of Donna Draper for conspiracy to import heroin, an illegal substance, the prosecution offered the testimony of Sergeant Edward Conley concerning a nine-year-old German shepherd named Bosco. Sergeant Conley testified that Bosco was trained to detect narcotics by smell. Sergeant Conley further testified that he took Bosco to a room in a bank in which a bag containing $9,000 was located, and, when he instructed Bosco to search for drugs, the dog "showed a strong, positive aggressive alert, shaking the bag, ripping it apart, grabbing the money in his mouth, and ripping the money." Other evidence establishes that the currency to which Bosco reacted had been brought to the bank by Draper in order to purchase cashier's checks. Should this evidence be excluded on the ground that it is hearsay? On any other ground?

8.25. Return to Problem 4.28 at page 221. Is Ensign Chandler's testimony about the display on the GPS screen hearsay?

8.26. In the prosecution of Clive Bailey for conspiracy to possess marijuana with the intent to distribute, the prosecution offered the testimony of the arresting officer. The officer testified that a Ms. Washington had been caught collecting a shipment of a barrel of marijuana. Washington agreed to cooperate with the government by having agents accompany her to deliver the barrel to the intended recipient. She then drove her van to her residence, with two task force agents hiding in the back, and placed a phone call, punching in a code. Fifteen minutes later, Clive came up to the van, opened the back of the van, and fled upon seeing the agents, but was apprehended. The agents recovered his pager, which reflected receipt of the call from Ms. Washington's telephone and the code she had entered. Is any of this testimony hearsay?

7.   Utterances Relevant for the Truth of the Declarant's Unstated Beliefs

Verbal conduct, that is, oral or written words of a declarant, often expresses the belief of a declarant explicitly. But sometimes, the beliefs of the declarant that generate verbal conduct are not stated explicitly but can be inferred from the words that are spoken or written. Is verbal conduct hearsay when offered to prove the truth of the unstated (inferred) beliefs? To answer this question we must first address the relevancy of such utterances.

a. The Relevancy of Unstated Beliefs

Here are some examples of utterances that can be relevant only if they are offered to prove beliefs that the declarant holds but does not state explicitly. In our hypothetical case brought by the pedestrian against the driver of the gray SUV, suppose that Sally says to George "That SUV driver must be drunk" just after the pedestrian is struck. And suppose that the pedestrian is *not* trying to prove that the driver was drunk. The relevance of Sally's statement would depend on the inference that Sally has an unstated belief that the driver of the gray SUV was driving in a careless or wrongful manner when his car hit the pedestrian. The pedestrian would offer Sally's statement to prove that this *unstated belief is true*. The fact of consequence is that the driver was driving carelessly or wrongfully. Under this theory, the relevance of the statement depends on all of Sally's testimonial qualities, thus requiring a complete trip around the testimonial triangle, as Diagram 8-8 illustrates:

Diagram 8-8

B
Declarant Belief:
Sally believes driver's driving was careless

Narration-Ambiguity,
Sincerity

Perception,
Memory

Issue

A
Declarant's
Utterance:
Sally says "Driver must be drunk"

C
Event:
Driver was
careless

Further inferences to reach the issue in the pedestrian's case will involve deciding what kind of wrongful driving Sally perceived. Other facts about the incident will show that Sally was probably referring to the driver's failure to stop at the red light.

In the hypothetical about Jim Harris's prosecution for battery, suppose that the woman said to Jim "get out of here quick" just after the police officer asked who had thrown the first punch. Or, a man said, "Jim Harris ought to confess." These statements might be relevant to the prosecution's case, but not to prove that Jim ought to get out or confess. The relevance of the statements would depend on an inference that the woman and the man held the belief that Jim had thrown the first punch. Again, this belief is unstated, but the prosecution would be offering the two statements to prove that this unstated belief is true. And again, this theory of relevance requires reliance on all of the testimonial qualities of the woman and man.

It may occur to you to ask why the pedestrian would want to use Sally's out-of-court statement when questioning Sally at trial would reveal with more certainty what she believed about the accident. The same is true for the woman and man in the bar. Why not call them as witnesses and ask them whether they saw Jim throw the first punch? The answer is that sometimes declarants cannot be called as witnesses — they are unavailable, unwilling, or forgetful. Their out-of-court statements are the best source of their knowledge and beliefs, even if those beliefs are unstated.

One final example will help to make this point. In State v. Dullard, 668 N.W.2d 585 (Iowa 2003), Brent Dullard was convicted of possession of the precursor materials with intent to manufacture methamphetamine, a controlled substance. On a tip, police had conducted a legal search of the house and garage that Dullard shared with his mother. In the garage, police found materials that are potential precursors of methamphetamine (ephedrine and ether) plus items commonly used in the manufacture of methamphetamine. Under Iowa law, Dullard and his mother had joint possession of the garage where all of the substances were found. Thus, the prosecution had to prove Dullard's "actual knowledge or circumstances from which a jury could infer knowledge" in order to establish his possession of the precursors. This led the prosecution to offer into evidence a small spiral notebook found in a wooden desk in the garage that contained a handwritten note from an unknown person. The note read:

> B-
> I had to go inside and pee + calm my nerves somewhat down. When I came out to go get Brian I looked over to the street North of here + there sat a black + white w/ the dude out of his car facing our own direction — no one else was with him

The prosecution contended that the note was intended for Dullard ("B") and that it was relevant to show the writer's belief that Dullard needed to be told about the policeman because he was involved in, and had actual knowledge of, the drug activity in the garage. This relevant belief was unstated; and, the unknown writer was not available as a witness.

You can see that, just as with the hypothetical statements of Sally and about Jim Harris discussed above, inferences about all of the unknown writer's testimonial qualities are necessary to the relevancy of the note. Perhaps the author knew that Brent Dullard was ignorant of the contents of his garage and wanted to misrepresent his involvement (a sincerity risk); perhaps the author mistakenly wrote "B" and intended the note for "E" (a narration risk); perhaps the author had misperceived or forgotten about Brent's actual conduct and was mistaken about Brent's involvement (perception and memory risks). Even if all of these risks, or some of them, seem small to you, their existence implicates hearsay policy. If you were the attorney for Dullard, you would certainly want the opportunity to cross-examine the author of the note.

b.   Application of FRE 801(a) and (c)

Courts and commentators have struggled for two centuries with the problem of how the rule against hearsay should classify the kinds of utterances that we have been discussing. The Iowa Supreme Court posed the question of whether this implied, unstated belief — which it also called an "implied assertion" using the terminology of the common law — is a hearsay statement under the definition contained in the Iowa rule of evidence identical to FRE 801(a) and (c).

   i.   The Literal Approach.   FRE 801(a) defines a "statement" as "a person's oral assertion, [or] written assertion." FRE 801(c) defines hearsay as a "statement [of a declarant] that a party offers in evidence to prove the truth of the matter asserted in the statement." Taking these terms literally, the declarant's written assertions in the note in *Dullard* were not offered to prove the truth of the matters or propositions that they assert. Instead, the Court wrote, "the handwritten note is offered solely to show the declarant's belief, implied from the words and the message conveyed" that Dullard, the alleged recipient, had knowledge and thus possession of the drug lab materials. 668 N.W.2d at 591.

   Under a literal approach to FRE 801(a) and (c), since that relevant belief was not stated as an assertion in the note, the note could not be a statement that was offered to prove the truth of the matter it asserted. The same result would be reached if these definitions were applied to Sally's statement that the "driver must be drunk" and to the statements that Jim Harris should "get out quick" or "ought to confess" in the hypotheticals we have just discussed. These utterances would not be hearsay because they are not offered to prove the truth of the matters they explicitly and literally assert.

   ii.   The Common Law Approach.   At common law, courts used the phrase *implied assertions* to identify those utterances that were relevant not for the stated beliefs but for the implied unstated beliefs of the declarant. The Iowa Supreme Court in *Dullard* treated the note as containing an "implied assertion" of the author's belief that Dullard had knowledge and possession of the drug lab materials. The court described the common law approach:

> The starting point for the common law approach to implied assertions inevitably begins with the celebrated and durable case of Wright v. Tatham, 112 Eng. Rep. 488 (Ex. Ch. 1837). The case involved an action to set aside a will based on the incompetency of the testator . . . . At trial, the proponents of the will offered several letters written to the testator by various individuals concerning a variety of business and social subjects . . . . The purpose of the letters was to show the absent declarants must have believed the testator was able to engage in intelligent discourse on the various topics discussed in the letters . . . . This belief, therefore, constituted evidence of the testator's competency. [668 N.W. 2d at 591.]

The opinion in *Wright* became the general rule at common law. The court analogized the written letters to nonverbal conduct, the relevance of which depends on the belief of the actor. It held that "assertions that are relevant only as implying a statement or opinion of the absent declarant on the matter at issue constitute hearsay in the same way the actual statement or opinion of the absent declarant would be inadmissible hearsay."

   If the goal of a definition of hearsay is to identify those out-of-court utterances that require evaluation of *all* of the declarant's testimonial qualities — where the trip around the complete testimonial triangle is required — then the holding in *Wright* makes sense. All of the examples of utterances relevant to prove unstated beliefs that we have discussed so far (which the common law would call implied assertions) require inferences about *all* of the declarants' testimonial qualities. Under hearsay policy, this justifies requiring oath, demeanor, and cross-examination. Professor Roger Park labeled this common law risk analysis a "declarant-oriented" test for hearsay; a test that "focuses on whether the use of the utterance will require reliance on the credibility of the out-of-court declarant." Roger C. Park, McCormick on Evidence and the Concept of Hearsay: A Critical Analysis Followed by Suggestions to Law Teachers, 65 Minn. L. Rev. 423, 424 (1981).

iii.   FRE 801(a)-(c) Rejects the Common Law Approach.   The Advisory Committee Note to FRE 801(a) states that certain utterances are removed from the definition of hearsay, even though their relevance depends on the testimonial qualities of the declarant. This rejection of the "declarant-oriented" common law approach is briefly stated and sparingly justified as follows:

> [S]ituations giving rise to [nonassertive] . . . conduct are such as virtually to eliminate questions of sincerity. Similar considerations govern nonassertive verbal conduct and verbal conduct which is assertive but offered as a basis for inferring something other than the matter asserted, also excluded from the definition of hearsay by the language of subdivision (c).

The Note relies on an analogy between nonassertive *conduct*, defined as not hearsay by FRE 801(a), and two kinds of *verbal utterances*. The first sentence states that evidence of an actor's nonassertive conduct involves no sincerity danger. Why? Because the actor has no intent to use his conduct to communicate his belief. Think back to the earlier examples of nonassertive conduct admitted as not hearsay under FRE 801(a). Without the intent to communicate, there is no opportunity for the actor to lie, that is, to decide to communicate false information through conduct. In the next sentence, the Note implies that the risk of insincerity is also nonexistent for *all* "nonassertive verbal conduct and verbal conduct which is assertive but offered as a basis for inferring something other than the matter asserted" and that therefore such utterances should also be defined as not hearsay.

"Nonassertive verbal conduct" may refer to hortatory declarations, instructions and commands. The exclamation "Jim, get out quick" would be an example of this type of utterance. Assertive verbal conduct "offered as the basis for inferring something other than the matter asserted" may refer to assertions like the note in *Dullard* — utterances relevant for unstated beliefs that still bear hearsay dangers. The Note does not explain or give examples of either kind of statement, however, so its meaning is somewhat ambiguous. Furthermore, "nonassertive verbal conduct" is an oxymoron, for virtually all conscious utterances are efforts to assert something. Nonetheless, when utterances are offered as relevant to prove the declarant's unstated beliefs, the Advisory Committee appears to reject the common law approach to the definition of hearsay.

8.   Elaboration of FRE 801: Courts Reject the Literal Approach and Apply an "Intent" Test

Many federal courts faced with a choice between the literal approach of FRE 801(c) and the common law approach to statements relevant for unstated beliefs have rejected both. Instead, they have sought to identify those statements that bear the highest risk of insincerity and to exclude only those statements as hearsay. This approach rests on the understanding that words may be spoken or written with the *intent* to communicate something different from, or in addition to, what the words themselves formally articulate. People use language in many different ways to communicate. If the man stating "Jim Harris ought to confess" is intending to communicate his unstated belief that Jim threw the first punch by using this form of speech, it follows that he could choose to "lie" by communicating false information about Jim. When a speaker intends to communicate an unstated belief, there is enhanced danger of insincerity.

a.   The Judicially Created Intent Test

The test used by courts to identify those statements with the greatest sincerity danger has been articulated in different ways. Some courts have read "matter asserted" broadly enough to include matters that are *intentionally implied*, as well as explicitly stated — hence the label "implied assertions" for this type of hearsay. In Park v. Huff, 493 F.2d 923, 927 (5th Cir.), *rev'd on other grounds*, 506 F.2d 849 (5th Cir. 1974) (en banc), the court said that a declarant's statements implying that the defendant was financing a murder conspiracy are hearsay when there is a "possibility that the declarant intended to leave a particular impression." The court in United States v. Zenni, 492 F. Supp. 464, 468-469 and n.21 (E.D. Ky. 1980) acknowledged that FRE 801(a) "does not seem to require a preliminary determination by the trial court whether verbal conduct is intended as an assertion" but the court held that such a determination of intent would be required to include some "implied assertions" within the definition.

This intent test has been a judicial creation. Prior to the restyling of the Federal Rules, FRE 801(a)(1), defined verbal assertions as "statements" and did not contain an intent test, in contrast to the definition of nonverbal conduct as "statements" in FRE 801(a)(2), which did.[3] In creating this test, courts relied on the somewhat backhanded language of the Advisory Committee Note to FRE 801(a) that does emphasize that an intent to assert is critical to identifying hearsay: "The key to the definition is that nothing is an assertion unless intended to be one." Conversely, it would seem that if there is intent to assert, there is hearsay. Many evidence commentators agree:

> A number of scholars have advocated using the declarant's intent, or some objective manifestation of it, in determining what the declarant's statement asserts. Some version of an intent test seems necessary to keep the assertion definition [the literal truth-of-the-matter-asserted test] from being wholly arbitrary. [Roger C. Park, "I Didn't Tell Them Anything About You": Implied Assertions as Hearsay Under the Federal Rules of Evidence, 74 Minn. L. Rev. 783, 800 (1990).]

b.   The Difficulties of Applying an Intent Test

An intent test might be stated as follows: *When an out-of-court utterance is relevant to prove the truth of a belief that is different from or more than the truth of the*

---

3.   But see the text of the restyled FRE 801(a):"Statement" means a person's oral assertion, written assertion, or nonverbal conduct, if the person intended it as an assertion. Could it be argued that the "it" in the final clause refers to oral and written assertions, as well as conduct, and thus the Rule itself applies the intent test to verbal statements of unstated belief as well? Probably not, as this would be a substantive change in the Rule.

declarant's literal utterance, the evidence is hearsay if the declarant is intending to communicate the truth of the unstated belief that is critical to the relevance of the evidence.

One problem with such a test is that it is not clear what the meaning of "intent" is. When people speak, they have many beliefs in mind all at the same time. How central to the declarant's consciousness or thinking does a matter have to be for it to qualify as an "intended" communication? Consider Jill's statement to a friend of hers to whom she has been complaining about one of her coworkers, Mary. Jill says: "Well, at least I never stole from the company!" It seems clear from the context of the conversation that Jill has the specific intent to communicate to her friend the specific unstated proposition that Mary *did* steal from her employer. Jill has chosen a somewhat unusual way of expressing that proposition, but this does not diminish any of the hearsay dangers, including the danger of insincerity. Since she is intending to make an implicit communication, Jill has the opportunity to imply deliberately and falsely that Mary steals. The same analysis would seem to apply to the man's statement "Jim Harris ought to confess" in our hypothetical about who started the fight in the bar.

But while Jill's intent, and the man's intent, may be reasonably clear, in many cases it may be quite difficult to determine whether specific intent exists to communicate an unstated proposition. Consider the following:

> During the search of [codefendant] Mayfield's apartment, the telephone rang, and a police officer answered it. An unidentified female voice asked to speak with "Keith." The officer replied that Keith was busy. The caller then asked if Keith "still had any stuff." The officer asked the caller what she meant, and the caller responded "a fifty." The officer said "yeah." [United States v. Long, 905 F.2d 1572, 1579 (D.C. Cir. 1990).]

The defendant, Keith Long, was charged with possession of cocaine with intent to distribute. The caller's questions were clearly based on her belief that Keith was a drug-seller and had sold her drugs in the past. But what was the declarant intending to communicate? It may be that the declarant was simply intending to express her desire for drugs and not trying to assert the proposition "Keith is a drug-seller." Nonetheless, the declarant, at some level of consciousness, is basing her conduct on her knowledge that Keith has sold to her in the past and that her questions will communicate this fact. The declarant's out-of-court utterance was admitted at trial and Long was convicted. On appeal, Long argued that "the questions plainly revealed assumptions that are the functional equivalent of direct assertions . . . . [T]he caller, through her questions, in effect asserted that 'Keith ha[d] crack and s[old] it out of Mayfield's apartment.'" Id. The appellate court disagreed that "intent" was involved:

> With our inquiry focused on the *intent* of the caller, we have little trouble disposing of Long's theory about implied assertions. Long has not provided any evidence to suggest that the caller, through her questions, intended to assert that he was involved in drug dealing. The caller may indeed have conveyed messages about Long through her questions, but any such messages were merely incidental and not intentional. [Id. at 1580.]

Do you agree with the court's conclusion? Is the caller's statement more like Jill's "at least I never stole from the company" or like the statement of the note writer in *Dullard*?

To make an accurate decision about a speaker's intent, the jury will require sufficient factual information. Out-of-court utterances are typically described to the jury by someone who overheard them. Testimony from this witness about the immediate context in which the utterance was made may be the only information available to the jury. If the utterance was written, the document, and the witness authenticating it, may provide even less information pertinent to intent. 3 Stephen A. Saltzburg, Michael M. Martin and Daniel J. Capra, Federal Rules of Evidence Manual 1473 (7th ed. 1998), suggests that factual difficulties in applying an "actual intent" test can be adequately handled by an objective, rather than subjective, test of intent: "The question should be whether a reasonable person making a statement such as the declarant made would have intended to communicate the implied assertion that the proponent is offering for its truth."

Finally, which party should bear the burden of persuading the judge as to whether the declarant has or does not have the requisite intent? The traditional legal device for dealing with uncertainty about factual issues is allocating the burden of proof. By assigning the burden of proving intent, or lack thereof, the risk of erroneous decisions can be assigned to one party instead of the other to further evidentiary policy. Most proposed intent tests do place the burden to prove intent on the opponent of the evidence. "As with conduct, the burden should be placed on the non-offering party to show that the declarant had the intent to communicate the implied assertion." 3 Stephen A. Saltzburg, Michael M. Martin, and Daniel J. Capra, Federal Rules of Evidence Manual at 1473.

c.   *Some Courts Still Adhere to the Common Law Approach*

The Iowa Supreme Court in *Dullard* rejected both the literal approach and an intent test, and adopted the common law's "declarant-oriented" approach to the definition of hearsay. The court held that the note written by the unknown declarant was hearsay, even if its author did not intend to assert that Brent Dullard had knowledge of and possession of the substances in his garage.

> The distinction drawn between intended and unintended conduct or speech only implicates the danger of sincerity . . . other 'hearsay dangers remain viable, giving rise to the need for cross-examination. Moreover, even the danger of insincerity may . . . be present . . . . where the reliability of the direct assertion . . . is insincere . . . . Implied assertions can be no more reliable than the predicate expressed assertion. [668 N.W.2d at 594-595.]

Two years after *Dullard*, the Maryland Court of Appeals made a thorough analysis of the common law approach and the federal intent test, as well as much of the scholarly literature. It broadened the meaning of "matter asserted" and held that

> where the probative value of words, as offered, depends on the declarant *having communicated a factual proposition*, the words constitute an "assertion" of that proposition. The declarant's intent . . . is irrelevant. If the words are . . . offered in court to prove the truth of the [communicated] proposition — *i.e.* of the "matter asserted" — they are hearsay under our rules. [Stoddard v. State, 887 A.2d 564, 577 (Md. 2005) (emphasis added).]

Some federal circuit courts also seem to have applied the common law approach by excluding statements that are relevant only for the declarant's unstated belief without making any finding that the declarant intended to assert that belief. See Weinstein and Berger, Weinstein's Federal Evidence §801.10[2][c], at 801-10 to 801-12 nn.13,

15 (McLaughlin ed., 2d ed. 2003); Callen, Hearsay and Informal Reasoning, 47 Vand. L. Rev. 43, 47-48 n.18 (1994). Nevertheless, it is fair to say that the prevailing judicial practice is to admit as not hearsay statements relevant for unstated beliefs when the declarant did not intend to assert those beliefs, and to apply an intent test to exclude those statements that appear to bear significant sincerity danger due to opportunity to fabricate.

KEY POINTS

1. The Advisory Committee Note to FRE 801 construes FRE 801(a) and (c) as excluding oral and written utterances that are offered to prove a declarant's unstated beliefs from the definition of hearsay. Such utterances are not offered to prove the truth of the literal matters they assert.

2. The relevancy of these utterances still depends on the declarants' testimonial qualities. However, when the declarant is not intending to communicate the unstated belief, the sincerity danger may be minimal, and the utterance is analogous to nonassertive conduct.

3. In the majority of jurisdictions, if a court finds that the declarant specifically intends to communicate an unstated belief, it will usually exclude the utterance as hearsay.

4. Intent to communicate may be difficult to prove either because of factual uncertainty or because of ambiguity in the meaning of intent.

NOTES AND QUESTIONS

1. Ever since Wright v. Tatham, there has been a continued practical and academic debate about whether these utterances — also called "implied assertions" — should be classified as hearsay or as not hearsay, and about the most effective doctrinal test for accomplishing this. An informative contribution to this debate is the Symposium on Hearsay and Implied Assertions: How Would (or Should) the Supreme Court Decide the *Kearley* Case?, 16 Miss. C. L. Rev. 1 (1995). Other articles include Michael S. Pardo, Testimony, 82 Tul. L. Rev. 119 (2007); Michael H. Graham, Handbook of Federal Evidence Section 801.7, at 73-77 (5th ed. 2001); Craig R. Callen, Hearsay and Informal Reasoning, 47 Vand. L. Rev. 43 (1994); Paul S. Milich, Re-examining Hearsay Under the Federal Rules: Some Method for the Madness, 39 Kan. L. Rev. 893 (1991); Roger C. Park, "I Didn't Tell Them Anything About You": Implied Assertions as Hearsay Under the Federal Rules of Evidence, 74 Minn. L. Rev. 783 (1990). In 1992, a case before the Law Lords in the English House of Lords reaffirmed the common law approach to implied assertions set forth in Wright v. Tatham. Regina v. Kearley, 2 App. Cas. 228 (1992). However, some 10 years later, section 115 of the Criminal Justice Act of 2003 rejected this approach. The key text is that the definition of hearsay includes only those statements where "the purpose of, or one of the purposes, of the person making the statement appears to the court to have been (a) to cause another person to believe the matter, or (b) to cause another person to act . . . on the basis that the matter is as stated." Would the note in *Dullard* be hearsay under this test?

PROBLEMS

8.27. Return to Problem 8.13 at page 426, supra. To prove that there was ketchup on the floor where she fell, Sondra Evers presents Joel as a witness who will testify that shortly before Sondra's fall he heard another customer say, "Watch out for that ketchup!" Joel was standing in an aisle and did not see what the customer was looking at. Is it hearsay?

8.28. Return to Problem 3.4, State v. Blair, at page 137 supra. In Norma's private diary, on a page dated the day before the attack on her, Norma has written:

> Jimmy has really hurt me this time. He is getting more violent when I tell him I want to leave. I don't want anyone to read this and I am going to burn this diary when I leave for L.A.

Hearsay?

8.29. Victim was alone with Fred and Stanley when he was shot. To prove Fred shot the victim, the prosecution offers the following:

(a) The victim's statement immediately thereafter: "Help me, Stanley, I've got a bullet in me."

(b) The victim's statement at the hospital: "Whatever you do, don't let Fred in here. He wants to hurt me."

8.30. Fred and John have just been arrested by the police for a robbery. Fred says to John: "Don't worry, I didn't tell them anything about you." Hearsay if offered to prove John participated in the robbery?

8.31. Roger was arrested in the parking lot of a shopping center after selling two golf ball-sized packages of heroin to an undercover police agent. Roger told police that Frank was acting as his look-out during the transaction and was circling the parking lot in a blue van. The police questioned Frank, who insisted he knew nothing about a drug deal and denied that he had been circling the parking lot. Frank is now on trial for conspiracy to distribute heroin. Evidence is presented that while the police were talking to Frank, his cell phone rang repeatedly. An officer answered the cell phone 10 times and each time the caller "was someone requesting heroin." There is no evidence as to what the anonymous callers actually said to the officer. The court held that the calls were not hearsay:

> Even if the calls included assertions, the government offers them, not for their truth, but for the fact they were made. The fact that Frank received ten successive solicitations for heroin is probative circumstantial evidence of his involvement in a conspiracy to distribute heroin. The defense argues that the calls contain implicit factual assertions about the callers' belief that the defendant could supply the desired heroin. But the government did not offer the calls to prove the truth of these implicit assertions. Even if the callers had no real desire for the drug, and no faith that Frank could deliver it, the fact that he received ten of these calls is still evidence of his participation in a heroin distribution conspiracy.

What do you think of the court's reasoning? Why would anyone make such a call if he had no desire for the drug or belief that Frank could supply it? Could the reasoning be the same if Frank had received only one call? What result if the court had applied the "intent" test?

9.   Reflection on the Definition of Hearsay: Should FRE 801 Be Revised?

The goal of a definition of hearsay is at least twofold. It should advance hearsay policy by identifying evidence that should be subject to the hearsay prohibition of FRE 802. It should also provide rules that are as clear and as simple as possible for judges to apply quickly in the charged atmosphere of an ongoing trial. Thus, it may be undesirable to burden the definition of hearsay with an intent test, both in terms of time and fact-finding competence. If so, must intent be ignored and the identification of hearsay remain focused solely on the literal content of the words uttered to see whether the evidence was offered to prove the truth of those words?

An alternative is, of course, the "declarant-oriented" approach to defining hearsay adopted in *Dullard*. This approach would define all of these problematic utterances as hearsay without the necessity of any "intent" test at all. The result would be wholesale exclusion of utterances whenever relevance depends on the complete trip around the testimonial triangle.

There are other options for the definition. In Tex. R. Crim. Evid. 801(c) and Tex. R. Civ. Evid. 801(c), Texas has adopted a definition of "matter asserted" that focuses on the use of utterances to prove the beliefs of the declarant. "Matter asserted" includes "any matter explicitly asserted, and any matter implied by a statement, if the probative value of the statement as offered flows from declarant's belief in the matter." Professor Michael Graham proposes a similar definition that focuses on the presence of a necessary inference of sincerity:

> "Hearsay" is a statement offered in evidence, other than one made by the declarant while testifying at the trial or hearing, to the extent relevance depends upon (1) the truth of the matter asserted or (2) the declarant's belief in the truth or falsity of the matter asserted. [Michael Graham, "Stickperson Hearsay": A Simplified Approach to Understanding the Rule Against Hearsay, 1982 U. Ill. L. Rev. 887, 921 (1982).]

In practice, judges probably apply the truth-of-the-matter-asserted language of FRE 801(c) in a literalistic fashion, until they are confronted with an out-of-court utterance where the declarant's specific intent to communicate an unstated belief is clear. Then they craft some kind of intent test to exclude it. Is such muddling through acceptable? Professor Roger Park contends that judges are doing fine with the current rule:

> A review of the published caselaw does not reveal any obvious signs of injustice . . . . The cases generally involve utterances classed as [not hearsay] that raise no real insincerity dangers affecting the purpose for which they are being used . . . . [F]ederal courts are reaching fair results in resolving implied assertion problems under the existing assertion definition. [Park, 74 Minn. L. Rev. at 836-838.]

It would be possible to abandon the categorical thinking that underlies the truth-of-the-matter asserted test, the intent test, and the declarant-oriented test. The definition could focus on the more functional question whether the utterance is one that, from its content or context, appears to raise few sincerity risks. Professor Paul Milich suggests a specific test that would require judicial appraisal of the risk of insincerity:

> If it appears from the circumstances and the language used that the declarant probably would not have used that particular locution to lie about the fact in question, then the

reduced risk of insincerity frees the evidence from the definition of assertion and the federal definition of hearsay. [Paul S. Milich, Re-examining Hearsay Under the Federal Rules: Some Method for the Madness, 39 Kan. L. Rev. 893, 909 (1991).]

A shift in the definition toward an explicit appraisal of sincerity risk on a case-by-case basis affords the trial judge more discretion in applying the basic hearsay rule of exclusion. Lack of sincerity danger would be a stand-in for greater probative value, and out-of-court utterances would escape the definition because trial judges evaluate them as more probative. If appellate courts defer to this evaluation, then there could be less appellate review than is currently afforded under any of the more categorical "truth of the matter asserted," "intent" and "declarant-oriented" definitions.

We have discussed here only a fraction of the academic ink that has been spilled on the question of the definition of hearsay. As we stated at the beginning of this chapter, a brief doctrinal definition can only imperfectly capture all of the reasons for the hearsay prohibition. Any test of hearsay that focuses solely on identifying sincerity danger reflects a choice to ignore perception and memory dangers. This reflects a compromise with other values at stake in our system of trial, including the efficiency of trials, confidence in jury fact-finding, the role of the trial judge and the nature of appellate review. Different definitions reflect a difference in thinking about where the compromise should be drawn. After you have studied the exemptions and exceptions to the general rule of exclusion, we will again examine some of the current and diverse thinking on the meaning, function, and future of the entire hearsay rule.

B.   A GENERAL APPROACH TO THE ADMISSION OF HEARSAY UNDER THE EXEMPTIONS AND EXCEPTIONS

Many out-of-court statements, although they are hearsay, are admitted into evidence to prove the truth of the matters they assert. FRE 801(d) *exempts* eight types of out-of-court statements from the definition of hearsay, and FRE 803, 804, and 807 create 29 explicit *exceptions* to FRE 802's rule of exclusion. In terms of the process by which judges admit these various statements, there is no difference between an FRE 801(d) hearsay exemption and an FRE 803, FRE 804, or FRE 807 hearsay exception. We treat them separately in the sections of this chapter only as a matter of organizational convenience.

1.   Justification for the Exemptions and Exceptions

There are differences, however, in the justifications for admitting all these different types of hearsay statements. The drafters of the Federal Rules created the new status of *exemption* under FRE 801(d) to admit hearsay statements whose principal rationale for admission is the possibility for cross-examining the declarant. Most hearsay *exceptions* admitted under FRE 803, 804 and 807 are justified by the presence of circumstances that tend to minimize one or more of the hearsay dangers, making these statements perhaps more "trustworthy" than other hearsay. Thus, there would be, in theory, less reason for concern about the absence of cross-examination.

We analyze these justifications in more detail in each of the following sections in this chapter, and you should ask yourself how persuasive you think they are. After you have spent considerable time and effort on identifying hearsay and on understanding how and why hearsay policy operates to exclude it, it may come as something of a shock to see how freely a lot of hearsay is admitted through the exemptions and exceptions.

2.   The Categorical Approach

FRE 801(d), FRE 803, and FRE 804 all apply a categorical approach to the admission of hearsay. FRE 807 applies a noncategorical "trustworthiness" approach, which will be discussed separately in Section F. By "categorical approach" we mean that the rules establish specific categories of out-of-court statements that can be admitted for their truth. These categories are sometimes defined by who the declarant is, sometimes by the content of the statement, and sometimes by the circumstances in which the statement was made. You should read through these rules now to get a general sense of what these categories are like.

3.   The Process of Admission

The process of admission under FRE 801(d), FRE 803, and FRE 804 goes something like this: A proponent typically offers to prove a declarant's out-of-court statement through the testimony of a witness who overheard it or through an exhibit that contains it, such as a document in which the statement is written or a tape or some other recording of it. The opponent typically objects on grounds of hearsay. In order to rule on this objection, the judge must decide whether the statement is hearsay under FRE 801(a)-(c). If it is, then the burden is on the proponent of the statement to produce foundational evidence — typically evidence of who the declarant is, or what the content of the statement is, or the out-of-court circumstances in which the hearsay statement was made — that satisfies the categorical terms of a specific exemption or exception. The doctrinal terms of the exemption or exception tell you what foundational evidence needs to be produced. The judge then decides whether the proffered statement fits within the specific categorical exemption or exception.

4.   The Foundational Requirements

We call this foundational evidence *foundation facts*. You saw in Chapter Four that the proponent of an exhibit must produce foundation facts that satisfy the standard for authentication and identification set by FRE 901(a). In the same way, under FRE 801(d), FRE 803, and FRE 804, the proponent must produce foundation facts that satisfy the standards set by the categorical subsections of those rules. Typically, this will mean that the proponent must produce a witness who can testify about these foundation facts. We call this witness a *foundation witness*.

Take as one example a witness, Joe, who testifies in court and identifies Sam, the defendant, as the perpetrator of a crime or tort. At a lineup held at a police station just a few days after the crime or accident, Joe made a statement that the perpetrator was Peter, not Sam. Sam, the defendant, would obviously want to offer this prior statement into evidence to prove that he was *not* the perpetrator. Can Joe's prior statement be admitted for the truth of the matter it asserts? Yes, if it fits within a categorical exemption or exception. By reading FRE 801(d)(1)(A), you will see that the foundational requirements for it are as follows:

- the statement was made by a declarant who is now testifying in court as a witness;
- the declarant is subject to cross-examination about the statement;
- the contents of the statement are inconsistent with testimony given at trial;
- the statement was made under penalty of perjury; and
- the statement was made at a trial, hearing, other proceeding, or in a deposition.

Focusing for now just on the fourth requirement, the proponent will have to produce foundational evidence as to whether the statement was made under penalty of perjury. A foundation witness who can present foundation facts that Joe made his statement subject to a formal oath or attestation might be Joe himself; it might be the police officer at the lineup; or, it could be anyone else who observed Joe and who could describe the oath or attestation. After hearing this foundational testimony, the judge will decide whether the categorical requirement has been satisfied. This is a preliminary question that is necessary to the application of an evidence rule. FRE 104 governs such questions, as you know. Applying the policies underlying Rule 104 you should be able to determine whether the judge applies Rule 104(a) or (b). As a general principle, FRE 104(a) applies unless the facts listed above as foundational requirements are necessary to the out-of-court statement's relevancy. Are they? You can see that they are not. Joe's prior statement would be relevant to prove that Sam was *not* the perpetrator whether or not it was under penalty of perjury. This requirement is, instead, a matter of hearsay policy. Thus, the judge would have to be persuaded by a preponderance of the evidence, pursuant to FRE 104(a), that the foundational requirement was satisfied. This is the proponent's burden, and it is the key to the admission of hearsay. We will have more to say about this judicial decision-making process as we discuss Rules 801(d), 803, and 804 in greater detail.

5. Multiple Exemptions and Exceptions May Apply

As you study the hearsay exemptions and exceptions, keep in mind that an out-of-court statement may sometimes be admissible pursuant to more than one of them. For example, the deposition testimony given by a party who is now testifying as a witness could be admissible against the party as an admission under FRE 801(d)(2)(A) or as a prior inconsistent statement under oath under FRE 801 (d)(1)(A); a statement may be both a present sense impression under FRE 803(1) and an excited utterance under FRE 803(2); a document may qualify for admission as a public record under FRE 803(8) and as a business record under FRE 803(6). When this is the case, it is sufficient to overcome a hearsay objection to show that the evidence falls within one exemption or exception. Similarly, except in one context that we will consider later, the fact that evidence does *not* quite fit within a particular exemption or exception does not prevent its admission under a different one.

6.   The Confrontation Clause

There is one more introductory point to be made. In criminal prosecutions, defendants have a right "to be confronted with the Witnesses against them," which is protected by the Sixth Amendment to the U.S. Constitution. This right has been recently construed by the Supreme Court to mean that so-called testimonial hearsay statements may not be used by the prosecution at all in criminal trials. Crawford v. Washington, 541 U.S. 36 (2004). We will discuss the meaning given to the term *testimonial* and the complexities of applying the testimonial standard in Section G of this chapter. *Crawford* affects some, but not all, of the hearsay exceptions, and there are also exceptions to its prohibition, including that the declarant is testifying as a witness at the trial. We raise the confrontation issue now because some of the hearsay statements that you will find to be admissible under a hearsay exemption or exception must still be tested under the interpretation of the confrontation clause in *Crawford* as well. We raise the *Crawford* issue explicitly at a few points in Sections C, D, E, and F.

C.   HEARSAY EXEMPTIONS

FRE 801(d) exempts certain types of out-of-court statements from the definition of hearsay. These statements are admissible to prove the truth of the matters they assert, assuming that they are otherwise unobjectionable. FRE 801(d)(1) exempts certain kinds of statements previously made out of court by a testifying witness. FRE 801(d)(2) exempts out-of-court statements made by a party or by persons affiliated with a party, so long as the statements are offered *against* that party. Reading the Advisory Committee Notes to FRE 801(d) will give you some idea of the controversy surrounding the hearsay status of these two broad categories of out-of-court statements.

1.   FRE 801(d)(1) and (2)

RULE 801.   Definitions

(d) *Statements That Are Not Hearsay*. A statement that meets the following conditions is not hearsay:

(1) A *Declarant-Witness's Prior Statement*. The declarant testifies and is subject to cross-examination about a prior statement, and the statement:

(A) is inconsistent with the declarant's testimony and was given under penalty of perjury at a trial, hearing, or other proceeding or in a deposition;

(B) is consistent with the declarant's testimony and is offered to rebut an express or implied charge that the declarant recently fabricated it or acted from a recent improper influence or motive in so testifying; or

(C) identifies a person as someone the declarant perceived earlier.

(2) *An Opposing Party's Statement.* The statement is offered against an opposing party and:

(A) was made by the party in an individual or representative capacity;

(B) is one the party manifested that it adopted or believed to be true;

(C) was made by a person whom the party authorized to make a statement on the subject;

(D) was made by the party's agent or employee on a matter within the scope of that relationship and while it existed; or

(E) was made by the party's co-conspirator during and in furtherance of the conspiracy.

The statement must be considered but does not by itself establish the declarant's authority under (C); the existence or scope of the relationship under (D); or the existence of the conspiracy or participation in it under (E).

2.   Interpretation and Illustration of FRE 801(d)(1): The Testifying Declarant Must Be "Subject to Cross-examination About a Prior Statement"

FRE 801(d)(1) admits statements made outside of court by a hearsay declarant who is testifying as a witness at trial. With the declarant-witness in court, subject to cross-examination, you might think that *all* of that witness's out-of-court statements should be admitted as exempt from the hearsay rule of exclusion. This is not the case, however, as the rule admits only three categories of prior statements. There are two basic requirements that apply to all three categories:

- the out-of-court declarant is testifying at trial; and
- the declarant is subject to cross-examination about the prior statement.

Consider the example presented on page 447, supra: Joe is an eyewitness to a crime or accident and he testifies in a criminal or civil case brought against Sam, the alleged wrongdoer. At trial, Joe identifies Sam as the wrongdoer. Suppose that Joe had been brought to a police lineup that included Sam just a few days after the incident. After viewing the lineup Joe identified Peter, not Sam, as the perpetrator. Sam would like to offer evidence of this prior statement in his own defense. Would it be admissible under FRE 801(d)(1)(A), or (B), or (C)?

a.   Preliminary Fact-finding

i.   The Declarant Is Testifying at Trial.   The first foundational requirement is that the person testifying — Joe — be identified as the same person — Joe — who made the proffered out-of-court statement. United States v. Byrd, 210 Fed. Appx. 101 (2d Cir. 2006) (defendant's offer of his probation officer's testimony about statements made by defendant himself was inadmissible because defendant did not testify). The proponent of Joe's hearsay statement can fulfill this requirement through Joe's own acknowledgment that he made the out-of-court statement, or through the testimony of another witness who can say that the witness Joe was the out-of-court speaker.

ii. Examination Concerning the Statement.   Then the judge must determine that Joe is *subject to cross-examination about the prior statement*. The opponent's opportunity to cross-examine the declarant-witness is, as we have said, the principal justification for admitting Rule 801(d)(1) statements. Although the rule speaks in terms of *cross-examination* only, it has been construed to mean redirect examination as well. Thus, either party may introduce a prior statement of a witness, either on direct or cross-examination, and the opposing party must then have the opportunity to examine the witness about the statement. Prior statements can also be admitted after the witness has testified. The declarant-witness must still be available in court or subject to recall by the opposing party to satisfy the requirement of cross-examination *about* the statement, if the witness was not asked about it during the original examination by the opponent.[4]

Remember that the declarant-witness's prior hearsay statement is now being offered for its truth. Thus, the opponent of the statement will want to examine the declarant-witness *about* the hearsay statement in order to expose reasons why it should not be relied on by the jury. If the declarant-witness remembers both making the prior statement and the events that are the subject of the statement, the cross-examiner can elicit information pertinent to evaluating the declarant-witness's testimonial qualities at the time the statement was made. If the declarant-witness denies the truth of the prior statement, or attempts to explain it, the jury will decide what weight to give it. If the witness adopts as true the contents of a prior inconsistent statement, there is then no hearsay problem because the adopted inconsistency corrects and becomes a part of the witness's in-court testimony. United States v. Lopez-Lopez, 282 F.3d 1, 17 (1st Cir. 2000) (witness adopted prior statement that he had observed defendant for "only two or three seconds" as opposed to his trial testimony of "four or five" seconds; "adoption bypasses . . . the entire hearsay problem"). But "adoption" of a prior *consistent* statement does not eliminate the hearsay problem.

iii. Denial of, or Inability to Remember, the Prior Statement.   What if the witness denies making or cannot remember making the prior statement? If the prior statement is an authenticated writing or recording, there may be little doubt that it was made. If the prior statement was not recorded, then it will be the subject of testimony from someone who was present at the time — the police officer, for example, who was with Joe at the police lineup when Joe identified Peter and not Sam. At trial, if Joe denies that he made the prior inconsistent identification, he will still be considered to be a witness *subject to cross-examination about the statement*. But how would you cross-examine him? There is likely to be nothing more than a swearing contest between two witnesses, such as Joe and the police officer, about whether the statement was made.

iv. Inability to Remember the Underlying Events.   It may also happen that the witness cannot remember the underlying event that is the subject of the statement. If this seems far-fetched to you, consider United States v. Owens, 484 U.S. 554 (1988), in which a battery victim's prior statement identifying defendant Owens as his assailant was admitted under FRE 801(d)(1)(C). At trial, the victim had no memory

---

4.   Note that this protection of the right of the opponent to examine the witness concerning the prior statement under FRE 801(d) is equivalent to the protection afforded under FRE 613(b) when a witness's prior inconsistent statement is offered only for impeachment, as discussed in Chapter Seven, page 384.

of seeing the assailant. He could remember the attack and making the prior identification of Owens at the hospital, but he could not recall how he knew it was Owens
who attacked him. How would you cross-examine this victim about his perception or
memory of the assailant? Should the victim be considered to be a witness *subject to
cross-examination about the statement*, in fulfillment of FRE 801(d)(1)?

In *Owens*, the Supreme Court rejected both a confrontation clause and a Rule
801(d)(1) challenge to the admission of the prior statement of identification. With
respect to the adequacy of cross-examination under FRE 801(d)(1) the Court said:

> Ordinarily a witness is regarded as "subject to cross-examination" when he is placed on
> the stand, under oath, and responds willingly to questions. Just as with the constitutional
> prohibition, limitations on the scope of examination by the trial court or assertions of
> privilege by the witness may undermine the process to such a degree that meaningful
> cross-examination within the intent of the rule no longer exists. But that effect is not
> produced by the witness's assertion of memory loss — which . . . is often the very result
> sought to be produced by cross-examination, and can be effective in destroying the force
> of the prior statement. Rule 801(d)(1)(C), which specifies that cross-examination need
> only "concer[n] the statement," does not on its face require more. [Id. at 561-562.]

Owens thus imposes a minimal requirement of what it means to cross-examine a
witness "concerning" a prior statement, which was the applicable term prior to the
restyling of the rule. There is no reason to think that the new text — "about" the
statement — changes its meaning. Under *Owens*, it does not matter that the witness
denies making, or cannot remember, either the prior statement or the underlying
event, or perhaps even both. United States v. Harty, 476 F. Supp. 2d 17, 25 (D. Mass.
2007) (witness's hearsay identification of defendant's photograph admissible under
FRE 801(d)(1)(C) despite the witness's inability to remember the alleged crime, to
recognize the photo currently, and to remember why he had picked out defendant's
photo originally).

Lower courts following *Owens* have applied this minimalist position to statements governed by FRE 801(d)(1)(A). In United States v. Milton, 8 F.3d 39 (D.C.
Cir. 1993), the court held that a witness who claimed to have forgotten both the
underlying events and the making of the prior inconsistent statement was nevertheless
subject to cross-examination concerning it:

> When a witness has forgotten the basis for and the giving of testimony under oath in an
> earlier proceeding and that testimony is then introduced into evidence, defense ques-
> tioning, though impaired, is not futile for the reasons given in Owens. It is still possible
> to bring out on cross-examination the "witness' bias, his lack of care and attentiveness . . .
> and even (what is often a prime objective of cross-examination) the very fact that he has a
> bad memory." And that is precisely what took place in this case. Defense counsel elicited
> testimony from Jones that tended to discredit her grand jury testimony. She admitted that
> when she appeared before the grand jury she was addicted to drugs, was suffering from
> withdrawal and was on the verge of a nervous breakdown. [Id. at 46-47.]

In United States v. Keeter, 130 F.3d 297 (7th Cir. 1997), the defendant claimed that
the witness was feigning a loss of memory of both the litigated event and the prior
statement, and thus could not be cross-examined. The Seventh Circuit, relying on
Owens, held that the "Supreme Court's point was that the confrontation clause (and
the rule) are satisfied when the witness must look the accused in the eye in court;
shortcomings in the declarant's memory may be made known to the jury." Id. at 302.

v.   Personal Knowledge Is Required.   The Ninth Circuit opinion in *Owens*, 789 F.2d 750 (9th Cir. 1986), also discussed the requirement of personal knowledge. Courts and commentators are agreed that the requirement applies to statements admitted under FRE 801(d)(1). Thus, in *Owens*, where the witness-declarant could not remember seeing his assailant at the time of the attack, the defendant Owens argued that personal knowledge had not been shown. The appellate court concluded that it could not say whether the district court had actually decided the personal knowledge issue. Most courts have applied FRE 104(a) to the personal knowledge requirement for hearsay declarants. This requires a higher threshold of proof to be met by proponents, and requires a decision by the judge under the preponderance of the evidence standard. In cases of failed memory, such a decision may be difficult to make.

b.   Other Justifications for the FRE 801(d)(1) Exemptions

In addition to the witness-declarant being subject to some form of cross-examination, the foundational requirements of prior statements admitted under subsections (A), (B) and (C) may make those statements more reliable than other hearsay.

3.   Interpretation and Illustration of FRE 801(d)(1)(A): Prior Inconsistent Statements

a.   Preliminary Fact-finding

The foundational requirements for FRE 801(d)(1)(A) are:

- the contents of the statement are inconsistent with testimony given at trial;
- the statement was given under the penalty of perjury; and
- the statement was made at a trial, hearing, other proceeding, or in a deposition.

i.   Inconsistency.   In the example of Joe's prior identification of Peter, the foundational requirement of its inconsistency with his in-court identification of Sam is determined by comparing the contents of the two statements. Generally, the inconsistency will appear from the contents alone, particularly when the statements are diametrically opposed such that the truth of one implies the falsity of the other. But inconsistency is not limited to such opposition; "any substantive divergence between two statements" will permit use of the prior statement. United States v. Jasin, 215 F. Supp. 2d 552, 591 (E.D. Pa. 2002) (citing Weinsten's Federal Evidence §801.21(2) (b)). Sometimes there may be doubt about the fact of inconsistency, particularly if the allegedly inconsistent statement is ambiguous. The judge should make an FRE 104(a) determination of inconsistency — under the higher standard of preponderance of the evidence. The relevancy of the prior statement is to prove the truth of its own content; relevancy is not dependent on whether the statement is actually inconsistent with the witness's trial testimony.

ii. Inconsistency Due to Evasion. Some courts have found inconsistency when a witness claims a loss of memory of relevant events while testifying at trial, but had previously testified in detail about them before a grand jury. "We have previously concluded that a witness's 'feigned' memory loss can be considered inconsistent under the Rule, for 'the unwilling witness often takes refuge in a failure to remember.'" United States v. Cisneros-Gutierrez, 517 F.3d 751, 757 (5th Cir. 2008). Inconsistency may be found in evasive answers, silence, or changes in position. United States v. Iglesias, 535 F.3d 150, 159 (3d Cir. 2008) (prior testimony from a suppression hearing admitted when, just two days later, witness's testimony "included one word admissions, evasive and rambling responses, and equivocations").

iii. Under Penalty of Perjury and at a Trial, Hearing, or Other Proceeding. The circumstances in which the inconsistent statement was made are also part of the FRE 801(d)(1)(A) foundation. The proponent must show that the statement was made under penalty of perjury and that the statement was made in a trial, hearing, deposition, or other proceeding. These foundation facts are relatively easy to prove, although you can see that Joe's prior inconsistent statement, made at the lineup, would not satisfy the requirement of being made at a hearing. But is a lineup an *other proceeding* that would satisfy the rule's requirement? Typically, statements made in the course of interviews and lineups are held not to be within the meaning of "other proceedings." They are not under penalty of perjury, and the formality of trials, hearings, and depositions is thought to be conducive to reliability and truthfulness; the informality of most other interrogations is not. In United States v. Perez, 870 F.2d 1222 (7th Cir. 1989), the transcript of defense counsel's pretrial interview with an adverse government witness was not admissible under FRE 801(d)(1)(A). The statement was under oath and recorded by a court reporter. But it did not meet the requirements of a deposition under the Federal Rules of Criminal Procedure. The government was not present and the court did not authorize the interview. Some interrogations by immigration officers have been held to be "other proceedings." United States v. Castro-Ayon, 537 F.2d 1055, 1058 (9th Cir. 1976) (interrogation bore "many similarities to a grand jury proceeding; both are investigatory, ex parte, inquisitive, sworn, basically prosecutorial . . . recorded, and held in circumstance of some legal formality.").

b. Justification for the FRE 801(d)(1)(A) Limitations

The Advisory Committee originally proposed that *all* prior inconsistent statements could be used for their truth, as is true in California under Evidence Code §1235. Because such statements are closer in time to the events they relate to, and the declarant-witness is testifying before the jury, hearsay dangers are diminished. The House of Representatives, however, decided that admissibility should be limited to statements made under oath and *subject to cross-examination at the time they were made*. The final version of FRE 801(d)(1)(A) represents a compromise between these two positions: A witness's inconsistent statement may be used for its truth only if made at a trial, hearing, other proceeding, or in a deposition, but without the requirement of cross-examination. The compromise permits admission of statements made to grand juries under FRE 801(d)(1)(A), used most commonly when government witnesses change their stories at trial or claim not to remember the facts about the defendant's culpability to which they testified previously.

Most hearings or other proceedings are likely to be transcribed, so the fact that the prior statement was made at all will be easier to prove. Both sides to the debate over FRE 801(d)(1)(A), reported in the Advisory Committee Note, also used arguments about the reliability of prior inconsistent statements. The potential penalty of perjury, and the requirement of being made at a hearing, were intended to increase the trustworthiness of the statement. As we have said before, admitting hearsay for such reasons of increased trustworthiness is typical under the hearsay exceptions.

c.   *Prior Inconsistent Statements Not Within FRE 801(d)(1)(A)*

At common law, any prior inconsistent statement could be admitted, but only as nonhearsay to impeach the testifying witness, not for its truth. Today, an allegedly inconsistent statement that does not fit within FRE 801(d)(1)(A) may still be admitted just to show that the witness has said inconsistent things and should not be relied on. The use of prior inconsistent statements for this impeachment purpose was discussed in Chapter Seven.

4.   Interpretation and Illustration of FRE 801(d)(1)(B): Prior Consistent Statements

a.   *Preliminary Fact-finding*

In our previous example, Joe might have told the police the license plate number of the car involved in the crime or tort and then testified to this same number at trial. The statement to the police could be admissible for its truth as a prior consistent statement if the requirements of FRE(d)(1)(B) are satisfied. These requirements are:

> the statement . . . is consistent with the declarant's testimony and is offered to rebut an express or implied charge that the declarant recently fabricated it or acted from a recent improper influence or motive in so testifying.

The consistency of Joe's two statements would be apparent. If there are doubts about consistency, the preliminary question would be decided similarly to the question of inconsistency, discussed above.

i.   An Express or Implied Charge of Recent Fabrication or Improper Influence or Motive.   It seems obvious that parties would find it advantageous to present their witnesses' prior consistent statements to the jury for their truth. But FRE 801(d)(1)(B) applies only if the credibility of the testifying witness has been attacked in the particular way spelled out in the rule. Proof of such attack will be apparent to the judge from the opponent's cross-examination of the witness or from the admission of other impeaching evidence. Prior consistent statements should not be admitted for their truth until such an attack has actually occurred. The kinds of impeachment techniques that qualify as charges of *recent fabrication or improper influence or motive* are analyzed in Chapter Seven. A common example of a motive to fabricate arises in criminal cases where confederates of the defendant negotiate a plea bargain and then testify against the defendant. The defense will seek to impeach such witnesses with the suggestion that they have received favorable treatment from the government in exchange for testimony inculpating the defendant. United States v. Washington, 462 F.3d 1124, 1135 (9th Cir. 2006) (defense counsel accused witnesses of colluding with each other, because of their plea agreements, "to make up stories implicating [defendant] in the bank robbery.").

   ii.   To "Rebut" the Charge.   In Tome v. United States, 513 U.S. 150 (1995), the question was raised whether the consistent statement could *rebut* the charge of improper influence or motive, as required by Rule 801(d)(1)(B), only if it was made *prior* to the date at which the improper influence or motive allegedly arose. In *Tome*, a child witness testified in court about acts of sexual assault by her father. After cross-examination, several of her prior statements making the same accusations were then admitted under FRE 801(d)(1)(B) to rebut the implicit charge that the child's in-court testimony was fabricated and was motivated by a desire to live with her mother. The child's out-of-court accusations had been made, however, *after* the child's motive to fabricate arose; that is, *after* primary custody had been awarded to the father. The Supreme Court majority held that the prior accusations did not, therefore, fall within the meaning of *rebut* under subsection (B). The majority reasoned first that the term meant rebutting a specific charge, not just bolstering credibility:

> [T]he question is whether A.T.'s out-of-court statements rebutted the alleged link between her desire to be with her mother and her testimony, not whether they suggested that A.T.'s in-court testimony was true. The Rule speaks of a party rebutting an alleged motive, not bolstering the veracity of the story told. [Id. at 157-158.]

The majority noted that this same common law meaning of "to rebut" had been adopted by the Advisory Committee in its Note to FRE 801(d)(1)(B), limiting the scope of subsection (B) to statements made *before* the motive to fabricate arose. Only pre-motive statements could *rebut* an improper motive because their consistency would show that the in-court testimony was not tainted by that motive. Four dissenting Justices read the term *rebut* as raising a relevance issue rather than a rigid pre-motive timing requirement. In their view, not only pre-motive but some post-motive consistent statements might be relevant to rebut a charge of recent fabrication or improper influence or motive, and should be admitted under the rule.
   Cases decided since *Tome* raise the question as to when a motive to fabricate arises. When several persons are complicit in a crime, each may seek to cooperate with the government in order to receive more lenient treatment. Typically, cooperation involves giving incriminating testimony against others. Does the motive to fabricate arise at the time of arrest? United States v. Trujillo, 376 F.3d 593, 611 (6th Cir. 2004) (it is not believable that "a day or two after [declarant-witnesses] were stopped with more than fifty kilograms of marijuana in their car and were subsequently arrested, they did not have a motive to lie, regarding the source of the marijuana, to get lenient treatment"). Or, not until discussions begin about what benefits, if any, are to be received in exchange for cooperation? Several Circuit Courts have refused to hold that a motive to fabricate always attaches upon arrest and require the trial court to make a finding about motive on the specific facts:

> [S]tatements made after arrest are not automatically and necessarily contaminated by a motive to fabricate in order to curry favor with the government. Indeed, we recognize

that a variety of motives may drive a person's decision to disgorge the details of a crime he has committed . . .

But given the complexity of the human psyche, we agree with the Fourth, Seventh, and Eighth Circuits that whether a witness had a motive to fabricate when prior consistent statements were made is plainly a question of fact to be resolved by the trial court based precisely on the particular circumstances of an individual case. Quite simply, the trial court is in the best position to make that determination and its determination deserves great deference. [United States v. Prieto, 232 F.3d 816, 820-821 (11th Cir. 2000).]

Do you think fact-finding about the motives of the human psyche is possible? Would a bright-line legal rule about when a motive to fabricate will be held to have arisen in plea bargaining situations be preferable?

b.   Justification for the FRE 801(d)(1)(B) Limitation

At common law, it was clear that only consistent statements made *before* the motive to fabricate arose were admissible. Broader admissibility, it was thought, would create a risk of admitting manufactured consistent statements, and could unfairly surprise the opponent. The majority in *Tome* adopted this common law justification and relied heavily on the intent of the Advisory Committee as expressed in its Note to Rule 801(d)(1)(B) in doing so.

c.   Prior Consistent Statements Not Within FRE 801(d)(1)(B)

Consistent statements that do not fall within FRE 801(d)(1)(B) may still be relevant to bolster credibility on other grounds. They are, however, not admissible for their truth. In Chapter Seven, we discussed whether or not prior consistent statements not within FRE 801(d)(1)(B) are admissible not for their truth but for the nonhearsay purpose of bolstering the witness.

5.   Interpretation and Illustration of FRE 801(d)(1)(C): Prior Statements of Identification

a.   Preliminary Fact-finding

In our lineup example, now assume that Joe identified Sam at the lineup as the perpetrator of the crime or tort and also identified Sam when testifying in court. Statements identifying a person are admitted under FRE 801(d)(1)(C) without any necessary predicate testimony from the declarant-witness that is consistent or inconsistent with the out-of-court identification. The foundational requirements are:

- the statement identifies a person; and
- the statement identifies that person as someone the declarant perceived earlier.

You can see that these foundation requirements are minimal. Joe's identification of either Sam or Peter at the lineup clearly qualifies. Indeed, the statement may be made in contexts other than lineups, and no oath is required. Thus, FRE 801(d)(1) (C) adds to what may be admitted under (A) and (B). A prior identification that is *consistent* with in-court testimony (Joe's identification of Sam) can be admitted without proof of any attack on Joe's sincerity. And it can be admitted even if Joe has forgotten the underlying event and cannot make an in-court identification at all. If a pretrial identification is *inconsistent* with in-court testimony (Joe's identification of Peter), it can be admitted even if not admissible under FRE 801(d)(1)(A) because not made under oath or at a hearing. The jury as fact finder determines the accuracy of the out-of-court identification. The inability or hesitancy of a witness to make an in-court identification, recantation of a prior identification, or discrepancies in the descriptions given of the person identified, are all "customary grist for the jury mill." Manson v. Braithwaite, 432 U.S. 98, 116 (1977).

i. The Statement Identifies a Person as Someone the Derclarant Perceived Earlier. According to the Advisory Committee Note, FRE 801(d)(1)(C) was intended to include statements of identification made at traditional lineups and show ups. The declarant would be reperceiving the person whom the declarant had seen previously committing a crime or participating in some other disputed event. But the language used in the rule is not limited to *reperceptions at lineups*. Subsection (C) has been interpreted very broadly to include statements that identify a person seen after the disputed event in a chance encounter; that identify the photograph of the person; and that identify a police artist sketch of the person. It has also been held to permit the admission of hearsay statements that identify people (for example in surveillance photos) who are known to the declarant, but when the declarant did not perceive the underlying disputed event.

The Third Circuit has held that a statement to police, made on the day after a series of home invasions in a neighborhood, that the witness "had seen three of the defendants in the area of the crime during the time the homes were invaded" was admissible under FRE 802(d)(1)(C). United States v. Lopez, 271 F.3d 472, 485 (3d Cir. 2001). This statement was made without reperception of the defendants, and was acknowledged by the court to be simply "a person coming forward after a crime is committed and saying he saw particular persons at a certain place and time." This "Lopez rule" was rejected and, in our view, soundly criticized as contrary to the meaning of "identification" as had been used in Rule 801(d)(1)(C) prior to the restyling. United States v. Kaquatosh, 242 F. Supp. 2d 562, 566-567 (E.D. Wis. 2003) (statement of identification requires designation of a particular person (or photo) upon reperception as being the same as the person previously perceived). If reperception is not required, subsection (C) allows admission of out-of-court statements that identify perpetrators of crimes but are really nothing but accusations that have no particular indicia of reliability. Federal case law has not taken up the *Lopez/Kaquatosh* debate, but the majority of state courts that have cited it hold with the *Lopez* view that subsection (C) statements are not limited to those made at formal lineups, etc., and, if made by a person who knows the subject of the identification, can be made in police interviews without reperception. Commonwealth v. Adams, 941 N.E.2d 1127, 1130-1133 (Mass. 2011) (defendant's younger brother identified defendant as a shooter in two police interviews). The restyling of subsection (C) — that the statement "identifies a person as someone the declarant perceived earlier" — does not either explicitly support or reject the *Lopez* view.

A similar split in authority exists as to whether a physical description of a person given by the declarant to the police, also without any reperception of the person, fits within FRE 801(d)(1)(C). United States v. Brink, 39 F.3d 419 (3d Cir. 1994) (admitting bank teller's statement to police, on the day following a bank robbery, that the robber had dark-colored eyes); Puryear v. State, 810 So. 2d 901 (Fla. 2002) (excluding robbery victim's statement to police that assailant was a black male, missing every other tooth, and had body odor). Case law in state courts continues to reflect this split.

Our concern is that statements of accusation and description are usually admitted under the hearsay exceptions for spontaneous and excited statements under FRE 803(1) and (2), which we discuss on pages 486-493, infra. If they are admitted instead under FRE 801(d)(1)(C), it is without any of the limits of timing and stressful circumstances that those exceptions impose, although subsection (C) does require that the declarant testify as a witness and be subject to cross-examination. Whether such statements are "testimonial" and whether they are subject to exclusion in criminal trials under the confrontation clause as interpreted by Crawford v. Washington is discussed in Section G, infra.

ii.   Identifies a Person.   As drafted, subsection (C) appears to be limited to statements about the physical characteristics of persons. Why should identifications of persons but not, for example, automobiles be admissible? If that seems too far an extension of the exemption, what about descriptions of the clothing worn by the person? The answer to how narrowly or broadly to construe the language of subsection (C) lies in the justification for the admission of prior statements identifying people. In gray areas, one should be able to state the reasons for the exemption and argue by analogy for exclusion or admission of a particular piece of evidence.

b.   Justifications for the Admissibility of Prior Statements of Identification

Remember that the basic justification for the FRE 801(d)(1) exemptions is the opportunity to cross-examine the witness-declarant. But since *all* prior statements are not admitted, why are prior statements of identification included within the exemption?

Subsection (C) is justified by the *need* for prior identification testimony. Although it applies to both civil and criminal actions, this exemption is of primary benefit to prosecutors in criminal proceedings. The Advisory Committee Note describes identifications made in court as "unsatisfactory and inconclusive . . . as compared with those made at an earlier time under less suggestive conditions." In some cases, the prosecutor's use of the prior statement of identification for its truth may be essential to avoid a directed verdict of acquittal. Some witnesses may have genuinely lost the ability to make an in-court identification, as occurred in the *Owens* case discussed at page 450, supra. In this situation, neither a prior inconsistent nor a prior consistent statement would be admissible without subsection (C). There is also a risk that a prosecution witness may testify falsely at trial because of intimidation or threats to self or family members. The categorical approach to admission, however, does not permit such a case-by-case assessment of need. If the out-of-court statement satisfies the categorical requirements, it is admissible.

It is not clear that the reliability of the declarant's testimonial qualities is enhanced by the subsection (C) foundational requirements. The out-of-court statement may be more reliable because it was made closer in time to the event in which the person identified participated. On the other hand, an oath is not required, the setting may be quite informal, and no circumstance decreases the risk of improper motive for making the identification. Moreover, when the statement is made in the context of a police-arranged lineup, neither the witness nor even the police officers who arranged for the identification may have been aware of possible subtle suggestive factors that could have influenced it. Studies have demonstrated that individuals' memories fade quickly. For an excellent summary of the psychological data bearing on the reliability of eyewitness identification testimony, see Brian L. Cutler and Steven D. Penrod, Mistaken Identifications: The Eyewitness, Psychology, and the Law (1995). Thus, the argument for the admission of prior identifications is strongest with respect to identifications made soon after the perception of the person identified. Would it be desirable to amend subsection (C) to provide that the statement of identification must be made "soon" or "shortly" after the witness perceived the person identified?

c. *Constitutional Concerns*

In addition to the hearsay issue, there is a substantial body of case law that focuses on whether a prior identification violated a criminal defendant's constitutional right to counsel or due process of law. See, e.g., Gilbert v. California, 388 U.S. 263 (1967) (criminal defendant has right to counsel at postindictment confrontation between witness and defendant; denial of right to counsel requires exclusion of pretrial identification evidence); Manson v. Brathwaite, 432 U.S. 98 (1977) (due process requires exclusion of unnecessarily suggestive pretrial identification if identification is likely to be unreliable).

KEY POINTS

1. The prior out-of-court statement of a testifying witness may be admitted for the truth of the matter it asserts if it is (A) inconsistent with the witness's testimony, (B) consistent with the witness's testimony and rebuts a charge of recent fabrication or improper influence or motive, or (C) a statement of identification of a person, made after perceiving that person.

2. The judge must be persuaded, pursuant to FRE 104(a), that the foundational requirements are satisfied prior to admitting the statements.

3. The witness must be subject to cross-examination concerning the statement by answering questions willingly; the witness need not necessarily remember the underlying event or making the prior statement.

PROBLEMS

8.32. Esther Kingsley and Robert Roby were riding in a car that crossed the median strip on a two-lane highway and collided with a pickup truck driven by William Burditt. Esther was killed in the crash and the executor of her estate is suing Robert for wrongful death, alleging that he was driving the car and that his negligence caused the accident. Robert claims that Esther was driving and that the accident was her fault.

(a)   Several hours after the accident, William Burditt told a state trooper that "a man was driving." Two days later Burditt told a friend "the woman was not driving the car." Called by the plaintiff executor to testify at trial, Burditt testifies "I have a picture in my mind that the woman was behind the wheel. It seems when we hit, she was on the driver's side." Can the plaintiff use Burditt's prior statements to prove that Robert was driving? To impeach Burditt's credibility? If there is no other evidence that Robert was driving, will the judge grant a directed verdict against the plaintiff?

(b)   What if Burditt's deposition had been taken by plaintiff and Burditt said "a man was driving" — admissible? For what purpose?

(c)   What if there was no deposition but Burditt had previously submitted a sworn affidavit that said "a man was driving" in support of plaintiff's motion for summary judgment against Robert? Admissible? For what purpose?

(d)   Assume that the statements in (a) are admitted to impeach Burditt. Plaintiff also asks Burditt: "Isn't it true that Robert paid you for the extensive damage done to your truck in the collision, just a week before this trial?" Burditt answers "Yes." Relevant? Admissible?

(e)   Assume that the evidence in (d) is admitted. Robert then offers the testimony of Burditt's coworker that, on the day before the trial started, Burditt said: "You know, I think that it was the woman driving." Relevant? Admissible?

(f)   Assume that two *men* — Edwin and Robert — were in the car that collided with Burditt's truck. Edwin was killed in the crash and his estate sues Robert for wrongful death, claiming that Robert was driving. Robert says that Edwin was driving. Plaintiff offers testimony that Burditt said to a state trooper, just after the accident, "that man there was driving" and then pointed at Robert. Admissible? For what purpose?

(g)   Same facts as (f). What if, several days after the accident, Burditt said to a friend, "It was the man with black hair and the blue jacket who was driving." (Robert has black hair and was wearing a blue jacket on the day of the accident.)

8.33 Return to Problem 3.3, United States v. Ray, at page 136, supra. At Ray's trial, in February of 2011, Beth Barker testifies for the prosecution on direct examination that she remembers June Jacobs giving her the March 14, 2010 memorandum written by the outside auditor Andrews. She further testifies that she placed it in Ray's "in box" on that same day, March 14, and then removed it the next day, March 15, from his "out box." She also remembers that Ray's initials were on the memorandum.

(a)   On cross-examination, defense counsel asks the following:

Q: Ms. Barker, you testified at a preliminary hearing on December 1, 2010, in this case, did you not?
A: Yes.
Q: And I asked you some questions at that time, do you recall that?
A: Yes.
Q: Isn't it true that I asked you the following questions, and you gave the following answers: [reading from transcript]
      "Q: When did June Jacobs give you the auditor's memo?
      A: I believe it was March 18."

Is Barker's answer from the preliminary hearing transcript admissible, over the prosecutor's hearsay objection, to prove that June Jacobs delivered the auditors' memo to
Ray's office on March 18?,

   (b)   Defense counsel next offers Exhibit B into evidence, an authenticated writ-
         ten affidavit signed by Beth Barker dated December 19, 2010, which states
         (in pertinent part):

         I, Beth Barker, declare:

              On March 18, 2010, June Jacobs personally handed me a copy of
         Andrews' auditor's memo and said "Mr. Ray needs to see this." I remem-
         ber this incident because it was unusual for Ms. Jacobs to deliver a docu-
         ment for Mr. Ray personally.
              I declare under penalty of perjury that the foregoing is true and cor-
         rect to the best of my knowledge.

                                                               [signed] Beth Barker

Is this affidavit admissible, over the prosecutor's hearsay objection, to prove that June
Jacobs delivered the auditors' memo to Ray's office on March 18?

   (c)   On cross examination, defense counsel asks Barker the following questions:

         Q: Ms. Barker, on January 20, 2011, you were arrested for embezzling
              $250 from a petty cash fund, while employed at Rundown?
         A: Yes.
         Q: And that alleged embezzlement occurred on January 5, 2011, isn't that
              so?
         A: I believe so.
         Q: Ms. Barker, isn't it a fact that you made up the testimony you gave today
              about removing the March 14, 2010, auditor's memorandum, with Mr.
              Ray's initials on it, from Mr. Ray's out box on March 15, 2010 in order to
              get a deal from the prosecutor on your embezzlement charge?
         A: No, that's not true.
         DEFENSE COUNSEL: I have no further questions.

     The prosecutor then calls an FBI agent who will testify that in June of 2010 he
interviewed Beth Barker and she told him that she remembered removing a memorandum dated March 14, 2010, written by the outside auditor Andrews, from Mr.
Ray's out box on March 15, 2010. She also told the agent that it had Mr. Ray's initials
on it, and that she filed it. Is this testimony admissible over defense counsel's hearsay
objection?
     8.34. Ed Larson is being prosecuted for armed robbery of a bank. Terry Davis,
an alleged accomplice, pleaded guilty to the same charge and is currently serving a
20-year sentence. Davis admitted that he was involved in the robbery, but he claimed
that he could not remember whether he had a partner or, if he did have one, who
the partner might have been. He also claimed not to remember ever having made a
statement to anyone about having a partner. To prove that Larson committed the robbery with Davis the prosecutor offers (a) a transcript of Davis's grand jury testimony

describing Larson's participation in the robbery and (b) the testimony of a police officer to the effect that following Davis's arrest several days after the robbery, he confessed to the crime and named Larson as his accomplice. The defendant has objected to both pieces of evidence. What result?

8.35. Larry Emerson is being tried for arson. The government's key witness, Alice Hastings, testified under a grant of immunity that she had cooperated with Larry in planning the arson, but then had withdrawn from the scheme. On cross-examination, defense counsel inquired about promises made to Hastings in return for her testimony and suggested that she was testifying against Emerson in order to shift responsibility for the crime from herself. The government then calls a police officer who was present at Hastings's arrest to testify that Hastings voluntarily began talking to the police; that she did not ask any questions about what benefits she might obtain; that another officer informed Hastings that her cooperation would be brought to the attention of the District Attorney; and that before any other statements about cooperation were made, Hastings identified Larry Emerson as the arsonist. Is this testimony admissible under FRE 801(d)(1)(B)?

8.36. A fight broke out between Defendant and Joe Williams in a nightclub. Williams lay collapsed on the floor and Defendant was ejected from the club. It is alleged that Defendant returned with a gun and shot Williams. Although the alleged murder weapon was never recovered, Defendant is charged in federal court with the crime of unlawful possession of a firearm and ammunition by a convicted felon. At trial, Holmes, a friend of Williams, testified that he witnessed the fight and the shooting committed by Defendant. Williams's girlfriend arrived at the club after the shooting, having been called by her nephew and told that Williams was lying on the floor after the fight. The girlfriend testifies that when she arrived at the club 30 minutes later, she met Holmes in the parking lot. She further testifies:

> I asked Holmes, "What happened, what happened?" Holmes said, "He shot him." I said, "Who shot him?" Holmes said, "Defendant shot him."

Was it error for the trial court to admit this testimony under FRE 801(d)(1)(A)?

6. Interpretation and Illustration of FRE 801(d)(2): Party Admissions in General

Each subsection of FRE 801(d)(2) defines a specific type of out-of-court statement made by a declarant who is either a party in the case or has a particular type of affiliation with a party. The foundational requirements of subsections (A)-(E) focus primarily on the relationship between the party and the declarant. The single common requirement for all the subsections is that the proponent must offer the declarant's statement *against* the opposing party. It is the proponent's choice whether or not to use an opposing party's own statements, or statements of affiliates, to prove the case *against* that party at trial.

Before we discuss each FRE 801(d)(2) subsection in detail, you should read through them all again briefly:

> (d) *Statements That Are Not Hearsay.* A statement that meets the following conditions is not hearsay:

(2) *An Opposing Party's Statement.* The statement is offered against an opposing party and:

(A) was made by the party in an individual or representative capacity;

(B) is one the party manifested that it adopted or believed to be true;

(C) was made by a person whom the party authorized to make a statement on the subject;

(D) was made by the party's agent or employee on a matter within the scope of that relationship and while it existed; or

(E) was made by the party's co-conspirator during and in furtherance of the conspiracy.

The statement must be considered but does not by itself establish the declarant's authority under (C); the existence or scope of the relationship under (D); or the existence of the conspiracy or participation in it under (E).

We will use the following example to illustrate subsections (A)-(E):

> Suppose that Day and Moore are partners in a business. They are being tried jointly for preparing and filing a false partnership income tax return in 1999. The government's evidence tends to show that Day and Moore diverted income from the partnership to themselves by cashing checks made out to the partnership. The government claims that Day and Moore did not account for the proceeds in either the partnership or their own income tax returns. At trial, Moore testifies in his own defense and denies all knowledge of and participation in such a scheme. The government then seeks to introduce against both Day and Moore a properly authenticated tape recording of a statement that Moore made, unbeknownst to Day, in an interview with an Internal Revenue Service agent who was investigating the 1999 partnership return. Moore's recorded statement implicates both Day and Moore in the income diversion and tax evasion scheme. It was not made under oath, however, and would not be admissible as a prior inconsistent statement under FRE 801(d)(1)(A).

Would Moore's recorded statement be admissible against Moore under FRE 801(d)(2)(A)? Would it be admissible against Day? Would the statement be admissible against Day under FRE 801(d)(2)(B), (C), (D), or (E)? If you can fit the statement under (A) against Moore, or under (B), (C), (D), or (E) against Day, then although it is offered for the truth of the matter it asserts — that Moore and Day both participated in the illegal scheme to file a false tax return — it will be exempt from the definition of hearsay and will be admissible as substantive evidence for its truth.

7. Interpretation and Illustration of FRE 801(d)(2)(A): A Party's Own Statements

a. Preliminary Fact-finding

The foundational requirements for a party admission are:

- the statement is made by a party; and
- the statement is offered against that party.

This is perhaps the simplest foundation of all the hearsay exemptions and exceptions. Moore's recorded statement easily satisfies it, so long as it is offered against Moore himself. *Any* out-of-court statement made in *any* context by *any* party (whether plaintiff or defendant) to *any* action (whether civil or criminal) may be admissible, unless otherwise objectionable, if offered *against* that party. In Jewell v. CSX Transportation, Inc., 135 F.3d 361, 364-365 (6th Cir. 1998), the statement of a six-year-old plaintiff, made after she had suffered brain damage when the car in which she was riding was hit by a train, was admitted to prove that the car's driver had not been keeping a proper lookout. The court stated that "[t]rustworthiness is not a separate requirement for admission under FRE 801(d)(2)(A)." Id. at 365.

The party's statement must of course be relevant and not subject to exclusion under other rules of evidence. Guilty pleas, depositions, personal documents, and prepared charts, as well as conversational oral statements, have all been admitted for their truth under FRE 801(d)(2)(A). Trull v. Volkswagen of America, Inc., 187 F.3d 88, 98 (1st Cir. 1999) (plaintiffs' diagram from a prior lawsuit, showing a different version of the collision in question, was admitted against them in their suit against the manufacturer of their van). If a party's nonverbal conduct is hearsay under FRE 801(a) because it is intended as an assertion, it is a statement for the purposes of this or any other hearsay exception or exemption. A nod of assent in response to an incriminating question, for example, would be admissible as an admission against a defendant in a subsequent prosecution.

If a proponent offers a Rule 801(d)(2)(A) statement *against* a party at trial, the proponent must think that the statement is adverse to the interest of that party. For this reason, party admissions are sometimes referred to as "admissions against interest." We strongly urge you to avoid the phrase "admission against interest." First, the foundational requirements for the admissions exemption *do not require that the statement be "against interest" when it is made, nor that the person making the statement think that it is.* Sometimes a party's statement attains its "against interest" significance long after it is made. Second, as you will see, there is a completely distinct exception to the hearsay rule for "declarations against interest." Getting used to referring to admissions simply as admissions should help to avoid confusion between declarations against interest and admissions.

b.   *Individual and Representative Capacity*

FRE 801(d)(2)(A) controls the admission of statements made by an individual person that are offered against that same individual person at trial. But a person can speak, and can be a party, either as an individual or as a representative — a trustee, executor, or guardian — of some other entity or individual. The rule provides for the admission of statements against the individual person even if those statements were made when the individual was speaking as a representative outside of court. In re Special Federal Grand Jury Empanelled Oct. 31, 1985 Impounded, 819 F.2d 56, 59 (3d Cir. 1987) (statements made to a grand jury solely in the declarant's capacity as an agent for a corporation is admissible against him as an individual). And statements made outside of court by a person, whether as an individual or as a representative, will be admissible against that person if he appears as a party solely in a representative capacity. Estate of Shafer v. Commissioner, 749 F.2d 1216, 1219 (6th Cir. 1984) (letter written by son of a decedent admissible against him as coexecutor of his father's estate, whether it was written by the son as an individual or in his capacity as executor). When an entity such as a corporation is a party, the statements of its representatives can be admitted against the entity under FRE 801(d)(2)(C) or (D), but not pursuant to FRE 801(d)(2)(A), as we will discuss at pages 472-473, infra.

c.   *Admissions, Personal Knowledge, and Lay Opinions*

In two respects the admissions exemption operates differently from other hearsay exceptions. First, there is *no* requirement that a party admission be based on firsthand knowledge. This is in contrast to all other hearsay exceptions and Rule 801(d)(1) statements. The Advisory Committee Note to FRE 801(d)(2)(a) states that admissions of a party-opponent are free from "the restrictive influences of the opinion rule and the rule requiring first hand knowledge . . . ." McCormick offers the following justification for dispensing with the personal knowledge requirement for a party's own admissions:

> [T]he vast majority of admissions that become relevant in litigation concern some matter of substantial importance to declarants upon which they would likely have informed themselves. As a result, most admissions possess greater reliability than the general run of hearsay, even when not based on firsthand observation. Moreover, the possibility is substantial that the declarant may have significant information that the opponent cannot prove. [McCormick on Evidence, Vol. 2 §255, at 183 (Kenneth S. Broun, ed., 6th ed. 2006).]

Do you find this justification convincing? Is there some other justification for dispensing with the requirement? Would the proponent of the admission find it easy to prove what a party opponent knows about the facts of their dispute without using the party's out-of-court statements?

Second, courts have tended to be liberal in admitting statements of opinion if the evidence is an admission. Since the party against whom an admission is offered can take the witness stand and explain the basis for the opinion, declining to exclude the lay opinion rule in this context seems reasonable. Combining freedom from the personal knowledge requirement and the lay opinion rule means that a party's admissions may be based on hearsay statements of others, or the party's inferences from circumstances.

8.   Elaboration of FRE 801(d)(2)(A): Justifications for the Admissibility of Party Admissions

As you can see from the breadth of Rule 801(d)(2)(A), the justification for its admissibility cannot rest on a claim of enhanced reliability. There are no limitations in the rule concerning the content of the out-of-court statement or the circumstances in which it was made. We emphasize again that it need not have been "against interest" when made. Instead, all five of the subsections of FRE 801(d)(2) are justified by considerations relating to the adversarial system of trial and to values of freedom of choice and personal responsibility in our larger society. These considerations operate most powerfully as justifications for the admissibility of a party's own statements under subsection (A). As we will see in succeeding sections of this chapter, these justifications become less powerful as the relationship between the party and the declarant becomes weaker. Then circumstances that may increase the need for or the reliability of the out-of-court statement are added to the foundational requirements of each subsection.

a.   The Opportunity to Explain

Hearsay is excluded primarily because the opponent lacks the opportunity to expose weaknesses in the declarant's narration, sincerity, perception, and memory through cross-examination. In civil cases, however, parties to an action cannot reasonably complain about the lack of an opportunity for cross-examining themselves. There is a viable alternative. If a party's hearsay statement has been admitted against him, he can take the stand in rebuttal and have a full opportunity to explain any difficulties with the accuracy of the statement. In short, it seems absurd for a party who is directly affected by the outcome in the case, and who is sitting in the courtroom, to complain about not being able to cross-examine herself.

b.   Fifth Amendment Concerns

In criminal cases, while it is true that the criminal defendant has the same right as any other litigant to testify, it is also true that the criminal defendant has the Fifth Amendment right to refuse to testify. Admitting a criminal defendant's statements under FRE 801(d)(2)(A) may put some pressure on the defendant to abandon that right.

Any number of factors may make a defendant feel pressured to testify, and only some of these factors raise constitutional problems. At one extreme, a direct threat of punishment for refusing to testify would be regarded as a violation of the Fifth Amendment right not to testify. At the other extreme, the defendant may feel pressure to testify simply because of the nature or strength of the prosecutor's case, and this type of pressure does not raise constitutional problems. It is well settled that the FRE 801(d)(2)(A) exemption applies to criminal defendants as well as to all other parties to actions.

c.   Responsibility for One's Own Statements and Fairness

Professors Lempert, Gross, and Liebman offer a moral responsibility rationale for the admissions exception:

> The law recognizes in the hearsay rule the fact that people do not always speak the truth, but recognizing this does not mean that parties before the court will be assumed to have failed in their moral duty to tell the truth or be relieved of the responsibility for their actions if they have failed. [Richard O. Lempert, Samuel R. Gross, and James Liebman, A Modern Approach to Evidence 537 (3d ed. 2000).]

Consider whether this is a viable theory. Even if one concedes that there are general and generally accepted moral norms of personal accountability and honesty, do they extend to mandating that a litigant's statements be used to work a legal deprivation against the litigant? Why should somebody who perhaps quite unwillingly becomes a litigant be required to shoulder this particular responsibility?

One answer might be based on the norms of fairness in a free society. People who choose to speak usually do so in their own self-interest. The party's own out-of-court statement presumably served that party's interest when it was made. Moreover, others may have taken action in reliance on the statement. There is a common law notion of fairness, enforced as a principle of estoppel, that operates to prevent people from switching positions they have taken cost-free. With benefits come burdens. A party is not irrevocably bound by a prior out-of-court statement if the party later wants to claim that it was inaccurate. But the party at least has to account for it when it is offered against him in court. This is a minimal burden.

Adversarial fairness is also a justification for admitting party admissions. The proponent may want to use as evidence what the opponent knows about the facts that are in dispute. But the civil party may not want to call the opponent to the witness stand during the case-in-chief. The civil plaintiff, for example, cannot prepare the defendant as a witness, thus what the defendant might say is unknown and could be harmful. And, of course, the prosecutor *cannot* call the criminal defendant to the stand because of the Fifth Amendment. Offering the opponent's hearsay statements thus may be the fairest way — and in a criminal case the only way, thus adding the element of necessity — for the proponent to prove what the opposing party knows.

9. Further Elaboration of FRE 801(d)(2)(A)

a. Preliminary Fact-finding on the Identity of the Declarant

The foundational requirements for all hearsay exceptions and exemptions are preliminary questions of fact subject to FRE 104, and are typically for the judge to decide pursuant to FRE 104(a). These requirements are imposed by hearsay policy; they do not establish the relevance of the out-of-court statement. But consider a case in which relevancy and hearsay policy are determined by the same question of fact. Suppose that it is alleged that the defendant started a fight with a coworker. The defendant denies starting the fight. What if the coworker had previously received an unsigned letter expressing great animosity toward the coworker? The coworker claims that the defendant wrote this letter and that the animosity is relevant to prove that defendant started the fight. The defendant denies sending the letter. Since the letter is hearsay, the coworker offers it under FRE 801(d)(2)(A) against the defendant. Should FRE 104(a) or (b) control the judge's fact-finding on whether the defendant wrote the letter?

In this case, this same fact is necessary both to the relevance (and authentication) of the letter under FRE 401 and to the admissibility of the hearsay statement under FRE 801(d)(2)(A). FRE 104(b) governs the relevance and the authentication questions; FRE 104(a) governs the hearsay policy question. Which should control? The difference between them would be that under FRE 104(b), the judge would have to admit the letter with less foundational evidence — only evidence sufficient to support a finding — that the defendant wrote it. Under FRE 104(a), the judge should admit the letter only if the judge is actually persuaded by a preponderance of the evidence that the defendant wrote it.

In this example, the letter *can only be relevant and harmful* to the defendant if the defendant in fact wrote it. If the defendant did not write the letter, the animosity it expresses *could not* rationally be used in a way that is harmful to the defendant.

Therefore, since the Federal Rules of Evidence favor greater admissibility of relevant evidence, it would seem that the question should be decided under Rule 104(b) as a matter of relevance policy. It would be much easier for the coworker to meet the FRE 104(b) standard and to get the letter admitted than if FRE 104(a) were to apply. Of course, the defendant can still deny being the author and the jury will ultimately decide the question. The crucial point is that if the jury finds that it was not written by the defendant, we are fairly confident that the jury can disregard the letter as irrelevant.

b.   Admissibility of Party Admissions in Multiparty Cases: The Bruton Problem

In some cases, there are multiple plaintiffs or defendants. One party's party admission is not admissible against anyone other than the party who made the statement. The potential for improper use against another party would be resolved under FRE 403. But in criminal cases, there is a potential violation of the confrontation clause.

In Bruton v. United States, 391 U.S. 123 (1968), Bruton and Evans were tried jointly for armed robbery. Evans did not testify but was in court. The prosecution introduced into evidence an earlier confession by Evans that implicated both Evans and Bruton. Since the confession was admissible as a party admission only against Evans, the trial court instructed the jury that it could consider the confession as evidence only against Evans. Because Evans did not testify, Bruton could not cross-examine him. The Supreme Court, relying in part on the probable inability of the jury to limit its consideration of the confession to Evans, held that introduction of the confession had violated Bruton's confrontation right. Thus, whenever one declarant-defendant's confession implicates another codefendant, Bruton may preclude admission unless the declarant-defendant can be cross-examined.

Another way to accommodate the Bruton problem is to sever the trials of the codefendants. This, however, is an expensive remedy and prosecutors have sought other solutions. If all specific references to the codefendant are redacted from the declarant-defendant's statement, it may then be offered only against the declarant-defendant. Richardson v. Marsh, 481 U.S. 200 (1987). Confessions redacted by substituting a single codefendant's name with blank spaces or symbols have been held to be incriminating of the codefendant and inadmissible under Bruton. Gray v. Maryland, 523 U.S. 185 (1998). Substitution of names with neutral pronouns such as "other guys" or "persons" has been held not to incriminate specific codefendants when there are several of them, and therefore not to violate Bruton. United States v. Molina, 407 F.3d 511 (1st Cir. 2005). But in United States v. Lujan, 529 F. Supp. 2d 1315 (D.N.M. 2007), the court held that the sheer magnitude of the incriminating statements (265 pages from two defendants other than Lujan), the difficulty of the redaction in statements referring to all three defendants, the risk of distorting certain statements that might be exculpatory to one defendant, and the confusion resulting from replacing names with pronouns, compelled the findings that redaction would not cure the confrontation problem and that the trials must be severed.

10. Interpretation and Illustration of FRE 801(d)(2)(B): Adoptive Admissions

a. Preliminary Fact-finding

The foundational requirements for an adoptive admission are:

- a statement has been made;
- the party has done something to manifest adoption of the statement or belief in its truth; and
- the statement is offered against the party.

Under FRE 801(d)(2)(B), there is no limitation on who may make the statement that is subsequently offered against a party. It is thus not an exemption based on a relationship between the declarant and the party. Rather, it is based on the party's own conduct.

In the false partnership tax return example, for the government to use subsection (B) to secure the admission of Moore's recorded statement for its truth against Day, it would first have to prove that Day had heard Moore's statement or knew of it, and that he appeared to adopt it or to accept it as true. If the recording had been played to Day and he nodded "yes," or said, "That's right," the government could argue that these words satisfied the foundational requirements of subsection (B).

A party may manifest adoption of a statement in any number of ways, including through words, conduct, or silence. United States v. Jinadu, 98 F.3d 239 (6th Cir. 1996) (defendant answered "yes" during interrogation to question "you know that's China White heroin"); United States v. Pulido-Jacobo, 377 F.3d 1124, 1132 (10th Cir. 2004) (to prove truth of contents of a document, mere possession does not constitute adoption but "surrounding circumstances can tie the possessor and the document together in a meaningful way," e.g., by accepting the document and acting upon it); United States v. Joshi, 896 F.2d 1303, 1311 (11th Cir. 1990) (party nodded head after statement by another, and made a sound of agreement); Wagstaff v. Protective Apparel Corp., 760 F.2d 1074, 1078 (10th Cir. 1985) (party used for its own advantage a written statement prepared by another); Pillsbury Co. v. Cleaver-Brooks Div. of Aqua-Chem, Inc., 646 F.2d 1216, 1218 (8th Cir. 1981) (party signed statement prepared by another); United States v. Weaver, 565 F.2d 129, 135 (8th Cir. 1977) (party repeated statement of another); United States v. Safavian, 435 F. Supp. 2d 36, 43 (D.D.C. 2006) (party's words "manifested an adoption or belief" in the truth of the statements of other people as he forwarded their e-mails). If ambiguous, the meaning of a party's behavior is ultimately for the jury to assess after determination of this preliminary question by the judge. State v. Carlson, 808 P.2d 1002 (Or. 1991). However, courts appear to disagree as to whether these preliminary questions are decided pursuant to FRE 104(a) or 104(b). Id. at 1006-1009 (holding that Rule 104(a) applies after a thorough discussion of the precedent and policy).

b. Justification for the Admissibility of Adoptive Admissions

If a party has done something to manifest adoption or belief in the truth of an uncross-examined statement made by another, an inference can be drawn that the party knows that the contents of the statement are accurate, or thinks that the person speaking is reliable and knowledgeable. The party can still dispute these inferences, and the statement's accuracy, at trial. The party can explain why the statement was unreliable and why, at the time, the party did not repudiate the statement. If the party in fact knew nothing about what the statement asserted, then the party went along with it presumably to get some advantage, or induce some reliance. This makes it fair to admit the statement against the party at trial.

c. Adoption by Silence

A common type of adoptive admission is the admission by silence. In United States v. Duval, 496 F.3d 64 (1st Cir. 2007), Duval was convicted of possession of a firearm by a convicted felon. To prove possession, the prosecution offered the testimony of an undercover informant. The informant testified at trial that while Duval and his companion were staying at the informant's apartment, the companion stated that he and Duval wanted to sell firearms that were in their possession. The prosecution claimed that the companion's incriminating statement implicated Duval because he was present when the statement was made but did not attempt to disassociate himself from it.

A problem with using nonresponsiveness or silence as the basis for an inference of a subsection (B) admission is the ambiguity of the party's conduct. What does it mean if someone fails to respond to a statement? To a letter? Or to the calculation of a bill? These ambiguities are resolved by preliminary fact-finding on the question of whether the party's conduct "manifests" adoption or belief. "[T]he burden is on the proponent to convince the judge [under FRE 104(a)] that in the circumstances . . . a failure to respond is so unnatural that it supports the inference that the party acquiesced in the statement." Weston-Smith v. Cooley Dickinson Hospital, Inc., 282 F.3d 60, 67 (1st Cir. 2002). The judge considers the nature of the statement, the audience, and the surrounding circumstances. For example, in Weston-Smith, failure to respond to an accusatory statement made at a social occasion, when the party did not have information necessary to assess the accusation's truthfulness, was held not to be an adoptive admission. Id. at 68. The court's decision calls for an evaluation of probable human behavior. The party who opposes the admissibility of the statement can of course offer evidence on the preliminary fact questions as part of the judge's fact-finding process. This evidence may be re-submitted to the jury to reduce the probative value of the statement, if it is admitted.

In United States v. Duval, supra, Duval contended that the facts described were insufficient to prove that he had *actually heard* the companion's statement, which was necessary to the prosecution's showing under FRE 801(d)(2)(B) that he could have adopted the statement or believed the truth of it. Duval offered the testimony of a fourth person present who testified that he had not heard the statement himself. The appellate court upheld the finding of the district judge that, based on testimony that the conversation took place in a small room, and that Duval was in that room, the foundation was adequate to admit the companion's statement. This decision should be made under FRE 104(a). This preliminary fact is solely a matter of hearsay policy, not of relevancy, because evidence of the companion's statement would be relevant and harmful to Duval whether or not Duval heard it.

11. Interpretation and Illustration of FRE 801(d)(2)(C) and (D): Admissions by Agents, Servants, and Employees

a. Preliminary Fact-finding

The foundational requirements for authorized admissions under subsection (C) are:

- the statement is on a subject;
- the statement was made by person whom a party authorized to make a statement on that subject; and
- the statement is offered against that party.

In the example of the false partnership tax return, Moore's recorded statement could only be admitted against Day under subsection (C) if the government had evidence showing that Day had given Moore authority to make the recorded statement on Day's behalf. FRE 801(d)(2) also states that the contents of the statement itself may be used to prove the issue of authority (if Moore stated on the tape that Day had asked him to speak with the government about their scheme, for example) but that other independent evidence of authority is also required. The foundational requirements for admissions by agents and employees under subsection (D) focus on the existence of the agency or employee relationship and do not require any showing of authority:

- the declarant is an agent or employee of a party;
- the statement was made while this relationship existed;
- the statement is on a matter within the scope of the agency or employment relationship; and
- the statement is offered against that party.

Under subsection (D), Moore's statement might be admitted against Day if a principal-agent or employer-employee relationship existed between them. Partners are treated as agents of the partnership; but are partners agents of each other? An agency relationship is typically defined by *control*; that is, the principal having "the right to control the manner and method in which the work is carried out by the alleged agent." Chemtool, Inc. v. Lubrication Technologies, Inc., 148 F.3d 742, 745 (7th Cir. 1998). United States v. Saks, 964 F.2d 1514, 1523 (5th Cir. 1992) (The general rule is that the declarations of one partner about the partnership's affairs are admissible against the other partners.).

In addition, the proponent would need to prove that the statement was made during the relationship and that it was on a matter within Moore's duties as an agent of Day. The contents of the statement itself may be used to prove the fact of agency and the scope thereof, but the *statement alone is not sufficient* under FRE 801(d)(2). Gomez v. Rodriguez, 344 F.3d 103, 117 (1st Cir. 2003) (statement by mayor's wife that she was interviewing employment applicants for him and applying "political" criteria, held inadmissible as statement of an agent, since no independent evidence in the record supported the existence of the agency relationship).

i. Statements by Attorneys. Many of the cases involving authorized admissions offered under subsection (C) concern statements made by attorneys on behalf of their clients. When an attorney represents a party in litigation, statements of facts made in formal litigation documents — pleadings, answers to interrogatories, responses to requests for documents, briefs — and in opening and closing statements at trial may all be found to be within the scope of the attorney's authority even though there is no specific grant of authority to make the particular statement. In other settings, the scope of an attorney's representation of the party, and the specific tasks undertaken by the attorney or other agent, create *implied* authority to speak on the party's behalf. Whether or not such authority exists is a preliminary question for the judge to decide under FRE 104(a).

ii.   Other Specifically Authorized Statements.   Some agents would ordinarily be viewed as having authority from a party to make statements that are necessary to the performance of their duties; for example, minutes taken by the secretary at a school board would be admissible as authorized statements under FRE 801(d)(2) (C) if offered against the board. Other employees of a party may be given specific authority to speak on a one-time basis, or to speak on a topic not within their normal relationship with the party. Subsection (C) may also apply to authorized statements made by persons in relationships with the party that are not within the definition of agency, such as employer-independent contractor, or parent-child.

iii.   Statements Made During the Relationship On a Matter Within the Scope of an Agent's Employment.   Subsection (D) does not require that the declarant have specific authority to speak. Nor does it require that the statement be made on the job, that is, *within* the scope of the agent's duties. Rather, subsection (D) focuses on subject matter: The statement must be *on* a matter within the scope of the employment or agency relationship.

Prior to the restyling of the FRE, subsection (D) required that the statement "concern" a matter within the scope of the employment or agency. The term "concern" was interpreted as meaning the statement must "relate to" the scope of employment or agency, or the subject matter of the statement must "match" the subject matter of the employee's or agent's job description. Since the restyling is not intended to change the substance of any rule, we assume that the term "on" will be given the same meaning as "concern."

Typical cases have involved agents speaking about their own job performance or about events that happened on the job that would be of legitimate concern to the speaker. For example, statements by superiors to company employees concerning the employee's standing in the company may be within subsection (D), depending on the superior's job, duties, and role in relation to the employee. In Carter v. University of Toledo, 349 F.3d 269, 271-272 (6th Cir. 2002), the plaintiff, an African-American professor, sued the defendant for failure to renew her contract because of her race. The plaintiff sought to testify that the University's Vice-Provost had said to her that the Dean who had refused the renewal was "trying to whitewash the college of education" and "was trying to get rid of black professors." The appellate court held that while the Vice-Provost was not a "direct decision-maker" concerning the plaintiff's employment, he did have "oversight of the affirmative action process at the University" and thus his statements concerned a matter within his authority. Statements have been excluded as not concerning a matter within the scope of the agency when the declarant is like a bystander eyewitness who describes an event perceived at work that has no relation to the job or the concerns of the speaker. Wilkinson v. Carnival Cruise Lines, 920 F.2d

1560 (11th Cir. 1991) (statement by cabin steward about previous problems with sliding glass door in ship's swimming pool area did not concern a matter within scope of steward's employment since his job involved no responsibilities in the engineering department or for the swimming pool). Since the contents of the hearsay statement alone are not sufficient to prove the scope of authority, the proponent must present corroborating evidence. Mercado v. City of Orlando, 407 F.3d 1152, 1156 (11th Cir. 2005).

The proponent of a statement under subsection (D) must also provide evidence that the statement was made while the principal-agent relationship existed. This does not mean that the statement must be made "on the job" or during the performance of duties. Rule 801(d)(2)(D) abandons the common law requirement that agents must be *acting* within the scope of their authority when they make the statement. The exemption thus includes statements made away from the workplace to third parties uninvolved in the speaker's work. Kraus v. Sobel Corrugated Containers, Inc., 915 F.2d 227, 230-231 (6th Cir. 1990) (statement praising job performance of plaintiff shortly before her termination, made by a department manager during holiday dinner at the home of the plaintiff, would be admissible against the defendant in an age discrimination case).

Statements of employees are admitted not only against employer corporations but also against their corporate supervisors if direct supervision and control is proved. United States v. Agne, 214 F.3d 47, 55 (1st Cir. 2000) (statements admissible against the president of a corporation under FRE 801(d)(2)(D), because evidence showed that the declarant, an employee of the corporation's wholly-owned company, was directly responsible to the president and often acted for him).

b.   *Justification for the Admissibility of Statements Under FRE 801(d)(2)(C) and (D): Necessity, Fairness, and Reliability*

Under both subsections (C) and (D), there is no guarantee that the declarant will be available to testify at trial. Thus, the principal rationale for admitting statements under subsections (A) and (B) — that the party can choose to explain the statement — may not apply. If the declarant is out of the country or otherwise unavailable, and the party had little or no knowledge of the statement when made, the justification that cross-examination is unnecessary because the party can explain the declarant's statement seems particularly weak.

Instead, other values justify these exemptions (and other exceptions) to the hearsay rule: necessity, fairness, and reliability. Necessity stems from the fact that individuals, corporations, and other institutional entities conduct their affairs through authorized representatives, agents and employees. These persons constitute a primary source of information about corporate activities. Such information is necessary to impose liability on corporate and institutional entities. And, as a matter of substantive law, individual and corporate or institutional parties are legally responsible for the activities of their authorized representatives, employees, and agents. It is probably essential for the proper functioning of this liability scheme for these declarants' statements to be admissible against principals and employers. Permitting the use of hearsay statements by these representatives, agents and employees can also be justified on grounds of fairness. If proponents cannot use this hearsay, they would either have to call the declarants as hostile witnesses or forgo the information altogether if the declarant has disappeared. Parties gain advantages by being able to conduct their business affairs through their representatives, agents, and employees. Moreover, third parties rely on statements of these people when doing business with the principal. The advantages obtained and the reliance incurred make it seem fair to place some burden of accountability for such out-of-court statements onto the principal. When an agent's hearsay is admitted under subsection (D), the principal is not irrevocably bound by it but does bear the burden of contesting its reliability, if the principal does not want the jury to use it. While it may be difficult for the party to obtain the information necessary to explore weaknesses in the declarant's statement, the party is probably better able to do so, and to do so more efficiently, than the proponent of the statement.

In addition, the foundational requirements of FRE 801(d)(2)(C) and (D) generate some inferences about the reliability of the declarants' testimonial qualities. To state the strongest case, if a statement is authorized, it may be reasonable to infer that the principal selected a trustworthy and reliable spokesperson. Second, if a statement is authorized or is about a matter central to the activities of the agent, the declarant may have a solid basis for making the statement, and if central, the statement may be made carefully and accurately. Third, if the declarant is an agent at the time of the statement, it may be inferred that the declarant is loyal to the interests of the principal and would not lie to injure the principal.

c.   Personal Knowledge and Lay Opinions

Many courts dispense with the personal knowledge requirement and the lay opinion rule under FRE 801(C) and (D) as well as (A) and (B). It is thus possible to admit a representative's or agent's conclusory statement that is based only on hearsay and rumor. This puts the principal under a heavy burden of disproving the reliability of the statement. Abandoning the personal knowledge requirement for a party's own admissions under subsection (A) may be justified because parties can impeach their own out-of-court statements by establishing their own lack of firsthand knowledge. But the principal may not be so easily able to show lack of firsthand knowledge in an employee's statement, particularly in a far-flung corporate context and particularly if the employee is not available. Again, necessity and fairness must justify abandoning the personal knowledge requirement. Abandoning the requirement means that more hearsay will be admitted and that corporate parties will bear the burden of impeaching its reliability or will suffer the risk of being unable to do so. Do you think that this result strikes the proper balance of necessity and fairness?

d.   Admissions by Government Employees

When can statements made by government employees be offered against the government in civil or criminal cases? Some courts adhere to the traditional common law position that the answer is never, based on the rationale that no individual can bind the sovereign. Courts adhere to this principle in criminal cases. United States v. Evans, 1990 WL 32581 (6th Cir. 1990) (excluding testimony about an out-of-court statement made by the assistant U.S. Attorney on the case to the effect that Evans did not have the requisite intent to be guilty of the crime charged); United States v. Yildiz, 355 F.3d 80, 82 (2d Cir. 2004) (out-of-court statements of a government informant are not admissible in a criminal trial under FRE 801(d)(2)(D)). But some courts have admitted statements of prosecutors made in court and in pleadings. United States v. Bakshinian, 65 F. Supp. 2d 1104, 1106 (C.D. Cal. 1999) (prosecutors have the power to bind the sovereign and are not disinterested in the outcome).

In civil cases, government manuals, sworn affidavits submitted to a judge, depositions and prior testimony given by government employees have been admitted under subsection (D). Timber Products Co. v. United States, 2010 U.S. Claims LEXIS 5 (Fed. Cl. 2010) (prior testimony by a litigation coordinator for the Forest Service concerning the Service's decision-making process admissible against the government under (D) in a suit for breach of contract by the Service). In C & H Commercial Contractors v. United States, 35 Fed. Cl. 246, 256 (1996), a highly relevant memorandum by a government contracting officer that recited damaging representations made by government officials to a private contractor was admitted under subsection (D) without hesitation.

12. Interpretation and Illustration of FRE 801(d)(2)(E): Co-conspirators' Admissions

a. *Preliminary Fact-finding*

The foundational requirements for co-conspirators' admissions are:

- the declarant and the party against whom the statement is offered were both members of the same conspiracy;
- the statement was made during the conspiracy; and
- the statement was made in furtherance of the conspiracy.

The typical co-conspirator statement is offered by the government against a criminal defendant to prove that defendant's criminal conduct. The recorded statement by Moore in the false partnership tax return hypothetical would not be admissible against Day under subsection (E), even if the government had evidence that Moore and Day were co-conspirators. Statements made to tax investigators, after the tax return has been filed, would not be considered to be made *during* or *in furtherance of* a conspiracy.

Consider also the following example, which is a typical situation in which the government seeks to use subsection (E):

A government informer has infiltrated a drug-selling ring. He speaks and works only with a few people involved in the ring, and never sees or talks to the boss. The people he deals with, however, make many statements about the boss, such as "he gets the best stuff" or "he sold this for $100 per gram." These out-of-court statements, if true, are evidence of the boss's drug-selling activities.

If the boss is charged with selling drugs and with conspiracy to sell drugs, may the informant testify that the out-of-court statements about the boss were made by the various "small fry" in the drug ring?

i.   Proof of Co-membership.   First, the proponent of a co-conspirator's statement under FRE 801(d)(2)(E) must prove that a conspiracy exists and that both the declarant (the "small fry") and the party (the boss) are members of it. Membership in a conspiracy requires a meeting of the minds to join an enterprise with others with the aim of accomplishing a specific purpose, sometimes phrased as "specific intent to further a common objective [which is usually, although not always, unlawful], and knowing and voluntary participation." The conspirators do not have to have contact with, or ever know, all of the other conspirators, but "[n]o one can join a conspiracy without knowledge of its existence . . . [and] the aim to forward or assist" it. United States v. Garcia-Torres, 280 F.3d 1, 4 (1st Cir. 2002). A conspiracy can be "a joint venture for an illegal purpose, or for a legal purpose using illegal means." United States v. Gil, 604 F.2d 546, 549 (7th Cir. 1979). There does not have to be a formal charge of conspiracy for the co-conspirators' admissions exception to apply. Indeed, the exception is not limited to use in criminal prosecutions. As a practical matter, however, the exception is most frequently invoked by prosecutors in criminal cases. Our discussion here reflects this common usage.

ii.   During the Course of the Conspiracy.   Statements made to the government informant in the drug ring example will satisfy this requirement if the conspiracy was ongoing when they were made. Statements made prior to a defendant's joining the conspiracy may not be used to prove the defendant's participation, but may be admissible to show the nature of the illegal enterprise and its preparations. United States v. Segura-Gallegos, 41 F.3d 1266 (9th Cir. 1994). And statements about events that occurred prior to the defendant's joining a conspiracy are admissible so long as these events were part of a "single, overarching" conspiracy and not multiple, independent conspiracies. United States v. Handlin, 366 F.3d 584, 591 (7th Cir. 2004). A defendant must affirmatively withdraw from a conspiracy for statements of co-conspirators no longer to be admissible against him. United States v. Robinson, 390 F.3d 853, 882 (6th Cir. 2004) (arrest or incarceration does not qualify as affirmative withdrawal).

The principal issue with respect to the *during* requirement is whether it extends to statements made in the so-called concealment phase of the conspiracy, after the objectives of the conspiracy have been either met or thwarted. If the conspiracy is terminated, it is usually by arrest or failure. United States v. Osorio-Soto, 1998 U.S. App. LEXIS 1950 (10th Cir. 1998) (government seizure of the illegal drug ended the conspiracy because it was no longer possible to achieve its objectives). If statements made during a police investigation or after an arrest cast blame on others, perhaps the declarant is lying in order to shift the blame away from him- or herself. There is a greater likelihood that each co-conspirator will be primarily concerned with self-protection. The majority position is that statements made during this phase are not within the scope of the exemption, as was true regarding Moore's recorded statement to the tax investigator. But if some activities of the conspiracy are still ongoing, and can be covered up, statements in furtherance of those concealment activities may be admissible. United States v. Gajo, 290 F.3d 922, 928 (7th Cir. 2002) ("concealment is . . . one of the main criminal objectives of an arson-for-profit scheme because it facilitates the primary objective of fraudulently acquiring insurance proceeds"); United States v. Urrego-Linares, 879 F.2d 1234, 1240 (4th Cir. 1989) (statements by co-conspirator on a monitored telephone call to the defendant who had already been arrested held to still be in the course of the conspiracy).

iii.   In Furtherance of the Conspiracy.   Statements that further the common objectives of the conspiracy, or set in motion transactions that are part of it, will satisfy the "in furtherance" requirement. Statements naming the drug ring boss in order to secure a sale, or to confirm lines of command, seem to further the goals of the illegal enterprise. "Idle chatter" and statements among conspirators that merely narrate past events have been held not to satisfy the requirement. United States v. Cornett, 195 F.3d 776, 783 (5th Cir. 1999). But statements that inform new conspirators, or keep co-conspirators informed, of significant events and problems have been held admissible, even though they do not actually further the enterprise. United States v. Jefferson, 215 F.3d 820, 823 (8th Cir. 2000) (conversations among three alleged co-conspirators concerning their botched attempt to murder their target by arson, and the resulting deaths of five others, admitted as in furtherance). Statements to customers, and to outsiders from whom the co-conspirator seeks help, may or may not further the conspiracy. In United States v. Urbanik, 801 F.2d 692 (4th Cir. 1986), casual conversation about weightlifting followed a drug purchase, during which the seller described the defendant to the buyer both as an excellent weightlifter and as the supplier of drugs. This was held not admissible against defendant because it was not in furtherance of the conspiracy. In United States v. Lee, 374 F.3d 637 (8th Cir. 2004) a co-conspirator's confession of murder to his brother (not a co-conspirator) to enlist his aid in selling weapons stolen from the murder victim was admitted as in furtherance of the conspiracy to use ill-gotten proceeds to fund a white supremacist group.

b.   Justification for the Admissibility of Co-conspirators' Admissions

One largely artificial rationale for the co-conspirators' admissions exemption is that each co-conspirator authorizes (or is deemed to have authorized) the statements of other co-conspirators. A more practical rationale is necessity: Conspiracies tend to be secret enterprises. The criminal activities, particularly of the leadership, are very difficult to prove. Some of the best evidence — and perhaps essential evidence if a prosecutor is to prove a defendant's guilt beyond a reasonable doubt — will be statements about the conduct of other co-conspirators. Thus, it is arguably appropriate to burden a person who chooses to engage in a conspiracy (particularly as an organizer or leader) with the risk that false or inaccurate co-conspirators' statements will be used against that person.

There is also a somewhat weak reliability rationale for the exception: To the extent that the *during* and *in furtherance of the conspiracy* requirements are taken seriously, co-conspirators' declarations may tend to be trustworthy because they advance the interest of the speaker in the success of the criminal enterprise.

13.   Elaboration of FRE 801(d)(2)(E): Applying FRE 104 to the Co-conspirator Exemption

Since it is the co-conspirator relationship that justifies the admission of co-conspirator hearsay, much attention has been paid to the process of proving this relationship.

a.   Bourjaily v. United States

In 1987, the Supreme Court in Bourjaily v. United States, 483 U.S. 171 (1987), held that all of the preliminary facts necessary to admit hearsay under FRE 801(d)(2)(E), including the co-conspirator relationship, are FRE 104(a) questions for the judge to decide by a preponderance of the evidence. The judge will *not* instruct the jury to decide the relationship issue as a necessary precondition to using the statement for its truth. This conclusion seems to be quite sound. The foundational question of co-membership in a conspiracy is a hearsay policy issue, not a relevance issue. Thus, *Bourjaily's* adoption of the FRE 104(a) test for deciding this question seems desirable.

Bourjaily also held that it is appropriate for the judge to consider the content of the hearsay statement itself in deciding whether the foundational requirements have been satisfied:

> Rule 104(a) provides: "In making its [preliminary fact] determination [the court] is not bound by the rules of evidence except those with respect to privileges." Similarly, Rule 1101(d)(1) states that the Rules of Evidence (other than with respect to privileges) shall not apply to "[t]he determination of questions of fact preliminary to admissibility of evidence when the issue is to be determined by the court under rule 104." . . . The Rule on its face allows the trial judge to consider any evidence whatsoever, bound only by the rules of privilege . . . .
>
> It is sufficient for today to hold that a court, in making a preliminary factual determination under Rule 801(d)(2)(E), may examine the hearsay statements sought to be admitted. As we have held in other cases concerning admissibility determinations, "the judge should receive the evidence and give it such weight as his judgment and experience counsel." [Id. at 178-181.]

Bourjaily's decision that the hearsay statement itself may "bootstrap" the statement's admissibility is reasonable and consistent with the terms of FRE 104(a). But since there may be reasons to distrust the reliability of alleged co-conspirators' statements, it may well be that it would be unwise to rely on *nothing* but the statement at issue to establish the foundational requirement of the party's membership in the conspiracy.

b.   The Amendment to FRE 801(d)(2): The Requirement of Additional Evidence

The Supreme Court promulgated an amendment, effective in December 1997, that added the following language to FRE 801(d)(2):

> The statement must be considered but does not by itself establish the declarant's authority under (C); the existence or scope of the relationship under (D); or the existence of the conspiracy or participation in it under (E).

This language does not specify what kind of additional proof is needed, nor how much. Most courts post-*Bourjaily* had required some additional evidence from a source *independent* of the co-conspirator's hearsay statement to corroborate the defendant's membership in the conspiracy. The Advisory Committee Note to the amendment, however, appears to contemplate that evidence of the identity of the speaker and the context in which statement was made, as well as corroboration, might suffice. As we have noted previously, the requirement of additional evidence also applies to the key foundational issues under subsections (C) and (D) as well.

Prior to this amendment, courts found the requirement of independent evidence to be satisfied by behavior of the defendant that established a connection to the conspiracy: the defendant's own statements or statements of others that the defendant adopts; presence at locations where the co-conspirator said the defendant would be; attempts to silence the victim of the conspiracy; frequent phone contact with co-conspirators; or presence at drug deliveries. "Mere association" was held to be insufficient evidence of membership, but repeated meetings that coincide with large-scale drug deliveries were held sufficient. United States v. Ammar, 714 F.2d 238, 250 (3d Cir. 1983).

Reported cases since the amendment have continued to enforce the requirement of evidence corroborating the defendant's participation in the conspiracy's activities. "The quantum of independent evidence needed to corroborate the existence of a conspiracy necessarily is dependent on the totality of circumstances, including the strength of the hearsay statements themselves." United States v. Abu-Jihaad, 531 F. Supp. 2d 289, 296 (D. Conn. 1998). Here, the court found no independent evidence of the formation of the conspiracy prior to the co-conspirator statements offered against the defendant and wrote: "[T]his case is precisely what [those] requirements are designed to catch." Id. at 289.

Examples of cases in which independent corroboration has been found include: United States v. Sudeen, 434 F.3d 385 (5th Cir. 2005) (co-conspirator received and deposited a check for defendant, received a commission from defendant, and explained delays to defendant's customers); United States v. Capelton, 350 F.3d 231 (1st Cir. 2003) (defendant possessed marked bills from drug transaction and was on the scene during the transaction); United States v. Stotts, 323 F.3d 520 (7th Cir. 2003) (defendant accompanied brother, who actually sold the drugs, to and from the sale, gestured for the buyer to follow him in her car, and nodded in agreement for her to inspect the drugs before paying).

c.   Process for Admission of a Co-conspirator's Statement

It is well settled that the trial court has discretion to use the tool of conditional admissibility with respect to a co-conspirator's statements. "A court may conditionally admit a challenged statement subject to later proof to satisfy the co-conspirator rule and defer a final ruling on admissibility until after hearing the relevant evidence." United States v. Roach, 164 F.3d 403, 409 (8th Cir. 1998). Should the judge give any instruction to the jury when conditionally admitting the co-conspirator's statement? The judge could say something like, "I am provisionally admitting these hearsay statements pursuant to what is called the co-conspirator admission provision. If the prosecutor does not introduce sufficient independent evidence of the existence of a conspiracy, I may ask you later to disregard these hearsay statements." Would this be a good idea? What are the risks?

However, once a judge has conditionally admitted a co-conspirator's statements, the judge may be reluctant to find that the FRE 104(a) preliminary fact standard has not been satisfied. Such a finding would require the judge either to instruct the jury to disregard the co-conspirator's statement or to declare a mistrial. The instruction to disregard is not a realistic solution in many cases. Can the jury be expected to be able to obey it? And because the prosecutor will have presented all — or at least a substantial part — of the state's case before it becomes clear that the foundational requirements cannot be satisfied, the mistrial alternative will frequently be quite expensive. For these reasons, it may be wise for the judge to insist on proof of the foundational facts before proof of the co-conspirator's statement. United States v. Saneaux, 365 F. Supp. 2d 493, 502 (S.D.N.Y. 2005) (paucity of government's proof that statements were "in furtherance" at motion in limine held to preclude conditional admission; government should place before the jury all evidence it relies on to satisfy the required foundation before jury may hear the recorded co-conspirator statements).

KEY POINTS

1. Under FRE 801(d)(2)(A), any statement made out of court by a party may be used against that party to prove the truth of the matter it asserts, so long as it is relevant and not otherwise objectionable.

2. FRE 801(d)(2) also provides a hearsay exemption for: (B) statements about which the party manifests adoption or belief their truth; (C) statements authorized by the party; (D) certain statements made by an agent or employee of the party during the relationship on matters within the scope of the agent's employment; and (E) certain statements made by a co-conspirator of the party during the conspiracy and in furtherance of it.

3. The judge must be persuaded, pursuant to FRE 104(a), that the foundational requirements for each of these exemptions are satisfied. The judge may use the statement itself in deciding the preliminary questions, but other evidence is necessary to find authority, agency and a co-conspirator relationship.

4. The primary justification for the FRE 801(d)(2) exemptions is that the party cannot fairly complain about the loss of cross-examination of the declarant because the party can explain the unreliability in the statement, or because it is necessary and fair to impose on the party the risk and burden of not being able to do so.

PROBLEMS

8.37. Return to Problem 3.3, United States v. Ray, at page 136. The prosecution offers the following evidence. Defense counsel objects to each piece of evidence as hearsay. How should the court rule?

(a) A Rundown V.P. to testify: "On March 15, 2010, Bernard Ray said to me that he had just read a memo from his auditor, Andrews, and Rundown stock was going to take a beating."

(b) A senior VP at Andrews's accounting firm to testify: "On March 16, 2010, I spoke with Bernard Ray at our club. I said, 'Bernard, I hear that Rundown is going to project big losses in a few days. I assume you've already dumped most of your holdings.' Then Bernard said, 'Don't worry about me — I'm all set.'"

(c) The prosecution offers an authenticated copy of the March 14, 2010 outside auditor's memo to prove that Andrews in fact projected Rundown losses for the second quarter of 2004.

8.38. Daniel Mahlandt has sued the Wild Canid Survival & Research Center, Inc. and its director of education, Kenneth Poos, for injuries sustained when Daniel was allegedly bitten by a wolf named Sophie. Sophie was owned by the Center but lived temporarily at the Poos home. She was enclosed in the yard by a five-foot chain link fence and was chained to the fence with a six-foot-long chain. Daniel, who was three-and-a-half years old at the time of the alleged biting, was found bleeding and hysterical inside the yard with Sophie. There were no eyewitnesses as to how Daniel got into the yard or whether Sophie bit him. One witness testified that she heard a child's screams and observed Daniel on the ground with Sophie straddling him. Sophie's face was near Daniel's, and Sophie was wailing. Kenneth Poos's son found Daniel and carried him into the house.

Kenneth Poos will testify that Sophie had been hand raised by humans since birth, has been very gentle, and that he takes her to various schools and institutions as part of his educational program for the Center. A defense witness, an expert on animal behavior, will testify that when a wolf licks a child's face, that is a sign of care; that a wolf's wail is a sign of compassion; and that Daniel's particular injuries were not consistent with a wolf attack.

Mr. Poos arrived at his home shortly after the incident. After seeing that Daniel was taken to a hospital, Mr. Poos talked to his son about what happened and then went to the Center to report the incident to the Center's president. The president was not in, so Mr. Poos left the following note on his door: "Please call me at home. Sophie bit a child that came into our backyard. All has been taken care of. I need to convey to you what happened. KP." Several weeks later there was a meeting of the Board of Directors of the Center. Mr. Poos was not present. The minutes of that meeting state that there was a "great deal of discussion about the incident of Sophie biting the child and its legal aspects." Plaintiff has offered into evidence against both Mr. Poos and against the Center (a) the note written by Mr. Poos and (b) the foregoing passage from the minutes of the board meeting. Both defendants have objected on hearsay grounds to the admission of both pieces of evidence. With respect to each defendant, what result?

8.39. Tom Hay went to the emergency room (ER) complaining of chest pains and excessive sweating. Standard ER tests were run by Dr. Gatwick. These tests ruled out a recent heart attack but did not rule out cardiovascular disease as the cause of his symptoms. Two weeks later Hay suffered a heart attack and died.

Plaintiff, Hay's wife Barbara, has filed suit against Dr. Gatwick for medical malpractice seeking damages for her loss of consortium and support. It is agreed that the prevailing standard of care is that Gatwick should have advised Hay, his patient, to agree to enter the hospital for observation and additional tests. There is evidence suggesting that Hay's heart disease might have been treatable had it been discovered by further tests that can be administered only to a hospitalized patient. Gatwick asserts that he gave the required advice, and that Hay left the hospital that day *against* medical advice.

At trial, Plaintiff testifies that she arrived at the ER as Hay was leaving, and that Hay said, "The doctor told me that I was lucky and could safely leave." She further testifies that Gatwick was standing close enough that, in her opinion, he could have heard Hay's statement. Is Plaintiff's testimony admissible?

8.40. The United States is suing the Sheriff of Paxton County, Virginia, for refusing to consider women for a deputy sheriff (patrol) position in violation of Title VII, 42 U.S.C. §§2000 et seq. The government offered the testimony of an equal opportunity employment investigator who was investigating complaints against the Sheriff. The investigator recited the contents of a conversation with Mr. Giana, the county attorney who was representing the Sheriff regarding the discrimination claim:

> Mr. Giana: "The sheriff wants big tall men for that job [patrolman], that could defend themselves and be somewhat imposing. Females don't have a chance in this position."

Are Mr. Giana's statements admissible against the Sheriff?

8.41. Return to Problem 4.5 on page 191. The prosecution wants to argue that Bonds authorized his trainer, Greg Anderson, to speak to the BALCO lab on his behalf. Recall that when Anderson delivered urine samples to BALCO, he allegedly told Valente that the samples were from Barry Bonds. The government concedes that it cannot prove that Bonds gave specific authority to Anderson, but that by allowing Anderson to have the samples tested, Bonds *impliedly* authorized Anderson to identify them to BALCO. What do you think of this argument? Could any section of FRE 801(d)(2) be used to admit Anderson's hearsay statements against Bonds?

8.42. Return to Problem 3.2, Pedroso v. Driver, on page 136. Paul's mother testifies for plaintiffs that Paul's teacher told her, several weeks after the accident, that Driver's supervisor had told the teacher that, in his opinion, Driver was not keeping a proper lookout before the accident. Defendants object on grounds of hearsay. Admissible?

8.43. Plaintiff, an African-American employee of Johnson Welding, filed an EEOC complaint for hostile work environment on the job. After the complaint was filed, plaintiff contends, the company retaliated by intentionally isolating him from other employees, instructing them not to talk with him, and moving plaintiff's work station to the "back" of the welding facility. After trial, the jury awarded plaintiff both compensatory and punitive damages. On appeal, Johnson Welding claims error in the admission of testimony by one of plaintiff's witnesses, Alan Mason. Mason was a coworker of plaintiff at Johnson Welding. Mason testified as follows:

> At a barbecue at my home, my brother-in-law, David, made a statement to me. David works at Johnson also. David said that Tom (plaintiff's supervisor) told David that "some bad stuff is going to happen in the back" and that "David should tell Mason that he should stay out of it unless he wants to be fired."

Plaintiff claims this testimony was relevant to show Johnson Welding's vindictive state of mind toward him and that its treatment of him was retaliatory. Was it error to admit Mason's testimony?

8.44. Seven members of the Gangster Disciples (GD), a street gang (6,000 members) that operated a massive drug distribution business in the Chicago area, are being prosecuted for drug, weapons, and money-laundering offenses. The leader of the GD is known to be Larry Hoover, who for years ran the gang from inside of various prisons. His female partner owned a legitimate business called Save the Children Promotions. In an authorized IRS search of the Save the Children offices, agents found a document in a folder marked "L.H./Sr." The document was a list describing the hierarchical and territorial organization of the entire GD operation. In some taped conversations, Hoover had mentioned his desire to develop such a document to keep track of gang members and their payments to GD. All seven defendants are mentioned in the list. On what basis can they object to admission of the list against them at trial? What result?

8.45. In the prosecution of a wealthy show horse owner for insurance fraud, the government seeks to prove that the owner conspired to have one of his horses, Charisma, killed in order to collect insurance proceeds. The person who was hired to kill Charisma, Burns, was hired by Marty, the owner's horse trainer, and told that "the owner wanted it done on December 15 because he was in Asia, and because Charisma was scheduled to travel from New York to Florida on December 16." Marty paid Burns to do the job. Can the government use Burns's testimony about Marty's statements against the owner? Suppose that the government has independent proof that the owner was indeed in Asia on December 15, and that Charisma was scheduled to travel to Florida on December 16? What result? Suppose that the government can also prove that, after Charisma's death, the owner intentionally lied to the insurance company about who was allowed to ride Charisma, in order to avoid one of the insurance policy's exceptions?

D.   HEARSAY EXCEPTIONS NOT REQUIRING THE UNAVAILABILITY OF THE DECLARANT

FRE 803 excepts 23 different types of hearsay statements from the general rule of exclusion. There is no requirement in this rule that the declarant be unavailable to testify as a witness. Thus, the justifications for admitting this much hearsay are especially important for your overall evaluation of the hearsay rule in practice. Some of the FRE 803 exceptions are legacies of almost 300 years of common law development and are rarely used in modern federal litigation. We will focus primarily on the exceptions that are most used today.

The premise of all FRE 803 exceptions is that these types of statements are reliable enough to be used in the jury's fact-finding even without cross-examination of the declarant by the opponent. In the words of the Advisory Committee Note, these kinds of statements "possess circumstantial guarantees of trustworthiness sufficient to justify nonproduction of the declarant in person at the trial even though he may be available." This means that something about the hearsay statement—its content, its source, the circumstances in which it was made—reveals something "trustworthy" about the declarant's testimonial qualities. This is the "reliability approach" to the admission of hearsay that we already saw at work in FRE 801(a) and (c) and in the FRE 801(d) exemptions as well.

The Rule 803 exceptions are categorical. They each define a specific type of out-of-court statement that may be admitted for the truth of the matter it asserts, and they each establish foundational requirements that the proponent must satisfy pursuant to the process described above in Section B. In this section, we now examine the categorical foundational requirements of the FRE 803 exceptions, and the reliability rationale underlying the more important ones. Remember that other rules may operate to exclude a hearsay statement even if it fits within a Rule 803 exception—relevancy, authentication, best evidence, the relevancy rules such as the character prohibitions, privilege, and, of course, FRE 403, may all have to be applied as well.

Two other general points apply to all Rule 803 (and Rule 804) exceptions. Because the declarant's statement is offered for its truth, the declarant is a source of knowledge for the jury, analogous to a witness testifying at trial. Therefore, the fundamental requirement that witnesses must speak from personal knowledge applies as well to hearsay declarants under FRE 803 and FRE 804. The Advisory Committee Note to Rule 803 makes this clear:

> In a hearsay situation, the declarant is, of course, a witness, and neither this rule nor Rule 804 dispenses with the requirement of firsthand knowledge. It may appear from his statement or be inferable from circumstances. See Rule 602.

In addition, the opponent to an item of hearsay can attack the credibility of hearsay declarants in most of the ways that witnesses can be attacked. FRE 806 makes this clear:

RULE 806. ATTACKING AND SUPPORTING THE DECLARANT'S CREDIBILITY

When a hearsay statement — or a statement described in Rule 801(d)(2)(C), (D), or (E) — has been admitted in evidence, the declarant's credibility may be attacked, and then supported, by any evidence that would be admissible for those purposes if the declarant had testified as a witness. The court may admit evidence of the declarant's inconsistent statement or conduct, regardless of when it occurred or whether the declarant had an opportunity to explain or deny it. If the party against whom the statement was admitted calls the declarant as a witness, the party may examine the declarant on the statement as if on cross-examination.

It is more difficult, of course, to impeach a hearsay declarant without the tool of cross-examination. Issues regarding impeachment under FRE 806 are discussed in Margaret Meriwether Cordray, Evidence Rule 806 and the Problem of Impeaching the Nontestifying Declarant, 56 Ohio St. L.J. 495 (1995).

1.   FRE 803

RULE 803.   EXCEPTIONS TO THE RULE AGAINST HEARSAY—REGARDLESS OF WHETHER THE DECLARANT IS AVAILABLE AS A WITNESS

The following are not excluded by the rule against hearsay, regardless of whether the declarant is available as a witness:

(1) *Present Sense Impression.* A statement describing or explaining an event or condition, made while or immediately after the declarant perceived it.

(2) *Excited Utterance.* A statement relating to a startling event or condition, made while the declarant was under the stress of excitement that it caused.

(3) *Then-Existing Mental, Emotional, or Physical Condition.* A statement of the declarant's then-existing state of mind (such as motive, intent, or plan) or emotional, sensory, or physical condition (such as mental feeling, pain, or bodily health), but not including a statement of memory or belief to prove the fact remembered or believed unless it relates to the validity or terms of the declarant's will.

(4) *Statement Made for Medical Diagnosis or Treatment.* A statement that:

(A) is made for — and is reasonably pertinent to — medical diagnosis or treatment; and

(B) describes medical history; past or present symptoms or sensations; their inception; or their general cause.

(5) *Recorded Recollection.* A record that:

(A) is on a matter the witness once knew about but now cannot recall well enough to testify fully and accurately;

(B) was made or adopted by the witness when the matter was fresh in the witness's memory; and

(C) accurately reflects the witness's knowledge.

If admitted, the record may be read into evidence but may be received as an exhibit only if offered by an adverse party.

(6) *Records of a Regularly Conducted Activity.* A record of an act, event, condition, opinion, or diagnosis if:

(A) the record was made at or near the time by — or from information transmitted by — someone with knowledge;

(B) the record was kept in the course of a regularly conducted activity of a business, organization, occupation, or calling, whether or not for profit;

(C) making the record was a regular practice of that activity;

(D) all these conditions are shown by the testimony of the custodian or another qualified witness, or by a certification that complies with Rule 902(11) or (12) or with a statute permitting certification; and

(E) neither the source of information nor the method or circumstances of preparation indicate a lack of trustworthiness.

(7) *Absence of a Record of a Regularly Conducted Activity*. Evidence that a matter is not included in a record described in paragraph (6) if:

(A) the evidence is admitted to prove that the matter did not occur or exist;

(B) a record was regularly kept for a matter of that kind; and

(C) neither the possible source of the information nor other circumstances indicate a lack of trustworthiness.

(8) *Public Records*. A record or statement of a public office if:

(A) it sets out:

(i) the office's activities;

(ii) a matter observed while under a legal duty to report, but not including, in a criminal case, a matter observed by law-enforcement personnel; or

(iii) in a civil case or against the government in a criminal case, factual findings from a legally authorized investigation; and

(B) neither the source of information nor other circumstances indicate a lack of trustworthiness.

(9) *Public Records of Vital Statistics*. A record of a birth, death, or marriage, if reported to a public office in accordance with a legal duty.

(10) *Absence of a Public Record*. Testimony — or a certification under Rule 902 — that a diligent search failed to disclose a public record or statement if the testimony or certification is admitted to prove that:

(A) the record or statement does not exist; or

(B) a matter did not occur or exist, if a public office regularly kept a record or statement for a matter of that kind.

(11) *Records of Religious Organizations Concerning Personal or Family History*. A statement of birth, legitimacy, ancestry, marriage, divorce, death, relationship by blood or marriage, or similar facts of personal or family history, contained in a regularly kept record of a religious organization.

(12) *Certificates of Marriage, Baptism, and Similar Ceremonies*. A statement of fact contained in a certificate:

(A) made by a person who is authorized by a religious organization or by law to perform the act certified;

(B) attesting that the person performed a marriage or similar ceremony or administered a sacrament; and

(C) purporting to have been issued at the time of the act or within a reasonable time after it.

(13) *Family Records*. A statement of fact about personal or family history contained in a family record, such as a Bible, genealogy, chart, engraving on a ring, inscription on a portrait, or engraving on an urn or burial marker.

(14) *Records of Documents That Affect an Interest in Property*. The record of a document that purports to establish or affect an interest in property if:

(A) the record is admitted to prove the content of the original recorded document, along with its signing and its delivery by each person who purports to have signed it;

(B) the record is kept in a public office; and

(C) a statute authorizes recording documents of that kind in that office.

(15) *Statements in Documents That Affect an Interest in Property*. A statement contained in a document that purports to establish or affect an interest in property if the matter stated was relevant to the document's purpose — unless later dealings with the property are inconsistent with the truth of the statement or the purport of the document.

(16) *Statements in Ancient Documents*. A statement in a document that is at least 20 years old and whose authenticity is established.

(17) *Market Reports and Similar Commercial Publications*. Market quotations, lists, directories, or other compilations that are generally relied on by the public or by persons in particular occupations.

(18) *Statements in Learned Treatises, Periodicals, or Pamphlets.* A statement contained in a treatise, periodical, or pamphlet if:

(A) the statement is called to the attention of an expert witness on cross-examination or relied on by the expert on direct examination; and

(B) the publication is established as a reliable authority by the expert's admission or testimony, by another expert's testimony, or by judicial notice.

If admitted, the statement may be read into evidence but not received as an exhibit.

(19) *Reputation Concerning Personal or Family History.* A reputation among a person's family by blood, adoption, or marriage — or among a person's associates or in the community — concerning the person's birth, adoption, legitimacy, ancestry, marriage, divorce, death, relationship by blood, adoption, or marriage, or similar facts of personal or family history.

(20) *Reputation Concerning Boundaries or General History.* A reputation in a community — arising before the controversy — concerning boundaries of land in the community or customs that affect the land, or concerning general historical events important to that community, state, or nation.

(21) *Reputation Concerning Character.* A reputation among a person's associates or in the community concerning the person's character.

(22) *Judgment of a Previous Conviction.* Evidence of a final judgment of conviction if:

(A) the judgment was entered after a trial or guilty plea, but not a nolo contendere plea;

(B) the conviction was for a crime punishable by death or by imprisonment for more than a year;

(C) the evidence is admitted to prove any fact essential to the judgment; and

(D) when offered by the prosecutor in a criminal case for a purpose other than impeachment, the judgment was against the defendant.

The pendency of an appeal may be shown but does not affect admissibility.

(23) *Judgments Involving Personal, Family, or General History or a Boundary.* A judgment that is admitted to prove a matter of personal, family, or general history, or boundaries, if the matter:

(A) was essential to the judgment; and

(B) could be proved by evidence of reputation.

2.   Interpretation and Illustration of FRE 803(1): Present Sense Impressions

There are two exceptions that provide for the admission of two different kinds of spontaneous hearsay statements—present sense impressions and excited utterances. The categorical requirements for each are somewhat different. FRE 803(1) provides:

(1) *Present Sense Impression.* A statement describing or explaining an event or condition, made while or immediately after the declarant perceived it.

a.   *Preliminary Fact-finding*

The foundational requirements for present sense impressions are:

- the occurrence of an event or condition;
- the contents of the statement describe or explain the event or condition; and

- the declarant made the statement while or immediately after perceiving the event or condition.

Think back to the first illustration of an out-of-court statement that we used in this chapter. We found that Sally's statement "the gray SUV ran the red light and hit a pedestrian" would be hearsay, if reported by George at trial. But Sally's statement might have been made to George either while Sally was seeing the SUV, or within seconds or minutes of seeing it. Thus, it might be admissible hearsay, if it qualifies as a present sense impression. The pedestrian, the proponent of the statement, must present evidence to show that it falls within the categorical terms of FRE 803(1). These are preliminary questions for the judge to determine pursuant to FRE 104(a). The court should be convinced by a preponderance of the evidence that there was an event occurring just before Sally's statement was made, and that Sally's statement describes it.

Many present sense impressions are presented in court through the testimony of witnesses who also perceived the event or condition themselves. If George saw the accident, he would be the foundation witness who could provide evidence showing that the event occurred and that Sally made the statement contemporaneously with it. The judge can determine whether the statement describes or explains the event or condition from the contents of the statement itself.

b. Justification for the Admissibility of Present Sense Impressions

The primary justification for admitting present sense impressions is that the contemporaneity of the statement and the event it is offered to prove tends to ensure the declarant's sincerity. This rationale falls squarely within the reliability theory advanced for admitting trustworthy hearsay. It is based on the generalization that contemporaneity between statement and event means that the statement is spontaneous rather than premeditated. If the statement is spontaneous, there is no time to develop the intent to fabricate. If there is no time or opportunity to fabricate, the statement is sincere. Additionally, the contemporaneity of the statement and the event virtually eliminates any memory problem.

3. Interpretation and Illustration of FRE 803(2): Excited Utterances

FRE 803(2) provides:

(2) *Excited Utterance.* A statement relating to a startling event or condition, made while the declarant was under the stress of excitement that it caused.

a. Preliminary Fact-finding

The foundational requirements for excited utterances are:

- the occurrence of a startling event or condition;
- the statement relates to the startling event or condition;

- the statement was made by the declarant while under stress of excitement; and
- the stress of excitement was caused by the startling event or condition.

Sally's statement to George might also be an excited utterance. Again, the proponent must present evidence to satisfy the foundational requirements, and the judge will decide the preliminary questions pursuant to FRE 104(a). The judge may conclude that an SUV running through a red light and hitting a pedestrian is a *startling* event. Again, George would be the foundation witness to testify that the event occurred and that Sally was under stress of excitement when she made the statement. How might George describe Sally's behavior to prove that she was *under stress of excitement*? George might also establish that Sally's stress was caused by the startling event, if he said, "She was perfectly calm before the accident." In Boucher v. Grant, 74 F. Supp. 2d 444, 450 (D.N.J. 1999), the court held that declarant Grant's hearsay statement was admissible under the following analysis:

> An automobile accident and a contemporaneous statement by an individual involved in that accident concerning its cause undoubtedly satisfy the first three elements of the excited utterance hearsay exception. The question becomes, then, whether the hearsay statements meet the last condition of admissibility, namely, spontaneity. . . .
>
> Boucher testified that his exchange with Grant occurred "within a minute" of the accident . . . Grant himself testified that as a result of the crash, he was "scared . . . shaken up." . . . The brief lapse of time coupled with Grant's mental state cannot give rise to a finding of conscious reflection. Therefore, I conclude that the statement was made while Grant was still in an excited state and before he could reflect and fabricate.

Many factors are relevant to the question of whether the defendant was under stress of excitement from the startling event at the time the statement was made:

> [W]e consider . . . the lapse of time between the startling event and the statement, whether the statement was made in response to an inquiry, the age of the declarant, the physical and mental condition of the declarant, the characteristics of the event, and the subject matter of the statement. [United States v. Wilcox, 487 F.3d 1163, 1170 (8th Cir. 2007).]

b.   Justification for the Admissibility of Excited Utterances

The justification for the exception is similar to the argument that present sense impressions are reliable. A statement made under the stress of a startling event or condition is likely to be spontaneous, and a person under stress is not likely to develop the intent to fabricate. If there is no opportunity to fabricate, the statement is likely to be sincere. Notice, however, that there is no foundational requirement of "contemporaneity" between the event and the statement. Stress of excitement is the substitute for contemporaneity. A longer time lag will not defeat application of the FRE 803(2) exception if the declarant remains under stress. So long as stress is operative, there is assumed to be no opportunity to plan to make a false statement and thus the statement is likely to be sincere. United States v. DeMarce, 564 F.3d 989, 997 (8th Cir. 2009) ("The rationale of the excited utterance exception is that 'stress of nervous excitement or physical shock stills the reflective faculties, thus removing an impediment to truthfulness.'"). In *De Marce*, the plaintiff in an attempted sexual assault case initially fabricated a story about tripping in the hallway to explain why she had a bloody lip. Then she returned and told her mother about the attempted assault. The court held that her statements "demonstrate a level of reflection that prohibit their admission as an 'excited utterance.'"

Since the duration of the declarant's stress of excitement is likely to be relatively short, memory danger may also be lessened. However, as commentators have long recognized, the stress that decreases the sincerity danger may increase perception dangers and memory dangers, and perhaps even narration dangers as well. Consider the effects of seeing someone hit by a car—how carefully and accurately are you able to perceive and recount the details of such an event? These risks are discussed in Robert M. Hutchins and Donald Slesinger, Some Observations on the Law of Evidence: Spontaneous Exclamations, 28 Colum. L. Rev. 432 (1928); Fredric D. Woocher, Note, Did Your Eyes Deceive You? Expert Psychological Testimony on the Unreliability of Eyewitness Identification, 29 Stan. L. Rev. 969, 975-988 (1977). Nonetheless, the exception is well established in the Federal Rules and in most jurisdictions.

Compare the concern for contemporaneity or spontaneity under FRE 803(1) and (2) with the lack of such requirements for statements identifying a person admitted under FRE 801(d)(1)(C). We noted on page 458 that application of this exemption to statements not made at lineups and other formal opportunities for re-perception, but rather after a lapse of time and in the absence of stress, undermines the potential reliability of such statements.

4.   Elaboration of FRE 803(1) and (2): Effects of the Categorical Approach

a.   *The Categories Determine Admissibility*

Do you agree that the probability of Sally's sincerity in making her statement about the gray SUV is increased by the fact that her statement was made contemporaneously with seeing the SUV? Or by the fact that it was made under stress of a startling event? Analyzing this question requires you to think in terms of generalizations about large groups of out-of-court declarants who share either the FRE 803(1) or the FRE 803(2) characteristic in common. How can we be sure that everyone within this large group does have enhanced sincerity? The answer is, we cannot be sure. Even more troubling, how do we know that Sally has good eyesight and could perceive the SUV from the distance at which she was standing, or could perceive that the light was red? The answer is, we do not know. The only facts about Sally's testimonial qualities that FRE 803(1) and (2) require to be presented to the jury are the facts about spontaneity that satisfy the categorical requirements of the exceptions.

The effects of this categorical approach are twofold. First, if a statement clearly fits within the broad categorical generalizations of the specific exception, it must be admitted (unless there is some other objection to its admissibility unrelated to hearsay). "If a declaration comes within a category defined as an exception, the declaration is admissible without any preliminary credibility finding by the judge. . . . " United States v. DiMaria, 727 F.2d 265, 272 (2d Cir. 1984). Except for the three specific exceptions (FRE 803(6), 803(8), and 804(b)(3)), there is no explicit judicial discretion to *exclude* a particular statement that fits within a categorical exception because the judge doubts the sincerity, perception, memory, or narration of the hearsay declarant. United States v. Perkins, 1999 WL 506980 (6th Cir. 1999) (declarant, a police informant, had the opportunity to deliberately mislead the police in reporting the contents of a series of phone calls made over an extended period of time with defendant; nevertheless, declarant's statements fit within present sense impression exception). Second, if a judge thinks that a hearsay statement seems to be particularly trustworthy but it is neither contemporaneous with an event (it was made an hour later) nor made under the stress of excitement (it was made calmly), the judge has no explicit discretion under FRE 803(1) or (2) to admit it. The categorical requirements of each exception determine admissibility. Only FRE 807 permits the *admission* of hearsay based on judicial determinations that it is trustworthy.

b.   The Categorical Terms Require Judicial Interpretation

Although there is no explicit discretion in most of the hearsay exceptions, judges do have some leeway when they interpret and apply the categorical terms of the exceptions to particular statements. How long a time lag is permitted by the term "immediately thereafter" in FRE 803(1)? Just what is "stress" in FRE 803(2), and how long does it last? There are no clear-cut answers to these questions in some cases. You will see in many of the Rule 803 and Rule 804 exceptions that there is considerable room for judicial interpretation. Since the categorical requirements are determinative of admissibility, judicial interpretation of these requirements is crucial to the administration of hearsay policy. These requirements are intended to ensure the trustworthiness of one or more of the declarant's testimonial qualities. It follows that judges should interpret and apply the doctrinal terms with the awareness that different interpretations can either increase or decrease the apparent trustworthiness of admitted hearsay statements.

i.   **Time Lapse Between Event and Statement.**   Not all seemingly contemporaneous statements are really spontaneous. They might have been thought up in advance, if the declarant had any foreknowledge that the relevant event might occur. And a time lapse of more than a few minutes may be plenty of time to think up something self-serving to say. Particularly if a statement is obviously self-serving, one may doubt its spontaneity and, therefore, its sincerity. Rigorous application of the contemporaneity requirement of FRE 803(1) would reduce this problem. Many courts have interpreted "immediately after" in FRE 803(1) to mean within a matter of seconds, or as soon as is possible. United States v. Shoup, 476 F.3d 38, 42 (1st Cir. 2007) (911 phone call made "only one or two minutes . . . immediately following" event). Some courts, however, have stretched the interpretation of that doctrinal phrase to admit apparently spontaneous statements made 10 to 15 minutes after the event they describe or explain. See, e.g., United States v. Obayagbona, 627 F. Supp. 329 (E.D.N.Y. 1985) (statement made by undercover police officer about a drug transaction, made 14 minutes afterward, "was as spontaneous as possible" since it could not be made until after the arrest.) Courts also look to the context within which the statement was given, and any intervening events. United States v. Ramos, 397 Fed. Appx. 767, 771 (3d Cir. 2010) (statement inadmissible when 20 minutes had elapsed between event and statement and declarant was securely detained within police car; requirement of "no time to fabricate or misrepresent" not satisfied).

FRE 803(2) places no specific time restraint on the scope of the exception. The temporal gap is therefore not dispositive, but is a relevant consideration in determining whether the statement is made while the declarant is still under stress. "Our cases do not demand a precise showing of the lapse of time . . . The exception may be based solely on '[t]estimony that the declarant still appeared nervous or distraught and that there was a reasonable basis for continuing [to be] emotional[ly] upset.'" United States v. Davis, 577 F.3d 660, 669 (6th Cir. 2009). Other relevant factors include the characteristics of the event; the subject matter of the statement; whether the statement was made in response to an inquiry; and the declarant's age, motive to lie and physical and mental condition. "It is the totality of the circumstances . . . that determine whether a hearsay statement was an excited utterance." United States v. Belfast, 611 F.3d 783, 817 (11th Cir. 2010). United States v. Alexander, 331 F.3d 116, 123 (D.C. Cir. 2003). In cases where the event is less startling, courts tend to require a shorter time lapse between event and statement.

Statements of young children about incidents of sexual abuse are frequently made hours or even days after the alleged incident occurred. Some courts admit these statements under FRE 803(2) citing various justifications—"first real opportunity" to speak to an adult or caregiver, or fear and guilt causing child to delay reporting, or lack of capacity to fabricate—while other courts are suspicious of such lengthy delays. Reed v. Thalacker, 198 F.3d 1058, 1062 (8th Cir. 1999) ("distorted recollection . . . can occur through deliberate coaching, inadvertent suggestion, confusion of fact and fantasy, or a simple defect in memory"). For a teenager, a time lapse of three hours has been held to be too long to reduce the risk of deliberate fabrication, particularly when the declarant had not appeared to be stressed in the interim. Stress can be rekindled by events that remind the declarant of the startling event or that generate additional anguish. United States v. Lossiah, 129 Fed. Appx. 434 (10th Cir. 2005) (child under age of 12 saw defendant at her school and "ran to tell" her teacher "Don't let him check me out . . . he raped me"; alleged attack had occurred two months before, but caused child to be fearful when she saw defendant at school).

Cases involving domestic violence may also justify courts in extending the period of time during which the declarant is under stress: "trauma and anxiety prompted by a spousal assault—which form the predicate for calling something an excited utterance—do not suddenly dissipate when the assailant leaves the scene." United States v. Green, 125 Fed. Appx. 659, 662 (6th Cir. 2005). Excited utterances about criminal activity made to 911 operators and police present challenging issues under Crawford v. Washington's holding that the confrontation clause applies to "testimonial" statements. See Section G, infra.

ii.   Content of the Statement.   The FRE 803(1) requirement that the declaration be one *describing or explaining an event or condition* is intended to be a limitation that is consistent with the exception's underlying rationale. United States v. Ferber, 966 F. Supp. 90 (D. Mass. 1997) (handwritten notes reciting what someone said at a meeting fall within the exception). The Advisory Committee Note explains that the language of FRE 803(2) — *relating to a startling even or condition—* "affords a broader scope of subject matter coverage." But the Advisory Committee does not elaborate on the meaning of the terms *describing, explaining,* and *relating,* and it is not intuitively obvious how broadly or narrowly they should be defined. The Note does cite two cases that apparently, in the view of the Advisory Committee, would fall within the meaning of *relating to* but not *describing or explaining*:

> See Sanitary Grocery Co. v. Snead, 67 App. D.C. 129, 90 F.2d 374 (1937), slip-and-fall case sustaining admissibility of clerk's statement, "That has been on the floor for a couple of hours," and Murphy Auto Parts Co. v. Ball, 101 U.S. App. D.C. 416, 249 F.2d 508 (1957), upholding admission, on issue of driver's agency, of his statement that he had to call on a customer and was in a hurry to get home.

Why do these statements relate to but not describe or explain an event or condition? The first statement refers to a past historical fact about the offending condition, and does not express just a *present* description of the floor. The second refers to the driver's purpose in driving his truck, and does not describe the event or condition—the accident—that was the subject of his statement. Why should statements encompassing this broader range of facts be admissible under FRE 803(2) but not FRE 803(1)? There are limits, however, to how broadly the term "relating to" will be applied. United States v. Alarcon-Simi, 300 F.3d 1172, 1176 (9th Cir. 2002) (defendant sought admission of his own exculpatory statement made just after the "traumatic incident" of being arrested for fraudulent check-cashing; statement that "he didn't know about [it]" held inadmissible as not "relating to" what "occurred *at the time of his arrest*" but to earlier events).

c.   Use of the Statement Itself in Preliminary Fact-finding

FRE 104(a) governs the judge's preliminary fact-finding necessary to apply the categorical terms of the FRE 803 exceptions. FRE 104(a) permits the judge to use inadmissible evidence, and thus would permit use of the hearsay statement itself. This is the same "bootstrapping" issue that we discussed in the context of the Rule 801(d)(2)(E) co-conspirators' exemption.

This issue frequently arises with regard to present sense impressions and excited utterances when the proponent wants to use the content of these statements to prove that an event (or a startling event) actually occurred. Other witnesses, including the foundation witness who testifies about the out-of-court statement, may be able to testify that the event occurred. But often, such independent evidence will not be available. For example, if Sally was speaking to George on her car phone when she said "a gray SUV just ran the red light and hit a pedestrian," George cannot provide independent evidence that the event described by Sally actually occurred. Statements admitted under FRE 803(1) and (2) can also be in writing, so there may be no other person present to verify either the event or when the written statement was made. The contents of the statement itself may be used by the judge to decide that an event occurred, when it occurred, and what kind of an event it was. United States v. Arnold, 486 F.3d 177, 180 (6th Cir. 2007) (to establish a startling event, court relied on declarant's statement during 911 call that defendant had just threatened her with a gun).

May the statement alone satisfy the Rule 104(a) burden of proving that an event occurred? Yes, according to the Advisory Committee Note. "[A]n excited utterance may of itself be sufficient to establish the occurrence of the startling event." Most federal courts agree although as a practical matter, there will often be independent evidence that a startling event occurred. The nature of the event is likely to attract attention; and even if there are no eyewitnesses, the declarant's nervousness or injuries or quivering voice would constitute at least some independent evidence of a startling event. A vigorous dissent in *Arnold*, however, contended that reliance solely on the hearsay statement would vitiate the underlying reliability theory of the exception: "[A]nyone could contrive a fact that — if real — would cause excitement, and state it in an exclamatory manner. To hold that such a statement, standing alone, is admissible for the truth of the matter asserted stands the hearsay rule on its head." Id. at 208.

Courts are no longer hesitant in admitting excited utterances made by unidentified bystanders. United States v. Montero-Camargo, 177 F.3d 1113, 1123 (9th Cir. 1999) ("trustworthiness of the statement is bolstered by the declarant's status as a mere bystander with no apparent motivation for providing false information."); Miller v. Crown Amusements, Inc., 821 F. Supp. 703 (S.D. Ga. 1993) (unidentified 911 caller).

d.   Proof of Personal Knowledge

The proponent of a present sense impression or excited utterance must show that "the declarant had personally perceived the event or condition about which the statement is made." United States v. Mitchell, 145 F.3d 572, 575 (3d Cir. 1998). The content of the statement, and the circumstances surrounding the making of it, may be sufficient, even when the declarant is unidentified. In Miller v. Keating, 754 F.2d 507 (3d Cir. 1985), an unidentified bystander ran up to the parties involved in an automobile collision and exclaimed that one car (the defendant's) had cut into the line of traffic, thus causing the accident. The appellate court reversed the trial court's admission of this statement:

> When there is no evidence of personal perception, apart from the declaration itself, courts have hesitated to allow the excited utterance to stand alone as evidence of the declarant's opportunity to observe . . . In some cases, however, the substance of the statement itself does contain words revealing perception. A statement such as, "I saw that blue truck run down the lady on the corner," might stand alone to show perception if the trial judge finds, from the particular circumstances, that he is satisfied by a preponderance that the declarant spoke from personal perception . . . [Id. at 511-512.]

The court in *Miller* found no evidence to support an inference that the declarant actually saw what had happened, that he could have seen it, or that he was excited. The court treated the issue of personal knowledge as an FRE 104(a) issue for the judge. Most other opinions on this point agree. Miller v. Crown Amusements, Inc., supra, 821 F. Supp. at 705-706 ("the Court finds by a preponderance of the evidence that the declarant observed the accident. The caller specifically stated, '[W]e *noticed* [the truck sideswipe a person]' thus indicating actual perception.").

KEY POINTS

1. Generalizations about the lack of sincerity and memory dangers provide the justification for the present sense impression and excited utterance exceptions, but

statements falling within these exceptions remain untested with regard to perception and narration dangers.

2. The rigor with which courts interpret and apply the terms defining the time lapse between the event or condition and the statement itself affects the degree of sincerity danger in both exceptions.

3. The judge may use the statement itself to determine whether and when the event or condition occurred pursuant to FRE 104(a), and in some cases may require no independent evidence.

PROBLEMS

8.46. In the case involving the pedestrian suing the driver of the SUV (pages 408-409), George would testify to the following: (Each statement is an alternative, not cumulative.)

(a) Sally was standing right next to me on the street corner, and she said, "That gray SUV just ran a red light and hit a pedestrian." I looked up and saw the SUV stopped near a person lying on the street.

(b) I was at my desk when Sally came running into the office, out of breath and very agitated. She said, "You won't believe what I just saw. A gray SUV ran a red light and hit a pedestrian!"

(c) Sally came back to the office from lunch and calmly stated, "I was on my way back from lunch when I saw yet another SUV running a stoplight and knocking someone down. Go figure. I spoke with the police for 30 minutes."

8.47. Victor was arrested by a group of law enforcement officers who burst into the apartment, guns drawn, in which Victor was meeting with others. The officers shouted at the group to "show their hands"; asked, "Is this dope, is this dope"; and pointed to money inside a car seat and asked, "Is that money? How much?" Victor responded, "I was buying a truck, man." Victor offers the officers' authenticated tape recording of his statement at his trial. Admissible?

8.48. Return to Problem 3.2, Pedroso v. Driver, at page 136. A teacher at Paul's school testifies for plaintiffs that Ann, who was on the school bus with Paul, was playing during recess in the schoolyard several days after the accident. Ann suddenly started to cry and exclaimed, "That's the bus driver who hit Paul on the side of the road" just as Denise Driver was walking by. Admissible?

8.49. Defendant Louis D'Onofrio is charged with illegal possession of a firearm as a convicted felon and two counts of brandishing a deadly weapon, one occurring on January 24 and one on January 26.

(a) A 911 call was made by Mrs. D'Onofrio from her home at 2:15 A.M. on January 26. She told the operator that her husband, Louis, was drunk and threatening to shoot her. The operator could hear Louis yelling loudly, but she heard no threats. The operator asked whether her husband had a weapon. Mrs. D'Onofrio said that he has a gun and is pointing it at her. Can the tape recording of this conversation be admitted at defendant's trial?

(b)   Police officers arrived at the D'Onofrio home at 2:30 A.M. Louis D'Onofrio had just left the house with the gun, according to Mrs. D'Onofrio, who was upset and crying. She stated that she and Louis had been arguing on the evening of January 24; that he held the gun and threatened to kill her during the argument; that when she returned from work on January 25, Louis had the gun and killed the family cat; that he spent the evening of January 25 drinking and that she had called 911 at 2:15 A.M. when he began to make more threats. Mrs. D'Onofrio consented to a search for a gun, but none was found. Defendant had no gun in his possession when he was arrested. Mrs. D'Onofrio now refuses to testify, claiming spousal privilege, and there is no other evidence that defendant possessed a firearm. Can the officers testify about her statements at defendant's trial?

8.50. Defendant Jack Jordan is charged with arson as a result of a fire that destroyed his clothing store and the apartments above it. The prosecution claims that Jack employed his brother Mark and friend Thomas Telford to commit the deed and gave them a key to the store, which had not been broken into. The fire was ablaze by 11:00 P.M. and, apparently, Telford remained at the scene. He was told by tenants exiting the building that there might be other people trapped inside. At 2:00 A.M., Telford knocked on the window of his friend Larry's apartment, appeared "all hyped up" and "nervous" according to Larry, and told Larry that "Mark and I lit a building for Jack." Can Larry testify as to Telford's statement in Jack Jordan's trial?

8.51. After a morning of skiing at Timber Mountain, Joe and his wife, both intermediate skiers, had lunch and then rode the Wolf chairlift to the top of Red Run. Red Run is a groomed, intermediate-level run below the Wolf chair. As Joe skied down first, he was spotted by an off-duty Timber Mountain Lodge employee who was on the Wolf chairlift. The employee witnessed Joe skiing down Red Run, then lose control and crash headfirst into a tree near the edge of the run. There was a partially exposed tree stump near the area where Joe had lost control and crashed.

The employee skied down to Joe in five minutes, after having alerted Timber Mountain Ski Patrol about the accident. By that time, Joe's wife was also present. Joe was unconscious, bleeding from the mouth, and turning blue. Joe's wife was screaming for help. A vacationing nurse stopped and administered CPR to Joe. When the ski patrol arrived, Joe's wife overheard the employee say, "What took you so long? Someone might die here." The ski patrol asked the employee, "What happened?" Joe's wife claims that she overheard the employee tell the ski patrol that he had seen Joe hit a stump, then crash into a tree, hitting his head on the tree.

Joe is partially disabled from the accident and cannot remember what happened. He and his wife have sued Timber Mountain for negligence in maintaining a hazardous condition, the stump, on Red Run. Timber Mountain defends on the basis that Joe was an inexperienced skier and crashed into the tree on his own. At trial, the court excludes the wife's testimony about the employee's statements for the following reasons: that they were made 15 or 20 minutes after witnessing Joe's fall; that they were made in response to the ski patrol's inquiry and not spontaneously; and that the employee and Joe were strangers. If Joe and his wife lose at trial, what would you argue on appeal to overturn the trial court's exclusion of the wife's testimony?

5.   Interpretation and Illustration of FRE 803(3): State-of-Mind Declarations

FRE 803(3) states:

(3) *Then-Existing Mental, Emotional, or Physical Condition.* A statement of the declarant's then-existing state of mind (such as motive, intent, or plan) or emotional, sensory, or physical condition (such as mental feeling, pain, or bodily health), but not including a statement of memory or belief to prove the fact remembered or believed unless it relates to the validity or terms of the declarant's will.

a.   Preliminary Fact-finding

The foundational requirements for statements of state of mind are:

- the contents of the statement express the declarant's state of mind that is currently existing at the time of the statement;
- state of mind may include motive, intent, plan; emotional, sensory, or physical condition; mental feeling, pain or bodily health; and
- a state of mind of memory or belief may not be used to prove the fact remembered or believed unless it relates to the validity or terms of the declarant's will.

As with all exceptions that depend on content as a categorical requirement, the judge can determine content from proof of the statement itself. Thus, the statements "I like Harold the best of all my children" or "I am miserably unhappy at work" fall within the FRE 803(3) exception, and will be admissible for their truth, if those current feelings are relevant. No other foundational facts concerning the declarant or the circumstances within which the statement was made are required.

Notice that Rule 803(3) defines *state of mind* broadly to include any sensation present in the mind of declarant. The state of mind of a party, or of any person who becomes involved in litigated events, may be relevant at trial: For example, a criminal defendant's state of mind of "love" or "hate" can be relevant to show motive for the crime; a civil defendant's state of mind of "knowledge" can be relevant to prove notice; and in any type of case, a witness's state of mind of "bias" or "malice" toward one of the parties can be relevant to impeach the witness's credibility. Statements of an official representative of a corporate or governmental entity are admissible under FRE 803(3) to prove the motives underlying the business decisions of the entity. Municipal Revenue Service, Inc. v. Xspand, Inc., 700 F. Supp. 2d 692, 705-706 (M.D. Pa. 2010).

But the scope of the FRE 803(3) exception is specifically limited. Statements of memory or belief may be used to prove a declarant's then-existing relevant state of mind, but may not be admitted to prove the fact remembered or believed, unless that fact relates to the terms or validity of declarant's will. Thus, the statement of belief "I believe my brakes are bad," or the statement of memory "I remember that my brakes squeaked yesterday," may be used to prove the declarant's current state of mind of knowledge (notice), *but not the fact that the brakes are bad.* In contrast, the statement "I want Harold to inherit all of my estate so I have left it all to him in my will" is admissible to prove the state of mind of the declarant *as well as the terms of the declarant's will*.

b.   Justification for the State-of-Mind Exception

A statement relevant to prove the declarant's current state of mind requires inferences about the declarant's sincerity and narration. The fact of consequence is what is going on inside the mind of the declarant, and the declarant's statement must sincerely and accurately express what that is. The declarant is not perceiving anything outside the declarant's own mind, so there is no traditional risk of misperception. And, since the statement expresses the *then-existing* mental state, there is no memory problem. Thus, the primary rationale for the state-of-mind exception is that there are no perception or memory dangers. Under the reliability rationale of the Rule 803 exceptions, the absence of these dangers provides circumstantial guarantees of trustworthiness, and thus diminishes the importance of cross-examining the declarant.

There is, however, a weakness in the trustworthiness justification for the state-of-mind exception. Although it has been said that statements that express a present state of mind are likely to be spontaneous and therefore sincere, there is no independent requirement of proving spontaneity and there is no limit to the circumstances in which such statements can be made. The statement "I love my spouse" may be spontaneous, or it may be calculated to mislead if the declarant has a reason to want to create the false impression of affection. There are no definitive means of proving that the declarant really has the mental state that is being spoken about. Thus, the sincerity risks in FRE 803(3) statements are substantial. If the statement is not spontaneous, then the declarant has the opportunity to fabricate. In United States v. DiMaria, 727 F.2d 265, 271-272 (2d Cir. 1984), the defendant's statement during his arrest "I only came here to get some cheap cigarettes" was offered by the defense to rebut a presumption of guilty knowledge raised by defendant's possession of cigarettes that were in fact stolen. The prosecution contended that this statement should not be admitted under FRE 803(3) as "an absolutely classic false exculpatory statement." The court acknowledged that a declaration of a mental state by an accused can readily be trumped up, but held that since it fell within FRE 803(3) "its truth or falsity was for the jury to determine." Some courts, however, have added a requirement to their application of FRE 803(3) that the declarant "must not have had time to reflect and to fabricate or misrepresent the state of mind being expressed." United States v. Secor, 73 Fed. Appx. 554, 566-567 (4th Cir. 2003) (treating FRE 803(3) as a subset of FRE 803(1)). These cases usually involve offers by criminal defendants of their own statements made either long after the crime committed, when their current states of mind may no longer be relevant, or after they suspect they are under investigation and have a clear motive to represent their current mental state of "innocence."

Necessity may justify the admission of state-of-mind statements despite their sincerity risks. Mental states are a pervasive part of our substantive law and a person's own statements are a primary source of evidence about mental states. However, the state-of-mind exception is used beyond its necessity in proving essential elements, and people's conduct can be more probative than people's words in assessing mental states.

Statements of memory or belief used to prove facts concerning the validity and terms of declarant's will do require reliance on the declarant's memory and perception, as well as sincerity and narrative ability. Making a will is an external event that the declarant has perceived, and remembers. Admission of these statements is justified by the likelihood that persons will speak carefully about their wills and the necessity that arises from the unavailability of the declarant.

c.   *State-of-Mind Utterances Are Classified as Either Direct or Circumstantial*

Some utterances directly assert the declarant's mental state. For example, to prove that a witness has a motive to lie in favor of plaintiff, the defendant could offer evidence that the witness once said, "I can't stand the defendant." This is a direct statement of the witness's feelings and state of mind. But what if the witness said, "The defendant is a vile person who has done me great harm"? This statement is not a direct assertion of a mental state, but it probably reflects a state of mind of intense dislike. Because the mental state is not directly asserted, courts and commentators call this type of statement "circumstantial evidence" of the witness's state of mind.

Utterances that are circumstantial evidence of the declarant's state of mind are not offered to prove the truth of the literal matters they assert. The witness's statement is not offered to prove that the defendant is vile, or that the defendant has done great harm to the witness. Thus, some courts and commentators have taken the position that utterances that are circumstantial evidence of state of mind are nonhearsay. But unlike the categories of nonhearsay that we discussed at pages 421-423, supra—*effect on listener* and *legally operative facts*—the relevancy of state-of-mind utterances *does* involve potential sincerity and narration risks. If the witness in our hypothetical is lying or joking, and does not sincerely believe that the defendant is vile and has done wrong, then the witness's statement is not relevant to prove a motive to lie in favor of plaintiff. Therefore, utterances that are circumstantial evidence of state of mind are not a true nonhearsay category.

FRE 803(3) provides such a broad hearsay exception for statements of a declarant's then-existing state of mind that labeling them as direct or circumstantial, hearsay or nonhearsay, is purely academic in terms of admissibility under the Federal Rules. United States v. Quinones, 511 F.3d 289, 312 (2d Cir. 2007) (under either theory, a state of mind can be proved circumstantially by statements that are not intended to assert the truth of the fact being proved).

6.   Elaboration of FRE 803(3): Relevant Uses of State-of-Mind Evidence

a.   *Future and Past State of Mind of the Declarant*

A declarant's current statement of state of mind may be just one step in the inferential process to establish some fact of consequence. Frequently, inferences both forward and backward in time are made from statements of currently existing mental states. For example, consider a case in which a criminal defendant wishes to establish that some third person had a motive for killing the victim and that the third person was in fact the killer. The third person's statement, "I hate the victim," made a week *before* the killing, is admissible under FRE 803(3) to prove that one week before the killing the third person hated the victim. From hatred at that time we infer a future state of mind—there was probably still hatred a week later, when the killing occurred. The inference is based on the generalization that strong emotional feelings about an individual are not likely to change over a relatively short period of time. Hatred a week later is relevant to show a motive to harm the victim, and from motive we infer the possibility that the third person killed the victim.

State of mind can also be used to prove a past state of mind without relying on the declarant's perception or memory. Consider in the preceding murder case that the third person said two days *after* the murder, "The thought of the victim fills me with rage." The present state of mind of "rage" would be relevant to prove that declarant was probably also angry at the victim two days earlier, again because of a generalization about the stability of such states of mind. If angry two days earlier, the declarant may have had a motive to kill the victim at that time.

In these cases, the court will examine the circumstances to decide whether the inference of continuity of state of mind is reasonable.

> Some expressions of emotion last a lifetime, while others may be unlikely to persist long after their triggering events. Some professions of state of mind may be too vague or tenuous to support an inference of continuity, particularly where there is a significant lapse of time between the declaration and the *mens rea* at issue. Intervening events may also signal a possible change in the declarant's state of mind." [United States v. Farhane, 634 F.3d 127, 173 (2d Cir. 2011).]

Statements made months after the time at which the declarant's state of mind was relevant have been held too remote to be probative. United States v. Reyes, 239 F.3d 722, 743 (5th Cir. 2001).

b. Future Conduct of the Declarant

Mary's statement on Monday "I plan to leave on my vacation to Hawaii on Tuesday" may be relevant to prove that she in fact left on Tuesday, and that she went to Hawaii. We first must infer the truth of the matter she asserts—that on Monday, Mary sincerely planned to leave on Tuesday for her vacation in Hawaii. Then, from this state of mind, we can infer that she probably had the same intent on Tuesday and, then, that she carried it out and did go to Hawaii.

The generalizations underlying the inference from Mary's state of mind to her future conduct concern the behavior of people; for example, that people with intentions or plans of the type that Mary had are not likely to change, or that people generally do the things that they intend or plan to do. The probability of each inference from intent to future conduct will vary depending on the nature of the intended activity and the time lag involved. In some situations, intent may be stated so far in advance, or may be so contingent, that there is little probative force to the generalization that people act in conformity with intent. What is important is that the inferences from Mary's state of mind to her conduct do not require any further evaluation of Mary's testimonial qualities. FRE 803(3) can be used to admit Mary's statement of intent to show that she had that same intent at some future time and that she acted on it. *Staelens ex rel. Estate of Staelens v. Staelens,* 677 F. Supp. 2d 499, 503 (D. Mass. 2010) (decedent's statement that he continued to name his former wife as the beneficiary to his 401(k) account because he wanted to be sure she would be okay admissible to prove that naming her was not a mistake).

c.   *Evidence of State of Mind Used to Prove Past Facts*

FRE 803(3) provides that statements of memory or belief to prove the fact remembered or believed may not be admitted through the state-of-mind exception (unless they concern wills). It is common that past facts are asserted in the context of state-of-mind evidence; but proof of the truth of the past facts is not an acceptable use of FRE 803(3). To show the bias of Emily, a witness against John, evidence is offered that Emily said outside of court, "I am angry at John because he stole all of my money last year." The statement about the theft is a statement of memory or belief. FRE 803(3) could not be used if the statement is offered to prove that John did steal the money, the fact remembered or believed. Why? The past fact of theft is an event outside Emily's mind. Her accurate perception and memory would be necessary to the statement's relevance. Since the justification for the FRE 803(3) exception is that these risks are nonexistent, the exception cannot be used when those risks are present. The same is true if Emily, the declarant, said, "I believe that John stole all my money last year."

All statements about past facts contain an implicit "I think" or "I believe." Admitting such statements as expressing a state of mind of "belief" would swallow the hearsay prohibition. *United States v. Mandel,* 437 F. Supp. 262 (D. Md. 1977) (admission of statements that refer to a relevant present state of mind but also past conduct of declarant and others would threaten continued existence of hearsay rule).

It is possible that if the past fact of theft is not relevant to the litigation, then the declarant's entire statement might be admissible simply to prove the relevant fact — Emily's anger at John. Theft would be a good reason to feel angry and it makes her statement all the more probative of her relevant state of mind of bias against John. Indeed, the past fact of theft need not even be true; if Emily believes it, however, her state of mind of anger is more probable. FRE 403 might be the basis for objection if the statement about the theft raises dangers of unfair prejudice against a party or confusion of the issues.

d.   *The Hillmon Case*

Prior to the Federal Rules of Evidence, some courts applied the state-of-mind exception more broadly (and some courts still do). One of the leading state-of-mind cases, *Mutual Life Insurance Co. of New York v. Hillmon,* 145 U.S. 285 (1892), presents a challenging interpretation of the exception. *Hillmon* was an action by Sallie Hillmon to recover the proceeds of life insurance policies on the life of her husband John Hillmon, who, she alleged, died in Crooked Creek, Colorado, on March 17, 1879. The principal issue in the case was whether a body found in Crooked Creek was Hillmon's. The plaintiff contended that it was. The defendant insurance companies tried to establish that Hillmon was not dead. They alleged that a man named Walters had traveled to Crooked Creek with Hillmon and that the body was Walters's, not Hillmon's. Their evidence included the contents of a letter Walters had written to his sister:

> Dear sister and all: I now in my usual style drop you a few lines to let you know that I expect to leave Wichita on or about March the 5th, with a certain Mr. Hillmon, a sheeptrader, for Colorado or parts unknown to me. I expect to see the country now. News are of no interest to you, as you are not acquainted here. I will close with compliments to all inquiring friends. Love to all. I am truly your brother, Fred. Adolph Walters. [Id. at 288.]

The trial court excluded proof of this and a similar letter from Walters as hearsay, and the jury found in favor of Sallie Hillmon. In reversing this judgment, the Supreme Court explained why proof of the letters was admissible:

> The letters in question were competent, not as narratives of facts communicated to the writer by others, nor yet as proof that he actually went away from Wichita, but as evidence that, shortly before the time when other evidence tended to show that he went away, he had the intention of going, *and of going with Hillmon*, which made it more probable both that he did go *and that he went with Hillmon*, than if there had been no proof of such intention. In view of the mass of conflicting testimony introduced upon the question whether it was the body of Walters that was found in Hillmon's camp, this evidence might properly influence the jury in determining that question. [Id. at 295-296 (emphasis added).]

i. Walters's Future Conduct.   It is correct that Walters's statement in his letter is relevant to prove his own intent to leave Wichita and to go to Colorado. The Court held as much in the same paragraph — Walters's statement would be admissible to prove his own intent and his own future conduct.

ii. Hillmon's Future Conduct.   Some courts, in apparent reliance on the italicized portions of the above quotation, have interpreted *Hillmon* to stand for the proposition that Walters's letters could also be used to show Hillmon's future conduct—that Hillmon went to Crooked Creek with Walters. As a result, these courts have used a declarant's statement about what a third person plans to do to prove what that third person in fact did, and they have justified admission of these statements under the state-of-mind exception. See United States v. Pheaster, 544 F.2d 353 (9th Cir. 1976) (statement of declarant's intent to meet Angelo to get drugs admissible to show that declarant did meet Angelo); People v. Alcalde, 148 P.2d 627 (Cal. 1944) (victim's statement of intent to go out with Frank admissible to prove that Frank went out with victim and thus had the opportunity to commit murder).

Such use of this exception is problematic, however, because the relevance of Walters's assertion about Hillmon is necessarily dependent on Walters's belief about *Hillmon's state of mind* to travel to Colorado and to travel with Walters. Moreover, Walters's belief must be accurate, based on Walters's perception and memory of some past fact—something that Hillmon said or did to indicate that he was going to Colorado and wanted to travel with Walters. Otherwise, Walters's statement about leaving Wichita with Hillmon for Colorado is sheer speculation and cannot be relevant. Thus, all hearsay dangers are potentially present. If Walters's letter directly expressed the fact on which his knowledge of Hillmon's intent was based (e.g., Hillmon had invited Walters to go with him), such an additional statement would be a statement of memory or belief, offered to prove the fact believed. FRE 803(3) may not be used to admit such a past fact, as we know. United States v. Cohen, 631 F.2d 1223 (5th Cir. 1980) (the exception "does not permit a declarant to relate . . . why he held the particular state of mind, or what he might have believed that would have induced the state of mind").

In Walters's letter, past facts about Hillmon's past state of mind and conduct are implied, not expressed, by Walters's plan to travel "with Hillmon." Still, the relevance of Walters's own state of mind to prove the state of mind of another person (Hillmon's intent to travel) or the future conduct of another person (Hillmon did travel to Crooked Creek) depends on an inference about Walters's perception and memory of some past fact about that other person. Permitting the state-of-mind exception to admit statements for purposes that so clearly depend on the declarant's perception and memory of past facts would undermine the policies of the rule.

iii.   Recent Interpretations of *Hillmon*.

iii.   Recent Interpretations of *Hillmon*.   A number of federal courts have held that FRE 803(3) does not support the use of a declarant's state-of-mind declaration to prove the conduct of a third person. The House Judiciary Committee approved the Rule 803(3) exception under the explicit assumption that the rule would limit the *Hillmon* doctrine to use of the declarant's state of mind to prove only the declarant's own future conduct. Other courts, however, have admitted declarants' statements of intent to travel with or to meet a third person against that third person, to prove that the declarant and that person *did in fact travel together or meet*. United States v. Barraza, 576 F.3d 798, 805 (8th Cir. 2010) (admitting statement in declarant's diary that she intended to travel to Mexico with Barraza); United States v. Johnson, 354 F. Supp. 2d 939, 962 (N.D. Iowa 2005) (discussing collected cases). Most of these decisions have required independent corroboration of the third person's conduct. See, e.g., United States v. Sperling, 726 F.2d. 69, 73-74 (2d Cir. 1984) (declarant's statement that she would meet with her drug source at noon that day was admissible to prove Sperling's participation in a drug conspiracy where agents observed Sperling meet with the declarant at noon). See Joseph A. Devall, Jr., Comment, 78 Tul. L. Rev. 911 (2004) for a survey of the split in state court authority on whether the state-of-mind exception permits statements of intent to prove the conduct of third persons. If we commit to the trial judge's discretion the evaluation of the reliability of an inference from intent (or belief) backward to a third person's past act that caused the intent (or belief), we are abandoning FRE 803(3) as we know it in favor of judicial discretion.

Another possible scenario in cases like *Hillmon* is to rely on the declarant's intent to act *only* if a specific person acts as well. For example, would it be appropriate to infer that Walters planned to leave Wichita and travel *only* if he went with Hillmon? If so, since Walters was not in Wichita, the inference could be made, without reliance on Walters's perception or memory, that Hillmon must have decided to leave and travel with Walters. Another ingenious solution to the problem of using state-of-mind statements to prove the conduct of third persons was upheld in United States v. Persico, 2011 WL 1661420, at *12-13 (2d Cir.). In a prosecution for murder, the court upheld the admission of testimony by the victim's wife that, on the day he disappeared, the victim telephoned her to say that he "was going to meet" the defendant Persico [the alleged murderer] later that day. This statement, the court held,

> was in no way offered to show that in fact "Persico met [the victim] at the Shore Road location". . . rather, that statement was properly admitted to show [victim's] intent to

meet Persico there and to support an inference that [victim] acted in furtherance of that intent, from which the jury could reasonably infer that [victim] had communicated to Persico that [victim] would be at Shore Road expecting to meet Persico there.

Which inference do you think is more likely? That Persico had engaged in some past act to lure his victim to Shore Road? Or that the unsuspecting victim set up the meeting on his own?

KEY POINTS

1. Statements expressing a declarant's current state of mind, both directly and circumstantially, are admissible under FRE 803(3) to prove that state of mind, if it is relevant in the case. Although sincerity and narration dangers are present, there are no perception and memory dangers.

2. State-of-mind evidence may not be admitted under FRE 803(3) if its relevancy is to prove an historical event or condition, typically the fact that caused the state of mind. If statements of state of mind were used to prove past facts, or to prove the conduct of third persons, perception and memory dangers would be involved. Some courts do permit statements of a declarant's intent to be used to prove the future conduct of a third person, as well as the declarant's conduct, if there is corroboration.

3. Statements of past state of mind and past fact relating to the validity and terms of declarant's will may, however, be admitted under FRE 803(3).

PROBLEMS

8.52. David White has been sued by the driver of an automobile that was hit by David's car, a blue Mazda, driven by David's wife Brenda White. Brenda was allegedly driving 100 MPH on a freeway between her home in the country and Central City. Is the following testimony admissible?

(a) W_1 testifies that on the morning of the accident, Brenda White said, "I love to drive my car at 100 MPH." *ok, win 403*

(b) W_2 testifies that on the morning of the accident, Brenda White said, "I intend to speed all the way to Central City." *ok, plan*

(c) A bystander testifies that two miles before the accident a hitchhiker said, "I believe that blue car just sped right by me going 100 MPH."

(d) A bystander testifies that, at the scene of the accident, a hitchhiker said, "I remember that blue car sped right by me going 100 MPH."

8.53. The United States has filed an interpleader action to determine the true owner of the boxing championship belts awarded to boxer Roberto Duran. Duran claims they were stolen from his house by his brother-in-law in 1993. The FBI recovered the belts in 2003 from businessman Louis Baez, who claimed that the belts were not stolen. To prove theft, Duran and a number of witnesses would testify that in 2000, the brother-in-law apologized to Duran for stealing the belts. Admissible? Would the statement of apology alone be admissible?

8.54. Plaintiffs run a political advocacy group that is distributing pamphlets and soliciting signatures for a petition in Anderson County. Plaintiffs are suing a group of county officials, alleging that the officials have abridged Plaintiffs' First Amendment rights by actively encouraging residents to file criminal complaints for harassment against them. Ellen, a county resident, did file such a complaint. Defendants offer the testimony of Ellen's neighbor that, on the morning before Ellen went to the police station to file her complaint, she told the neighbor that she wanted to file a criminal complaint against Plaintiffs because she was so upset by their harassment. Plaintiffs object on grounds of hearsay. What result?

8.55. Return to Problem 8.39 on page 481. To prove that he gave proper advice to his patient, Tom Hay, Defendant Dr. Gatwick offers a cab driver who picked up a man and woman at the ER at the time Tom and Barbara Hay were leaving the hospital. The cab took them to a home address that admissible evidence will show is the home of Tom and Barbara Hay. The cab driver will testify that he overheard the man say to the woman: "I don't care what the doctor said, I hate hospitals." Is the cab driver's testimony admissible?

8.56. Lyons Partnership owns all of the intellectual property rights to the character "Barney," the well-stuffed Tyrannosaurus Rex with a green chest and stomach, green spots on its back, and yellow "toeballs." Barney is readily recognizable to young children. The *Barney and Friends* TV show is viewed weekly by 14 million children, and over 50 million copies of Barney-related videos have been sold. Lyons controls the "live" appearances of the Barney character played by adults in costume, and Lyons does not license Barney costumes.

Lyons filed suit against Nelson Costumes, alleging trademark infringement arising out of rental of Nelson's costume, "Duffy the Dragon," to the public. Lyons had to prove, under the Lanham Act, that the defendant is infringing its valid mark by creating consumer confusion. Proof of *actual confusion* is often paramount to the success of such a claim. Lyons offered three types of evidence of confusion at trial, all of which the district court excluded as "unreliable hearsay." Was this error? The evidence offered was as follows:

(a)   Testimony from parents that when they rented the Duffy costume for their children's birthday parties, they were confused because the costume looked just like Barney.

(b)   Testimony from a principal of an elementary school that when she wore the Duffy costume at a school rally, the children shouted, "Barney, Barney, Barney!"

(c)   The results of a survey conducted by Lyons at several shopping malls. Shoppers were shown a photograph of the Duffy costume and asked whether they could identify the character. Fifty percent identified the character as Barney; 50 percent had no idea who the character was.

8.57. Oscar Small is charged with the kidnapping and murder of Spenser Reed, who has disappeared. The prosecution claims Small is engaged in extensive cocaine trafficking; that Small hired Reed to do house cleaning for him; that Reed stole cocaine from Small's house; and that Small found this out and retaliated by snatching Reed off the street, forcing Reed into his car, and murdering him. Small explains the presence of Reed's fingerprints in the car by claiming that Reed came over to his house, they took a friendly drive together, and Reed then left. The prosecutor calls several friends of Reed to testify as follows. Is their testimony admissible?

(a)   W$_1$: "On the Saturday he disappeared, Reed looked very nervous. He said to me, 'I'm afraid of seeing Small.'"
(b)   W$_2$: "A week before he disappeared, Reed said, 'I don't ever want to see Small again.'"
(c)   W$_3$: "A few days before he disappeared. Reed said to me, 'I'm afraid of Small because he got really violent with me when he found out about the cocaine I took.'"
(d)   W$_4$: "A few days before he disappeared, Reed said to me, 'I think Small is going to kill me.'"

8.58. Return to Problem 3.2, Pedroso v. Driver, at page 136. Joan testifies for defendants that she also rode the same school bus as Paul and Tom, and that Paul and Tom always got off at the same stop. On the day of the accident, Tom said to Joan, "Paul and I are going to play tag when we get off the bus today." Admissible?

8.59. Frank Jackson is charged with the murder of Steve Smart, whose body was found in a public park on Sunday, April 4.

(a)   The prosecution offers the following testimony of Barbara Berry: "When I spoke to Steve on Saturday, April 3, he said, 'I'm meeting Frank Jackson later tonight.'"
(b)   Instead of (a), the prosecution offers the following testimony of Carl Cole: "I spoke with Steve on the afternoon of April 3. He said he had to work at home all weekend to finish a report that was due Monday and that he was stuck in his apartment working unless Frank Jackson was available to meet him for a few hours."

NOTE

The *Hillmon* case has fascinated evidence law specialists for years. But never has it aroused more interest than recently, due to the efforts of Professor Marianne Wesson to determine, once and for all, whose body was buried at Crooked Creek. Her history of the dispute over the proceeds of Hillmon's insurance policy is fascinating, as reported at www.thehillmoncase.com/index.html.

7.   Interpretation and Illustration of FRE 803(4): Statements Made for Medical Diagnosis or Treatment

FRE 803(4) states:

> (4) *Statement Made for Medical Diagnosis or Treatment.* A statement that:
>   (A) is made for — and is reasonably pertinent to — medical diagnosis or treatment; and
>   (B) describes medical history; past or present symptoms or sensations; their inception; or their general cause.

a.   Preliminary Fact-finding

The foundational requirements for FRE 803(4) statements are:

- the statement must be made for the purpose of medical diagnosis or treatment;
- the statement must describe medical history, past or present symptoms or sensations, or the inception or the general cause of the symptoms or sensations; and
- the statement is reasonably pertinent to diagnosis or treatment.

There is some overlap between this exception and statements of mental state admitted under FRE 803(3). A patient's description of currently existing sensation ("I feel dizzy") could fall within both. But FRE 803(4) also admits statements to prove current symptoms that exist outside the mind of the declarant ("The thermometer says I have a temperature of 102") and to prove past symptoms as well ("I had a runny nose yesterday, and I coughed a lot"). The relevance of these statements depends upon the accuracy of the declarant's perception and memory, as well as sincerity and narration; thus a complete trip around the testimonial triangle is required. The well-established test of trustworthiness is that the declarant's motive in making the statement must be consistent with the purposes of promoting treatment.

FRE 803(4) does not specify that the declarant be the patient, relating the declarant's own medical history and symptoms. Family, friends, nurses and other medical personnel may convey information for purposes of medical treatment that will be admitted under FRE 803(4). Campos v. MTD Products, Inc., 2009 WL 425012, at *12 (M.D. Tenn.) (statements by immediate family members included under this exception). Even an unidentified declarant speaking to an ambulance crew may qualify under the exception if the court is persuaded that the declarant spoke for purposes of securing medical care for the patient. Bucci v. Essex Ins. Co., 393 F.3d 285, 299 (1st Cir. 2005). And if the patient is speaking to an intermediary—a child to a parent, for example, so that the parent can relate the symptoms to a doctor—the terms of the exception could still apply so long as the purpose of seeking medical help exists.

There is also recent case law that the rule covers statements made to psychotherapists, social workers, pharmacists, and other health care personnel, not just physicians and nurses. "[A]dmissibility . . . is based, not on the person to whom made, but on the purpose for which they are made, which gives rise to the presumption of reliability." Williams v. Virgin Islands, 271 F. Supp. 2d 696, 704-705 (D.V.I. 2003). However, FRE 803(4) has been interpreted to apply only to statements by persons *seeking* care, not *giving* care. Thus, statements made by doctors to patients, by consulting physicians to treating physicians, are not within the FRE 803(4) exception. Field v. Trigg County Hosp., Inc., 386 F.3d 729, 735-736 (6th Cir. 2004).

b.   Justification for the Admissibility of Statements for Medical Purposes

The justification for this exception rests on the declarant's "selfish motive to be truthful" in making the statement. The assumption is that a person seeking medical diagnosis and treatment is highly motivated to speak carefully and honestly about symptoms and conditions in order to receive effective medical care. Thus, even though the declaration may not be spontaneous, and even though there may be perception and memory risks when past conditions and causes are related, the statement bears less danger of insincerity and inaccuracy. Statements not so motivated by this self-interested motive are not within the exception. Brown v. Smithkline Beecham Corp., 2008 WL 205410 (N.D. Ill.) (statement to adult children by father that he had taken cold medicine for a cold inadmissible); Phillips v. Potter, 2009 WL 3271238, at *3-4 (journal entries made at the direction of therapist, as a "therapeutic exercise" to assist in plaintiff's treatment, are not statements made in order to obtain a diagnosis or treatment, and the incentive for truthfulness underlying the exception is absent).

Can a motive to be truthful when speaking with a physician always be assumed? According to some surveys, between 13 and 32 percent of patients lie or stretch the truth to their doctor, in particular about smoking, risky sex, alcohol and drug use, and taking medications as prescribed. http://www.newsweek.com/2009/01/07/little-white-coat-lies.html.

c.   *Statements About the Cause or External Source Must Be "Pertinent"*

It is common for persons seeking medical treatment to describe how their injury occurred ("I was hit from behind while sitting in my car, and my neck aches terribly"). FRE 803(4) explicitly includes such hearsay statements to prove the truth of the matters they assert (the declarant was hit from behind in her car) if they are "reasonably pertinent to diagnosis or treatment." Sanders v. The Ritz-Carlton Hotel Co., 2008 WL 4155635, at *2 (S.D.N.Y.) (plaintiff statement in his medical records that he "tripped" rather than "slipped" when he injured his ankle describe the general cause of his injury). But sometimes, patients' statements make more specific attributions of causation, naming specific persons or entities that caused them harm. Should these statements also be admitted by FRE 803(4)?

In general, pertinence is determined from testimony of the medical professional as to the type of information reasonably relied on by a physician in treatment or diagnosis. If the declarant's statements are not medically pertinent, there is some reason to suspect the declarant's motivation in speaking and thus to suspect lack of sincerity. Thus, a statement such as "I was hit from behind by a red Mustang, with license plate number 445HCN, while I was sitting in my car" is not likely to fall within Rule 803(4).

The issue of pertinence frequently arises in cases of child abuse and molestation when the victim names the abuser to the health care professional. In United States v. Tome, 61 F.3d 1446 (10th Cir. 1995), the child declarant's statements identifying her father as the abuser were held to fall within the "pertinence" requirement. Quoting its own precedent, the court reasoned that

> [a]ll victims of domestic sexual abuse suffer emotional and psychological injuries, the exact nature and extent of which depend on the identity of the abuser. The physician generally must know who the abuser was in order to render proper treatment because the physician's treatment will necessarily differ when the abuser is a member of the victim's family or household. In the domestic sexual abuse case, for example, the treating physician may recommend special therapy or counseling and instruct the victim to remove

herself from the dangerous environment by leaving the home and seeking shelter elsewhere. [Id. at 1450.]

In the Tenth Circuit, the identity of the abuser is pertinent in domestic abuse cases, and the definition of who is a member of the family or household is quite broad. United States v. Pacheco, 154 F.3d 1236, 1240-1241 (10th Cir. 1998) (defendant was not victim's natural father but had an intermittent relationship with victim's mother, and both victim and her mother stayed in his family home several months each year). This issue is not resolved in other Circuits and many state courts.

Statements made by adult victims of domestic violence have also been admitted by some courts when the identity of the abuser is stated to a treating physician. United States v. Hall, 419 F.3d 980 (9th Cir. 2005) (statements to doctor that live-in boyfriend caused patient's injuries admissible). Other past facts about causation of physical and mental problems are also subject to the dual test of "motivation" and "pertinence." Willingham v. Crooke, 412 F.3d 553, 561-562 (4th Cir. 2005) (plaintiff's description of her arrest, including a gun being pointed at her, was admissible for diagnosis and treatment of her emotional trauma and physical injuries); McCollum v. McDaniel, 32 Fed. Appx. 49, 55 (4th Cir. 2002) (statement that injuries were caused by "assault" were admissible as statements relating to cause more than to fault).

d.   Requiring Proof of Medical Purpose

Courts are likely to assume that adults, and even teenagers, understand the purpose for which they are asked to give information to medical personnel. With young children being examined for sexual abuse, however, many courts have rejected this assumption and require that the child's treatment motive be established on the record. In the Eighth Circuit, identifications of abusers by child abuse victims are admissible only "where the physician makes clear to the victim that the inquiry into the identity of the abuser is important to diagnosis and treatment, and the victim manifests such an understanding." Olsen v. Class, 164 F.3d 1096, 1098 (8th Cir. 1999). The Ninth and Tenth Circuits, however, have rejected the Eighth Circuit's requirement of such a specific showing. In the Tenth Circuit, there need only be a showing that the declarant made the statement for the purpose of diagnosis or treatment, not that the declarant understood that the statements must be truthful to have medical importance for care. United States v. Wilson, 2010 WL 3023035, at *11 (D.N.M.).[1]

e.   Statements Made for Diagnostic Evaluations for Litigation

The sincerity rationale, of course, may not apply when a statement of physical condition is made for the purpose of diagnosis in preparation for litigation. The treatment motive that tends to ensure sincerity is lacking. Moreover, the possibility of receiving a high damage award is an incentive to exaggerate present and past symptoms or suffering. For this reason, the common law physical condition exception did

---

1.   Most cases brought in federal court alleging crimes of child abuse are within the Eighth, Ninth and Tenth Circuits because federal jurisdiction is limited to offenses committed on federal lands, such as Native American territories.

not apply to declarations made for the purpose of diagnosis in preparation for litigation. FRE 803(4), however, specifically abandons this common law limitation. Most courts have held that admission of statements made to physicians only for the purpose of providing expert testimony is now permitted by the rule.

8.   Elaboration of FRE 803(4): Patients' Statements as the Basis for Expert Opinion

FRE 803(4)'s admission of statements made to testifying experts may not be justified by the reliability of such statements, but it is understandable when one considers this exception in conjunction with the rules regulating expert opinion testimony. When a person's physical condition is at issue, there frequently will be an expert witness to testify about the nature of the condition, likely based at least in part on the basis of what the person said outside of court about present and past symptoms. At common law, such self-serving hearsay statements of physical condition admissible and expert witnesses had to base their opinions solely on admissible evidence. This required the patient to testify about the physical condition at issue and then the treating physicians to testify (and be cross-examined) about the patient's treatment. The expert would then be asked to offer an opinion in response to a hypothetical question that incorporated the information already described in court.

Well aware of the problems with hypothetical questions, the drafters of the Federal Rules consciously sought to avoid them in providing for the presentation of expert information. See FRE 702, 703, and 705, discussed in Chapter Nine. A medical expert who has been consulted for diagnosis in preparation for litigation is almost certainly going to rely on the patient's statements about past and present symptoms and will want to recite these statements when explaining the diagnosis. FRE 803(4) takes full advantage of the information that medical experts can supply by making statements of physical condition fully admissible.

KEY POINTS

1. Statements describing medical history and symptoms are admissible under FRE 803(4) even though they involve inferences about all four of the declarant's testimonial qualities. The context of speaking for the purpose of medical treatment reduces the sincerity danger, and people may take care in perceiving and reporting their medical symptoms.

2. The statements may be made by the patient or by others seeking care by providing medical information about the patient.

3. If the statement contains information about the external cause or source of the medical condition, there must be evidence that such information is reasonably pertinent to treatment or diagnosis. Such evidence is typically supplied by the physician seeking the information.

4. Statements made for purposes of medical diagnosis only, including a diagnosis undertaken in preparation for litigation, are included within the FRE 803(4) exception.

PROBLEMS

8.60. Consider whether the following declarations would be admissible in a personal injury action if made to the declarant's spouse, to the declarant's physician for treatment, or to a physician consulted for the purpose of giving expert testimony at trial:

(a) "I have a severe headache."
(b) "Yesterday, I had a severe headache."
(c) "I was hit in the head with a baseball bat."
(d) "John Jones hit me in the head with a baseball bat."

8.61. Return to Problem 8.4, Broadback v. Trapp, at page 419. Are any of the statements made to the ambulance driver admissible under FRE 803(4)?

8.62. Jenkins, a federal prison inmate, is charged with committing an assault resulting in serious bodily injury to another inmate. At trial, an emergency room physician who treated the victim testified on direct that "there was reportedly—and I got this second- or thirdhand as I often do in the ER—a loss of consciousness in the ambulance." Admissible?

8.63 Return to Problem 3.4, State v. Blair, at page 137. Norma's doctor would testify that during a routine medical examination in 2009, Norma explained some bruising on her ribs. She told the doctor that her boyfriend had hit her in the middle of an argument. The doctor then recommended a local counseling program for victims of domestic violence to her. Would the doctor's testimony be admissible? What if it is mandatory under state law for a doctor to report, to local law enforcement, injuries that are reasonably suspected to be related to domestic violence?

8.64. Defendant is charged with sexually abusing his nine-year-old stepson. When the alleged child victim was being examined by Dr. Wolfe, he denied that defendant was abusing him. Victim's mother then asked to speak to Dr. Wolfe and told the doctor that defendant had "brainwashed" the victim and that the victim had been abused by defendant. At defendant's trial, may Dr. Wolfe testify as to what the mother said?

9.   Interpretation and Illustration of FRE 803(5): Past Recollection Recorded

FRE 803(5) states:

(5) *Recorded Recollection.* A record that:
    (A) is on a matter the witness once knew about but now cannot recall well enough to testify fully and accurately;
    (B) was made or adopted by the witness when the matter was fresh in the witness's memory; and
    (C) accurately reflects the witness's knowledge.

If admitted, the record may be read into evidence but may be received as an exhibit only if offered by an adverse party.

a.   Preliminary Fact-finding

The foundational requirements for the past recollection recorded exception are:

- the declarant is testifying as a witness;
- the statement is in the form of a record;
- the statement is on a matter about which the witness once had personal knowledge;
- the witness cannot remember the matter sufficiently to testify fully and accurately;
- the statement was made or adopted by the witness when the matter was fresh in the witness's memory; and
- the statement accurately reflects the witness's knowledge.

Written or recorded memoranda or notes about events are often a substitute for failed memory in our everyday lives. Try to remember something you once knew but now are unable to remember—say, whether a particular case was assigned in your Torts class during your first year of law school. You kept notes of all your first year law school assignments. Could these notes fulfill the foundational requirements of FRE 803(5)? Or, when people pack their household belongings for a cross-country move, they often keep detailed lists of objects placed in particular moving boxes. What questions would you ask to elicit the required foundation for admission of such a list under FRE 803(5)?

i.   The Contents of the Statement.   FRE 803(5) places no limit on the subject matter or contents of a statement admitted as a past recollection recorded. The notes and lists discussed above could qualify. So could any form of record of any sort of event that later becomes relevant in litigation. United States v. Cash, 394 F.3d 560 (7th Cir. 2005) (record of a threatening phone call from a veteran written by a Veterans' Administration representative); United States v. Jones, 601 F.3d 1247 (11th Cir. 2010) (video recording of witness's interview with a police detective). Cases also include the use of diaries, police arrest and booking forms, and transcripts of wiretapped phone calls. If the record is a regular part of a business or governmental function, the exceptions for business and public records may also be available and the more onerous foundational requirements of FRE 803(5) would not need to be satisfied.

ii.   The Declarant Must Be a Witness with Failed Memory.   FRE 803(5) is unique in the Rule 803 exceptions in that it requires the presence of the declarant in court, as a witness. In this respect, therefore, the exception is analogous to the Rule 801(d)(1) exemptions for prior statements of a witness. Under FRE 803(5), however, it is categorically required that the witness *not* have sufficient memory of the underlying events that are the subject of the out-of-court statement, and that the statement must be in written or recorded form. United States v. Burke, 2009 WL 173829, at *17 (E.D. Cal.) (documents not admissible under FRE 803(5) because witness testified about the specific subjects he states are covered by the documents). Thus, in one sense the witness is both available (on the witness stand) and unavailable (no adequate current memory of the events recorded).

iii.   Made with Personal Knowledge and Fresh Memory.   There is an explicit requirement of a showing that the witness "once knew" the matter recorded. Prior to restyling, FRE 803(5) similarly required *personal knowledge* of the matter when the record was made (as under FRE 602), and a showing that the record was made when that knowledge was "fresh" in the witness's memory. Typically, if the witness remembers making the record, the witness will be able to testify about what he had knowledge of and the circumstances in which the record was created. In United States v. Cash, the VA representative testified that she documents phone conversations while she is speaking with each veteran who calls her because she gets another call as soon as she hangs up, and she includes exact questions and quotations from the veteran. 394 F.3d at 561. If the witness cannot remember making the written record, then the record's own contents, or the testimony of someone who saw the record being made, or other circumstantial evidence, would be used to satisfy the requirement of personal knowledge and fresh memory.

Notice that the record can either be *made* or *adopted* by the witness. Thus, if the witness did not actually write or record the statement, but read over and adopted the written statements made by another, the requirement can be satisfied. Plaza-Bonilla v. Cortazzo, 2009 WL 605909, at *2, n.4 (E.D. Pa.) (witness to an alleged incident of excessive force by police "provided the statement just a couple of hours after the incident took place . . . initialed each and every answer he provided, signed the bottom of every page, and subscribed the last page, on which he indicated that he had been given 'the chance to read, correct, and initial [his] statement' and that 'everything in this statement [was] true and correct.'"). That the contents of the record reflected what the witness knew from firsthand knowledge would still have to be shown.

Courts have not adopted a bright-line rule to determine whether the witness's memory was "fresh" when the record was made. Statements recorded years after the events described in them have been rejected. One court stated "it would seem difficult for a memorandum drafted by a witness either one month or three months after the fact" to be deemed "fresh." SEC v. Johnson, 534 F. Supp. 2d 63, 66 n.4 (D.D.C. 2008). Other courts are more generous. United States v. Green, 258 F.3d 683, 689 (7th Cir. 2001) ("the trial court may consider the lapse of time along with other circumstances that may be relevant in determining [whether] the witness had an accurate memory," citing cases where a three-year and 15-month delay were held not excessive under the circumstances). Additional evidence, such as clarity of statement, richness of detail, making changes and corrections, can show that the witness's recollection was still vital. Time lapses between a witness making a statement and later adopting its recorded version may also be lengthy, creating risks that inaccuracies in the record would not be spotted. United States v. Lewis, 954 F.2d 1386, 1394 (7th Cir. 1992) (trial court is in the best position to gauge the significance of these difficulties, and this is why arbitrary time limitations are inappropriate).

iv.   The Record Reflects the Witness's Knowledge Accurately.   Some evidence that the statement is an accurate reflection of knowledge and memory—that is, both sincerely and accurately recorded—is required. The typical question asked is whether the contents are "true and accurate." United States v. Jones, supra, at 1262. But if the witness cannot adequately remember the events recorded, it may be impossible for the witness to testify truthfully that the record is an accurate reflection of what the witness knew when the record was made. What may often happen is that the witness-declarant simply answers "yes" to the typical question asked and the basis for the witness's ability to so testify is not probed. In some cases, there are circumstances from which accuracy can be inferred. Erasures and corrections in the list may indicate care about accuracy. Or a written statement signed by a suspect in criminal custody could contain the language, "This is an accurate statement to the best of my recollection." And, the witness can testify as to why the statement is *likely to have been accurate* at the time that it was made. As a law student, you could testify that you had strong motivation to record your Torts assignments accurately. As we have stated before, these foundational requirements are FRE 104(a) questions for the judge to decide.

v. **The Record May Only Be Read to the Jury.** FRE 803(5) limits the use of a past recollection recorded statement. It may be read to the jury, but may not be received as an exhibit (unless it is the opponent who wants it to be). Thus, it may not be handed around by the jury or taken into the jury room for deliberations, "for fear that a factfinder would be unduly influenced by the document rather than the testimony." United States v. Cuesta, 2007 WL 2729853, at *19 (E.D. Cal.). When testimony in a deposition is admitted into evidence, it is typically treated in the same manner: The contents of the deposition are read to the jury, but the deposition is not itself admitted as an exhibit, or at least is not allowed into the jury room, unlike other admissible documents or records. If for some tactical reason of advantage the opponent wishes to have the FRE 803(5) record before the jury as a document, the opponent may offer it as an exhibit.

b. Justification for the Admissibility of Past Recollection Recorded

The absence of adequate memory creates the need for the admission of statements that record a witness's past recollection. In addition, the Rule 803(5) foundational requirements tend to indicate the record's increased trustworthiness. Obviously, if the record was made when the matter was fresh in the witness's mind, memory problems may be minimized. The requirement of accuracy provides information concerning the witness's sincerity and care in recording the statement. The foundational requirements do not address the accuracy of the witness's perception of the matter reported in the statement, but the witness's current availability for general cross-examination may furnish information pertinent to perception ability and opportunity. These requirements are only effective, however, if trial courts apply them strictly. For example, if the trial judge does not probe the basis for a witness's testimony that a written memo is "true and accurate," we cannot be sure that sincerity and narration dangers are decreased.

10. Elaboration of FRE 803(5)

a. Past Recollection Recorded Can Be Created by Multiple Declarants

Sometimes one person observes events and tells them to a second person who then makes a record based on what was said. When that occurs, there are two levels of hearsay contained in one document. For example, John might do the packing of his household goods and then call out what he puts into each box while a second person, Bob, makes the list. There are two declarants in this situation: the observer, John, who has observed the event (what item is packed where), and the recorder, Bob, who transfers information obtained from the observer into the record. If the observer does not check and adopt these lists, then the observer cannot later say in court that the lists correctly reflect what the observer saw. Therefore, the observer alone cannot provide a complete Rule 803(5) foundation. There are many other possible examples of this scenario. Employers may make oral statements that are recorded and transcribed by secretarial staff; people make statements at group meetings where one of the group members takes notes.

FRE 803(5) does not specifically address the effect of multiple person involvement in making the record. The Advisory Committee Note to FRE 803(5) states, "Multiple person involvement in the process of observing and recording . . . is entirely consistent with the exception." McCormick addresses the multiple person involvement issue as follows:

> A . . . type of cooperative report is involved when one person orally reports facts to another person, who writes them down. A store clerk or timekeeper, for example, may report information to a bookkeeper. In this situation, courts have held the written statement admissible if the person reporting the facts testifies to the correctness of the oral report (although at the time of the testimony, the detailed facts cannot be remembered) and the recorder of that statement testifies to faithfully transcribing that oral report. [McCormick on Evidence, Vol. 2 §283, at 300 (Kenneth S. Broun ed., 6th ed. 2006).]

The proponent of the cooperative report can satisfy all of the FRE 803(5) requirements only if both out-of-court declarants—the original observer of the information and the later recorder of the information—testify about the observing and recording process. This also gives the opposing party the opportunity to cross-examine both the observer and the recorder about their part in the creation of the record. Thus, if the proponent relies solely on Rule 803(5) to admit a record produced by multiple declarants, each declarant in the hearsay chain must be presented as a witness. United States v. Green, 258 F.3d at 689 ("both the witness and the one transcribing the statement must testify"). This can be a cumbersome process for the proponent, and some of the declarants may not be available.

b.   Multiple Hearsay Requires a Hearsay Exception or Exemption for Each Level

There are other strategies to admit a cooperative report created by multiple declarants. FRE 805 provides as follows:

> Hearsay within hearsay is not excluded by the rule against hearsay if each part of the combined statements conforms with an exception to the rule.

This means that whenever multiple layers of hearsay and multiple declarants are identified, *each declarant's hearsay statement must fall within either an FRE 801(d) exemption or an FRE 803, 804, or 807 exception.* The burden is on the proponent of multiple hearsay to satisfy the foundational requirements of all of the rules being used. Any combination of exceptions, exemptions, and nonhearsay statements is permitted. For example, suppose several friends help John pack up his household goods, and each one tells the recorder what is in each box. The recorder later compiles a list based on their hearsay statements. All of the friends are not available to testify, but their statements are probably present sense impressions within FRE 803(1). The combination of this exception for the friends and the past recollection recorded exception for the recorder who will testify in court will satisfy FRE 805 and overcome any multiple hearsay objection. Other combinations are also possible, if the record is made of an excited utterance or an admission by a party opponent, for example. United States v. Cuesta, 2007 WL 2729853, at *19 (ranger's citation that recorded defendant's date of birth from a driver's license was admitted under FRE 803(5); the date of birth on the license is an official record or adoptive admission).

If the recorder is not available, or has no memory of the accuracy of the particular recording, another exception might apply to the recorder, such as FRE 803(1) or the exception for business records, FRE 803(6). It is important in applying the past recollection recorded exception that the recorder be truly recording, as opposed to interpreting or editing, what the witness was saying and has now forgotten. The absence of interpretation ensures that it is the observer's perception and memory, not the recorder's consciously altered version, that is recorded.

c.   *Present Recollection Refreshed*

The past recollection recorded exception should not be confused with the process of refreshing memory (sometimes referred to as "refreshing recollection" or "present recollection refreshed"). When a witness initially cannot recall something, it may be possible to refresh the witness's memory by presenting that witness with a document or something else that the examiner thinks, or that the witness suggests, may jog the witness's memory. John, for example, might remember actually packing the objects that he placed in a particular box if he looks briefly at a packing list. Use of this list to "refresh" would be permissible because, under the Federal Rules of Evidence, there are no substantive limits on the type of item that may be used to refresh recollection. The view of most courts is more akin to that of Baker v. State:

> Although the use of a memorandum of some sort will continue quantitatively to dominate the field of refreshing recollection, we are better able to grasp the process conceptually if we appreciate that the use of a memorandum as a memory aid is not a legal phenomenon unto itself but only an instance of a far broader phenomenon. In a more conventional mode, the process might proceed, "Your Honor, I am about to show the witness a written report, ask him to read it and then inquire if he can now testify from his own memory thus refreshed." In a far less conventional mode, the process could as well proceed, "Your Honor, I am pleased to present to the court Miss Rosa Ponselle who will now sing 'Celeste Aida' for the witness, for that is what was playing on the night the burglar came through the window."[2] Whether by conventional or unconventional means, precisely the same end is sought. One is looking for the effective elixir to revitalize dimming memory and make it live again in the service of the search for truth. [35 Md. App. 593, 604-605, 371 A.2d 699, 705-706 (1977).]

If some physical object, like a document, is used to refresh memory, it will first be marked as an exhibit for the purpose of identifying it in the transcript. Use of the object to refresh memory, however, is *not using the document as evidence*. Rather, the object is only a device to try to jog the witness's memory. If the witness's memory

---

2.   [Do you think Rosa Ponselle ever sang "Celeste Aida"—except perhaps in the shower?—Eds.]

is refreshed, the witness will then proceed to testify on the basis of current (revived) recollection, and there will be no need for further reference to the object that revived the witness's memory. In the case of John's refreshed memory, it will be for the court to decide whether John can actually remember packing the objects or whether he is simply testifying from the packing list. If John is testifying from the list, then it must itself be admissible into evidence under a hearsay exception. Any exception would suffice, including FRE 803(5). Indeed, a standard (but not absolutely required) way to satisfy the FRE 803(5) foundational requirement of insufficient current memory is to show the witness the record, ask if it refreshes the witness's memory, and offer it if the memory is not refreshed. United States v. Weller, 238 F.3d 1215 (10th Cir. 2001) (not error for trial court to prohibit witness's use of an appraisal list of objects to refresh recollection where the judge believed that the list would be the source of direct testimony).

If the object is a writing that refreshes the witness's memory, the opposing party is entitled to inspect the document and to introduce into evidence "those portions which relate to the testimony of the witness." FRE 612. If the writing has refreshed the witness's memory, however, it will probably contain information that corroborates what the witness has said. Thus, it is unlikely that the opposing party would want to introduce it into evidence. If the object does not revive the witness's memory, there will be no further occasion to refer to the object, unless the object happens to have some independent relevance to the lawsuit.

d.   The Impact of FRE 612 on Refreshing Recollection

With a friendly witness, the process of refreshing memory is likely to take place outside the courtroom while discussing and rehearsing the direct and anticipated cross-examination. If during this or any other preparation for courtroom or deposition testimony the witness uses a writing to refresh memory, the opposing party may be entitled to inspect the writing. This is because FRE 612 provides as follows:

RULE 612.   WRITING USED TO REFRESH A WITNESS'S MEMORY

(a) *Scope*. This rule gives an adverse party certain options when a witness uses a writing to refresh memory:

(1) while testifying; or

(2) before testifying, if the court decides that justice requires a party to have those options.

(b) *Adverse Party's Options; Deleting Unrelated Matter*. Unless 18 U.S.C. §3500 provides otherwise in a criminal case, an adverse party is entitled to have the writing produced at the hearing, to inspect it, to cross-examine the witness about it, and to introduce in evidence any portion that relates to the witness's testimony. If the producing party claims that the writing includes unrelated matter, the court must examine the writing in camera, delete any unrelated portion, and order that the rest be delivered to the adverse party. Any portion deleted over objection must be preserved for the record.

(c) *Failure to Produce or Deliver the Writing*. If a writing is not produced or is not delivered as ordered, the court may issue any appropriate order. But if the prosecution does not comply in a criminal case, the court must strike the witness's testimony or — if justice so requires — declare a mistrial.

FRE 612 may be the most important rule for you to remember after this class. It is not merely a rule of admissibility; it is also a rule of discovery. And one of the things it means is that any documents that a person looks at in preparing for a deposition may be discoverable by the opposing party—including perhaps documents that would otherwise be protected by the work-product doctrine or some privilege. Since many of you are likely to become involved in the process of taking depositions long before you are responsible for a trial, we urge you to find a special place in your memory for FRE 612.

KEY POINTS

1. Recorded statements concerning any relevant matters may be admissible for their truth under FRE 803(5) if the declarant testifies as a witness and is not able to fully recollect those matters, and if the foundation regarding the freshness and accuracy of the statement is satisfied.

2. FRE 805 provides that each part of a multiple hearsay statement must conform to a hearsay exception or exemption.

3. If a statement is the product of reporting and recording by two or more out-of-court declarants, then all declarants must testify if FRE 803(5) is the sole hearsay exception relied on to admit the statement. FRE 803(5) can be used in combination with other exemptions and exceptions to admit statements containing multiple levels of hearsay.

PROBLEMS

8.65. Plaintiff Rhoda Bolt, a CPA and Chief Auditor for Aquatic Marine Corp. (AMC), has filed suit against AMC for sexual harassment and wrongful discharge due to AMC's creation of a hostile work environment. She alleges that the harassment, consisting of overtly sexual and demeaning comments and behavior from other employees, began in July 2007; that the atmosphere in the Auditing Department was overtly hostile to her; that this affected her ability to perform her job; and that she was wrongfully discharged in 2010.

(a) At trial, Plaintiff will offer notes that she wrote outlining many specific incidents of harassment that she cannot entirely recall. She testifies that she is not sure when she began taking notes on the incidents, but that it was some time in 2008; that she made the notes at home, usually but not always on the same day as the incident reported; and that the only reason she made the notes was to accurately record what happened and when. The notes terminate in 2010 when she was discharged by AMC. Are Bolt's notes admissible to prove a hostile work environment?

(b) Defendant AMC will offer the personal notes made by Leveritt Darnell, Chief Financial Officer of AMC and Bolt's supervisor. Darnell testifies that after Bolt made several complaints about the problems and hostile work environment in the Auditing Department, he became concerned about Bolt's job performance. He says he wrote these notes for his own reference for a period of several months in 2010, before he discharged Bolt. The notes describe Darnell's analysis of accounting mistakes made in accounting documents written by Bolt in her role as Chief Auditor, dating back as early as 2007. The notes were not shown to Bolt nor to anyone else, but were placed by Darnell into his file on Bolt. Are Darnell's notes admissible if Darnell has insufficient memory to testify fully and accurately?

8.66. While Andrew was crossing an intersection, he was hit by an automobile, which fled the scene of the accident. Sadie, Andrew's companion, rushed to his side, and asked, "Are you okay?" Andrew, who was still conscious, responded, "I don't know, but I got the license number of the car that hit me. It was 879-ACY. Write it down so we won't forget." Sadie had nothing to write on, so she kept repeating the license number to herself. When she got home, a few hours later, she wrote down the number. Andrew has brought an action for personal injuries against Roland Bowers, who is the registered owner of a green Plymouth with the license number 879-ACY. Neither Andrew nor Sadie remembers the license number now. Is Sadie's record of it admissible under any hearsay exceptions? Which ones?

11. Interpretation and Illustration of FRE 803(6): Records of a Regularly Conducted Activity

FRE 803(6) Provides:

(6) *Records of a Regularly Conducted Activity.* A record of an act, event, condition, opinion, or diagnosis if:

(A) the record was made at or near the time by — or from information transmitted by — someone with knowledge;

(B) the record was kept in the course of a regularly conducted activity of a business, organization, occupation, or calling, whether or not for profit;

(C) making the record was a regular practice of that activity;

(D) all these conditions are shown by the testimony of the custodian or another qualified witness, or by a certification that complies with Rule 902(11) or (12) or with a statute permitting certification; and

(E) neither the source of information nor the method or circumstances of preparation indicate a lack of trustworthiness.

a. *Preliminary Fact-finding*

The foundation requirements for business records are:

- the statement is a record;
- the record is of an act, event, condition, opinion, or diagnosis;
- the record was made at or near the time of the act, etc.
- the record was made by someone with knowledge of the act, etc.; or
- the record was made from information transmitted by someone with knowledge;
- the record was kept in the course of a regularly conducted activity of a business, organization, occupation, or calling, whether or not for profit;
- it was a regular practice of that activity to make the record.

In addition to these requirements, FRE 803(6) also contains two unique features. It requires the proponent to produce a "custodian or other qualified witness" to testify about the foundational requirements or to present a written declaration certifying such foundation facts pursuant to FRE 902(11) or (12). FRE 803(6)(E) also permits the judge to exclude a record that otherwise fits the exception, if "the source of information [or] the method or circumstances of preparation indicate a lack of trustworthiness."

i.   The Broad Scope of FRE 803(6)(B).

i.   **The Broad Scope of FRE 803(6)(B).**   No business or other organized entity can survive in today's world without keeping records of its activities. And there is very little civil litigation that does not use some type of record as evidence. Prior to the restyling, FRE 803(6) used the term "business records" and defined "business" very broadly. Now, the Rule explicitly includes records of organizations, occupations and callings, whether or not for profit. Thus, the records of groups that do not seem to be businesses, such as the expense records of a Scout Troop, or records of expenses kept by students working on a student law journal or other student organization, easily fall within Rule 803(6)(B). When record-keeping activity assumes a public role, or provides a function within an "organization," the terms of the exception apply.

You might wonder what kinds of records would *not* fall within its terms. Probably your notes as a student do not, nor would casual records you keep of your household expenses. But there are cases in which a person's own records of expenses, or income, kept for business reasons such as balancing bank accounts, maintaining a budget, or preparing tax returns can qualify under FRE 803(6) so long as they are "systematically checked and regularly and continually maintained." Keogh v. IRS, 713 F.2d 496, 499 (9th Cir. 1983). Your receipts and bills for goods and services that you purchase are business records of the seller or the credit card company, but they are not your business records. Courts do not treat people as being in the business of being a consumer.

The term *record* has also been interpreted to include a broad range of documents—memoranda, reports, records, or data compilations. The distinguishing feature of the FRE 803(6) records is that information about acts and events, etc., has been stored somewhere outside of the human mind and can be recalled in some form other than oral testimony. The permissible contents of these records are likewise broad, and include acts, events, conditions, opinions, or diagnoses—so long as they are topics that are regularly recorded as part of the regular activity of the author.

The more than 30 years of existing case law that we draw on to interpret and apply the provisions of FRE 803(6) has focused primarily on the records of "businesses." We thus use the "business" terminology of this existing case law in the text below. But remember that the records that are admitted under FRE 806(6) extend beyond a for-profit, business context.

ii.   Personal Knowledge and Near Contemporaneity Are Required.

ii.   **Personal Knowledge and Near Contemporaneity Are Required.**   The original source of a FRE 803(6) record is like the observer discussed in regard to FRE 803(5). This original source must have personal knowledge of a matter and must start the process of making a record of that matter. The source may make the written record, or may transmit information orally or in some written format to a series of other people who record the information in various formats. FRE 803(6) also requires that the original source start this process of record-keeping at or near the time that the source observed the matter. An example will help to illustrate these requirements. In a suit for breach of contract, the purchaser claims that goods purchased from the seller were delivered in a damaged condition. To prove damaged condition, the purchaser offers a document entitled "Damage Report." It identifies the shipment of goods as coming from the seller and describes the damaged condition of the items. Joan, the purchaser's employee who wrote the report, has left the company and cannot testify. Since the report is offered to prove the truth of the matters it asserts—that the boxes were labeled as coming from seller, and that the goods were damaged—it is hearsay. To fit within the business record exception, the proponent must prove that Joan had personal knowledge of the matters described and that she wrote the report or transmitted her knowledge close in time to her observation of the shipment. The judge must be persuaded, under FRE 104(a), by a preponderance of the evidence that these requirements are fulfilled.

It is important to identify the activity with which the record should be contemporaneous. In *In Re WorldCom, Inc. Securities Litigation*, 2005 U.S. Dist. LEXIS 2215, at *24-25 (S.D.N.Y. 2005), the consolidated securities class action arising out of the collapse of the telecommunications giant WorldCom, one of the defendants filed a motion in limine to exclude the Restatement of WorldCom's 2000 and 2001 financial statements. The Restatement was issued in 2004. It revealed an overstatement of WorldCom's net income by $74 billion in those two years. It was produced by a WorldCom's successor corporation, MCI, and audited by KPMG, Inc. In response to the claim that the Restatement was not contemporaneous with the financial events of 2000-2001, the court held that a financial statement is never created contemporaneously with the underlying business records; " . . . it is filed months after the end of the fiscal year . . . a restatement is the result of a process of review . . . that reflects the accounting work done [by the reviewer] 'at or near the time' that the report [Restatement] was created."

iii. Made Pursuant to a "Business Duty." Unlike the past recollection recorded exception, FRE 803(6) does not require testimony as to the accuracy of the contents of the record. *United States v. Scholl*, 166 F.3d 964, 978 (9th Cir. 1999) (estimates made by a casino floor walker of a particular gambler's winnings and losses need not be proven to be accurate before they are admitted). Trustworthiness is inferred from the two foundational requirements that contain the word *regular*. The record must be shown to be kept in the course of *regular* "business" activity, meaning an activity within the customary purposes of the enterprise. Compare *United States v. Skeddle*, 981 F. Supp. 1069, 1072 (N.D. Ohio 1997) (customary for an accounting firm employee to take notes at client meetings, place them in the client files, and refer to them at a later time; therefore, notes were kept as part of the regular course of business) with *AgriBioTech, Inc. v. Thomas*, 2005 U.S. Dist. LEXIS 6465 (D. Nev. 2005) (document entitled "Trott conference" appears to be notes of a meeting but no evidence offered that employee regularly took notes at meetings, or that it was his practice to make such notes, or that he was under any "business" duty to report his notes of the events of the meeting). That the declarant had a *business duty* to keep the record is a term often used to describe a regular "business" activity. Here are two examples of judicial consideration of the "business duty" issue. In *United States v. Kaiser*, 609 F.3d 556, 574 (2d Cir. 2010), a participant in the fraudulent business scheme charged against defendant made notes in his "business planner" concerning telephone calls during which defendant asked him to send letters confirming financial obligations that were false. The court held that "part of the participant's business was to sign these confirmations, and these are records of conversations he had in connection with that part of his business . . . [they are] unquestionably business records." In AAMCO Transmissions, Inc. v. Baker, 591 F. Supp. 2d 788 (E.D. Pa. 2008), AAMCO offered a memorandum written by the supervisor of AAMCO's consumer affairs department concerning defendant's operations of his AAMCO franchise. The supervisor testified that he prepared the memorandum about the defendant Baker "basically giving me — providing myself with my own understanding of the history of my experiences with Mr. Baker in the shop in Tallahassee . . . Just probably to get my thoughts in order on the point of bringing him in getting him to meet with us." The court excluded this memorandum as not within the regular course of business.

In addition, the exception requires a showing that it was a *regular* practice to make the record, meaning that making such a record, or records like it, happens systematically or repeatedly. In the *Kaiser* case described above, Kaiser argued that the participant's note-taking was too sporadic and selective to meet the standard of "regular practice," and that the participant stated on cross-examination that he only wrote down "highlights" and what he thought was important. The court held that these objections failed.

> The selectivity that Kaiser points out, however, is the nature of all note-taking. A business record need not be mechanically generated to be part of a "regular practice." . . . [The participant's] contact log is different in kind from the types of "miscellaneous jottings" that courts have found inadmissible under this exception, because it was maintained in a consistent way and was focused on a certain range of issues that were relevant to his business. *Cf. United States v. Ramsey*, 785 F.2d 184, 192 (7th Cir. 1986) ("Occasional desk calendars, in which entries may or may not appear at the whim of the writer, do not have the sort of regularity that supports a reliable inference.") [Id. at 575.]

iv.   Custodian or Other Qualified Witness.   Courts have interpreted the language in FRE 803(6)(D) to require that the custodian of the record or some other qualified witness be able to explain the record-keeping procedures of the organization. Personal knowledge of the specific records at issue is not required:

> Rule 803(6) does not require that the custodian personally gather, input, and compile the information memorialized in a business record. The custodian . . . need not be in control of or have individual knowledge of the particular corporate records, but need only be familiar with the company's recordkeeping practices. [Guillermety v. Secretary of Education, 341 F. Supp. 2d 682, 690 (E.D. Mich. 2003).]

The foundation witness need not be an employee of the organization, so long as there is a showing of the witness's familiarity with the record-keeping system. And the end custodian of data may testify as to the process by which the data was generated, and transmitted by, other entities. Houston v. Smith, 2010 U.S. Dist. LEXIS 118135 (W.D. Pa.) (satellite data generated by a computer and processed by Qualcomm and then used and stored by defendant corporation was shown to be transmitted from the other entities in the regular course of business by the testimony of defendant's witness).

FRE 803(6), together with FRE 902(11) and (12), now permit the foundation for business records to be provided by a written declaration, rather than a live testifying witness. While the foundational requirements for the hearsay exception remain the same, it appears from some cases that the declarations speak in wholly conclusory terms: "[T]he records were made and kept in the course of business by an employee who had personal knowledge of the facts recorded . . . This is sufficient." Spurlock v. Commissioner, T.C. Memo 2003-124 (U.S. Tax Ct.). In such a case, neither the opponent nor the jury is provided with any detailed, context-specific information with which to evaluate the reliability of the record. The notice requirement is intended to give the opponent the opportunity to take discovery to test the adequacy of the foundation in the declaration, but this results in increasing the costs of the opponent's pretrial discovery. United States v. Klinzing, 315 F.3d 803 (7th Cir. 2003) (defendant had right to depose record keepers or call them to the stand for cross-examination).

b.   Justification for the Admissibility of Records of Regularly Conducted Activities

Like many other exceptions, the admissibility of FRE 803(6) records is justified on the grounds of necessity and reliability. The necessity is twofold. First, there is frequently multiple person involvement in the production of these records. It would be time-consuming, inconvenient, and perhaps not possible to call each individual who had a part in generating the record as a witness. Second, even if the people who were responsible for making the record were on the witness stand, they might not have any present memory of matters contained in the record. With respect to routine matters recorded in the ordinary course of business, all they can testify about is their routine practice in making such a record. The record itself is the only accurate source of the substantive information.

The reliability rationale for the exception is based on several factors. The requirement that the record be made at or near the time of the matter recorded minimizes any memory problem; a person who makes a record in the regular course of activity has an incentive to be honest and accurate in order to advance within an organization or business; the fact that the record is kept in the regular course suggests that it may be relied on or checked for accuracy, which provides an added guarantee of trustworthiness and an incentive for the record maker to be accurate in the first place; the routine nature of many records that are made and kept in the regular course of organized activity suggests that there is not likely to be an incentive to lie about routine matters; and finally, the regularity of the record-making process often gives the record maker some expertise in record-making that tends to ensure accuracy. Many of these generalizations might not apply to the kinds of personal records described on page 519 that may not qualify as FRE 803(6) records.

12. Elaboration of FRE 803(6)

Not all records that are made and kept in the regular course of business or organized activities are reliable. Consider, for example, records that are created for self-serving purposes, such as for promotion and public relations, or in preparation for litigation. You might think differently about the reliability of a discussion of the safety of an automobile braking system contained in a company's testing report, as opposed to a discussion in a report prepared to defend against a lawsuit. Or consider the difference between job site accident reports filed by injured employees or by an official public investigator.

a.   *Exclusion for Untrustworthiness*

FRE 803(6)(E) permits the judge to exclude a record if "the source of information [or] the method or circumstances of preparation indicate a lack of trustworthiness." This exclusionary clause is based on a concern articulated by the Supreme Court in Palmer v. Hoffman, 318 U.S. 109 (1943). The plaintiff, who was injured in a railroad grade crossing accident, claimed that the railroad was negligent in that the engineer failed to ring a bell, blow a whistle, or have a light burning in the front of the train. The defendant offered into evidence as a business record an accident report made by the engineer, who died before the trial. The Supreme Court, interpreting the then-existing federal business record statute, upheld exclusion of the record as not made "in the regular course of business."

> [I]t is manifest that in this case those reports are not for the systematic conduct of the enterprise as a railroad business. Unlike payrolls, accounts receivable, accounts payable, bills of lading and the like, these reports are calculated for use essentially in the court, not in the business. Their primary utility is in litigating, not in railroading. [Id. at 113-114.]

The approach of Palmer v. Hoffman is to interpret narrowly what constitutes regular business conduct and would eliminate documents prepared with a self-interested business or personal motivation such as, in our hypothetical, the Damage Report prepared by Joan about the damaged shipment. Yet it could be a regular practice of a company to prepare such reports, and it would serve a regular business interest to do so. The approach of FRE 803(6) is to permit the judge to deal with the risk of untrustworthiness on a case-by-case basis.

   i.   Burden of Persuasion.   Prior to the restyling of FRE 803(6), courts determined that the opponent to the proffered record has the burden of persuading the judge that a record lacks trustworthiness. Thus, the seller of the damaged goods would attack Joan's self-interest (on behalf of her employer) in writing the Damage Report, and could question her method of preparing it. That the custodian or other qualified witness does not know whether the records are complete, or completely accurate, did not establish untrustworthiness. The opponent must produce "specific and credible" evidence of untrustworthiness. Morris v. B.C. Olympiakos, SFP, 721 F. Supp. 2d 546 (S.D. Tex. 2010). Of course, the proponent of the record must be prepared to respond to the opponent's attack with facts that show trustworthiness.
   Could the restyled structure of FRE 803(6)(E) be read as imposing the initial burden on the *proponent* of the record to prove that "neither the source of information nor the method or circumstances of preparation indicate a lack of trustworthiness." This would be a significant change in the substance of the Rule which, as you know, the restyling project sought to avoid.

   ii.   Circumstances Indicating Lack of Trustworthiness.   The greatest concern about trustworthiness focuses on sincerity dangers, such as the motivation of the preparer. The purpose of the record is central; records specifically prepared for litigation are viewed as infused with a motive to distort the truth. Certain Underwriters at Lloyd's, London v. Sinkovich, 232 F.3d 200, 205 (4th Cir. 2000) (report of an insurance investigator hired by plaintiff Underwriters was inadmissible as prepared in anticipation of litigation, even though the investigator regularly prepared such reports in the regular course of his business; the primary motive was to prepare for litigation). Where accident reports are prepared pursuant to a statutory duty, or a regular business routine, they may be found not oriented toward litigation. Other motives may also affect trustworthiness. Opponents charged that the Restatement prepared in the *WorldCom* case was unreliable because the preparers were motivated to maximize the restatement adjustments for tax purposes. The court held that this possible motive did not justify exclusion of the Restatement as untrustworthy, since it was required to comply with GAAP; was under intense scrutiny from the courts, the SEC, and the parties; and was created by scores of people, making any plan of manipulation exceedingly difficult. In re WorldCom, Inc. Securities Litigation, 2005 U.S. Dist. LEXIS 2215, at *26-27. Where the original source of the information or the method of preparation of the record is unclear or unknown, courts may find untrustworthiness. Kay v. Lamar Advertising of South Dakota, Inc., 2009 WL 2731054 (D.S.D.) (in an personal injury case, speed of plaintiffs' motorcycle appearing in ambulance report untrustworthy; source of the statement not identified or explained; no evidence showing it was given in a routine, business manner). It has been held that when the author of the record is testifying as a witness, "the degree of reliability for admission is greatly reduced." United States v. Kaiser, 609 F.3d at 576.

b.   *Opinions and Diagnoses*

FRE 803(6) states that opinions and diagnoses contained within records of regular activities are admissible, while some states do not extend the exception so far. Cal. Evid. Code §1271, for example, covers only records of "an act, condition, or event." In re WorldCom, Inc. Securities Litigation, 2005 U.S. Dist. LEXIS 2215, at *26 (a Restatement of financial statements "reflects accounting judgments to the same extent that any financial statement does"; it cannot be suggested that financial statements are not business records).

The difficulty with admitting opinions and diagnoses is that there will not necessarily be an opportunity to cross-examine the person who made these statements. The opponent will be less able to explore the underlying factual bases for the opinion or diagnosis and, in the case of expert opinions, to explore the purported expert's degree of expertise. In some cases, information about the expert or about the factual support for the opinion may be available from the foundation witness or may be contained in the document itself. To the extent that such information is not available, the party against whom the evidence is offered can argue for exclusion on several possible grounds such as the source has not been qualified as an expert (FRE 702), or the bases for the expert opinion cannot be disclosed (FRE 703). Van der AA v. Commissioner, 2005 U.S. Tax Ct. LEXIS 21 (U.S. Tax Ct.) (the business record rule does not override the rules governing opinion testimony; court would not admit valuation report into evidence without the availability of the author for cross-examination). Most courts treat these issues as a question of lack of trustworthiness under FRE 803(6), Aumand v. Dartmouth Hitchcock Medical Center, 611 F. Supp. 2d 78, 86 (D.N.H. 2009) (rather than seek exclusion of an opinion in a medical report, the "adverse party bears the burden to show . . . lack of trustworthiness"), or an issue under FRE 403 that the probative value of the evidence is substantially outweighed by the risk that, in the absence of critical evaluation, the jury will be misled and will give undue weight to the opinion. These concerns are particularly significant "if the opinion involves difficult matters of interpretation and a central dispute in the case, such as causation." McCormick on Evidence, Vol. 2 §293, at 322 (Kenneth S. Broun ed., 6th ed. 2006).

c.   Records Containing Multiple Levels of Hearsay

If several people contribute to the creation of FRE 803(6) records, then there are multiple levels of hearsay in the document. Under FRE 805, each level must fit within a hearsay exception or exemption. If only FRE 803(6) is used to admit the entire document, then *all* declarants must be shown to satisfy *all* of its foundational requirements. For example, in the case of the Damage Report just discussed, Joan may have inspected the damaged goods and written notes about them; then her assistant, Linda, may have entered the contents of the notes onto a company Damage Form; and Eileen, the manager of the division, may have actually written the Damage Report based on the Damage Form. Each of these declarants perceived something as part of their regular business duty: Joan perceived the damaged goods, Linda perceived the notes, and Eileen perceived the Damage Form. If the information is transmitted along this business chain with near contemporaneity, then its final incarnation as the Damage Report may fall within FRE 803(6). The actual maker of the record, Eileen, does not have to have personal knowledge of the damaged goods. Rather, it is sufficient, according to the language of the rule, that the record was made at or near the time by — or from information transmitted by — someone with knowledge. The custodian or other foundation witness would be required to testify (or submit a declaration) about the process by which the information was transmitted and the record was created.

Records containing multiple levels of hearsay are created in a wide variety of situations: A recording secretary may take notes on what happened at a board meeting and give those notes to a stenographer to transcribe; a doctor may orally recite her observations about a patient, which are then recorded by a medical assistant; an employee of a seller may report shipping information to an employee of a purchaser, who then records it. In testifying about how third-party cost estimates were incorporated into his own business records, a witness testified that he would receive outside estimates, incorporate them into his project file on his computer, do a scope comparison to see that the estimate was what he requested, check the reasonableness of the estimate, and look for mistakes or omissions. BP Amoco Chemical Co. v. Flint Hills Resources, LLC, 697 F. Supp. 2d 1001, 1021-1022 (N.D. Ill. 2010).

At each level, there is of course some risk that the declarants may fabricate, misunderstand, or incorrectly remember the events reported or recorded. It is the belief that, in general, routinely prepared records are accurate that justifies admission of the documents.

i.   **Sources of Information with No Business Duty.**   What if the original source of the information recorded in a business record is not acting in the regular course of business—that is, has no business duty to report on the events observed. In the preceding hypothetical concerning the Damage Report, that Joan's Damage Report contains the following statement: "Just after delivery, Bystander reported to me that he had seen the seller's delivery truck in a rear-end collision on the highway an hour previously." If the Damage Report is offered to prove that the rear-end collision caused the damage to the delivered goods while in seller's custody, there is now an additional hearsay step in the record—from Bystander to Joan. It is the truth of Bystander's statement that the record is offered to prove. Bystander has no business duty to observe or report this accident, or to ensure the accuracy of Joan's record. Thus, the rationale for the business records exception is not applicable to Bystander's statement to Joan. Yet the record was made "from information transmitted by . . . a person [Bystander] with knowledge." FRE 803(6), if read literally, would appear to make the record admissible.

According to the Advisory Committee Note, however, the intent was to exclude, without regard to the trustworthiness clause, statements from persons with no business duty to transmit information to the record keeper:

> If . . . the supplier of the information does not act in the regular course [of business activity], an essential link is broken; the assurance of accuracy does not extend to the information itself, and the fact that it may be recorded with scrupulous accuracy is of no avail. An illustration is the police report incorporating information obtained from a bystander: the officer qualifies as acting in the regular course but the informant does not. The leading case, Johnson v. Lutz, 253 N.Y. 124, 170 N.E. 517 (1930), held that a report thus prepared was inadmissible.

In light of the legislative background to FRE 803(6), the rule has been interpreted consistently with the Advisory Committee's comments: Any declarant to whom this exception applies must transmit knowledge in the course of a regular activity—that is, an activity that imposes a duty to make the out-of-court statement. If not, Rule 803(6) may not be used to admit the recorded statement. United States v. Patrick, 959 F.2d 991 (D.C. Cir. 1992) (no business duty to supply name and address when purchasing a television, thus receipt with defendant's name and address on it was not an admissible business record). If information is provided by outside persons not acting within a business duty, the exception may still apply if it is the business's standard practice to verify or otherwise assure the accuracy of the information transmitted. United States v. Sokolow, 91 F.3d 396, 403 (3d Cir. 1996) (proof of claim forms submitted by insurance claimants were verified and audited before being incorporated into the insurance adjuster's records).

ii.   Use of Multiple Exceptions and Exemptions.   The source of information in a FRE 803(6) record may be a declarant whose statement falls within *another hearsay exception or exemption.* If Bystander's statement to Joan had been, "I just saw that truck in a rear-end collision," it might have been admissible under FRE 803(1), the present sense impression exception. If so, combining that exception for Bystander's statement with FRE 803(6) for the other hearsay steps would make the entire record admissible, assuming that Joan has a duty to report that a Bystander's statement was made to her. What if a doctor's record describing a patient's symptoms includes the patient's statement, "My arm is broken because I was assaulted by Paul"? The patient's statements about the general cause of injury may fit within FRE 803(4), the exception for statements made for medical treatment. Naming the assailant, however, is not likely to be pertinent to diagnosis or treatment. Therefore, FRE 803(4) would probably not be available to admit the name of the alleged attacker. And, the information about who is responsible for the patient's injury is arguably not pertinent to treatment, therefore the doctor may have no professional duty to record such information. Or, the potential risks become a basis for arguing that the recording of the statement about Paul lacks trustworthiness.

Customer surveys are often taken by market research companies to generate a report about what customers believe about products or about their relationship with suppliers. The customers are not acting within a business duty when they respond to a survey, but their statements are usually admitted as "state of mind" under FRE 803(3) as long as they are not used to prove *facts* remembered or believed. DeBeans Cone Co., LLC v. Norse Dairy Systems, LLC, 678 F. Supp. 2d 883 (N.D. Iowa 2009) (categorizations of survey responses and conclusions in the report are within the regular business activity of the survey firm).

d.   Computer Documents and Electronic Data

FRE 803(6) also permits reliance on computer, electronic and website documents. See the Advisory Committee Note to FRE 803:

> The form which the "record" may assume under the rule is described broadly . . . The expression "data compilation" is used as broadly descriptive of any means of storing information other than the conventional words and figures in written or documentary form. It includes, but is by no means limited to, electronic computer storage.

Some computer documents, such as accounting records, represent the storage and sorting of declarations of fact that are entered by persons into the system. The process by which the data were input and used must be pursuant to a regular duty in accordance with regular practice. Some courts have also insisted on evidence concerning procedures for input control, including tests to insure accuracy and reliability. United States v. Scholle, 553 F.2d 1109 (8th Cir. 1997). Other computer documents, such as telephone records, are automatically generated by the computerized system without any human input of underlying data. These records may not be hearsay at all because there is no human declarant making a statement, but the accuracy of the process by which they are produced is still necessary for authentication under FRE 901(b)(9). Houston v. Smith, 2010 U.S. Dist. LEXIS, at *10-12 (satellite tracking data processed through a computer authenticated by testimony of data recipient).

Many businesses and organizations publish internal information about their activities on Web sites. Every digital data entry is a record of such information, and provided that all of the requirements are satisfied, each printout of this information would be admitted under FRE 803(6). For both computer and Web documents, if the data was collected and entered into the computer or onto the Web site in the regular course of business, then printing out a document for purposes of litigation does not trigger the untrustworthiness concerns of Palmer v. Hoffman. Documents culled from a business's data base by a query that selects a smaller subset of data is within the FRE 803(6) exception. Health Alliance Network, Inc. v. Continental Casualty Ins. Co., 245 F.R.D. 121 (S.D.N.Y. 2007).

E-mail documents may also qualify as FRE 803(6) records if it can be shown that it was the regular practice of employees to write and maintain such e-mails. An exchange of e-mails between people in different companies may also be admissible under FRE 803(6) if adequate declarations as to business duty are provided by both businesses. DirecTV v. Murray, 307 F. Supp. 2d 764 (D.S.C. 2004). In United States v. Ferber, 966 F. Supp. 90 (D. Mass. 1997), the government sought the admission of an e-mail sent from the employee of an investment banking firm to his superior, recounting an inculpatory conversation that the employee had had with the defendant. The defendant's statements were, of course, FRE 801(d)(2)(A) admissions, but the employee's recounting of the conversation in an e-mail was claimed to be a business record. The employee testified that it was his regular practice to send such e-mails to coworkers after important telephone conversations with clients. The court refused to admit the e-mail, however, finding that there was no evidence that Merrill Lynch, the employer, required such records to be maintained:

> [I]n order for a document to be admitted as a business record, there must be some evidence of a business duty to make and regularly maintain records of this type . . . Were it otherwise, virtually any document found in the files of a business which pertained in any way to the functioning of that business would be admitted willy-nilly as a business record. This is not the law." [Id. at 98-99.]

Other courts admit e-mails prepared by employees "during the ordinary course of business" but decline to require an employer-imposed business duty to make and maintain e-mails. Pierre v. RBC Liberty Life Ins., 2007 WL 2071829 (M.D. La.) Why should an employer-imposed duty be an element of FRE 803(6) regarding e-mails?

KEY POINTS

1. FRE 803(6) requires testimony from a foundational witness (or a written declaration) to provide evidence of the foundation requirements for the exception. Once these requirements are satisfied, to obtain exclusion the opponent bears the burden of submitting evidence to show the record's lack of trustworthiness, arising from the record's sources of information or the method or circumstances of its preparation.

2. Each link in the chain of supplying and recording the information contained in the record must have personal knowledge of the underlying event or have perception of the information transmitted about it, and must be acting in the course of a regular activity in passing the information on or recording it. If information is supplied by or recorded by a declarant with no regular or "business" duty, the information must be either verified or the FRE 803(6) exception alone cannot be used to admit the record. Any other hearsay exemption or exception may be used for that declarant, however, and the record may be admitted using a combination of exceptions and exemptions.

PROBLEMS

8.67. Return to Problem 8.65, at page 517. The notes written by Leveritt Darnell are offered as business records under FRE 803(6) because Darnell is unavailable to testify. Who might serve as the foundation witness for these notes? What questions should be asked to satisfy FRE 803(6)? Will they be admitted?

In addition, Defendant AMC will also offer a memorandum evaluating Bolt's job performance that was written by Darnell approximately five months after Bolt was terminated. Darnell based the memorandum on (1) his own notes in Problem 8.65(b), and (2) interviews that he conducted with employees in the Auditing Department who worked under Bolt. The employees told him that from 2007 to 2010, Bolt kept interfering in their assigned tasks, and that she refused to delegate appropriate tasks to them. In this memorandum, Darnell expresses his opinion that it was proper to discharge Bolt (1) because of her lack of expertise in accounting principles and (2) because she failed to manage her staff effectively. He admits that this document was written to "express management's perspective" in the face of an impending EEOC investigation of Bolt's complaint. Is this memorandum admissible as a business record under FRE 803(6)?

8.68. Plaintiff Narr has filed an employment discrimination complaint against Columbia Community College for refusing to renew her teaching contract on grounds of her national origin. The College defends on the ground that the failure to renew was based on Narr's poor teaching performance and the numerous administrative problems that she caused. Plaintiff has filed a motion in limine to exclude the following exhibits, properly authenticated documents written prior to the decision not to renew Narr, offered by the College:

(a) Handwritten notes signed by students criticizing Narr's teaching over the course of the semester.

(b) Anonymous handwritten comments by students on the formal course evaluation forms for Narr's classes that are distributed by Columbia at the end of each semester and kept in the regular course of the college's business.

(c) Two e-mails written by one of Narr's departmental colleagues describing his observation of Narr's failure to follow important departmental policies. One e-mail was addressed to Narr, and the other to Narr's department chair.

(d) Another e-mail by the same colleague to the chair describing a student's complaints about Narr's ineffectual teaching and poor attitude toward students.

(e) A memorandum to the department chair from an administrative assistant in the department chronicling years of complaints from faculty about Narr and her own problems with Narr.

(f) A log recorded by the department chair of the numerous issues faculty members have raised about Narr, written at the request of Columbia's Director of Human Resources.

How should the court rule on Narr's motion? Consider all applicable evidence rules. If you were the judge, would you want to request additional information from the parties before ruling on the motion?

8.69. Return to Problem 8.39 on page 481. To prove that he gave proper advice to his patient, Tom Hay, Defendant Dr. Gatwick will offer the properly authenticated hospital chart of Hay's visit to the ER. Dr. Gatwick will testify that during and immediately after an ER exam he always dictates notes for the chart to the ER nurse who is also attending the patient. He testifies that the nurse always makes handwritten notes in the chart while he is dictating. The handwritten notes in Hay's chart state: "Hospital tests advised. Patient refusing to be admitted to Hospital." Are these notes in the chart admissible?

8.70. Plaintiff is suing Chem-Clean manufacturing company for personal injuries resulting from his use of a Chem-Clean household cleaning product. Plaintiff was taken to the hospital emergency room. Plaintiff's medical records contain the following notation made by the emergency room physician: "Burn appears to be second degree. Covers area approximately 6 inches in diameter. Patient said he was using

Chem-Clean cleaning product when he got burned. " Can Plaintiff obtain the admission of this entire record without the testimony of the physician? Using what hearsay exceptions? What if plaintiff were suing Clean-rite company instead, and alleged that he had been using a Clean-rite product. Could Clean-rite obtain the admission of the entire medical record? Using what exceptions?

8.71. Ronald has been diagnosed with chronic pulmonary disease and has been hospitalized several times. He has filed suit against the manufacturer of the butter flavorings used at his place of employment, the American Popcorn Factory. He claims that exposure to the chemical ingredients in defendant's flavorings has caused his illness. Ronald has filed a motion in limine to prevent defendant's use of certain statements in his own medical files kept by his own treating physician, Dr. Farr. Ronald seeks to exclude the following statements:

(1) With regard to his [Ronald's] pulmonary status, he has improved significantly since being here. His daughter states that their house is basically, the word they have used to describe it is filthy, which may be contributing somewhat to his pulmonary problems. Daughter has insisted that he will not be going home until the house is thoroughly cleaned.

(2) Apparently, his home environment is quite dirty with animal feces, etc., in the house.

(3) He has had long-standing problems with his lungs. Actually, this was improved through hospitalization, and the daughters feel that this may be due to his home environment, which they call filthy.

Ronald admits that these statements are in Dr. Farr's handwriting and that Dr. Farr was in charge of Ronald's medical care when he wrote the notes. Ronald objects to defendant's use of these statements on grounds of FRE 401, 602, 801, and 403.

8.72. Mary is suing Pam for personal injuries resulting from an automobile accident. As part of her case, Mary calls Frank Williams, a bystander who observed the accident. He testifies that Pam ran a red light and collided with Mary. As part of her defense, Pam offers a properly authenticated police report, which contains the following statement: "Bystander Frank Williams stated that Mary ran red light." Should Mary's hearsay objection to this evidence be sustained?

8.73. Joseph Reyes is charged with multiple counts of racketeering, murder, assault, firearms, and narcotics violations, as well as conspiracy charges, for the role he played as the head of a large drug distribution organization. At the time of these crimes, Reyes was confined in a state prison where he was visited by Ralph Vargas and others to receive instructions. Vargas became a cooperating witness and testified about his meetings with Reyes in prison and the orders he received to commit murders. To corroborate this testimony, the government offers the visitor logbook from the prison, which indicated that Vargas and other gang members visited Reyes on several occasions, including on days close in time to several murders. The coordinator of inmate records at the prison, who has overall responsibility for storing and maintaining the logbooks, testified that visitors must sign the logbooks in the prison lobby when they enter the building and that they are required to show identification to the lobby officer. The coordinator testified that she observed her own visitors sign the books; that she had no personal knowledge whether all visitors showed identification or whether the lobby officer checked the identification against the log entry, but that these were procedures that were supposed to be followed. The logbooks themselves reflect irregularities such as missing names, missing addresses, and different names in the same handwriting. Reyes also contends that visitors of inmates have an incentive to provide misinformation to avoid monitoring of their contacts.

What arguments would you make on behalf of Reyes to exclude the logbooks under FRE 803(6)? As the government, how would you respond? What result?

13. Interpretation and Illustration of FRE 803(8): Public Records and Reports

Every jurisdiction permits certain public records and reports to be admitted into evidence for their truth. The exception for public records has common law origins, but there are also many statutes governing the admissibility of particular kinds of public records. FRE 803(8) provides for the admission of three types of records:

> (8) *Public Records.* A record or statement of a public office if:
>   (A) it sets out:
>   (i) the office's activities;
>   (ii) a matter observed while under a legal duty to report, but not including, in a criminal case, a matter observed by law-enforcement personnel; or
>   (iii) in a civil case or against the government in a criminal case, factual findings from a legally authorized investigation; and
>   (B) neither the source of information nor other circumstances indicate a lack of trustworthiness.

a. Preliminary Fact-finding

The basic foundation requirements for public records under FRE 803(8) are:

- the statement is in the form of a record or statement of a public office;
- the contents set out the following:
  - the activities of that office;
  - matters observed under a duty imposed by law to report, but not a matter observed by law enforcement in criminal cases; or
  - factual findings from a legally authorized investigation, if in a civil case or against the government in a criminal case.

Unlike FRE 803(6), a qualified witness is not required to lay this foundation. Some public records, if identified and authenticated, can satisfy the foundational requirements with their contents alone. Like FRE 803(6), this exception does include a general exclusionary clause that permits the judge to exclude public records if the sources of information or other circumstances indicate lack of trustworthiness.

i. Activities of the Office. Subsection A(i) is generally interpreted to admit records pertaining to a public office's own internal "housekeeping" functions such as its own personnel records and budgetary information. It also includes records of official activities of the office that are necessary to the performance of its public duties independent of any specific investigation or litigation. In the *Johnson* case, the "C" file on defendant Johnson contained records of Johnson's movements into and out of the California Department of Corrections, which set out the official activities of the CDC—housing and transporting prisoners. United States v. Clarke, 628 F. Supp. 2d 15, 19 (D.D.C. 2009) (certificate of naturalization sets out the activity of the INS, that is, a granting of a petition for naturalization by the Attorney General).

ii.   Matters Reported Pursuant to a Legal Duty, Excluding Matters Observed by Law-Enforcement Personnel in Criminal Cases.   Records that report what public employees have observed pursuant to their public duties are admitted under subsection (A)(ii) upon a minimal foundation. Consider the differences between these public reports and the records admitted under FRE 803(6). The foundation for business and other records of regular activities requires evidence of near contemporaneity and regularity—circumstances that increase the trustworthiness of the records. These indicia of reliability are not required by FRE 803(8)(A)(ii).

Observing and reporting matters under a legal duty to report rarely requires independent proof of the pertinent law. Duty is presumed from the legal purpose of the public office itself and the scope of employment of the public employee. Such public records span many fields, and may include weather reports, police reports, records of border crossings, and accident scene investigations. Many public records and reports are the product of multiple levels of hearsay, when one public employee observes and reports observations to a colleague or subordinate who is also a public employee, and who then records them. As long as each link in the chain bears a public duty, FRE 803(8)(A)(ii) encompasses the entire report.

The exclusionary terms of subsection (A)(ii) apply to criminal cases and operate against the admission of reports of matters observed by "law-enforcement personnel." Reports authored by police officers are readily identifiable as law enforcement. We will discuss at pages 534-536, infra, how courts have applied this term to other public employees. Despite the text of the rule, it has been held in most Circuits that *criminal defendants may offer FRE 803(8)(B) records against the government.* United States v. Carneglia, 256 F.R.D. 384 (E.D.N.Y. 2009).

iii.   Factual Findings in Investigative Reports.   A wide range of government investigative reports have been admitted in civil cases pursuant to the precursor of the restyled subsection (A)(iii): findings of official misconduct, accident reports of police or incident reports by specialized agencies, safety and diagnostic studies relating to public health issues, and reports and studies on housing and employment discrimination. Such reports are powerful evidentiary tools, both because of the allegedly neutral weight of government investigation behind them and because of the persuasive impact of their findings and conclusions.

In 1988, the U.S. Supreme Court ended over 10 years of debate among the Circuit courts as to whether the evaluative opinions and conclusions contained in public investigative reports should be admitted as "factual findings" under this subsection. In Beech Aircraft Corp. v. Rainey, 488 U.S. 153, 170 (1988), the Court held: "As long as the conclusion is based on a factual investigation and satisfies the Rule's trustworthiness requirement, it should be admissible along with other portions of the report." *Beech* involved the crash of a Navy training aircraft that caused the death of two pilots onboard. The suit against the manufacturer of the aircraft, Beech Aircraft Corp., was based on an alleged defect in the aircraft's fuel control system that may have caused a loss in engine power. The defendant relied on a report prepared by an investigating officer authorized by the Judge Advocate General's (JAG) Office of the Navy. This report concluded that "[t]he most probable cause of the accident was the pilots [sic] failure to maintain proper interval." Id. at 159. The Supreme Court upheld the trial court's decision to admit this evaluative conclusion. Its broad interpretation of the "factual finding" language noted the analytic difficulty of drawing a line between "fact" and "opinion" and the opportunity for exclusion of opinions and conclusions that lack trustworthiness under the exclusionary clause of FRE 803(8).

The scope of "factual finding" is not unlimited, however, as shown by the following judicial applications of that term. Preliminary or interim evaluative opinions of agency staff, interim reports, and preliminary memoranda do not satisfy this requirement of FRE 803(8)(C). Smith v. Isuzu Motors Ltd., 137 F.3d 859 (5th Cir. 1998). The National Institute of Justice's Status Reports to the Attorney General regarding the safety of using "Zylon" fabric in soft body armor were not interim, internal work products "because they are the result of scientific studies conducted by the NIJ and then published by the agency for public use or reliance." Boyd v. Toyobo Am., Inc., 421 B.R. 823, 831 (Bankr. W.D. Mich. 2010). A report that is nothing more than interview notes of statements of potential witnesses is not a "factual finding." Roxbury-Smellie v. Florida Dept. of Corrections, 324 Fed. Appx. 783 (11th Cir. 2009). While factually based conclusions and opinions are included under (A)(iii) by *Beech Aircraft*, pure legal conclusions are not admissible. Sullivan v. Dollar Tree Stores, Inc., 623 F.3d 770 (9th Cir. 2010) (that defendant is a "successor in interest" is a pure legal conclusion). It is clear from its language that FRE 803(8)(A)(iii) permits use of factual findings only in civil cases and against the government in criminal cases. The prohibition against use against criminal defendants is grounded on concern that multiple, potentially inadmissible hearsay sources in such reports could run afoul of the Sixth Amendment confrontation clause that protects a criminal accused's right to confront and cross-examine witnesses.

iv. Exclusion for Lack of Trustworthiness. The exclusionary clause for lack of trustworthiness of FRE 803(8)(B) applies to all three subsections of (A)(iii). Like FRE 803(6), the burden is on the opponent to persuade the judge as to its application. Weinstein v. Stevens, 2010 WL 4824952 (E.D. Mich. 2010) (documents that fall under the public records exception are presumed admissible, placing the burden of establishing untrustworthiness on the opponent). The proponent must also be prepared to respond by citing factors that show trustworthiness. Under FRE 803(B), the focus of most challenges is on the hearsay nature of the underlying sources and the circumstances surrounding the factual investigation. The Advisory Committee Note emphasizes the timeliness of the report; the skill, expertise, and motivation of the investigator; and the procedures followed in preparation of the record. Desrosiers v. Flight International of Florida, Inc., 156 F.3d 952, 962 (9th Cir. 1998) (JAG report containing opinions regarding the cause of an air crash was partially redacted as untrustworthy because the author was not shown to be an expert, had not attended accident reconstruction school, had no formal training in investigation of aircraft accidents, and had not previously written such reports). It has been held that the subsection (B) should be applied "in a common sense manner . . . in determining whether the hearsay document . . . has sufficient independent indicia of reliability to justify its admission." Hickson Corp. v. Norfolk Southern Railway Co., 124 Fed. Appx. 336, 345 (6th Cir. 2005).

b.   Justification for the Admissibility of Public Records

The rationale for the public records exception—at least with respect to routine matters—is virtually identical to the rationale for the FRE 803(6) records exception: The inconvenience of calling public officials to testify and the likelihood that public officials may not recall the information in the records create the need for the exception. United States v. Midwest Fireworks Mfg. Co., 248 F.3d 563, 567 (6th Cir. 2001) (the public records exception "is a practical necessity [for] . . . government officers 'who have made in the course of their duties thousands of similar written hearsay statements'"). The public official's duty and the likelihood that public access to the records will reveal inaccuracies tend to ensure the records' reliability. As with all hearsay exceptions, there must be a sufficient showing of personal knowledge in subsection (A)(i) and (ii) records. There are no specific foundational requirements, however, that the record be made at or near the time of the event or that it be a regular practice of the public agency to make the record. Opinions and conclusions admitted under subsection (A)(iii) may, as we shall see, rest on information outside the investigator's own firsthand knowledge. "It is the methodology of factual investigation which provides a threshold safeguard against untrustworthiness." Ariza v. City of New York, 139 F.3d 132, 133 (2d Cir. 1998).

14.   Elaboration of FRE 803(8)(A)(ii): The Meaning of "Law-Enforcement Personnel"

a.   The Meaning of Law-Enforcement Personnel

An early Circuit court opinion, United States v. Oates, 560 F.2d 45 (2d Cir. 1977), was influential in adopting a broad reading of who counted as "law-enforcement" personnel under subsection (A)(ii). At issue in *Oates* were two public records—the handwritten worksheet and the official report of a Customs Service chemist. These documents recorded the testing procedure and test results on a white powder seized from one of the defendants, found to be heroin. The examining chemist did not testify due to illness, and there were inconsistencies between the two documents regarding the chain of custody. On appeal from appellant's conviction for possession of heroin with intent to distribute, the Second Circuit held that the reports were hearsay and were "factual findings" under FRE 803(8)(A)(iii), thus inadmissible against a criminal defendant. The court also considered whether the documents were admissible under FRE 803(8)(A)(ii). It construed "'law-enforcement personnel' to include, at the least, any officer or employee of a governmental agency which has law enforcement responsibilities" and then elaborated on the extensive role Customs Service chemists play in the development of evidence for criminal prosecutions. Id. at 67-68. In the more than 30 years since *Oates*, most courts have interpreted "law-enforcement" more narrowly. Obviously, police officers fall within that term. The question is, who else?[3]

---

3.   Prior to the restyling, subsection (B) of FRE 803(8) excluded matter observed by "police and law enforcement." The "police" has been dropped and "law-enforcement personnel" stands on its own as the term of exclusion. We assume that all prior case law interpreting the "law-enforcement" term will now apply to subsection (A)(ii).

i. **Prosecutorial Function.** Courts have included within this exclusionary language public officers whose functions are similar to police officers. This includes public employees who perform a "prosecutorial" or investigative function in specific cases. In part, courts are responding to Congress's concern that it might violate a defendant's confrontation right to use a police report *instead of the live testimony of a police officer*, particularly when the report contained the police officer's eyewitness account of criminal conduct. The same concern would extend to other public officials who are investigating specific cases of criminal conduct, such as customs inspectors and border patrol agents. It also became clear that "law-enforcement," as interpreted by *Oates*, would exclude too much, such as statements by those who are not responsible for enforcing the criminal law, who perform administrative duties in a regulatory scheme, make administrative decisions, or seek compliance with fines and citations. In an early case that controverted the holding in *Oates*, the court in United States v. Rosa, 11 F.3d 315 (2d Cir. 1993), upheld admission of the factual observations contained in autopsy reports from the medical examiner's office because the employees of the office had no responsibilities for enforcing the law. The conclusions in the report as to the manner and cause of death, however, would be excluded under FRE 803(8)(A)(iii).

In a more recent case, an interview conducted by an official of the Immigration and Naturalization Service (INS) resulted in the prosecution of the defendant for having entered into a fraudulent marriage and for lying on an immigration document. The Ninth Circuit in United States v. Orellana-Blanco, 294 F.3d 1143, 1150 (9th Cir. 2002), overturned the trial court's admission of defendant's statement, written by the official but signed by the defendant, under FRE 803(B), now (A)(ii):

> An interview such as the one in the exhibit is adversarial in nature. [Defendant] was separated from his wife, obviously so that they could not coordinate their stories as they told them, and put under oath. Numerous cases treat INS officers and agents as "law enforcement" personnel, which are covered by the exclusion to the hearsay exception. Though the interview might not have been used for law enforcement purposes had the INS officer been satisfied, it was in fact used for that purpose, and in the natural course would be, if the INS was unsatisfied. Because [defendant] was put under oath and then charged with lying under oath on the form, the interview itself, at the INS office, was the "scene of the crime," and Officer Kendall's notes were in fact his subjective recordation of his aural observations at the scene of the crime as it took place.

In criminal cases, the focus on admissibility of many types of public records now includes the question of whether such reports and records are "testimonial" statements of the declarant under the interpretation of the confrontation clause set forth in Crawford v. Washington. See Section G., infra.

ii. **Routine and Regular Activities.** It is now well established that routine, bureaucratic and nonadversarial reports made by law enforcement personnel, and even by police officers, do not fall within the subsection (A)(ii) exclusion. Thus, courts have admitted records kept in an automated data base kept by the California Department of Justice of firearms purchases from information provided by firearms dealers; a federal Secret Service data base identifying counterfeit currency by denomination, serial number, and date and location of its seizure; a warrant of deportation, which records deportation of aliens; reports of the time and date of crimes, but not the facts and circumstances involved; a log of all 911 calls; stolen vehicle reports;

and records relating to the regular maintenance checks of a breathalyzer unit. All of these records were considered reliable because they were routine and ministerial, that is, not made in an adversarial setting. Two recent cases appear to be somewhat more problematic in holding that records are not made by "law-enforcement" personnel: United States v. Dowdell, 595 F.3d 50 (1st Cir. 2010) (arrest booking sheets containing identifying information about the person arrested, including photograph and description of clothing later used in an identification by an eyewitness); United States v. Reyes, 2009 WL 3273896 (S.D. Fla.) (a Situation Report of the names of persons taken on board a Coast Guard cutter, according to standard practice, from a capsized ship smuggling illegal aliens into the United States). Again, even for routine reports, the question remains whether the statements made therein are "testimonial" under *Crawford*.

b.   The Relationship Between FRE 803(8)(A)(ii)) and (iii), and Other Exceptions

The court in *Oates* also considered whether the two chemist's reports could have been admitted as business records pursuant to FRE 803(6):

> [T]he government argues . . . that the chemist's report and worksheet in the case at bar fall clearly within the literal terms of . . . FRE 803(6) . . . [W]e assume for purpose of argument here, that . . . the chemist's report and worksheet might fall within the literal language of FRE 803(6) . . . This would not be the first time that a court has encountered a situation pitting some literal language of a statute against a legislative intent that flies in the face of that literal language. Our function as an interpretive body is, of course, to construe legislative enactments in such a way that the intent of the legislature is carried out . . . .
>
> [P]olice and valuative reports not satisfying the standards of FRE 803(8)(B) and (C) [now restyled as (A)(ii) and (iii)] may not qualify for admission under FRE 803(6) or any of the other exceptions to the hearsay rule. . . . [560 F.2d at 73-77.]

Under *Oates*, if a document is inadmissible under FRE 803(8) because of the specific exclusionary terms in subsections (A)(ii) and (iii), it would be a subversion of the legislative intent to permit the document to be used as an FRE 803(6) business record. The justifications for admitting business and public records are, after all, very similar. In addition, it should not be permissible to circumvent the specific limitations on the scope of FRE 803(8) by resorting to the residual exception FRE 807. However, some Courts of Appeals have admitted lab reports identifying illegal substances as FRE 803(6) business records. United States v. Roulette, 75 F.3d 418, 421 (8th Cir. 1999).

We do not believe, however, that the *Oates* dictum prohibiting resort to *all* other exceptions is sound. FRE 803(5), for example, requires the attendance of the author of the public record as a witness. If the police or law-enforcement officer does testify and is available for cross-examination, a court should not forbid the use of FRE 803(5) by the government in criminal cases because the recorded recollection also happens to be in a public record made by law-enforcement personnel. United States v. Sawyer, 607 F.2d 1190 (7th Cir. 1979) (document falling within the law-enforcement exclusionary provision of FRE 803(8) admissible under FRE 803(5)).

Some records of a governmental entity may contain information that is neither a "matter observed" nor a "factual finding," and therefore, cannot fall within the exclusionary terms of FRE 803(8)(A)(ii) or (iii). Thus, it would not be a subversion of those limitations to resort to FRE 803(6) or to any other hearsay exception.

15. Elaboration of FRE 803(8)(C): The Problem of Multiple Hearsay Sources Within Investigative Reports

a. Is the Report Itself Admissible?

Many investigations that result in factual findings are based on hearsay information. Factual findings might be based on interviews of witnesses conducted by the investigator or on research evaluating both public and private records. In the *Beech* case, for example, the investigator relied on eyewitness accounts of the plane crash and reports analyzing the condition of the aircraft after the crash. Subsection (A)(iii) clearly contemplates that the investigator may use those sources, evaluate them, and then reject them or rely on them in making factual findings. Thus, unlike records under FRE 803(6) and public records under FRE 803(8)(A)(ii), where all sources must be operating under a "business" or organizational or legal duty to conform to the requirement of the exceptions, *sources relied on under FRE 803(8)(A)(iii) need not be operating under any sort of public duty in relaying information to the investigator.* In re September 11 Litigation, 621 F. Supp. 2d 131, 156 (S.D.N.Y. 2009) ("relevant and appropriate findings made by the Commission are potentially trustworthy and admissible. . . . The Commission heard 160 witnesses, was free from bias, and conducted public hearings that were the adequate equivalent of cross-examination. . . . ").

Some hearsay sources may fall within their own exception or exemption to the rule of exclusion—for example, excited utterances, statements of parties, or business records. This would satisfy FRE 805 and would also provide some circumstantial guarantees of trustworthiness. Weinstein v. Stevens, 2010 WL 4824952, at *5 (E.D. Mich. 2010) (third-party witness statements were defendants' employees, authorized to speak on the subject or speaking about matters within the scope of their employment, thus entirely admissible). If the underlying hearsay sources are not admissible, one safeguard may be the public agency's ability to evaluate such sources before it decides to rely on them. If the original source has personal knowledge and no reason to misrepresent the information to the public official, under the circumstances, then the public report may be admitted. In re Air Disaster at Lockerbie Scotland on December 21, 1988, 37 F.3d 804 (2d Cir. 1994) (investigation of air crash relied in part on computerized records of passenger baggage based on hearsay reports from passengers' and crew members' friends and relatives).

But if factual findings are based on hearsay sources that are unidentified or that the court finds to be unreliable, the report itself may be excluded as lacking in trustworthiness. Lang v. Cullen, 725 F. Supp. 2d 925, 959 (C.D. Cal. 2010) (presentence report inadmissible under FRE 803(8) because the sources are not subject to evidentiary standards and may also contain factual errors); Hickman v. Norfolk Southern Railway Co., 124 Fed. Appx. at 346 (unknown source reporting a toxic leak, transmitted by multiple levels of hearsay through state agencies and resulting in an erroneous time of occurrence, lacked "the necessary indicia of reliability"); Miller v. Field, 35

F.3d 1088 (6th Cir. 1994) (judgment for defendants reversed on grounds of erroneous admission of official report disputing alleged inmate rape of plaintiff, since report was based on inadmissible hearsay statements of the assailants and the local prosecutor).

b.   Are Otherwise Inadmissible Hearsay Sources Admissible?

FRE 803(A)(iii) does not admit otherwise inadmissible hearsay sources for the truth of the matters they assert, even if they are relied on by the author of the report. In re September 11 Litigation, 621 F. Supp. 2d at 157: "The statements of the terrorists, even though found in The 9/11 Report, cannot qualify as factual findings [and] . . . will be excluded." If inadmissible sources appear in the text of the public report, the jury might decide to use them anyway, in violation of the basic principle of the hearsay rule of exclusion. Thus, there is a conflict between admitting the investigator's entire report—including the substantive contents of *all* of its sources—and keeping inadmissible hearsay from the jury. A similar conflict exists when opinions of testifying expert witnesses are admitted together with all of the expert's underlying, potentially inadmissible sources, as will be discussed in Chapter Nine. FRE 703 now provides its own approach to this conflict, as we will discuss on page 690, infra. It seems possible that the balancing test provided in Rule 703 could be applied to subsection (A)(iii) reports as well. The jury would be instructed that the underlying hearsay sources are admitted not for their truth but in order for the jury to evaluate the basis for the investigation's findings. Otherwise, the hearsay sources would be redacted from the report, or application of the untrustworthiness clause of Rule 803(8) could be used to exclude the report altogether.

c.   Administrative Findings

It is well established that the findings and conclusions that result from judicial proceedings do not fall within FRE 803(8)(A)(iii). Nipper v. Snipes, 7 F.3d 415, 417 (4th Cir. 1993) ("a judge in a civil trial is not an investigator"). However, agency hearings within the executive branch, even those presided over by officials called Administrative Law Judges, do qualify as investigations. In a case involving a trial-type hearing, the presentations of witnesses, cross-examination and a review of records and tests, the ALJ issued a decision with detailed factual findings concerning the airworthiness of an airplane for purposes of suspending the aircraft's National Transportation Safety Board certificate of airworthiness. These findings and decision were later admitted in a trial for breach of contract against the company that had attempted to restore the aircraft to airworthy condition. Zeus Enterprises, Inc. v. Alphin Aircraft, Inc., 190 F.3d 238 (4th Cir. 1999). Such findings are not automatically admissible, however. The trial judge has discretion pursuant to FRE 403 to assess the probative value of such reports and findings, as well as their Rule 403 dangers:

> The party against whom such a determination is admitted must attempt to expose the weaknesses of the report . . . an effort that may well confuse or mislead the jury and result in an undue waste of time . . . We believe that the district court is in the best position to consider the quality of the report, its potential impact on the jury, and the likelihood that the trial will deteriorate into a protracted and unproductive struggle over how the

evidence admitted at trial compared to the evidence considered by the agency. [Paolitto v. John Brown E.&C., Inc., 151 F.3d 60, 65 (2d Cir. 1998).]

16. Other Exceptions for Records Under FRE 803

In addition to the business and official records exceptions, FRE 803 contains a variety of exceptions for other types of records. You should read FRE 803(9), (11), (12), (13), (14), (15), (16), and (17) at least once. These exceptions for the most part are based on the notion that the records are likely to be reliable because of the nature of the entity preparing them, the routine nature of their preparation, and their subject matter. The scope and operation of these exceptions should be easily discernable from the language of the rule and the Advisory Committee Notes.

FRE 803(7) and FRE 803(10) set forth hearsay exceptions for the *absence of* entries in business, organizational and public records, offered for the purpose of proving the nonoccurrence or nonexistence of a matter if that matter was of a kind that was regularly recorded if it occurred or existed. As the Advisory Committee noted, it is unlikely that the failure to make the entry is the result of a conscious intent to assert that an event did not occur. Thus, the failure to make an entry may not constitute a hearsay "statement" in the first place. The exceptions exist, according to the Advisory Committee, "[i]n order to set the question at rest in favor of admissibility. . . ." The search for public records must be diligent, and a showing must be made that the documents searched are proper FRE 803(6) or public records. The results of such a search have been held *not* to be excluded in criminal cases by the exclusionary clauses of subsections FRE 803(8)(a)(ii) and (iii). United States v. Mendez, 514 F.3d 1035, 1044-1045 (10th Cir. 2008) (search in U.S. Central Index System containing regularly reported data on legal entries into the United States did not disclose defendant's name, indicating he had not entered the country legally; absence of public record admissible pursuant to FRE 803(10) and not excluded as created with an eye toward litigation by FRE 803(8)(B), now (A)(ii)).

KEY POINTS

1. FRE 803(8) provides for the admission of (A)(i) records of the activities of public offices and agencies, of (A)(ii) matters observed pursuant to public duty to report by employees of public offices, and of (A)(iii) public investigative reports, including factual findings. The testimony of a foundation witness may be necessary, but is not required by FRE 803(8).

2. All public records are subject to exclusion by the trial court for lack of trustworthiness.

3. In criminal cases, the prosecution may not use FRE 803(8)(A)(ii) to admit reports of matters observed by law-enforcement officials against criminal defendants. This limitation may not apply to records of public officers not engaged in the investigation or prosecution of individual criminal cases, nor to routine and regular records kept by law enforcement personnel.

4. Under FRE 803(8)(A)(iii), factual findings include opinions and conclusions. Investigative reports and factual findings may not be used by the prosecutor against

defendants in criminal cases. Multiple hearsay contained in such reports may be used as the basis for the findings, but unless it falls within an exemption or exception, is not admitted for its truth. Courts may also exclude factual findings as lacking trustworthiness because of reliance on inadmissible and unreliable hearsay.

PROBLEMS

8.74. A defendant in a criminal case, charged with kidnapping and assault, has filed a Motion to Suppress statements made by him to three law enforcement officers following his indictment, arrest, and request for assistance of counsel. The defendant claims that continued questioning by the three officers violated his right to counsel under the Sixth Amendment. At the suppression hearing, the prosecution offers the report of FBI Agent Peters, who observed the defendant's arrest and questioning. The report was prepared several weeks after the defendant's Motion was filed. It includes Peters's own recollection of events, including that he, and the three other officers whom he interviewed, never heard the defendant say that he wanted to speak to an attorney.

(a) Can the prosecution secure the admission of this report under any Rule 803 hearsay exception? Could the officers use this report if the defendant were pursuing a civil rights claim against them for money damages?

(b) Could the defendant secure the admission of a written finding made by a police department review board, after a full hearing, that a year ago the same three officers had denied an arrestee the assistance of counsel by ignoring her requests for an attorney?

8.75. In the *Johnson* case, each correctional officer prepared a CDC 115 Report of his own observations of the incident involving inmate Johnson. These reports, as described on page 17, supra, may lead to officer or inmate discipline. Can the prosecution use Walker's CDC 115 Report to prove Walker's version of the incident? Could defendant Johnson offer the report in his own defense?

8.76. Return to Problem 3.2, Pedroso v. Driver, on page 136. The defendants offer a police report filed on the day of the accident by Officer Rojas who arrived at the scene five minutes after the accident. The report describes the location and position of the school bus after the impact. It states that Driver said, "Paul ran out unexpectedly." It also states "Officer Nelson arrived at the scene a few minutes after I did. She interviewed children who had witnessed the incident. She reports that several of them claimed that the boy ran in front of the bus, and that although they were very distressed, they seemed to be reliable." In the space for "Conclusions," Officer Rojas wrote "No apparent violation." How much of the police report can the defendants introduce against plaintiffs? Must Officer Rojas testify as a witness in order to secure the report's admission?

8.77. Harris, on trial for possession of crack cocaine with intent to sell, claims in his defense that the drugs were planted in his apartment by a police detective who had a vendetta against him and had harassed him three times while Harris was on parole. Harris claims that he called Wilkins, his parole officer, as he was required to do, each time he had an encounter with the detective. Wilkins has retired. The prosecution offers the testimony of Wilkins's replacement to testify that "it is normal policy for probation officers to make an entry in a probationer's file for each contact with the probationer, and there are no notations in Harris's file indicating that he contacted Wilkins." Is this testimony admissible to prove that Harris did not tell Wilkins about any alleged police harassment?

8.78. A Liberian corporation, Bridgeton, seeks to enforce in federal court the final judgment rendered in its favor by the Supreme Court of Liberia against Citibank. Citibank is defending against the enforcement action by challenging the legitimacy of the Liberian judicial system, claiming that Liberia's courts do not constitute a system of jurisprudence likely to secure an impartial judgment, and thus Bridgeton's judgment is unenforceable in the United States. As proof of its claim, Citibank offers the U.S. State Department Country Reports for Liberia for the years 1994-1997. Country Reports are prepared annually by area specialists at the Department of State and report on human rights conditions prevailing in the subject country. Federal law requires their annual submission to Congress. In describing their preparation, the State Department says that "[w]e have given particular attention to attaining a high standard of consistency despite the multiplicity of sources and the obvious problems related to varying degrees of access to information, structural differences in political and social systems, and trends in world opinion regarding human rights practices in specific countries." Are the Country Reports admissible?

17.   Interpretation and Illustration of FRE 803(22): Judgment of Previous Conviction

A judgment on the merits in a criminal or civil action is relevant to prove the actual occurrence of the facts essential to support the judgment. The judgment is hearsay evidence of those facts. Indeed, it may be multiple hearsay. A defendant's plea of guilty is itself a hearsay statement, and a judge's or a jury's conclusions about the evidence presented in a trial or summary proceeding are offered to prove the truth of those conclusions.

FRE 803(22) provides for the use of criminal felony convictions:

> (22) *Judgment of a Previous Conviction.* Evidence of a final judgment of conviction if:
>   (A) the judgment was entered after a trial or guilty plea, but not a nolo contendere plea;
>   (B) the judgment was for a crime punishable by death or by imprisonment for more than a year;
>   (C) the evidence is admitted to prove any fact essential to the judgment; and
>   (D) when offered by the prosecutor in a criminal case for a purpose other than impeachment, the judgment was against the defendant.
> The pendency of an appeal may be shown but does not affect admissibility.

a.   Preliminary Fact-finding

The foundational requirements for the use of a final judgment of conviction are as follows:

- the judgment must follow a criminal trial or guilty plea;
- the judgment must be for a crime punishable by death or more than one year's imprisonment;
- the judgment must be offered to prove any fact essential to the judgment; and
- a judgment offered against a criminal defendant must be a judgment entered against that defendant, unless it is offered only for impeachment.

The relevance of a judgment to prove underlying events requires a determination as to what "essential" facts were necessarily decided by the judge or jury. Also keep in mind that the judgment serves only as *some evidence* of those facts. The exception does not raise issues of the possible *binding* effect of a prior judgment—a matter to be resolved under principles of collateral estoppel or issue preclusion.

b.   Justification for the Admissibility of Criminal Judgment

FRE 803(22) reflects confidence that a judgment of guilt in a criminal felony case is reliable proof of the facts essential to sustain the judgment. The high standard of proof—beyond a reasonable doubt—is probably the strongest argument in favor of reliability. The exclusion of judgments entered after a plea of nolo contendere is based on the fact that a nolo plea, which can be entered only with the leave of the court, is specifically designed to resolve a criminal matter without the expense of a trial or the defendant's acknowledgment of guilt. Evidence of judgments entered against persons other than the defendant are excluded from criminal trials, unless used for impeachment, because of concern about the defendant's right to confront and cross-examine those adverse witnesses whose testimony provided the basis for judgment. United States v. Austin, 786 F.2d 986 (10th Cir. 1986) (marijuana convictions reversed because government informed jury that 10 co-conspirators had already been convicted for participating in the same alleged conspiracy). Confidence in the reliability of judgments in civil cases is not so deeply felt. When claims involve substantial monetary damages or important principles, it is reasonable to believe that the parties will put forth their best efforts in trying to vindicate their positions. Nevertheless, the standard of persuasion—a preponderance of the evidence—is significantly lower than in criminal cases. If the stakes are small, a litigant may not have a serious interest in devoting the resources that would be necessary to vindicate the litigant's position. Even if one wanted to include judgments from major civil cases, any attempt to define the difference between major and minor cases would probably seem quite arbitrary.

c.   The Admission of Misdemeanor Convictions
for Impeachment

The most frequent use of judgments is to impeach testifying witnesses pursuant to FRE 609. As we noted on page 378, supra, courts invariably admit misdemeanor convictions for *crimen falsi* to impeach witnesses pursuant to FRE 609(a)(2), even though misdemeanors are not included within FRE 803(22).

E.   HEARSAY EXCEPTIONS REQUIRING THE UNAVAILABILITY OF THE DECLARANT

FRE 804 provides five categorical hearsay exceptions that may be used only when the hearsay declarant is unavailable—former testimony, dying declarations, declarations against interest, statements of personal and family history, and statements offered against a party whose wrongdoing procured the unavailability of the declarant as a witness.

Why unavailability is a requirement for only these five categorical exceptions is by no means clear. The Advisory Committee Note to FRE 803 suggests that unavailability is not required for the FRE 803 exceptions because they are reliable hearsay and, therefore, as acceptable as live testimony. By contrast, according to the Advisory Committee, hearsay falling within an FRE 804 exception "is not equal in quality to testimony of the declarant on the stand. . . . " These hearsay statements are admissible only as a last resort; that is, only if the declarant is unavailable to testify in person.

We urge you to question whether there is a significant "reliability difference" between the Rule 803 and the Rule 804 exceptions. At the same time, we caution you against trying too hard to come up with an overarching theory to rationalize the existing law. The earliest common law exceptions—former testimony and dying declarations—were both premised on arguments of necessity because of death. It may be that historical precedent is the best explanation for the current state of the unavailability requirement.

1.   FRE 804

RULE 804.   EXCEPTIONS TO THE RULE AGAINST HEARSAY — WHEN THE DECLARANT IS UNAVAILABLE AS A WITNESS

(a) *Criteria for Being Unavailable*. A declarant is considered to be unavailable as a witness if the declarant:

(1) is exempted from testifying about the subject matter of the declarant's statement because the court rules that a privilege applies;

(2) refuses to testify about the subject matter despite a court order to do so;

(3) testifies to not remembering the subject matter;

(4) cannot be present or testify at the trial or hearing because of death or a then-existing infirmity, physical illness, or mental illness; or

(5) is absent from the trial or hearing and the statement's proponent has not been able, by process or other reasonable means, to procure:

(A) the declarant's attendance, in the case of a hearsay exception under Rule 804(b)(1) or (6); or

(B) the declarant's attendance or testimony, in the case of a hearsay exception under Rule 804(b)(2), (3), or (4).

But this subdivision (a) does not apply if the statement's proponent procured or wrongfully caused the declarant's unavailability as a witness in order to prevent the declarant from attending or testifying.

(b) *The Exceptions*. The following are not excluded by the rule against hearsay if the declarant is unavailable as a witness:

(1) *Former Testimony*. Testimony that:

(A) was given as a witness at a trial, hearing, or lawful deposition, whether given during the current proceeding or a different one; and

(B) is now offered against a party who had — or, in a civil case, whose predecessor in interest had — an opportunity and similar motive to develop it by direct, cross-, or redirect examination.

(2) *Statement Under the Belief of Imminent Death.* In a prosecution for homicide or in a civil case, a statement that the declarant, while believing the declarant's death to be imminent, made about its cause or circumstances.

(3) *Statement Against Interest.* A statement that:

(A) a reasonable person in the declarant's position would have made only if the person believed it to be true because, when made, it was so contrary to the declarant's proprietary or pecuniary interest or had so great a tendency to invalidate the declarant's claim against someone else or to expose the declarant to civil or criminal liability; and

(B) is supported by corroborating circumstances that clearly indicate its trustworthiness, if it is offered in a criminal case as one that tends to expose the declarant to criminal liability.

(4) *Statement of Personal or Family History.* A statement about:

(A) the declarant's own birth, adoption, legitimacy, ancestry, marriage, divorce, relationship by blood, adoption, or marriage, or similar facts of personal or family history, even though the declarant had no way of acquiring personal knowledge about that fact; or

(B) another person concerning any of these facts, as well as death, if the declarant was related to the person by blood, adoption, or marriage or was so intimately associated with the person's family that the declarant's information is likely to be accurate.

(5) *[Other Exceptions.]* [Transferred to Rule 807.]

(6) *Statement Offered Against a Party That Wrongfully Caused the Declarant's Unavailability.* A statement offered against a party that wrongfully caused — or acquiesced in wrongfully causing — the declarant's unavailability as a witness, and did so intending that result.

Our initial discussion focuses on FRE 804(a). We discuss the remainder of the rule later in the chapter.

2.   Interpretation and Illustration of FRE 804(a): Grounds for a Finding of Unavailability

FRE 804(a) contains a broad, reasonable definition of unavailability that applies to the exceptions under FRE 804(b)(1)-(4), though not to FRE 804(b)(6). Before the adoption of the Federal Rules, what constituted unavailability would vary among jurisdictions and even among hearsay exceptions within a single jurisdiction. For some exceptions, a claim of privilege or absence from the jurisdiction or, occasionally, even absence from the courtroom would suffice. For dying declarations, death was the only acceptable type of unavailability. Now, any of the five subparts may be used for any of the 804(b)(1)-(4) exceptions.

a.   Preliminary Fact-finding

As is generally true in applying the hearsay exceptions, these preliminary questions are to be decided by the judge pursuant to FRE 104(a). Representations of counsel have been held sufficient to establish the absence or unavailability of a witness under FRE 804(a)(5), so long as good-faith efforts have been made to secure the witness, including requests for voluntary attendance and subpoenas. But when the issue is a witness's claim of privilege under FRE 804(a)(1), some courts hold that statements from counsel are insufficient to show that the witness *actually* will not testify. In other words, the witness must claim the privilege in court. Invocation of FRE 804(a)(2) requires the witness's presence in court and a court order directing the witness to testify; FRE 804(a)(3) requires testimony from the witness as to failed memory but not a court order. Evidence that a mental or physical infirmity (confined to home because of heart condition, unable to walk because of back condition, incapacitated by a stroke) will continue for some length of time is usually necessary under FRE 804(a)(4); otherwise, the court may seek a continuance in order to call a witness who is merely ill, if the testimony is significant. United States v. Amaya, 533 F.2d 188 (5th Cir. 1976) (FRE 804(a) requirement of unavailability satisfied by probability that the duration of illness or loss of memory will be long enough so that the trial cannot be postponed).

b.   Preference for Former Testimony or Deposition

FRE 804(a)(5) states a preference for former testimony that applies when the declarant is absent (not deceased). The purpose of FRE 804(a)(5)(B) is to make clear that the proponent of an absent declarant's dying declaration, declaration against interest, or declaration of pedigree must first use the declarant's former testimony or deposition; if none exists, the proponent must make *reasonable efforts to obtain the declarant's deposition testimony* (and seek the declarant's attendance as a witness) as a precondition to the declarant being held to be unavailable. The preference for former testimony, and the requirement of an attempt to depose a declarant, may reflect even stronger suspicion about the reliability of FRE 804(b)(2), (3), and (4) exceptions. After studying these exceptions, you can decide whether this suspicion makes sense.

Unfortunately, this preference sometimes produces problematic results. Where the absent declarant has flatly denied wrongdoing in a deposition taken for a tort case, but has made inculpatory hearsay statements to various people that the defendant seeks to admit, it has been held that the deposition must be used pursuant to FRE 804(a)(5) and that the oral statements are inadmissible for their truth (though, presumably, they could be used to impeach). Campbell v. Coleman Co., 786 F.2d 892 (8th Cir. 1986).

c.   Reasonable Means to Procure Attendance

"Reasonable means" to procure the attendance of an absent witness under FRE 804(a)(5) requires a good-faith effort on the part of the proponent of hearsay, but not the doing of a futile act. In the Ninth Circuit, when the government has the name and address of a foreign witness, some effort must be made to contact that witness in the witness's native country or else a finding of unavailability will be error. United States v. Pena-Gutierrez, 222 F.3d 1080, 1086 (9th Cir. 2000). Offers from the government to pay airfare, met with refusal by the foreign witness, has been held to be a reasonable effort. United States v. Siddiqui, 253 F.3d 1318, 1323-1324 (11th Cir. 2000).

A decision by the government not to personally serve subpoenas on two allegedly unavailable witnesses until after the first day of trial was found not to be "reasonable" absent further extenuating facts. United States v. Pluta, 176 F.3d 43, 48 (2d Cir. 1999); compare United States v. Olafson, 213 F.3d 435 (9th Cir. 2000) (in a criminal case, district court has broad discretion under Fed. R. Crim. P. 15(a) in deciding whether to order a deposition, and it is not unreasonable to refuse to do so when conditions in Mexico make it unsafe for American prosecutors, and there is no indication that the unavailable witnesses would cooperate).

There are also constitutional issues in criminal cases. In Barber v. Page, 390 U.S. 719 (1968), the hearsay declarant was in federal prison in another state, but there was a federal policy to honor subpoenas issued for witnesses to testify. Thus, even though the declarant was technically beyond the subpoena power of the state, it was likely that the prosecutor could have secured the declarant's attendance. The introduction of the declarant's former testimony in these circumstances, the Court held, violated the defendant's Sixth Amendment right to confront witnesses. But in Mancusi v. Stubbs, 408 U.S. 204 (1972), the hearsay declarant was out of country and, unlike the declarant in *Page*, had been extensively cross-examined at an earlier proceeding. The failure to try to contact him before the use of his former testimony was held not to violate the confrontation clause.

d.   *Unavailability Caused by the Proponent*

If a witness is unable to, or refuses to, testify *because of the conduct of the proponent* of the hearsay statement, FRE 804(a) directs that the witness not be found to be unavailable. Proof of threats made against a witness are not enough; there must be an actual finding of presumptive unavailability. United States v. Pizarro, 717 F.2d 336 (7th Cir. 1983). There must also be a finding of "purpose" underlying the proponent's conduct. The government's carelessness in losing custody of a witness, or an inability to keep track of a witness, may not qualify as procurement or wrongdoing that would prevent a finding of unavailability. It has also been held that the government's refusal to grant immunity to a witness who exercises a Fifth Amendment right not to testify is neither "procurement" nor "wrongdoing" and does not negate the witness's status as "unavailable" under FRE 804(a)(1), so that prior testimony may be admissible. United States v. Dolah, 245 F.3d 98, 103 (2d Cir. 2001).

PROBLEM

8.79. Consider which of the following may be sufficient to constitute unavailability for the purposes of satisfying FRE 804(a). What other steps might the proponent have to take before unavailability is adequately proved?

(a)   A criminal defendant asserts the Fifth Amendment privilege not to testify at trial and the defense offers the defendant's own prior testimony.

(b)   A witness invokes the Fifth Amendment privilege against self-incrimination in court.

(c)   The party offering the hearsay evidence submits his or her attorney's affidavit stating that the declarant is in another state beyond the subpoena power of the court.

(d)   The party offering the hearsay evidence submits the declarant's affidavit stating that the declarant does not recall the events in question.

(e)   The hearsay declarant is on the witness stand and claims to have no current memory of the events in question, and the judge believes this testimony.

(f)   The hearsay declarant is on the witness stand and claims to have no current memory of the events in question, and the judge does not believe this testimony.

3.   Interpretation and Illustration of FRE 804(b)(1): Former Testimony

FRE 804(b)(1) states:

(b) *The Exceptions.* The following are not excluded by the rule against hearsay if the declarant is unavailable as a witness:

(1) *Former Testimony.* Testimony that:

(A) was given as a witness at a trial, hearing, or lawful deposition, whether given during the current proceeding or a different one; and

(B) is now offered against a party who had — or, in a civil case, whose predecessor in interest had — an opportunity and similar motive to develop it by direct, cross-, or redirect examination.

a.   *Preliminary Fact-finding*

The foundational requirements for former testimony are:

- the statement must be in the form of testimony given at a hearing or in a "lawful" deposition;
- in a criminal case, the party against whom the statement is being offered must have had an opportunity and similar motive to develop the testimony at the prior hearing or deposition by direct, cross- or redirect examination; and
- in a civil case, either the party against whom the statement is being offered, or a predecessor in interest to that party, must have had an opportunity and similar motive to develop the testimony at the prior hearing or deposition by direct, cross- or redirect examination.

   i.   **"Trial, Hearing or Lawful Deposition."**   This phrase broadly includes transcripts or other recordings of sworn testimony given at a formal adversarial proceeding before a person authorized to administer oaths. It thus includes trials, evidentiary hearings in court, adversarial administrative hearings, and "lawful deposition[s]." This latter phrase simply means a deposition taken in conformity with a procedural code applicable to the proceeding in which the deposition was taken. See, e.g., Fed. R. Civ. P. 30. The former testimony need not have been given in the same case in which the former testimony is currently being offered. In other words, in the case at hand, a party could use FRE 804(b)(1) to offer a transcript of testimony from a prior trial or a deposition taken in a wholly different case. The former trial or deposition might even be from a case in a different court system (such as a state court).

ii.   Opportunity to Develop by Same Party or a Predecessor in Interest. Former testimony of a witness who has become unavailable can be offered against a criminal defendant in the current case so long as that defendant is the one who had the earlier opportunity and similar motive to "develop" that former testimony. It does not matter whether the *former* proceeding in which the testimony was given was criminal or civil.

Where the former testimony of a now-unavailable witness is offered in a *current civil case*, the party against whom the former testimony is being offered need not be the same one who had the earlier opportunity and motive to develop the former testimony. It is permissible if a third-party "precedessor in interest" developed the former testimony. Again, that former testimony may have been given in either a civil or a criminal proceeding. Concern with a criminal defendant's personal opportunity to confront and cross-examine witnesses underlies this FRE 804(b)(1)'s differing treatment of criminal and civil cases.

iii.   Opportunity and Similar Motive. Consider the following example:

> Paula has sued Drew for personal injuries caused in an automobile accident. Wilma, a passenger in Drew's car, testifies for Paula that Drew was drunk at the time and had been driving on the wrong side of the road. There is a judgment for Paula, but the judgment is reversed on appeal because of improper jury instructions and a new trial is ordered. Wilma dies before the retrial, so Paula offers a transcript of Wilma's testimony from the first trial.

Even though Wilma's former testimony is hearsay, it will be admissible against Drew in the retrial under FRE 804(b)(1). All of the foundational requirements are satisfied. Wilma's statement was given at the first trial, obviously a *hearing*. Drew was the adverse party at that trial. Because exactly the same factual issues about which Wilma testified are disputed in the retrial, Drew's *motive* to develop the testimony fully was as great at the first trial as it is now. Moreover, Drew had an *opportunity* to develop the testimony through cross-examination. And it is clear that opportunity is enough, even if Drew did not take advantage of it. Nor is it necessary that the former testimony have been given in a trial or formal hearing: So long as the opportunity and similar motive requirements are satisfied, testimony taken in Wilma's deposition during discovery could be admitted under FRE 804(b)(1) as well.

Similar motive does not mean identical motive, thus a factual inquiry is required. Courts have identified several factors to be considered in determining whether a prior party, in a prior proceeding, had a sufficiently similar motive to develop the testimony of a witness. Most plainly, the questioner must be on the same side of the same issue at both proceedings, and must have a substantially similar interest in asserting and prevailing on the issue. United States v. DiNapoli, 8 F.3d 909, 912 (2d Cir. 1993). In addition:

> Circumstances or factors which influence motive to develop testimony include "(1) the type of proceeding in which the testimony [was] given, (2) trial strategy, (3) the potential penalties or financial stakes, and (4) the number of issues and parties." [United States v. Reed, 227 F.3d 763, 768 (7th Cir. 2000).]

Similarity between the factual issues in dispute in the first and second proceedings also influence a party's motive to develop the witness's testimony. For example, in

McKnight v. Johnson Controls, Inc., 36 F.3d 1396 (8th Cir. 1994), a personal injury case against the manufacturer of a car battery that exploded, the deposition testimony from another suit against the manufacturer, given by a witness who had been injured by a similar explosion, was properly admitted under FRE 804(b)(1). In Schmidt v. Duo-Fast Corp., 1976 U.S. Dist. LEXIS 6106 (E.D. Pa. 1996), however, a witness's testimony from a prior suit against the defendant that was based on a "ricochet" accident involving defendant's pneumatic nailer machine was not admitted into a later case based on a "bumpfire" accident involving the same machine. The differing nature of the two accidents may have affected trial strategy and thus the defendant did not have a similar motive to examine that witness in the two cases.

   iv.   **No Opportunity.**   In some proceedings where the former testimony was given, a party had no meaningful opportunity to examine the witness. In United States v. Deeb, 13 F.3d 1532 (11th Cir. 1994), defendant was a fugitive from justice, tried in absentia, and was not represented. Testimony taken against him was not admissible in a later proceeding under FRE 804(b)(1). If the former testimony is taken at a proceeding where, due to its nature or due to the conduct of the judge, a party was present but had no meaningful opportunity to develop testimony, courts have held that the prior testimony is inadmissible under FRE 804(b)(1). In re Paducah Towing Co., 692 F.2d 412 (6th Cir. 1982) (Coast Guard employee did not have necessary skills to test an expert witness's qualifications at the first hearing, and was not permitted to impeach the witness; held, no adequate opportunity to examine the witness).

   v.   **No Requirement of "Offered on Same Issue."**   Before FRE 804(b)(1), some cases articulated a requirement that the evidence had to be offered on the same *legal* issue. Apart from ensuring that the motive to develop the testimony is the same, however, there is no reason to insist that the legal issue be precisely the same. Assume, for example, that the judgment in our Paula v. Drew hypothetical was reversed because the jury was instructed to apply a gross negligence rather than a negligence standard to the defendant's conduct. Wilma's former testimony should not be precluded at the second trial because the issue to which the testimony relates is now somewhat different. The testimony is undoubtedly still relevant, and it is difficult to believe that the motive of the parties to develop the testimony is any different because of the different legal standard against which the defendant's culpability will be measured. Appropriately, FRE 804(b)(1) makes no reference to an "offered on same legal issue" requirement.

b.   *Justification for the Admissibility of Former Testimony*

   A principal justification for admitting former testimony under FRE 804(b)(1) is necessity. Since Wilma is dead, the choice is not between live testimony or hearsay, but rather hearsay or nothing. This all-or-nothing choice, of course, always exists when the hearsay declarant is unavailable (although there may sometimes be other relevant evidence on the same point, so the need for the hearsay will in fact vary from case to case). Although perhaps the law should be otherwise, the all-or-nothing choice is not itself enough to justify the admission of hearsay evidence. There must also be circumstantial guarantees of trustworthiness or some other reasons to justify the loss of the opportunity for cross-examination.

The *prior* opportunity and motive to develop testimony are important justifications for the lack of present cross-examination. If Drew's cross-examination of Wilma had cast any doubt on the truth of what Wilma said, Drew could introduce relevant parts of the cross-examination at the retrial. In fact, given the oath, courtroom formalities and the prior opportunity to develop testimony, prior testimony seems far closer to live testimony than any of the Rule 803 exceptions.

Yet the reason for imposing an unavailability limitation on use of former testimony is readily apparent. Without such a limitation, parties could make wholesale substitutions of former trial transcripts for live testimony in cases retried after a hung jury, mistrial, or reversal on appeal. Indeed, depositions or preliminary hearing transcripts could be substituted wholesale for live witness testimony in the initial trial. Plainly, the drafters of the rule wished to avoid such eventualities.

4.   Elaboration of FRE 804(b)(1)

Variations on the Paula v. Drew lawsuit illustrate additional applications of FRE 804(b)(1).

a.   *The Opportunity to Develop Testimony*

Although usually thought of as cross-examination, the requirement of an opportunity to develop testimony has a broader meaning:

> Wilma, called as a witness by Paula at the first trial, surprised Paula by testifying on direct examination that Paula had been speeding and that Paula drove across the center line and hit Drew's car. At the second trial, Drew offers this former testimony, and Paula objects on the ground that she did not have an opportunity to cross-examine Wilma.

Under FRE 804(b)(1), it does not matter that Paula did not have an opportunity to "cross-examine" Wilma. It is sufficient, in the language of the exception, that Paula had the opportunity and similar motive "to develop the testimony by *direct*, cross, or *redirect* examination" (emphasis added). FRE 804(b)(1) specifically permits a party to impeach the credibility of any witness, including a witness called by the party, under FRE 607. And, as we discussed in Chapter Two on pages 91-100, supra, FRE 611 sets forth general guidelines for the "mode and order" of presenting evidence and provides sufficient flexibility for Paula to develop fully and to explore weaknesses in Wilma's testimony. Thus, unless the trial judge unduly restricted Paula's direct and redirect examination, she has nothing about which to complain.

b.   *Identity of Parties*

Returning to the original hypothetical in which Wilma testifies for Paula and adversely to Drew, what if another party, not Paula, offers Wilma's testimony against Drew at another proceeding?

> Rhoda, another passenger in Paula's car, has sued Drew for her own personal injuries. By the time Rhoda's case goes to trial, Wilma has died, and Rhoda offers Wilma's

testimony from the first Paula v. Drew trial about Drew's being drunk and driving on the wrong side of the road.

Some of the older former testimony cases speak of an "identity of parties" requirement. Under FRE 804(b)(1), however, there is no requirement that the party *offering the former testimony* must have been a party to the original proceeding in which the testimony was given. Rather, it is sufficient if the party *against whom the evidence is offered* had an opportunity to develop the testimony. In our hypothetical, since Drew had an opportunity to develop the testimony, it does not matter that the person now offering the testimony is Rhoda rather than Paula as long as the "similar motive" requirement is also satisfied.

c.   Former Testimony Offered Against a Party Who Was Not a Party to the Original Action

What if Paula offers Wilma's testimony against a new party—someone who was an outsider to the original Paula v. Drew trial?

> Paula now sues Barney to recover damages for her injuries in the accident with Drew. Barney is the owner of the tavern where Drew had been drinking before the accident. Wilma has died, and Paula offers Wilma's testimony from the first Paula v. Drew trial about Drew's being drunk and driving on the wrong side of the road.

We know that in a criminal case, former testimony cannot be offered under FRE 804(b)(1) against a defendant who was not a party to the first proceeding. Offering Wilma's testimony against Barney, even in a civil case, is somewhat troublesome. Here, Barney did not have an opportunity to develop Wilma's testimony when it was given. He was not a party to that proceeding. Of course Barney can use the prior cross-examination of Wilma from the first trial. But this is, in effect, to impose upon him Drew's selection of counsel. If Drew was represented by a mediocre attorney who did not do a good job of cross-examining Wilma, Barney would be stuck with that result even though his attorney might have done a substantially better job of discrediting Wilma. On the other hand, Drew did have the opportunity to develop the testimony and to discredit Wilma's opinion that Drew was drunk, and his motive for doing so was identical to Barney's. Given the fact that the alternative is to forgo highly relevant evidence, whatever Drew's lawyer accomplished with the cross-examination of Wilma is arguably sufficient to permit admission of the evidence against Barney. Moreover, as a practical matter, Drew himself may not have been aware of the skills or able to control the actions of his attorney. Thus, while it may at first blush sound unfair to characterize use of the evidence against Barney as sticking Barney with Drew's choice of an attorney, it may be no more "unfair" to do this than to stick Drew with the choice of attorney that he initially made and that he may later regret.

i.   In a Civil Case, the Party in the Former Proceeding May Also Be a Predecessor in Interest.   The Federal Rules as originally promulgated by the Supreme Court permitted the use of former testimony *whenever* the party against whom the evidence is offered *or some third person with a similar motive* had the opportunity to develop the testimony. The Judiciary Committee of the House of Representatives, however, took the view that

> it is generally unfair to impose upon the party against whom the hearsay evidence is being offered responsibility for the manner in which the witness was previously handled by another party. The sole exception to this, in the Committee's view, is when a party's predecessor in interest in a civil action or proceeding had an opportunity and similar motive to examine the witness.

As a result, the existing language of Rule 804(b)(1) regarding development of testimony by a *predecessor in interest* was added.

ii.   What Is a Predecessor in Interest?   Is Drew a *predecessor in interest* to Barney? Cases decided soon after the enactment of FRE 804(b)(1) interpreted the statutory language and legislative history in, broadly speaking, three different ways. Some interpreted the term *predecessor in interest* narrowly, to include only relationships in which individuals stand in privity to each other in some traditional property or contract law sense. Under this view, Drew would not be a predecessor in interest to Barney. Other courts expanded the notion of privity somewhat more broadly to include, for example, subsidiary and parent corporations, or co-employees such as a district attorney and a city solicitor. More recently, courts have adopted the more liberal approach of equating *interest* with *motive*, just as the rule was originally drafted: Any party to an earlier proceeding who had a similar motive to develop the testimony fully is a predecessor in interest. Under this interpretation, since the same factual issues are in dispute in both the first and the second proceeding, and Drew and Barney are on the same side of those issues with the same interest in discrediting Wilma's opinion, Drew would have had a similar motive to develop Wilma's testimony and would be considered a predecessor in interest to Barney.

d.   Lack of Similar Motive Due to Difference in Procedural Context

In some procedural contexts, parties do not have the same motive to develop a witness's testimony that they will have later at a full trial on the merits. United States v. Powell, 894 F.2d 895 (7th Cir. 1990) (no error to exclude criminal defendant's offer of former testimony given by the witness at his guilty plea hearing; the government's motive to test the voluntariness of the plea, and its factual basis, is not the same as at a trial).

In United States v. Salerno, 505 U.S. 317 (1992), the Supreme Court considered the question whether grand jury testimony could be offered *by a criminal defendant*, against the government, when grand jury witnesses were unavailable due to an assertion of privilege. The witnesses DeMatteis and Bruno had been presented to the grand jury by a member of the prosecution team. Their grand jury testimony, however, tended to exculpate the defendant. The prosecutor, presumably, then had a motive to develop their testimony—that is, to impeach or challenge it. At trial, the defendant sought to use the former testimony of DeMatteis and Bruno in his own defense. The government admitted that it was the "same party," but contended that it had not had, and would indeed never have, a "similar motive" to develop testimony at a grand jury proceeding as it would at trial: "A prosecutor . . . must maintain secrecy during the investigatory stages of the criminal process and therefore may not desire to confront grand jury witnesses with contradictory evidence . . . [A] prosecutor may not know, prior to indictment, which issues will have importance at trial. . . . " Id. at 325. The Supreme Court held that this argument had to be addressed and remanded the case to the Second Circuit.

On remand, the court held en banc that the grand jury testimony should not have been admitted under FRE 804(b)(1):

> The proper approach . . . [to similarity of motive] must consider whether the party resisting the offered testimony at a pending proceeding has at a prior proceeding an interest of substantially similar intensity to prove (or disprove) the same side of a substantially similar issue. The nature of the two proceedings—both what is at stake and the applicable burden of proof—and, to a lesser extent, the cross-examination at the prior proceeding—both what was undertaken and what was foregone—will be relevant though not conclusive on the ultimate issue of similarity of motive. [United States v. DiNapoli, 8 F.3d 909 (2d Cir. 1993).]

The Second Circuit believed that the government had no motive to press these particular witnesses at the grand jury hearing because the defendants had already been indicted. Because the grand jury was already persuaded that a conspiracy existed, the government had little incentive to attack DeMatteis's and Bruno's exculpating testimony. The prosecutor did attack them somewhat, by accusing them of lying and confronting them with contradictory evidence. The court held that this was not full-blown cross-examination, and that the questions were carefully limited to matters already publicly disclosed. Thus, no secret information was used, as it might be at trial.

In light of the holdings in *Salerno* and *DiNapoli*, perhaps the admissibility of preliminary hearing testimony given by a government witness against a criminal defendant should be rethought. Traditionally, preliminary hearing testimony can be admitted under FRE 804(b)(1) against the defendant later at trial, despite the fact that the defendant had little actual motive to develop the testimony fully at the preliminary hearing. However,

> (1) the preliminary hearing is at such an early stage of the proceedings that the defendant may not have sufficient information to cross-examine the witness adequately; (2) like the prosecutor at the grand jury, the defendant at the preliminary hearing has no wish to "tip his hand" by aggressive cross-examination, and would much prefer to attack the witness at trial; and (3) because of the minimal standard of proof, it is often a foregone conclusion that the defendant will lose at the preliminary hearing, so that any attempted cross-examination or impeachment of inculpatory witnesses will be so much wasted effort at that point . . . [Stephen A. Saltzburg, Michael M. Martin and Daniel J. Capra, Federal Rules of Evidence Manual 1838 (7th ed. 1998).]

These concerns about the adequacy of opportunity to cross-examine will also affect the defendant's right to confrontation under *Crawford* if preliminary hearing testimony is offered at trial. See Section G, infra.

e.   Method of Introducing Former Testimony

When former testimony is admissible, any witness with present knowledge of the content of the former testimony can relate what was said. In theory, this could be someone who heard the testimony in person at the former proceeding. However, by far the most common method of getting former testimony before the fact finder is to introduce a properly authenticated transcript of the testimony. Use of a transcript for this purpose actually involves multiple hearsay. First, there is the out-of-court statement of the now unavailable witness; second, there is the activity of the court reporter in taking down what the witness says; and third, there is the activity of the court reporter in making a transcript of the testimony. The business or official records exceptions of FRE 803(6) and (8) will generally apply to the court reporter's hearsay.

Courts generally allow counsel to use varying methods to introduce former testimony. If the former testimony was videotaped, the relevant portion of the video can simply be played for the jury.

f.   Objections to the Contents of the Former Testimony

Regardless of what method is used to introduce former testimony, there is a possibility that the former testimony may itself be objectionable for some reason. For example, the former testimony may have been elicited in response to a leading question; it may have contained an impermissible lay opinion; it may have been privileged; or it may recite inadmissible hearsay. In these types of situations, the question arises whether objections can be made to exclude former testimony that meets all the requirements of the former testimony exception. The Federal Rules do not address this issue. McCormick, after noting that some courts say always and other courts say never, states:

> The more widely approved view, however, is that objections which go merely to the form of the testimony—as on the ground of leading questions, unresponsiveness, or opinion—must be made at the original hearing when they can be corrected. On the other hand, objections that go to the relevancy or the competency of the evidence may be asserted for the first time when the former testimony is offered at the present trial. [McCormick on Evidence, Vol. 2 §306, at 358 (Kenneth S. Broun, ed. 6th ed. 2006).]

KEY POINTS

1. Assuming unavailability, testimony given at a prior hearing (or deposition) may be admitted against a civil party or a criminal party if that party was present at the prior hearing, had a meaningful opportunity to examine the witness, and had the same motive to examine the witness as at the current trial.

2. The party may not have had the same motive at the prior hearing if different facts are at issue in the two proceedings, or if the procedural context in the prior hearing eliminated the party's incentive to fully examine the witness.

3. Testimony given at a prior hearing (or deposition) may also be admitted against a civil party if a predecessor in interest to that party—someone with the same motive because disputing the same factual issues—had the opportunity to examine the witness at the prior hearing.

PROBLEMS

8.80. David Bond and his parents have sued David's treating physicians and their practice group for medical malpractice in failing to diagnose David's extremely rare form of encephalitis. Defendants noticed a deposition of plaintiffs' expert witness,

Dr. Lakeman, whose test of David's cerebral spinal fluid was positive for this disease whereas defendants' test, administered one day previously, was negative. At trial, Dr. Lakeman is unavailable and plaintiffs seek the admission of his deposition pursuant to FRE 804(b)(1). Defendants object on the grounds that they did not have a "similar motive" to develop Lakeman's testimony because Lakeman's deposition was a "discovery" deposition. They intended to discover Lakeman's opinions and the basis for those opinions; they asked open-ended questions to produce answers to submit to their own experts for review; and they were not prepared and did not cross-examine Lakeman to challenge or discredit his opinions. What result?

8.81. Alex and Brenda Dawson are suing the Delta Insurance Company for the loss they sustained when a warehouse they jointly owned was destroyed in a fire. Delta has refused payment because a clause in the policy precludes recovery in the event that either owner is responsible for damage to the property. The insurance company claims that Alex arranged to have Eddy Hall burn the building. Eddy pleaded guilty to arson and testified against Alex at Alex's arson trial, which resulted in a hung jury. Eddy falls ill in prison and is not available to testify in the current action. Delta offers a properly authenticated transcript of Eddy's testimony at Alex's arson trial. Alex objects on the ground that he now has new evidence with which to impeach Eddy; Brenda objects on the ground that she did not have any opportunity to cross-examine Eddy. How should the court rule?

8.82. Defendant was charged with interstate transmission of child pornography via computer. At trial, after the government rested its case, defendant sought the admission of the transcript of a witness's grand jury testimony in lieu of live testimony. The court found the witness to be unavailable. In the grand jury proceeding, the following had occurred: The witness testified that she resided with defendant during the time of his alleged illegal activity, that she had access to his computer with his own password, and that she never saw any child pornography. The prosecutor had then asked about her opportunity for observing the pornography, whether she had seen a particular digital image, and then explored the witness's relationship with defendant and their living arrangements.

The government objects to the admission of the grand jury testimony on the basis of United States v. Salerno, page 552, supra. What result?

5.   Interpretation and Illustration of FRE 804(b)(2): Dying Declarations

FRE 804(b)(2) provides:

(b) *The Exceptions.* The following are not excluded by the rule against hearsay if the declarant is unavailable as a witness:

. . .

(2) *Statement Under the Belief of Imminent Death.* In a prosecution for homicide or in a civil case, a statement that the declarant, while believing the declarant's death to be imminent, made about its cause or circumstances.

a.   Preliminary Fact-finding

The foundational requirements for dying declarations are:

- the statement concerns the cause or circumstances of what the declarant believes is impending death;

- the statement is made while the declarant believes death to be imminent; and
- the statement is offered in a homicide prosecution or a civil case.

Statements concerning the cause or circumstances of the declarant's death include identifications of the perpetrator and descriptions of accidents and of past events that led up to the mortal injury or disease. Even though the belief in imminent death may *generally* enhance a declarant's sincerity, contents other than the cause or circumstances of death are not included within the exception. Does the hearsay statement have to concern the cause of only the declarant's death, or could it extend to the cause of death of another? The language of FRE 804(b)(2) appears to be ambiguous on this point, but presumably it means the declarant's *own* death.

A belief in imminent death means the lack of hope of recovery—"a settled hopeless expectation that death is near at hand and what is said must have been spoken in the hush of its impending presence." Shepard v. United States, 290 U.S. 96, 100 (1933). This state of mind can be shown by the declarant's own statement, by circumstances such as the nature of the declarant's wound, by evidence that the declarant was told that death was imminent, or by the opinion of a physician. Vazquez v. National Car Rental System, Inc., 24 F. Supp. 2d 197 (D.P.R. 1998). This preliminary question is to be decided by the judge, pursuant to FRE 104(a). Thus, the jury is not instructed that it must find the declarant's belief in imminent death before it may consider the statement, but evidence that tends to show that the declarant did not have this belief may be used by the opponent to argue to the jury that the statement is not reliable.

Note that the relevant inquiry is the declarant's subjective belief of imminent death: It need not be shown that the declarant in fact died. McCormick on Evidence, Vol. 2, §310, at 367 (Kenneth S. Broun ed., 6th ed. 2006) ("The Federal Rules do not require that the declarant must be dead, only unavailable."). This is implicit in FRE 804(a)(5)(B), which contemplates situations in which a "dying declarant" is unavailable because "absent from the trial or hearing." That form of unavailability is distinguished from absence due to death or physical incapacity in FRE 804(a)(4).

Homicide defendants have invoked the dying declaration exception in homicide cases to show that some third person committed the murder. As a practical matter, however, it will usually be prosecutors who want to take advantage of the dying declaration exception.

b.   *Justification for the Admissibility of Dying Declarations*

The dying declaration exception is one of the oldest common law exceptions to the rule excluding hearsay. It is also one of the most problematic in terms of the soundness of its underlying rationale. The necessity rationale for the exception is twofold. As usual, the unavailability of the declarant means that there may not be another means of obtaining the same or similar evidence. Reliability inheres in the notion that people who realize that death is imminent will be especially likely to be sincere, since their condition obviates any motive to misstate the truth. Or, declarants may believe it is in their interest to "meet their maker" with clean hands, or least with hands that have not recently been soiled by falsehood.

However, both the necessity and reliability justifications for this exception are subject to criticism. It is not clear that the need for a dying declarant's statement about the cause or circumstances of death is any greater than the need for the statements of any unavailable witness. There may be an absence of available eyewitnesses to all sorts of events; and there may be alternative forms of evidence available to prove the cause of death in a homicide or civil case.

The notion that dying declarations are likely to be reliable is also suspect. The proposition that individuals who believe death is imminent are particularly likely to be sincere is sheer speculation. There is no requirement that dying declarants be shown to be religious, and no requirement of other circumstances that reduce a motive to misrepresent the cause of death. Furthermore, even if one assumes that dying declarants are likely to be sincere, the circumstances surrounding a dying declaration may exacerbate other hearsay dangers. If the declarant is the victim of a sudden attack, there is reason to question the accuracy of the victim's perceptions. Additionally, an individual who is suffering enough to believe that death is imminent may have somewhat reduced capacities for narration and memory.

There are additional indications of doubt about the justifications for the admission of dying declarations. In some jurisdictions the party against whom a dying declaration is admitted is entitled to a jury instruction that these statements are to be considered with caution. And the limitation to homicide cases was generated by the concern of the House Judiciary Committee: "The Committee did not consider dying declarations as among the most reliable forms of hearsay. Consequently, it amended the provision to limit their admissibility in criminal cases to homicide prosecutions, where exceptional need for the evidence is present." What this means, of course, is that we are willing to use evidence whose reliability we question in order to obtain criminal convictions that carry the most severe sanctions!

KEY POINT

Assuming unavailability, statements made by a declarant who believes that death is imminent are admissible in civil cases and in homicide cases so long as the contents of the statement concern the cause or circumstances of the declarant's impending death.

6.   Interpretation and Illustration of FRE 804(b)(3): Declarations Against Interest

FRE 804(b)(3) states:

(b) *The Exceptions.* The following are not excluded by the rule against hearsay if the declarant is unavailable as a witness:

. . .

(3) *Statement Against Interest.* A statement that:

(A) a reasonable person in the declarant's position would have made only if the person believed it to be true because, when made, it was so contrary to the declarant's proprietary or pecuniary interest or had so great a tendency to invalidate the declarant's claim against someone else or to expose the declarant to civil or criminal liability; and

(B) is supported by corroborating circumstances that clearly indicate its trustworthiness, if it is offered in a criminal case as one that tends to expose the declarant to criminal liability.

a. Preliminary Fact-finding

The foundational requirements for declarations against interest are:

- the content of the statement, at the time the statement was made, was
  - against the pecuniary or proprietary interest of the declarant;
  - could subject the declarant to civil or criminal liability; or
  - could render invalid a claim held by the declarant;
- the statement was against any of the above interests of the declarant to an extent great enough such that a reasonable person, in declarant's position, would not have made such a statement unless it was true; and
- if the statement exposes the declarant to criminal liability and is offered to exculpate the accused, evidence of corroborating circumstances that clearly indicate the trustworthiness of the statement must be offered.

i. Content Against Interest. The focus of the *against-interest* requirement is usually on the content of the statement. This content must be contrary to one of the specific interests of the declarant identified in the rule when the statement is made. At trial, the statement is offered to prove the truth of those facts. Assume, for example, that Mark tells a friend that he owes a lot of money to Ryan. The fact of owing money is against Mark's *pecuniary* interest. Suppose Mark told his friend that he had robbed a convenience store in order to pay the debt. This statement could subject Mark to criminal liability and thus would be against Mark's *penal* interest. We assume that people in general have an interest in maintaining ownership of their money as well as their possessions, so Mark's statement that he owes money should qualify as contrary to his proprietary interest as well.

To be against a declarant's pecuniary, penal, or civil claim interests, a statement under FRE 804(b)(3) need not have been said in the face of immediate adverse consequences. For instance, the rule does not require that Mark's admission of robbing the store have been made to a police officer; conversely, Mark's belief that his friend would keep his statements confidential does not alter their against-interest quality. A better test is whether the statements would harm Mark's interest if disclosed publicly or to the relevant authorities.

Nevertheless, in other respects the context of the statement does matter: Sometimes a statement that on its face appears to be against interest is not in fact against the declarant's interest because of the surrounding circumstances. A statement by Mark that he owes Ryan $500 may not be against Mark's interest if Mark knows that Ryan claims that the debt is really $2,000. If the facts in the statement can no longer cause trouble for the declarant (e.g., he has been convicted of the crime whereof he speaks) then the against-interest element may not be satisfied. And as we discuss on page 560, infra, if the context within which the statement is made gives the declarant a strong self-serving motive, then the exception may not apply. On the other hand, although one might confess a crime to a spouse or close friend and expect the confession never to be disclosed, in admitting such statements courts typically focus and rely on the against-interest content of the facts disclosed.

ii.   Ascertaining the Declarant's Knowledge.   The declarant's knowledge comes up in two different senses under FRE 804(b)(3). Like other FRE 803 and 804 exceptions, FRE 804(b)(3) requires a showing that the declarant (Mark) had personal knowledge of the against-interest fact when the statement was made.

In addition, FRE 804(b)(3) applies only if Mark knows (or reasonably should know) that the fact is against his interest. If particular facts affect the declarant's assessment of what is against interest, then these facts will be taken into account. FRE 804(b)(3) calls for evaluation of the probable understanding of an individual by asking what a reasonable person in that individual's position would be thinking; and we typically apply "objective," reasonable person standards in light of the circumstances and facts known to the particular individual whose conduct or statement is at issue. In most cases, it will be relatively easy to determine that the declarant knows the statement is "against interest."

iii.   Distinct from Party Admission.   It is important, as we suggested earlier, not to confuse FRE 801(d)(2)(A) admissions of a party with declarations against interest. You can see that FRE 804(b)(3) requires many more foundational requirements. It also applies to statements made by anyone, not just a party, and is typically not offered against the person who made the statement (and who is unavailable) but against someone else.

b.   Justification for the Admissibility of Declarations Against Interest

The content of Mark's statement that he owes money reflects damage to his pecuniary interest. This against-interest factor is thought to give the statement a sufficient circumstantial guarantee of trustworthiness to warrant admissibility, at least if the alternative is forgoing the evidence altogether, which it is since the exception requires unavailability. The underlying theory of human behavior is that most people generally tell the truth in the absence of a motive to lie, and motivations to lie are nearly always self-serving: statements against interest, which are the opposite of self-serving by definition, are thus seen as reflecting an absence of a motive to lie. Such a statement is therefore likely to be reliable, even though oath and cross-examination are lacking. The other types of interests that are included within the exception—not being subjected to civil and criminal liability, possessing valid claims against others—are also assumed to be important enough that people should have no reason to lie if they say something that reflects badly on such interests. Some courts speak of a requirement to show that the declarant did not have a motive to lie, but this is not an independent requirement for the exception.

7.   Elaboration of FRE 804(b)(3)

a.   Doubts About the Underlying Rationale for the Exception

The most serious problem with the declaration against interest exception, in our view, is its empirical assumptions. The first premise underlying the exception, with which we agree, is that people seldom intentionally state facts that truly reflect against their interest. We find troublesome, however, the next inference: that if such statements are made they would not be lies, and therefore are likely to be trustworthy. It seems much more likely that a statement that appears to be against interest is in fact not against interest, but reflects an ulterior motive that may be difficult to discern.

Most statements that are characterized as declarations against interest are likely to fall into one of two categories:

i. Mixed Motive Statements. "Mixed motive" statements *appear* to be against interest but have a high risk of being unreliable if there was an ulterior self-interested motive for making the statement. For example, a declarant might say he owes money in order to justify asking the listener for a loan; the declarant may "admit" robbing a convenience store or dealing drugs to impress the listener. Numerous criminal cases involve statements to law enforcement officials made by declarants who both admit culpability while also blaming others in order to curry favor with the authorities, or to secure immunity from prosecution.

Sometimes, however, there may not be much available information bearing on the real motivation of the declarant and the court may fail to see that the declarant also had a self-serving reason to make the statement. Examples of cases in which conflicting motives were recognized are Donovan v. Crisostomo, 689 F.2d 869 (9th Cir. 1982) (statements of foreign employees that they did not work overtime were not declarations against their pecuniary interest, because they may have been motivated to make the statements to avoid being sent back to their country of origin), and United States v. Bobo, 994 F.2d 524 (8th Cir. 1993) (in a prosecution for possession of a firearm, no error to exclude the defendant's brother's statement that a gun was his, and not the defendant's; court distrusted the brother's motive and the timing of the statement just before trial). If courts do not discern such mixed motives, untrustworthy statements may be admitted.

ii. Statements Made with No Motive to Lie. The second type of admitted statements are reliable statements whose reliability has more to do with lack of motivation to lie and less to do with their against-interest characterization. Mark's statement that he owes money may be, to him, merely a neutral recitation of a fact. The fact that the statement may be characterized as being against interest may have nothing to do with its sincerity. In this respect the statement is no different from many other hearsay statements that do not fall within the declaration against interest (or any other hearsay) exception.

b.   Requirement of Corroboration for Statements Against Penal Interest Offered to Exculpate the Accused

FRE 804(b)(3) imposes special corroboration requirements on declarations against penal interest that are offered by defendants in criminal cases to exculpate themselves. In such cases, an out-of-court declarant has made a statement assuming criminal responsibility for the crime with which the defendant is charged. The requirement is framed in terms of "corroborating circumstances" that "clearly indicate the trustworthiness of the statement." See United States v. Vega, 221 F.3d 789 (5th Cir. 2000). Courts look to circumstances that corroborate either the content of the statement (other evidence that the facts that exculpate the defendant are true) or the trustworthiness of the declarant (voluntariness, lack of motive to curry favor, lack of subsequent inconsistent statements). Recantation of exculpatory statements, and assertions of the Fifth Amendment privilege have been held to weigh against trustworthiness. United States v. Davis, 2001 WL 524374 (D.C. Cir. 2001).

Prior to an amendment in 2001, FRE 804(b)(3) was written to require corroboration only of exculpatory statements against interest offered by an accused. Classic examples would include purported admissions of guilt by declarants other than the defendant who had since died, disappeared, or asserted the privilege against self-incrimination. The drafters of the original version of the rule were undoubtedly concerned about the fabrication of exculpatory evidence in criminal cases. Without the corroboration requirement, it could arguably be relatively easy for someone (most likely a convicted criminal) to make a false confession to the defendant's crime in order to help a friend who has not yet been convicted. Similarly, the drafters may have been concerned about the ease with which a made-up confession could be attributed to a declarant known to be unavailable—perhaps one who has absconded or died. Strictly speaking, this concern is not a hearsay problem. The witness whom the drafters fear will fabricate the against-interest statement of an unavailable declarant will himself be on the witness stand and subject to cross-examination. Nevertheless, the corroboration requirement is part of the rule.

Notwithstanding these concerns, and the corroboration requirement for the particular category of statements against interest, doubts about the credibility of the testifying witness should not be a factor in assessing the trustworthiness of the *declarant's* statement. United States v. Atkins, 558 F.2d 133 (3d Cir. 1977).

c.   *Statements That Inculpate Accomplices*

Mixed motive statements raise special, recurring problems in criminal cases. Consider a case in which prosecutors have charged two defendants, Worrell and Holmes, with robbing a bank. Holmes makes a written confession to the crime at the police station and in the confession names Worrell as his accomplice. At Worrell's separate trial, Holmes successfully asserts his Fifth Amendment right not to testify and is therefore unavailable. The prosecutors offer Holmes's written confession against Worrell, arguing that it is a statement against the penal interest of the declarant, Holmes under FRE 804(b)(3).

A key question presented in cases of potential statements against penal interest that inculpate the defendant in addition to the hearsay declarant will be whether the statement constitutes "testimonial" hearsay under Crawford v. Washington. If it does, then the statement is barred by the confrontation clause, unless the defendant had a prior opportunity to cross-examine the declarant and the declarant is currently unavailable. Inadmissibility under the confrontation clause cuts off any inquiry into whether the statement qualifies for admission under FRE 804(b)(3). Any statement given under police questioning at the station house, whether a written confession as in the Worrell-Holmes hypothetical or tape recorded interview, as in *Crawford* itself, plainly falls within the core application of the *Crawford* definition. But what about more casual hearsay statements? Lower courts have recently begun to struggle with the contours of the "testimonial" definition, as will be discussed in Section G, infra.

If the hearsay offered under FRE 804(b)(3) is held to be not testimonial, then it is necessary to analyze whether a mixed motive statement like Holmes's is truly against the declarant's interest. Pre-*Crawford* authorities analyzing this question in the context of statements made to law enforcement have held that FRE 804(b)(3) should not allow admission of statements that inculpate purported accomplices unless they also specifically self-inculpate the declarant as well. A broad narrative that is only generally self-inculpatory might not be found to be sufficiently against interest, while statements that intertwine self-inculpation could be genuinely against the interest of the declarant; for example, "I hid the gun in Joe's apartment" could show both self-incrimination and Joe's involvement. See Williamson v. United States, 512 U.S. 594 (1994); United States v. McClesky, 228 F.3d 640, 643 (6th Cir. 2000); United States v. Westmoreland, 240 F.3d 618, 626 (7th Cir. 2001).

d.   The Corroboration Requirement as Applied to Inculpatory Statements

Critics of the original corroboration requirement in FRE 804(b)(3), which applied only to exculpatory statements, argued that if penal interest statements are less reliable and require corroboration, there is no reason to limit the requirement solely to exculpatory statements. In 2001, FRE 804(b)(3) extended the corroboration requirement for penal interest statements that inculpate and are offered by the prosecution against the accused. Note that such statements would necessarily take the form of mixed motive statements by a declarant other than the accused, as described in the previous section. This is so because inculpatory admissions by an accused would be admissible as an opposing party's own statement under FRE 801(d)(1)(A). If such a mixed motive statement were found to have been made in an informal, spontaneous setting to someone unconnected with law enforcement, there is an argument that the statement is nontestimonial and thus falls outside *Crawford*. (See confrontation clause discussion, infra, section G.) In such a case, it would presumably be governed by the corroboration requirement.

KEY POINTS

1. Assuming unavailability, statements that are against the declarant's pecuniary, proprietary, penal, or civil liability interest may be admissible. The statement must be so far against that interest that a reasonable person would not be lying when making that statement.

2. In order to determine whether the statement is against interest, the court should examine the situation and motives of the declarant.

3. Statements of fact that inculpate others, made in the context of a self-inculpating statement, are admissible only if each specific statement is against the declarant's interest. Courts are divided as to whether such statements, made in custody, can be admitted as against the declarant's interest.

4. Statements against penal interest offered by a criminal defendant for exoneration must be corroborated as to contents, the trustworthiness of the declarant, or both.

8.   Interpretation and Illustration of FRE 804(b)(4): Statements of Personal or Family History

FRE 804(b)(4) provides:

(b) *The Exceptions.* The following are not excluded by the rule against hearsay if the declarant is unavailable as a witness:

. . .

(4) *Statement of Personal or Family History.* A statement about:
(A) the declarant's own birth, adoption, legitimacy, ancestry, marriage, divorce, relationship by blood, adoption, or marriage, or similar facts of personal or family history, even though the declarant had no way of acquiring personal knowledge about that fact; or
(B) another person concerning any of these facts, as well as death, if the declarant was related to the person by blood, adoption, or marriage or was so intimately associated with the person's family that the declarant's information is likely to be accurate.

a.   Preliminary Fact-finding

The foundational requirements for statements of personal or family history are:

- the content must concern the declarant's own personal or family history; or
- the statement concerns the personal or family history of one to whom the declarant is related or was intimately associated.

i.   Personal Knowledge of One's Own Personal and Family History.   FRE 804(b)(4)(A), like the common law pedigree exception, does not require that the declarant have personal knowledge. Obviously, a declarant has no personal recollection of birth or place of birth. United States v. Hernandez, 105 F.3d 1330, 1832 (9th Cir. 1997) (statement that declarant was born in Mexico admissible without personal knowledge). However, any declarant meeting the requirements of subsection (A) is inevitably going to have knowledge of circumstantial evidence of personal and family relationships.

ii.   Statements of Relations and Intimate Associates.   The common law also required that a declarant speaking about the pedigree of another be related by blood or marriage to the person about whom the declaration is made. FRE 804(b)(4)(B) expands the common law pedigree exception to close family members and intimate associates so long as the relationship is such that the declarant would have accurate information about the family history. Do the reasons for eliminating the personal knowledge requirement in subsection (A) also apply to the declarants listed in subsection (B)? Independent evidence may be required that the declarant was a family member or so intimately associated with a family as to be knowledgeable.

iii.   Concerning Personal History.   The exception is limited to past facts and events of an objective, rather than subjective, nature. Statements as to motives or purpose for marriage are beyond the scope of FRE 804(b)(4). United States v. Carvalho, 742 F.2d 146 (4th Cir. 1984) (statements from former spouses as to the defendants' previous motives to marry in order to obtain citizenship were admitted in error).

b.   Justification for the Admissibility of Statements of Personal or Family History

Statements about the declarant's own pedigree are assumed to be reliable enough to be admitted if the declarant is unavailable. No special assurances of reliability are required. The common law hearsay exception required that the declaration be made prior to the time of the controversy that is the subject of the litigation. The Advisory Committee Note to FRE 804(b)(4) explains the absence of this requirement on the ground that the timing of the statement has a "bearing more appropriately on weight than admissibility."

KEY POINTS

1. Assuming unavailability, a statement asserting the declarant's own family history may be admitted without a showing of personal knowledge.
2. A statement asserting the family history of another person may be admitted if the declarant had accurate knowledge as a result of being related to or intimately associated with the other person's family.

PROBLEMS

8.83. A doctor, dying from non-Hodgkins lymphoma, brought a strict product liability suit against the manufacturer of an herbicide containing 2, 4-D acid, which he alleged was the cause of his disease. After his death, the doctor's wife, as executor of his estate, was substituted as plaintiff. Eight days after filing the complaint, the doctor gave a sworn, videotaped statement to the effect that in the 1940s, when he was a teenager, he worked for a crop dusting service in Montana mixing 2, 4-D herbicide products and loading them into crop dusting aircraft. He stated that he recalled the labels on the 2, 4-D barrels and that the defendant, Dow Chemical, was the manufacturer. He also stated that his lymphoma was in "stage four," the disease's final incurable stage. Based upon his experience with patients, he stated that he might survive three months.

In fact, the doctor's condition did worsen and he died in two months. In the intervening time, he and his wife traveled to Yugoslavia on a religious pilgrimage, which he believed was the last resort to receiving healing. May his recorded statement be admitted pursuant to FRE 804(b)(2)?

8.84. Fueled by alcohol, rivalry, and the desire for the victim's new car, five men hatched a plot to carjack an acquaintance of theirs and murder him. Three of them carried out the plan. In his dying moments, the victim identified by name the three who attacked him. Unfortunately, he was wrong about two of them, which the government's own proof substantiates. The government nevertheless seeks to use the dying statement against the third attacker who, it claims, was accurately named. May this defendant prevent the admission of the dying declaration? On what grounds? May a fourth defendant, who the government claims did participate in the attack but who was not named by the victim, use the dying declaration at trial to show that he was not an attacker?

8.85. Hanna Mason has sued the Acme Rental Company for personal injuries that she sustained as a pedestrian when she was hit by an Acme truck driven by James Lowe, an Acme employee. Lowe was fired the day after the accident, and six months later moved to Acapulco. Just before leaving the country, Lowe told his friend, Andy Becker, that he had been drinking at the time of the accident and had failed to stop at a stop sign. Lowe also made the same statement in a deposition taken during the discovery phase of the current lawsuit. Lowe has refused to respond to plaintiff's letter requesting that he return to the United States to testify. At trial, Hanna calls Andy Becker to testify about Lowe's statement. Is the evidence admissible?

8.86. Cosimo Demasi sued the Whitney Trust & Savings Bank for $6,500 dollars that the plaintiff claimed the bank held in a joint savings account that he maintained with his wife. The bank defended on the ground that all but $700 had been withdrawn by the plaintiff's daughter with the consent of Mr. or Mrs. Demasi. A judgment for the defendant was reversed on appeal, and before the new trial Mrs. Demasi sought to withdraw the $700 that the bank conceded remained in the account. In order to receive the money, the bank required that Mrs. Demasi sign an affidavit indicating that she had consented to the prior withdrawals. Mrs. Demasi signed the affidavit, withdrew the $700, and died before the second trial began. At the retrial, the bank offers her affidavit. Should it be admitted?

8.87. Burton is charged with robbery and use of a firearm during a crime of violence, both in connection with the robbery of an Oriental rug store, Carpets of Asia, in Carmel, California. The government's theory is that the robbery was masterminded by Wilson, who was also charged but who remains at large. Wilson's girlfriend, Carla, was a U-Haul employee who rented out trucks illegally used by Wilson in other rug store robberies. Carla was arrested and charged with conspiracy to rob a rug store. Unbeknownst to Wilson, she then began to cooperate with the FBI once she was out on bail. Over the next six months, Carla surreptitiously tape recorded numerous conversations with Wilson. In one recording, Wilson gave a detailed account of the Carmel rug store robbery. Wilson said that he recalled how he told the others that they probably only had five minutes for the robbery due to the store alarm timer, which would probably automatically reset itself and notify the police. He recalled how Burton had shown "a lot of heart" during the robbery and had told a female customer who had wandered into the store during the robbery that the store was closed for remodeling. He told Carla that money from the robbery had been used to pay her bail. Alleging that Wilson is unavailable, the government offers Carla's tape recording in evidence against Burton. What result?

8.88. John Bowman has filed an action in probate court, claiming to be the closest kin—a nephew—of the wealthy decedent, George Bowman. George died intestate and had no children or surviving spouse. To establish his claim, John offers the affidavit of one Jacob Bowman, John's father, who John claims is brother to George. Jacob is now deceased. In this affidavit, Jacob states that he and George are brothers and that they emigrated to the United States together from Germany in 1905. John offers no other evidence of a family relationship. Another distant relative who claims the estate offers an authenticated letter from Emily Bowman, deceased wife of Jacob. The letter states that her husband, Jacob, was bribed by John to make the affidavit and that, to her knowledge, George and Jacob were not brothers. Is Jacob's affidavit admissible? Is Emily's letter admissible?

8.89. Plaintiff Maureen Sullivan has sued No-State Life Insurance Company for failure to pay benefits due upon the death of her husband, Stephen. One of the disputed issues is Stephen's age at the time of death. On direct examination of Maureen, her attorney asks her:

Q: What is your husband's date of birth?
DEFENSE COUNSEL: Objection, hearsay. This witness has no firsthand knowledge and could only know based on what someone told her.
BY PLAINTIFF'S COUNSEL: Ms. Sullivan, did your husband ever tell you what his birthdate was?
DEFENSE COUNSEL: Hearsay, Your Honor. Her husband cannot possibly have remembered firsthand, as a newborn baby, the date of his own birth. He could only know this by being told.

What should plaintiff's counsel argue?

8.90. Joshua Thomas has been charged for his alleged role in arson and vandalism of an SUV dealership, destroying a number of Hummers and doing other property damage. Thomas denies any involvement in the act. A group called the Environmental Liberation Front (ELF) claimed responsibility for the act shortly after it occurred. The city newspaper reported that an anonymous source communicated with reporter Bob Adams, the author of the news story, in three e-mails and two telephone interviews, claiming to be responsible for the arson and vandalism, while indicating that Thomas is innocent. Consider whether defense counsel for Thomas, preparing his case for trial, can introduce this information as evidence. What form would this evidence take? What witnesses would the defense need to call? What objections would the prosecution make, and how would the defense respond? What further investigation would defense counsel have to undertake in order get this evidence in admissible form?

9.   Interpretation and Illustration of FRE 804(b)(6): Forfeiture by Wrongdoing

FRE 804(b)(6) provides:

(b) *The Exceptions.* The following are not excluded by the rule against hearsay if the declarant is unavailable as a witness:

. . .

(6) *Statement Offered Against a Party That Wrongfully Caused the Declarant's Unavailability.* A statement offered against a party that wrongfully caused — or acquiesced in wrongfully causing — the declarant's unavailability as a witness, and did so intending that result.

This exception, added to the Federal Rules in 1997, codified a line of cases beginning with United States v. Mastrangelo, 693 F.2d 269 (2d Cir. 1982), in which key prosecution witnesses would "suddenly" became unavailable due to violence or intimidation allegedly perpetrated against them by the defendants against whom they were to testify. Admission of the unavailable witnesses' hearsay statements was justified on a theory of waiver. *Mastrangelo* held that although a criminal defendant's Sixth Amendment right of confrontation "is an essential trial right, it may be waived by the defendant's misconduct." United States v. Dhinsa, 243 F.3d 635, 651 (2d Cir. 2001). This waiver-by-misconduct rule permitted the admission of the hearsay statements of unavailable witnesses when the defendant had "wrongfully procured the witnesses' silence through threats, actual violence or murder," id., despite the lack of confrontation. See Section G infra for discussion of this waiver rule under Crawford v. Washington. The waiver principle was then extended to include the hearsay rule — waiver of confrontation rights simultaneously waived "the right to object on hearsay grounds to the admission of [the] out-of-court statements." United States v. Houlihan, 92 F.3d 1271, 1281 (1st Cir. 1996). The Advisory Committee Note to FRE 804(b)(6) makes it clear that the new hearsay exception was intended to implement *Mastrangelo* and its progeny.

a.   Preliminary Fact-finding

The foundational requirements for forfeiture-by-wrongdoing statements are:

- the party engaged or acquiesced in wrongdoing;
- the wrongdoing was intended to procure the unavailability of the declarant as a witness against the party;
- the wrongdoing did render the declarant unavailable as a witness; or
- the declarant's statement is offered against the party.

i.   The Declarant Was a Witness or a Potential Witness Against a Party.   It is clear from the case law that the purpose of FRE 804(b)(6) is to secure the admission at trial of hearsay statements made by unavailable declarants who were serving as witnesses against a party, for example by giving grand jury testimony or by being scheduled to appear in an upcoming trial. If there was instead only an ongoing criminal investigation, declarants are *potential* witnesses if they are assisting in this investigation. Both prior to and after FRE 804(b)(6), courts have held that the forfeiture rule applies to wrongdoing against both actual and potential witnesses. United States v. Houlihan, 92 F.3d 1271, 1279 (1st Cir. 1996) ("We see no [difference] between a defendant who assassinates a witness on the eve of trial and a potential defendant who assassinates a potential witness before charges have officially been brought.").

ii.   The Party Engaged in Wrongdoing That Did Procure the Unavailability of the Declarant.   The party against whom the declarant's statements are offered must be shown to have "procured" the unavailability of the declarant by engaging in or acquiescing in "wrongdoing." The proponent of the statements must persuade the judge by a preponderance of the evidence, pursuant to FRE 104(a), that the party did so act. In general, wrongdoing is defined broadly to mean threats, intimidation, kidnapping, hiding, acts of violence and, ultimately, murder to secure the silence of the then-unavailable declarant. Engaging in wrongdoing means "he or she participated directly in planning or procuring the declarant's unavailability." United States v. Cherry, 217 F.3d 811, 820 (10th Cir. 2000) (defendant's obtaining the car used in the declarant's murder under false pretenses, and her apparent proximity to the actual murderer around the time of the murder, might be sufficient circumstantial evidence that she participated in the planning of the murder).

Evidence used to prove the party's engagement in wrongdoing may include the declarant's hearsay statements. As we know from the Supreme Court's opinion in *Bourjaily*, discussed on page 478, supra, FRE 104(a) permits the court to "bootstrap" a finding of a foundational fact by relying on the contested hearsay statement itself. Should courts impose a requirement, similar to the language in FRE 801(d)(2), that the contested hearsay statement may be used but is not sufficient to prove the party's wrongdoing?

iii.   Intent to Procure the Declarant's Unavailability as a Witness.   To admit a statement under this exception, the trial court must specifically find that the party acted with the intention of making the declarant unavailable as a witness. Giles v. California, 554 U.S. 353, 367 (2008) (FRE 804(b)(6) codifies a common law rule forfeiting hearsay objection by party who intentionally procured declarant's unavailability); United States v. Dhinsa, 243 F.3d at 652 ("government has the burden of proving by a preponderance of the evidence that . . . the . . . party against whom the out-of-court statement is offered . . . acted with the intent of procuring the declarant's unavailability as an actual or potential witness"). The Supreme Court held in *Giles* that the confrontation clause requires this specific intent element for the forfeiture by wrongdoing exception to apply in criminal cases. On that ground, the Court rejected a state law rule that applied the state's hearsay forfeiture exception to admit statements made by a murder victim without requiring a finding that the defendant had killed the victim with a specific intent to make her unavailable as a witness; the fact that the defendant had made the witness unavailable by murdering her did not suffice to establish forfeiture in a manner that would satisfy the confrontation clause. Even in criminal prosecutions, however, it does not appear to be necessary "to show that the defendant's sole motivation was to procure the declarant's absence; rather, [the prosecution] need only show that the defendant was motivated *in part* by a desire to silence the witness." United States v. Dhinsa, 243 F.3d at 652. In *Giles*, for example, the defendant Giles had been convicted of first degree murder of his girlfriend based on evidence that included hearsay testimony from the victim that Giles had beaten and threatened to kill her three weeks before the murder. The testimony had been offered to establish his intent to kill and to rebut Giles's claim of self-defense. The Supreme Court vacated the conviction and remanded the case to the state courts to determine whether Giles intended to make the victim unavailable as a witness. According to the Court, the prior incident of domestic violence would be relevant to that inquiry:

> Acts of domestic violence often are intended to dissuade a victim from resorting to outside help, and include conduct designed to prevent testimony to police officers or cooperation in criminal prosecutions. Where such an abusive relationship culminates in murder, the evidence may support a finding that the crime expressed the intent to isolate the victim and to stop her from reporting abuse to the authorities or cooperating with a criminal prosecution — rendering her prior statements admissible under the forfeiture doctrine. [554 U.S. at 377.]

iv.   Content of Declarant's Statement.   In the classic forfeiture by wrongdoing case, the unavailable declarant's statements pertain to past events or offenses (such as racketeering or drug sales) that the declarant could have testified about at the time the declarant was silenced by the defendant's wrongdoing. The statements are then admitted against the defendant to prove these past offenses. Increasingly, however, the government prosecutes the defendant for the act of wrongdoing—typically murder—that has made the declarant unavailable. The content of some of the declarant's hearsay statements may concern the murder itself, not the defendant's past offenses as to which the declarant would have been a witness or potential witness.

Defendants have argued that this is an improper extension of the forfeiture-by-wrongdoing principle since the declarant's status as "witness" is not related to the content of the out-of-court statements. But courts have unanimously declined to impose any limit on the application of Rule 804(b)(6), holding that its broad terminology includes within its reach the admission of statements by the declarant when the murder of the declarant is the crime charged. *Dhinsa*, 243 F.3d at 652. Of course, the rule still requires that the intent of the defendant be *at least in part* to prevent the declarant from testifying in some other proceeding; thus, the requirement that there be some other on-going criminal investigation or legal dispute in which the declarant might participate must still be satisfied. United States v. Lentz, 2005 WL 2124104, at *8 (E.D. Va.) (husband and wife involved in bitter custody dispute; husband charged with wife's murder motivated "at least in part" to procure her unavailability as a witness).

b.   Justification for the Admissibility of Forfeiture by Wrongdoing Statements

The justification for the admissibility of forfeiture by wrongdoing statements is straightforward: "[T]he law [will not] allow a person to take advantage of his own wrong." *Mastrangelo*, 693 F.2d at 272. An oft-quoted explication of this policy was stated in United States v. White, 116 F.3d 903, 911 (D.C. Cir. 1997):

> . . . It is hard to imagine a form of misconduct more extreme than the murder of a potential witness. Simple equity supports a forfeiture principle, as does a common sense attention to the need for fit incentives. The defendant who has removed an adverse witness is in a weak position to complain about losing the chance to cross-examine him. And where a defendant has silenced a witness through the use of threats, violence or murder, admission of the victim's prior statements at least partially offsets the perpetrator's rewards for his misconduct.

There is no reliability inquiry authorized by FRE 804(b)(6). The trial court need not look for indicia of trustworthiness under either the hearsay rule or the confrontation clause. Once the defendant has waived these rights, the court "is not required to assess independently the reliability of those statements." United States v. Dhinsa, 243 F.3d at 655.

c.   Acquiescence in Wrongdoing

One of the principal concerns voiced to the Advisory Committee as it was considering the adoption of FRE 804(b)(6) was the breadth of the term "*acquiesced in wrongfully causing . . . the declarant's unavailability.*" The Tenth Circuit in United States v. Cherry, supra, interpreted the rule (in its original form, prior to the 2011 restyling) to permit its application to co-conspirators who did not plan or in any way participate in wrongdoing that caused the unavailability of the declarant:

> [T]he use of the words "engaged or acquiesced in wrongdoing" lends support to the government's assertion that, at least for purposes of the hearsay rules, waiver can be imputed under an agency theory of responsibility to a defendant who "acquiesced" in

the wrongful procurement of a witness's unavailability but did not actually "engage" in wrongdoing apart from the conspiracy itself. [217 F.3d at 816.]

Cherry involved five defendants charged with a drug conspiracy. Much of the evidence against them came from Mr. Lurks, a cooperating witness who was murdered by one of the five prior to trial. The district court rejected the use of FRE 804(b)(6) against three of the defendants, finding that there was "absolutely no evidence" that the three "had actual knowledge of, agreed to or participated in the murder of . . . Lurks." Id. at 820. The government took an interlocutory appeal, since exclusion of Lurks's statements against the three would destroy its case.

The majority applied the principles of conspiratorial liability enunciated in *Pinkerton v. United States*, 328 U.S. 640 (1946) to define "acquiescence":

> . . . A defendant may be deemed to have waived his or her Confrontation Clause rights (and, a fortiori, hearsay objections) if a preponderance of the evidence establishes . . . [that] the wrongful procurement [of the defendant's unavailability] was in furtherance, within the scope, and reasonably foreseeable as a necessary or natural consequence of an ongoing conspiracy . . . Actual knowledge is not required for conspiratorial waiver by misconduct if the[se] elements . . . are satisfied . . . We note that the scope of the conspiracy is not necessarily limited to a primary goal—such as bank robbery—but can also include secondary goals relevant to the evasion of apprehension and prosecution for that goal—such as escape, or, by analogy, obstruction of justice . . . We further reiterate that . . . a defendant is not responsible for the acts of co-conspirators if that defendant meets the burden of proving he or she took affirmative steps to withdraw from the conspiracy before those acts were committed. [217 F.3d at 820.]

d.   *Application of FRE 403*

Admission of the unavailable declarant's statements is not automatic, however, as the court must still perform the balancing test under FRE 403. Prior to the adoption of FRE 804(b)(6), this inquiry included evaluation of the reliability of the declarant's statement to avoid the admission of "facially unreliable hearsay." *Dhinsa*, 243 F.3d at 655. Now that the specific exception is in place, however, it would be highly unusual for the court to exclude a statement that falls within the categorical exception on the basis of "low probative value" based on the court's doubts about its reliability. However, since FRE 804(b)(6) is a categorical exception that requires absolutely no indicia of reliability, perhaps Rule 403's balancing test should take reliability into account. There also remains the danger of ambiguity, confusion, and undue prejudice from the inflammatory nature of the evidence or its context for the court to consider.

e.   *Is an FRE 104(c) Hearing Required?*

Several courts have ruled specifically that the district court must hold an evidentiary hearing, outside the presence of the jury, in which the government has the burden of proving by a preponderance of the evidence that the defendant did procure the unavailability of the declarant by wrongdoing, and did intend to do so to prevent the declarant from being an actual or potential witness. *Dhinsa*, 243 F.3d at 653. The Eighth Circuit, however, has held that the trial court can admit the hearsay evidence at trial, in the presence of the jury, "contingent upon proof of the underlying murder by a preponderance of the evidence." *United States v. Emery*, 186 F.3d 921, 926 (8th Cir. 1999). The court in *Emery* analogized this process to that used to admit the statements of co-conspirators pursuant to FRE 801(d)(2)(E), and noted that "the repetition necessarily inherent with a preliminary hearing would amount to a significant waste of judicial resources." Id. Consider, however, whether the jury could adhere to the admonition of the judge to ignore a contingently admitted hearsay statement of a murder victim, in a case that the judge still thinks sufficiently strong that a reasonable jury *could* find the defendant guilty of the charged act of murder beyond a reasonable doubt.

KEY POINTS

1. If a party has procured the unavailability of a hearsay declarant by wrongdoing, and intended to do so to prevent the declarant from being an actual or potential witness, then the declarant's statements are admissible against that party.

2. The party's conduct may have involved planning of, participation in, or acquiescence in the wrongdoing.

PROBLEMS

8.91. Raymond Ochoa is charged with conspiracy to commit mail fraud for filing a false insurance claim on his automobile, which he falsely reported as stolen. The prosecution learned that Ochoa's former tenant, Dave McLaughlin, had put Ochoa in touch with a "chop shop," which would help him dispose of his allegedly stolen car. McLaughlin was approached by an FBI agent who told McLaughlin that he would benefit from talking to the FBI. McLaughlin made statements to the agent describing his role in the conspiracy and implicating Ochoa in the plan to dispose of the car and make the false claim. On the very next day, the FBI attempted to serve McLaughlin with a subpoena; McLaughlin's current landlord said he had left town "for Maryland" with all his belongings.

The FBI agent also visited McLaughlin's employer looking for him. He learned that McLaughlin had stopped coming to work but was owed his last paycheck. On the day after the FBI's visit, McLaughlin actually called the employer to ask for his paycheck. When he hung up, the employer used caller ID and determined that the call was made from Ochoa's home phone number. Phone records later revealed that seven phone calls were made from Ochoa's phone number to McLaughlin's employer during the next two days. McLaughlin then apparently disappeared and was never found, despite good-faith efforts by the government. May the government use McLaughlin's hearsay statements against Ochoa pursuant to FRE 804(b)(6)? By what process should the foundational facts be determined?

8.92. Return to Problem 3.4, State v. Blair, at page 137. Police investigation reveals that several weeks before the attack on Norma, she filed a complaint against Jimmy for assault and battery. A police officer then interviewed both Jimmy and Norma; Norma told the officer she wanted to drop the charges. Since the attack, Norma is still unable to remember anything about what happened that night, and she says she is unwilling to testify against Jimmy. The prosecutor wants to know whether, if Norma is called to the stand as a witness, all of the entries in her diary that describe Jimmy's violent temper and his beating of her over the past three years can be admitted under FRE 804(b)(6). What issues in the application of this exception are raised in this case? What would have to happen at trial for the diary to be admitted?

F.   THE RESIDUAL EXCEPTION

The Federal Rules of Evidence as originally promulgated by the Supreme Court provided a broad residual exception in both FRE 803 and FRE 804 for a "statement not specifically covered by any of the foregoing exceptions but having comparable circumstantial guarantees of trustworthiness." Effective December 1, 1997, the Rules were amended to eliminate the two subsections and to add a single, identical residual hearsay exception as FRE 807. In case law prior to 1997, remember that the residuals are FRE 803(24) and 804(b)(5).

1.   FRE 807

RULE 807.   RESIDUAL EXCEPTION

(a) *In General.* Under the following circumstances, a hearsay statement is not excluded by the rule against hearsay even if the statement is not specifically covered by a hearsay exception in Rule 803 or 804:
    (1) the statement has equivalent circumstantial guarantees of trustworthiness;
    (2) it is offered as evidence of a material fact;
    (3) it is more probative on the point for which it is offered than any other evidence that the proponent can obtain through reasonable efforts; and
    (4) admitting it will best serve the purposes of these rules and the interests of justice.
(b) *Notice.* The statement is admissible only if, before the trial or hearing, the proponent gives an adverse party reasonable notice of the intent to offer the statement and its particulars, including the declarant's name and address, so that the party has a fair opportunity to meet it.

2.   Interpretation and Illustration of FRE 807

The foundational requirements for FRE 807 are:

- the statement must have circumstantial guarantees of trustworthiness;
- these guarantees should be "equivalent" to the exceptions in Rules 803 and 804;
- the statement is offered to prove a material fact;
- the statement is more probative on the point for which it is offered than any other evidence that can be obtained through reasonable efforts;
- admission will serve the general purposes of the rules and the interests of justice; and
- notice is given to the opponent.

a.   Preliminary Fact-finding

The first thing to notice about FRE 807 is that it is not a categorical exception. There are no categorical requirements concerning the identity of the declarant, the content of the statement, or the circumstances in which the statement was made.

There is no categorical requirement that the declarant be unavailable. Instead, the principal requirements for admission are that the statement has "circumstantial guarantees of trustworthiness" and that it is "more probative" than other reasonably available evidence — clearly individualized judgments to be made by the trial judge. These two requirements reflect the two primary justifications for admitting hearsay under the categorical system of hearsay exceptions: reliability and necessity.

The following example illustrates some of the major preliminary fact-finding issues in applying the residual exception:

> Ed Barns has sued Acme Used Cars for injuries that he sustained when he and a friend were examining a used car at the Acme lot. The car would not start, so Fred Anders, an Acme mechanic, offered his assistance. Barns was pouring gasoline from a small can into the carburetor while his companion attempted to start the engine. The engine backfired and ignited the can, and Barns suffered severe burn injuries. At trial, Barns claimed that he was acting pursuant to Fred Anders's instructions to pour the gasoline directly into the carburetor. Acme claimed that, to the contrary, Anders warned Barns to stop what he was doing.
>
> Anders died before the trial. Acme offers into evidence Exhibit B, an authenticated handwritten statement signed by Anders that describes the incident and states that he warned Barns not to pour the gasoline. Acme offers the foundational testimony of Anders's supervisor, Georgia Breen:
>
>> I learned of the accident within several hours of its occurrence. I immediately instructed Fred Anders to go into a room, not to talk to anyone else, and to write down everything that happened. Anders obeyed my instruction and came back with a handwritten statement within 30 minutes. I recognized his handwriting and he signed the document in my presence. I recognize Exhibit B as that document.

You can see that Exhibit B does not fall within any of the categorical exceptions under FRE 803 and FRE 804. Should it be admitted into evidence under FRE 807?

b.   *Circumstantial Guarantees of Trustworthiness*

Looking at Exhibit B, what foundation facts would you use to argue that Anders's statement bears "circumstantial guarantees of trustworthiness"? Case law has established two principal means of establishing trustworthiness.

i.   Reliability of Testimonial Qualities.   The most common means of satisfying the trustworthiness requirement is to show that one or more of Anders's testimonial qualities appears to be reliable because of the circumstances within which it was made.

> [A]ll of the traditional hearsay exceptions minimize one or more of the four hearsay risks: (1) insincerity; (2) faulty perception; (3) faulty memory; and (4) faulty narration...the Court must determine the relative degree to which the [proffered item] is prone to the hearsay risks, and if any of the risks are minimized by circumstantial guarantees of trustworthiness. [United States v. Southern Indiana Gas and Electric Co., 258 F. Supp. 2d 884, 890 (S.D. Ind. 2003).]

Facts relating to the identity, knowledge, qualifications, and motivation of the declarant; the content of the statement; and the circumstances in which it was made are all considered for their effect on testimonial qualities.

For example, in United States v. Tome, 61 F.3d 1446, 1453 (10th Cir.1995), the Tenth Circuit considered the admissibility under the residual exception of statements made by defendant's daughter concerning acts of alleged sexual abuse. Statements made to a social worker were considered to be trustworthy because the social worker was trained in interviewing children and used open-ended, nonleading questions (context promotes sincerity), and the declarant used childish language while describing the abuse with specificity and detail (content indicates sincerity and memory). Other circumstances, however, cast doubt on the statement's trustworthiness: The statement was not spontaneous because the declarant knew that she was taken to the social worker in order to say what the defendant had done to her (context provides opportunity for insincerity); it was made a year after the events described (context affects memory); and it was made when the declarant arguably had a motive to lie because she wanted to live with her mother, not her father (identity of declarant provides motive to lie). The court held that the statement did not qualify for the residual exception because of these equivocal circumstances. Other factors relevant to reliability would be the length of time between the incident and making the hearsay statement, and whether the child made the same statements consistently to adults.

Motive and incentive to lie commonly figure in evaluations of trustworthiness: United States v. Walker, 410 F.3d 754 (5th Cir. 2005) (interview at police station, not under oath, facing the threat of criminal charges); United States v. Wright, 363 F.3d 237 (3d Cir. 2004) (self-serving statements made when declarant knew he was under investigation); Land Grantors v. United States, 86 Fed. Cl. 35, 42 (Fed. Cl. 2009) (direct interest in mineral rich land indicated guarantees of trustworthiness were lacking). Other courts mention factors relating to perception and memory: New Colt Holding Corp. v. RJG Holdings of Fla., Inc, 312 F. Supp. 2d 195, 223 (D. Conn. 2004) ("A methodologically sound survey can reduce . . . the danger of insincerity and faulty narration [and] . . . a particular memory survey which . . . relates to events that were learned by direct perception and are unlikely to be forgotten, can . . . minimize all five of the classes of risk ordinarily associated with survey evidence."); In re Columbia Securities Litigation, 155 F.R.D. 466, 475 (S.D.N.Y. 1994) ("Unless their author is available for cross-examination, newspaper stories generally will present a blank face that gives little clue as to the reliability of the reporter's perception, memory, narration, or sincerity, and in addition facts to disclose how the article was changed in the editing process").

In the hypothetical case against Acme Used Cars, what circumstances bear on the reliability of Anders's testimonial qualities? You should by now be able make arguments both for and against trustworthiness.

ii.   Independent Corroboration.   The second means of establishing trustworthiness is to show by way of independent corroborating evidence that the facts asserted in the particular hearsay statement are probably accurate. Larez v. City of Los Angeles, 946 F.2d 630, 643 & 643 n.6 (9th Cir. 1991) (news account of a specific quotation from the defendant met "circumstantial guarantees of trustworthiness" requirement when three independent newspapers attributed similar quotations to defendant). Testimony given before a grand jury was frequently admitted under the residual exception when its contents were corroborated. Under the Supreme Court opinion in Crawford v. Washington, however, grand jury testimony qualifies as a "testimonial" statement. Because the criminal defendant is not present during the grand jury proceeding and cannot cross-examine the witnesses there, the prosecution is prohibited from using grand jury testimony under the confrontation clause in criminal cases, unless the declarant also testifies. It is possible, however, that this testimony might still be admitted under the residual exception in a civil case.

c.   Equivalency

FRE 807 also requires that the guarantees of trustworthiness be "equivalent," presumably to the guarantees in FRE 803 and FRE 804. Since the apparent trustworthiness of the hearsay admitted under all 28 categorical exceptions varies widely in both kind and degree, it is impossible to identify a single standard, and a rigorous showing of "equivalence" is not required. But courts sometimes do analogize the hearsay sought to be admitted to the indicia of trustworthiness of some categorically admitted hearsay, such as spontaneity, against interest, or careful routine. United States v. Perez, 217 F.3d 323, 329 (5th Cir. 2000) (statements by illegal immigrants "bore . . . indicia of reliability equivalent to declarations against interest" because made to agency responsible for their deportation and possible prosecution; however, inadmissible because made not under oath and in an informal interview); Conoco, Inc. v. Department of Energy, 99 F.3d 387, 392 (Fed. Cir. 1997) (purchase summaries do not have same indicia of reliability as commercial publications).

d.   Near Miss

A "near miss" occurs when a hearsay statement almost, but not quite, fits within one of the categorical hearsay exceptions and would thus be inadmissible but for the residual exception. The majority of Circuits now agree that the language of FRE 807 — "not specifically covered by a hearsay exception in Rule 803 or 804" — means that statements found to be inadmissible under the Rule 803 and 804 categories may still be considered under Rule 807. That a statement "almost fits" into other hearsay exceptions can be held to favor admissibility under FRE 807, but that factor is not determinative and does not alone compel admission. United States v. Bonds, 608 F.3d 495, 501 (9th Cir. 2010).

e.   Offered to Prove a Material Fact

Subsection (a)(2) requires that the proponent must show that the statement is offered as evidence of a "material" fact. Typically, this term means nothing more than that the statement is relevant, but it has been used to protect against overuse of the residual exception to prove minor points or points on which the statement has low probative value. Cook v. Miss. Dept. Human Servs., 108 Fed. Appx. 852, 856 (5th Cir. 2004) (statement of belief that person was hired because of his race "not so material that it must have been admitted in the interests of justice" because it could not by itself raise a genuine issue of discrimination).

f.   More Probative on the Point Than Other Reasonably Available Evidence

Subsection (a)(3) requires a showing that the proponent has been reasonably diligent in attempting to secure evidence — witnesses or other kinds of hearsay — that would substitute for hearsay admitted under the residual exception. Courts have required parties to produce an available hearsay declarant as a witness. United States v. Patrick, 248 F.3d 11, 25 (1st Cir. 2001) (affidavit inadmissible since officer who conducted the search described in the affidavit was available); to present the declarant through affidavits or depositions, Andrekus v. Board of Educ., 2004 U.S. Dist. LEXIS 19388, at *28 (N.D. Ill.) (affidavits and depositions rather than hearsay note are "better evidence" for summary judgment proceedings); and to produce original records underlying secondary evidence such as summaries, Conoco Inc. v. Department of Energy, 99 F.3d 387, 393 (Fed. Cir. 1997) (original underlying records of purchases of crude oil were more probative than summaries and DOE made no showing that reasonable efforts would not produce them).

If the declarant is deceased and once had knowledge about a central fact that would be otherwise unavailable, courts weigh this need heavily in making the Rule 807 decision. Bohler-Udderholm Am., Inc. v. Ellwood Group, Inc., 247 F.3d 79 (3d Cir. 2001) (affidavit of deceased representative of plaintiff at a crucial board of directors' meeting was the only available source to contradict defendant's version of what was said at the meeting). If diligence in seeking alternative proof can be demonstrated, and nothing better is available, then the proponent has a legitimate case of need to use the residual.

g.   Serve the General Purposes of the Rules and Interests of Justice

Because of the generality in which these lofty ideals are expressed in subsection (a)(4), they are not likely to be of much assistance to the trial judge in deciding whether to admit individual items of hearsay. In re Drake, 786 F. Supp. 229, 233 (E.D.N.Y. 1992) (the third factor "is so abstruse in formulation as to constitute little guidance for the court").

h.   Notice

The proponent is required by FRE 807(b) to inform the opponent of the intent to use the residual exception, and of the particulars of the statement and location of the declarant. This enables the opponent to prepare in order to argue more effectively against admission. And it serves as a limit both on the last-minute creativity of lawyers and on the susceptibility of judges to accede to lawyers' last-minute protestations of need. The requirement that notice be given *before trial* is, however, far from absolute. Some courts have interpreted the requirement liberally, upholding admission if the hearsay statement was disclosed within sufficient time — even on the first day of trial — to permit the opponent to prepare to contest the use of the statement. A continuance may be granted to permit the opponent to meet the evidence. In United States v. Panzardi-Lespier, 918 F.2d 313, 316-318 (1st Cir. 1990), the court discussed the conflicting case law on the strict versus the flexible approach to pretrial notice. It held that even in a criminal case, notice on the first day of trial was sufficient where seven days elapsed before the statement was actually offered into evidence. There was no surprise to its content, and opposing party had ample time to review it and prepare its defense. And if the proponent could not have reasonably anticipated the need for the residual exception, the notice requirement may be excused altogether by the judge. There are limits, however, even to this flexible approach. In United States v. Coney, 51 F.3d 164 (8th Cir. 1995), it was held to be not an abuse of the trial court's discretion to refuse admission to a report offered by the defendant under the residual exception 45 minutes before she wanted to introduce it. If the opponent knows of the existence of the hearsay statement before trial, and of the proponent's intent to use it, courts have applied the notice requirement flexibly where there is no prejudice.

3. Elaboration of FRE 807: How Much Hearsay Is Admitted Under the Residual Exception?

The trial judge's decision whether to admit Anders's statement under FRE 807 might be influenced by the general policy underlying the residual exception. Is the residual exception — which is, after all, a radical departure from the strict categorical approach of the common law — to be used frequently or rarely? Liberally or sparingly? According to the Senate Judiciary Committee:

> It is intended that the residual hearsay exceptions will be used very rarely, and only in exceptional circumstances. The committee does not intend to establish a broad license for trial judges to admit hearsay statements that do not fall within one of the other exceptions contained in rules 803 and 804(b). The residual exceptions are not meant to authorize major judicial revisions of the hearsay rule, including its present exceptions. Such major revisions are best accomplished by legislative action.

There is language in appellate opinions in most of the Circuits that FRE 807 was designed for "exceptional" circumstances, and Circuit courts have given district courts wide discretion in its application. In a study of reported decisions from 1975 through 1991, the following kinds of statements were most frequently admitted under the residual exceptions (also called "catchall" exceptions):

> Prosecutors attempted to introduce grand jury testimony in thirty-seven cases pursuant to the 804(b)(5) catchall exception. In twenty-nine of these cases, the court admitted the hearsay. Another hidden catchall category encompasses written and oral statements made to law enforcement officials which are prior consistent or inconsistent statements [of a testifying witness] not fitting the Rule 801 criteria. A growing number of cases appear to include statements to law enforcement officials by declarants not present at trial. Such declarants have ranged from accomplices to spouses, victims, and truly disinterested individuals. [Myrna S. Raeder, Commentary: A Response to Professor Swift, 76 Minn. L. Rev. 507, 514-516 (1992).]

Professor Raeder expressed concern that such decisions "permit the total erosion of the hearsay rule by judicial discretion." Id. at 517. We will see in Section G, infra, that the application of the confrontation clause following Crawford v. Washington will change these results in criminal cases. Grand jury testimony and statements made to law enforcement may be excluded, although all prior statements of a testifying witness would be admitted. Concern has also been expressed that undue focus on whether a statement is or is not a "near miss" has distracted courts from careful evaluation of the "equivalency" of the circumstantial guarantees of trustworthiness required by FRE 807. Elizabeth DeCoux, Textual Limits on the Residual Exception to the Hearsay Rule: The "Near Miss" Debate and Beyond, 35 S.U. L. Rev. 99 (2007).

KEY POINTS

1. Under FRE 807, the judge has discretion to admit hearsay statements that appear to be reliable; that is, they have circumstantial guarantees of trustworthiness either because the circumstances indicate that the declarant has reliable testimonial qualities or because the contents of the statement are corroborated.

2. The statement must also be more probative than other available evidence, typically because the hearsay declarant is unavailable.

3. The proponent of the statement must also notify the opponent of the intent to invoke the residual exception, preferably before trial but not in cases of necessity.

PROBLEMS

8.93. Return to Problem 8.49 at page 494. At 3:00 A.M. on January 26, Mrs. D'Onofrio was asked to complete and sign a complaint form by one of the police officers. She repeated, in writing, the statements she had made earlier concerning her husband's behavior on January 24, 25 and 26. She signed her name twice, acknowledging that the police officer was relying upon her allegations to establish probable cause to arrest Louis D'Onofrio for brandishing a weapon, and affirming that her statements were true. This form, as well as the hearsay statements in Problem 8.49, are the only proof that Louis D'Onofrio had a gun in his possession and threatened her with it. At trial, Mrs. D'Onofrio asserts her marital privilege, which prevents the government from calling her as a witness against her husband. Is the written statement admissible into evidence?

8.94. David Dixon has been charged with conspiracy to sell and with selling heroin. Two alleged co-conspirators, Brown and Green, were granted immunity and were prepared to testify against Dixon. Since Green had a long history of involvement with drugs and several drug-related convictions, the prosecution planned to make Brown the star witness. Brown, however, died of a heart attack several days before the trial. At Dixon's trial the prosecution authenticates and offers into evidence a letter from Brown to his mother, telling her that he is feeling sick, that he thinks he is about to die, and that he wants to confess to her. The letter then describes his drug dealings with Dixon. What arguments can be made for and against admission under FRE 807? How should the court rule?

8.95. In preparing the prosecution of Barry Bonds, Problem 4.5 on page 191, the government contended that the statements made by Bonds's trainer Greg Anderson to James Valente at BALCO identifying the urine samples as coming from Bonds were admissible under FRE 807. The government based its argument on these statements "nearly missing" admissibility as statements against interest under FRE 804(b)(3), and being "exactly the type of scenario" FRE 807 was intended to remedy when Anderson refused to testify. Should Anderson's statements be admitted under the residual exception? Consider *all* of its terms in constructing your argument.

8.96. Four victims of abduction and brutal torture during the reign of terror conducted by El Salvadoran Security Forces in 1979 are suing two El Salvadoran military commanders. The suit is filed in federal court in Florida, where the two defendants reside, and seeks compensatory and punitive damages pursuant to federal and state law. One element of plaintiffs' claim requires proof that the defendants had actual or constructive knowledge of ongoing criminal conduct by troops over which they had command.

To prove actual or constructive knowledge, plaintiffs seek to introduce a properly authenticated English language translation of a tape-recorded diary kept by the Archbishop of El Salvador, Oscar Arnulfo Romero. Romero kept this diary from March 1978 until his assassination in 1980 while conducting a Mass. He created the diary by making notes throughout each day of events connected with his ministry, including meetings and conversations with various individuals. Later that same day he would dictate a narrative version of these notes into a portable tape recorder. These tapes (but not the notes) were preserved, copied, transcribed and translated, as can be proved by authenticating witnesses. Their contents were not made public until 1990. An early entry in the diary states that "I want this diary to be a record of the chancery team and of the life of the archdiocese." Entries in the diary state that meetings were held between the archbishop and both of the defendants in 1978 and 1979. The diary states that human rights abuses, the acts of violence committed by the security forces, the need for remedial action, and even the archbishop's public denunciation of one of the defendants were discussed. Both defendants deny ever meeting with the archbishop. There is also evidence that the archbishop made statements critical of the defendants and the security forces during his "homilies" that were broadcast throughout the country. The defendants deny hearing the homilies.

Is the Romero diary admissible under FRE 807? What other hearsay exceptions might apply?

G.   HEARSAY AND THE CONFRONTATION CLAUSE

The confrontation clause in the Sixth Amendment to the United States Constitution states: "In all criminal prosecutions, the accused shall enjoy the right . . . to be confronted with the Witnesses against him." The meaning of this terse phrase is far from clear: There is virtually no legislative history shedding light on the Framers' intent, and the words themselves are subject to a number of possible interpretations. When the prosecution presents a *witness* at trial, the Supreme Court's most frequently cited analysis is that the clause requires

> a personal examination and cross-examination of the witness in which the accused has the opportunity, not only of testing the recollection and sifting the conscience of the witness, but of compelling him to stand face to face with the jury in order that they may look at him, and judge by his demeanor upon the stand and the manner in which he gives his testimony whether he is worthy of belief. [Mattox v. United States, 156 U.S. 237, 242-243 (1895).]

As you know, most hearsay admitted through the exceptions and exemptions does not require the presence of the hearsay declarant as a witness in court. Thus, the admission of hearsay presents an immediate threat to the criminal defendant's confrontation right. A literal reading of the clause, however, might hold that it operates *only* when the prosecutor calls witnesses. *All* hearsay could be admitted without regard to confrontation rights. Or, "witnesses" might be interpreted more broadly to include all individuals who provide evidence against the defendant. *All* hearsay would then be within the reach of the clause and *no* hearsay could be admitted without confrontation and cross-examination.

In Crawford v. Washington, 541 U.S. 124 (2004), the U.S. Supreme Court provided a new interpretation of criminal defendants' confrontation right. In keeping with its own past opinions, the Court held that the confrontation clause bars the use of some, but not of all, hearsay against criminal defendants. It provided a new set of standards by which to test when the confrontation right is violated, and left open some important questions in the administration of those standards. The *Crawford* opinion will concern us throughout this section because it purports to include within its scope the two recurring situations in which the prosecution introduces hearsay against a criminal defendant: hearsay admitted under an exemption or exception, and hearsay admitted as a prior statement of a testifying witness. We begin our discussion with a brief analysis of the Court's interpretation of the confrontation clause prior to *Crawford*. The approach developed in Ohio v. Roberts, 448 U.S. 56 (1980), is important for understanding the Court's critique of *Roberts*, its new stance in *Crawford*, and its evolving development of the confrontation right.

1. Ohio v. Roberts

In *Roberts*, the Supreme Court had seemed to establish a two-pronged test—unavailability and reliability—for satisfying the accused's confrontation right when hearsay is admitted but the declarant does not testify:

> The Confrontation Clause operates in two separate ways to restrict the range of admissible hearsay. First, in conformity with the Framers' preference for face-to-face accusation, the Sixth Amendment establishes a rule of necessity. In the usual case (including cases where prior cross-examination has occurred), the prosecution must either produce, or demonstrate the unavailability of, the declarant whose statement it wishes to use against the defendant . . . . The second aspect operates once a witness is shown to be unavailable. Reflecting its underlying purpose to augment accuracy in the factfinding process by ensuring the defendant an effective means to test adverse evidence, the Clause countenances only hearsay marked with such trustworthiness that "there is no material departure from the reason of the general rule." The Court has applied this "indicia of reliability" requirement principally by concluding that certain hearsay exceptions rest upon such solid foundations that admission of virtually any evidence within them comports with the "substances of the constitutional protection." [Mattox v. United States, 156 U.S. 237, 244 (1895).] . . . In sum, when a hearsay declarant is not present for cross-examination at trial, the Confrontation Clause normally requires a showing that he is unavailable. Even then, his statement is admissible only if it bears adequate "indicia of reliability." Reliability can be inferred without more in a case where the evidence falls within a firmly rooted hearsay exception. In other cases, the evidence must be excluded, at least absent a showing of particularized guarantees of trustworthiness. [448 U.S. at 65-66.]

Twelve years later, in White v. Illinois, 502 U.S. 346, 354 (1992), the Court virtually abandoned the unavailability requirement by limiting it to statements admitted as former testimony under FRE 804(b)(1).

Thus, for most hearsay, the confrontation clause under *Roberts* imposed only an inquiry whether the hearsay statement fits within a "firmly rooted" exception and, if it does not, whether there are "particularized guarantees" of the statement's trustworthiness.

a. Firmly Rooted Hearsay Exceptions

Most of the exceptions under FRE 803 and 804 were then found to be "firmly rooted." In *Roberts*, the Court stated that exceptions for business records, dying declarations, and public records are firmly rooted. Co-conspirator statements were found to be firmly rooted in Bourjaily v. United States 483 U.S. 171, 182 (1987) (with vigorous dissent); and statements falling within the traditional exceptions for present sense impression, excited utterances, statements of state of mind, and past recollection recorded survived challenge under the confrontation clause. This meant that the legislatively drawn categorical hearsay exceptions of the Federal Rules stood in for judicial analysis of the right to confrontation in most cases.

b. Not Firmly Rooted Exceptions Require "Particularized Guarantees of Trustworthiness"

A Supreme Court plurality in Lilly v. Virginia, 527 U.S. 116 (1999), held that statements against penal interest, admitted under FRE 804(b)(3), are not firmly rooted. The Court had previously discussed the "particularized guarantees of trustworthiness" test in Idaho v. Wright, 497 U.S. 805 (1990), when it held that the residual exception (now FRE 807) was not firmly rooted. In *Wright*, the Court characterized "particularized guarantees of trustworthiness" as the inherent trustworthiness of the declarant's statement, to be found in the circumstances that "surround the making of the statement." Id. at 821. The Court specifically prohibited the consideration of corroboration, that is, independent evidence that corroborates the contents of the statement itself. Courts had come to rely on corroboration to satisfy the residual exception's requirement of "circumstantial guarantees of trustworthiness," particularly in admitting statements of grand jury witnesses, which often bore few indicia of inherent trustworthiness. Under *Wright*, the use of corroboration was prohibited to satisfy the "particularized" trustworthiness standard for all not firmly rooted hearsay.

Also in Lilly v. Virginia, Justices Scalia and Thomas each wrote separately to state their views that the proper scope of the confrontation right was more limited than the Court's opinions in *Roberts*, *Wright*, and *Lilly* had held. That right, they asserted, "is implicated by extra judicial statements only insofar as they are contained in formalized testimonial material, such as affidavits, depositions, prior testimony or confessions." 527 U.S. at 365. Justice Breyer wrote in his separate concurrence that *Roberts*'s linkage of the confrontation right so closely to the "firmly rooted" provisions of the hearsay rule was both too broad and too narrow a standard, and that this linkage was an open question to be considered at another time. In *Crawford*, five years after *Lilly*, that time had come.

2. Crawford v. Washington

CRAWFORD v. WASHINGTON
541 U.S. 36 (2004)

Justice Scalia delivered the opinion of the Court, in which Stevens, Kennedy, Souter, Thomas, Ginsburg, and Breyer, JJ., joined. Rehnquist, C.J., filed an opinion concurring in the judgment, in which O'Connor, J., joined.

Petitioner Michael Crawford stabbed a man who allegedly tried to rape his wife, Sylvia. At his trial, the State played for the jury Sylvia's tape-recorded statement to the police describing the stabbing, even though he had no opportunity for cross-examination. The Washington Supreme Court upheld petitioner's conviction after determining that Sylvia's statement was reliable. The question presented is whether this procedure complied with the Sixth Amendment's guarantee that, "[i]n all criminal prosecutions, the accused shall enjoy the right . . . to be confronted with the witnesses against him."

I

On August 5, 1999, Kenneth Lee was stabbed at his apartment. Police arrested petitioner later that night. After giving petitioner and his wife *Miranda* warnings, detectives interrogated each of them twice.[6] Petitioner eventually confessed that he and Sylvia had gone in search of Lee because he was upset over an earlier incident in which Lee had tried to rape her. The two had found Lee at his apartment, and a fight ensued in which Lee was stabbed in the torso and petitioner's hand was cut.

Petitioner gave the following account of the fight:

"Q. Okay. Did you ever see anything in [Lee's] hands?
"A. I think so, but I'm not positive.
"Q. Okay, when you think so, what do you mean by that?
"A. I coulda swore I seen him goin' for somethin' before, right before everything happened. He was like reachin', fiddlin' around down here and stuff . . . and I just . . . I don't know, I think, this is just a possibility, but I think, I think that he pulled somethin' out and I grabbed for it and that's how I got cut . . . but I'm not positive. I, I, my mind goes blank when things like this happen. I mean, I just, I remember things wrong, I remember things that just doesn't, don't make sense to me later." (punctuation added).

Sylvia generally corroborated petitioner's story about the events leading up to the fight, but her account of the fight itself was arguably different—particularly with respect to whether Lee had drawn a weapon before petitioner assaulted him:

"Q. Did Kenny do anything to fight back from this assault?
"A. (pausing) I know he reached into his pocket . . . or somethin' . . . I don't know what.
"Q. After he was stabbed?
"A. He saw Michael coming up. He lifted his hand . . . his chest open, he might [have] went to go strike his hand out or something and then (inaudible).
"Q. Okay, you, you gotta speak up.
"A. Okay, he lifted his hand over his head maybe to strike Michael's hand down or something and then he put his hands in his . . . put his right hand in his right pocket . . . took a step back . . . Michael proceeded to stab him . . . then his hands were like . . . how do you explain this . . . open arms . . . with his hands open

---

6. Petitioner Michael Crawford's and his wife Sylvia's interrogations were tape recorded by the Olympia Police Department.—EDS.

and he fell down . . . and we ran (describing subject holding hands open, palms toward assailant).

"Q. Okay, when he's standing there with his open hands, you're talking about Kenny, correct?

"A. Yeah, after, after the fact, yes.

"Q. Did you see anything in his hands at that point?

"A. (pausing) um um (no)." (punctuation added).

The State charged petitioner with assault and attempted murder. At trial, he claimed self-defense. Sylvia did not testify because of the state marital privilege, which generally bars a spouse from testifying without the other spouse's consent. In Washington, this privilege does not extend to a spouse's out-of-court statements admissible under a hearsay exception, so the State sought to introduce Sylvia's tape-recorded statements to the police as evidence that the stabbing was not in self-defense. Noting that Sylvia had admitted she led petitioner to Lee's apartment and thus had facilitated the assault, the State invoked the hearsay exception for statements against penal interest, Wash. Rule Evid. 804(b)(3) (2003).

Petitioner countered that, state law notwithstanding, admitting the evidence would violate his federal constitutional right to be "confronted with the witnesses against him." Amdt. 6. According to our description of that right in Ohio v. Roberts, 448 U.S. 56 (1980), it does not bar admission of an unavailable witness's statement against a criminal defendant if the statement bears "adequate 'indicia of reliability.'" To meet that test, evidence must either fall within a "firmly rooted hearsay exception" or bear "particularized guarantees of trustworthiness." The trial court here admitted the statement on the latter ground, offering several reasons why it was trustworthy: Sylvia was not shifting blame but rather corroborating her husband's story that he acted in self-defense or "justified reprisal;" she had direct knowledge as an eyewitness; she was describing recent events; and she was being questioned by a "neutral" law enforcement officer. The prosecution played the tape for the jury and relied on it in closing, arguing that it was "damning evidence" that "completely refutes [petitioner's] claim of self-defense." The jury convicted petitioner of assault.

The Washington Court of Appeals reversed. It applied a nine-factor test to determine whether Sylvia's statement bore particularized guarantees of trustworthiness, and noted several reasons why it did not: The statement contradicted one she had previously given; it was made in response to specific questions; and at one point she admitted she had shut her eyes during the stabbing. The court considered and rejected the State's argument that Sylvia's statement was reliable because it coincided with petitioner's to such a degree that the two "interlocked." The court determined that, although the two statements agreed about the events leading up to the stabbing, they differed on the issue crucial to petitioner's self-defense claim: "[Petitioner's] version asserts that Lee may have had something in his hand when he stabbed him; but Sylvia's version has Lee grabbing for something only after he has been stabbed."

The Washington Supreme Court reinstated the conviction, unanimously concluding that, although Sylvia's statement did not fall under a firmly rooted hearsay exception, it bore guarantees of trustworthiness: "'[W]hen a codefendant's confession is virtually identical [to, *i.e.*, interlocks with,] that of a defendant, it may be deemed reliable.'" The court explained:

"Although the Court of Appeals concluded that the statements were contradictory, upon closer inspection they appear to overlap . . . .

"[B]oth of the Crawfords' statements indicate that Lee was possibly grabbing for a weapon, but they are equally unsure when this event may have taken place. They are also equally unsure how Michael received the cut on his hand, leading the court to question when, if ever, Lee possessed a weapon. In this respect they overlap.

"[N]either Michael nor Sylvia clearly stated that Lee had a weapon in hand from which Michael was simply defending himself. And it is this omission by both that interlocks the statements and makes Sylvia's statement reliable."[7]

We granted certiorari to determine whether the State's use of Sylvia's statement violated the Confrontation Clause.

II

The Sixth Amendment's Confrontation Clause provides that, "[i]n all criminal prosecutions, the accused shall enjoy the right . . . to be confronted with the witnesses against him." We have held that this bedrock procedural guarantee applies to both federal and state prosecutions. Pointer v. Texas, 380 U.S. 400 (1965). As noted above, *Roberts* says that an unavailable witness's out-of-court statement may be admitted so long as it has adequate indicia of reliability—*i.e.*, falls within a "firmly rooted hearsay exception" or bears "particularized guarantees of trustworthiness." Petitioner argues that this test strays from the original meaning of the Confrontation Clause and urges us to reconsider it.

A

The Constitution's text does not alone resolve this case. One could plausibly read "witnesses against" a defendant to mean those who actually testify at trial, those whose statements are offered at trial, see 3 J. Wigmore, Evidence §1397, p 104 (2d ed. 1923) (hereinafter Wigmore), or something in-between. We must therefore turn to the historical background of the Clause to understand its meaning.

The right to confront one's accusers is a concept that dates back to Roman times. The founding generation's immediate source of the concept, however, was the common law. English common law has long differed from continental civil law in regard to the manner in which witnesses give testimony in criminal trials. The common-law tradition is one of live testimony in court subject to adversarial testing, while the civil law condones examination in private by judicial officers. See 3 W. Blackstone, Commentaries on the Laws of England 373-374 (1768).

Nonetheless, England at times adopted elements of the civil-law practice. Justices of the peace or other officials examined suspects and witnesses before trial. These examinations were sometimes read in court in lieu of live testimony, a practice that "occasioned frequent demands by the prisoner to have his 'accusers,' *i.e.* the witnesses against him, brought before him face to face." 1 J. Stephen, History of the Criminal Law of England 326 (1883). In some cases, these demands were refused. See 9 W.

---

7. The court rejected the State's argument that guarantees of trustworthiness were unnecessary since petitioner waived his confrontation rights by invoking the marital privilege. It reasoned that "forcing the defendant to choose between the marital privilege and confronting his spouse presents an untenable Hobson's choice." The State has not challenged this holding here. The State also has not challenged the Court of Appeals' conclusion (not reached by the State Supreme Court) that the confrontation violation, if it occurred, was not harmless. We express no opinion on these matters.

Holdsworth, History of English Law 216-217, 228 (3d ed. 1944); *e.g.*, Raleigh's Case, 2 How. St. Tr. 1, 15-16, 24 (1603).

Pretrial examinations became routine under two statutes passed during the reign of Queen Mary in the 16th century. These Marian bail and committal statutes required justices of the peace to examine suspects and witnesses in felony cases and to certify the results to the court. It is doubtful that the original purpose of the examinations was to produce evidence admissible at trial. Whatever the original purpose, however, they came to be used as evidence in some cases, see M. Hale, Pleas of the Crown 284 (1736), resulting in an adoption of continental procedure.

The most notorious instances of civil-law examination occurred in the great political trials of the 16th and 17th centuries. One such was the 1603 trial of Sir Walter Raleigh for treason. Lord Cobham, Raleigh's alleged accomplice, had implicated him in an examination before the Privy Council and in a letter. At Raleigh's trial, these were read to the jury. Raleigh argued that Cobham had lied to save himself: "Cobham is absolutely in the King's mercy; to excuse me cannot avail him; by accusing me he may hope for favour." 1 D. Jardine, Criminal Trials 435 (1832). Suspecting that Cobham would recant, Raleigh demanded that the judges call him to appear, arguing that "[t]he Proof of the Common Law is by witness and jury: let Cobham be here, let him speak it. Call my accuser before my face . . . ." The judges refused, and, despite Raleigh's protestations that he was being tried "by the Spanish Inquisition," the jury convicted, and Raleigh was sentenced to death.

One of Raleigh's trial judges later lamented that "'the justice of England has never been so degraded and injured as by the condemnation of Sir Walter Raleigh.'"; Through a series of statutory and judicial reforms, English law developed a right of confrontation that limited these abuses. For example, treason statutes required witnesses to confront the accused "face to face" at his arraignment. Courts, meanwhile, developed relatively strict rules of unavailability, admitting examinations only if the witness was demonstrably unable to testify in person. Several authorities also stated that a suspect's confession could be admitted only against himself, and not against others he implicated.

One recurring question was whether the admissibility of an unavailable witness's pretrial examination depended on whether the defendant had had an opportunity to cross-examine him. In 1696, the Court of King's Bench answered this question in the affirmative, in the widely reported misdemeanor libel case of King v. Paine. The court ruled that, even though a witness was dead, his examination was not admissible where "the defendant not being present when [it was] taken before the mayor . . . had lost the benefit of a cross-examination."

Paine had settled the rule requiring a prior opportunity for cross-examination as a matter of common law, but some doubts remained over whether the Marian statutes prescribed an exception to it in felony cases. The statutes did not identify the circumstances under which examinations were admissible, and some inferred that no prior opportunity for cross-examination was required . . . .

B

Controversial examination practices were also used in the Colonies. Early in the 18th century, for example, the Virginia Council protested against the Governor for having "privately issued several commissions to examine witnesses against particular men *ex parte*," complaining that "the person accused is not admitted to be confronted with, or defend himself against his defamers." A decade before the Revolution, England gave jurisdiction over Stamp Act offenses to the admiralty courts, which followed civil-law rather than common-law procedures and thus routinely took testimony by deposition or private judicial examination. Colonial representatives protested that the Act subverted their rights "by extending the jurisdiction of the courts of admiralty beyond its ancient limits." Resolutions of the Stamp Act Congress §8th (Oct. 19, 1765). John Adams, defending a merchant in a high-profile admiralty case, argued: "Examinations of witnesses upon Interrogatories, are only by the Civil Law. Interrogatories are unknown at common Law, and Englishmen and common Lawyers have an aversion to them if not an Abhorrence of them." Draft of Argument in Sewall v. Hancock (1768-1769).

Many declarations of rights adopted around the time of the Revolution guaranteed a right of confrontation. The proposed Federal Constitution, however, did not. At the Massachusetts ratifying convention, Abraham Holmes objected to this omission precisely on the ground that it would lead to civil-law practices: "The mode of trial is altogether indetermined; . . . whether [the defendant] is to be allowed to confront the witnesses, and have the advantage of cross-examination, we are not yet told . . . . [W]e shall find Congress possessed of powers enabling them to institute judicatories little less inauspicious than a certain tribunal in Spain, . . . the *Inquisition*." 2 Debates on the Federal Constitution 110-111 (J. Elliot 2d ed. 1863). Similarly, a prominent Antifederalist writing under the pseudonym Federal Farmer criticized the use of "written evidence" while objecting to the omission of a vicinage right: "Nothing can be more essential than the cross examining [of] witnesses, and generally before the triers of the facts in question. . . . [W]ritten evidence . . . [is] almost useless; it must be frequently taken ex parte, and but very seldom leads to the proper discovery of truth." R. Lee, Letter IV by the Federal Farmer (Oct. 15, 1787). The First Congress responded by including the Confrontation Clause in the proposal that became the Sixth Amendment . . . .

III

This history supports two inferences about the meaning of the Sixth Amendment.

A

First, the principal evil at which the Confrontation Clause was directed was the civil-law mode of criminal procedure, and particularly its use of *ex parte* examinations as evidence against the accused. It was these practices that the Crown deployed in notorious treason cases like Raleigh's; that the Marian statutes invited; that English law's assertion of a right to confrontation was meant to prohibit; and that the founding-era rhetoric decried. The Sixth Amendment must be interpreted with this focus in mind.

Accordingly, we once again reject the view that the Confrontation Clause applies of its own force only to in-court testimony, and that its application to out-of-court statements introduced at trial depends upon "the law of Evidence for the time being." 3 Wigmore §1397, at 101; accord, Dutton v. Evans, 400 U.S. 74, 94 (Harlan, J., concurring in result). Leaving the regulation of out-of-court statements to the law of evidence would render the Confrontation Clause powerless to prevent even the most flagrant inquisitorial practices. Raleigh was, after all, perfectly free to confront those who read Cobham's confession in court.

This focus also suggests that not all hearsay implicates the Sixth Amendment's core concerns. An off-hand, overheard remark might be unreliable evidence and thus a good candidate for exclusion under hearsay rules, but it bears little resemblance to the civil-law abuses the Confrontation Clause targeted. On the other hand, *ex parte* examinations might sometimes be admissible under modern hearsay rules, but the Framers certainly would not have condoned them.

The text of the Confrontation Clause reflects this focus. It applies to "witnesses" against the accused—in other words, those who "bear testimony." 1 N. Webster, An American Dictionary of the English Language (1828). "Testimony," in turn, is typically "[a] solemn declaration or affirmation made for the purpose of establishing or proving some fact." *Ibid.* An accuser who makes a formal statement to government officers bears testimony in a sense that a person who makes a casual remark to an acquaintance does not. The constitutional text, like the history underlying the common-law right of confrontation, thus reflects an especially acute concern with a specific type of out-of-court statement.

Various formulations of this core class of "testimonial" statements exist: "*ex parte* in-court testimony or its functional equivalent—that is, material such as affidavits, custodial examinations, prior testimony that the defendant was unable to cross-examine, or similar pretrial statements that declarants would reasonably expect to be used prosecutorially," Brief for Petitioner 23; "extrajudicial statements . . . contained in formalized testimonial materials, such as affidavits, depositions, prior testimony, or confessions," White v. Illinois, 502 U.S. 346 (1992) (Thomas, J., joined by Scalia, J., concurring in part and concurring in judgment); "statements that were made under circumstances which would lead an objective witness reasonably to believe that the statement would be available for use at a later trial," Brief for National Association of Criminal Defense Lawyers et al. as *Amici Curiae* 3. These formulations all share a common nucleus and then define the Clause's coverage at various levels of abstraction around it. Regardless of the precise articulation, some statements qualify under any definition—for example, *ex parte* testimony at a preliminary hearing.

Statements taken by police officers in the course of interrogations are also testimonial under even a narrow standard. Police interrogations bear a striking resemblance to examinations by justices of the peace in England. The statements are not *sworn* testimony, but the absence of oath was not dispositive. Cobham's examination was unsworn, see 1 Jardine, Criminal Trials, at 430, yet Raleigh's trial has long been thought a paradigmatic confrontation violation. Under the Marian statutes, witnesses were typically put on oath, but suspects were not. Yet Hawkins and others went out of their way to caution that such unsworn confessions were not admissible against anyone but the confessor.

That interrogators are police officers rather than magistrates does not change the picture either. Justices of the peace conducting examinations under the Marian statutes were not magistrates as we understand that office today, but had an essentially investigative and prosecutorial function. England did not have a professional police force until the 19th century, so it is not surprising that other government officers performed the investigative functions now associated primarily with the police. The involvement of government officers in the production of testimonial evidence presents the same risk, whether the officers are police or justices of the peace.

In sum, even if the Sixth Amendment is not solely concerned with testimonial hearsay, that is its primary object, and interrogations by law enforcement officers fall squarely within that class.[8]

B

The historical record also supports a second proposition: that the Framers would not have allowed admission of testimonial statements of a witness who did not appear at trial unless he was unavailable to testify, and the defendant had had a prior opportunity for cross-examination. The text of the Sixth Amendment does not suggest any open-ended exceptions from the confrontation requirement to be developed by the courts. Rather, the "right . . . to be confronted with the witnesses against him," Amdt. 6, is most naturally read as a reference to the right of confrontation at common law, admitting only those exceptions established at the time of the founding. As the English authorities above reveal, the common law in 1791 conditioned admissibility of an absent witness's examination on unavailability and a prior opportunity to cross-examine. The Sixth Amendment therefore incorporates those limitations. The numerous early state decisions applying the same test confirm that these principles were received as part of the common law in this country.[9]

[This] is not to deny, as the Chief Justice notes, that "[t]here were always exceptions to the general rule of exclusion" of hearsay evidence. Several had become well established by 1791. See 3 Wigmore §1397, at 101. But there is scant evidence that exceptions were invoked to admit *testimonial* statements against the accused in a *criminal* case.[10] Most of the hearsay exceptions covered statements that by their nature were not testimonial-for example, business records or statements in furtherance of a conspiracy. We do not infer from these that the Framers thought exceptions would apply even to prior testimony. Cf. Lilly v. Virginia, 527 U.S. 116 (1999) (plurality opinion) ("[A]ccomplices' confessions that inculpate a criminal defendant are not within a firmly rooted exception to the hearsay rule").[11]

---

8. We use the term "interrogation" in its colloquial, rather than any technical legal, sense. Cf. Rhode Island v. Innis, 446 U.S. 291, 300-301 (1980). Just as various definitions of "testimonial" exist, one can imagine various definitions of "interrogation," and we need not select among them in this case. Sylvia's recorded statement, knowingly given in response to structured police questioning, qualifies under any conceivable definition.

9. The Chief Justice claims that English law's treatment of testimonial statements was inconsistent at the time of the framing, but the examples he cites relate to examinations under the Marian statutes. As we have explained, to the extent Marian examinations were admissible, it was only because the statutes *derogated* from the common law[.]

10. The one deviation we have found involves dying declarations[.] Although many dying declarations may not be testimonial, there is authority for admitting even those that clearly are. We need not decide in this case whether the Sixth Amendment incorporates an exception for testimonial dying declarations. If this exception must be accepted on historical grounds, it is *sui generis*.

11. []Involvement of government officers in the production of testimony with an eye toward trial presents unique potential for prosecutorial abuse—a fact borne out time and again throughout a history with which the Framers were keenly familiar. This consideration does not evaporate when testimony happens to fall within some broad, modern hearsay exception, even if that exception might be justifiable in other circumstances.

IV

. . .

Our cases have . . . remained faithful to the Framers' understanding: Testimonial statements of witnesses absent from trial have been admitted only where the declarant is unavailable, and only where the defendant has had a prior opportunity to cross-examine.[12]

V

Although the results of our decisions have generally been faithful to the original meaning of the Confrontation Clause, the same cannot be said of our rationales. *Roberts* conditions the admissibility of all hearsay evidence on whether it falls under a "firmly rooted hearsay exception" or bears "particularized guarantees of trustworthiness." 448 U.S., at 66. This test departs from the historical principles identified above in two respects. First, it is too broad: It applies the same mode of analysis whether or not the hearsay consists of *ex parte* testimony. This often results in close constitutional scrutiny in cases that are far removed from the core concerns of the Clause. At the same time, however, the test is too narrow: It admits statements that *do* consist of *ex parte* testimony upon a mere finding of reliability. This malleable standard often fails to protect against paradigmatic confrontation violations.

Members of this Court and academics have suggested that we revise our doctrine to reflect more accurately the original understanding of the Clause. They offer two proposals: First, that we apply the Confrontation Clause only to testimonial statements, leaving the remainder to regulation by hearsay law—thus eliminating the overbreadth referred to above. Second, that we impose an absolute bar to statements that are testimonial, absent a prior opportunity to cross-examine—thus eliminating the excessive narrowness referred to above.

In *White*, we considered the first proposal and rejected it. Although our analysis in this case casts doubt on that holding, we need not definitively resolve whether it survives our decision today, because Sylvia Crawford's statement is testimonial under any definition. This case does, however, squarely implicate the second proposal.

A

Where testimonial statements are involved, we do not think the Framers meant to leave the Sixth Amendment's protection to the vagaries of the rules of evidence, much less to amorphous notions of "reliability." Certainly none of the authorities discussed above acknowledges any general reliability exception to the common-law rule. Admitting statements deemed reliable by a judge is fundamentally at odds with the right of confrontation. To be sure, the Clause's ultimate goal is to ensure reliability of evidence, but it is a procedural rather than a substantive guarantee. It commands, not that evidence be reliable, but that reliability be assessed in a particular manner: by testing in

---

12.   [W]e reiterate that, when the declarant appears for cross-examination at trial, the Confrontation Clause places no constraints at all on the use of his prior testimonial statements. See California v. Green, 399 U.S. 149 (1970). The Clause does not bar admission of a statement so long as the declarant is present at trial to defend or explain it. (The Clause also does not bar the use of testimonial statements for purposes other than establishing the truth of the matter asserted.)

the crucible of cross-examination. The Clause thus reflects a judgment, not only about the desirability of reliable evidence (a point on which there could be little dissent), but about how reliability can best be determined. Cf. 3 Blackstone, Commentaries, at 373 ("This open examination of witnesses . . . is much more conducive to the clearing up of truth"); M. Hale, History and Analysis of the Common Law of England 258 (1713) (adversarial testing "beats and bolts out the Truth much better").

The *Roberts* test allows a jury to hear evidence, untested by the adversary process, based on a mere judicial determination of reliability. It thus replaces the constitutionally prescribed method of assessing reliability with a wholly foreign one. In this respect, it is very different from exceptions to the Confrontation Clause that make no claim to be a surrogate means of assessing reliability. For example, the rule of forfeiture by wrongdoing (which we accept) extinguishes confrontation claims on essentially equitable grounds; it does not purport to be an alternative means of determining reliability. See Reynolds v. United States, 98 U.S. 145, 158-159.

The Raleigh trial itself involved the very sorts of reliability determinations that *Roberts* authorizes. In the face of Raleigh's repeated demands for confrontation, the prosecution responded with many of the arguments a court applying *Roberts* might invoke today: that Cobham's statements were self-inculpatory, that they were not made in the heat of passion, and that they were not "extracted from [him] upon any hopes or promise of Pardon." It is not plausible that the Framers' only objection to the trial was that Raleigh's judges did not properly weigh these factors before sentencing him to death. Rather, the problem was that the judges refused to allow Raleigh to confront Cobham in court, where he could cross-examine him and try to expose his accusation as a lie.

Dispensing with confrontation because testimony is obviously reliable is akin to dispensing with jury trial because a defendant is obviously guilty. This is not what the Sixth Amendment prescribes.

B

The legacy of *Roberts* in other courts vindicates the Framers' wisdom in rejecting a general reliability exception. The framework is so unpredictable that it fails to provide meaningful protection from even core confrontation violations. Reliability is an amorphous, if not entirely subjective, concept.

. . .

The unpardonable vice of the *Roberts* test, however, is not its unpredictability, but its demonstrated capacity to admit core testimonial statements that the Confrontation Clause plainly meant to exclude. Despite the plurality's speculation in *Lilly*, 527 U.S., at 137, that it was "highly unlikely" that accomplice confessions implicating the accused could survive *Roberts*, courts continue routinely to admit them. One recent study found that, after *Lilly*, appellate courts admitted accomplice statements to the authorities in 25 out of 70 cases — more than one-third of the time. Kirst, Appellate Court Answers to the Confrontation Questions in *Lilly v. Virginia*, 53 Syracuse L. Rev. 87, 105 (2003). Courts have invoked *Roberts* to admit other sorts of plainly testimonial statements despite the absence of any opportunity to cross-examine. See[, e.g.,] United States v. Aguilar, 295 F.3d 1018, 1021-1023 (CA9 2002) (plea allocution showing existence of a conspiracy); United States v. Papajohn, 212 F.3d 1112, 1118-1120 (CA8 2000) (grand jury testimony).

To add insult to injury, some of the courts that admit untested testimonial statements find reliability in the very factors that *make* the statements testimonial. As noted
earlier, one court relied on the fact that the witness's statement was made to police
while in custody on pending charges—the theory being that this made the statement
more clearly against penal interest and thus more reliable. Other courts routinely rely
on the fact that a prior statement is given under oath in judicial proceedings, [e.g.,
plea allocution, grand jury testimony]. That inculpating statements are given in a testimonial setting is not an antidote to the confrontation problem, but rather the trigger
that makes the Clause's demands most urgent. It is not enough to point out that most
of the usual safeguards of the adversary process attend the statement, when the single
safeguard missing is the one the Confrontation Clause demands.

C

Roberts' failings were on full display in the proceedings below. [The Court recounted
the lower courts' reliance on conflicting factors indicating that Sylvia Crawford's
recorded statement was both seemingly unreliable and reliable as an example of
Roberts''s "unpredictable and inconsistent application."]

. . .

We readily concede that we could resolve this case by simply reweighing the "reliability factors" under *Roberts* and finding that Sylvia Crawford's statement falls short.
But we view this as one of those rare cases in which the result below is so improbable
that it reveals a fundamental failure on our part to interpret the Constitution in a way
that secures its intended constraint on judicial discretion. Moreover, to reverse the
Washington Supreme Court's decision after conducting our own reliability analysis
would perpetuate, not avoid, what the Sixth Amendment condemns. The Constitution
prescribes a procedure for determining the reliability of testimony in criminal trials,
and we, no less than the state courts, lack authority to replace it with one of our own
devising.

We have no doubt that the courts below were acting in utmost good faith when
they found reliability. The Framers, however, would not have been content to indulge
this assumption. They knew that judges, like other government officers, could not
always be trusted to safeguard the rights of the people; the likes of the dread Lord
Jeffreys were not yet too distant a memory. They were loath to leave too much discretion in judicial hands. Cf. U.S. Const., Amdt. 6 (criminal jury trial); Amdt. 7 (civil
jury trial). By replacing categorical constitutional guarantees with open-ended balancing tests, we do violence to their design. Vague standards are manipulable, and, while
that might be a small concern in run-of-the-mill assault prosecutions like this one, the
Framers had an eye toward politically charged cases like Raleigh's—great state trials
where the impartiality of even those at the highest levels of the judiciary might not
be so clear. It is difficult to imagine *Roberts'* providing any meaningful protection in
those circumstances.

. . .

Where nontestimonial hearsay is at issue, it is wholly consistent with the
Framers' design to afford the States flexibility in their development of hearsay
law—as does *Roberts*, and as would an approach that exempted such statements
from Confrontation Clause scrutiny altogether. Where testimonial evidence is at
issue, however, the Sixth Amendment demands what the common law required:

unavailability and a prior opportunity for cross-examination. We leave for another day any effort to spell out a comprehensive definition of "testimonial." Whatever else the term covers, it applies at a minimum to prior testimony at a preliminary hearing, before a grand jury, or at a former trial; and to police interrogations. These are the modern practices with closest kinship to the abuses at which the Confrontation Clause was directed.

In this case, the State admitted Sylvia's testimonial statement against petitioner, despite the fact that he had no opportunity to cross-examine her. That alone is sufficient to make out a violation of the Sixth Amendment. *Roberts* notwithstanding, we decline to mine the record in search of indicia of reliability. Where testimonial statements are at issue, the only indicium of reliability sufficient to satisfy constitutional demands is the one the Constitution actually prescribes: confrontation.

The judgment of the Washington Supreme Court is reversed, and the case is remanded for further proceedings not inconsistent with this opinion.

It is so ordered.

Chief Justice REHNQUIST, with whom Justice O'CONNOR joins, concurring in the judgment.

I dissent from the Court's decision to overrule Ohio v. Roberts [. . . .] It is a change of course not in the least necessary to reverse the judgment of the Supreme Court of Washington in this case. The result the Court reaches follows inexorably from *Roberts* and its progeny without any need for overruling that line of cases. In Idaho v. Wright, 497 U.S. 805, 820-824 (1990), we held that an out-of-court statement was not admissible simply because the truthfulness of that statement was corroborated by other evidence at trial. [T]he Supreme Court of Washington gave decisive weight to the "interlocking nature of the two statements." No re-weighing of the "reliability factors," which is hypothesized by the Court, is required to reverse the judgment here. A citation to Idaho v. Wright, *supra*, would suffice.

KEY POINTS

1. In *Crawford*, the Supreme Court held that the confrontation clause of the Sixth Amendment applies to the government's use of "testimonial" hearsay statements against a criminal defendant. The Court based its holding on what it considered to be the core value of the clause, which is to protect the criminal defendant's right to cross-examination.

2. The Court did not establish a single definition of "testimonial," but stated three possible definitions. At its core, according to the Court, "testimonial" means a statement made when the declarant is acting like a witness who "bears testimony," further defined as a "solemn declaration or affirmation made for the purpose of establishing or proving some fact."

3. Testimonial hearsay statements may be admitted at trial against a criminal defendant only if the declarant is unavailable and the defendant has had a prior opportunity to cross-examine the declarant. In addition, the government's use of all hearsay statements made by a testifying witness does not violate the defendant's confrontation right. And, admission of nontestimonial hearsay against the defendant does not violate that right.

PROBLEMS

8.97. Return to Problem 3.4, State v. Blair, at page 137. The prosecutor seeks to admit the following out-of-court statements by Norma. The court cites three different doctrinal definitions of "testimonial" statements from three different sources. How do they differ in application to Norma's statements? Do the different tests identify different concerns about "testimonial" statements?

    (a)   A friend of Norma's says that a month before the attack, Norma told the friend, "Last week I told Jimmy that I was going to break up with him and leave the Bay Area soon. Jimmy was furious."

    (b)   Inside the locked drawer in which police found photographs of Norma showing severe bruising and date-stamped July 25, 2009, a handwritten diary was also found. On the page dated July 21, 2009, it stated: "Jimmy beat me after an argument."

    (c)   On August 1, 2009, Norma filed a formal complaint against Blair for assault and battery at the local police station. A week later she withdrew the complaint.

8.98. Return to Problem 8.49 on page 494. Are Mrs. D'Onofrio's statements during the 911 call "testimonial" under *Crawford*? Are her subsequent statements to the police officers "testimonial" under *Crawford*? (Assume that both sets of statements would be admissible under the hearsay rule.)

NOTES

1. The *Crawford* opinion suggests that statements falling within the hearsay exceptions for dying declarations and the doctrine of forfeiture by wrongdoing might be excepted from the ban on testimonial statements due to their historical pedigree. Both exceptions are discussed in Section 7 starting on page 621, infra.

2. In dicta, the Court also indicates that certain types of hearsay are not testimonial, including business records and co-conspirators' statements. Unless "testimonial" is given the most narrow definition of formalized testimonial materials, this seems plainly wrong. Both types of statements could certainly fit within the "reasonable expectations" test. Government business records are often created just for that purpose, as courts have had to acknowledge. See page 612, infra.

3. Note that the Supreme Court did not review the holding below that Sylvia Crawford was unavailable due to the defendant's invocation of the state marital privilege. Doesn't it seem a bit peculiar to think of Mrs. Crawford as constitutionally unavailable for cross-examination by her husband when it is her husband's choice to keep her off the stand?

4. The new approach to confrontation announced in *Crawford* was applied to cases that were currently pending in both federal and state courts. In Whorton v. Bockting, 549 U.S. 406 (2007), the Supreme Court decided that *Crawford* was not retroactive, meaning that it is not applicable to pre-*Crawford* convictions under habeas corpus review in federal courts. State courts, however, could choose to give broader effect to new rules of constitutional criminal procedure. In Danforth v. Minnesota,

552 U.S. 264 (2008), the Court held that the federal doctrine of nonretroactivity was intended to limit the authority of federal courts to overturn state convictions, not to limit a state court's authority to grant relief for violations of new rules of constitutional law when reviewing its own state convictions.

5. The Supreme Court held in its next major confrontation clause opinion, Davis v. Washington, 547 U.S. 813 (2006), that if a statement is nontestimonial, the confrontation clause has no bearing on its admissibility. Id. at 824. Thus, the reliability inquiry of Ohio v. Roberts is now completely obsolete except in post-conviction review to which *Crawford* does not apply. See, e.g., United States v. Watson, 525 F.3d 583, 588-589 (7th Cir. 2008).

6. One of the definitions of *testimonial* offered by the Supreme Court was that proposed by Justices Scalia and Thomas in White v. Illinois — "extrajudicial statements . . . contained in formalized testimonial materials, such as affidavits, depositions, prior testimony, or confessions," 502 U.S. at 346. And in *Crawford* itself, the majority concluded its opinion by stating that, at a minimum, "testimonial" applies to "prior testimony at a preliminary hearing, before a grand jury, or at a former trial; and to police interrogations." 541 U.S. at 68. Courts have readily adopted these categories. United States v. Bruno, 383 F.3d 65, 78 (2d Cir. 2004) (plea allocution transcripts and grand jury testimony of unavailable witnesses are testimonial). The Court itself applied the "formalized testimonial materials" standard in Melendez-Diaz v. Massachusetts, 129 S. Ct. 2527 (2009). See page 612, infra.

7. Another of the definitions of testimonial statements mentioned, but not explicitly adopted, in *Crawford* was statements "made under circumstances which would lead an objective witness reasonably to believe that the statement would be available for use at a later trial." After *Crawford*, lower courts started to apply a similar definition, usually using "reasonable expectations" terminology to exclude statements they found to be testimonial. United States v. Cromer, 389 F.3d 662, 674-678 (6th Cir. 2004) (statements given by confidential informants to police that implicated others in criminal activities); United States v. Summers, 414 F.3d 1287, 1302 (10th Cir. 2005) (statement by declarant in custody but not during interrogation); United States v. Hinton, 423 F.3d 355, 360 (3d Cir. 2005) (victim made identification while riding in police car). The *Summers* court stated the justification for this standard:

> It is the reasonable expectation that a statement may be later used at trial that distinguishes the flippant remark, proffered to a casual acquaintance . . . from the true testimonial statement. Certain factual circumstances surrounding the out-of-court statement give rise to just such an expectation. . . . We further reject a narrow approach that would limit testimonial statements to those made by witnesses "who testify . . . via government-prepared affidavits, depositions, videotapes, and the like." [Id. at 1302.]

3.   The Definition of Testimonial Statements After Crawford v. Washington: Statements Made During Questioning by Police

Many police interrogations are like that of Mrs. Crawford. They are formal, recorded, consist of structured questions, and have a law enforcement purpose. Such interrogations lie at the core of concern about a defendant's confrontation right. But a difference of opinion quickly emerged after *Crawford* as to how broadly this core concern extends. Some courts defined "interrogation" to include most statements made in response to police questions. Other courts held that responses to initial police inquiries at a crime scene are typically not testimonial. In 2006, the Supreme Court addressed this split of opinion in two companion cases, Davis v. Washington and Hammon v. Indiana.

a.   The "Primary Purpose" Test: Davis v. Washington

DAVIS v. WASHINGTON, HAMMON v. INDIANA
547 U.S. 813 (2006)

Justice SCALIA delivered the opinion of the Court, in which ROBERTS, C.J., STEVENS, KENNEDY, SOUTER, GINSBURG, BREYER, and ALITO, JJ., joined. THOMAS, J., filed an opinion concurring in the judgment in part and dissenting in part.

These cases require us to determine when statements made to law enforcement personnel during a 911 call or at a crime scene are "testimonial" and thus subject to the requirements of the Sixth Amendment's Confrontation Clause.

I

A

The relevant statements in Davis v. Washington, No. 05-5224, were made to a 911 emergency operator on February 1, 2001. When the operator answered the initial call, the connection terminated before anyone spoke. She reversed the call, and Michelle McCottry answered. In the ensuing conversation, the operator ascertained that McCottry was involved in a domestic disturbance with her former boyfriend Adrian Davis, the petitioner in this case:

"911 Operator: Hello.
"Complainant: Hello.
"911 Operator: What's going on?
"Complainant: He's here jumpin' on me again.
"911 Operator: Okay. Listen to me carefully. Are you in a house or an apartment?
"Complainant: I'm in a house.
"911 Operator: Are there any weapons?
"Complainant: No. He's usin' his fists.
"911 Operator: Okay. Has he been drinking?
"Complainant: No.
"911 Operator: Okay, sweetie. I've got help started. Stay on the line with me, okay?
"Complainant: I'm on the line.
"911 Operator: Listen to me carefully. Do you know his last name?
"Complainant: It's Davis.
"911 Operator: Davis? Okay, what's his first name?
"Complainant: Adran.
"911 Operator: What is it?
"Complainant: Adrian.

"911 Operator: Adrian?

"Complainant: Yeah.

"911 Operator: Okay. What's his middle initial?

"Complainant: Martell. He's runnin' now."

As the conversation continued, the operator learned that Davis had "just run out the door" after hitting McCottry, and that he was leaving in a car with someone else. McCottry started talking, but the operator cut her off, saying, "Stop talking and answer my questions." She then gathered more information about Davis (including his birthday), and learned that Davis had told McCottry that his purpose in coming to the house was "to get his stuff," since McCottry was moving. McCottry described the context of the assault, after which the operator told her that the police were on their way. "They're gonna check the area for him first," the operator said, "and then they're gonna come talk to you."

The police arrived within four minutes of the 911 call and observed McCottry's shaken state, the "fresh injuries on her forearm and her face," and her "frantic efforts to gather her belongings and her children so that they could leave the residence."

The State charged Davis with felony violation of a domestic no-contact order. "The State's only witnesses were the two police officers who responded to the 911 call. Both officers testified that McCottry exhibited injuries that appeared to be recent, but neither officer could testify as to the cause of the injuries." McCottry presumably could have testified as to whether Davis was her assailant, but she did not appear. Over Davis's objection, based on the Confrontation Clause of the Sixth Amendment, the trial court admitted the recording of her exchange with the 911 operator, and the jury convicted him. The Washington Court of Appeals affirmed. The Supreme Court of Washington, with one dissenting justice, also affirmed, concluding that the portion of the 911 conversation in which McCottry identified Davis was not testimonial, and that if other portions of the conversation were testimonial, admitting them was harmless beyond a reasonable doubt.

In Hammon v. Indiana, No. 05-5705, police responded late on the night of February 26, 2003, to a "reported domestic disturbance" at the home of Hershel and Amy Hammon. They found Amy alone on the front porch, appearing "'somewhat frightened,'" but she told them that "'nothing was the matter.'" She gave them permission to enter the house, where an officer saw "a gas heating unit in the corner of the living room" that had "flames coming out of the . . . partial glass front. There were pieces of glass on the ground in front of it and there was flame emitting from the front of the heating unit."

Hershel, meanwhile, was in the kitchen. He told the police "that he and his wife had 'been in an argument' but 'everything was fine now' and the argument 'never became physical.'" By this point Amy had come back inside. One of the officers remained with Hershel; the other went to the living room to talk with Amy, and "again asked [her] what had occurred." Hershel made several attempts to participate in Amy's conversation with the police, but was rebuffed. The officer later testified that Hershel "became angry when I insisted that [he] stay separated from Mrs. Hammon so that we can investigate what had happened." After hearing Amy's account, the officer "had her fill out and sign a battery affidavit." Amy handwrote the following: "Broke our Furnace & shoved me down on the floor into the broken glass. Hit me in the chest and threw me down. Broke our lamps & phone. Tore up my van where I couldn't leave the house. Attacked my daughter."

The State charged Hershel with domestic battery and with violating his probation. Amy was subpoenaed, but she did not appear at his subsequent bench trial. The
State called the officer who had questioned Amy, and asked him to recount what Amy
told him and to authenticate the affidavit. Hershel's counsel repeatedly objected to the
admission of this evidence. At one point, after hearing the prosecutor defend the affidavit because it was made "under oath," defense counsel said, "That doesn't give us the
opportunity to cross examine [the] person who allegedly drafted it. Makes me mad."
Nonetheless, the trial court admitted the affidavit as a "present sense impression," and
Amy's statements as "excited utterances" that "are expressly permitted in these kinds of
cases even if the declarant is not available to testify." The officer thus testified that Amy

> "informed me that she and Hershel had been in an argument. That he became
> irrate [sic] over the fact of their daughter going to a boyfriend's house. The argu-
> ment became . . . physical after being verbal and she informed me that Mr.
> Hammon, during the verbal part of the argument was breaking things in the liv-
> ing room and I believe she stated he broke the phone, broke the lamp, broke the
> front of the heater. When it became physical he threw her down into the glass of
> the heater . . . . She informed me Mr. Hammon had pushed her onto the ground,
> had shoved her head into the broken glass of the heater and that he had punched
> her in the chest twice I believe."

The trial judge found Hershel guilty on both charges, and the Indiana Court of
Appeals affirmed in relevant part. The Indiana Supreme Court also affirmed, concluding that Amy's statement was admissible for state-law purposes as an excited utterance;
that "a 'testimonial' statement is one given or taken in significant part for purposes of
preserving it for potential future use in legal proceedings," where "the motivations of
the questioner and declarant are the central concerns"; and that Amy's oral statement
was not "testimonial" under these standards. It also concluded that, although the affidavit was testimonial and thus wrongly admitted, it was harmless beyond a reasonable
doubt, largely because the trial was to the bench. We granted certiorari.

II

The Confrontation Clause of the Sixth Amendment provides: "In all criminal prosecutions, the accused shall enjoy the right . . . to be confronted with the witnesses
against him." In Crawford v. Washington, we held that this provision bars "admission
of testimonial statements of a witness who did not appear at trial unless he was unavailable to testify, and the defendant had had a prior opportunity for cross-examination."
A critical portion of this holding, and the portion central to resolution of the two cases
now before us, is the phrase "testimonial statements . . . ."
    Our opinion in Crawford set forth "various formulations" of the core class of
"'testimonial'" statements . . . . Among those, we said, were "statements taken by
police officers in the course of interrogations." The questioning that generated the
deponent's statement in Crawford — which was made and recorded while she was in
police custody, after having been given Miranda warnings as a possible suspect herself — "qualifies under any conceivable definition" of an "interrogation." We therefore did not define that term, except to say that "we use [it] . . . in its colloquial, rather
than any technical legal, sense," and that "one can imagine various definitions . . . ,
and we need not select among them in this case." The character of the statements in

the present cases is not as clear, and these cases require us to determine more precisely which police interrogations produce testimony.

Without attempting to produce an exhaustive classification of all conceivable statements — or even all conceivable statements in response to police interrogation — as either testimonial or nontestimonial, it suffices to decide the present cases to hold as follows: Statements are nontestimonial when made in the course of police interrogation under circumstances objectively indicating that the primary purpose of the interrogation is to enable police assistance to meet an ongoing emergency. They are testimonial when the circumstances objectively indicate that there is no such ongoing emergency, and that the primary purpose of the interrogation is to establish or prove past events potentially relevant to later criminal prosecution.[13]

III

A

. . .

The question before us in *Davis*, then, is whether, objectively considered, the interrogation that took place in the course of the 911 call produced testimonial statements. When we said in *Crawford*, that "interrogations by law enforcement officers fall squarely within [the] class" of testimonial hearsay, we had immediately in mind (for that was the case before us) interrogations solely directed at establishing the facts of a past crime, in order to identify (or provide evidence to convict) the perpetrator. . . . A 911 call, on the other hand, and at least the initial interrogation conducted in connection with a 911 call, is ordinarily not designed primarily to "establish or prove" some past fact, but to describe current circumstances requiring police assistance.

The difference between the interrogation in *Davis* and the one in *Crawford* is apparent on the face of things. In *Davis*, McCottry was speaking about events *as they were actually happening*, rather than "describing past events." Sylvia Crawford's interrogation, on the other hand, took place hours after the events she described had occurred. Moreover, any reasonable listener would recognize that McCottry (unlike Sylvia Crawford) was facing an ongoing emergency. Although one *might* call 911 to provide a narrative report of a crime absent any imminent danger, McCottry's call was plainly a call for help against a bona fide physical threat. Third, the nature of what was asked and answered in *Davis*, again viewed objectively, was such that the elicited statements were necessary to be able to *resolve* the present emergency, rather than simply to learn (as in *Crawford*) what had happened in the past. That is true even of the operator's effort to establish the identity of the assailant, so that the dispatched officers might know whether they would be encountering a violent felon. And finally, the difference in the level of formality between the two interviews is striking. Crawford was responding calmly, at the station house, to a series of questions, with the officer-interrogator taping and making notes of her answers; McCottry's frantic answers were

13. This is not to imply, however, that statements made in the absence of any interrogation are necessarily nontestimonial. The Framers were no more willing to exempt from cross-examination volunteered testimony or answers to open-ended questions than they were to exempt answers to detailed interrogation. . . . And of course even when interrogation exists, it is in the final analysis the declarant's statements, not the interrogator's questions, that the Confrontation Clause requires us to evaluate.

provided over the phone, in an environment that was not tranquil, or even (as far as any reasonable 911 operator could make out) safe.

We conclude from all this that the circumstances of McCottry's interrogation objectively indicate its primary purpose was to enable police assistance to meet an ongoing emergency. She simply was not acting as a *witness*; she was not *testifying*. What she said was not "a weaker substitute for live testimony" at trial, like Lord Cobham's statements in *Raleigh's Case . . .* , or Sylvia Crawford's statement in *Crawford*. In each of those cases, the *ex parte* actors and the evidentiary products of the *ex parte* communication aligned perfectly with their courtroom analogues. McCottry's emergency statement does not. No "witness" goes into court to proclaim an emergency and seek help.

. . .

This is not to say that a conversation which begins as an interrogation to determine the need for emergency assistance cannot, as the Indiana Supreme Court put it, "evolve into testimonial statements," once that purpose has been achieved. In this case, for example, after the operator gained the information needed to address the exigency of the moment, the emergency appears to have ended (when Davis drove away from the premises). The operator then told McCottry to be quiet, and proceeded to pose a battery of questions. It could readily be maintained that, from that point on, McCottry's statements were testimonial, not unlike the "structured police questioning" that occurred in *Crawford*. This presents no great problem . . . . [T]rial courts will recognize the point at which, for Sixth Amendment purposes, statements in response to interrogations become testimonial. Through *in limine* procedure, they should redact or exclude the portions of any statement that have become testimonial, as they do, for example, with unduly prejudicial portions of otherwise admissible evidence. Davis's jury did not hear the *complete* 911 call, although it may well have heard some testimonial portions. We were asked to classify only McCottry's early statements identifying Davis as her assailant, and we agree with the Washington Supreme Court that they were not testimonial. That court also concluded that, even if later parts of the call were testimonial, their admission was harmless beyond a reasonable doubt. Davis does not challenge that holding, and we therefore assume it to be correct.

B

Determining the testimonial or nontestimonial character of the statements that were the product of the interrogation in *Hammon* is a much easier task, since they were not much different from the statements we found to be testimonial in *Crawford*. It is entirely clear from the circumstances that the interrogation was part of an investigation into possibly criminal past conduct — as, indeed, the testifying officer expressly acknowledged. There was no emergency in progress; the interrogating officer testified that he had heard no arguments or crashing and saw no one throw or break anything. When the officers first arrived, Amy told them that things were fine, and there was no immediate threat to her person. When the officer questioned Amy for the second time, and elicited the challenged statements, he was not seeking to determine (as in *Davis*) "what is happening," but rather "what happened." Objectively viewed, the primary, if not indeed the sole, purpose of the interrogation was to investigate a possible crime — which is, of course, precisely what the officer *should* have done.

It is true that the *Crawford* interrogation was more formal. It followed a *Miranda* warning, was tape-recorded, and took place at the station house. While these features certainly strengthened the statements' testimonial aspect — made it more objectively apparent, that is, that the purpose of the exercise was to nail down the truth about past criminal events — none was essential to the point. It was formal enough that Amy's interrogation was conducted in a separate room, away from her husband (who tried to intervene), with the officer receiving her replies for use in his "investigation." What we called the "striking resemblance" of the *Crawford* statement to civil-law *ex parte* examinations, is shared by Amy's statement here. Both declarants were actively separated from the defendant — officers forcibly prevented Hershel from participating in the interrogation. Both statements deliberately recounted, in response to police questioning, how potentially criminal past events began and progressed. And both took place some time after the events described were over. Such statements under official interrogation are an obvious substitute for live testimony, because they do precisely *what a witness does* on direct examination; they are inherently testimonial.

Both Indiana and the United States as *amicus curiae* argue that this case should be resolved much like *Davis*. For the reasons we find the comparison to *Crawford* compelling, we find the comparison to *Davis* unpersuasive. The statements in *Davis* were taken when McCottry was alone, not only unprotected by police (as Amy Hammon was protected), but apparently in immediate danger from Davis. She was seeking aid, not telling a story about the past. McCottry's present-tense statements showed immediacy; Amy's narrative of past events was delivered at some remove in time from the danger she described. And after Amy answered the officer's questions, he had her execute an affidavit, in order, he testified, "to establish events that have occurred previously."

Although we necessarily reject the Indiana Supreme Court's implication that virtually any "initial inquiries" at the crime scene will not be testimonial, we do not hold the opposite — that *no* questions at the scene will yield nontestimonial answers. We have already observed of domestic disputes that "officers called to investigate . . . need to know whom they are dealing with in order to assess the situation, the threat to their own safety, and possible danger to the potential victim. Such exigencies may *often* mean that "initial inquiries" produce nontestimonial statements. But in cases like this one, where Amy's statements were neither a cry for help nor the provision of information enabling officers immediately to end a threatening situation, the fact that they were given at an alleged crime scene and were "initial inquiries" is immaterial.[12]

IV

Respondents in both cases, joined by a number of their *amici*, contend that the nature of the offenses charged in these two cases — domestic violence — requires greater flexibility in the use of testimonial evidence. This particular type of crime

---

12.   Police investigations themselves are, of course, in no way impugned by our characterization of their fruits as testimonial. Investigations of past crimes prevent future harms and lead to necessary arrests. While prosecutors may hope that inculpatory "nontestimonial" evidence is gathered, this is essentially beyond police control. Their saying that an emergency exists cannot make it be so. The Confrontation Clause in no way governs police conduct, because it is the trial *use* of, not the investigatory *collection* of, *ex parte* testimonial statements which offends that provision. But neither can police conduct govern the Confrontation Clause; testimonial statements are what they are.

is notoriously susceptible to intimidation or coercion of the victim to ensure that she does not testify at trial. When this occurs, the Confrontation Clause gives the criminal a windfall. We may not, however, vitiate constitutional guarantees when they have the effect of allowing the guilty to go free. But when defendants seek to undermine the judicial process by procuring or coercing silence from witnesses and victims, the Sixth Amendment does not require courts to acquiesce. While defendants have no duty to assist the State in proving their guilt, they *do* have the duty to refrain from acting in ways that destroy the integrity of the criminal-trial system. We reiterate what we said in *Crawford*: that "the rule of forfeiture by wrongdoing . . . extinguishes confrontation claims on essentially equitable grounds. That is, one who obtains the absence of a witness by wrongdoing forfeits the constitutional right to confrontation."

We have determined that, absent a finding of forfeiture by wrongdoing, the Sixth Amendment operates to exclude Amy Hammon's affidavit. The Indiana courts may (if they are asked) determine on remand whether such a claim of forfeiture is properly raised and, if so, whether it is meritorious.

. . .

We affirm the judgment of the Supreme Court of Washington in No. 05-5224. We reverse the judgment of the Supreme Court of Indiana in No. 05-5705, and remand the case to that Court for proceedings not inconsistent with this opinion.

It is so ordered.

Justice THOMAS, concurring in the judgment in part and dissenting in part.

In Crawford v. Washington, we abandoned the general reliability inquiry we had long employed to judge the admissibility of hearsay evidence under the Confrontation Clause, describing that inquiry as *"inherently*, and therefore *permanently*, unpredictable." Today, a mere two years after the Court decided *Crawford*, it adopts an equally unpredictable test, under which district courts are charged with divining the "primary purpose" of police interrogations. Besides being difficult for courts to apply, this test characterizes as "testimonial," and therefore inadmissible, evidence that bears little resemblance to what we have recognized as the evidence targeted by the Confrontation Clause . . . . [T]he plain terms of the "testimony" definition we endorsed necessarily require some degree of solemnity before a statement can be deemed "testimonial."

This requirement of solemnity supports my view that the statements regulated by the Confrontation Clause must include "extrajudicial statements . . . contained in formalized testimonial materials, such as affidavits, depositions, prior testimony, or confessions." Affidavits, depositions, and prior testimony are, by their very nature, taken through a formalized process. Likewise, confessions, when extracted by police in a formal manner, carry sufficient indicia of solemnity to constitute formalized statements and, accordingly, bear a "striking resemblance," to the examinations of the accused and accusers under the Marian statutes . . . . In *Crawford*, for example, the interrogation was custodial, taken after warnings given pursuant to Miranda v. Arizona. *Miranda* warnings, by their terms, inform a prospective defendant that "'anything he says can be used against him in a court of law.'" This imports a solemnity to the process that is not present in a mere conversation between a witness or suspect and a police officer.

. . .

B

. . .

The Court's determination that the evidence against Hammon must be excluded extends the Confrontation Clause far beyond the abuses it was intended to prevent. When combined with the Court's holding that the evidence against Davis is perfectly admissible, however, the Court's *Hammon* holding also reveals the difficulty of applying the Court's requirement that courts investigate the "primary purposes" of the investigation . . . . [T]he fact that the officer in *Hammon* was investigating Mr. Hammon's past conduct does not foreclose the possibility that the primary purpose of his inquiry was to assess whether Mr. Hammon constituted a continuing danger to his wife, requiring further police presence or action. It is hardly remarkable that Hammon did not act abusively towards his wife in the presence of the officers, and his good judgment to refrain from criminal behavior in the presence of police sheds little, if any, light on whether his violence would have resumed had the police left without further questioning, transforming what the Court dismisses as "past conduct" back into an "ongoing emergency." Nor does the mere fact that McCottry needed emergency aid shed light on whether the "primary purpose" of gathering, for example, the name of her assailant was to protect the police, to protect the victim, or to gather information for prosecution. In both of the cases before the Court, like many similar cases, pronouncement of the "primary" motive behind the interrogation calls for nothing more than a guess by courts.

II

Because the standard adopted by the Court today is neither workable nor a targeted attempt to reach the abuses forbidden by the Clause, I concur only in the judgment in Davis v. Washington, and respectfully dissent from the Court's resolution of Hammon v. Indiana.

KEY POINTS

1. In cases involving statements made during the course of police questioning, a key issue is whether the statement is made in which the circumstances, viewed objectively, indicate that the primary purpose of the questioning is to enable police assistance to meet an ongoing emergency. Such statements are nontestimonial. Statements are testimonial when circumstances objectively indicate that there is no ongoing emergency and that the primary purpose of the questioning is to establish or prove past facts potentially relevant to later criminal prosecution.

2. Several factors bear on this objective inquiry: Is the declarant speaking about events as they are actually happening or describing past events? Is the declarant facing an ongoing emergency? Is the content of the questions and answers necessary to resolve a present emergency or simply to learn what happened in the past? Is the level of formality in the questioning indicative of an emergency or a structured interrogation?

PROBLEM

8.99. H.D. was convicted by a jury of possession of a firearm by a felon pursuant to 18 U.S.C. §922(g)(1). It is undisputed that H.D. is a "felon" under this statute. Officer Carlton testified at trial for the prosecution as follows:

> I observed the defendant on Elm Street pushing another man in a wheelchair. I exited my squad car and headed in defendant's direction. Defendant looked at me, took a gun from his waistband, and fled on foot. I chased him on foot and I observed a gun in his right hand. I ran at him full speed, crashed into him, subdued him on the ground and seized the gun. The gun was not fired.

H.D. made no objection to this testimony. However, H.D. denies that he possessed a gun and claims that Officer Carlton lied about the gun during his testimony. It is undisputed that H.D. was the person chased and knocked down by Officer Carlton. The gun that Officer Carlton said he seized from H.D.'s possession was not offered into evidence at trial because it could not be located. H.D. did not testify.

The court permitted Officer Carlton to testify as follows just prior to his statements quoted above. Does admission of this testimony violate the confrontation clause?

> I answered the phone at the police station. The caller refused to identify herself. She spoke in a calm and quiet voice. She said: "The neighborhood bully is just walking by on Elm Street, pushing a man in a wheelchair." I asked her what the problem was. She said: "I see a gun stuck into his pants." Then she hung up. I immediately left the station and drove my squad car to Elm Street. We have been unable to determine who this caller was.

NOTES AND QUESTIONS

1. Does the objective "primary purpose" test, and the factors laid out in *Davis*, make a wholly formal distinction between the statements of Michelle McCottry and Amy Hammon? Does the distinction function to sort out hearsay risks generated by the conduct of police interrogators or by the mental state of the person making the statement? Does the Court explicitly hold whose "primary purpose" is dispositive of the status of the statement — the police interrogator's or the hearsay declarant's?

2. Finally, is the distinction between statements made for the purpose "to enable police assistance in an ongoing emergency" versus "to establish or prove past events potentially relevant to later criminal prosecution" a bright-line rule? Is it easy to apply or are there difficult line-drawing questions? What about the police asking a crime victim who is lying, bleeding, on the ground "who did this?" versus "is the person who did this still around?" What about a frightened and emotional statement made by a woman to her best friend telling the friend that she was violently assaulted the day before by her boyfriend? What is her purpose in making this statement? To seek emotional support or to create a record should anything happen to her? Courts seem to be fairly consistent in their analysis of fact patterns that are easily analogized to the facts in *Davis/Hammon* fact patterns, whereas they are decidedly more varied when considering fact patterns far outside the scope of 911 calls or emergency situations involving police.

3. Although the Court's opinion contained no factual basis for inferring that either of the defendants in *Davis* and *Hammon* had induced the hearsay declarants not to testify in their respective cases, the Court nevertheless closed Part IV with a discussion of the doctrine of forfeiture by wrongdoing. The Court seems to endorse the use of the preponderance of the evidence standard to find the facts necessary to forfeiture, as well as the use of hearsay in this fact-finding process. It makes no comment on the critical issue of whether the purpose of the defendant's wrongdoing must be to prevent the declarant from testifying against the defendant. This issue was addressed in 2008 in Giles v. California, 554 U.S. 353 (2008), as will be discussed starting on page 622, infra.

4. Lower court decisions, both state and federal, have indicated a growing consensus that statements establishing the identity of a perpetrator when made in informal settings during the immediate aftermath of a crime can be nontestimonial if the court finds that an "ongoing emergency" exists. See, e.g., State v. Calhoun, 657 S.E.2d 424 (N.C. App. 2008) (finding that in an interrogation with the primary purpose of enabling police assistance to deal with an ongoing emergency, permissible questions may "'establish the identity of the assailant, so that the dispatched officers might know whether they would be encountering a violent felon'") (quoting *Davis*); State v. Slater, 939 A.2d 1105 (Conn. 2008) (holding that a rape victim's statements to bystanders who inquired about her distress were nontestimonial because the victim "clearly was seeking aid" and the men responded with "no indication that their primary purpose was to do anything but aid her").

b.   The "Primary Purpose" Test: *Michigan v. Bryant*

In 2011, the Supreme Court decided its second case involving statements made during police questioning. In Michigan v. Bryant, 131 S. Ct. 1143 (2011), the Court applied the primary purpose test in a context very different from the domestic violence situations in *Davis* and *Hammon*. In *Bryant*,

> Around 3:25 a.m. on April 29, 2001, Detroit, Michigan police officers responded to a radio dispatch indicating that a man had been shot. At the scene, they found the victim, Anthony Covington, lying on the ground next to his car in a gas station parking lot. Covington had a gunshot wound to his abdomen, appeared to be in great pain, and spoke with difficulty.
>
> The police asked him "what had happened, who had shot him, and where the shooting had occurred." . . . Covington stated that "Rick" shot him at around 3 a.m. . . . He also indicated that he had a conversation with Bryant, whom he recognized based on his voice, through the back door of Bryant's house. Covington explained that when he turned to leave, he was shot through the door and then drove to the gas station, where police found him.
>
> Covington's conversation with the police ended within 5 to 10 minutes when emergency medical services arrived. Covington was transported to a hospital and died within hours. The police left the gas station after speaking with Covington, called for backup, and traveled to Bryant's house. They did not find Bryant there but did find blood and a bullet on the back porch and an apparent bullet hole in the back door. Police also found Covington's wallet and identification outside the house. [Id. at 1150.]

Covington's statements were admitted against the defendant Bryant at his trial on charges of second degree murder. Bryant was convicted, and the Michigan Court

of Appeals upheld the trial court's determination that these statements were nontestimonial, made for the purpose of resolving an ongoing emergency. The Michigan
Supreme Court reversed, applying the *Davis* factors and holding that Covington's
statements were testimonial and thus, Bryant's confrontation right had been violated:

> These statements related solely to events that had occurred in the past and at a different
> location. None of these statements referred to events occurring at the time the state-
> ments were made, none alleged any ongoing threat, and none asserted the possible pres-
> ence of the alleged perpetrator. The circumstances, in our judgment, clearly indicate
> that the "primary purpose" of the questioning was to establish the facts of an event that
> had already occurred; the "primary purpose" was not to enable police assistance to meet
> an ongoing emergency. . . . The police asked the victim what had happened in the past,
> not what was currently happening. That is, the "primary purpose" of the questions asked,
> and the answers given, was to enable the police to identify, locate, and apprehend the
> perpetrator. [People v. Bryant, 768 N.W.2d 65 (Mich. 2009).]

The Supreme Court granted certiorari, and a five-Justice majority held as
follows:

> [T]he circumstances of the interaction between Covington and the police objectively
> indicate that the "primary purpose of the interrogation" was "to enable police assistance
> to meet an ongoing emergency." *Davis,* 547 U.S., at 822. Therefore, Covington's iden-
> tification and description of the shooter and the location of the shooting were not testi-
> monial statements, and their admission at Bryant's trial did not violate the Confrontation
> Clause.

The majority opinion was written by Justice Sotomayor, joined by Chief Justice
Roberts, and Justices Kennedy, Breyer, and Alito. Justice Thomas's concurrence was
grounded on the same position he had asserted in *Davis,* that questioning by police
lacked sufficient formality and solemnity for Covington's statements to be considered
to be testimonial. Justices Scalia and Ginsburg filed dissenting opinions, discussed
below, and Justice Kagan took no part in the consideration of the case. The effect of
the majority view is, of course, to permit the conviction of Bryant to stand, grounded
as it was on the hearsay statements of the deceased victim of the crime who was never
cross-examined by the defendant.

The majority opinion reviewed the Court's confrontation jurisprudence starting with *Crawford* and continuing through *Davis,* citing the factors that the *Davis*
Court had developed to determine the primary purpose of statements made during
police questioning. Justice Sotomayor took issue with the Michigan Supreme Court's
finding of no ongoing emergency. The opinion found that the Michigan court had
focused too narrowly on whether there was an emergency because of an ongoing
threat to the victim, and it had ignored the ongoing threat that an unknown shooter
with a gun posed both to the police themselves and to the public. This emergency,
the Justice wrote, "stretches more broadly" than those in *Davis* and *Hammon.* The
majority opinion continued:

> We reiterate, moreover, that the existence *vel non* of an ongoing emergency is not the
> touchstone of the testimonial inquiry; rather, the ultimate inquiry is whether the "pri-
> mary purpose of the interrogation [was] to enable police assistance to meet [the] ongo-
> ing emergency." *Davis,* 547 U.S., at 822. We turn now to that inquiry, as informed by
> the circumstances of the ongoing emergency just described. The circumstances of the

encounter provide important context for understanding Covington's statements to the police. When the police arrived at Covington's side, their first question to him was "What happened?" Covington's response was either "Rick shot me" or "I was shot," followed very quickly by an identification of "Rick" as the shooter. In response to further questions, Covington explained that the shooting occurred through the back door of Bryant's house and provided a physical description of the shooter. When he made the statements, Covington was lying in a gas station parking lot bleeding from a mortal gunshot wound to his abdomen. His answers to the police officers' questions were punctuated with questions about when emergency medical services would arrive. He was obviously in considerable pain and had difficulty breathing and talking. From this description of his condition and report of his statements, we cannot say that a person in Covington's situation would have had a "primary purpose" "to establish or prove past events potentially relevant to later criminal prosecution."

For their part, the police responded to a call that a man had been shot. As discussed above, they did not know why, where, or when the shooting had occurred. Nor did they know the location of the shooter or anything else about the circumstances in which the crime occurred. The questions they asked — "what had happened, who had shot him, and where the shooting occurred," — were the exact type of questions necessary to allow the police to "'assess the situation, the threat to their own safety, and possible danger to the potential victim'"[15] and to the public, including to allow them to ascertain "whether they would be encountering a violent felon," In other words, they solicited the information necessary to enable them "to meet an ongoing emergency."

Nothing in Covington's responses indicated to the police that, contrary to their expectation upon responding to a call reporting a shooting, there was no emergency or that a prior emergency had ended. Covington did indicate that he had been shot at another location about 25 minutes earlier, but he did not know the location of the shooter at the time the police arrived and, as far as we can tell from the record, he gave no indication that the shooter, having shot at him twice, would be satisfied that Covington was only wounded. In fact, Covington did not indicate any possible motive for the shooting, and thereby gave no reason to think that the shooter would not shoot again if he arrived on the scene. As we noted in *Davis*, "initial inquiries" may "*often* . . . produce nontestimonial statements." The initial inquiries in this case resulted in the type of nontestimonial statements we contemplated in *Davis*.

Finally, we consider the informality of the situation and the interrogation. This situation is more similar, though not identical, to the informal, harried 911 call in *Davis* than to the structured, station-house interview in *Crawford*. As the officers' trial testimony reflects, the situation was fluid and somewhat confused: the officers arrived at different times; apparently each, upon arrival, asked Covington "what happened?"; and, contrary to the dissent's portrayal, (opinion of Scalia, J.), they did not conduct a structured interrogation.

. . .

Because the circumstances of the encounter as well as the statements and actions of Covington and the police objectively indicate that the "primary purpose of the interrogation" was "to enable police assistance to meet an ongoing emergency," Covington's identification and description of the shooter and the location of the shooting were not testimonial hearsay. The Confrontation Clause did not bar their admission at Bryant's trial. [Id. at 1165-1167.]

The method of the majority deserves some further comment. The majority employed what the opinion calls a "combined" approach to determining the primary

---

15.   [References to the *Davis/Hammon* opinion and other cases are omitted. — Eds.]

purpose of the police interrogation. That is, in applying the factors outlined in *Davis*, a court must look to the circumstances in which an encounter between police and declarant occurs; the statements and actions of both the declarant and the interrogators; the nature (content) of what was asked and answered; acknowledge the possibility of mixed motives on the part of both police and declarant; and not look for "purpose" by looking solely at one participant. In short, a court must arrive at an objective determination of the primary purpose of "the interrogation" itself by examining its contents and the combined circumstances of the participants.

More startling is the majority's explicit reference to the "reliability" of statements, such as Covington's, made during ongoing emergencies:

> The existence of an ongoing emergency is relevant to determining the primary purpose of the interrogation because an emergency focuses the participants on something other than "prov[ing] past events potentially relevant to later criminal prosecution." *Davis*, 547 U.S., at 822. Rather, it focuses them on "end[ing] a threatening situation." *Id.*, at 832. Implicit in *Davis* is the idea that because the prospect of fabrication in statements given for the primary purpose of resolving that emergency is presumably significantly diminished, the Confrontation Clause does not require such statements to be subject to the crucible of cross-examination.
>
> This logic is not unlike that justifying the excited utterance exception in hearsay law. Statements "relating to a startling event or condition made while the declarant was under the stress of excitement caused by the event or condition," Fed. Rule Evid. 803(2); see also Mich. Rule Evid. 803(2) (2010), are considered reliable because the declarant, in the excitement, presumably cannot form a falsehood. See Idaho v. Wright, 497 U.S. 805, 820 (1990) ("The basis for the 'excited utterance' exception . . . is that such statements are given under circumstances that eliminate the possibility of fabrication, coaching, or confabulation . . . . An ongoing emergency has a similar effect of focusing an individual's attention on responding to the emergency").[16] [*Id.* at 1157.]

This astounding departure from the philosophy and methodology of *Crawford*, and its seeming invitation to return to the reliability rationale of *Roberts*, has confounded the legal academy and was received with scathing criticism from Justice Scalia in dissent:

> The Court attempts to fit its resurrected interest in reliability into the *Crawford* framework, but the result is incoherent. Reliability, the Court tells us, is a good indicator of whether "a statement is . . . an out-of-court substitute for trial testimony." That is patently false. Reliability tells us *nothing* about whether a statement is testimonial. Testimonial and nontestimonial statements alike come in varying degrees of reliability. An eyewitness's statements to the police after a fender-bender, for example, are both reliable and testimonial. Statements to the police from one driver attempting to blame the other would be similarly testimonial but rarely reliable. [*Id.* at 1175.]

Justice Scalia's dissenting opinion finds that Covington's statements were testimonial, and in this conclusion he was joined by Justice Ginsburg. In *Davis*, the

---

16.   Many other exceptions to the hearsay rules similarly rest on the belief that certain statements are, by their nature, made for a purpose other than use in a prosecution and therefore should not be barred by hearsay prohibitions. See, e.g., Fed. Rule Evid. 801(d)(2)(E) (statement by a co-conspirator during and in furtherance of the conspiracy); 803(4) (Statements for Purposes of Medical Diagnosis or Treatment); 803(6) (Records of Regularly Conducted Activity); 803(8) (Public Records and Reports); 803(9) (Records of Vital Statistics); 803(11) (Records of Religious Organizations); 803(12) (Marriage, Baptismal, and Similar Certificates); 803(13) (Family Records); 804(b)(3) (Statement Against Interest).

majority opinion, written by Justice Scalia, has refused to give primacy to any one of the factors it considered in finding "primary purpose," including whether the purpose of the police or the declarant counted for more. In *Bryant*, Justice Scalia made clear that he believes that it is the declarant's intent and understanding that counts:

> *Crawford* and *Davis* did not address whose perspective matters — the declarant's, the interrogator's, or both — when assessing "the primary purpose of [an] interrogation." In those cases the statements were testimonial from any perspective. I think the same is true here, but because the Court picks a perspective so will I: The declarant's intent is what counts. In-court testimony is more than a narrative of past events; it is a solemn declaration made in the course of a criminal trial. For an out-of-court statement to qualify as testimonial, the declarant must intend the statement to be a solemn declaration rather than an unconsidered or offhand remark; and he must make the statement with the understanding that it may be used to invoke the coercive machinery of the State against the accused. See Friedman, Grappling with the Meaning of "Testimonial," 71 Brooklyn L. Rev. 241, 259 (2005). That is what distinguishes a narrative told to a friend over dinner from a statement to the police. The hidden purpose of an interrogator cannot substitute for the declarant's intentional solemnity or his understanding of how his words may be used.
>
> A declarant-focused inquiry is also the only inquiry that would work in every fact pattern implicating the Confrontation Clause. The Clause applies to volunteered testimony as well as statements solicited through police interrogation. An inquiry into an officer's purposes would make no sense when a declarant blurts out "Rick shot me" as soon as the officer arrives on the scene. I see no reason to adopt a different test — one that accounts for an officer's intent — when the officer asks "what happened" before the declarant makes his accusation. (This does not mean the interrogator is irrelevant. The identity of an interrogator, and the content and tenor of his questions, can bear upon whether a declarant intends to make a solemn statement, and envisions its use at a criminal trial. But none of this means that the interrogator's purpose matters.) [Id. at 1168-1169.]

Justice Scalia is certainly correct that the majority opinion requires judges to conduct an open-ended inquiry into the totality of the circumstances surrounding a police interrogation in order to determine its "primary purpose." This inquiry would still be framed by the factors outlined in *Davis*. If conflicting purposes are inferred, some type of "balancing test" might have to be applied to determine primacy. To what extent "reliability" will seep into that determination remains to be seen.

PROBLEMS

8.100. Father is charged with the crime of aggravated assault and battery on his 15-year-old son, Joe, who suffered a slash wound on his cheek and neck. The prosecution claims that Father and Joe got into an argument at home; Father pushed Joe; Joe fell onto a glass coffee table and smashed the glass top; Father grabbed a very sharp piece of glass from the coffee table and deliberately cut Joe. Father's defense is that Joe accidentally fell over the glass coffee table and cut his face on the shattered glass.

Immediately after he was injured, Joe ran out of the house. A neighbor had heard the father and son yelling and had called 911 to report a domestic disturbance. Police Officer Mullin went to Father's home, saw blood on the floor, and saw Father cleaning up broken glass from the smashed coffee table top. Father told Mullin that Joe had fallen onto the table and cut himself, but that Joe was OK. The neighbor who called 911 told Mullin that Joe and his father were always fighting.

One hour later, Mullin was sent to a location a mile away where a male youth was sitting on a curb, his face slashed. Mullin asked the youth for his name, and learned that he was Father's son, Joe. Mullin called for emergency medical personnel to take Joe to a hospital. Mullin then asked Joe, "What happened between you and your father?" Joe said: "I got into an argument with my father; he pushed me and I fell over the coffee table. The glass top broke. My father picked up a piece of glass and cut me." The emergency medical team arrived and Mullin asked no further questions.

Joe has disappeared. If Joe is not available to testify at Father's trial, Officer Mullin would testify as to what Joe said in response to his question. Officer Mullin would also testify that his own primary purpose in his questioning of Joe was to assess whether there was an ongoing emergency in Joe's home. Would Joe's statement to Mullin about the cause of his injury be admissible under the confrontation clause?

8.101. Hannah owns a small accessories store on a busy shopping street. She was robbed at gunpoint as she stood behind the counter of her store. The robber took cash from the cash box and her purse. Immediately after the robber left her store, Hannah ran outside and asked a bystander to observe the license plate number of the car that she had seen the robber get into and start to drive away. The bystander did so, and wrote the license number on a piece of paper. He gave the paper to Hannah, who gave it to the investigating police officer. The license number was registered to a car owned by defendant. The bystander is not available to testify at defendant's trial for the robbery of Hannah's store, and the bystander was never cross-examined by the defendant. May the piece of paper be admitted against the defendant? Consider all possible objections.

NOTES AND QUESTIONS

1. The split of opinions in *Bryant* reveals that Justice Scalia has lost his ability to control the implementation of the "testimonial" standard, at least insofar as the "primary purpose" test is concerned. It would seem that application of the multi-factor "combined approach" of the majority could lead to future differences in outcomes as well. Remember that in *Crawford* the Court roundly criticized the prior "reliability" approach to the confrontation right in Ohio v. Roberts as amorphous, indeterminate, and unpredictable. In *Bryant*, hasn't the testimonial standard revealed the same weaknesses? Justice Scalia criticizes the combined approach of the majority on those grounds:

> The only virtue of the Court's approach (if it can be misnamed a virtue) is that it leaves judges free to reach the "fairest" result under the totality of the circumstances. If the dastardly police trick a declarant into giving an incriminating statement against a sympathetic defendant, a court can focus on the police's intent and declare the statement testimonial. If the defendant "deserves" to go to jail, then a court can focus on whatever perspective is necessary to declare damning hearsay nontestimonial. And when all else fails, a court can mix-and-match perspectives to reach its desired outcome. Unfortunately, under this malleable approach "the guarantee of confrontation is no guarantee at all." [Id. at 1170.]

2. How realistic is it to search for a "primary" purpose of police questioning of victims at or near a potential crime scene? When asked, police officers will tell you

that they have two equally powerful motives — to define and resolve any emergency situation and to gather evidence for future prosecution. Is it sensible for a legal doctrine to require courts to struggle so hard to construct an alternate reality?

c.   Medical Interviews and Examinations

When medical interviews and examinations are made by nongovernment employees, courts have engaged in a fact-intensive analysis as to whether the questioning is the "functional equivalent of a police interrogation." Hernandez v. State, 946 So. 2d, 1284-1285 (Fla. App. 2007) (court applied a four-factor test that included (1) the legal status of the examining entity as an arm of law enforcement, (2) the involvement of law enforcement in the production of the statements, (3) the purpose of the exam conducted by the nurse, and (4) the absence of any ongoing emergency). In *Hernandez*, the court focused on the purpose of the examiner in conducting the interview:

> Ms. Shulman regularly appeared in court to give testimony about the results of the examinations that she performed on children. She told the jury that she had been qualified as an expert in the area of child assault medical examinations "[w]ell over a hundred times" and had testified as an expert witness in Hillsborough, Pinellas, Pasco, and Dade counties. Based on Ms. Shulman's background and her focus on forensic issues, there is no doubt that Ms. Shulman reasonably expected that she would be appearing in court to testify against Mr. Hernandez about the results of her examination and the statements made by the child and her parents during the course of the examination.

See also United States v. Bordeaux, 400 F.3d 548, 556 (8th Cir. 2005) ("The purpose of the interview (and by extension, the purpose of the statements) is disputed, but the evidence requires the conclusion that the purpose was to collect information for law enforcement.").

Other courts since *Davis* have focused on the declarant's knowledge and purpose. See, e.g., Blount v. Hardy, 337 Fed. Appx. 271 (4th Cir. 2009) (holding that admission at trial of out-of-court statements made by a three-year-old victim to therapists, where the victim did not know or have reason to know that her statements would be used against the defendant at trial, did not violate defendant's confrontation clause rights).

And in the context of nongovernment interviews, courts have recognized that statements may have multiple purposes. In State ex rel. Juvenile Dept. of Multnomah County v. S.P., 215 P.3d 847 (Or. 2009), the court found that an organization whose purpose was the diagnosis and treatment of child abuse served as a "proxy" for police, a fact that weighed in favor of finding that the victim's statements were testimonial. The court noted that the organization's questioning process served multiple purposes: first, the nontestimonial purpose of determining whether a child has been sexually abused for the purpose of providing effective medical and psychological treatment to the child, and second, the testimonial purpose of enabling police and child welfare authorities to obtain credible evidence of abuse. Id. at 864. Because these purposes were concurrent and coequal, both were "primary" in the sense that neither took precedence over the other. Finally, the S.P. court noted that the purposes of both the questioner and the declarant were relevant in determining whether statements are testimonial.

Other courts have found that statements made during medical examinations that result in immediate treatment, without the involvement of police, are for the primary purpose of treatment and are nontestimonial.

> [W]hen John [the declarant] was seen by Dr. Russell, he needed immediate acute treatment for a five- or six-inch laceration on the side of his face and neck. As Dr. Russell explained, his sole object in asking John "what happened" was to determine, in accordance with his standard medical procedure, the exact nature of the wound, and thus the correct mode of treatment. The question was neutral in form, and though John responded by identifying defendant as his assailant, Dr. Russell did not pursue that avenue further. Objectively viewed, the primary purpose of the question, and the answer, was not to establish or prove past facts for possible criminal use, but to help Dr. Russell deal with the immediate medical situation he faced. It was thus akin to the 911 operator's emergency questioning of Michelle McCottry in *Davis*. [People v. Cage, 155 P.3d 205, 218-220 (Cal. 2007).]

4. The Definition of Testimonial Statements After Crawford v. Washington: Government Forensic Reports

Application of the confrontation clause to routine governmental reports, prepared by public employees who are not directly involved in crime investigation and law enforcement, has presented a dilemma for courts making the transition from the "reliability" theory of Ohio v. Roberts to the "testimonial statement" theory of *Crawford*. Under *Roberts*, routine noninvestigative factual reports were often treated as business or public records, thus admissible under "firmly-rooted" hearsay exceptions. In addition, after *Roberts*, many states enacted special legislation providing that official reports of standardized chemical tests analyzing narcotics and other drugs, prepared and submitted under oath by the proper governmental analyst, were admissible as prima facie evidence of the chemical composition of the tested substance without the testimony of the analyst in court. See, e.g., Mass. Gen. Laws, ch. 111, §13. Routine and regularized data collection, and the application of standardized tests, were held to provide sufficient reliability to dispel the need for confrontation and cross-examination of both types of documents.

After *Crawford*, some courts still held that government documents that were routine and objective cataloging of unambiguous factual matters, not made in anticipation of litigation, were nontestimonial. Examples include a certificate of no record (CNR), reporting that a diligent search of appropriate records indicated no license to carry a weapon issued to defendant; a warrant of deportation recording that deportee actually left the country; raw data generated by diagnostic machines; and even the conclusion drawn from standardized laboratory test despite the author's knowledge that the report would be used by the prosecution. In June of 2009, the Supreme Court decided Melendez-Diaz v. Massachusetts, 129 S. Ct. 2527 (2009), a case that impacted the admissibility of many types of these governmental forensic reports.

a. *Melendez-Diaz v. Massachusetts*

Defendant Melendez-Diaz was charged with distributing and trafficking in cocaine. At issue was the admissibility of three "certificates of analysis," which stated that the substance in the bags found in defendant's possession was cocaine. These certificates had been prepared pursuant to the special Massachusetts statute cited above, and their admission into evidence at defendant's trial had been upheld.

Justice Scalia, writing for a five-Justice majority that included Justices Stevens, Thomas, Souter, and Ginsburg, found these certificates to be testimonial and held that their admission against Melendez-Diaz was error, thus requiring reversal and remand of the judgment against him. On this point, the majority opinion was brief.

The Sixth Amendment to the United States Constitution, made applicable to the States via the Fourteenth Amendment, Pointer v. Texas, 380 U.S. 400, 403 (1965), provides that "[i]n all criminal prosecutions, the accused shall enjoy the right . . . to be confronted with the witnesses against him." In *Crawford*, after reviewing the Clause's historical underpinnings, we held that it guarantees a defendant's right to confront those "who 'bear testimony'" against him. 541 U.S., at 51. A witness's testimony against a defendant is thus inadmissible unless the witness appears at trial or, if the witness is unavailable, the defendant had a prior opportunity for cross-examination. *Id.*, at 54.

Our opinion described the class of testimonial statements covered by the Confrontation Clause as follows:

"Various formulations of this core class of testimonial statements exist: *ex parte* in-court testimony or its functional equivalent — that is, material such as affidavits, custodial examinations, prior testimony that the defendant was unable to cross-examine, or similar pretrial statements that declarants would reasonably expect to be used prosecutorially; extrajudicial statements . . . contained in formalized testimonial materials, such as affidavits, depositions, prior testimony, or confessions; statements that were made under circumstances which would lead an objective witness reasonably to believe that the statement would be available for use at a later trial." *Id.*, at 51-52 (internal quotation marks and citations omitted).

There is little doubt that the documents at issue in this case fall within the "core class of testimonial statements" thus described. Our description of that category mentions affidavits twice. See also White v. Illinois, 502 U.S. 346, 365, (1992) (Thomas, J., concurring in part and concurring in judgment) ("[T]he Confrontation Clause is implicated by extrajudicial statements only insofar as they are contained in formalized testimonial materials, such as affidavits, depositions, prior testimony, or confessions"). The documents at issue here, while denominated by Massachusetts law "certificates," are quite plainly affidavits: "declaration[s] of facts written down and sworn to by the declarant before an officer authorized to administer oaths." Black's Law Dictionary 62 (8th ed. 2004). They are incontrovertibly a "'solemn declaration or affirmation made for the purpose of establishing or proving some fact.'" *Crawford, supra*, at 51 (quoting 2 N. Webster, An American Dictionary of the English Language (1828)). The fact in question is that the substance found in the possession of Melendez-Diaz and his codefendants was, as the prosecution claimed, cocaine — the precise testimony the analysts would be expected to provide if called at trial. The "certificates" are functionally identical to live, in-court testimony, doing "precisely what a witness does on direct examination." Davis v. Washington, 547 U.S. 813, 830 (2006) (emphasis deleted).

Here, moreover, not only were the affidavits "'made under circumstances which would lead an objective witness reasonably to believe that the statement would be available for use at a later trial,'" *Crawford, supra*, at 52, but under Massachusetts law the *sole purpose* of the affidavits was to provide "prima facie evidence of the composition, quality, and the net weight" of the analyzed substance, Mass. Gen. Laws, ch. 111, §13. We can safely assume that the analysts were aware of the affidavits' evidentiary purpose, since that purpose — as stated in the relevant state-law provision — was reprinted on the affidavits themselves.

In short, under our decision in *Crawford* the analysts' affidavits were testimonial state-ments, and the analysts were "witnesses" for purposes of the Sixth Amendment. Absent a showing that the analysts were unavailable to testify at trial *and* that petitioner had a prior opportunity to cross-examine them, petitioner was entitled to "'be confronted with'" the analysts at trial. *Crawford, supra,* at 54. [129 S. Ct. at 2531-2532.]

Justice Thomas, once again, filed a short concurrence to note that his position, advanced in his opinions since 1992, is that "the Confrontation Clause is implicated by extrajudicial statements only insofar as they are contained in formalized testimo-nial materials, such as affidavits, depositions, prior testimony, on confessions." He joined the majority opinion because, in his words, the "documents at issue in this case 'are quite plainly affidavits'... [that] 'fall within the core class of testimonial state-ments' governed by the Confrontation Clause." 129 S. Ct. at 2543.

In the following excerpt from the dissent, Justice Kennedy, joined by Justices Breyer and Alito and Chief Justice Roberts, leveled a direct attack on Justice Scalia's formal approach to defining "testimonial statements" in *Crawford, Davis,* and now *Melendez-Diaz,* as well as on the majority's holding in the case, and makes a series of attacks on the outcome of the majority opinion as well.

II.

The Court's fundamental mistake is to read the Confrontation Clause as referring to a kind of out-of-court statement — namely, a testimonial statement — that must be excluded from evidence. The Clause does not refer to kinds of statements. Nor does the Clause contain the word "testimonial." The text, instead, refers to kinds of persons, namely, to "witnesses against" the defendant. Laboratory analysts are not "witnesses against" the defendant as those words would have been understood at the framing. There is simply no authority for this position.

Instead, the Clause refers to a conventional "witness" — meaning one who witnesses (that is, perceives) an event that gives him or her personal knowledge of some aspect of the defendant's guilt. Both *Crawford* and *Davis* concerned just this kind of ordinary wit-ness — and nothing in the Confrontation Clause's text, history, or precedent justifies the Court's decision to expand those cases.

A

The Clause states: "In all criminal prosecutions, the accused shall enjoy the right . . . to be confronted with the witnesses against him." U.S. Const., Amdt. 6. Though there is "virtually no evidence of what the drafters of the Confrontation Clause intended it to mean,"...it is certain the Framers did not contemplate that an analyst who conducts a scientific test far removed from the crime would be considered a "witnes[s] against" the defendant.

The Framers were concerned with a typical witness — one who perceived an event that gave rise to a personal belief in some aspect of the defendant's guilt. There is no evidence that the Framers understood the Clause to extend to unconventional witnesses. As discussed below, there is significant evidence to the contrary. . . . In these circum-stances, the historical evidence in support of the Court's position is "'too meager . . . to form a solid basis in history, preceding and contemporaneous with the framing of the Constitution." . . . The Court goes dangerously wrong when it bases its constitutional interpretation upon historical guesswork.

The infamous treason trial of Sir Walter Raleigh provides excellent examples of the kinds of witnesses to whom the Confrontation Clause refers . . . see *Crawford*, 541 U.S., at 44-45 (Raleigh's trial informs our understanding of the Clause because it was, at the time of the framing, one of the "most notorious instances" of the abuse of witnesses' out-of-court statements); *ante*, at 9 (same). Raleigh's accusers claimed to have heard Raleigh speak treason, so they were witnesses in the conventional sense. We should limit the Confrontation Clause to witnesses like those in Raleigh's trial.

The Court today expands the Clause to include laboratory analysts, but analysts differ from ordinary witnesses in at least three significant ways. First, a conventional witness recalls events observed in the past, while an analyst's report contains near-contemporaneous observations of the test. An observation recorded at the time it is made is unlike the usual act of testifying. A typical witness must recall a previous event that he or she perceived just once, and thus may have misperceived or misremembered. But an analyst making a contemporaneous observation need not rely on memory; he or she instead reports the observations at the time they are made. We gave this consideration substantial weight in *Davis*. There, the "primary purpose" of the victim's 911 call was "to enable police assistance to meet an ongoing emergency," rather than "to establish or prove past events potentially relevant to later criminal prosecution." 547 U.S., at 822, 827 . . . . The Court cites no authority for its holding that an observation recorded at the time it is made is an act of "witness[ing]" for purposes of the Confrontation Clause.

Second, an analyst observes neither the crime nor any human action related to it. Often, the analyst does not know the defendant's identity, much less have personal knowledge of an aspect of the defendant's guilt. The analyst's distance from the crime and the defendant, in both space and time, suggests the analyst is not a witness against the defendant in the conventional sense.

Third, a conventional witness responds to questions under interrogation. But laboratory tests are conducted according to scientific protocols; they are not dependent upon or controlled by interrogation of any sort. Put differently, out-of-court statements should only "require confrontation if they are produced by, or with the involvement of, adversarial government officials responsible for investigating and prosecuting crime." . . . There is no indication that the analysts here — who work for the State Laboratory Institute, a division of the Massachusetts Department of Public Health — were adversarial to petitioner. Nor is there any evidence that adversarial officials played a role in formulating the analysts' certificates.

Rather than acknowledge that it expands the Confrontation Clause beyond conventional witnesses, the Court relies on our recent opinions in *Crawford* and *Davis*. . . . The Court assumes, with little analysis, that *Crawford* and *Davis* extended the Clause to any person who makes a "testimonial" statement. But the Court's confident tone cannot disguise the thinness of these two reeds. Neither *Crawford* nor *Davis* considered whether the Clause extends to persons far removed from the crime who have no connection to the defendant. Instead, those cases concerned conventional witnesses. *Davis*, *supra*, at 826-830 (witnesses were victims of defendants' assaults); *Crawford*, *supra*, at 38 (witness saw defendant stab victim).

It is true that *Crawford* and *Davis* employed the term "testimonial," and thereby suggested that any testimonial statement, by any person, no matter how distant from the defendant and the crime, is subject to the Confrontation Clause. But that suggestion was not part of the holding of *Crawford* or *Davis*. Those opinions used the adjective "testimonial" to avoid the awkward phrasing required by reusing the noun "witness." The Court today transforms that turn of phrase into a new and sweeping legal rule, by holding that anyone who makes a formal statement for the purpose of later prosecution — no matter how removed from the crime — must be considered a "witness against" the defendant. The Court cites no authority to justify this expansive new interpretation.

NOTES

1. The dissent contended that confrontation and cross-examination are not effective ways to detect errors in scientific tests. Instead, the dissent suggested that new tests should be conducted, or the defendant may call his own expert "to explain to the jury the test's flaws and the dangers of relying on it . . . ," or the defendant may subpoena the government's analyst himself. Moreover, according to the dissent, defendants' objections to the results of the laboratory tests will be "formalistic and pointless" since there are rarely (as evidenced by the *Melendez-Diaz* case itself) any significant challenges made to the accuracy of such standardized, routine procedures.

The majority replied by pronouncing its view of the core concept of the confrontation clause:

> Converting the prosecution's duty under the Confrontation Clause into the defendant's privilege under state law or the Compulsory Process Clause shifts the consequences of adverse-witness no-shows from the State to the accused. More fundamentally, the Confrontation Clause imposes a burden on the prosecution to present its witnesses, not on the defendant to bring those adverse witnesses into court. Its value to the defendant is not replaced by a system in which the prosecution presents its evidence via *ex parte* affidavits and waits for the defendant to subpoena the affiants if he chooses. [129 S. Ct. at 2540.]

2. Several types of government reports found to be nontestimonial under *Crawford* have been reclassified by courts applying *Melendez-Diaz*. Many certificates of no result (CNRs) have been found testimonial when they "are not routinely produced in the course of government business but are generated exclusively for use at trial." United States v. Martinez-Rios, 595 F.3d 581 (5th Cir. 2010). Other more routine and objective governmental reports have been found to be nontestimonial. United States v. Caraballo, 595 F.3d 1214 (11th Cir. 2010) (INS forms that record biographical information required of every entrant are nontestimonial); United States v. Mashek, 606 F.3d 922 (8th Cir. 2010) (records from local pharmacies that defendant had made frequent pseudoephedrine purchases, purportedly used to manufacture methamphetamine, are not testimonial).

3. Forensic reports other than drug analyses have been found testimonial, which requires the prosecution to produce the author of the report. Wood v. State, 299 S.W.2d 200 (Tex. Ct. App. 2009) (autopsy report); State v. Locklear, 681 S.E.2d 293 (N.C. 2009) (reports of nontestifying forensic pathologist and forensic dentist identifying the remains of the victim); State v. Dilboy, 2010 WL 1541447 (N.H. 2010) (blood and urine tests); Government of Virgin Islands v. Vicars, 340 Fed. Appx. 807 (3d Cir. 2009) (physician's report of a rape examination); Commonwealth v. Loadholt, 923 N.E.2d 1037 (Mass. 2010) (ballistics certificate stating that a weapon was a "firearm" and that bullets were "ammunition").

b.   Bullcoming v. New Mexico

Adhering closely to *Melendez-Diaz*, a new five-Justice majority of the Supreme Court held in Bullcoming v. New Mexico, 131 S. Ct. 2705 (2011), that a forensic report stating a defendant's blood alcohol content was the testimonial statement of the analyst who had run the underlying test and signed the report. As such, its use at trial without the appearance of the analyst as a witness violated Bullcoming's confrontation right. The New Mexico Supreme Court had acknowledged that the report was testimonial, but had held that in-court testimony from a knowledgeable laboratory official provided the defendant with an adequate opportunity for cross-examination in satisfaction of the *Melendez-Diaz* and *Crawford* standards.

The majority opinion, written by Justice Ginsburg and joined in its significant holdings by Justices Scalia, Thomas, Sotomayor, and Kagan, expressed no doubt that the analyst's certification of the test results, written for the purpose of proving a particular fact in court, was testimonial. That Justice Thomas agreed indicates that his "solemnity" and "formality" tests were passed despite the fact that the certification was not a sworn affidavit, as the report in *Melendez-Diaz* had been. The majority noted that the report also contained statements of the analyst about the procedures he had followed, and that the operation of the gas chromatograph machine generates at least some risk of human error. In footnote 6, which Justice Thomas did not join, the opinion applied the "primary purpose" test of *Davis*: "To rank as 'testimonial,' a statement must have a 'primary purpose' of 'establish[ing] or prov[ing] past events potentially relevant to later criminal prosecution."

The majority further held that the testimony of the surrogate witness could not fulfill the defendant's confrontation right for two reasons. First, the surrogate had not supervised or observed any of the testing involved in this case and could not have answered any questions on cross-examination about the particular test of Bullcoming's blood alcohol content; the surrogate could not be cross-examined on why the missing analyst was on "unpaid leave" from his job and was not himself testifying; and the surrogate did not assert his own independent opinion concerning the alcohol content of Bullcoming's blood. More importantly, the majority held, the Sixth Amendment does not itself suggest such an open-ended exception to its terms, nor should a court create such an exception because it believes that the underlying "values" of the confrontation clause are fulfilled:

> [T]he Clause does not tolerate dispensing with confrontation simply because the court believes that questioning one witness about another's testimonial statements provides a fair enough opportunity for cross-examination. [Id. at 2716]

The *Bullcoming* opinion thus puts an end to speculation about whether the majority that followed Justice Scalia in *Melendez-Diaz* would survive the retirement of Justices Stevens and Souter. The dissenters in *Melendez-Diaz* dissented again, making the argument that the analyst in this case was even less of a "witness" against the defendant and played even less of a role in the generation of the inculpating evidence against him than had the analysts in *Melendez-Diaz*. Given the testimony of the surrogate witness concerning all of the laboratory's protocols and procedures, the dissenters rejected the majority's insistence that the analyst be available for cross-examination as a "hollow formality."

PROBLEM

8.102. Prosecution of Jones for unlawful possession of a firearm by a convicted felon. The prosecution offers a firearm, in a plastic bag with a tag attached to it, into evidence as an exhibit. To admit the exhibit, the prosecution must produce evidence sufficient to support a finding that the firearm was in the possession of Jones.

For the prosecution, Police Officer Green testifies as follows:

On January 10, 2011, I arrested Jones in his apartment. I seized a firearm from his jacket pocket and placed it in a plastic evidence bag with a label that I wrote identifying it as the firearm seized from Jones. Later that day, I took the firearm to the evidence storage room in the Police Department. I gave the plastic bag containing the firearm that I seized from Jones to the custodian of the storage room. The custodian wrote on a tag, and attached the tag on the plastic bag with the firearm in it. It is the regular and customary practice of the evidence custodian to fill out a property receipt for any type of evidence that is stored in the storage room and to state the source of the evidence.

Officer Green further testifies that she cannot identify the firearm offered by the prosecution as the weapon she seized from Jones. She acknowledges that the plastic bag does not have any label on it that she wrote. However, she recognizes the handwriting on the tag as the handwriting of the custodian. The custodian is now deceased.

The tag on the firearm reads:

PROPERTY RECEIPT:

Firearm received from Office Green.

DATE: January 10, 2010

SIGNED: A. Adams, Custodian

Is the receipt admissible to prove that the firearm offered by the prosecution is the firearm that Officer Green seized from Jones? Consider all possible objections.

8.103. Prosecution of defendant for murder. The state offers a qualified expert witness to testify to all of the following:

(1) The expert is employed by the state forensic laboratory. She herself obtained a sample of defendant's saliva for purposes of DNA testing. After performing the proper test procedures (extraction, amplification, detection of genetic type), the expert obtained a DNA profile of the defendant.

(2) The expert then performed the same proper test procedures on a blood sample, and obtained a DNA profile of the blood sample.

(3) According to Report A, written by a police forensic specialist, the specialist had retrieved this blood sample from the clothes of the murder victim and had delivered it to the state forensic laboratory for testing.

(4) The expert then compared the DNA profile of the blood sample to the defendant's DNA profile and declared that they match.

Would the expert's testimony be admissible under the Confrontation Clause? Would the police forensic specialist have to testify? What if the DNA profile of the blood sample had been obtained after testing at Cellmark Laboratory, a private testing lab? Could the expert rely on the profile obtained by Cellmark to declare a match?

NOTES

1. The dissent in *Bullcoming* also takes aim at the overall methodology of the Court's confrontation opinions since *Crawford*. The dissent noted the "weaving in

and out" of concerns for reliability and for solemnity; the elusive distinction between a primary purpose of proving past facts and resolving an emergency; the failure to state a clear rule on what witnesses were required to render a scientific report admissible; the failure to command a clear set of common principles in applying *Crawford*; and in particular, the "amorphous" and "highly context-dependant" "combined approach" of *Bryant*, a majority opinion in which, it must be noted, all of the *Bullcoming* dissenters had joined.

The inability of the seven Justices in the *Crawford* majority to agree on a single definition of "testimonial" has led to the current state of doctrinal complexity and disarray. Perhaps the four dissenters are indicating that they have had enough of the definitionless limbo into which *Crawford* plunged the Court. The dissenters express some nostalgia for returning to the "basic purpose" of the confrontation clause: "to bar admission of out-of-court statements obtained through formal interrogation in preparation for trial" which may be unreliable, are untested, might not have been uttered at all, and might not have been true — a purpose that they believe did not apply to the lab report in this case.

2. In her concurring opinion, Justice Sotomayor stated her view as to what other facts, if added to the scenario in *Bullcoming*, might possibly change the outcome: (1) a report also created for the alternate purpose of medical treatment; (2) admission of a report accompanied by testimony at trial from a surrogate expert who had reviewed, supervised, or been otherwise involved in the report at issue; (3) a surrogate expert witness who would testify to an independent opinion based on test results generated by other analysts that were not admitted into evidence; (4) submission only of raw data from the testing equipment itself. Lower courts have been presented with such alternate scenarios and, in many cases, admitted the report and/or testimony as fulfilling the defendant's confrontation right. What do you think of permitting an expert to offer an opinion based solely on reports that would violate the confrontation clause unless their authors testified? This issue, and FRE 703 which may permit this practice, are discussed in Chapter Nine at pages 690-691, infra.

Several days after the release of the *Bullcoming* opinion, the Court granted certiorari in Illinois v. Williams, 939 N.E.2d 268 (Ill. 2010), in which the Illinois Supreme Court upheld, against a confrontation challenge, the testimony of an expert witness concerning DNA match evidence. The expert based her opinion solely on the test results obtained by the lab analyst who had performed the DNA testing. The report of the analyst was not itself admitted into evidence. As stated above, Rule 703 can permit this strategy as a matter of policy regarding the proper basis for an expert opinion, but whether it will withstand challenge under *Crawford*, *Melendez-Diaz*, and *Bullcoming* remains to be seen. Other state supreme courts have rejected this strategy as a violation of the defendant's confrontation right if the testifying expert refers to the results of the missing analyst's tests. Commonwealth v. Bizanowicz, 945 N.E.2d 356, 365 (Mass. 2011).

3. The majority and dissent also engaged in a dispute over whether requiring the test analyst to appear in court was having disastrous practical consequences for governments' ability to prosecute. Both opinions cite data presented to the Court in amicus briefs, and in Part IV of the majority opinion, joined only by Justice Scalia, Justice Ginsburg takes note of a variety of ways in which the burden on prosecutors is and can be reduced. 131 S. Ct. at 2717-2719.

5. "Nontestimonial" Statements After *Crawford*

The Supreme Court asserted in *Crawford* that there are certain types of hearsay statements, corresponding to specific hearsay exceptions, that are simply not testimonial "by their nature" and thus not within the scope of the confrontation clause. 541 U.S. at 1367. Courts have relied on this seeming "categorical" approach. For example, statements not intended as assertions (such as questions) may escape the definition of hearsay and thus the reach of the confrontation clause. Other such types mentioned in *Crawford* include casual remarks to acquaintances, business and public records, and co-conspirator statements in furtherance of a conspiracy.

Business and governmental records are now potentially testimonial under the *Melendez-Diaz* test. In its recent opinion in Giles v. California, the majority reiterated that "[s]tatements to friends and neighbors about abuse and intimidation, and statements to physicians in the course of receiving treatment" would not be testimonial and "would be excluded, if at all, only by hearsay rules . . . ." 554 U.S. 353 (2008). Some lower courts have adopted a categorical approach, Doan v. Carter, 548 F.3d 449 (6th Cir. 2008) (statements of victim about abuse to friends and family were nontestimonial), while others apply a declarant-oriented test, Rice v. Hudson, 2009 U.S. Dist. Lexis 67592, at *5 (N.D. Ohio 2009) ("victim's statements to her mother about the abuse are nontestimonial . . . because a reasonable four-year-old would not expect her statements to be used in legal proceedings…). Finally, courts do state categorically that statements made between co-conspirators in furtherance of a conspiracy are not testimonial. United States v. King, 541 F.3d 1143 (5th Cir. 2008).

6. Testimonial Statements That Satisfy the Confrontation Right

Under *Crawford*, testimonial statements can satisfy the confrontation right in two ways: (1) if the declarant testifies as a witness at trial and thus is available for cross-examination by the defendant, and (2) if the declarant is unavailable at trial but the defendant has previously had the opportunity to cross-examine the declarant. Existing case law has established the parameters of these requirements, and the Court in *Crawford* gave no indication that their meaning was to change.

a. The Declarant Testifies

The Supreme Court stated in *Crawford* that

> [w]hen the declarant appears for cross-examination at trial, the Confrontation Clause places no constraints at all on the use of his prior testimonial statements. See California v. Green, 399 U.S. 149 (1970). The Clause does not bar admission of a statement so long as the declarant is present at trial to defend or explain it. [541 U.S. at 59, n.9.]

The prior statements must, of course, fall within a hearsay exception; the confrontation right may not coincide precisely with the hearsay rule.

The issue of the adequacy of cross-examination of the declarant, such as when the declarant is unable to recall the events that are the subject of the hearsay statement, appears to be well settled under United States v. Owens, 484 U.S. 554 (1988), as discussed on pages 450-451, supra. United States v. Ghilarducci, 480 F.3d 542, 549 (7th Cir. 2007) (declarant did not claim a "total loss of memory regarding the events"); United States v. Harty, 476 F. Supp. 2d 17, 25 (D. Mass. 2007) (witness's lack of recollection of reasons why he had selected defendant's photograph did not violate confrontation clause); Yanez v. Minnesota, 562 F.3d 958, 963 (8th Cir. 2009) (holding that a child witness's faulty memory did not deprive defendant of the ability to cross-examine where the defendant could remind the jury of the witness's "inability to recall the abuse or any details related to the criminal acts and thus call into question her reliability.").

b. Unavailability and Prior Opportunity for Cross-examination

The Court in *Crawford* stated that the Framers would not have permitted the admission of testimonial statements *unless* the declarant "was unavailable to testify and the defendant had had a prior opportunity for cross-examination." 541 U.S. at 57. Prior cross-examination can thus satisfy the confrontation right, if the declarant is unavailable at trial.

i. Unavailability. Typically, the federal or state requirements of "unavailability" under the hearsay rule, such as FRE 804(a), will be used to determine unavailability for confrontation clause purposes as well, with one addition. In Barber v. Page, 390 U.S. 719 (1968), the Supreme Court held that the Sixth Amendment requires the prosecution to demonstrate in court that it had made a good-faith effort to produce the hearsay declarant, even if its effort was unsuccessful. There is also Supreme Court precedent that does not permit the prosecution to offer a testimonial statement when the unavailability of the declarant was caused by the prosecution's own negligence. Motes v. United States, 178 U.S. 458, 474 (1900). The *Crawford* opinion does not mention *Barber* or *Motes*, although in the circumstances of Crawford's exercise of his spousal privilege, there was no need to do so. State courts have help that prior standards of good faith and reasonable diligence are still applicable after *Crawford*. United States v. Tirado-Tirado, 563 F.3d 117, 120 (5th Cir. 2009).

ii. Prior Opportunity for Cross-examination. Where defendant had strong motive and a full opportunity to cross-examine the declarant at a prior trial, the requirements of *Crawford* have been found to be satisfied. Romans v. Berghuis, 2007 U.S. Dist. LEXIS 88905 (E.D. Mich. 2007).

In Ohio v. Roberts, the Supreme Court approved the admission of statements made by the declarant at a preliminary hearing when the defendant's counsel had engaged in cross-examination. However, as we stated on page 553, a criminal defendant may lack motivation to cross-examine witnesses vigorously at preliminary hearings, due to an inability to prepare adequately and a reluctance to reveal strategy. There are also states in which preliminary hearings are truncated proceedings, and cross-examination is fruitless because the court will not weigh the credibility of witnesses. See People v. Fry, 92 P.3d 970 (Colo. 2004). See also Beasley v. State, 258 S.W.3d 728, 731-735 (Ark. 2007) (exclusion of testimony at bond reduction hearing where defendant did not have strong motive to cross-examine the witness).The

Roberts Court left open the question whether opportunity alone, or merely cursory questioning, would satisfy the confrontation requirement. The Court in *Crawford* wrote in terms of "opportunity" but did not discuss the issue fully.

7.   Exceptions to the Requirement of Confrontation

The *Crawford* opinion mentioned two possible exceptions to the confrontation requirement under which testimonial statements could be admitted. The first is an exception for dying declarations, grounded on the historical admission of such statements during the time when the right to confrontation was developed. 541 U.S. at 56, n.6. The second is an exception based on a defendant's "forfeiture" of the right to confrontation based on wrongful conduct that has made the declarant unavailable to testify. 541 U.S. at 62.

a.   *Dying Declarations*

In *Crawford*, *Giles*, and *Bryant*, the Supreme Court has suggested that dying declarations, even if testimonial, may be admitted as an historically incorporated exception to the requirement of confrontation. Michigan v. Bryant, 131 S. Ct. at 1151, n.1. State supreme courts and other lower courts have admitted dying declarations as nontestimonial. People v. D'Arcy, 226 P.3d 040, 971-973 (Cal. 2010); Commonwealth v. Nesbitt, 829 N.E.2d 299, 309-312 (Mass. 2008); Gilmore v. Lafler, 2010 U.S. Dist. Lexis 59488, at *26-31 (E.D. Mich. 2010) (on habeas review, held that admitting a dying declaration is not contrary to Supreme Court precedent).

b.   *"Forfeiture-by-Wrongdoing"*

As explained on page 566, supra, a theory of "forfeiture" of a defendant's confrontation right developed from the holding in United States v. Mastrangelo, 693 F.2d 269 (2d Cir. 1982), that this right may be waived by the defendant's misconduct in making the hearsay declarant unavailable. The Supreme Court accepted this doctrine explicitly in *Crawford*:

> The rule of forfeiture by wrongdoing (which we accept) extinguishes confrontation claims on essentially equitable grounds; it does not purport to be an alternative means of determining reliability. [541 U.S. at 62.]

And again in *Davis*, the Court explicitly approved the use of this doctrine against defendants who act "in ways that destroy the integrity of the criminal-trial system." See page 601, supra.

A key issue in forfeiture doctrine, however, is whether the *purpose* of the defendant's wrongdoing must be *to prevent the declarant from testifying against the defendant*. This requirement is explicit in the hearsay exception for forfeiture, FRE 804(b)(6). But immediately following *Crawford*, several courts held such a purpose was not necessary to justify forfeiture of the constitutional right to confrontation. See, e.g.,

United States v. Garcia-Meza, 403 F.3d 364, 370-371 (6th Cir. 2005) (holding that
the motive for the defendant's wrongdoing is irrelevant, since "the forfeiture doctrine's
equitable basis, as enunciated in *Crawford*, prevent[s] the defendant from benefiting
in any way from his wrongdoing . . . ").

Dispensing with the "purpose" requirement expanded forfeiture doctrine considerably. The expanded doctrine was frequently applied in cases involving domestic
violence, such as in *Garcia-Meza* where the defendant was charged with the murder
of his wife. The court upheld admission of the wife's statements to police, made after
being assaulted by her husband five months previously, that her husband was becoming violent toward her because she had spoken to a former boyfriend. Since many
victim statements in domestic violence and child abuse cases are found to be "testimonial" and would have been excluded under *Crawford*, the forfeiture exception
became an important component of these prosecutions.

However, in Giles v. California, 554 U.S. 353 (2008), the Supreme Court
rejected this broadened interpretation of constitutional forfeiture doctrine. In that
case, Dwayne Giles was charged and tried for the murder of his ex-girlfriend Brenda
Avie. Giles claimed self-defense, asserting that Avie was jealous and violent. On the
day of her death, she threatened him and charged at him, causing him to close his eyes
and shoot to defend himself. At trial, the prosecution introduced statements that Avie
had made to a police officer responding to a domestic violence report three weeks earlier. Avie had accused Giles of choking her, punching her, and threatening to kill her
with a knife if she ever cheated on him. These statements describing threats of physical injury were admissible hearsay under a California statute. Giles was convicted of
first degree murder. On appeal, the California Supreme Court upheld Giles's conviction. The court assumed that Avie's statements were testimonial but held that they did
not violate the confrontation clause because *Crawford* had recognized a doctrine of
forfeiture, and that Giles's intentional act had made Avie unavailable to testify.

i.   The Majority Opinion in *Giles*.   The Supreme Court granted Giles's petition for certiorari to determine whether this broadened scope of constitutional forfeiture doctrine was legitimate: "We held in *Crawford* that the Confrontation Clause
is 'most naturally read as a reference to the right of confrontation at common law,
admitting only those exceptions established at the time of the founding . . . .' We therefore ask whether the theory of forfeiture by wrongdoing accepted by the California
Supreme Court is a founding-era exception to the confrontation right." 554 U.S. at
358. The majority opinion, authored by Justice Scalia, thus focused on whether the
early common law forfeiture doctrine had required proof that the defendant's purpose
in making a declarant unavailable was to prevent the declarant from testifying.

The Court concluded that forfeiture doctrine required at common law, and thus
must require today, that defendant's purpose in making a declarant unavailable was to
prevent his testimony.

> In sum, our interpretation of the common-law forfeiture rule is supported by (1) the
> most natural reading of the language used at common law; (2) the absence of common-
> law cases *admitting* prior statements on a forfeiture theory when the defendant had not
> engaged in conduct designed to prevent a witness from testifying; (3) the common law's
> uniform exclusion of unconfronted inculpatory testimony by murder victims (except tes-
> timony given with awareness of impending death) in the innumerable cases in which the
> defendant was on trial for killing the victim, but was not shown to have done so for the

purpose of preventing testimony; (4) a subsequent history in which the dissent's broad forfeiture theory has not been applied. The first two and the last are highly persuasive; the third is in our view conclusive. [Id. at 368.]

Six Justices joined in this conclusion as to the proper scope of forfeiture doctrine. The Court vacated the judgment of the California Supreme Court and remanded the case for further proceedings on the question whether defendant had the requisite intent to prevent Avie from reporting abuse or cooperating with authorities when he killed her.

ii.   The Concurring Opinion of Justices Souter and Ginsburg. Justices Souter and Ginsburg joined in a separate concurrence[17] that agreed that the majority opinion was right about the scope of the confrontation right at the time of the Framing and ratification of the Sixth Amendment:

[It] was subject to exception on equitable grounds for an absent witness's prior relevant, testimonial statement, when the defendant brought about the absence with intent to prevent testimony. It was, and is, reasonable to place the risk of untruth in an unconfronted, out-of-court statement on a defendant who meant to preclude the testing that confrontation provides. [Id. at 379.]

But for Justices Souter and Ginsburg, the equitable, rather than the historical, basis for forfeiture doctrine was primary. It was the defendant's intent to prevent testimony that made it fair to place this risk of unconfronted hearsay on the defendant through forfeiture of the confrontation right. Otherwise, they seemed to say, admitting a victim's statement in a murder trial to prove the murder solely on the ground that the defendant probably committed the killing was too close to "question begging":

The only thing saving admissibility and liability determinations from question begging would be (in a jury case) the distinct functions of judge and jury: judges would find by a preponderance of evidence that the defendant killed (and so would admit the testimonial statement), while the jury could so find only on proof beyond a reasonable doubt. Equity demands something more than this near circularity before the right to confrontation is forfeited, and more is supplied by showing intent to prevent the witness from testifying. [Id.]

iii.   The Dissenting Opinion in *Giles*. Three dissenters, Justices Breyer, Stevens, and Kennedy, argued against the majority's conclusion on the historical record. They claimed that "the language that courts have used in setting forth the exception is broad enough to cover the wrongdoing in the present case (murder) and much else besides" and that the basic equitable "purposes and objectives" of forfeiture doctrine — to prevent the defendant from gaining an advantage from his own evil practices — applied to Giles. Their principle dispute with the majority focused on the element of "intent" that had been found against Giles, which they considered sufficient to prove that it was fair to require forfeiture of his confrontation right. Justice Breyer's dissent strongly objected to the majority opinion's seeming substitution of *purpose* or *motive* for the element of intent.

---

17.   Justices Thomas and Alito also wrote brief concurrences stating their doubts that Avie's statements to the police were "testimonial" at all, but acknowledging that this issue was not before the Court.

As to the historical record found in seventeenth-, eighteenth-, and nineteenth-century evidence law, the dissent claimed that

> a review of the cases set forth [by the majority] makes clear that no case limits forfeiture to instances where the defendant's *purpose* or *motivation* is to keep the witness away. . . . Rather . . . , the relevant cases suggest that the forfeiture rule would apply where the witness' absence was the *known consequence* of the defendant's intentional wrongful act. [Id. at 389-392.]

NOTES AND QUESTIONS

1. Only by reading the full majority and dissenting opinions can one appreciate the difficulty of analyzing the historical record in order to determine the precise scope of forfeiture doctrine "at the time of the Framing and the adoption of the Sixth Amendment." When the historical record is in doubt, at least five of the Justices are willing to turn to constitutional, evidentiary, and common law policies to interpret the confrontation right. Only four Justices appear to agree that parsing the historical record is the only legitimate inquiry to make in interpreting the confrontation clause today.

2. The *Giles* opinions acknowledge that *Crawford* has a special impact on cases involving vulnerable victims who will not or cannot testify, or who cannot be effective as witnesses. Some commentators believe that police practices will change to accommodate the change in law, in particular by creating more informal questioning opportunities that do not cry out "interrogation" under *Davis*, by creating more opportunities for pretrial cross-examination in pretrial hearings or depositions; and by working closely with fearful witnesses to enable them to testify. Commonwealth v. Wholaver, 989 A.2d 883 (Pa. 2010) (defendant had adequate opportunity to confront his two daughters at his preliminary hearing; after murder of the two girls, forfeiture doctrine was not needed).

Articles that discuss the effects of *Crawford* on these kinds of prosecutions include Robert P. Mosteller, Crawford v. Washington: Encouraging and Ensuring the Confrontation of Witnesses, 39 U. Rich. L. Rev. 511 (2005); Tom Lininger, Prosecuting Batterers After *Crawford*, 91 Va. L. Rev. 747 (2005); Celeste E. Byrom, The Use of the Excited Utterance Hearsay Exception in the Prosecution of Domestic Violence Cases After Crawford v. Washington, 23 Rev. Litig. 409 (2005).

Child witnesses may testify by closed circuit television, pursuant to the narrow exception established in Maryland v. Craig, 497 U.S. 836 (1990), to protect the physical and psychological well-being of the child. When they do, it has been held, prior to *Crawford*, that this counts as an in-court appearance for purposes of admitting their other hearsay statements, so long as the specific finding of necessity mandated in *Craig* is satisfied. United States v. Turning Bear, 357 F.3d 730, 738 (8th Cir. 2004).

Recent articles include David A. Sklansky, Hearsay's Last Hurrah, 2009 Sup. Ct. Rev. 1 (2010); Jay A. Abarbanel, In Light of Crawford v. Washington and the Difficult Nature of Domestic Violence Prosecutions, Maryland Should Adopt Legislation Making Admissible Prior Acts of Domestic Violence in Domestic Violence Prosecutions, 39 U. Balt. L. Rev. 467 (2010); Brian Fox, *Crawford* at Its Limits: Hearsay and Forfeiture in Child Abuse Cases, 46 Am. Crim. L. Rev. 1245 (2009); Aiysha Hussain, Reviving Hope for Domestic Violence Prosecutions: Giles v. California, 46 Am. Crim. L. Rev. 1301 (2009).

H.   REFLECTION ON THE HEARSAY RULE

Critics of the hearsay rule are plentiful. Their criticisms focus primarily on the complexity of the categorical structure of the exemptions and exceptions and on whether such an elaborate structure is necessary to fulfill hearsay policy. This, in turn, raises the deeper question of what hearsay policy should be in the context of modern litigation.

1.   The Traditional Goals of Hearsay Policy

We presented the traditional formulation of the policy excluding hearsay in Section A of this chapter: A witness's oath, demeanor, and cross-examination are thought to reduce testimonial dangers and make in-court testimony *more* reliable than out-of-court statements. A somewhat stronger version of this policy would state that hearsay is inherently weak evidence, that juries cannot properly evaluate it, that verdicts should not be based on hearsay, and that excluding hearsay protects against fraudulent evidence. A thorough analysis and critique of this traditional policy can be found in Paul S. Milich, Hearsay Antinomies: The Case for Abolishing the Rule and Starting Over, 71 Or. L. Rev. 723 (1992).

Based on this view of the weaknesses of hearsay evidence, the two primary justifications for admitting it through categorical exceptions and exemptions are *reliability* and *necessity*: The goal of traditional hearsay policy is to admit hearsay that is more reliable than run-of-the mill hearsay, or that seems necessary to the rational resolution of litigated disputes. This "reliability theory" of the hearsay exceptions presumes that reliable hearsay can be identified in advance by identifying those circumstances that may reduce some risks of insincerity, to a lesser extent risk of loss of memory, and only occasionally a risk of inaccurate perception.

2.   The Reliability Theory Does Not Work

It is easy to criticize the reliability theory of the traditional hearsay rule. We have done so implicitly throughout this chapter by pointing out where the foundational requirements of the categorical exceptions and exemptions fail to fulfill their goal. Much seemingly unreliable hearsay is admitted, and it may be that much that seems reliable is excluded. Even the Advisory Committee's Introductory Note to Article VIII of the Federal Rules of Evidence acknowledges these criticisms:

> The solution evolved by the common law has been a general rule excluding hearsay but subject to the numerous exceptions under circumstances supposed to furnish guarantees of trustworthiness. Criticisms of this scheme are that it is bulky and complex, fails to screen good from bad hearsay realistically, and inhibits the growth of the law of evidence.

A similar critique is found in Michael Seigel, Rationalizing Hearsay: A Proposal for a Best Evidence Hearsay Rule, 72 B.U. L. Rev. 893, 912-913 (1992):

> Sadly, our current system employs the *least rational* means of evaluating the reliability of hearsay evidence: preconceived categories. Each categorical exception is theoretically supported by an initial inductive hypothesis about human behavior that, if true, reduces

the probability that an out-of-court statement falling within the category suffers from
one of the hearsay dangers. Accordingly, any such statement is deemed reliable and,
therefore, admissible. However, even assuming the accuracy of the categories' foundation hypotheses, an out-of-court statement's reliability is simply not measurable through
what is, in effect, an unidimensional test. A statement may be grossly unreliable despite
the fact that it falls within the bounds of a categorical exception, in light of other information in the case. This more specific information may demonstrate that the category's
behavioral assumption is inapplicable to the particular statement at issue; or the statement may present a danger not accounted for by the assumption underlying the specific
exception; or other more definitive evidence might make the accuracy of the hearsay
suspect. At the same time, the categorical exceptions are not comprehensively inclusive;
the facts surrounding excluded hearsay may indicate that it is reliable even though it fails
to meet the strictures of any given exception.

The trouble is, there is not much agreement on an alternative approach to determining the reliability of the hearsay that should be admitted.

3.   A Rule of Discretion

One option is to change the rule to a Rule 403-type of balancing test, whereby
the trial judge would be given discretion to admit hearsay that the judge thinks is
more probative because it is more credible, and to exclude hearsay that is less probative because less credible. Under the categorical approach, the credibility of hearsay
evidence is not to be weighed by the judge. The advantages of a discretionary rule
were forcefully argued in Jack B. Weinstein, The Probative Force of Hearsay, 46 Iowa
L. Rev. 331 (1961). A discretionary approach was also described, but rejected, in the
Advisory Committee's Introductory Note:

> Admissibility would be determined by weighing the probative force of the evidence
> against the possibility of prejudice, waste of time, and the availability of more satisfactory
> evidence. The bases of the traditional hearsay exceptions would be helpful in assessing
> probative force . . . . Procedural safeguards would consist of notice of intention to use
> hearsay, free comment by the judge on the weight of the evidence, and a greater mea-
> sure of authority in both trial and appellate judges to deal with evidence on the basis of
> weight. The Advisory Committee has rejected this approach to hearsay as involving too
> great a measure of judicial discretion, minimizing the predictability of rulings, enhanc-
> ing the difficulties of preparing for trial, adding a further element to the already over-
> complicated congeries of pretrial procedures, and requiring substantially different rules
> for civil and criminal cases.

According to Professor Seigel, a discretionary rule would vest considerably more
authority over the outcomes of trials in the judge:

> Simply put, the power to exclude evidence is the power to determine the outcome of
> cases. If truly discretionary—in other words, if not subject to appellate review—this
> power is too great to vest in individual trial judges. Moreover, absent clear guide-
> lines defining reliable hearsay, the exclusionary process would be akin to a game of
> roulette. On the other hand, imposing clear guidelines and enforcing them through
> appellate review would cause the standard of reliability to evolve slowly into a set of
> rules. The final outcome would be the recreation of what existed prior to codifica-
> tion of the rules of evidence: an ad hoc common law hearsay regime. [Seigel, 72
> B.U. L. Rev. at 914.]

4. Abolition

The more extreme option would be to abandon the search for reliability and abolish the rule of exclusion altogether. The admission of hearsay would be governed only by its relevance under FRE 401 and its risks of FRE 403 dangers, which should not include concerns about the credibility of the declarant. Under a truly *abolitionist* regime, exclusion would depend solely on the judge's estimation of Rule 403 dangers that might negatively affect the jury's ability to evaluate the credibility of hearsay.

What might be the consequences of an abolitionist regime? An article by Professor Eleanor Swift, Abolishing the Hearsay Rule, 75 Cal. L. Rev. 495 (1987), predicted that potentially admissible hearsay would raise three kinds of problems: (1) statements by unidentified persons about whom very little is known, so that the jury has little factual basis on which to apply its own general knowledge and experience; (2) statements that bear obvious risks, in particular a declarant's motive to misrepresent, requiring the jury to make hard choices between conflicting inferences; and (3) statements presented in documentary form without any witness to supply information about them, thus permitting the proponent to avoid presenting either the declarant or a foundation witness for cross-examination.

The Advisory Committee rejected an abolitionist regime on grounds that it "has been unconvinced of the wisdom of abandoning the traditional requirement of some particular assurance of credibility as a condition precedent to admitting the hearsay declaration of an unavailable declarant."

5. Reformulating Hearsay Policy

a. *Is There a Need for a Hearsay Rule in Modern Civil Litigation?*

In his article The Evolution of the Hearsay Rule to a Rule of Admission, 76 Minn. L. Rev. 797, 797-801 (1992), Professor Ronald Allen describes why the hearsay rule of exclusion is no longer important in civil litigation due to prevalent use of discovery depositions, party admissions, and the numerous exceptions and exemptions. His concern is that its continued existence imposes too great a cost:

> My instinct is that . . . [g]iven all the inroads into the rule, it no longer can seriously be contended that the rule contributes in any robust way to substantial justice.[18] To be sure, an occasional case will turn on hearsay, and occasionally justice might be done because of exclusion for reason of hearsay, but against this must be balanced the probability that without a hearsay rule the evidence would have been excluded under some other rule, most likely relevancy. Further to be considered in the balance are cases of injustice resulting from the exclusion of hearsay as well as the astounding cost of maintaining the rule.
>
> The cost of maintaining the rule is not just a function of its contribution to justice. It also includes the time spent on litigating the rule. And of course that is not just a cost voluntarily borne by the parties, for in our system virtually all the cost of the court—salaries, administrative costs, and capital costs—are borne by the public. As expensive as litigation is for the parties, it is supported by an enormous public subsidy. Each time a hearsay question is litigated, the public pays. The rule imposes other costs as well.

---

18. I put aside Confrontation Clause questions in criminal cases.

Enormous time is spent teaching and writing about the hearsay rule, which are both costly enterprises. In some law schools, students spend over half their time in evidence classes learning the intricacies of the hearsay rule, and . . . enormous academic resources are expended on the rule.

   Like other social practices, the hearsay rule should be required to pull its own freight; only if its costs are justified should it be maintained.

b.   Regulation Premised on the Excesses of the Adversary System

One justification for regulating the admission of hearsay derives from the excesses of the adversary system of proof.

> Consider for instance, the possibility that a hearsay declarant might be a bad witness, or . . . might be shown incredible on cross-examination. A party might prefer to offer the [hearsay statement] rather than to call the declarant to the stand. In effect, such a choice would be a deliberate choice to mislead the factfinder, because the hearsay would not be accompanied by information that would enable the jury to evaluate the evidence properly. [Craig R. Callen, Foreword to the First Virtual Forum: Wallace Stevens, Blackbirds and the Hearsay Rule, 16 Miss. Col. L. Rev. 1, 10 (1995).]

Hearsay policy could be premised on mitigating this adversarial tactic. Professor Seigel proposes a principle for admitting hearsay only when it is the "best evidence" available from a particular declarant source. Seigel, 72 B.U. L. Rev. at 930-938. Professor Swift proposes that admission of hearsay be based on the production of a foundation witness who would be able to present information that the jury needs to evaluate the hearsay statement. Eleanor Swift, A Foundation Fact Approach to Hearsay, 75 Cal. L. Rev. 1339 (1987).

c.   Notice-based Admission in Civil Cases: Reliance on the Adversary System

Several proposals have been made to admit hearsay more freely in civil cases, premised on sufficient notice to the opponent. Professor Roger Park recommends a notice-based residual exception that makes no provision for reliability screening by judges in A Subject Matter Approach to Hearsay Reform, 86 Mich. L. Rev. 51 (1987). The proponent of hearsay would state whether the declarant is available or unavailable. Then, the opponent could demand that the declarant be produced and examined by the proponent and be available for cross-examination. In certain circumstances, the trial judge would be authorized to shift costs of production to the opponent. In the view of Professor Milich, all that is needed is notice of an intent to offer information from a source *not* to be called to testify at trial. The notice would include the name and location of the source so that the opponent could interview, depose, or produce the source if desired. Milich, 71 Or. L. Rev. at 774-776.

d.   Why Hearsay Should Be Treated Differently in Criminal Cases

The confrontation clause does place a constraint on hearsay reform in criminal cases. Most legislators, courts, attorneys, and commentators agree that the criminal defendant's interest in personal liberty does weigh more heavily in favor of a requirement that the prosecution's use of hearsay be limited. Eileen A. Scallen, Constitutional Dimensions of Hearsay Reform: Toward a Three-Dimensional Confrontation Clause, 76 Minn. L. Rev. 623 (1992). The approach in *Crawford* is to identify what might be thought of as the most *unreliable* categories of hearsay — testimonial statements — and to exclude them unless confrontation is or has been provided. These same risks of unreliability were identified previously by Professor Park in recommending that a categorical approach to admitting hearsay in criminal cases be maintained:

> Generally, out-of-court statements relevant to criminal cases are made, in the broadest sense, with a view to litigation, or at least with knowledge that the legal process may be brought to bear on the matter being described. . . . Moreover, many of the declarants' statements are taken by police, often under interrogation — a process essential in producing investigative leads but not calculated to elicit spontaneous statements that spring from a spirit of candor. [Park, A Subject Matter Approach to Hearsay, 86 Mich. L. Rev. at 94-97, 99.]

Under *Crawford*, prosecutors will remain constrained in their use of hearsay even should the hearsay rule itself be changed and further liberalized.

e.   Conclusion

This debate over hearsay reform should convince you of at least one thing: Hearsay evidence presents fundamental challenges to the values that underlie our system of trial proof-reliance on the inferential reasoning of lay fact finders, adversarial control of proof, and relaxed judicial control. Despite the liberalization of proof under the Federal Rules of Evidence, hearsay is treated with suspicion and remains subject to judicial regulation. None of the commentators discussed herein favors total abolition of the general rule against hearsay offered against criminal defendants.

CHAPTER NINE

LAY OPINIONS AND
EXPERT WITNESSES

Recall the following portion of the *Johnson* transcript (direct examination of Officer Huston by Mr. Cummings):

Q: At some point in time it became clear to you that inmate Johnson was not going to slide the trays through the food port door.

A: No. When he picked up the trays and brought them to the food port it was not subtle, I guess. He didn't say anything, he was calm, walked up to the door and held the tray.

Q: At that point in time did somebody order the door be opened?

A: Yes. Officer Smith.

Q: And is that an appropriate method to get back the trays?

A: Yes.

MR. DEEMER: Excuse me. A, lack of qualifications; B, lack of foundation; and, C, it's leading.

THE COURT: Are you asking for an expert opinion, Mr. Cummings?

Q. BY MR. CUMMINGS: Officer Huston, you stated that you have worked as a correctional officer at Pelican Bay for six years?

A: Yes.

Q: And during those six years, did you receive special education and training for your job?

A: Yes.

Q: What was that?

A: There are training manuals, and training courses for correctional officers on-site and throughout the state that we attend.

Q: And does this training include the handling of specific problems that inmates sometimes cause?

A: Yes, it does.

Q: And based on this training, do you have an opinion on the proper means to handle situations like inmate Johnson's, that is, on whether it is appropriate to open the cell door? Just tell us whether you have an opinion.

A: Yes, I do.

MR. CUMMINGS: I would offer Officer Huston's opinion now as based on his special experiences and training at Pelican Bay.

THE COURT: You may answer.

Q.   BY MR. CUMMINGS: Is opening the cell door an appropriate way to get back the food trays?

A: Yes, on the General Population side it is. If the inmates are General Population inmates so they are out of their cells a lot of the time and if they are, what we say, programmed and everything else and they seem calm and everything else, well, we — yeah, we get the trays that way, especially when they have more than two trays or have two trays with garbage on the top . . . .

Q: Was the door opened?

A: Yes, the door was opened.

Q: What happened when the door opened?

A: Inmate Johnson — when the door was opened up inmate Johnson immediately instantly dropped the food trays. He was standing just inside the door, up next to the door. Dropped the food trays immediately and bowed his head, brought up his fists and just tried to come through the door and hit Officer Walker in the chest.

Q: Where did Officer Walker make contact or where did Johnson make contact with Walker?

A: In the door. In the doorway after the door was opened. Officer Walker was on the outside of the cell . . . .

Q: What happened when Johnson charged the officers and made contact with Walker?

A: Officer Walker immediately grabbed him and pushed him inside the cell and inmate Johnson fell back up against the desk area, which is approximately three feet inside the cell.

Q: What was inmate Johnson doing at that time?

A: *Combative*

MR. DEEMER: One moment, Your Honor. I am going to object to that term. It's conclusionary.

THE COURT: Overruled.

Q.   BY MR. CUMMINGS: Describe for me what you mean by "combative"?

A: Swinging his arms, not complying with orders, using his strength.

This short excerpt contains examples of two different kinds of opinions. The reference to Johnson as "combative" is a lay opinion. It relates not what the witness *observed,* but instead a *conclusion or inference* about a situation. In this case, the witness inferred from the observation of Johnson's "[s]winging his arms, not complying with orders, using his strength" that Johnson was primed for a fight and physically resisting the authority of the guards. He added to the testimony of his observations a summary of what he believed their import to be; he expressed an opinion, in other words. Witnesses are allowed, but not encouraged, to give lay opinions. Opinions always rest on underlying generalizations, and the value of the opinion is in direct proportion to the reliability of the underlying generalization. In this sense, the structure of lay opinions is identical to that of relevancy discussed in Chapter Three. It is the fact finder's task to determine the pertinent underlying generalizations and the extent to which they should be credited; it is the witness's task to provide an accurate recitation of what was observed. The lay opinion rule polices this boundary.

Often the boundary does not need formal policing. Note in the transcript that the direct examiner, Mr. Cummings, asked the witness to describe the factual basis of his conclusion, even though the judge let the witness testify in conclusory terms. This is because facts are usually more persuasive than opinions, and in this case the underlying factual predicate was not difficult to extract. In cases like this, the opinion rule is self-policing; the self-interest of the parties will generate the proper result.

Officer Huston also offered an "expert opinion" about the proper manner to retrieve trays. This opinion was based on his special training and experience as a correctional officer, which includes information not within the general run of human knowledge and experience. When such knowledge exists and would be helpful to a fact finder, it may be presented either through a description of the relevant knowledge or through the offering of expert opinions in the fashion of Officer Huston's testimony. Often experts provide information and opinions about scientific matters; but as this example demonstrates, expert testimony is not limited to science. It can extend to any knowledge that might be helpful but is not likely to be possessed by the fact finder.

In this chapter, we examine the various issues involved in the offering of opinions at trial, both lay and expert; we also examine the implications of the law's need for information from other disciplines that possess specialized knowledge. If the trial judge determines that a witness is offering a lay opinion, FRE 701 applies, as is discussed in Section A where we examine what lay opinions are and when they may be offered at trial.

If the judge determines a witness is offering an expert opinion or testifying about specialized knowledge, the remainder of Article VII, (FRE 702-706), applies. Section B examines expert testimony and the conditions under which specialized evidence may be adduced at trial. Section C addresses briefly the recurring problem of opinions being offered on ultimate issues of fact. Section D discusses the use of court appointed experts. Section E presents a number of areas involving scientific evidence and expert testimony in which there have been recent developments.

A. LAY OPINIONS

1. FRE 701

RULE 701. OPINION TESTIMONY BY LAY WITNESSES

If a witness is not testifying as an expert, testimony in the form of an opinion is limited to one that is:

(a) rationally based on the witness's perception;

(b) helpful to clearly understanding the witness's testimony or to determining a fact in issue; and

(c) not based on scientific, technical, or other specialized knowledge within the scope of Rule 702.

2. Interpretation and Illustration of FRE 701

FRE 701 captures the common law rule concerning lay opinions. Like its common law counterpart, the rule states a preference for witnesses not to testify in the form of opinions. In the traditional language of the common law, witnesses were to testify to what they observed (i.e., "facts") rather than to any inferences about, summaries of, or conclusions of fact, all of which together were referred to as "opinions." Notwithstanding the rule, testimony in the form of opinions is common at trial, largely because it is common in our conventional manner of speaking. In a sexual harassment suit, for example, testimony that the defendant "winked" expresses a summary of observations in the form of a conclusion, which is to say an opinion. Consider another example: testimony concerning the speed of a car. A witness testifying that a car was going "approximately 60 miles an hour" is actually testifying about the conclusion of an unconscious calculation that computes the speed from watching the car pass a certain distance over a certain time. In the subsections below, we examine when such conclusory testimony is allowed and when it will likely be forbidden, and why.

a.   Fact Versus Opinion

Some commentators believe that FRE 701 is more liberal than its common law counterparts, but generalizations are difficult because the line between "fact" and "opinion" is unclear. As early as 1878, a court commented that lay opinions were admissible on a wide variety of topics, including

> identity, handwriting, quantity, value, weight, measure, time, distance, velocity, form, size, age, strength, heat, cold, sickness, and health; questions also concerning various mental and moral aspects of humanity, such as disposition and temper, anger, fear, excitement, intoxication, veracity, general character, and particular phases of character, and other conditions and things, both moral and physical, too numerous to mention. [Hardy v. Merrill, 56 N.H. 227, 22 Am. Rep. 441 (1878).]

The line between what is a fact and what is an "opinion" is unclear because the distinction is not an analytical one; it is a question of degree. All testimony involves "opinions." Consider the testimony of a witness that the blue car ran the red light. There is no scientific or analytical standard being applied here by the witness concerning what a "blue car" or a "red light" is. Rather, the witness is offering an "opinion" of what the witness thinks was observed. What this witness calls red, someone else may call green, and what this witness calls blue somebody else may call black. This may not convince you (although we think that on further reflection it will). Consider, then, that the witness will not be testifying to what happened but instead as to what the witness believes was observed. The witness's perspective may have been bad, whether known to the witness or not, and memory may have decayed. These points — observational and memory problems, whether realized or not — are unavoidable and make it clear that every word uttered at trial is an "opinion" of the person uttering the word.

If the distinction between "fact" and "opinion" is analytically untenable, you may be wondering why the rules of evidence nonetheless insist on making the distinction. Good question. The answer is that doing so pushes witnesses toward relating sensory impressions that are less rather than more thickly varnished. Testimony can be more or less loaded with opinions (inferences, summaries, and conclusions), and we prefer to have less rather than more. Even though relating sensory impressions ("I saw the blue car run the red light") involves opinions ("I *believe* I saw . . ."), the more testimony concentrates on relating sensory impressions, the easier it is for the fact finder to mediate among conflicting versions from the various witnesses, and thus to decide what actually happened almost as though the juror had access to the inner workings of the witnesses' minds. The juror is aided in this task by quite liberal rules of cross-examination that allow the cognitive and affective states of witnesses to be examined thoroughly for whatever clues they may yield as to why the witnesses testified as they did.

The question of how to distinguish between allowable and inappropriate lay opinions remains, but very little more can be suggested than a reliance on common sense, which is precisely what many common law courts appeared to do by applying an "I know it when I see it" standard for defining opinions. Thus, virtually all judges would agree that the statement "the platform was dangerous" is an opinion whereas the assertions "John shot me" or "the object is a chair" are statements of fact. The difficulty, of course, is that this does not provide much guidance for classifying statements. For example, what about a statement that the defendant was "speeding" or was driving "recklessly" or was driving "too fast given the weather conditions"? Moreover, even supposedly clear examples may be unclear in some contexts. Is the statement "John shot me" one of fact or opinion if we know that John and Jim are identical twins?

Although relying on "common sense" is often problematic, here there is no plausible alternative. The legitimate concern underlying the prohibition against lay opinions, upon which common sense will operate, is that we do not want witnesses to substitute their conclusions for facts that would be helpful to the jury. Thus, in the dangerous platform case, we would prefer to have the witness describe to the jury the condition of the platform in some detail. Without the detailed information about the condition of the platform, the jury's only choice would be whether to rely on the conclusion of the witness, and the condition of the platform most likely will not defy straightforward description. With the detailed information the jurors would be in a better position to determine for themselves whether the platform was dangerous, and this is what we want them to do. Similarly, in the identical twin case, we would prefer to have the victim describe the particular characteristics of the assailant or the prior encounters with John that led the victim to conclude that the assailant was John rather than Jim, which should be relatively easy to do. In short, in cases like these, sustaining a lay opinion objection rather obviously, "commonsensically," forces the witness to articulate the underlying details that gave rise to their "opinion" without impeding the efficient flow of the trial.

b.   Rationally Based on the Perception of the Witness

Bear in mind that the lay opinion rule does not excuse or substitute for the requirement of firsthand knowledge; indeed, section (a) of FRE 701 restates the firsthand knowledge requirement. The rule merely allows firsthand knowledge to be summarized in the form of an opinion. For a good example of the import of this point, see Alexis v. McDonald's Restaurants of Mass., Inc., 67 F.3d 341 (1st Cir 1995). In *Alexis*, the plaintiff got into an argument with a McDonald's employee. The manager asked the plaintiff to leave. She refused and was arrested. Later she filed a civil rights action alleging racial discrimination. On motion for summary judgment, she offered depositions of eyewitness family members and an unrelated eyewitness that contained opinions to the effect that the plaintiff would have been treated differently had she been "a rich white woman." The only bases for these opinions were that the McDonald's staff had reacted angrily toward the plaintiff, with "a negative tone," and were generally unfriendly and impolite. As the court pointed out in affirming exclusion of the evidence, such actions may be consistent with racial discrimination, but they do not demonstrate it. The opinions to the contrary, in short, were not rationally based on firsthand knowledge.

You must bear in mind how case specific these rulings are. In Bohannon v. Pegelow, 652 F.2d 729 (7th Cir. 1981), the plaintiff filed a civil rights action alleging wrongful arrest. The trial court allowed, and the Seventh Circuit affirmed, testimony from a friend of the plaintiff that the arrest was motivated by racial prejudice, despite the fact that the rest of the witness's testimony did not contain any facts indicating prejudice. The court rejected the argument that the testimony could not have been rationally based on the perception of the witness. The court said it was enough that the witness had observed the arrest: "When, as here, the witness observes first hand the altercation in question, her opinions on the feelings of the parties are based on her personal knowledge and rational perceptions and are helpful to the jury." The appellate court believed this to be similar to the cases that admitted lay opinions concerning the state of another, such as United States v. Lawson, 653 F.2d 299 (7th Cir. 1981), admitting the FBI agent's testimony that the defendant was sane. In your judgment, what is the lesson here? Is it that few generalizations will operate in this context? That the rulings will be radically case specific? That *Alexis* and *Bohannon* are inconsistent? It is impossible to say from the cold appellate record. The conclusion of a trial judge to permit opinion testimony is conditioned by all the events at trial, including behavioral cues from the witnesses that are not reflected in the record. This in turn means that trial court decisions on lay opinions are largely unreviewable. We know the proper question: Is the witness testifying rationally from firsthand knowledge? But there are virtually no standards available to systematically judge the answer given.

c. Helpful to Clearly Understanding the Witness's Testimony or to Determining a Fact in Issue

If a judge is convinced that a witness is testifying from firsthand knowledge, even though expressed in the form of an opinion (e.g., "The defendant was belligerent"), the judge may allow the testimony if it is "helpful to clearly understanding the witness's testimony or to determining a fact in issue." When is that? Again, it is very difficult to say in a systematic way, which means that once more trial judges will be invested with substantial discretion. The pertinent concerns are easily identifiable, however. The purpose of the lay opinion rule is to facilitate a certain mode of proceeding at trial. The more opinions are allowed, the more the witness usurps the role of the fact finder. The fact finder is the one charged to draw inferences; the witnesses are to relate factual observations, leaving to the fact finder the inferences to be drawn from those factual observations. This point is illustrated in Lynch v. City of Boston, 180 F.3d 1, 16 (1st Cir. 1999). Helen Lynch sued the City of Boston alleging that she was wrongfully terminated from her position with the City's "Can Share" hunger program. At trial, Lynch sought admission of the testimony of one of her coworkers, Michael Devlin, on the specific question of whether her work was adequate. Specifically, Lynch sought to have Devlin answer the question: "In the time that you worked in the Can Share program, who would you say was responsible for the success and growth the program had?" Though Devlin had years of experience working with Lynch, the trial court ruled his testimony on this question inadmissible, stating

> Even though rationally based on the witness's personal perception, lay opinion testimony will be excluded if it is not "helpful" to the trier of fact. . . . Lay opinions are not helpful when the jury can readily draw the necessary inferences and conclusions without the aid of the opinion. . . . Here, as Lynch herself points out, Devlin testified at some length concerning his personal observation of Lynch's excellent organizational skills, her proficiency at long-term program planning, her "phenomenal" ability to recruit participants from the business community, her "incredible" motivational skills, and her ability to communicate clearly. Devlin testified that Lynch's ability to recruit in the business community "brought in a lot of people to take part in the campaign fully." Contrary to Lynch's assertion that the jury could not determine "how effective plaintiff was in her job" without Devlin's lay opinion, the jury, unaided by Devlin's opinion, could readily have drawn the inference from Devlin's detailed factual account of Lynch's exceptional work at Can Share that Lynch was quite effective in her position and was responsible for the success and growth of the Can Share program during the time she and Devlin worked together. . . . Hence the district court may well have believed — in finding the opinion not to pertain to an appropriate subject for lay opinion testimony — that it would simply not be helpful. [Citations omitted.]

In a similar case, the court excluded, and its opinion was upheld on appeal, testimony from a son and former wife that a person in a photograph was the father/former husband. United States v. Dixon, 413 F.3d 540 (6th Cir. 2005). There was testimony that the defendant's physical appearance had not changed from the time of the photograph to the time of trial, the photo was of good quality, and thus the jury would not be helped by the testimony of the son and former wife.

"Helpfulness" has two sides to it. In addition to being helpful to the fact finder, presenting lay opinions can be helpful to the orderly presentation of testimony by permitting individuals to testify consistent with their normal use of language. If insisting on testimony about "facts" rather than "opinions" proves difficult if not impossible, and impedes rather than facilitates inquiry at trial, lay opinions should be allowed. In many instances, the underlying generalization or the very observations themselves defy articulation by the witness, or the elaboration of such generalizations would be a waste of time. When either is the case, the purposes of trial are advanced by allowing the "lay opinion." Earlier, we gave the statement that the defendant winked at the plaintiff as an example of an opinion testimony in a harassment suit. "Winking" is a summary of a complex physical act. A witness could be required to describe scrunching up one's nose and closing an eyelid while leaning forward with a provocative look on one's face (but what is a "provocative look"?), but no obvious benefit would come from imposing this requirement on the witness. Thus, virtually all judges would allow the lay opinion about a wink. Consider also the example of testimony about the speed of a car. Forcing witnesses to testify about such matters in a nonconclusory fashion — to make them testify about observations of distance divided by time and to forbid them from testifying that the car was going approximately 60 miles an hour — would make it virtually impossible to get useful information from them. Similarly, when a witness identifies another person with whom the witness is acquainted, the witness can just say "That's John," rather than say "John has a certain facial structure just like the person you are asking me to identify," and so on. In such cases, FRE 701 permits testimony in the form of an opinion.

Compare testimony about winking or the speed of a car to testimony that a person observed by a witness was drunk. Like testimony that a person winked at somebody, testimony that a person was drunk is a summary of observations such as lack of balance, fumbling around, slurred speech, and odor of alcohol. Unlike testimony about speed of cars or winking, these matters can be testified to fairly easily. Thus, many courts would exclude testimony that a person was "drunk," and instead insist that the witness relate the observations on which that conclusion was based.

There is a line of cases that fairly directly indicates that FRE 701 permits the trial courts to align testimony at trial with our normal conventions of both observing and relating what we observe. Appraising the state of mind of another person is something that is done constantly in life, but often is done on the basis of nonverbal cues that are difficult to describe. Think of your use of the word "impression." When you have an "impression" that someone is upset, angry, or depressed, what exactly do you mean? When you express such a view, and a friend queries you about it, do you normally respond by shrugging your shoulders and saying, "I don't know, I just had the impression that . . . . " Not surprisingly, in similar situations courts often admit lay opinions. For example, in United States v. Garcia, 982 F. Supp. 112 (D.P.R. 1997), the court admitted lay opinion testimony that the defendant did not seem mentally retarded and that she "appeared to be logical." Though witnesses should not be forced to break their testimony into the smallest component parts, judges must be watchful and prevent witnesses from, either purposely or carelessly, drawing conclusions that they are no more qualified than the jury to reach. Witnesses were held to this standard even before the passage of the Federal Rules of Evidence. In Tyndall v. Harvey, 226 N.C. 620 (1946), the court found that the trial court had erred by allowing a nonexpert witness who had arrived at the scene in the aftermath of an accident, to testify about the speed of one of the cars involved. The witness testified about the position of the car and the skid marks left on the pavement and then deduced the car's speed. On appeal, the court explained:

> [O]ne who did not see a vehicle in motion will not be permitted to give an opinion as to its speed. The "opinion" must be a fact observed. The witness must speak of facts within his knowledge. He cannot, under the guise of an opinion, give his deductive conclusion from what he saw and knew. [Id. at 624.]

This standard did not substantially change with the adoption of the Federal Rules nor has it changed over the subsequent 30 years.

Of course, the benefits of opinion testimony must be balanced by its risks, but in general these are small. Judge Learned Hand explained why there need be no great fear about lay opinion testimony in United States v. Cotter, 60 F.2d 689, 693-694 (2d Cir. 1932):

> No rule is subject to greater abuse [than the opinion testimony rule]; it is frequently an obstacle to any intelligible account of what happens. Most witnesses will tell their story in colloquial speech which skips the foundations and runs in terms of the "ultimate facts." Ordinarily, they tell it much more plainly in this way, and the warrant for what they say can be perfectly probed by cross-examination.

d.   Not Based on Scientific, Technical, or Other Specialized Knowledge Within the Scope of Rule 702

Section (c) of FRE 701 was added as an amendment in 2000. To understand fully its significance requires you to first work through the remainder of the material in this chapter. In brief, this is what you will find. The Supreme Court has interpreted FRE 702 to require trial judges to act as gatekeepers to the admissibility of expert testimony. The trial judge must be convinced that the expert is testifying on the basis of knowledge acquired in a reliable way and applied appropriately to the case at hand. The form of knowledge most likely to meet such standards is the results of controlled scientific studies, but the scope of expert testimony, as you will soon see, reaches far beyond "scientific knowledge" to "scientific, technical, or other specialized knowledge." FRE 702. The Supreme Court also instructed the lower courts that "technical or other specialized knowledge" must be justified in ways at least roughly analogous to the justifications for the admissibility of "scientific knowledge." This increased the difficulty of gaining admission of certain forms of testimony that previously had passed muster under FRE 702. In response, trial lawyers began offering such testimony as "lay opinions" under FRE 701, directly contravening the Supreme Court's interpretation of the rules. See, e.g., Asplundh Mfg. Div. v. Benton Harbor Eng., 57 F.3d 1190 (3d Cir. 1995) (courts have "commonly interpreted [Rule 701] to permit individuals not qualified as experts but possessing experience or specialized knowledge about particular things, to testify about technical matters that might have been thought to lie within the exclusive province of experts."). The rule was amended to put a stop to that practice. As the Advisory Committee commented:

> Rule 701 has been amended to eliminate the risk that the reliability requirements set forth in Rule 702 will be evaded through the simple expedient of proffering an expert in lay witness clothing. Under the amendment, a witness' testimony must be scrutinized under the rules regulating expert opinion to the extent that the witness is providing testimony based on scientific, technical, or other specialized knowledge within the scope of Rule 702. By channeling testimony that is actually expert testimony to Rule 702, the amendment also ensures that a party will not evade the expert witness disclosure requirements set forth in Fed. R. Civ. P. 26 and Fed. R. Crim. P. 16.

A few trial court decisions have been reversed under Rule 701(c), but it is unlikely that such reversals will ever become common. More than as a change in the law, this amendment should be understood as an admonition to trial judges that they must conscientiously apply the rule appropriate to a situation and limit testimony to that which a witness, as designated, is qualified to offer. But see, e.g., JGR, Inc. v. Thomasville Furniture Indus., 370 F.3d 519 (6th Cir. 2004) (vacating damage award where award was based on improper admission of accountant's testimony under FRE 701 and accountant should have been classified as expert under FRE 702); Bank of China v. NBM LLC, 359 F.3d 171 (2d Cir. 2004) (ruling that admission of bank employee's testimony on bank practice, which spanned several days of trial, was erroneous under FRE 701 but might be admissible under FRE 702).

Even prior to the revision to Rule 701(c), many courts recognized a rigid division between expert and lay testimony. See, e.g., Certain Underwriter's at Lloyd's, London v. Synkovich, 232 F.3d 200 (4th Cir. 2000) ("This rule . . . generally does 'not permit a lay witness to express an opinion as to matters which are beyond the realm of common experience and which require the special skill and knowledge of an expert witness.'") (citing Randolph v. Collectramatic, Inc., 590 F.2d 844, 846 (10th Cir. 1979)). This amendment allows judges much discretion to tailor a ruling on the admissibility of testimony to the qualifications and the extent of firsthand knowledge of an individual witness. See, e.g., United States v. Ayala-Pizarro, 407 F.3d 25 (1st Cir. 2005) (law enforcement agent allowed to testify about nature of drug distribution

points and what occurs there without being qualified as expert, because knowledge
of points was gained through firsthand observation). Rules 701 and 702 distinguish
between expert and lay testimony rather than expert and lay witnesses and so it is possible for the same witness to provide both lay and expert testimony in a single case.
See, e.g., United States v. Figueroa-Lopez, 125 F.3d 1241, 1246 (9th Cir. 1997) (law
enforcement agents allowed to testify that the defendant was acting suspiciously, without being qualified as experts; however, the rules on experts were applicable where
the agents testified on the basis of extensive experience that the defendant was using
code words to refer to drug quantities and prices). This allows judges to faithfully follow the letter and spirit of Rule 702 and yet not be forced into formulaic exclusions of
testimony. We are about to turn to expert testimony. When you have finished studying that material, you will be in a better position to appraise the significance of this
amendment and may want to return to this section to reconsider its implications.

3.   Elaboration of FRE 701: Trial Court Discretion

As we have tried to show, FRE 701 basically stands as an admonition to the trial
judge to preserve the role of the fact finder, but not to impede significantly the progress of the trial. Little more can be said about the matter, as indicated by the small
number of appellate cases finding trial courts' decisions under FRE 701 to be reversible error. Because it is largely an admonition, its implementation is left largely to the
discretion of the trial judges. This does not mean that the rule is of no consequence.
Rather, it means that its importance lies primarily in its implications for trial preparation and strategy for the opposing attorneys.

Interestingly, there is no logical need for a special evidentiary provision dealing
with lay opinions. A court could rely on FRE 402 and FRE 403 to exclude opinions
or conclusions that are not helpful to the fact finder. However, the absence of a lay
opinion provision in a general codification of evidentiary rules would be ambiguous.
It might suggest that the common law prohibition against opinions should not be
disturbed or equally plausible, that it had been rejected. Perhaps the primary utility
of FRE 701 is simply to indicate that the Federal Rules maintain the common law's
approach to opinions.

Although the vast run of cases indicates the breadth of discretion vested in trial
courts, on occasion the failure to exclude a lay opinion will be reversible error. An
example is United States v. Forrester, 60 F.3d 52 (2d Cir. 1995), holding that the
trial court's allowance of a lay opinion concerning the credibility of another witness
was reversible error. In *Forrester*, two men were indicted for conspiracy to distribute
cocaine. At trial, an acquaintance of the two men testified that she had smuggled
drugs for them and that she had so informed an FBI agent when interviewed by him.
She also testified that she had identified one of the men from a photograph during
that same interview. Neither of these allegations appeared in the agent's report. Later,
the FBI agent was called to testify about his investigation of the case. The agent's
report, made during the investigation, showed that the witness had identified one of
the men, but not the other, as the only person who had asked her to smuggle drugs.
The agent was then read the witness's earlier testimony, and was asked whether her
testimony was in any way "inconsistent" with what she had previously told him. Over
the defense's objection, the agent was allowed to testify that he "didn't find her testimony to be inconsistent." The government tried to justify the agent's testimony on the

grounds that he was the only person present for both the interview and the witness's trial testimony, and thus that his testimony would be "helpful" to the jury. The trial court, while allowing the testimony, gave a special jury instruction: "In light of [the agent's] testimony regarding the testimony of another witness here today, I want to remind the members of the jury, and I instruct the members of the jury, that it is the function of the jury to determine the credibility of each witness." The judge's instruction and the government's contention were not enough in the eyes of the appellate court. The court stated that, as a matter of law, the credibility of witnesses is exclusively for the determination of the jury, and witnesses cannot express their opinion as to the credibility of other witnesses. "Far from being helpful," the court said, the agent's testimony "invaded the traditional province of the jury." The court also felt that the government was trying to "cloak" the witness's testimony with the "heightened credibility" some jurors afford testimony given by government witnesses.

Although there are cases like *Forrester* requiring the exclusion of lay opinions, courts operating under the Federal Rules have been fairly liberal in overruling objections based on FRE 701. In United States v. Skeet, 665 F.2d 983 (9th Cir. 1982), the court gave as examples of permissible lay opinions: the mental or physical condition of a person, his or her character or reputation, emotions manifested by the person's acts, speed of a moving object, size, height, odor, flavor, color, and heat. However, the same court approved the trial court's refusal to permit an opinion that a shooting was accidental, indicating again the trial judge's discretion over these matters. Similarly, United States v. Lawson, 653 F.2d 299 (7th Cir. 1981), affirmed admission of the opinions of FBI agents that the defendant was "sane." Compare Gorby v. Schneider Tank Lines, 741 F.2d 1015 (7th Cir. 1984), upholding a trial court's exclusion of an opinion in a suit arising out of a collision between a truck and a semitanker that the driver of the tanker "did everything he could to avoid this accident." These cases also demonstrate how case-specific rulings on opinions are. In some instances, the underlying facts might be easy to describe, whereas in others it would be quite difficult. Trial judges have a great deal of discretion in deciding which is the case, and rarely are their determinations reversed on appeal.

An example of how case-specific rulings on lay opinions can be is a series of cases dealing with whether a police detective can testify about the identity of a person in surveillance photographs taken during robberies. Compare two, United States v. Henderson, 68 F.3d 323 (9th Cir. 1995), and United States v. Lapierre, 998 F.2d 1460 (9th Cir. 1993). In *Lapierre*, the court ruled that the officer's testimony was inadmissible because he had not known the defendant before the robbery investigation, and thus had no substantial previous contact with him. His only knowledge of the defendant's appearance came from photographs or from eyewitness descriptions. Consequently, the court concluded that his testimony would not be "helpful" to the jury, and would invade the jury's role. The court stated that there were two cases where this sort of identification would be allowed — where the identifying officer had had substantial contact with the defendant, and where the defendant's appearance had changed from the time the surveillance photographs were taken and the time the defendant was on trial.

In *Henderson*, the court allowed the officer's testimony, stating that it did "not require a showing of both sustained contact and special knowledge as prerequisites to a lay witness giving identification testimony." Even though the court held that "specialized knowledge" of the defendant was not required, in this particular case the witness had such knowledge, because he had seen the defendant wearing a heavy overcoat, of the same sort worn by the robber in the bank's photographs. The jury had not seen the defendant wearing the coat, which the court felt could lead to an incorrect conclusion regarding his "weight and bulk." The *Henderson* court also noted that the witness had known the defendant for over 15 years and was thus "more likely" than the jury to make a correct identification of him.

The common law prohibition against lay opinions was informed by one other concern, which is the desire to forbid witnesses from expressing an opinion on the ultimate issue in the case. Interestingly, even though FRE 704 has eliminated the common law prohibition of opinions on ultimate issues, it remains true that the more germane an opinion is to an ultimate issue, the more likely the courts seem to be to require a recitation of the facts underlying the opinion. As one court said, "the closer the subject of the opinion gets to critical issues, the likelier the judge is to require the witness to be more concrete." United States v. Allen, 10 F.3d 405, 414 (7th Cir. 1993). We discuss FRE 704 in Section C, infra.

KEY POINTS

1. The concern underlying the prohibition against lay opinions is that a witness's opinion (inferences, summaries, or conclusions) may sometimes deprive the jurors of important data they need to perform their fact-finding role.

2. Whether a jury is deprived of important data does not depend on an *a priori* distinction between fact and opinion. It depends instead on an assessment of what information will be optimally helpful to jurors in their fact-finding role in the context of a particular case.

3. If a summary or conclusion that forgoes underlying details will be adequate for the jury's purposes, the testimony in that form should be admissible. If, to the contrary, the jurors need underlying details and it is feasible to provide them, the witness should be required to provide those details rather than the witness's own summary or conclusion.

PROBLEMS

9.1. Defendant was driving his car, and crashed into Plaintiff's car at an intersection. Plaintiff alleges that Defendant was driving over the speed limit, was intoxicated, and ran a red light. To establish these facts, Plaintiff wants to call W_1, who was at the scene and will testify that Defendant, when he exited his car, was wobbly and looked like he was drunk, and that the smell of alcohol was detectable. W_2 will testify that he was getting his hair cut in a barber shop about a mile away from the accident and observed Defendant's car "whiz by the barber shop going about 70 miles an hour." W_3 will testify that she heard the squeal of tires that could only be made by a car greatly exceeding the speed limit trying to stop quickly, that she looked up and "thought she saw Defendant's car enter the intersection while the light was against him" but she "can't be positive that's so." W_4, also at the scene, will testify that the first thing Defendant did when he got out of his car after the wreck is walk toward Plaintiff's car, trip over a small piece of wire, get up, and say, "My God, I need another drink," although W_4 isn't absolutely sure that Defendant said "another." Can all these witnesses testify accordingly?

9.2. In his capacity as an auto parts delivery driver, Jack Miller delivered metal tubing to Prairie Center Muffler. Miller was directed to place the tubing on a storage rack inside Prairie Center. The storage rack had been constructed by Prairie Center a number of years prior and was not affixed to the wall or the floor.

Miller alleges that while loading the tubing onto the storage rack, both the metal tubing and the storage rack fell onto him, causing him to fall to the ground and be seriously injured. Miller alleges that by constructing the rack to hold metal tubing, but failing to secure the rack to the wall, Prairie Center created and maintained an unreasonably dangerous condition, which ultimately caused the rack, with the metal tubing, to fall over on him and to cause him serious injury.

Miller concedes that he did not see the rack fall because he had his back to the rack when it allegedly fell over. He would testify as follows:

> The rack had approximately six levels of support arms on which the tubing was to be stacked. The support arms were made of either metal rods or metal tubing. I placed the various diameters of tubing on the various support arms and turned my back to the rack. When I was 4 or 5 feet away from the rack, with my back to it, the rack tipped over and one of the metal support arms struck me on my left upper back/left shoulder, dug into my left upper back, left shoulder, and left arm, and threw me to the floor.
>
> I have been a weightlifter all my life and am familiar with weights and forces. I also had extensive experience handling, lifting, and carrying the tubing that I was placing on the rack. The force and weight of what hit me was such that I know it was the rack — it could not have only been the metal tubing. Had the metal tubing fallen off the rack and hit me, it would not have had the weight or the force to have dug into my back, shoulder and arm nor would it have had the weight or the force to have thrown me to the ground.
>
> Further, I know that the rack tipped over because of the distance I was from the rack when it hit me and threw me to the ground. Had the metal tubing rolled off the support arms, they would have cascaded downward like a waterfall. They would not have flown horizontally across the room, five or six feet above the ground, and struck me in the upper back and shoulder. Nor would the tubing have had the force necessary to push me to the ground. On the other hand, the rack tipping over would have reached me, where I stood, and would have had the force to have knocked me to the ground.

Should Miller's testimony be admissible lay opinion under Rule 701? Argue for and against admissibility.

9.3. Mr. Sheley regularly abused his wife, violently beating her, running her over with a car, and threatening her with a gun and other deadly weapons. Though Mrs. Sheley had never before responded with force, she killed him during one of his brutal attacks. On that occasion, Mrs. Sheley shot and killed her husband with a handgun while Mr. Sheley threatened her and her daughters with a shotgun.

Mr. Sheley had previously purchased a life insurance policy that provided for double benefits in the case of accidental death. Under Georgia law, the death of an insured spouse during a domestic dispute is considered accidental for the purposes of redeeming life insurance if the decedent reasonably believed that his wife would not respond to his aggression with force. Gail, Mrs. Sheley's daughter, testified that she believed that Mr. Sheley never thought that Mrs. Sheley would shoot him. After the jury found the death to have been accidental, the insurance company appealed. It argued that Gail's testimony should not have been admitted under Rule 701 because Gail could not have had personal knowledge of Mr. Sheley's subjective state of mind and that Gail's opinions were therefore not rationally based upon her perceptions. Should the appellate court reverse?

9.4. In a real estate deal gone sour, several hotel chains were sued for breach of contract by DIJO, Inc., the real estate developer for a project in Tunica, MI. The project never got beyond the planning stages. During the portion of the trial on lost profits, Kerry Skinner (a lay witness, representing DIJO's potential lender and otherwise uninvolved in the project) testified that "based on projected earnings of $1 million per year, the value of the Project to DIJO was $8,000,007." Skinner was a knowledgeable financial consultant, but his testimony revealed that he had little significant actual knowledge about DIJO and its operations. The jury later returned an $8 million plaintiff's verdict. Should Skinner's testimony have been permitted?

9.5. Police officers in New Bern, North Carolina, found Eddie Roberts on his kitchen floor, dead from a bullet wound to the head. At the trial of Don Duncan, a witness, Dove, testified that he saw a man fire a rifle into Roberts's kitchen. "It was dark, but the man looked to be about the same size and height of Don Duncan." The witness was familiar with Duncan's appearance because he was acquainted with Duncan and had seen him earlier on the day of the murder. Again explaining what he had witnessed, the witness stated:

> I couldn't tell what kind of clothes he had on. The rifle sounded like a .22 — in my opinion, it was a .22. I had a chance to see the man, but I couldn't tell who he was. After he shot the rifle, he climbed over the fence and crossed Broad Street. He was about the same size and height of Don. I am not willing to identify any man that I couldn't see his face. There are hundreds of people in town who are the same height and I have seen a lot of people in this town who are the same size.

Is all of Dove's testimony admissible?

9.6. On April 12, 1964, Texas Gulf Sulfur Company issued an optimistic press release about the results of its recent exploratory drilling in Timmins, Ontario. The press release led to a substantial increase in the price of the company's stock, benefiting several corporate officials who had purchased large quantities of the stock only days before. The SEC filed charges of insider trading against the corporate officials and charged the company with making a misleading statement that might make reasonable investors rely on it. The SEC introduces several investors who testified as lay witnesses that the press release created erroneous impressions. Should this testimony be allowed?

9.7. Annie Hester worked in the BIC Corporation's order-processing department for seven years before BIC merged its order-processing department with its customer service department. Beck, the manager of the new department, may have shown favoritism to those employees from the old customer service department and thus there was some tension in the new group. Despite Beck's recommendation of an employee from the old customer service department, Hester was promoted to a group leadership position for which she was well qualified. After only a few months in the new position, customers began complaining about Hester's performance and Beck transferred her to another department. Hester sued BIC for race discrimination, alleging that Beck had given white Group Leaders additional training and feedback and had promoted a white employee with fewer qualifications than Hester to replace her. Hester called four lay witnesses who were prepared to testify to the following:

(1) Mary Ende, a white file clerk, believed that Beck treated those from the customer service department like "stepchildren." She did not know anything about

Hester's performance as a Group Leader. (2) Darlene Miller, a white employee who had worked with Hester prior to the merging of the two departments, felt that Beck "was mean to everyone in order-processing, but she was more mean to Hester." Like Ende, Miller admitted that she, too, had no personal knowledge of Hester's job performance. (3) Patricia Wright, an African-American receptionist who had been fired from BIC, had had the chance to observe Beck's treatment of Hester but was more eager to testify that her own termination had been because of race and that she had received mysterious racist phone calls around the time of her dismissal. (4) Lillian Turner, an African-American employee, had observed on two or three occasions Beck treating Hester with "borderline disrespect and condescension" but had never seen Beck treating white employees in this way. Turner was herself suing BIC for racial discrimination and wished to explain that, absent any other reason, she believed she must have been treated poorly because of her race.

How, if at all, should the trial judge limit this testimony?

9.8. Two former corporate executives of Cal Micro, Henke and Douglas, were accused of being part of a false revenue reporting conspiracy that portrayed the company as a good investment option when in reality it was struggling. Proving that Henke and Douglas had knowledge of the false reporting scheme was critical to the government's case. To do this, it called Wade Meyercord, Douglas's replacement as Chairman of Cal Micro's Board of Directors, and asked him about the Board's reasons for terminating the defendants:

Q. [Prosecution]:   What happened next . . . ?
A. [Meyercord]:   There was another Board meeting in October of '94, so that the — later that month. I don't recall the exact date. At which time, if I recall correctly, we removed Mr. Douglas as Chairman of the company, and I was elected Chairman.
Q. Why did you remove — yeah, why did you remove Mr. Douglas?
[Defense counsel]:   Objection, Your Honor.
The court: You can rephrase that, counsel.
Q. [Prosecution]:   If you know, what — how did the Board reach that decision?
[Defense counsel]:   Your Honor, that's simply an opinion that they reached — conclusion that they reached.
The court: Well, no. I think the witness can testify as to the understanding that he has of the reason that the Board took that action. That's, I think, the appropriate question. All right? With that in mind, Mr. Meyercord, what is your understanding of the reason that the Board took the action which you did in removing Mr. Douglas as Chairman of the Board?
A. Because we felt there was — we removed Mr. Douglas as Chairman because we felt there was a high probability that he knew that the revenues had been misstated and that we could not in good conscience leave him in that position . . . .
Q. [Prosecution]:   Did Mr. Henke resign around this time period?
A. [Meyercord]:   Yes, he did.
Q. And was — were you aware of the fact that he had negotiated a severance package with Mr. Douglas?
A. I became aware later, yes.
Q. Well, Mr. Meyercord, did the Board accept this severance packet?
A. No, we did not.
Q. Why not?

[Defense counsel]:   Well, I object to it, Your Honor, on the same grounds that we've objected to the other documents, that it's prejudicial, and it's — actually this is testimony.

The court: Well, now, no speaking objections, Mr. Hallinan. What's the basis of the objection?

[Defense counsel]:   Well, first of all, under the circumstances, it's so prejudicial. That's one. Second of all, there's no basis for it, doesn't show any special knowledge. And third of all, it calls for an opinion of this witness.

The court: Overruled. The witness may testify as to his understanding of the reason that the Board took the action which it did.

[Meyercord]:   The Board — the Board did not feel that a severance package for Mr. Henke was appropriate given the evidence we had in front of us.

Q.   What evidence was that?

[Defense counsel]:   Well, there, Your Honor. Object to that.

The court: Objection overruled.

A.   The evidence that the revenue had been misstated.

Q.   Did you have an understanding as a Board — did you learn as a Board member what Mr. Henke's role was in that?

[Defense counsel]:   Your Honor, what relevance — ?

The court: Objection overruled.

Q.   Did you learn in the investigation — ?

The court: What was the witness's understanding of the facts?

[Prosecution]:   Right.

Q.   What was your understanding of the facts as they concerned Mr. Henke?

A.   My understanding of the facts were that Mr. Henke must have known about this — about the revenue misstatements.

[Defense counsel]:   Well, I'll move to strike that. That is just an opinion, he "must have known." That shouldn't even be before the jury, Your Honor.

The court: Objection overruled.

[Prosecution]:   No further questions, Your Honor.

The defendants appealed the conviction. Should the court have excluded the opinion testimony that the defendants "must have known"?

9.9. A police officer investigating a murder found a hatchet near the scene of the crime. In the trial of the accused, should the officer be allowed to testify to his estimation of how long the hatchet had rested in that spot? Or, should the officer be required to describe that the area where he found the hatchet contained old, brown, moist grass in the late stages of decomposition, and that when he retrieved the hatchet, its face was caked with moist, decomposing grass? Or both?

B.   EXPERT WITNESSES

Expert witnesses present evidence based on knowledge acquired through specialized study or unusual training and experience that permits them to generate, piece together, or interpret data in a manner that would not be readily apparent to the fact finder. Experts can be useful at every stage of the fact-finding process:

(1)   Experts can generate evidentiary facts themselves. An example is a chemist who has analyzed a substance in a case in which the chemical makeup of the substance matters, such as in litigation over water pollution or a criminal drug charge. Another example is the medical worker who does blood or tissue analysis. Such individuals provide basic facts for the fact finder.

(2)   Experts can educate the jury regarding specialized or scientific information that is needed to draw inferences about evidentiary facts. For example, with respect to the safety of a car's construction, an engineer may testify to the tensile strength of its component metals. Another example is a medical specialist who educates the fact finder about the implications of symptoms of disease.

(3)   Most prevalent, and in our view least justifiable, experts may present inferences and conclusions to which fact finders may defer. A psychiatrist who testifies about the sanity of a criminal defendant is an example; a scientist who testifies that water pollution caused a person's health problems is another. A fact finder may have to rely on little more than a hunch when choosing to defer, and accept as accurate, the scientifically sophisticated conclusions of one of two conflicting experts.

Given the many roles they can play, it is not surprising that experts are ubiquitous in both state and federal trials today.

SAMUEL GROSS, EXPERT EVIDENCE
1991 Wis. L. Rev. 1113, 1118-1120

There is next to nothing to be learned from published data on the use of experts in American litigation. A few patchy studies report that experts are used in a sizeable minority of felony prosecutions, and that they are more likely to be called by the prosecution. There are no systematic studies of the use of experts in civil cases. The data described here will begin to fill that gap. They are based on reports on 529 civil trials that led to jury verdicts in California State Superior Courts in 1985 and 1986 . . . .

1. *The frequency of expert testimony.* Experts testified in 86% of these civil jury trials. Overall, there were an average of 3.3 experts per trial; in the trials in which any experts appeared, there were an average of 3.8. Most trials with experts had two, three, four or five of them. Plaintiffs called more expert witnesses than defendants — about 64% of the total.

2. *The specialties of expert witnesses.* Half of the experts in our data were medical doctors, and an additional 9% were other medical professionals — clinical psychologists, rehabilitation specialists, dentists, etc. Engineers, scientists and related experts made up the next largest category, nearly 20% of the total. The only other sizeable categories were experts on various aspects of business and finance (11%), and experts in reconstruction and investigation (8%).

3. *The cases in which experts appear.* Over 70% of these trials concerned claims of wrongful death or personal injury. As a group, these trials involved more experts than the remainder. There were expert appearances in nearly 95% of the personal injury or death trials, an average of 3.8 witnesses per case. Looking at smaller categories, the highest rates of use were in: (i) medical malpractice cases (97% of trials, an average of five witnesses per trial), where almost all the witnesses were medical experts and (ii) products liability

cases (100% of trials, an average of 4.7 witnesses per trial), where an unusually high proportion of the witnesses (1.8 per trial) were engineers, scientists and the like.

4. *Conflicts between opposing experts.* In nearly three-quarters of the trials in which experts testified (or 63% of all trials) there were experts on both sides. In two-thirds of the trials with expert testimony (57% of all trials) there were opposing experts in the same general area of expertise — most often, opposing medical experts. Similarly, for over two-thirds of the appearances by expert witnesses, there were opposing experts in the same general area. Again, such conflicts were particularly common for medical witnesses — their testimony was opposed by other medical witnesses 78% of the time. In sum, most expert witnesses were disputed by similar experts for the opposing side, and most juries had to resolve such disputes.

5. *The testimonial experience of expert witnesses.* Most expert testimony is given by repeat players. Nearly 60% of the appearances by expert witnesses in California Superior Court civil jury trials were by witnesses who testified in such cases at least two times over a six-year period. For a particular appearance before a jury, the average number of times the same expert testified over a six-year period was 9.4; the median was 2.2. It is important to note that these numbers greatly underrepresent the experts' total experience in litigation. They do not, for instance, include testimony in criminal trials or in civil trials in courts other than California State Superior Courts. More important, the numbers do not catch the many cases in which the same experts were consulted, wrote reports, or even testified in depositions, but failed to testify in court because the cases were settled or dismissed before trial.

One way to put the trial experience of witnesses in perspective is to compare it to that of trial lawyers. Judging from the 1985-1986 cases, when an attorney examines an expert witness in a civil jury trial in California, the expert is twice as likely to have testified in another such case in the preceding six months as the attorney is to have tried one (42% to 21%).

CAROL KRAFKA ET AL., JUDGE AND ATTORNEY EXPERIENCES, PRACTICES, AND CONCERNS REGARDING EXPERT TESTIMONY IN FEDERAL CIVIL TRIALS

Federal Judicial Center (2002)

Questions that remain about expert evidence far outnumber those that research has begun to address. . . . What types of cases, for instance, are most likely to involve expert testimony? What types of experts testify, how frequently do they appear, and on whose behalf are they testifying? What issues do the experts address? . . . The research we report here involved [three] surveys of judges and attorneys. Data sources included a 1998 survey of [303 U.S. district court] judges, a 1991 survey of [335 U.S. district court] judges, and a 1999 survey of [302] attorneys [involved in district court cases presided over by the aforementioned judges]. The most frequent types of [federal] trials involving experts — 45% of the 299 trials reported — were tort cases, primarily those involving personal injury or medical malpractice. Tort cases were followed in frequency by civil rights cases (23%); contract cases (11%); intellectual property cases, primarily patent cases (10%); labor cases (2%); prisoner cases (2%); and other civil cases (8%).

To gauge whether expert testimony is differentially associated with certain case types, we compared the distribution of sample cases to the distribution of all federal civil cases terminating during or after a bench or jury trial in the year before and year of our survey. Compared to all civil trials, experts were overrepresented in tort cases (which constituted only 26% of all civil trials) and intellectual property cases (3% of all civil trials). Experts were underrepresented in contract cases (14% of all civil trials); labor cases (4% of all civil trials); general (nonprisoner) civil rights cases (31% of all civil trials); and prisoner cases, nearly all of which are civil rights actions (14% of all civil trials). In cases classified as "other" civil trials, experts were represented in equal proportion to the general case type (8%).

Ninety-two percent of reported trials involved expert testimony by plaintiffs, and 79% of trials involved expert testimony by defendants. Seventy-three percent of the trials had experts testifying for both plaintiffs and defendants. These figures are comparable to statistics from 1991, when 95% of trials involved expert testimony for the plaintiff, 81% involved expert testimony for the defendant, and 76% had experts testifying on both plaintiff and defendant side. Seventy-seven percent of the civil trials we surveyed in 1998 were conducted before juries. . . . The jury trial rate for cases with expert evidence is somewhat higher than for cases as a whole — in 1998 jury trials accounted for 64% of all civil trials — suggesting that experts appear with somewhat disproportionate frequency in jury trials.

The average number of experts testifying for plaintiffs was 2.47, compared to 1.85 for defendants. Tort cases had the highest mean number of testifying experts — an average of 3.11 experts testified for plaintiffs, with 2.28 testifying for defendants. Civil rights cases averaged 1.81 experts for the plaintiff and 1.24 experts for the defense; case types that fell into the "other" category averaged 2.70 and 2.00 experts, respectively. . . . The mean number of testifying experts in 1998 was 4.31 per trial. This figure is somewhat lower than in 1991, when cases averaged 4.80 experts per trial. . . .

In both the judge and attorney surveys, respondents were asked to describe the types of experts who testified and the issues addressed by their testimony . . . Medical and mental health specialists were the most frequently presented category of experts, accounting for more than 40% of the experts presented overall. The medical profession, representing many types of specialists, collectively accounted for about one-third of all testifying experts. This showing is not surprising, given that 45% of the survey trials were tort cases. Specialists from business, law, and financial worlds accounted for another 25% of experts. This category includes the most frequently heard professional, the economist, representing almost 12% of all experts. Engineers and other safety, or process, specialists registered close behind experts from the business/ law/ financial sector. These professionals accounted for about 22% of all experts. Individuals representing scientific fields such as chemistry, ballistics, toxicology, and metallurgy accounted for only a small percentage, less than 8%, of testifying experts.

1.   FRE 702

RULE 702.   TESTIMONY BY EXPERT WITNESSES

A witness who is qualified as an expert by knowledge, skill, experience, training, or education may testify in the form of an opinion or otherwise if:

(a) the expert's scientific, technical, or other specialized knowledge will help the trier of fact to understand the evidence or to determine a fact in issue;

(b) the testimony is based on sufficient facts or data;

(c) the testimony is the product of reliable principles and methods; and

(d) the expert has reliably applied the principles and methods to the facts of the case.

2.   Interpretation and Illustration of FRE 702

a.   *Scientific, Technical, or Other Specialized Knowledge*

FRE 702 makes admissible a broad array of testimony from a multitude of sources covering an enormous range of affairs. It includes scientific, technical, and medical experts, but its pragmatic phrase "other specialized knowledge" extends the scope of the rule far beyond those confines. In the words of the Advisory Committee:

> The rule is broadly phrased. The fields of knowledge which may be drawn upon are not limited merely to the "scientific" and "technical" but extend to all "specialized" knowledge. Similarly, the expert is viewed, not in a narrow sense, but as a person qualified by "knowledge, skill, experience, training, or education." Thus within the scope of the rule are not only experts in the strictest sense of the word, e.g. physicians, physicists, and architects, but also the large group sometimes called "skilled" witnesses, such as bankers or landowners testifying to land values.

Consistent with the Advisory Committee's views, the cases admit a vast array of expert testimony. A person experienced in the practices of a particular business or industry can testify about those practices. Courts regularly admit comparison ballistics and fingerprint evidence, expert testimony about valuation in a condemnation proceeding, and expert medical testimony about a criminal defendant's competence to stand trial or insanity at the time of the alleged crime. On the other hand, courts have traditionally been reluctant to admit, in the absence of prior stipulation by the parties, the results of lie detector tests, and most courts have traditionally excluded expert testimony about the vagaries of eyewitness identification, although this seems to be changing. A court would almost certainly exclude an astrologer's or palm reader's "expert" testimony about an individual's violent tendencies or life expectancy. Cf. United States v. Tranowski, 659 F.2d 750 (9th Cir. 1981) (excluding testimony on photograph dating using astronomy charts).

b.   *Help the Trier of Fact*

Any knowledge that is not likely to be possessed by the fact finder qualifies for admission under this rule, no matter how the knowledge is obtained. A person possessing a "skill" can testify to it and its implications, even if the skill was gained through experience rather than traditional formal study. Moreover, the knowledge that qualifies for admission is relative to the fact finder. If a potential witness possesses knowledge that the fact finder is not likely to possess, even though some other fact finder somewhere else might, the testimony is admissible. For example, if the qualities of nitrogen fertilizer are relevant to a case in New York City, a farmer from Iowa knowledgeable of the matter through years of experience would qualify as an expert, even though the farmer had never formally studied the matter. If the trial were held in an Iowa farming community, quite possibly no expert testimony would be admissible because the fact finder's common knowledge and experience might very well extend to the relevant issues. It is these two factors — (1) specialized knowledge relative to the fact finder (2) gained by experience — that explain the court's decision in *Johnson* permitting Officer Huston to give an expert opinion about tray collection from inmates.

The helpfulness component of FRE 702 is not superfluous. Courts historically were reluctant, for example, to admit expert testimony on the limits of eyewitness identifications because the jury may already sufficiently understand the point. If the jurors already are appropriately skeptical of eyewitness identifications, putting an expert on the stand to discourage the jury from believing eyewitness testimony may result in an erroneous verdict through increasing the already appropriate level of skepticism of the jurors. See, e.g., United States v. Smith, 122 F.3d 1355 (11th Cir. 1997) (holding expert testimony on the reliability of eyewitness identification inadmissible, because not helpful to jury); United States v. Hall, 165 F.3d 1095 (7th Cir. 1998) (". . . expert testimony relating to eyewitness identification is strongly disfavored."). To be confident that such testimony is "helpful," one must know the reliability of the information presented and how it is likely to affect the fact finder, which includes knowing the baseline from which the fact finder is presently operating. This judicial attitude is changing, however, as most courts find that such evidence is admissible in certain circumstances. See, e.g., United States v. Rodriguez-Berrios, 573 F.3d 55 (1st Cir. 2009) (affirming that admission of expert testimony on the flaws inherent in eyewitness identification "is a matter of case-by-case discretion"); United States v. Brownlee, 454 F.3d 131 (3d Cir. 2006) (holding that expert testimony on eyewitness identification would have been helpful to trier of fact and exclusion of expert was reversible error); United States v. Smithers, 212 F.3d 306 (6th Cir. 2000) (exclusion of expert on eyewitness identification reversible error); United States v. Brien, 59 F.3d 274 (1st Cir. 1995) (holding the exclusion of such evidence discretionary, not per se inadmissible); United States v. Rodrigues-Felix, 450 F.3d 1117 (10th Cir. 2006) (collecting cases). Admissibility of such testimony is favored by some legal scholars as well. See Harvey Gee, Eyewitness Testimony and Cross-Racial Identification, 35 New Eng. L. Rev. 835 (2001) (reviewing Elizabeth Loftus, Eyewitness Testimony (1996)); Jennifer L. Devenport, Steven D. Penrod, and Brian L. Cutler, Eyewitness Identification Evidence: Evaluating Commonsense Evaluations, 3 Psy. Pub. Poly. & L. 338 (1997); Michael R. Leippe, The Case for Expert Testimony About Eyewitness Memory, 1 Psy. Pub. Poly .& L. 909 (1995). In any event, the person offering an expert witness must be prepared to qualify the witness as having knowledge that the jury lacks that would be helpful to its decision.

c. A Witness Qualified as an Expert

If specialized information will help the trier of fact, the trial judge must then determine whether the person offered to present the information is qualified to do so. As we previously indicated, the qualifications need not include formal education in the subject matter. Rather, as FRE 702 provides, one can be qualified as an expert based on "knowledge, skill, experience, [or] training," as well as education. As a result, courts admit an extremely wide variety of testimony on this basis. FBI agents have been permitted to testify to the structure of various criminal schemes based on their law enforcement experience. Farmers have testified to the likely value of their ruined crops, and so on. The crucial questions are whether the proposed witness has specialized knowledge, however obtained, and whether it would be helpful to the jury.

Qualifying an expert involves a voir dire of the witness that brings out the person's expertise. If there is no reasonable doubt about the expertise, the opposing party may try to stipulate to it. Wise counsel usually reject the stipulation because they want the fact finder to hear the credentials of the witness. The opposing party can object to qualifying the witness as an expert, and can also voir dire the witness in an effort to show that the witness is not qualified or has nothing of relevance to add to the trial. The trial judge then decides if the person qualifies as an expert pursuant to FRE 104(a).

d.   FRE 403 and Litigation Incentives

As the foregoing illustrations suggest, whether scientific or specialized evidence should be admitted turns on an evaluation of the relevance of the evidence and the countervailing FRE 403 factors. Some purportedly specialized evidence may appear to have no probative value. Evidence with slight probative value arguably should be excluded because of FRE 403 concerns: The evidence may be misleading if scientific jargon gives the evidence an aura of legitimacy that it does not deserve; the complexity of the evidence may tend to confuse rather than help jurors; and perhaps most important, the speculative nature or low probative value of some specialized evidence may not warrant spending the time, first, to demonstrate the possible relevance of the evidence and, second, to explore all of the possible weaknesses in the evidence.

Perhaps FRE 401-403 are adequate tools for dealing with the potential problems raised by scientific and specialized evidence, and perhaps courts should be especially reluctant to exclude specialized evidence pursuant to these rules, for there are at least three factors inherent in the litigation process that may inhibit parties from procuring unreliable specialized evidence.

First, the attorney will need to develop some familiarity with any specialization about which the attorney desires to interrogate a witness, and the specialist is likely to demand a fee for preparing for the litigation and testifying. These expenditures of time and money are likely to make the cost of procuring specialized evidence higher than the cost of procuring other evidence.

Second, the seemingly bizarre nature of some specialized evidence may lead jurors to reject it out of hand. Even if there appears to be an initial aura of legitimacy to the specialized evidence, opposing counsel will have the opportunity through cross-examination and rebuttal to demonstrate the irrelevance or low probative value of the evidence. In either situation, jurors' skepticism about the specialized evidence may lead them not merely to reject the specialized evidence; it may lead them to draw an inference similar to the inference that one can draw from the exposure of an attempt to bribe a witness or the knowing presentation of perjured testimony: If the party must resort to this type of unreliable evidence, the party's case must be a weak one.

Third, perhaps the nature of scientific evidence increases the possibility that unreliable evidence will be exposed on cross-examination. The probative value of specialized evidence is likely to depend in large measure on the rationality and methodology of allegedly scientific processes. These are matters that can be extensively explored during the examination of witnesses. The witnesses, of course, may be lying or may have misperceived or forgotten something that will not come to light during the examination. We can think of no reason, however, why this problem is likely to be any greater with purported specialists than with other witnesses.

Admittedly, these factors will not ensure the reliability of all specialized evidence, and quite frankly we cannot say how significant these factors are. Particularly in the context of a criminal prosecution, where discovery may not be readily available, opposing counsel may not be sufficiently knowledgeable about the specialty or adequately prepared to cross-examine specialists and offer opposing experts. Additionally, a litigant with a weak case may decide that the best chance of prevailing is through attempting to sow confusion by the presentation of unreliable or extremely complex specialized evidence, and we do not really know how effective this tactic is. Moreover, it is arguably inappropriate to place on opposing counsel the burden of having to respond to specialized evidence unless the offering party first demonstrates that it has a relatively high degree of probative value. Finally, perhaps some jurors will be impressed by even bizarre specialized evidence merely because the evidence is presented to them: They may think, *Why would the judge let us hear this evidence if it were not relevant?* Again, we do not know the extent of this phenomenon, just as we do not know the extent to which jurors reject specialized evidence because it appears to them bizarre.

There is one other factor to take into account in deciding how receptive the law should be to specialized evidence: A judge's proclivity to exclude unusual types of specialized evidence can prevent litigants from taking advantage of innovative, highly probative information and, as a result, detract from the search for truth. See, e.g., E.S. Lander and B. Budowle, DNA Fingerprinting Dispute Laid to Rest, 371 Nature 735 (1994) (discussing the initial controversy over the use of DNA fingerprinting); United States v. Martinez, 3 F.3d 1191 (8th Cir. 1993) (discussion of admissibility of DNA evidence).

e.   *Summary Witnesses*

Summary witnesses represent a blurring of the line between who qualifies as an "expert witness" and who remains a "lay witness." In some trials, usually those involving large amounts of evidence or extraordinarily complicated evidence, a lay witness will be permitted to testify as to what the aggregate of the evidence shows — in other words, to summarize the evidence. Because the witness is simply serving as a human "tape recorder," the witness need not be qualified as an expert to provide this summary. However, if the witness draws conclusions from this evidentiary summation for the purposes of assisting the jury, it is probable that the witness should be certified as an expert. See, e.g., United States v. Pree, 408 F.3d 855, 869 (7th Cir. 2005) (admission of summary witness testimony regarding the tax consequences of a series of complicated stock sales in a fraud case). For more on summary witnesses, see D. Michael Risinger, Preliminary Thoughts on a Functional Taxonomy of Expertise for the Post-Kumho World, 31 Seton Hall L. Rev. 508 (2000).

3.   Elaboration of "Scientific Evidence" Under FRE 702: Frye and Daubert

a.   *From Frye to Daubert*

You have probably noticed that we have not yet discussed subsections b, c, and d of FRE 702. They are additions to FRE 702, added in the aftermath of the *Daubert* case, which is reproduced later in this section, and the *Kumho Tire* case, reproduced in the following section. To understand the amendments, you need to understand these two cases. To understand the cases in turn, you must understand Frye v. United States, 293 F. 1013 (D.C. Cir. 1923). In *Frye*, the federal circuit court for the District of Columbia adopted a special rule for the admissibility of scientific evidence. The defendant, Frye, sought to introduce into evidence the results of an early type of lie detection device — a systolic blood pressure test. In upholding the trial court's exclusion of the evidence the Court of Appeals stated:

> Just when a scientific principle or discovery crosses the line between the experimental and demonstrable stages is difficult to define. Somewhere in this twilight zone the evidential force of the principle must be recognized, and while courts will go a long way in admitting expert testimony deduced from well-recognized scientific principle or discovery, the thing from which the deduction is made must be sufficiently established to have gained general acceptance in the particular field in which it belongs. [Id. at 1014.]

The *Frye* opinion is unclear about whether "the thing" that must have gained "general acceptance" is the relationship between truth-telling and blood pressure, or the ability of an expert to measure and interpret the changes in blood pressure, or both. Despite this ambiguity and despite the court's failure to explain further or to cite precedent for its holding, a number of courts adopted the "general acceptance" test, commonly referred to as the "*Frye* test":

> Polygraphy, graphology, hypnotic and drug induced testimony, voice stress analysis, voice spectrograms, various forms of spectroscopy, infrared sensing of aircraft, retesting of breath samples for alcohol content, psychological profiles of battered women and child abusers, post traumatic stress disorder as indicating rape, penile plethysmography as indicating sexual deviancy, astronomical calculations, blood group typing, and DNA testing all have fallen prey to its influence. [McCormick on the Evidence §203, at 306 (John William Strong, ed., 5th ed. 1999).]

Particularly in recent years the *Frye* test has been the subject of extensive criticism, primarily because a rigorous application of the test prevents use of scientific evidence based on emerging disciplines or cross-disciplinary studies. The Federal Rules make no reference to the "general acceptance" standard. Consider again the language of FRE 702:

> If scientific, technical, or other specialized knowledge will assist the trier of fact to understand the evidence or to determine a fact in issue, a witness qualified as an expert by knowledge, skill, experience, training, or education, may testify thereto in the form of an opinion or otherwise.

On its face, the "assist the trier of fact" criterion appears to be nothing more than an incorporation of the basic relevance concepts embodied in FRE 401-403. Given the language of FRE 702, some commentators took the position that the Federal Rules rejected the *Frye* test. E.g., 3 Jack Weinstein and Margaret Berger, Weinstein's Evidence ¶702[03], at 702-716 (1982). Lower courts divided on the issue. E.g., compare United States v. Brown, 557 F.2d 541 (6th Cir. 1977) (applying *Frye*) with United States v. Williams, 583 F.2d 1194 (2d Cir. 1978). If the *Frye* test is abandoned, should there be some substitute test for the admissibility of scientific and specialized evidence that is more rigorous than the standards embodied in FRE 401-403? Less rigorous? Instead of focusing on standards of admissibility, would it be desirable for there to be some

mandatory process — perhaps implemented through discovery and pretrial conferences — that would ensure that both the lawyers and the judge were sufficiently versed
in the specialty to address questions of admissibility in a reasonable and helpful way?
Should there be a panel of experts either to make decisions about the admissibility
of specialized evidence, or perhaps even to make the ultimate factual determination
of questions that turn on the evaluation of scientific evidence? The Supreme Court
addressed a number of these issues, including the continuing viability of the *Frye* rule:

DAUBERT v. MERRELL DOW PHARMACEUTICALS, INC.
509 U.S. 579 (1993)

Justice BLACKMUN delivered the opinion of the Court.

In this case we are called upon to determine the standard for admitting expert
scientific testimony in a federal trial.

I

Petitioners Jason Daubert and Eric Schuller are minor children born with serious
birth defects. They and their parents sued respondent in California state court, alleging that the birth defects had been caused by the mothers' ingestion of Bendectin, a
prescription anti-nausea drug marketed by respondent. Respondent removed the suits
to federal court on diversity grounds.

After extensive discovery, respondent moved for summary judgment, contending
that Bendectin does not cause birth defects in humans and that petitioners would be
unable to come forward with any admissible evidence that it does. In support of its
motion, respondent submitted an affidavit of Steven H. Lamm, physician and epi-
demiologist, who is a well-credentialed expert on the risks from exposure to various
chemical substances.[1] Doctor Lamm stated that he had reviewed all the literature
on Bendectin and human birth defects — more than 30 published studies involving
over 130,000 patients. No study had found Bendectin to be a human teratogen (i.e.,
a substance capable of causing malformations in fetuses). On the basis of this review,
Doctor Lamm concluded that maternal use of Bendectin during the first trimester of
pregnancy has not been shown to be a risk factor for human birth defects.

Petitioners did not (and do not) contest this characterization of the published
record regarding Bendectin. Instead, they responded to respondent's motion with the
testimony of eight experts of their own, each of whom also possessed impressive credentials.[2] These experts had concluded that Bendectin can cause birth defects. Their

1.   Doctor Lamm received his master's and doctor of medicine degrees from the University of
Southern California. He has served as a consultant in birth-defect epidemiology for the National Center
for Health Statistics and has published numerous articles on the magnitude of risk from exposure to various chemical and biological substances.

2.   For example, Shanna Helen Swan, who received a master's degree in biostatics from Columbia
University and a doctorate in statistics from the University of California at Berkeley, is chief of the section of the California Department of Health and Services that determines causes of birth defects, and has
served as a consultant to the World Health Organization, the Food and Drug Administration, and the
National Institutes of Health. Stewart A. Newman, who received his master's and a doctorate in chemistry
from Columbia University and the University of Chicago, respectively, is a professor at New York Medical
College and has spent over a decade studying the effect of chemicals on limb development. The credentials of the others are similarly impressive.

conclusions were based upon "in vitro" (test tube) and "in vivo" (live) animal studies that found a link between Bendectin and malformations; pharmacological studies of the chemical structure of Bendectin that purported to show similarities between the structure of the drug and that of other substances known to cause birth defects; and the "reanalysis" of previously published epidemiological (human statistical) studies.

The District Court granted respondent's motion for summary judgment. The court stated that scientific evidence is admissible only if the principle upon which it is based is "sufficiently established to have general acceptance in the field to which it belongs." The court concluded that petitioners' evidence did not meet this standard. Given the vast body of epidemiological data concerning Bendectin, the court held, expert opinion which is not based on epidemiological evidence is not admissible to establish causation. Thus, the animal-cell studies, live-animal studies, and chemical-structure analyses on which petitioners had relied could not raise by themselves a reasonably disputable jury issue regarding causation. Petitioners' epidemiological analyses, based as they were on recalculations of data in previously published studies that had found no causal link between the drug and birth defects, were ruled to be inadmissible because they had not been published or subjected to peer review.

The United States Court of Appeals for the Ninth Circuit affirmed. Citing Frye v. United States, the court stated that expert opinion based on a scientific technique is inadmissible unless the technique is "generally accepted" as reliable in the relevant scientific community. The court declared that expert opinion based on a methodology that diverges "significantly from the procedures accepted by recognized authorities in the field . . . cannot be shown to be generally accepted as a reliable technique." The court emphasized that other Courts of Appeals considering the risks of Bendectin had refused to admit reanalyses of epidemiological studies that had been neither published nor subjected to peer review. Those courts had found unpublished reanalyses "particularly problematic in light of the massive weight of the original published studies supporting [respondent's] position, all of which had undergone full scrutiny from the scientific community." Contending that reanalysis is generally accepted by the scientific community only when it is subjected to verification and scrutiny by others in the field, the Court of Appeals rejected petitioners' reanalyses as "unpublished, not subjected to the normal peer review process and generated solely for use in litigation." The court concluded that petitioners' evidence provided an insufficient foundation to allow admission of expert testimony that Bendectin caused their injuries and, accordingly, that petitioners could not satisfy their burden of proving causation at trial.

We granted certiorari in light of sharp divisions among the courts regarding the proper standard for the admission of expert testimony.

II

A

In the 70 years since its formulation in the *Frye* case, the "general acceptance" test has been the dominant standard for determining the admissibility of novel scientific evidence at trial. Although under increasing attack of late, the rule continues to be followed by a majority of courts, including the Ninth Circuit.

The *Frye* test has its origin in a short and citation-free 1923 decision concerning the admissibility of evidence derived from a systolic blood pressure deception test, a crude precursor to the polygraph machine. In what has become a famous (perhaps infamous) passage, the then Court of Appeals for the District of Columbia described the device and its operation and declared:

> Just when a scientific principle or discovery crosses the line between the experimental and demonstrable stages is difficult to define. Somewhere in this twilight zone the evidential force of the principle must be recognized, and while courts will go a long way in admitting expert testimony deduced from a well-recognized scientific principle or discovery, the thing from which the deduction is made must be sufficiently established to have gained general acceptance in the particular field in which it belongs.

Because the deception test had "not yet gained such standing and scientific recognition among physiological and psychological authorities as would justify the courts in admitting expert testimony deduced from the discovery, development, and experiments thus far made," evidence of its results was ruled inadmissible.

The merits of the *Frye* test have been much debated, and scholarship on its proper scope and application is legion. Petitioners' primary attack, however, is not on the content but on the continuing authority of the rule. They contend that the *Frye* test was superseded by the adoption of the Federal Rules of Evidence. We agree.

We interpret the legislatively-enacted Federal Rules of Evidence as we would any statute. Beech Aircraft Corp. v. Rainey, 488 U.S. 153, 163 (1988). Rule 402 provides the baseline: "All relevant evidence is admissible, except as otherwise provided by the Constitution of the United States, by Act of Congress, by these rules, or by other rules prescribed by the Supreme Court pursuant to statutory authority. Evidence which is not relevant is not admissible." "Relevant evidence" is defined as that which has "any tendency to make the existence of any fact that is of consequence to the determination of the action more probable or less probable than it would be without the evidence." Rule 401. The Rule's basic standard of relevance thus is a liberal one.

Frye, of course, predated the Rules by half a century. In United States v. Abel, 469 U.S. 45 (1984), we considered the pertinence of background common law in interpreting the Rules of Evidence. We noted that the Rules occupy the field, id. at 49, but, quoting Professor Cleary, the Reporter, explained that the common law nevertheless could serve as an aid to their application:

> In principle, under the Federal Rules no common law of evidence remains. "All relevant evidence is admissible, except as otherwise provided . . . ." In reality, of course, the body of common law knowledge continues to exist, though in the somewhat altered form of a source of guidance in the exercise of delegated powers.

Id., at 51-52.

We found the common-law precept at issue in the *Abel* case entirely consistent with Rule 402's general requirement of admissibility, and considered it unlikely that the drafters had intended to change the rule. In Bourjaily v. United States, 483 U.S. 171 (1987), on the other hand, the Court was unable to find a particular common-law doctrine in the Rules, and so held it superseded.

Here there is a specific Rule that speaks to the contested issue. Rule 702, governing expert testimony, provides:

> If scientific, technical, or other specialized knowledge will assist the trier of fact to understand the evidence or to determine a fact in issue, a witness qualified as an expert by

knowledge, skill, experience, training, or education, may testify thereto in the form of an opinion or otherwise.*

Nothing in the text of this Rule establishes "general acceptance" as an absolute prerequisite to admissibility. Nor does respondent present any clear indication that Rule 702 or the Rules as a whole were intended to incorporate a "general acceptance" standard. The drafting history makes no mention of *Frye*, and a rigid "general acceptance" requirement would be at odds with the "liberal thrust" of the Federal Rules and their "general approach of relaxing the traditional barriers to 'opinion' testimony." Beech Aircraft Corp. v. Rainey, 488 U.S. at 169 (citing Rules 701 to 705). Given the Rules' permissive backdrop and their inclusion of a specific rule on expert testimony that does not mention "general acceptance," the assertion that the Rules somehow assimilated *Frye* is unconvincing. *Frye* made "general acceptance" the exclusive test for admitting expert scientific testimony. That austere standard, absent from and incompatible with the Federal Rules of Evidence, should not be applied in federal trials.

B

That the *Frye* test was displaced by the Rules of Evidence does not mean, however, that the Rules themselves place no limits on the admissibility of purportedly scientific evidence. Nor is the trial judge disabled from screening such evidence. To the contrary, under the Rules the trial judge must ensure that any and all scientific testimony or evidence admitted is not only relevant, but reliable.

The primary locus of this obligation is Rule 702, which clearly contemplates some degree of regulation of the subjects and theories about which an expert may testify. "If scientific, technical, or other specialized knowledge will assist the trier of fact to understand the evidence or to determine a fact in issue" an expert "may testify thereto." The subject of an expert's testimony must be "scientific . . . knowledge."[3] The adjective "scientific" implies a grounding in the methods and procedures of science. Similarly, the word "knowledge" connotes more than subjective belief or unsupported speculation. The term "applies to any body of known facts or to any body of ideas inferred from such facts or accepted as truths on good grounds." Webster's Third New International Dictionary 1252 (1986). Of course, it would be unreasonable to conclude that the subject of scientific testimony must be "known" to a certainty; arguably, there are no certainties in science. But, in order to qualify as "scientific knowledge," an inference or assertion must be derived by the scientific method. Proposed testimony must be supported by appropriate validation — i.e., "good grounds," based on what is known. In short, the requirement that an expert's testimony pertain to "scientific knowledge" establishes a standard of evidentiary reliability.[4]

---

* [This is the prior version of FRE 702, which was restyled but with no substantive changes. — EDS.]

3.   Rule 702 also applies to "technical, or other specialized knowledge." Our discussion is limited to the scientific context because that is the nature of the expertise offered here.

4.   We note that scientists typically distinguish between "validity" (does the principle support what it purports to show?) and "reliability" (does application of the principle produce consistent results?). See Black, A Unified Theory of Scientific Evidence, 56 Ford. L. Rev. 595, 599 (1988). Although "the difference between accuracy, validity, and reliability may be such that each is distinct from the other by no more than a hen's kick," Starrs, Frye v. United States Restructured and Revitalized: A Proposal to Amend Federal Evidence Rule 702, 26 Jurimetrics J. 249, 256 (1986), our reference here is to evidentiary reliability — that is, trustworthiness. Cf., e.g., Advisory Committee's Notes on Fed. Rule Evid. 602 ("'[T]he rule requiring that a witness who testifies to a fact which can be perceived by the senses must have had an opportunity to observe, and must have actually observed the fact' is a 'most pervasive manifestation' of

Rule 702 further requires that the evidence or testimony "assist the trier of fact to understand the evidence or to determine a fact in issue." This condition goes primarily to relevance. "Expert testimony which does not relate to any issue in the case is not relevant and, ergo, non-helpful." 3 Weinstein & Berger ¶702[02], p. 702-18. See also United States v. Downing, 753 F.2d 1224, 1242 (C.A.3 1985) ("An additional consideration under Rule 702 — and another aspect of relevancy — is whether expert testimony proffered in the case is sufficiently tied to the facts of the case that it will aid the jury in resolving a factual dispute"). The consideration has been aptly described by Judge Becker as one of "fit." Ibid. "Fit" is not always obvious, and scientific validity for one purpose is not necessarily scientific validity for other, unrelated purposes. The study of the phases of the moon, for example, may provide valid scientific "knowledge" about whether a certain night was dark, and if darkness is a fact in issue, the knowledge will assist the trier of fact. However (absent creditable grounds supporting such a link), evidence that the moon was full on a certain night will not assist the trier of fact in determining whether an individual was unusually likely to have behaved irrationally on that night. Rule 702's "helpfulness" standard requires a valid scientific connection to the pertinent inquiry as a precondition to admissibility.

That these requirements are embodied in Rule 702 is not surprising. Unlike an ordinary witness, see Rule 701, an expert is permitted wide latitude to offer opinions, including those that are not based on first-hand knowledge or observation. See Rules 702 and 703. Presumably, this relaxation of the usual requirement of first-hand knowledge — a rule which represents "a 'most pervasive manifestation'" of the common law insistence upon 'the most reliable sources of information,'" Advisory Committee's Notes on Fed. Rule Evid. 602 — is premised on an assumption that the expert's opinion will have a reliable basis in the knowledge and experience of his discipline.

C

Faced with a proffer of expert scientific testimony, then, the trial judge must determine at the outset, pursuant to Rule 104(a),[5] whether the expert is proposing to testify to (1) scientific knowledge that (2) will assist the trier of fact to understand or determine a fact in issue.[6] This entails a preliminary assessment of whether the reasoning or methodology underlying the testimony is scientifically valid and of whether that reasoning or methodology properly can be applied to the facts in issue. We are confident that federal judges possess the capacity to undertake this review. Many factors will bear on the inquiry, and we do not presume to set out a definitive checklist or test. But some general observations are appropriate.

Ordinarily, a key question to be answered in determining whether a theory or technique is scientific knowledge that will assist the trier of fact will be whether it can

---

the common law insistence upon 'the most reliable sources of information.'" (citation omitted)); Advisory Committee's Notes on Art. VIII of the Rules of Evidence (hearsay exceptions will be recognized only "under circumstances supposed to furnish guarantees of trustworthiness"). In a case involving scientific evidence, evidentiary reliability will be based upon scientific validity.

5. These matters should be established by a preponderance of proof.

6. Although the *Frye* decision itself focused exclusively on "novel" scientific techniques, we do not read the requirements of Rule 702 to apply specially or exclusively to unconventional evidence. Of course, well-established propositions are less likely to be challenged than those that are novel, and they are more handily defended. Indeed, theories that are so firmly established as to have attained the status of scientific law, such as the laws of thermoydnamics, properly are subject to judicial notice under Fed. Rule Evid. 201.

be (and has been) tested. K. Popper, Conjectures and Refutations: The Growth of Scientific Knowledge 37 (5th ed. 1989) ("[T]he criterion of the scientific status of a theory is its falsifiability, or refutability, or testability").

Another pertinent consideration is whether the theory or technique has been subjected to peer review and publication. Publication (which is but one element of peer review) is not a sine qua non of admissibility; it does not necessarily correlate with reliability, see S. Jasanoff, The Fifth Branch: Science Advisors as Policymakers 61-76 (1990), and in some instances well-grounded but innovative theories will not have been published, see Horrobin, The Philosophical Basis of Peer Review and the Suppression of Innovation, 263 J. Am. Med. Assn. 1438 (1990). Some propositions, moreover, are too particular, too new, or of too limited interest to be published. But submission to the scrutiny of the scientific community is a component of "good science," in part because it increases the likelihood that substantive flaws in methodology will be detected. The fact of publication (or lack thereof) in a peer-reviewed journal thus will be a relevant, though not dispositive, consideration in assessing the scientific validity of a particular technique or methodology on which an opinion is premised.

Additionally, in the case of a particular scientific technique, the court ordinarily should consider the known or potential rate of error, and the existence and maintenance of standards controlling the technique's operation.

Finally, "general acceptance" can yet have a bearing on the inquiry. A "reliability assessment does not require, although it does permit, explicit identification of a relevant scientific community and an express determination of a particular degree of acceptance within that community." United States v. Downing, 753 F.2d, at 1238. Widespread acceptance can be an important factor in ruling particular evidence admissible, and "a known technique that has been able to attract only minimal support within the community," Downing, supra, may properly be viewed with skepticism.

The inquiry envisioned by Rule 702 is, we emphasize, a flexible one. Its overarching subject is the scientific validity — and thus the evidentiary relevance and reliability — of the principles that underlie a proposed submission. The focus, of course, must be solely on principles and methodology, not on the conclusions that they generate.

Throughout, a judge assessing a proffer of expert scientific testimony under Rule 702 should also be mindful of other applicable rules. Rule 703 provides that expert opinions based on otherwise inadmissible hearsay are to be admitted only if the facts or data are "of a type reasonably relied upon by experts in the particular field in forming opinions or inferences upon the subject." Rule 706 allows the court at its discretion to procure the assistance of an expert of its own choosing. Finally, Rule 403 permits the exclusion of relevant evidence "if its probative value is substantially outweighed by the danger of unfair prejudice, confusion of the issues, or misleading the jury . . . ." Judge Weinstein has explained:

> Expert evidence can be both powerful and quite misleading because of the difficulty in evaluating it. Because of this risk, the judge in weighing possible prejudice against probative force under Rule 403 of the present rules exercises more control over experts than over lay witnesses.

Weinstein, 138 F.R.D., at 632.

III

We conclude by briefly addressing what appear to be two underlying concerns of the parties and amici in this case. Respondent expresses apprehension that abandonment of "general acceptance" as the exclusive requirement for admission will result in a "free-for-all" in which befuddled juries are confounded by absurd and irrational pseudoscientific assertions. In this regard respondent seems to us to be overly pessimistic about the capabilities of the jury, and of the adversary system generally. Vigorous cross-examination, presentation of contrary evidence, and careful instruction on the burden of proof are the traditional and appropriate means of attacking shaky but admissible evidence. Additionally, in the event the trial court concludes that the scintilla of evidence presented supporting a position is insufficient to allow a reasonable juror to conclude that the position more likely than not is true, the court remains free to direct a judgment, Fed. Rule Civ. Proc. 50(a), and likewise to grant summary judgment, Fed. Rule Civ. Proc. 56. These conventional devices, rather than wholesale exclusion under an uncompromising "general acceptance" test, are the appropriate safeguards where the basis of scientific testimony meets the standards of Rule 702.

Petitioners and, to a greater extent, their amici exhibit a different concern. They suggest that recognition of a screening role for the judge that allows for the exclusion of "invalid" evidence will sanction a stifling and repressive scientific orthodoxy and will be inimical to the search for truth. It is true that open debate is an essential part of both legal and scientific analyses. Yet there are important differences between the quest for truth in the courtroom and the quest for truth in the laboratory. Scientific conclusions are subject to perpetual revision. Law, on the other hand, must resolve disputes finally and quickly. The scientific project is advanced by broad and wide-ranging consideration of a multitude of hypotheses, for those that are incorrect will eventually be shown to be so, and that in itself is an advance. Conjectures that are probably wrong are of little use, however, in the project of reaching a quick, final, and binding legal judgment — often of great consequence — about a particular set of events in the past. We recognize that in practice, a gatekeeping role for the judge, no matter how flexible, inevitably on occasion will prevent the jury from learning of authentic insights and innovations. That, nevertheless, is the balance that is struck by Rules of Evidence designed not for the exhaustive search for cosmic understanding but for the particularized resolution of legal disputes.

IV

To summarize: "general acceptance" is not a necessary precondition to the admissibility of scientific evidence under the Federal Rules of Evidence, but the Rules of Evidence — especially Rule 702 — do assign to the trial judge the task of ensuring that an expert's testimony both rests on a reliable foundation and is relevant to the task at hand. Pertinent evidence based on scientifically valid principles will satisfy those demands.

The inquiries of the District Court and the Court of Appeals focused almost exclusively on "general acceptance," as gauged by publication and the decisions of other courts. Accordingly, the judgment of the Court of Appeals is vacated and the case is remanded for further proceedings consistent with this opinion.

It is so ordered.

Chief Justice REHNQUIST, with whom Justice STEVENS joins, concurring in part and dissenting in part.

The petition for certiorari in this case presents two questions: first, whether the rule of Frye v. United States, remains good law after the enactment of the Federal Rules of Evidence; and second, if *Frye* remains valid, whether it requires expert scientific testimony to have been subjected to a peer-review process in order to be admissible. The Court concludes, correctly in my view, that the *Frye* rule did not survive the enactment of the Federal Rules of Evidence, and I therefore join Parts I and II-A of its opinion. The second question presented in the petition for certiorari necessarily is mooted by this holding, but the Court nonetheless proceeds to construe Rules 702 and 703 very much in the abstract, and then offers some "general observations." "General observations" by this Court customarily carry great weight with lower federal courts, but the ones offered here suffer from the flaw common to most such observations — they are not applied to deciding whether or not particular testimony was or was not admissible, and therefore they tend to be not only general, but vague and abstract. This is particularly unfortunate in a case such as this, where the ultimate legal question depends on an appreciation of one or more bodies of knowledge not judicially noticeable, and subject to different interpretations in the briefs of the parties and their amici. Twenty-two amicus briefs have been filed in the case, and indeed the Court's opinion contains no less than 37 citations to amicus briefs and other secondary sources.

The various briefs filed in this case are markedly different from typical briefs, in that large parts of them do not deal with decided cases or statutory language — the sort of material we customarily interpret. Instead, they deal with definitions of scientific knowledge, scientific method, scientific validity, and peer review — in short, matters far afield from the expertise of judges. This is not to say that such materials are not useful or even necessary in deciding how Rule 703 should be applied; but it is to say that the unusual subject matter should cause us to proceed with great caution in deciding more than we have to, because our reach can so easily exceed our grasp.

But even if it were desirable to make "general observations" not necessary to decide the questions presented, I cannot subscribe to some of the observations made by the Court. In Part II-B, the Court concludes that reliability and relevancy are the touchstones of the admissibility of expert testimony. Federal Rule of Evidence 402 provides, as the Court points out, that "[e]vidence which is not relevant is not admissible." But there is no similar reference in the Rule to "reliability." The Court constructs its argument by parsing the language "[i]f scientific, technical, or other specialized knowledge will assist the trier of fact to understand the evidence or to determine a fact in issue . . . an expert . . . may testify thereto . . . ." Fed. Rule Evid. 702. It stresses that the subject of the expert's testimony must be "scientific . . . knowledge," and points out that "scientific" "implies a grounding in the methods and procedures of science," and that the word "knowledge" "connotes more than subjective belief or unsupported speculation." From this it concludes that "scientific knowledge" must be "derived by the scientific method." Proposed testimony, we are told, must be supported by "appropriate validation." Indeed, . . . the Court decides that "[i]n a case involving scientific evidence, evidentiary reliability will be based upon scientific validity." Questions arise simply from reading this part of the Court's opinion, and countless more questions will surely arise when hundreds of district judges try to apply its teaching to particular offers of expert testimony. Does all of this dicta apply to an expert seeking to testify on the basis of "technical or other specialized knowledge" — the other types of expert knowledge to which Rule 702 applies — or are the "general observations" limited only to "scientific knowledge"? What is the difference between scientific knowledge and technical knowledge; does Rule 702 actually contemplate that the phrase "scientific, technical, or other specialized knowledge" be broken down into numerous subspecies of expertise, or did its authors simply pick general descriptive language covering the sort of expert testimony which courts have customarily received? The Court speaks of its confidence that federal judges can make a "preliminary assessment of whether the reasoning or methodology underlying the testimony is scientifically valid and of whether that reasoning or methodology properly can be applied to the facts in issue." The Court then states that a "key question" to be answered in deciding whether something is "scientific knowledge" "will be whether it can be (and has been) tested." Following this sentence [is a] quotation . . . which states that "the criterion of the scientific status of a theory is its falsifiability, or refutability, or testability." I defer to no one in my confidence in federal judges; but I am at a loss to know what is meant when it is said that the scientific status of a theory depends on its "falsifiability," and I suspect some of them will be, too. I do not doubt that Rule 702 confides to the judge some gatekeeping responsibility in deciding questions of the admissibility of proffered expert testimony. But I do not think it imposes on them either the obligation or the authority to become amateur scientists in order to perform that role. I think the Court would be far better advised in this case to decide only the questions presented, and to leave the further development of this important area of the law to future cases.

NOTES AND QUESTIONS

1. The *Daubert* opinion is curious in many respects. Although the majority in *Daubert* purported to bury *Frye*, the case was not long interred; immediately following the announcement of its demise came the resurrection. To say that "scientific knowledge" that may be helpful to the trier of fact is admissible is not to say what "scientific knowledge" is. In its examination of the meaning of "scientific knowledge" and the *Frye* rule, the Court noted four factors that will help guide the lower courts in making determinations of the admissibility of proffered expert testimony. Three of them either restate or are derivative of *Frye*, and the fourth is merely a quite sensible admonition that is consistent with, even if not strictly derivable from, *Frye*.

The first factor is whether the subject matter may be tested, but attempts to falsify propositions take place virtually exclusively within normal scientific endeavors, which means within the context of generally accepted scientific canons. The Court's second factor is "whether the theory or technique has been subjected to peer review and publication." In addition to ruling out almost all legal knowledge (although perhaps it is "specialized"), this guide line again will tend to limit material to that which is generally accepted; rarely does unaccepted "science" get published. Third, in determining whether data is sufficiently reliable to be admitted, a court may also look to general acceptance. The first two standards restate general acceptance; the third adopts it explicitly. The fourth is merely that rate of error in scientific techniques is a prudential consideration to be taken into account in the admissibility determination, a factor that if not taken into account by "scientists" would seriously undermine the "general acceptance" of their work.

2. Even though *Frye* apparently lives, although in the guise of "guidelines" rather than "rule," the immediate reaction to *Daubert* was that it loosened the standards of admissibility for expert testimony through its conclusion that the *Frye* test was not a necessary condition of admissibility. Interestingly, the lower federal courts saw in *Daubert* the justification to take long, hard looks at expert witnesses being proffered, and they have increasingly declined to admit the testimony. See Section E, infra. It is not too much to say that *Daubert* has prompted a revolution in the manner in which expert testimony is being treated by the lower courts.

3. Although the lower courts have become much more active in policing the admissibility of expert testimony, and are making serious efforts to grapple with the various problems presented, the difficulty remains that the trial judges remain scientific amateurs. The deeper problem is that the Court's opinion simply ignored the issue that is presently informing the use of and fueling the controversy over expert testimony. That issue is the tension between the conventional understanding of trials that demands that fact finders be educated about the relevant facts and the use of experts that introduce a large dose of deference. The most regrettable aspect of the Court's opinion in *Daubert* is that it lost an opportunity to discuss this legal issue. Having not discussed the issue that drives contemporary problems, the Court's decision will largely leave those problems unaffected and undisturbed. We discuss the distinction between education and deference, and its implications for expert testimony, in greater detail in subsection 5, infra.

The Court did emphasize, although in difficult to follow language, that scientific evidence must be relevant, which includes a "helpfulness" component. What is "helpful" depends on the task. If the task is simply to decide a case, there need be no means of connecting scientific (or any other) evidence to the understanding of the jurors. Providing an opinion or conclusion to defer to would suffice nicely (as would providing the jurors a coin to flip). However, if the task is to decide rationally, then any scientific evidence will have to be sufficiently explained so that the jurors have a reasonable chance of understanding it. If this is what the Court meant, then *Daubert* could eventually revolutionize in a second direction the area of scientific and expert testimony by its rejection of the deference approach and its embrace of the educational model.

4. Whatever the precise standards for the admission of specialized testimony, the evidentiary principles involved in dealing with the evidence are quite simple and straightforward: They are, as we have suggested, the principles embodied in FRE 401-403 and 104. What is not simple and what is by far the most important aspect of dealing with specialized evidence is that the attorney must have a solid working grasp of the specialized or scientific principles to which the testimony relates, for it is the attorney who will be responsible for developing and refuting the information through the direct and cross-examination of witnesses. In short, the attorney must be an expert.

5. The actual holding in *Frye* excluding the result of lie detector tests became for a time the universal rule in this country. This rule began to slowly change in the mid-1990s with several decisions allowing polygraph evidence coming in the wake of *Daubert*. A number of jurisdictions began admitting the evidence, probably because a per se rule of exclusion seemed contradictory to the new statement of the standard which was enunciated in *Daubert*. For an influential, pre-*Daubert* decision, see, e.g., United States v. Piccinonna, 885 F.2d 1529 (11th Cir. 1989). *Piccinonna* held that polygraph results would be admissible to impeach or corroborate testimony if three

conditions were met: (1) notice of intent to use the evidence must be given to the opposition; (2) the opposing side must be given an opportunity to administer its own test; and (3) admissibility of the evidence is to be governed by the normal rules for the admissibility of corroboration and impeachment evidence, so that, for example, corroborating evidence would not be admissible until a witness's character for truthfulness has been attacked under FRE 608. The 11th Circuit has continued to adhere to these three conditions post-*Daubert*. See United States v. Henderson, 409 F.3d 1293 (11th Cir. 2005) (stating that *Piccinonna's* ruling is still valid post-*Daubert*). In United States v. Posado, 57 F.3d 428 (5th Cir. 1995), the court held that the results of polygraph examinations may be admissible in certain criminal cases regardless of stipulations (here one was offered but rejected). The court read *Daubert* as liberalizing the admission of scientific evidence, and concluded that the 70 percent to 90 percent accuracy rate now achieved with polygraphs exceeded the level of reliability of much evidence presently admitted. The court expressed concern about the prejudicial effect of such evidence, but found it not to be a problem here because the issue was who to believe, the state or the defendants, at a suppression hearing where dramatically different stories were being told and where other evidence cast doubt on the state's version of events. In any event, the evidence was not going to be heard by a jury. Admissibility was taken a step further in United States v. Galbreth, 908 F. Supp. 877 (D.N.M. 1995). *Galbreth* involved a prosecution for tax evasion. The defendant moved to admit a polygraph examination that showed that he was telling the truth in stating that he did not realize he had underreported his income. The court found the technique valid and the operator qualified, and admitted the evidence.

Despite these decisions, courts in some jurisdictions are still regularly excluding polygraph evidence. In United States v. Gill, 513 F.3d 836 (8th Cir. 2008), the court, noting numerous cases that denied admitting polygraph evidence, explained that "polygraph evidence is disfavored." The court in United States v. Prince-Oyibo, 320 F.3d 494 (4th Cir. 2003), stated that they would continue to adhere to a per se inadmissibility standard for polygraph results, despite more lenient standards in other courts. See also United States v. Thomas, 167 F.3d 299, 308 (6th Cir. 1999) ("[This Court does] . . . generally disfavor admitting the results of polygraph examinations."); United States v. Benavidez-Benavidez, 217 F.3d 720 (9th Cir. 2000) (upholding the exclusion of unstipulated polygraph evidence and the conviction of the defendant). See also United States v. Gill, 513 F.3d 836 (8th Cir. 2008), noting numerous cases that denied admitting polygraph evidence on the ground that "polygraph evidence is disfavored."

The Supreme Court has spoken on the issue a few times, but rather than clarifying the issue, has merely reiterated the aura of skepticism that surrounds polygraph evidence. In Wood v. Bartholomew, 516 U.S. 1 (1995), the Court held that the prosecutor has no constitutional duty ever to disclose to a criminal defendant the fact that a witness has "failed" a polygraph test. United States v. Scheffer, 523 U.S. 303 (1998), seems to have merely revealed the Court's hesitance about seeing polygraphs become commonplace, stating that because there is no consensus about the reliability of polygraph tests, there is no violation of rights where a per se rule against admitting polygraphs is applied. The gatekeeping role for trial judges created in *Daubert* makes it difficult on appeal to find that an exclusion of expert testimony was in error. Still, the Supreme Court's finding of "no consensus" makes it sound like a stricter test is applied to polygraph tests than to other expert evidence. It may make sense, however, that judges instinctively require a higher level of reliability for assessments of witness veracity. A judge may, in a given case, simply rely on a Rule 403 exclusion of overly prejudicial evidence if she is concerned that the jury may confuse evidence of veracity for proof of accuracy. See, e.g., United States v. Lea, 249 F.3d 632 (7th Cir. 2001) ("[A] district court need not conduct a full *Daubert* analysis in order to determine the admissibility of standard polygraph evidence, and instead may examine the evidence under a Rule 403 framework."). Still, it is not clear how polygraph tests, if found to be generally admissible, can be allowed in any fewer than all cases. Whenever there is witness testimony, the truthfulness of that witness is relevant. For a discussion of the slippery slope into the world of mandatory polygraph tests for all witnesses during the discovery stage of all civil and criminal trials, see D. Michael Risinger, Navigating Expert Reliability: Are Criminal Standards of Certainty Being Left on the Dock?, 64 Alb. L. Rev. 99 (2000). For an assessment of the present state of polygraph techniques and a précis of the scientific literature on the subject, see David C. Raskin, et al., The Scientific Status of Research on Polygraph Techniques: The Case for Polygraph Tests, 19-2.0, in 1 Modern Science Evidence: The Law and Science of Expert Testimony (David L. Faigman, David H. Kaye, Michael J. Saks, and Joseph Sanders eds., 2002 & Supp. 2003). For a general review, see National Research Council, Committee to Review the Scientific Evidence on the Polygraph. 2003. The Polygraph and Lie Detection. Washington, DC: The National Academies Press.

6. Note that in *Daubert* the Court said that in determining admissibility of expert testimony the "focus, of course, must be solely on principles and methodology, not on the conclusions that they generate." Can this distinction be maintained? Should it be maintained? What if an expert applies a reliable methodology but draws an unsupportable inference? In General Electric Co. v. Joiner, 522 U.S. 136 (1997), the Court essentially rejected this distinction. "But nothing in either *Daubert* or the Federal Rules of Evidence requires a district court to admit opinion evidence that is connected to existing data only by the *ipse dixit* of the expert. A court may conclude that there is simply too great an analytical gap between the data and the opinion proffered." The *Joiner* Court also clarified that the standard of review was abuse of discretion, thus making it difficult for courts of appeals to overturn trial court decisions either way on the admissibility of expert testimony. Under such a standard, trial courts have tremendous leeway and can in essence fashion a test more or less "austere" despite *Daubert*'s warning that the liberality of the Federal Rules of Evidence must be preserved. The result may be that each jurisdiction, or even each judge, may develop a habit, supported by growing bodies of precedent, of accepting or excluding specific types of expert testimony. The *Daubert* court would not disagree that two judges, applying substantially the same test, might reach two different decisions on admissibility without abusing their discretion. See Jerome P. Kassirer and Joe S. Cecil, Inconsistency in Evidentiary Standards for Medical Testimony, 288 JAMA 1382, 1384-1385 (2002) (discussing the different admissibility standards across jurisdictions for similar medical testimony). If two judges routinely reach divergent decisions, this may lead to what is known as "forum shopping." Litigants may try to bring their suits in specific jurisdictions, or even before specific judges, in the hopes of a favorable ruling on the admissibility of expert testimony. Appellate courts have little power to create a consistent standard because of the difficulty of finding abuse of discretion.

7. On remand, the Ninth Circuit, now applying *Daubert*, reached the same conclusion it had previously that the evidence was inadmissible. Daubert v. Merrell Dow Pharmaceuticals, Inc., 43 F.3d 1311 (9th Cir. 1995). In reaching that conclusion, however, the court also considered a number of factors in addition to the Supreme

Court's list. One was whether the expert was testifying on the basis of research conducted independently of the litigation. How important is this criterion? The Ninth Circuit is concerned about the biasing effects of research conducted for hire, but how much research is now conducted for hire in one way or another? As the Advisory Committee Note to the amendments to FRE 702 following *Daubert* pointed out:

> Courts both before and after *Daubert* have found other factors relevant in determining whether expert testimony is sufficiently reliable to be considered by the trier of fact. These factors include:
>
> (1) Whether experts are "proposing to testify about matters growing naturally and directly out of research they have conducted independent of the litigation, or whether they have developed their opinions expressly for purposes of testifying." Daubert v. Merrell Dow Pharmaceuticals, Inc., 43 F.3d 1311, 1317 (9th Cir. 1995).
>
> (2) Whether the expert has unjustifiably extrapolated from an accepted premise to an unfounded conclusion. See General Elec. Co. v. Joiner, 522 U.S. 136, 146 (1997) (noting that in some cases a trial court "may conclude that there is simply too great an analytical gap between the data and the opinion proffered").
>
> (3) Whether the expert has adequately accounted for obvious alternative explanations. See Claar v. Burlington N.R.R., 29 F.3d 499 (9th Cir. 1994) (testimony excluded where the expert failed to consider other obvious causes for the plaintiff's condition). Compare Ambrosini v. Labarraque, 101 F.3d 129 (D.C. Cir. 1996) (the possibility of some uneliminated causes presents a question of weight, so long as the most obvious causes have been considered and reasonably ruled out by the expert).
>
> (4) Whether the expert "is being as careful as he would be in his regular professional work outside his paid litigation consulting." Sheehan v. Daily Racing Form, Inc., 104 F.3d 940, 942 (7th Cir. 1997). See Kumho Tire Co. v. Carmichael, 119 S. Ct. 1167, 1176 (1999) (*Daubert* requires the trial court to assure itself that the expert "employs in the courtroom the same level of intellectual rigor that characterizes the practice of an expert in the relevant field").
>
> (5) Whether the field of expertise claimed by the expert is known to reach reliable results for the type of opinion the expert would give. See Kumho Tire Co. v. Carmichael, 119 S. Ct. 1167, 1175 (1999) (*Daubert's* general acceptance factor does not "help show that an expert's testimony is reliable where the discipline itself lacks reliability, as, for example, do theories grounded in any so-called generally accepted principles of astrology or necromancy."); Moore v. Ashland Chemical, Inc., 151 F.3d 269 (5th Cir. 1998) (en banc) (clinical doctor was properly precluded from testifying to the toxicological cause of the plaintiff's respiratory problem, where the opinion was not sufficiently grounded in scientific methodology); Sterling v. Velsicol Chem. Corp., 855 F.2d 1188 (6th Cir. 1988) (rejecting testimony based on "clinical ecology" as unfounded and unreliable).

8. *Daubert* stimulated, and continues to stimulate, an avalanche of academic writing on the topic of scientific evidence. See, e.g., Ronald J. Allen and Esfand Nafisi, *Daubert* and Its Discontents, 76 Brook. L. Rev. 131 (2010); Edward K. Cheng and Albert H. Yoon, Does *Frye* or *Daubert* Matter? A Study of Scientific Admissibility Standards, 91 Va. L. Rev. 471 (2005); Jennifer L. Groscup et al., The Effects of *Daubert* on the Admissibility of Expert Testimony in State and Federal Criminal Cases, 8 Psy. Pub. Poly. & L. 339 (2002); Joseph Sanders et al., Legal Perceptions of Science and Expert Knowledge, 8 Psy. Pub. Poly. & L. 139 (2002); Jeffrey L. Harrison, Reconceptualizing the Expert Witness: Social Cost, Current Controls and Proposed Responses, 18 Yale J. on Reg. 253 (2001); Brandon L. Jensen, Litigating the Crossroads Between *Sweet Home* and *Daubert*, 24 Va. L. Rev. 169 (2000); Derek L. Mogck, Are We There Yet? Refining the Test for Expert Testimony Through *Daubert, Kumho Tire* and Proposed

Federal Rule of Evidence 702, 33 Conn. L. Rev. 303 (2000); Navigating Uncertainty: Gatekeeping in the Absence of Hard Science, 113 Harv. L. Rev. 1467 (2000); Symposium, At the *Daubert* Gate: Managing and Measuring Expertise in an Age of Science, Specialization, and Speculation, 57 Wash. & Lee L. Rev. 661 (2000) (with articles by David L. Faigman, David S. Caudill, and Richard E. Redding, D. Michael Risinger, Roger D. Blair and Jill Boylston Herndon, Andrew I. Gavil, Michael J. Saks, John Monahan, and Christopher Slobogin); Erica Beecher-Monas, A Ray of Light for Judges Blinded by Science: Triers of Science and Intellectual Due Process, 33 Ga. L. Rev. 1047 (1999); Improving Judicial Gatekeeping: Technical Advisors and Scientific Evidence, 110 Harv. L. Rev. 941 (1997); Ronald J. Allen, Expertise and the *Daubert* Decision, 84 J. Crim. L. & Criminology 1157 (1994); Burt Black et al., Science and the Law in the Wake of *Daubert*: A New Search for Scientific Knowledge, 72 Tex. L. Rev. 715 (1994); Developments in the Law, Confronting the New Challenges of Scientific Evidence, 108 Harv. L. Rev. 1481 (1995); Edward J. Imwinkelried, The Meaning of "Facts or Data" in Federal Rule of Evidence 703: The Significance of the Supreme Court's Decision to Rely on Federal Rule 702 in Daubert v. Merrell Dow Pharmaceuticals, Inc., 54 Md. L. Rev. 352 (1995).

4.   Elaboration of Technical or Other Specialized Knowledge Under *Kumho Tire*

Daubert explicitly dealt only with scientific evidence. Immediately following the case, the circuits split on how, or whether, *Daubert* applied to "technical or other specialized knowledge." The Court addressed this issue in the following case involving a tire blowout. A purported expert was willing to testify on the basis of a highly subjective methodology that the cause of the blowout was a manufacturing defect. The trial judge applied *Daubert* and excluded the evidence. The court of appeals reversed, holding that *Daubert* only applies to scientific evidence and not to "technical or otherwise specialized knowledge," which it claimed was involved in this case. The Supreme Court reversed, and also expanded on the meaning of the "abuse of discretion" standard.

KUMHO TIRE COMPANY, LTD. v. CARMICHAEL
526 U.S. 137 (1999)

Justice BREYER delivered the opinion of the Court.

. . . This case requires us to decide how *Daubert* applies to the testimony of engineers and other experts who are not scientists. We conclude that *Daubert*'s general holding — setting forth the trial judge's general "gate-keeping" obligation — applies not only to testimony based on "scientific" knowledge, but also to testimony based on "technical" and "other specialized" knowledge. See Fed. Rule Evid. 702. We also conclude that a trial court may consider one or more of the more specific factors that *Daubert* mentioned when doing so will help determine that testimony's reliability. But, as the Court stated in *Daubert*, the test of reliability is "flexible," and *Daubert*'s list of specific factors neither necessarily nor exclusively applies to all experts or in every case. Rather, the law grants a district court the same broad latitude when it decides how to determine reliability as it enjoys in respect to its ultimate reliability determination. See General Electric Co. v. Joiner, 522 U.S. 136, 143 (1997) (courts of appeals are to apply "abuse of discretion" standard when reviewing district court's reliability determination). Applying these standards, we determine that the District Court's decision in this case — not to admit certain expert testimony — was within its discretion and therefore lawful . . . .

II

A

In *Daubert*, this Court held that Federal Rule of Evidence 702 imposes a special obligation upon a trial judge to "ensure that any and all scientific testimony . . . is not only relevant, but reliable." The initial question before us is whether this basic gatekeeping obligation applies only to "scientific" testimony or to all expert testimony. We, like the parties, believe that it applies to all expert testimony. For one thing, Rule 702 itself says:

> If scientific, technical, or other specialized knowledge will assist the trier of fact to understand the evidence or to determine a fact in issue, a witness qualified as an expert by knowledge, skill, experience, training, or education, may testify thereto in the form of an opinion or otherwise.*

This language makes no relevant distinction between "scientific" knowledge and "technical" or "other specialized" knowledge. It makes clear that any such knowledge might become the subject of expert testimony. In *Daubert*, the Court specified that it is the Rule's word "knowledge," not the words (like "scientific") that modify that word, that "establishes a standard of evidentiary reliability." Hence, as a matter of language, the Rule applies its reliability standard to all "scientific," "technical," or "other specialized" matters within its scope. We concede that the Court in *Daubert* referred only to "scientific" knowledge. But as the Court there said, it referred to "scientific" testimony "because that was the nature of the expertise" at issue.

Neither is the evidentiary rationale that underlay the Court's basic *Daubert* "gatekeeping" determination limited to "scientific" knowledge. *Daubert* pointed out that Federal Rules 702 and 703 grant expert witnesses testimonial latitude unavailable to other witnesses on the "assumption that the expert's opinion will have a reliable basis in the knowledge and experience of his discipline." 509 U.S. at 592 (pointing out that experts may testify to opinions, including those that are not based on firsthand knowledge or observation). The Rules grant that latitude to all experts, not just to "scientific" ones.

Finally, it would prove difficult, if not impossible, for judges to administer evidentiary rules under which a gatekeeping obligation depended upon a distinction between "scientific" knowledge and "technical" or "other specialized" knowledge. There is no clear line that divides the one from the others. Disciplines such as engineering rest upon scientific knowledge. Pure scientific theory itself may depend for its development upon observation and properly engineered machinery. And conceptual efforts to distinguish the two are unlikely to produce clear legal lines capable

---

*[This is the old rule, which has been replaced by a restyled rule with no substantive changes. — EDS.]

of application in particular cases. Cf. Brief for National Academy of Engineering as Amicus Curiae 9 (scientist seeks to understand nature while the engineer seeks nature's modification); Brief for Rubber Manufacturers Association as Amicus Curiae 14-16 (engineering, as an "applied science," relies on "scientific reasoning and methodology"); Brief for John Allen et al. as Amici Curiae 6 (engineering relies upon "scientific knowledge and methods").

Neither is there a convincing need to make such distinctions. Experts of all kinds tie observations to conclusions through the use of what Judge Learned Hand called "general truths derived from . . . specialized experience." Hand, Historical and Practical Considerations Regarding Expert Testimony, 15 Harv. L. Rev. 40, 54 (1901). And whether the specific expert testimony focuses upon specialized observations, the specialized translation of those observations into theory, a specialized theory itself, or the application of such a theory in a particular case, the expert's testimony often will rest "upon an experience confessedly foreign in kind to [the jury's] own." Ibid. The trial judge's effort to assure that the specialized testimony is reliable and relevant can help the jury evaluate that foreign experience, whether the testimony reflects scientific, technical, or other specialized knowledge.

We conclude that *Daubert*'s general principles apply to the expert matters described in Rule 702. The Rule, in respect to all such matters, "establishes a standard of evidentiary reliability." 509 U.S. at 590. It "requires a valid . . . connection to the pertinent inquiry as a precondition to admissibility." 509 U.S. at 592. And where such testimony's factual basis, data, principles, methods, or their application are called sufficiently into question, the trial judge must determine whether the testimony has "a reliable basis in the knowledge and experience of [the relevant] discipline." 509 U.S. at 592.

B

The petitioners ask more specifically whether a trial judge determining the "admissibility of an engineering expert's testimony" may consider several more specific factors that Daubert said might "bear on" a judge's gate-keeping determination. These factors include:

— Whether a "theory or technique . . . can be (and has been) tested";
— Whether it "has been subjected to peer review and publication";
— Whether, in respect to a particular technique, there is a high "known or potential rate of error" and whether there are "standards controlling the technique's operation"; and
— Whether the theory or technique enjoys "general acceptance" within a "relevant scientific community." 509 U.S. at 592-594.

Emphasizing the word "may" in the question, we answer that question yes.

Engineering testimony rests upon scientific foundations, the reliability of which will be at issue in some cases. See, e.g., Brief for Stephen Bobo et al. as Amici Curiae 23 (stressing the scientific bases of engineering disciplines). In other cases, the relevant reliability concerns may focus upon personal knowledge or experience. As the Solicitor General points out, there are many different kinds of experts, and many different kinds of expertise. See Brief for United States as Amicus Curiae 18-19, and n.5 (citing cases involving experts in drug terms, handwriting analysis, criminal modus operandi, land valuation, agricultural practices, railroad procedures, attorney's fee valuation, and others). Our emphasis on the word "may" thus reflects *Daubert*'s description of the Rule 702 inquiry as "a flexible one." *Daubert* makes clear that the factors it mentions do not constitute a "definitive checklist or test." And *Daubert* adds that the gatekeeping inquiry must be "'tied to the facts'" of a particular "case." We agree with the Solicitor General that "the factors identified in *Daubert* may or may not be pertinent in assessing reliability, depending on the nature of the issue, the expert's particular expertise, and the subject of his testimony." The conclusion, in our view, is that we can neither rule out, nor rule in, for all cases and for all time the applicability of the factors mentioned in *Daubert*, nor can we now do so for subsets of cases categorized by category of expert or by kind of evidence. Too much depends upon the particular circumstances of the particular case at issue.

Daubert itself is not to the contrary. It made clear that its list of factors was meant to be helpful, not definitive. Indeed, those factors do not all necessarily apply even in every instance in which the reliability of scientific testimony is challenged. It might not be surprising in a particular case, for example, that a claim made by a scientific witness has never been the subject of peer review, for the particular application at issue may never previously have interested any scientist. Nor, on the other hand, does the presence of *Daubert*'s general acceptance factor help show that an expert's testimony is reliable where the discipline itself lacks reliability, as, for example, do theories grounded in any so-called generally accepted principles of astrology or necromancy.

At the same time, and contrary to the Court of Appeals' view, some of *Daubert*'s questions can help to evaluate the reliability even of experience-based testimony. In certain cases, it will be appropriate for the trial judge to ask, for example, how often an engineering expert's experience-based methodology has produced erroneous results, or whether such a method is generally accepted in the relevant engineering community. Likewise, it will at times be useful to ask even of a witness whose expertise is based purely on experience, say, a perfume tester able to distinguish among 140 odors at a sniff, whether his preparation is of a kind that others in the field would recognize as acceptable.

We must therefore disagree with the Eleventh Circuit's holding that a trial judge may ask questions of the sort *Daubert* mentioned only where an expert "relies on the application of scientific principles," but not where an expert relies "on skill- or experience-based observation." We do not believe that Rule 702 creates a schematism that segregates expertise by type while mapping certain kinds of questions to certain kinds of experts. Life and the legal cases that it generates are too complex to warrant so definitive a match. To say this is not to deny the importance of *Daubert*'s gatekeeping requirement. The objective of that requirement is to ensure the reliability and relevancy of expert testimony. It is to make certain that an expert, whether basing testimony upon professional studies or personal experience, employs in the courtroom the same level of intellectual rigor that characterizes the practice of an expert in the relevant field. Nor do we deny that, as stated in *Daubert*, the particular questions that it mentioned will often be appropriate for use in determining the reliability of challenged expert testimony. Rather, we conclude that the trial judge must have considerable leeway in deciding in a particular case how to go about determining whether particular expert testimony is reliable. That is to say, a trial court should consider the specific factors identified in *Daubert* where they are reasonable measures of the reliability of expert testimony.

C

The trial court must have the same kind of latitude in deciding how to test an expert's reliability, and to decide whether or when special briefing or other proceedings are needed to investigate reliability, as it enjoys when it decides whether that expert's relevant testimony is reliable. Our opinion in *Joiner* makes clear that a court of appeals is to apply an abuse-of-discretion standard when it "reviews a trial court's decision to admit or exclude expert testimony." 522 U.S. at 138-139. That standard applies as much to the trial court's decisions about how to determine reliability as to its ultimate conclusion. Otherwise, the trial judge would lack the discretionary authority needed both to avoid unnecessary "reliability" proceedings in ordinary cases where the reliability of an expert's methods is properly taken for granted, and to require appropriate proceedings in the less usual or more complex cases where cause for questioning the expert's reliability arises. Indeed, the Rules seek to avoid "unjustifiable expense and delay" as part of their search for "truth" and the "just determination" of proceedings. Fed. Rule Evid. 102. Thus, whether *Daubert's* specific factors are, or are not, reasonable measures of reliability in a particular case is a matter that the law grants the trial judge broad latitude to determine. And the Eleventh Circuit erred insofar as it held to the contrary.

III

[The Court then reviewed the basis of the expert's testimony, and decided that the District Court was acting within its discretion in excluding the testimony, and thus that the Court of Appeals erred in reversing.]

. . . In sum, Rule 702 grants the district judge the discretionary authority, reviewable for its abuse, to determine reliability in light of the particular facts and circumstances of the particular case. The District Court did not abuse its discretionary authority in this case. Hence, the judgment of the Court of Appeals is Reversed.

NOTE

We said earlier, at page 654, that to understand the amendments to FRE 702 that added the three subsections to the rule, you have to understand *Daubert* and *Kumho Tire*. The reason for this is now obvious. The amendments requiring the testimony to be the product of reliable principles and methods and to be based upon sufficient facts and data, and requiring a showing that the witness has reliably applied the principles and methods to the facts of the case, are an effort to embody in the rule the essence of the cases.

KEY POINTS

1. FRE 702 adopts a functional approach to the meaning of "scientific," "technical," and "specialized" knowledge. If a witness possesses knowledge, however obtained, that would be helpful to the jury, the witness may testify to that knowledge.

2. The *Frye* test has been replaced with the requirement that "scientific" evidence be reliable and relevant, which essentially means scientifically valid and helpful to the jury.

3. *Kumho* extends *Daubert's* reach to technical and other specialized knowledge, and also extends *Joiner's* articulation of the discretionary authority of trial judges by emphasizing that it is up to the trial judges to decide how best to fulfill their gatekeeping function.

4. *Kumho* also modifies the central meaning of *Daubert* through its conversion of the "*Daubert* criteria" into the *Daubert* "neither necessary nor sufficient" list of possibly relevant factors.

PROBLEMS

9.10. A jury found that ABC Radio breached its contract with Children's Radio and misappropriated trade secrets. During the trial, the judge allowed economist Stephen Willis to testify that, absent ABC's damaging conduct, Children's Radio would have been valued at $30 million. On defendant's post-trial motion, the judge ruled that Willis's testimony should not have been admitted because, although he applied an "uncontroversial accounting method," his ultimate opinions were dubious. On appeal, Children's Radio argued that, under *Daubert*, a court can review only the methodology of the expert, not his or her conclusions. Is it within the trial court's discretion to exclude expert testimony on this ground?

9.11. Ms. Elcock fell and was injured while shopping in a Kmart store. In her suit against the Kmart Corporation, Dr. Copemann, a vocational rehabilitationist, testified that through his evaluation and treatment of Ms. Elcock he found her to be depressed and suffering from disorders linked to her pain and inability to adapt, and that all of her ailments were brought on by her fall at Kmart. He went on to opine that Ms. Elcock would never recover and would always be 50 percent to 60 percent vocationally disabled. Copemann testified that he valued Elcock's injuries using the Fields (comparing pre- and post-injury access to labor market) and Gamboa (more holistic approach, examining extent of injury and client's perceptions among other factors) analyses. The jury returned a verdict in favor of the plaintiff and awarded her $650,000. The Kmart Corporation appealed. In reviewing the trial record the appellate court found that Dr. Copemann was adequately qualified to testify, but it also noted that his testimony failed to meet several of the *Daubert* factors. First, the court found that Copemann had not provided "an inkling as to the standards controlling his method — i.e., how he excludes for other variables, such as Elcock's pre-existing injuries or job limitations — an expert trying to reproduce Copemann's method would be lost." Second, the plaintiff introduced evidence that both the Gamboa approach and the Fields approach to vocational rehabilitation assessments have received general acceptance in the field. Dr. Copemann, however, had testified that he used a "hybrid methodology," employing some aspects of both techniques. There was no evidence demonstrating that this "hybrid" had reached a level of general acceptance. Are these shortcomings in Dr. Copemann's testimony sufficient for a finding of abuse of discretion? How should the appellate court rule?

9.12. Rhonda Woods and Darla Burns worked as operators of a specially designed forklift called the TSP. Both Woods and Burns were injured on the job when they were struck by empty wooden pallets while driving the TSP down narrow warehouse aisles. Both sued the manufacturer of the TSP, alleging negligence in the design, maintenance, and operational warnings. Daniel Pacheco, who had a B.S. degree in mechanical engineering and had been a registered Professional Engineer for 30 years, was prepared to testify for the plaintiffs. Everyone agreed that Pacheco's credentials were adequate. In his investigation prior to trial, Pacheco read the depositions of the plaintiffs and 10 other people who had knowledge relevant to the incidents, he reviewed the defendant's manufacturing and service documents for the TSP, and he read the TSP's sales brochures, a training manual, and engineering drawings. Pacheco explained that he had seen photographs of the TSP and had read the manufacturer's literature but had never operated or observed another person operating the TSP. Despite this, he was prepared to testify that it was his opinion that an extension of the existing wire mesh guard would have prevented the plaintiffs' injuries and that an alternative warning would have been more effective to this end as well. At the time of the pretrial hearing to determine the admissibility of his testimony, he had not drafted such an alternative warning to present to the court. Should Pacheco be allowed to testify to both or either of these opinions?

9.13. Soon after Kenneth Goodwin purchased a MTD lawnmower, he suffered an eye injury while cutting the grass in front of his home. He had to undergo eye surgery for a cut in his cornea and sued MTD Products for the dangerous and defective design of its mower. During the trial, Goodwin testified that he had been mowing about five feet from his house when he felt something hit his left eye. He stated that when he later returned to the spot, he found a plastic wing nut with a slice mark in it. Goodwin proposed to the jury the theory that the mower was defective in that the motor's vibrations had loosened the wing nut, allowing it to fall into the cutting blades. The nut then shot out at about 190 mph and ricocheted off the plaintiff's house and into his left eye.

In support of this theory, lawn mower experts testified about the manufacture, design, and condition of the mower, and medical experts testified about his eye injury. To rebut this evidence, MTD called Gunter Plamper, its vice president in charge of product development and safety. Plamper explained why he felt MTD's mower was safe but when he tried to explain that it was impossible for a wing nut to cause Goodwin's eye injury, the attorney for the plaintiff objected. What were the best grounds for this objection and how should the judge rule?

Later, the defense attorney tried to elicit from Plamper his expert opinion about whether he believed Goodwin when he stated that he was in the operator's zone behind the lawnmower with the discharge chute facing down when he was injured. The plaintiff's attorney again objected. How should the court rule?

9.14. Officer Muirhead was sued for use of excessive force by Mr. Nimely, who was rendered paraplegic when Muirhead shot him after an armed chase on foot. During the trial, the plaintiff offered the testimony of several experts to the extent that Muirhead's shot was fired while Nimely was facing away from him, fleeing. The defense countered with the testimony of Dr. Stuart Dawson, a consulting expert in forensic pathology. Dawson testified that regardless of the actual course of events, Muirhead probably perceived Nimely as turning to face him as Muirhead fired; thus Muirhead's use of force would have been justified (since Nimely was armed at the time). Dawson's testimony on the "misperception" of Officer Muirhead was based in part on his review of Muirhead's pre-trial deposition, in which Muirhead related his belief that Nimely was turned to face him when the shot was fired. Dawson further testified that he based his expert opinion on his independent conclusion that

Muirhead must not have been lying in his account of the course of the events leading up to the shot:

Q: Now, Doctor Dawson, did you also review the deposition testimony of Police Officers Muirhead and McCarthy?
A: Yes.
Q: Was there testimony about what Mr. Nimely was doing at the time Sergeant Muirhead thought he shot him consistent with your findings?

. . .

A: Well, yes and no. There was testimony that Mr. Nimely was turning, but taken literally, the testimony wasn't consistent with the facts because the literal testimony was that the officer felt that he shot directly in front of the chest of Mr. Nimely but he did say that Mr. Nimely was in the process of turning, so in effect my analysis considered both of those aspects and realized they could basically be synthesized in something reasonable.
Q: In doing your analysis, in light of — what you described as the entrance and exit wound and trajectory of the bullet, did you consider that the police officer who said that he shot him straight in the chest wasn't telling the truth?
A: That certainly is one of the considerations that goes through your mind, is perhaps the officer is simply lying about the incident. I considered that possibility and — but fairly quickly rejected it as being the less likely of the things that happened.
Q: Why did you reject it? . . .
A: Well, I rejected it because, you know, in — it's generally an acceptable concept that police officers aren't going to discharge their weapons —
MR. KELTON: Judge, I object to what is an acceptable concept of what police officers will do.
THE COURT: Overruled. The witness is explaining his answer. He may complete it.
A: Thank you, Judge. What it boils down to is police officers don't discharge weapons lightly because the discharge of a weapon creates all kinds of problems . . .
THE COURT: . . . You may continue with your answer.
A: Thank you. It causes problems of criminal litigation, civil litigation, et cetera. The other thing is, it's reasonable to infer that a police officer is going to know that whenever a discharge does occur, there is going to be a big investigation and that will include forensic examination of wounds, so it didn't make much sense to me that the police officer would say that the person was shot in the front if it would be obvious to the police officer that an investigation would be done and that would show the person was shot in the back.

The jury found for the defense. Should Dawson's testimony have been permitted?

9.15. In a personal injury suit (a "slip and fall case") against a grocery store, Maxine Black sought to introduce the testimony of Dr. Reyna, her algologist (a doctor who treats persistent pain). Ms. Black developed fibromyalgia (a nonspecific, chronic-pain illness) after the accident. At trial, Dr. Reyna testified that she fully apprised herself of Ms. Black's prior medical history before the accident, that she determined that no post-accident incident was an intervening cause for the onset of Ms. Black's fibromyalgia, and that no other factors — based upon her review of tests performed prior to accepting Ms. Black as a patient, as well as those tests which Dr. Reyna, herself, directed to be made — contributed to Ms. Black's fibromyalgia. Reyna acknowledged that fibromyalgia has no known etiology (i.e., medical science does not know whether the cause of the condition is muscle, nerve, or hormone damage); but she was willing to testify that the fall contributed to the development of Ms. Black's condition. Should Dr. Reyna be allowed to testify?

9.16. The defendant, Mr. Salimonu, is being tried for conspiracy to import heroin, a federal offense. As one of the elements of the crime, the prosecution has the burden of proving that Mr. Salimonu knew, and was in contact with, another member of the conspiracy. To this end, it presented tape recordings of incriminating conversations between "Laddie" and McKinnon and between "Laddie" and Petrosino. McKinnon and Petrosino are alleged co-conspirators. A voice exemplar that contains a recording of Salimonu's voice was also played for the jury for purposes of comparison. The prosecution seeks to convince the jury that "Laddie" was in fact Mr. Salimonu.

To refute this argument, Salimonu wishes to introduce the testimony of two expert witnesses to establish that Laddie's voice and Salimonu's voice on the exemplar are different. Robert Berkovitz, the developer of a spectogram computer program that plots the frequency and magnitude of speech signals, is prepared to testify that substantial differences between the spectograms of the two voices indicate that the tapes are of two different people. Dr. Stephen Cushing, a linguist, has listened to the tapes and, based on this, is willing to testify that the two voices were different.

In the voir dire, Dr. Cushing states that he has listened to the tapes several times and has distinguished 14 differences between the two voices. Cushing admits that he has had no training or special certification in voice identification or comparison, and that he has only engaged in voice recognition procedures two or three times before. He also concedes that a person may be able to disguise his voice and that he does not know whether the voice in this exemplar is disguised. Finally, Cushing states that a layperson without training in linguistics would be able to discern the same differences that he has by listening to the tapes. Should the trial judge allow both experts to testify?

9.17. As part of a conspiracy trial, the government called a handwriting analyst to testify to the identity of persons who had addressed an envelope containing illegal drugs. The analyst, Dr. Learned, had attended courses and seminars on handwriting identification, was employed by the secret service as a handwriting expert, and had testified in over 100 court cases. Handwriting analysis essentially involves comparing a known sample of a person's writing with the writing on the document sought to be identified. The analyst compares the characteristics of the writing, including the slant of the writing, the height and shape of the letters, and the spacing between letters and words.

After the court ruled that Dr. Learned's testimony was admissible, the defense tried to call Lou Bowden, a law professor who had no formal training in handwriting analysis and who lacked practical experience in the field. Bowden nevertheless had published an article in a well-respected law review, criticizing the field of handwriting analysis and its use in litigation. Bowden's main critique of this type of analysis was that it lacked standards to guide experts in weighing the match or nonmatch of particular handwriting characteristics.

The trial court ruled Bowden's testimony inadmissible. Was the court correct?

5.   Reflection on Scientific Evidence and the *Daubert* Case

Trials in the Anglo-American tradition were originally the means by which conventional disputes were resolved. The original mode of trial gathered together individuals with knowledge of local affairs to decide notorious disputes. The existence of disputes was part of conventional knowledge, as was the knowledge necessary to resolve them. The local conventions determining borders or access to bodies of water or the proper maintenance of property were truly conventions, and thus known throughout the relevant community. As times changed, various forces coalesced that required modification in the self-informing aspect of juries, with the result that the knowledge of jurors was supplemented with the testimony of other members of the community, but disputes were for the most part still conventional ones requiring primarily the judgment of responsible members of the community for decision.

Over time litigated matters became more complex, and the gap of ignorance separating the fact finders from the witnesses increased. More and more frequently what witnesses said had to be explained to make it understandable. A case may depend on the conventions of a certain business or industry rather than the conventions of the society at large, and jurors will often need to be informed of those conventions. A witness may not speak English, and thus the testimony must be translated.[7] The case may involve a technical vocabulary that, like a foreign vocabulary, must be made accessible to those lacking the technical training. As such cases became more common, the traditional model of fact-finding was largely followed. The parties were merely obligated to explain a little bit more, to put the juror in a position to understand what the witnesses were saying, and thus to decide the case in an intelligent fashion.

Are there any cases that cannot be accommodated within the traditional model? Do some cases present issues for decision that defy the ability of fact finders to understand them? Perhaps the answer to these questions is no. Perhaps with enough time and resources, jurors can be sufficiently informed so that they can decide intelligently all litigated cases. Yet now another set of questions lurks in the shadows: At what cost is this knowledge purchased, and is the bargain a wise one? Would resources be better used elsewhere? Who should decide on what "better" use of resources may be available?

The answer to the first question, whether there are cases that defy the ability of fact finders to understand them, seems clear enough upon reflection, even though it may be counterintuitive, and the answer is surely no. The deficits of juridical fact finders are not primarily cognitive; they are informational. Judges and jurors lack knowledge about various branches of human inquiry, as we all do, but there is little reason to believe that, with instruction, they could not adequately master the relevant fields. Ironically, and again counterintuitively, jurors, because they sit on juries, are possibly better able to master the relevant subjects than judges. The issue is not whether every single juror understands adequately every single issue, but whether the jury adequately understands. The question is not whether each of the jurors ends up understanding all there is to know about a field, or even knows as much as does any particular expert. The question is whether the jury collectively knows or can learn

---

7.   Apparently a party can insist on its being translated. In Hernandez v. New York, 500 U.S. 352 (1991), the Supreme Court upheld the exclusion of Spanish-speaking jurors in a case in which some witnesses would testify in Spanish on the ground that the jurors might not accept the translator's rendition of the testimony.

enough for rational deliberation. With the wealth of talent almost always contained in even a randomly selected group of six to 12 individuals, it would be a remarkable case that truly defied their collective cognitive abilities. Moreover, that experts like witnesses know more than they can communicate does not disprove this point. Experts may very well develop intuitive skills that could not be imparted to a jury. Still, the question is whether those skills matter for rational decision in any particular litigated case. If deciding a case is actually reduced to a choice between the hunches of experts that cannot be further explained, the case most likely does not belong in the courts.

The argument that there are cases that defy the ability of fact finders to understand them may not be just counterintuitive; it may appear to be disproved by common experience. Many ideas, especially in their youth, are extremely difficult to grasp. A good example is Einsteinian relativity theory, which was understood by only a small handful of individuals for a considerable time following its creation. But we do not know of any case that required for decision an understanding of general relativity theory, nor of an analogous case, one involving string theory, for example. Perhaps there is one, but again it would be the exception that proves the rule.

General relativity theory is not the only difficult idea to grasp. Many individuals find calculus and probability theory obscure, for example, and both are often integral to trials. But many people do not find mathematics at this level obscure. In determining whether a jury possessed the necessary tools for rational decision, again the question is not whether all jurors do; it is whether the jury does. Nor is the question whether the jury already knew enough about calculus or probability; it is whether they could learn enough. Furthermore, if a case posed an issue requiring a certain technical or mathematical capacity, that capacity could be a condition of serving on the jury. This would make the seating of a jury no more difficult than doing so in a notorious case.[8] The real objection to the argument for educating juries is not that it is wrong; the real objection is that it would be too costly. No doubt educating jurors adequately to decide intelligently cases with complicated issues would be costly. In many instances, the jurors would literally have to go to school, or the school brought to them. One can easily imagine cases that would require months of evidence before jurors would be competent to decide intelligently. It is, however, much more difficult to find cases that would defy this educational process, which brings us full circle.

But the circle reveals a paradox. There are many cases that do not involve scientific or technical questions but do require months of instruction so that the jury can understand them. In these cases we do not permit juror deference to juridical outsiders such as experts; we require the parties to connect the case through evidence to the experience of the jurors. Why, then, do we flirt with, and perhaps adopt, a more deferential mode when something comes into court labeled "expert testimony"? The cognitive questions are highly similar, even if not identical, in both sets of cases. The

8. In some cases, this could run up against the notion that defendants must be tried by a jury of their peers. Though not explicit in the Seventh Amendment or elsewhere in the Constitution, the Supreme Court has often reiterated that the doctrine should not be abandoned in criminal cases. See, e.g., Apprendi v. New Jersey, 530 U.S. 466, 548 (2000). The requirement has also been codified in federal law. See, e.g., 28 U.S.C.S. 1861 (2001) ("It is the policy of the United States that all litigants in Federal courts entitled to trial by jury shall have the right to grand and petit juries selected at random from a fair cross section of the community in the district or division wherein the court convenes."). A jury comprised of the highly educated would neither represent a fair cross-section nor would it provide a poor defendant with a jury of his peers. If juries were to be selected by their level and area of knowledge this could be a significant concern, but the essence of this problem may already exist where juries defer to experts, allowing them to decide crucial issues. When a jury defers, an expert who is likely not the defendant's peer in several respects, essentially tries the defendants.

economic questions are truly identical. In all cases, parties must take into account the costs of presenting their cases and responding to their opponents' cases in determining their optimal strategy. This variable is independent of the distinction between conventional and expert testimony. The economics of public subsidy are also highly analogous, if not identical. All trials have public subsidies, such as the cost of the courthouse and various governmental salaries. From the public point of view, a subsidy to a six-month trial that involved educating the jury about calculus is no different from the subsidy to a six-month bank fraud trial. If there is a difference, it favors the subsidy in support of the instruction in calculus, as that might lead to social benefits that are very difficult to see flowing from the educational effort directed toward the jury in a bank fraud case.

Perhaps the difference between complex conventional cases and cases that call for expert testimony is that the latter demand expertise that is missing from the former. People do possess specialized nonconventional knowledge about mathematics, economics, toxicology, oncology, and so on. Perhaps no one possesses expertise about complex conventional cases such as bank fraud or criminal conspiracies. Perhaps so, but this argues not for our current system of presenting competing versions of expertise at trial, but instead for a form of judicial notice (see FRE 201, discussed in Chapter Eleven, infra).

If expertise exists and can be identified with the certainty that the existence of Lake Michigan bordering the city of Chicago can be, trials should not pause over it. Its lessons should be taken as true, and the fact finder so constricted. Whether in any particular case there is expertise in this sense should be easy to determine by judges or legislatures, and its implications mined for what they are worth. We would defer to such knowledge just as we defer to the indisputable knowledge that Lake Michigan borders Chicago. We would not litigate whether Lake Michigan does; that would simply waste resources. If expertise does exist, we waste resources each time (at least beyond the first or unless conditions have changed) that we litigate the issue.

We not only waste time when we litigate the existence of expertise; we also deliberately engage in nonsensical activity. One of the reasons to litigate the existence of expertise is to provide opinions to which jurors can defer. This is the opposite of education, of course. Jurors are not expected to understand the relevant fields of inquiry; they are simply to decide which expert to believe. How is this to be done intelligently without understanding the relevant fields? This question, which reverberates over the increasing use of expertise at trial, has no satisfactory answer, precisely because the two points cannot be reconciled. Though it is true that juries routinely evaluate the credibility of witnesses and the veracity of their statements, the senses and instincts useful in judging the testimony of an eyewitness are useless when contrasting the credentials of two experts or the scientific likelihood of the theories they propound. It is painfully obvious that jurors (and judges) who do not know enough about the relevant fields of knowledge to decide intelligently cannot decide intelligently which expert to believe among those providing competing versions of that field. Consequently, even if our view of the cognitive capacity of juries is rejected, the present system still is nonrational, and the central problem remains. Obversely, if jurors can decide intelligently about which expert to believe, they can with a little more education reason intelligently about the matters in issue, so that deference to the expert is not necessary.

Deference and education are not analytically distinct entities; they are opposite points on a spectrum. Jurors will virtually never see true "raw" data at trial. Deference occurs to some extent whenever a jury decides whether a witness has testified truthfully.

Still, the extent of deference, or of education, is a variable; one can have more of one and less of the other. This is particularly obvious when one considers a case involving not just reporting of sensory experience ("the light was red") but the drawing of inferences ("in light of these studies, I am of the opinion that Bendectin causes birth defects"). In the typical case, the jury is supposed to be able to understand the reasoning process that led the witness from observation to conclusion. Understanding may bring either acceptance or rejection, of course, and the decision will be made by the jury's own lights. Often with experts there is no expectation that the reasoning process can be understood. Acceptance or rejection cannot occur by the jury's own lights, and thus we see a much larger dose of deference. How well a witness's analytical process can be understood is again clearly a variable. Some can be understood completely, some partially, and some not at all. The legal question is the significance of this variable.

Out of this cauldron of concerns emerge three competing methods of handling expert testimony, each with its own strengths and weaknesses:

The Normal, Educational Approach. Expert testimony can be treated just like any other testimony, which means for it to be relevant it must be understandable by the fact finder. To make an expert's testimony understandable will require the jury to be educated about the relevant matters, and thus the "normal approach" collapses into adopting an education model. The difficulty is cost, especially the fact that cost may skew decision toward those with greater resources. The more impecunious a party, the less able the party will be to provide the necessary educative function or to respond to an opponent's case. The latter point is another detrimental aspect of our system's failure to make parties bear the true cost of their cases, which includes the opponent's cost of responding. Without cost shifting, a wealthier party can make the cost of suit too high for the opponent. Adopting the normal approach to expert testimony would exacerbate this problem by tending to make cases involving expertise more protracted. Offsetting this factor in part is that higher costs are a laudable disincentive to sue or an equally laudable incentive to agree to resolution in other, less costly forums.

The Deference Model. Fact finders can be required to defer to established expertise, as occurs whenever experts are required to testify in hypothetical question format. The advantages are obvious. Those with the ability to decide rationally make the decision, costs are reduced, and consistency in decision is advanced. If the decisions about expertise are correct, accuracy in decision should be advanced as well. The disadvantage is the resultant extension of official orthodoxy, which removes decision from the jury and trial judge to some higher level court or legislature. Also, if the decision about expertise is incorrect, consistency of decision will remain, but the decisions will be consistently wrong.

The Adversary Model. Parties can choose either to educate the jury with the assistance of expert testimony or to convince the jury to defer to an expert's opinion. This leaves the whole matter up to the parties, save only for the admissibility decision of judges. That admissibility decision, in turn, would have to be made in anticipation of either education or a request for deference. Again, the advantages are obvious. The parties know their dispute and their resources better than anyone else, and are in the best position to make choices that optimize their interests. The difficulties are that the cost of education will tend to make deference more attractive and that deference cannot occur rationally with any great frequency. The reduction in the likelihood of rationality is at odds with the essence of the common law mode of trial, that is, the pursuit of factual accuracy through rational deliberation. Indeed, there is a high irony here: in a case in which the parties employ a deference mode, the mere admission by the trial judge of competing expert views without requiring full explanation of those views, including instruction on the underlying field of inquiry, ensures that a decision will be nonrational if not irrational. Only if a juror could see clearly that one side was right and the other wrong would nonrationality be avoided; but if that were so, the judge would admit only the one version and exclude the other. If reasonable people could rationally disagree about which expert is right, they in addition would be able to understand the underlying dispute, and thus deference would not be needed. Note also what a dramatic qualification of the normal rules of relevancy deference entails. Normally, a party must explain the relevance of evidence by adequately connecting the evidence to the fact finder's understanding. With experts in a deferential model, one party can shift that cost of explanation to the opponent by producing an unexplained opinion.

As this brief presentation demonstrates, the use of expert testimony poses fundamental challenges to the common law system of adjudication. Experts are often expert because of years of specialized training, and thus there often will be formidable barriers to educating the fact finder about the relevant issues at trial. Hence, pressure arises to defer to the expertise of experts as a means of keeping trials to a manageable length, but the pressure to defer constitutes a challenge to the core concept of trials, and puts into issue our basic commitment to decisions based on rational deliberation on the evidence. This explains in part the remarkable controversy over expert testimony even as expert testimony is becoming ever more prevalent at trial, for lurking here is the fundamental question of the nature of litigation: To what extent is rational deliberation the hallmark of adjudication?

The *Daubert* case presented these issues to the Court, but its opinion did not address them. The opinion offered no recognition that what was at stake was not just a technical rule of evidence but a conception of trial, and thus the implications of its decision for rational deliberation were not addressed. The Court focused on two other matters that formed the basis of the lower court's ruling in favor of the defendants: First, that the general acceptance standard of *Frye* governed the admissibility of expert testimony in federal court, and second that the standard could not be met with evidence of reanalyses of data that had not previously been published and subjected to peer review. The deep conceptual issue of the defining characteristics of litigation was overlooked in the Court's unenlightening, but thankfully not positively harmful, discussion of the general acceptance standard.

The Court's failure to deal with the core issues presented to it in *Daubert* is all the more unfortunate because still operating are the pressures that over time have resulted in modification of the litigation process to permit large amounts of deference to experts. First is the added cost of educating fact finders so that they may follow the reasoning of the expert in the same way the fact finders can follow the reasoning of a lay witness (thus essentially converting an expert into a lay witness). There is in addition the lottery effect. If reasons for opinions need not be given in detail, one has an increased chance of a lottery-effect jury verdict if the trial judge qualifies a witness as an expert. One effect of *Daubert* has been to transmute the mechanical invocation of the *Frye* test by the trials courts into a more ostensibly subtle but in fact largely identical process of qualification of expert witnesses. What else can they do? The Supreme Court did not take its opportunity to tell trial judges to admit purported expertise only if the basis of the expertise were understandable, as it could and should have done. Trial judges will thus continue to look for a justification to defer to expertise, and they will continue to find it in the general acceptance of that expertise in generally accepted bodies of knowledge.

Telling the lower courts not to invoke mechanically "general acceptance" may prove marginally helpful, but none of the important questions in the case were addressed. In particular, the conflict between the demands of education and deference was ignored. Indeed, if anything the dichotomy between deference and education was reinforced by the Court's opinion. The list of criteria provided by the Court is only relevant to a system willing to defer; by providing the list, the Court, although surely unintentionally, gave sustenance to deference. This is also why the Court's limitation of its discussion to "scientific" evidence is not problematic. The other kinds of information listed in Rule 702 are unlikely to require deference; information of those types can be explained. A car mechanic can qualify as an expert under the rule, but few would claim that such expertise would defy the cognitive capacity of fact finders. As you saw in *Kumho*, however, the Court has proved even more willing to perpetuate the tendency to allow deference than some critics initially thought.

The most regrettable aspect of *Daubert* is that the Court seemed quite unaware of the implications of admitting data without a basis for believing that the data can be understood. By doing so, it seems to be putting its stamp of approval on undeliberative and nonrational legal decision-making, which are the antitheses of the law's aspirations. Jurors or judges who cannot understand the reasoning of a witness can only accept or reject the witness's conclusions, but neither acceptance nor rejection will occur rationally. The choice will not be made because a fact finder understands the reasoning and sees either its cogency or its flaws; it will be made for some other reason. And the set of "some other reasons" is, from the point of view of the law's aspirations, filled with unsavory characters.

Yet another interesting aspect of the expert evidence area that may remain undisturbed by *Daubert* is the special treatment that expert testimony gets with regard to the distinction between sufficiency and admissibility. Often trial courts seem to make a sufficiency determination in the guise of an admissibility determination. The explanation, we think, is that trial judges are admitting evidence that they know they and jurors cannot be expected to understand. Such evidence should not be admitted unless the trial judge is willing to let a verdict rest on it, and so the admissibility decision becomes a sufficiency decision. This all confirms the entrenchment of a deference mode of decision at the trial court level.

Perhaps there is no feasible alternative. Perhaps the cost of truly educating the fact finders would be too high in some cases, or perhaps our skepticism about the point does not dispose of concerns about the cognitive capacity of fact finders. If either is true, the answer again is obvious: Unless we are also wrong that the core aspiration of litigation is decision through rational deliberation, the common law form of decision-making should not be employed for those cases.

6.   FRE 705

RULE 705.   DISCLOSURE OF THE FACTS OR DATA UNDERLYING AN EXPERT'S OPINION

Unless the court orders otherwise, an expert may state an opinion — and give the reasons for it — without first testifying to the underlying facts or data. But the expert may be required to disclose those facts or data on cross-examination.

7.   Interpretation and Illustration of FRE 705

At common law, once a witness was qualified to testify as an expert it was necessary to elicit the basis for the opinion before asking the witness about the opinion. This
requirement, coupled with the requirement that opinions be based on admissible
evidence, tended to force reliance on the use of hypothetical questions. Experts typically were asked long and involved questions containing the evidence as summarized
by the examiner. An opinion was then offered on that basis. Use of the hypothetical
question approach ensured that the premises of an opinion had been the subject of
earlier testimony and that the factual basis of an opinion had been set forth before the
opinion being given, but it also created a significant artificiality in trials. The most
important innovation of FRE 705 is its elimination of the requirement of experts testifying in the form of a response to a hypothetical question.

FRE 705 gives the direct examiner the flexibility to elicit the opinion or conclusion before developing all the details that support it. The rule goes further, however, and permits the opinion without requiring the proponent ever to produce the
underlying basis. The advantage to this approach is that it permits the proponent
of the evidence to structure its case most effectively. If the proponent is concerned
that the fact finders will not pay careful attention without having the summarizing
opinion of the expert already before them, the opinion can be introduced early in
the expert's testimony. If the proponent believes that laying the foundation first and
then bringing out the opinion is optimal, that approach is permissible, also. There is
one disadvantage to FRE 705's loose structuring of the evidentiary process. If there
is reason to suspect that the information on which the expert bases the opinion is so
unreliable that it may be appropriate to exclude the opinion altogether, the opponent will often desire to test that suspicion before rather than after the jury hears the
opinion. By explicitly giving the judge authority to require that the basis for an opinion be elicited before the opinion is given, FRE 705 provides a reasonable means for
solving this type of problem. See, e.g., United States v. Brien, 59 F.3d 274 (1st Cir.
1995) (holding that the defense was not entitled to offer expert testimony without disclosing the underlying data, leaving it to be developed on cross-examination; rather
the data must be supplied to the judge upon demand and may be used in making a
preliminary ruling on admissibility). Neither the rule nor the Advisory Committee
Note suggests any criteria for the judge to apply in deciding whether to require that
the basis for the opinion precede the opinion. And for good reason, this is a matter
that could not easily be reduced to rules, and thus is best left to the discretion of the
trial judge.

An unsubstantiated opinion is not likely to impress the jury as much as one
that has a demonstrably solid basis. Thus, as a matter of strategy, the direct examiner is likely to explore the bases for an expert's opinion sometime during the direct
examination. There may be times, however, when the attorney's voluntary exploration
of the basis for the testimony on direct examination is less than complete or when
there is no substantial basis for the opinion. Rather than ensuring in every case that
direct examination will reveal the basis for an opinion, FRE 705 leaves these matters
to cross-examination. See, e.g., Smith v. Ford Motor Co., 626 F.2d 784, 793 (10th
Cir. 1980) (the effect of Rule 705 is to "place the full burden of exploration of the
facts and assumptions underlying the testimony of an expert witness squarely on the
shoulders of opposing counsel's cross-examination"). In some cases, the information
revealed upon cross-examination can be quite damaging to the party that proffered

the evidence, either because it weakens the expert's credibility or because it muddles the story the jury hears. In Skidmore v. Precision Printing & Packaging, Inc., 188 F.3d 606 (5th Cir. 1999), the plaintiff sued her employer for sexual harassment by a coworker that damaged her mental and physical health. The plaintiff introduced her psychiatrist who testified to his diagnosis that the plaintiff suffered from posttraumatic stress disorder and depression brought on by the coworker's conduct. When pressed, under Rule 705, to reveal the underlying facts upon which he had relied, it became clear that he had relied on facts in conflict with the plaintiff's own testimony. The jury was then free to consider the likelihood of the accuracy of the expert's diagnosis in this light.

The Advisory Committee explained the role of cross-examination as follows:

> If the objection is made that leaving it to the cross-examiner to bring out the supporting data is essentially unfair, the answer is that he is under no compulsion to bring out any facts or data except those unfavorable to the opinion. *The answer assumes that the cross-examiner has the advance knowledge which is essential for effective cross-examination.* This advance knowledge has been afforded, though imperfectly, by the traditional foundation requirement. *Rule 26(b)(4) of the Rules of Civil Procedure, as revised, provides for substantial discovery in this area, obviating in large measure the obstacles which have been raised in some instances to discovery of findings, underlying data, and even the identity of the experts.* [Emphasis added.]

The Advisory Committee's answer to bringing out supporting data may be sufficient for civil cases. In criminal cases, where discovery traditionally has been more limited, the cross-examiner may be at a serious disadvantage if the underlying facts and data are not revealed on direct examination. In such a case it would be appropriate for the trial judge to require that the bases for the opinion be elicited on direct examination.

8.   FRE 703

RULE 703.   Bases of an Expert's Opinion Testimony

An expert may base an opinion on facts or data in the case that the expert has been made aware of or personally observed. If experts in the particular field would reasonably rely on those kinds of facts or data in forming an opinion on the subject, they need not be admissible for the opinion to be admitted. But if the facts or data would otherwise be inadmissible, the proponent of the opinion may disclose them to the jury only if their probative value in helping the jury evaluate the opinion substantially outweighs their prejudicial effect.

9.   Interpretation and Illustration of FRE 703

In a crucial sense, the primary point of this chapter is to examine the implications of the proposition that to decide some cases correctly requires access to specialized bodies of knowledge. The law needs the knowledge that other disciplines possess, but there is a problem. The knowledge of other disciplines — medicine is a good example — is not organized according to legal requirements. In particular, many disciplines do quite well without the hearsay rule, as when the night nurse informs the day nurse who informs the doctor that the patient vomited during the evening, and the doctor prescribes action in part on the basis of that report. Another example: The surgeon is operating to remove cancerous tissue. In order to determine whether enough tissue has been removed, samples are sent to pathology for immediate evaluation. Reports come back, and on that basis decisions are made whether to remove more tissue. In preparing for trial, an expert witness will "review the file" and formulate an opinion in part on the hearsay contained in the file.

When faced with a conflict between the legal requirements concerning evidence, such as the hearsay rule, and the conventions of other disciplines, such as the reliance on hearsay accounts in a hospital setting, the common law tended to demand that witnesses from other disciplines conform their practice to ours (although some federal circuits adopted a rule allowing physicians to testify on the basis of information from nurses, radiologists, pathologists, and the like; see the discussion in Zenith Radio Corp. v. Matsushita Elec. Indus. Co., 505 F. Supp. 1313, 1322-1323 (E.D. Pa. 1980), *rev'd on other grounds*, 723 F.2d 238 (3d Cir. 1983)). That meant that they could testify but only on the basis of admissible evidence. This, in large measure, was the point of the hypothetical question mode of proceeding. The disadvantage of requiring other disciplines to conform to the legal requirements is that it can make obtaining good and reliable evidence more difficult and costly. The drafters of the Federal Rules rejected this aspect of the common law in FRE 703, providing that experts can testify on the basis of data that would be legally inadmissible, so long as "experts in the particular field would reasonably rely on those kinds of facts or data in forming an opinion on the subject." Thus, under FRE 703 experts no longer must conform their practices to the law's conventions, but rather the law bends to accommodate the practices of the other disciplines. This is most significant for experts, such as medical personnel, who take action and make decisions on the basis of reliable hearsay. FRE 703 makes clear that expert testimony based on such otherwise inadmissible evidence is permissible, notwithstanding the lack of symmetry between the law's rules about evidence and medicine's practices. Thus, the nurse's observations written on the patient's chart, radiological and pathological evaluations, lab reports, and so on may legitimately form the basis of an expert testifying at trial.

Though the law bends to accommodate other disciplines, judges are not obligated to bend over backward. The "would reasonably rely on" requirement is taken seriously by courts and can be a basis for finding an expert's testimony inadmissible. In Redman v. John D. Brush & Co., 111 F.3d 1174 (4th Cir. 1997), a burglary victim brought a products liability suit against the manufacturer of the safe from which his coin collection had been stolen. A metallurgic engineer testified for the plaintiff about the failure analysis he had conducted on the safe. From this analysis he had learned what materials the safe was made of and how those materials were assembled. He also reached the conclusion that the burglar broke into the safe by prying the door open. Based on his findings, he opined that the safe was not "burglar deterrent." The expert, however, admitted that he had never before analyzed a safe, engaged in the design or manufacture of safes, received any special training in regard to safes, and was not personally familiar with the standards and rating systems used in the safe industry for burglary protection capacity. In order to reach the conclusion that the defendant's safe was not "burglar deterrent," the expert relied upon the hearsay of store personnel to ascertain the meaning of "burglar deterrent." The plaintiff did not call those employees as witnesses nor did he attempt to qualify them as witnesses. Discussing the "would reasonably rely on" requirement, the appellate court noted:

> In this case an expert in the relevant field would be familiar with the design and manufacture of safes and the industry standards regarding safes. There is no proof and no reason to believe that such an expert would rely upon conversations with store personnel to identify a standard of burglar protection capacity. Thus, [the plaintiff's] expert should not have been permitted to rely on the inadmissible hearsay of the store personnel for the purpose of establishing a purported industry standard. [Ill. F.3d at 1179.]

In contrast, in Sphere Drake Insurance PLC v. Trisko, 226 F.3d 951 (8th Cir. 2000), the court affirmed the lower court's admission of expert testimony that had been objected to on Rule 703 grounds. Here, a jeweler's jewelry went missing from the trunk of the car he was traveling in, although he was in the car the whole time. His insurance policy covered lost or damaged jewelry but excepted "unexplained loss" or a "mysterious disappearance." At trial, the jeweler called a police detective as an expert witness to give testimony about crime patterns in the Miami area, including the covert *modi operandi* of jewel thieves. The detective testified that two unidentified informants had reported to him that someone had paid two persons $20,000 each to steal the jewelry. Though the informants were not available for cross-examination and there was no evidence as to their credibility, the detective was permitted to opine that someone had probably stolen the jewelry and it was thus not a "mysterious disappearance." On appeal, the court held that since the detective testified that he "regularly relied on the statements of informants," he should also be allowed to do so in forming the basis of his expert opinion.

In addition to accommodating the practices of other disciplines, FRE 703 solves another problem. Latent in the common law's opposition to inadmissible evidence forming the basis of expert opinion is a subtle but important fraud. What makes an expert an expert in many instances is a heavy dose of book learning. To the extent that an expert relies on academic study (books and treatises and the like) or on conversations with others such as occur during "rounds" at teaching hospitals, the expertise is based on hearsay, much of which would be inadmissible or too costly to produce at trial. The common law courts overlooked this point. Thus, even though the common law courts "purported" to require a basis in admissible evidence for an expert's opinion, opinions remained admissible even though they relied heavily on knowledge gained through a form of inadmissible, or at least unadmitted, hearsay. Under FRE 703, this is not a problem.

10. Elaboration of FRE 703: Opinions Based on Otherwise Inadmissible Evidence

You may have noted a peculiarity in FRE 703 and in our discussion above. FRE 703 makes admissible an opinion based on inadmissible evidence, if it is the type of facts or data that an "expert in the particular field would reasonably rely on," but, as a consequence of the last sentence of the rule, the proponent of the opinion may not present to the jury the evidence the expert reasonably is relying upon unless a reverse FRE 403 standard is met ("probative value . . . substantially outweighs . . . prejudicial effect."). Even then, the admission is limited to "helping the jury evaluate the [expert] opinion," rather than admitted substantively for its truth. This sentence was added to the rule in the 2000 amendments to clear up a controversy over the rule's meaning. While the controversy has been resolved, there is considerable doubt whether the resolution makes any sense.

When an expert bases an opinion in whole or in part on inadmissible evidence, there is an inevitable tension between whatever rule makes the evidence inadmissible and FRE 703. As we discussed above, most often this is a tension between FRE 703 and 705 and the hearsay rule, but data on which an opinion is based may be inadmissible for other reasons as well. For example, the expert may have relied on the oral recitation of the contents of an X-ray, whereas the best evidence rule would require reliance on the X-ray itself; or the expert may have relied on writings that have been insufficiently authenticated. Prior to the amendment to FRE 703, this potential conflict in the rules posed an important question: Does FRE 703 operate as a rule of admission that can take precedence over various specific exclusionary rules, or does it merely permit an expert to express and explain an opinion based on inadmissible evidence? May, in other words, the fact finder rely on the data to draw inferences concerning the material propositions in the case? Or is it "admissible" only to help the fact finder understand the opinion that is based on it? And if the latter is true, to what extent can the fact finder rely on the opinion in deciding the case? Only to the extent that independent admissible evidence of the basis of the opinion is produced?

Courts had taken inconsistent approaches to the problem. Some restricted the otherwise inadmissible data to be used solely to help the fact finder appraise the opinion. Some permitted the underlying data to be used substantively. An example of the former is United States v. Madrid, 673 F.2d 1114 (10th Cir. 1982), where the jury was instructed: "I have instructed you as to opinions by experts and that they may state their reasons for such opinions. You are not to consider such evidence for any other purpose than in evaluating the expert testimony." Unfortunately, the *Madrid* court did not explain how the jurors can consider the opinion unless they consider the basis of the opinion, and it is a puzzle. The jury can consider whether the opinion makes sense in light of its basis, but only if the basis is true will an opinion relate to the case at hand. This approach to the problem of FRE 703, while the typical response of the courts, makes very little sense. For other examples of this approach, see Sphere Drake Insurance PLC v. Trisko, 226 F.3d 951 (8th Cir. 2000) (affirming the jury instruction to "give no weight to the statements of [the informants] in the consideration of the issues in this case. You are to consider that testimony only in developing what [the expert witness] did in the course of his investigation."); United States v. Affleck, 776 F.2d 1451 (10th Cir. 1985).

An example of a court seeing that the typical response to this issue makes little sense is In re Melton, 597 A.2d 892 (D.C. 1991). In *Melton*, psychiatrists offered opinions concerning whether the respondent was a danger to himself or others. The opinions were based in part on accounts of the respondent's behavior given by his mother to the psychiatrists. In an interesting passage, the court captured the dilemma we are discussing:

> We begin by noting that the testimony by Dr. Byrd and Dr. Cornet as to what they learned from others was not admitted in order to prove the truth of the matter asserted. The trial judge specifically instructed the jury that any out-of-court statements by third parties which were reported in the experts' testimony were to be considered only "for the purpose of evaluating the reasonableness and correctness of the doctors' conclusions," and not "to establish the truth of the matters asserted by [the declarants]." As the court

explained in United States v. Williams, 447 F.2d 1285, 1290 (5th Cir. 1971) (en banc), *cert. denied*, 405 U.S. 954 (1972),

> an expert's opinion is derived not only from records and data, but from education and from a lifetime of experience. Thus, when the expert witness has consulted numerous sources, and uses that information, together with his own professional knowledge and experience, to arrive at his opinion, that opinion is regarded as evidence in its own right and not as hearsay in disguise.

The problem raised by Melton cannot, however, be avoided simply by calling the evidence expert testimony rather than hearsay. Labels cannot perform juridical alchemy. By resort[ing] to expert testimony, the District was able to bring to the jury's attention matters that could obviously prejudice Melton, including, e.g., reports that he had punched his mother, and that on an earlier occasion he had threatened his sister with a screwdriver. Melton was never able to cross-examine those who accused him of these anti-social acts. Such a procedure presents obvious problems of basic fairness. Courts are not blind to these concerns and have attempted to fashion rules which afford reasonable latitude to expert witnesses but simultaneously protect the rights of litigants against whom expert testimony has been offered. The tension between these competing interests is at the heart of this case.

The problem in *Melton* was exacerbated because the trial court gave its instruction four days after the evidence was admitted. Consequently, the appellate court treated the case as one in which no limiting instruction was given:

> Even if, as we have concluded, the psychiatric witnesses testified on the basis of the kind of data on which experts in their field reasonably rely, we have some concern for another reason about the admission and use of the evidence. If we look at the substance rather than the form of what occurred, the secondhand testimony about Melton having punched his mother came to the jurors' attention in such a way that they might well have considered it for the truth of the out-of-court statement. This may also have occurred with respect to some other incidents.

On October 17, 1985, Dr. Byrd testified that Melton "became impulsive and lost control of his temper, which is a characteristic of a schizophrenic. And he punched his mother in the nose and became very angry with her." The trial judge gave no contemporaneous instruction as to the purpose for which this testimony was received. It was not until four days later, during his final instructions, that the judge told the jurors, with respect to testimony by Dr. Byrd and Dr. Cornet as to information given to them by other individuals, that:

> these statements are admitted only to demonstrate the information relied upon by the doctors in forming their conclusion. They are to be considered by you only for the purpose of evaluating the reasonableness and correctness of the doctors' conclusions. They are not to be considered by you as actual proof of the incidents described. They are hearsay and as such are not admissible to establish the truth of the matters asserted by them.

This court has since noted that some students of the law of evidence consider the distinction sought to be articulated in such a "limiting" instruction as "most unlikely to be made by juries." In re Samuels, 507 A.2d 150 (D.C. 1986). As Judge Salzman aptly remarked for the court in that case, "conceptual problems are bound to arise when a judge tells a jury that the jury may consider psychiatric diagnoses based on medical records customarily relied on in professional practice, but then tells the jury that it may not consider the 'truthfulness' of those records for any other purpose." Id. With his customary eloquence, Justice Cardozo made a similar point for the Court in a somewhat different context in Shepard v. United States, 290 U.S. 96 (1933): "Discrimination so subtle is a feat beyond the compass of ordinary minds. The reverberating clang of those accusatory words would drown all weaker sounds. It is for ordinary minds, and not for psychoanalysts, that our rules of evidence are framed." The "conceptual" problems to which we referred in *Samuels* are especially serious with respect to a discreet dramatic act like punching one's mother on the nose. To tell the jurors that they are to consider the testimony about the punch as a basis for the expert's finding of dangerousness, but not with respect to whether Mr. Melton punched his mother, may call for mental gymnastics which only the most pristine theoretician could perform. We suspect that the reaction of that elusive individual, the reasonable person, would be that you cannot believe that the testimony about the punch tends to show that Melton is dangerous unless you first believe that he actually punched his mother. Since the expert apparently believed that he punched her, the jury was likely to believe it too. The distinction sought to be made may therefore become ephemeral.

The problem is a perplexing one, because it is difficult to articulate reasonable or workable limits on any rule which would exclude testimony of the kind here at issue and still vindicate the policies underlying Rule 703.

As the *Melton* court so aptly put it, "you cannot believe that the testimony about the punch tends to show that Melton is dangerous unless you first believe that he actually punched his mother." The restrictive approach exemplified above by the jury instruction from *Madrid* quite literally makes no sense. By contrast, permitting the admission of otherwise inadmissible evidence would not create a dangerous loophole in the rules for unreliable evidence (although there is some disagreement about this among the authors of this text). First, the admitted data would have to be data on which one could reasonably rely. If the data in question is reasonably reliable, even though it may be technically improper, accurate outcomes at trial are likely to be advanced by its admission. To admit data that is likely to advance accuracy hardly sounds like the creation of a regrettable loophole. See Boim v. Holy Land Foundation, 549 F.3d 685 (7th Cir. 2008) (allowing expert opinion based on unauthenticated websites and documents that "have long been accepted by security experts as valid, important, and indeed indispensable sources of information"). Indeed, the kind of information that would be admitted pursuant to a liberal reading of FRE 703 is likely to be significantly more reliable than other forms of admissible evidence under the rule. Reflect on our discussion at page 532, supra, of Beech Aircraft Corp. v. Rainey. As you recall, *Beech Aircraft Corp.* interpreted FRE 803(8)(c), which makes admissible over a hearsay objection "reports . . . setting forth . . . factual findings resulting from an investigation made pursuant to authority granted by law, unless the sources of information or other circumstances indicate lack of trustworthiness." The Court held that the phrase "factual findings" included opinions or inferences based on observations made during the investigation. In *Beech Aircraft Corp.*, the report in question contained the assertion that "[t]he most probable cause of the accident was the pilot's failure to maintain proper interval." If FRE 803(8)(c) indicates a baseline of reliability for the admission of evidence over technical objections such as hearsay or opinion, evidence reasonably relied on by experts in other disciplines clearly meets the test for admissibility.

Second, bear in mind that FRE 703 does not provide the only basis for excluding unreliable opinion testimony. FRE 702 requires that the subject matter be one that requires specialized knowledge to be understood, that the purported expert have that knowledge, and that the expert's opinion be of assistance to the fact finder. In addition, FRE 403 permits the exclusion of evidence whose probative value is substantially outweighed by various countervailing concerns of unreliability and inefficiency.

In any event, the amendment to FRE 703 resolves these matters in favor of the largely incoherent view that an opinion can be understood and credited independently of the basis for that opinion. This will leave intact the prior practice of most courts of excluding reference to the underlying data or giving juries an incomprehensible instruction concerning the use of the otherwise inadmissible evidence. It will also leave intact a practice that cannot conceivably advance the objective of rational decision-making. Quite remarkably, the Advisory Committee in its Note on this amendment failed even to address, let alone attempt to respond to in a coherent fashion, this fundamental point.

The amendment to FRE 703 adopts a balancing test that the proponent of the opinion (and thus the underlying facts) must meet before otherwise inadmissible facts that the expert "reasonably rel[ied] on" may be disclosed to the jury. This amendment does not eliminate, indeed may exacerbate, the conceptual confusion at the heart of the rule. It perpetuates the myth that one can appraise the expert's opinion without regard to the truth of facts relied upon by the expert, which is plainly false (as in *Melton*, he either hit his Mom or he didn't). Given that the amended rule remains so confused, it is perhaps not surprising that what it might possibly mean for the "probative value" of the underlying facts to "substantially outweigh their prejudicial effect" is completely opaque. Not surprisingly, the Advisory Committee's Note to the 2000 Amendment is rather sparse in this regard, noting only that "an adversary's attack on an expert's basis will often open the door to a proponent's rebuttal," and "in some circumstances the proponent might wish to disclose information that is relied upon by the expert in order to 'remove the sting' from the opponent's anticipated inference." The amendment to the rule was not necessary to permit a fair response. This suggests that the only example the Advisory Committee could come up with where the amendment to the rule would make a difference and that meets this "balancing" test is one in which the underlying facts were helpful to the opponent of the testimony. See McDevitt v. Guenther, 522 F. Supp. 2d 1272 (D. Haw. 2007) (holding it is permissible to base opinion on inadmissible hearsay, but reciting hearsay statements on the record — when statements related to facts disputed in the case — was in violation of FRE 703 because probative value was outweighed by prejudicial effect). Cf., Turner v. Burlington Northern Santa Fe RR, 338 F.3d 1058, 1062 (9th Cir. 2003) (applying balancing test to exclude evidence where underlying were facts helpful to proponent of testimony). But see Lexcel Solutions, Inc. v. Mastercard Intl, Inc., 2005 WL 5976566 (D. Ariz. 2005) (allowing the expert to testify about inadmissible evidence because it was not being offered for substance). Some courts, however, have allowed facts helpful to the proponent to be disclosed on direct. For example, in Mactec, Inc. v. Bechtel Jacobs Co., 346 Fed. Appx. 59 (6th Cir. 2009), the court allowed an expert to introduce into evidence interviews and other secondhand data when there was substantial evidence that such information was routinely used by experts in the field and the opponent had ample opportunity to challenge its credibility on cross. Nonetheless, what the cases will make of this mess of a rule, more generally, remains to be seen. If, for example, this rule applied to the *Melton* case, we have no idea how the case would have come out.

A new wrinkle is added to the implications of FRE 703 by way of *Crawford* and *Melendez-Diaz*, which are reproduced and discussed at greater length at pages 581-615. At least one case has held that statements to psychiatrists are testimonial, thus triggering the *Crawford* analysis. People v. Goldstein, 843 N.E.2d 727 (N.Y. 2005). Similarly, the Second Circuit did not allow an expert on gang culture to describe specific information related to gang procedures because the information was gathered through custodial interrogations with informants, and thus based on testimonial out-of-court statements. United States v. Mejia, 545 F.3d 179 (2d Cir. 2008). Other courts, however, have restricted the application of both *Crawford* and *Melendez-Diaz*. For example, the Seventh Circuit allowed the unit head in a drug testing facility to testify about work completed by an employee, when he had reviewed the findings and signed off on the results. The court emphasized that, unlike in *Melendez-Diaz*, the report in question was not admitted into evidence or presented in the form of a sworn affidavit. Instead, the unit head testified "as an expert witness presenting his own conclusions about the substances in question to the jury." Thus, because *Melendez-Diez* "did not do away with [FRE] 703," the testimony was admissible. United States v. Turner, 591 F.3d 928 (7th Cir. 2010) (internal citations omitted). See also United States v. Ayala, 601 F.3d 256 (4th Cir. 2010) ("[T]he question when applying *Crawford* to expert testimony is whether the expert is, in essence, giving an independent judgment or merely acting as a transmitter for testimonial hearsay.") (internal quotations omitted); United States v. Henry, 472 F.3d 910 (D.C. Cir. 2007) ("*Crawford*, however, did not involve expert witness testimony and thus did not alter an expert witness's ability to rely on (without repeating to the jury) otherwise inadmissible evidence in formulating his opinion under Federal Rule of Evidence 703."); United States v. Forstell, 656 F. Supp. 2d 578 (E.D. Va. 2009) (holding *Melendez-Diaz* does not apply to every person involved in establishing chain of custody or accuracy of testing devices). For more information see Julie A. Seaman, *Triangular Testimonial Hearsay: The Constitutional Boundaries of Expert Opinion Testimony*, 96 Geo. L.J. 827 (2008).

KEY POINTS

1. Under FRE 702, an expert is simply a person with knowledge not likely to be possessed by the fact finder, and they may testify to basic facts, general principles, or inferences to be drawn from the basic facts.

2. The Federal Rules have eliminated the necessity, but not the possibility, of testifying in the form of an answer to a hypothetical question. Under FRE 705, an expert may give an opinion before the basis of the opinion is offered into evidence.

3. FRE 703 allows opinions based on reasonably reliable but otherwise inadmissible data. The underlying data normally is not admitted at trial. On occasion it is admitted but only for purposes of appraising the opinion, even though the data only matters for that purpose if true.

PROBLEMS

9.18. Wally Daniels is charged with murder and arson. The prosecution's theory is that Wally killed his wife and then, at about 7:00 P.M., set fire to the house in order to make the death look like an accident. Wally claims that he was not near the house at the relevant times and that the fire was the result of bad electrical wiring. The prosecutor's expert, a fire marshal, offers to testify that in his opinion the fire was the result of arson. The fire marshal is prepared to testify about the bases for his opinion, which include, inter alia, the following:

(a)   interviews with next door neighbors, John and Wilma Smith, who say they saw Wally running from the house at about 7:00 P.M. shortly before they noticed the fire;

(b)   a written police report prepared by Officer June Adkins, stating that she was patrolling the area shortly before the fire was discovered and that she observed an adult male running from the defendant's house at about 7:00 P.M.; and

(c)   the fact that Wally had twice previously been convicted of arson.

Wally has objected to all of this evidence. To support the objection, he offers to prove that John Smith is an alcoholic who almost daily is in an alcohol-induced stupor from 3:00 P.M. until midnight. What result?

9.19. Waitress Tina Brennan received an electric shock from a coffee maker while working and allegedly developed fibromyalgia as a result. Ms. Brennan brought a personal injury suit against Reinhart Corp., the manufacturer and installer of the coffee maker. At trial, her vocational rehabilitation counselor Mr. Ostrander testified that in his opinion Ms. Brennan's fibromyalgia would be a permanent condition. As part of the basis for this conclusion, Ostrander stated that Ms. Brennan's rheumatologist had reported that the plaintiff had "permanent partial impairment of 11 percent of the whole person" and that her specialist in physical medicine and rehabilitation had also examined the patient and agreed with Ostrander's analysis. The defense objected to Ostrander's use of out-of-court hearsay, pointing out that both the rheumatologist and the specialist would be unavailable for cross-examination and, although the rheumatologist had given testimony by deposition, he had not mentioned the 11 percent impairment conclusion. The jury returned a verdict for the plaintiff and the defendant appealed, maintaining that the trial court erred in allowing Ostrander to summarize the opinions of others. Should the appellate court reverse?

9.20. A year after Jimmy Boyd complained about a racial slur made by his supervisor, he received an unfavorable performance review and subsequently remained absent from work for over five weeks. He was terminated after his psychologists reported that his leave was not medically required. Boyd brought suit under the Family Medical Leave Act (FMLA).

During the initial hearing, the employer offered the depositions of Boyd's treating physicians, neither of whom supported Boyd's claim that his absence, purportedly due to the stress and anxiety of his job, constituted protected leave under the FMLA. Boyd responded with the affidavit testimony of his expert witness, Dr. Emory:

> Based upon my review of the records and my examination of Mr. Boyd, it is my professional opinion that Mr. Boyd's health condition rendered him unable to perform his job, and in fact left him disabled. Continued work would have increased his health problems and, in my professional opinion, the only solution to Mr. Boyd's medical condition would have been a leave of absence. At a minimum, Mr. Boyd required a leave of absence to obtain treatment for his condition.

The district court excluded the affidavit, finding that it was "vague and conclusory," provided no foundation for Dr. Emory's conclusions, and spoke only in general terms. On appeal, Boyd argued that Dr. Emory's affidavit should not have been excluded because Rule 705 permitted Dr. Emory to give his opinion without prior disclosure of the underlying facts and data. If allowed, Dr. Emory's statements would create a genuine issue of fact as to whether he suffered a serious health condition under FMLA. Should the court admit Dr. Emory's testimony?

9.21. David Ricci was an environmental engineer doing testing on defendant companies' biomass smoke stack when he fell to his death from a platform surrounding the stack. The platform was about 80 feet from the ground and a ladder ran up the stack's side to the platform. No eyewitnesses saw the fall but Ricci's father inferred that his son inadvertently stepped through the platform ladderway opening that admittedly was missing safety guards, and sued the stack's owner based on this theory. Defendants inferred that the fall occurred as the son descended the ladder.

A safety inspector was qualified as an expert for the plaintiff and testified at trial that it was more probable than not that Ricci had inadvertently fallen through the ladderway opening. This opinion was based in part on statements from Ricci's father and coworkers that Ricci was always careful and that it was his practice to wear gloves while climbing. The defense objected. Do you think the father's and coworkers' testimonials are of the type of data "reasonably relied upon by experts in the particular field"?

9.22. In a criminal trial, the defendant pleaded not guilty by reason of insanity. The prosecution called a psychiatrist as an expert witness to testify to an opinion that the defendant was sane at the time he committed the criminal act. During direct examination, the witness was asked how confident he was in his opinion. He responded: "Very confident. Indeed, I called Dr. Smith, the world's leading expert in this particular area. I explained the case and my diagnosis to him, and he concurred in my conclusions." The defense counsel objected and moved to strike this answer. Should it be stricken?

C.   OPINIONS ON AN ULTIMATE ISSUE

In the most radical rejection of the common law dealing with opinion testimony, the Federal Rules explicitly permit opinion on ultimate issues in all save one situation.

1.   FRE 704

RULE 704.   OPINION ON AN ULTIMATE ISSUE

(a) *In General* — Not Automatically Objectionable. An opinion is not objectionable just because it embraces an ultimate issue.

(b) *Exception*. In a criminal case, an expert witness must not state an opinion about whether the defendant did or did not have a mental state or condition that constitutes an element of the crime charged or of a defense.

2.   Interpretation and Illustration of FRE 704(a)

In the nineteenth and early twentieth century a number of courts adopted the rule that witnesses — lay as well as expert — could not offer opinions on an ultimate issue in a case. The typical rationale for this rule was that such an opinion would invade the province of the jury. As Wigmore pointed out, it is not clear how or why an opinion on an ultimate issue "invades the province of the jury." 7 John Henry Wigmore, Evidence §1920 at 18 (James Chadbourn rev. 1978). Indeed, it is not entirely clear what constitutes an opinion on an ultimate issue. Consider a case in which the defendant is charged with possessing drugs with the intent to sell them. Presumably, it would be an opinion on an ultimate issue for a narcotics officer to testify that the amount of drugs possessed by the defendant indicated that the defendant intended to sell the drugs. But would it be an opinion on an ultimate issue for the officer (1) to testify that the amount possessed was far in excess of what one would possess for personal use or (2) to offer her opinion about how much of the particular drug a typical user or addict is likely to consume in a given period of time? If not, the prohibition against opinions on an ultimate issue would appear to be more one of form than of substance.

The foregoing example illustrates both the benefit and one of the potential problems with opinions about matters that are, or are closely related to, ultimate issues in a lawsuit. Jurors unfamiliar with the use of drugs may not know what quantities of a particular drug individuals are likely to possess for personal use. Thus, the narcotics officer's testimony can be helpful — indeed, perhaps critical — to the jury's evaluation of the defendant's intent. The narcotics officer's testimony would be most helpful if the jury were assured of learning the basis for the officer's opinion, for example, how much of the particular drug a person can be expected to use in a given period of time and the habits of drug users with respect to stockpiling. Yet the prosecutor may fail to bring out all of the underlying data on direct examination for fear of running afoul of the "ultimate opinion" rule, and defense counsel may be reluctant to explore the matter on cross-examination for fear of bolstering the officer's testimony. If the subject matter of the opinion testimony is not critical to the resolution of the lawsuit, the failure to develop the underlying facts may not be a problem of major concern. It is particularly important, however, that jurors have as much detailed factual information as possible on the ultimate issues in a lawsuit, for the resolution of those issues is their primary responsibility.

There are at least two other potential problems with opinions about ultimate issues. First, even if jurors have all of the underlying facts and data and are fully capable of resolving the ultimate issues, the mere fact that they hear witnesses express opinions on those issues may mislead them into believing that they should give some special deference to the opinions. Why else would the evidence be presented to them? Second, if an opinion on an ultimate issue embraces a legal concept or conclusion, there may be uncertainty about whether the expert is using that concept in the same manner in which the law uses it.

Adequate means exist for dealing with these potential problems without altogether prohibiting opinions on an ultimate issue. The judge has the discretion to exclude opinions that are not helpful (see, e.g., FRE 701 and 702) or whose probative value is substantially outweighed by the possibility of confusing or misleading the jury (see, e.g., FRE 403). If there is a concern that the underlying facts and data may not be forthcoming, the judge can require that they be set forth before the opinion is offered (see, e.g., FRE 705); and if there is concern that the expert's use of a particular term may differ from the legal definition of a term, the judge can deal with this possibility in the instructions to the jury.

During the last several decades a number of courts have rejected an absolute prohibition against opinions on ultimate issues, but at the same time courts generally prohibit opinions on questions of law. If by "questions of law" one means questions that are for the judge rather than the jury to decide, it is obviously appropriate that jurors not hear evidence on the issue in any form. The evidence from their perspective would be irrelevant. On the other hand, if the issue is one for the jury to decide, there would appear to be no sound reason to prohibit an opinion merely because one can characterize the issue as embodying "law" or a "legal concept." Indeed, to have a rule that prohibits opinions on jury issues that are characterized as questions of law — or, as some courts have said, "mixed questions of law and fact"[9] — and, at the same time, to permit opinions about ultimate issues of "fact" may lead to an abstract, meaningless debate about whether the issue is one of "fact" or "law."[10] There may, of course, be times when an opinion embracing a legal concept would be confusing (e.g., if the witness were using the term differently from the manner in which the law used it) or not very helpful (e.g., if it were a substitute for the underlying facts and data). Courts can deal adequately with these problems on a case-by-case basis, just as they can deal adequately on a case-by-case basis with opinions on ultimate issues of "fact." Regardless of how one characterizes the issue to which the opinion is directed, the critical question should be whether the opinion will be helpful to the jury.

3. Interpretation and Illustration of FRE 704(b)

FRE 704, as promulgated by the Supreme Court and initially adopted by Congress, followed the lead of those courts that had rejected the prohibition against opinions on an ultimate issue. FRE 704 provided that there was no such general prohibition for opinions on an "ultimate issue to be decided by the trier of fact." According to the Advisory Committee:

> The older cases often contained strictures against allowing witnesses to express opinions upon ultimate issues. . . . The rule was unduly restrictive, difficult of application, and generally served only to deprive the trier of fact of useful information. . . . Efforts to meet the felt needs of particular situations led to odd verbal circumlocutions which were said not to violate the rule. Thus a witness could express his estimate of the criminal responsibility of an accused in terms of sanity or insanity, but not in terms of ability to tell right from wrong or other more modern standard. And in cases of medical causation, witnesses were sometimes required to couch their opinions in cautious phrases of "might or could," rather than "did," though the result was to deprive many opinions of the positiveness to which they were entitled, accompanied by the hazard of a ruling of insufficiency to support a verdict. In other instances the rule was simply disregarded, and, as concessions to need, opinions were allowed upon such matters as intoxication, speed, handwriting, and value, although more precise coincidence with an ultimate issue would scarcely be possible.

---

9.   See, e.g., Grismore v. Consolidated Products Co., 232 Iowa 328, 5 N.W.2d 646 (1942) (opinions on ultimate questions of fact permissible, but opinions on questions of law or questions of mixed fact and law not permissible).

10.   See, e.g., State v. Ogg, 243 N.W.2d 620 (Iowa 1976) (in prosecution for possession of LSD with intent to distribute, prosecution witness testified that in his opinion the amount of drugs possessed by defendant far exceeded the amount one would possess for personal use; majority and dissent disagree on whether witness's testimony is impermissible opinion of law, with majority labeling opinion as one of law).

In 1984, in the aftermath of John Hinckley's acquittal on insanity grounds of the attempt to assassinate President Reagan, there was substantial public debate about and criticism of the insanity defense. Congress enacted legislation that for the first time provided a federal statutory definition for insanity and that made insanity an affirmative defense that must be proved by the defendant. As part of that legislation, Congress amended FRE 704 to add FRE 704(b).

According to the Report of the House Judiciary Committee (quoting an earlier Senate Judiciary Committee Report):

> The purpose of this amendment is to eliminate the confusing spectacle of competing expert witnesses testifying to directly contradictory conclusions as to the ultimate legal issue to be found by the trier of fact. Under this proposal, expert psychiatric testimony would be limited to presenting and explaining their diagnoses, such as whether the defendant had a severe mental disease or defect and what the characteristics of such a disease or defect, if any, may have been . . . .
>
> Moreover, the rationale for precluding ultimate opinion psychiatric testimony extends beyond the insanity defense to any ultimate mental state of the defendant that is relevant to the legal conclusion sought to be proven. The Committee has fashioned its Rule 704 provision to reach all such "ultimate" issues, e.g., premeditation in a homicide case, or lack of predisposition in entrapment.

In support of this view, the Committee quoted from the American Psychiatric Association's Statement on the Insanity Defense (1982):

> [I]t is clear that psychiatrists are experts in medicine, not the law. As such, it is clear that the psychiatrist's first obligation and expertise in the courtroom is to "do psychiatry," i.e., to present medical information and opinion about the defendant's mental state and motivation and to explain in detail the reason for his medical-psychiatric conclusions. When, however, "ultimate issue" questions are formulated by the law and put to the expert witness who must then say "yea" or "nay," then the expert witness is required to make a leap in logic. He no longer addresses himself to medical concepts but instead must infer or intuit what is in fact unspeakable, namely, the probable relationship between medical concepts and legal or moral constructs such as free will. These impermissible leaps in logic made by expert witnesses confuse the jury. Juries thus find themselves listening to conclusory psychiatric testimony that defendants are either "sane" or "insane" or that they do or do not meet the relevant legal test for insanity. This state of affairs does considerable injustice to psychiatry and, we believe, possibly to criminal defendants. In fact, in many criminal insanity trials both prosecution and defense psychiatrists do agree about the nature and even the extent of mental disorder exhibited by the defendant at the time of the act.
>
> Psychiatrists, of course, must be permitted to testify fully about the defendant's diagnosis, mental state and motivation (in clinical and common sense terms) at the time of the alleged act so as to permit the jury or judge to reach the ultimate conclusion about which they and only they are expert. Determining whether a criminal defendant was legally insane is a matter for legal fact finders, not for experts.

Do you think that jurors may sometimes have difficulty relating a psychiatrist's diagnosis to the legal standard for insanity without some expert assistance? If so, does the problem lie with the amendment to FRE 704 or with the legal definition of insanity or both?

Even if a witness cannot offer an opinion about a defendant's "sanity," "premeditation," "predisposition," or other mental state, is it likely that jurors will be unaware of what the witness feels about such an issue? If not, of what practical benefit is the amendment to FRE 704? Keeping in mind that FRE 403, 701, 702, and 705 are available to regulate opinion testimony about ultimate issues, do you believe that the amendment to FRE 704 improved the Federal Rules of Evidence?

Note again how the crucial issue is the unstated distinction between education and deference. Provisions like FRE 704(b) only matter in a system willing to defer to the opinions of experts. In a system that required the expert to play an educational role, FRE 704(b) would be superfluous. Even if an opinion were offered, the fact finder would be in a position to appraise it rather than simply defer to or reject it. Only if we fear silly or capricious opinions to which fact finders might defer because of ignorance do provisions like FRE 704(b) make sense. If that is the case, however, the problem lies in the structure of litigation that allows the responsibility for deliberate, rational decision to be transferred from the juridical fact finder, judge or jury, to third party "experts."

KEY POINT

The Federal Rules have rejected the common law limitation forbidding opinions on ultimate issues, except for opinions concerning the mental states of criminal defendants.

PROBLEMS

9.23. Reconsider the narcotics possession hypothetical set forth at page 694, supra. To what extent and in what manner does the amendment to FRE 704 restrict the ability of the narcotics officer from offering helpful evidence about the defendant's intent?

9.24. Edward Santos is being tried for threatening to kill President Bill Clinton. In its attempts to prove the mental element of the crime, the prosecution elicits testimony from a psychiatric expert that Santos's efforts to "throw people off his trail" indicate that he "knew what he was doing was wrong." As an attorney for the defense, make an objection. Do you think you will be able to persuade the judge that the statements should be stricken from the record?

9.25. Taxpayer D was accused of making erroneous deductions from his taxable income. The government claimed that he owed over $200,000. The tax court in which the case was heard excluded two letters from certified public accountants that contained analyses that led to the conclusion that the law did not preclude Taxpayer D from making these deductions. Taxpayer D appealed, arguing that Rule 704(a) supports the admission of these reports. Did the court err?

9.26. Corey Boyd was convicted by a jury in the United States District Court for the District of Columbia for possession with intent to distribute crack cocaine. Boyd was arrested after police officers briefly spotted him on the street holding a plastic bag between himself and another individual. The officers observed the two men for only a couple of seconds, so they could not see precisely what Boyd and his compatriot were doing, nor could they tell who controlled the plastic bag that was between them. Neither Boyd nor his compatriot was heard to say anything, nor seen to do anything (other than look into the plastic bag), and no money or drug paraphernalia was seen or found. Both men ran upon being spotted by the police, Boyd with the plastic bag still in hand. While being chased, he threw the bag under a truck, and it was recovered by the police. During his trial, the government introduced the expert testimony of Officer Stroud, who testified that, on the basis of a "hypothetical situation" exactly mirroring the facts of Boyd's arrest, in his opinion, the hypothetical facts showed possession with intent to distribute. Is there a problem with, or an appropriate objection to, this testimony?

9.27. Latana Slayton worked as a corrections officer for the Ohio Department of Youth Services with her coworker Corry Appline. In a suit against her employer, Slayton alleged that the DYS maintained a hostile work environment in which she was required to endure routine sexual harassment. Appline, she claimed, encouraged the young men to drop their towels while Slayton was on shower duty, sent her to check on an inmate who he knew was masturbating at the time, and provided the inmates with sexually explicit movies and music that referred to women as "bitches." On several occasions, Slayton sought redress from her superiors, who never took any action to remedy the situation. During the jury trial, the judge permitted the lay opinions of Slayton's supervisors that the alleged conduct violated its internal sexual harassment policy. During the testimony of one of the supervisors, the judge interrupted to ask: "Hypothesize that the plaintiff's testimony is true. In your view does that constitute under the terms of your policy, the state's policy, does that constitute sexual harassment in the workplace?" The supervisor answered that it would. After a verdict for the plaintiff, the defense appealed claiming that the lay opinions of the supervisors were inadmissible because they spoke to the ultimate issue. Was the trial judge right to allow the testimony?

9.28. Joe, a United States citizen of Filipino dissent, is suing his employer for discrimination. Joe asserts that he was denied a promotion because of his national origin. His employers counter that they decided to hire from outside the company because of certain perceived dissension within the ranks of its present employees. The employers called one of their directors, Mr. Queeg, to the witness stand. Queeg had taken part in the hiring of the new employee. Defense counsel asked Queeg, "Is it true that you did not believe that Joe had been discriminated against in the interview process because of his national origin?" Over the defense's objection, Queeg was allowed to answer that counsel's statement was correct. Should Queeg's opinion testimony have been allowed before the jury?

9.29. Mark Bruck's business was failing when he purchased additional insurance to cover a building into which he moved equipment and highly flammable substances. The building burned down and Bruck was charged with arson and bank fraud. At trial, the prosecution called an expert who testified as follows:

Q: (By Asst. U.S. Attorney Kinder). Based on the training and experience you have had in arson investigations, have you learned that there's certain indicators in an arson for profit scheme that you look for?
MR. MURRAY [Defense counsel]:   Objection.
THE COURT: He may testify.
A: Yes.
Q: Did you find any of those indicators for the investigation of the Advance Resins' fire?
A: Yes, I did.

Q: What were they?
A: The fire was deliberately set in multiple locations. The fire was set for economic —
MR. MURRAY: I object and move to strike. That is a conclusion left to the jury's determination, not this agent's.
THE COURT: Well, he may give his opinion based on his experience, background and training, and on the number of fires he's investigated, teaching experience and so forth. Based on that, he may give his opinion as to whether or not it was a set fire and to show how he determined it.

After his conviction, Bruck argued on appeal that the expert's testimony was inadmissible under Rule 704(b). Was it error for the court to allow the expert to testify in this way?

D. COURT APPOINTED EXPERTS

1. FRE 706

RULE 706. COURT APPOINTED EXPERT WITNESSES

(a) *Appointment Process.* On a party's motion or on its own, the court may order the parties to show cause why expert witnesses should not be appointed and may ask the parties to submit nominations. The court may appoint any expert witness that the parties agree on and any of its own choosing. But the court may only appoint someone who consents to act.

(b) *Expert's Role.* The court must inform the expert of the expert's duties. The Court may do so in writing and have a copy filed with the clerk or may do so orally at a conference in which the parties have an opportunity to participate. The expert:

(1) must advise the parties of any findings the expert makes;
(2) may be deposed by any party;
(3) may be called to testify by the court or any party; and
(4) may be cross-examined by any party, including the party that called the expert.

(c) *Compensation.* The expert is entitled to reasonable compensation, as set by the court. The compensation is payable as follows:

(1) in a criminal case or in a civil case involving just compensation under the Fifth Amendment, from any funds that are provided by law; and

(2) in any other civil case, by the parties in the proportion and at the time that the court directs — and the compensation is then charged like other costs.

(d) *Disclosing the Appointment to the Jury.* The court may authorize disclosure to the jury that the court appointed the expert.

(e) *Parties' Choice of Their Own Experts.* This rule does not limit a party in calling its own experts.

2. Interpretation and Illustration of FRE 706

FRE 706 permits courts to appoint their own experts. The advantage in doing so is the securing of disinterested, objective testimony concerning the issues in the case. This can provide a fact finder with important information when the adversarial system fails to bring the two sides of an issue to light. See, e.g., Grove v. Principle Mutual Life Insurance Co., 200 F.R.D. 434 (S.D. Iowa 2001) (appointing two experts to assist the court where both parties in a class action suit supported a settlement agreement but what was missing was someone to play the "devil's advocate"). The disadvantage is that many disciplines have internal disputes so that any expert selected by the court would not be truly "objective," but instead would be testifying from the perspective of one not universally shared view of the field. A good example of this is psychiatry. Freudian psychiatrists are called as expert witnesses, yet very little within the field has been empirically verified. As a consequence, psychiatry as a field is moving away from Freudian concepts, yet Freudian concepts still have their adherents.[11] The choice of an "expert" in psychiatry must thus resolve the contested issue of the validity of these concepts. As a consequence of problems like this, courts have essentially refused to take advantage of the power given them by this rule, leaving it a functional dead letter and the parties to fight out among themselves basic disciplinary disputes when necessary for the adjudication of a case. The lawyers view this favorably, for they are disinclined to have judges interfere with their presentation of the case. Our view is that this is regrettable, and leads to such spectacles as juries rejecting the implications of DNA testing or accepting explanations of pertinent matters that are virtually without any rational support. At least one Circuit court agrees. In DeKoven v. Plaza Associates, the Seventh Circuit pointed out that a neutral expert in a Fair Debt Collection Case could be a "possible alternative to the often unedifying spectacle of a battle of party-appointed experts," and suggested that, at least in such cases, "[d]istrict judges may want to consider exercising the clearly authorized but rarely exercised option of appointing their own expert." 599 F.3d 578 (7th Cir. 2010). The best that can be said to the contrary is that the refusal of judges to employ this rule reduces somewhat the tendency toward the creation of an official orthodoxy, thus leaving all factual matters constantly open for reconsideration. Such epistemological modesty has its virtues, but also its price. For a discussion of court-appointed expert panels, see Karen Butler Reisinger, Court-Appointed Expert Panels: A Comparison of Two Models, 32 Ind. L. Rev. 225 (1998).

Rule 706 did come into use in one area: the litigation of silicone breast implant tort claims. U.S. District Judge Robert E. Jones, while he was overseeing all federal breast implant litigation in Oregon, noted that "litigation over the ability of silicone gel breast implants to cause disease in women has been chaotic in its results" and thus appointed a panel of independent experts to review all of the scientific evidence supporting the plaintiffs' claim that breast implants have caused serious diseases in women. See Hall v. Baxter Healthcare Corp., 947 F. Supp. 1387 (1996). In this decision, however, Judge Jones made the interesting decision to appoint the panel under FRE 104 (Preliminary Questions) rather than under FRE 706. He appointed a panel of "technical advisors," representing the fields of epidemiology, rheumatology, immunology, toxicology, and polymer chemistry, but refrained from designating them as court appointed experts "[t]o keep the advisors independent of any ongoing proceedings." Faced with the daunting task of evaluating extensive scientific evidence in silicone breast implant cases, other courts followed suit. U.S. District Judges Jack Weinstein and Harold Baer, Jr., who managed all breast implants cases in the U.S. District Courts for the Eastern and Southern Districts of New York respectively, came

---

11.   For an interesting review of the status of Freudian psychiatry, see Frederick Crews, The Memory Wars (1997).

up with a similar plan but named a team of three special masters to help determine the types of expertise that would be needed in a Rule 706 panel. See Mark Hansen, Panel to Examine Implant Evidence: Unusual Move by Two New York Federal Judges Could be Copied Elsewhere, A.B.A. J., June 1996, at 34.

The most far-reaching order was issued by Judge Samuel Pointer of the U.S. District Court for the Northern District of Alabama, who was at the time coordinating about 21,000 cases on a pretrial basis. In a two-step plan, Judge Pointer appointed a "Selection Panel" whose duty it would be to recommend to the court the names of "neutral, impartial persons," qualified to sit on the "Science Panel" and "review, critique, and evaluate exiting scientific literature, research, and publications — addressing such matters as the meaning, utility, significance, and limitations of such studies — on topics as, from time to time, may be identified by the Court as relevant in breast-implant litigation, particularly on issues of 'general causation.'" Order No. 31 (May 31, 1996). As Judge Pointer envisioned it, the appointments would be made on a national basis "for potential use in all federal courts and as permitted in state courts." Though both the attorneys for the plaintiffs and for the defendants expressed some trepidation about the process, Rule 706 preserves a party's right to call its own expert witnesses and to cross-examine the court appointed experts. The four member panel of scientists eventually appointed by Judge Pointer, issued a report in December of 1998, after two years of investigation, concluding that the evidence had not yet shown that silicone breast implants caused disease, though the connection might still be established in the future. By all accounts, the report was very damaging to plaintiffs, who now found themselves in a disadvantaged position for settlement and with diminished prospects for success at trial. In the years since the report was issued, judges from many jurisdictions have cited the panel's findings as support for exclusion of expert testimony intended to prove a causal link between implants and disease. See, e.g., Pozefsky v. Baxter Healthcare Corp., 2001 U.S. Dist. LEXIS 11813 (N.D.N.Y. Aug. 16, 2001); Havard v. Baxter International Inc., 2000 U.S. Dist. LEXIS 21316 (N.D. Ohio, July 21, 2000); Toledo v. Medical Engineering Corp., 50 Pa. D. & C.4th 129 (C.P. Ct. Phila. Cnty., Dec. 29, 2000). Though the courts succeeded in adopting a more efficient system of hearing expert testimony, do you think that one court should be able to exercise so great an influence over the success of cases in so many jurisdictions?

E.   RECENT CONTROVERSIES IN FORENSIC SCIENCE AND VARIETIES OF SCIENTIFIC EVIDENCE AND EXPERT TESTIMONY

1.   Problems in Forensic Science

Herein we examine different kinds of scientific evidence and expert testimony that have, for one reason or another, caused difficulties for the courts. Interestingly, it was only recently that DNA evidence was regularly questioned by defendants and courts. Now, while it seems that the acceptance of most DNA evidence is firmly rooted in the judicial system, more traditional methods of forensic science are causing controversy because they lack the theoretical scientific basis of DNA.

The concerns about the dearth of detailed analysis outside of DNA lead Congress to authorize a study of forensic sciences. In 2009, under the supervision of the National Academy of Sciences (NAS), members of the forensic community, including crime laboratories, legal experts, and medical examiners, published a report on the serious problems present in the traditional forensic science fields as well as recommendations on how best to solve them. Selected excerpts from the report follow.[12]

CHALLENGES FACING THE FORENSIC SCIENCE COMMUNITY

For decades, the forensic science disciplines have produced valuable evidence that has contributed to the successful prosecution and conviction of criminals as well as to the exoneration of innocent people. Over the last two decades, advances in some forensic science disciplines, especially the use of DNA technology, have demonstrated that some areas of forensic science have great additional potential to help law enforcement identify criminals. Many crimes that may have gone unsolved are now being solved because forensic science is helping to identify the perpetrators.

Those advances, however, also have revealed that, in some cases, substantive information and testimony based on faulty forensic science analyses may have contributed to wrongful convictions of innocent people. This fact has demonstrated the potential danger of giving undue weight to evidence and testimony derived from imperfect testing and analysis. Moreover, imprecise or exaggerated expert testimony has sometimes contributed to the admission of erroneous or misleading evidence.

Further advances in the forensic science disciplines will serve three important purposes. First, further improvements will assist law enforcement officials in the course of their investigations to identify perpetrators with higher reliability. Second, further improvements in forensic science practices should reduce the occurrence of wrongful convictions, which reduces the risk that true offenders continue to commit crimes while innocent persons inappropriately serve time. Third, any improvements in the forensic science disciplines will undoubtedly enhance the Nation's ability to address the needs of homeland security.

. . .

PROBLEMS RELATING TO THE INTERPRETATION OF FORENSIC EVIDENCE

Often in criminal prosecutions and civil litigation, forensic evidence is offered to support conclusions about "individualization" (sometimes referred to as "matching" a specimen to a particular individual or other source) or about classification of the source of the specimen into one of several categories. With the exception of nuclear DNA analysis, however, no forensic method has been rigorously shown to have the capacity to consistently, and with a high degree of certainty, demonstrate a connection between evidence and a specific individual or source. In terms of scientific basis, the analytically based disciplines generally hold a notable edge over disciplines based on expert interpretation. But there are important variations among the disciplines relying on expert interpretation. For example, there are more established protocols and available research for fingerprint analysis than for the analysis of bite marks. There also are significant variations within each discipline. For example, not all fingerprint evidence is equally good, because the true value of the evidence is determined by the quality of the latent fingerprint image. These disparities between and within the forensic science disciplines highlight a major problem in the forensic science community: The simple reality is that the interpretation

---

12.   The National Academies, Strengthening Forensic Science in the United States: A Path Forward (2009) [hereinafter NAS Report 2009].

of forensic evidence is not always based on scientific studies to determine its validity. This is a serious problem. Although research has been done in some disciplines, there is a notable dearth of peer-reviewed, published studies establishing the scientific bases and validity of many forensic methods.

. . .

THE ADMISSION OF FORENSIC SCIENCE EVIDENCE IN LITIGATION

Forensic science experts and evidence are used routinely in the service of the criminal justice system. DNA testing may be used to determine whether sperm found on a rape victim came from an accused party; a latent fingerprint found on a gun may be used to determine whether a defendant handled the weapon; drug analysis may be used to determine whether pills found in a person's possession were illicit; and an autopsy may be used to determine the cause and manner of death of a murder victim. In order for qualified forensic science experts to testify competently about forensic evidence, they must first find the evidence in a usable state and properly preserve it. A latent fingerprint that is badly smudged when found cannot be usefully saved, analyzed, or explained. An inadequate drug sample may be insufficient to allow for proper analysis. And, DNA tests performed on a contaminated or otherwise compromised sample cannot be used reliably to identify or eliminate an individual as the perpetrator of a crime. These are important matters involving the proper processing of forensic evidence. The law's greatest dilemma in its heavy reliance on forensic evidence, however, concerns the question of whether — and to what extent — there is *science* in any given forensic science discipline.

Two very important questions should underlie the law's admission of and reliance upon forensic evidence in criminal trials: (1) the extent to which a particular forensic discipline is founded on a reliable scientific methodology that gives it the capacity to accurately analyze evidence and report findings and (2) the extent to which practitioners in a particular forensic discipline rely on human interpretation that could be tainted by error, the threat of bias, or the absence of sound operational procedures and robust performance standards. These questions are significant. Thus, it matters a great deal whether an expert is qualified to testify about forensic evidence and whether the evidence is sufficiently reliable to merit a fact finder's reliance on the truth that it purports to support. Unfortunately, these important questions do not always produce satisfactory answers in judicial decisions pertaining to the admissibility of forensic science evidence proffered in criminal trials.

In 1993, in Daubert v. Merrell Dow Pharmaceuticals, Inc.,[13] the Supreme Court ruled that, under Rule 702 of the Federal Rules of Evidence (which covers both civil trials and criminal prosecutions in the federal courts), a "trial judge must ensure that any and all scientific testimony or evidence admitted is not only relevant, but reliable."[14] The Court indicated that the subject of an expert's testimony should be scientific knowledge, so that "evidentiary reliability will be based upon scientific validity."[15] The Court also emphasized that, in considering the admissibility of evidence, a trial judge should focus "solely" on the expert's "principles and methodology," and "not on the conclusions that they generate."[16] In sum, *Daubert*'s requirement that an expert's testimony pertain to "scientific knowledge" established a standard of "evidentiary reliability."[17]

13.   509 U.S. 579 (1993).
14.   Ibid., p. 589.
15.   Ibid., pp. 590 and 591 n.9 (emphasis omitted).
16.   Ibid., p. 595. In General Electric Co. v. Joiner, 522 U.S. 136, 146 (1997), the Court added: "[C]onclusions and methodology are not entirely distinct from one another. Trained experts commonly extrapolate from existing data. But nothing in *Daubert* or the Federal Rules of Evidence requires a district court to admit opinion evidence that is connected to existing data only by the *ipse dixit* of the expert."
17.   *Daubert*, 509 U.S. at 589, 590 n.9, 595.

In explaining this evidentiary standard, the *Daubert* Court pointed to several factors that might be considered by a trial judge: (1) whether a theory or technique can be (and has been) tested; (2) whether the theory or technique has been subjected to peer review and publication; (3) the known or potential rate of error of a particular scientific technique; (4) the existence and maintenance of standards controlling the technique's operation; and (5) a scientific technique's degree of acceptance within a relevant scientific community.[18] In the end, however, the Court emphasized that the inquiry under Rule 702 is "a flexible one."[19] The Court expressed confidence in the adversarial system, noting that "[v]igorous cross-examination, presentation of contrary evidence, and careful instruction on the burden of proof are the traditional and appropriate means of attacking shaky but admissible evidence."[20] The Supreme Court has made it clear that trial judges have great discretion in deciding on the admissibility of evidence under Rule 702, and that appeals from *Daubert* rulings are subject to a very narrow abuse-of-discretion standard of review.[21] Most importantly, in Kumho Tire Co., Ltd. v. Carmichael, the Court stated that "whether *Daubert*'s specific factors are, or are not, reasonable measures of reliability in a particular case is a matter that the law grants the trial judge broad latitude to determine."[22]

Daubert and its progeny have engendered confusion and controversy. In particular, judicial dispositions of *Daubert*-type questions in criminal cases have been criticized by some lawyers and scholars who thought that the Supreme Court's decision would be applied more rigorously.[23] If one focuses solely on reported federal appellate decisions, the picture is not appealing to those who have preferred a more rigorous application of *Daubert*. Federal appellate courts have not with any consistency or clarity imposed standards ensuring the application of scientifically valid reasoning and reliable methodology in criminal cases involving *Daubert* questions. This is not really surprising, however. The Supreme Court itself described the *Daubert* standard as "flexible." This means that, beyond questions of relevance, *Daubert* offers appellate courts no clear substantive standard by which to review decisions by trial courts. As a result, trial judges exercise great discretion in deciding whether to admit or exclude expert testimony, and their judgments are subject only to a highly deferential "abuse of discretion" standard of review. Although it is difficult to get a clear picture of how trial courts handle *Daubert* challenges, because many evidentiary rulings are issued without a published opinion and without an appeal, the vast majority of the *reported* opinions in criminal cases indicate that trial judges rarely exclude or restrict expert testimony offered by prosecutors; most *reported* opinions also indicate that appellate courts routinely deny appeals contesting trial court decisions admitting forensic evidence against criminal defendants.[24] But the reported opinions do not offer in any way a complete sample of federal trial court dispositions of *Daubert*-type questions in criminal cases.

The situation appears to be very different in civil cases. Plaintiffs and defendants, equally, are more likely to have access to expert witnesses in civil cases, while prosecutors usually have an advantage over most defendants in offering expert testimony in criminal cases. And, ironically, the appellate courts appear to be more willing to second-guess trial

18.   Ibid., pp. 593-94.
19.   Ibid., p. 594. In Kumho Tire Co., Ltd. v. Carmichael, 526 U.S. 137 (1999), the Court confirmed that the *Daubert* factors do not constitute a definitive checklist or test. *Kumho Tire* importantly held that Rule 702 applies to both scientific and nonscientific expert testimony; the Court also indicated that the *Daubert* factors might be applicable in a trial judge's assessment of the reliability of nonscientific expert testimony, depending upon "the particular circumstances of the particular case at issue." Ibid., at 150.
20.   *Daubert*, 509 U.S. at 596.
21.   See Gen. Elec. Co. v. Joiner, 522 U.S. 136, 142-143 (1997).
22.   *Kumho Tire*, 526 U.S. at 153.
23.   See, e.g., P.J. Neufeld. 2005. The (near) irrelevance of *Daubert* to criminal justice: And some suggestions for reform. *American Journal of Public Health* 95(Supp.1):S107.
24.   Ibid., p. S109.

court judgments on the admissibility of purported scientific evidence in civil cases than in criminal cases.[25]

Prophetically, the *Daubert* decision observed that "there are important differences between the quest for truth in the courtroom and the quest for truth in the laboratory. Scientific conclusions are subject to perpetual revision. Law, on the other hand, must resolve disputes finally and quickly."[26] But because accused parties in criminal cases are convicted on the basis of testimony from forensic science experts, much depends upon whether the evidence offered is reliable. Furthermore, in addition to protecting innocent persons from being convicted of crimes that they did not commit, we are also seeking to protect society from persons who have committed criminal acts. Law enforcement officials and the members of society they serve need to be assured that forensic techniques are *reliable*. Therefore, we must limit the risk of having the reliability of certain forensic science methodologies judicially certified before the techniques have been properly studied and their accuracy verified by the forensic science community. "[T]here is no evident reason why ['rigorous, systematic'] research would be infeasible."[27] However, some courts appear to be loath to insist on such research as a condition of admitting forensic science evidence in criminal cases, perhaps because to do so would likely "demand more by way of validation than the disciplines can presently offer."[28]

The adversarial process relating to the admission and exclusion of scientific evidence is not suited to the task of finding "scientific truth." The judicial system is encumbered by, among other things, judges and lawyers who generally lack the scientific expertise necessary to comprehend and evaluate forensic evidence in an informed manner, trial judges (sitting alone) who must decide evidentiary issues without the benefit of judicial colleagues and often with little time for extensive research and reflection, and the highly deferential nature of the appellate review afforded trial courts' *Daubert* rulings. Given these realities, there is a tremendous need for the forensic science community to improve. Judicial review, by itself, will not cure the infirmities of the forensic science community.[29] The development of scientific research, training, technology, and databases associated with DNA analysis have resulted from substantial and steady federal support for both academic research and programs employing techniques for DNA analysis. Similar support must be given to all credible forensic science disciplines if they are to achieve the degrees of reliability needed to serve the goals of justice. With more

25.   See, e.g., McClain v. Metabolife Int'l, Inc., 401 F.3d 1233 (11th Cir. 2005); Chapman v. Maytag Corp., 297 F.3d 682 (7th Cir. 2002); Goebel v. Denver & Rio Grande W. R.R. Co., 215 F.3d 1083 (10th Cir. 2000); Smith v. Ford Motor Co., 215 F.3d 713 (7th Cir. 2000); Walker v. Soo Line R.R. Co., 208 F.3d 581 (7th Cir. 2000); 1 D.L. Faigman, M.J. Saks, J. Sanders, and E.K. Cheng. 2007-2008. *Modern Scientific Evidence: The Law and Science of Expert Testimony*. Eagan, MN: Thomson/West, §1.35, p. 105 (discussing studies suggesting that courts "employ *Daubert* more lackadaisically in criminal trials — especially in regard to prosecution evidence — than in civil cases — especially in regard to plaintiff evidence").

26.   *Daubert*, 509 U.S. at 596-97.

27.   J. Griffin and D.J. LaMagna. 2002. *Daubert* challenges to forensic evidence: Ballistics next on the firing line. *The Champion*, September-October:20, 21 (quoting P. Giannelli and E. Imwinkelried. 2000. Scientific evidence: The fallout from Supreme Court's decision in *Kumho Tire. Criminal Justice Magazine* 14(4):12, 40).

28.   Ibid. See, e.g., United States v. Crisp, 324 F.3d 261, 270 (4th Cir. 2003) (noting "that while further research into fingerprint analysis would be welcome, to postpone present in-court utilization of this bedrock forensic identifier pending such research would be to make the best the enemy of the good." (internal quotation marks omitted)).

29.   See J.L. Mnookin. Expert evidence, partisanship, and epistemic competence. 73 Brook. L. Rev. 1009, 1033 (2008) ("[S]o long as we have our adversarial system in much its present form, we are inevitably going to be stuck with approaches to expert evidence that are imperfect, conceptually unsatisfying, and awkward. It may well be that the real lesson is this: those who believe that we might ever fully resolve — rather than imperfectly manage — the deep structural tensions surrounding both partisanship and epistemic competence that permeate the use of scientific evidence within our legal system are almost certainly destined for disappointment.").

and better educational programs, accredited laboratories, certified forensic practitioners, sound operational principles and procedures, and serious research to establish the limits and measures of performance in each discipline, forensic science experts will be better able to analyze evidence and coherently report their findings in the courts. The current situation, however, is seriously wanting, both because of the limitations of the judicial system and because of the many problems faced by the forensic science community.

The NAS report is thoroughly discussed in Symposium: Forensic Science for the 21st Century, 50 Jurimetrics J. 1-146 (2009).

2.   Some Specific Controversies

In part because *Daubert* has given trial judges such broad discretion in their role as "gatekeepers," inconsistent rulings on admissibility are not uncommon when a new type of "scientific" evidence first begins appearing in court. There is often significant disagreement even between experts within a field, thus making it almost impossible for a fact finder using the deference model to reach a rational conclusion. We have already mentioned the ongoing debates surrounding polygraph testing, see note 5, page 664, supra, and the vagaries of eyewitness identification, see page 651, supra. The following discussion highlights a few more of these hot topics.

a.   *Recent Debates in DNA Testing*

Courts and commentators are currently debating the extent to which trawling DNA databases to find a match to a sample taken at a crime scene could result in a false match. The likelihood of a false match is highly contested, and defendants prosecuted based on these matches have argued that the lack of an agreement in the scientific community should prevent courts from admitting the evidence. Nonetheless, courts faced with the question have allowed the DNA evidence to be admitted, and as governments and various organizations establish DNA databases, law enforcement officials are increasingly able to solve both old and new cases after finding a DNA match in a database. For more information on the current debate and an argument courts should continue to allow the DNA evidence, see David H. Kaye, Rounding Up the Usual Suspects: A Legal and Logical Analysis of DNA Trawling Cases, 87 N.C. L. Rev. 425 (2009).

b.   *Psychological and Behavioral Sciences*

Following some widely publicized convictions based on syndrome evidence and repressed memory, courts recognize that such "scientific evidence," if misused, can be a dangerous tool. "Syndromes" are collections of symptoms that occur together and characterize a particular abnormality. Experts frequently are offered at trial for information and opinions about syndromes of various kinds. In medical science, the term tends to be used to refer to a set of symptoms whose underling etiology was not fully understood at the time the syndrome was identified, as is the case, for example, with Down Syndrome. The knowledge of experts in the relevant medical areas frequently is based on carefully controlled studies (Down's Syndrome is again a good example), and can be valuable in litigation. In a medical malpractice suit alleging a mistake involving amniocentesis leading to the birth of a seriously disabled child, medical testimony concerning Down's Syndrome and its detectability through amniocentesis will be crucial.

Over the last few decades, syndrome evidence of a different kind has emerged. Battered woman syndrome, posttraumatic stress disorder, post-Vietnam syndrome, rape trauma syndrome, and child sexual abuse accommodation syndrome, are just a few. As the diagnosis of these syndromes began producing therapeutic successes and thus respectability, experts were permitted to testify that a person has suffered some legally cognizable harm, such as child or sex abuse, based on various symptoms that the alleged victim possesses.[30] These claims were often coupled with testimony that the victim repressed memory of the traumatic event for a considerable period of time, in many instances stretching into decades.

When a therapist diagnoses a patient with a psychological syndrome, the therapist is making a decision to use certain methods of treatment that have been beneficial to patients with like symptoms. The diagnostic process may not reveal any of the causes of the patient's symptoms and a therapist's speculative opinions about such causes may be highly prejudicial. Though syndrome evidence is usually inadequate for proof of causation, it can be effectively and appropriately used as rebuttal evidence. An example is in rape prosecutions where the victim has delayed reporting the crime. The defense may present this fact as an indication of a false charge. It may be helpful to the fact finder in such a case to be educated about the frequency of delayed reports among rape victims. See, e.g., United States v. Simmons, 470 F.3d 1115 (5th Cir. 2006) (finding no error in admitting such evidence even though not all *Daubert* factors were satisfied); People v. Hampton, 746 P.2d 947 (Colo. 1987) (admitting such evidence). For a more detailed examination of the controversy surrounding this and other types of psychological and behavioral evidence, see Henry F. Fradella et al., The Impact of *Daubert* on the Admissibility of Behavioral Science Testimony, 30 Pepp. L. Rev. 403 (2003) (studying *Daubert's* application to psychological expert testimony); Christopher Slobogin, Doubts About *Daubert*: Psychiatric Anecdata as a Case Study, 57 Wash. & Lee L. Rev. 919 (2000) (arguing that opinion testimony from psychologists and psychiatrists concerning past mental state and proffered by criminal defendants, should be admissible under *Daubert-Kumho* though it may be considered "unreliable"); Rosemary L. Flint, Child Sexual Abuse Accommodation Syndrome: Admissibility Requirements, 23 Am. J. Crim. L. 171 (1995).

c. Toxic Tort Causation

A toxic tort . . . is a cause of action that arises when a plaintiff has developed a disease following long-term exposure to a physical agent — either a chemical or a form of energy such as electromagnetic fields (EMFs). Typically, the defendant's economic activity resulted in the plaintiff's exposure to the agent. Courts essentially must determine whether the plaintiff's exposure and subsequent disease are causally related, as that

---

30. See Robert Rosenthal, State of New Jersey v. Margaret Kelly Michaels: An Overview, 1 Psychol., Pub. Poly. & L. 246 (1995) for a description of the prosecution of Margaret Kelly Michaels for child abuse on the basis of repressed memory.

relationship is defined by the applicable law, or whether the exposure and disease are associated merely by chance. For example, did the asbestos inhaled by the plaintiff cause his lung cancer? Did the radar gun used by the traffic control officer cause his testicular cancer? Did the Bendectin taken by the plaintiff cause the birth defects that occurred thereafter? Traumatic injury occurs instantaneously, but disease develops over a period of time. The cause of disease, therefore, cannot be the direct object of the senses and can only be inferred. [Andrew A. Marino and Lawrence E. Marino, The Scientific Basis of Causality in Toxic Tort Cases, 21 Dayton L. Rev. 1, 2 (1995).]

You will recall that *Daubert* addressed the admissibility of expert testimony in a case in which a family alleged that their children's birth defects had been caused by the mothers' ingestion of Bendectin during pregnancy. The defendant, Merrell Dow Pharmaceuticals, Inc., argued that the plaintiffs could not prove that the prescription antinausea drug had caused the defects.[31] It is not surprising that such a seminal case should grow out of a dispute about toxic tort causation. As a central element of all toxic tort claims and one about which most fact finders know little, proving causation can be extremely difficult and often requires the plaintiff to call numerous expert witnesses.

The expert in a toxic tort case must rationalize an assertion that the plaintiff's disease and the dosage of the toxin received were causally related and not merely a chance association. For example, in the case of a traffic control officer who used a radar gun and developed cancer, the plaintiff's exposure to electromagnetic fields and his disease occurred in the context of many factors, among others: the plaintiff ate peanuts; smoked cigarettes; wore blue socks; drove a motorcycle; lifted weights; collected coins; lived near a superhighway; and had arthritic knees. The question arises, therefore, why the expert singled out electromagnetic fields as the causative agent, as opposed to myriad other co-existing circumstances. [Andrew A. Marino and Lawrence E. Marino, The Scientific Basis of Causality in Toxic Tort Cases, 21 Dayton L. Rev. 1, 21 (Fall, 1995).]

Since it is unlikely that the mechanism by which an agent causes a disease will be known in a toxic tort case, to be able to opine that the agent "caused" the disease, the expert will have to express why this explanation is more likely than other possible explanations. It may be that this logical gap, inherent in evidence of a toxic tort, creates a certain uneasiness among trial courts and leads them to decide cases one at a time, making it difficult for observers to predict the outcomes.

In Wright v. Willamette Industries, Inc., 91 F.3d 1105 (8th Cir. 1996), the appellate court asked whether sufficient evidence had been offered at trial to support the plaintiffs' claim that the formaldehyde emitted by the defendant's fiberboard manufacturing plant had caused the plaintiffs' headaches, sore throats, watery eyes, running noses, dizziness, and shortness of breath. The jury found for the plaintiffs and awarded compensatory damages of $226,250.00. The court reversed, explaining that, although the plaintiffs had proved their exposure to the defendant's emissions, they had failed to prove that their level of exposure was hazardous and that the defendant's emissions probably caused their particular ailments. The court characterized the expert testimony that had been offered in the following way:

Their experts' information on this subject was simply insufficient. Dr. Fred Fowler, an industrial hygienist, and Dr. Jimmie Valentine, a pharmacologist, did offer testimony

31. For a thorough look at the steady stream of Bendectin cases that began in 1977, see Joseph Sanders, Bendectin on Trial: A Study of Mass Tort Litigation (Ann Arbor: The University of Michigan Press, 1998).

about the levels of gaseous formaldehyde that might be expected to cause symptoms like the ones that plaintiffs claim to have experienced. But the Wrights do not claim to have been injured from breathing gaseous formaldehyde, and they make no reference to any studies that reveal the levels of exposure to wood fibers impregnated with formaldehyde that are likely to produce adverse consequences. It is true that Dr. Frank Peretti, after a great deal of prodding, testified that the Wrights' complaints were more probably than not related to exposure to formaldehyde, but that opinion was not based on any knowledge about what amounts of wood fibers impregnated with formaldehyde involve an appreciable risk of harm to human beings who breathe them. The trial court should therefore have excluded Dr. Peretti's testimony, as Willamette requested it to do, because it was not based on scientific knowledge. See Daubert v. Merrell Dow Pharmaceuticals, Inc., 509 U.S. 579, 589-91 (1993); Fed. R. Evid. 702; Federal Judicial Center, Reference Manual on Scientific Evidence 47-48 (1994). Dr. Peretti's testimony regarding the probable cause of the Wrights' claimed injuries was simply speculation. [Wright v. Willamette Industries, Inc., 91 F.3d 1105, 1107-1108 (8th Cir. 1996).]

Thus, the court accepted scientific testimony that "gaseous formaldehyde" could cause the types of ailments suffered by the plaintiffs but it distrusted the experts' opinion that formaldehyde carried by particulate matter could have the same effect. For a critique of *Wright*, see Erica Beecher-Monas, The Heuristics of Intellectual Due Process: A Primer for Triers of Science, 75 N.Y.U. L. Rev. 1563 (2000).

In Zuchowicz v. United States, 140 F.3d 381 (2d Cir. 1998), the United States appealed an unfavorable decision in which the district court held that the plaintiff's wife's fatal lung condition was the result of the government's negligence in prescribing an overdose of the drug Danocrine. There was no question that the government had erred in its prescription or that the plaintiff's wife died from primary pulmonary hypertension (PPH). The only question before the trial court had been whether the one had caused the other. The trial court found that Danocrine had been extensively studied and prescribed for many years and that even though the Food and Drug Administration had approved it for use in dosages not exceeding 800 mg/day, the plaintiff's wife was accidentally instructed to take 1,600 mg/day. At the time of the trial, there had been no formal studies of effects of such high doses of Danocrine and it was thought that very few women had ever taken so much. Despite the plaintiff's inability to close this gap, his experts were permitted to testify that, although all of the other possible causes of the plaintiff's wife's PPH could not be excluded, the experts were "confident to a reasonable medical certainty that the Danocrine caused Mrs. Zuchowicz's PPH." There are many more examples of courts being more or less demanding of a plaintiff's experts in toxic tort litigation. With the great discretion accorded to trial judges within this area, it will take some time for courts to begin reaching more consistent conclusions. But cf. Plourde v. Gladstone, 190 F. Supp. 2d 708, 721 (D. Vt. 2002) (discussing some factors considered in admissibility of expert testimony in toxic tort cases); see also Williams v. Utica College, 453 F.3d 112 (2d Cir. 2006) (distinguishes *Zuchowicz* based on factors, found in *Zuchowicz* but absent in the present case, that make the causal inference reliable).

d.   Traditional Law Enforcement Investigative Tools

Recently, several types of evidence that have been used for years in U.S. courtrooms have been questioned anew. The renewed scrutiny of handwriting identification, fingerprint identification, and comprehensive bullet lead analysis (CBLA) may be attributed to a belated recognition that "new" scientific techniques are not the only ones that should be subject to a *Daubert* analysis. As a result, the use of each of these techniques, though not novel, is less settled now than 10 or even five years ago.

     i. Handwriting Identification.   According to the thorough history provided in D. Michael Risinger, Mike P. Denbeaux, and Michael J. Saks, Exorcism of Ignorance as a Proxy for Rational Knowledge: The Lessons of Handwriting Identification "Expertise," 137 U. Pa. L. Rev. 731, 762 (1988), by 1925 all but five jurisdictions in the United States had declared handwriting expertise permissible. Despite its early and continued[32] recognition, some courts can still be persuaded to exclude handwriting identification evidence. In United States v. Saelee, 162 F. Supp. 2d 1097 (D. Alaska 2001), the defendant, charged with three counts of importing opium in violation of federal drug laws, sought to exclude the testimony of John W. Cawley, III, a forensic document analyst with the U.S. Postal Service. After concluding that the 2000 amendments to FRE 702 required a *Daubert* hearing on the admission of Mr. Cawley's testimony, as it was based on "technical or other specialized knowledge," the court concluded that testimony on handwriting identification was unreliable for several reasons:

> [Reliability in this case may be determined by asking] whether the theories and techniques of handwriting comparison have been tested, whether they have been subjected to peer review, the known or potential error rate of forensic document examiners, the existence of standards in making comparisons between known writings and questioned documents, and the general acceptance by the forensic evidence community [of handwriting analysis]. [United States v. Saelee, 162 F. Supp. 2d 1097, 1101 (D. Alaska 2001).]

    After concluding that the field of handwriting analysis failed to meet the first four of these requirements, the court examined the fifth and ultimately excluded the evidence, stating:

> Finally, the evidence does indicate that there is general acceptance of the theories and techniques involved in the field of handwriting analysis among the closed universe of forensic document examiners. This proves nothing. Testimony from these experts has, until recently, been uncritically accepted as reliable in the courts. Having previously testified somewhere as an expert document examiner was usually sufficient qualification. "Courts have long received handwriting analysis testimony as admissible evidence." United States v. Paul, 175 F.3d 906, 910 n.2 (11th Cir. 1999). However, the fact that this type of evidence has been generally accepted in the past by courts does not mean that it should be generally accepted now, after *Daubert* and *Kumho*. [United States v. Saelee, 162 F. Supp. 2d 1097, 1104-1105 (D. Alaska 2001).]

    Nonetheless, one commentator points out: "Even when the most vulnerable forensic sciences — [including] handwriting — are attacked, the courts routinely affirm

---

    32.   Many courts continue to allow handwriting identification evidence. See D. Michael Risinger, Navigating Expert Reliability: Are Criminal Standards of Certainty Being Left on the Dock?, 64 Alb. L. Rev. 99, 140 n.161 (2000) for an extensive list which includes: United States v. Battle, No. 98-3246, 188 F.3d 519 (10th Cir. Aug. 6, 1999) (rejecting the defendant's challenge to the testimony of a qualified document examiner who testified that the defendant had forged the signature of another individual); United States v. Paul, 175 F.3d 906, 911 (11th Cir. 1999) (affirming the trial court's decision to allow an FBI document examiner to testify that the defendant authored an extortion note); United States v. Jones, 107 F.3d 1147, 1161 (6th Cir. 1997) (upholding the admissibility of a United States Postal Service forensic document analyst's testimony that the defendant's signature was on various documents related to a stolen credit card).

admissibility citing earlier decisions rather than facts established at a hearing. Defense lawyers generally fail to build a challenge with appropriate witnesses and new data. Thus, even if inclined to mount a *Daubert* challenge, they lack the requisite knowledge and skills, as well as the funds, to succeed."[33] The NAS Committee Report agrees that "[t]he scientific basis for handwriting comparisons needs to be strengthened." However, while concerned that research to quantify the "reliability and replicability" of handwriting analysis is limited, the Committee acknowledged that "recent studies have increased [the scientific community's] understanding of handwriting," and that "there may be a scientific basis for handwriting comparison."[34]

   ii.   Fingerprint Identification.   The *Saelee* court's statement to the fact that handwriting analysis evidence "has been generally accepted in the past . . . does not mean that it should be generally accepted now" might just as well be applied to a recent decision on fingerprint analysis, which seemed to be well-settled evidence until United States v. Plaza, 179 F. Supp. 2d 492 (E.D. Pa. 2002), *vacated*, 188 F. Supp. 2d 549 (E.D. Pa. 2002). In *Plaza*, the defendant moved to exclude testimony on FBI fingerprint analysis (ACE-V) for failure to meet the criteria set forth in *Daubert* and *Kumho*. After a lengthy consideration of the history of the use of fingerprint evidence in U.S. courts and the science behind such evidence, the court ruled that "no expert witness for any party will be permitted to testify that, in the opinion of the witness, a particular latent print is — or is not — the print of a particular person." *Plaza*, 179 F. Supp. 2d at 518. The reasoning for the ruling was stated as follows:

> The court finds that ACE-V does not adequately satisfy the "scientific" criterion of testing (the first *Daubert* factor) or the "scientific" criterion of peer review (the second *Daubert* factor). Further, the court finds that the information of record is unpersuasive, one way or another, as to ACE-V's "scientific" rate of error (the first aspect of *Daubert*'s third factor), and that, at the critical evaluation stage, ACE-V does not operate under uniformly accepted "scientific" standards (the second aspect of *Daubert*'s third factor). [United States v. Plaza, 179 F. Supp. 2d 492, 517 (E.D. Pa. 2002).]

   Though the court later reversed its decision in light of new evidence on the reliability of the ACE-V methodology, the *Plaza* case marked the first time that fingerprint evidence had been rejected under a *Daubert* analysis. Subsequent cases have generally admitted testimony on fingerprint identification. See, e.g., United States v. Mitchell, 365 F.3d 215 (3d Cir. 2004) (admitting fingerprint identification testimony after extensive Daubert hearing); United States v. Crisp, 324 F.3d 261 (4th Cir. 2003), *cert. denied*, 540 U.S. 888 (2003); United States v. George, 363 F.3d 666 (7th Cir. 2004); United States v. Janis, 387 F.3d 682 (8th Cir. 2004); United States v. Abreu, 406 F.3d 1304 (11th Cir. 2005). However, after *Plaza*, exclusion of fingerprint evidence is now at the district court's discretion in at least one jurisdiction. See Jacobs v. Virgin Islands, 53 Fed. Appx. 651 (3d Cir. 2002) (affirming exclusion of fingerprint evidence as within district court's discretion).

   For current views on the issue, it is once again useful to turn to the NAS Committee Report:

> Over the years, the courts have admitted fingerprint evidence, even though this evidence has "made its way into the courtroom without empirical validation of the

---

33.   NAS Report 2009, citing P.J. Neufeld. 2005. The (near) irrelevance of *Daubert* to criminal justice: And some suggestions for reform. American Journal of Public Health 95 (Supp. 1): S107, S110.
   34.   NAS Report 2009 (internal citations omitted).

underlying theory and/or its particular application."[35] The courts sometimes appear to assume that fingerprint evidence is irrefutable. For example, in United States v. Crisp, the court noted that "[w]hile the principles underlying fingerprint identification have not attained the status of scientific law, they nonetheless bear the imprimatur of a strong general acceptance, not only in the expert community, but in the courts as well."[36] The court went on to say:

> [E]ven if we had a more concrete cause for concern as to the reliability of fingerprint identification, the Supreme Court emphasized in *Daubert* that "[v]igorous cross-examination, presentation of contrary evidence, and careful instruction on the burden of proof are the traditional and appropriate means of attacking shaky but admissible evidence." *Daubert*, 509 U.S. at 596. Ultimately, we conclude that while further research into fingerprint analysis would be welcome, "to postpone present in-court utilization of this bedrock forensic identifier pending such research would be to make the best the enemy of the good."[37]

Opinions of this sort have drawn sharp criticism:

> [M]any fingerprint decisions of recent years . . . display a remarkable lack of understanding of certain basic principles of the scientific method. Court after court, for example, [has] repeated the statement that fingerprinting met the *Daubert* testing criterion by virtue of having been tested by the adversarial process over the last one-hundred years. This silly statement is a product of courts' perception of the incomprehensibility of actually limiting or excluding fingerprint evidence. Such a prospect stilled their critical faculties. It also transformed their admissibility standard into a *Daubert*-permissive one, at least for that subcategory of expertise.[38]

This is a telling critique, especially when one compares the judicial decisions that have pursued rigorous scrutiny of DNA typing with the decisions that have applied less stringent standards of review in cases involving fingerprint evidence.

In holding that fingerprint evidence satisfied *Daubert*'s reliability and relevancy standards for admissibility, the Fourth Circuit's decision in *Crisp* noted approvingly that "the Seventh Circuit [in United States v. Havvard, 260 F.3d 597 (7th Cir. 2001)] determined that *Daubert*'s 'known error rate' factor was satisfied because the expert in *Havvard* had testified that the error rate for fingerprint comparison was 'essentially zero.'"[39] This statement appears to overstate the expert's testimony in *Havvard*, and gives fuel to the misconception that the forensic discipline of fingerprinting is infallible. The *Havvard* opinion actually described the expert's testimony as follows:

> [The expert] testified that the error rate for fingerprint comparison is essentially zero. Though conceding that a small margin of error exists because of differences in individual examiners, he opined that this risk is minimized because print identifications are typically confirmed through peer review. [The expert] did acknowledge that fingerprint examiners have not adopted a single standard for determining when a fragmentary latent fingerprint is sufficient to permit a comparison, but he suggested that the unique nature of fingerprints is counterintuitive to the establishment of such a standard and that through experience each examiner develops a comfort level for deciding how much of a fragmentary print is necessary to permit a comparison.[40]

This description of the expert's equivocal testimony calls into question any claim that fingerprint evidence is infallible.

---

35.   M.A. Berger. Procedural paradigms for applying the *Daubert* test. 78 Minn. L. Rev. 1345, 1354 (1994).

36.   324 F.3d 261, 268 (4th Cir. 2003).

37.   Ibid., pp. 269-70 (second alteration in original) (other internal citation omitted).

38.   1 Faigman et al., op. cit., supra note 1, §1:1, p. 4; see also J.J. Koehler. Fingerprint error rates and proficiency tests: What they are and why they matter. 59 Hastings L.J. 1077 (2008).

39.   324 F.3d at 269 (quoting *Havvard*, 260 F.3d at 599).

40.   *Havvard*, 260 F.3d at 599. The *Havvard* decision is sharply criticized by 1 Faigman et al., op. cit., supra note 1, §1:30, pp. 86-89.

The decision in *Crisp* also pointed out that "[f]ingerprint identification has been admissible as reliable evidence in criminal trials in this country since at least 1911."[41] The court, however, pointed to no studies supporting the reliability of fingerprint evidence. When forensic DNA first appeared, it was sometimes called "DNA fingerprinting" to suggest that it was as reliable as fingerprinting, which was then viewed as the premier identification science and one that consistently produced irrefutable results. During the effort to validate DNA evidence for courtroom use, however, it became apparent that assumptions about fingerprint evidence had been reached without the scientific scrutiny being accorded DNA. When the Supreme Court decided *Daubert* in 1993, with its emphasis on validation, legal commentators turned their attention to fingerprinting and began questioning whether experts could match and attribute fingerprints with a zero error rate as the FBI expert claimed in *Havvard*, and whether experts should be allowed to testify and make these claims in the absence of confirmatory studies. As noted above, most of these challenges have thus far failed, but the questions persist.

The 2004 Brandon Mayfield case refueled the debate over fingerprint evidence. The chronology of events in the Mayfield case is as follows:

> March 11, 2004: Terrorists detonate bombs on a number of trains in Madrid, Spain, killing approximately 191 people, and injuring thousands more, including a number of United States citizens.
>
> May 6, 2004: Brandon Bieri Mayfield, a 37-year-old civil and immigration lawyer, practicing in Portland, Oregon, is arrested as a material witness with respect to a federal grand jury's investigation into that bombing. An affidavit signed by FBI Special Agent Richard K. Werder, submitted in support of the government's application for the material witness arrest warrant, [avers] that Mayfield's fingerprint has been found on a bag in Spain containing detonation devices similar to those used in the bombings, and that he has to be detained so that he cannot flee before the grand jury has a chance to obtain his testimony.
>
> May 24, 2004: The government announces that the FBI has erred in its identification of Mayfield and moves to dismiss the material witness proceeding.[42]

In March 2006, the Office of the Inspector General of the U.S. Department of Justice issued a comprehensive analysis of how the misidentification occurred.[43] And in November 2006, the federal government agreed to pay Mayfield $2 million for his wrongful jailing in connection with the 2004 terrorist bombings in Madrid.[44] The Mayfield case and the resulting report from the Inspector General surely signal caution against simple, and unverified, assumptions about the reliability of fingerprint evidence.

In Maryland v. Rose, a Maryland State trial court judge found that the Analysis, Comparison, Evaluation, and Verification (ACE-V) process [] of latent print identification does not rest on a reliable factual foundation.[45] The opinion went into considerable detail about the lack of error rates, lack of research, and potential for bias.

---

41. *Crisp*, 324 F.3d at 266. The decision cites a number of other legal references, including, *inter alia*: People v. Jennings, 96 N.E. 1077 (1911); J.L. Mnookin. Fingerprint evidence in an age of DNA profiling. 67 Brook. L. Rev. 13 (2001) (discussing history of fingerprint identification evidence).

42. S.T. Wax and C.J. Schatz. 2004. A multitude of errors: The Brandon Mayfield case. *The Champion*. September-October, p. 6. The facts of the case and Mayfield's legal claims against the government are fully reported in Mayfield v. United States, 504 F. Supp. 2d 1023 (D. Or. 2007).

43. Office of the Inspector General, Oversight and Review Division, U.S. Department of Justice. 2006. *A Review of the FBI's Handling of the Brandon Mayfield Case*. Available at www.usdoj.gov/oig/special/s0601/exec.pdf.

44. E. Lichtblau. 2006. "U.S. Will Pay $2 Million To Lawyer Wrongly Jailed." *New York Times*. November 30, at A18.

45. Maryland v. Rose, Case No. K06-0545, mem. op. at 31 (Balt. Cnty. Cir. Ct. Oct. 19, 2007) (holding that the ACE-V methodology of latent fingerprint identification was "a subjective, untested, unverifiable identification procedure that purports to be infallible" and therefore ruling that fingerprint evidence was inadmissible). The ACE-V process is described in Chapter Five.

The judge ruled that the State could not offer testimony that any latent fingerprint matched the prints of the defendant. The judge also noted that, because the case involved the possibility of the death penalty, the reliability of the evidence offered against the defendant was critically important.[46]

iii. **Compositional Analysis of Bullet Lead.** Another previously well-settled area of expert testimony that has been largely discredited is Compositional Analysis of Bullet Lead (CABL or CBLA), a method by which bullets used in the commission of a crime are compared with bullets found in the possession of a suspect. In such an analysis, metal from the bullets at the scene is compared on a molecular level with metal from bullets possessed by the suspect; if the bullets are sufficiently similar in composition, the bullets are deemed to be from the same lot and the suspect may be charged accordingly. This method of analysis has been used by law enforcement since the 1960s.[47] Courts have traditionally admitted CABL. However, in the wake of a number of recent reports calling into question the reliability of CABL as a methodology,[48] courts subject the method to increased scrutiny and, in some cases, exclude expert testimony on CABL for failure to meet *Daubert* criteria. In United States v. Mikos, 2003 U.S. Dist. LEXIS 22069 (N.D. Ill. Dec. 5, 2003), the defendant moved to exclude CABL expert testimony that a bullet recovered from the body of a murder victim matched bullets found in the defendant's possession. The reasoning of the court in that case reflects the skepticism in CABL as a scientific technique:

> We understand that the FBI Laboratory has performed comparative bullet lead analysis (CBLA) for many years. Furthermore, we understand that persons from the FBI Laboratory . . . have for years been allowed to testify at trials as to their opinions regarding the source of tested bullets based on CBLA. In our opinion, however, the required

---

46. Professor Jennifer Mnookin has also highlighted an important concern over "the rhetorical dimensions of the testimony . . . provide[d] in court" by members of the fingerprint community:

> At present, fingerprint examiners typically testify in the language of absolute certainty. Both the conceptual foundations and the professional norms of latent fingerprinting prohibit experts from testifying to identification unless they believe themselves certain that they have made a correct match. Experts therefore make only what they term "positive" or "absolute" identifications — essentially making the claim that they have matched the latent print to the one and only person in the entire world whose fingertip could have produced it. In fact, if a fingerprint examiner testifies on her own initiative that a match is merely "likely" or "possible" or "credible," rather than certain, she could possibly be subject to disciplinary sanction! Given the general lack of validity testing for fingerprinting; the relative dearth of difficult proficiency tests; the lack of a statistically valid model of fingerprinting; and the lack of validated standards for declaring a match, such claims of absolute, certain confidence in identification are unjustified, the product of hubris more than established knowledge. Therefore, in order to pass scrutiny under *Daubert*, fingerprint identification experts should exhibit a greater degree of epistemological humility. Claims of "absolute" and "positive" identification should be replaced by more modest claims about the meaning and significance of a "match."

J.L. Mnookin, The Validity of Latent Fingerprint Identification: Confessions of a Fingerprinting Moderate. Law, Probability and Risk 7(2):127 (2008); see also Koehler, supra note 38.

47. See Committee on Scientific Assessment of Bullet Lead Elemental Composition Comparison, National Research Council: Forensic Analysis: Weighing Bullet Lead Evidence (2004).

48. See, e.g., Michael O. Finkelstein and Bruce Levin, Compositional Analysis of Bullet Lead as Forensic Evidence, 13 J.L. & Poly. 119 (2005); William A. Tobin, Comparative Bullet Lead Analysis: A Case Study In Flawed Forensics, 28 Champ. 12 (July 2004); Edward J. Imwinkelried and William A. Tobin, Comparative Bullet Lead Analysis (CBLA) Evidence: Valid Inference or Ipse Dixit?, 28 Okla. City U. L. Rev. 43 (2003); William A. Tobin and Wayne Duerfeldt, How Probative Is Comparative Bullet Lead Analysis?, 17 Crim. Just. 26 (2002); Robert D. Koons and Diana M. Grant, Compositional Variation in Bullet Lead Manufacture, 47 J. Foren. Sci. 950 (2002); Erik Randich et al., A Metallurgical Review of the Interpretation of Bullet Lead Compositional Analysis, 127 Foren. Sci. Intl. 174 (2000).

standard of scientific reliability is met only as to the proposed opinion testimony that the elements composition of the bullets recovered from the body is indistinguishable from the composition of the bullets found in the Defendant's car. There is no body of data to corroborate the government's expert's further opinion that from this finding it follows that the bullets must or even likely came from the same batch or melt. The motion to exclude the expert testimony . . . relating to comparative bullet lead analysis is therefore granted. [United States v. Mikos, 2003 U.S. Dist. LEXIS 22069, at *18 (N.D. Ill. Dec. 5, 2003).]

In contrast to fingerprint evidence, which is still generally believed to be reliable despite recent findings to the contrary, CABL evidence is beginning to be viewed with disfavor in many jurisdictions, to the point that some courts have reversed previous convictions that were based on CABL evidence. See, e.g., State v. Behn, 375 N.J. Super. 409 (N.J. Super. Ct. App. Div. 2005) (reversing conviction and remanding for new trial where defendant was convicted on the basis of unreliable CABL testimony). See also Ragland v. Commonwealth, 191 S.W.3d 569 (Ky. 2006) (disallowing CABL evidence and describing scholarship that criticizes CABL).

Perhaps most pertinently, in 2004, at the request of the FBI, the National Academies of Science completed a study on the reliability of CABL as a technique, concluding:

The available data do not support any statement that a crime bullet came from a particular box of ammunition. In particular, references to "boxes" of ammunition in any form should be avoided as misleading under Federal Rule of Evidence 403.

Compositional analysis of bullet lead data alone also does not permit any definitive statement concerning the date of bullet manufacture.

Detailed patterns of the distribution of ammunition are unknown, and as a result, experts should not testify as to the probability that the crime scene bullet came from the defendant. Geographic distribution data on bullets and ammunition are needed before such testimony can be given.

It is the conclusion of the committee that, in many cases, CABL is a reasonably accurate way of determining whether two bullets could have come from the same compositionally indistinguishable volume of lead. It may thus in appropriate cases provide additional evidence that ties a suspect to a crime, or in some cases evidence that tends to exonerate a suspect. CABL does not, however, have the unique specificity of techniques such as DNA typing to be used as standalone evidence. It is important that criminal justice professionals and juries understand the capabilities as well as the significant limitations of this forensic technique.

QUESTION

The above discussion touches only a few of the more controversial types of scientific evidence. Debates also surround statistics, survey research, horizontal gaze nystagmus (the observation of eye tremors as a method for gauging intoxication), the estimation of economic losses in damages awards, identification through bite marks, *modus operandi*, and the outer reaches of medical testimony. Though each type of scientific evidence raises unique questions, can you articulate a systematic approach for determining whether a given piece of expert testimony will be admissible under the Federal Rules and *Daubert/Kumho*? Do you have a sense of the concerns, either enunciated by judges or not, that will lead courts to exclude probative evidence?

CHAPTER TEN

THE PROCESS OF PROOF IN CIVIL AND CRIMINAL CASES:
Burdens of Proof, Judicial Summary and Comment, and Presumptions

We have studied in great detail the proof process at the level of individual elements and items of evidence. We turn now to aspects of the process of proof that affect the structure of trials and the sufficiency of evidence as a whole. The roles of the judge and the jury and their relationship to each other continue to be a central focus of our inquiry.

Even if all the evidence each party wishes to produce is admitted into evidence, the role of the trial judge is not at an end. Just as the trial judge must make a preliminary determination concerning the logical force of any offered evidence, the judge must also make a preliminary determination of the overall strength of each party's case. The judge is empowered to issue rulings that terminate the litigation at various stages in the proceedings based in large measure on the judge's assessment as to how reasonable people would analyze the evidence offered at trial. In civil cases, judges may issue a summary judgment before trial, Fed. R. Civ. P. 56, or a judgment as a matter of law at or after trial, Fed. R. Civ. P. 50, if no reasonable jury could find for one side or the other. Similarly, courts may dismiss a criminal case, Fed. R. Crim. P. 29, or overturn a criminal conviction, Jackson v. Virginia, 443 U.S. 307 (1979), if no reasonable jury could find guilt beyond a reasonable doubt. Judges must also instruct juries about what standard of proof to apply in assessing the evidence.

In addition to evaluating the sufficiency of the evidence and instructing the jury about the standard of proof, the trial judge has various means to influence the jury's deliberations. We have already encountered one indirect instance of such power. By ruling on the admissibility of specific proffers, the judge can dramatically influence the jury's perspective. For example, if a judge finds that a proposed witness lacks personal knowledge and thus cannot be placed on the stand, the jury will not have before it that witness's testimony. Suppose that witness would have contradicted an important witness of the adversary. By excluding the testimony, the judge affects the proof process by constraining the jury's perspective. Thus, the judge, by deciding questions of the admissibility of evidence, has significant power to influence the deliberative process. As we will see, the judge may also influence the deliberative process by summarizing or commenting on the evidence.

We first discuss the process of proof in civil cases and then discuss the process of proof in criminal cases. We treat them separately because of the different standards and constitutional issues that arise in criminal cases. First understanding how the various evidentiary devices operate in civil cases will allow you to better understand the additional complexities that arise in criminal cases. Although our primary focus will be on jury trials, many of the same principles, issues, and devices also arise in bench trials.

A.   THE PROCESS OF PROOF IN CIVIL CASES

In this section we discuss three related aspects of the process of proof in civil cases: the burdens of proof, judicial summary of and comment on the evidence, and evidentiary presumptions.

1.   The Burdens of Proof in Civil Cases

A critical part of evaluating the parties' evidence is the application of rules governing the burden of proof. There are two aspects to the burden of proof — the burden of persuasion and the burden of production. For the burden of persuasion, there are decision rules that the jury must apply in evaluating the evidence. For most civil cases the decision rule is a "preponderance of the evidence." For example, a plaintiff in a negligence action must persuade the jury by a preponderance of the evidence that the defendant negligently injured the plaintiff. In some civil actions the standard is "clear and convincing evidence." The second aspect of the burden of proof is the production burden or the burden of producing evidence. For the burden of production, the judge applies rules to determine whether a party has produced enough evidence to avoid an adverse judgment. If a party fails to meet its production burden prior to trial, the judge will issue a summary judgment for the other side. Fed. R. Civ. P. 56. If a party fails to meet a production burden at trial, the judge will issue a judgment as a matter of law for the other side. Fed. R. Civ. P. 50. We first discuss the burden of production and then the burden of persuasion.

a.   The Burden of Production

i.   The Role of and Rationale for Production Burdens.   Our system of civil litigation does not give each party the automatic right to proceed through the entire trial process and have the jury resolve the case on the basis of whatever evidence the parties choose to introduce. Rather, in order to proceed to that stage a party must produce evidence that satisfies a burden of production.

Each issue to be litigated, whether it is an element or an affirmative defense, has a burden of production associated with it that requires one party or the other to produce evidence relevant to the particular issue. If the party with a burden of production fails to produce sufficient evidence on a particular issue, the judge will not permit the issue to go to the jury. Thus, the burden of production informs the parties how issues will be decided if no evidence is produced.

How, though, is one to know when a party with a burden of production has produced sufficient evidence to avoid a ruling that would decide an issue for the other side? A burden of production is satisfied when the underlying purpose of the requirement is met. In civil cases, the primary purpose of a burden of production is to ensure that there are issues in the case that need to be resolved by the jury. Issues need to be resolved by juries when there could be reasonable disagreement about which party should prevail. If there could be no reasonable disagreement, there is no reason to go to the expense and trouble of a trial, or to risk the possibility that the jury will render an irrational verdict. In such a case, the judge should, and will, render a judgment for the appropriate party. Thus, the failure to satisfy a burden of production will result in the adversary's prevailing on that particular issue. For this reason the burden of production is sometimes referred to as the *risk of nonproduction*.

ii.   The Relationship Between Production Burdens and Persuasion Burdens.
To decide if there could be reasonable disagreement about which party should prevail, the judge must consider the burden of persuasion. Assume, for example, that the plaintiff must prove a particular fact by a preponderance of the evidence, a standard commonly understood to mean the disputed fact is "more likely true than not." The plaintiff will satisfy the burden of production by presenting enough evidence to create a jury issue regarding that fact. In other words, the plaintiff must produce enough evidence so that a jury could find that the fact is "more likely true than not." If no reasonable person could conclude that the plaintiff has satisfied the relevant burden of persuasion, then there is no reason to prolong the proceedings on that issue. The judge should terminate the proceedings with respect to the fact in favor of the defendant. Similarly, if the plaintiff's evidence is so overwhelming that any reasonable jury would find the fact is more likely true than not, and if the defendant does not challenge or rebut the plaintiff's evidence, the judge should terminate the proceedings with respect to that fact in favor of the plaintiff. In short, the burden of production is a function of the burden of persuasion. John T. McNaughton, Burden of Production of Evidence: A Function of a Burden of Persuasion, 68 Harv. L. Rev. 1382 (1955). The test to determine if a burden of production has been met is whether, in light of the evidence, there could be reasonable disagreement over which party should win. If there could be such disagreement, a jury question has been generated and the case should proceed.

iii.   The Relationship Between the Burden of Production and the Burden of Persuasion Illustrated.
The relationship between burdens of production and burdens of persuasion may be understood in more detail by reflecting on the burdens in terms of probabilities. Jurors evaluate evidence by making rough estimates of the likelihood that facts are true. In other words, although jurors may not articulate or even tacitly assign specific quantified degrees of probability to their conclusions, they make factual assessments that may be expressed as probabilities. We may also express burdens of persuasion in terms of probabilities — for example, the preponderance standard could be taken to mean "more than 50 percent likely." For purposes of

illustration only, assume that jurors do think in roughly probabilistic terms and that a preponderance of the evidence means more than a 50 percent chance of the relevant fact being true.

Under these assumptions, one may diagram the evidentiary process in such a way as to highlight the relationship between burdens of production and burdens of persuasion. Assume that the party with a burden of production produces some evidence. That evidence will indicate that there is a certain chance that the relevant facts are true. However, the evidence is likely to be not perfectly clear as to what probability it generates. Looking at that evidence, reasonable people could disagree about the probability to which the evidence establishes some necessary fact. Does that mean that every time evidence is produced a jury issue is generated because there always will be reasonable disagreement about its implications? No; a jury issue will be generated only when there is disagreement about which party should win, and that requires referring to the burden of persuasion. Consider now the three possibilities charted in Diagram 10-1:

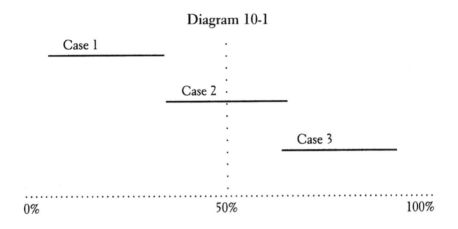

Diagram 10-1

After a party produces evidence on an issue, this chart reflects the three relevant possibilities in terms of the implications of the evidence. First, the evidence produced may not be very convincing. A reasonable person looking at it may conclude that it has some persuasive force, but not very much. That possibility is represented by Case 1. It indicates that, given the evidence, the probability of the relevant fact being true ranges from about 10 to 35 percent (we could have drawn that line segment anywhere between 0 and 50 percent, just so long as it did not exceed 50 percent). In this case, the burden of production has not been satisfied. Since no reasonable person could conclude that the party producing the evidence should win, there is no reason to send this issue to the jury. In Case 2, the evidence has generated a jury issue. The evidence indicates a range of reasonable persuasiveness from about 40 to 60 percent (here we could have drawn the line segment in any fashion so long as it ranged over 50 percent). Since reasonable people could disagree about the implications of the evidence in this case, the issue will be sent to the jury. Case 3 is similar to Case 1 in that again no reasonable disagreement could exist as to the implications of the evidence. The evidence indicates somewhere between a 65 and 90 percent chance of the relevant fact being true (here the line could be drawn anywhere to the right of 50 percent).

Case 3 is different from Case 1 in one respect. We have been assuming that the party with the burden of production has produced evidence. In Case 1, the burden has not been met, and thus there is no reason to proceed further. In Case 2, the burden of production has been met, and the case will proceed. In Case 3, the burden has not only been met, but exceeded. No reasonable person could disagree about who should win. This conclusion, though, is based solely on the evidence produced by one party. Case 3 differs from Case 1 in that rather than the judge disposing of the issue, Case 3 requires that the adversary be given a chance to produce contrary evidence in order to demonstrate that there is a reasonable dispute about the relevant fact. In Case 1, there is no reason to have the adversary proceed because the party's evidence itself indicates that the relevant fact cannot be established. Having the adversary produce still more information substantiating that conclusion would be a waste of time and money. In Case 3, however, the adversary has not yet been heard and may be in possession of information that would affect the analysis of how likely the relevant fact is, given all the evidence (including the adversary's). Accordingly, in Case 3, the judge will not dispose of the relevant issue. The party with the initial burden of production cannot prevail before the adversary has an opportunity to respond. After the adversary responds — and each side has had a chance to rebut evidence submitted by the other side — one or both parties may ask the judge to rule on the sufficiency of the evidence.

   iv.   Procedural Mechanisms for Enforcing Burdens of Production.   The manner in which a party asks a judge to determine whether the opponent has met a production burden depends on the time at which the judge is asked to make such a ruling, and here we see the interaction between the rules of evidence and civil procedure. One possibility is that before any evidence is produced a party can move for summary judgment. Fed. R. Civ. P. 56. The judge will grant the motion if it can be determined from the pleadings and any supporting documentation that there are no issues in need of judicial resolution in the case. Such a decision, however, is equivalent to saying that either Case 1 or Case 3 in the Diagram 10-1 is present — either the party with the burden of production will not be able to meet it, or the adversary will not be able to show that the party's evidence does not justify taking the case away from a jury. If Case 2 is present, the judge will deny the motion for summary judgment (by either party) and the litigation will proceed.
   Another possibility is that, if a case goes to trial, the judge may be asked to test the strength of the evidence by a motion for judgment as a matter of law at the end of a party's case. Fed. R. Civ. P. 50. The analysis is similar to the analysis of summary judgment. For both summary judgment and judgment as a matter of law, the judge's decision will rest on the ability of a party to meet its burden of production and the adversary's ability to respond with sufficient evidence to justify taking the issue to a jury. As the Supreme Court observed in Anderson v. Liberty Lobby, Inc., 477 U.S. 242, 252 (1986):

> [T]he inquiry involved in a ruling on a motion for a summary judgment . . . necessarily implicates the substantive evidence standard of proof that would apply at trial on the merits. . . . The judge's inquiry, therefore, invariably asks whether reasonable jurors could find by a preponderance of the evidence that the plaintiff is entitled to a verdict.

See also Reeves v. Sanderson Plumbing Prods., Inc., 530 U.S. 133, 150 (2000) (explaining that the standard for judgment as a matter of law "mirrors" the standard for summary judgment). In short, the burden of production and the motions for summary judgment and judgment as a matter of law are functions of the burden of persuasion. For further discussion of the relationships between these procedural devices and the evidentiary proof process, see Michael S. Pardo, Pleadings, Proof, and Judgment: A Unified Theory of Civil Litigation, 51 B.C. L. Rev. 1451 (2010).

v.   **The Allocation of Burdens of Production.**   Typically, the pleading or moving party bears both the burden of pleading and the burden of production. In general, whoever is asking the courts to modify the status quo, which is either the plaintiff or a party who has made a motion for some sort of relief, must introduce sufficient evidence of the relevant factual claims to justify a finding of fact consistent with those claims. Thus, who bears the burden of production will normally be a function of the position of the parties. If X sues Y over a contract, X will bear the burden of production on most factual issues. If, by contrast, Y sues X in a declaratory judgment action, Y will bear the burden of production on most of the identical factual issues. In most instances there will be well-established precedent allocating the burden of production. If there is no such precedent, however, there is "no satisfactory test" for allocating the burden of production. Fleming James Jr., Burdens of Proof, 47 Va. L. Rev. 58, 58 (1961).

KEY POINTS

1. Every factual element of a claim or a defense has a production burden associated with it.

2. The purpose of the production burden is to require the party who has it to present enough evidence to create a jury question.

3. The failure to satisfy the burden of production will result in a judgment against the party with the burden.

4. The party with the burden of pleading a matter typically has the burden of production with respect to that matter.

b.   The Burden of Persuasion

The skeptic will say that we can know nothing with certainty (although one might ask how the skeptic knows that). Even if there are matters that we can know with certainty, disputes at trial typically do not fall into that category. Indeed, without some uncertainty cases would not make it to trial in the first place. Jurors (or judges in bench trials) will usually be less than certain about the determinations they are called upon to make. There may be credible, conflicting accounts about what happened; there may be uncertainty about how much weight to give scientific evidence; or there may be conflicting views about how much weight to give a circumstantial inference. For example, in the *Johnson* case, to what extent does evidence of Officer Walker's character for violence suggest that he may have been the first aggressor?

i.   **Burdens of Persuasion Are Decision Rules That Manage Uncertainty.**   A burden of persuasion is a rule of decision that informs the jury how to decide a case in light of the uncertainties that inevitably will accompany the presentation of evidence. For example, one possible rule of decision is that a plaintiff should prevail only if the evidence establishes the plaintiff's case to a 95 percent certainty. This rule would require a verdict for the defendant if there were more than a slight doubt about the truth of the facts that the plaintiff must establish.

Such a rule may initially seem to have an intuitive appeal — people (defendants) should not be required to pay unless they have done something wrong. Notwithstanding this intuitive appeal, it is not the rule generally found in civil litigation because it would put plaintiffs at a serious disadvantage. Requiring plaintiffs to meet such a high burden, it is believed, would result in a disproportionate number of wrongful verdicts for defendants at the expense of deserving plaintiffs. The opposite rule — requiring defendants to show to a 95 percent certainty that they should not be held liable — would have the opposite effect. Rather than adopt either of these two extremes, the virtually uniform practice in civil litigation is to define the burden of persuasion as a preponderance of the evidence. Plaintiffs must prove each of their necessary factual claims to a preponderance of the evidence, and defendants must establish affirmative defenses by the same standard. Accordingly, judges instruct juries in civil cases to analyze the evidence and render a verdict for the party in whose favor the evidence "preponderates." As we noted earlier, preponderance is usually defined as meaning "more likely true than not." Thus, the task for juries is to determine whether the evidence makes the plaintiff's story appear more likely true than not with respect to the factual elements of a cause of action and to determine whether the evidence makes the defendant's story appear more likely true than not with respect to affirmative defenses.

ii. **The Premises Underlying the Preponderance Rule.** The preponderance rule incorporates an underlying assumption concerning the participants in litigation: Plaintiffs as a class and defendants as a class generally ought to be treated equivalently. The reason for this assumption is that before a case is resolved, one cannot know who should win; it is as likely that the defendant should win as the plaintiff. Assume that the plaintiff is suing the defendant for $200 allegedly owed under a contract. Before the parties to this dispute produce evidence relevant to its resolution, how should we conceptualize the case — as one in which the plaintiff is trying to get $200 of the defendant's money, as a case in which the defendant is wrongfully refusing to pay, or as a case in which two individuals are contesting whose $200 it is? The last view is intuitively most compelling. Without knowing the facts, it seems just as likely that the defendant is refusing to pay what is owed as that the plaintiff is attempting to obtain an undeserved benefit.

One implication of the equivalency notion is that there should be roughly the same number of errors made for plaintiffs as for defendants. The preponderance standard may implement this result if certain conditions exist. First, assume that in the set of all cases going to trial there are approximately as many deserving plaintiffs as deserving defendants. Second, assume further that the jury will make a rough probability assessment of the strength of each case presented by the parties. Presumably, those probability assessments will range from 0.0 to 1.0. Now compare the set of cases in which plaintiffs deserve to win to the set of cases in which defendants deserve to win. It is not unreasonable to suppose that in most of the cases in which plaintiffs deserve to win the facts will support that conclusion, thus creating a probability assessment of more than .5, which will result in a verdict for the plaintiff. Only in those cases in which the probability assessment is .5 or less will there be wrongful verdicts for defendants. This supposition is equally applicable to the set of cases that defendants deserve to win: Presumably the evidence in most of these cases will demonstrate that the defendant deserves to win, thus creating a probability assessment of .5 or less. Only in those cases in which the probability assessment is more than .5 will there be wrongful verdicts for plaintiffs. If one assumes that the probability assessments for these two sets are in a normal distribution over the range of 0.0 to 1.0, then the number of errors made for plaintiffs will approximate the number of errors made for defendants, and the preponderance of the evidence standard will have done its job.

Diagram 10-2 demonstrates this proposition geometrically.[1] The horizontal axis is the probability that juries assign to cases, and the vertical axis is the number of cases assigned a particular probability. Graph I is the set of cases in which defendants deserve to win (which means if we knew all the facts to certainty, the defendant would win); graph II is the set of cases in which plaintiffs deserve to win.

Diagram 10-2

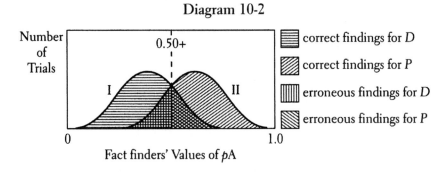

In graph I all of those cases to the right of the .5 level, which is the heavily shaded area, are errors. In graph II all of the cases to the left of the .5 level, which is again the heavily shaded area, are errors. The larger the heavily shaded areas are, the more errors there are; the smaller the heavily shaded areas are, the fewer errors there are. So long as the heavily shaded areas under the two graphs are of approximately equal size, then the preponderance standard will have done its appointed task of equalizing errors among plaintiffs and defendants. Note, however, that this equalization will occur only if three conditions are met: The relevant areas under the two graphs are roughly the same size; the evidence presented in the cases is a good indicator of which party deserves to win; and the juries properly interpret the evidence. If any of these conditions are not met, errors may not be allocated equally.

iii.   Higher Burdens of Persuasion.   We can use these same graphs to demonstrate why alternative, higher burdens of persuasion are occasionally relied on in civil cases. Many jurisdictions require allegations in civil cases of fraud or of activity that would be criminal to be proven by clear and convincing evidence. See also Addington v. Texas, 411 U.S. 418 (1979) (civil commitment requires clear-and-convincing-evidence standard). Because of the seriousness of such allegations, errors should favor the person against whom such allegations are made (which also explains the higher

---

1. We are indebted for what follows, including the graphs, to Richard S. Bell, Decision Theory and Due Process: A Critique of the Supreme Court's Lawmaking for Burdens of Proof, 78 J. Crim. L. & Criminology 557 (1987).

burden of persuasion in criminal cases). Making the same assumptions as we did above, we illustrate the effect of raising the burden of persuasion from a preponderance to "clear and convincing" evidence in Diagram 10-3. The shaded area again represents errors, and the effect of raising the burden of proof is obvious. Errors favoring defendants increase and errors favoring plaintiffs decrease, which is precisely the effect that the higher burden of persuasion is designed to accomplish. Again, though, bear in mind that the actual distribution of errors will depend on the accuracy of the assumptions we are making.

Diagram 10-3

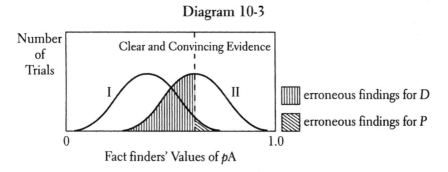

Although our primary concern here is with civil cases, note that Diagram 10-3 can also explicate the proof beyond reasonable doubt requirement in criminal cases: Assume that the horizontal and vertical axes retain the same significance and simply move somewhat to the right the vertical line representing the burden of persuasion standard.

iv. **The Meaning of "Preponderance of the Evidence" in Practice.** Burdens of persuasion, or at least the preponderance burden, may not operate as they are intended. In an interesting study, Professors Rita James Simon and Linda Mahan obtained data indicating that jurors may understand "preponderance of the evidence" to mean a probability somewhere between .7 and .8, while judges consistently indicate that it means slightly more than .5. Rita James Simon and Linda Mahan, Quantifying Burdens of Proof, 5 Law & Soc. Rev. 319 (1971). In this study, jurors were asked to translate the phrase *preponderance of the evidence* into a probability assessment rather than being informed that the phrase means "50 percent plus." When so informed, however, there is data indicating that individuals can follow such instructions. Dorothy K. Kagehiro and W. Clark Stanton, Legal v. Quantified Definitions of Standards of Proof, 9 Law & Hum. Behav. 159 (1985). As we discussed in Chapter Two, there is also empirical evidence that jurors decide cases by constructing and evaluating overarching stories or theories of what happened, often selecting among one of the two presented by the parties. See pages 113-116, supra. Thus, in practice, the preponderance standard will often be implemented by selecting which version of what happened jurors find to be more plausible, rather than by making explicit probability assessments. For further discussion, see Michael S. Pardo, Second-Order Proof Rules, 61 Fla. L. Rev. 1083 (2009).

v. **The Relative Nature of the Burden of Persuasion.** From the standpoint of the parties to an action, any burden of persuasion is relative. If the plaintiff has a greater than 50 percent burden of persuasion, the defendant will lose unless the jury can be convinced by at least a 50 percent probability that the plaintiff's version of the facts is untrue. If the defendant does not carry that burden, the inevitable logical result will be that the jury believes that the plaintiff's version of the facts is more than 50 percent likely to be true. Thus, to say that the plaintiff has a greater than 50 percent burden of persuasion is to say that the defendant has a 50 percent burden of persuasion. Similarly, to say that a plaintiff has a 70 percent burden of persuasion is to say that a defendant has a greater than 30 percent burden of persuasion.

vi.   **The Allocation of the Burden of Persuasion.**   As is true of production burdens, a burden of persuasion for each necessary element of a cause of action must be allocated to one party or the other. Usually, the law is clear on which party has the burden of persuasion. Plaintiffs typically bear the burden to prove by a preponderance all of the elements of their claims, and defendants bear the burden of persuasion for the elements of "affirmative defenses." If the law is not clear on this issue, however, there is no very helpful formula or litmus test for determining who should have the burden. Courts may consider a variety of factors, including (1) which party has better access to evidence; (2) "the extent to which a party's contention departs from what would be expected in light of ordinary human experience"; (3) "a feeling that a charge of wrongdoing should in fairness be proven by the party making it"; and (4) "real or supposed reasons of policy [for which] the law sometimes disfavors claims or defenses which it nevertheless allows." Fleming James Jr., Burdens of Proof, 47 Va. L. Rev. 58-59 (1961).

In general, states are free to allocate burdens of proof in civil cases virtually any way they like. Lavine v. Milne, 424 U.S. 577, 585 (1976) ("Outside the criminal area, where special concerns attend, the locus of the burden of persuasion is normally not an issue of federal constitutional concern."). For example, a state may require one party to bear a burden of production on an issue and the other party to bear the burden of persuasion on that issue. States on occasion exercise the power to allocate the burdens of proof in interesting ways. Consider the following case.

SCHECHTER v. KLANFER

321 N.Y.S.2d 99, 28 N.Y.2d 228, 269 N.E.2d 812 (1971)

BREITEL, Judge.

In this negligence action for personal injuries, the issue is whether the jury should have been instructed to hold plaintiff, who had by amnesia lost his memory of the events causing his injury, to a lesser degree of proof than a plaintiff who could have testified to the events.

Upon the trial, a verdict in favor of defendants was returned. The trial court initially instructed the jury to hold plaintiff to a lesser degree of proof if it found his amnesia to be genuine. Upon defendants' objection, however, the charge was withdrawn, plaintiff taking exception.

There should be a reversal and a new trial in order that the jury may consider whether plaintiff should be held to a lesser degree of proof.

Robert Schechter and his companion, Alice Stone, were involved in a motorboat collision on the night of August 25, 1964. Both were then 14 years old. They had left a party at a lakeshore home and, with Robert operating his father's boat, had begun motoring across the lake. Alice sat in the front seat, to the left of Robert. Alice testified that the night was clear and moonlit, that the boat's lights were on, and that Robert was taking a straight course at about four miles an hour. They had not gone far, Alice continued, when she looked to her right and saw a motorboat some 50 feet distant heading towards them, its bow out of water. About one second later, she estimated, the other boat, operated by defendant Robert Klanfer, struck the Schechter boat near the driver's seat. Alice estimated that the Klanfer boat was traveling at 30 miles an hour. The nighttime speed limit on the lake was 10 miles an hour. The defendants disputed Alice's testimony as to the speed of their boat and the lighting of the Schechter boat. Robert testified but not as to the accident, claiming that, as a result of the collision, he had no memory of the events. He had sustained a fractured skull, fractured arm, fractured jaw, and other physical injuries. He had been comatose for several days. Plaintiff's medical expert testified that Robert had suffered severe emotional shock and psychiatric change, including amnesia, due to brain damage.

The rule providing when a plaintiff may prevail on a lesser degree of proof was best crystallized in Noseworthy v. City of New York, 80 N.E.2d 744. The court there held that "in a death case a plaintiff is not held to as high a degree of proof of the cause of action as where an injured plaintiff can himself describe the occurrence." Moreover, despite some contrary notions, the rule has been applied in wrongful death cases where the plaintiff has called an eyewitness. . . .

The Committee on Pattern Jury Instruction of the Association of Supreme Court Justices recommends, in a pattern instruction, that the amnesiac plaintiff be held to a lesser degree of proof if the jury is satisfied from medical and other evidence that plaintiff is suffering from loss of memory and that the injuries plaintiff incurred were a substantial factor in causing plaintiff's loss of memory (PJI 1:62).[2] In a thoughtful and well-documented comment to the instruction, the committee explains: "The limitation that the accident must have been a substantial factor in causing the loss of memory is predicated on the rationale of the *Noseworthy* case, which is not merely plaintiff's inability to present proof, but the unfairness of allowing the defendant, who has knowledge of the facts, to benefit by standing mute when plaintiff's inability *results from defendant's acts*." (1 N.Y. PJI 36, emphasis in original).

Of course, an amnesiac plaintiff can no more "describe the occurrence" that produced his injury than can a plaintiff's decedent, a toddler or an imbecile. Other States, faced with an analogous choice of extending to amnesiac plaintiffs a "presumption of due care" normally accorded plaintiffs' decedents, have reasoned that the amnesiac's inability to testify entitles him to the preferential rule.

The rule even as applied to amnesiacs does not, however, shift the burden of proof or eliminate the need for plaintiffs to introduce evidence of a *prima facie* case. The jury must rest its findings on some evidence to establish negligence and also the absence of contributory negligence. In this case, however, plaintiff did introduce evidence to make out a *prima facie* case, so that there was an opportunity to apply the lesser burden of persuasion. If the jury had been told to apply a lesser burden of persuasion, it could have and, therefore, might have found plaintiff free from contributory negligence. The circumstances testified to by Alice Stone that Robert drove the

---

2. "If, however, you are satisfied from the medical and other evidence presented that plaintiff is suffering from a loss of memory that makes it impossible for him to recall events at or about the time of the accident and that the injuries plaintiff incurred in the accident were a substantial factor in causing his loss of memory, the plaintiff is not held to as high a degree of proof as would be a plaintiff who can himself describe the occurrence."

boat in a straight line, at a speed of four miles an hour, and with the boat lights on, were relevant on the issue of contributory negligence. It also could have found defendants negligent upon Alice's testimony of the speed and course of the Klanfer boat.

The danger is, of course, that amnesia is easily feigned. The dangers may be ameliorated. Plaintiff has the burden of proof on the issue of amnesia as on other issues. A jury should be instructed that before the lesser burden of persuasion is applied, because of the danger of shamming, they must be satisfied that the evidence of amnesia is clear and convincing, supported by the objective nature and extent of any other physical injuries sustained, and that the amnesia was clearly a result of the accident.

The above is undoubtedly a more severe test than that suggested by the Pattern Jury Instructions. Yet it would seem a small price to pay for a liberal rule treating amnesiac plaintiffs on a par with the representatives of decedents in death actions. The reasons for so treating amnesiacs are similar to those advanced for representatives of persons silenced in fatal accidents, but the risk and ease of shamming are measurably greater.

Accordingly, the order of the Appellate Division should be reversed and a new trial ordered, with costs to abide the event.

Order reversed, etc.

NOTES AND QUESTIONS

1. According to the *Schechter* court, the plaintiff must present a prima facie case of negligence in order to be in a position to get the benefit of the reduced burden of proof rule. What is a prima facie case? The *Schechter* court does not tell us, but usually courts use that term to describe the production burden that a party must meet. If that is what the court means here, and it seems likely that it is, the plaintiff must introduce enough evidence of the defendant's negligence to raise a jury issue. In other words, in holding that the plaintiff had presented a prima facie case, the court, in effect, was saying that the evidence of the defendant's negligence resembled Case 2 in Diagram 10-1 on page 720, supra.

2. Could or should the *Schechter* court have been more precise in articulating how amnesia could affect the plaintiff's burden of proof? The court stated that in the case of amnesia caused by the defendant the plaintiff "is not held to as a high a degree of proof as would be a plaintiff who can himself describe the occurrence," and the court also stated that "the rule even as applied to amnesiacs does not . . . shift the burden of proof." If the plaintiff's ordinary burden of persuasion is just slightly greater than 50 percent, and if that burden is lessened, how is the burden of persuasion not shifted to the defendant?

3. What justification is there for giving a reduced burden of persuasion to a plaintiff with amnesia? The *Schechter* court's answer to this question was to quote with approval a statement from the recommendations of the New York Supreme Court Justices Committee on Pattern Jury Instructions:

> The limitation that the accident must have been a substantial factor in causing the loss of memory is predicated on the rationale of the *Noseworthy* case, which is not merely plaintiff's inability to present proof, but the unfairness of allowing the defendant, who has knowledge of the facts, to benefit by standing mute when plaintiff's inability results from defendant's acts.

Consider what this statement means and what relationship it has to the facts of *Schechter*. With respect to the plaintiff's possible "inability to present proof," the plaintiff in *Schechter* produced his boating companion as an eyewitness.

What is the court's concern when it refers to the "unfairness of allowing the defendant, who has knowledge of the facts, to benefit by standing mute"? If standing mute with knowledge is "unfair," is it unfair, as the court suggests, only when the defendant is the cause of plaintiff's amnesia? In any event, the defendant in *Schechter* did not stand mute, and other defendants are not likely to stand mute — unless the plaintiff's amnesia prevents the plaintiff from meeting the initial production burden. But if the plaintiff has not met the production burden, the case will not go to the jury, so there will be no occasion to apply a reduced burden of proof!

Are there other justifications for applying a burden-of-persuasion rule favorable to a plaintiff who suffers amnesia as a result of the defendant's conduct? If so, what do you think of the requirement that the plaintiff must establish the amnesia by clear and convincing evidence?

4. If burdens of persuasion operate as they are intended to operate, precisely what cases would come out differently under a rule that allocated the preponderance burden of persuasion to one party instead of the other? Is not the answer only those cases in which the jury is in equipoise and is unable to say whether the burden of persuasion is met or not? How large a class of cases do you think that is likely to be? Changing a burden of persuasion from preponderance to clear and convincing evidence, by contrast, is more likely to affect the results in cases, again assuming burdens of persuasion operate roughly as intended.

Consider the implication of these observations in the context of *Schechter*. If holding the plaintiff with amnesia to a lower standard of persuasion than other plaintiffs means that the plaintiff's burden is reduced slightly from the preponderance standard, the effect is to make the plaintiff's burden something less than 50-plus percent — say, 49 percent. This is the equivalent of saying that the burden of persuasion shifts to the defendant to persuade the jury by a 51-plus percent preponderance that the defendant is not negligent. Thus, contrary to the court's assertion, the amnesia rule does shift the burden of proof to the defendant (unless, of the course, the fact finder understands preponderance to mean more than 50-plus percent). Such a shift, however, is unlikely to affect many cases. The practical impact of the amnesia rule lies not in the question whether there is a shifting of the preponderance burden but rather in how much of a shift the amnesia rule creates.

5. In Santosky v. Kramer, 455 U.S. 745, 757 (1982), the Supreme Court explained that the applicable standard of proof will depend on the general type of case at issue, and is not something to be allocated on a case-by-case basis, because "litigants and the factfinder must know at the outset of a given proceeding how the risk of error will be allocated." Is *Schechter* consistent with this principle?

6. There are statements in many cases that the "burden of proof never shifts; it always rests with the party to whom it was originally allocated." For the most part this statement is true, but it is more misleading than helpful. Reconsider Diagram 10-1, page 720, supra. When a party has demonstrated such a strong case that no reasonable person could disagree that the party deserves on the evidence so far produced to win, a judgment will be entered unless the adversary produces more evidence that lowers the probabilities to a point where reasonable people could disagree. In such a case, the adversary bears a functional burden of production; the adversary can produce evidence or lose. In this sense, the "burden of production" can shift numerous times during the course of a trial.

7. There are various policies that could be pursued through different choices concerning burdens of persuasion. We have mentioned some, such as error equalization over parties. Others include the reduction of erroneous determinations of liability, reduction of total dollars wrongfully allocated as a result of trial, and the minimization of large mistakes. Different burden of proof rules may serve these various policies better than others. Neil Orloff and Jery Stedinger, A Framework for Evaluating the Preponderance-of-the-Evidence Standard, 131 U. Pa. L. Rev. 1159 (1983).

KEY POINTS

1. A burden of persuasion is a procedural rule of decision that requires a party to persuade the fact finder of a proposition to a specified degree of certainty.

2. The usual burden of persuasion in civil cases is a "preponderance of the evidence," which is generally understood as meaning "more likely true than not"; in some types of civil cases the burden of persuasion is "clear and convincing evidence."

3. From the perspective of the parties to the action, the burden of persuasion is relative: To say that the plaintiff must prove some proposition to be true by greater than 50 percent in order to win is to say that the defendant must prove that proposition to be false by 50 percent.

4. The burden of persuasion is usually on the party who has the burdens of pleading and production on the matter.

2.   Judicial Summary and Comment in Civil Cases

At common law, trial judges had the power to sum up the evidence at the close of the trial and to comment on its implications. The power to sum up the evidence allows the judge to review for the jury all the evidence that the parties presented. The value of summary is that it gives the jury an impartial review of the evidence. The power to comment on the evidence goes considerably further. It permits the court to express its own views on the implications of the evidence, thus injecting the judge's personal opinion into the litigation.

The drafters of the Federal Rules proposed the following rule:

SUMMING-UP AND COMMENT BY JUDGE

After the close of the evidence and arguments of counsel, the judge may fairly and impartially sum up the evidence and comment to the jury upon the weight of the evidence and the credibility of the witnesses, if he also instructs the jury that they are to determine for themselves the weight of the evidence and the credit to be given to the witnesses and that they are not bound by the judge's summation or comment.

According to the commentary to the proposed rule, the intent was to codify the common law in the federal courts. Congress rejected the rule on the ground that such a rule is more properly one of procedure than evidence. The intention, though, was not to affect or change the existing power of the trial judge.

Many states have rejected the common law relating to summary and comment. Indeed, some states still have constitutional or statutory provisions prohibiting summary or comment, or both. Curtis Wright Jr., Instructions to the Jury: Summary Without Comment, 1954 Wash. U. L.Q. 177; Curtis Wright Jr., The Invasion of the Jury: Temperature of the War, 27 Temple L.Q. 137 (1953).

a.   The Advantages and Disadvantages of Permitting Summary and Comment

The attractiveness of comment and summary is that it may inject into the trial process a disinterested element that is valuable to the jury in its appraisal of the evidence. To the extent one believes that there is such a thing as a "disinterested observer," and to the extent one distinguishes the "evidence" presented at trial from "inferences" one draws from the evidence, one may be convinced that summary and comment are laudable features of trials. Both of these points have another side to them, however.

Trial judges certainly are disinterested in some respects, but they, like the rest of us, have their own way of looking at things that undoubtedly affects both what they observe and retain as well as what inferences they draw from evidence. Reconsider the discussion of relevancy in Chapter Three. Fact finders evaluate evidence in the context of their belief systems — the way they look at the world. Suppose, for example, that a person returns home one night and before entering the house wonders if her husband is at home. She notices that the evening paper is not on the doorstep and that the deadbolt on the front door is unlocked. Moreover, she knows from prior experience that when her husband returns home he invariably picks up the paper and leaves the deadbolt unlocked after entering the house. She also knows that she has a reliable paper delivery service. By comparing what she observes — no newspaper and deadbolt unlocked — she can infer that her spouse has already arrived home.

Of course, the inference she has drawn may be erroneous. It is possible, for example, that the paper blew away or was not delivered that day and that she or her husband inadvertently left the deadbolt unlocked in the morning. These matters, too, might be considered in light of observations made at the time, which would also be compared to previous experience. Is it a windy day? What happens to the paper on such a day? How often is the deadbolt inadvertently unlocked? The process of inference, in short, requires that evidence be compared to previous experience. That is what jurors do when they consider evidence, and indeed it explains in large measure why we cherish the jury system. In deciding the facts of a case, we want a representative mix of the population to bring their differing views to bear on the question of what inferences may be drawn from evidence.

This inevitable reliance on personal experience in fact-finding explains in large measure the resistance to judicial comment on the evidence, and to some extent summary as well. Judges commenting on the implications of evidence are, in a very real sense, commenting on their previous experience, and the injection of their previous experience into the fact-finding process may have an unwarranted influence. Trial judges, like all of us, have individual biases and prejudices that may affect how they summarize or comment on the evidence. In addition, there may be a kind of group bias stemming from the common, not particularly diverse backgrounds that judges to a substantial extent share. Judges as a class tend to be well educated, educated in a similar manner, economically comfortable, and accustomed to respect in the community. In addition, judges still tend to be predominantly white and male and from middle- or upper-class backgrounds. Any small and coherent group, such as trial judges were and probably still are, tends to share beliefs and attitudes that may affect how they perceive evidence as well as what inferences they draw from that evidence. Allowing judges to summarize and comment on the evidence permits their beliefs and attitudes to creep into the fact-finding process, skewing it in favor of the interests of this particular elite group. J. Willard Hurst, The Growth of American Law: The Lawmakers, 97-98, 104, 145, 351-352 (1940).

b.   The Criteria for Evaluating Judicial Summary and Comment

In federal court, summary and comment are appropriate "to assist [the jury] in arriving at a just conclusion." Vicksburg & M.R.R. v. Putnam, 118 U.S. 545, 553 (1886). The difficulty is that the criteria for determining what properly assists a jury — and what goes too far — are not clear.

Consider Nunley v. Pettway Oil Co., 346 F.2d 95 (6th Cir. 1965), where the jury was unable to decide if the plaintiff had been an invitee or a licensee. In order to encourage the jury to break the impasse, the judge gave the jury the following instruction during a break from deliberations:

> Now, the jury of course is the sole and exclusive judge of the facts in this lawsuit. It is appropriate that the court in an effort to be possibly of some help to the jury may comment upon the evidence. I refrain from doing that and have refrained until this time from doing it in this case. However, in an effort to be of some possible assistance to you I think that I should under these circumstances make some comment upon the evidence upon this issue of invitee-licensee. I want you to understand, however, that in making these comments that you are not in any degree, in any respect, obligated to receive or accept or agree with what I may say. It is your duty to accept what I say with regard to the law in the case, but it is not your duty to accept any comment that I may make or any evaluation that I make or conclusion that I might reach on the evidence. That is solely your responsibility and solely your duty. But, with that understanding, it is the opinion of the court in this case that, from all the evidence upon the issue of invitee or licensee, that the evidence will establish that at the time and place of the accident the plaintiff was a licensee and not an invitee. Now, I say that just for the purpose, as I say, of possibly being of some help to you, but I want you to understand that making that comment you are not obligated whatsoever to accept that comment as your comment or as your opinion in the case, because it is your job and your responsibility to resolve that issue. I only make that with the thought and the hope that it may be of some possible assistance to you. At any rate, I want to ask you once again to retire and consider your verdict and see if you cannot come to some agreement, some verdict that will reflect the views of all of the jurors. Have respect for the views of your fellow jurors. If you find there are jurors that have different views from you, don't hesitate to change your mind if you should be persuaded by reason and logic to accept a different view. Attempt if you can in good conscience to arrive at a unanimous verdict. After you have considered the views of all others you shouldn't give up a firm conviction that you have just for the purpose of arriving at a unanimous verdict, but see if you cannot resolve this issue. Make one more effort, please. [Id. at 98.]

In reversing a judgment for the defendant, the court of appeals said that "the trial judge's opinion on the licensee-invitee issue was an opinion on an ultimate fact question peculiarly for jury consideration and amounted to an instructed verdict as to defendant. . . ." Id. Do you agree?

c. *Standardized Comments*

Perhaps in response to restraints on the power to summarize and comment, a practice of providing "standardized inferences" has developed. These are instructions that inform the jury that proof of one fact gives rise to an inference of another fact. Such instructions come in a variety of forms. For examples, see Longenecker v. General Motors, 594 F.2d 1283 (9th Cir. 1979) (inference of a defect from a product failure); Ina Aviation Corp. v. United States, 468 F. Supp. 695 (E.D.N.Y.), *aff'd*, 610 F.2d 806 (1st Cir. 1979) (inference that evidence in a party's control but not produced at trial would have been unfavorable to that party). For a discussion, see 2 McCormick on Evidence §342, at 496-497 n.9, 497-498 (Kenneth S. Broun ed., 6th ed. 2006).

The sources of a standardized inference can be statutory or common law. When the source is the common law, the standardized inference is, in essence, a summary of collected judicial wisdom with respect to a certain matter. Such a standardized inference may be preferable to a normal comment on the evidence because the personal views of the trial judge are relegated to a lesser role. To some extent the same is true of standardized inferences that are authorized by statute, except that the source of the inference is legislative rather than judicial wisdom. On the other hand, because instructions on standardized inferences typically do not incorporate references to specific evidence in the case and because they sometimes contain excessive legal jargon, they may not convey information to the jury as well as individualized comments. Charles T. McCormick, Charges on Presumptions and Burdens of Proof, 5 N.C. L. Rev. 291, 299-301 (1972).

d. *The Relationship Between Comments on the Evidence and the Burden of Persuasion*

When a comment has its intended effect, it inevitably has the consequence of shifting the relative burdens of persuasion of the parties in the case. Consider, for example, a comment that is favorable to the plaintiff, who has the persuasion burden of proving fact X by a preponderance of the evidence. If there were no comment, the plaintiff in order to prevail would have to introduce enough evidence to convince the jury that fact X is 50-plus percent likely to be true; the defendant in order to prevail would have to convince the jury that there was at least a 50-50 chance that fact X is untrue. With a comment favorable to the plaintiff, the plaintiff will have to do less to persuade the jury that fact X is true, and the defendant will have to do more to persuade the jury that fact X is untrue. For example, the plaintiff's evidence standing alone may convince the jury that there is only a 45 percent probability that X is true, but the evidence along with the comment may convince the jury by a greater than 50 percent probability that X is true. In such a case, the effect of the comment is to permit the plaintiff to prevail even though the plaintiff has introduced evidence to satisfy only a 45 percent persuasion burden. The defendant, in order to prevail in the case, would have had to introduce enough evidence to convince the jury by a 55-plus percent probability that X was untrue.

KEY POINTS

1. Judicial summary of and comment on the evidence are permissible in federal courts, but many states prohibit judicial comment or summary or both.

2. If summary or comment is permissible, an important criterion for evaluating the propriety of a particular summary or comment should be its accuracy.

3. Unless a summary or comment merely states the obvious to the jury, the summary or comment will inevitably be helpful to one party and harmful to the other, thereby shifting the parties' relative burdens of persuasion.

NOTES AND QUESTIONS

1. Reconsider the *Schechter* case at page 726, supra. Try to formulate a comment on the evidence that would have roughly the equivalent effect of the burden-reducing amnesia instruction that the court approved.

2. Would a comment of the type contemplated in Note 1 be permissible? If the answer is yes, which device — the comment or the explicit burden-reducing instruction — is preferable? If the answer is no, why should it be permissible to reduce the plaintiff's burden of persuasion in one way but not the other?

3.   Presumptions in Civil Cases

Presumption is a term that courts and commentators use to describe rules that regulate the process of proof by creating a special *legal* relationship between one fact, A, a proven fact that gives rise to the presumption, and another fact, B, the presumed fact. For example, many jurisdictions have a rule that on proof of the fact that a person has been missing for seven years (fact A), there is a presumption that the person is dead (fact B). Typically, this rule or presumption means that proof of fact A (e.g., that a person has not been heard from in seven years) *requires* a finding of fact B (e.g., that the person is dead) unless the party against whom the presumption operates adequately rebuts fact B.

There almost always will be some *inferential* relationship between a presumed fact and the fact that gives rise to the presumption. For example, in the presumption-of-death example, proof of fact A (not heard from in seven years) provides some inferential support for fact B (death). Indeed, in some cases a reasonable fact finder may be warranted in finding fact B on proof only of fact A even if there were no presumption. The significance of saying that proof of fact A gives rise to a presumption of fact B is that the presumption connotes some special *legal* relationship between the two facts. There is, however, no unique evidentiary device or concept referred to by the term *presumption*. Rather, *presumption* is a label that courts, legislatures, and commentators attach to a variety of devices that manipulate the process of proof. It would be possible to describe those manipulations specifically and directly and to eliminate the term *presumption* from legal discourse. Morejon v. Rais Constr. Co., 851 N.E.2d 1143 (N.Y. 2006) ("The dizzying array of formulations (from mandatory inferences to permissive presumptions), however, suggests that things would be far less complicated if we viewed [the issue] without undue emphasis on labels and pigeonholes."). Indeed, as the materials throughout this section imply, such a reform would be desirable.

Presumptions come in different shapes and forms. Some are irrebuttable or conclusive, and some are rebuttable. Some rebuttable presumptions affect only the burden of production, and some affect the burden of persuasion. Some rebuttable presumptions are mandatory, in the sense that they require a finding of the presumed fact in the absence of sufficient rebuttal. Other rebuttable presumptions are permissive. They permit but do not require a finding of the presumed fact even if there is no rebuttal. The use of term *presumption* is therefore often ambiguous, and when it is not clear from the context which type is being referred to this ambiguity creates confusion.

As we will explain, presumptions fall into four main types or categories: (1) conclusive presumptions, (2) production-burden presumptions, (3) persuasion-burden presumptions, and (4) permissive presumptions. After discussing examples of these four types of presumptions, we will explore some further complexities in presumption analysis. We will then consider and critique the approach to presumptions in the Federal Rules of Evidence.

As we begin the consideration of presumptions, you should keep in mind two issues that affect the operation of presumptions.

First, who has what burden of persuasion with respect to the facts that give rise to presumptions? In other words, in order for the aforementioned presumption of death (fact B) to come into play, who has what burden of persuasion with respect to proof that the individual has not been heard from in seven years (fact A)? The *who* part of this question is not controversial: The person who wishes to take advantage of the presumption has the burden of establishing the facts that give rise to the presumption. The answer to the *what* part of the question is likely to be a preponderance of the evidence, which is the common although seldom articulated standard of proof for most preliminary facts. There may be instances, however, in which a court sets forth a higher standard. Cf. Schechter v. Klanfer at page 726, supra (to get advantage of reduced burden of proof plaintiff must prove amnesia by clear and convincing evidence).

Second, who decides whether the party wishing to take advantage of a presumption has satisfied the appropriate burden of persuasion with respect to the facts that give rise to the presumption? Assume, for example, that a woman wishes to take advantage of the presumption of death (fact B) with respect to her husband. If there is conflicting evidence about whether he has been heard from within seven years (fact A), does the judge decide or does the jury decide that question? We will elaborate on this issue in the context of our discussion of the different types of presumptions.

a.   Irrebuttable or Conclusive Presumptions

Some presumptions are conclusive or irrebuttable. In other words, once there is proof of fact A, the fact giving rise to the presumption, fact B, the presumed fact, is conclusively established. The party against whom the presumption operates is not allowed to present evidence of non-B. The Federal Coal Mine Health and Safety Act of 1969, which entitles totally disabled coal miners to compensation creates such an irrebuttable or conclusive presumption. Upon proof by X-ray or other clinical evidence that a miner has complicated pneumoconiosis (fact A), the law conclusively presumes that the miner is totally disabled (fact B) and, therefore, entitled to compensation. 30 U.S.C. §921(c) (1994). In other words, if the miner can establish fact A, the miner is entitled to compensation; the mine owner is not permitted to try to prove that the miner may not in fact be totally disabled (fact B).

A conclusive presumption is nothing more than a somewhat awkwardly worded substantive rule of law: If the law states that a plaintiff must prove fact B to prevail and if, on proof of fact A, fact B is conclusively presumed to exist, the rule of law really is that the plaintiff will prevail by proving *either* fact A *or* fact B. Usery v. Turner Elkhorn Mining Co., 428 U.S. 1 (1976); Wiehe v. Kissick Constr. Co., 232 P.3d 866 (Kan. App. 2010) (irrebuttable presumption of impairment under workers' compensation statute if employee tests above a specified level for alcohol or drugs).

As long as the classification created by a conclusive presumption is not so arbitrary or irrational that it raises due process or equal protection concerns, there is no valid basis for objecting to it. For example, if, as the Court held in *Usery*, Congress could have enacted a statute specifically providing that the two categories of miners were entitled to compensation, there should be no reason to object to the statute merely because Congress utilized presumption jargon to accomplish this objective. On the other hand, if a court were to conclude that a legislative classification is so arbitrary or irrational that it is unconstitutional, the classification should be unconstitutional regardless of whether the legislature used presumption language to create the categories. In re Adoption of Doe, 2008 WL 5070056 (Fla. Cir. Ct. Aug. 29, 2008) (irrebuttable presumption that "it is never in the best interest of any adoptee to be adopted by a homosexual" held unconstitutional). In short, what should matter is not the manner in which the legislature chooses to formulate its categories, but rather whether the categories themselves present constitutional issues.

Because a conclusive presumption is nothing more than a substantive rule of law, the question whether the facts giving rise to a conclusive presumption exist is, as it should be, one for the jury to decide. To put the matter somewhat differently, a conclusive presumption is nothing more than a somewhat awkward way of stating that identical legal ramifications follow from two classifications (fact B, which may be proved without regard to the presumption, and fact A, which by virtue of the conclusive presumption is legally indistinguishable from fact B). If the jury is the decision maker with respect to fact B, the jury should also be the decision maker with respect to fact A.

KEY POINTS

1. A conclusive presumption is a somewhat awkward way of stating a substantive rule of law.

2. As long as it is constitutionally permissible to attribute the same legal consequences to the presumed fact and the fact giving rise to the conclusive presumption, there should be no reason for objecting to a conclusive presumption.

PROBLEMS

10.1. Casanova, a life beneficiary, and Linus and Lucy, two remaindermen of a testamentary trust, seek to accelerate and thereby terminate the trust. They argue that the class of remaindermen who are the issue of Casanova has been effectively closed by reason of a vasectomy performed on Casanova, which rendered him sterile. The Trustee defends on the ground that there is in this jurisdiction an irrebuttable presumption that a man or woman irrespective of his or her age or physical capacity is conclusively presumed to be capable of producing children. Moreover, the Trustee argues the vasectomy may be reversible. The Trustee moves for a directed verdict. Should it be granted?

10.2. Husband is being sued by Wife for support for a child born to Wife during the marriage to Husband. The marriage has since ended in divorce, and Husband defends on the ground that he and his wife had not had sexual relations for two years before the birth of the child. Wife asks the trial judge to instruct the jury on the irrebuttable presumption that a child born during wedlock is presumed to belong to the husband. Should such an instruction be given, assuming that the law is as Wife asserts? Would it make any difference if Husband could prove beyond any doubt, based on blood test for example, that he is not the father of the child?

b. Mandatory Rebuttable Presumptions

Mandatory rebuttable presumptions create special burden of proof rules for designated situations. The particular rationale for a special burden of proof rule — like the rationales for general allocations of production and persuasion burdens — is often elusive. Nonetheless, it is fair to say that in general the purpose for creating special burden of proof rules is to fine-tune the process of proof in order to advance the goal of rational and accurate fact-finding or other goals related to the allocation of burdens of proof. See Notes 4 and 7 at pages 729 and 730, supra. Because of the complexity and confusion in the analysis of presumptions, however, the use of presumptions often detracts from rather than advances these goals.

i. Mandatory Rebuttable Presumptions That Shift a Burden of Production. Some presumptions create a mandatory relationship between fact A, the proved fact, and fact B, the presumed fact, that affects only the burden of producing evidence. Once a party establishes fact A, there *must* be finding of fact B unless the party against whom the presumption operates produces evidence of non-B. In other words, if the party against whom the presumption operates fails to produce evidence of the presumed fact, the party will lose on that fact. If the party meets the production burden, the presumption has no further impact on the case. Courts and commentators, following the lead of Professor Thayer, commonly refer to this type of presumption as a "bursting bubble" presumption. Once the party against whom the presumption operates produces sufficient evidence, the presumption — the bubble — disappears or bursts. See James B. Thayer, A Preliminary Treatise on Evidence at Common Law 336-337 (1898).

Consider a case in which, in the absence of any presumption, the plaintiff would have to establish that the defendant received a letter in order to prevail. Assume that there is a mandatory production burden presumption that on proof of mailing (fact A) receipt of the letter (fact B) is presumed. In re Yoder Co., 758 F.2d 1114 (6th Cir. 1985); City & County of Denver v. East Jefferson County Sanitation District, 771 P.2d 16 (Colo. App. 1988); Winkfield v. American Continental Insurance Co., 110 Ill. App. 2d 156, 249 N.E.2d 174 (1969) (all dealing with the presumption of receipt on proof of mailing). In order to take advantage of the presumption, the person in whose favor the presumption operates must establish that the facts giving rise to the presumption exist. Thus, in our example, to take advantage of the presumption the plaintiff must establish that the letter was mailed. If the plaintiff fails to do so and if there is no other evidence of receipt, the plaintiff will lose. If the plaintiff establishes that the letter was mailed (fact A) and if the defendant produces no evidence of nonreceipt (non-B), the court will direct a verdict in favor of the plaintiff on the receipt issue regardless of the strength or weakness of inference of receipt in the particular case; the presumption mandates that result. On the other hand, if the defendant meets the production burden, the presumption disappears and the case will proceed as if there had been no presumption in the first place. Typically, this means that the judge will send the case to the jury with the instruction that the plaintiff, in order to prevail, must convince the jury by a preponderance of the evidence that the defendant received the letter (fact B). In any particular instance, however, whether the judge should send the matter to the jury or issue a judgment as a matter of law for one of the parties should depend on which Case in Diagram 10-1 at page 720, supra, accurately represents the totality of the evidence. In re Estate of Wood, 374 Mich. 278, 132 N.W.2d 35 (1965).

As the preceding discussion demonstrates, a mandatory production burden presumption is in effect a specialized judgment-as-a-matter-of-law rule. As such, it has two consequences. First, establishing the facts that give rise to such a presumption will require the court to render a judgment as a matter of law on the presumed fact against an opposing party who fails to meet the production burden mandated by the presumption. Second, establishing the facts that give rise to a mandatory production burden presumption protects the party in whose favor the presumption operates from a judgment as a matter of law, at least until the opposing party produces evidence: Since proof of fact A requires a finding of fact B in the absence of rebuttal, it would be improper, before rebuttal, to issue a judgment against the person invoking the presumption regardless of how weak the inference from fact A to fact B may be.

NOTES AND QUESTIONS

1. Courts rarely focus in detail on how much evidence a party must produce to burst the bubble of a mandatory production burden presumption. Courts use phrases like "some evidence" or "any evidence" or "credible evidence" to describe what the presumption demands, but whether a party's evidence meets the articulated standard is seldom an issue. Graham C. Lilly, An Introduction to the Law of Evidence 68-71 (3d ed. 1996). In our view, the evidence necessary to rebut a production burden presumption should be no different from the evidence required to satisfy other production burdens. The question should be whether the party who has the production burden has produced enough evidence to create a jury issue on the nonexistence of the presumed fact. See Diagram 10-1 and accompanying discussion at pages 719-721, supra.

2. Even if there are instances in which special production burden rules seem appropriate, it is important to note that there is no need to resort to the rhetoric of presumption to accomplish the desired end. One can simply and directly allocate the production burden.

KEY POINTS

1. A mandatory production burden presumption is the equivalent of a specialized judgment-as-a-matter-of-law rule.

2. Once a party establishes facts giving rise to a mandatory production burden presumption, the presumption requires a finding of the presumed fact in the absence of any rebuttal of the presumed fact.

3. Establishing the facts that give rise to a mandatory production burden presumption also protects a party in whose favor the presumption works from an opponent's request for a judgment as a matter of law — at least before any rebuttal of the presumed fact.

ii. Mandatory Rebuttable Presumptions That Shift the Burden of Persuasion.

Some mandatory rebuttable presumptions shift the burden of persuasion to the party against whom they operate. Consider, for example, a case in which the plaintiff wishes to establish that the defendant, her former husband, is the father of her child. Normally, the plaintiff as the moving party would have both the burden of introducing sufficient evidence of paternity and the burden of persuading the fact finder that the defendant was the father. Assume, though, that there is a mandatory rebuttable presumption in the jurisdiction that a child born or conceived during a valid marriage relationship is the child of the husband. Assume further that this presumption shifts the burden of persuasion to the person against whom it operates. Cal. Fam. Code §7611. To take advantage of the presumption the plaintiff will have to establish that she was legally married (fact A_1) to the defendant (fact A_2) at the time of the child's conception or birth (fact A_3). If the plaintiff can establish these facts, the fact finder must find that the defendant is the father (fact B) unless the defendant rebuts the presumption. One possible strategy for the defendant in this case is to attack one or more of the facts giving rise to the presumption, facts A_1, A_2, and A_3. If the plaintiff cannot establish by the requisite degree of proof — probably a preponderance of the evidence — that they exist, there is no presumption in the case, and the plaintiff retains the burden of persuading the fact finder that the defendant is the father of the child. (Even if there were doubts about whether the child was born or conceived during the marriage relationship, the plaintiff may be able to establish with blood test or other evidence that the defendant is probably the father.) Another, not mutually exclusive, strategy for the defendant is to attack the presumed fact, paternity, directly. For example, the defendant might present witnesses to testify that he was out of the country during the possible time of conception and, therefore, could not be the father. If the plaintiff can establish facts A_1, A_2, and A_3, the reasonable inference of paternity that one can draw from these facts is sufficiently strong, without regard to the presumption, to permit the fact finder to find paternity. Regardless of the strength of this inference, however, the mandatory persuasion burden presumption means, at a minimum, that the defendant must persuade the jury that he is not the father of the child.

A persuasion burden presumption is similar to an *affirmative defense,* the term used to describe the direct placement of a persuasion burden on a defendant. Fed. R. Civ. P. 8(c) (listing a number of affirmative defenses that must be proven by defendants). Consider, for example, the persuasion burden presumption of paternity that arises on proof of conception during a valid marriage. To say that there is a "presumption of paternity that allocates or shifts the burden of persuasion" to the defendant and that there is an "affirmative defense of nonpaternity" that requires the defendant to prove the fact is to make functionally identical statements. There is nothing in the concept of a presumption that facilitates the allocation of a burden of persuasion. Rather, presumptions that shift the burden of persuasion are simply affirmative defenses created for the same reasons of policy that generally inform the decision to allocate burdens of persuasion.

NOTES AND QUESTIONS

1. What is the justification for allocating the burden of persuasion to a (former) husband in a paternity action?

2. As we pointed out in our initial discussion of burdens of persuasion, shifting the preponderance burden from one party to another may not have an impact on very many cases, at least if the jury understands preponderance to mean 50-plus percent.

KEY POINTS

1. A mandatory persuasion burden presumption requires the party against whom the presumption operates to carry the burden of persuasion on the issue.

2. A mandatory persuasion burden presumption is the functional equivalent of an affirmative defense.

iii.   Decision-making with Respect to the Facts Giving Rise to Mandatory Presumptions.   Despite the functional equivalence of mandatory rebuttable presumptions and direct allocations of burdens of proof, courts tend to implement the presumptions differently from the manner in which they implement direct allocations of burdens of proof. If there is a question about who has the "normal" burden of proof with respect to an issue, there is general agreement that the question is one for the court or legislature to determine. By contrast, when the burden of proof rule depends on proof of some particular fact, which is of course always the situation with presumptions, the question whether that fact exists typically is one for the jury.

Consider, for example, the preceding mailing and receipt example. If the defendant produces sufficient evidence of nonreceipt to satisfy the production burden created by the presumption, there is no need to deal further with the presumption; the bubble has burst. Indeed, it is not necessary even to consider whether the presumption arose in the first place. If the defendant produces no evidence of nonreceipt, however, it will be necessary to determine whether the plaintiff should have the benefit of the presumption. In such a situation, the jury typically decides whether the plaintiff has established the fact of mailing (fact A), which gives rise to the presumption of receipt (fact B). If there were no evidence of receipt other than the plaintiff's evidence of mailing, the court would instruct the jury that it must find for the plaintiff if it finds that the plaintiff mailed the letter.

KEY POINT

Typically, the jury decides whether the facts giving rise to a mandatory rebuttable presumption exist.

PROBLEMS

10.3. Plaintiff sues Defendant and one element of Plaintiff's claim is fact B. In the absence of any presumption, Plaintiff would have to prove fact B by a preponderance of the evidence. There is a presumption in the jurisdiction that if fact A is proven, fact B is presumed to exist. It is a mandatory *production* burden presumption.

Assume that Plaintiff introduces no direct evidence of fact B, but that Plaintiff introduces sufficient evidence of fact A to create a jury issue over whether fact A exists. Assume further that the inference from fact A to fact B is sufficiently strong that if fact A exists, a reasonable juror could find that fact B exists. Finally, assume that there is nothing in the evidence or common experience that would permit a finding of fact B in the absence of fact A.

(a) At the close of Plaintiff's case, both parties move for judgment as a matter of law. What result?

(b) Assume that there is no motion for judgment as a matter of law at the close of Plaintiff's case and that Defendant rests without presenting any evidence. Now both parties move for judgment as a matter of law. Should either party's motion be granted? If not, what should the judge tell the jury about how to decide the case? In answering this question assume alternatively (1) that Plaintiff's evidence of fact A is so overwhelming that no reasonable person could disbelieve it and (2) that reasonable people could disagree about the existence of fact A.

(c) Assume that Defendant introduces evidence of only non-A before resting and that reasonable people viewing all of the evidence could disagree about the truth of both fact A and fact B. What should the judge tell the jury about how to decide the case?

(d) Assume that Defendant introduces evidence of only non-B before resting and that reasonable people could disagree about the truth of both fact A and fact B. What should the judge tell the jury about how to decide the case?

(e) Assume that Defendant introduces evidence of both non-A and non-B before resting and that reasonable people could disagree about the truth of both fact A and fact B. What should the judge tell the jury about how to decide the case?

10.4. Assume the same facts and alternative possibilities as in Problem 10.3 except now the mandatory rebuttable presumption is one that places the burden of *persuasion* on the party against whom it operates.

c. Permissive or "Weak" Presumptions

Sometimes the law creates a special relationship between two facts — fact A, the proven fact, and fact B — but makes that relationship permissive rather than mandatory. In other words, on proof of fact A the fact finder may but is not required to find fact B even if the opponent makes no effort to rebut fact B. Commentators refer to these permissive relationships variously as permissive presumptions, "weak" presumptions, or "inferences."

The most common permissive presumption is res ipsa loquitur. Although the content and impact of res ipsa loquitur vary somewhat among the jurisdictions, a fair statement of the doctrine is this: If the plaintiff proves that the plaintiff was injured by an act that would normally not occur without negligence (fact A_1), that the defendant was in exclusive control of the instrumentality that caused the act (fact A_2), and that the plaintiff was not contributorily negligent (fact A_3), the fact finder may (but is not required to) find that the defendant negligently caused the defendant's injury (fact B). Although facts A_1, A_2, and A_3 standing alone create a fairly strong inference of fact B without regard to the res ipsa doctrine, the significance of res ipsa is that the judge in a special instruction will commend the relationship among these facts to the jury. In other words, to say that there is a permissive presumption from fact A to fact B is to say that the judge will instruct the jury that if they find fact A to be true the law permits them to infer fact B. At the same time, the judge will tell the jury that the law does not require a finding of fact B on proof of fact A and that the jury still must be convinced by the requisite burden of persuasion that fact B exists.

Even if the term *permissive presumption* is new to you, the foregoing explanation and illustration of what constitutes a permissive presumption should sound familiar. A permissive presumption is a standardized comment on the evidence. See the discussion at page 733, supra.

KEY POINTS

1. Permissive presumptions — sometimes referred to as "weak" presumptions or inferences — are the equivalent of standardized comments on the evidence.

2. Standardized comments couched in presumption language are not likely to advance reasoned decision-making because such comments typically do not inform the jury of reasons why the court is commending certain facts to the jury.

d.   The Complexity of Presumptions

Despite the intricacies in the foregoing material, the presentation thus far has been a somewhat oversimplified glimpse of the world of presumptions. The reality is considerably more complex for a variety of reasons. Sometimes the complexity is simply a function of the difficult proof problems in complex litigation, Usery v. Turner Elkhorn Mining Co., 428 U.S. 1 (1976), but presumptions can create difficult problems even in relatively simple litigation. For example, it may not be clear from the existing law what impact the presumption is supposed to have, and there may sometimes be "conflicting" presumptions, see 2 McCormick on Evidence §344, at 510-12 (Kenneth S. Broun ed., 6th ed. 2006). In at least some cases, the problem seems to be that the court is grappling with a tension between its assumption that the term *presumption* connotes something important and the reality that a typical production burden presumption frequently has no impact on litigation or the litigants. See Note 4 at page 729, supra. The result is confusing jury instructions that attempt to transform production burden presumption rhetoric into what becomes in effect a not very comprehensible comment on the evidence.

NOTES AND QUESTIONS

1. The Supreme Court has recognized that legislatures have wide latitude in allocating burdens of proof as they like. Lavine v. Milne, 424 U.S. 577, 585 (1976)

("Outside the criminal law area, where special concerns attend, the locus of the burden of persuasion is normally not an issue of federal constitutional moment."). Thus, one would think that the use of a presumption to allocate a burden of production or burden of persuasion should give rise to no special difficulty. Nonetheless, in dealing with rebuttable presumptions, the Supreme Court has stressed the need for a rational relationship between the proven fact that gives rise to a presumption and the presumed fact. Consider, for example, Usery v. Turner Elkhorn Mining Co., 428 U.S. 1 (1976), where the Court upheld several production burden presumptions set forth in the Federal Coal Mine Health and Safety Act of 1969. One of the presumptions provided that upon proof that a coal miner with 10 years of employment in the mines had pneumoconiosis, it was presumed that the miner contracted the disease from employment. According to the Court:

> We have consistently tested presumptions arising in civil statutes such as this, involving matters of economic regulation, against the standard articulated in Mobile, J. & K.C.R. Co. v. Turnipseed, 219 U.S. 35, 43 (1910):
>
>> That a legislative presumption of one fact from evidence of another may not constitute a denial of due process of law or a denial of the equal protection of the law it is only essential that there shall be some rational connection between the fact proved and the ultimate fact presumed, and that the inference of one fact from proof of another shall not be so unreasonable as to be a purely arbitrary mandate.
>
> Moreover, as we have recognized:
>
>> The process of making the determination of rationality is, by its nature, highly empirical, and in matters not within specialized judicial competence or completely commonplace, significant weight should be accorded the capacity of Congress to amass the stuff of actual experience and cull conclusions from it. United States v. Gainey, 380 U.S. 63, 67 (1965).
>
> Judged by these standards the . . . [presumption is] constitutionality valid . . . . [I]t is agreed here that pneumoconiosis is caused by breathing coal dust, and that the likelihood of a miner's developing the disease rests upon both the concentration of dust to which he was exposed and the duration of his exposure. Against this scientific background, it was not beyond Congress' authority to refer to exposure factors in establishing a presumption that throws the burden of going forward on the operators. And in view of the medical evidence before Congress indicating the noticeable incidence of pneumoconiosis in cases of miners with 10 years' employment in the mines, we cannot say that it was "purely arbitrary" for Congress to select the 10-year figure as a point of reference for these presumptions. No greater mathematical precision is required. [428 U.S. at 28-29.]

Perhaps an allocation of a burden of proof — whether by way of presumption or otherwise — could be so arbitrary or unreasonable as to raise a constitutional issue. If the implications of *Lavine* are correct, however, Congress seemingly could enact — without regard to any medical evidence — a compensation scheme for coal miners that did not mention presumptions that placed on coal mine operators the burden of coming forward with evidence that a miner's pneumoconiosis was not contracted during employment. If that is correct, why is the Court concerned, as it was in *Usery*, about the empirical relationship between a proven fact and presumed fact when Congress uses presumption language to allocate a burden of production?

    2. Compare *Usery* with the following passage from Lavine v. Milne, supra. In *Lavine*, the Court considered the constitutionality of a statute that "deemed" persons applying for welfare within 75 days after voluntarily terminating their employment or reducing their earning capacity to have done so "for the purpose of qualifying for such

assistance or a larger amount thereof, in the absence of evidence to the contrary. . . . N.Y. Soc. Serv. Law §131(11)":

> Although the District Court found this [provision] to be an unconstitutional "rebuttable presumption," the sole purpose of the provision is to indicate that, as with other eligibility requirements, the applicant rather than the State must establish that he did not leave employment for the purpose of qualifying for benefits. The provision carries with it no procedural consequence; it shifts to the applicant neither the burden of going forward nor the burden of proof, for he appears to carry the burden from the outset.
>
> The offending sentence could be interpreted as a rather circumlocutory direction to welfare authorities to employ a standardized inference that if the Home Relief applicant supplies no information on the issue, he will be presumed to have quit his job to obtain welfare benefits. However, such an instruction would be superfluous for the obvious reason that the failure of an applicant to prove an essential element of eligibility will always result in a nonsuit. The only "rebuttable presumption" — if, indeed, it can be so called — at work here is the normal assumption that an applicant is not entitled to benefits unless and until he proves his eligibility.
>
> Despite the rebuttable presumption aura that the second sentence of §131(11) radiates, it merely makes absolutely clear the fact that the applicant bears the burden of proof on this issue, as he does on all others. And since appellees do not object to the substantive requirement that Home Relief applicants must be free of the impermissible benefit-seeking motive, their underlying complaint may be that the burden of proof on this issue has been unfairly placed on welfare applicants rather than on the State[, a complaint that the Court rejected]. [424 U.S. at 583-585.]

Note that the Court said that there was no "procedural consequence," as though it is one thing to structure burdens of proof before any evidence is heard, and another to provide for burdens of proof to shift after evidence is heard. Can you make any sense out of that distinction?

3. In St. Mary's Honor Center v. Hicks, 509 U.S. 502 (1993), a racial discrimination case brought under Title VII of the Federal Civil Rights Act of 1964, the Supreme Court elaborated on the nature of a rebuttable presumption that it had created to help resolve discrimination claims. The *Hicks* Court began with a description of the prior law:

> With the goal of "progressively . . . sharpening the inquiry into the elusive factual question of intentional discrimination," Texas Dept. of Community Affairs v. Burdine, 450 U.S. 248, 255 n.8 (1981), our opinion in McDonnell Douglas Corp. v. Green, 411 U.S. 792 (1973), established an allocation of the burden of production and an order for the presentation of proof in Title VII discriminatory-treatment cases. The plaintiff in such case, we said, must first establish, by a preponderance of the evidence, a "prima facie" case of racial discrimination . . . .
>
> . . . "[E]stablishment of the prima facie case in effect creates a presumption that the employer unlawfully discriminated against the employee." To establish a "presumption" is to say that a finding of the predicate fact (here, the prima facie case) produces "a required conclusion in the absence of explanation" (here, the finding of unlawful discrimination). Thus, the *McDonnell Douglas* presumption places upon the defendant the burden of producing an explanation to rebut the prima facie case — i.e., the burden of "producing evidence" that the adverse employment actions were taken "for a legitimate, nondiscriminatory reason." [509 U.S. at 506-507.]

There was no dispute in *Hicks* that the defendant had established a prima facie case by proving "(1) that he is black, (2) that he was qualified for the position of shift commander, (3) that he was demoted from that position and ultimately discharged, and (4) that the position remained open and was ultimately filled by a white man." Id. at 506. There was also no dispute that upon adequate rebuttal the plaintiff retained the burden of persuasion. The issue involved the adequacy of the defendant's rebuttal:

> The District Court, acting as trier of fact in this bench trial, found that the reasons petitioners gave [severity and accumulation of rule violations] were not the real reasons for respondent's demotion and discharge. . . . It nonetheless held that respondent had failed to carry his ultimate burden of proving that his race was the determining factor in petitioners' decision first to demote and then to dismiss him. In short, the District Court concluded that "although [respondent] has proven the existence of a crusade to terminate him, he has not proven that the crusade was racially rather than personally motivated." The Court of Appeals set this determination aside on the ground that "once [respondent] proved all of [petitioners'] proffered reasons for the adverse employment actions to be pretextual, [respondent] was entitled to a judgment as a matter of law. [Id. at 508.]

A majority of the Supreme Court, in an opinion by Justice Scalia, agreed with the district court and reversed the judgment of the court of appeals. Justice Souter, in a dissent joined by Justices White, Blackmun, and Stevens, agreed with the court of appeals.

4. Neither opinion in *Hicks* is right or wrong as far as presumptions in the abstract are concerned. *Presumption*, after all, is only a term used to describe various rules that modify or fine-tune general burden of proof rules. Once the plaintiff establishes a prima facie case, it is analytically coherent, as the majority holds, to have a burden of proof rule that merely requires the defendant to come forward with some evidence of nondiscrimination and that has no other impact on the case. Similarly, it is analytically coherent to have a burden of proof rule that, on proof of a prima facie case, treats the defendant's rejected reasons as the equivalent of failing to produce evidence. This latter approach, as the *Hicks* dissent points out, has the effect of focusing the inquiry on the legitimacy of the defendant's reasons. The plaintiff's burden of persuasion, once the prima facie case is established, is to show the falsity of the defendant's proffered reasons. The ultimate question should be which burden of proof rule better serves the objectives of Title VII of the Civil Rights Act.

5. In defense of its position that offering disbelieved reasons was adequate to rebut the presumption in *Hicks* Justice Scalia wrote:

> We have no authority to impose liability upon an employer for alleged discriminatory employment practices unless an appropriate factfinder determines, according to proper procedures, that the employer has unlawfully discriminated. We may, according to traditional practice, establish certain modes and orders of proof, including an initial rebuttable presumption of the sort . . . [that we hold applies in this case]. But nothing in law would permit us to substitute for the required finding that the employer's action was the product of unlawful discrimination, the much different (and much lesser) finding that the employer's explanation of its action was not believable. [Id. at 514-515.]

If the Court can, as the *Hicks* majority conceded, hold the nonresponding employer liable regardless of how weakly the plaintiff's prima facie case may suggest discrimination, why should the Court not be able to require that the employer's explanation be believable? Indeed, is it not true, as the dissent maintained, that the majority's approach substantially undermines the purpose for placing a production burden on the employer in the first place?

6. In Reeves v. Sanderson Plumbing Prods, Inc., 530 U.S. 133 (2000), the Supreme Court again addressed the relationship between production burdens and the burden of persuasion in Title VII cases. The jury returned a verdict in favor of the plaintiff on his age discrimination claim after the plaintiff proved a prima facie case and offered sufficient evidence that explanations the defendant produced in response were "pretextual" (i.e., not the real reasons for its conduct toward the plaintiff). The defendant argued that this was insufficient evidence to get to a jury and that it was entitled to judgment as a matter of law. In other words, the defendant argued that the plaintiff — who bore the burden of persuasion — needed additional evidence to meet its burden of production. The Supreme Court disagreed. While noting that the plaintiff did have additional evidence, the Court explained that in Title VII cases proof of a prima facie case, along with disproving the defendant's proffered explanations, may be sufficient evidence from which a reasonable jury could find for the plaintiff.

e.   *The Federal Rules Approach to Presumptions*

Congress attempted to deal with the problem of presumptions in FRE 301, which provides that the effect of a presumption is to place a burden of production on the party against whom the presumption operates:

> In a civil case, unless a federal statute or these rules provide otherwise, the party against whom a presumption is directed has the burden of producing evidence to rebut the presumption. But this rule does not shift the burden of persuasion, which remains on the party who had it originally.

The exception for what is otherwise provided in "these rules" is an apparent cross-reference to FRE 302:

> In a civil case, state law governs the effect of a presumption regarding a claim or defense for which state law supplies the rule of decision.

For similar deferrals to state law, see FRE 501 (privileges) and FRE 601 (competency).

Despite the seemingly straightforward language of FRE 301, the rule is fraught with difficulties. We touch briefly on two of them here. For a more comprehensive analysis of FRE 301's deficiencies, see Ronald J. Allen, Presumptions, Inferences and Burdens of Proof in Federal Civil Actions — An Anatomy of Unnecessary Ambiguity and a Proposal for Reform, 76 Nw. L. Rev. 892 (1982).

i.   The "Federal Statute" Exception.   What are the criteria for determining whether a federal statute "provide[s] otherwise"? Nothing in the rule or its legislative history specifically addresses this question. As a result, it is not clear whether, for example, this category includes presumptions that do not directly shift the burden of persuasion but that have been interpreted as doing so. Similarly, it is not clear whether the language extends to all of the variations of language that Congress has chosen to employ in formulating evidentiary burdens created by statute. Poncy v. Johnson & Johnson, 460 F. Supp. 795, 803 (D.N.J. 1978) (FRE 301 applies to federal statute containing provision for a prima facie case).

If FRE 301 does not apply to a wide variety of statutes and is limited only to those that clearly allocate burdens of production, then it is superfluous. If, by contrast, it has a wider application, Congress has significantly changed federal law in the form of a simple rule of evidence. Courts that have wanted a presumption to have a greater effect than merely shifting a production burden have not found FRE 301 to be a constraint. Hood v. Knappton Corp., 986 F.2d 329 (9th Cir. 1993); American Coal Co. Benefits Review Board, 738 F.2d 387 (10th Cir. 1984).

ii.   The Relationship Between FRE 301 Presumptions and Other Means of Allocating Burdens of Proof.   FRE 301 does not address presumptions and their relationships to a judge's authority to allocate burdens of production and persuasion, to instruct the jury on inferences, or to comment on the evidence. Yet, as we have seen, the word *presumption* is merely a label applied to various manipulations of these other judicial prerogatives. Any attempt to define the scope of presumptions without dealing with these related areas was thus doomed to fail. The dominant judicial response to FRE 301with regard to these issues has been to ignore it. The Supreme Court has noted the impotency of FRE 301 in this context. In National Labor Relations Board v. Transportation Management Corp., 462 U.S. 393 (1983), the Court reviewed a change in NLRB rules that required employers to bear the burden of persuasion on the issue whether discharge of an employee was for a permissible reason. The employer argued that this shift in the burden of persuasion was in contravention of FRE 301. The Court concluded to the contrary, but in such a way that demonstrates the insignificance of FRE 301: "The Rule merely defines the term 'presumption.' It in no way restricts the authority of a court or an agency to change the customary burdens of persuasion in a manner that otherwise would be permissible." Id. at 403 n.7.

KEY POINTS

1. FRE 301 purports to make federal presumptions production burden presumptions unless Congress has otherwise provided.

2. Because of the uncertain scope of the "provide otherwise" clause, and because FRE 301 fails to address devices other than statutory presumptions that allocate burdens of proof, FRE 301 provides little guidance for or constraint on judicial decision-making.

B.   THE PROCESS OF PROOF IN CRIMINAL CASES

The process of proof in criminal cases is similar but not identical to the process of proof in civil cases. As in civil cases, the law determines what facts need to be proven in order to establish that a crime has occurred. The criminal law also possesses virtually the same rules for the allocation of burdens of proof as in civil cases. The "plaintiff," which is the state, must plead and prove the necessary elements of the crime, and in many jurisdictions there are affirmative defenses that defendants must plead and with respect to which defendants bear the burden of production or persuasion.

The primary differences between the civil and criminal arenas are that the burden of persuasion in criminal cases is proof beyond reasonable doubt and that as a result of In re Winship, 397 U.S. 358 (1970), the prosecution always carries that burden with respect to the necessary elements of the offense.

In this section, as with the process of proof in civil cases, we first discuss the burdens of proof and then discuss comments on the evidence and presumptions.

1.   The Burdens of Proof in Criminal Cases

a.   The Burden of Persuasion: In re Winship's Mandate of Proof Beyond a Reasonable Doubt

Because the proof beyond a reasonable doubt rule has been so uniformly accepted as the standard of proof for criminal cases, the Supreme Court did not have occasion specifically to address the question whether due process required that standard of proof until 1975 in In re Winship. Even then, the immediate issue for the Court was not whether a criminal defendant was entitled to have guilt proven beyond a reasonable doubt. Rather, *Winship* was a challenge to the New York rule utilizing the preponderance standard in juvenile delinquency cases. The Court affirmed its prior dictum that due process required the proof beyond a reasonable doubt standard in adult criminal prosecutions and went on to hold that due process required the same standard in delinquency adjudications based on conduct that would be criminal if committed by an adult. According to the Court:

> The requirement that guilt of a criminal charge be established beyond a reasonable doubt dates at least from our early years as a Nation. The "demand for a higher degree of persuasion in criminal cases was recurrently expressed from ancient times, [though] its crystallization into the formula 'beyond a reasonable doubt' seems to have occurred as late as 1789. It is now accepted in common law jurisdictions as the measure of persuasion by which the prosecution must convince the trier of all the essential elements of guilt." Although virtually unanimous adherence to the reasonable-doubt standard in common-law jurisdictions may not conclusively establish it as a requirement of due process, such adherence does "reflect a profound judgment about the way in which law should be enforced and justice administered." . . .
>
> The reasonable-doubt standard plays a vital role in the American scheme of criminal procedure. It is a prime instrument for reducing the risk of convictions resting on factual error. The standard provides concrete substance for the presumption of innocence — that bedrock "axiomatic and elementary" principle whose "enforcement lies at the foundation of the administration of our criminal law." . . .
>
> The requirement of proof beyond a reasonable doubt has this vital role in our criminal procedure for cogent reasons. The accused during a criminal prosecution has at stake interests of immense importance, both because of the possibility that he may lose his liberty upon conviction and because of the certainty that he would be stigmatized by the conviction. Accordingly, a society that values the good name and freedom of every individual should not condemn a man for commission of a crime when there is reasonable doubt about his guilt. As we said in Speiser v. Randall[, 357 U.S. 513, 525-526 (1958)]: "There is always in litigation a margin of error, representing error in factfinding, which both parties must take into account. Where one party has at stake an interest of transcending value — as a criminal defendant his liberty — this margin of error is reduced as to him by the process of placing on the other party the burden of . . . persuading the

factfinder at the conclusion of the trial of his guilt beyond a reasonable doubt. Due process commands that no man shall lose his liberty unless the Government has borne the burden of . . . convincing the factfinder of his guilt." To this end, the reasonable-doubt standard is indispensable, for it "impresses on the trier of fact the necessity of reaching a subjective state of certitude of the facts in issue." Dorsen & Rezneck, In re Gault and the Future of Juvenile Law, 1 Family Law Quarterly, No. 4, pp. 1, 26 (1976).

Moreover, use of the reasonable-doubt standard is indispensable to command the respect and confidence of the community in applications of the criminal law. It is critical that the moral force of the criminal law not be diluted by a standard of proof that leaves people in doubt whether innocent men are being condemned. It is also important in our free society that every individual going about his ordinary affairs have confidence that his government cannot adjudge him guilty of a criminal offense without convincing a proper factfinder of his guilt with utmost certainty.

Lest there remain any doubt about the constitutional stature of the reasonable-doubt standard, we explicitly hold that the Due Process Clause protects the accused against conviction except upon *proof beyond a reasonable doubt of every fact necessary to constitute the crime with which he is charged.* [397 U.S. at 362-364 (emphasis added).]

NOTES AND QUESTIONS

1. Despite the wide acceptance and the familiarity of the reasonable doubt standard, its precise meaning remains elusive. Although the due process clause requires courts to apply the beyond a reasonable doubt standard, "the Constitution neither prohibits trial courts from defining reasonable doubt nor requires them to do so as a matter of course." Victor v. Nebraska, 511 U.S. 1, 8 (1994). Consider the following three attempts to define proof beyond a reasonable doubt:

a. A reasonable doubt is one that is founded upon a real tangible substantial basis and not upon mere caprice and conjecture. It must be such doubt as would give rise to a grave uncertainty, raised in your mind by reasons of the unsatisfactory character of the evidence or lack thereof. A reasonable doubt is not a mere possible doubt. It is an actual substantial doubt. It is a doubt that a reasonable man can seriously entertain. What is required is not an absolute or mathematical certainty, but a moral certainty.

b. A defendant in a criminal action is presumed to be innocent until the contrary is proved, and in case of a reasonable doubt whether his guilt is satisfactorily shown, he is entitled to a verdict of not guilty. This presumption places upon the State the burden of proving him guilty beyond a reasonable doubt.

Reasonable doubt is defined as follows: It is not a mere possible doubt; because everything relating to human affairs, and depending on moral evidence, is open to some possible or imaginary doubt. It is that state of the case which, after the entire comparison and consideration of all the evidence, leaves the minds of the jurors in that condition that they cannot say they feel an abiding conviction, to a moral certainty, of the truth of the charge.

c. The burden is always on the state to prove beyond a reasonable doubt all of the material elements of the crime charged, and this burden never shifts.

"Reasonable doubt" is such a doubt as would cause a reasonable and prudent person, in one of the graver and more important transactions of life, to pause and hesitate before taking the represented facts as true and relying and acting thereon. It is such a doubt as will not permit you, after full, fair, and impartial consideration of all the evidence, to have an abiding conviction, to a moral certainty, of the guilt of the accused. At the same time, absolute or mathematical certainty is not required. You may be convinced of the truth of a fact beyond a reasonable doubt and yet be fully aware that possibly you may be mistaken. You may find an accused guilty upon the strong probabilities of the case, provided such probabilities are strong enough to exclude any doubt of his guilt that is reasonable. A reasonable doubt is an actual and substantial doubt arising from the evidence, from the facts or circumstances shown by the evidence, or from the lack of evidence on the part of the state, as distinguished from a doubt arising from mere possibility, from bare imagination or from fanciful conjecture.

In Cage v. Louisiana, 498 U.S. 39 (1990) (per curiam), the Supreme Court held that instruction (a) above violated the defendant's right to due process. The Court concluded that "a reasonable juror could have interpreted the instruction to allow a finding of guilt based on a degree of proof below that required by the Due Process Clause." Id. at 41. Instructions (b) and (c) were before the Court in Victor v. Nebraska, supra. The *Victor* Court distinguished *Cage* and held that the instructions were constitutional. What precisely is there in instructions (b) and (c) that suggests the requirement of a higher degree of proof than the first instruction? Are any of the instructions likely to be helpful to the jury? Or is that question impossible to answer until we have clearer guidance as to what the legal meaning of "beyond a reasonable doubt" in fact is?

2. Is the notion of reasonable doubt sufficiently difficult to define that we would be better off not trying to define it for jurors? No, according to Justice Ginsburg in her separate opinion in *Victor*:

> Because the trial judges in fact defined reasonable doubt in both jury charges we review, we need not decide whether the Constitution required them to do so. Whether or not the Constitution so requires, however, the argument for defining the concept is strong. While judges and lawyers are familiar with the reasonable doubt standard, the words "beyond a reasonable doubt" are not self-defining for jurors. Several studies of jury behavior have concluded that "jurors are often confused about the meaning of reasonable doubt," when that term is left undefined. Note, Defining Reasonable Doubt, 90 Colum. L. Rev. 1716, 1723 (1990) (citing studies). Thus, even if definitions of reasonable doubt are necessarily imperfect, the alternative — refusing to define the concept at all — is not obviously preferable. Cf. Newman, Beyond "Reasonable Doubt," 68 N.Y.U. L. Rev. 979, 984 (1993) ("I find it rather unsettling that we are using a formulation that we believe will become less clear the more we explain it.") [511 U.S. at 43.]

Justice Ginsburg then endorsed the following reasonable doubt instruction:

> The government has the burden of proving the defendant guilty beyond a reasonable doubt. Some of you may have served as jurors in civil cases, where you were told that it is only necessary to prove that a fact is more likely true than not true. In criminal cases, the government's proof must be more powerful than that. It must be beyond a reasonable doubt.
>
> Proof beyond a reasonable doubt is proof that leaves you firmly convinced of the defendant's guilt. There are very few things in this world that we know with absolute certainty, and in criminal cases the law does not require proof that overcomes every possible doubt. If, based on your consideration of the evidence, you are firmly convinced that the defendant is guilty of the crime charged, you must find him guilty. If on the other hand, you think there is a real possibility that he is not guilty, you must give him the benefit of the doubt and find him not guilty. [Id. at 44, quoting Federal Judicial Center, Pattern Criminal Jury Instructions 17-18 (1987) (instruction 21).]

3. Commentators have also lamented the lack of clarity surrounding "beyond a reasonable doubt." See Larry Laudan, Truth, Error, and Criminal Law: An Essay in Legal Epistemology 31 (2006) ("The most earnest jury, packed with twelve people desirous of doing the right thing and eager to see that justice is done, are left dangling with respect to how powerful a case is required before they are entitled to affirm that they believe the guilt of the defendant beyond a reasonable doubt. In such circumstances, simply muddling on is not an attractive prospect.").

4. The criminal proof standard is sometimes explained and justified based on the idea that it is designed to produce a certain ratio of false acquittals to false convictions. The common source cited for this idea is William Blackstone's adage that it is better for 10 guilty men to go free than for one innocent man to be convicted, although several other sources and ratios may be found. See Alexander Volokh, n Guilty Men, 146 U. Pa. L. Rev. 173 (1997). This idea may be more misleading than it is enlightening, however. A ratio of 10 to one, for example, would be satisfied by a decision rule that in 100 cases produced (1) 90 false acquittals; (2) nine false convictions; and (3) one accurate verdict. We obviously care about accurate verdicts — acquittals and convictions — as much as we care about errors. For further discussion, see Ronald J. Allen and Larry Laudan, Deadly Dilemmas, 41 Tex. Tech. L. Rev. 65 (2008).

KEY POINT

In a criminal prosecution, due process requires proof beyond a reasonable doubt of every fact necessary to constitute the crime charged.

b.   The Scope of Winship: Explicit Shifts in the Burden of Persuasion and Other Matters

i.   The *Mullaney* Decision.   Mullaney v. Wilbur, 421 U.S. 684 (1975), involved a homicide defendant who claimed that he killed his victim in the heat of passion provoked by a homosexual assault. The issue was the applicability of *Winship* to a Maine homicide statute that placed the burden of persuasion on the defendant to prove that a killing was "in the heat of passion on sudden provocation" in order to reduce the crime from murder to manslaughter. The Supreme Court affirmed the granting of a writ of habeas corpus to the defendant:

> After reading the statutory definitions of both offenses [murder and manslaughter], the court charged that "malice aforethought is an essential and indispensable element of the crime of murder," without which the homicide would be manslaughter. The jury was further instructed, however, that if the prosecution established that the homicide was both intentional and unlawful, malice aforethought was to be conclusively implied unless the defendant proved by a fair preponderance of the evidence that he acted in the heat of passion on sudden provocation. The court emphasized that "malice aforethought and heat of passion on sudden provocation are two inconsistent things"; thus, by proving the latter the defendant would negate the former and reduce the homicide from murder to manslaughter. . . .
> . . . Felonious homicide is punished as murder — i.e., by life imprisonment — unless the defendant proves by a fair preponderance of the evidence that it was committed in the heat

of passion on sudden provocation, in which case it is punished as manslaughter — i.e., by a fine not to exceed $10,000 or by imprisonment not to exceed 20 years. . . .

[T]he fact at issue here — the presence or absence of the heat of passion on sudden provocation — has been, almost from the inception of the common law of homicide, the single most important factor in determining the degree of culpability attaching to an unlawful homicide. And . . . the clear trend has been toward requiring the prosecution to bear the ultimate burden of proving this fact. . . .

Petitioners . . . note that as a formal matter the absence of the heat of passion on sudden provocation is not a "fact necessary to constitute the crime" of felonious homicide in Maine. This distinction is relevant, according to petitioners, because in *Winship* the facts at issue were essential to establish criminality in the first instance . . . . [H]ere . . . , petitioners maintain, the defendant's critical interests in liberty and reputation are no longer of paramount concern since, irrespective of the presence or absence of the heat of passion on sudden provocation, he is likely to lose his liberty and certain to be stigmatized. . . .

Maine has chosen to distinguish those who kill in the heat of passion from those who kill in the absence of this factor. Because the former are less "blameworth[y]," they are subject to substantially less severe penalties. By drawing this distinction, while refusing to require the prosecution to establish beyond a reasonable doubt the fact upon which it turns, Maine denigrates the interests found critical in *Winship*.

. . . [W]hen viewed in terms of the potential difference in restrictions of personal liberty attendant to each conviction, the distinction established by Maine between murder and manslaughter may be of greater importance than the difference between guilt or innocence for many lesser crimes.

Moreover, if *Winship* were limited to those facts that constitute a crime as defined by state law, a State could undermine many of the interests that decision sought to protect without effecting any substantive change in its law. It would only be necessary to redefine the elements that constitute different crimes, characterizing them as factors that bear solely on the extent of punishment. [Id. at 696-698.]

Mullaney, which was a unanimous decision, generated considerable litigation challenging state rules placing burdens of persuasion on the defendant. The Court revisited the issue only two years later in Patterson v. New York, 432 U.S. 197 (1977). Although the Patterson Court purported to distinguish *Mullaney*, *Patterson* in fact overrules *Mullaney* in all but the most formalistic sense. As you will see, however, that formalistic sense appears to retain considerable importance.

ii.   The *Patterson* Decision.   Patterson was convicted of murdering the partner of his estranged wife. The killing took place after the defendant had "observed his wife through a window in a state of semiundress" with the victim. The New York homicide statute defined the elements of murder as an "intent to cause the death of another person" and "causing the death of such person." New York also recognized as an affirmative defense acting "under the influence of extreme emotional disturbance for which there was a reasonable explanation or excuse." Extreme emotional distress reduced murder to manslaughter, and the burden of persuasion with respect to this affirmative defense rested with the defendant.

In rejecting Patterson's contention that placing the burden of proof with respect to extreme emotional distress on him was unconstitutional the Court observed that

1.   "dealing with crime is much more the business of the States than it is of the Federal Government";

2.   the New York "extreme emotional distress" defense is "a considerably expanded version of the common-law defense of heat of passion on sudden provocation";
3.   subsequent to *Mullaney* the Court in Rivera v. Delaware, 429 U.S. 877 (1976), reaffirmed that placing the burden of proof with respect to insanity on the defendant did not violate due process; and
4.   states may be reluctant to create or expand defenses if they have to disprove the defenses beyond a reasonable doubt.

Mullaney, according to the Court, was not controlling for the following reasons:

The crime of murder [in New York] is defined by statute . . . as causing the death of another person with intent to do so. The death, the intent to kill, and causation are the facts that the State is required to prove beyond a reasonable doubt if a person is to be convicted of murder. No further facts are either presumed or inferred in order to constitute the crime. The statute does provide an affirmative defense [of extreme emotional disturbance] . . . which, if proved by a preponderance of the evidence would reduce the crime to manslaughter, an offense defined in a separate section of the statute. It is plain enough that if the intentional killing is shown, the State intends to deal with the defendant as a murderer unless he demonstrates the mitigating circumstances. . . .

In *Mullaney* . . . the Maine statute defined [murder] as the unlawful killing of a human being "with malice aforethought, either express or implied." The trial court instructed the jury that the words *malice aforethought* were most important because "malice aforethought is an essential and indispensable element of the crime of murder." . . . The instructions emphasized that "malice aforethought and 'heat of passion on sudden provocation are two inconsistent things.'" . . .

The Maine Supreme Judicial Court held that murder and manslaughter were varying degrees of the crime of felonious homicide and that the presumption of malice arising from the unlawful killing was a mere policy presumption operating to cast on the defendant the burden of proving provocation if he was to be found guilty of manslaughter rather than murder. . . .

This Court . . . unanimously agreed with the Court of Appeals [in *Mullaney*] that [the defendant's] due process rights had been invaded by the presumption casting upon him the burden of proving by a preponderance of the evidence that he had acted in the heat of passion upon sudden provocation.

Mullaney's holding, it is argued, is that the State may not permit the blameworthiness of an act or the severity of punishment authorized for its commission to depend on the presence or absence of an identified fact without assuming the burden of proving the presence or absence of that fact, as the case may be, beyond a reasonable doubt. In our view, the *Mullaney* holding should not be so broadly read. . . .

Mullaney surely held that a State must prove every ingredient of an offense beyond a reasonable doubt, and that it may not shift the burden of proof to the defendant by presuming that ingredient upon proof of the other elements of the offense. . . . Such shifting of the burden of persuasion with respect to a fact which the State deems so important that it must be either proved or presumed is impermissible under the Due Process Clause.

It was unnecessary to go further in *Mullaney*. . . . [A] killing became murder in Maine when it resulted from a deliberate, cruel act committed by one person against another, "suddenly without any, or without a considerable provocation." . . . [M]alice, in the sense of absence of provocation, was part of the definition of that crime. Yet malice, i.e., lack of provocation, was presumed and could be rebutted by the defendant only by proving by a preponderance of the evidence that he acted with heat of passion upon sudden provocation. . . .

As we have explained, nothing was presumed or implied against Patterson. [432 U.S. at 205-206, 212-216.]

iii.   The Functional Equivalence of *Mullaney* and *Patterson*.   Except for the fact that New York's "extreme emotional distress" defense is somewhat broader than the Maine "heat of passion" defense, *Mullaney* and *Patterson* are functionally identical. In both cases to obtain a murder conviction the state had to prove an intentional killing beyond a reasonable doubt, and in both cases proof of provocation made a killing, that would otherwise be murder, manslaughter. The only difference between the two cases is in the language that the state legislatures used to achieve this gradation in homicide crimes. Maine defined the critical element of murder as "malice aforethought," a concept that encompassed the absence of provocation. Maine then created a rule that proof of intent gave rise to a presumption or mandatory finding of malice unless the defendant proved provocation by a preponderance of the evidence. New York defined murder initially as requiring only proof that the defendant intentionally killed a person and then defined provocation as an affirmative defense for the defendant to prove by a preponderance of the evidence. Admittedly, the New York formulation is less cumbersome than the Maine formulation. As long as the formulation is not so confusing or incomprehensible to raise void-for-vagueness types of concerns, however, the language that the legislature uses to define crimes should not raise a due process issue and certainly not a *Winship* issue.

iv.   *Mullaney*'s Departure from *Winship*.   In one respect *Mullaney* is a significant departure from *Winship*. The *Winship* Court observed that the universal acceptance of the beyond a reasonable doubt standard strongly implied the necessity of employing that standard to protect a fundamental value — preferring errors benefitting the accused over those favoring the prosecution. The Court then supplemented its analysis by articulating the interests that this value preference protects — principally the accused's liberty and good name — in order to demonstrate that they were of sufficient magnitude to justify including the procedure safeguarding them among the elements of due process. In *Mullaney*, by contrast, the Court reversed its order of reasoning, concentrating almost exclusively on the interests protected by the reasonable doubt standard rather than on whether Maine's statute was consistent — which it was — with common practices in the states.

In short, *Mullaney* invoked *Winship* to invalidate a practice long accepted throughout the country, whereas *Winship* relied on the "traditions and conscience of our people" to hold that due process required application of the proof beyond a reasonable doubt standard. Thus, *Mullaney*, which purported to "apply" *Winship*, drastically altered that case from one that looks to traditional practice and prevailing usage by the states to aid in due process analysis to one that frees the federal courts to impose their own view about the appropriate use of the reasonable doubt standard on the states notwithstanding widely shared views to the contrary.

v.   Evaluating *Mullaney* and *Patterson*: The Theory That the Greater Includes the Lesser.   The fact that *Mullaney* is a departure from *Winship* in the sense just described does not necessarily lead to the conclusion that *Patterson* rather than *Mullaney* is the correct decision. Whenever a defendant fails to establish an affirmative defense, the possibility is presented that, had the prosecution been required to disprove the defense beyond reasonable doubt, the trier of fact would have either convicted the defendant of a lesser offense or acquitted altogether. Such verdicts would expose the defendant to a lesser punishment or no punishment at all. Thus, affirmative defenses undeniably affect the interests articulated in *Winship*. Yet one cannot jump from this fact alone to the conclusion that requiring the prosecutor to disprove affirmative defenses beyond a reasonable doubt serves the due process interest. Assuming that the punishment for the higher offense is constitutionally acceptable, *given what the prosecution must prove beyond a reasonable doubt,* the allocation of the persuasion burden of the mitigating factor has no bearing on whether the defendant suffers unconstitutional punishment.

An example may help to clarify this point. Consider a state with an intentional homicide statute that punishes every intentional homicide with 30 years of imprisonment; if the state proves that the defendant intentionally killed the victim, then a flat sentence of 30 years is imposed regardless of the presence of any mitigating factor. *Assume* that such a statute is constitutional. Now consider how the constitutionality of that statute is affected if we simply add to it a provision that no more than 20 years of imprisonment may be imposed when defendants prove by a preponderance of the evidence that they acted under the influence of extreme emotional disturbance. If the constitutional interest in the reasonable doubt standard centers on liberty deprivation, the addition of a chance to mitigate a constitutionally valid punishment cannot invalidate the statute. To put it another way, if a state may constitutionally imprison all intentional killers for 30 years by proving beyond reasonable doubt only intent and causation, then whatever liberty interest defendants constitutionally possess in the context of homicide prosecutions surely is fully accommodated by such a statute. The addition of a mitigating circumstance in the form of an affirmative defense — a factor that reduces punishment — cannot violate the already fully accommodated interest.

According to this theory — sometimes referred to as the theory that "the greater includes the lesser" — the analysis of the constitutionality of an affirmative defense must proceed to another level. One must ask whether the greater punishment — the punishment authorized in the event the defendant fails to establish the affirmative defense — is constitutional. In other words, one must ask how to give content to *Winship*'s command that the state "prove beyond a reasonable doubt every fact necessary to constitute the crime." To state the matter in terms of the issue in *Mullaney* and *Patterson*: Is it constitutionally permissible for Maine or New York to impose its penalty for nonprovoked or nonemotionally distressed intentional killings on individuals whose killings are the result of extreme provocation or extreme emotional distress? In the next subsection we discuss several possible tests for resolving this issue.

   vi.   Giving Content to *Winship*: Tests for Assessing the Validity of Affirmative Defenses.

   (1)   ***The Elements Test.***   Pursuant to the elements test, the state must prove beyond reasonable doubt whatever factual issues it labels as elements of the offense. A component of this test is the "physical location" rule, a rule of statutory construction providing that a particular factual issue is an element of an offense only if it is incorporated into the text of the basic statute describing the offense.

At various points throughout the *Patterson* opinion the Court alluded to the elements test, most explicitly in the statement that the Court "will not disturb the balance struck in previous cases holding that the Due Process Clause requires the prosecution to prove beyond reasonable doubt all of the elements included in the definition of the offense of which the defendant is charged." 432 U.S. at 210. Both examples given by the Court of unconstitutional burden shifts also tend to support this view. The Court noted that the legislature cannot declare an individual guilty or presumptively guilty, nor can it declare that the finding of an indictment or proof of the identity of the accused shall create a presumption of the existence of all the facts essential to guilt. These are situations in which no elements are included within the definition of "crime," which may suggest that any affirmative defense will be sustained so long as the legislature does not drain all substantive content from a crime's definition.

It is difficult to see what constitutional interest is served by the elements test. The physical location rule is obviously an arbitrary means of determining the "definition" of an offense. The legislature may wish to "define" an offense in one way but determine the elements of the prosecution's case in another, and either could be considered the "definition" of the crime. There is no reason why the validity of a state statute placing the burden of proving provocation on the defendant should depend on whether the state "defines" murder (1) as intent, causation, and no provocation in one statute and in another places the burden of proving provocation on the defendant, or simply (2) as intent and causation with another statute authorizing provocation as an affirmative defense.

(2)   The Political Compromise Test.   A second standard that has been proposed for judging the validity of an affirmative defense, while somewhat more sophisticated than the elements test, is no more persuasive. This is the "political compromise" test, which permits affirmative defenses that result from the compromise of competing forces in the legislature. This test responds to the fear that states may be unwilling to provide certain affirmative defenses if they cannot place on the defendant the burden of proof for the factual issue created. Commentators have often pointed out that a decision like *Mullaney*, if followed, would likely inhibit experimentation with new affirmative defenses. To avoid that harsh irony, the political compromise test looks to whether the legislature would have refused to adopt the defense but for the provision imposing the burden of proof on the defendant.

The most disturbing feature of this test is its paradoxical quality. It is paradoxical in the sense that if the only justification for allowing affirmative defenses is that otherwise the legislature will be forced to choose between two diametrically opposed but constitutional alternatives, then the argument implicitly assumes the unconstitutionality of affirmative defenses. The real point, in other words, is that affirmative defenses are unconstitutional but that such a conclusion may result in an unfortunate legislative choice, and thus the better tack is to permit an unconstitutional choice as an expedient.

(3)   The Proportionality Test.   Within the last century the cruel and unusual punishment clause of the Eighth Amendment[3] has been interpreted to require a rough proportionality between the culpability of an offense and the punishment that is imposed. This requirement of proportionality provides the method of testing the constitutionality of affirmative defenses, and it also provides the means of delineating the extent of the federal interest in the reasonable doubt standard. Reconsider the intentional homicide hypothetical in subsection 1.b.5, supra. If the courts conclude that a given punishment (30 years in the hypothetical) is not disproportional to what

---

3. U.S. Const. amend. VIII ("Excessive bail shall not be required, nor excessive fines imposed, or cruel and unusual punishment inflicted.").

the state has proved beyond reasonable doubt (intentional killing), notwithstanding the presence or absence of any mitigating factors, then a defendant's liberty interest would obviously be satisfied by a statute that required proof of only those elements and that imposed that particular punishment. Accordingly, the mere addition to that statute of an affirmative defense, which after all could constitutionally be ignored, should be equally satisfactory. The import of the proportionality principle is, then, that the state should be required to prove enough to justify the imposition of the maximum sentence permissible under the statute. Once that is accomplished, the accused has been fully protected against an unwarranted deprivation of liberty, and the state should be permitted to elaborate on the basic statute as it sees fit.

The thesis that due process requires proof beyond a reasonable doubt only with respect to those elements of the offense that are "essential" by virtue of the Eighth Amendment concretely expresses the role of the reasonable doubt standard. Due process and the Eighth Amendment protect criminal defendants from unwarranted deprivations of liberty by requiring the state to establish sufficient factual elements to justify the allotted punishment and by requiring the state, in establishing those elements, to minimize the risk of error adverse to the defendant. Once the overriding constitutional command is satisfied, however, the need for the protective procedure is likewise satisfied, and the traditional state power should reassert itself, permitting the states to allocate burdens of proof as they desire.

The theoretical appeal of the proportionality test, in our view, is compelling. The inherent vagueness of the notion of proportionality, however, may lead courts to impinge on legislative judgments about affirmative defenses. Alternatively, the vagueness may lead courts to defer to legislative judgments except in the most extreme cases. Indeed, the Supreme Court, particularly in recent years, has upheld against proportionality challenges quite severe penalties for relatively minor misconduct. Hutto v. Davis, 454 U.S. 370 (1982) (upholding 40-year prison term for possession and distribution of approximately nine ounces of marijuana); Rummell v. Estelle, 445 U.S. 263 (1980) (upholding constitutionality of a recidivist statute under which defendant received mandatory life sentence for three crimes of fraud that netted a total sum of less than $230). But see Solem v. Helm, 463 U.S. 277 (1983) (striking down life sentence for uttering "no-account" check for less than $100). In the civil context, however, the Supreme Court has been more willing to impose constitutional proportionality limits in cases involving punitive damages. See State Farm v. Campbell, 538 U.S. 408 (2003); BMW v. Gore, 517 U.S. 559 (1996).

(4) ***Justice Powell's Two-Part Test.***   In his *Patterson* dissent, Justice Powell suggested a two-part test for determining whether it is unconstitutional to place the burden of persuasion on the defendant. First, the facts must make "a substantial difference in punishment of the offender and in the stigma associated with the conviction." Second, in the Anglo-American legal tradition the facts must historically have had "that level of importance." If, but only if, both of these things are true — as Justice Powell argued they were with respect to extreme emotional distress, it is unconstitutional to place the burden of proof on the defendant.

vii.   Affirmative Defenses After *Patterson*.   *Patterson* did not adopt either the proportionality test or Justice Powell's two-part test for determining what the state must prove beyond a reasonable doubt. *Patterson*, however, did acknowledge, as *Mullaney* pointed out earlier, that reliance solely on the elements test creates the possibility that states can undermine *Winship* by making most factors critical to the imposition or degree of punishment affirmative defenses. Moreover, the *Patterson* Court stated that "there are obviously constitutional limits beyond which the States may not go in this regard." What might those limits be?

MARTIN v. OHIO
480 U.S. 228 (1987)

Justice WHITE delivered the opinion of the Court.

The Ohio Code provides that "(e)very person accused of an offense is presumed innocent until proven guilty beyond a reasonable doubt, and the burden of proof for all elements of the offense is upon the prosecution. The burden of going forward with the evidence of an affirmative defense, and the burden of proof by a preponderance of the evidence, for an affirmative defense, is upon the accused." Ohio Rev. Code Ann. §2901.05(A) (1982). An affirmative defense is one involving "an excuse or justification peculiarly within the knowledge of the accused, on which he can fairly be required to adduce supporting evidence." Ohio Rev. Code Ann. §2901.05(C)(2) (1982). The Ohio courts have "long determined that self-defense is an affirmative defense," and that the defendant has the burden of proving it as required by §2901.05(A).

As defined by the trial court in its instructions in this case, the elements of self-defense that the defendant must prove are (1) that the defendant was not at fault in creating the situation giving rise to the argument; (2) the defendant had an honest belief that she was in imminent danger of death or great bodily harm and that her only means of escape from such danger was in the use of such force; and (3) the defendant must not have violated any duty to retreat or avoid danger. The question before us is whether the Due Process Clause of the Fourteenth Amendment forbids placing the burden of proving self-defense on the defendant when she is charged by the State of Ohio with committing the crime of aggravated murder, which, as relevant to this case, is defined by the Revised Code of Ohio as "purposely, and with prior calculation and design, caus[ing] the death of another." Ohio Rev. Code Ann. §2903.01 (1982).

The facts of the case, taken from the opinions of the courts below, may be succinctly stated. On July 21, 1983, petitioner Earline Martin and her husband, Walter Martin, argued over grocery money. Petitioner claimed that her husband struck her in the head during the argument. Petitioner's version of what then transpired was that she went upstairs, put on a robe, and later came back down with her husband's gun which she intended to dispose of. Her husband saw something in her hand and questioned her about it. He came at her, she lost her head and fired the gun at him. Five or six shots were fired, three of them striking and killing Mr. Martin. She was charged with and tried for aggravated murder. She pleaded self-defense and testified in her own defense. The judge charged the jury with respect to the elements of the crime and of self-defense and rejected petitioner's Due Process Clause challenge to the charge placing on her the burden of proving self-defense. The jury found her guilty.

Both the Ohio Court of Appeals and the Supreme Court of Ohio affirmed the conviction. . . . We granted certiorari, and affirm the decision of the Supreme Court of Ohio.

In re Winship declared that the Due Process Clause "protects the accused against conviction except upon proof beyond a reasonable doubt of every fact necessary to constitute the crime with which he is charged." A few years later, we held that *Winship*'s mandate was fully satisfied where the State of New York had proved beyond reasonable doubt, each of the elements of murder, but placed on the defendant the burden of proving the affirmative defense of extreme emotional disturbance, which, if proved, would have reduced the crime from murder to manslaughter. Patterson v. New York[, 432 U.S. 197 (1977)]. . . . Referring to Leland v. Oregon, 343 U.S. 790, and Rivera v. Delaware, 429 U.S. 877, we added that New York did no more than *Leland* and *Rivera* permitted it to do without violating the Due Process Clause and declined to reconsider those cases. It was also observed that "the fact that a majority of the States have now assumed the burden of disproving affirmative defenses — for whatever reasons — [does not] mean that those States that strike a different balance are in violation of the Constitution." As in *Patterson*, the jury was here instructed that to convict it must find, in light of all the evidence, that each of the elements of the crime of aggravated murder must be proved by the State beyond reasonable doubt and that the burden of proof with respect to these elements did not shift. To find guilt, the jury had to be convinced that none of the evidence, whether offered by the State or by Martin in connection with her plea of self-defense, raised a reasonable doubt that Martin had killed her husband, that she had the specific purpose and intent to cause his death, or that she had done so with prior calculation and design. It was also told, however, that it could acquit if it found by a preponderance of the evidence that Martin had not precipitated the confrontation, that she had an honest belief that she was in imminent danger of death or great bodily harm, and that she had satisfied any duty to retreat or avoid danger. The jury convicted Martin.

We agree with the State and its Supreme Court that this conviction did not violate the Due Process Clause. The State did not exceed its authority in defining the crime of murder as purposely causing the death of another with prior calculation or design. It did not seek to shift to Martin the burden of proving any of those elements, and the jury's verdict reflects that none of her self-defense evidence raised a reasonable doubt about the state's proof that she purposefully killed with prior calculation and design. She nevertheless had the opportunity under state law and the instructions given to justify the killing and show herself to be blameless by proving that she acted in self-defense. The jury thought she had failed to do so, and Ohio is as entitled to punish Martin as one guilty of murder as New York was to punish Patterson.

It would be quite different if the jury had been instructed that self-defense evidence could not be considered in determining whether there was a reasonable doubt about the state's case, i.e., that self-defense evidence must be put aside for all purposes unless it satisfied the preponderance standard. Such instruction would relieve the state of its burden and plainly run afoul of *Winship*'s mandate. The instructions in this case could be clearer in this respect, but when read as a whole, we think they are adequate to convey to the jury that all of the evidence, including the evidence going to self-defense, must be considered in deciding whether there was a reasonable doubt about the sufficiency of the state's proof of the elements of the crime.

We are thus not moved by assertions that the elements of aggravated murder and self-defense overlap in the sense that evidence to prove the latter will often tend to negate the former. It may be that most encounters in which self-defense is claimed arise suddenly and involve no prior plan or specific purpose to take life. In those cases, evidence offered to support the defense may negate a purposeful killing by prior calculation and design, but Ohio does not shift to the defendant the burden of disproving any element of the state's case. When the prosecution has made out a *prima facie* case and survives a motion to acquit, the jury may nevertheless not convict if the evidence offered by the defendant raises any reasonable doubt about the existence of any fact necessary for the finding of guilt. Evidence creating a reasonable doubt could easily fall far short of proving self-defense by a preponderance of the evidence. Of course, if such doubt is not raised in the jury's mind and each juror is convinced that the defendant purposely and with prior calculation and design took life, the killing will still be excused if the elements of the defense are satisfactorily established. We note here, but need not rely on it, the observation of the Supreme Court of Ohio that "Appellant did not dispute the existence of [the elements of aggravated murder], but rather sought to justify her actions on grounds she acted in self-defense." Petitioner submits that there can be no conviction under Ohio law unless the defendant's conduct is unlawful and that because self-defense renders lawful what would otherwise be a crime, unlawfulness is an element of the offense that the state must prove by disproving self-defense. This argument founders on state law, for it has been rejected by the Ohio Supreme Court and by the Court of Appeals for the Sixth Circuit. White v. Arn, 788 F.2d 338, 346-347 (6th Cir. 1986); State v. Morris, 8 Ohio App. 3d 12, 18-19, 455 N.E.2d 1352, 1359-1360 (1982). It is true that unlawfulness is essential for conviction, but the Ohio courts hold that the unlawfulness in cases like this is the conduct satisfying the elements of aggravated murder — an interpretation of state law that we are not in a position to dispute. The same is true of the claim that it is necessary to prove a "criminal" intent to convict for serious crimes, which cannot occur if self-defense is shown: the necessary mental state for aggravated murder under Ohio law is the specific purpose to take life pursuant to prior calculation and design.

As we noted in *Patterson*, the common law rule was that affirmative defenses, including self-defense, were matters for the defendant to prove. "This was the rule when the Fifth Amendment was adopted, and it was the American rule when the Fourteenth Amendment was ratified." Indeed, well into this century, a number of States followed the common law rule and required a defendant to shoulder the burden of proving that he acted in self-defense. We are aware that all but two of the States, Ohio and South Carolina, have abandoned the common law rule and require the prosecution to prove the absence of self-defense when it is properly raised by the defendant. But the question remains whether those States are in violation of the Constitution; and, as we observed in *Patterson*, that question is not answered by cataloging the practices of other States. We are no more convinced that the Ohio practice of requiring self-defense to be proved by the defendant is unconstitutional than we are that the Constitution requires the prosecution to prove the sanity of a defendant who pleads not guilty by reason of insanity. We have had the opportunity to depart from Leland v. Oregon but have refused to do so. Rivera v. Delaware, 429 U.S. 877 (1976). These cases were important to the *Patterson* decision and they, along with *Patterson*, are authority for our decision today.

The judgment of the Ohio Supreme Court is accordingly affirmed.

NOTES AND QUESTIONS ON MARTIN

1. Consider carefully the relationship between self-defense and the "prior calculation and design" element of aggravated murder. In a dissenting opinion, Justice Powell argued that "prior calculation" and self-defense were mutually exclusive. Thus, he regarded self-defense as negating one of the elements of murder. The defendant,

however, apparently disagreed. As the majority pointed out, the defendant did not dispute the existence of the elements of aggravated murder.

To the extent that Justice Powell's characterization of the relationship between "prior calculation" and self-defense is correct, the principal problem with *Martin*, as Justice Powell pointed out, is a potentially confusing jury instruction: "It makes no sense to say that the prosecution has the burden of proving an element beyond a reasonable doubt and that the defense has the burden of proving the contrary by a preponderance of the evidence." On the other hand, if the mens rea for aggravated murder is not inconsistent with self-defense, *Martin* is a much more troubling decision. Assume for the sake of argument that "prior calculation and design" means no more forethought than would typically go into a decision to kill in self-defense or under extreme emotional distress. Now compare a killing allegedly committed under extreme emotional distress with a killing allegedly committed in self-defense. Reasonable people may differ about whether extreme emotional distress is sufficiently mitigating that the defendant should not be punished as a *murderer* unless the prosecution disproves the extreme emotional distress claim beyond a reasonable doubt. The defendant who kills under the influence of extreme emotional distress will be punished, however. The killing is a culpable, criminal act; the extreme emotional distress mitigates the crime but does not justify or excuse it. By contrast, the person who kills in self-defense has not committed a crime; the killing is justified. Thus, when the central issue in a case is self-defense, the entire question whether there was culpable criminal conduct turns on a resolution of that issue. To convict a person claiming self-defense of aggravated murder — a capital offense in Ohio — without requiring the prosecution to disprove self-defense beyond a reasonable doubt is to convict someone for whom there has been no proof beyond a reasonable doubt of culpable conduct!

2. Unfortunately, the broad, troublesome implications of *Martin* appear to be the correct ones. The *Martin* majority's superficial analysis did not move beyond the fact that Ohio proved beyond a reasonable doubt the elements that it had included in its murder statute. Moreover, White v. Arn, 788 F.2d 338 (6th Cir. 1986), one of the cases setting forth constitutional interpretations of Ohio law that the *Martin* majority was "not in a position to dispute," involved self-defense and nonaggravated murder. In that case, there was no plausible inconsistency between having the mental state defined in the murder statute (purposefulness) and having the mental state required for self-defense. In other words, there could be a purposeful killing in self-defense. Indeed, *White* specifically relied on this lack of inconsistency to hold that proof of self-defense does not negate purposefulness and, therefore, that it was not unconstitutional to place the burden of proof with respect to self-defense on the defendant. Id. at 346.

3. After *Martin*, is it still true, as the *Patterson* majority claimed, that "there are obviously constitutional limits beyond which the States may not go"? Could a state constitutionally define murder simply as "causing the death of another human being." How would that statute differ from what the Court approved in *Martin*?

KEY POINTS

1. Courts interpret the *Winship* mandate as a requirement that the prosecution prove beyond a reasonable doubt each fact listed in the statutory definition of the crime.

2. It is permissible to place the burden of persuasion on the defendant with respect to affirmative defenses such as extreme emotional distress or self-defense, as long as the state categorizes them as affirmative defenses rather than elements of the crime.

3. There are some unspecified limits beyond which the states may not go in creating affirmative defenses that limit the *Winship* proof beyond a reasonable doubt mandate.

NOTES AND QUESTIONS ON THE APPLICATION OF WINSHIP IN OTHER CONTEXTS

1. Winship *and Sentencing*. In Apprendi v. New Jersey, 530 U.S. 466 (2000), the defendant was convicted of weapons offenses as a result of his shooting a gun into the home of an African-American family that had recently moved into a previously all-white neighborhood. The maximum sentence for Apprendi's offenses was 10 years, but a separate New Jersey statute — a "hate crimes" statute — permitted adding up to 10 additional years to the sentence if the judge found by a preponderance of the evidence that the crime was racially motivated. At Apprendi's sentencing, the judge made the requisite finding and sentenced Apprendi to 12 years imprisonment. The Supreme Court held that the sentencing violated Apprendi's constitutional rights. According to the Court, any fact increasing the penalty beyond the prescribed statutory maximum (here 10 years), other than the fact of a prior conviction, must be submitted to the jury and proven beyond a reasonable doubt.

Apprendi, like Mullaney v. Wilbur, page 751, supra, unleashed a flood of litigation. Would *Apprendi* apply if, for example, (a) the hate-crime provision had been part of the same statute that was the basis for Apprendi's conviction, (b) the judge did not exceed the statutory maximum but gave an unusually harsh sentence on the basis of facts found by a preponderance of the evidence at sentencing, or (c) the judge relied on sentencing guidelines to increase a defendant's sentence? In the last case, would it matter if the guidelines were mandatory or discretionary?

Patterson v. New York, page 752, supra, resolved many of the uncertainties created by *Mullaney* with its adoption of the "elements" test for determining what the prosecution must prove beyond a reasonable doubt. Similarly, United States v. Booker, 543 U.S. 220 (2005), appears to have resolved many of the constitutional uncertainties created by *Apprendi*.

Booker was convicted of possessing with the intent to distribute over 50 grams of cocaine. The statutory penalty for the offense was 10 years to life imprisonment. The Federal Sentencing Guidelines, however, required a sentence of between 17 and 22 years in the absence of any aggravating or mitigating factors. The sentencing judge found by a preponderance of the evidence that Booker had obstructed justice and had possessed an additional 566 grams of cocaine. With these aggravating factors, the Federal Sentencing Guidelines mandated a sentence of between 30 years and life. The judge imposed a 30-year sentence — 12 years longer than the sentence that could have been imposed on the basis of facts found by the jury beyond a reasonable doubt.

The same five-Justice majority that had upheld Apprendi's claim (Stevens, Souter, Scalia, Thomas, and Ginsburg) held that *Apprendi* applied to mandatory sentencing guidelines: The judge cannot impose a sentence that exceeds the maximum authorized by the jury's finding or a guilty plea, regardless of whether the maximum is created by statute or sentencing guideline. All nine Justices agreed that in the absence of statutory or guideline mandates, there would be no constitutional problem. In other words, if there had been no guidelines or only voluntary guidelines and a statutory penalty of 10 years to life, the trial judge could have given Booker any sentence within the statutory range — even if the judge chose a relatively high sentence on the basis of a preponderance finding that Booker obstructed justice and possessed additional amounts of cocaine! In short, the *Booker* "solution" to the *Apprendi* problem is as formalistic and artificial as is the *Patterson* solution to the *Mullaney* problem. In one case it is a matter of statutory "elements," and in the other it is a matter of mandatory sentencing limits.

In one important respect, though, *Booker* is quite different from *Patterson*. *Patterson*'s elements test has the effect of deferring to legislative judgments about how to define crimes. By contrast, *Booker* interferes with legislative judgments about how to regulate sentencing: Mandatory sentencing guideline systems, which a number of jurisdictions had adopted to regulate sentencing disparity, are now unconstitutional. Unregulated sentence discretion, on the other hand, is alive and well. What values protected by the *Winship* reasonable doubt requirement and the Sixth Amendment jury trial right justify this type of interference with legislative judgments?

2. *Winship* problems may arise when a state permits the jury to convict the defendant of a single crime without necessarily agreeing on the facts that support the conviction or when a jury convicts a defendant of a greater crime (for which there is reasonable doubt) because they were not given the option of convicting for a lesser crime (for which there is proof beyond a reasonable doubt). See Schad v. Arizona, 501 U.S. 624 (1991) (upholding first degree murder conviction under jury instructions that did not require jury to distinguish between felony-murder and premeditated murder); Beck v. Alabama, 477 U.S. 625 (1980) (holding unconstitutional a statute that prohibited instructions for lesser included offenses in criminal cases).

3. In Montana v. Egelhoff, 518 U.S. 37 (1996), a murder prosecution, the Supreme Court upheld a Montana statute that made evidence of voluntary intoxication inadmissible "in determining the existence of a mental state which was an element of the offense." According to Justice Scalia's plurality opinion, this restriction on the right to introduce evidence did not violate a "'fundamental principle of justice.'" Id. at 42.

The defendant had argued, inter alia, that the statute had the effect of reducing the state's burden of proof on the mens rea element in violation of *Winship*. The Montana Supreme Court had agreed, relying on the following passage from Martin v. Ohio:

> It would be quite different if the jury had been instructed that self-defense evidence could not be considered in determining whether there was a reasonable doubt about the State's case, i.e., that self-defense evidence must be put aside for all purposes unless it satisfied the preponderance standard. Such instruction would relieve the State of its burden and plainly run afoul of *Winship*'s mandate. The instructions in this case . . . are adequate to convey to the jury that all of the evidence, including the evidence going to self-defense, must be considered in deciding whether there was a reasonable doubt about the sufficiency of the State's proof of the elements of the crime. [480 U.S. at 233-234.]

Justice Scalia's response to the *Winship-Martin* argument was as follows:

> This passage can be explained in various ways — e.g., as an assertion that the right to have a jury consider self-defense evidence (unlike the right to have a jury consider evidence of

voluntary intoxication), is fundamental, a proposition that the historical record may support. But the only explanation needed for present purposes is the one given in Kokkonen v. Guardian Life Ins. Co., 511 U.S. 375, 379 (1994): "It is to the holdings of our cases, rather than dicta, that we must attend." [518 U.S. at 56.]

What do you think of the defendant's *Winship* argument? Of Justice Scalia's response?

Justice Ginsburg, concurring in the judgment, maintained that the Montana statute should be understood as redefining mens rea, not as restricting evidence:

> Beneath the labels (rule excluding evidence or redefinition of the offense) lies the essential question: Can a State, without offense to the Federal Constitution, make the judgment that two people are equally culpable where one commits an act stone sober, and the other engages in the same conduct after his voluntary intoxication has reduced his capacity for self-control? [Id. at 57.]

What do you think of Justice Ginsburg's formulation of the issue? Of her affirmative answer? See Ronald J. Allen, Forward: Montana v. Egelhoff — Reflections on the Limits of Legislative Imagination and Judicial Authority, 87 J. Crim. L. & Criminology 633 (1997).

4. In Clark v. Arizona, 548 U.S. 735 (2006), the Supreme Court upheld a state statute that limited a defendant's psychiatric expert testimony about his mental illness to the affirmative defense of insanity — an issue the defendant needed to prove by clear and convincing evidence — and excluded this evidence on the issue of mens rea. The defendant, who was convicted of first degree murder for intentionally killing a police office, argued that expert testimony about his schizophrenia showed that he was acting out of delusions caused by his mental illness and not with the requisite intent. By upholding the state statute limiting the use of this evidence, is the Court in effect saying that it is constitutional to make defendants prove lack of mens rea when they wish to introduce expert testimony on the issue? If states may shift the burden of persuasion on the issue of mens rea (at least with regard to mentally ill defendants), we ask once again: What are the constitutional limits on what states may do? For further discussions of *Clark*, see Ronald J. Allen, Clark v. Arizona: Much (Confused) Ado About Nothing, 4 Ohio St. J. Crim. L. 135 (2006); Peter Westen, The Supreme Court's Bout with Insanity: Clark v. Arizona, 4 Ohio St. J. Crim. L. 143 (2006).

c.   The Burden of Production in Criminal Cases

As we discussed in Section A, at pages 718-722, supra, the primary significance of a production burden is that the failure to meet it will preclude the party who has that burden from presenting the matter to the jury. The court will resolve the issue against the party with the production burden. For example, if the prosecution fails to present sufficient evidence to permit a finding beyond a reasonable doubt of each element of the crime, the court will direct a verdict of acquittal for the defendant.

It is frequently said that because of a criminal defendant's constitutional right to a jury trial, it is impermissible to direct a verdict against a criminal defendant. In fact, however, courts commonly engage in activity that is the equivalent of directing verdicts against criminal defendants. Consider, for example, the refusal of a judge to instruct the jury on a particular defense or lesser included offense on the grounds that insufficient evidence of that defense has been produced, a practice approved by the Supreme Court in United States v. Bailey, 444 U.S. 394 (1980).

Bailey involved defendants' challenges to their convictions for escaping from a federal institution. In upholding the convictions, the Court rejected claims that the trial court erred in failing to instruct the jury on the common law defenses of duress and necessity. The defendants testified that their actions were motivated by death threats, and they requested an instruction on duress or necessity. The Court concluded that even if Congress intended to allow such defenses, a point left undecided, the defendants failed to make a sufficient showing of duress or necessity to justify a jury instruction. The defendants, in other words, failed to meet a burden of production, and the district court directed a verdict on their defense by refusing to instruct on it.

NOTES AND QUESTIONS

1. What the *Bailey* Court did not do, unless it did so implicitly, was to inquire into the constitutional necessity of establishing the fact in issue — in this case, whether or not the defendants had acted under duress or necessity. Without that inquiry, the Court's analysis is incomplete. If the fact in issue was one that must be established in order to justify the potential sanction, then permitting the district court to remove that issue from the case resulted in a conviction when one essential fact had not been proven beyond reasonable doubt to the jury's satisfaction, which is inconsistent with *Winship*.

2. If the fact in issue does not need to be established beyond a reasonable doubt, then *Bailey* provides an acceptable, if not ideal, analysis of burdens of production on nonessential elements. The analysis is not ideal because of the majority's position that personal testimony of the defendants did not justify a jury instruction. 444 U.S. at 415. The Court is playing the role of fact finder with such a test and concluding that the defendants' testimony is incredible. As a matter of policy, such questions should be left to the jury even on nonessential issues.

Analyzing burdens of production in this fashion not only tidies up the analytical scheme, it also has significant pragmatic appeal. The rules governing the placement of burdens of production are not altogether clear, but analyzing burdens of production functionally provides a clear articulation of the appropriate question: whether the Constitution requires that the fact in issue be proven by the prosecution.

KEY POINTS

1. Courts typically refuse to give instructions on defenses and lesser included offenses on the ground that the defendant has produced insufficient evidence to warrant such instructions. These rulings are the equivalent of directed verdicts against criminal defendants.

2. Although the Supreme Court has not addressed the issue, refusing to give such an instruction has the potential for undermining *Winship*.

2.   Judicial Summary and Comment on the Evidence in Criminal Cases

In the criminal context, courts apply a similar standard for evaluating summary and comment as in civil cases. See our discussion of summary and comment in civil cases in Section A.2, supra. For example, in Quercia v. United States, 289 U.S. 466, 468-469 (1933), the trial judge instructed the jury in the following manner:

> And now I am going to tell you what I think of the defendant's testimony. You may have noticed, Mr. Foreman and gentlemen, that he wiped his hands during his testimony. It is rather a curious thing, but that is almost always an indication of lying. Why it should be so we don't know, but that is the fact. I think that every single word that man said, except when he agreed with the Government's testimony, was a lie.
>
> Now, that opinion is an opinion of evidence and is not binding on you, and if you don't agree with it, it is your duty to find him not guilty.

In reversing the ensuing conviction, the Supreme Court stated:

> This privilege of the judge to comment on the facts has its inherent limitations. His discretion is not arbitrary and uncontrolled, but judicial, to be exercised in conformity with the standards governing the judicial office. In commenting upon testimony he may not assume the role of a witness. He may analyze and dissect the evidence, but he may not either distort it or add to it. His privilege of comment in order to give appropriate assistance to the jury is too important to be left without safeguards against abuses. . . .
>
> Nor do we think that the error was cured by the statement of the trial judge that his opinion of the evidence was not binding on the jury and that if they did not agree with it they should find the defendant not guilty. His definite and concrete assertion of fact, which he had made with all the persuasiveness of judicial utterance, as to the basis of his opinion, was not withdrawn. [Id. at 469, 472.]

NOTES AND QUESTIONS

1. Courts regularly cite and quote from *Quercia* in cases involving challenges to judicial summary and comment. In most of these cases, the judge's statements to the jury are not as extreme as the remarks in *Quercia*. United States v. Maguire, 918 F.2d 254, 268-269 (1st Cir. 1990) (instruction summarizing government's theory of the case proper); United States v. Paiva, 892 F.2d 148, 159 (1st Cir. 1989) (judge's explanation of what a field test for cocaine is went beyond proper bounds of judicial comment since there had not been testimony about what a field test was or involved, but error was harmless).

2. Is the standard implicit in *Quercia* inherently inconsistent? How can one "analyze and dissect the evidence" without "adding to it"? For a discussion, see Ronald J. Allen, More on Constitutional Process-of-Proof Problems, 94 Harv. L. Rev. 1795 (1981); and Charles R. Nesson, Rationality, Presumptions, and Judicial Comment: A Response to Professor Allen, 94 Harv. L. Rev. 1574, 1589-1590 (1981).

3. A judicial comment will either be obvious or not obvious to the jury. If it is obvious, the reiteration of the obvious by the trial judge should not be grounds for

reversal. If the judge's comment is not obvious, a critical question should be whether the comment is accurate:

> Consider a murder trial where the defendant has injected the "defense" of alibi. Assume that on the basis of the evidence adduced without judicial comment, a well-informed, rational jury would conclude that there is a 15 per cent chance that the facts of the alibi story are true. The verdict would be not guilty, since a 15 per cent chance of error surely is a "reasonable doubt." First, take the case in which the trial judge comments on the evidence tending to prove or disprove the alibi and assume that the comment is factually inaccurate. Assume further that as a result of the inaccurate comment, the same jury would conclude that there is only a very small chance that the alibi is true. The verdict, then, all other things remaining the same, would be guilty. In order to escape the guilty verdict, and the effect of the trial judge's comments, the defendant would unfairly be forced to produce stronger, more persuasive evidence of the alibi. In effect, his burden of persuasion has been increased beyond that of merely raising a reasonable doubt.
>
> Now consider the case where the judge's comments on the evidence are accurate. Assume again that the comments caused the jury to discredit the alibi sufficiently to render a guilty verdict. Once again, the defendant's burden of persuasion has been increased — he would have to present stronger evidence to gain an acquittal — but this time the defendant has no constitutional grounds to complain. By altering the jury's factual matrix to one more in accordance with reality, the judicial comment has enabled the jury to perceive that guilt was indeed proven beyond a reasonable doubt.
>
> The example illustrates that inaccurate judicial comment detrimental to the defendant, on an issue that constitutionally must be included in a state's definition of a crime, violates the mandate of In re Winship by effectively lowering the state's burden of proving guilt beyond a reasonable doubt. . . . Accurate comment, on the other hand, can prevent an erroneous verdict when the jury is unable to appreciate the implications of certain facts proven at trial. [Ronald J. Allen, Structuring Jury Decisionmaking in Criminal Cases: A Unified Constitutional Approach to Evidentiary Devices, 94 Harv. L. Rev. 321, 348-349 (1980).]

3. Presumptions in Criminal Cases: The Impact of *Winship*

Review the discussion of *Mullaney* and *Patterson* at pages 751-755, supra. A presumption that explicitly shifts the burden of persuasion to the defendant is obviously unconstitutional if the presumed fact is one that the prosecution must prove beyond a reasonable doubt. For example, the Court in *Mullaney*, beginning with the premise that the prosecution must establish malice aforethought beyond a reasonable doubt, held unconstitutional the "conclusive inference" of malice from proof of an unlawful, intentional killing. This "conclusive inference," which *Patterson* characterized as a presumption, was indeed a traditional mandatory persuasion burden presumption. See pages 753-754, supra.

Patterson, of course, called into question the underlying premise that the state had to prove malice (i.e., the absence of provocation) beyond a reasonable doubt. As we suggested in Section B, however, the Supreme Court has relied primarily on how a state chooses to define a crime as the basis for determining what the state must prove beyond a reasonable doubt. Thus, *Mullaney* apparently stands for the proposition that once a state includes a fact as part of the definition of a crime, the state cannot create a presumption that shifts the burden of persuasion on that fact. Similarly, the state cannot create a conclusive or irrebuttable presumption that an element of a crime exists. Sandstrom v. Montana, 442 U.S. 510 (1979). Unless we state otherwise, we will assume in the ensuing discussion that we are dealing with facts that the state has defined as elements of offenses and that must, therefore, be proven beyond a reasonable doubt.

It is by no means clear that one can reconcile the Supreme Court's cases dealing with presumptions in criminal cases. Many commentators think that the cases are hopelessly at odds with one another. Peter Lushing, Faces Without Features: The Surface Validity of Criminal Inferences, 72 J. Crim. L. & Criminology 82 (1981). For an elaboration on many of the issues created by the Court's criminal presumption cases, see Ronald J. Allen and Lee Ann DeGrazia, The Constitutional Requirement of Proof Beyond Reasonable Doubt in Criminal Cases: A Comment upon Incipient Chaos in the Lower Courts, 20 Am. Crim. L. Rev. 1 (1982). Here, we put those problems aside and attempt to describe the most salient features of current constitutional law regarding *Winship* and presumptions.

In order to avoid a *Mullaney*-type conflict with *Winship*, presumptions in criminal cases are typically permissive rather than mandatory: If the fact finder believes the facts giving rise to the presumption, the fact finder may but is not required to find the presumed fact. The fact finder must be convinced of the presumed fact beyond a reasonable doubt. Merely making the presumption permissive, however, does not necessarily eliminate *Winship* problems.

To determine whether a jury instruction about a presumption violates *Winship*, it is important to focus on the language of the instruction itself. If jurors could reasonably understand the instruction as permitting proof of the presumed fact by less than beyond a reasonable doubt, the instruction is unconstitutional. Sandstrom v. Montana, 442 U.S. at 510. According to County Court of Ulster County v. Allen, 442 U.S. 140 (1979), a permissive presumption instruction with respect to an element of an offense is constitutional (1) if the instructions as a whole make it clear that the jury must be convinced of each element of the crime beyond a reasonable doubt and (2) if there is a "more likely than not" relationship between the proven facts and the presumed fact. In deciding whether the relationship exists, the primary focus is on the evidence in the case, not on whether the relationship exists in the abstract.

A production burden presumption — that is, a presumption informing the jury that a presumption exists with respect to some element of the crime unless the defendant produces evidence to rebut the presumed fact — may or may not be constitutional. The best guide for dealing with this type of presumption is dictum in *Ulster County*. If jurors could reasonably understand such an instruction as requiring them to find the presumed fact unless the defendant produces a certain amount of evidence, the instruction is probably unconstitutional. In essence it permits conviction because of the defendant's failure to come forward with evidence, regardless of whether the jury is convinced beyond a reasonable doubt that the fact exists. On the other hand, if the instruction makes it clear that the defendant's obligation is minimal and if the instructions as a whole stress the *Winship* beyond-a-reasonable-doubt mandate, the instruction may be tantamount to a permissive presumption — at least if it is clear that the defendant has in fact produced some evidence. Such an instruction would apparently be constitutional if the presumption met the "more likely than not" requirement for permissive presumptions. *Ulster County*, 442 U.S. at 157 n.16.

NOTES AND QUESTIONS

1. In criminal cases prior to *Ulster County*, the Supreme Court had assessed the constitutionality of presumptions primarily in terms of the empirical relationship between the presumed facts and the facts giving rise to the presumption. The recurring issue was whether the relationship had to exist beyond a reasonable doubt or whether a more-likely-than-not relationship was sufficient. Barnes v. United States, 412 U.S. 837 (1973); Turner v. United States, 396 U.S. 398 (1970). *Ulster County* resolved the issue for permissive presumptions by settling on the more-likely-than-not standard. In addition, dictum in *Ulster County* suggests that a presumption shifting the burden of persuasion to the defendant may be constitutional if the facial (as opposed to case-specific) relationship between the proven fact and the presumed facts exists beyond a reasonable doubt. 442 U.S. at 157-159 and nn.16-17. Sandstrom v. Montana, however, makes no reference to this dictum in holding unconstitutional a presumption instruction that could have been understood as shifting the burden of persuasion to the defendant.

2. Why should it matter what the empirical relationship is between facts that give rise to a presumption and the presumed fact? As we have pointed out, instructions on inferences and presumptions are either awkward methods of allocating burdens of proof or comments on the evidence designed to inform the jury of the inferential relationship between facts.

If an instruction allocates a burden of persuasion to the defendant, the issue should be whether *Winship* requires the fact finder to prove that fact beyond a reasonable doubt. How, if at all, is the nature of the empirical relationship between the facts that the prosecution must prove and the facts that the defendant must prove important to the resolution of the *Winship* issue?

If an instruction is a comment on the evidence, it may be a comment on an ultimate fact or it may be a comment on an evidentiary fact. It may accurately point out that one fact may be inferred from another beyond reasonable doubt or it may, just as accurately, point out that one fact may be inferred from another without meeting the reasonable doubt standard. Alternatively, a comment could be inaccurate, but in such a way as to be helpful to either the prosecution or the defense. The empirical relationship tests employed in *Ulster County* and its predecessors are inadequate to deal with these and other nuances.

3. For a discussion of the criteria that should be used in evaluating presumptions in criminal cases, see Ronald J. Allen, Structuring Jury Decisionmaking in Criminal Cases: A Unified Constitutional Approach to Evidentiary Devices, 94 Harv. L. Rev. 321 (1980).

KEY POINTS

1. In assessing the constitutionality of a presumption instruction, it is important to focus on precisely what the court tells the jury. If the jury could understand the instruction in a manner that violates *Winship*, the presumption is unconstitutional.

2. Presumptions that make defined elements of crimes irrebuttable are unconstitutional.

3. Presumptions that shift the burden of persuasion to the defendant with respect to elements of offenses are also unconstitutional, except perhaps in cases in which the

general relationship between the proven facts and the presumed fact exists beyond a reasonable doubt.

4. Permissive presumptions are constitutional if the relationship between the proven facts and the presumed fact meets the "more likely than not" standard in light of the evidence in the case.

PROBLEMS

10.5. Defendant Morgan was convicted of driving under the influence of intoxicating beverages. Some 90 minutes after Morgan drove his vehicle off the road and through a fence, an officer interviewed him at a friend's home. According to the officer, Morgan appeared unsteady and smelled of alcohol, but Morgan claimed that he had not consumed any alcohol since the accident. A breathalyzer test at the time of the interview indicated that Morgan had a blood alcohol level of .14 percent. Morgan is 19 years old, 5 feet 10 inches tall, and weighs 190 pounds. In the instructions to the jury, the judge stated that Morgan was to be found guilty "if, and only if, you believe from all the evidence beyond reasonable doubt (a) that the defendant was driving a motor vehicle and (b) that while doing so he was under the influence of alcohol." The judge also read verbatim to the jury the following statutory language and told the jury to "consider this as evidence in the case":

(a) In any criminal prosecution in which the defendant is charged with having operated a vehicle while under the influence of intoxicating beverages, the amount of alcohol in the defendant's blood as determined at the time of making an analysis of his blood, urine, breath, or other bodily substance, shall give rise to the following presumptions: (i) If there was .05 percent or less by weight of alcohol in such blood, it shall be presumed that the defendant was not under the influence of intoxicating beverages; (ii) If there was more than .05 percent but less than .10 percent by weight of alcohol in such blood, such fact shall not constitute a presumption that the defendant either was or was not under the influence of intoxicating beverages, but such fact may be considered together with other competent evidence, in determining the guilt or innocence of the defendant; (iii) If there was .10 percent or more by weight of alcohol in such blood, it shall be presumed that the defendant was under the influence of intoxicating beverages.

(b) The provisions of subsection (a) of this section shall not be construed as limiting the introduction of any other competent evidence bearing on the question whether the defendant was under the influence of intoxicating beverages.

Did the instruction violate the defendant's constitutional rights?

10.6. Davis, a union official, was convicted of lying to the grand jury. The allegedly false statement was his denial that he had accepted campaign contributions from an employer. The trial judge's jury instructions included the following:

Under federal law, it is improper for a union official to accept any union campaign contributions from any employer. Specifically, federal law provides that "no moneys of an employer shall be contributed or applied to promote the candidacy of any person in any election." This law applied even where the contribution may have been minimal.

I want to caution you that the defendant is not charged in this indictment with receiving improper payments of union campaign expenses. I want to instruct you that you may only consider this instruction in determining the defendant's intent and state of mind in answering questions before the grand jury.

The purpose of the instruction, according to the prosecution, was to suggest to the jury that Davis had a motive to lie to the grand jury: Because receiving such funds is illegal and because Davis presumably knew it was illegal, he had a motive to lie about whether he had received the funds. Davis, on the other hand, points out that the only sanction for receiving such funds would have been his removal from office for the one remaining month of his term. Avoiding such a minor sanction, he suggests, is not worth the risk of a possible criminal conviction for lying to the grand jury. He claims that the instruction was unconstitutional because it created for the jury either an irrational permissive inference or a mandatory presumption. What result?

10.7. Libby was convicted of murder for stabbing his victim to death in a fight. There were no eyewitnesses to the stabbing, but witnesses did testify that Libby had been seen carrying a knife before the stabbing, that he had been seen running away from the site of the fight with blood on his clothes, that he was seen holding a knife shortly after the stabbing, that he admitted having stabbed the victim, and that he threatened anyone who might "snitch" on him. There was also testimony that he stabbed the victim because he thought the victim was about to jump him from behind and because he believed the victim was beating up a third person. The trial judge instructed the jury with respect to murder and voluntary manslaughter. The murder instruction included the following:

> Murder is the killing of a human being without legal justification or without excuse or without such extenuating circumstances as may reduce the crime to manslaughter; but with what is called in the law malice aforethought.
>
> Any intentional killing of a human being without legal justification or excuse and with no extenuating circumstances sufficient in law to reduce the crime to manslaughter is malicious.
>
> If the wicked intent to do injury to another person precedes the act by which the injury was done, it is malice aforethought. If the homicide is committed without legal justification or, that is to say, without due authority of law and not in self defense, and there is no issue here of self defense, nor in the heat of passion on great provocation, but with the specific intent to take the life of the one killed, or an unlawful act, the natural consequence of which would be to deprive another person of life, it is murder.
>
> Malice is implied in every deliberate cruel act by one against another.

The judge then gave the manslaughter instruction explaining that a killing under the influence of extreme emotional distress was manslaughter and that if there were evidence of extreme emotional distress, the jury could convict the defendant only of manslaughter unless the prosecution proved beyond a reasonable doubt that the killing was not done under the influence of extreme emotional distress. The judge told the jury to consider first whether the defendant was guilty of murder and then to consider the manslaughter charge unless the jury agreed that the defendant was guilty of murder. The judge also told the jury that to find the defendant guilty of any crime the prosecution had to prove each element beyond a reasonable doubt.

What constitutional challenges can the defendant make to these instructions?

CHAPTER ELEVEN

JUDICIAL NOTICE

Consider a case in which a large-scale livestock operation is being sued for allowing agricultural wastes to run off the animal lot into nearby waterways. Suppose the plaintiff is required to establish, as part of its case, the amount of rainfall that fell in the area during the preceding year. It seems as though there should be a clear, undisputed answer to the rainfall question; yet for the plaintiff to prove the rainfall amount using the kinds of evidence you have studied thus far might be difficult or exceedingly costly. There is no percipient witness who could give precise eyewitness testimony about how many inches of rainfall occurred. The plaintiff might have to go to the trouble of retaining an expert simply to establish an undisputable fact.

Fortunately, the Federal Rules provide a procedure that might simplify proof in this situation, known as "judicial notice." The term *judicial notice* actually encompasses a range of situations in which judges take official cognizance of propositions of fact and of law. FRE 201, discussed in Section A, deals with judicial notice in the strict sense of a formal judicial determination that a particular "adjudicative" fact is "not subject to reasonable dispute." However, the term *judicial notice* is also often used more loosely to refer to other forms of judicial fact-finding not addressed by the Federal Rules of Evidence at all. These are discussed in Sections B and C.

A. *JUDICIAL NOTICE OF ADJUDICATIVE FACTS*

1. FRE 201

RULE 201. JUDICIAL NOTICE OF ADJUDICATIVE FACTS

(a) *Scope.* This rule governs judicial notice of an adjudicative fact only, not a legislative fact.

(b) *Kinds of Facts That May Be Judicially Noticed.* The court may judicially notice a fact that is not subject to reasonable dispute because it:

(1) is generally known within the trial court's territorial jurisdiction; or

(2) can be accurately and readily determined from sources whose accuracy cannot reasonably be questioned.

(c) Taking Notice. The court:

(1) may take judicial notice on its own; or

(2) must take judicial notice if a party requests it and the court is supplied with the necessary information.

(d) Timing. The court may take judicial notice at any stage of the proceeding.

(e) Opportunity to Be Heard. On timely request, a party is entitled to be heard on the propriety of taking judicial notice and the nature of the fact to be noticed. If the court takes judicial notice before notifying a party, the party, on request, is still entitled to be heard.

(f) Instructing the Jury. In a civil case, the court must instruct the jury to accept the noticed fact as conclusive. In a criminal case, the court must instruct the jury that it may or may not accept the noticed fact as conclusive.

2.   Interpretation and Illustration of FRE 201(a) and (b)

FRE 201 authorizes, and in some circumstances requires, the judge to instruct the jury to accept certain facts as true, if those facts are "not subject to reasonable dispute." The judge may make such a ruling whether requested or not, but must make such a ruling on request of a party who properly demonstrates the undisputable quality of the fact. In criminal cases, the judge must qualify the instruction by advising the jury that it "may," but need not, accept the fact as true.

a.   Types of Adjudicative Facts That Are Frequently Noticed

In theory, a court could take judicial notice of any evidentiary facts or propositions of background knowledge that meet the high standards of certainty required by FRE 201(b). In practice, the kinds of facts judicially noticed under this rule tend to fall into a predictable set of broad categories: business or government custom; calendar dates and time limits; product characteristics in copyright, patent, and trademark litigation; current events; general principles of economics and economic information; fees and salaries; geography; historical information; judicial records and proceedings; medical information; official records; scientific facts and principles, and performance of scientific equipment; and weather. See 1 Stephen A. Saltzburg, Michael M. Martin, and Daniel J. Capra, Federal Rules of Evidence Manual 132-148 (7th ed. 1998).

b.   The Scope of FRE 201(a): What Are Adjudicative Facts?

FRE 201(a) states that the rule applies only to those situations in which judges take official cognizance of "adjudicative facts," but the rule itself does not define that term. Adjudicative facts are those facts that the jury typically decides at trial. Adjudicative facts may be either the alleged facts of consequence that are the essential elements of a dispute under the substantive law or the evidentiary facts that are relevant to prove those facts of consequence. As described by the Advisory Committee Note to FRE 201(a):

> Adjudicative facts are simply the facts of the particular case . . . . [T]he adjudicative facts are those to which the law is applied in the process of adjudication. They are the facts that normally go to the jury in a jury case. They relate to the parties, their activities, their properties, their businesses. [2 Kenneth Davis, Administrative Law Treatise 353 (1958).]

You know by now from your study of evidence how broad this concept of adjudicative facts really is — potentially any fact relevant to a dispute under FRE 401 would be an adjudicative fact and *could be* subject to FRE 201. The real limits to the scope of this rule come from FRE 201(b).

c.   *The Scope of FRE 201(b): The Required State of Knowledge of Adjudicative Facts That May Be Judicially Noticed*

If a party requests the court to take judicial notice of an adjudicative fact pursuant to FRE 201, the party must persuade the court that the fact satisfies the standards of FRE 201(b). The fact must be indisputable as defined by the rule; it must not be subject to "reasonable dispute." That indisputability can be established through either of two means. First, the fact may be the kind of fact that is "generally known within the territorial jurisdiction of the trial court." For example, in Goldblatt v. Fed. Deposit Ins. Corp., 105 F.3d 1325, 1329 n.3 (9th Cir. 1999), the court took judicial notice of the interest bearing nature of money market accounts. By contrast, in Carley v. Wheeled Coach, 991 F.2d 1117, 1126 (3d Cir. 1993), the appellate court concluded that the trial court had erred in taking judicial notice of the "well known rollover propensities of vehicles having a high center of gravity." According to the court, "[m]ost people probably know little, if anything, about how high centers of gravity cause vehicular accidents." The parties thus had to produce evidence on this issue, and the jury would ultimately decide it.

The second way to establish indisputability is by reference to "sources whose accuracy cannot reasonably be questioned." For example, in United States v. Pozsgai, 999 F.2d 719, 731 (3d Cir. 1993), the appellate court held that the trial court had properly taken judicial notice of the fact that the Pennsylvania Canal was or could be used in interstate commerce. The status of the Canal in interstate commerce was established by two scholarly history books and a U.S. Army Corps of Engineers report. As a result, the parties needed to produce no evidence on this issue, and the jury was instructed as to its truth. If indisputability cannot be established under either of these standards, the factual issue is subject to proof at trial.

These two criteria significantly narrow the scope of facts subject to judicial notice from FRE 201(a)'s broad reference to "adjudicative facts." Facts that are "generally known" or that are established by "unquestionably accurate" sources tend to be what we would think of as "background information." Such facts may be highly relevant and indeed essential to a party's claim or defense, but they are probably not unique to the case.

3.   Elaboration of FRE 201(a) and (b)

a.   Further Illustration of 201(b) Standards

IN RE THIRTYACRE

154 B.R. 497 (Bankr. C.D. Ill. 1993)

WILLIAM V. ALTENBERGER, Bankruptcy Judge.

[In a bench trial, a judgment creditor sought a finding from the Bankruptcy Court that the debt was nondischargeable as a willful and malicious injury, because it was based on a state court judgment that the debtor Thirtyacre had assaulted the creditor. The debtor Thirtyacre's defense was that his mental capacity to form an intent to act in a willful and malicious manner was impaired because he had been taking the drug Pamelor and drinking alcohol at the time of the assault. Thirtyacre asked the court to take judicial notice of the effects of Pamelor.] . . .

The first evidentiary issue is whether this Court should take judicial notice of the drug manufacturer's pamphlet for the drug Pamelor. This pamphlet contains sections entitled: Description, Actions, Indications, Contraindications, Warnings, Precautions, Adverse Reactions, Dosage and Administration, and How Supplied. The Defendant [Mr. Thirtyacre] asked this Court to take judicial notice of the definition of Pamelor. In effect he was asking this Court to take judicial notice of the matters in the pamphlet, including that the drug when taken with an excessive consumption of alcohol may have adverse consequences.

Rule 201 of the Federal Rules of Evidence governs judicial notice of adjudicative facts . . . .

Clearly the pamphlet does not fall within the scope of the rule . . . .It cannot be said that the effects of Pamelor when taken with an excessive consumption of alcohol are generally known within the jurisdiction of this Court. As stated in McCormick on Evidence:

> [T]he more reflective opinions speak in terms of the knowledge of "most men," or of "what well-informed persons generally know," or "the knowledge that every intelligent person has."

The information contained in the pamphlet does not fall within those standards.

Nor can it be said that the effect of the drug when taken with an excessive consumption of alcohol can be accurately or readily determined by resorting to the pamphlet. It is appropriate to take judicial notice of a proposition of science, but the Defendant's request does not fall within that category. Rather, the Defendant asks this Court to take judicial notice from the pamphlet of the effect on the Defendant of his using the drug while drinking. It does not follow from the pamphlet what the specific effect of the Defendant's use while drinking might be.

As the court stated in Clark v. South Central Bell Tel. Co. . . . :

> F.R.E. 201 states that facts may be noticed if they are "capable of accurate and ready determination by resort to sources whose accuracy cannot reasonably be questioned." For a Court to notice facts judicially, if they are not matters of general knowledge, the sources of those facts must be placed before the Court. If a party places the source before the Court and requests judicial notice, the Court must take it if the facts are susceptible of judicial notice.

This standard of "indisputability" was discussed in Louisell & Mueller, Federal Evidence, §57, Rule 201, p.437:

> Facts may be indisputable within the meaning of Rule 201 because (even though not generally known) they can be verified by resort to sources whose accuracy cannot reasonably be questioned. At one time courts indulged in the obvious fiction of consulting sources to refresh recollection, but it is clear enough that courts in reality simply inform themselves of facts which nobody is likely to carry around in his head from whatever sources the trial judge deems to be unquestionably accurate. Almanacs, encyclopedias, calendars, historical works and charts tabulating information deduced from the application of the laws of physics form only a part of what must be a list too long to be worth enumerating of sources to which a court may in proper circumstances resort for the purpose of deriving judicially noticeable information.

If the Defendant had submitted information regarding Pamelor that had been obtained from the FDA or a medical dictionary (as he represented it was), then perhaps it would have been admissible. But for this Court to find that the manufacturer's own representations regarding the drug are "sources whose accuracy cannot reasonably be questioned" within the meaning of FRE 201(b) goes far beyond any reported application of that rule. There is no element of objectivity with such an application. In United States v. Houston, . . . the court held that judicial notice could be taken of a two-page publication setting out information pertaining to the background, pharmacological information, pattern of use, and subjective effects of the drug phencyclidine, finding that the information was factual and could be readily obtained from the National Institute of Drug Abuse. The court in that case was willing to go beyond the record and do its own independent verification. In this Court's view, the burden is on the party seeking to have the court take judicial notice of the fact to put the sources before the court and establish their complete accuracy.

NOTES AND QUESTIONS

1. As Thirtyacre's lawyer, how would you state the proposition of fact that you would ask the court to judicially notice? Why is this an adjudicative fact?

2. If you sought judicial notice of this fact on behalf of Thirtyacre, what kind of information might you have attempted to present to satisfy FRE 201(b)? What kind of instruction, in a jury trial, would you request from the court if you were able to satisfy FRE 201? And what would you do if the court refused to take judicial notice of this fact?

b. Sources of Information Under FRE 201

The *Thirtyacre* opinion lists the kinds of sources of information that judges typically use to satisfy the "general knowledge" and "accurate and ready determination" standards of FRE 201(b). The more specifically the facts concern the individual litigant, the more difficult it is to satisfy these standards. Storm Plastics, Inc. v. United States, 770 F.2d 148, 155 (10th Cir. 1985) (trial judge improperly took judicial notice of the quality of plaintiff's fishing lures, as this fact was not generally known in the community nor one capable of accurate determination by plainly accurate sources). If sources are used to establish propositions of generalized background knowledge, then they must be well recognized. United States v. Simon, 842 F.2d 552, 555 (1st Cir. 1988) (trial judge not required to take judicial notice of the fact that Rastafarians use marijuana as part of their religion because this fact is not generally known and the offered sources — a 1967 dissertation and a 1960 research paper — were "hardly sources whose accuracy cannot reasonably be questioned"). And if judges take judicial notice of adjudicative facts on the basis of their own personal experience, they are likely to be reversed. United States v. Lewis, 833 F.2d 1380, 1384 (9th Cir. 1987) (judge erred in finding a confession to be involuntary by taking judicial notice of the effects of general anesthetic following an operation, relying on his own personal experience).

4.   Interpretation and Illustration of FRE 201(c) and (e)

Subsection (c) of FRE 201 provides that a court *may* take judicial notice of a fact on its own initiative; the court may determine that a fact should be noticed, and it may obtain information from its own investigation to determine whether the standards of FRE 201(b) are met. The judge in *Thirtyacre* refused to engage in his own search for information concerning the indisputability of the Pamelor pamphlet. He held instead that "the burden is on the party seeking to have the court take judicial notice of the fact to put the sources before the court and establish their complete accuracy." This holding is consistent with FRE 201(c)(1) and (2), which plainly imply that a court is not required to take judicial notice on its own initiative. Under subsection (c)(2), the court *must* take judicial notice of an adjudicative fact *only* when the party seeking notice has provided the information necessary to satisfy FRE 201(b).

FRE 201 contains only minimal direction for the court on the process to be followed before notice of an adjudicative fact is taken. Because of the close connection of these facts to the matters in dispute, they will usually have an immediate impact on the litigants' case. Therefore FRE 201(e) provides that a party, upon timely request, has the right to be heard on the "propriety of taking judicial notice and the nature of the fact to be noticed." For example, if defendant Thirtyacre had produced scientific literature concerning the effects of taking Pamelor with alcohol, the plaintiff could have requested the opportunity to attack the accuracy of defendant's sources or to produce other contradictory information. This opportunity must be given upon the party's request whether the judicial notice was initiated by the opposing party under subsection (c)(1) or the judge under (c)(2). The "opportunity to be heard" does not necessarily mean the right to a formal hearing, but simply the right to object to judicial notice. See American Stores v. Commission of Internal Revenue Service, 170 F.3d 1267 (10th Cir. 1999).

5.   Interpretation and Illustration of FRE 201(d) and (f)

a.   *Judicial Notice of Adjudicative Facts in Civil Cases: Mini Directed Verdicts*

Judicial notice of adjudicative facts has two major effects on the civil trial process: (1) It simplifies the jury's fact-finding role because it removes a fact from dispute and (2) it relieves a party both from the burden of producing evidence of the noticed fact to the jury and from the threat of having the jury hear contradictory evidence from the opponent. Remember that the party must present evidence *to the judge* that satisfies the standards of FRE 201(b). Under the first sentence of FRE 201(f), once the judge decides that these standards are satisfied, the jury will be instructed that it must accept the noticed fact. The party's evidence need not be presented to the jury; the opponent may present no contradictory evidence; no closing argument need be made in support of the fact; and no argument can be made against it. In effect, the court is directing a verdict on the judicially noticed fact.

b. Judicial Notice of Adjudicative Facts in Criminal Cases: Judicial Comments

Judicial notice in criminal cases poses somewhat different problems from judicial notice in civil cases. The second sentence of FRE 201(f) provides: "In a criminal case, the court must instruct the jury that it *may or may not* accept the noticed fact as conclusive." (Emphasis added.) It may seem contradictory to tell the jury that it "may" accept a fact that has been judicially noticed. After all, judicial notice is supposed to dispose of issues. The explanation for this apparent incongruity is that juries are given greater deference in criminal cases than in civil. Indeed, it is frequently said that there are no directed verdicts against criminal defendants, and as we have just observed, to take binding judicial notice of a fact is to direct a verdict on that fact. Thus, treating judicial notice as binding would seem to conflict with the conventional view of the role of jurors in criminal cases. United States v. Mentz, 840 F.2d 315, 318 (6th Cir. 1988) (a conclusive instruction to the jury on a noticed fact in a criminal case is an error of constitutional magnitude). If the judge takes judicial notice in a criminal case, she will call the noticed fact to the jury's attention in something like the following terms:

> You may accept the court's declaration as evidence and regard as proved the fact or event which has been judicially noticed. You are not required to do so, however, since you are the sole judges of the facts.

United States v. Chapel, 41 F.3d 1338, 1339 (9th Cir. 1994). Such an instruction allows the judge, in effect, to make a nonbinding comment that the judicially noticed fact is obvious, generally known, or indisputable.

c. Timing of Judicial Notice

Pursuant to FRE 201(d), judicial notice may be taken at any time in the proceeding. This means that adjudicative facts may be noticed during pretrial proceedings, such as in a motion to narrow the scope of discovery or in a motion for directed verdict. In a jury trial, facts are usually noticed before the court gives its instructions so that the proper instructions may be given. In a bench trial, notice can be taken or refused at any time during the judge's deliberations, as was done in the *Thirtyacre* case.

 i. Judicial Notice to Preserve Civil Verdicts. At least in civil cases, courts may also take judicial notice after a case has been submitted to the jury, after the jury's verdict has been rendered, or on appeal, even if not requested during the trial. When there is a gap in a winning party's proof, judicial notice of that fact could be taken by either the trial court or the appellate court in order to protect the jury's verdict. If the gap in proof is discovered after a party moves for a directed verdict, the trial court might be persuaded to take judicial notice of the missing fact by the nonmoving party as a way to fend off the directed verdict. FRE 201(d) (formerly subsection (f)) has even been construed to allow an appellate court to take judicial notice where the other criteria for judicial notice are satisfied. See, e.g., Gustafson v. Cornelius Co., 724 F.2d 75, 79 (8th Cir. 1983) (appellate court took judicial notice of an unfair labor practice charge for the purpose of determining date at which a cause of action accrued); Havens Steel Co. v. Randolph Eng'g Co., 813 F.2d 186 (8th Cir. 1987) (appellate court took judicial notice of the average annual prime interest rate in rejecting the defendant's claim that the proof of damages at trial had been too imprecise); but see Colonial Leasing Co. v. Logistics Control Group Int'l, 762 F.2d 454, 461, modified, 770 F.2d 479 (5th Cir. 1985) (taking judicial notice after trial would raise due process concerns).

ii.   Judicial Notice to Preserve Criminal Verdicts.   Some courts have taken the same verdict-saving approach in criminal cases in which prosecutors have failed to prove the facts necessary for federal jurisdiction. United States v. Lavender, 602 F.2d 639 (4th Cir. 1979) (court took judicial notice that the Blue Ridge Parkway was located in federal territory); United States v. Piggie, 622 F.2d 486, 487-488 (10th Cir. 1980). Proponents of this approach argue that it is consistent with the spirit of judicial notice to promote judicial efficiency by obviating the need for evidentiary proof of irrefutable facts.

But such an approach seems to violate the clear intent of the second sentence of subsection (f), which prohibits binding judicial notice in criminal cases in order to preserve the jury's role to decide all issues of fact in criminal cases. See United States v. Dior, 671 F.2d 351, 358 n.11 (9th Cir. 1982); United States v. Jones, 580 F.2d 219 (6th Cir. 1978).

KEY POINTS

1. FRE 201 provides that courts may take judicial notice of adjudicative facts. Adjudicative facts are those facts that are usually decided by the jury.

2. Facts judicially noticed pursuant to FRE 201(b) must be established as certain beyond reasonable dispute, and this standard of certainty must be satisfied on the basis of general knowledge within the jurisdiction or from sources whose accuracy cannot reasonably be questioned.

3. In civil cases, the judge will instruct the jury that it must accept a judicially noticed fact as true. In criminal cases, the judge will instruct the jury that it may, but need not, accept the noticed fact as true.

4. Facts may be judicially noticed at any time, but if the winning party has failed to prove an essential element at trial, the taking of judicial notice to preserve the winning party's jury verdict may violate the constitutional rights of the opponent in both criminal and civil cases.

NOTES AND QUESTIONS

1. Although the second sentence of FRE 201(g) applies to criminal cases generally, the underlying concern is the supposed tension between binding judicial notice

and a *criminal defendant's* right to jury trial. Compare FRE 201(g) with Md. R. Evid. 5-201(g), which makes judicial notice nonbinding only when the noticed fact is "adverse to the defendant."

2. Particularly in light of the fact that courts regularly direct verdicts against criminal defendants by not instructing juries on defenses for which there is insufficient evidence, why is it arguably unconstitutional for courts to take binding judicial notice in criminal cases? Should it matter whether the noticed fact is a jurisdictional matter (e.g., the location of the crime) or a substantive element (e.g., the value of stolen goods)?

3. Even if binding judicial notice adverse to criminal defendants is not unconstitutional, one may for prudential reasons want to avoid restricting the scope of the jury's fact-finding role. If so, would it be preferable to ban any form of "judicial notice" that is adverse to criminal defendants? Consider whether a nonbinding judicial notice instruction like the one quoted at page 779, supra, is likely to contribute to the jury's rational decision-making.

4. Since the last sentence of FRE 201(g) calls for what is in effect judicial comment, does FRE 201 imply that all judicial comment in criminal prosecutions must satisfy the certainty requirements of FRE 201(b)?

PROBLEMS

11.1. Review the agricultural waste runoff hypothetical at the beginning of this chapter. What sources might the plaintiff rely upon to request that the court take judicial notice of the amount of rainfall that occurred in the region the year preceding the runoff event? Can the defendant object to judicial notice without having a reasonable basis to dispute the amount of rainfall asserted in plaintiff's request for judicial notice?

11.2. The ship *S.S. Norton* broke from its moorings and ran aground, releasing 200,000 barrels of crude oil into the ocean near Guam. The owner, Kramden, sued the captain and the charterers for negligence, arguing that mooring the ship in Guam during the month of November — the peak of the typhoon season — posed a great danger to both the cargo of oil and the environment. At trial, the judge is asked to take notice that Guam is seriously vulnerable to typhoons, and that the month of November is the peak of the typhoon season. Objection? What kind of sources might be found that would satisfy FRE 201(b)?

11.3. In imposing sanctions against an extremely litigious inmate and issuing an injunction against further filings without paying full filing fees, the trial judge made a finding of fact that the inmate had access to considerable sums of money. That finding was based in part on the judge's judicial notice of a local newspaper article describing the inmate as extremely wealthy and quoting him as saying that he had made thousands of dollars from his extortion activities in prison. Was taking judicial notice proper?

11.4. In an age discrimination suit against Acme Aircraft Corp., defendant claims that the reason plaintiff lost his job was inadequate performance and reduction in the workforce. To support the latter claim, the defendant presents the court with a newspaper article describing widespread layoffs at Acme and asks the court to take judicial notice of the contents of the article. What result?

11.5. In a suit against tobacco companies for injuries related to smoking, the defendants request that the court take judicial notice that since the late 1960s (when plaintiffs began smoking) the health hazards and the addictive nature of smoking have been common knowledge. Are these proper matters for judicial notice?

11.6. The United States brought a civil action against Dr. Jones to recover federal student loans that Jones had received from the National Health Service Corps. Dr. Jones allegedly breached his mandatory four-year contract of employment with a community health center. The issue at trial was whether Dr. Jones left the health center because of a salary dispute or whether he was terminated because of attendance and other problems, which would trigger an obligation to pay back his loans. The district court granted summary judgment in favor of the government by taking judicial notice of factual findings that Jones was terminated for attendance and other problems. These findings had been made in an order entered by another district court in a suit by Jones against the health center. Dr. Jones contests this result on appeal. What result?

11.7. Defendant is charged with assault within federal territory. After proof at trial that Raybrook Federal Prison was owned by the federal government, the district court gave the following instruction that removed the federal jurisdictional element from defendant's assault charge:

> The Government must prove the alleged assault took place within the special maritime and territorial jurisdiction of the United States. This simply means that the alleged assault must have occurred in any lands reserved or acquired for the use of the United States and under the exclusive or concurrent jurisdiction thereof. I charge you now that [Raybrook] is a place that falls within the territorial jurisdiction of the United States. Therefore, if you find beyond a reasonable doubt that the acted [sic] alleged occurred at [Raybrook], the sixth element of the offense has been met.

On appeal, defendant contends that this instruction violated FRE 201(g) and his constitutional right to be convicted by the jury on proof beyond a reasonable doubt. What result?

11.8. Plaintiff has sued defendants alleging that they participated in a scheme to defraud him through the fictitious sale of Nigerian crude oil. Plaintiff asks the trial court to take judicial notice of the following: (1) that at all times pertinent to the lawsuit, there were Nigerian fraud scams perpetrated on people in the United States and other countries in the world, and (2) that the fraud scams involved, among other things, oil deals that never materialized. To support this request for judicial notice plaintiff has provided the trial judge with a congressional report dated December 12, 1995, a Senate committee report, at least two newspaper articles, a videotape from the television news magazine "20/20," a videotape from the television news magazine "60 Minutes," and a videotape from the British Broadcasting Corporation. What result?

B.   JUDICIAL NOTICE AS PART OF JUDICIAL DECISION-MAKING

In performing their judicial function, judges must take official account of propositions of law, of generalized knowledge, and of specific facts in many different contexts. Although the types of propositions, the sources from which they are established, and the uses to which they are put in judicial decision-making vary enormously, all of these judicial behaviors are sometimes called "taking judicial notice," even though FRE 201 does not — and often, as a practical matter, could not — apply. For example, if preliminary facts necessary to make admissibility decisions had to meet the certainty standard of FRE 201(b), much currently admissible evidence would be inadmissible. Similarly, if the factual premises underlying a court's interpretation of law had to meet the FRE 201(b) standard, it would be virtually impossible for courts to engage in the process of law interpretation. This section briefly discusses some of the contexts in which judges take official account of facts and of law — sometimes, but not always, under the guise of taking "judicial notice" — without the necessity of complying with FRE 201. As you can imagine, this loose and inconsistent usage of the term *judicial notice* occasionally creates confusion.

A caveat is in order about the materials that follow. Outside the area of adjudicative facts, the term *judicial notice* is most commonly associated with "legislative facts," which we discuss in subsection 2, infra. Keep in mind, though, that (1) there is nothing analytically significant about the use of the term judicial notice for any of the fact finding that we discuss here and (2) there is nothing analytically significant about the distinct categories of judicial fact finding that we describe here. Rather, the controlling and only analytically significant issue should be whether the judge is making a factual finding that would normally be made by a jury or whether the judge is making the finding for some other purpose. In the former situation FRE 201 applies; in the latter, it does not. If there is uncertainty about whether the finding is an adjudicative fact — that is, a "jury issue" — the uncertainty has nothing to do with judicial notice. Rather, the uncertainty is about application of the criteria for allocating fact finding generally between judge and jury.

For the leading scholarly critique of the limited scope of FRE 201 in light of these broader notions of "judicial notice," see Kenneth C. Davis, Judicial Notice, 1969 Law and the Soc. Order 513 (1969); and Dennis J. Turner, Judicial Notice and Federal Rule of Evidence 201 — A Rule Ready for Change, 45 U. Pitt. L. Rev. 181 (1983).

1. Judicial Cognizance of Common Knowledge Without Formal Judicial Notice

a. *The Jury's General Background Knowledge*

We know that when juries decide questions of fact they must rely on their own generalized knowledge and experience to make the inferences necessary to jury reasoning. The jury's background knowledge and experience are largely unexamined by the judicial system. In a few contexts, however, judges do consider what common generalized knowledge the jury can be assumed to have. This is sometimes called taking judicial notice of such common knowledge, although FRE 201 does not apply and the propositions relied on could not possibly satisfy the rule's standards of certainty. For example, when judges rule on questions of relevance in admitting evidence, they will occasionally articulate the generalized background knowledge that they assume the jurors can use to make the necessary inferences. And when there is a gap in proof to sustain a verdict, the court may find that, based on all the evidence, the jury's background knowledge could fill the gap. In United States v. Luckenbill, 421 F.2d 849

(9th Cir. 1970), the defendant was charged with forcing an accomplice to forge an endorsement on a government check in Spokane, Washington. No evidence was presented that the crime occurred in Spokane, which was necessary for venue. However, references in testimony to areas called "Nine Mile" and "Seven Mile" (areas known to be close to Spokane) were sufficient, the court held, to justify the jury in finding that the crime took place in Spokane.

Consider also the problem of jurors relying on unique personal knowledge or their independent investigatory information. If such independently obtained information is not general or common enough for the judge to assume that reasonable jurors already share it, then its injection into the jury room may violate the principles of public, adversarial proof-taking. In Thomas v. Kansas Power & Light Co., 340 P.2d 379 (Kan. 1959), for example, the court granted a new trial when it discovered that a juror had borrowed a book on electricity and had shared information on the arcing characteristics of electricity with other jurors.

b.   Judges' Own Background Knowledge

When judges decide questions of fact, they must draw inferences on the basis of their own generalized knowledge and experience. Commentators sometimes refer to the process of using such background knowledge and experience as judicial notice:

> When the judge or jury use their pre-existing knowledge, they are said to be taking "judicial notice" of the facts thus utilized. Probably 99% of the judicial notice taken could be called "tacit" or "unconscious" judicial notice; that is, the process goes on without anyone being aware that reliance is being placed on extra-record facts. [21 Charles A. Wright and Kenneth W. Graham Jr., Federal Practice and Procedure §5102, at 460 (1990).]

As the Advisory Committee Note to FRE 201(a) makes clear, the rigors of FRE 201 do not apply: "It is apparent that this use of non-evidence facts in evaluating the adjudicative facts of the case is not an appropriate subject for a formalized judicial notice treatment." Unlike juries, however, judges must account for their decisions. Frequently, judges will articulate in their judicial opinions the background generalizations that they have used in their fact-finding. Since FRE 201 does not apply, these generalizations are reviewed on appeal for their reasonableness. If reasonable, appellate courts will defer to the trial court's use of them under the deferential standard of "abuse of discretion." But what if a judge's background or experience is relatively unusual, giving the judge a unique factual perspective on the case? Should it be sufficient that the judge's fact finding is reasonable, or should any unique factual assumptions have to satisfy the certainty criteria of FRE 201(b)? Some of these issues are raised in the following case.

IN RE MARRIAGE OF TRESNAK
297 N.W.2d 109 (Iowa 1980)

McCormick, Justice.
This appeal involves a parental dispute over custody of two sons, Rick, age eleven, and Ryan, age nine. The parents are Emil James Tresnak (Jim) and Linda Lou Tresnak (Linda) who were married in 1965. In the August 1979 decree dissolving

the marriage, the trial court awarded custody of the children to Jim. Linda appeals. We reverse and remand . . . .

In awarding custody of the children to Jim, the trial court said:

> The Petitioner at this time in life now desires to continue her education by attending law school at the University of Iowa. Although this is commendable insofar as her ambition for a career is concerned, in the opinion of the Court, it is not necessarily for the best interest and welfare of her minor children, who are now ten and eight years of age. Anyone who has attained a legal education can well appreciate the time that studies consume. Although the Petitioner, during her undergraduate work, was able to care for the children while attending the Northeast Missouri University at Kirksville by studying after the children were placed in bed, the study of law is somewhat different in that it usually requires library study, where reference material is required. Also, other than time in class during the day, there will be study periods during the day in the library necessary, as well as in the evening, and which would necessarily require the children being in the hands of a babysitter for many hours a day when not attending school. The weekends are usually occupied by study periods, and although the Petitioner has a high academic ability, she will find that by reason thereof there will be additional activities bestowed upon her, such as becoming a member of a law review, which is time-consuming. Although the Petitioner may believe that she would not have to engage in such, she by not doing so would be interfering with her own achievements for her own benefit and welfare in future years.

In challenging the trial court's reasoning, Linda contends no evidentiary support existed for the court's assumptions about law school and the children's activities. She also contends the assumed facts are not a proper subject of judicial notice. . . .

The only evidence about the demands of law school appeared in Linda's testimony. She acknowledged on cross-examination that law school would require many hours of study. However, she also said she did not expect to leave the children with babysitters often, she would take them to the library with her if necessary, and she did not believe her studies would interfere with her care of the children. Thus, while the record supports the trial court's inference that law school studies would occupy much of Linda's time, it does not lend much support to the court's statements about the necessity of library work away from the children, the likelihood of her involvement in extracurricular activities, or the effect of such factors on her care of the children.

Nor are these matters subject to judicial notice. "To be capable of being judicially noticed a matter must be of common knowledge or capable of certain verification." Motor Club of Iowa v. Department of Transportation, 251 N.W.2d 510, 517 (Iowa 1977). Courts are permitted to dispense with formal proof of matters which everyone knows. In this case, in overruling Linda's motion for new trial, the trial court defended its findings by asserting a "personal acquaintanceship with the studies of law school." However, judicial notice "is limited to what a judge may properly know in his judicial capacity, and he is not authorized to make his (personal) knowledge of a fact not generally or professionally known the basis of his action." Bervid v. Iowa State Tax Commission, 78 N.W.2d 812, 816 (1956). It is common knowledge in the legal profession that law school studies are demanding and time-consuming, but the requirements of a specific law school curriculum are not generally or professionally known.

The trial court's statements about the necessity of extensive library study and likelihood of Linda's work on the law review at the University of Iowa law school are not matters of common knowledge or capable of certain verification within the meaning of the judicial notice principle. Because the statements have only tenuous support in the evidence, they are entitled to little weight in evaluating the merits of the custody dispute. In saying this, however, we do not suggest the court could not consider the demands of law school which were shown in the evidence. . . .

Because either parent would be a good custodian of the children, the decision on the merits is difficult. Linda and Jim are stable and responsible persons who love their children and are capable of giving them adequate care. . . .

It is common knowledge that in many homes today both parents have demanding out-of-home activities, whether in employment, school or community affairs. Neither should necessarily be penalized in child custody cases for engaging in such activities. In this case, Linda seeks a legal education for self-fulfillment and as a means of achieving financial independence. These goals are not inimical to the children's best interests. Because the record shows she is capable of continuing to provide the children with the same high quality of care she has given them in the past, her attendance at law school should not disqualify her from having their custody. We perceive no reason for believing she will not give the children excellent care during her law school years and thereafter.

. . . We believe the long-range best interests of the children will be better served if Linda has their custody. Therefore we reverse the trial court and remand to permit the court to enter appropriate orders relating to child support and visitation.

Reversed and remanded.

NOTES AND QUESTIONS

The appellate court's reliance in *Tresnak* on "common knowledge" seems somewhat ironic, given its discussion of the trial court's decision. What kind of facts had the trial court judicially noticed? Can you tell, based on the appellate opinion, whether FRE 201 should have applied if the action were in federal court? Or was the court taking cognizance of propositions of fact that were not adjudicative facts? Would you say that the real lesson of cases like *Tresnak* is that trial judges should not explain the basis of their reasoning if they wish to avoid being reversed? Is that a disturbing commentary on the legal system?

2.   Judicial Cognizance of Legislative Facts

Courts must make factual assumptions to decide law. Thus, judges take cognizance of propositions of fact when they interpret statutes (facts about legislative history or policy, or about how the statute affects the population) and when they develop principles of common law (facts about changed societal or economic conditions that justify a new legal rule). As an example, the Advisory Committee Note to FRE 201(a) cites the Supreme Court case of Hawkins v. United States, 358 U.S. 74 (1958), in which the Court relied on the following proposition to uphold the spousal testimonial privilege: If spouses testify against each other this would "be likely to destroy almost any marriage." Id. at 78. Another frequently cited example is the social science research, showing that segregation creates a feeling of inferiority, relied on in Brown v. Board of Education, 347 U.S. 483, 494 n.11 (1954), to hold that segregated schools are inherently unequal. These propositions are rarely indisputable, and they are necessary for judges to make sense of most questions of legal policy. It is clear from the text of the rule, and from the Advisory Committee Note, that FRE 201 does not apply to judges' use of such facts; and even the rules of evidence do not limit the materials that courts can use to resolve disputed issues of legislative fact.

Judges obtain information about these empirical propositions from their own research and from the parties, either at trial or in briefs to the court. Thus, the parties often do have the opportunity to debate the propriety of the court's reliance on certain legislative facts. However, not all facts necessary to creating law or policy can be put "into a party-prepared record of evidence. Judges . . . cannot confine their thoughts to facts that parties have prepared in a formal record. . . ." 2 Kenneth C. Davis and Richard J. Pierce Jr., Administrative Law Treatise §10.5, at 142 (3d ed. 1994). When judicial use of disputable legislative facts is based on the judges' own independent research, the parties may be excluded from the decision-making process. Some commentators have found this to be troublesome:

> We do not claim that Judges cannot rely on a broad range of facts to force the law forward. We suggest only that the parties should be permitted to participate in the march. . . . If a fact or set of facts is likely to be critical to a decision on the law to be applied to parties, there is every reason to want the parties to be heard on the factual question. Evidence need not always be taken. Briefs may work better in many situations. But some chance for the parties to be heard on decisive legislative facts is desirable. [1 Stephen A. Saltzberg, Michael M. Martin and Daniel J. Capra, Federal Rules of Evidence Manual 125 (7th ed. 1998).]

Although the Federal Rules do not expressly authorize judicial notice of legislative facts, the reality that courts must make factual assumptions to decide legal questions — under the rubric of "legislative fact" — has been recognized in numerous judicial decisions. Therefore the distinction between "adjudicative" and "legislative" facts can have significant practical impact on whether and how a party meets its burden of proof. Consider United States v. Gould, 536 F.2d 216 (8th Cir. 1976), in which the prosecution's expert failed to provide testimony that the cocaine hydrochloride found in defendants' possession was a derivative of coca leaves, as required to establish a violation of the drug laws then in force. The appellate court affirmed the conviction on the ground that the trial judge had permissibly taken judicial notice of a legislative fact. Not only did this obviate the need for expert testimony linking cocaine hydrochloride to cocaine, but the court could simply issue a jury instruction permitting the jury to so find without going through the formalities of FRE 201, which apply only to adjudicative facts:

> The precise line of demarcation between adjudicative facts and legislative facts is not always easily identified[.] "Legislative facts . . . do not relate specifically to the activities or characteristics of the litigants. . . ." Legislative facts are established truths, facts or pronouncements that do not change from case to case but apply universally, while adjudicative facts are those developed in a particular case.
> . . . When a court attempts to ascertain the governing law in a case for the purpose of instructing the jury, it must necessarily rely upon facts which are unrelated to the activities of the immediate parties. These extraneous, yet necessary, facts fit within the definition of legislative facts and are an indispensable tool used by judges when discerning the applicable law through interpretation. The District Court, therefore, was judicially noticing such a legislative fact when it recognized that cocaine hydrochloride is derived from coca leaves. . . . [536 F.2d at 219-220.]

NOTES AND QUESTIONS

1. Was the result in *Gould* correct, or was the court struggling to resolve the tension created when indisputable facts are essential elements in criminal cases? How does one determine whether a fact is legislative or adjudicative? Should the result in *Gould* depend upon the generality or universality of the fact that cocaine hydrochloride is a derivative of coca leaves, the incongruity of giving a nonbinding judicial notice instruction, the intent of congress, or something else?

2. Reconsider the instruction given in Problem 11.7 at page 782. Is this instruction a violation of FRE 201(g)? Is the federal status of Raybrook prison an adjudicative or a legislative fact?

3. In United States v. Dior, 671 F.2d 351 (9th Cir. 1982), the court considered whether the American-Canadian exchange rate could be classified as a legislative fact. Should it be under *Gould*? If not, then could the jurors be permitted to find that the illegally imported goods (worth $13,690 in Canadian dollars) were worth $5,000 or more in U.S. currency, based on their own generalized knowledge? The dissent in *Dior* suggested they could:

> [T]he only issue is whether the jurors could find beyond a reasonable doubt that $13,690 Canadian dollars equaled $5,000 American dollars at the time of the theft.
>
> Seattle, the place of trial, is approximately 100 miles from the long Canadian border. The two countries share a long history of cultural, personal and trade relations sustained and encouraged by easy and warm reciprocal travel on many levels. They interconnect by multi-lane superhighways. Out of this proximity and close relationship the jurors, as people of both countries everywhere, could easily have possessed the elementary and practical knowledge of the worth of Canadian currency. [671 F.2d at 359.]

4. What if a frustrated juror deciding the *Dior* case looked up the American-Canadian exchange rate for the date of the alleged crime and reported this fact to the rest of the jury during deliberations? If Dior is convicted, is the juror's conduct grounds for a new trial? Would your answer be the same if the trial judge in a bench trial had looked up the exchange rate?

3.   Judicial Notice of Substantive Law

A court may "judicially notice," or is "presumed to know," the law of its own jurisdiction, which governs the cases before it. Obviously the judge investigates such law through traditional legal research. Questions of sister state and foreign law, however, have proved more troublesome. Common law rules required parties to plead and prove the content of such law. This requirement has been eliminated in the federal courts by Fed. R. Civ. P. 44.1 and Fed. R. Crim. P. 26.1, which commit the question of foreign law to the judge, whose "determination shall be treated as a ruling on a question of law," but many states still possess the common law rule.

KEY POINT

Courts use propositions of generalized knowledge in their own fact-finding. Courts also use propositions of specific or general fact when interpreting legal standards and applying and developing rules of law. FRE 201 does not apply to judicial use of facts in these contexts.

PROBLEMS

11.9. To establish the unavailability for the purpose of offering testimony pursuant to the declaration against interest exception to the hearsay rule, the defendant offers affidavits of several individuals who state that the declarant is living someplace in Milan. In ruling that the hearsay testimony is admissible the trial judge states, "On the basis of the uncontested affidavits I find that the declarant is living in Milan, and I take judicial notice of the fact that Milan is in Italy, far beyond the jurisdiction of this court." Following a verdict for the defendant, the plaintiff appeals on the ground that the trial judge's taking of judicial notice was improper. According to the plaintiff, the declarant's unavailability is subject to reasonable dispute because "Milan" could refer to the small farming community of Milan (pronounced MY-lan), which is only several miles away. Assuming that the hearsay testimony is critical to the defendant's defense, what result?

11.10. The local M&P Grocery Store has sued Harold Hays for food purchased on credit by his estranged wife, Stella. M&P bases its claim on a state statute that makes husbands liable for all "necessaries" purchased by their wives. It is clear from the statute that food falls within the category of necessaries. At trial M&P establishes that Stella did in fact make the purchases and that she was married to Harold at the time. Harold establishes that he did not authorize or benefit from any of the purchases. The judge takes the matter under advisement and eventually issues the following opinion:

> The statute was enacted at a time when husbands were the primary breadwinners; its purpose was to ensure that merchants would not deny wives the necessities of life. Today, we live in a much different world. I take judicial notice that the statute in question actually perpetuates the stereotypical notions of women as second class citizens. As a result I declare the statute unconstitutional under the state constitution's due process and equal protection provisions.

On appeal the plaintiff claims that the judicial notice was improper because the matter noticed does satisfy the certainty criteria in FRE 201(b). Plaintiff further claims that because there was no mention of the statute's possible unconstitutionality or the judicially notice fact at trial, plaintiff was denied the FRE 201(e) opportunity to be heard. What result?

11.11. Reconsider Problem 11.8 at page 782, where the plaintiff asked the court to take judicial notice of Nigerian fraud scams throughout the world. The problem is based on Qualley v. Clo-Tex Int'l, Inc., 212 F.3d 1123 (8th Cir. 2000). The trial judge granted the judicial notice request, and the jury returned a verdict for the plaintiff. The court of appeals, relying on *Gould* and quoting a portion of the excerpted passage, supra, held that the facts were legislative facts:

> The facts of which the trial court took judicial notice did not specifically concern the parties before the court. The trial court acknowledged that the evidence underlying the noticed facts "[had] to do with the pretty much universal publicity that was out about what Nigeria was doing. . . ." The videotapes contained nothing involving anyone with

whom [plaintiff] had communicated. Nor were the other exhibits considered "specific to ... others [involved in the scheme ...]." ... Thus ... [the facts] were "legislative" rather than "adjudicative," and were therefore outside the scope of [FRE 201]. [212 F.3d at 1128.]

The court of appeals then concluded that the trial judge's action was prejudicial error:

> [B]oth during the trial and in the final instructions, the trial court instructed the jury pursuant to Federal Rule of Evidence 201(g) that it must accept the judicially noticed facts as proven. Thus, the trial court injected legislative facts — facts not within the jury's fact-finding province — into the jury's deliberations by telling the jury that they must treat those facts as conclusively proven. [Id. at 1132.]

What do you think of the court's reasoning? The result?

11.12. Perez, an illegal alien, is seeking review of his denial of political asylum. The asylum request is based on his claim that if he is returned to his native country, he will be persecuted because of his religious affiliation. He claims to be a Jehovah's Witness. The immigration judge rejected Perez's asylum request on the ground that Perez had failed to establish the sincerity of his claim to religion and membership in the Jehovah's Witnesses. The judge's decision rested in part on the following: "In this proceeding Perez took the standard oath to testify truthfully. I take judicial notice that Jehovah's Witnesses are prohibited from swearing under oath." The judge went on to explain that "many Jehovah's Witnesses who have appeared before this court have declined to take the oath and have indicated that it is prohibited by their religion to swear under God or swear under oath." Was the judge's action proper?

11.13. In United States v. Jakobetz, 955 F.2d 786, 799-800 (2d Cir. 1992), the district court had conducted an extended hearing on the admissibility of DNA evidence against the defendant. The court heard nine experts, five for the government and four for the defense. The appellate court held:

> Given the findings made by the district court, and after careful consideration and review by this court, it appears that in future cases with a similar evidentiary issue, a court could properly take judicial notice of the general acceptability of the general theory and the use of these specific [laboratory] techniques. . . . Beyond such judicial notice, the threshold for admissibility should require only a preliminary showing of reliability of the particular data to be offered. . . .

Is this a proper application of FRE 201? Is the "general acceptance" (under *Frye*) or the "validity" (under *Daubert*) of the basic scientific theory and techniques underlying DNA profiling an adjudicative fact?

11.13. Lewis was convicted of carjacking in the Virgin Islands. The statute is applicable only to motor vehicles that have been "transported, shipped, or received in interstate or foreign commerce." To establish this element the prosecution relied on the testimony of Edgar Ames. Ames described himself as a police officer and lifelong resident of the Virgin Islands. He testified that no motor vehicles are manufactured in the Virgin Islands that all motor vehicles have to be shipped to the islands. On appeal Lewis claims that there is insufficient evidence of interstate or foreign commerce. He argues that Ames was not qualified to testify to this element merely because he was a lifelong resident of the Virgin Islands and that no foundation was laid for his testi-mony. In affirming the conviction, the court of appeals stated:

> We take judicial notice of the fact that the United States Virgin Islands consist of three main islands, which are closely grouped and have an area of only 136 square miles. We further take judicial notice of the fact that a police officer and life long resident of a place of this size has a sufficient basis to testify as to whether any motor vehicle manufacturing facilities are located there.

Was the court's action proper?

CHAPTER TWELVE

PRIVILEGES

A. *THE LAW OF PRIVILEGE*

1.   A General Introduction

Most rules of evidence are designed to facilitate the fact-finding process, but rules creating evidentiary privilege are different. For the most part, they exclude relevant evidence in order to promote extrinsic policies unrelated to accurate fact-finding. Their primary aim is to protect certain relationships and interests in the world outside the courtroom that are deemed of sufficient importance to justify the costs imposed on the judicial process through the loss of useful evidence.

The scope of privilege law is quite broad. Some privileges have a direct constitutional basis; examples are the Fifth Amendment privilege against self-incrimination (the Fourth Amendment exclusionary rule for evidence obtained as the result of an illegal search and seizure has aspects of a privilege) and the executive privilege claimed by various presidents of the United States. These rules typically are considered in criminal procedure and constitutional law courses and they will be addressed in this chapter only where they intersect with nonconstitutional privileges. Our main focus will be on evidentiary privileges with common law or statutory origins. Many of these privileges are designed to protect confidential communications, thereby encouraging the free flow of information in certain relationships. This group includes the most prevalent privileges: the attorney-client, physician-patient, priest-penitent, and marital communications privilege. Still other privileges are intended to prevent interference with certain favored relationships, such as the marital testimonial privilege. Finally, privileges also exist to protect against the disclosure of specific types of information, such as privileges for the identity of news reporters' sources, diplomatic secrets, and other sensitive government information (the identity of informants is an example).

The traditional justification for rules of privilege is the utilitarian argument espoused by Dean Wigmore. This argument has been most commonly advanced in support of the confidential communication privileges. It is based on an underlying, untested empirical assumption: The benefit derived from recognizing a privilege — such as open communication between attorney and client or between spouses — outweighs the cost of barring relevant evidence. The argument rests on an empirical assumption about how the existence of the privilege affects individual behavior. Without the protection of the privilege, Wigmore argued, communication will be impeded and certain relationships, such as attorney-client and physician-patient, will be jeopardized. This justification has been widely accepted by the courts and has greatly influenced the development of the law of privilege. Wigmore's conditions for the establishment of a privilege flow directly from his justification for privileges: (1) the communications must originate in a *confidence* that they will not be disclosed; (2) the element of *confidentiality must be essential* to the full and satisfactory maintenance of the relation between the parties; (3) the *relation* must be one that in the opinion of the community ought to be *sedulously fostered*; and (4) the injury that would inure to the relation by the disclosure of the communications must be *greater than the benefit* thereby gained for the correct disposal of the litigation. 8 John Henry Wigmore, Evidence §2285, at 527 (John T. McNaughton ed., rev. ed. 1961).

A distinct privacy-based rationale has also emerged for certain privileges. Rather than focus on the inducement of conduct in certain relationships, the privacy argument emphasizes the protection that privileges afford to individual privacy. According to this rationale, the confidentiality of communications is a privacy interest that itself acts as a legitimate constraint on the truth-finding function of trial. An advocate of the privacy rationale would argue, for example, that the existence of a marital communications privilege may have little if any impact on the extent to which spouses engage in confidential communications; nonetheless, the privilege is desirable because it provides some recognition of and protection for the privacy of intimate aspects of the marital relationship. For an argument reconciling the traditional utilitarian justification and the privacy rationale, see Developments in the Law — Privileged Communications, 98 Harv. L. Rev. 1450, 1481-1486 (1985).[1] The existence and scope of privileges vary from jurisdiction to jurisdiction. Under FRE 501 (reproduced in subsection 3, infra), federal common law governs the privileges applicable in federal question and criminal cases, while state law determines the privileges applicable in diversity actions. In state courts and in federal cases applying state law, the law of privilege is a varied collection of rules, created mostly by the state legislatures.

2.   The Unique Operation of Privilege Rules

Regardless of the particular justification, rules of privilege operate differently from other rules of evidence in at least two and sometimes three respects. First, since the objective of the privilege would be frustrated by forced disclosure of privileged information at any time, the rules of privilege apply to all stages of judicial proceedings. Other rules of evidence are designed primarily to enhance the accuracy of fact-finding, particularly in jury trials, and they therefore do not apply to various preliminary or relatively informal aspects of the adjudicatory process. For example, FRE 1101 provides that the rules of evidence, other than those relating to privileges, do not apply to FRE 104(a) preliminary fact determinations, grand jury proceedings, and other specified, relatively informal proceedings.

Second, the person who can claim or invoke a rule of privilege to exclude evidence will not necessarily be one of the litigants. Because the rules of evidence other than the

---

1.   In Chapter Four we noted that similar utilitarian and nonutilitarian justifications provide partial support for some of the relevance rules. See pages 240-242, supra.

rules of privilege are designed to enhance the fact-finding process, they exist for the benefit of and may be invoked only by the parties to the dispute. By contrast, rules of privilege exist for the benefit of the persons whose communications or actions are covered by a privilege. Only these intended beneficiaries of a privilege (or persons acting on their behalf), who need not be parties to the action, can claim or forgo a privilege.

The third way in which rules of privilege sometimes differ — and perhaps should always differ — from other evidentiary rules relates to the impact on appeal of an erroneous trial court decision regarding admissibility of allegedly privileged information. If the trial judge erroneously excludes the evidence, the party who would have benefited from the evidence will be able to raise the improper exclusion on appeal. As is true whenever a judge erroneously excludes relevant evidence, the exclusion deprives the fact finder of information that would have enhanced the likelihood of a factually accurate result; this type of error, if serious enough, can be cured on appeal by reversal and retrial. And if a trial judge erroneously admits evidence, inflammatory character evidence for example, the result often is to interject prejudicial or misleading information into the trial.

By contrast, a trial judge's erroneous admission of privileged information results in the jurors having before them more relevant, helpful information than they would otherwise have had. The only impact of such an error is to enhance the likelihood of a factually accurate result. Thus, even if the person entitled to invoke the privilege happens to be one of the litigants, the injury from the erroneous admission of the evidence does not adversely affect the person's legitimate interests *as a litigant*. Moreover, the injury caused by the wrongful denial of the privilege is complete at the time the privileged information is presented to the fact finder. Reversal on appeal cannot unring the bell. Unless there is reason to believe that the possibility of reversal on appeal is a desirable way to make litigants and trial judges more sensitive to and more prone to accept claims of privilege, the error should not be grounds for reversal. And if the erroneous denial of a privilege claim is recognized as a possible ground for reversal on appeal, it should make no difference whether the person entitled to claim the privilege happens to be one of the litigants. Nonetheless, appellate courts on occasion entertain such grounds for reversal, particularly in situations in which the appellant is also the primary beneficiary of the privilege, but they typically do not analyze carefully what interests are being vindicated.

A similar question relates to the timing of an appeal. In Mohawk Industry Inc. v. Carpenter, the District Court found that Mohawk had waived the attorney-client privilege, and Mohawk sought to appeal that decision through a collateral order before proceeding with the remainder of the trial. After dismissal at the appellate level, the Supreme Court addressed whether an allegedly erroneous admission of evidence, specifically when adverse to the attorney-client privilege, "qualifies for immediate appeal under the collateral order doctrine." 130 S. Ct. 599 (2009). Justice Sotomayor wrote that "[it does] not. Postjudgment appeals, together with other review mechanisms, suffice to protect the rights of litigants and preserve the vitality of the attorney-client privilege." The Court did not address the effect its decision would have on litigants and trial judges, but instead focused on the effects delayed review would have on the privilege versus the cost of allowing immediate appeal. In denying review, the Court reasoned that *ex ante* incentives for clients to have open conversations with counsel are not reduced by deferring review until final judgment, while the cost on the system of allowing immediate appeal would be significant.

3.　Historical Background and Current Status of Privilege Rules

The earliest recognized privileges, the attorney-client and marital privileges, were judge-made.[2] The attorney-client privilege, which has Roman law roots, finds its first expressions in the common law in the sixteenth century. The privilege of a witness spouse not to testify against a party spouse, which we will refer to as the marital testimonial privilege, also dates back to the sixteenth century. The origins of this privilege are obscure, although the privilege is frequently associated with the general common law rule of competency that prevented interested parties from testifying as witnesses. By contrast, the privilege for confidential communications between spouses received wide recognition in the latter part of the nineteenth century, and it is frequently said to have common law origins. The privilege, however, received substantial support and recognition through legislative action both in this country and in England. We discuss these two privileges in Section D at page 856, infra.

During the last half of the nineteenth century, courts became increasingly reluctant to expand existing privileges or to create new ones. Since that time the fashioning of privileges has become primarily — but not exclusively — a legislative matter. For example, both the physician-patient and the priest-penitent privileges are creatures of the legislature, not the common law. As a result of such statutory revision of evidence law, privilege law varies widely from state to state.

Significantly, a detailed law of privileges has not been codified by the Federal Rules of Evidence. As drafted by the Advisory Committee and proposed by the Supreme Court, the Proposed Federal Rules of Evidence set forth nine discrete privileges governing: (i) required reports; (ii) attorney-client confidential communications; (iii) psychotherapist-patient confidential communications; (iv) prevention of spousal testimony; (v) clergy-communicant confidential communications; (vi) political vote; (vii) trade secrets; (viii) state secrets and other official information; and (ix) the identity of an informer.[3] Noticeably absent were the physician-patient, marital confidential communication, and journalist's privileges. Moreover, Proposed FRE 501 made it clear that, in the absence of a constitutional mandate, courts were not at liberty to alter the list.

Once submitted to Congress, the proposed rules excited considerable controversy and criticism, culminating in a congressional decision to delete the proposed rules relating to privilege. In its place, Congress enacted one general privilege rule, FRE 501, updated in 2009 to read:

> The common law — as interpreted by United States courts in the light of reason and experience — governs a claim of privilege unless any of the following provides otherwise:
>
> * the United States Constitution;
> * a federal statute; or
> * rules prescribed by the Supreme Court.
>
> But in a civil case, state law governs privilege regarding a claim or defense for which state law supplies the rule of decision.

At the same time, Congress revoked the Supreme Court's rule-making power with respect to rules of privilege. This new Enabling Act stated that "[a]ny . . . amendment

2.　For a more comprehensive historical analysis, see 21 Charles A. Wright and Kenneth W. Graham Jr., Federal Practice and Procedure: Evidence §5001-5005 (1977 & Supp. 2001), and Lawrence Meir Friedman, A History of American Law 134-137 (1973).

3.　See Proposed FRE 502-510 and Advisory Committee Notes, 51 F.R.D. 360-380 (1971).

creating, abolishing, or modifying a privilege shall have no force or effect unless it shall be approved by act of Congress." 28 U.S.C. §2076 (1976). Thus, FRE 501 created a bifurcated system of privilege rules. In the situations in which state law supplies the rule of decision, such as diversity cases, state rules of privilege apply even though the case is in federal district court. In the situations in which federal law governs, the common law determines the applicable rules of privilege.

This system is designed to protect state policies concerning privilege, but it does so only to a degree. If a case is not based on state law, state privileges do not apply, and information that a state would immunize from disclosure will be disclosed unless there is a corresponding federal privilege (which often times there is not). For an example, see United States v. Schoenheinz, 548 F.2d 1389 (9th Cir. 1977) (holding that an employer-stenographer privilege available under Oregon law did not apply to a proceeding to enforce an IRS summons). Cases involving supplemental jurisdiction (pendent and ancillary jurisdiction) can pose particular problems, because the same case will have both federal and state claims. The typical resolution is to apply federal privilege law to all claims. See Hancock v. Hobbs, 967 F.2d 462 (11th Cir. 1992).

In contrast to the proposed rules, FRE 501 provides for fluidity in the federal law of privilege. FRE 501's reference to "principles of the common law . . . interpreted . . . in light of reason and experience" grants courts discretion both to modify common law privileges and to create new ones:

> In rejecting the proposed rules and enacting Rule 501, Congress manifested an affirmative intention not to freeze the law of privilege. Its purpose rather was to "provide the courts with the flexibility to develop rules of privilege on a case-by-case basis" and to leave the door open to change. [Trammel v. United States, 445 U.S. 40, 47 (1980), quoting Statement by Representative Hungate, 120 Cong. Rec. 40,891 (1974).]

In accordance with this mandate the Supreme Court, as we shall see shortly, has substantially narrowed the scope of one common law privilege,[4] and the Supreme Court and lower courts have recognized new privileges.[5] Although courts have referred to the proposed rules in deciding privilege questions, such rules have not controlled the development of the federal law of privileges. Although well over half of the states, 41 to date, have adopted rules of evidence modeled after the Federal Rules, the failure of Congress to enact specific rules of privilege has contributed to less uniformity among the states in this area of evidence law. Approximately one-third of the states that have promulgated rules of evidence since the adoption of the Federal Rules have followed their lead and omitted specific privilege provisions. In these states the preexisting statutory and common law rules of privilege govern. Most of the remaining states have tended to use as models the Proposed Federal Rules relating to privilege or the privilege provisions in the Revised Uniform Rules of Evidence (1974). The Revised Uniform Rules are themselves based on the Proposed Federal Rules, but the

---

4. See Trammel v. United States, page 862, infra.
5. See, e.g., Jaffee v. Redmond, 518 U.S. 1 (1996) (recognizing psychotherapist-patient privilege — *Jaffee* is reproduced at page 872, infra); In re Grand Jury Investigation, 918 F.2d 374 (3d Cir. 1990) (recognizing clergy-communicant privilege; Cusumano v. Microsoft Corp., 162 F.3d 708 (1st Cir. 1998) (acknowledging similarity of academic research and work product of journalists, thus recognizing limited scholar's privilege); In re Zuniga, 714 F.2d 632 (6th Cir. 1983) (acknowledging but not applying psychotherapist-patient privilege); In re Agosto, 553 F. Supp. 1298 (D. Nev. 1983) (recognizing parent-child privilege).

Revised Uniform Rules differ in some important respects.[6] States using either model have not been reluctant to deviate from it.[7] Within the fluid, bifurcated system of privilege rules, new privileges can spread among jurisdictions, gradually gaining or losing recognition over time. An interesting example of a privilege not recognized at common law but slowly gaining acceptance is the parent-child privilege. Under Wigmore's utilitarian test and the privacy-based rationale discussed above, this privilege has obvious appeal. There is currently no federal parent-child privilege but a few states recognize some form of the privilege and it seems to be gaining support with federal legislators. See Section G at page 897, infra, for a discussion of the evolution of the parent-child privilege.

B.   GENERAL STRUCTURE OF PRIVILEGES

1.   Holder of the Privilege

A critically important concept in dealing with rules of privilege is that of the "holder" of a privilege — the person to whom in a sense the privilege "belongs." Since the attorney-client relationship exists for the benefit of the client, for example, the client is the holder of the privilege. The holder is entitled to claim the privilege and only the holder may waive a privilege. Once the holder has waived a privilege, no other person can invoke it.

The person who holds a privilege will not necessarily be one of the litigants. Nonparty witnesses may hold privileges that allow them to withhold evidence. Jurisdictions sometimes differ as to who holds a given privilege. Within the marital privilege, for example, the holder may be the spouses jointly, the communicating spouse, the witness spouse, or the party spouse. Section D at page 856, infra, discusses some of the reasons behind, and the implications of, locating the marital privilege with one or both spouses.

2.   Invocation

A person other than the holder may be able to invoke the privilege on the holder's behalf. For example, a nonparty eyewitness to the event that is the subject of litigation may have made a confidential communication to his or her attorney for the purpose of obtaining legal advice about the event. The out-of-court communication of some historical fact, of course, is hearsay, but the communication may fall within a hearsay exception. Assume, for example, that the declaration is an excited utterance, or that the declarant is presently unavailable and the communication is a declaration against interest. The nonparty declarant may invoke the privilege; and in the absence of the

---

6.   See generally 3 Jack B. Weinstein and Margaret A. Berger, Weinstein's Federal Evidence §§501.02-501.04 (Joseph M. McLaughlin ed., 2d ed. 1997).

7.   See generally 1 Gregory P. Joseph and Stephen A. Saltzburg, Evidence in America: The Federal Rules in the States ch. 23-24 (1987).

declarant, the declarant's attorney may invoke the privilege *on behalf of* the declarant. If the declarant has expressed a desire not to claim the privilege, however, nobody can invoke the privilege.

Typically, if the holder of a privilege is unavailable to claim the privilege, individuals acting on behalf of the holder or the holder's estate, such as the holder's conservator or guardian, may claim the privilege. In the case of privileges covering conversations between a patient or client and a professional, the professional may claim the privilege on behalf of the patient or client. For example, in the physician-patient relationship, if the patient-holder has not specifically waived the privilege, the doctor may be able to claim the privilege on the patient's behalf. In some instances, as in the attorney-client relationship, the professional is obligated by rules of professional conduct to maintain confidentiality where the client has not expressed an intent to waive his privilege. In addition, there is precedent permitting the trial judge to invoke a privilege on behalf of an absent holder.[8] Interesting questions sometimes arise when the holder of the privilege is an entity, such as a corporation or governmental agency, rather than an individual. In Nixon v. Administrator of General Services, 433 U.S. 425 (1977), the former President sought to invoke the executive privilege "against the very Executive Branch in whose name the privilege is invoked." The Presidential Recordings and Materials Preservation Act required the former President to deliver presidential papers and tape recordings to an archivist of the Executive Branch to be screened and cataloged. Nixon resisted turning the materials over and invoked the presidential privilege. The Supreme Court held that the "privilege survives the individual President's tenure" but that the expectation of the confidentiality of executive communications is "subject to erosion over time after an administration leaves office." Though the Court allowed Nixon to invoke the privilege on behalf of the government, it upheld the Act as facially constitutional because the screening by the archivist would be but a "limited intrusion by personnel in the Executive Branch sensitive to executive concerns." It is unclear whether the former President would have been allowed to invoke the privilege if the Office of the President had attempted to waive it.

In the corporate setting, some courts have struggled with whether an attorney may invoke the attorney-client privilege on behalf of the client-corporation when shareholders seek disclosure of communications between corporate officers and corporate attorneys. In Fausek v. White, 965 F.2d 126 (6th Cir. 1992), the defendant and majority shareholder of the corporation, Robert E. White, appealed from a district court judgment denying his claim of attorney-client privilege in an action alleging securities violations. The plaintiffs, former shareholders, brought suit against White alleging that he had abused his position to their financial detriment. The plaintiffs subpoenaed the corporation's attorney to testify about communications he had had with White but the attorney resisted, asserting the attorney-client privilege on behalf of the corporation. The appellate court affirmed the lower court, holding that the corporation could not claim the attorney-client privilege because it owed fiduciary duties to the plaintiffs and the latter had shown "good cause" for not permitting defendant to rely on the privilege.

---

8.   See, e.g., Coles v. Harsch, 129 Or. 11, 30-31, 276 P.2d 248, 255 (1929). Judge Weinstein and Professor Berger have suggested that this is an inherent judicial power that is not abrogated by the failure of a rule specifically to mention the authority of the judge to act on the holder's behalf. 3 Jack B. Weinstein and Margaret A. Berger, Weinstein's Federal Evidence §503.20[3] (Joseph M. McLaughlin ed., 2d ed. 1997).

The court provided a long list of factors for determining whether there is "good cause" to recognize an exception to the attorney-client privilege, including the

> number of shareholders and the percentage of stock they represent; . . . the nature of the shareholders' claim and whether it is obviously colorable; the apparent necessity or desirability of the shareholders having the information and the availability of it from other sources; . . . the extent to which the communication is identified versus the extent to which the shareholders are blindly fishing; the risk of revelation of trade secrets or other information in whose confidentiality the corporation has an interest for independent reasons.

The Fifth Circuit took a similar approach in Garner v. Wolfinbarger, 430 F.2d 1093 (5th Cir. 1970), and Ward v. Succession of Freeman, 854 F.2d 780 (5th Cir. 1988), but the Ninth Circuit drew a distinction between derivative suits brought by current shareholders and class actions brought by past shareholders and refused to recognize the exception in Weil v. Investment/Indicators, Research & Management, 647 F.2d 18 (9th Cir. 1981). For further discussion, see Keith W. Johnson, Fausek v. White: The Sixth Circuit Garners Support for a Good Cause Exception to the Attorney-Client Privilege, 18 Dayton L. Rev. 313 (1993). For more discussion on the derivative suit distinction, see Paul R. Rice, Attorney-Client Privilege in the U.S., Cause to overcome privilege — Limitations on applicability of *Garner* — Must the action be derivative for *Garner* rule to apply? ACPRIV-FED §8:20 (2010).

Another related subtlety of privileges is the ability of third parties to invoke them after the holder's death. Though confidential communications privileges are generally thought to survive the death of a holder, they may not always be invoked. The personal representative of the deceased, for example, may choose not to invoke the privilege; or an attorney may be deprived of the opportunity to invoke a privilege by the commonly recognized exception to the attorney-client privilege for communications "relevant to an issue between parties who claim through the same deceased client." Proposed FRE 503(d)(3).

The Supreme Court acknowledged the importance of maintaining the attorney-client privilege after a client's death in Swidler & Berlin v. United States, 524 U.S. 399 (1998). The Court allowed Deputy White House Counsel Vince Foster's attorney to invoke the attorney-client privilege on Foster's behalf after Foster committed suicide. The government sought to obtain notes from Foster's attorney that were taken in a meeting between the two, nine days before Foster's death. The Court held that an attorney's notes from his meeting with his client are privileged and immune to a federal grand jury subpoena. The dissent agreed that attorney-client privilege ordinarily survives the death of the client, but emphasized that the common law also dictates that privileges should be construed narrowly. In this criminal investigation into wrongdoings in the White House, the dissent stated, the "paramount value" of our criminal justice system — the protection of an innocent defendant — should "outweigh a deceased client's interest in preserving confidence." For further discussion of the case, see Michael Stokes Plausen, Dead Man's Privilege: Vince Foster and the Demise of Legal Ethics, 68 Fordham L. Rev. 807 (1999) (arguing that the Supreme Court ignored the complexity of the case and instituted a broader rule than is supported by policy or precedent).

3.   Scope and Limits

Each privilege has a particularized scope; it covers some things but not others. The confidential communications privileges, for example, extend only to confidential communications. If an unnecessary third party is present during a conversation between lawyer and client or husband and wife, the conversation will not be privileged. Another example: The attorney-client privilege extends only to communications for purposes of obtaining legal advice. If a person who happens to be, or who becomes, a client communicates with a lawyer for some other purpose, the communication is not privileged. Similarly, conversations between clergy and their flock are only privileged if in a confessional, or perhaps counseling, situation.

Privileges may also be limited by the potential benefit and harm to the litigants. While most of the confidential communications privileges are immune to claims of need by the opposing party, privileges to protect disclosure of specific types of information are often less secure. When considering whether to protect the identity of an informant, for example, a court may balance the importance to the defendant of the informant's testimony against the government's interest in resisting disclosure. See United States v. Fischer, 531 F.2d 783 (5th Cir. 1976). Similarly, scholars enjoy a privilege limited by a party's nonfrivolous claim of need and inability to otherwise obtain the information. See Cusumano v. Microsoft Corp., 162 F.3d 708 (1st Cir. 1998).[9]

4.   Waiver

The holder of a privilege may waive the privilege in at least four different ways. First, the holder may indicate through words or conduct a desire to forgo the privilege. Second, if the holder refrains from invoking the privilege, the failure to assert the privilege typically will be regarded as a waiver. However, newly enacted FRE 502, discussed infra page 809, addresses the effects of waiver when communication or information protected by the attorney-client privilege and the work-product doctrine is inadvertently disclosed; the rule generally limits the effect of such disclosure. Third, the voluntary disclosure of the confidential communication, such as a client discussing legal advice he received from his attorney with a third person, will constitute a waiver. Voluntary disclosure of a confidential communication in the context of another privileged communication will not result in waiver. For instance, if a person, in the presence of his spouse, made a confidential statement to his attorney that was covered under the attorney-client privilege, the marital communication privilege would preclude the waiver of the attorney-client privilege. Proposed FRE 511 captured well this aspect of the common law:

> A person upon whom these rules confer a privilege against disclosure of the confidential matter or communication waives the privilege if he or his predecessor while holder of the privilege voluntarily discloses or consents to disclosure of any significant part of the matter or communication. This rule does not apply if the disclosure is itself a privileged communication.

---

9. See also Nixon v. United States, 418 U.S. 683 (1974) (claim of absolute executive privilege for presidential communications will not prevail over demonstrated need for particular evidence); Dellwood Farms v. Cargill, Inc., 128 F.3d 1122 (7th Cir. 1997) (law enforcement investigatory privilege not absolute, rather surmountable by strong showing of need).

With respect to waiver by disclosure, it is important to note that the voluntary disclosure must be a disclosure of *the confidential communication itself*. A voluntary statement — either as a witness or in a casual conversation — of facts that were the subject of the communication is not a waiver of the privilege. The privilege protects solely the confidential communication, not the facts. For example, if a patient discussed a crime that she had committed in a confidential session with her psychotherapist, but she later voluntarily confessed the facts of the crime to a third party, the communication with the psychotherapist would still be privileged, as long as she did not disclose what she had actually communicated to the therapist.

Fourth, waiver may also occur through asserting a claim based on privileged information. "Waiver by claim assertion" of privileged materials has been generally recognized as requiring disclosure when a party "asserts a claim that in fairness requires examination of protected communications." United States v. Bilzerian, 926 F.2d 1285, 1292 (2d Cir. 1991). For example, in In re Grand Jury Proceedings, 350 F.3d 299, 305 (2d Cir. 2003), the Second Circuit held that where a letter was sent by a corporation to a U.S. attorney explaining that it had been told by federal agents that its actions were legal, there was no unfairness to the government and thus the company did not waive its privilege as a result of placing its claims at issue. In contrast, a party who asserts that action was taken on the advice of counsel waives the attorney-client privilege with respect to those communications. For example, in United States v. Cohn, 303 F. Supp. 2d 672, 681 (D. Md. 2003), the court held that an investment company indicted for mail and wire fraud waived its attorney-client privilege after its general counsel raised an advice of counsel defense in his opening statement at trial.

5. Exceptions

Each privilege has a set of exceptions that are derived from the underlying policies the particular privilege is created to serve. For example, the attorney-client privilege does not extend to communications in furtherance of a crime or fraud. The purpose of the privilege is to facilitate the giving of legal advice with respect to presently existing legal problems and to assist a client in conforming to the dictates of the law; its purpose is not to facilitate transgressions of the law. Similarly, the marital privileges do not apply in cases of alleged spousal abuse and the priest-penitent privilege does not apply when child abuse has been alleged. Again, these privileges are designed to preserve relationships, not to encourage assaultive behavior.

6. Drawing Adverse Inferences from Invoking a Privilege

In Griffin v. California, 380 U.S. 609 (1965), the Supreme Court held that allowing comment on the defendant's decision not to testify violated his Fifth Amendment privilege against self-incrimination "by making its assertion costly." Proposed FRE 513 applied the *Griffin* rationale to the law of privileges generally:

> (a) Comment or inference not permitted. The claim of a privilege, whether in the present proceeding or upon a prior occasion, is not a proper subject of comment by judge or counsel. No inference may be drawn therefrom.

(b) Claiming privilege without knowledge of jury. In jury cases, proceedings shall be conducted, to the extent practicable, so as to facilitate the making of claims of privilege without knowledge of the jury.

(c) Jury instructions. Upon request, any party against whom the jury might draw an adverse inference from a claim of privilege is entitled to an instruction that no inference may be drawn therefrom.

Presently, there appears to be no general *constitutional* rule barring comment on a party's invocation of a confidential communications privilege, and the case law is divided[10] as to the propriety of comment about invoking privileges outside the *Griffin* context.[11] Cases allowing comment frequently draw an analogy to the long-established practice of permitting comments on and drawing adverse inferences from the destruction of evidence or the failure to produce available witnesses or documents. In contrast, cases barring comment echo *Griffin*'s concern that comment or adverse inferences undermine the privilege.

7. Constitutional Limitations on Privilege

The Sixth Amendment creates constitutional limits on privileges in criminal prosecutions. If a privilege is claimed by a witness from whom a criminal defendant seeks to elicit testimony, the privilege directly conflicts with the defendant's rights under the compulsory process and confrontation clauses. Various Supreme Court decisions have explored whether a claim of privilege must yield when a defendant either needs to present the privileged evidence in his defense or needs to introduce the privileged evidence to impeach the government's testimony; other opinions have explored the limits of privilege, such as the executive privilege, when opposed to a legitimate governmental investigation.[12] Privileges that impede a defendant's rights or governmental investigation may be unconstitutional, in violation of the Sixth Amendment or the due process clause of the Fourteenth Amendment,[13] or not recognized as a matter of the common law development of privileges.

---

10. See 3 Jack B. Weinstein and Margaret A. Berger, Weinstein's Federal Evidence §513.04 (Joseph M. McLaughlin ed., 2d ed. 1997).

11. *Griffin* itself applies only to comments regarding a criminal defendant's invocation of the privilege in a criminal prosecution. See Baxter v. Palmigiano, 425 U.S. 308 (1976); Brink's, Inc. v. City of New York, 717 F.2d 700 (2d Cir. 1983).

12. See Nixon v. United States, 418 U.S. 683 (1974) (claim of absolute executive privilege for general presidential communications will not prevail over demonstrated need for specific evidence); Nixon v. Administrator of General Services, 433 U.S. 425 (1977) (former President directed to deliver presidential papers and tape recordings to an official of the Executive Branch for the creation of public access under the Presidential Recordings and Materials Preservation Act, held to be facially constitutional and not violative of the presidential privilege doctrine); Davis v. Alaska, 415 U.S. 308 (1974) (defendant's right to confront and cross-examine key prosecution witness includes right to bring out witness's juvenile record despite state statute privileging those records); Washington v. Texas, 388 U.S. 14 (1967) (state statute prohibiting individuals charged with participating in same crime from testifying for one another violates right to compulsory process).

13. See Pennsylvania v. Ritchie, 480 U.S. 39 (1987).

C.   THE ATTORNEY-CLIENT PRIVILEGE

1.   Elements of the Privilege

A good statement of the modern attorney-client privilege is contained in Proposed FRE 503:

(a) *Definitions*. As used in this rule:

(1) A "client" is a person, public officer, or corporation, association, or other organization or entity, either public or private, who is rendered professional legal services by a lawyer, or who consults a lawyer with a view to obtaining professional legal services from him.

(2) A "lawyer" is a person authorized, or reasonably believed by the client to be authorized, to practice law in any state or nation.

(3) A "representative of the lawyer" is one employed to assist the lawyer in the rendition of professional legal services.

(4) A communication is "confidential" if not intended to be disclosed to third persons other than those to whom disclosure is in furtherance of the rendition of professional legal services to the client or those reasonably necessary for the transmission of the communication.

(b) *General Rule of Privilege*. A client has a privilege to refuse to disclose and to prevent any other person from disclosing confidential communications made for the purpose of facilitating the rendition of professional legal services to the client,

(1) between himself or his representative and his lawyer or his lawyer's representative, or

(2) between his lawyer and the lawyer's representative, or

(3) by him or his lawyer to a lawyer representing another in a matter of common interest, or

(4) between representatives of the client or between the client and a representative of the client, or

(5) between lawyers representing the client.

(c) *Who May Claim the Privilege*. The privilege may be claimed by the client, his guardian or conservator, the personal representative of a deceased client, or the successor, trustee, or similar representative of a corporation, association, or other organization, whether or not in existence. The person who was the lawyer at the time of the communication may claim the privilege but only on behalf of the client. His authority to do so is presumed in the absence of evidence to the contrary.

(d) *Exceptions*. There is no privilege under this rule:

(1) Furtherance of crime or fraud. If the services of the lawyer were sought or obtained to enable or aid anyone to commit or plan to commit what the client knew or reasonably should have known to be a crime or fraud; or

(2) Claimants through same deceased client. As to a communication relevant to an issue between parties who claim through the same deceased client, regardless of whether the claims are by testate or intestate succession or by *inter vivos* transaction; or

(3) Breach of duty by lawyer or client. As to a communication relevant to an issue of breach of duty by the lawyer to his client or by the client to his lawyer; or

(4) Document attested by lawyer. As to a communication relevant to an issue concerning an attested document to which the lawyer is an attesting witness; or

(5) Joint clients. As to a communication relevant to a matter of common interest between two or more clients if the communication was made by any of them to a lawyer retained or consulted in common, when offered in an action between any of the clients.

As Proposed FRE 503 suggests, much of the law governing the attorney-client privilege is quite straightforward. The attorney-client privilege originally was based on the theory that it would be unprofessional for the lawyer to reveal confidential communications from the client. Thus, the lawyer was the holder of the privilege. Today, jurisdictions uniformly recognize that the attorney-client privilege exists for the benefit of the client, who is thus now the holder of the privilege. The privilege may be claimed on the client's behalf by various individuals representing the client. If the client waives the privilege, the attorney cannot refuse to reveal the confidential communications. Although Proposed FRE 503 does not treat the matter, the client alone may waive the privilege by disclosing the information, and Proposed FRE 503(d) lists the standard exceptions to the attorney-client privilege.

The primary difficulty is determining the scope of the privilege. The following sections discuss which communications are and which are not covered by the privilege.

a.   Communications with a Lawyer or Representative of a Lawyer

The attorney-client privilege applies to any communication between client and lawyer made for the purpose of securing legal advice. If a person approaches someone reasonably believed to be an attorney for the purpose of obtaining legal advice, confidential communications between the two are privileged even if the person is mistaken in the belief, unless one of the exceptions applies. The privilege also attaches to preliminary discussions with an attorney, even if the attorney is not ultimately retained. Moreover, the presence of third parties who are necessary or useful to the objective of rendering legal advice, such as translators, does not destroy confidentiality. The attorney-client privilege applies not only to communications between the attorney and the client but also to communications between the client and a representative of the attorney, which is defined as a person who is "employed to assist the lawyer in the rendition of professional services." Proposed FRE 503(a)(3). But how far does the privilege extend over employees of a law firm who are not attorneys? In United States v. Kovel, 296 F.2d 918 (2d Cir. 1961), Judge Friendly wrote an influential opinion discussing the issue. In *Kovel*, an accountant was employed by a law firm specializing in tax law. Id. at 919. Although Kovel was not an attorney, he met with clients to discuss complex tax issues. Id. The suit involved Kovel's refusal to reveal communications with one of his clients when subpoenaed by a grand jury, invoking the attorney-client privilege. Id. The court held that the attorney-client privilege extends to nonlawyer employees of a law firm so long as the communications relate to legal advice. Id. at 922. The court justified extending the privilege as follows:

> [T]he complexities of modern existence prevent attorneys from effectively handling clients' affairs without the help of others. . . . "The assistance of these agents being indispensable to his work and the communications of the client being often necessarily committed to them by the attorney or by the client himself, the privilege must include all the persons who act as the attorney's agents." 8 Wigmore, Evidence, §2301. [Id. at 921.]

The court in *Kovel* further stated that the privilege exists if the lawyer has directed the client to tell his story to an accountant in order to provide better advice. Id. at 922.

The notorious prosecution of Martha Stewart for obstructing justice raised an interesting twist on the *Kovel* situation. In re Grand Jury Subpoenas Dated March 24, 2003, 265 F. Supp. 2d 321 (S.D.N.Y. 2003), dealt with "the troublesome question whether and to what extent the attorney-client privilege and the protection afforded to work product extend to communications between and among a prospective defendant in a criminal case, her lawyers, and a public relations firm hired by the lawyers to aid in avoiding an indictment." Martha Stewart and her lawyers had hired a public relations firm, and the grand jury subpoenaed communications between Stewart, the lawyers, and the firm. Discovery was resisted on the ground that the public relations firm had been hired as part of Stewart's legal defense. In particular, Stewart claimed that the "unbalanced and often inaccurate press reports about Target created a clear risk that the prosecutors and regulators conducting the various investigations would feel public pressure to bring some kind of charge against her," and the public relations firm was hired to help redress the purported imbalance in the media. In an interesting opinion that relied heavily on *Kovel*, the court concluded that:

> This Court is persuaded that the ability of lawyers to perform some of their most fundamental client functions — such as (a) advising the client of the legal risks of speaking publicly and of the likely legal impact of possible alternative expressions, (b) seeking to avoid or narrow charges brought against the client, and (c) zealously seeking acquittal or vindication — would be undermined seriously if lawyers were not able to engage in frank discussions of facts and strategies with the lawyers' public relations consultants. For example, lawyers may need skilled advice as to whether and how possible statements to the press — ranging from "no comment" to detailed factual presentations — likely would be reported in order to advise a client as to whether the making of particular statements would be in the client's legal interest. And there simply is no practical way for such discussions to occur with the public relations consultants if the lawyers were not able to inform the consultants of at least some non-public facts, as well as the lawyers' defense strategies and tactics, free of the fear that the consultants could be forced to disclose those discussions. In consequence, this Court holds that (1) confidential communications (2) between lawyers and public relations consultants (3) hired by the lawyers to assist them in dealing with the media in cases such as this (4) that are made for the purpose of giving or receiving advice (5) directed at handling the client's legal problems are protected by the attorney-client privilege.

The court did note that, notwithstanding the formalism of it all, had Stewart hired the public relations firm herself, the privilege would not apply, and further that any communications for purposes other than legal advice would not be covered by the privilege. For a critical appraisal of the case, see Ann M. Murphy, Spin Control and the High-Profile Client — Should the Attorney-Client Privilege Extend to Communications with Public Relations Consultants?, 55 Syracuse L. Rev. 545 (2005).

A difficult question is whether the privilege covers communications between a criminal defendant and psychiatric experts retained by defense counsel, where the defendant asserts an insanity defense. The rule noted above that the attorney-client privilege applies to communications between a client and agents retained by defense counsel usually is extended to include psychiatrists. See Ballew v. State, 640 S.W.2d 237 (Tex. Crim. App. 1982); United States v. Talley, 790 F.2d 1468, 1470-1471 (9th Cir. 1986) (recognizing "attorney-psychotherapist-client privilege" based in common law); but see Colo. Rev. Stat. §13-90-107(3) (scope of attorney-client privilege does not cover communications between a psychiatrist and a criminal defendant who asserts an insanity defense). However, some jurisdictions consider an insanity defense a waiver of the privilege through the assertion of a claim based on privileged information. This "waiver by claim assertion" of privileged materials has been generally recognized as requiring disclosure when a party "asserts a claim that in fairness requires examination of protected communications." United States v. Bilzerian, 926 F.2d 1285, 1292 (2d Cir. 1991). Compare Gray v. District Court, 884 P.2d 286, 292 (Colo. 1994) (holding that a defendant waives the right to claim the attorney-client and psychiatrist-patient privileges if mental condition is an issue), with People v. Knuckles, 165 Ill. 2d 125, 140, 650 N.E.2d 974, 981 (1995) (holding that there was no waiver of the attorney-client privilege with respect to communications between a defendant who raises an insanity defense and a psychiatrist employed by defense counsel to aid in the preparation of the defense). Also, Sixth Amendment challenges may arise from a state's limiting of the scope of the attorney-client privilege with respect to defense psychiatrists. However, the majority rule is that the Sixth Amendment is not violated by denying the privilege. See, e.g., Lange v. Young, 869 F.2d 1008, 1013 (7th Cir. 1989), *aff'g* State v. Lange, 126 Wis. 2d 513, 376 N.W.2d 868 (1985).

b.   Communications for the Purpose of Legal Service

The person invoking the privilege bears the burden of proof to show that the attorney was contacted for a legal professional purpose. If the attorney was contacted for some other purpose, the privilege does not apply. For example, if the client solicits business or financial advice, or sees a lawyer about an accounting issue rather than legal matters, any communications between them are not protected by the privilege. See, e.g., In re Grand Jury Testimony of Attorney X, 621 F. Supp. 590, 592 (E.D.N.Y. 1985) ("where attorney is a mere 'conduit' the client may not invoke the privilege"); United States v. Woodruff, 383 F. Supp. 696, 698 (E.D. Pa. 1974) (attorney-client communication regarding time of trial not privileged). It can be a challenge to distinguish a "legal" purpose from another purpose, such as business or financial advice. In Georgia-Pacific Corp. v. GAF Roofing Manufacturing Corp., 1996 U.S. Dist. LEXIS 671 (S.D.N.Y. Jan. 24, 1996), GAF's in-house counsel, Scott, was asked to review certain environmental provisions of a proposed asset purchase agreement. He then negotiated the provisions of the agreement, and after execution of the agreement, he negotiated related matters. After the agreement was terminated, his testimony was needed to determine whether GAF agreed to assume certain environmental risks. Scott asserted the attorney-client privilege to avoid disclosure, stating that he had merely provided legal advice to management. The court held that, as a negotiator for GAF, Scott was acting in a business capacity, and with no litigation in sight, he was not giving legal advice. Therefore, no attorney-client privilege applied.

Proposed FRE 503(d)(5) implies that in a joint client situation, communications between an attorney and either of his joint clients are privileged against outsiders, which is the standard rule. Where two different parties have different representation, courts typically extend the privilege to cover what is called "common interest" or "joint defense" situations, as again Proposed FRE 503(b)(3) indicates. United States v. Schwimmer, 892 F.2d 237 (2d Cir. 1989). Problems arise when the joint defense breaks down and the previous cooperating parties become adversaries. Some courts take the position that in such circumstances a lawyer may not use against the now adverse party any confidences disclosed while the parties were cooperating, at least if their agreement so specifies. See, e.g., United States v. Anderson, 790 F. Supp. 231 (W.D. Wash. 1992).

c.   The Scope of Confidential Communications
Included in Privilege

Confidential conversations between an attorney and client are covered, so long as the conversations relate to legal advice. However, what about non-verbal communications, or documents exchanged between an attorney and client? In In re Navarro, 93 Cal. App. 3d 325, 155 Cal. Rptr. 522 (1979), the court considered whether an attorney's act of handing a police report to his client was a "communication" within the attorney-client privilege. In *Navarro*, an attorney was subpoenaed and refused to answer whether or not she showed a police report to her client, invoking the privilege. The court stated that the privilege covers "information transmitted between a client and his lawyer," and thus even turning over to the client a public document, such as the police report in question, if given as part of her legal advice or strategy, is covered by the privilege. Id. at 327.

Some courts have extended the privilege beyond mere communications. In State v. Meeks, 666 N.W.2d 859 (Wis. 2003), the Wisconsin Supreme Court held that an attorney's opinions and impressions of a former client's competence were protected by the attorney-client privilege. Although the attorney's opinion is not a communication, the court stated that "a lawyer's opinion about a client's competence or state of mind is inextricably mixed with the client's private communications." Id. at 870. However, a majority of courts have held that the attorney-client privilege does not protect an attorney's perceptions of a former client's mental competency unless relating the perceptions would reveal the substance of a confidential communication. See Darrow v. Gunn, 594 F.2d 767 (9th Cir. 1979).

For the privilege to attach, not only must the communication be confidential, but also clients must take "reasonable precautions" to ensure confidentiality. 3 Jack B. Weinstein and Margaret A. Berger, Weinstein's Federal Evidence, §503.15[3] (Joseph M. McLaughlin ed., 2d ed. 1997). See Suburban Sew 'N Sweep v. Swiss-Bernina, 91 F.R.D. 254 (N.D. Ill. 1981) (client who placed confidential documents in dumpster failed to take adequate precautions and lost protection of the privilege). Eavesdroppers present special problems for the privilege. The modern trend is to allow the claim of privilege to prevent testimony by the eavesdropper as long as the setting of the conversation suggests that the speakers intended the conversation to be confidential. Communicating in a public setting, for example, would tend to negate the claim that the participants intended the conversation to be confidential. Still, location is not dispositive. If the parties were speaking in hushed tones and thus not likely to be overheard, that their meeting took place in a public place would not automatically negate a claim of confidentiality. See, e.g., In re Sealed Case, 737 F.2d 94, 101-102 (D.C. Cir. 1984).

d.   Limitations on Waiver of the Privilege

What if confidential material is inadvertently disclosed, perhaps as a result of a clerical error during discovery? Whether inadvertent disclosure of privileged lawyer-client communications and attorney work product should operate as a waiver of the protected material is a question that has plagued courts for decades. The problem has grown exponentially worse since e-discovery has become prevalent in most major civil litigation. As vast amounts of electronic documents are exchanged, it is increasingly easy to disclose inadvertently protected materials.

Outdated legal precedents added uncertainty as to the results of such disclosure. Most courts provided some protection where inadvertent waivers have occurred in modern, document-intensive litigation if the party holding the privilege could show that it had not been careless with the privileged materials. See, e.g., Gray v. Bicknell, 86 F.3d 1472, 1484 (8th Cir. 1996). Some courts, however, continued to strictly find waiver in cases of inadvertent disclosure. See, e.g., Wichita Land & Cattle Co. v. American Federal Bank, F.S.B., 148 F.R.D. 456 (D.D.C. 1992) ("Disclosure of other-wise-privileged materials, even where the disclosure was inadvertent, serves as waiver of the privilege."). For a discussion, see Roberta M. Harding, Waiver: A Comprehensive Analysis of a Consequence of Inadvertently Producing Documents Protected by the Attorney-Client Privilege, 42 Cath. U. L. Rev. 465 (1993). Inadvertent waiver could be particularly harsh when conjoined with what is sometimes called subject matter waiver. Some courts held that disclosure of any aspect of privileged material resulted in a waiver of all privileged material related to the topic. For an excellent discussion of the general area of waiver, see Richard L. Marcus, The Perils of Privilege: Waiver and the Litigator, 84 Mich. L. Rev. 1605 (1986). As a result, large amounts of resources were dedicated to document reviews, and costs were frequently grossly disproportion-ate to the stakes of the litigation. Further, the in-depth review process itself impeded the efficient processing of cases through the system.[14]

Federal Rule 502, the first new rule concerning privileges since 1975, has been adopted to deal with this problem, among other issues.

RULE 502. Attorney-Client Privilege and Work Product; Limitations on Waiver

The following provisions apply, in the circumstances set out, to disclosure of a com-munication or information covered by the attorney-client privilege or work-product protection.

(a) *Disclosure Made in a Federal Proceeding or to a Federal Office or Agency; Scope of a Waiver*

When the disclosure is made in a federal proceeding or to a federal office or agency and waives the attorney-client privilege or work-product protection, the waiver extends to an undisclosed communication or information in a federal or state proceeding only if:

(1) the waiver is intentional;

(2) the disclosed and undisclosed communications or information concern the same subject matter; and

(3) they ought in fairness to be considered together.

(b) *Inadvertent disclosure*

When made in a federal proceeding or to a federal office or agency, the disclosure does not operate as a waiver in a federal or state proceeding if:

(1) the disclosure is inadvertent;

(2) the holder of the privilege or protection took reasonable steps to prevent dis-closure; and

(3) the holder promptly took reasonable steps to rectify the error, including (if appli-cable) following Federal Rule of Civil Procedure 26(b)(5)(B).

(c) *Disclosure Made in a State Proceeding*

---

14. See Remarks made to the House of Representatives by Congresswoman Jackson-Lee of Texas; H7818 Congressional Record — House September 8, 2008.

When the disclosure is made in a State proceeding and is not the subject of a state-court order concerning waiver, the disclosure does not operate as a waiver in a federal proceeding if the disclosure:

(1) would not be a waiver under this rule if it had been made in a federal proceeding; or

(2) is not a waiver under the law of the state where the disclosure occurred.

(d) *Controlling Effect of a Court Order*

A federal court may order that the privilege or protection is not waived by disclosure connected with the litigation pending before the court — in which event the disclosure is also not a waiver in any other federal or state proceeding.

(e) *Controlling Effect of a Party Agreement*

An agreement on the effect of disclosure in a federal proceeding is binding only on the parties to the agreement, unless it is incorporated into a court order.

(f) *Controlling Effect of this Rule*

Notwithstanding Rules 101 and 1101, this rule applies to state proceedings and to federal court-annexed and federal court-mandated arbitration proceedings, in the circumstances set out in the rule. And notwithstanding Rule 501, this rule applies even if state law provides the rule of decision.

(g) *Definitions*

In this rule:

(1) "attorney-client privilege" means the protection that applicable law provides for confidential attorney-client communications; and

(2) "work-product protection" means the protection that applicable law provides for tangible material (or its intangible equivalent) prepared in anticipation of litigation or for trial."

e.   *Interpretation of the New Rule*[15]

i.   Purpose of FRE 502.   According to the Advisory Committee Notes:

This new rule has two major purposes:

1) It resolves some longstanding disputes in the courts about the effect of certain disclosures of communications or information protected by the attorney-client privilege or as work product — specifically those disputes involving inadvertent disclosure and subject matter waiver.

2) It responds to the widespread complaint that litigation costs necessary to protect against waiver of attorney-client privilege or work product have become prohibitive due to the concern that any disclosure (however innocent or minimal) will operate as a subject matter waiver of all protected communications or information.

The rule seeks to provide a predictable, uniform set of standards under which parties can determine the consequences of a disclosure of a communication or information covered by the attorney-client privilege or work-product protection. Parties to litigation need to know, for example, that if they exchange privileged information pursuant to a confidentiality order, the court's order will be enforceable. Moreover, if a federal court's confidentiality order is not enforceable in a state court then the burdensome costs of privilege review and retention are unlikely to be reduced.[16]

---

15.   Much of this subsection compresses, summarizes, and paraphrases materials from the Advisory Committee's Notes.

16.   Explanatory Note on Evidence Rule 502 Prepared by the Judicial Conference Advisory Committee on Evidence Rules (Revised 11/28/2007).

ii.   Limitation to FRE 502.   The new rule does not alter federal and state law governing whether information is protected under the attorney-client privilege or the work-product doctrine. Similarly, while the rule establishes exceptions, it does not displace applicable waiver doctrines. Its application is limited to attorney-client privilege and work-product protected information. The effect of disclosure of information protected by other evidentiary privileges continues to be a question of federal common law.[17]

f.   Aspects of the New Rule

i.   Scope of Waiver Under FRE 502(a) and Subject Matter Waiver.   Inadvertent disclosure of privileged information will never result in a subject matter waiver. Similarly, when intentional disclosure of privileged information is found to waive the protection, the waiver is only applied to the disclosed information. The important exception to this rule is when protected information is intentionally disclosed in a selective or misleading manner to disadvantage the adversary. Under such circumstances, a judge may find that fairness requires further disclosure of related, protected information (e.g., a subject matter waiver). Note the similarity of the language to Rule 106. The principle behind the "ought in fairness" language is the same under both rules. According to the Committee, "Under both Rules, a party that makes a selective, misleading presentation that is unfair to the adversary opens itself to a more complete and accurate presentation."[18]

Subsection (a) also stipulates that a waiver decision made under FRE 502 "extends to an undisclosed communication or information in a federal or state proceeding." Thus, the federal ruling on waiver of a particular disclosure governs in subsequent state proceedings. As will become apparent below, the rule and the official commentary frequently refer to the relationship between federal rulings on waiver and its implication in future proceedings and to third parties. As a practical matter, this scope is necessary to assure protection and predictability in the rule's application.

ii.   When Does an Inadvertent Disclosure Waive Protection Under FRE 502(b)?   The privilege is waived when the holder of the privilege does not take reasonable steps to prevent disclosure and does not take reasonable steps to rectify the error. This position "opts for the middle ground" historically taken by the Circuits on whether inadvertent disclosure is a waiver. However, while the "middle ground," it is having a dramatic effect in many Circuits. See Silverstein v. Federal Bureau of Prisons, 2009 U.S. Dist. LEXIS 121753 (D. Co. Dec. 14, 2009) ("Rule 502 clearly abrogates previous Tenth Circuit law concerning subject matter waivers on disclosed documents otherwise protected by attorney-client privilege and work-product protection."); Amobi v. D.C. Dept. of Corr., 262 F.R.D. 45 (D.D.C. Dec. 8, 2009) ("Just over a year ago, parties in defendants' position in this Circuit would have no argument to protect against waiver").

Reasonableness will be decided on the particular facts of each case. The Advisory Committee Notes clarify that factors previously employed by the courts to determine

---

17.   See Advisory Committee Notes.
18.   See Advisory Committee Notes.

the reasonableness of disclosure can still be persuasive. Specifically, the Advisory Committee Notes state that:

> [Various cases] set out a multifactor test for determining whether inadvertent disclosure is a waiver. The stated factors (none of which is dispositive) are the reasonableness of precautions taken, the time taken to rectify the error, the scope of discovery, the extent of disclosure and the overriding issue of fairness. The rule does not explicitly codify that test, because it is really a set of non-determinative guidelines that vary from case to case. The rule is flexible enough to accommodate any of those listed factors. Other considerations bearing on the reasonableness of a producing party's efforts include the number of documents to be reviewed and the time constraints for production. Depending on the circumstances, a party that uses advanced analytical software applications and linguistic tools in screening for privilege and work product may be found to have taken "reasonable steps" to prevent inadvertent disclosure. The implementation of an efficient system of records management before litigation may also be relevant.
>
> The rule does not require the producing party to engage in a post-production review to determine whether any protected communication or information has been produced by mistake. But the rule does require the producing party to follow up on any obvious indications that a protected communication or information has been produced inadvertently.

iii.   If Disclosure Is Made in a State Proceeding, the More Protective Law Will Apply Under FRE 502(c).   This section addresses the problems that arise when disclosure is made in a state proceeding and that same information or communication is offered as evidence in a subsequent federal proceeding. If the state and federal laws are inconsistent, the federal court will apply the law most protective of the protection. The reason for this rule is laid out in the Advisory Committee Notes:

> If the state law is more protective (such as where the state law is that an inadvertent disclosure can never be a waiver), the holder of the privilege or protection may well have relied on that law when making the disclosure in the state proceeding. Moreover, applying a more restrictive federal law of waiver could impair the state objective of preserving the privilege or work-product protection for disclosures made in state proceedings. On the other hand, if the federal law is more protective, applying the state law of waiver to determine admissibility in federal court is likely to undermine the federal objective of limiting the costs of production.

Note that this rule is not intended to change the effect of a state court order concerning waiver. The Advisory Committee Notes point out that under existing law (28 U.S.C. §1738) and principles of federalism and comity, a state court order continues to be generally enforceable in a subsequent federal proceeding. However, this enforceability is "not absolute." See Tucker v. Ohtsu Tire & Rubber Co., 191 F.R.D. 495, 499 (D. Md. 2000). Under certain circumstances, federal courts will modify or circumvent a state court order. Thus, it may be the case that after FRE 502 federal court orders will have greater consequences in state courts than state court orders have in federal courts.

iv.   Controlling Effect of a Court Order Under FRE 502(d).   This subsection allows parties to "opt out" of the default standard set in subdivision (b). It provides that disclosure, made under any standard of care, will not result in a waiver, *if that* *standard is memorialized in a court order.*[19] According to the Advisory Committee Notes, "[t]he rule provides that when a confidentiality order governing the consequences of disclosure in that case is entered in a federal proceeding, its terms are enforceable against non-parties in any federal or state proceeding."

This subsection recognizes that confidentiality orders are frequently used to reduce the cost of privilege review during discovery. However, confidentiality orders can reduce costs effectively only if they provide protection in subsequent suits and against third parties. Without such predictability, parties will not limit their privilege review. Note, however, that there is no requirement that the confidentiality order memorialize an agreement among the parties to the litigation. Thus, a federal judge can create a confidentiality order without assent by the parties.

Orders issued under this subsection govern *only* documents that are disclosed in connection with federal proceedings (whether during discovery or at other times). While this subsection dictates that disclosure protected in federal court cannot be used by a third party or in a state court, it does *not* address waiver effects of separate disclosures (even of the same information) made in other proceedings, state or federal. Disclosures made in state proceedings are subject to either a state court order, or if no order has been entered, to FRE 502(c).

v.   Controlling Effect of a Party Agreement Under FRE 502(e).   This subsection codifies the well-established practice of using party agreements to limit the effect of waiver by disclosure. It is important because of its relationship to FRE 502(d). An agreement under this subsection applies only to the documents exchanged between and among the parties and binds *only* the parties to the agreement. The Advisory Committee Notes make clear that parties who seek protection against nonparties must make the agreement pursuant to a court order under FRE 502(d).

vi.   Controlling Effect of FRE 502.   According to the Advisory Committee Notes, subsection (f) clarifies that (1) FRE 502 protection against waiver must be applicable in subsequent state proceedings, and (2) FRE 502 "applies to state law causes of action brought in federal courts." The first part reiterates subsection (d) and implies that privileged communication or information disclosed in a federal proceeding, and not waived due to application of FRE 502, cannot be used in a subsequent state proceeding. The second part simply dictates that FRE 502 will be followed even if state law provides the rule of decision. Additionally, subsection (f) makes clear that FRE 502 should not be limited by FRE 101 and FRE 1101, which could otherwise be seen as in tension with this rule.

g.   Additional Concerns Raised by FRE 502

i.   The Rule Does Not Eliminate the Need to Review Documents Prior to Disclosure.   As noted above, the rule applies only to information and communication protected by the attorney-client privilege or the work-product doctrine. However, documents are reviewed during discovery for various reasons other than fear of waiving these protections. For example, rules of professional conduct, privacy laws, or

---

19.   Martin R. Lueck and Patrick M. Arenz, Federal Rule of Evidence 502(d) and Compelled Quick Peek Productions, 10 Sedona Conference J. 229, 299 (2009).

confidentiality agreements may prohibit lawyers from breaching confidentiality or waiving the attorney-client privilege. Failure to review documents during discovery will also potentially produce documents protected by other privilege doctrines (e.g., settlement negotiations and self-evaluative documents). FRE 502 does not extinguish an attorney's responsibilities under the lawyer's code of conduct or other legal standards, nor does it protect information and communication protected by other privileges.

Furthermore, disclosure of protected information has the potential to severely prejudice a case, even if the information cannot be used directly by the receiving party. Once a receiving party has read privileged information, the court can only prohibit its use in trial; it cannot force the attorney to unlearn the information. The document itself may reveal strategy or thinking about the case. It may contain business-sensitive documents, such as trade secrets or processes that should not be revealed to a competitor. The document may expose the client to additional unrelated claims, or allow the receiving attorney to formulate further discovery requests that will target critical information. For all these reasons, attorneys and their clients may find that extensive document review is necessary, notwithstanding FRE 502.

ii. The Constitutionality of the Rule's Application to State Court Proceedings.

Constitutional concerns arise because FRE 502, a federally created rule, directs state courts on how to handle potential evidence. As Henry Noyes points out, FRE 502 may face a constitutional challenge because it is a federal action that causes a "direct loss of state control over the operation of the state courts."[20] FRE 502 was passed under Congress's power to regulate activity that substantially affects interstate commerce. However, the rule regulates all attorney-client or work-product material; it is not limited to information that relates to interstate commerce. Cf. Pierce Country v. Guillen, 537 U.S. 129 (2003), page 907, infra (holding a federal statute, protecting information relating to highway safety from discovery in state courts, constitutional under Congress's commerce clause power, because it addressed the channels and instrumentalities of interstate commerce). Further, while Congress passed FRE 502 to make the discovery process more efficient and cost-effective, there are no findings about the burden and cost of privilege review on interstate commerce. For additional discussion on the possible unconstitutional nature of FRE 502, see Henry S. Noyes, Federal Rule of Evidence 502: Stirring the State Law of Privilege and Professional Responsibility with a Federal Stick, 66 Wash. & Lee L. Rev. 673 (2009).

iii. The Rule May Not Significantly Reduce the Cost of Discovery.

One of the admitted goals of FRE 502 is to reduce the cost of discovery. The theory is that limiting the necessity for pre-disclosure review will significantly reduce cost. However, under FRE 502(b), pre-disclosure review must be "reasonable" to prevent waiver; without further elaboration of this requirement, attorneys may continue to impose extensive reviews to ensure the process is considered reasonable. There are two additional problems with this contention. First, as discussed above, there are numerous reasons why parties will continue to engage in intensive pre-disclosure review. Second, if the parties are not concerned with negative implications of disclosing documents, the new rule may encourage parties to turn over too much information. These "data dumps" shift the cost of discovery from the disclosing party to the receiving party. Importantly,

---

20. Henry S. Noyes, Federal Rule of Evidence 502: Stirring the State Law of Privilege and Professional Responsibility with a Federal Stick, 66 Wash. & Lee L. Rev. 673, 727 (2009).

the overall cost likely increases as well, because the receiving party is likely to be less efficient at sorting through the documents.

iv.   The Rule May Jeopardize the Attorney-Client Privilege.   As mentioned above, the FRE 502 order can be initiated by a judge without the consent of the parties. A short time-frame imposed on discovery requests combined with a mandated 502 order may effectively force attorneys to hand over confidential information. However, the attorney-client privilege exists for the benefit of the client and is beneficial because it creates incentives to disclose information to the lawyer. If FRE 502 damages the confidentiality of the relationship, it may have significant, counterproductive, long-term consequences.

KEY POINTS

1. The attorney-client privilege extends to confidential communications between an attorney and client made for the purpose of obtaining legal advice. The privilege does not cover communications made to a lawyer for the purpose of obtaining any other kind of advice, such as business or tax advice. Determining which is which is not always easy.

2. The client is the holder of the privilege, but the privilege may be claimed on behalf of the client by the attorney and other individuals responsible for the client's interests.

3. The privilege extends over communications between joint clients and their attorney, and also covers "common interest" or "joint defense" cases, in which multiple parties and multiple attorneys are involved.

4. A communication does not necessarily have to be verbal. However, reasonable precautions must be taken by the parties to ensure confidentiality for the privilege to attach.

5. The privilege is not waived due to inadvertent disclosure in a federal proceeding if reasonable steps were taken to prevent disclosure.

NOTES AND QUESTIONS

1. The fact that FRE 502 is limited to attorney-client and work-product-protected information may have a significant impact on the effectiveness of the rule. Do you understand why a protective order under FRE 502 may not entice lawyers to forgo pre-disclosure document review?

2. Under FRE 502(a), a party that intentionally produces a privileged document may face a subject matter waiver. However, a party that unintentionally produces a privileged document will never face a subject matter waiver and will only be found to waive the privilege as to the disclosed document if the steps taken to protect the document and to rectify the error were unreasonable. Thus, FRE 502(b) requires courts to determine whether disclosure was "inadvertent" and whether "reasonable steps" were taken. How much room does this leave for courts to determine the definition of "inadvertent"? See Silverstein v. Federal Bureau of Prisons, 2009 U.S. Dist. LEXIS 121753 (D. Colo. Dec. 14, 2009) (finding that 502(b) covers "unintended,

rather than mistaken, disclosure," and disclosure was not inadvertent when document was mislabeled). Similarly, after reading the Advisory Committee Notes for subsection (b), are you confident that you can employ "reasonable steps" to prevent waiving the privilege through unintentional disclosure? What does it mean to take "reasonable steps"? How much is still left to the discretion of the judge? See Amobi v. D.C. Dept. of Corr., 262 F.R.D. 45 (D.D.C. 2009) (finding that reasonable steps were not taken when procedures were not described to the court and there was "no indication of what specific efforts were taken to prevent disclosure"); Rhoads Industries, Inc. v. Building Materials Corp., 254 F.R.D. 216 (E.D. Pa. 2008) (finding steps taken to prevent disclosure were not reasonable after reviewing multiple factors and specifically concerned that party claiming privilege did not prepare for discovery sufficiently far in advance). Do you think that a judge's definition of "reasonable" or "inadvertent" may be affected by the old waiver rules in his or her Circuit?

3. FRE 502 frequently refers to "subsequent state and federal proceedings," specifically indicating that the federal ruling governs subsequent determinations on the scope of a waiver. The Advisory Committee Notes indicate that this is necessary "to assure protection and predictability." Why is this so? Does it help if you know that plaintiff groups frequently share documents that are produced during a lawsuit? Would the rule be effective if protective orders ceased at the end of trial? How much confidence would an FRE 502 order give defendants if it was not enforceable in subsequent procedures and against third parties?

4. As a defense attorney, do you want the judge to unilaterally impose an FRE 502 order?

PROBLEMS

12.1. Brent Carson and Gloria Green were charged with importing cocaine, and retained separate counsel. At a meeting involving Brent, Gloria, and Gloria's attorney, Gloria supposedly said that Brent did not know anything about the plan to import cocaine. Gloria subsequently fled the jurisdiction, and Brent is now on trial. He calls Gloria's attorney to testify about her statement that he was not involved in the cocaine scheme. The prosecutor has objected to this testimony and asserted the attorney-client privilege on behalf of Gloria. How should the court rule?

12.2. Metro Display Advertising, Inc. (MDA) was in the business of buying and selling advertising space on bus stop shelters before it was forced to declare bankruptcy in the aftermath of an SEC investigation. The government has charged Munoz, one of MDA's independent sales agents, with mail fraud and has subpoenaed Sherron to testify against him. Sherron was once Munoz's attorney in an unrelated matter prior to either's employment with MDA. Subsequently, Sherron was retained by MDA. Munoz communicated to Sherron about the current charges against him, mistakenly believing that Sherron was representing him as well as MDA. Munoz now seeks to prevent Sherron from testifying about his damaging statements by invoking his attorney-client privilege. Should the court allow Sherron's testimony?

12.3. Ed Brown has been charged with assault. At a pretrial hearing to determine Brown's competence to stand trial, the attorney called himself as a witness for the purpose of explaining how difficult it was to communicate with Brown. The attorney's testimony included the details of three quite different stories that Brown had told at various times about the incident in question. The court found Brown competent to stand trial. At trial, where Brown was represented by a different attorney, the prosecutor called the former attorney to testify about Brown's earlier inconsistent statements regarding the crime. Brown has objected on the ground that his statements are protected by the attorney-client privilege. What result?

12.4. Dunlap was the director of the Lincoln Challenge Project, a betterment program for teenaged high school dropouts. In 1994, he hired Peters to teach in the program, requiring him to consent to criminal and educational background checks as a condition of his employment. When Peters sought to have his contract renewed in 1996, Dunlap informed him that he would be required to sign a much broader release consenting to, among other things, the full and complete disclosure of the records of attorneys, whether representing him or another person, in any case in which Peters has had an interest. Peters refused to sign the release and his employment contract was not renewed. Peters sued Dunlap. Can an employer require an employee to waive all attorney-client privileges as a condition of employment? Could any constitutional argument(s) be made by Peters to protect the privileged information?

12.5. Suburban Sew 'N Sweep is a retail store selling sewing machines manufactured and distributed by Fritz, Inc. A few years ago Suburban began suspecting that Fritz was engaging in unlawful price discrimination and conspiring to restrain trade in violation of the Clayton Act and the Sherman Antitrust Act. To confirm its suspicions, Suburban began regularly searching the Dumpster behind Fritz's office. Over the course of two years, Suburban found hundreds of relevant documents, many of which were confidential correspondences between Fritz's officers and Fritz's corporate counsel. It is uncontested that the documents were intended to be confidential and would be protected by attorney-client privilege if they had not been discovered by Suburban. Are these documents privileged?

12.6. Connolly was laid off as a part of a reduction in workforce by his employer, Athens Enterprises. He sued the company, alleging that it discriminated against him on the basis of race, in violation of federal and state law. Connolly, who is white, offered evidence that the company considered federal Equal Employment Opportunity reasons when it reduced its workforce, specifically that it targeted white employees for elimination while keeping less qualified minorities. Davis, an in-house attorney for Athens, advised the company regarding the layoffs. He prepared a memo from the law department on proposed guidelines for implementing the cutbacks. In addition, he advised the company regarding possible legal problems with the lists of employees the company proposed to fire. Connolly moved to compel the production of these documents, arguing that they were not privileged because they were prepared in the ordinary course of business, and not for the purpose of giving legal advice. Should the documents be produced? With regard to the lists, would it make a difference if they were prepared at the request of the law department?

12.7. Habs Brewing Company brought suit against Blue Jay Importers, alleging patent and trademark infringement resulting from Blue Jay's marketing of "dry" beer. Blue Jay motioned the court to compel production of certain documents, which Habs claims are protected by the attorney-client privilege. The 15 documents for which the plaintiffs are asserting the privilege were initiated by or received by Beardsley. Beardsley is a member of the legal department of Habs, and serves as their Intellectual Property Officer. Although not an attorney, Beardsley is registered as a patent agent before the U.S. Patent and Trademark Office. The Patent office allows nonlawyer patent agents to perform certain legal tasks before it, such as giving patent advice and preparing patent applications. Patent agents do not have any corresponding authorization to practice trademark law. Can Habs successfully assert the attorney-client privilege with respect to the communications by and to Beardsley? Does it make a difference whether such communications involved patent or trademark law?

NOTE ON THE ATTORNEY-CLIENT PRIVILEGE, THE WORK-PRODUCT DOCTRINE, AND THE ETHICAL DUTY OF CONFIDENTIALITY

Three sources protect confidentiality in the attorney-client relationship: the attorney-client privilege, the work-product doctrine, and the ethical duty of confidentiality. While the attorney-client privilege and work-product doctrine find their source in the law of evidence, the duty of confidentiality is grounded in the code of professional ethics.

The work-product doctrine often overlaps or supplements the attorney-client privilege. Protection for the "work product" of an attorney or party has been codified under Fed. R. Civ. P. 26(b)(3). Under Rule 26(b)(3), a party may obtain discovery of documents and tangible things prepared "in anticipation of litigation" by an attorney or representative of the opposing party only on a showing of "substantial need" and on a showing that the party seeking discovery is unable, without undue hardship, to obtain the substantial equivalent from alternative means. Furthermore, even if the required showing is put forth, the court must protect against disclosure of "the mental impressions, conclusions, opinions, or legal theories of an attorney or other representative of a party concerning the litigation." While both the attorney-client privilege and work-product doctrine act as a bar to discovery, there exist some crucial distinctions between the two. First, the work-product doctrine recognizes a qualified privilege, while the attorney-client privilege is usually considered absolute, although this is slowly beginning to change. See, for example, Greater Newburyport Clamshell Alliance v. Public Service Co. of N.H., 838 F.2d 13, 19 (1st Cir. 1988) (in civil damages action, "fairness requires that the privilege holder surrender the privilege to the extent that it will weaken, in a meaningful way, the defendant's ability to defend"); In re Grand Jury Proc., Des Moines, Iowa, 568 F.2d 555, 557 (8th Cir. 1977) (opponent's need relevant to a determination of privilege). At least with respect to discovery of "documents and tangible things," as opposed to "mental impressions, conclusions, opinions, or legal theories of an attorney," work-product protection is subject to a substantial need test. By contrast, if the attorney-client privilege is applicable, a showing of need will typically not overcome the privilege.

Second, whereas the work-product doctrine applies only to information prepared "in anticipation of litigation," the attorney-client privilege protects confidential communications, regardless of whether litigation is expected. Although the scope of work-product protection may seem unduly limited by the litigation requirement, in reality the work-product doctrine covers a much larger category of material than the attorney-client privilege. The work-product doctrine applies to all information collected by the attorney or the agent of the client insofar as it is gathered in anticipation of litigation. Most Circuits hold that a document is prepared in "anticipation of litigation" if the document is prepared "because of" the upcoming litigation. See United States v. Adlman, 134 F.3d 1194 (2d Cir. 1998). However, the Fifth Circuit applies a narrower "primary purpose" test — protecting a document only if the primary purpose of the document is to prepare for litigation. *United States v. El Paso Co.*, 682 F.2d 530 (5th Cir. 1982). Under both standards, the protection applies not only to information passing from client to attorney, but to information from outside sources as well, such as a statement of a nonparty witness to an attorney as well as work compiled by an investigator, without the attorney's participation. In contrast, the attorney-client privilege applies solely to confidential communications between attorney and client, or representatives on either party's behalf.

A third source for the protection of confidentiality in attorney-client relations is the ethical duty of a lawyer to keep confidential matters about a client's affairs. The American Bar Association's Model Rules of Professional Conduct set forth this obligation in Rule 1.6, which as amended in 2005 now states:

> (a) A lawyer shall not reveal information relating to the representation of a client unless the client gives informed consent, the disclosure is impliedly authorized in order to carry out the representation or the disclosure is permitted by paragraph (b).
>
> (b) A lawyer may reveal information relating to the representation of a client to the extent the lawyer reasonably believes necessary:
>
> (1) to prevent reasonably certain death or substantial bodily harm;
>
> (2) to prevent the client from committing a crime or fraud that is reasonably certain to result in substantial injury to the financial interests or property of another and in furtherance of which the client has used or is using the lawyer's services;
>
> (3) to prevent, mitigate or rectify substantial injury to the financial interests or property of another that is reasonably certain to result or has resulted from the client's commission of a crime or fraud in furtherance of which the client has used the lawyer's services;
>
> (4) to secure legal advice about the lawyer's compliance with these Rules;
>
> (5) to establish a claim or defense on behalf of the lawyer in a controversy between the lawyer and the client, to establish a defense to a criminal charge or civil claim against the lawyer based upon conduct in which the client was involved, or to respond to allegations in any proceeding concerning the lawyer's representation of the client; or
>
> (6) to comply with other law or a court order.

Comment Two accompanying Model Rule 1.6 provides the rationale behind the ethical obligation.

> A fundamental principle in the client-lawyer relationship is that, in the absence of the client's informed consent, the lawyer must not reveal information relating to the representation. . . . This contributes to the trust that is the hallmark of the client-lawyer relationship. The client is thereby encouraged to seek legal assistance and to communicate fully and frankly with the lawyer even as to embarrassing or legally damaging subject matter. The lawyer needs this information to represent the client effectively and, if necessary, to advise the client to refrain from wrongful conduct. . . .

The duty of confidentiality is an important mechanism by which the rules of ethics protect these interests. The rule was relaxed slightly in the 2005 update, now allowing the lawyer to breach confidentiality to prevent any reasonably certain bodily harm, no longer limited to harm caused by a client's criminal act. Further, in the wake of financial scandals such as Enron, the updated rule allows for a breach of confidentiality to prevent a client's crime or fraud from causing harm to financial interests or property. Despite these few exceptions, the ethical duty of confidentiality remains essential to the protection of the client-lawyer relationship. Violation of Rule 1.6 may lead to professional censure and possible suspension or loss of license.

Comment Three to Rule 1.6 clarifies the distinction between evidentiary privileges and the ethical duty of confidentiality:

> The principle of client-lawyer confidentiality is given effect by related bodies of law: the attorney-client privilege, the work product doctrine and the rule of confidentiality established in professional ethics. The attorney-client privilege and work-product doctrine apply in judicial and other proceedings in which a lawyer may be called as a witness or otherwise required to produce evidence concerning a client. The rule of client-lawyer confidentiality applies in situations other than those where evidence is sought from the lawyer through compulsion of law. The confidentiality rule, for example, applies not only to matters communicated in confidence by the client but also to all information relating to the representation, whatever its source. A lawyer may not disclose such information except as authorized or required by the Rules of Professional Conduct or other law. . . .

The duty of confidentiality covers much more than the privilege — it covers all communications between a client and an attorney, including those that are not specifically tied to seeking legal advice, and those that are not meant to be confidential. The duty of confidentiality also covers more than just verbal communications, unlike the attorney-client privilege. However, a lawyer can still be called on to testify regarding these communications, so the protection afforded by the duty of confidentiality may not be as great as that afforded by the privilege.

An interesting empirical question is whether the lawyer's ethical obligation to maintain confidentiality is sufficiently analogous to the privilege to encourage communications between client and attorney. If clients can be encouraged by the attorney's ethical obligation not to disclose information, then the attorney-client privilege may not be needed. See, in this regard, ABA Code of Professional Responsibility, Ethical Consideration 4-1:

> A lawyer should be fully informed of all the facts of the matter he is handling in order for his client to obtain the full advantage of our legal system. It is for the lawyer in the exercise of his independent professional judgment to separate the relevant and important from the irrelevant and unimportant. The observance of the ethical obligation of a lawyer to hold inviolate the confidences and secrets of his client not only facilitates the full development of facts essential to proper representation of the client but also encourages laymen to seek early legal assistance.

NOTES AND QUESTIONS

1. How absolute should the protection be for a client's confidential communications or a lawyer's thought processes and other creative efforts? Even if the existence of rules of confidentiality produce benefits, isn't it conceivable in a particular case that their costs would exceed their benefits? What should happen in such cases? In thinking about this issue, do not neglect the costs of deciding on a case-by-case basis if the costs of confidentiality exceed the benefits. If a witness uses a document protected by the attorney-client privilege or the work-product doctrine to refresh the witness's memory before testifying, should the judge be able to order production of the document pursuant to FRE 612?

2. The American Bar Association's Model Code of Professional Responsibility, the predecessor to the Model Rules of Professional Conduct, included a similar confidentiality provision. ABA Model Code of Professional Responsibility Disciplinary

Rule 4-101. The exception for contemplated criminal conduct by a client, however, extended to *all* crimes, and there was also an exception permitting a lawyer to reveal confidences "when required by law or court order." With respect to the omission of this latter exception in the Model Rules, the Comment accompanying Rule 1.6 states: "Whether another provision of law supersedes Rule 1.6 is a matter of interpretation beyond the scope of these Rules, but a presumption should exist against such a supersession." How compelling a case for confidentiality does the Comment to Rule 1.6 make? Do the rule and commentary deal adequately with the relationship between the ethical obligation of confidentiality and the attorney-client privilege? Is Rule 1.6's permission for a lawyer to disclose a client's contemplated criminal conduct too narrow? Why should there be a "presumption" that provisions of law mandating disclosure do not supersede Rule 1.6's obligation of confidentiality?

3. There is one situation in which the Model Rules of Professional Conduct specifically provide that the rule of confidentiality is superseded. See Model Rule 3.3:

> (a) A lawyer shall not knowingly:
>   (1) make a false statement of material fact or law to a tribunal;
>   (2) fail to disclose a material fact to a tribunal when disclosure is necessary to avoid assisting a criminal or fraudulent act by the client;
>   (3) fail to disclose to the tribunal legal authority in the controlling jurisdiction known to the lawyer to be directly adverse to the position of the client and not disclosed by opposing counsel; or
>   (4) offer evidence that the lawyer knows to be false. If a lawyer has offered material evidence and comes to know of its falsity, the lawyer shall take reasonable remedial measures.
> (b) The duties stated in paragraph (a) continue to the conclusion of the proceeding, and apply even if compliance requires disclosure of information otherwise protected by Rule 1.6.
> (c) A lawyer may refuse to offer evidence that the lawyer reasonably believes is false.

4. For further discussion of the relation between the attorney-client privilege and the ethical rules of confidentiality, see Harry Schaffner, Reconciling Attorney-Client Privilege with the Rules of Professional Conduct, 81 Ill. Bus. J. 410 (1993); see also Fred C. Zacharias, Harmonizing Privilege and Confidentiality, 41 S. Tex. L. Rev. 69 (1999).

PROBLEMS

12.8. Al Driver, who is suspected of bank robbery, tells his attorney, George Shippers, where to locate the mask and gun used in the robbery. Shippers retrieves the mask and gun and places them in the office safe. Has Shippers acted unethically? What disclosures about the gun and mask is he now permitted or required to make?

What if it had been Shippers's secretary who had, without Shippers's permission, retrieved the mask and gun? In either case, should it matter (a) whether the police or some third person would have been likely to find the mask and gun or (b) whether the initial information about the mask and gun came from some person other than the client?

After Shippers first learned about the mask and gun, what would have been the appropriate course of action for him to take?

12.9. Sarah Johnson, an attorney, represents Oscar Rivers, who has been charged with murder. Rivers and his girlfriend, Elsie Lewis, are both prepared to testify that they were together at Elsie's apartment at the time of the killing. Oscar has consistently told Sarah this alibi story; Elsie, however, has confided in Sarah that she was not with Oscar at the time of the killing and that Oscar admitted to her that he was the murderer. The only eyewitness to the killing, Elvira Dugan, is an elderly woman with failing eyesight.

What should Sarah do if both Oscar and Elsie are adamant about testifying that they were together at Elsie's apartment when the murder was committed? Does your answer depend on whether Sarah believes Oscar or Elsie?

Sarah is convinced that she can neutralize Elvira Dugan's eyewitness testimony during cross-examination. Is there any problem with her doing so if she is convinced that Oscar is guilty and that Elvira's identification is in fact accurate?

2.   The Corporate Client

The attorney-client privilege extends not only to individual clients but also to corporate and other organizational clients. Application of the privilege in this context has proved troublesome because an organization can make confidential communications only through individual members. Thus, the question necessarily arises: Who can speak for the organization for the purposes of the attorney-client privilege? Or to phrase the issue in terms of the language of Proposed FRE 503: Who is a "representative of the client"?

Courts are divided as to the extent of the privilege in the corporate context. As the law has evolved on the subject, three approaches can be discerned. Under the early decisions, any officer, employee, or member of an organization was a representative of the organization. See, e.g., United States v. United Shoe Mach. Corp., 89 F. Supp. 357 (D. Mass. 1950). Although this definition had the advantage of ease in application, it was widely criticized for being too broad.

A second approach to defining representative of the client was the "control group" test. See City of Philadelphia v. Westinghouse Elec. Corp., 210 F. Supp. 483 (E.D. Pa. 1962). According to this test an employee's communication is privileged only if the employee "is in a position to control or even to take a substantial part in a decision about any action which the corporation may take upon the advice of the attorney." Although widely adopted, the control group test was subject to criticism on two grounds. First, it was unclear precisely to whom the privilege would apply, and this lack of certainty would inhibit candid communication. Second, because the control group test tended to limit the attorney-client privilege to communications by upper level management, the test did not go far enough in protecting communications of employees who might have information that would be critical in order for the attorney to give sound legal advice to the organization.

A third approach to defining representative of the client was the "subject matter" test. See Harper & Row Publishers, Inc. v. Decker, 423 F.2d 487 (7th Cir. 1970), *aff'd mem.*, 400 U.S. 955 (1971). Under this test an employee's communication is privileged if the employee "makes the communication at the direction of his superiors" and the subject matter of the communication "is the performance by the employee of the duties of his employment." This test avoids both the problem of bringing within the scope of the privilege communications by any and all employees and the problem of limiting the privilege to communications from members of the control group. But is the subject matter test itself too broad? Would the first prong of the test be satisfied if every employee were routinely directed to channel all business reports through corporate counsel? See Note, Evidence — Privileged Communications — The Attorney-Client Privilege in the Corporate Setting: A Suggested Approach, 69 Mich. L. Rev. 360 (1970). Would the first prong be satisfied if *any* superior for *any* reason directed the employee to communicate with the attorney?

The drafters of the Federal Rules chose not to define "representative of the client." Without elaboration, the Advisory Committee concluded that the matter was "too hot to handle" and "better left to resolution on a case-by-case basis."[21] The Supreme Court addressed the issue in *Upjohn*.

UPJOHN CO. v. UNITED STATES
449 U.S. 383 (1981)

Justice REHNQUIST delivered the opinion of the Court.

We granted certiorari in this case to address important questions concerning the scope of the attorney-client privilege in the corporate context and the applicability of the work-product doctrine in proceedings to enforce tax summonses. . . . We . . . conclude that the attorney-client privilege protects the communications involved in this case from compelled disclosure and that the work-product doctrine does apply in tax summons enforcement proceedings.

I

Petitioner Upjohn Co. manufactures and sells pharmaceuticals here and abroad. In January 1976 independent accountants conducting an audit of one of Upjohn's foreign subsidiaries discovered that the subsidiary made payments to or for the benefit of foreign government officials in order to secure government business. The accountants so informed petitioner Mr. Gerard Thomas, Upjohn's Vice President, Secretary, and General Counsel. Thomas is a member of the Michigan and New York Bars, and has been Upjohn's General Counsel for 20 years. He consulted with outside counsel and R. T. Parfet, Jr., Upjohn's Chairman of the Board. It was decided that the company would conduct an internal investigation of what were termed "questionable payments." As part of this investigation the attorneys prepared a letter containing a questionnaire which was sent to "All Foreign General and Area Managers" over the Chairman's signature. The letter began by noting recent disclosures that several

---

21. See Hearings on Proposed Rules of Evidence Before the Special Subcommittee on Reform of Federal Criminal Laws of the House Committee on the Judiciary, 93d Cong., 1st Sess. 524 (1973) (testimony by Professor Cleary). In earlier drafts the Advisory Committee had included a version of the control group test in the definition section of Proposed FRE 503. Prior to the final draft, however, the Supreme Court affirmed by an equally divided vote the decision that had announced the subject matter test. Harper & Row Publishers v. Decker, 400 U.S. 348 (1970). As Weinstein and Berger noted: The Advisory Committee recognized that lack of consensus in the Supreme Court precluded the possibility of drafting a rule satisfactory to a majority of the justices. Consequently, the Committee eliminated the definition of "representative of the client" in subdivision (a) of the rule. [3 Jack B. Weinstein and Margaret A. Berger, Weinstein's Federal Evidence §503 App.01[2] (Joseph M. McLaughlin ed., 2d ed. 1997).]

American companies made "possibly illegal" payments to foreign government officials and emphasized that the management needed full information concerning any such payments made by Upjohn. The letter indicated that the Chairman had asked Thomas, identified as "the company's General Counsel," "to conduct an investigation for the purpose of determining the nature and magnitude of any payments made by the Upjohn Company or any of its subsidiaries to any employee or official of a foreign government." The questionnaire sought detailed information concerning such payments. Managers were instructed to treat the investigation as "highly confidential" and not to discuss it with anyone other than Upjohn employees who might be helpful in providing the requested information. Responses were to be sent directly to Thomas. Thomas and outside counsel also interviewed the recipients of the questionnaire and some 33 other Upjohn officers or employees as part of the investigation.

On March 26, 1976, the company voluntarily submitted a preliminary report to the Securities and Exchange Commission on Form 8-K disclosing certain questionable payments. A copy of the report was simultaneously submitted to the Internal Revenue Service, which immediately began an investigation to determine the tax consequences of the payments. Special agents conducting the investigation were given lists by Upjohn of all those interviewed and all who had responded to the questionnaire. On November 23, 1976, the Service issued a summons pursuant to 26 U.S.C. sec. 7602 demanding production of:

> All files relative to the investigation conducted under the supervision of Gerard Thomas to identify payments to employees of foreign governments and any political contributions made by the Upjohn Company or any of its affiliates since January 1, 1971 and to determine whether any funds of the Upjohn Company had been improperly accounted for on the corporate books during the same period.
>
> The records should include but not be limited to written questionnaires sent to managers of the Upjohn Company's foreign affiliates, and memorandums or notes of the interviews conducted in the United States and abroad with officers and employees of the Upjohn Company and its subsidiaries. . . .

The company declined to produce the documents specified in the second paragraph on the grounds that they were protected from disclosure by the attorney-client privilege and constituted the work product of attorneys prepared in anticipation of litigation. . . . [T]he United States filed a petition seeking enforcement of the summons . . . in the United States District Court for the Western District of Michigan. That court adopted the recommendation of a Magistrate who concluded that the summons should be enforced. Petitioners appealed to the Court of Appeals for the Sixth Circuit which rejected the Magistrate's finding of a waiver of the attorney-client privilege, . . . but agreed that the privilege did not apply "[t]o the extent that the communications were made by officers and agents not responsible for directing Upjohn's actions in response to legal advice . . . for the simple reason that the communications were not the client's." . . . The court reasoned that accepting petitioners' claim for a broader application of the privilege would encourage upper-echelon management to ignore unpleasant facts and create too broad a "zone of silence." Noting that Upjohn's counsel had interviewed officials such as the Chairman and President, the Court of Appeals remanded to the District Court so that a determination of who was within the "control group" could be made. In a concluding footnote the court stated that the work-product doctrine "is not applicable to administrative summonses issued under 26 U.S.C. sec. 7602." . . .

II

. . . The attorney-client privilege is the oldest of the privileges for confidential communications known to the common law. . . . Its purpose is to encourage full and frank communication between attorneys and their clients and thereby promote broader public interests in the observance of law and administration of justice. The privilege recognizes that sound legal advice or advocacy serves public ends and that such advice or advocacy depends upon the lawyer's being fully informed by the client. [I]n Fisher v. United States, 425 U.S. 391, 403 (1976), we recognized the purpose of the privilege to be "to encourage clients to make full disclosure to their attorneys." This rationale for the privilege has long been recognized by the Court. . . . Admittedly complications in the application of the privilege arise when the client is a corporation, which in theory is an artificial creature of the law, and not an individual; but this Court has assumed that the privilege applies when the client is a corporation, . . . and the Government does not contest the general proposition.

The Court of Appeals, however, considered the application of the privilege in the corporate context to present a "different problem," since the client was an inanimate entity and "only the senior management, guiding and integrating the several operations, . . . can be said to possess an identity analogous to the corporation as a whole." . . . The first case to articulate the so-called "control group test" adopted by the court below, Philadelphia v. Westinghouse Electric Corp., 210 F. Supp. 483, 485 (ED Pa.), *petition for mandamus and prohibition denied sub nom.* General Electric Co. v. Kirkpatrick, 312 F.2d 742 (CA3 1962), *cert. denied*, 372 U.S. 943 (1963), reflected a similar conceptual approach:

> Keeping in mind that the question is, Is it the corporation which is seeking the lawyer's advice when the asserted privileged communication is made?, the most satisfactory solution, I think, is that if the employee making the communication, of whatever rank he may be, is in a position to control or even to take a substantial part in a decision about any action which the corporation may take upon the advice of the attorney, . . . then, in effect, *he is (or personifies) the corporation* when he makes his disclosure to the lawyer and the privilege would apply. (Emphasis supplied [by the Court].)

Such a view, we think, overlooks the fact that the privilege exists to protect not only the giving of professional advice to those who can act on it but also the giving of information to the lawyer to enable them to give sound and informed advice. The first step in the resolution of any legal problem is ascertaining the factual background and sifting through the facts with an eye to the legally relevant. See ABA Code of Professional Responsibility, Ethical Consideration 4-1:

> A lawyer should be fully informed of all the facts of the matter he is handling in order for his client to obtain the full advantage of our legal system. It is for the lawyer in the exercise of his independent professional judgment to separate the relevant and important from the irrelevant and unimportant. The observance of the ethical obligation of a lawyer to hold inviolate the confidences and secrets of his client not only facilitates the full development of facts essential to proper representation of the client but also encourages laymen to seek early legal assistance.

. . . In the case of the individual client the provider of information and the person who acts on the lawyer's advice are one and the same. In the corporate context, however, it will frequently be employees beyond the control group as defined by the court below — "officers and agents . . . responsible for directing [the company's] actions in response to legal advice" — who will possess the information needed by the corporation's lawyers. Middle-level — and indeed lower-level — employees can, by actions within the scope of their employment, embroil the corporation in serious legal difficulties, and it is only natural that these employees would have the relevant information needed by corporate counsel if he is adequately to advise the client with respect to such actual or potential difficulties. . . .

The control group test adopted by the court below thus frustrates the very purpose of the privilege by discouraging the communication of relevant information by employees of the client to attorneys seeking to render legal advice to the client corporation. The attorney's advice will also frequently be more significant to noncontrol group members than to those who officially sanction the advice, and the control group test makes it more difficult to convey full and frank legal advice to the employees who will put into effect the client corporation's policy. See, e.g., Duplan Corp. v. Deering Milliken, Inc., 397 F. Supp. 1146, 1164 (S.C. 1974) ("After the lawyer forms his or her opinion, it is of no immediate benefit to the Chairman of the Board or the President. It must be given to the corporate personnel who will apply it").

The narrow scope given the attorney-client privilege by the court below not only makes it difficult for corporate attorneys to formulate sound advice when their client is faced with a specific legal problem but also threatens to limit the valuable efforts of corporate counsel to ensure their client's compliance with the law. In light of the vast and complicated array of regulatory legislation confronting the modern corporation, corporations, unlike most individuals, "constantly go to lawyers to find out how to obey the law," Burnham, The Attorney-Client Privilege in the Corporate Arena, 24 Bus. Law. 901, 913 (1969), particularly since compliance with the law in this area is hardly an instinctive matter, see, e.g., United States v. United States Gypsum Co., 438 U.S. 422, 440-441 (1978) ("the behavior proscribed by the [Sherman] Act is often difficult to distinguish from the gray zone of socially acceptable and economically justifiable business conduct").[22] The test adopted by the court below is difficult to apply in practice, though no abstractly formulated and unvarying "test" will necessarily enable courts to decide questions such as this with mathematical precision. But if the purpose of the attorney-client privilege is to be served, the attorney and client must be able to predict with some degree of certainty whether particular discussions will be protected. An uncertain privilege, or one which purports to be certain but results in widely varying applications by the courts, is little better than no privilege at all. The very terms of the test adopted by the court below suggest the unpredictability of its application. The test restricts the availability of the privilege to those officers who play a "substantial role" in deciding and directing a corporation's legal response. Disparate decisions in cases applying this test illustrate its unpredictability. Compare, e.g., Hogan v. Zletz, 43 F.R.D. 308, 315-316 (ND Okla. 1967), aff'd in part sub nom. Natta v. Hogan, 392 F.2d 686 (CA10 1968) (control group includes managers and assistant managers of patent division and research and development department), with Congoleum Industries,

---

22. The Government argues that the risk of civil or criminal liability suffices to ensure that corporations will seek legal advice in the absence of the protection of the privilege. This response ignores the fact that the depth and quality of any investigations to ensure compliance with the law would suffer, even were they undertaken. The response also proves too much, since it applies to all communications covered by the privilege: an individual trying to comply with the law or faced with a legal problem also has strong incentive to disclose information to his lawyer, yet the common law has recognized the value of the privilege in further facilitating communications.

Inc. v. GAF Corp., 49 F.R.D. 82, 83-85 (E.D. Pa. 1969), aff'd, 478 F.2d 1398 (CA3 1973) (control group includes only division and corporate vice presidents, and not two directors of research and vice president for production and research).

The communications at issue were made by Upjohn employees[23] to counsel for Upjohn acting as such, at the direction of corporate superiors in order to secure legal advice from counsel. As the Magistrate found, "Mr. Thomas consulted with the Chairman of the Board and outside counsel and thereafter conducted a factual investigation to determine the nature and extent of the questionable payments *and to be in a position to give legal advice to the company with respect to the payments.*" (Emphasis supplied [by the Court].). . . . Information, not available from upper-echelon management, was needed to supply a basis for legal advice concerning compliance with securities and tax laws, foreign laws, currency regulations, duties to shareholders, and potential litigation in each of these areas. The communications concerned matters within the scope of the employees' corporate duties, and the employees themselves were sufficiently aware that they were being questioned in order that the corporation could obtain legal advice. The questionnaire identified Thomas as "the company's General Counsel" and referred in its opening sentence to the possible illegality of payments such as the ones on which information was sought. . . . A statement of policy accompanying the questionnaire clearly indicated the legal implications of the investigation. The policy statement was issued "in order that there be no uncertainty in the future as to the policy with respect to the practices which are the subject of this investigation." It began "Upjohn will comply with all laws and regulations," and stated that commissions or payments "will not be used as a subterfuge for bribes or illegal payments" and that all payments must be "proper and legal." Any future agreements with foreign distributors or agents were to be approved "by a company attorney" and any questions concerning the policy were to be referred "to the company's general Counsel." . . . This statement was issued to Upjohn employees worldwide, so that even those interviewees not receiving a questionnaire were aware of the legal implications of the interviews. Pursuant to explicit instructions from the Chairman of the Board, the communications were considered "highly confidential" when made, . . . and have been kept confidential by the company. Consistent with the underlying purposes of the attorney-client privilege, these communications must be protected against compelled disclosure.

The Court of Appeals declined to extend the attorney-client privilege beyond the limits of the control group test for fear that doing so would entail severe burdens on discovery and create a broad "zone of silence" over corporate affairs. Application of the attorney-client privilege to communications such as those involved here, however, puts the adversary in no worse position than if the communications had never taken place. The privilege only protects disclosure of communications; it does not protect disclosure of the underlying facts by those who communicated with the attorney. . . . Here the Government was free to question the employees who communicated with Thomas and outside counsel. Upjohn has provided the IRS with a list of such employees, and the IRS has already interviewed some 25 of them. While it would probably be more convenient for the Government to secure the results of petitioner's internal investigation by simply subpoenaing the questionnaires and notes taken by

---

23. Seven of the eighty-six employees interviewed by counsel had terminated their employment with Upjohn at the time of the interview. . . . Petitioners argue that the privilege should nonetheless apply to communications by these former employees concerning activities during their period of employment. Neither the District Court nor the Court of Appeals had occasion to address this issue, and we decline to decide it without the benefit of treatment below.

petitioner's attorneys, such considerations of convenience do not overcome the policies served by the attorney-client privilege. . . .

Needless to say, we decide only the case before us, and do not undertake to draft a set
of rules which should govern challenge to investigatory subpoenas. Any such approach
would violate the spirit of Federal Rule of Evidence 501. See S. Rep. No. 93-1277, p.13
(1974) ("the recognition of a privilege based on a confidential relationship . . . should
be determined on a case-by-case basis"). . . . While such a "case-by-case" basis may to
some slight extent undermine desirable certainty in the boundaries of the attorney-client
privilege, it obeys the spirit of the Rules. At the same time we conclude that the narrow
"control group test" sanctioned by the Court of Appeals in this case cannot, consistent
with "the principles of the common law as . . . interpreted . . . in the light of reason and
experience," Fed. Rule Evid. 501, govern the development of the law in this area.

III

Our decision that the communications by Upjohn employees to counsel are covered
by the attorney-client privilege disposes of the case so far as the responses to the questionnaires and any notes reflecting responses to interview questions are concerned.
The summons reaches further, however, and Thomas has testified that his notes and
memoranda of interviews go beyond recording responses to his questions. . . . To the
extent that the material subject to the summons is not protected by the attorney-client
privilege as disclosing communications between an employee and counsel, we must
reach the ruling by the Court of Appeals that the work-product doctrine does not
apply to summonses issued under 26 U.S.C. sec. 7602.[24] The Government concedes,
wisely, that the Court of Appeals erred and that the work-product doctrine does apply
to IRS summonses. . . . This doctrine was announced by the Court over 30 years
ago in Hickman v. Taylor, 329 U.S. 495 (1947). In that case the Court rejected "an
attempt, without purported necessity or justification, to secure written statements, private memoranda and personal recollections prepared or formed by an adverse party's
counsel in the course of his legal duties." Id., at 510. The Court noted that "it is essential that a lawyer work with a certain degree of privacy" and reasoned that if discovery
of the material sought were permitted

> much of what is now put down in writing would remain unwritten. An attorney's thoughts,
> heretofore inviolate, would not be his own. Inefficiency, unfairness and sharp practices
> would inevitably develop in the giving of legal advice and in the preparation of cases for
> trial. The effect on the legal profession would be demoralizing. And the interests of the
> clients and the cause of justice would be poorly served. [Id., at 511.]

The "strong public policy" underlying the work-product doctrine was reaffirmed
in United States v. Nobles, 422 U.S. 225, 236-240 (1975), and has been substantially
incorporated in Federal Rule of Civil Procedure 26(b)(3).[25]

---

24.   The following discussion will also be relevant to counsel's notes and memoranda of interviews
with the seven former employees should it be determined that the attorney-client privilege does not apply
to them. See n.[23], supra.

25.   This provides, in pertinent part:

> [A] party may obtain discovery of documents and tangible things otherwise discoverable under
> subdivision (b)(1) of this rule and prepared in anticipation of litigation or for trial by or for another

. . . While conceding the applicability of the work-product doctrine, the Government asserts that it has made a sufficient showing of necessity to overcome its protections. The Magistrate apparently so found. . . . The Government relies on the following language in *Hickman*:

> We do not mean to say that all written materials obtained or prepared by an adversary's counsel with an eye toward litigation are necessarily free from discovery in all cases. Where relevant and nonprivileged facts remain hidden in an attorney's file and where production of those facts is essential to the preparation of one's case, discovery may properly be had. . . . And production might be justified where the witnesses are no longer available or can be reached only with difficulty. [*Hickman*, 329 U.S., at 511.]

The Government stresses that interviewees are scattered across the globe and that Upjohn has forbidden its employees to answer questions it considers irrelevant. The above-quoted language from *Hickman*, however, did not apply to "oral statements made by witnesses . . . whether presently in the form of [the attorney's] mental impressions or memoranda." Id., at 512. As to such material the Court did "not believe that any showing of necessity can be made under the circumstances of this case so as to justify production. . . . If there should be a rare situation justifying production of these matters, petitioner's case is not of that type." Id., at 512-513. . . . Forcing an attorney to disclose notes and memoranda of witnesses' oral statements is particularly disfavored because it tends to reveal the attorney's mental processes, 329 U.S., at 513 ("what he saw fit to write down regarding witnesses' remarks"); id., at 516-517 ("the statement would be his [the attorney's] language, permeated with his inferences") (Jackson, J., concurring).[26] Rule 26 accords special protection to work product revealing the attorney's mental processes. The Rule permits disclosure of documents and tangible things constituting attorney work product upon a showing of substantial need and inability to obtain the equivalent without undue hardship. This was the standard applied by the Magistrate. . . . Rule 26 goes on, however, to state that "[i]n ordering discovery of such materials when the required showing has been made, the court shall protect against disclosure of the mental impressions, conclusions, opinions or legal theories of an attorney or other representative of a party concerning the litigation." Although this language does not specifically refer to memoranda based on oral statements of witnesses the *Hickman* court stressed the danger that compelled disclosure of such memoranda would reveal the attorney's mental processes. It is clear that this is the sort of material the draftsmen of the Rule had in mind as deserving special protection. See Notes of Advisory Committee on 1970 Amendment to Rules, 28, U.S.C. App., p.442 ("The subdivision . . . goes on to protect against disclosure the mental impressions, conclusions, opinions, or legal theories . . . of an attorney or other representative of a

---

party or by or for that other party's representative (including his attorney, consultant, surety, indemnitor, insurer, or agent) only upon a showing that the party seeking discovery has substantial need of the materials in the preparation of his case and that he is unable without undue hardship to obtain the substantial equivalent of the materials by other means. In ordering discovery of such materials when the required showing has been made, the court shall protect against disclosure of the mental impressions, conclusions, opinions, or legal theories of an attorney or other representative of a party concerning the litigation.

26.   Thomas described his notes of the interviews as containing "what I considered to be the important questions, the substance of the responses to them, my beliefs, as to the importance of these, my beliefs as to how they related to the inquiry, my thoughts as to how they related to other questions. In some instances they might even suggest other questions that I would have to ask or things that I needed to find elsewhere." . . .

party. The *Hickman* opinion drew special attention to the need for protecting an attorney against discovery of memoranda prepared from recollection of oral interviews. The courts have steadfastly safeguarded against disclosure of lawyers' mental impressions and legal theories. . . . ").

Based on the foregoing, some courts have concluded that *no* showing of necessity can overcome protection of work product which is based on oral statements from witnesses. . . . Those courts declining to adopt an absolute rule have nonetheless recognized that such material is entitled to special protection. . . .

We do not decide the issue at this time. It is clear that the Magistrate applied the wrong standard when he concluded that the Government had made a sufficient showing of necessity to overcome the protections of the work-product doctrine. The Magistrate applied the "substantial need" and "without undue hardship" standard articulated in the first part of Rule 26(b)(3). The notes and memoranda sought by the Government here, however, are work product based on oral statements. If they reveal communications, they are, in this case, protected by the attorney-client privilege. To the extent they do not reveal communications, they reveal the attorneys' mental processes in evaluating the communications. As Rule 26 and *Hickman* make clear, such work product cannot be disclosed simply on a showing of substantial need and inability to obtain the equivalent without undue hardship.

While we are not prepared at this juncture to say that such material is always protected by the work-product rule, we think a far stronger showing of necessity and unavailability by other means than was made by the Government or applied by the Magistrate in this case would be necessary to compel disclosure. . . . [W]e . . . reverse the judgment of the Court of Appeals for the Sixth Circuit and remand the case to it for such further proceedings in connection with the work-product claim as are consistent with this opinion. . . .

Chief Justice Burger, concurring in part and concurring in the judgment.

I join in Parts I and III of the opinion of the Court and in the judgment. As to Part II, I agree fully with the Court's rejection of the so-called "control group" test, its reasons for doing so, and its ultimate holding that the communications at issue are privileged. As the Court states, however, "if the purpose of the attorney-client privilege is to be served, the attorney and client must be able to predict with some degree of certainty whether particular discussions will be protected." . . . For this very reason, I believe that we should articulate a standard that will govern similar cases and afford guidance to corporations, counsel advising them, and federal courts.

The Court properly relies on a variety of factors in concluding that the communications now before us are privileged. . . . Because of the great importance of the issue, in my view the Court should make clear now that, as a general rule, a communication is privileged at least when, as here, an employee or former employee speaks at the direction of the management with an attorney regarding conduct or proposed conduct within the scope of employment. The attorney must be one authorized by the management to inquire into the subject and must be seeking information to assist counsel in performing any of the following functions: (a) evaluating whether the employee's conduct has bound or would bind the corporation; (b) assessing the legal consequences, if any, of that conduct; or (c) formulating appropriate legal responses to actions that have been or may be taken by others with regard to that conduct. . . . Other communications between employees and corporate counsel may indeed be privileged . . . but the need for certainty does not compel us now to prescribe all the details of the privilege in this case.

Nevertheless, to say we should not reach all facets of the privilege does not mean that we should neglect our duty to provide guidance in a case that squarely presents the question in a traditional adversary context. Indeed, because Federal Rule of Evidence 501 provides that the law of privileges "shall be governed by the principles of the common law as they may be interpreted by the courts of the United States in the light of reason and experience," this Court has a special duty to clarify aspects of the law of privileges properly before us. Simply asserting that this failure "may to some slight extent undermine desirable certainty" . . . neither minimizes the consequences of continuing uncertainty and confusion nor harmonizes the inherent dissonance of acknowledging that uncertainty while declining to clarify it within the frame of issues presented.

KEY POINTS

1. The attorney-client privilege extends to corporations, but there is not a simple test to determine whether a communication is covered by the privilege. If an employee makes a communication to a lawyer at the direction of a superior for the purpose of obtaining legal advice for the corporation about a matter relevant to the scope of the employee's corporate duties, the communication is likely to be privileged.

2. Privileging the communication to the attorney does not privilege the underlying facts. The employee may be deposed and must answer truthfully and fully about the relevant matter, but may not be asked "What did you say to corporate counsel?"

NOTES AND QUESTIONS

1. *Upjohn* involved application of the work-product doctrine in addition to the attorney-client privilege. The Supreme Court initially announced the doctrine, now codified in Fed. R. Civ. P. 26(b)(3), in Hickman v. Taylor, 329 U.S. 495, 511 (1947):

> Proper preparation of a client's case demands that [the lawyer] assemble information, sift what he considers to be the relevant from the irrelevant facts, prepare his legal theories and plan his strategy without undue and needless interference. . . .
> . . . This work is reflected, of course, in interviews, statements, memoranda, correspondence, briefs, mental impressions, personal beliefs, and the countless other tangible and intangible ways — aptly though roughly termed by the Circuit Court of Appeals in this case as the "work product of the lawyer." Were such materials open to opposing counsel on mere demand, much of what is now put down in writing would remain unwritten. An attorney's thought, heretofore inviolate, would not be his own. Inefficiency, unfairness and sharp practices would inevitably develop in the giving of legal advice and in preparation of cases for trial. The effect on the legal profession would be demoralizing. And the interests of the clients and the cause of justice would be poorly served.

Although the Court's rhetoric may be a bit extreme, this language suggests a rationale for the work-product doctrine that is similar to that often suggested for the attorney-client privilege.

2. Should corporations possess an attorney-client privilege? How do they differ in relevant respects from individuals? In thinking about this, is it pertinent that

corporations cannot claim the Fifth Amendment privilege against self-incrimination? Is it sensible to speak of a corporation's "expectation of privacy"?

3. What are the consequences of permitting assertion of the privilege in *Upjohn*? What would have been the consequences of forbidding it? How costly would discovery have been? How costly do you think the litigation trying to avoid discovery was? How do these costs relate to the policies of the privilege?

4. Where does the law stand in the aftermath of *Upjohn*? The Court rejected the control group test, but refused to replace it with a new test, electing instead to determine on a case-by-case basis whether the privilege exists. See page 828, supra. How clear is the Court's opinion? Could it have been clearer? Should it have been? Where does the subject matter test stand in the wake of *Upjohn*?

5. When new management take over a corporation, they, not the previous management, are the holders of the corporation's privilege, and may decide whether to assert or waive it, even with respect to statements made by previous management. Commodity Futures Trading Comm'n v. Weintraub, 470 U.S. 1026 (1985).

6. One issue that often arises is whether a corporation waives its attorney client privilege when it conducts an internal investigation of corporate wrongdoing. In In re Woolworth Corp. Securities Class Action Litig., 1996 U.S. Dist. LEXIS 7773 (S.D.N.Y. June 6, 1996), the court held that an internal investigative report prepared jointly by attorneys and accountants was protected by the attorney-client privilege. Relying on *Upjohn*, the court stated that where counsel had been retained by upper management to conduct an internal investigation, notes and memoranda reflecting communications between a corporation's employees and counsel were protected by the attorney-client privilege. The court also stated that strong public policy considerations militated against a broad finding of waiver with regard to the investigator's underlying notes and memoranda, when the investigative report was given to the SEC and released to the public: "A finding that publication of an internal investigative report constitutes waiver might well discourage corporations from taking the responsible step of employing outside counsel to conduct an investigation when wrongdoing is suspected." In contrast, in In re Kidder Peabody Securities Litigation, 168 F.R.D. 459 (S.D.N.Y. 1996), the court held that a securities firm waived the attorney-client privilege by publicly releasing an internal investigative report and by attempting to use the favorable report as a "sword" in litigation. The securities firm had invoked the privilege with respect to notes from interviews of individuals who were employed by the firm at the time of the interview. Relying on In re von Bulow, 828 F.2d 94, 100-103 (2d Cir. 1987), the court said that the scope of any waiver by virtue of disclosure was to be defined by the so-called fairness doctrine, which turns on the circumstances of the disclosure. The court said that disclosure in a "judicial" setting does trigger a waiver by implication for related and otherwise privileged materials. It held that, under the particular facts of the case, Kidder had waived its privilege by repeated injection of the substance of the investigative report into "this and other litigations" and into related litigation contexts. The offer of the Kidder report to the SEC was said to represent Kidder's continuing effort to influence the outcome of pending or anticipated litigations and agency investigations. It is not clear how this case would be treated under the new FRE 502; however, if the disclosure was intentional, the "ought in fairness" language of FRE 502(a) would likely lead the court to similar results. In re Omnicom Group Securities Litigation, 233 F.R.D. 400, 406-409 (S.D.N.Y. 2006), has a lengthy discussion of relatively current views on the matter.

7. Some critics express concern that privilege challenges and crime-fraud proceedings are undermining the ability of corporate defendants to protect legitimate claims of privilege, especially in highly regulated industries where product liability litigation has been significant. In one example, the State of Minnesota and Blue Cross and Blue Shield of Minnesota brought suit against 11 tobacco manufacturers for reimbursement of Medicaid costs related to the treatment of smoking-related illnesses in State by Humphrey v. Philip Morris, Inc., 1998 Minn. App. LEXIS 431 (Minn. Ct. App. Mar. 17, 1998), *stay denied*, 523 U.S. 1056 (1998). The plaintiffs used broad allegations of fraud and conspiracy in its production requests, which ultimately resulted in the production of more than 33 million pages and privilege logs identifying more than 200,000 privileged documents. The Minnesota district court found that an *in camera* review of the privileged documents was required after the plaintiff's prima facie showing of crime-fraud.

To facilitate the massive task of reviewing the documents, the court instituted a system of random review or spot checking. The defendants were ordered to separate the privileged documents into 16 categories. To determine where there was privilege, the special master reviewed documents from each category. He eventually reviewed approximately 800 of the 200,000 documents and made his recommendation based on this "illustrative" sample. The court held that four categories of documents were not privileged, releasing approximately 39,000 documents to the plaintiffs. Privilege challenges, it has been argued, are becoming a more common trial strategy for plaintiffs who are unburdened by massive production requests that drain the resources of corporate defendants. For an in-depth discussion of the problem, see John J. Mulderig, Leslie Wharton, and Cynthia S. Cecil, Tobacco Cases May Be Only the Tip of the Iceberg for Assaults on Privilege, 67 Def. Counsel J. 16 (2000); David J. Fried, Too High a Price for Truth: The Exception to the Attorney-Client Privilege for Contemplated Crimes and Frauds, 64 N.C. L. Rev. 443 (1986). The privilege as it relates to crime-fraud proceedings is discussed more fully in the section "Exceptions to the Privilege," beginning on page 836, infra. It is mentioned here to sensitize you to one of the problems with the attorney-client privilege that occurs within the corporate context.

PROBLEMS

12.10. Defendant Admiral Insurance Co. has filed a petition for writ of mandamus directing the district court to vacate its order compelling production of communications secured by Admiral's counsel in anticipation of a securities fraud suit. In June 1987, counsel for Admiral had interviewed the two Admiral executives who were most informed about Admiral's allegedly fraudulent transactions in Arizona properties. The two executives resigned soon after the interviews. When plaintiffs, individuals injured by the transactions, scheduled the former executives for deposition, counsel for the two executives responded that they would invoke the Fifth Amendment. Plaintiffs seek production of the statements on the basis that the information is unavailable from any other source. Admiral argues that these statements are protected from disclosure by the attorney-corporate client privilege. How should the court rule?

12.11. Plaintiffs have moved to compel the production of a diary written by Jeanette Curry while she was an employee of defendant Dayco Corporation. Jeanette compiled the diary at the direction of outside counsel to her employer. The diary chronicled events that form the basis for part of the present securities litigation. Plaintiffs contend that any privilege that might protect the contents of the diary has been waived since a newspaper reporter obtained a copy of the diary from an unidentified source. The defendants (Dayco and Jeanette) argue that the contents are protected by the attorney-corporate client privilege and work-product doctrine. They argue that since Jeanette did not authorize disclosure, there has been no waiver. What result?

12.12. Employees of several Chemical Bank branches under the supervision of Demauro were investigated for violation of the Bank Secrecy Act, which makes "laundering" money (exchanging large denomination bills for small ones) illegal. Demauro gave false testimony to a grand jury about his knowledge of the violations and has been charged with perjury. To establish that he knowingly made false statements to the grand jury, the prosecution seeks to introduce the testimony of Chemical Bank's attorney, Martin. When Chemical Bank became aware of the criminal investigation, it asked Martin to conduct an internal investigation into employee wrongdoing. In the course of the investigation, Martin interviewed Demauro in his capacity as Vice President in charge of 23 branches. Demauro insists that his communications with Martin are protected by attorney-client privilege. Should the judge allow Martin's testimony?

12.13. Chicago Police Officer Rehling was injured and had part of one leg amputated after an automobile ran him down several years ago. Rehling finished a long period of medical leave and then requested reassignment on a limited duty basis to District 16, his former assignment. He worked for a few months processing citations at District 16 before he was transferred to the Alternative Response Unit, where officers handle incoming requests for the dispatch of squad cars. Rehling was unhappy with the transfer and sued the city under the American's with Disabilities Act, claiming discrimination against him due to his disability and failure to provide him with a reasonable accommodation. The City made a motion in limine to bar the testimony of Zoufal, General Counsel to the Superintendent of Police, based on their attorney-client privilege. Zoufal had allegedly stated that the Chicago Police Department could not have a "cripple" in a position where he would interact with the public because of the likelihood of the negative reaction it would draw. Rehling has argued that Zoufal, in his "business capacity as a decision-maker," decided to have him transferred out of District 16. The city has countered by asserting that Zoufal was giving legal advice when he encouraged ranking members of the Police Department to order the transfer. Is Zoufal's testimony privileged?

3. The Government Client

The attorney-client privilege extends to entity clients other than corporations. Federal courts generally agree that the government, as client, should be afforded the protection of the attorney-client privilege. Some of the same difficulties that arise in regards to corporate clients are also present when the client is the government: Who exactly is the client? Who may invoke and waive the privilege? What is required to maintain a privilege's requirement of confidentiality? And, what constitutes a waiver? Since there has been no equivalent to *Upjohn* to define the parameters of the governmental attorney-client privilege, courts have tended to follow the law of corporate privilege. See, e.g., Galarza v. United States, 179 F.R.D. 291 (S.D. Cal. 1998).

In In re Grand Jury Subpeona Duces Tecum, 112 F.3d 910 (8th Cir. 1997), *cert. denied sub nom.* Office of the President v. Office of the Independent Counsel, 521 U.S. 1105 (1997), the court held that the White House may not use a governmental attorney-client privilege to withhold potentially relevant information from a federal grand jury. The strong public interest in honest government and in exposing wrongdoing by public officials, it said, would be ill-served by the use of a governmental attorney-client privilege in criminal proceedings.

In so deciding, the court highlighted two important distinctions between corporate and governmental clients. The White House, unlike private corporations, is not subject to any criminal liability and all government agents have a public duty to report wrongdoing. There seems to be an intuitive problem, the court said, with allowing the government to conceal evidence from a court, especially in criminal cases.

Only a year later, the Independent Counsel moved to compel the grand jury testimony of Deputy White House Counsel Bruce Lindsey after he declined to answer certain questions based on the governmental attorney-client privilege in In re Lindsey (Grand Jury Testimony), 158 F.3d 1263 (D.C. Cir. 1998). Like the Eighth Circuit, the court abrogated the governmental attorney-client privilege in criminal grand jury proceedings. Both cases clearly rejected the privilege in criminal proceedings only, leaving the governmental attorney-client privilege intact in civil cases. The Seventh Circuit also has rejected the privilege. In re Witness Before the Special Grand Jury 2000-2, 288 F.3d 289 (7th Cir. 2002) (holding that no attorney-client privilege existed between a state officer and government lawyer in context of federal criminal investigation).

However, the Second Circuit declined to follow *Lindsey*, in In re Grand Jury Investigation, 399 F.3d 527 (2d Cir. 2005), holding that the privilege exists and is enforceable in criminal proceedings as well. The court held that the Connecticut governor's office could invoke the attorney-client privilege against federal grand jury inquiries into conversations with former legal counsel, which were sought in connection with a federal bribery investigation. Id. at 536. The court reasoned that "[u]pholding the privilege furthers a culture in which consultation with government lawyers is accepted as a normal, desirable, and even indispensable part of conducting public business." Id. at 534. Although federal law applied in the case, the court gave weight to the fact that Connecticut had enacted a statute granting the privilege, noting that "the people of Connecticut, acting through their representatives, concluded that the public interest is advanced by upholding a governmental privilege even in the face of a criminal investigation." Id. For further discussion see Bryan S. Gowdy, Note, Should the Federal Government Have an Attorney-Client Privilege?, 51 Fla. L. Rev. 695 (1999). The Second Circuit recently took a similarly expansive view of the scope of privilege in civil cases. In In re County of Erie, 473 F.3d 413 (2d Cir. 2007), the court addressed whether the attorney-client privilege protects e-mails passed between a government lawyer and a public official, when the e-mails assessed "the legality of a policy and propose[d] alternative policies in that light." While the trial judge had denied protection of the e-mails because they went "beyond rendering legal advice," the court of appeals relied on In re Grand Jury Investigation, 399 F.3d 527 (2d Cir. 2005), and applied the attorney-client privilege. Specifically, the court emphasized that legal considerations should play a role in government policy-making and when a lawyer is assessing compliance with legal requirements "the lawyer's recommendation of a policy that complies (or better complies) with the legal obligation . . . is legal advice." Id. at 422.

4. Exceptions to the Privilege

There are four main exceptions to the attorney-client privilege:

a. Breach of Duty by a Lawyer or Client

The first exception applies to controversy between attorney and client. If a client sues for damages for the attorney's negligence or the attorney sues for fees due, the client may not invoke the privilege to bar admission of relevant evidence. Though the attorney-client communications remain protected against disclosure to outsiders, as between attorney and client the privilege is inapplicable. McCormick argues that the exception is premised on the "practical necessity that if effective legal service is to be encouraged the privilege must not stand in the way of the lawyer's just enforcement of his rights to be paid a fee and to protect his reputation." Kenneth S. Broun et al., McCormick on Evidence §91, at 143 (5th ed. 1999). Is that persuasive to you? Why is "encouraging effective legal service" important enough to pierce the veil of confidentiality, but determining, say, who committed a murder is not?

b. Document Attested by a Lawyer

A second exception concerns the attorney who acts as attesting witness on a document executed by the client. The exception is most commonly applied in will contests between the heirs or personal representatives of the deceased client. Although the privilege generally survives the death of a client, if an attorney acts as attesting witness to his client's will, the attorney is permitted to testify regarding the validity or interpretation of the will.

c. Identity of Client, Fee Information, and Related Matters

The third exception, which is the subject of increasing controversy in the courts, denies the privilege for certain fundamental information about the attorney-client relationship, such as the identity of the client, the client's address and occupation, and the attorney's fee arrangement. The exception is supported by some courts on the ground that such information does not involve a confidential communication. See In the Matter of Witnesses Before the Special March 1980 Grand Jury Appeal of United States, 729 F.2d 489 (7th Cir. 1984). Other courts have argued that such matters are not privileged because they are "preliminary, by their nature, establishing only the existence of the relation between client and counsel." In re Grand Jury Subpoenas (United States v. Hirsch), 803 F.2d 493, 496 (9th Cir. 1986).

Notwithstanding such arguments, courts have created three exceptions to the traditional rule that attorney's fees and client identity are not privileged. The first exception, known as the "legal advice" exception, holds that such information is protected by the privilege where there is a strong likelihood that disclosure would implicate the client in the very matter for which legal advice was sought. See In re Grand Jury Proceedings (Twist), 689 F.2d 1351, 1352 (11th Cir. 1982). The second exception, known as the "communication rationale" exception, holds that identity and fee information are privileged if disclosure would connect the client with a previously disclosed and independently privileged communication. See In re Shargel, 742 F.2d 61, 64 (2d Cir. 1984). The third exception privileges identity and fee information if it provides the "last link" in a chain of incriminating evidence that could result in criminal prosecution of the client. See In re Grand Jury Proceedings (Pavlick), 680 F.2d 1026, 1027 (5th Cir. 1982) (en banc), *rev'g* 663 F.2d 1057 (5th Cir. 1981); Baird v. Koerner, 279 F.2d 623, 633 (9th Cir. 1960) (attorney made payment to IRS of back taxes for client but refused to reveal name of client). These exceptions have not been uniformly approved by the courts. In fact, after a small burst of enthusiasm for them following the seminal decision in Baird v. Koerner, the courts have become disenchanted. For example, the Ninth Circuit, which decided *Baird*, now takes the position that only the "communications rationale" exception remains good law. Tornay v. United States, 840 F.2d 1424 (9th Cir. 1988). Much more typical of the current judicial attitude toward these matters is In re Grand Jury Investigation 83-2-35 (Durant), 723 F.2d 447 (6th Cir. 1983). In *Durant*, checks had been stolen from IBM and deposited in various bank accounts. Durant, an attorney, had been paid for legal services out of one of these accounts. Thus, identifying the client who had paid him would probably identify a person involved with the thefts. Durant was required to disclose that information. For an argument that exceptions to the privilege should focus exclusively on the client's intent, see Developments in the Law — Privileged Communications, 98 Harv. L. Rev. 1501 (1985).

d.   *Communication in Furtherance of a Crime or Fraud*

Though communications regarding a past crime or fraud are privileged, communications in furtherance of an ongoing or future illegality are not. The rationale behind the exception is that where a client seeks advice to aid a crime or fraud, the client does not retain an attorney in his professional capacity. In order to defeat the privilege, the party seeking disclosure bears the burden of bringing the communication within the crime-fraud exception.

In applying the crime-fraud exception, many courts follow the intent-based test announced in Clark v. United States, 289 U.S. 1 (1933). Under this test, the party invoking the exception must make a prima facie showing that the attorney-client communications were made for the purpose of furthering the commission of a future or present crime or fraud. The test focuses strictly on the client's intent. Thus, even if the attorney acted in good faith and was unaware of the wrongdoing, the privilege may be lost. For an example, see In re Grand Jury Proceedings No. 96-55344, 87 F.3d 377 (9th Cir. 1996). The Second Circuit has referred to the burden in terms of a probable cause showing to believe that the client consulted the attorney for the purpose of furthering wrongful conduct. See In re Grand Jury Subpoena Duces Tecum Dated Sept. 15, 1983, 731 F.2d 1032, 1039 (2d Cir. 1984). Other courts have defined the evidentiary standard differently. For example, in In re Grand Jury Investigation, 842 F.2d 1223 (11th Cir. 1987), the court used a two-part test to decide whether the crime-fraud exception applied to an attorney-client communication, not only requiring the prima facie showing of crime-fraud purpose, but also "showing that the attorney's assistance was obtained in furtherance of the criminal or fraudulent activity or was closely related to it." Id. at 1226. The correct answer should be that the finding is governed by FRE 104(a), and thus that its necessary conditions must be found by a preponderance of the evidence.

Remember that privileges do apply in preliminary fact-finding. Under what circumstances, then, may allegedly privileged material be consulted to determine if it is privileged? This was the question facing the Court in United States v. Zolin, 491 U.S. 554 (1989). The Court held that before engaging in *in camera* review of the allegedly privileged material to decide the privilege question, the trial court "should require a factual basis adequate to support a good faith belief by a reasonable person" that *in camera* review would establish that the crime-fraud exception applies and that the communication would be admitted. Id. at 572. The court concluded that the evidentiary threshold could be satisfied by any relevant evidence, whether or not it was independent of the allegedly privileged communication. Id. at 574. For further discussion of the effect of *Zolin* on the crime-fraud exception, see Christopher Paul Galanek, Note, The Impact of the *Zolin* Decision on the Crime-Fraud Exception to the Attorney-Client Privilege, 24 Ga. L. Rev. 1115 (1990).

The crime-fraud exception applies both to the attorney-client privilege and to the attorney's ethical duty of confidentiality. See Rules 1.2(d) and 1.6(b) in the ABA's Model Rules of Professional Conduct (2005) for provisions dealing with a client's illegal conduct. Is an attorney ethically obligated to report future crimes on the part of a client? What about past crimes? Compare ABA Model Rules of Professional Conduct, Rule 1.6(b), with ABA Model Code of Professional Responsibility, DR 4-101(C).

The crime-fraud exception has also been applied to the work-product privilege. In In re Murphy, 560 F.2d 326, 328 (8th Cir. 1977), the court applied a two-part test to determine which work-product documents would be admitted into evidence. Under the test, the party must (1) make a prima facie showing of crime or fraud; and (2) show a relationship between the illegal conduct and the attorney's work product. This test has been criticized on the ground that it disregards the client's intent. See, e.g., In re International Sys. & Controls Corp Sec. Litig., 693 F.2d 1235, 1243 (5th Cir. 1982).

For further discussion of the crime-fraud exception, see generally David J. Fried, Too High a Price for Truth: The Exception to the Attorney-Client Privilege for Contemplated Crimes and Frauds, 64 N.C. L. Rev. 443 (1986); Ann M. St. Peter-Griffith, Abusing the Privilege: The Crime-Fraud Exception to Rule 501 of the Federal Rules of Evidence, 48 U. Miami L. Rev. 259 (1993).

PROBLEMS

12.14. A federal grand jury indicted Edwin Lewis and three others with conspiring to violate federal immigration laws. The indictment alleged that Lewis had falsely held himself out to be an attorney, and had filed fraudulent amnesty applications with the Immigration and Naturalization Service (INS) on behalf of over 100 clients. A search warrant allowed the government to seize client files from Lewis's office. The files contained four types of documents: (1) completed INS forms; (2) forms prepared in house by the law firm (forms designed to elicit information for the applications); (3) materials designed to corroborate the information contained in the INS forms; and (4) notes apparently prepared by agents of the law firm. Some of the other items seized from the offices included blank boarding passes; blank stationery from airlines and blank stationery from various Consulates General, presumably used to create false evidence of foreign travel; and blank pay receipts from various businesses, presumably used to create false evidence of employment.

Some of Lewis's clients had filed for amnesty with the INS, while others had sought his legal advice regarding amnesty but had not filed applications at the time Lewis was arrested. The only way the government can find out the identity of these latter clients is by looking at Lewis's files. What arguments can the government make that they are entitled to all of the evidence seized from Lewis's office? Are there any special problems they might run into regarding the anonymous clients?

12.15. The government obtained a warrant and seized files and materials from a law firm that is the subject of a criminal proceeding. The files are currently sealed by court order, pending a decision as to whether the files should be protected by the attorney-client privilege. The government concedes that the firm has the right to invoke the privilege on behalf of its clients but contends that the crime-fraud exception removes these materials from the scope of the privilege. Should the crime-fraud exception apply where the alleged criminality being investigated is solely that of the law firm? If so, the government will be given access to the confidential files of innocent clients. If not, the law firm will be able to hinder an investigation of its own alleged criminal conduct by asserting a privilege designed to protect clients. Should the court allow the files to be unsealed?

12.16. Ralls was paid by a client/fee-payer to defend Bonnette against criminal charges connected to Bonnette's attempt to transport 300 pounds of cocaine from Arizona to California. The government sought to discover the name of the person who hired Ralls and the amount and method of payment. Ralls moved to quash the government's grand jury subpoena on the basis of attorney-client privilege. The district court ordered Ralls to testify as to the client's identity and the fee arrangements but held that the conversations between Ralls and the client were privileged. Should an appellate court affirm this decision?

12.17. Elsa and Arlen were in the midst of a messy divorce. During a custody fight over their two sons, Lars and Herbie, Elsa met with her attorney, Friedman. Elsa was convinced that Arlen had been sexually abusing the children. Friedman invited Elsa's friend, Margie, to be present in order to have a "cool head" in the room. While in front of Friedman, Elsa and Margie began discussing ways of killing Arlen or hurting the children and framing Arlen for it. Friedman, afraid that Elsa and Margie might be serious, informed a judge. The judge announced the substance of Friedman's disclosure at the custody hearing, and Arlen was granted custody, while Friedman's appearance as Elsa's counsel was stricken. Margie later broke into Arlen's house carrying a gun, found him asleep in his bed, and fired two shots, hitting him once in the leg. Margie was arrested and pled guilty to a series of assault related crimes. Elsa is now on trial for conspiracy to commit murder and conspiracy to commit assault. The prosecution has called Friedman to testify to the conspiracy related communications that he witnessed between Elsa and Margie in his office, but Elsa has asserted the attorney-client privilege to bar his testimony. What result?

5.   Reflection on the Attorney-Client Privilege

The attorney-client privilege is the oldest of the confidential communication privileges. Still, debate has continued over why the privilege should exist. Such debate has often focused on the costs that the privilege entails. One argument, employing a micro-economic perspective, has been made that the attorney-client privilege has benefits that justify its costs. The following excerpt discusses these and other related matters:

RONALD J. ALLEN, MARK F. GRADY, DANIEL D. POLSBY, AND MICHAEL S. YASHKO, A POSITIVE THEORY OF THE ATTORNEY-CLIENT PRIVILEGE AND THE WORK PRODUCT DOCTRINE

19 J. Legal Stud. 359 (1990)

I.   INTRODUCTION

Protecting the confidentiality of legal information is an odd goal in a judicial system that values openness as highly as ours does. In some litigation settings we make a fetish out of free access to all information. Modern discovery rules can require parties to exchange boxcars of records with one another, and attorneys are under an obligation to disclose cases that run against the arguments that they make. The argument for openness is in principle strong. When there are no surprises at trial, the parties more likely will join issue on the real questions of fact and law — those that properly should determine case outcomes.

Why, then, do the confidentiality doctrines remain? The conventional response quickly runs up against an insoluble dilemma. It accepts the aspirations of modern discovery systems, including the one forbidding counsel from participating in perjurious efforts; it posits costless rules of confidentiality that have no effect on the opponent's ability to obtain information; and then it asserts that these supposedly costless rules nonetheless create incentives for clients to disclose information to counsel.[27] How can this be? If confidentiality rules do not increase the cost of obtaining information once it is in the lawyer's possession, and if the lawyer must rigorously police the client's responses to the opponent to ensure no prevarication or sleight of hand, then the client will have no incentive to disclose unfavorable information to the lawyer.

Because of the tension between the conventional view of the confidentiality rules and their purported consequences, some scholars have recognized that the justifications for the rules are insubstantial,[28] but they have not examined the assumption that confidentiality rules are costless.[29] This failure may be a testament to the strength of the commitment to openness in the legal process. To admit that the rules of confidentiality are costly requires one to recognize that they do indeed constrain openness. If confidentiality rules impose costs, and we assert that they do, the effect is

---

27.   See for example Stephen A. Saltzburg, Corporate and Related Attorney-Client Privilege Claims: A Suggested Approach, 12 Hofstra L. Rev. 279, 283-284 (1984).

28.   It is this recognition that makes explaining such matters as waiver under the privilege so difficult. See, for example, Richard Marcus, The Perils of Privilege: Waiver and the Litigator, 84 Mich. L. Rev. 1605, 1619-1622 (1986).

29.   Yet other scholars, convinced that the rules of confidentiality impose greater costs than they secure benefits, argue for eliminating some or all of the rules. See, for example, Marvin Frankel, Partisan Justice (1980). For a discussion, see Albert Alschuler, The Preservation of a Client's Confidences: One Value Among Many or a Categorical Imperative?, 52 Colo. L. Rev. 349 (1981).

to.increase the cost to the opponent of securing the relevant information, whatever it may be. Because of the confidentiality rules, for example, rather than simply asking the attorney to turn over the entire case file, the opponent must secure that information in other ways, such as deposing the client. That in itself may increase costs, and in addition the client will have the aid of counsel before and at the deposition, which may make the opponent's task of extracting the information more difficult and thus more costly still. After all, merely having to ask two questions instead of one to get the requested information increases costs. Under our theory, however, the costs of confidentiality are not regrettable; rather, they are the conditions that create incentives to disclose to the lawyer: the more costly an opponent's efforts to obtain information disclosed to the lawyer, the less likely the opponent will secure that information, and the greater the corresponding incentive to disclose it to the lawyer. Once the information is in the lawyer's possession, the lawyer may guide the litigation in directions unanticipated by the client, and here lie the benefits of the confidentiality rules that justify their costs.

We develop these points here and propose a positive theory that explains the confidentiality rules. Two doctrines authorize or mandate lawyers to preserve the confidentiality of their clients' legal affairs. The attorney-client privilege exempts from discovery and production at trial confidential communications from client to lawyer, and confidential communications from lawyer to client that may expose a client's confidential communication, if made for the purpose of securing legal advice.[30] The work product doctrine exempts from production material generated by the attorney in anticipation of litigation.[31] These doctrines affect decision making on two margins. The expectation of confidentiality can affect a client's decision concerning how much unfavorable information to divulge to a lawyer and, at a limit, whether to go to a lawyer at all. Without legal protection, a client might otherwise anticipate that divulging information to a lawyer would reduce an opponent's cost of acquiring it. Thus, contrary to the conventional theory of the privilege, one of effects of the privilege must be to raise — or at least not lower — the cost of obtaining useful information once it is in the hands of the attorney. Confidentiality can also affect the amount of information produced by the lawyer. When lawyers cannot produce favorable information without also producing unfavorable information, lack of confidentiality would reduce the amount of favorable information that lawyers would produce.[32] In brief, our argument is that the attorney-client privilege and the work product doctrine offer two perspectives on a larger goal, which is to increase the amount of information available to courts about disputes and to work against the disincentives to the production

---

30. John Henry Wigmore, 4 Evidence §§2285-2292 (1905). We are relying on the 1905 edition of Wigmore because we are more interested in his views than his subsequent compilers. See also Developments in the Law: Privileged Communications, 98 Harv. L. Rev. 1450, 1501 (1985).

31. Hickman v. Taylor, 329 U.S. 495 (1947); Fed. Rule Civil Proc. 26(b)(3).

32. Ethical rules also comprise a form of legally mandated confidentiality. The lawyer's ethical obligations pose the problem of how to prevent the agent from expropriating the principal — the lawyer could threaten to inform on his client and thereby get a payment from him. The other two rules — the attorney-client privilege and the work product doctrine — address a different problem: how much information about legal disputes will clients and lawyers produce. Accordingly, the ethical obligations of lawyers are beyond the scope of this Article. . . .

We also put aside the question of the implications of the privilege for nonlitigation oriented activity. The problem there, again, does not center on the production of legal information. Instead, it centers on providing the optimum incentives to ensure compliance with the law. For a preliminary exploration of that issue, see Ronald J. Allen and Cynthia M. Hazelwood, Preserving the Confidentiality of Internal Corporate Investigations, 12 J. Corp. L. 355 (1987).

of that information which would otherwise exist. In our legal system, lawyers are both conduits of information from their clients to the courts and independent producers of information for the same audience. The attorney-client privilege takes the client's perspective and establishes the level of confidentiality needed to get the client to consult a lawyer and to divulge the optimum amount of information to him. The work product doctrine then takes the attorney's perspective and provides the level of confidentiality needed to induce the attorney to perform the optimal amount of legal investigation. . . .

II. THE ATTORNEY-CLIENT PRIVILEGE AND THE CONTINGENT CLAIM THEORY . . .

A. THEORIES ABOUT THE ATTORNEY-CLIENT THEORY

1. *The Contingent Claim Theory*

In contrast to some contemporary theories of the privilege, ours assumes that it must impose some costs upon the adversary. If a person believes that disclosure of an unfavorable fact to an attorney could reduce the other side's costs to discover it, this belief may deter the party from divulging the fact to his lawyer. And without a privilege, a party may very well believe that disclosure to an attorney would reduce his opponent's cost of discovery. The attorney is a repeat player in the legal system, and so is likely to co-operate with other repeat players. Moreover, the attorney is ethically bound to respect the system's rules. Accordingly, a client reasonably could believe that in the absence of a privilege an attorney would truthfully answer the question: "What has your client told you?" A client left entirely to his own, by contrast, may feel that he has more room to maneuver. Thus, one might expect a client to conclude that, absent a privilege, divulging information to a lawyer will reduce his opponent's costs of discovering information.

The existence of a privilege changes things. The privilege at a minimum does not decrease the adversary's costs in obtaining information, and in fact it may increase them. There is no decrease because the adversary must still obtain information from the client, just as he would have been required to do had the client never consulted an attorney. Costs may increase because the lawyer may give the client guidance in how to respond honestly but craftily to an interrogatory, thus making the adversary's task of obtaining complete information more difficult. In any event, if the privilege does not increase the other side's discovery costs, there is no conceivable reason for it, a point that Kaplow and Shavell have made before us.[33] Moreover, there is evidence suggesting that the privilege does increase discovery costs. The most telling datum may be the continuing existence of attorney-client privilege cases. If opponents could acquire information just as cheaply by alternative means, there would be little reason for them to litigate whether that same information is protected by the privilege. In addition, studies indicate that lawyers often assert after trial that the other side did not acquire all the relevant unfavorable facts. Some of these unfavorable facts must be privileged under the current rules, which is one reason they never see the light.

---

33.   Louis Kaplow and Steven Shavell, Legal Advice About Information to Present in Litigation: Its Effects and Social Desirability, 102 Harv. L. Rev. 565, 570 (1989).

Moreover, notwithstanding the ostensible dedication of the legal system to open discovery, the attorney is not in fact expected to act as a policeman regulating in detail the forthrightness of the client's responses to an opponent. Perjury is a limit, but there is a large gap between absolute candor and perjury. As the activity of the client moves towards the perjurious pole, the chances increase that a court will hold there to be no privilege, but there nonetheless remains a large area within which clients and attorneys may maneuver while blanketed with the protections of the privilege.[34] It is here that the actual incentives created by the privilege become clear, and they entail the possibility that the privilege will detract from, rather than just be neutral with respect to, the objective of openness in the system.

Given that the privilege must entail costs — and the enormous volume of litigation over the privilege could hardly be explained unless it were pretty clear that the privilege did impede full discovery — it is necessary to understand the benefits it provides. Existing theories of the privilege do not answer this question. In fact, two benefits result. First, the privilege facilitates the examination of contingent claims and in so doing furthers the values served by those claims. Second, it reduces perjury in the system as a whole. We discuss these points in turn.

Many legal claims depend on facts that may appear to the lay person as unfavorable to the party asserting the legal claim. For example, a party's defense of contributory negligence often entails the concession of his own negligence. Similarly, for a party to claim that he was incompetent to enter a contract often involves conceding that an agreement was reached.

This contingent structure of the law may be the most visible remnant of the old system of special pleading.[35] Under common law pleading requirements, the parties pleaded against each other until they joined issue on a question of law or fact. Each time one party pleaded, the other would have an opportunity either to demur, or to deny the truth of his opponent's allegations, or to introduce new matter and thus to confess and avoid it.[36] In the earliest days of the common law, unlike our modern era, the two were strict alternatives. The common law's nurturance of special pleas made contingent claims common. Parties could and frequently did confess and avoid the pleas of their opponents. Thus, if a party pleaded the making of a contract, his opponent could specially plead that he was incompetent to contract because of age or some other reason. If a party pleaded that the defendant struck him, his opponent could specially plead that he was acting in self defense. A special plea (confession and avoidance) by the defendant would open the door to further special pleading by the plaintiff, for instance, that the defendant used more force than was necessary to defend himself. Ultimately special pleading made lawsuits depend on narrow issues of

34.   The formal rules of confidentiality actually protect a certain amount of evasion by the attorney. For example, the Model Rules of Professional Conduct, in a Comment to rules on "Candor Toward the Tribunal," state that "An advocate . . . is usually not required to have personal knowledge of matters asserted in [pleadings and other litigation documents], for litigation documents ordinarily present assertions by the client, or by someone on the client's behalf, and not assertions by the lawyer." Rule 3.3, Comment, Representations by a Lawyer [2] (1984). Creating a distinction between the client's and the lawyer's knowledge encourages lawyers to learn of the client's information without fully "knowing" it for purposes of the ethical rules.

35.   See Richard A. Epstein, A Theory of Strict Liability, 2 J. Legal Stud. 151 (1973); Richard A. Epstein, Defenses and Subsequent Pleas in a System of Strict Liability, 3 J. Legal Stud. 165 (1974).

36.   See Thomas Chitty, Treatise on Pleading with Precedents and Forms (13th ed. 1859); James Fitzjames Stephen, A Treatise on the Principles of Pleading in Civil Actions (Tyler ed. 1882); Joseph H. Koffler and Alison Reppy, Common Law Pleading 433-531 (1969); Richard A. Epstein, Pleadings and Presumptions, 40 U. Chi. L. Rev. 556 (1973).

fact or law, a result that seems alien to our civil procedure. Nonetheless, the hierarchical imprint and doctrinal structure both remain.

Our theory proceeds on the assumption that a modern litigant, like his common law ancestors, still has two main strategies for defeating an adverse claim. He can deny the claim in its own terms or defeat it with an affirmative defense, or some similar contingent claim. In the driver-pedestrian example, the driver can deny he was negligent or prove that the pedestrian was contributorily negligent. However, and this is the heart of the matter, a potential client ignorant of the law has one option and not two. He must deny the claim against him in its own terms. Of course if potential clients were always honest, they would never deceitfully deny claims. We assume that individuals will sometimes be dishonest in pursuit of their self-interest. However — and this is the second crucial component of our argument — a legal regime that reduces the costs of information about contingent claims should facilitate their examination and consequently reduce the amount of perjury. Reducing the cost of litigating contingent claims gives potential clients an incentive to substitute away from dishonest denials. Even a client inclined to commit perjury about whether he was in the intersection against the light will have less reason to do so if he can easily learn from his lawyer that the plaintiff's claim can be defeated honestly — by proving that the plaintiff was contributorily negligent in jumping out into the intersection so soon after the light changed, and without looking for opposing traffic.

In sum, by increasing the adversary's costs of obtaining information about communications between lawyers and clients, the privilege facilitates inquiry into legal claims beyond the ken of lay persons. By doing so, the values that underlie contingent claims are furthered, and contingent claims, no less than others, produce real benefits. For instance, if contributory negligence were less often interposed as a defense, it would reduce the incentives of potential victims to use the proper amount of precaution.[37] This praiseworthy result is also accompanied by a decrease in fraud in the system, which occurs each time an individual who otherwise would have committed fraud in litigation is channeled to litigate a truthful contingent claim. Under our theory, then, the ultimate justification for the privilege lies in the improvements in behavior that result from the increased availability of contingent claims.

The foregoing discussion has emphasized how "No, I didn't" and "Yes, but" can be substituting strategies for defendants. What about plaintiffs' claims, though? A plaintiff's original claim may appear to be uncontingent, depending only on facts favorable to it, but even plaintiffs' claims can become contingent when defendants oppose them. For instance, a plaintiff's claim that he lent the defendant money, which the defendant never repaid, begins life in an entirely uncontingent form, as every prima facie showing does. Nonetheless, if the defendant maintains that he was underage at the time he borrowed, the plaintiff's claim changes character, because it can then depend on whether he made the loan so that the defendant could purchase "necessities." Similarly a plaintiff who originally pleads that the defendant was negligent may find that his ultimate claim depends on whether he or the defendant had the last clear chance.

Contingent claims are not strictly affirmative defenses. Suppose that someone has promised that he will put X's first born daughter through college. Making his communication with his lawyer confidential would increase the odds that he would

---

37.   See for example Richard Posner, A Theory of Negligence, 1 J. Legal Stud. 29 (1973); John Prather Brown, Toward An Economic Theory of Liability, 2 J. Legal Stud. 323 (1973); Mark Grady, Common Law Control of Strategic Behavior: Railroad Sparks and the Farmer, 17 J. Legal Stud. 15 (1988).

truthfully claim that there was no consideration and reduce the odds that he would falsely claim that he never said it. So long as there is any set of facts more favorable to the party than those which a typical lay person would think necessary to secure a claim or defense, the contingent claim theory would predict a privilege. To give a different example, a plaintiff in a contracts case may think that all contracts have to be in writing to be enforceable, and thus is willing to assert falsely that a writing has been destroyed in order to win a case in which there was an oral promise in front of a witness. Encouraging the plaintiff to be truthful with the lawyer will lead the lawyer to direct the litigation toward the enforceable oral contract. Similarly, if a plaintiff is unaware of the nature of executory contracts, he may falsely assert reliance; but if he fully discloses to counsel, the litigation can be channeled in the proper direction.

Because both plaintiffs' and defendants' claims are or can become contingent in the litigation process, we would expect that the privilege would apply to both types. If by contrast defendants simply denied claims made against them in precisely the same form originally used by plaintiffs, or if plaintiffs' claims were not or could not become contingent, we would not predict a privilege, even though we would predict that clients would still hire lawyers. . . .

The legal system might, but does not, make confidentiality depend on whether the client's communication actually bore on a denial or a contingent claim. It would be difficult, even after litigation, to sort communications so strictly; so much more while litigation is still in progress. Moreover, a strict privilege would neglect the fact that the critical incentives must exist at a time when the reluctant client is still ill-informed about the law. Thus, if a hypothetical client would assess some nontrivial probability that a communication would be helpful in devising a contingent claim, we would expect that the communication would be privileged (unless the opponent's costs of self-production by other means are very high). If the privilege were narrower, some contingent claims would be lost. Our theory thus predicts a broad privilege, but not an unlimited one. When the lawyer could not possibly use information to develop a contingent claim, and even a relatively ignorant client would know it, our theory predicts that the client's communication would not be privileged. Many cases bear out this hypothesis.

Our theory also predicts that the privilege does not reduce the cost of making a dishonest contingent claim.[38] We will return to this point when we examine the cases, because it is critical to our theory. Nonetheless, even if the privilege did to some extent reduce the cost of dishonest contingent claims, there would still be the question of which effect dominates: whether the privilege prevents more dishonest denials or induces more dishonest contingent claims.

In sum, the real question raised by the attorney-client privilege is virtually the opposite of the one posed by the many scholars who have criticized it. The question is not whether the privilege increases perjury, but whether the increased costs created by the privilege can be justified by the *reduced* perjury that the privilege brings about and the greater number of contingent claims that it allows to be litigated, with their beneficial real-world effects.

This perspective also provides a powerful ordering principle for the privilege. As a result of failing properly to perceive the incentive structure that underlies the

---

38. This prediction is confirmed in cases such as Nix v. Whiteside, [475] U.S. [157] (1986), in which the Supreme Court held that the attorney acted properly in refusing to permit the client to testify falsely about a claim of self-defense.

privilege, traditional theorists such as Wigmore have promulgated a general "absolute" rule followed by a welter of apparently ad hoc case law exceptions. Under our theory, the appropriate question would always remain the same: Would providing a privilege advance the exploration of contingent claims at trial? Cases finding no privilege can best be understood as expressing conclusions to the contrary.[39]

Numerous critics have charged that the attorney-client privilege encourages perjury and reduces the deterrent power of the law. We think these theories are wrong, and examine the best known ones here.

2. *The Morgan Theory*

Edmund Morgan's argument against the privilege was that its only practical consequence is to protect perjurers. Morgan thought that the complexity of modern law cases oblige lay persons to seek legal counsel.[40] Such persons could choose either to reveal all their facts to their lawyer or to suppress some. Called as a witness at the subsequent trial, the client would be positioned thus:

> If he told his lawyer the truth, he must now tell the same thing from the witness box. If he told his lawyer a lie and sticks to it, he will tell the same story at the trial or hearing. If he told his lawyer the truth and now tells a lie, why should he be protected from exposure? Is the privilege retained in order to protect perjurers? How can that either directly or indirectly further the administration of justice?[41]

Morgan's primary error was to use the average case to discredit the marginal one. When the marginal case is considered, it becomes evident that instead of increasing perjury, the attorney-client privilege reduces it. Typically, a client will be motivated to commit perjury when someone has made a claim against him. Even if Morgan was correct that people with legal problems will usually consult lawyers, it does not follow that therefore a client will necessarily disclose to his lawyer all unfavorable facts about himself. On the margin, he will be less likely to do so as the costs associated with disclosure increase. The defendant who is unaware of the defense of contributory negligence is that much less likely to admit his own negligence.

Morgan thought, mistakenly, that the law can reduce perjury only by using sticks; he did not think of carrots. But it makes perfect sense to conceive of confidentiality as a carrot to induce people to refrain from lying; when the attorney-client privilege reduces the cost of contingent claims, it should also reduce the amount of perjury.

---

39.   The prediction of the contingent claim theory that the privilege is best understood as a qualified rather than an absolute bar to discovery is beginning to be explicitly expressed in the cases. See, for example, Greater Newburyport Clamshell Alliance et al. v. Public Service Co. of N.H., 838 F.2d 13, 19 (1st Cir. 1988); In re Grand Jury Proc., Des Moines, Iowa, 568 F.2d 555, 557 (8th Cir. 1977) (opponent's need relevant to a determination of privilege).

40.   Edmund M. Morgan, Forward to the American Law Institute's Model Code of Evidence 25 (1942).

41.   Id. at 26-27. Morgan's theory was foreshadowed by Whiting v. Barney, 30 N.Y. 330, 332 (1864), in which Judge Selden stated that the original purpose of the privilege came from the ancient rule of procedure that parties could not be compelled to testify. As the rules of litigation became more complex, lawyers became necessary, but "as parties were not then obliged to testify in their own cases, and could not be compelled to disclose facts known only to themselves, they would hesitate to employ professional men, and make the necessary disclosures to them, if the facts thus communicated were thus within the reach of their opponent." Id. at 333. Judge Selden then wondered whether legislation placing parties under obligations to testify had removed the reason for the privilege. Id. at 342.

3. *The Bentham-Kaplow-Shavell Theory*

Jeremy Bentham's argument against the attorney-client privilege has been taken up and extended by Professors Louis Kaplow and Steven Shavell. According to Bentham, the attorney-client privilege reduces the deterrent effect of the law by giving lawbreakers the hope that the unfavorable information that they reveal to their attorneys would never be presented against them in a court of law. With his characteristic flair, he wrote,

> "A counselor, solicitor, or attorney, cannot conduct the cause of his client," (it has been observed) "if he is not fully instructed in the circumstances attending it; but the client" (it is added) "could not give the instructions with safety, if the facts confided to his advocate were to be disclosed." Not with safety? So much the better. To what object is the whole system of penal law directed, if it be not that no man shall have it in his power to flatter himself with the hope of safety, in the event of his engaging in the commission of an act which the law, on account of its supposed mischievousness, has thought fit to prohibit? The argument employed as a reason against the compelling such disclosure, is the very argument that pleads in favour of it. . . .
>
> [T]o the man who, having no guilt to disclose, has disclosed none to his lawyer, nothing could be of greater advantage than that this should appear; as it naturally would if the lawyer were subject to examination.[42]

Kaplow and Shavell make the same point, albeit with a much more elaborate model.[43] Kaplow and Shavell posit that lawyers act as filters for the information that triers of fact ultimately receive. When the lawyer is effective, the trier of fact receives less unfavorable information and more favorable information about the client and so is more likely to decide in his favor. According to this theory, the primary effect of the privilege is to reduce the expected sanction that a party faces for a possibly unlawful act. Hence, the privilege ought to be regarded as counterproductive whenever the client is factually liable, excepting only the case where the sanctions for the individual's act are too high. Deterrence would therefore increase, and that would be undesirable only in cases in which the law had established excessive sanctions in the first place. In such a case, the proper reform would be to correct the sanction rather than extend a privilege to suppress evidence.

Although superficially attractive, the Bentham-Kaplow-Shavell theory proves too much. By the same reasoning, for example, people should not be allowed to have lawyers at all. Kaplow and Shavell give no account of the good that the privilege might do, other than acknowledging that the privilege makes it easier for the innocent to escape liability. Under a normative interpretation of their theory, the privilege should be available only to individuals who have been mistakenly (or maliciously) accused of wrongdoing; or, put differently, that people charged with wrongdoing should not be able to consult lawyers unless they are in fact innocent. But of course if we could tell how cases ought to be decided dehors the legal process there would be little reason to have a legal process, or indeed to have lawyers.[44] Kaplow and Shavell's argument fails

---

42.   Jeremy Bentham, 7 The Rationale of Evidence, b. 9, 4, ch. 5 at 474 et seq. (Bowring ed. 1827).

43.   Kaplow and Shavell, supra [note 33]. The basic model employed by Kaplow and Shavell in large measure is an elaboration of a model first proposed by B. Peter Pashigian, Regulation, Preventive Law, and the Duties of Attorneys, 21-25, in William J. Carney, ed., The Changing Role of the Corporate Attorney (1982).

44.   It is unclear precisely of what the Kaplow/Shavell theory of the attorney-client privilege consists. Theories are generally tested by their predictive power. The only prediction that seems to emerge from the

because it ignores the useful role lawyers play in helping clients to develop contingent claims. To recur to our example, the absence of the attorney-client privilege would make some pedestrians a little more eager to step out into traffic without looking, even though the average pedestrian would not be affected. When clients are deterred from asserting contingent claims, because they are reluctant to reveal the bad facts upon which such claims may depend, society loses the benefit of whatever interest the contingent claim is supposed to serve. Kaplow-Shavell miss this effect, as did Bentham before them.

4. The Wigmore Theory

John Henry Wigmore defended the theory of the privilege against Bentham's attack, declaring: "In order to promote freedom of consultation of legal advisers by clients, the apprehension of compelled disclosure by the legal advisers must be removed; and hence the law must prohibit such disclosure by the legal advisers except on the client's consent.[45] Bentham's argument was that the privilege operates as a mere filter that would encourage unlawful acts. As Wigmore pointed out, this argument erroneously assumed that "all the acts and facts on one side have been wholly right and lawful and all of those on the other wholly wrong and unlawful."[46] But in a large proportion of cases, each party would have something to fear. Without a privilege, "a person who has a partly good cause would often be deterred from consultation by virtue of the bad part or of the part that might possibly (to his notion) be bad."[47] Wigmore's idea that the privilege is needed to ensure full disclosure — still the dominant theme in the literature — adumbrates the contingent claim theory by recognizing that the facts and law will not uniformly favor either party. Nevertheless, this idea is too simple to explain the cases. This is particularly evident in the famous Wigmore gloss upon the privilege. According to Wigmore, the conditions for the privilege are:

> Where legal advice of any kind is sought (2) from a professional legal adviser in his capacity as such, (3) the communications relevant to that purpose, (4) made in confidence (5) by the client, (6) are at his instance permanently protected (7) from disclosure by himself or by the legal adviser, (8) except the client waives the protection.[48]

The critical ingredient missing from his exegesis, which has exposed it to the contemporary attack, is any recognition of the relevance of behavioral incentives. Even if each of Wigmore's conditions is met, it would be senseless to provide confidentiality if the privilege would not advance the exploration of contingent claims. Courts have intuited this point, and have often refused to recognize a privilege, even when the Wigmore conditions have clearly been met, where doing so would not advance the exploration of contingent claims. Of course, courts have not formulated the issue in this way, but have simply engrafted upon Wigmore a long list of ad hoc exceptions. The contingent claim theory explains the cases more parsimoniously than Wigmore's ideas do because it focuses explicitly on the relevant incentives, and it gives a more satisfactory account of the beneficial purposes that the privilege seeks to advance.

Kaplow/Shavell theory is that lawyers should only be provided for innocent individuals, if sanctions are set at the appropriate levels. This prediction is falsified by the facts.

45.   Wigmore, supra note [30], §2991, at 3196.
46.   Id. at 3202.
47.   Id.
48.   Wigmore, supra note [30], §2292, at 3204.

5. Rights-Based Theories

Several commentators have proposed that under some circumstances it would be wrong — immoral — for the legal system to force the disclosure of attorney-client communications. David Louisell, for example, has urged that respect for privacy could adequately explain the privilege.[49] Charles Fried, on another tack, has defended the privilege as necessary to allow people in legal scrapes to discover what their rights are.[50] Neither of these theories adequately explains the privilege.

(a) Privacy

Louisell's notion that the privilege is founded on privacy leaves one to ponder: what is privacy founded upon? The legal system has routinely sacrificed the privacy of litigants to the interests of justice. A litigant can be obliged to reveal the most sordid and intimate details of his marriage or even to pull his pants down in front of the jury. Of course one could say that the system respects privacy, not absolutely, but only to the extent that it respects privacy. Surely a useful theory requires a deeper tread.

(b) Adjective Right

According to Fried, the attorney-client privilege is rooted in the sense of personal autonomy that legal systems must respect.[51] "[I]t is immoral for society to limit [a person's] liberty other than according to the rule of law," and is therefore "immoral for society to constrain anyone from discovering what the limits of its power over him are." Similarly, it is "immoral for society to constrain anyone from informing another [about] those limits. . . ."[52] Supposing that certain attorney-client communications would be less likely to occur in the absence of the privilege, Fried must explain why refusing to recognize the privilege ought to count as a morally unacceptable "constraint." Not every change in the world that makes a certain end state more or less likely qualifies as a "constraint." When government subsidizes a certain activity (or refuses to subsidize it) it makes the activity more or less likely to occur without "constraining" that result. But even if denial of the privilege is a constraint, the question of justification must be addressed by more than mere assertion. Again some inquiry into the particular consequences and their desirability is required.[53] . . .

---

49.   Louisell has written:

[T]here are things more important to human liberty than accurate adjudication. One of them is the right to be left by the state unmolested in certain human relations. . . . It is the historic judgment of the common law . . . that whatever handicapping of the adjudicatory process is caused by recognition of the privilege, it is not too great a price to pay for secrecy in certain communicative relations. . . .

David Louisell, Confidentiality, Conformity and Confusion: Privileges in Federal Court Today, 31 Tul. L. Rev. 101, 110 (1956).

50.   Charles Fried, Correspondence, 86 Yale L.J. 573, 586 (1977).

51.   Id. at 586.

52.   Id.

53.   Some commentators have justified the privilege on the grounds that individuals in trouble with the law are in need of a friend. Albert Alschuler, The Preservation of a Client's Confidences: One Value Among Many or a Categorical Imperative?, 52 Colo. L. Rev. 349 (1981). The cases do not support such a theory. See for example U.S. v. Tedder, 801 F.2d 1437 (4th Cir. 1986). Indeed, in Morris v. Slappy, 461 U.S. 1 (1983), the Supreme Court held that the sixth amendment does not guarantee a "meaningful relationship" between attorney and client. Nor are people in trouble with the law the only ones in need of friends. The point, in short, has little explanatory power.

III.   THE WORK PRODUCT DOCTRINE AND THE JOINT PRODUCTION THEORY

A. INTRODUCTION

The work product doctrine has proven to be as puzzling as the attorney-client privilege. The doctrine was first articulated in 1947, in Hickman v. Taylor,[54] where the Supreme Court held that there is a qualified immunity from discovery for attorney work product prepared in anticipation of litigation. The plaintiff had brought suit to recover for the death of a seaman in the sinking of the defendants' tug. The defendants' attorney had interviewed all of the survivors of the sinking and taken statements from them. The plaintiff sought copies of these statements in discovery, and the district court held the attorney in contempt for failing to provide them. The Supreme Court reversed, holding that the statements that the plaintiff sought were protected from discovery as attorney's work product. In so holding, the Court did not rely upon the Federal Rules of Civil Procedure — though after the Hickman case an explicit work product provision was added[55] — but instead found an analogy in the English practice of protecting from discovery "all documents prepared by or for counsel with a view to litigation." Two opinions were filed in the case, that of the Court, authored by Justice Murphy, and a concurring opinion by Justice Jackson (in which Justice Frankfurter joined). The Murphy opinion stressed that the plaintiff's attorney could have acquired similar statements directly from the witnesses themselves, since they were all still alive, and asserted that the purpose of the doctrine is to protect the privacy of the lawyer's thoughts. He worried that, if the plaintiff won, lawyers would be deterred from writing down their thoughts. He also predicted that "Inefficiency, unfairness and sharp practices would inevitably develop in the giving of legal advice and in the preparation of cases for trial," presumably because in the absence of a work product doctrine lawyers would seek other ways to keep the relevant material out of the hands of their opponents.[56] The Jackson approach had a different emphasis: that discovery of work product would be inconsistent with the adversary system and would allow a lawyer to live on "wits borrowed from the adversary."[57] Modern scholars have disagreed on both the merits of the doctrine and its justification.[58] The best explanatory account now available is Judge Easterbrook's. He argues that the work product doctrine operates in much the same way as other rights restricting the use of intellectual property.[59] Just as too few songs would be written if there were no copyrights, too little legal information would be produced in the absence of the work product doc-

---

54.   329 U.S. 495 (1947).

55.   See Fed. Rule Civil Proc. 26.

56.   *Hickman*, 329 U.S. at 511. Murphy wrote: "[T]he general policy against invading the privacy of an attorney's course of preparation is so well recognized and so essential to an orderly working of our system of legal procedure that a burden rests on the one who would invade that privacy to establish adequate reasons to justify production through a subpoena or court order." *Hickman*, 329 U.S. at 512.

57.   Id. at 516. Jackson also worried that a contrary decision would allow witnesses to be impeached with opposing counsel's summaries of their pre-trial statements and that in many cases opposing counsel himself would have to be called as a witness.

58.   As even those who provide the justifications acknowledge. See, for example, Kevin Clermont, Surveying Work Product, 68 Corn. L. Rev. 755 (1983): "As proof of [the] difficulty [of the work product doctrine], I note — without insult by citation — the serious shortcomings of almost all of that commentary."

59.   Frank Easterbrook, Insider Trading, Secret Agents, Evidentiary Privileges, and the Production of Information, 1981 Sup. Ct. Rev. 309. See also Richard Posner, The Economics of Justice 244 (1983) ("the attorney-work product doctrine is, I think, best understood as the use of secrecy to protect the lawyer's (and hence client's) investment in research and analysis of a case").

trine.[60] Although we rely on Easterbrook's argument that the work product doctrine is essentially a property-right system in some ways similar to copyright,[61] we think he missed the essential idea that makes it important for the law to enforce these property rights. Easterbrook suggests that the doctrine protects and nurtures lawyer creativity; we think that it mainly protects and encourages something different but just as important — lawyer perseverance.

B. Theories About the Work Product Doctrine

1. *The Joint Production Theory*

Most litigation activity involves a form of "joint production," whereby the lawyer cannot get information helpful to his side of the case without also producing information helpful to the other side. In order to get helpful information (of which more is preferred to less), he has to take harmful information (of which less is preferred to more). Both a trial lawyer's factual investigations and the resulting legal theorizing are subject to joint production. It is difficult to generate helpful legal theories and useful "facts" without also generating theories and facts more helpful to the other side. In many factual investigations, the same conditions apply. It is often impossible to interview witnesses to find facts helpful to one's own side without discovering facts helpful to the other side.[62] A lawyer will normally want to consider carefully the strongest positions that could be asserted by an opponent, and this may oblige an attorney to think about a case from the opponent's point of view.

As Gordon Tullock has pointed out, the private and social value of the investment in lawyering activity may be significantly out of line with each other.[63] Tullock hypothesized that the net benefits from litigation would often appear higher to private litigants than they would to society, giving private parties an incentive to overinvest. In the context of much of lawyering activity, however, the reverse may be true. If a legal investigation is subject to joint production, it can be quite easy for the expected private value of the information generated to be zero, even when its expected social value is large. In such a case, there would be inadequate private incentive to undertake such investigations even when they are socially valuable. To the extent this is true, the concern is the opposite of Tullock's; it is not that too much will be invested in the resolution of "private" disputes but rather too little. The work product rule is a solution to this problem. Under this doctrine, attorneys are allowed to hold the detrimental results of their joint production investigations in confidence from the other

---

60. See generally Edmund Kitch, The Law and Economics of Rights in Valuable Information, 9 J. Legal Stud. 683 (1980); Edmund Kitch, The Nature and Function of the Patent System, 20 J. L. and Econ. 265 (1977).

61. The first suggestion of this idea in the literature is in Richard Posner, Privacy, Secrecy, and Reputation, 28 Buff. L. Rev. 1, 11 (1979), although the idea is not developed.

62. Wigmore writes, "Men do not gather grapes of thorns, nor figs of thistles; yet they may enter one and the same field and find diverse fruits." Wigmore, supra note [30], §2295, at 3212. He makes little of this insight however.

It should be noted that whether evidence is helpful or not is a function of at least two variables: its absolute value, that is, does it tend to confirm or deny the party's allegations, and its relative value, that is, its value given the evidence already known. Indeed, there are further complexities, for the attorney must make at least two different assessments: 1. what probability range will the jury assign to the evidence; 2. what is the probability that further investigation will turn up information that will affect the probability range the jury would assign. These matters are beyond the scope of the present article.

63. Gordon Tullock, Trial on Trial: The Pure Theory of Legal Procedure 154-158 (1980).

side, thus lowering the private costs of the lawyering effort.[64] This strategy has social costs, however, which we predict are reflected in the rules themselves. The principal one is the duplication of production. An optimal rule of confidentiality would seek to maximize the private incentive to undertake socially valuable joint production investigation subject to the constraint of duplication. Formally stated, a party should be able to suppress disclosure up to the point where the value of the increased information produced is equal to the increased cost of duplicative effort. In addition, under our theory no valuable incentive is lost by requiring a party to disclose information favorable to his case, so we would expect that such information would be discoverable even when it was produced under conditions of joint production. It is coerced disclosure of unfavorable information and ambiguously favorable information (for example, early drafts of legal briefs) that would reduce the private incentive for joint production, so it is here that the courts should be especially protective if they are deciding cases in a way explained by our theory.

We do not claim that courts have adopted the joint production theory in their opinions, but only that this theory gives a better account of their actual results in work product cases than their stated theories. The privacy theory that Murphy emphasized in Hickman is both too broad and too narrow when measured against the subsequent case results that define the doctrine, including the Court's own. Nonetheless, it is probably no accident that the Court found the Hickman facts to be an especially appealing basis for the doctrine. In terms of our theory, the documents that the plaintiff sought were the quintessential result of joint production. When the defendants' attorney interviewed the accident survivors, no one knew the cause of the tug's sinking. Ex ante, the lawyer would have predicted that the interviews would reveal both favorable and unfavorable information about why the tug sank. In this situation, if the defendants' lawyer knew that he would have to disclose to his opponent all the information that he acquired, he would have less incentive to conduct the interviews in the first place. The consequence would be a reduction in the amount and quality of information available at trial.

Indeed, Murphy's opinion may be read to suggest the joint production theory, although one almost needs a microscope to find it. Recall that Murphy predicted that without the doctrine lawyers would not write things down and "inefficiency, unfairness and sharp practices" would result. Perhaps what he meant was that in the absence of the work product doctrine lawyers would still be reluctant to disclose the unfavorable information yielded by their joint production activities. Hence, lawyers would be reluctant to record this unfavorable information, because this would make it more accessible to their opponents. By extension, if lawyers had to constantly cull their records to ensure that they contained nothing unfavorable to their side, it would certainly be inefficient, and for lawyers to suppress unfavorable information (in the absence of the doctrine's protection) may be the sharp practice that Murphy

---

64.   The typical criticism of the work product doctrine is to the effect that lawyers will investigate and prepare their cases even in the absence of the doctrine. See for example Kathleen Waits, Work Product Protection for Witness Statements: Time for Abolition, 1985 Wisc. L. Rev. 305, 331 ("Because preparation increases the chances of a favorable outcome, it is its own reward. This remains true even if some of the preparatory documents must be shared with the other side. We therefore should not fear that abolition of work product would cause parties to abandon all investigative efforts."). This is another lump-up argument. The concern is not whether all investigative efforts will be abandoned but rather with the scale of the efforts that are undertaken. Disincentives to such efforts are likely to reduce their scale.

envisioned. Hence, what the Court wrote in Hickman is consistent with the joint production theory.

2. The Easterbrook Theory

Frank Easterbrook stresses that our legal system relies on the attorney's self-interest to stimulate the production of legal goods or "lawyering." If such goods are to be produced, it will be necessary to allow the producer to profit from the production or otherwise to subsidize the production of such goods. If producers cannot derive any special benefits from their creation, if nonproducers are welcome to use them without having to pay for or contribute to their creation, there is a substantial risk that not enough of the good will be produced. Under Easterbrook's theory, the work product doctrine is analogous to copyright protection. Just as the creative efforts of artists must be protected in order to induce the optimal scale of them, so must be the creative efforts of lawyers.

The copyright theory of the work product doctrine places the wrong stress on the legal production process. The work product doctrine protects not so much legal inspiration, but legal perspiration. Thomas Edison would maintain that the two are related, and so do we. Nonetheless, instead of merely protecting the lawyer's creative inspirations as such, the work product doctrine protects a broader class of information: the results of investigations that can yield both favorable and unfavorable information. Of course, even legal inspiration may be produced under joint production conditions. In simply thinking about the theory of a case, a lawyer may produce insights more helpful to the other side than to his own. In this situation, both our theory and Easterbrook's predict that the unfavorable insight would be protected by the work product doctrine.

The joint production theory includes legal creativity as a subset. When lawyer-produced information involves no legal creativity, we would predict that the work product doctrine would nonetheless protect it if the information is produced under joint conditions. Thus, interviewing witnesses in an accident case certainly involves little legal creativity — indeed, the lawyer may often delegate the task to an investigator for this reason — but the results of the interviews should nonetheless be protected, at least if courts accept the joint production theory. The reason is simple: interviewing witnesses can just as easily yield unfavorable as favorable information.

We have one further disagreement with Judge Easterbrook's analysis. Easterbrook, elaborating on a model first suggested by Tullock, suggests that litigation is often a "fight over spilt milk" where the outcome of the case may have little influence on how the parties behave in the future. If litigation has only a stakes dividing function, it is socially desirable to restrict as much as possible the expenditure of resources resolving the dispute. Thus, any incentives to expend resources on such an effort — such as those created by the work product doctrine — would be, as Tullock points out, socially perverse. The error in this argument is that it overlooks the intimate relationship between accurate stakes dividing and rule enforcement. If cases are not accurately decided, the underlying rules will not be implemented, with a corresponding loss in the deterrent function of those rules. Thus, by offsetting disincentives to the production of legal information, the work product doctrine advances rather than retards the social interest, which explains its persistence in the cases.

In any event, whether the better account of the doctrine is Easterbrook's theory or our own is something that ultimately must be determined by looking at the cases.

NOTES AND QUESTIONS

1. One of the many interesting facets of the attorney-client privilege is that even its friends have serious doubts about it. Among the strongest advocates of the privilege, Dean Wigmore stated:

> [T]he privilege remains an exception to the general duty to disclose. Its benefits are all indirect and speculative; its obstruction is plain and concrete. . . . It is worth preserving for the sake of a general policy, but is nonetheless an obstacle to the investigation of the truth. It ought to be strictly confined within the narrowest possible limits consistent with the logic of its principle. [8 John Henry Wigmore, Evidence §2291, at 554 (1905).]

Similarly, in United States v. Nixon, 418 U.S. 683 (1974), the Supreme Court addressed the scope of privileges generally, specifically referring to the attorney-client privilege:

> [T]he public . . . has a right to every man's evidence, except for those persons protected by a constitutional, common-law, or statutory privilege, [citing precedents]. . . . And, generally, an attorney . . . may not be required to disclose what has been revealed in professional confidence. . . . [P]rivileges against forced disclosure . . . [a]s exceptions to the demand for every man's evidence are not lightly created nor expansively construed, for they are in derogation of the search for truth. [Id. at 709-710.]

Thus, the Supreme Court seems to be in accord with the view that the privilege should be narrowly construed. The reason for this is that the costs of privilege are obvious, while the benefits obscure. Do the contingent claim and joint production theories redress this imbalance? Are they persuasive? Plausible?

2. Recall that the Supreme Court in *Upjohn* took a somewhat different view of the privilege than that expressed in *Nixon*. There the Court said: "Application of the attorney-client privilege to communications such as those involved here, however, puts the adversary in no worse position than if the communication had never taken place. The privilege only protects disclosure of communications; it does not protect disclosure of the underlying facts by those who communicated with the attorney." Is this correct? In large measure it depends on what the baseline is, doesn't it? If the baseline is the cost of securing information from the opposing client, the Court might be right, but why is that the correct baseline? Why isn't it instead the cheapest cost of obtaining the information, which obviously is from the attorney, once the attorney is in possession of the relevant information? Rather than depose the client, the adversary need merely ask the attorney for copies of the attorney's files. So, we are back to the same question: What justifies the increased cost of obtaining the relevant information? In addition, do you believe that putting the information in the hands of the attorney will not increase the adversary's costs of obtaining that information from the client? Isn't it obvious that part of what counsel will do is advise how to answer discovery requests in a legal, but as unhelpful as possible, manner?

Last, don't arguments like the Court's in *Upjohn* suggest that counsel will not engage in behavior that raises the costs of their adversary? But what exactly does that mean? Suppose a client says X to its lawyer, but Y at a deposition. Must the lawyer correct this misimpression? If so, as the conventional arguments for the privilege implicitly suggest, isn't it obvious that the privilege provides no incentive to disclose? Isn't it thus obvious that we do not expect attorneys to police their clients in this fashion? Isn't it thus obvious that one thing that must be explained is why such tactics are tolerated, and that naive statements such as the Court's in *Upjohn* dramatically miss the point of what is going on? Again, how do the contingent claim and joint production theories measure up here?

3. In thinking about the contingent claim theory, remember that its predictions and Wigmore's are largely consistent. The difference lies in Wigmore's need to create numerous ad hoc exceptions. The central argument of the contingent claim theory is that it captures the essence of what the cases do without the need for exceptions.

4. In the Allen et al. article from which the preceding excerpt is taken, the authors proceed to discuss numerous cases in an effort to show that their theories better explain the cases than any of the alternatives. We cannot reproduce the detailed arguments here, but urge you to consult that discussion. To whet your appetite, consider two matters:

(a) The contingent claim theory predicts that the privilege will become qualified rather than absolute. This is a somewhat bold prediction, but in fact cases are beginning to adopt this view. See, e.g., Greater Newburyport Clamshell Alliance v. Public Service Co. of N.H., 838 F.2d 13, 20 (1st Cir. 1988) (in civil damages action, "fairness requires that the privilege holder surrender the privilege to the extent that it will weaken, in a meaningful way, the defendant's ability to defend"); In re Grand Jury Proceedings, Des Moines, Iowa, 568 F.2d 555, 557 (8th Cir. 1977) (opponent's need relevant to a determination of privilege).

(b) Also, consider the following from the same article:

> The theory has a number of other predictions that are borne out by the cases. First, when a client consults a lawyer to perform some function that could not possibly lead to a contingent claim, the client's communications ought not to be privileged. In this type of case, the client's expectation that he would be conveying unfavorable information to the lawyer could not deter him from obtaining the lawyer's advice about a contingent claim, since that is not his purpose. Accordingly, we find in the cases that the privilege does not apply when the attorney has been retained as an agent to procure a loan, when the attorney is asked to witness a deposition, and in similar cases.
>
> Our core proposition is that the purpose of the privilege is to encourage clients to divulge unfavorable information to their attorneys upon which contingent claims might rest. It follows that there is no need for the privilege when a regulatory agency or some other binding authority has obliged the client to hire an attorney and divulge unfavorable information to him. The cases bear out this prediction.
>
> An Eighth Circuit case, Simon v. G.D. Searle & Co., 816 F. 2d 397 (8th Cir. 1987), provides yet another demonstration of the explanatory power of the contingent claim theory. The case involved litigation over Searle's intrauterine contraceptive device. During discovery, Searle refused to turn over certain documents prepared by its risk management department. This department monitors the company's products liability litigation and analyzes its litigation reserves. In doing so, the department utilizes individual case reserves determined by the assessment of the company's legal staff. Relying on various arguments of Wigmore, the court held that the attorney-client privilege did not protect the documents prepared by the risk management department. The court asserted that these documents did not embody communications relevant to obtaining legal advice and that the documents related to business rather than legal matters.
>
> In dissent, Judge Gibson politely noted the court's opinion verged on the incoherent: "Only by concluding that Searle is in the business of litigation can the court convert these

litigation-oriented documents into business planning documents." Judge Gibson's lament is correct, but so too is the majority's result. No contingent claim could conceivably rest upon the information collected and utilized by the risk management department and the company's lawyers. The result reached, then, is perfectly in accord with the predictions of the contingent claim theory, even though, as Judge Gibson rightly says, the court's opinion is virtual nonsense if analyzed from the perspective of the conventional explanations of the privilege. [Allen et al. supra, 19 J. Legal Stud. at 382-383.]

5. If Allen et al. are correct, and the work-product doctrine protects and encourages lawyer perseverance, how expansively should the doctrine be interpreted? While the doctrine only protects documents that are prepared "in anticipation of litigation," courts are divided as to the proper definition of the term. In a recent case heard en banc by the First Circuit, the court found that notes and memoranda drafted by in-house tax attorneys were not protected by the doctrine. The majority believed the documents were independently required by the IRS and would not be used in litigation, thus denying protection. The dissent, pointing out that the documents would not have been prepared if litigation was not anticipated, vigorously argued that the documents should have been protected. See United States v. Textron, 577 F.3d 21 (1st Cir. 2009), *petition for cert. filed*, 2009 WL 5115221 (U.S. Dec. 24, 2009) (No. 09-750). Which side is correct? Given the reason for the work-product doctrine, should dual purpose documents — documents that analyze future litigation possibilities, but are used primarily to make a business or tax decision — be protected? Should "in anticipation of litigation" be interpreted to mean prepared "because of" litigation or prepared for the "primary purpose of" litigation? See also *G.D. Searle & Co*, supra Note 4, finding that the risk management documents were not prepared for purposes of litigation, and thus not protected by the work-product doctrine, but noting that the documents "may be protected from discovery to the extent that they disclose the individual case reserves calculated by Searle's attorneys, [because such] figures reveal the mental impressions, thoughts, and conclusions of an attorney in evaluating a legal claim." Id. at 401.

D. THE MARITAL PRIVILEGES

There are two distinct marital privileges, the marital communications privilege and the marital testimonial privilege: The *marital communications privilege* protects confidential communications between spouses; the *marital testimonial privilege* (usually applicable only in phases of criminal prosecutions) prevents a witness spouse from testifying against the party spouse. A particular jurisdiction may have either or both privileges. Prior to the adoption of the Federal Rules of Evidence, federal courts recognized both privileges. In drafting the Proposed Federal Rules on privilege, the Advisory Committee included only the marital testimonial privilege. Subsequently, the Supreme Court in Trammel v. United States, 445 U.S. 40, 51 (1980), indicated in dictum that it would continue to apply the marital confidential communications privilege as well. *Trammel* is reproduced in subsection 2, infra.

1. The Marital Communications Privilege

a. *Elements of the Privilege and Its Justifications*

The marital communications privilege has three requirements: (1) the privilege extends only to words or acts that are communications to the other spouse, (2) the communication must have been made during a valid marriage, and (3) the communication must have been made with the intent that it remain confidential. See United States v. Marashi, 913 F.2d 724, 729 (9th Cir. 1990). The party asserting the privilege has the burden of proving that disclosure would reveal words or acts "intended as communications." The party also has the burden of proving that the communication was made during a valid marriage. If these two elements are established, then the final element of confidentiality is presumed. See United States v. Hamilton, 19 F.3d 350, 354 (7th Cir. 1994). The party opposing the privilege can overcome this presumption by showing that the communication in question was not intended to be confidential.

Similar to the justifications that have been offered for the attorney-client privilege, two justifications are commonly offered for the marital communication privilege: (1) to encourage open and frank discussions between spouses and (2) regardless of the privilege's encouraging effect, to protect the privacy of intimate spousal communications. Consistent with both these rationales, the marital communications privilege applies to communications that take place during the marriage relationship, and the privilege does not end with the termination of the marriage.

b. *Holder*

Jurisdictions differ as to who holds this privilege. The holder may be the spouses jointly, the communicating spouse, the witness spouse who heard the communication, or the spouse who is also a party. Most federal courts have held that the privilege is held by both spouses and that each can invoke the privilege to prevent the other from testifying about spousal communications. See United States v. 281 Syosset Woodbury Rd., 71 F.3d 1067 (2d Cir. 1995). In criminal cases, some courts have held that the exclusive holder of the privilege is the defendant. See, e.g., United States v. Acker, 52 F.3d 509 (4th Cir. 1995). This permits the defendant to compel the spouse to testify about spousal communications, if such evidence can exculpate the defendant. In cases where both spouses are holders of the privilege, one but not the other may have waived it. Can a nonwaiving witness or party subsequently claim the privilege? The cases have been split on this issue.

c. *Scope of the Privilege*

As with all privileges, the marital communications privilege is limited by judicial interpretation of its requirements.

i. Valid Marriage. The party who asserts the privilege must prove that a valid marriage existed at the time the communication was made. If the parties were separated, the privilege technically still applies, but many courts refuse to uphold the privilege in such circumstances. Some courts adopt a categorical rule rejecting the privilege in such circumstances. United States v. Fulk, 816 F.2d 1202 (7th Cir. 1987). More commonly, courts use a balancing test to determining whether upholding the privilege will serve the purpose of promoting full communication between spouses. In United States v. Roberson, 859 F.2d 1376 (9th Cir. 1988), the court upheld the district court's ruling that the privilege did not apply because the couple was "irreconcilably" separated at the time of their confidential communications. In future cases, the court said, judges should consider whether, at the time of the communication, a divorce action had been filed, as well as other relevant evidence: for example, whether there were statements by either party regarding irreconcilability; or whether there were allegations of gross misconduct or grievances stretching back over a period of years. Such evidence "may distinguish the failed marriage from the occasional disharmony that sometimes accompanies these relationships." Id. at 1380. How well suited do you think courts are to make these kinds of determinations? The *Roberson* court also said that the inquiry should address the interest society has in preserving the confidentiality of marriages generally, not the confidentiality of the couple before the court. Does a categorical rule better achieve this purpose?

For the most part, courts construe the marriage requirement very narrowly. For instance, neither federal nor state courts have extended the protection of the privilege to unmarried opposite-sex couples who cohabitate. United States v. Acker, 52 F.3d 509 (4th Cir. 1995) (finding no valid marriage where the heterosexual couple involved had been living together for 25 years in two states that did not recognize common law marriage). But see In re Grand Jury Proceedings Witness Ms. X, 562 F. Supp. 486 (N.D. Cal. 1983) (stating in dicta that it might be appropriate to allow unmarried opposite-sex partners to invoke the marital communication privilege). The reason for this refusal to recognize unmarried partnerships rests on two grounds. First, courts point to the benefits of a bright-line rule that does not require an inquiry into the details of the relationship. United States v. Acker, 52 F.3d at 515 (discussing the administrative difficulty of determining what relationships would qualify as "de facto" marriages). Second, some courts also have stated that the privilege should not extend to unmarried cohabitants because they have not assumed the responsibilities of marriage. Id.

In the case of same-sex couples, the idea that couples are intentionally avoiding the responsibilities of marriage does not hold true, as until recently such individuals were legally prevented from obtaining valid marriages in every state. However, in a landmark 1999 case, the Supreme Court of Vermont held that excluding same-sex couples from the benefits and protections incident to marriage violated the State Constitution. Baker v. State, 744 A.2d 864, 886 (Vt. 1999). This ruling paved the way for Vermont's statute recognizing same-sex civil unions. Vt. Stat. Ann. tit. 15, §1201 (2002). The statute provides parties to a civil union with "immunity from compelled testimony and the marital communication privilege." Id. at §1204(e)(15). See also N.J. Stat. Ann. §26:8A (West Supp. 2005) (recognizing domestic partnerships between same-sex couples). Massachusetts became the first state to allow same-sex marriage, when the Supreme Judicial Court of Massachusetts held that denying same-sex couples the right to marriage was a violation of the state's constitution. Goodridge v. Dept. of Pub. Health, 798 N.E.2d 941 (Mass. 2003). As Massachusetts now allows same-sex marriage, the marriage communication privileges should be applicable to married same-sex couples in the state. Although a few states have granted marriage benefits to same-sex couples, the majority of states remain opposed to the idea, and several states have even passed constitutional amendments banning same-sex marriage. Nonetheless, the issue of same-sex marriage and the application of the spousal communication privilege to such relationships remain open questions, as a recent decision by the Eighth Circuit highlights. While the district court in Citizens for Equal Protection, Inc. v. Bruning, 368 F. Supp. 2d 980 (D. Neb. 2005), held that the state's ban on same-sex marriage violated equal protection and the First Amendment, the ruling was reversed by the Eighth Circuit. The appeals court held that the ban was rationally related to a legitimate state interest "to encourage heterosexual couples to bear and raise children in committed marriage relationships," and did not violate equal protection or the First Amendment. 455 F.3d 859 (8th Cir. 2006). See Developments in the Law — Privileged Communications, 98 Harv. L. Rev. 1563, 1589 (1985), for argument that same-sex relationships should have the benefit of the "marital" communication privilege.

ii. Confidentiality. It is a near universal rule that all marital communications will be treated as confidential unless the party seeking to introduce the evidence shows that the communication was not intended to be, or should not be, considered confidential. The presence of third persons is an almost certain indication that the requisite intent of confidentiality is lacking. Wolfle v. United States, 291 U.S. 7, 16 (1934) (use of stenographer destroyed the privilege). If a child is old enough to comprehend what is being said, spousal statements made in the presence of the child — at the dinner table, for example, or on a drive in the family automobile — will typically not be privileged. Chamberlain v. State, 348 P.2d 280, 286 (Wyo. 1960). Sometimes courts will find that a third party is constructively present if the spouse made the same communication to a third party on another occasion. People v. Burton, 286 N.E.2d 792, 798 (Ill. Ct. App. 1972). The location in which the communication is made also is probative as to whether the spouse intended a confidential communication. State of Maine v. Smith, 384 A.2d 687, 691 (1978) (finding that communicating in a public location does not necessarily mean that the communication was not confidential; rather, the inquiry should focus on the spouse's reasonable expectation of confidentiality).

iii. What Is a "Communication"? An issue that often arises in cases involving the marital communications privilege is whether conduct — acts and gestures — is protected by the privilege. Courts are required to distinguish between noncommunicative behavior and conduct that has communicative content. For example, testimony from a wife identifying a pair of pants as being the style and size worn by her husband was admitted as involving no communication at all. United States v. Bolzer, 556 F.2d 948 (9th Cir. 1977); similarly, in United States v. Lefkowitz, 618 F.2d 1313 (9th Cir. 1980), testimony concerning the fraudulent nature of documents turned over to the IRS, and the location of other records, was found to be based on the personal observations of the wife, not on any communicative conduct of the husband. Other acts observed by spouses, however, have been found by some courts to be communicative and thus privileged:

> [W]hen the defendant revealed the stolen objects [a gun and camera] to his wife he was imparting a confidence as clearly as if he had told his wife, "I have stolen a gun and a camera." . . . Where as here conduct by a spouse can be reasonably interpreted

as intending to convey a message to the other spouse, a marital communication has occurred. [State v. Smith, 384 A.2d 687, 690 (Me. 1978).]

The "intent to communicate" test as to whether spousal conduct should be privileged replicates the test provided under FRE 801(a)(2) to determine whether conduct is hearsay or not. Some courts, however, adopt a broader test. In People v. Daghita, 299 N.Y. 194, 86 N.E.2d 172 (N.Y. 1949), the court held that it was a violation of the confidential communications privilege to admit a wife's testimony that her husband hid proceeds of a theft under the bed:

> [T]he term communication . . . includes knowledge derived from the observance of disclosive acts done in the presence or view of one spouse . . . because of the confidence existing between them by reason of the marital relation. . . . [The husband] was, in a word, confiding in her the information disclosed by his conduct. [Id. at 198-199.]

Contrast *Daghita* with the holding in United States v. Estes, 793 F.2d 465, 467 (2d Cir. 1986), that "counting, hiding and laundering of the money conveyed no confidential message. . . . Acts do not become privileged communications simply because they are performed in the presence of the actor's spouse." Which do you think is the better result?

d. Exceptions

Like the attorney-client privilege, there is an exception to the marital communications privilege that permits the admission — by a willing spousal witness — of statements made in the course of, or concerning, ongoing criminal activity between the spouses. In *Estes*, the first communications from the husband to the wife that first disclosed his crime to her were privileged; only those communications made after she became an accessory were excepted from the privilege. Id. at 466.

At common law, the privilege did not apply to spousal communications in specific kinds of litigation. Although there is variation from state to state, the privilege is most frequently inapplicable in prosecutions for crimes committed by one spouse against the other or against children of either, and in actions by one spouse against the other, typically divorce. McCormick on Evidence, Vol. 1, §84, 131 (5th ed. 1999).

The Supreme Court of Pennsylvania has held that a defendant's communications to his spouse were not subject to the spousal communication privilege where the statements were intended to create or further marital discord. Commonwealth v. Spetzer, 572 Pa. 17, 813 A.2d 707 (Pa. 2002). In *Spetzer*, the defendant admitted to his wife that he had raped his stepdaughter, detailed plans for future abuse, and attempted to intimidate his wife. 572 Pa. at 39. The court noted that the communications were not of the "marital harmony-inspiring" type envisioned by the common law or the Pennsylvania General Assembly:

> Certainly the persistent and sadistic statements at issue here, concerning a husband's actual and contemplated crimes against his wife and her children, cannot rationally be excluded on the pretext that "considerations of domestic peace and harmony of the marital relation forbid their disclosure." *Seitz*. It would be perverse, indeed, to indulge a fiction of marital harmony to shield statements which prove the declarant spouse's utter contempt for, and abuse of, the marital union. Accordingly, we hold that here, as

in *Seitz*, the challenged communications "did not arise from the confidence existing between the parties, but from the want of it," *id.*, and, as such, the communications were admissible. [*Spetzer*, 572 Pa. at 40.]

PROBLEMS

12.18. Randy Dwayne Hurley was charged and convicted of armed robbery, felony murder, and first degree murder. On appeal, the defendant objects to the trial court's admission of letters containing incriminating information that were written from him to his wife on the ground that the letters should have been protected by the marital confidential communications privilege. Hurley, who had married his wife after the arrest but prior to trial, had written the letters to his wife from jail. At the time of the trial, however, the two were separated. The wife was a willing witness. What result?

12.19. Jim Montague and his sister Mary O'Connell are charged with conspiracy to commit mail fraud and several counts of mail fraud for mishandling reservations of rentals by their property management company and sidetracking money from the owners of the units by not reporting reservations. Jim's wife, Louise, also was an owner but agreed to cooperate with the government and to testify against Jim and Mary. The prosecution is seeking to present as evidence a letter that Louise wrote Jim and left for him on the kitchen counter in their home. The letter discussed Mary's fraudulent activities and stated that Louise wanted Jim to confront Mary. Louise testified that she did not intend the information in the letter to remain private, as she hoped that Jim would communicate it to Mary. Jim and Louise had children residing in the house at the time the letter was left on the kitchen counter. Jim has asserted the spousal communication privilege to prevent the letter, or testimony about its contents, from being used in the trial. Was the communication privileged? If so, can Louise waive the privilege?

12.20. Craig Klaxon is charged with mail fraud and wire fraud for filing a fraudulent insurance claim for a $4,000 silver tray that he listed as having been stolen. Klaxon's wife, Connie, is prepared to testify that she and her husband never owned a silver tray and that she refused, when her husband had asked her (when both Klaxon and the insurance agent were on the phone) to sign the insurance claim. Would this testimony be excluded by the marital communications privilege?

12.21. Chester Newman is being prosecuted for arson, burglary, and theft. An investigation had uncovered that a fire at the Good Times Club was a result of arson and that stereo equipment owned by the club was missing. Defendant's wife, Catherine Newman, is prepared to testify about certain events involving her husband on the night of the fire. Catherine will testify that on the night in question her husband returned home from the Good Times Club with a set of expensive stereo equipment. She then accompanied her husband to sell the stereo equipment to John Palmer, a potential purchaser. Communications concerning the source of the equipment — that it had been "snatched" from the Club — took place during the negotiation and sale of the equipment. Defendant filed a motion to suppress his wife's testimony on the ground that such conversations constituted privileged confidential communications. Should this testimony be admissible over Chester's objection?

12.22. Arlene is suing the Major League Broadcasting Corp. (MLBC) for employment discrimination. She alleges violations of the Equal Pay and Fair Labor Standards Act and of Title VII. MLBC has subpoenaed Arlene's husband, Fred, to give deposition testimony that might involve conversations he had with the plaintiff. Specifically,

MLBC wants to ask Fred about the following: (1) Fred's assistance with his wife's job search following her departure from MLBC; (2) his observation of injuries suffered by his wife in an automobile accident that may bear on injuries allegedly suffered in this case; (3) Fred's conversations with his wife concerning incidents of harassment allegedly occurring at MLBC; (4) miscellaneous areas including his knowledge of Arlene's work habits, what her last evaluation at MLBC was before she lost her job, and her claim against MLBC; and (5) his knowledge of Arlene's confrontation with her supervisor at her new job. Can Fred claim marital communications privilege?

Prior to her husband's deposition, Arlene asserts the marital communications privilege to block his testimony regarding these conversations. Should the court uphold the privilege as to each of the areas MLBC wants to discover?

2.   The Marital Testimonial Privilege

a.   Elements of the Privilege and Its Justifications

The modern justification for the marital testimonial privilege is that it exists to promote harmony in an ongoing marriage relationship; without the privilege, one spouse could be required to testify against the other in a criminal proceeding, bringing disharmony to the marriage. Consistent with this rationale, the privilege is not limited to testimony about confidential communications, and for the privilege to apply the witness and the party must be married at the time the privilege is invoked. See United States v. Bolzer, 556 F.2d 948 (9th Cir. 1977).

In contrast to the marital communications privilege, the marital testimonial privilege generally applies only in criminal actions. In federal courts, it is now well established that the testifying spouse holds the privilege and may waive it in order to testify. The Supreme Court addressed this issue, and the scope of the privilege, in the following case:

TRAMMEL v. UNITED STATES
445 U.S. 40 (1980)

Mr. Chief Justice BURGER delivered the opinion of the Court. . . .

I

On March 10, 1976, petitioner Otis Trammel was indicted with two others, Edwin Lee Roberts and Joseph Freeman, for importing heroin into the United States from Thailand and the Philippine Islands and for conspiracy to import heroin in violation of 21 U.S.C. sec. 952(a), 962(a), and 963. The indictment also named six unindicted co-conspirators, including petitioner's wife Elizabeth Ann Trammel.

According to the indictment, petitioner and his wife flew from the Philippines to California in August 1975, carrying with them a quantity of heroin. Freeman and Roberts assisted them in its distribution. Elizabeth Trammel then traveled to Thailand where she purchased another supply of the drug. On November 3, 1975, with four ounces of heroin on her person, she boarded a plane for the United States. During a routine customs search in Hawaii, she was searched, the heroin was discovered, and she was arrested. After discussions with Drug Enforcement Administration agents, she agreed to cooperate with the Government.

Prior to trial on this indictment, petitioner moved to sever his case from that of Roberts and Freeman. He advised the court that the Government intended to call his wife as an adverse witness and asserted his claim to a privilege to prevent her from testifying against him. At a hearing on the motion, Mrs. Trammel was called as a Government witness under a grant of use immunity. She testified that she and petitioner were married in May 1975 and that they remained married.[65] She explained that her cooperation with the Government was based on assurances that she would be given lenient treatment.[66] She then described, in considerable detail, her role and that of her husband in the heroin distribution conspiracy.

After hearing this testimony, the District Court ruled that Mrs. Trammel could testify in support of the Government's case to any act she observed during the marriage and to any communication "made in the presence of a third person"; however, confidential communications between petitioner and his wife were held to be privileged and inadmissible. The motion to sever was denied.

At trial, Elizabeth Trammel testified within the limits of the court's pretrial ruling; her testimony, as the Government concedes, constituted virtually its entire case against petitioner. He was found guilty on both the substantive and conspiracy charges and sentenced to an indeterminate term of years pursuant to the Federal Youth Corrections Act, 18 U.S.C. sec. 5010(b). . . . [The Court of Appeals affirmed the conviction.]

II

The privilege claimed by petitioner has ancient roots. Writing in 1628, Lord Coke observed that "it hath been resolved by the Justices that a wife cannot be produced either against or for her husband." 1 E. Coke, A Commentarie upon Littleton 6b (1628). See, generally, 8 J. Wigmore, Evidence sec. 2227 (McNaughton rev. 1961). This spousal disqualification sprang from two canons of medieval jurisprudence: first, the rule that an accused was not permitted to testify in his own behalf because of his interest in the proceeding; second, the concept that husband and wife were one, and that since the woman had no recognized separate legal existence, the husband was that one. From those two now long-abandoned doctrines, it followed that what was inadmissible from the lips of the defendant-husband was also inadmissible from his wife.

Despite its medieval origins, this rule of spousal disqualification remained intact in most common-law jurisdictions well into the 19th century. . . . Indeed, it was not until 1933, in Funk v. United States, 290 U.S. 371, that this Court abolished the testimonial disqualification in the federal courts, so as to permit the spouse of a defendant to testify in the defendant's behalf. *Funk*, however, left undisturbed the rule that either

---

65.   In response to the question whether divorce was contemplated, Mrs. Trammel testified that her husband had said that "I would go my way and he would go his."

66.   The Government represents to the Court that Elizabeth Trammel has not been prosecuted for her role in the conspiracy.

spouse could prevent the other from giving adverse testimony. Id., at 373. The rule thus evolved into one of privilege rather than one of absolute disqualification. . . .

The modern justification for this privilege against adverse spousal testimony is its perceived role in fostering the harmony and sanctity of the marriage relationship. Notwithstanding this benign purpose, the rule was sharply criticized. Professor Wigmore termed it "the merest anachronism in legal theory and an indefensible obstruction to truth in practice." 8 Wigmore sec. 2228, at 221. The Committee on Improvements in the Law of Evidence of the American Bar Association called for its abolition. 63 American Bar Association Reports 594-595 (1938). In its place, Wigmore and others suggested a privilege protecting only private marital communications, modeled on the privilege between priest and penitent, attorney and client, and physician and patient. See 8 Wigmore sec. 2332 et seq.[67] . . .

In Hawkins v. United States, 358 U.S. 74 (1958), this Court considered the continued vitality of the privilege against adverse spousal testimony in the federal courts. There the District Court had permitted petitioner's wife, over his objection, to testify against him. With one questioning concurring opinion, the Court held the wife's testimony inadmissible; it took note of the critical comments that the common-law rule had engendered, . . . but chose not to abandon it. Also rejected was the Government's suggestion that the Court modify the privilege by vesting it in the witness-spouse, with freedom to testify or not independent of the defendant's control. The Court viewed this proposed modification as antithetical to the widespread belief, evidenced in the rules then in effect in a majority of the States and in England, "that the law should not force or encourage testimony which might alienate husband and wife, or further inflame existing domestic differences." Id., at 79.

Hawkins, then, left the federal privilege for adverse spousal testimony where it found it, continuing "a rule which bars the testimony of one spouse against the other unless both consent." Id., at 78. . . . However, in so doing, the Court made clear that its decision was not meant to "foreclose whatever changes in the rule may eventually be dictated by 'reason and experience'." [Id.], at 79.

III

. . . The Federal Rules of Evidence acknowledge the authority of the federal courts to continue the evolutionary development of testimonial privileges in federal criminal trials "governed by the principles of the common law as they may be interpreted . . . in the light of reason and experience." Fed. Rule Evid. 501. . . .

Although Rule 501 confirms the authority of the federal courts to reconsider the continued validity of the *Hawkins* rule, the long history of the privilege suggests that it ought not to be casually cast aside. That the privilege is one affecting marriage, home, and family relationships — already subject to much erosion in our day — also counsels caution. At the same time, we cannot escape the reality that the law on occasion adheres to doctrinal concepts long after experience suggests the need for change. . . .

---

67.   This Court recognized just such a confidential marital communications privilege in Wolfle v. United States, 291 U.S. 7 (1934), and in Blau v. United States, 340 U.S. 332 (1951). In neither case, however, did the Court adopt the Wigmore view that the communications privilege be substituted *in place of* the privilege against adverse spousal testimony. The privilege as to confidential marital communications is not at issue in the instant case; accordingly, our holding today does not disturb *Wolfle* and *Blau*.

Since 1958, when *Hawkins* was decided, support for the privilege against adverse spousal testimony has been eroded further. Thirty-one jurisdictions, including Alaska and Hawaii, then allowed an accused a privilege to prevent adverse spousal testimony. . . . The number has now declined to 24. In 1974, the National Conference on Uniform State Laws revised its Uniform Rules of Evidence, but again rejected the *Hawkins* rule in favor of a limited privilege for confidential communications. See Uniform Rules of Evidence, Rule 504. That proposed rule has been enacted in Arkansas, North Dakota, and Oklahoma — each of which in 1958 permitted an accused to exclude adverse spousal testimony.[68] The trend in state law toward divesting the accused of the privilege to bar adverse spousal testimony has special relevance because the laws of marriage and domestic relations are concerns traditionally reserved to the states. . . .

Testimonial exclusionary rules and privileges contravene the fundamental principle that "'the public . . . has a right to every man's evidence.'" United States v. Bryan, 339 U.S. 323, 331 (1950). As such, they must be strictly construed and accepted "only to the very limited extent that permitting a refusal to testify or excluding relevant evidence has a public good transcending the normally predominant principle of utilizing all rational means for ascertaining truth." Elkins v. United States, 364 U.S. 206, 234 (1960) (Frankfurter, J., dissenting). . . . Here we must decide whether the privilege against adverse spousal testimony promotes sufficiently important interests to outweigh the need for probative evidence in the administration of criminal justice.

It is essential to remember that the *Hawkins* privilege is not needed to protect information privately disclosed between husband and wife in the confidence of the marital relationship. . . . Those confidences are privileged under the independent rule protecting confidential marital communications. . . . The *Hawkins* privilege is invoked, not to exclude private marital communications, but rather to exclude evidence of criminal acts and of communications made in the presence of third persons.

No other testimonial privilege sweeps so broadly. The privileges between priest and penitent, attorney and client, and physician and patient limit protection to private communications. These privileges are rooted in the imperative need for confidence and trust. The priest-penitent privilege recognizes the human need to disclose to a spiritual counselor, in total and absolute confidence, what are believed to be flawed acts or thoughts and to receive priestly consolation and guidance in return. The lawyer-client privilege rests on the need for the advocate and counselor to know all that relates to the client's reasons for seeking representation if the professional mission is to be carried out. Similarly, the physician must know all that a patient can articulate in order to identify and to treat disease; barriers to full disclosure would impair diagnosis and treatment.

---

68. In 1965, California took the privilege from the defendant-spouse and vested it in the witness-spouse, accepting a study commission recommendation that the "latter [was] more likely than the former to determine whether or not to claim the privilege on the basis of the probable effect on the marital relationship." See Cal. Evid. Code Ann. sec. 970-973 (West 1966 and Supp. 1979) and 1 California Law Revision Commission, Recommendation and Study relating to The Marital "For and Against" Testimonial Privilege, at F-5 (1956). See also 6 California Law Revision Commission, Tentative Privileges Recommendation — Rule 27.5, pp.243-244 (1964).

Support for the common-law rule has also diminished in England. In 1972, a study group there proposed giving the privilege to the witness-spouse, on the ground that "if [the wife] is willing to give evidence . . . the law would be showing excessive concern for the preservation of marital harmony if it were to say that she must not do so." Criminal Law Revision Committee, Eleventh Report, Evidence (General) 93.

The *Hawkins* rule stands in marked contrast to these three privileges. Its protection is not limited to confidential communications; rather it permits an accused to exclude all adverse spousal testimony. As Jeremy Bentham observed more than a century and a half ago, such a privilege goes far beyond making "every man's house his castle," and permits a person to convert his house into "a den of thieves." 5 Rationale of Judicial Evidence 340 (1827). It "secures, to every man, one safe and unquestionable and ever ready accomplice for every imaginable crime." Id., at 338.

The ancient foundations for so sweeping a privilege have long since disappeared. Nowhere in the common-law world — indeed in any modern society — is a woman regarded as chattel or demeaned by denial of a separate legal identity and the dignity associated with recognition as a whole human being. Chip by chip, over the years those archaic notions have been cast aside so that "[n]o longer is the female destined solely for the home and the rearing of the family, and only the male for the marketplace and the world of ideas." Stanton v. Stanton, 421 U.S. 7, 14-15 (1975).

The contemporary justification for affording an accused such a privilege is also unpersuasive. When one spouse is willing to testify against the other in a criminal proceeding — whatever the motivation — their relationship is almost certainly in disrepair; there is probably little in the way of marital harmony for the privilege to preserve. In these circumstances, a rule of evidence that permits an accused to prevent adverse spousal testimony seems far more likely to frustrate justice than to foster family peace.[69] Indeed, there is reason to believe that vesting the privilege in the accused could actually undermine the marital relationship. For example, in a case such as this, the Government is unlikely to offer a wife immunity and lenient treatment if it knows that her husband can prevent her from giving adverse testimony. If the Government is dissuaded from making such an offer, the privilege can have the untoward effect of permitting one spouse to escape justice at the expense of the other. It hardly seems conducive to the preservation of the marital relation to place a wife in jeopardy solely by virtue of her husband's control over her testimony.

IV

Our consideration of the foundations for the privilege and its history satisfy us that "reason and experience" no longer justify so sweeping a rule as that found acceptable by the Court in *Hawkins*. Accordingly, we conclude that the existing rule should be modified so that the witness-spouse alone has a privilege to refuse to testify adversely; the witness may be neither compelled to testify nor foreclosed from testifying. This modification — vesting the privilege in the witness-spouse — furthers the important public interest in marital harmony without unduly burdening legitimate law enforcement needs.

Here, petitioner's spouse chose to testify against him. That she did so after a grant of immunity and assurances of lenient treatment does not render her testimony involuntary. . . . Accordingly, the District Court and the Court of Appeals were correct in rejecting petitioner's claim of privilege, and the judgment of the Court of Appeals is affirmed.

[The concurring opinion of Justice Stewart is omitted.]

---

69.   It is argued that abolishing the privilege will permit the Government to come between husband and wife, pitting one against the other. That, too, misses the mark. Neither *Hawkins* nor any other privilege prevents the Government from enlisting one spouse to give information concerning the other to aid in the other's apprehension. It is only the spouse's testimony in the courtroom that is prohibited.

NOTES AND QUESTIONS

1. Consider carefully the last footnote in *Trammel*. As the Court acknowledged early in its opinion, Mrs. Trammel was heavily involved in drug trafficking and thus faced the possibility of serious criminal penalties. Thus, the government's offer of immunity to her was a substantial incentive for her to testify against her husband. Perhaps the Trammels' marriage was likely to end regardless of the immunity, and perhaps she would have been willing to testify against her husband in any event. If it were clear that she would have testified without a grant of immunity, however, it seems unlikely that the prosecutor would have offered her immunity. In any event, if we are serious about trying to preserve marital harmony — as recognizing the testimonial privilege suggests we are — why should we formulate the privilege in a way that encourages prosecutors to pressure one spouse into testifying against the other? If the accused spouse could claim the privilege, the government, as the Court recognized, would have no incentive to try to drive a wedge between the husband and wife with an offer of leniency or immunity in cases where the spouses were cohorts in crime or by trying to pit an innocent spouse against the charged spouse. On the other hand, in states where the accused spouse holds the privilege, prosecutors may not be able to compel testimony from the victim spouse in domestic violence cases. Malinda L. Seymore, Isn't It a Crime: Feminist Perspectives on Spousal Immunity and Spousal Violence, 90 Nw. L. Rev. 1032, 1036 (1996).

2. The privilege may not apply if the marriage relationship is no longer viable at the time the testimony is sought. Should courts focus on whether the marriage is in a state of "disrepair" when the testimonial privilege is claimed? In United States v. Brown, 605 F.2d 389 (8th Cir. 1979), the Eighth Circuit reversed its prior approach and premised its rejection of the privilege primarily upon its opinion of the health of the marriage. Noting that the husband and wife had not seen each other for eight months, the court stated that is was "difficult to visualize" how protection of the marital bond "would have required the total exclusion of Mrs. Clincy from the witness stand." Should courts have the discretion to make such judgments? Some don't think so. See United States v. Lilley, 581 F.2d 182 (8th Cir. 1978).

3. Like the marital communications privilege, the testimonial privilege is construed narrowly to prevent fraud. Courts are reluctant to apply the privilege when it appears that the marriage was entered into solely for the purpose of preventing testimony. As stated by the Supreme Court in Lutwak v. United States, 344 U.S. 604, 614-615 (1953):

> When the good faith of the marital relation is pertinent and it is made to appear . . . that the relationship was entered into with no intention of the parties to live together as husband and wife but only for the purpose of using the marriage ceremony in a scheme to defraud, the ostensible spouses are competent to testify against each other.

However, the "sham marriage" doctrine is not easy to apply. See, for example, In re Grand Jury Subpoena, 884 F. Supp. 188 (D. Md. 1995) (holding that, while the marriage may have been primarily intended to prevent adverse testimony from one spouse against the other, there was evidence to suggest the marriage was in fact genuine); and Glover v. State, 816 N.E.2d 1197 (Ind. App. 2004) (refusing to recognize fraudulent marriage exception, as state's statutory scheme docs not permit the exception).

Most federal courts hold that the privilege applies only to testimony by the spouse and does not block admission of out-of court statements when such statements are admissible under the hearsay rule. In United States v. Chapman, 866 F.2d 1326 (11th Cir. 1986), a bank robbery case, the out-of-court statements made by the defendant's spouse were held to be admissible hearsay. The requirement of unavailability was met because the out-of-court declarant was unavailable in that she refused, on the basis of her marital privilege, to give any substantive testimony. The court also held that the out-of-court statements bore sufficient indicia of reliability to be admissible. In holding the marital testimonial privilege to be inapplicable, the court relied on the Supreme Court's statement in *Trammel* that nothing in the law of privileges "prevents the Government from enlisting one spouse to give information concerning the other or to aid in the other's apprehension. It is only the spouse's testimony in the courtroom that is prohibited." Id. at 1333. In United States v. James, 128 F. Supp. 2d 291 (D. Md. 2001), the district court upheld the admissibility of the defendant's wife's call to the 911 operator, stating that her husband had assaulted her, as an excited utterance.

State courts, however, are split on whether the privilege prevents admission of out-of-court statements. The Ohio Supreme Court recently found that a recording between a criminal defendant and his or her spouse is admissible despite the testimonial privilege, because the statute establishing the privilege precludes only "spouse's testimony," not "communication through other means." Ohio v. Perez, 920 N.E.2d 104 (Ohio 2009). Michigan, Minnesota, Nevada, North Dakota, and Arkansas follow the same general approach, while Illinois and North Carolina have extended the privilege to outside recordings.

4. The marital privileges may attach to common-law marriages, provided that the law of the domicile state recognizes them and that the marriage itself is legally valid under state law. See United States v. Lustig, 555 F.2d 737, 747-748 (9th Cir. 1978), (both of the marital privileges were lost because Alaska did not recognize common law marriages).

However, neither federal nor state courts have extended the protection of the privilege to unmarried cohabitants. See, e.g., United States v. Acker, 52 F.3d 509 (4th Cir. 1995) (finding no valid marriage where the heterosexual couple involved had been living together for 25 years in states that do not recognize common law marriage).

5. As with the marital communications privilege, the marital testimonial privilege, as applied to same-sex couples, now exists in a few states. As discussed on page 858, supra, recent developments in state law, such as the creation of same-sex civil unions in Vermont and New York, and the acceptance of same-sex marriage by Massachusetts courts, require that same-sex couples be given the same benefits and privileges as other married couples. However, most states do not recognize same-sex unions of any kind, and thus provide no marital testimonial privileges to such individuals.

6. For further discussion on the marital privileges generally, see Regan, Spousal Privilege and the Meanings of Marriage, 81 Va. L. Rev. 2045 (1995).

b. Exceptions

It is well established that the marital testimonial privilege does not apply when one spouse is prosecuted for a crime against the person or property of the other. Some states extend this exception to charges of crimes committed against family members or cohabitants. For example, Cal. Evid. Code §972(e)(1) (West 1995) provides:

> A married person does not have a privilege under this article in: (e) A criminal proceeding in which one spouse is charged with: (1) A crime against the person or property of the other spouse or of a child, parent, relative, or cohabitant of either, whether committed before or during marriage.

In People v. Bogle, 41 Cal. App. 4th 770, 782 (1995), the court said that "cohabitant" should be interpreted broadly, because "individuals are uniquely vulnerable in their domestic environment." In *Bogle*, the court applied this exception to the privilege and upheld the wife's ability to testify against her husband in his trial for murder of the wealthy couple with whom he lived as a boarder, even though he was not related to them. More commonly, of course, the exception is applied where the defendant is charged with a crime against his spouse or against their children. If the crime is one of domestic violence, then the witness spouse can be compelled to testify despite her assertion of the privilege. But even where this exception exists, "married women [are left] unprotected by the legal system because of very narrow and uninformed views of what constitutes spousal violence." Malinda L. Seymore, Isn't It a Crime: Feminist Perspectives on Spousal Immunity and Spousal Violence, 90 Nw. L. Rev. 1032, 1036 (1996).

There is a split among federal circuits as to whether there is a "joint participants in crime" exception to the testimonial privilege. Some courts require the witness spouse to testify when the spouses have engaged in joint illegal behavior. United States v. Clark, 712 F.2d 299 (7th Cir. 1983). Others still apply the privilege, reasoning that the policy of *Trammel* to protect the marriage is not outweighed and that compelled testimony would "undermine the marriage precisely in the manner that the privilege is designed to prevent." Appeal of Malfitano, 633 F.2d 276, 279 (3d Cir. 1980). See also In re Grand Jury Subpoena United States, 755 F.2d 1022 (2d Cir. 1985), *vacated on other grounds sub nom.* United States v. Koecher, 475 U.S. 133 (1986) ("In light of [the testimonial privilege's] existence since the early days of the common law and of the importance of the interests which the marital privilege serves, we would leave the creation of exceptions to the Supreme Court or to Congress."); United States v. Ramos-Oseguera, 120 F.3d 1028 (9th Cir. 1997) (citing language in *Trammel* to find no exception, despite acknowledging an exception to the marital communication privilege when the communication relates to present or future crimes in which both spouses are participants).

The marital testimonial privilege also does not apply to prosecutions under the Mann Act, where a wife is transported across state lines by her husband for the purpose of prostitution. Wyatt v. United States, 362 U.S. 525, 530 (1960).

KEY POINTS

1. Two privileges relate to the marital relationship. One immunizes confidential communications made during the marriage from disclosure; it applies in civil and criminal cases. The other permits a spouse not to testify (or permits the accused spouse from stopping the other spouse from testifying) against the accused spouse in a criminal case.

2. The confidential communications privilege survives the marriage; the testimonial privilege does not.

3. Neither privilege applies in litigation between the spouses, or involving accusations of criminal acts of one spouse against the other.

PROBLEMS

12.23. Ellen Graves has been subpoenaed to provide a handwriting exemplar and fingerprints to the grand jury, which is investigating the filing of false joint income tax returns by Ms. Graves and her husband. Ms. Graves moves to quash the subpoena on the ground that compliance would violate her privilege not to testify against her husband. What result?

12.24. Ms. Witness's husband is the target of a grand jury investigation into illegal drug trafficking. Ms. Witness has been summoned to appear before the grand jury to testify about her own bank accounts and financial history both before and after they were married. The government's purpose is to determine whether her accounts were used for money laundering from illegal drug sales. Ms. Witness refuses to testify and seeks to invoke the marital testimonial privilege. Should she be compelled to testify? What if the government asserts that since its questions are about her personal financial history, they should be asked, answered, and examined on a question-by-question basis to determine whether the information elicited is "adverse" to the husband?

E.   THE PHYSICIAN-PATIENT AND PSYCHOTHERAPIST-PATIENT PRIVILEGES

Neither the physician-patient privilege nor the psychotherapist-patient privilege existed at common law. The physician-patient privilege was first recognized in the United States by an 1828 New York statute that granted a testimonial privilege to physician-patient communications. In contrast, the psychotherapeutic privileges did not gain approval until the 1950s, when the fields of psychology and psychotherapy were first accorded professional recognition. The traditional justification for both privileges is the standard utilitarian argument that the privilege is necessary to encourage the patient to disclose information for the proper diagnosis and treatment of illness. By protecting the patient from the disclosure of potentially incriminating or liability-related information in court, the privilege helps to ensure the provision of effective medical or therapeutic treatment.

The utilitarian justification for the physician-patient privilege has been roundly criticized on the ground that patients will communicate all information that may aid in proper diagnosis and treatment whether or not a privilege exists. In contrast, the psychotherapist-patient privilege has received approval by both courts and commentators. Advocates argue that some form of protection is necessary in the psychotherapist-patient context because the communications usually involve matters that a patient regards as extremely personal.

We examine these two privileges in the next two subsections.

1. The Physician-Patient Privilege

The Proposed Federal Rules of Evidence did not recognize a physician-patient privilege. The Advisory Committee's Note to Proposed FRE 504 observed:

> While many states have by statute created the [physician-patient] privilege, the exceptions which have been found necessary in order to obtain information required by the public interest or to avoid fraud are so numerous as to leave little if any basis for the privilege. . . . California, for example, excepts cases in which the patient puts his condition in issue, all criminal proceedings, will and similar contests, malpractice cases, and disciplinary proceedings. . . . [Cal. Evid. Code §§990-1007.]

To this should be added the point noted above that the behavioral incentives typically are not needed in this context. For both reasons, most federal courts have rejected a physician-patient privilege. See United States v. Bercier, 848 F.2d 917, 920 (8th Cir. 1988) ("[b]ecause no physician privilege existed at common law . . . federal courts do not recognize the physician-patient privilege" . . . under federal common law); Patterson v. Caterpillar, 70 F.3d 503, 506 (7th Cir. 1995) (stating unequivocally that federal common law does not recognize this privilege).

Over three-quarters of the states have enacted statutes recognizing a physician-patient privilege. Most state statutes refer generally to "physicians" or "physicians or surgeons" to denote the type of health care providers covered by the statute. The Arizona physician-patient privilege statute is typical:

> In a civil action a physician or surgeon shall not, without the consent of his patient . . . be examined as to any communication made by his patient with reference to any physical or mental disease or disorder . . . or as to any such knowledge obtained by personal examination of the patient. [Ariz. Rev. Stat. Ann. sec. 12-2235 (West 2003).]

Some state statutes, however, are more expansive, such as the Minnesota privilege statute which includes "dentists, chiropractors, and registered nurses" within the protection of the privilege. Minn. Stat. Ann. §§595.02(1)(d), (g) (West 2000).

Typically, the patient is the holder, and the privilege covers confidential communications made for the purpose of, or in connection with, obtaining medical assistance or advice. Such information could be obtained through conversation with the patient or through the physician's physical examination. The privilege is also sometimes extended to "[a] record of identity, diagnosis, evaluation, or treatment of a patient by a physician that is created or maintained by a physician." Tex. Occ. Code §159.002(b) (Vernon 2004). Similar to the attorney-client privilege, the facts that a patient has consulted a physician, has been treated by him, and the number and dates of the visits, are not covered by the privilege. In some states, the physician-patient privilege applies only to judicial proceedings and does not prohibit defense counsel from engaging in ex parte communications with plaintiff's physicians. Steinberg v. Jensen, 534 N.W.2d 361, 370 (Wis. 1995).

Waiver occurs in the normal manner through disclosure or putting physical condition into issue in litigation. Carson v. Fine, 867 P.2d 610 (Wash. 1994) (privilege waived as to fact and opinion information held by all physicians when plaintiff filed malpractice action). A patient may expressly waive his privilege by authorizing the release of medical information. A patient may also impliedly waive the privilege by either voluntarily disclosing such medical information to an outside party or through partial disclosure in a judicial proceeding. In Ziegler v. Department of Fire, 426 So. 2d 311, 313 (La. Ct. App. 1983), a patient's failure to assert the privilege in objection to a physician's testimony at trial resulted in a waiver for all later trials.

The presence of third persons may destroy the required confidentiality of a physician-patient communication. However, if the third person is a necessary participant to the consultation, such as a nurse acting under the direction of the physician, the privilege may remain intact. Sims v. Charlotte Liberty Mut. Ins. Co., 125 S.E.2d 326, 331 (N.C. 1962) (records made by "nurses, technicians, and others" may be included under the privilege statute if they are acting under a physician or surgeon).

In addition, state statutes commonly require physicians to report certain information related to public health and safety, such as information regarding child abuse, venereal disease, and gunshot injury. In the absence of the statutes, this information would generally be protected by the privilege. In most instances, the reporting systems expressly prohibit public release of the information obtained.

2.   The Psychotherapist-Patient Privilege

a.   *Jaffee v. Redmond*

In 1996, the U.S. Supreme Court established the psychotherapist-patient privilege under FRE 501 in the case of Jaffee v. Redmond, 518 U.S. 1 (1996). This privilege had been included as Rule 504 in the Proposed Federal Rules of Evidence, and each state has a version of the privilege. The existence of this privilege is thus well established, but it is by no means free from controversy; nor is its scope entirely clear. Our study of this privilege begins with *Jaffee*, which thoroughly canvasses the then-existing law and the relevant policy justifications.

JAFFEE v. REDMOND
518 U.S. 1 (1996)

Justice STEVENS delivered the opinion of the Court.

After a traumatic incident in which she shot and killed a man, a police officer received extensive counseling from a licensed clinical social worker. The question we address is whether statements the officer made to her therapist during the counseling sessions are protected from compelled disclosure in a federal civil action brought by the family of the deceased. Stated otherwise, the question is whether it is appropriate for federal courts to recognize a "psychotherapist privilege" under Rule 501 of the Federal Rules of Evidence.

I

Petitioner is the administrator of the estate of Ricky Allen. Respondents are Mary Lu Redmond, a former police officer, and the Village of Hoffman Estates, Illinois, her employer during the time that she served on the police force. Petitioner commenced this action against respondents after Redmond shot and killed Allen while on patrol duty. On June 27, 1991, Redmond was the first officer to respond to a "fight in progress" call at an apartment complex. As she arrived at the scene, two of Allen's sisters ran toward her squad car, waving their arms and shouting that there had been a stabbing in one of the apartments. Redmond testified at trial that she relayed this information to her dispatcher and requested an ambulance. She then exited her car and walked toward the apartment building. Before Redmond reached the building, several men ran out, one waving a pipe. When the men ignored her order to get on the ground, Redmond drew her service revolver. Two other men then burst out of the building, one, Ricky Allen, chasing the other. According to Redmond, Allen was brandishing a butcher knife and disregarded her repeated commands to drop the weapon. Redmond shot Allen when she believed he was about to stab the man he was chasing. Allen died at the scene. Redmond testified that before other officers arrived to provide support, "people came pouring out of the buildings," and a threatening confrontation between her and the crowd ensued.

Petitioner filed suit in Federal District Court alleging that Redmond had violated Allen's constitutional rights by using excessive force during the encounter at the apartment complex. At trial, petitioner presented testimony from members of Allen's family that conflicted with Redmond's version of the incident in several important respects. They testified, for example, that Redmond drew her gun before exiting her squad car and that Allen was unarmed when he emerged from the apartment building. During pretrial discovery petitioner learned that after the shooting Redmond had participated in about 50 counseling sessions with Karen Beyer, a clinical social worker licensed by the State of Illinois and employed at that time by the Village of Hoffman Estates. Petitioner sought access to Beyer's notes concerning the sessions for use in cross-examining Redmond. Respondents vigorously resisted the discovery. They asserted that the contents of the conversations between Beyer and Redmond were protected against involuntary disclosure by a psychotherapist-patient privilege. The district judge rejected this argument. Neither Beyer nor Redmond, however, complied with his order to disclose the contents of Beyer's notes. At depositions and on the witness stand both either refused to answer certain questions or professed an inability to recall details of their conversations. In his instructions at the end of the trial, the judge advised the jury that the refusal to turn over Beyer's notes had no "legal justification" and that the jury could therefore presume that the contents of the notes would have been unfavorable to respondents. The jury awarded petitioner $45,000 on the federal claim and $500,000 on her state-law claim. The Court of Appeals for the Seventh Circuit reversed and remanded for a new trial. Addressing the issue for the first time, the court concluded that "reason and experience," the touchstones for acceptance of a privilege under Rule 501 of the Federal Rules of Evidence, compelled recognition of a psychotherapist-patient privilege. . . .

The Court of Appeals qualified its recognition of the privilege by stating that it would not apply if "in the interests of justice, the evidentiary need for the disclosure of the contents of a patient's counseling sessions outweighs that patient's privacy interests." . . . [T]he court concluded that the trial court had erred by refusing to afford protection to the confidential communications between Redmond and Beyer.

The United States courts of appeals do not uniformly agree that the federal courts should recognize a psychotherapist privilege under Rule 501.

II

. . . The common-law principles underlying the recognition of testimonial privileges can be stated simply. "'For more than three centuries it has now been recognized as a fundamental maxim that the public . . . has a right to every man's evidence. When we come to examine the various claims of exemption, we start with the primary assumption that there is a general duty to give what testimony one is capable of giving, and that any exemptions which may exist are distinctly exceptional, being so many derogations from a positive general rule.'" United States v. Bryan, 339 U. S. 323, 331 (1950) (quoting 8 J. Wigmore, Evidence §2192, p. 64 (3d ed. 1940)).[70] See also United States v. Nixon, 418 U. S. 683, 709 (1974). Exceptions from the general rule disfavoring testimonial privileges may be justified, however, by a "'public good transcending the normally predominant principle of utilizing all rational means for ascertaining the truth.'" *Trammel*, 445 U.S., at 50.

Guided by these principles, the question we address today is whether a privilege protecting confidential communications between a psychotherapist and her patient "promotes sufficiently important interests to outweigh the need for probative evidence. . . ." Both "reason and experience" persuade us that it does.

III

Like the spousal and attorney-client privileges, the psychotherapist-patient privilege is "rooted in the imperative need for confidence and trust." *Trammel*, 445 U.S., at 51. Treatment by a physician for physical ailments can often proceed successfully on the basis of a physical examination, objective information supplied by the patient, and the results of diagnostic tests. Effective psychotherapy, by contrast, depends upon an atmosphere of confidence and trust in which the patient is willing to make a frank and complete disclosure of facts, emotions, memories, and fears. Because of the sensitive nature of the problems for which individuals consult psychotherapists, disclosure of confidential communications made during counseling sessions may cause embarrassment or disgrace. For this reason, the mere possibility of disclosure may impede development of the confidential relationship necessary for successful treatment.[71] As the Judicial Conference Advisory Committee observed in 1972 when it recommended that Congress recognize a psychotherapist privilege as part of the Proposed Federal Rules of Evidence, a psychiatrist's ability to help her patients:

> "is completely dependent upon [the patients'] willingness and ability to talk freely. This makes it difficult if not impossible for [a psychiatrist] to function without being able to assure . . . patients of confidentiality and, indeed, privileged communication. Where there may be exceptions to this general rule . . . , there is wide agreement that confidentiality is a sine qua non for successful psychiatric treatment." Advisory Committee's Notes to Proposed Rules, 56 F.R.D. 183, 242 (1972) (quoting Group for Advancement

---

70.   The familiar expression "every man's evidence" was a well-known phrase as early as the mid-18th century. Both the Duke of Argyll and Lord Chancellor Hardwicke invoked the maxim during the May 25, 1742, debate in the House of Lords concerning a bill to grant immunity to witnesses who would give evidence against Sir Robert Walpole, first Earl of Orford. 12 T. Hansard, Parliamentary History of England 643, 675, 693, 697 (1812). The bill was defeated soundly. Id., at 711.

71.   See studies and authorities cited in the Brief for American Psychiatric Association et al. as Amici Curiae 14-17, and the Brief for American Psychological Association as Amicus Curiae 12-17.

of Psychiatry, Report No. 45, Confidentiality and Privileged Communication in the Practice of Psychiatry 92 (June 1960)).

By protecting confidential communications between a psychotherapist and her patient from involuntary disclosure, the proposed privilege thus serves important private interests.

Our cases make clear that an asserted privilege must also "serve public ends." . . . The psychotherapist privilege serves the public interest by facilitating the provision of appropriate treatment for individuals suffering the effects of a mental or emotional problem. The mental health of our citizenry, no less than its physical health, is a public good of transcendent importance.[72] In contrast to the significant public and private interests supporting recognition of the privilege, the likely evidentiary benefit that would result from the denial of the privilege is modest. If the privilege were rejected, confidential conversations between psychotherapists and their patients would surely be chilled, particularly when it is obvious that the circumstances that give rise to the need for treatment will probably result in litigation. Without a privilege, much of the desirable evidence to which litigants such as petitioner seek access — for example, admissions against interest by a party — is unlikely to come into being. This unspoken "evidence" will therefore serve no greater truth-seeking function than if it had been spoken and privileged.

That it is appropriate for the federal courts to recognize a psychotherapist privilege under Rule 501 is confirmed by the fact that all 50 States and the District of Columbia have enacted into law some form of psychotherapist privilege. We have previously observed that the policy decisions of the States bear on the question whether federal courts should recognize a new privilege or amend the coverage of an existing one. See *Trammel*, 445 U.S., at 48-50. . . . Because state legislatures are fully aware of the need to protect the integrity of the fact-finding functions of their courts, the existence of a consensus among the States indicates that "reason and experience" support recognition of the privilege. In addition, given the importance of the patient's understanding that her communications with her therapist will not be publicly disclosed, any State's promise of confidentiality would have little value if the patient were aware that the privilege would not be honored in a federal court.[73] Denial of the federal privilege therefore would frustrate the purposes of the state legislation that was enacted to foster these confidential communications.

It is of no consequence that recognition of the privilege in the vast majority of States is the product of legislative action rather than judicial decision. Although common-law rulings may once have been the primary source of new developments in federal privilege law, that is no longer the case. In Funk v. United States, 290 U.S. 371 (1933), we recognized that it is appropriate to treat a consistent body of policy

---

72.   This case amply demonstrates the importance of allowing individuals to receive confidential counseling. Police officers engaged in the dangerous and difficult tasks associated with protecting the safety of our communities not only confront the risk of physical harm but also face stressful circumstances that may give rise to anxiety, depression, fear, or anger. The entire community may suffer if police officers are not able to receive effective counseling and treatment after traumatic incidents, either because trained officers leave the profession prematurely or because those in need of treatment remain on the job.

73.   At the outset of their relationship, the ethical therapist must disclose to the patient "the relevant limits on confidentiality." See American Psychological Association, Ethical Principles of Psychologists and Code of Conduct, Standard 5.01 (Dec. 1992). See also National Federation of Societies for Clinical Social Work, Code of Ethics V(a) (May 1988); American Counseling Association, Code of Ethics and Standards of Practice a.3.a (effective July 1995).

determinations by state legislatures as reflecting both "reason" and "experience." That rule is properly respectful of the States and at the same time reflects the fact that once a state legislature has enacted a privilege there is no longer an opportunity for common-law creation of the protection. . . .[74] The uniform judgment of the States is reinforced by the fact that a psychotherapist privilege was among the nine specific privileges recommended by the Advisory Committee in its proposed privilege rules. . . . In rejecting the proposed draft that had specifically identified each privilege rule and substituting the present more open-ended Rule 501, the Senate Judiciary Committee explicitly stated that its action "should not be understood as disapproving any recognition of a psychiatrist-patient . . . privilege contained in the [proposed] rules." Because we agree with the judgment of the state legislatures and the Advisory Committee that a psychotherapist-patient privilege will serve a "public good transcending the normally predominant principle of utilizing all rational means for ascertaining truth," *Trammel*, 445 U.S., at 50, we hold that confidential communications between a licensed psychotherapist and her patients in the course of diagnosis or treatment are protected from compelled disclosure under Rule 501 of the Federal Rules of Evidence.[75]

IV

All agree that a psychotherapist privilege covers confidential communications made to licensed psychiatrists and psychologists. We have no hesitation in concluding in this case that the federal privilege should also extend to confidential communications made to licensed social workers in the course of psychotherapy. The reasons for recognizing a privilege for treatment by psychiatrists and psychologists apply with equal force to treatment by a clinical social worker such as Karen Beyer.[76] Today, social workers provide a significant amount of mental health treatment. Their clients often include the poor and those of modest means who could not afford the assistance of a psychiatrist or psychologist, but whose counseling sessions serve the same public goals. Perhaps in recognition of these circumstances, the vast majority of States explic-

74. Petitioner acknowledges that all 50 state legislatures favor a psychotherapist privilege. She nevertheless discounts the relevance of the state privilege statutes by pointing to divergence among the States concerning the types of therapy relationships protected and the exceptions recognized. A small number of state statutes, for example, grant the privilege only to psychiatrists and psychologists, while most apply the protection more broadly. Compare Haw. Rules Evid. 504, 504.1 and N.D. Rule Evid. 503 (privilege extends to physicians and psychotherapists), with Ariz. Rev. Stat. Ann. §32-3283 (1992) (privilege covers "behavioral health professionals"); Tex. Rule Civ. Evid. 510(a)(1) (privilege extends to persons "licensed or certified by the State of Texas in the diagnosis, evaluation or treatment of any mental or emotional disorder" or "involved in the treatment or examination of drug abusers"); Utah Rule Evid. 506 (privilege protects confidential communications made to marriage and family therapists, professional counselors, and psychiatric mental health nurse specialists). The range of exceptions recognized by the States is similarly varied. Compare Ark. Code Ann. §17-46-107 (1987) (narrow exceptions); Haw. Rules Evid. 504, 504.1 (same), with Cal. Evid. Code Ann. §§1016-1027 (West 1995) (broad exceptions); R.I. Gen. Laws §5-37.3-4 (1956) (same). These variations in the scope of the protection are too limited to undermine the force of the States' unanimous judgment that some form of psychotherapist privilege is appropriate.

75. Like other testimonial privileges, the patient may of course waive the protection.

76. If petitioner had filed her complaint in an Illinois state court, respondents' claim of privilege would surely have been upheld, at least with respect to the state wrongful death action. An Illinois statute provides that conversations between a therapist and her patients are privileged from compelled disclosure in any civil or criminal proceeding. Ill. Comp. Stat., ch. 740, §110/10 (1994). The term "therapist" is broadly defined to encompass a number of licensed professionals including social workers. Ch. 740, §110/2. Karen Beyer, having satisfied the strict standards for licensure, qualifies as a clinical social worker in Illinois. . . .

itly extend a testimonial privilege to licensed social workers. We therefore agree with the Court of Appeals that "drawing a distinction between the counseling provided by costly psychotherapists and the counseling provided by more readily accessible social workers serves no discernible public purpose." We part company with the Court of Appeals on a separate point. We reject the balancing component of the privilege implemented by that court and a small number of States. Making the promise of confidentiality contingent upon a trial judge's later evaluation of the relative importance of the patient's interest in privacy and the evidentiary need for disclosure would eviscerate the effectiveness of the privilege. As we explained in *Upjohn*, if the purpose of the privilege is to be served, the participants in the confidential conversation "must be able to predict with some degree of certainty whether particular discussions will be protected. An uncertain privilege, or one which purports to be certain but results in widely varying applications by the courts, is little better than no privilege at all." These considerations are all that is necessary for decision of this case. A rule that authorizes the recognition of new privileges on a case-by-case basis makes it appropriate to define the details of new privileges in a like manner. Because this is the first case in which we have recognized a psychotherapist privilege, it is neither necessary nor feasible to delineate its full contours in a way that would "govern all conceivable future questions in this area."[77]

V

The conversations between Officer Redmond and Karen Beyer and the notes taken during their counseling sessions are protected from compelled disclosure under Rule 501 of the Federal Rules of Evidence. The judgment of the Court of Appeals is affirmed.

It is so ordered.

Justice SCALIA, with whom THE CHIEF JUSTICE joins as to Part III, dissenting.

The Court has discussed at some length the benefit that will be purchased by creation of the evidentiary privilege in this case: the encouragement of psychoanalytic counseling. It has not mentioned the purchase price: occasional injustice. That is the cost of every rule which excludes reliable and probative evidence — or at least every one categorical enough to achieve its announced policy objective. In the case of some of these rules, such as the one excluding confessions that have not been properly "Mirandized," see Miranda v. Arizona, 384 U.S. 436 (1966), the victim of the injustice is always the impersonal State or the faceless "public at large." For the rule proposed here, the victim is more likely to be some individual who is prevented from proving a valid claim — or (worse still) prevented from establishing a valid defense. The latter is particularly unpalatable for those who love justice, because it causes the courts of law not merely to let stand a wrong, but to become themselves the instruments of wrong.

In the past, this Court has well understood that the particular value the courts are distinctively charged with preserving — justice — is severely harmed by contravention

---

77. Although it would be premature to speculate about most future developments in the federal psychotherapist privilege, we do not doubt that there are situations in which the privilege must give way, for example, if a serious threat of harm to the patient or to others can be averted only by means of a disclosure by the therapist.

of "the fundamental principle that "the public . . . has a right to every man's evidence."
. . . The Court today ignores this traditional judicial preference for the truth, and ends
up creating a privilege that is new, vast, and ill-defined. I respectfully dissent.

I

The case before us involves confidential communications made by a police officer
to a state-licensed clinical social worker in the course of psychotherapeutic counseling. Before proceeding to a legal analysis of the case, I must observe that the Court
makes its task deceptively simple by the manner in which it proceeds. It begins by
characterizing the issue as "whether it is appropriate for federal courts to recognize
a 'psychotherapist privilege,'" and devotes almost all of its opinion to that question.
Having answered that question (to its satisfaction) in the affirmative, it then devotes
less than a page of text to answering in the affirmative the small remaining question
whether "the federal privilege should also extend to confidential communications
made to licensed social workers in the course of psychotherapy." Of course the pro-
totypical evidentiary privilege analogous to the one asserted here — the lawyer-client
privilege — is not identified by the broad area of advice-giving practiced by the person
to whom the privileged communication is given, but rather by the professional status of that person. Hence, it seems a long step from a lawyer-client privilege to a tax
advisor-client or accountant-client privilege. But if one recharacterizes it as a "legal
advisor" privilege, the extension seems like the most natural thing in the world. That
is the illusion the Court has produced here: It first frames an overly general question
("Should there be a psychotherapist privilege?") that can be answered in the negative only by excluding from protection office consultations with professional psychiatrists (i.e., doctors) and clinical psychologists. And then, having answered that in the
affirmative, it comes to the only question that the facts of this case present ("Should
there be a social worker-client privilege with regard to psychotherapeutic counseling?") with the answer seemingly a foregone conclusion. At that point, to conclude
against the privilege one must subscribe to the difficult proposition, "Yes, there is a
psychotherapist privilege, but not if the psychotherapist is a social worker." Relegating
the question actually posed by this case to an afterthought makes the impossible possible in a number of wonderful ways. For example, it enables the Court to treat the
Proposed Federal Rules of Evidence developed in 1972 by the Judicial Conference
Advisory Committee as strong support for its holding, whereas they in fact counsel
clearly and directly against it. The Committee did indeed recommend a "psychotherapist privilege" of sorts; but more precisely, and more relevantly, it recommended a
privilege for psychotherapy conducted by "a person authorized to practice medicine"
or "a person licensed or certified as a psychologist," Proposed Rule of Evidence 504,
56 F.R.D. 183, 240 (1972), which is to say that it recommended against the privilege
at issue here. That condemnation is obscured, and even converted into an endorsement, by pushing a "psychotherapist privilege" into the center ring. The Proposed
Rule figures prominently in the Court's explanation of why that privilege deserves
recognition, and is ignored in the single page devoted to the sideshow which happens
to be the issue presented for decision.

This is the most egregious and readily explainable example of how the Court's
misdirection of its analysis makes the difficult seem easy; others will become apparent
when I give the social-worker question the fuller consideration it deserves. My initial

point, however, is that the Court's very methodology — giving serious consideration only to the more general, and much easier, question — is in violation of our duty to proceed cautiously when erecting barriers between us and the truth.

II

To say that the Court devotes the bulk of its opinion to the much easier question of psychotherapist-patient privilege is not to say that its answer to that question is convincing. At bottom, the Court's decision to recognize such a privilege is based on its view that "successful [psychotherapeutic] treatment" serves "important private interests" (namely those of patients undergoing psychotherapy) as well as the "public good" of "the mental health of our citizenry." I have no quarrel with these premises. Effective psychotherapy undoubtedly is beneficial to individuals with mental problems, and surely serves some larger social interest in maintaining a mentally stable society. But merely mentioning these values does not answer the critical question: are they of such importance, and is the contribution of psychotherapy to them so distinctive, and is the application of normal evidentiary rules so destructive to psychotherapy, as to justify making our federal courts occasional instruments of injustice? On that central question I find the Court's analysis insufficiently convincing to satisfy the high standard we have set for rules that are in derogation of the search for truth.

When is it, one must wonder, that the psychotherapist came to play such an indispensable role in the maintenance of the citizenry's mental health? For most of history, men and women have worked out their difficulties by talking to, inter alios, parents, siblings, best friends and bartenders — none of whom was awarded a privilege against testifying in court. Ask the average citizen: Would your mental health be more significantly impaired by preventing you from seeing a psychotherapist, or by preventing you from getting advice from your mom? I have little doubt what the answer would be. Yet there is no mother-child privilege. How likely is it that a person will be deterred from seeking psychological counseling, or from being completely truthful in the course of such counseling, because of fear of later disclosure in litigation? And even more pertinent to today's decision, to what extent will the evidentiary privilege reduce that deterrent? The Court does not try to answer the first of these questions; and it cannot possibly have any notion of what the answer is to the second, since that depends entirely upon the scope of the privilege, which the Court amazingly finds it "neither necessary nor feasible to delineate." If, for example, the psychotherapist can give the patient no more assurance than "a court will not be able to make me disclose what you tell me, unless you tell me about a harmful act," I doubt whether there would be much benefit from the privilege at all. That is not a fanciful example, at least with respect to extension of the psychotherapist privilege to social workers.

Even where it is certain that absence of the psychotherapist privilege will inhibit disclosure of the information, it is not clear to me that that is an unacceptable state of affairs. Let us assume the very worst in the circumstances of the present case: that to be truthful about what was troubling her, the police officer who sought counseling would have to confess that she shot without reason, and wounded an innocent man. If (again to assume the worst) such an act constituted the crime of negligent wounding under Illinois law, the officer would of course have the absolute right not to admit that she shot without reason in criminal court. But I see no reason why she should be enabled both not to admit it in criminal court (as a good citizen should), and to get the benefits of psychotherapy by admitting it to a therapist who cannot tell anyone else. And even less reason why she should be enabled to deny her guilt in the criminal trial — or in a civil trial for negligence — while yet obtaining the benefits of psychotherapy by confessing guilt to a social worker who cannot testify. It seems to me entirely fair to say that if she wishes the benefits of telling the truth she must also accept the adverse consequences. To be sure, in most cases the statements to the psychotherapist will be only marginally relevant, and one of the purposes of the privilege (though not one relied upon by the Court) may be simply to spare patients needless intrusion upon their privacy, and to spare psychotherapists needless expenditure of their time in deposition and trial. But surely this can be achieved by means short of excluding even evidence that is of the most direct and conclusive effect. . . .

The Court suggests one last policy justification: since psychotherapist privilege statutes exist in all the States, the failure to recognize a privilege in federal courts "would frustrate the purposes of the state legislation that was enacted to foster these confidential communications." . . . Since, as I shall discuss, state policies regarding the psychotherapist privilege vary considerably from State to State, no uniform federal policy can possibly honor most of them. If furtherance of state policies is the name of the game, rules of privilege in federal courts should vary from State to State, a la *Erie*.

The Court's failure to put forward a convincing justification of its own could perhaps be excused if it were relying upon the unanimous conclusion of state courts in the reasoned development of their common law. It cannot do that, since no State has such a privilege apart from legislation. . . . The Court concedes that there is "divergence among the States concerning the types of therapy relationships protected and the exceptions recognized." To rest a newly announced federal common-law psychotherapist privilege, assertable from this day forward in all federal courts, upon "the States' unanimous judgment that some form of psychotherapist privilege is appropriate," is rather like announcing a new, immediately applicable, federal common law of torts, based upon the States' "unanimous judgment" that some form of tort law is appropriate. In the one case as in the other, the state laws vary to such a degree that the parties and lower federal judges confronted by the new "common law" have barely a clue as to what its content might be.

III

Turning from the general question that was not involved in this case to the specific one that is: The Court's conclusion that a social-worker psychotherapeutic privilege deserves recognition is even less persuasive. In approaching this question, the fact that five of the state legislatures that have seen fit to enact "some form" of psychotherapist privilege have elected not to extend any form of privilege to social workers, ought to give one pause. So should the fact that the Judicial Conference Advisory Committee was similarly discriminating in its conferral of the proposed Rule 504 privilege. The Court, however, has "no hesitation in concluding . . . that the federal privilege should also extend" to social workers — and goes on to prove that by polishing off the reasoned analysis with a topic sentence and two sentences of discussion, as follows (omitting citations and nongermane footnote):

> "The reasons for recognizing a privilege for treatment by psychiatrists and psychologists apply with equal force to treatment by a clinical social worker such as Karen Beyer.

Today, social workers provide a significant amount of mental health treatment. Their clients often include the poor and those of modest means who could not afford the assistance of a psychiatrist or psychologist, but whose counseling sessions serve the same public goals."

So much for the rule that privileges are to be narrowly construed.

Of course this brief analysis — like the earlier, more extensive, discussion of the general psychotherapist privilege — contains no explanation of why the psychotherapy provided by social workers is a public good of such transcendent importance as to be purchased at the price of occasional injustice. Moreover, it considers only the respects in which social workers providing therapeutic services are similar to licensed psychiatrists and psychologists; not a word about the respects in which they are different. A licensed psychiatrist or psychologist is an expert in psychotherapy — and that may suffice (though I think it not so clear that this Court should make the judgment) to justify the use of extraordinary means to encourage counseling with him, as opposed to counseling with one's rabbi, minister, family or friends. One must presume that a social worker does not bring this greatly heightened degree of skill to bear, which is alone a reason for not encouraging that consultation as generously. Does a social worker bring to bear at least a significantly heightened degree of skill — more than a minister or rabbi, for example? I have no idea, and neither does the Court. The social worker in the present case, Karen Beyer, was a "licensed clinical social worker" in Illinois, a job title whose training requirements consist of "master's degree in social work from an approved program," and "3,000 hours of satisfactory, supervised clinical professional experience." . . . But the rule the Court announces today — like the Illinois evidentiary privilege which that rule purports to respect, — is not limited to "licensed clinical social workers," but includes all "licensed social workers." "Licensed social workers" may also provide "mental health services" as described in §20/3(5), so long as it is done under supervision of a licensed clinical social worker. And the training requirement for a "licensed social worker" consists of either (a) "a degree from a graduate program of social work" approved by the State, or (b) "a degree in social work from an undergraduate program" approved by the State, plus "3 years of supervised professional experience." With due respect, it does not seem to me that any of this training is comparable in its rigor (or indeed in the precision of its subject) to the training of the other experts (lawyers) to whom this Court has accorded a privilege, or even of the experts (psychiatrists and psychologists) to whom the Advisory Committee and this Court proposed extension of a privilege in 1972. Of course these are only Illinois' requirements for "social workers." Those of other States, for all we know, may be even less demanding. Indeed, I am not even sure there is a nationally accepted definition of "social worker," as there is of psychiatrist and psychologist. It seems to me quite irresponsible to extend the so-called "psychotherapist privilege" to all licensed social workers, nationwide, without exploring these issues.

Another critical distinction between psychiatrists and psychologists, on the one hand, and social workers, on the other, is that the former professionals, in their consultations with patients, do nothing but psychotherapy. Social workers, on the other hand, interview people for a multitude of reasons. The Illinois definition of "licensed social worker," for example, is as follows:

"Licensed social worker" means a person who holds a license authorizing the practice of social work, which includes social services to individuals, groups or communities in any one or more of the fields of social casework, social group work, community organization for social welfare, social work research, social welfare administration or social work education.

Thus, in applying the "social worker" variant of the "psychotherapist" privilege, it will be necessary to determine whether the information provided to the social worker was provided to him in his capacity as a psychotherapist, or in his capacity as an administrator of social welfare, a community organizer, etc. Worse still, if the privilege is to have its desired effect (and is not to mislead the client), it will presumably be necessary for the social caseworker to advise, as the conversation with his welfare client proceeds, which portions are privileged and which are not.

Having concluded its three sentences of reasoned analysis, the Court then invokes, as it did when considering the psychotherapist privilege, the "experience" of the States — once again an experience I consider irrelevant (if not counter-indicative) because it consists entirely of legislation rather than common-law decision. It says that "the vast majority of States explicitly extend a testimonial privilege to licensed social workers." There are two elements of this impressive statistic, however, that the Court does not reveal.

First — and utterly conclusive of the irrelevance of this supposed consensus to the question before us — the majority of the States that accord a privilege to social workers do not do so as a subpart of a "psychotherapist" privilege. The privilege applies to all confidences imparted to social workers, and not just those provided in the course of psychotherapy. . . .

Second, the Court does not reveal the enormous degree of disagreement among the States as to the scope of the privilege. . . . In Illinois and Wisconsin, the social-worker privilege does not apply when the confidential information pertains to homicide, and in the District of Columbia when it pertains to any crime "inflicting injuries" upon persons. In Missouri, the privilege is suspended as to information that pertains to a criminal act, and in Texas when the information is sought in any criminal prosecution. In Kansas and Oklahoma, the privilege yields when the information pertains to "violations of any law," in Indiana, when it reveals a "serious harmful act," and in Delaware and Idaho, when it pertains to any "harmful act." In Oregon, a state-employed social worker like Karen Beyer loses the privilege where her supervisor determines that her testimony "is necessary in the performance of the duty of the social worker as a public employee." In South Carolina, a social worker is forced to disclose confidences "when required by statutory law or by court order for good cause shown to the extent that the patient's care and treatment or the nature and extent of his mental illness or emotional condition are reasonably at issue in a proceeding." The majority of social-worker-privilege States declare the privilege inapplicable to information relating to child abuse. And the States that do not fall into any of the above categories provide exceptions for commitment proceedings, for proceedings in which the patient relies on his mental or emotional condition as an element of his claim or defense, or for communications made in the course of a court-ordered examination of the mental or emotional condition of the patient.

Thus, although the Court is technically correct that "the vast majority of States explicitly extend a testimonial privilege to licensed social workers," that uniformity exists only at the most superficial level. No State has adopted the privilege without restriction; the nature of the restrictions varies enormously from jurisdiction to jurisdiction; and 10 States, I reiterate, effectively reject the privilege entirely. It is fair to say that there is scant national consensus even as to the propriety of a social-worker psychotherapist privilege, and none whatever as to its appropriate scope. In other words, the state laws to which the Court appeals for support demonstrate most convincingly that adoption of a social-worker psychotherapist privilege is a job for Congress. . . .

The question before us today is not whether there should be an evidentiary privilege for social workers providing therapeutic services. Perhaps there should. But the question before us is whether (1) the need for that privilege is so clear, and (2) the desirable contours of that privilege are so evident, that it is appropriate for this Court to craft it in common-law fashion, under Rule 501. Even if we were writing on a clean slate, I think the answer to that question would be clear. But given our extensive precedent to the effect that new privileges "in derogation of the search for truth" "are not lightly created," United States v. Nixon, 418 U.S., at 710, the answer the Court gives today is inexplicable.

In its consideration of this case, the Court was the beneficiary of no fewer than 14 amicus briefs supporting respondents, most of which came from such organizations as the American Psychiatric Association, the American Psychoanalytic Association, the American Association of State Social Work Boards, the Employee Assistance Professionals Association, Inc., the American Counseling Association, and the National Association of Social Workers. Not a single amicus brief was filed in support of petitioner. That is no surprise. There is no self-interested organization out there devoted to pursuit of the truth in the federal courts. The expectation is, however, that this Court will have that interest prominently — indeed, primarily — in mind. Today we have failed that expectation, and that responsibility. It is no small matter to say that, in some cases, our federal courts will be the tools of injustice rather than unearth the truth where it is available to be found. The common law has identified a few instances where that is tolerable. Perhaps Congress may conclude that it is also tolerable for the purpose of encouraging psychotherapy by social workers. But that conclusion assuredly does not burst upon the mind with such clarity that a judgment in favor of suppressing the truth ought to be pronounced by this honorable Court. I respectfully dissent.

NOTES AND QUESTIONS

1. Who has the better of the argument, the majority or the dissent? Could you have written a more persuasive majority opinion? Could you have responded more effectively to the dissent?

2. One of the concerns is that embarrassing revelations are frequently made in therapeutic sessions, and the Court is certainly correct that the possibility of exposing such matters will be a disincentive to their creation. Still, is the patient's knowledge that there is a privilege necessary to effective mental health counseling? To support the argument of necessity, the majority relied heavily on amicus briefs filed by various organizations that promote psychotherapy. Careful analysis of the studies relied on in these briefs, however, shows that they "do not substantiate the empirical claim that the typical patient is so concerned about the prospect of litigation that the . . . privilege will significantly affect his or her willingness to seek treatment or make necessary revelations to a therapist." Edward Imwinkelried, The Rivalry Between Truth and Privilege: The Weakness of the Supreme Court's Reasoning in Jaffee v. Redmond, 518 U.S. 1 (1996), 49 Hastings L.J. 969, 980 (1998). Should courts require that the utilitarian justification for privileges be empirically valid? How can courts, as opposed to legislatures, obtain empirical data?

3. Is the majority's policy analysis satisfactory? Reflect back on the contingent claim theory about the attorney-client privilege. Like there, isn't the question here the marginal gains and losses under two different regimes: one with a privilege and one without a privilege? And if that data is not available in some form (including judicial experience), should a court create a privilege? In this respect, is the legislative process fundamentally different from the judicial process?

4. The majority purports to establish an absolute privilege in *Jaffee*; that is, it rejected the balancing component that the Seventh Circuit Court of Appeals believed necessary to evaluate the patient's interest in autonomy and privacy versus the evidentiary need for disclosure. Yet, in its final footnote, the majority acknowledges that "there are situations in which the privilege must give way" and cites as an example the situation in which disclosure is the only means to protect the patient or others from the serious threat of harm by the patient. See page 877 n.77, supra. We discuss below the circumstances under which federal courts have found that the privilege must "give way." See generally Christopher B. Mueller, The Federal Psychotherapist-Patient Privilege After *Jaffee*: Truth and Other Values in a Therapeutic Age, 49 Hastings L.J. 945 (1998).

b.   Scope of the Privilege After Jaffee

In the years since *Jaffee* was decided, the scope of the psychotherapist privilege has been tested in federal litigation. The privilege has developed on a case-by-case basis, since the Court did not spell out its full contours.

i.   Who Is a Psychotherapist?   The psychotherapist-patient privilege in Proposed FRE 504 includes "a person authorized to practice medicine" — in other words, all physicians — and "a person licensed or certified as a psychologist" within the definition of psychotherapist. Since *Jaffee*, courts have also included licensed social workers and other mental health workers within the privilege. For example, rape crisis counselors who are not licensed but who have undergone special training and work under the direct control and supervision of social workers or psychotherapists were included in United States v. Lowe, 948 F. Supp. 97, 99 (D. Mass. 1996), citing the fact that a majority of states have a privilege for rape counseling communications. But see Jane Student 1 v. Williams, 206 F.R.D. 306 (S.D. Ala. 2002) (holding that the psychotherapist-patient privilege does not extend to unlicensed professional counselors).

In Oleszko v. State Compensation Insurance Fund, 243 F.3d 1154, 1158 (9th Cir. 2001), the Ninth Circuit extended the privilege to unlicensed counselors employed by an Employee Assistance Program, which provides worksite assistance, including mental health counseling. The court cited *Jaffee* in noting:

> [T]he provision of mental health services has significantly changed in the last quarter century. EAPs embody what may be viewed as a team approach to providing mental health services. Thus, although EAP personnel do not engage in psychotherapy themselves, they serve as a primary link between the troubled employee and psychotherapeutic treatment. [Id.]

Some courts are also willing to consider licensed marriage, family and child counselors as within the privilege. Speaker v. County of San Bernadino, 82 F. Supp.

2d 1105, 1109 (C.D. Cal. 2000). In Carman v. McDonnell Douglas Corp., 114 F.3d 790, 793 (8th Cir. 1997), however, the Eighth Circuit held that communications to an ombudsman employed to resolve workplace disputes without litigation were not protected by the psychotherapist privilege because the assistance was limited to dealing with workplace disputes, not mental health problems.

   ii.   Communications.   Communications falling within the privilege must be made in the course of or for the purpose of obtaining mental health services. For example, Proposed FRE 504 limits the psychotherapist-patient privilege to confidential communications "made [by the patient] for the purpose of diagnosis or treatment of his mental or emotional condition, including drug addiction." See Doe v. Ensey, 220 F.R.D. 422, 425 (M.D. Pa. 2004). California's psychotherapist-patient privilege is unusual in that it extends the privilege to communications made "for the purpose of scientific research on mental or emotional problems." Cal. Evid. Code §1011. Information that does not reveal the client's confidential communications — such as identity of therapist and client, occurrence of psychotherapy and dates of treatment — are not privileged. See, e.g., Vinson v. Humana, Inc., 190 F.R.D. 624, 626-627 (M.D. Fla. 1999); and Merrill v. Waffle House, Inc., 2005 WL 928602 (N.D. Tex. Feb. 5, 2005).

   In situations where employees, such as police officers, are required to undergo psychological evaluations regarding fitness for duty and the results are disclosed to employers, it has been held that a psychotherapist privilege is not established because there is no treatment involved and there is no expectation of confidentiality. Kemper v. Gray, 182 F.R.D. 597, 599 (E.D. Mo. 1998). But where only a general conclusion is disclosed to the employer and the employee has been assured of confidentiality, the privilege has attached and prevents disclosure. See, e.g., Caver v. City of Trenton, 192 F.R.D. 154, 162 (D.N.J. 2000).

   iii.   Waiver.   As with the physician-patient privilege, the patient is the holder of the psychotherapist-patient privilege. Thus, the privilege may be waived only by the patient or an authorized representative on the patient's behalf. Parents can assert or waive the privilege on behalf of their minor children. But courts may find that invocation of the privilege may not be in the "best interests" of the child, for example in custody disputes where there are allegations of child abuse. Ellison v. Ellison, 919 P.2d 1, 8 (Okla. 1996).

   Taking a broad view of waiver, some courts have held that a patient impliedly waives the psychotherapist privilege by raising the patient's mental condition as an element of the claim or defense; generally, by making any claims for mental and emotional distress. See, e.g., Maday v. Public Libraries of Saginaw, 480 F.3d 815 (6th Cir. 2007) ("[W]hen [plaintiff] put her emotional state at issue in the case, she waived [the psychotherapist-patient privilege], and the records may come in, subject to what appears to have been reasonable Rule 403 balancing by the district judge."); Doe v. Oberweis Dairy, 456 F.3d 704 (7th Cir. 2006) (seeking damages for emotional distress places psychological state in issue and waives privilege); Schoffstall v. Henderson, 223 F.3d 818 (8th Cir. 2000) (same); Utah v. Worthen, 222 P.3d 1144 (Utah 2009) (hatred toward defendant was emotional condition, represented an element of defense's theory, and triggered exception in psychotherapist-patient privilege). A more restrictive view of waiver, however, has been taken by other courts. This narrower view requires that the privilege holder make an affirmative use of the privileged material by calling the therapist as a witness or putting specific communications at issue. See, e.g., Fitzgerald

v. Cassil, 216 F.R.D. 632 (N.D. Cal. 2003) (arguing that a narrow exception is more consistent with *Jaffee* and a broad approach is not necessary to achieve fairness for defendant); Vanderbilt v. Town of Chilmark, 174 F.R.D. 225, 230 (D. Mass. 1997) (noting that privilege is waived when substance of privileged communication is used by the party invoking the privilege); United States v. Sturman, 1998 U.S. Dist. LEXIS 3488 (S.D.N.Y. Mar. 9, 1998) (a criminal defendant's intention to use psychiatric testimony to negate the government's proof of specific intent does not waive the privilege prior to trial; defendant bears no burden on the issue of intent and does not put his mental condition "at issue" until he uses the testimony at trial).

A useful summary of this split in federal court opinions is contained in Fritsch v. City of Chula Vista, 187 F.R.D. 614 (S.D. Cal. 1999). The Supreme Court in *Jaffee* gave no guidance on this point. Indeed, the Supreme Court rejected the balancing test proposed by the Seventh Circuit Court of Appeals, but acknowledged that there would be circumstances in which the privilege must give way. See page 877, n.77, supra. Thus, both sides of this split of opinion are able to rely on policies discussed in *Jaffee* to justify their positions. The narrow view, requiring what amounts to actual waiver, protects the patient's imperative need for confidentiality and prevents post hoc balancing of the importance of privacy versus the evidentiary need for disclosure. Id. at 630. The broader view has been justified by the need for a fair discovery process when a patient "desires the jury to compensate for damage to her emotional condition . . . defendant is entitled to explore the circumstance [that] caused that injury." Id. at 569. See generally Melissa Nelkin, The Limits of the Privilege: The Developing Scope of Federal Psychotherapist-Patient Privilege Law, 20 Rev. Litig. 1 (2000).

Many decisions regarding the waiver of the privilege are made during the discovery phase of trial when one party seeks to compel production of medical records or to depose a psychotherapist. Some courts require the party seeking discovery to show cause why the "intrusion into the therapeutic relationship is the only possible means to obtain relevant information" and to narrowly tailor discovery requests to information directly relevant to the lawsuit. Vasconcellos v. Cybex International, Inc., 962 F. Supp. 701, 709 (D. Md. 1997).

Due to the prevalence of group counseling sessions, several courts have held that the psychotherapist-patient privilege is not waived when statements are made by patients in the presence of others in the group. The rationale is that the joint therapy comprises part of the treatment. See, e.g., State v. Andring, 342 N.W.2d 128, 133-134 (Minn. 1984). However, the statements are not privileged in joint litigation between the patients. Redding v. Virginia Mason Medical Ctr., 878 P.2d 483 (Wash. Ct. App. 1994).

c. *Exceptions to the Privilege*

Although the Court in *Jaffee* rejected an outright balancing test, there are several exceptions to the privilege where the need for probative evidence is great or the interests underlying the privilege are nonexistent.

i. Constitutional Limits.   Doe v. Diamond, 964 F.2d 1325 (2d Cir. 1992), decided prior to *Jaffee*, involved a criminal defendant's request for the psychiatric records of a victim, Doe, who had initiated the criminal charges, and who would be a witness against him. Consider the following excerpt from the opinion, and pay close attention to the significance of the confrontation clause to the analysis. The confrontation clause may often mandate discovery regardless of the parameters of a privilege:

> Although appellant's [Doe's] psychiatric files do contain material that squarely implicates his privacy interests, the balance in this case weighs overwhelmingly in favor of allowing an inquiry into his history of mental illness. Appellant is not only the person who initiated the criminal investigation against Diamond [the criminal defendant] but also a witness whose credibility will be the central issue at trial. He has a long history of emotional illness, and there is expert psychiatric opinion in the record that this history is relevant to his credibility. That opinion includes the observation that appellant's "interpretation of reality" might have been affected during times in which he was undergoing psychiatric treatment, as he was at the time of the events about which he is to testify. We agree with Chief Judge Platt that a preclusion of any inquiry into appellant's psychiatric history would violate the Confrontation Clause and vitiate any resulting conviction of Diamond.
>
> Appellant poses for us various hypotheticals concerning the disclosure of communications made to psychotherapists thirty years ago, destruction of the privacy interests of a third party, and the violation of the professional obligations of the psychotherapists involved. These matters are not before us, however. The questions that appellant declined to answer concerned times at which he received psychiatric treatment and the names of particular psychotherapists. They also concerned his refusal to consent to those psychotherapists being interviewed by counsel under the protective order. The hearing held by Chief Judge Platt was in camera, and appellant's answers to the questions and counsel's interviews of appellant's psychotherapists would have been subject to a protective order sufficient to prevent public revelation of confidential matters. His answers to the questions and consenting to the interests as an important factor to be weighed in the interviews would not, therefore, have resulted in the public disclosure of confidential matters. [Id. at 1329.]

In cases since *Jaffee*, courts have adhered to the reasoning in *Doe* and have held that a criminal defendant's Sixth Amendment rights to information that establishes an element of defense or impeaches a witness can justify discovery of a victim and/or witness's mental health records. United States v. Alperin, 128 F. Supp. 2d 1251, 1254 (N.D. Cal. 2001). But see United States v. Doyle, 1 F. Supp. 2d 1187 (D. Or. 1999) (victim's mental health records, relevant only to sentencing enhancement, need not be disclosed to already convicted defendant).

The psychotherapist-patient privilege can arise in criminal cases involving alleged child sexual abuse. If the child accuser confides his or her memories of abuse to a psychiatrist, the child may then assert the privilege when the accused attempts to discover the communications. See, e.g., Goldsmith v. State, 651 A.2d 866 (Md. 1995); State v. Speese, 545 N.W.2d 510 (Wis. 1996). The majority of courts hold that the defendant can have access to the psychiatric records of his accuser if the psychiatrist testifies at trial. Other concerns raised by these cases are whether courts should appoint counsel or guardians ad litem to assist minors in determining whether to assert or waive the privilege, whether the privilege should apply during discovery, and whether a person's refusal to waive the privilege should preclude that person from testifying at trial. Id. at 517.

ii.   Compelled Disclosures.   Statutory law typically abolishes the psychotherapist-patient privilege in proceedings to hospitalize the patient for mental illness, if the psychotherapist has determined that the patient is in need of hospitalization. And if a judge orders an examination of the mental or emotional condition of the patient, communications made in the course of the examination are not privileged with respect to the particular purpose for which the examination is ordered unless the judge orders otherwise. In many states, mental health professionals are also required to report their reasonable suspicions that children whom they treat have been abused, and some states create an exception to the privilege where child abuse is known or suspected. Note, Overriding the Psychologist-Patient Privilege in Child Custody Disputes: Are Anyone's Best Interests Being Served?, 68 UMKC L. Rev. 169 (1999) (critiquing the application of this exception in divorce and child custody cases where the use of psychotherapy records become a tool between battling parents).

iii. **Dangerous Patient.** In its concluding footnote, the majority opinion in *Jaffee* noted that "there are situations in which the privilege must give way, for example, if a serious threat of harm to the patient or to others can be averted only by means of a disclosure by the therapist." See page 877 n.77, supra. This footnote has generated some case law on whether threats made during therapy sessions can form the basis of prosecutions for violation of federal laws that define such threats as criminal conduct. In such instances, the therapist's testimony about the threats — in violation of the psychotherapist privilege — is the only evidence that the prosecutor has. Thus, the government has sought judicial recognition of a so-called dangerous patient exception. So far, federal courts have split on the question of whether the exception exists. The Sixth and Ninth Circuits have declined to adopt the dangerous patient exception. See United States v. Hayes, 227 F.3d 578 (6th Cir. 2000); and United States v. Chase, 340 F.3d 978 (9th Cir. 2003). Recognizing that psychotherapists have professional and ethical duties to protect potential victims when threats are made during therapy, the court in *Hayes* stated that these duties "may require, among other things, disclosure to third parties or testimony at an involuntary hospitalization proceeding." *Hayes*, 227 F.3d at 585. The court held, however, that "compliance with the professional duty to protect does not imply a duty to testify against a patient in criminal proceedings or in civil proceedings other than directly related to the patient's involuntary hospitalization, and such testimony is privileged and inadmissible if a patient properly asserts the psychotherapist/patient privilege." Id. The court reasoned that once the appropriate warning had been given, or proceedings initiated, it would be highly unlikely that the therapist's testimony in a criminal prosecution would be the only means of avoiding harm to others, which was the standard adverted to in *Jaffee*. Thus, the court in *Hayes* concluded the *Jaffee* footnote was no more than an aside

> to the effect that the federal psychotherapist/patient privilege will not operate to impede a psychotherapist's compliance with the professional duty to protect identifiable third parties from serious threats of harm. We think the *Jaffee* footnote was referring to the fact that psychotherapists will sometimes need to testify in court proceedings, such as those for the involuntary commitment of a patient, to comply with their "duty to protect" the patient or identifiable third parties. [Id. at 584.]

However, the Fifth Circuit recently found, in United States v. Auster, 517 F.3d 312, 319 (5th Cir. 2008), that when the psychiatrist had warned the patient that his professional duties would require him to report any threatening communication, the "patient [had] no reasonable expectation of confidentiality." While the court implied that an expectation that a psychiatrist will reveal threatening communication would generally lead "the cost-benefit scales [to] favor disclosure," it held that any threatening communication made with *actual knowledge* that it would not be kept confidential was not privileged. Id. In United States v. Glass, 133 F.3d 1356, 1360 (10th Cir. 1998), the Tenth Circuit stated that if the threat of harm was serious and could be averted only by disclosure, compelled disclosure may be warranted. For further discussion, see George C. Harris, The Dangerous Patient Exception to the Psychotherapist-Patient Privilege: The *Tarasoff* Duty and the *Jaffee* Footnote, 74 Wash. L. Rev. 33 (1999).

iv. Crime-Fraud Exception. In re Grand Jury Proceedings (Gregory P. Violette), 183 F.3d 71 (1st Cir. 1999), held that a "crime-fraud exception" applies to the psychotherapist patient privilege. The defendant was the target of a federal grand jury investigation focused on possible bank fraud crimes involving false claims of his disabilities. By analogy to the attorney-client privilege, the court found that the rationale for the privilege diminishes when communications made in therapy are in furtherance of crime. The exception will only apply, however, when the patient's purpose in making a communication is not therapy, but to promote a particular crime or fraud. It would not apply, for example, to a career criminal's confessions to his therapist even though the therapy may generally increase the patient's professional productivity. When the evidence indicates that defendant's communications to the therapists were made as part of a scheme to defraud lenders and/or disability insurers, the key ingredients of the crime-fraud exception are established.

KEY POINTS

1. Federal law recognizes a psychotherapist-patient privilege but not a physician-patient privilege. Most states recognize both privileges.

2. The federal psychotherapist-patient privilege has been extended to all physicians, psychologists, licensed social workers, and a variety of other mental health workers, when communications for the purpose of diagnosis or treatment of a mental or emotional condition are made with the reasonable expectation of confidence.

3. The privilege may not apply if disclosure of the communication is necessary to protect the Sixth Amendment rights of criminal defendants, if the patient has placed the patient's emotional or mental condition at issue in litigation, or if the communications are intended to promote a crime or fraud.

4. The courts are in disagreement over the existence of a dangerous patient exception.

PROBLEMS

12.25. At Alice Draper's prosecution for murder of a federal official, the prosecution offers to introduce the following evidence: Shortly after the victim's death, an individual called an Alcoholics Anonymous hotline manned by volunteers and asked to speak with a doctor. When the volunteer who had answered the phone asked what the problem was, the caller responded, "Murder. I just killed a man. I need help." Another volunteer called the police, and the police traced the telephone call to a telephone booth, where they found and arrested Draper. Draper has objected to evidence of what she said to the AA volunteer on the ground that her statements fall within the psychotherapist-patient privilege. What result? What additional facts might affect the outcome?

12.26. Plaintiff Peters brought an action in federal court against his employer for unlawful discrimination and violation of the Family Medical Leave Act due to his termination from employment on the basis of his mental illness. The defendant employer seeks discovery of a journal that Peters started keeping after losing his job, but which he has not shown to the doctor who is providing psychological counseling. The journal concerns the events that surrounded Peters's termination. Peters claims that the journal should be protected pursuant to the psychotherapist-patient privilege because he started keeping the journal when his doctor suggested that "writing down what happened can help you understand some of the situation." Is the journal privileged?

12.27. Plaintiff Salter has filed an action under the American with Disabilities Act (ADA) against her employer for unlawful discharge and failure to make reasonable accommodation for her clinical depression, which, she claims, required medication that caused her difficulty in waking up and chronic tardiness at work. The ADA requires the plaintiff to make a prima facie case of discrimination, which includes that she is a member of a protected category, which means a person with physical or mental impairment; a person with a record of such impairment; or a person being regarded as having such impairment. May plaintiff protect the release of her medical records of her treating psychiatrist pursuant to the psychotherapist-patient privilege?

12.28. Walter and Sarah Wong have sued Walter's tax preparer H&R Block, Inc. for breach of contract for its unauthorized disclosure in 1998 of Walter's tax return information, a disclosure that led to a criminal investigation and civil audits by the IRS. Plaintiffs allege that they incurred actual damages in the form of legal fees and "severe emotional distress, including physical mental suffering, shame, and humiliation." In 1998, prior to their marriage but after the conduct alleged in this suit, Walter and Sarah attended joint counseling sessions with a licensed social worker to help with the health of their relationship. In 1999, Sarah went for an initial consultation to a licensed psychologist. Defendant H&R Block has filed notices of taking depositions of both the social worker and psychologist. Defendant asserts that any psychotherapist-patient privilege was waived (1) by plaintiffs alleging serious claims for emotional distress and (2) through the revelation in their own depositions of the identities of their mental health providers, as well as the dates and costs of the sessions, and the purpose of the visits to the social worker. Plaintiffs contend that they have not waived the privilege because they have not alleged psychic injury or disease nor psychiatric injury or disease or disorder, and that no psychological testimony will be offered at trial. What result?

F.   THE CLERGY-COMMUNICANT PRIVILEGE

The priest-penitent privilege — now more commonly referred to as the clergy-communicant privilege — was not recognized at common law, largely because of the hostile climate in England toward the Roman Catholic Church during the Reformation. Today, however, its legitimacy is accepted by scholars and courts, at least to some degree. Indeed, every state has legislatively enacted some version of this privilege, and Proposed Federal Rule 506 specifically recognized a privilege protecting "confidential communication[s] by [a] person to a clergyman in his professional character as spiritual advisor." Pursuant to FRE 501, federal courts have recognized the existence of a clergy-communicant privilege as a matter of federal common law. See In re Grand Jury Investigation, 918 F.2d 374 (3d Cir. 1990); United States v. Dube, 820 F.2d 886 (7th Cir. 1987); United States v. Gordon, 655 F.2d 478 (2d Cir. 1981). See generally Whitaker, The Priest-Penitent Privilege: Its Constitutionality and Doctrine, 13 Regent U. L. Rev. 145 (2000-2001). The privilege is accepted in some form by all 50 states, but in the wake of the many high-profile cases involving child sexual abuse by clergy members in recent years, 40 states now require clergy members to report instances of child abuse as part of those states' mandatory reporting statutes, although many of those states provide exceptions for communications within the scope of the privilege. 1 David M. Greenwald et al., Testimonial Privileges §6:14 (Trial Practice Series, 3d ed. 2005).

1.   The Privilege and Its Justifications

The clergy-communicant privilege generally applies "to protect communications made (1) to a clergy person (2) in his or her spiritual and professional capacity (3) with a reasonable expectation of confidentiality." In re Grand Jury Investigation, 918 F.2d 374, 384 (3d Cir. 1990). The privilege has been justified in four ways: (1) The traditional utilitarian justification, that the privilege is necessary to preserve the confidential relationship between clergy person and communicant, is often given. In this respect the privilege is similar to the attorney-client, physician-patient, psychotherapist-patient, and marital communications privileges.

(2) Another justification is constitutional in origin, based upon the free exercise clause of the First Amendment. According to this argument, the clause prevents courts from compelling a priest to reveal confidential communications, where such disclosure would contradict their religious practice. Although the privilege is probably not mandated by the Constitution, the principle of religious freedom has historically offered compelling support for the privilege.

(3) The privacy rationale, emphasizing the private nature of religious worship, is occasionally invoked. By creating a zone of privacy and protecting spiritual counseling from disclosure, the privilege accords respect for the intimacy of the communicant's relationship to clergy. According to this rationale, confidentiality is a privacy interest that itself acts as a legitimate constraint on the truth-finding function of trial. This may be no more persuasive here than in the attorney-client context.

(4) Last, the privilege is said to protect the credibility of our judicial system by preventing controversial clashes between court and clergy. Advocates of this rationale contend that "the spectacle of courts imprisoning members of the clergy for refusing to violate confidences entrusted to them might tend to subvert public faith in the judicial process." Developments in the Law — Privileged Communications, 98 Harv. L. Rev. 1450, 1562 (1985). In this sense, the privilege accords respect to the separation between church and state.

2.   Scope of the Privilege

The most important issues in the interpretation of the clergy-communicant privilege are who counts as a clergy person, what kinds of communications are protected, and when does the presence of third persons waive the privilege. In most jurisdictions the holder of the privilege is the communicant, but a small minority of states grant the privilege and the decision to disclose communications to the clergy. Most state statutes, however, explicitly prohibit clergy from disclosing confidential communications without the communicant's consent. In a well-publicized case in New York, a priest revealed the confessional statement of a deceased parishioner, made 11 or 12 years earlier, that helped to exculpate two men wrongly convicted of the murder to which the deceased parishioner confessed. Such breach of confidence was proper, according to the priest and the Archdiocese of New York, because the confessional statement was not a formal confession within Catholic practice. Had the confession been formal, the priest would never have been able to reveal it, even after the parishioner's death. Morales v. Portuondo, 154 F. Supp. 2d 706, 714 (S.D.N.Y. 2001).

Even if the clergy person does not hold the privilege, the clergy have their own interests in protecting the privacy of their religious counseling. In Mockaitis v. Harcleroad, 104 F.3d 1522 (9th Cir. 1997), the court held that a tape-recorded conversation between a priest and a jail inmate — which the inmate knew was being taped by the state — was not privileged, but that disclosure would violate the priest's Fourth Amendment expectation of privacy and the federal Religious Freedom Restoration Act.

a.   Definition of Clergy

Proposed FRE 506(a)(1) defined a member of the clergy as "a minister, priest, rabbi, or other similar functionary of a religious organization, or an individual reasonably believed so to be by the person consulting him." This definition was adopted by the Third Circuit in In re Grand Jury Investigation, 918 F.2d 374, 384-385 (3d Cir. 1990). The "reasonably believed to be" a clergy person clause serves to protect the reasonable expectations of the individual. Some state statutes fail to provide any definition other than "clergyman or priest," while others provide very broad language in defining the individuals covered. See, e.g., 735 Ill. Comp. Stat. 5/8-803 (2002) (referring to "a clergyman or practitioner of any religious denomination accredited by the religious body to which he or she belongs"). Georgia explicitly delineates which members of the clergy are included, confining the privilege to "any Protestant minister of the Gospel, and any priest of the Roman Catholic faith, any priest of the Greek Orthodox Catholic faith, any Jewish rabbi, or to any Christian or Jewish minister, by whatever name called." Ga. Code Ann. §24-9-22 (West 2003).

One issue that often arises is whether the privilege extends to situations in which communicants receive spiritual advice from individuals who are not officially ordained members of the clergy. The Third Circuit foresaw this problem and stated, in dicta, that its adoption of the broad definition of clergy in Proposed Rule 506 did not imply "that the privilege should be interpreted to comprehend communications to and among members of sects that denominate each and every member as clergy." In re Grand Jury Investigation, 918 F.2d at 384 n.13. The burden is on the party asserting the privilege to show that the person to whom communications were made is regularly engaged in activities which conform generally to the conduct of Catholic priests, Jewish rabbis, or Protestant ministers. United States v. Napolean, 46 M.J. 279, 284-285 (Ct. App. A.F. 1997) (citing 2 S. Saltzburg and M. Martin, Federal Rules of Evidence Manual 601-602 (5th ed. 1990)). In In re Verplank, 329 F. Supp. 433, 435-436 (C.D. Cal. 1971), the court protected confidential communications made to nonordained counselors from disclosure, because the counselors' services sufficiently resembled acts performed by the ordained minister who supervised them. The complexity of this issue can be seen in Cox v. Miller, 154 F. Supp. 2d 787 (S.D.N.Y. 2001), where the district court dramatically expanded the privilege to include statements made at Alcoholics Anonymous (AA) meetings. In Cox, the defendant's confession to two murders, made to his fellow AA members, were covered by the privilege, as the court noted that the Second Circuit had held that AA *was a religion*, by reason of the religious nature of its "Twelve Steps of Recovery." Although the decision was subsequently reversed by the Second Circuit in Cox v. Miller, 296 F.3d 89 (2d Cir. 2002), the case indicates how the clergy-communicant privilege can be susceptible to a quite broad interpretation.

b.   Nature of the Communication

The clergy-communicant privilege applies only to communications made to a clergy person in that person's spiritual or professional capacity. Courts have interpreted this to mean that the communication is "related to a religious function. . . . [T]he communication must be essentially for an ecclesiastical and religious purpose." Ellis v. United States, 922 F. Supp. 539, 542 (D. Utah 1996). Such communications are to be distinguished from communications that simply advise clergy about events, as in *Ellis* (witness to a tragic accident at a church-sponsored outing informed church officials about the event for secular purposes), or that are made for emotional support and consolation rather than guidance and forgiveness as a formal act of religion or as a matter of conscience. United States v. Napolean, 46 M.J. at 285. A narrower view of the privilege — to apply only to acts of "confession" — could raise serious first amendment and equal protection concerns by limiting the privilege to certain religions.

c.   Expectation of Confidentiality

As is the case with the attorney-client privilege, the presence of third parties, if essential to and in furtherance of the communication, should not void the privilege. For example, transmission of the communications within a church hierarchy may remain privileged. In Scott v. Hammock, 133 F.R.D. 610 (D. Utah 1990), the court applied Utah law to hold that communications from the communicant to a clergy person, and then passed vertically from one religious authority up to another within the church hierarchy, were privileged because such communication was necessary to the carrying out of church discipline. If communications among the church officers themselves could be discovered, then the privilege would be destroyed and the communicant's confidence abridged.

In In re Grand Jury Investigation, the government sought to compel the disclosure of communications among several family members and their pastor on the grounds that a nonfamily member had also been present. The Third Circuit reasoned as follows:

> In essence, the government claims that persons who are not related by blood or by marriage cannot, under federal law, engage together in protected communications with a member of the clergy acting in a spiritual or professional capacity. . . .

The government is correct in observing that the traditional clergy-communicant privilege protected a penitential relationship in which a person privately confessed his or her sins to a priest, in order to receive some form of church sanctioned discipline or absolution. Neither family nor other types of group counseling fit neatly within this "one-to-one" model of the privilege. We have explained, however, that the modern view of the privilege is more expansive than the traditional one. We discern nothing in modern clergy-communicant privilege doctrine, as it finds expression in either proposed Rule 506 or the cases recognizing the privilege, that would limit the privilege's application solely to group discussions involving family members related by blood or marriage. Modern clergy-communicant privilege doctrine focuses, rather, on whether the presence of a third party is essential to or in furtherance of a communication to a member of the clergy. We think, consistent with the general constructional rule that evidentiary privileges should be narrowly construed, that recognition of the clergy-communicant privilege in this circumstance depends upon whether the third party's presence is essential to and in furtherance of a communication to a member of the clergy. As is the case with consultations between attorneys and clients, the presence of multiple parties, unrelated by blood or marriage, during discussions with a member of the clergy may, but will not necessarily, defeat the condition that communications be made with a reasonable expectation of confidentiality in order for the privilege to attach. [918 F.2d at 386.]

However, the appellate court also found that the district court had not developed adequate facts upon which to make the necessary finding that the family members reasonably expected that their communications to their pastor were confidential. It remanded the case to the district court "to determine whether the [family members] communicated with Pastor Knoche in his spiritual or professional capacity and with a reasonable expectation of confidentiality. . . ." Id. at 387. This might require an inquiry "into the nature of the communicants' relationship as well as the pastoral counseling practices of the relevant synod of the Lutheran church . . . whether the parties shared a commonality of interest at the time of the communication and, if so, in what respect . . . [and] a fuller record . . . as to [the third person's] role in the counseling session. In order to ascertain whether her presence worked to vitiate or to waive the privilege, the court will have to inquire into whether the other group members, who apparently are subjects of the grand jury investigation, reasonably required her presence at the counseling session, either in furtherance of their communications to the pastor or to protect their interests." Id. at 387-388. And the appellate court was well aware that such an inquiry might require some degree of disclosure from the pastor as to what was discussed in the group meeting. It left to the discretion of the district court how to ascertain this information; whether to use *in camera* hearings; whether or not parties and/or counsel should be present; and how to accommodate "delicate first amendment issues." Id. at 388.

d. Exceptions

The main exception to the clergy-communicant privilege in state statutes involves a clash between the privilege and state mandatory reporting statutes in the area of child abuse. Due to clergy child sex abuse scandals, public outrage has spurred state legislatures to act. "Every state has passed a statute requiring mandatory reporting of child abuse." 1 Greenwald et al., Testimonial Privileges §6:14. Some states have amended these mandatory reporting statutes by including clergy members in the list of groups required to report instances of child abuse. See, e.g., Mass. Gen. Laws Ann. ch. 119, §51A (West 2002); Ala. Code §26-14-3 (1992 & Supp. 2004). Currently, the mandatory reporting statutes of approximately 40 states require clergy to disclose known or suspected incidents of child abuse, either by specifically listing clergy members within the list of applicable groups, or by the use of a catchall phrase, such as "any person." Greenwald, et al. §6:4. However, the majority of the states that require clergy to report child abuse still maintain an exception in the case of the clergy-communicant privilege, protecting such communications from the mandatory reporting requirements. Id. For example, although Massachusetts has amended its mandatory reporting statute to include clergy members, the statute still provides the following exception:

> [A] . . . clergy member . . . shall report all cases of abuse under this section, but need not report information solely gained in a confession or similarly confidential communication in other religious faiths. Nothing in the general laws shall modify or limit the duty of a . . . clergy member . . . to report a reasonable cause that a child is being injured as set forth in this section when the . . . clergy member . . . is acting in some other capacity that would otherwise make him a reporter. [Mass. Ann. Laws ch. 119 §51A.]

Essentially, this means that, in many states, a clergy member is required to report suspected or known child abuse so long as doing so would not reveal the substance of a confession or an otherwise confidential communication with a penitent. A few states do the opposite, by specifically denying the privilege in their mandatory reporting statutes, see, e.g., Tex. Fam. Code Ann. §261.101 (Vernon 2002); N.H. Rev. Stat. Ann. §169-C:29 (2001), while others that require mandatory reporting do not mention its effect on the privilege. See, e.g., Ind. Code Ann. §31-33-5-1 (West 1999). For further discussion, see Norman Abrams, Addressing the Tension Between the Clergy-Communicant Privilege and the Duty to Report Child Abuse in State Statutes, 44 B.C. L. Rev. 1127 (2003); Christopher R. Pudelski, The Constitutional Fate of Mandatory Reporting Statutes and the Clergy-Penitent Privilege in a Post-*Smith* World, 98 Nw. U. L. Rev. 703, 706-707 (2004).

KEY POINTS

1. A clergy-communicant privilege has been recognized under federal law and in all state jurisdictions, though exceptions exist in several states for mandatory reporting of known or suspected child abuse.

2. Courts extend the privilege to communications made to ordained clergy or to people performing the same activities. The communications must be relevant to a religious function.

3. Communications made in the presence of third persons can be privileged if the third person's presence was essential to and in furtherance of the communication to the clergy.

PROBLEMS

12.29. Darlene is being tried for the crime of making threats through the U.S. mail. Darlene raises an insanity defense. The clergy person who leads Darlene's religious congregation testifies that during the time of Darlene's conduct, Darlene did "know right from wrong." The clergy person further states that this opinion is based on knowing Darlene, on observations of Darlene, and on speaking with Darlene during this period. Does this testimony violate the clergy-communicant privilege?

12.30. Jim Jones joined a mail order church for a fee of $100, which entitled him to the status of lay minister. The tenets of the church included a vow of poverty and the belief that personal income of ministers was not taxable by the federal government. Jones stopped paying income taxes and is now prosecuted for failure to file income tax returns from 1996 to 2000. In 1999, Jones also joined an established church and had several conversations with the minister concerning his beliefs about taxation. The government plans to call the minister who would testify that he advised Jones that his income was not exempt from taxation. Can Jones enforce the clergy-communicant privilege?

12.31. Sam Evans is being prosecuted for sexually assaulting his 12-year-old step-daughter. Shortly after the incident that is the subject of the prosecution, Sam and his wife were separated. Sam began seeing his minister for spiritual guidance. At one session, which concerned marriage counseling, Sam's wife was also present. At this session, Sam admitted that he had sexually assaulted the stepdaughter, and he said that he had told his wife this the night before. The prosecution plans to call Sam's wife, who is willing to testify about both of Sam's admissions. The prosecution also plans to call the minister and ask him about what Sam said at the counseling session. The minister, however, has expressed an unwillingness to testify about these matters, and the minister is disturbed that Sam's wife is willing to testify. Does the minister have any personal right not to testify or to prevent Sam's wife from testifying? What objections can Sam make to the testimony of his wife and the minister? What additional facts might be needed to answer these questions? How would they be determined?

G.   OTHER PRIVILEGES

1.   Other Professional-Client Relationships

Privileges are occasionally recognized for confidential communications to other professionals, such as accountants, teachers, family and marriage counselors, social workers, lay advocates, and private detectives who counsel, advise, or act on behalf of their clients. Statutes enacting such privileges have been passed in a minority of states. For example, an accountant-client privilege exists in approximately one-third of the states. One interesting issue relating to the accountant-client privilege is whether the privilege is waived for the underlying information that is used to develop a publicly disclosed financial report, such as an Annual Report prepared by independent auditors that is required by the SEC for public companies. If a state's law does not create an exception for the privilege in such a situation, then it is likely that the privilege will still be available for the underlying information. See, e.g., In re Hillsborough Holdings Corp., 176 B.R. 223, 237 (M.D. Fla. 1994). However, until relatively recently there was neither a privilege nor work-product protection for accountants in federal court. See United States v. Arthur Young & Co., 465 U.S. 805 (1984); Couch v. United

States, 409 U.S. 322 (1973). In 1998, 26 U.S.C. §7525 extended the attorney-client privilege to "a federally authorized tax practitioner," who is a nonlawyer authorized to practice before the Internal Revenue Service. Though work product is still not protected, the new privilege provides that "the same common law protections of confidentiality which apply to a communication between a taxpayer and an attorney shall also apply to a communication between a taxpayer and a federally authorized tax practitioner to the extent the communications would be considered a privileged communication if it were between a taxpayer and an attorney." §7525(a)(1).

Another example is that privileges for various counseling professionals may be recognized under a state's psychotherapist-patient privilege. *Psychotherapist* may be defined to include professionals other than psychiatrists, psychologists, and psychotherapists, such as social workers; psychiatric nurses; counselors of rape victims, battered women, and drug and alcohol abusers; as well as school, family, and marriage counselors whose functions are analogous to those of a psychotherapist. See Catharina J. H. Dubbleday, Comment, The Psychotherapist-Client Testimonial Privilege: Defining the Professional Involved, 34 Emory L.J. 777 (1985). Another "counseling privilege" that some states recognize is a sexual assault victim-counselor privilege. See, e.g., Cal. Evid. Code §1035-1036.2 (West 1995 & Supp. 2005); 735 Ill. Comp. Stat. 5/8-802.1 (2002); 42 Pa. Cons. Stat. Ann. §5945.1(b) (West 2000 & Supp. 2005) ("[n]o sexual assault counselor may, without the written consent of the victim, disclose the victim's confidential oral or written communications to the counselor nor consent to be examined in any court or criminal proceeding"). Some states, such as Massachusetts, provide for an absolute privilege, while others, such as California, have enacted a qualified privilege permitting disclosure under certain circumstances. For further discussion, see Euphemia B. Warren, She's Gotta Have It Now: A Qualified Rape Crisis Counselor-Victim Privilege, 17 Cardozo L. Rev. 141 (1995).

2. Parent-Child Privilege

A privilege for parent-child communications was not recognized at common law. Presently, five states, Colorado, Idaho, Massachusetts, Minnesota, and Washington, have enacted legislation adopting a parent-child confidential communications privilege, although in Colorado and Washington the privilege is limited to communications made to an attorney by a child while in the presence of a parent. In contrast, the majority of states have refused to adopt the privilege. See, e.g., People v. Dixon, 161 Mich. App. 388, 393, 411 N.W.2d 760, 763 (1987); In re Gail D., 217 N.J. Super. 226, 232, 525 A.2d 337, 340 (1987). A New York court recognized a parent-child privilege based on the constitutional right to privacy. People v. Fitzgerald, 101 Misc. 2d 712, 422 N.Y.S.2d 309 (Westchester County Ct. 1979). However, *Fitzgerald* has not been followed by any New York court decision, and has since been limited by People v. Harrell, 87 A.D.2d 21, 450 N.Y.S.2d 501, 504 (1982) and criticized in People v. Hilligas, 175 Misc. 2d 842, 670 N.Y.S.2d 744 (Erie County Ct. 1998), for its inappropriate extension of the privilege to adult children.

Prior to the passage of Washington's parent-child privilege statute, the Washington Supreme Court refused to adopt a general privilege. State v. Maxon, 110 Wash. 2d 564, 574, 756 P.2d 1297, 1302 (1988). As noted above, the Washington statute creates only a limited privilege, and as such the decision denying a general parent-child privilege in *Maxon* remains in effect, narrowing the scope of the privilege in Washington.

Addressing the constitutional claim for the privilege, the Washington Supreme Court stated:

> The Constitution does not mandate recognition of a parent-child privilege. The right of privacy line of cases gives no indication that the interest in confidential communications between parent and child qualifies as a fundamental right for the purpose of substantive due process analysis. Any infringement of this interest caused by nonrecognition of a parent-child privilege is indirect and incidental.

Maxon, supra, 756 P.2d at 1301 (quoting Donald Cofer, Comment, Parent-Child Privilege: Constitutional Right or Specious Analogy?, 3 U. Puget Sound L. Rev. 177, 210-211 (1979)).

In the absence of congressional action, federal courts have generally refused to recognize a parent-child privilege. Almost every circuit has ruled against such a privilege[78] but four of these courts noted in dicta that cases of adult and minor children are distinguishable and that they might be willing to recognize a parent-child privilege where an unemancipated minor confided in a parent.[79] Only a few federal district courts have recognized any form of the privilege. See In re Grand Jury Proceedings, Unemancipated Minor Child, 949 F. Supp. 1487 (E.D. Wash. 1996). In re Agosto, 553 F. Supp. 1298, 1325 (D. Nev. 1983); In re Greenburg, 11 Fed. R. Evid. Serv. 579, 582-584 (D. Conn. 1982). The *Agosto* court granted both parent and child the right to claim the privilege, in order to "protect communications made within an indissoluble family unit, bonded by blood, affection, loyalty and tradition." Courts that have rejected the privilege have found no "systematic regulation" of protected family interests that might give rise to a constitutional claim of privacy. United States v. Davies, 768 F.2d 893, 899-890 (7th Cir. 1985); see also In re Inquest Proceedings, 676 A.2d 790 (Vt. 1996).

An interesting issue raised by many courts presented with a claim of the privilege has been whether the privilege would apply solely to communications from child to parent or to communications from parent to child as well. Commentators argue that the privilege should apply solely to conversations from child to parent since the policy behind the privilege is to encourage the child to confide in the parent.

Though parent-child privileges have not gained widespread acceptance, their supporters often refer to what has been called the "cruel trilemma" that witnesses face. The first option for a testifying parent or child is to choose to commit perjury in order to protect a family member. Rather than implicate his father, a son in United States v. Ismail, 756 F.2d 1253 (6th Cir. 1985), perjured himself at a grand jury hearing. The son later broke down on the witness stand, admitting that he had lied to the grand jury and had considered suicide to avoid testifying against his father. The second option for a witness in this position is to tell the truth and face what damage may be done to the relationship and the guilt that will come from having hurt a loved one. Terry Nichols was convicted for his involvement in the 1995 Oklahoma City bombing after his son Josh, 13, was forced to testify before a grand jury. Josh's mother told reporters

---

78.   See, e.g., In re Grand Jury Proceedings of John Doe, 842 F.2d 244, 248 (10th Cir. 1988); United States v. Ismail, 756 F.2d 1253 (6th Cir. 1985); In re Santerelli, 740 F.2d 816 (11th Cir. 1984).

79.   See In re Erato, 2 F.3d 11, 16 (2d Cir. 1993); Port v. Heard, 764 F.2d 423, 430 (5th Cir. 1985); United States v. Ismail, 756 F.2d 1253, 1258 (6th Cir. 1985); United States v. Jones, 683 F.2d 817, 819 (4th Cir. 1982).

that her son suffered from nightmares as a result of testifying.[80] The third option is to refuse to testify and be found in contempt of court. In State v. DeLong, 456 A.2d 877 (Me. 1983), a 15-year-old girl who had been sexually abused by her adoptive father was sentenced to jail for refusing to testify against him.

Because of the difficulty of choosing to testify truthfully against a family member, many judges and prosecutors worry about the veracity of a parent's or child's testimony. Furthermore, the appeal of family privacy can make the support of a parent-child privilege politically attractive. The issue came under national scrutiny in February 1998 when Independent Counsel Kenneth Starr subpoenaed Marcia Lewis, mother of Monica Lewinsky, to testify before a grand jury about her daughter's relationship with President Clinton. In the 1998 and 1999 congressional sessions, the spectacle inspired three bills in the U.S. House of Representatives and one in the Senate,[81] each of which proposed the creation of a federal parent-child privilege. The "Confidence in the Family Act," 105 H.R. 3577 (1998), was rejected by the House Judiciary Committee for many reasons, including concern that the broad scope of the bill might cover natural parents as well a stepparents and grandparents, adult as well as minor children, and criminal as well as civil cases.[82] The three remaining bills did not emerge from the House and Senate Judiciary Committees. Representative Andrews, a Democrat from New Jersey, has repeatedly attempted to obtain legislative approval for a parent-child privilege statute, most recently introducing the Parent-Child Privilege Act of 2005, 109 H.R. 3443 (2005), though each attempt has been unsuccessful.

For further discussion, see generally Shonah P. Jefferson, The Statutory Development of the Parent-Child Privilege: Congress Responds to Kenneth Starr's Tactics, 16 Ga. St. U. L. Rev. 429 (1999); Yolanda L. Ayala and Thomas C. Martyn, To Tell or Not To Tell? An Analysis of Testimonial Privileges: The Parent-Child and Reporter's Privileges, 9 St. John's J. Legal Comment. 163 (1993); Note, Parent-Child Loyalty and Testimonial Privilege, 100 Harv. L. Rev. 910 (1987); Developments in the Law — Privileged Communications, 98 Harv. L. Rev. 1450, 1575 (1985).

3.   Communications Made in Settlement Negotiations

One emerging area of privilege law is that of settlement negotiations. As discussed in Chapter Six, FRE 408 precludes communications made in settlement negotiations from being used at trial as evidence of liability. However, "[t]he court may admit [such] evidence for another purpose, such as proving a witness's bias or prejudice, negating a contention of undue delay, or proving an effort to obstruct a criminal investigation or prosecution." Fed. R. Evid. 408. A question remains as to whether FRE 408 applies only to admissibility of evidence at trial, or whether it implies that

---

80.   See Lance Gay, Lewinsky's Mother Torn Between Law and Loyalty, *Times Union*, Feb. 14, 1998, at A1.

81.   See Confidence in the Family Act, 105 H.R. 3577 (1998) (amending Federal Rules of Evidence to include parent-child adverse testimonial privilege and confidential communications privilege in federal civil and criminal proceedings); Parent-Child Privilege Acts of 1998 and 1999, 105 H.R. 4286 (1998), 106 H.R. 522 (1999) (amending Federal Rules of Evidence establishing a parent-child privilege); Attorney General Guidelines for Familial Privacy, 105 S. 1721 (directing the Attorney General of the United States to develop guidelines for Federal prosecutors to protect familial privacy and communications between parents and children).

82.   The bill was ultimately rejected by a vote of 162 to 256. See 144 Cong. Rec. H2278 (daily ed. Apr. 23, 1998).

a privilege should exist to protect settlement communications from discovery. The primary justification for the privilege is the desire to promote settlements and the need for open discussion in settlement negotiations, including adopting hypothetical positions that may not be entirely self-interested in order to compromise effectively. If the statements made in settlement negotiations are not privileged, despite FRE 408 as a barrier to the use of the communications as evidence at trial, the statements could be subject to discovery, which could create a disincentive to open discussions during settlement negotiations.

The Sixth Circuit Court of Appeals held that a privilege does exist for communications made in furtherance of settlement negotiations, protecting them from third-party discovery. Goodyear Tire & Rubber Co. v. Chiles Power Supply, Inc., 332 F.3d 976 (6th Cir. 2003). In *Goodyear*, after the case was concluded, Chiles gave an interview in which settlement communications were improperly disclosed. Id. at 978. After learning about the communications, the plaintiffs in a separate lawsuit against both Goodyear and Chiles joined the suit and petitioned the district court to permit discovery of statements made in settlement negotiations. Id. at 979.

The Sixth Circuit relied heavily on the Supreme Court's decision in Jaffee v. Redmond, 518 U.S. 1 (1996), in discussing the parameters of a privilege. Id. at 979-980. The Sixth Circuit found a strong public policy interest in recognizing the privilege, as well as noting the tradition of confidentiality in settlement communications. Id. at 980. The court further concluded that information discovered from settlement negotiations was unlikely to be relevant:

> There exists a strong public interest in favor of secrecy of matters discussed by parties during settlement negotiations. This is true whether settlement negotiations are done under the auspices of the court or informally between the parties. The ability to negotiate and settle a case without trial fosters a more efficient, more cost-effective, and significantly less burdened judicial system. In order for settlement talks to be effective, parties must feel uninhibited in their communications. Parties are unlikely to propose the types of compromises that most effectively lead to settlement unless they are confident that their proposed solutions cannot be used on cross examination, under the ruse of "impeachment evidence," by some future third party. Parties must be able to abandon their adversarial tendencies to some degree. They must be able to make hypothetical concessions, offer creative quid pro quos, and generally make statements that would otherwise belie their litigation efforts. Without a privilege, parties would more often forego negotiations for the relative formality of trial. Then, the entire negotiation process collapses upon itself, and the judicial efficiency it fosters is lost. [Id. at 980.]

Although the Sixth Circuit has adopted the privilege, the issue has not yet been decided in other circuits. However, at least one district court has declined to follow the Sixth Circuit. In In re Subpoena Issued to Commodity Futures Trading Commission, 370 F. Supp. 2d 201 (D.D.C. 2005), the District Court for the District of Columbia held that it would not recognize a new settlement privilege to protect documents from third-party discovery. The court discussed several factors that the Supreme Court considers in assessing a potential privilege in reaching its decision. Id. at 208. The court noted that there is no broad consensus in federal courts, as few federal courts recognize the privilege, nor is there a consensus in state law supporting the privilege. Id. at 208-209. The court also reasoned that by enacting FRE 408, Congress chose to limit the admissibility of settlement matter rather than discoverability. Id. Last, the court opined that the proponents of the privilege had not made an adequate showing that the privilege would effectively advance a public good. Id. at 212.

For further discussion, see Jeffrey J. Lauderdale, A New Trend in the Law of Privilege: The Federal Settlement Privilege and the Proper Use of Federal Rule of Evidence 501 for the Recognition of New Privileges, 35 U. Mem. L. Rev. 255 (2005).

Another similar privilege is the mediation communications privilege. The mediation privilege protects from discovery communication and documentation related to mediation negotiations between parties. The mediation privilege was not recognized in common law, but every state has enacted some statutory form of the privilege. By passing the Alternative Dispute Resolution (ADR) Act in 1998, 28 U.S.C. §651, Congress requires federal district courts to authorize by local rule ADR programs for all civil litigation. The ADR Act requires ADR proceedings to be confidential and requires district courts to develop safeguards to protect the confidentiality of communications within these ADR proceedings. Id. at §652(d). Although the ADR Act did not actually create a privilege, some federal courts have adopted the privilege to protect the confidentiality of such mediation communications. See, e.g., Folb v. Motion Picture Industry Pension & Health Plans, 16 F. Supp. 2d 1164 (C.D. Cal. 1998); Sheldone v. Pennsylvania Turnpike Commission 104 F. Supp. 2d 511 (W.D. Pa. 2000). However, other federal courts have declined to adopt such a privilege without a clearer mandate from Congress. See FDIC. v. White, 76 F. Supp. 2d 736, 738 (N.D. Tex. 1999) ("[t]he [c]ourt does not read the ADR [Act] or its sparse legislative history as creating an evidentiary privilege"). For further discussion of the mediation privilege, see Ellen E. Deason, Predictable Mediation Confidentiality in the U.S. Federal System, 17 Ohio St. J. on Disp. Resol. 239 (2002).

4. Privileges Protecting Outside Sources of Information

A unique category of privileges exists to protect confidential sources of information. Three privileges of this type are the government informant's privilege, the journalist's privilege, and the scholar's privilege. These privileges can be distinguished from the confidential communications privileges, for rather than focusing on the communication's content, these privileges mainly focus on the protection of the source's identity. The common justification is that absent protection, the mere possibility of disclosure would disrupt the future flow of information and thereby "harm the public by impeding law enforcement efforts, the dissemination of news, or the advancement of knowledge." Developments in the Law — Privileged Communications, 98 Harv. L. Rev. 1592, 1594 (1985).

a. Government Informant's Privilege

The government informant's privilege protects the identities of individuals who provide the government with information regarding crimes or other suspect activity. Though the privilege was once recognized as absolute, it has been qualified due to concern for the constitutional rights of criminal defendants. In Roviaro v. United States, 353 U.S. 53, 62 (1957), the Supreme Court announced a test that "balanc[ed] the public interest in protecting the flow of information against the individual's right to prepare his defense." The informant's privilege arises most frequently in cases where a criminal defendant alleges that an informant's testimony is critical to his defense. In such circumstances, courts freely conduct *in camera* hearings with an informant to determine how the *Roviaro* balance should be struck. See, e.g., United States v. Anderson, 509 F.2d 724, 730 (9th Cir. 1974); United States v. Fischer, 531 F.2d 783 (5th Cir. 1976). The privilege is also frequently invoked in the context of a defendant's challenge to a search in which the government claims that the informant provided the basis for probable cause. The privilege has been applied in civil cases as well. In applying the *Roviaro* balancing test, some civil courts maintain that the "strength of the privilege is greater in civil litigation than in criminal," In re United States, 565 F.2d 19, 22 (2d Cir. 1978), while others adhere to the standard used in criminal cases, see, e.g., Hodgson v. Charles Martin Inspector of Petroleum, Inc., 459 F.2d 303, 305 (5th Cir. 1972).

b.   Journalist's Privilege

A privilege to protect journalists against the disclosure of the identities of their news sources has been consistently advocated by members of media organizations. Proponents assert a twofold justification for the privilege: (1) the privilege is necessary to encourage the flow of confidential information from external sources; and (2) the privilege protects the First Amendment guarantee of a free press. The constitutional argument was rejected by the Supreme Court in the 5 to 4 decision of Branzburg v. Hayes, 408 U.S. 665 (1972), which analyzed the privilege claim in the grand jury setting. Noting "the limited nature of the Court's holding," Justice Powell in his concurrence proposed a balancing test to determine journalist privilege claims. In line with Justice Powell's concurrence, many lower federal courts have recognized a qualified journalist's privilege based on the First Amendment. See, e.g., Continental Cablevision, Inc. v. Stores Broadcasting Co., 583 F. Supp. 427 (E.D. Mo. 1984); United States v. Burke, 700 F.2d 70 (2d Cir. 1983). But see Herbert v. Lando, 441 U.S. 153 (1979) (declining to recognize an editorial process privilege). In a recent decision, the D.C. Circuit reiterated *Branzburg* in rejecting a First Amendment challenge to a federal grand jury subpoena. In re Grand Jury Subpoena, Judith Miller, 397 F.3d 964 (D.C. Cir. 2005). In *Miller*, two reporters and Time, Inc., the parent company of Time Magazine, were subpoenaed to testify about sources used in their articles to a federal grand jury investigating the alleged leak of a CIA agent's identity by government officials. Id. at 966-968. The court held that the First Amendment does not grant journalists a right to refuse to divulge information about sources in the context of a grand jury subpoena, and further held that, even if there is a common law journalist privilege, which was not determined, the privilege would be qualified, and the government overcame any qualification. Id. at 972-973.

At least one federal court has specifically held that the reporter's privilege does not apply in grand jury proceedings. In re Grand Jury Proceedings (Scarce), 5 F.3d 397, 403 (9th Cir. 1993).

Efforts to enact a federal statutory privilege have not succeeded. However, most states have enacted shield laws that vary in levels of protection. When a reporter's sources are confidential, normally the plaintiff must make a more substantial showing of need in order to overcome the privilege. Mark v. Shoen, 48 F.3d 412 (9th Cir.

1995). New York law states that in order to overcome the privilege, the party seeking disclosure must make "a clear and specific showing that the news: (i) is highly material and relevant; (ii) is critical or necessary to the maintenance of a party's claim, defense or proof of an issue material thereto; and (iii) is not obtainable from any alternative source." N.Y. Civ. Rights Law §79-h(c) (McKinney 1992). See also In re Application to Quash Subpoena to National Broadcasting Co., Inc., 79 F.3d 346, 351 (2d Cir. 1996), where the court held that in order to find unpublished news to be critical or necessary, there must be a finding that the claim for which the information is to be used "virtually rises or falls with the admission or exclusion of the proffered evidence." In contrast, the test is much less stringent where the material is not confidential:

> [W]here information sought is not confidential, a civil litigant is entitled to requested discovery notwithstanding a valid assertion of the journalist's privilege by a nonparty only upon a showing the requested material is: (1) unavailable despite reasonable alternative sources; (2) noncumulative; and (3) clearly relevant to an important issue in the case. [Mark v. Shoen, 48 F.3d at 416.]

For further discussion of state press shield laws, see Theodore Campagnolo, The Conflict Between State Press Shield Laws and Federal Criminal Proceedings: The Rule 501 Blues, 38 Gonz. L. Rev. 445 (2002/03).

The application of this privilege in libel and slander cases has been limited. In Desai v. Hersh, 954 F.2d 1408 (7th Cir. 1992), the court held that the privilege could not be invoked by a libel defendant, because the plaintiff had the burden of proving actual malice on the part of the reporter. Proof of actual malice under New York Times v. Sullivan, 376 U.S. 254 (1964), depends on knowing the identity of a reporter's source, since a libel plaintiff needs to demonstrate that the source was unreliable or that the reporter failed to take sufficient steps to verify the factual accuracy of the story. Because of this, the general rule is that in defamation actions in which a plaintiff must establish actual malice the reporter's privilege must give way to disclosure. Miller v. Transamerican Press, Inc., 621 F.2d 721, 725-726 (5th Cir. 1980). But see Condit v. National Enquirer, Inc., 289 F. Supp. 2d 1175 (E.D. Cal. 2003) (wife of former Congressman Gary Condit sued tabloid for libel; court upheld privilege protecting confidential source, concluding that plaintiff did not investigate all reasonable alternative information sources).

c.   Scholar's (Academic Researcher's) Privilege

Academic researchers have advocated a privilege to protect the confidentiality of their research and the identity of their research subjects. Proponents advance two arguments to support their claim of the privilege. First, the scholar's privilege can arguably fall within the ambit of the more widely recognized journalist's privilege, particularly if the scholarly research is to result in publication. Second, proponents argue that academic freedom is a special concern of the First Amendment and that the privilege is necessary to protect the research process and encourage the flow of information from research subjects. In Cusumano v. Microsoft Corporation, 162 F.3d 708 (1st Cir. 1998), the court considered whether academic researchers who had interviewed over 40 current and former Netscape employees in preparation for a book could maintain the confidentiality of the interview notes, tapes, transcripts, and recordings. Microsoft moved to compel the surrender of the research materials after the researchers resisted a subpoena. The court held that academic researchers are analogous to journalists and that the First Amendment interest of preventing the "chilling effect on speech" mandates the protection of the scholar's sources as well as the journalist's. Without such a privilege, the court wrote, "an academician, stripped of sources, would be able to provide fewer, less cogent analyses" and thus would be less able to disseminate information to the public. The court found that Microsoft's need was not compelling when balanced against the First Amendment protection.

Other asserted bases for the privilege are that interference with ongoing research, especially scientific research, could occur if data were forced to be disclosed, and the potential for publishing research in peer reviewed or other scholarly publications could be harmed. This last asserted rationale has met with little success in the courts. See Burka v. United States Department of Health and Human Services, 87 F.3d 508 (D.C. Cir. 1996) (stating that there is not an established or well-settled practice of protecting research data on the ground that disclosure would harm a researcher's publication prospects).

Several federal and state statutes protect research and sources of academic researchers, although in limited areas, such as drug research. See, e.g., 21 U.S.C. §872(c) (2000) (drug research); Cal. Health & Safety Code §11603 (West 1991) (drug research); N.Y. Pub. Health Law §3371 (McKinney 2002, Supp. 2005) (drug research). Courts have generally been reluctant to recognize a scholar's privilege. See In re Grand Jury Subpoena, 750 F.2d 223 (2d Cir. 1984) (refusing to recognize scholar's privilege); In re Grand Jury Proceedings (Scarce), 5 F.3d 397 (9th Cir. 1993); United States v. Doe, 460 F.2d 328 (1st Cir. 1972). But see Richards of Rockford, Inc. v. Pacific Gas and Elec. Co., 71 F.R.D. 388 (N.D. Cal. 1976). For further discussion, see Howard Gray Curtis, Comment, Academic Researchers and the First Amendment: Constitutional Protection for Their Confidential Sources?, 14 San Diego L. Rev. 876 (1977); David A. Kaplan and Brian M. Cogan, The Case Against Recognition of a General Academic Privilege, 60 U. Det. J. Urb. L. 205 (1983).

5. Peer Review Privilege

A peer review privilege has been claimed by both academic institutions and hospitals to protect the confidentiality of the peer review process, a process that ultimately determines which candidates receive academic tenure and hospital privileges. The justification for the privilege is the standard argument that compelled disclosure of peer review evaluations would obstruct the free flow of information that is essential to the integrity of the peer review process. Without protection against disclosure, the quality of the critiques would decline and less qualified candidates would be promoted, with a resultant impact on the quality of our universities and hospitals.

Notwithstanding such arguments, in University of Pennsylvania v. EEOC, 493 U.S. 182 (1990), the Supreme Court refused to recognize a federal privilege protecting the confidentiality of academic peer review materials from disclosure. The claim arose out of a race and sex discrimination suit brought by an associate professor of the University of Pennsylvania. The Court held that the privilege would not be recognized under either common law or First Amendment grounds. The Court was "especially reluctant to recognize a [common law] privilege" in an area where Congress, under

Title VII, has balanced the problem of "invidious" discrimination in educational institutions against the interest of academic autonomy "but has not provided the privilege
itself." The Court refused to expand the protection of the First Amendment right of
academic freedom to embrace confidential peer review materials. Before the decision, a majority of federal courts of appeals had recognized a qualified peer review
privilege in the academic setting.

   In the hospital setting, federal and state courts have generally rejected claims of a
peer review privilege. See Memorial Hosp. v. Shadur, 664 F.2d 1058 (7th Cir. 1981);
Robinson v. Magovern, 83 F.R.D. 79 (W.D. Pa. 1979). Several states have enacted
statutes that accord protection to the hospital peer review process. See, e.g., Mich.
Comp. Laws Ann. §333.21515 (West 2001). Some states have included an exception
to provide for disclosure in the area of discrimination suits. See, e.g., Cal. Evid. Code
§1157(c) (West 1995). Even though some courts recognize the privilege, it has been
narrowly construed to allow plaintiffs to uncover evidence of wrongdoing. In Moretti
v. Lowe, 592 A.2d 855, 857 (R.I. 1991), the court held that while the internal communications and deliberative processes of a peer review committee were privileged,
the effect of those proceedings was not. Thus, the plaintiff in a medical malpractice
action could discover whether a particular nurse had been disciplined by her hospital
review committee. The court in *Moretti* also said that the privilege did not protect the
identity of persons who might serve on peer review committees or who have given
information to such committees.

   The privilege also does not protect pre-existing documents that have been turned
over to the peer-review committee. Roach v. Springfield Clinic, 157 Ill. 2d 29, 40-42,
623 N.E.2d 246, 251 (1993). In *Roach*, the court stated:

> If the simple act of furnishing a committee with earlier acquired information were suf-
> ficient to cloak that information with the statutory privilege, a hospital could effectively
> insulate from disclosure virtually all adverse facts known to its medical staff, with the
> exception of those matters actually contained in a patient's records.

For a decision upholding the privilege under difficult circumstances, see Jackson v.
Scott, 667 A.2d 1365 (D.C. Ct. App. 1995). In this case, the defendant hospital's
review of deaths during cardiac surgery revealed evidence of gross negligence. A confidential informant, who "had to [have been] in the operating room" during the surgery
performed on the plaintiff's wife, revealed that the surgery was "very mismanaged,"
resulting in the patient's death. The court upheld the hospital's claim of privilege
regarding its internal investigation of the death. Relying on the District of Columbia's
Health Care Peer Review Act of 1992, D.C. Code §§32-501 et seq., the court stated
that the privilege was unqualified. Defense witnesses testified, without mentioning
the internal report, that the hospital was not negligent in the patient's death. The
court nevertheless held that, under a plain reading of the statute, the report could not
be used for impeachment purposes.

   For further analysis of the peer review privilege, see David McMillin, University
of Pennsylvania v. EEOC and Dixon v. Rutgers: Two Supreme Courts Speak
on the Academic Freedom Privilege, 42 Rutgers L. Rev. 1089 (1990); Don Mark
North, University of Pennsylvania v. EEOC: The Denial of an Academic Freedom
Privilege, 18 Pepp. L. Rev. 213 (1990); Susan O. Scheutzow and Sylvia Lynn Gillis,
Confidentiality and Privilege of Peer Review Information: More Imagined Than Real,
7 J.L. & Health 169 (1992/ 1993).

6.   Self-evaluative Privilege

A privilege similar to the peer review privilege, the "self-critical analysis privilege" has been asserted in the corporate context. The privilege is often asserted by companies with affirmative action policies, to protect against disclosure of intracorporate communications made during the employee review process and against disclosure of compliance investigations done by the corporation. The asserted justification for the privilege is that forcing disclosure of these communications will have a chilling effect on compliance with equal employment opportunity laws. In Aramburu v. Boeing Co., 885 F. Supp. 1434 (D. Kan. 1995), the court refused to recognize the privilege in a Title VII case. Relying on University of Pennsylvania v. EEOC, the court stated that it was reluctant to recognize such a privilege when it appeared that Congress had considered the issue but had failed to provide for the privilege. 885 F. Supp. at 1440. Similarly, the court in Roberts v. Hunt, 187 F.R.D. 71 (W.D.N.Y. 1999), found that the Supreme Court, in rejecting a "peer review" privilege in *University of Pennsylvania*, implicitly rejected the rationale for a self-evaluation privilege and thus left the privilege unavailable under federal law. However, some lower federal courts have recognized this privilege. See, e.g., Troupin v. Metropolitan Life Insurance Company, 169 F.R.D. 546 (S.D.N.Y. 1996) (recognizing the privilege where "an intrusion into the self-evaluative analyses of an institution would have an adverse effect on the [evaluative] process, with a net detriment to a cognizable public interest"); Reichhold Chemicals, Inc. v. Textron, Inc., 157 F.R.D. 522 (N.D. Fla. 1994) (collecting cases recognizing self-critical analysis privilege); Banks v. Lockheed-Georgia Co., 53 F.R.D. 283 (N.D. Ga. 1971) (recognizing privilege in employment discrimination case). For a discussion, see Ronald J. Allen and Cynthia M. Hazelwood, Preserving the Confidentiality of Internal Corporate Investigations, 12 J. Corp. L. 355 (1987).

Congress has created a privilege for state and local governments, similar to the self-evaluative privilege, in the context of highway safety. In order to promote highway safety, in 1973 Congress created a hazard elimination program for public roadways, providing federal funds for states to identify, study, and eliminate hazardous conditions on the nation's roads. 23 U.S.C. §152. The program required the states to conduct surveys and collect data on accident statistics in order to identify potentially hazardous sites. Id. Although the program provided a mechanism to enhance highway safety, the information collected by the states became a potential liability, due to the threat of discovery in lawsuits against the states. In response to these threats and in the interest of obtaining the best possible information from the states to enhance highway safety, Congress enacted a statutory privilege similar to the self-evaluative privilege, protecting information collected by states for enhancing safety and improving hazardous roadways. 23 U.S.C. §409 (1995). The statute provides as follows:

> [R]eports, surveys, schedules, lists, or data compiled or collected for the purpose of identifying evaluating, or planning the safety enhancement of potential accident sites, hazardous roadway conditions, or railway-highway crossings, pursuant to sections 130, 144, and 152 of this title [23 U.S.C.S. §130, 144, and 152] or for the purpose of developing any highway safety construction improvement project which may be implemented utilizing Federal-aid highway funds shall not be subject to discovery or admitted into evidence in a Federal or State court proceeding or considered for other purposes in any action for damages arising from any occurrence at a location mentioned or addressed in such reports, surveys, schedules, lists, or data. [23 U.S.C. §409.]

Although the statute establishes a federal privilege, the statute was challenged in the case of Pierce County v. Guillen, 537 U.S. 129 (2003). In *Guillen*, a widower engaged in a negligence suit against a county government sought discovery of information obtained by the county relating to the intersection where his wife had been in an automobile accident. Id. The Supreme Court held that the statute was within the scope of Congress's power under the commerce clause, and that "§409 protects all . . . data actually compiled or collected for §152 purposes, but does not protect information that was originally compiled or collected for purposes unrelated to §152 and that is currently held by the agencies that compiled or collected it, even if the information was at some point 'collected' by another agency for §152 purposes." Id. at 144. Under this interpretation, an accident report collected only for law enforcement purposes and held by the county sheriff would not be protected under §409 in the hands of the county sheriff, even though that same report would be protected in the hands of the Public Works Department, so long as the department first obtained the report for §152 purposes. Id.

Although the development of a general self-evaluative privilege in the cases has been spotty, numerous statutes protecting discrete interests have been passed, particularly in the states. A good example is Oregon's environmental audit privilege for reports prepared as a result of voluntary environmental audits designed to assure compliance with the state's environmental laws. The privilege is thorough, protecting virtually all materials created for and during the audit, with no distinction between objective and subjective material. It protects the information from both private and governmental parties, even when filing a report is mandatory, and courts may not make case-by-case determinations whether disclosure would best serve the public interest. Similar, but sometimes less expansive, statutes have been passed in 10 other states. For a discussion, see Peter Gish, The Self-critical Analysis Privilege and Environmental Audit Reports, 25 Envtl. L. 73 (1995).

7.   Government Privileges — Executive Privilege

The Executive Branch has been the focus of most of the discussion of whether evidentiary privileges should be created to protect confidential communications within the government. But see United States v. Gillock, 445 U.S. 360 (1980) (holding that there is no privilege for state legislator in federal prosecution). The term *executive privilege* includes several different categories of privileges for governmental secrets. First, the state secrets privilege protects military, diplomatic, or sensitive national security secrets. Second, the qualified presidential communications privilege protects confidential conversations between the president and the president's advisers (e.g., the members of the cabinet). Last, there are privileges to protect a wide range of official information, such as law enforcement files and governmental agency deliberations.

a.   State Secrets Privilege

The state secrets privilege protects against the disclosure of highly secret military and diplomatic information. Here the concern is that the release of such information might endanger the public or harm the nation. The privilege has protected such information as FBI activities, see In re United States, 872 F.2d 472 (D.C. Cir.), *cert. dismissed sub nom.* United States v. Albertson, 493 U.S. 960 (1989); missile technology, see Bentzlin v. Hughes Aircraft Co., 833 F. Supp. 1486 (C.D. Cal. 1993); radar system capabilities, see Zuckerbraun v. General Dynamics Corp., 935 F.2d 544 (2d Cir. 1991); and diplomatic conversations, see Attorney Gen. v. Irish People, Inc., 502 F. Supp. 63, 64-65 (D.D.C. 1980).

In United States v. Reynolds, 345 U.S. 1 (1953), the Supreme Court provided a thorough examination of the state secrets privilege. According to the court, the government is the exclusive holder of the privilege. The privilege must be formally invoked by the head of the government department concerned, after "actual personal consideration" by that executive official. In deciding on a claim of the privilege, the standard to be applied is whether there is a reasonable danger that disclosure will harm national security. If the reasonable danger standard is met, the privilege is absolute. The court noted that "even the most compelling necessity cannot overcome the claim of privilege if the court is ultimately satisfied that military secrets are at stake." In Black v. United States, 62 F.3d 1115 (8th Cir. 1995), the court dismissed a harassment suit against federal intelligence agencies where litigation would necessarily breach the state secrets privilege. Black was an electrical engineer who had government security clearance to work on defense projects with various contractors. After a Soviet mathematician at a lecture in Zurich allegedly asked him suspiciously intrusive questions, Black reported the contact to the U.S. Consulate and soon thereafter his security clearance was "unplugged." He claimed that he was the victim of harassment and psychological attack and sued the United States for the actions of the CIA, FBI, and Department of State. R. James Woolsey, Director of the CIA, formally invoked the state secret privilege and asserted that litigation of the claim would result in the disclosure of highly sensitive names, dates, and locations of U.S. counterintelligence operations. The lower court reviewed the documents *in camera* and dismissed all of the claims. The Court of Appeals affirmed the decision, according the "utmost deference" to the executive's determination of the impact of disclosure.

Whether the privilege is claimed in a criminal or civil proceeding, the denial of discovery will dramatically affect the opposing party's preparation of the case. In both criminal and civil proceedings, the court may order dismissal as it did in *Black* or other less drastic relief, such as striking particular testimony of a witness or finding against the government on a particular issue.

The Classified Information Procedures Act (CIPA), 18 U.S.C.A. App. 3, §§1 et seq. (West 2001), grants statutory recognition to the state secrets privilege in the area of criminal proceedings. The act sets forth detailed procedures governing a criminal defendant's efforts to reveal or to obtain discovery of classified information and was passed by Congress in 1980 to address the defense tactic known as "graymail." The defendant who threatens to disclose classified information creates a dilemma for the government. It must either dismiss the charges against the defendant or allow the disclosure of sensitive information. The goal of CIPA is to provide pretrial procedures for the resolution of discovery and admissibility issues.

CIPA primarily functions in two ways. Section 5 requires defendants to notify the government of its intention to disclose classified information in the course of presenting a defense. Pretrial hearings on discovery and admissibility of evidence are governed by §§4 and 6. Section 4 expands on Federal Rule of Criminal Procedure 16 and permits courts to authorize the United States to delete specific classified information from documents, to substitute a summary of the information, or to substitute a statement admitting relevant facts that the classified information would tend to prove. Section 6 provides a pretrial hearing to determine relevance, §6(a), and a pretrial hearing to determine whether the substitutions offered in lieu of the classified documents provide the defendant with "substantially the same ability to make his defense as would disclosure of the specific classified information," §6(c).

"Graymail" may not be just a sneaky defense tactic but may be the result of legitimate efforts to prepare a criminal defense. Several high-profile defendants have raised the question of the constitutionality of CIPA because of the limitations it places on defendants' ability to launch effective defenses. In United States v. North, 708 F. Supp. 399 (D.D.C. 1988), the defendant, Oliver North, filed a written statement of relevant and material testimony he expected to disclose during the course of the trial for the court to consider in a pretrial hearing. North later objected to the fulfillment of the CIPA provision requiring the disclosure of the statement to the Independent Counsel on the grounds that it would violate his Fifth and Sixth Amendment rights. The court held that the Fifth Amendment due process claim was meritless because modern litigation involves extensive pretrial discovery and additionally, North had been given access to much of the government's information and witnesses. Similarly, the Sixth Amendment right to effective assistance of counsel argument was found by the court to be unpersuasive because North would still be able to call or not to call witnesses, and the tactical disadvantage of minimizing surprise would be "slight." The court held CIPA to be facially constitutional.

Since *North*, courts have consistently upheld the constitutionality of CIPA against arguments asserting the violation of due process, the Fifth Amendment privilege against self-incrimination and the right to remain silent unless and until one decides to testify, the Fifth and Sixth Amendment rights to testify in one's own defense, and the Sixth Amendment right to cross-examine witnesses. See United States v. McVeigh, 923 F. Supp. 1310 (D. Colo. 1996) (finding it unnecessary to reach the issue of the constitutionality of CIPA); United States v. Wen Ho Lee, 90 F. Supp. 2d 1324 (D.N.M. 2000) (denying the defendant's motion to find §§5 and 6 of CIPA unconstitutional); United States v. Bin Laden, 2001 U.S. Dist. LEXIS 719 (S.D.N.Y. Mar. 20, 2001) (denying the defendant's motion to find CIPA unconstitutional as it applies to him).

For further discussion of CIPA, see Tamanaha, a Critical Review of the Classified Information Procedures Act, 13 Am. J. Crim. L. 227 (1986); Salgado, Note, Government Secrets, Fair Trails, and the Classified Information Procedures Act, 98 Yale L.J. 427 (1988). For further discussion of the state secrets privilege generally, see J. Steven Gardner, The State Secret Privilege Invoked in Civil Litigation: A Proposal for Statutory Relief, 29 Wake Forest L. Rev. 567 (1994).

b.   Presidential Communications Privilege

President Jefferson first sought to maintain the confidentiality of presidential communications in United States v. Burr, 25 F. Cas. 187 (C.C. Dist. Va. 1807) when Chief Justice Marshall issued two subpoenas for letters written by General Wilkinson to the President. Jefferson asserted an exclusive right to the papers and resisted the subpoenas. Since that time, several presidents have invoked the privilege but United States v. Nixon provided the first clear description of its parameters.

In United States v. Nixon, 418 U.S. 683 (1974), the Supreme Court addressed whether a privilege exists to protect confidential communications between the president and the president's close advisors. President Nixon raised three claims: that the separation of powers doctrine precludes judicial review of a President's claim of privilege; that the Constitution provides an absolute privilege of confidentiality for all presidential communications; and alternatively, that the "presumptive" privilege for presidential communications should prevail over the subpoena in question. The Court, quoting Marbury v. Madison, reaffirmed that "it is the providence of this Court 'to say what the law is' with respect to the claim of privilege presented in this case," thus asserting the appropriateness of judicial review. The Court went on to recognize a constitutionally based privilege derived from the separation of powers, but noted that the presidential communications privilege is a qualified one. The Court stated that the privilege "must yield to the demonstrated, specific, need for evidence in a pending criminal trial."[83] In recognizing the qualified privilege, the Court noted that the presidential need for confidentiality justified a presumptive privilege for presidential communications. The burden rests with the person seeking discovery of the information to rebut the presumption of privilege. Moreover, in conducting an *in camera* inspection, the trial court must use "scrupulous protection" to ensure that presidential communications that are not relevant or admissible are not disclosed. The privilege may be stronger in civil proceedings. In Cheney v. U.S. Dist. Court for Dist. of Columbia, 542 U.S. 367 (2004), a case involving the assertion of executive privilege to prevent disclosure of the names of certain de facto members of the National Energy Policy Development Group, the court stated that "[t]he need for information for use in civil cases, while far from negligible, does not share the urgency or significance of the criminal subpoena requests in Nixon." Id. at 2589. For further discussion, see K. A. McNeely-Johnson, Comment, United States v. Nixon, Twenty Years After: The Good, the Bad and the Ugly — An Exploration of Executive Privilege, 14 N. Ill. U. L. Rev. 251 (1993). See also Mark J. Rozell, Symposium: Executive Privilege and the Clinton Presidency, 8 Wm. & Mary Bill of Rts. J. 541 (2000) (arguing that presidents should use the power only for the most compelling reasons and not to protect information that is merely embarrassing or politically damaging, and proposing that each administration adopt guidelines for its members with formal procedures for handling and resolving executive privilege issues).

In re Sealed Case, 121 F.3d 729 (D.C. Cir. 1997), provided the District of Columbia Court of Appeals with the opportunity to determine how far beyond direct communications with the President the presidential communications privilege might reach. As part of a grand jury investigation of former Secretary of Agriculture Mike Espy, the Office of the Independent Counsel tried to compel performance of a *subpoena duces tecum* issued by the grand jury and served on the Counsel to the President. The White House provided many of the requested documents but withheld 84 as privileged. The court held that the presidential privilege extends "down the line" from the President to his aides and advisors whenever they are in

---

83. Three years later the Court again declined to permit the executive privilege to prevent the release of information where an ex-president sought to invoke the privilege "against the very Executive Branch in whose name the privilege is invoked." Nixon v. Administrator of General Services, 433 U.S. 425 (1977) (former president directed to deliver presidential papers and tape recordings to an official of the Executive Branch for the creation of public access under the Presidential Recordings and Materials Preservation Act, held to be facially constitutional and not violative of the presidential privilege doctrine).

the "course of preparing advice" for the President even when they are not communicating directly with the President. The court found that all of the 84 documents — authored by White House Counsel, Deputy and Associate White House Counsel, legal externs to the White House Counsel's office, the Chief of Staff, the Press Secretary, and even three "no authored" documents — were privileged. The Office of the Independent Counsel, however, was given the opportunity on remand to demonstrate "sufficient need" in order to overcome the presidential communications privilege. The court sought to strike the "appropriate balance between openness and informed presidential deliberation."[84] In In re Sealed Case, 148 F.3d 1073 (D.C. Cir. 1998), *cert. denied sub nom.* Rubin v. United States 525 U.S. 990 (1998), the Government sought to extend the executive privilege to create a "protective function privilege" that would shield Secret Service agents from testifying. The Secret Service resisted the Independent Counsel's subpoena of 33 Secret Service officers to testify about their knowledge of President Clinton's affair with White House intern Monica Lewinsky. The Secret Service proposed an "absolute privilege that would preclude the OIC from compelling any testimony regarding information learned by Secret Service agents and officers while performing protective functions in physical proximity to the President where the information would tend to reveal the President's contemporaneous activities."[85] The court considered the three factors detailed by the Supreme Court in *Jaffee* (page 872, supra). It found that the privilege is not based in federal law[86] and Secret Service officers have testified previously;[87] the privilege is not supported by state precedents though the same need would presumably exist for state governors; and while there is a strong public policy interest in ensuring the safety of the President, the President will not resist the closeness of his protectors because of his own interest in his safety and because he is required by law to accept protection.[88] The court held that the absence of federal and state precedents and the Secret Service's failure to establish the need for the protective function privilege prevented its creation by the judiciary at this time. For further discussion of the case and an the argument that the D.C. Court of Appeals' discounting of the value of precedent in favor of policy arguments inappropriately relaxed the Supreme Court's standard that required more than a compelling public interest, see T. Spencer Crowley, Case Comment: Evidence: The Clinton Administration's Battle to Gain Evidentiary Privilege for Secret Service Agents — Another Tainted Legacy?, 51 Fla. L. Rev. 743 (1999).

---

84.   See Recent Case, 111 Harv. L. Rev. 861 (1998) (arguing that the court failed to recognize the difference in the privilege for the President and his advisors and disregarded other protections, such as the deliberative process privilege and statutory exceptions to the Freedom of Information Act, which would preserve the effectiveness of the executive branch).

85.   In re Grand Jury Proceedings, 1998 WL 272884 (D.D.C. May 22, 1998).

86.   There has been discussion in the Judiciary Committees of both the United States House of Representatives and the Senate about a potential protective function privilege. Senator Leahy introduced the Secret Service Protective Privilege Act of 1999, 106 S. 1360, which would prohibit testimony by Secret Service personnel or former personnel that was acquired during the performance of the protective function in physical proximity to the protectee. It was referred to the Senate Committee on the Judiciary but a report has not yet been issued.

87.   See In re Grand Jury Proceedings, 1998 WL 272884, at *3 (D.D.C. May 22, 1998) discussing President Nixon's taping system and John Hinckley's attempted assassination of President Reagan where the Secret Service did not assert a protective function privilege.

88.   18 U.S.C. §3056(a) mandates the protection of the President.

c.   *Official Information (Deliberative Process) Privilege*

The official information privilege exists to protect government deliberative processes and provides a limited executive privilege for executive officers other than the
President. Not surprisingly, the rationale is that compelled disclosure of such communications would inhibit the exchange of opinions and advice among executive
officials, and thereby impair the decision-making process. A related justification for
the privilege is that the judiciary is not authorized to probe the mental processes
of an executive or administrative officer. In re Franklin National Bank Securities
Litig., 478 F. Supp. 577, 580-581 (E.D.N.Y. 1979). The privilege is the government's.
Examples are government agency policy deliberations and law enforcement investigatory files. Both Proposed FRE 509 and the exemption provisions of the Freedom of
Information Act, 5 U.S.C. §552 (1994), address the need for protection of such official
information.

A qualified privilege protecting official information has been widely accepted
by the federal courts. See, e.g., Kelly v. City of San Jose, 114 F.R.D. 653 (N.D. Cal.
1987); United States v. Board of Educ. of City of Chicago, 610 F. Supp. 695 (N.D.
Ill. 1985); Kinoy v. Mitchell, 67 F.R.D. 1 (S.D.N.Y. 1975). In In re "Agent Orange"
Product Liability Litig., 97 F.R.D. 427, 434 (E.D.N.Y. 1983), the court described the
limited scope of the privilege:

> [The privilege] applies only to material reflecting [the] deliberative process — evalua-
> tions, expressions of opinions, and recommendations on policy matters. . . . Raw data
> and factual findings do not fall within the scope of the privilege because disclosures of
> facts, as opposed to opinions, would not hinder candor among government officials.

The D.C. Court of Appeals in In re Sealed Case, 121 F.3d 729 (1997), reiterated
this requirement that the material be "deliberative" and not merely factual and also
emphasized that it must be "predecisional." Furthermore, the court noted that the
privilege is not absolute and may be overcome by a showing that the need for evidence
in the specific case outweighs the harm that would result from disclosure. Quoting In
re Subpoena Served Upon the Comptroller of the Currency, 967 F.2d 630 (D.C. Cir.
1992), the court described the appropriate test:

> "Each time [the deliberative process privilege] is asserted the district court must under-
> take a fresh balancing of the competing interests," taking into account factors such as
> "the relevance of the evidence," "the availability of other evidence," "the seriousness of
> the litigation," "the role of the government," and the "possibility of future timidity by
> government employees."

In Dellwood Farms v. Cargill, Inc., 128 F.3d 1122 (7th Cir. 1997), private civil
plaintiffs sought materials gathered by the Department of Justice for use in criminal investigations. The FBI had been investigating charges of price fixing by Archer
Daniels Midland and other agricultural producers. The FBI recorded more than 150
hours of conversations within ADM and between ADM and its competitors. The government, without seeking any confidentiality agreement, played some of the recordings to the law firm representing ADM's outside directors to induce ADM to plead
guilty to the criminal antitrust offenses. The plaintiffs in this civil case subpoenaed the
tapes in the hope that they contained evidence of illegal conspiracy. The Department
of Justice attempted to block the subpoena with the law enforcement investigatory

privilege. The court held that the subpoena should be quashed because, though the privilege is not absolute and can be overridden through a showing of need, there ought to be a "pretty strong presumption" against lifting the privilege. It reasoned that crime investigation is the duty of the Executive Branch and it is inappropriate for the courts to be "thrust too deeply" into the process. Since the Freedom of Information Act would make the information available after the criminal trial is over, the court said, the civil suit could be postponed to await its release.

The plaintiffs additionally raised the issue of waiver since the Department of Justice had voluntarily played the recordings for ADM's lawyers. The court found that there had been a mere "selective waiver," described as the situation where, "having voluntarily disclosed privileged information to one person, the party who made the disclosure asserts the privilege against another person who wants the information." The court acknowledged that the government should have been more careful and obtained a protective order against further disclosure, as is normally required in selective disclosure cases. This error, however, the court said, should not be punished too harshly because there was no deliberate waiver of the privilege; to withhold the tapes from the plaintiffs and interference with criminal investigation would be an "excessive punishment."

The Supreme Court finally addressed the relationship between the official government information privilege and the Freedom of Information Act in United States v. Weber Aircraft Corp., 465 U.S. 792 (1984). The engine of an Air Force aircraft had failed, and the pilot was severely injured when he was ejected from the plane. He sued several entities responsible for the design and manufacture of his plane's ejection equipment. After the crash, the Air Force conducted both a "collateral investigation," designed to preserve evidence for use in whatever claims may ensue, and a "safety investigation," designed solely to permit corrective action to be taken in order to reduce the risk of similar occurrences. During safety investigations, witnesses are not sworn and are promised complete confidentiality. Lower courts had previously held the results of such investigations to be privileged from discovery, a holding the Supreme Court embraced. The plaintiff thus attempted to obtain the same information through a FOIA request, to which the Court responded:

> [R]espondents' contention that they can obtain through the FOIA material that is normally privileged would create an anomaly in that the FOIA could be used to supplement civil discovery. We have consistently rejected such a construction of the FOIA. We do not think that Congress could have intended that the weighty policies underlying discovery privileges could be so easily circumvented. [Id. at 801-802.]

After the passage of the Freedom of Information Act in 1967, many private litigants sought to use the new act rather than the normal rules of discovery to obtain information from the government in judicial proceedings. In NLRB v. Sears, Roebuck & Co., 421 U.S. 132 (1975), however, the Court examined the relationship between Exemption 5 of the FOIA and governmental privileges. The Court expressly found that Exception 5 contains a deliberative process privilege and a work product privilege and implied that a governmental attorney-client privilege should be recognized as well.

The Freedom of Information Act lists what each governmental agency must make available to the public and how the information is to be made accessible. There are several exceptions that allow agencies to maintain the confidentiality of some materials including those containing: matters of national defense or foreign policy,

internal personnel rules, privileged or confidential trade secrets or financial information, geological or geophysical information and data concerning wells, and records
or information compiled for law enforcement purposes to the extent that disclosure
would interfere with enforcement, deprive a person of the right to a fair trial, constitute an unwarranted invasion of personal privacy, reveal the identity of a confidential
source, endanger the life or physical safety of any individual, or disclose techniques
and procedures for law enforcement investigations or prosecutions.

Exception 5 to the FOIA, which excludes inter-agency or intra-agency communications, has allowed agencies to resist disclosure of information by claiming the
deliberative process privilege. The Supreme Court defined the deliberative process
as covering documents "reflecting advisory opinions, recommendations and deliberations comprising part of a process by which governmental decisions and policies are
formulated." NLRB v. Sears, Roebuck & Co., 421 U.S. 132, 150 (1975) (quoting Carl
Zeiss Stiftung v. V.E.B. Carl Zeiss, Jena, 40 F.R.D. 318, 324 (D.C. 1966)).

In Department of the Interior and Bureau of Indian Affairs v. Klamath Water
Users Protective Association, 532 U.S. 1 (2001), the Supreme Court addressed for the
first time the question of whether the deliberative process privilege could be extended
to cover communications between government agencies and "outsiders." The Klamath
Water Users, an association of water users in the Klamath River Basin, filed requests
under the FOIA for communications between the Bureau of Indian Affairs and the
Native American Tribes of the area, regarding the allocation of water. The Bureau
had consulted with the Tribes on the proposed Klamath Project Operation Plan in
efforts to assess the likely impact of the plan. The Bureau sought to invoke the deliberative process privilege of Exception 5 to resist the plaintiffs' request for information.
The Court acknowledged that courts have extended the privilege to communications
between governmental agencies and outside consultants[89] but rejected the Bureau's
portrayal of the Tribes as filling this sort of role. The Tribes, the Court found, had
communicated with the Bureau with their own interests in mind and had acted as
"self-advocates at the expense of others seeking benefits inadequate to satisfy everyone." The Court thus rejected the intra-agency nature of the communications and
held that they could not be exempted from discovery under Exception 5.

In the states, the extent of the protection afforded depends on the type of official
information at issue. For example, in the context of government agency deliberations, a majority of states have recognized a qualified privilege based on the federal
rule. In the context of law enforcement records, some states have enacted statutory
privileges to protect the information, while others have conferred some level of protection through the more general "classified" official information statutes. Where a
disclosure statute such as a state Freedom of Information Act is in effect, the statute
takes precedence in determining the scope of protection. For further discussion of
the various classes of official information, see 3 Jack B. Weinstein and Margaret A.
Berger, Weinstein's Evidence §§509.20-509.24 (Joseph M. McLaughlin ed., 2d ed.
1997).

---

89. See, e.g., Hoover v. Dept. of Interior, 611 F.2d 1132, 1138 (5th Cir. 1980) ("the government
may deem it necessary to seek the objective opinion of outside experts rather than rely solely on the opinions of government appraisers"); Lead Industries Assn. v. OSHA, 610 F.2d 70, 83 (2d Cir. 1979) (applying
Exemption 5 to cover draft reports "prepared by outside consultants who had testified on behalf of the
agency rather than agency staff"); Government Land Bank v. GSA, 671 F.2d 663, 665 (5th Cir. 1982)
("Both parties agree that a property appraisal, performed under contract by an independent professional,
is an 'intra-agency' document for purposes of the exemption").

In order to prevail on a claim of the official information privilege, the agency official asserting the privilege typically must specifically identify what government interest or privacy interest would be threatened by disclosure and describe how disclosure, even if made under a protective order, would create a substantial risk of harm. Chism v. County of San Bernadino, 159 F.R.D. 531, 534 (C.D. Cal. 1994). In *Chism*, the court held that a deputy sheriff's declaration failed to show that documents produced during an internal review of an allegedly unjustified shooting were protected by the official information privilege. The court said that a general assertion that the police department's internal investigatory system would be harmed by disclosure of its documents was insufficient. This information was presumptively discoverable because information in police files is often developed closer in time to the events in question, and therefore substantially comparable evidence is not available from other sources.

The official information privilege often arises in cases involving alleged violations of civil rights by police officers under 42 U.S.C. §1983 where plaintiffs want to discover the personnel records of police officer defendants. Despite the fact that many states have statutes protecting the confidentiality of these records, see, e.g., Kansas Open Records Act, Kan. Stat. Ann. §45-221(4) (2000); Cal. Penal Code §§832.7, 832.8 (Supp. 2005), and despite the fact that there are comparable confidentiality provisions for federal officers, 5 U.S.C. §552(b)(6) and (b)(7)(c), federal courts have been reluctant to recognize a privilege for police officer personnel records in §1983 cases. See, e.g., Mason v. Stock, 869 F. Supp. 828 (D. Kan. 1994); see also Welsh v. City and County of San Francisco, 887 F. Supp. 1293 (N.D. Cal. 1995).

8.   Miscellaneous Privileges

While the material above has covered the major privileges, there are in fact numerous other privileges found in case law and state statutes. This means that lawyers have to research, and research carefully, to see what privileges apply in their jurisdiction or that may be idiosyncratic to their case. Some state statutes affect the breadth of the otherwise general privileges discussed above. For example, statutes passed by some states to address domestic abuse victims effectively reduce the scope of the marital communication and physician-patient privileges that would otherwise be applicable. See, e.g., C.R.S. 18-6-401.1 (2009) ("The statutory privilege between the victim-patient and his physician and between the husband and the wife shall not be available for excluding or refusing testimony in any prosecution of an act of child abuse."). Other statutes are passed to reach discrete areas that may not otherwise be covered by general privileges. For example, Illinois protects information disclosed to a licensed genetic counselor, 225 Ill. Comp. Stat. 135/90 (2010); Delaware recognizes a specific type of self-evaluative privilege for hospitals, 16 Del. C. §1010A (2010); Connecticut privileges information gathered by mediators in labor disputes, Conn. Gen. Stat. §31-96 (2010); and Georgia does not require information gathered during the licensing stage of blasting operations to be turned over, Ga. Code Ann. §25-8-11 (2010). Case law similarly affects the privileges available in any jurisdiction. Two examples that have been accepted in some jurisdictions, and of which lawyers should be aware, are the common-interest or joint-defense privilege — protecting communications focused on creating a defense strategy with others who are similarly situated — and the absolute privilege protecting information disclosed in judicial proceedings. Many more privileges are potentially available in any litigation;

an attorney is well advised to check local statutes and case law before disclosing any document.

PROBLEMS

12.32. Michael McKinley is being prosecuted in Ireland for directing terrorism. He has asked the district court for an order to produce a tape recording that he believes will help him in cross-examining David Rogers, a key prosecution witness. The tape recordings are held by journalists who conducted interviews with Rogers for a contracted biography that they are writing. Rogers has not objected to the discovery, but the journalists have challenged, asserting the journalist's privilege. What result?

12.33. Ryan has lived with his grandmother for 15 years, all but a few months of his life, and she has always supported him financially and otherwise. Ryan has been charged with a crime and the prosecution is seeking to elicit the testimony of his grandmother about his statements to her following the alleged crime. Ryan's defense attorney objects on the ground that such statements were confidential and should be protected from disclosure under the parent-child privilege that is recognized in the state. Should the court permit testimony relative to statements made by Ryan to his grandmother?

12.34. All 230 persons aboard TWA flight 800 were killed when it exploded over the Atlantic Ocean on July 17th, 1996. The United States salvaged much of the wreckage and secured it in a building in Calverton, New York, to be used in the investigation of the accident. Sanders, an investigative journalist, pursued the hypothesis that a missile had caused the explosion and spoke with Captain Terrell, a senior 747 pilot with TWA who was involved in the investigation. Captain Terrell told Sanders that a "reddish" substance had been found on some of the seats that might be residue from an explosive. He later provided Sanders with a small portion of the substance that had been removed from the wreckage. Sanders wrote a book entitled The Downing of TWA Flight 800 in which he reported that this "reddish" substance tested consistent with the presence of solid rocket fuel. The FBI began investigating Sanders for violation of 49 U.S.C. §1155(b), which bans the unauthorized removal of "a part of a civilian aircraft involved in an accident." The government offered Sanders a nonprosecution agreement in exchange for the name of his confidential source but Sanders refused. After the government discovered his identity through other sources, Captain Terrell testified against Sanders in return for a reduction of his offense to a misdemeanor. Sanders argues that the journalist's privilege bars government coercion to disclose news sources and thus urges the court to use a balancing test weighing "the governmental interest served by prosecution" against "the detrimental impact of permitting such a prosecution to be used as a means of coercing disclosure of a journalist's source." Should the court hold that the journalist's privilege prevents prosecution from being used in this way?

12.35. Dr. Tambone has filed a complaint against Memorial Hospital for restraint of trade in violation of federal and state antitrust laws. He alleges that the physicians of Memorial Hospital have used the peer review and disciplinary process to exclude him from its medical staff, effectively destroying his practice. Dr. Tambone claims that he was the victim of a sham disciplinary proceeding that was used as a means of implementing the alleged restraint of trade. To prove this allegation he has sought discovery regarding the hospital's treatment of other doctors in comparable disciplinary proceedings. Can the hospital resist disclosure of the information under a peer review privilege?

12.36. The Federal Death Penalty Act of 1994 authorizes the death penalty for more than 40 crimes and sets the procedure for seeking the death penalty in federal cases. An Attorney General's Death Penalty Committee (DPC) reviews each case and conducts a meeting where the defendant's attorney may try to persuade the government not to seek the death penalty. The DPC then assists in advising the Attorney General as to the ultimate decision whether to pursue the death penalty. Defendant Jacobo is considered by the government to be a member of the "Mexican Mafia" and has been charged with murder in the furtherance of racketeering, an offence covered by the Federal Death Penalty Act. Jacobo has sought to discover information that might tend to mitigate the sentence in his case, including information from the DPC meetings and its completed "death penalty evaluation form." The government objects to the discovery request based on the deliberative process privilege. Should the court allow it to withhold this information from Jacobo?

12.37. USAID is a federal agency that oversees development projects under the government's foreign assistance program. USAID was involved in building a water treatment facility in Egypt, financing the project to be carried out by an Egyptian government agency. USAID hired a U.S. engineering firm, CDM, to design the project, while the construction contract was awarded to a joint venture (JV) between two companies. Under the contract, the builders deal directly with the host country, but USAID retains approval rights for significant changes and additional compensation.

The JV requested additional funds, but USAID refused after CDM assessed that the request should be much lower, and the parties have not been able to agree. USAID urged CDM to hire a consultant to evaluate the challenges to settlement. CDM hired Richard J. Roy, providing that a report of his findings was to be given only to USAID and the Egyptian government agency, without disclosure to other parties.

A Freedom of Information Act (FOIA) request was filed with USAID on behalf of the JV members for documents related to the dispute, including the Roy Report, which USAID refused to provide, arguing that the report was attorney work-product and was privileged under the attorney-client privilege. A FOIA lawsuit was filed in federal court alleging that USAID unlawfully withheld the report. What result?

Table of Cases

Principal cases are in italics.

AAMCO Transmissions, Inc. v. Baker, 521
Abel; United States v., 395, 396
Abreu; United States v., 188, 711
Abu-Jihaad; United States v., 479
Acevedo; United States v., 311
Acker; United States v., 857, 858, 868
Adair; United States v., 296, 298
Adams; Commonwealth v., 457
Adams; United States v., 395
Addington v. Texas, 724
Adlman; United States v., 818
Adoption of Doe, In re, 736
Ad-Vantage Tel. Directory Consultants, Inc. v. GTE
  Directories Corp., 363
Affleck; United States v., 687
"Agent Orange" Prod. Liab. Litig., In re, 912
Agne; United States v., 473
Agosto, In re, 797
AgriBio Tech, Inc. v. Thomas, 520
Air Crash Disaster, In re, 333
Air Disaster at Lockerbie Scotland on Dec. 21, 1988,
  In re, 537
Alarcon-Simi; United States v., 492
Albertson; United States v., 908
Alcalde; People v., 501
Alexander; United States v., 491
Alexis v. McDonald's Rests. of Mass., Inc., 635, 636
Allen; United States v. (540 F.3d 821), 370
Allen; United States v. (10 F.3d 405), 642
Allen J.; United States v., 178
Alperin; United States v., 887
Alvarez; United States v., 296, 298
Amachia; United States v., 377
Amaya; United States v., 545
American Coal Co. v. Benefits Review Bd., 747
American Stores Co. v. Commissioner of Internal
  Revenue, 778
Ammar; United States v., 479

Amobi v. D.C. Dep't of Corr., 811, 816
Anderson v. Liberty Lobby, Inc., 721
Anderson v. Malloy, 331
Anderson; United States v. (509 F.2d 724), 902
Anderson; United States v. (933 F.2d 1261), 229
Anderson; United States v. (790 F. Supp. 231),
  807
Andrekus v. Board of Educ., 576
Andrews v. State, 194
Andring; State v., 886
Ansaldi; United States v., 230, 231
Appeal of. *See name of party*
Application of. *See name of party*
Apprendi v. New Jersey, 678, 762, 763
Aramburu v. Boeing Co., 906
Ariza v. City of N.Y., 534
Armstrong; United States v., 219
Arnold; United States v., 492, 493
Arthur Young & Co.; United States v., 896
Asplundh Mfg. Div. v. Benton Harbor Eng'g, 639
Athey v. Farmers Ins. Exch., 336
Atkins; United States v., 561
Attorney Gen. v. Irish People, Inc., 908
Aumand v. Dartmouth Hitchcock Med. Ctr., 524
Auster; United States v., 888
Austin v. Hopper, 281
Austin; United States v., 542
Ayala; United States v., 691
Ayala-Pizarro; United States v., 639

Badgett v. Rent-Way, Inc., 219
Bailey; United States v., 765
Baird v. Koerner, 837
Baker v. State, 515, 858
Bakshinian; United States v., 475
Ballew v. State, 806
Bank of China v. NBM LLC, 639

919

Bankcard Am., Inc. v. Universal Bancard Sys., Inc., 336
Banks v. Lockheed-Georgia Co., 906
Barber v. Page, 546, 620
Barnes v. United States, 769
Barraza; United States v., 502
Batson v. Kentucky, 83
Battle; United States v., 710
Baxter v. Palmigiano, 803
Beasley v. State, 620
Beck v. Alabama, 763
Beech Aircraft Corp. v. Rainey, 532, 533, 537, 689
Beechum; United States v., 255
Behn; State v., 715
Belfast; United States v., 491
Bell; United States v., 143, 145
Benavidez-Benavidez; United States v., 665
Bensimon; United States v., 375
Bentzlin v. Hughes Aircraft Co., 908
Bercier; United States v., 871
Betts; United States v., 395
Big O Tire Dealers, Inc. v. Goodyear Tire & Rubber Co., 337
Bilderbeck; United States v., 255
Bilzerian; United States v., 802, 807
Bin Laden; United States v., 909
Bisbee; United States v., 209
Bizanowicz; Commonwealth v., 618
Black v. M & W Gear Co., 125
Black v. United States, 908
Blair; State v., 137, 204, 243, 250, 415, 443, 510, 571, 593
Blake v. Pellegrino, 140, 159
Blount v. Hardy, 610
Blu-J, Inc. v. Kemper C.P.A. Group, 337
BMW v. Gore, 757
Board of Educ. of Chicago; United States v., 912
Bobo; United States v., 560
Bogle; People v., 869
Bogosian v. Mercedes-Benz, Inc., 332
Bohannon v. Pegelow, 636
Bohler-Udderholm Am., Inc. v. Ellwood Group, Inc., 576
Boim v. Holy Land Found., 689
Bolick; United States v., 356
Bolzer; United States v., 859, 862
Bonds; United States v., 575
Booker; United States v., 762, 763
Bordeaux; United States v., 610
Boucher v. Grant, 488
Bourjaily v. United States, 225, 478, 568, 581
Bowie; United States v., 252
Boyd v. Toyobo Am., Inc., 533
BP Amoco Chem. Co. v. Flint Hills Res., LLC, 525
Brady v. Maryland, 365
Branzburg v. Hayes, 902
Bray; United States v., 218, 219
Bridges; United States v., 347
Brien; United States v., 651, 683
Brink; United States v., 457
Brink's, Inc. v. City of N.Y., 803
Broadback v. Trapp, 419, 510
Brocklesby v. United States, 336
Brooks v. Chrysler Corp., 280
Brooks; United States v., 252

Brown v. Board of Educ., 786
Brown v. Smithkline Beecham Corp., 507
Brown; United States v. (557 F.2d 541), 654
Brown; United States v. (605 F.2d 389), 867
Brownlee; United States v., 651
Brumley; United States v., 347
Bruno; United States v., 594
Bruton v. United States, 468
Bryant; Michigan v., 604, 608, 609, 621
Bryant; People v., 605
Bucci v. Essex Ins. Co., 506
Buchanan; United States v., 141
Buck; United States v., 219
Bullcoming v. New Mexico, 615, 616, 617, 618
Bunchan; United States v., 364
Burch; United States v., 348
Burchfield v. CSX Transp., Inc., 194
Burka v. United States Dep't of Health & Human Servs., 904
Burke; United States v. (700 F.2d 70), 902
Burke; United States v. (2009 WL 173829), 511
Burr; United States v., 909
Burton; People v., 859
Byrd v. Maricopa County Sheriff's Dep't, 154
Byrd; United States v., 449

CA, Inc. v. Simple, Inc., 185, 204
Cage v. Louisiana, 750
Cage; People v., 611
Calhoun; State v., 604
California v. Green, 92
Californian & Hawaiian Sugar Co. v. Kansas City Terminal Warehouse Co., 336
Call; United States v., 147
Campbell v. Coleman Co., 545
Campbell v. Greer, 375
Campos v. MTD Prods., Inc., 506
Candelaria-Silva; United States v., 151
C & E Serv., Inc. v. Ashland, Inc., 338–339
C & H Commercial Contractors v. United States, 475
Capelton; United States v., 479
Caraballo; United States v., 615
Carl Zeiss Stiftung v. V.E.B. Carl Zeiss, Jena, 914
Carley v. Wheeled Coach, 775
Carlson; State v., 227, 469
Carman v. McDonnell Douglas Corp., 885
Carneglia; United States v., 532
Carson v. Fine, 871
Carter v. University of Toledo, 472
Carvalho; United States v., 563
Cash; United States v., 511, 512
Cassidy; United States v., 178
Castillo; United States v., 308
Castro-Ayon; United States v., 453
Catalan-Roman; United States v., 401
Caver v. City of Trenton, 885
Certain Underwriters at Lloyd's, London v. Sinkovich, 523, 639
Chamberlain v. State, 859
Chapel; United States v., 779
Chapman; United States v., 868
Charmley v. Lewis, 270, 272
Chase v. General Motors Corp., 330

Chase; United States v., 888
Chemtool, Inc. v. Lubrication Techs., Inc., 471
Cheney v. U.S. Dist. Court for D.C., 910
Cherry; United States v., 567, 569, 570
Chism v. County of San Bernadino, 915
Chlopek v. Federal Ins. Co., 330
Cisneros-Gutierrez; United States v., 453
Citizens for Equal Prot., Inc. v. Bruning, 859
City & County of Denver v. East Jefferson County
    Sanitation Dist., 737
City of. *See specific city*
Clark v. Arizona, 764
Clark v. United States, 837
Clark; United States v., 869
Clarke; United States v., 532
Cleveland v. KFC Nat'l Mgmt. Co., 311, 314
Cohen; United States v., 502
Cohn; United States v., 802
Coles v. Harsch, 799
Coles v. Jenkins, 148
Collier; United States v., 374
Collins; United States v., 299
Colon; United States v., 254
Colonial Leasing Co. v. Logistics Control Group
    Int'l, 780
Columbia Sec. Litig., In re, 574
Commanche; United States v., 377
Commodity Futures Trading Comm'n v.
    Weintraub, 832
Commonwealth v. *See name of opposing party*
Conde v. Starlight I, Inc., 341
Condit v. National Enquirer, Inc., 903
Coney; United States v., 577
Conoco, Inc. v. Department of Energy, 575, 576
Continental Cablevision, Inc. v. Stores Broad. Co., 902
Cook v. Mississippi Dep't of Human Servs., 575
Cook v. Rockwell Int'l Corp., 341
Cornett; United States v., 477
Cotter; United States v., 638
Couch v. United States, 896–897
County Court of Ulster County v. Allen, 768, 769
Cox v. Miller, 893
Cox v. State, 316
Crawford v. Washington, 448, 458, 491, 535, 536,
    553, 561, 562, 567, 574, 577, 580, *581*, 592, 593,
    594, 605, 607, 609, 611, 613, 615, 616, 617, 618,
    619, 620, 621, 622, 624, 629, 690, 691
Cree v. Hatcher, 374
Crisp; United States v., 213, 711, 712, 713
Cromer; United States v., 594
Crosby; United States v., 146, 158
Croskey v. BMW of N. Am., Inc., 336
Cross v. United States, 212
Crowder; United States v., 167, 254, 255
Cuesta; United States v., 513, 515
Cusumano v. Microsoft Corp., 797, 801, 903

Daghita; People v., 860
Daly; State v., 379
Danforth v. Minnesota, 593
D'Arcy; People v., 621
Darrow v. Gunn, 808
Daubert v. Merrell Dow Pharm., Inc. (509 U.S. 579),
    653, 655, 663, 664, 665, 666, 667, 668, 672,

673, 681, 682, 706, 707, 708, 710, 711, 712, 713,
    714, 715, 790
Daubert v. Merrell Dow Pharm., Inc. (43 F.3d 1311),
    666–667
Davies; United States v., 898
Davis v. Alaska, 803
Davis v. State, 171
Davis v. Washington, 594, 595, 603, 604, 605, 606,
    607, 608, 610, 613, 616, 621
Davis; United States v. (183 F.3d 231), 363
Davis; United States v. (577 F.3d 660), 491
Davis; United States v. (2001 WL 524374), 561
DeBeans Cone Co., LLC v. Norse Dairy Sys., LLC, 527
DeBoer; United States v., 219
Deeb; United States v., 549
DeGeratto; United States v., 364
DeKoven v. Plaza Assocs., 700
DeLaurentis; United States v., 143
Dellwood Farms v. Cargill, Inc., 801, 912
DeLong; State v., 899
DeMarce; United States v., 488, 489
Demjanjuk; United States v., 202
Denton; United States v., 390
Desai v. Hersh, 903
DeSimone; United States v., 387
Desrosiers v. Flight Int'l of Fla., Inc., 533
Dhinsa; United States v., 567, 568, 569, 570
Diamond; Doe v., 886, 887
Diehl v. Blaw-Knox, 333
Dilboy; State v., 615
DiMaria; United States v., 489, 497
DiNapoli; United States v., 548, 553
Dior; United States v., 780, 788
DiPaola; United States v., 398
DirecTV v. Murray, 527
Dixon v. International Harvester Co., 331
Dixon; People v., 897
Dixon; United States v., 637
Doan v. Carter, 619
Doe v. *See name of opposing party*
Doe; In re Adoption of, 736
Doe; United States v. (460 F.2d 328), 904
Doe; United States v. (655 F.2d 920), 346
Dolah; United States v., 546
Donovan v. Crisostomo, 560
Dowdell; United States v., 536
Doyle; United States v., 887
Drake, In re, 576
Dring; United States v., 364
Dube; United States v., 891
Duffy; United States v., 218
Dullard; State v., 436, 437, 438, 440, 441, 442, 444
Duval; United States v., 470

Eagle; United States v., 310
EEOC v. *See name of opposing party*
Eichorn v. AT&T Corp., 219
El Paso Co.; United States v., 819
Elfgeeh; United States v., 154
Ellis v. United States, 893
Ellis; United States v., 390
Ellison v. Ellison, 885
Emery; United States v., 570, 571
Enjady; United States v., 308

Enron Creditors Recovery Corp., In re, 208
Ensey; Doe v., 885
Erato, In re, 898
Erie, In re County of, 835
Estate of. *See specific party*
Estes; United States v., 860
Evans; United States v., 413, 414, 474

Farhane; United States v., 499
Farrah; United States v., 202
Fasanaro v. Mooney Aircraft Corp., 330
Fausek v. White, 799
FDIC v. White, 901
Ferber; United States v., 491, 527
Ferreira; United States v., 128
Field v. Anderson, 427
Field v. Trigg County Hosp., Inc., 506
Figueroa; United States v., 359
Figueroa-Lopez; United States v., 640
First Sec. Bank v. Union Pac. R. Co., 280, 328
Fischer; United States v., 801, 902
Fitzgerald v. Cassil, 885–886
Fitzgerald; People v., 897
Flaminio v. Honda Motor Co., 328
Folb v. Motion Picture Indus. Pension & Health
    Plans, 901
Ford v. Schmidt, 330
Forrester; United States v., 640, 641
Forstell; United States v., 691
Four Corners Helicopters, Inc. v. Turbomeca, 280
Frank v. County of Hudson, 143, 310
Frank; United States v., 347
Franklin Nat'l Bank Sec. Litig., In re, 912
Fritsch v. City of Chula Vista, 886
Fry; People v., 620
Frye v. United States, 654, 655, 663, 664, 673,
    681, 790
Fulk; United States v., 858

Gabe; United States v., 310, 311
Gail D., In re, 897
Gajo; United States v., 476
Galarnyk v. Hostmart Mgmt., 339
Galarza v. United States, 834
Galbreth; United States v., 665
Gamerdinger v. Schaefer, 271
Garcia; United States v., 638
Garcia-Meza; United States v., 622
Garcia-Rosa; United States v., 151
Garcia-Torres; United States v., 476
Garner; People v., 248
Garner v. Wolfinbarger, 800
Gaskell; United States v., 194
General Elec. Co. v. Joiner, 666
General Signal Corp. v. MCI Telecomms. Corp., 148
General Wood Preserving Co.; NLRB v., 201
George; United States v., 711
Georgia-Pacific Corp. v. GAF Roofing Mfg. Corp.,
    807
Geston; United States v., 362
Ghilarducci; United States v., 620
Gierlinger v. Gleason, 230, 231, 233
Gil; United States v., 476

Gilbert v. California, 459
Gilbert; United States v., 371
Giles v. California, 568, 604, 619, 621, 622,
    623, 624
Gill; United States v., 665
Gillock; United States v., 907
Gilmore v. Lafler, 621
Gilmore; United States v., 370
Glass; United States v., 889
Glawson; United States v., 189
Glover v. State, 867
Goldblatt v. Federal Deposit Ins. Corp., 775
Goldsmith v. State, 887
Goldstein; People v., 691
Gomez v. Rodriguez, 471
Gonsalves; United States v., 144
Gonzalez v. Digital Equip. Corp., 151, 198
Gonzalez; United States v., 193
Gonzalez-Maldonado; United States v., 201
Goodridge v. Department of Pub. Health, 858
Goodyear Tire & Rubber Co. v. Chiles Power
    Supply, Inc., 900
Gorby v. Schneider Tank Lines, 641
Gordon; United States v., 891
Gould; United States v., 787, 788, 789
Government Land Bank v. GSA, 914
Government of. *See specific government*
Grady; United States v., 299
Grand Jury Investigation, In re (842 F.2d 1223), 837
Grand Jury Investigation, In re (918 F.2d 374), 797,
    891, 892, 893, 894
Grand Jury Investigation, In re (399 F.3d 527), 835
Grand Jury Investigation (Durant), In re, 837
Grand Jury Proceedings, In re (350 F.3d 299), 802
Grand Jury Proceedings, In re (1998 WL 272884),
    911
Grand Jury Proceedings (Des Moines, Iowa), In re,
    818, 855
Grand Jury Proceedings (Gregory P. Violette), In re,
    889
Grand Jury Proceedings (John Doe), In re, 898
Grand Jury Proceedings (Pavlick), In re, 837
Grand Jury Proceedings (Scarce), In re, 902, 904
Grand Jury Proceedings (Twist), In re, 836
Grand Jury Proceedings No. 96-55344, In re, 837
Grand Jury Proceedings Unemancipated Minor
    Child, In re, 898
Grand Jury Proceedings Witness Ms. X, In re, 858
Grand Jury Subpoena, In re (750 F.2d 223), 904
Grand Jury Subpoena, In re (884 F. Supp. 188), 867
Grand Jury Subpoena Dated March 24, 2003, In re,
    805
Grand Jury Subpoena Duces Tecum, In re, 835
Grand Jury Subpoena Duces Tecum Dated Sept. 15,
    1983, In re, 837
Grand Jury Subpoena, Judith Miller, In re, 902
Grand Jury Subpoena United States, In re, 869
Grand Jury Subpoenas (United States v. Hirsch), In
    re, 836
Grand Jury Testimony of Attorney X, In re, 807
Grant; United States v., 189
Gray v. Bicknell, 809
Gray v. District Court, 807
Gray v. Maryland, 468
Great Coastal Express, Inc. v. Atlanta Mut. Cos., 340

Greater Newburyport Clamshell Alliance v. Public Serv. Co. of N.H., 818, 855
Green; United States v., 491, 512, 514
Greenburg, In re, 898
Griffin v. California, 802, 803
Grismore v. Consolidated Prods. Co., 695
Grooms; United States v., 387, 401
Grove v. Principal Mut. Life Ins. Co., 700
Guardia; United States v., 308
Guillermety v. Secretary of Educ., 521
Gustafson v. Cornelius Co., 780
Guthrie; United States v., 198
Gutierrez-Rodriguez v. Cartagena, 422

Hall v. Baxter Healthcare Corp., 700
Hall v. Brannan, 198
Hall; United States v. (152 F.3d 381), 167
Hall; United States v. (165 F.3d 1095), 651
Hall; United States v. (419 F.3d 980), 508
Halvorsen v. Baird, 146
Hamama; United States v., 201, 202
Hamilton v. New York, 328
Hamilton; United States v., 857
Hammon v. Indiana, 595, 603, 604, 605, 606
Hammoud; United States v., 167
Hampton; People v., 707
Hampton; United States v., 208
Hancock v. Hobbs, 797
Handlin; United States v., 476
Hardwick; United States v., 348
Hardy v. Merrill, 634
Harper; United States v., 373
Harper & Row Publishers, Inc. v. Decker, 822
Harrell; People v., 897
Harrell v. State, 248
Harris; United States v. (130 F.3d 829), 167
Harris; United States v. (55 M.J. 433), 197
Hart; United States v., 213
Harty; United States v., 451, 620
Hauert; United States v., 336
Havard v. Baxter Int'l Inc., 701
Havens Steel Co. v. Randolph Eng'g Co., 780
Havvard; United States v., 712, 713
Hawkins v. United States, 786
Hayes; United States v., 888
Haywood; United States v., 151, 249
Health Alliance Network, Inc. v. Continental Cas. Ins. Co., 527
Henderson v. George Wash. Univ., 154
Henderson; United States v., 641, 642, 665
Henry; United States v., 691
Herbert v. Lando, 902
Hernandez v. New York, 677
Hernandez v. State, 610
Hernandez; United States v., 563
Hickman v. Taylor, 831
Hickson Corp. v. Norfolk S. Ry. Co., 533, 537
Higa; United States v., 387
Hill; United States v., 255
Hilligas; People v., 897
Hillsborough Holdings Corp., In re, 896
Hinkle v. City of Clarksburg, 195
Hinton; United States v., 594
Hitt; United States v., 109, *159*, 162, 195, 243

Hodgson v. Charles Martin Inspector of Petroleum, Inc., 902
Holden; United States v., 359
Holt; United States v., 363
Homestore.Com, Sec. Litig., In re, 203
Hometown Folks, LLC v. S&B Wilson, Inc., 178
Hood v. Knappton Corp., 747
Hoover v. Department of Interior, 914
Houlihan; United States v., 567
Houston v. Smith, 521, 527
Howard; United States v., 217
Howell; United States v., 373
Huddleston v. United States, 180, 230, 247, 248, 256, 309
Hull v. Chevron U.S.A., Inc., 330
Humphrey v. Philip Morris, Inc., 833
Hunziker v. Scheidemantle, 341
Hutto v. Davis, 757

Idaho v. Wright, 581
Iglesias; United States v., 453
Illinois v. Williams, 618
Ina Aviation Corp. v. United States, 733
Inquest Proceedings, In re, 898
International Sys. & Controls Corp. Sec. Litig., In re, 838
Ismail; United States v., 898

Jackim v. Sam's E., Inc., 217
Jackson v. Crews, 218
Jackson v. Scott, 905
Jackson v. Virginia, 717
Jackson; United States v., 201
Jacobs v. Virgin Islands, 711
Jaffee v. Redmond, 797, 872, 884, 886, 887, 888, 900, 911
Jakobetz; United States v., 790
James; United States v., 868
Jane Student 1 v. Williams, 884
Janis; United States v., 711
Jasin; United States v., 452
J.E.B. v. Alabama ex rel. T.B., 83
Jefferson; United States v. (215 F.3d 820), 477
Jefferson; United States v. (623 F.3d 227), 374
Jenkins; United States v., 254
Jensen; United States v., 362
Jenson v. Eveleth Taconite Co., 323
Jeter v. Commonwealth, 189
Jewell v. CSX Transp., Inc., 464
JGR, Inc. v. Thomasville Furniture Indus., 639
Jinadu; United States v., 469
Jinro Am. Inc. v. Secure Invs., Inc., 128
Johnson; People v., 1, 2, 79, 81, 83, 84, 85, 87, 92, 93, 98, 99, 102, 103, 106, 107, 109, 111, 113, 115, 116, 117, 123, 124, 125, 127, 129, 130, 131, 134, 135, 139, 141, 145, 146, 150, 177, 179, 184, 193, 196, 202, 208, 217, 227, 240, 241, 281, 285, 286, 287, 292, 294, 358, 359, 361, 366, 379, 381, 389, 395, 531, 540, 631, 651, 722
Johnson; SEC v., 512
Johnson; State v., 155
Johnson; United States v. (519 F.3d 478), 365
Johnson; United States v. (354 F. Supp. 2d 939), 502

Joint Asbestos Litig., In re, 330
Jones v. Ford Motor Co., 146
Jones v. Southern Pac. R.R. Co., 272
Jones; United States v. (580 F.2d 219), 780
Jones; United States v. (683 F.2d 817), 898
Jones; United States v. (107 F.3d 1147), 710
Jones; United States v. (601 F.3d 1247), 511, 512
Joon Kyu Kim; State v., 147
Jordan; United States v., 299
Joshi; United States v., 469
Juvenile Dep't of Multnomah County, State ex rel.,
   v. S.P., 610

Kaiser; United States v., 520, 521, 524
Kaquatosh; United States v., 457
Karmer; United States v., 374
Kately; State v., 273
Kay v. Lamar Adver. of S.D., Inc., 524
Keeter; United States v., 451
Kelly v. City of San Jose, 912
Kemper v. Gray, 885
Keogh v. IRS, 519
Kidder Peabody Sec. Litig., In re, 832
King; United States v., 619
Kinoy v. Mitchell, 912
Klinzing; United States v., 522
Knapp v. State, 131, 134
Knight v. Otis Elevator Co., 330
Knuckles; People v., 807
Koch, United States ex rel. v. Koch Indus., 273
Koecher; United States v., 869
Koenig; SEC v., 148
Kovacs v. Chesapeake & Ohio Ry., 270
Kovel; United States v., 805, 806
Kraus v. Sobel Corrugated Containers, Inc., 473
Krilich; United States v., 348
Kumho Tire Co. v. Carmichael, 654, 668, 672, 673,
   682, 707, 711, 715

Ladd; United States v., 190
Land Grantors v. United States, 574
Lang v. Cullen, 218, 537
Lange; State v., 807
Lange v. Young, 807
Lapierre; United States v., 641
Larez v. City of Los Angeles, 574
Larson; United States v., 310
Lavender; United States v., 780
Lavine v. Milne, 726, 742, 743
Lawson; United States v. (653 F.2d 299), 636, 641
Lawson; United States v. (494 F.3d 1046), 193
Lea; United States v., 666
Lead Indus. Ass'n v. OSHA, 914
LeCompte; United States v., 310, 311
Lee v. E.I. DuPont, 331
Lee; United States v. (374 F.3d 637), 477
Lee; United States v. (2011 WL 1832545), 218
Lefkowitz; United States v., 859
Lentz; United States v., 569
Levin v. United States, 271, 272
Levine; United States v., 217
Lewis v. Chicago Police Dep't, 145
Lewis; United States v. (833 F.2d 1380), 778

Lewis; United States v. (954 F.2d 1386), 512
Lexcel Solutions, Inc. v. Mastercard Int'l, Inc., 690
Lightfoot; United States v., 377
Lightly; United States v., 178
Lilley; United States v., 867
Lilly v. Virginia, 581
Lindsey (Grand Jury Testimony), In re, 835
Loadholt; Commonwealth v., 615
Locklear; State v., 615
Logan; United States v., 386
Long; United States v., 440
Longenecker v. General Motors, 733
Lopez; United States v., 457
Lopez-Lopez; United States v., 450
Lopez-Medina; United States v., 377
Lorraine v. Markel Am. Ins. Co., 185, 203
Lossiah; United States v., 491
Loughan v. Firestone Tire & Rubber Co., 273
Lowe; United States v., 884
Lowry's Reports, Inc. v. Legg Mason, Inc., 223
Lucas; United States v., 159
Luce v. United States, 379, 380
Luckenbill; United States v., 783
Lujan; United States v., 468
Lustig; United States v., 868
Lutwak v. United States, 867
Lynch v. City of Boston, 636

Mactec, Inc. v. Bechtel Jacobs Co., 690
Maday v. Public Libraries of Saginaw, 885
Maddox v. Los Angeles, 330
Madrid v. Gomez, 2, 76, 281
Madrid; United States v., 687, 689
Maguire; United States v., 766
Maine, State of v. Smith, 859
Malfitano, Appeal of, 869
Mancusi v. Stubbs, 546
Mandel; United States v., 500
Mann; United States v., 309
Manson v. Brathwaite, 457, 459
Marashi; United States v., 857
Marbury v. Madison, 910
Mark v. Shoen, 902, 903
Marriage of. *See name of party*
Martin v. Ohio, 758, 760, 761, 763
Martinez; United States v., 653
Martinez-Rios; United States v., 615
Maryland v. Craig, 624
Maryland v. Rose, 713
Mashek; United States v., 615
Mason v. Stock, 915
Mason v. Texaco, Inc., 377
Mastrangelo; United States v., 566, 567, 569, 621
Matter of. *See name of party*
Mattox v. United States, 579, 580
Maxon; State v., 897, 898
McCallum; United States v., 159
McClesky; United States v., 562
McCollum v. McDaniel, 508
McConnel; United States v., 379
McDevitt v. Guenther, 690
McGinnis; State v., 248
McKnight v. Johnson Controls, Inc., 549
McNaboe v. NVF Co., 422

McQueeney v. Wilmington Trust Co., 109, 153, 154, 159
McVeigh; United States v., 130, 153, 909
Meacham; United States v., 310
Medical Therapy Scis., Inc.; United States v., 359
Meeks; State v., 808
Mehojah v. Drummond, 333
Mejia; United States v., 691
Mejia-Alarcon; United States v., 374
Melendez-Diaz v. Massachusetts, 594, 611, 613, 615, 616, 618, 619, 690, 691
Melia; United States v., 365
Melton, In re, 687, 688, 689, 690
Memorial Hosp. v. Shadur, 905
Mendez; United States v., 539
Mentz; United States v., 779
Mercado v. City of Orlando, 473
Merino-Balderrama; United States v., 168
Merrill v. Waffle House, Inc., 885
Mezzanatto; United States v., 347, 348
Michelson v. United States, 295, 298, 299
Michigan v. Bryant, 604, 608, 609, 621
Midwest Fireworks Mfg. Co.; United States v., 534
Mikos; United States v., 714, 715
Millard; United States v., 347
Miller v. Crown Amusements, Inc., 493
Miller v. Field, 537
Miller v. Keating, 493
Miller v. Transamerican Press, Inc., 903
Miller; United States v., 390
Milton; United States v., 451
Mitchell; United States v. (145 F.3d 572), 493
Mitchell; United States v. (365 F.3d 215), 711
Mitchell; United States v. (633 F.3d 997), 348
Mockaitis v. Harcleroad, 892
Modena; United States v., 213
Mohawk Indus. Inc. v. Carpenter, 795
Molina; United States v., 468
Monell v. New York City Dep't of Soc. Servs., 281
Montana v. Egelhoff, 763
Montana; United States v., 422
Montero-Camargo; United States v., 493
Moore; United States v., 384
Morales v. Portuondo, 892
Morales-Evans v. Administrative Office of the Courts, 320
Morejon v. Rais Constr. Co., 734
Moreland, Estate of, v. Dieter, 158
Moretti v. Lowe, 905
Morgan; United States v., 347
Morris v. B.C. Olympiakos, SFP, 523
Morris v. Slappy, 849
Morris; United States v., 179
Morrison; United States v., 197
Morrow; United States v., 373
Morton v. Zidell Explorations, Inc., 341
Motes v. United States, 620
Mullaney v. Wilbur, 751, 752, 753, 754, 755, 756, 757, 762, 763, 767, 768
Municipal Revenue Serv., Inc. v. Xspand, Inc., 496
Munoz; United States v., 363
Murphy, In re, 838
Murphy Auto Parts Co. v. Ball, 492

Mutual Life Ins. Co. of New York v. Hillmon, 500, 501, 502, 505

Napolean; United States v., 892, 893
Napolitano v. Compania Sud Americana de Vapores, 158
National Broad. Co., In re Application to Quash Subpoena to, 903
Navarro, In re, 808
Neighbors Law Firm, P.C. v. Highland Capital Mgmt., L.P., 208
Nesbitt; Commonwealth v., 621
New Colt Holding Corp. v. RJG Holdings of Fla., Inc., 574
Newell v. Harold Shaffer Leasing Co., 341
New York Times v. Sullivan, 903
Nipper v. Snipes, 538
Nixon v. Administrator of Gen. Servs., 799, 803, 910
Nixon v. United States, 801, 803
Nixon; United States v., 854, 910
NLRB v. See name of opposing party
North; United States v., 909
Nunley v. Pettway Oil Co., 732

Oates; United States v., 534, 535, 536
Obayagbona; United States v., 490
Oberweis Dairy; Doe v., 885
Obrey v. Johnson, 148
Office of the President v. Office of the Indep. Counsel, 835
Ogg; State v., 695
Ohio v. Perez, 868
Ohio v. Roberts, 580, 581, 607, 611, 620, 621
Ohler v. United States, 379, 380
Olafson; United States v., 546
Old Chief v. United States, 162, 167, 246, 254, 255, 258
Oleszko v. State Comp. Ins. Fund, 884
Olsen v. Class, 508
Olsen v. Correiro, 345
Olsen; United States v., 347
Omnicom Group Sec. Litig., In re, 832
Orellana-Blanco; United States v., 535
Orr v. Albuquerque, 336
Osazuwa; United States v., 373, 377
Osorio-Soto; United States v., 476
Owens; United States v., 450, 451, 452, 458, 620

Pacheco; United States v., 508
Paducah Towing Co., In re, 549
Pageau; United States v., 197
Paiva; United States v., 766
Palmer v. Hoffman, 523, 527
Pandozzi; United States v., 377
Panzardi-Lespier; United States v., 576
Paoli R.R. Yard PCB Litig., In re, 147
Paolitto v. John Brown E. & C., Inc., 539
Park v. Huff, 439
Parker; United States v., 377
Patrick; United States v., 526, 576
Patterson v. Caterpillar, 871

Patterson v. New York, 752, 754, 755, 757, 758, 761, 762, 763, 767
Pau v. Yosemite Park & Curry Co., 333
Paul; United States v., 710
Peat, Inc. v. Vanguard Research, Inc., 213
Peays; United States v., 230, 231
Pedroso v. Driver, 136, 155, 204, 243, 250, 415, 426, 482, 494, 505, 540
Pena-Gutierrez; United States v., 545
Pennsylvania v. Ritchie, 803
Perez; Ohio v., 868
Perez; United States v. (870 F.2d 1222), 453
Perez; United States v. (217 F.3d 323), 575
Perkins; United States v., 490
Perry; United States v., 346
Persico; United States v., 502
Perzinski v. Chevron Chem. Co., 337
Peters; SEC v., 159
Pheaster; United States v., 501
Philadelphia, City of v. Westinghouse Elec. Corp., 822
Phillips v. Potter, 507
Piccinonna; United States v., 664
Pierce v. F.R. Tripler & Co., 338
Pierce County v. Guillen, 814, 907
Pierre v. RBC Liberty Life Ins., 528
Piggie; United States v., 780
Pillsbury Co. v. Cleaver-Brooks Div. of Aqua-Chem, Inc., 469
Pinkerton v. United States, 570
Pintar; United States v., 364
Pizarro; United States v., 546
Plaza; United States v., 711
Plaza-Bonilla v. Cortazzo, 512
Plourde v. Gladstone, 709
Pluta; United States v., 208, 546
Poncy v. Johnson & Johnson, 746
Port v. Heard, 898
Portrait of Wally; United States v., 202
Posado; United States v., 665
Powell; United States v., 552
Pozefsky v. Baxter Healthcare Corp., 701
Pozsgai; United States v., 775
Pree; United States v., 653
Pregeant v. Pan Am World Airways, 128
Prewitt; United States v., 338
Price; United States v., 365
Prieto; United States v., 456
Prince-Oyibo; United States v., 665
Pryce; United States v., 398
Pulido-Jacobo; United States v., 469
Puryear v. State, 458

Qualley v. Clo-Tex Int'l, Inc., 789
Queen Caroline's Case, 384
Quercia v. United States, 766
Quinones; United States v., 498
Quinto; United States v., 390

Racz v. R.T. Merryman Trucking, Inc., 195
Ragland v. Commonwealth, 715
Rambus, Inc. v. Infineon Techs. Ag, 208–209
Ramirez; United States v., 177

Ramos; United States v., 490
Ramos-Oseguera; United States v., 869
Randolph v. Collectramatic, Inc., 639
Rangel-Arreola; United States v., 269
Ray; United States v., 135, 155, 205, 220, 233, 243, 250, 275, 302, 415, 425, 460, 480
Rebbe; United States v., 348
Redding v. Virginia Mason Med. Ctr., 886
Redman v. John D. Brush & Co., 685
Reed v. Thalacker, 491
Reed; United States v., 548
Reese; United States v., 298, 366
Reeves v. Sanderson Plumbing Prods., Inc., 721, 746
Regina v. Kearley, 442
Reichhold Chems., Inc. v. Textron, Inc., 906
Reyes; United States v. (239 F.3d 722), 499
Reyes; United States v. (2009 WL 3273896), 536
Reynolds; United States v., 908
Rhoads Indus., Inc. v. Building Materials Corp., 816
Rice v. Hudson, 619
Richards of Rockford, Inc. v. Pacific Gas & Elec. Co., 904
Richardson v. Marsh, 151, 468
Rivera v. Delaware, 753
Roach v. Springfield Clinic, 905
Roach; United States v., 479
Roberson; United States v., 858
Roberts v. Hollocher, 398
Roberts v. Hunt, 906
Robinson v. Magovern, 905
Robinson; United States v. (390 F.3d 853), 476
Robinson; United States v. (583 F.3d 1265), 398
Rocky Mountain Helicopters, Inc. v. Bell Helicopters, 330
Rodrigues-Felix; United States v., 651
Rodríguez-Berrios; United States v., 651
Rodriguez-Cabrera; United States v., 142
Rogers; United States v., 374
Roland v. Johnson, 422
Romans v. Berghuis, 620
Rosa; United States v. (891 F.2d 1063), 363
Rosa; United States v. (11 F.3d 315), 535
Ross; United States v., 213
Roulette; United States v., 536
Roviaro v. United States, 902
Roxbury-Smellie v. Florida Dep't of Corr., 533
Ruberto v. Commissioner, 212
Rubin v. United States, 911
Rummell v. Estelle, 757

Saddey; United States v., 201
Saelee; United States v., 710, 711
Safavian; United States v., 469
St. Clair v. Johnny's Oyster & Shrimp, Inc., 203
St. Mary's Honor Ctr. v. Hicks, 744, 745
Saks; United States v., 471
Salerno; United States v., 552, 553, 555
Samaniego; United States v., 218
Samuels, In re, 688, 689
Sanchez v. Zabihi, 324
Sanders v. Ritz-Carlton Hotel Co., 507
Sandstrom v. Montana, 768, 769
Saneaux; United States v., 479
Sanitary Grocery Co. v. Snead, 492

Santerelli, In re, 898
Santobello v. New York, 346
Santosky v. Kramer, 729
Savoie v. Otto Candies, Inc., 340
Sawyer; United States v., 536
Sayakhom; United States v., 347
Schad v. Arizona, 763
Schechter v. Klanfer, 726, 728, 729, 734, 735
Scheffer; United States v., 665
Schmidt v. Duo-Fast Corp., 549
Schmude v. Tricam Indus., Inc., 375
Schoenheinz; United States v., 797
Schoffstall v. Henderson, 885
Scholl; United States v., 300, 520
Scholle; United States v., 527
Schultz; United States v., 185
Schwimmer; United States v., 807
Scott v. Hammock, 893
Scott; United States v., 363
Sealed Case, In re (737 F.2d 94), 808
Sealed Case, In re (121 F.3d 729), 910, 912
Sealed Case, In re (148 F.3d 1073), 911
Sears, Roebuck & Co.; NLRB v., 913, 914
SEC v. *See name of opposing party*
Secor; United States v., 497
Segura-Gallegos; United States v., 476
Seifert; United States v., 212
Seiler v. Lucasfilm, Ltd., 214, 222, 224
September 11 Litig., In re, 537, 538
Shafer, Estate of v. Commissioner, 464
Shargel, In re, 837
Shaw; United States v., 189
Sheffield v. Hilltop Sand & Gravel Co., 319–320
Sheldone v. Pennsylvania Tpk. Comm'n, 901
Shepard v. United States, 556, 689
Sheppard v. Union Pac. R.R. Co., 181
Sherrod v. Berry, 281
Shonubi; United States v., 129
Shores; United States v., 213
Shoup; United States v., 490
Siddiqui; United States v., 203, 545
Silverstein v. Federal Bureau of Prisons, 811, 815
Simmons; United States v., 707
Simon v. G.D. Searle & Co., 856
Simon; United States v., 778
Simplex Inc. v. Diversified Energy Sys., Inc., 272
Simpson; United States v., 203
Sims v. Charlotte Liberty Mut. Ins. Co., 872
Sinclair; United States v., 212
Sivils; United States v., 197
Skeddle; United States v., 520
Skeet; United States v., 641
Skidmore v. Precision Printing & Packaging,
    Inc., 684
Skipper; United States v., 184
Slater; State v., 604
Sliker; United States v., 218
Smith v. Ford Motor Co., 683
Smith v. City of Oakland, 145
Smith v. Isuzu Motors Ltd., 533
Smith; State v., 860
Smith; United States v., 651
Smithers; United States v., 651
Socks-Brunot v. Hirschvogel Inc., 319, 320
Sokolow; United States v., 526

Solem v. Helm, 757
Southern Ind. Gas & Elec. Co.; United States v., 573
Speaker v. County of San Bernadino, 884
Specht v. Google, Inc., 208
Specht v. Jensen, 330
Special Fed. Grand Jury Empanelled Oct. 31, 1985
    Impounded, In re, 464
Speese; State v., 887
Spell v. McDaniel, 336
Sperling; United States v., 502
Spetzer; Commonwealth v., 860, 861
Sphere Drake Ins. PLC v. Trisko, 686, 687
Sprint/United Mgmt. Co. v. Mendelsohn, 274, 279
Spurlock v. Commissioner, 522
Staelens ex rel. Estate of Staelens v. Staelens, 500
State v. *See name of opposing party*
State Farm v. Campbell, 757
Stein; United States v., 347
Steinberg v. Jensen, 871
Stephens v. Miller, 323
Stephens; United States v., 197, 198
Stern; United States v., 347
Stever; United States v., 132, 134
Stillis; United States v., 199
Stockman v. Oakland Dental Ctr., 151
Stoddard v. State, 441
Storm Plastics, Inc. v. United States, 777
Stotts; United States v., 479
Stout; United States v., 143
Stuart v. Unum Life Ins. Co., 423
Sturman; United States v., 886
Subpoena Issued to Commodity Futures Trading
    Comm'n, In re, 900
Suburban Sew 'N Sweep v. Swiss-Bernina, 808
Sudeen; United States v., 479
Sullivan v. Dollar Tree Stores, Inc., 533
Summers; United States v., 594
Sumner; United States v., 310
Subpoena Served upon the Comptroller of the
    Currency, In re, 912
Sutton; United States v., 386
Swidler & Berlin v. United States, 800
Sylvester; United States v., 348

Talley; United States v., 806
Talmage v. Harris, 422
Tarantino; United States v., 387
Taylor; United States v., 219
Textron; United States v., 856
Thirtyacre, In re, 776, 777, 778, 779
Thomas v. Kansas Power & Light Co., 784
Thomas; United States v. (167 F.3d 299), 665
Thomas; United States v. (321 F.3d 627), 257
Thompson; United States v., 201
Threadgill v. Armstrong World Indus., Inc., 202
Timber Prods. Co. v. United States, 475
Tinley v. Poly-Triplex Techs., Inc., 222
Tirado-Tirado; United States v., 620
Toledo v. Medical Eng'g Corp., 701
Tollardo; State v., 194
Tome v. United States (513 U.S. 150), 389, 455
Tome; United States v. (61 F.3d 1446), 507, 574
Tornay v. United States, 837
Torres; United States v., 362, 365

Towerridge, Inc. v. T.A.O., Inc., 338
Tracinda Corp. v. DaimlerChrysler AG, 217
Tracy; United States v., 226
Trammel v. United States, 797, 856, 862, 867, 868, 869
Tranowski; United States v., 650
Transportation Mgmt. Corp.; NLRB v., 747
Transportes Aereos Pegaso v. Bell Helicopter Textron, Inc., 423
Tresnak, In re Marriage of, 784, 786
Troupin v. Metropolitan Life Ins. Co., 906
Trujillo; United States v., 455
Trull v. Volkswagen of Am., Inc., 330, 464
Tucker v. Ohtsu Tire & Rubber Co., 812
Turner v. Burlington N. Santa Fe R.R., 690
Turner v. United States, 769
Turner; United States v., 691
Turning Bear; United States v., 159, 624
281 Syosset Woodbury Rd.; United States v., 857
Tyndall v. Harvey, 638

United Shoe Mach. Corp.; United States v., 822
United States v. *See name of opposing party*
United States, In re (565 F.2d 19), 902
United States, In re (872 F.2d 472), 908
University of Pa. v. EEOC, 904, 906
Upjohn Co. v. United States, 809, 823, 831, 832, 834, 854, 855
Urbanik; United States v., 477
Urrego-Linares; United States v., 476
Usery v. Turner Elkhorn Mining Co., 736, 742, 743
Utah v. Worthen, 885

Vaghari; United States v., 203
Vallejo; United States v., 167
Van der AA v. Commissioner, 524
Vanderbilt v. Town of Chilmark, 886
Varoudakis; United States v., 258, 265
Vasconcellos v. Cybex Int'l, Inc., 886
Vazquez v. National Car Rental Sys., Inc., 556
Vega; United States v., 560
Velarde; United States v., 362, 365
Velez; United States v., 348
Verplank, In re, 892
Viagra Prods. Liab. Litig., In re, 219
Vicksburg & M. R.R. v. Putnam, 732
Victor v. Nebraska, 749, 750
Vining, Vining ex rel. v. Enterprise Fin. Group, 273, 274
Vinson v. Humana, Inc., 885
Virgin Islands, Government of, v. Albert, 198
Virgin Islands, Government of, v. Vicars, 615
von Bulow, In re, 832

Wagner v. Firestone Tire & Rubber Co., 373
Wagstaff v. Protective Apparel Corp., 469
Walker v. Horn, 373
Walker; United States v., 178, 574
Wallace; United States v., 143
Ward v. Succession of Freeman, 800
Washington v. Texas, 803
Washington; United States v., 455

Watson; United States v. (669 F.2d 1274, 295
Watson; United States v. (525 F.3d 583), 594
Weaver; United States v., 469
Weber Aircraft Corp.; United States v., 913
Weil v. Investment/Indicators, Researchers & Mgmt., 800
Weil v. Seltzer, 272
Weinstein v. Stevens, 533, 537
Weinstock; United States v., 145
Welch; United States v., 197
Weller; United States v., 516
Wellons; United States v., 299
Wells; United States v., 356, 390
Welsh v. City & County of San Francisco, 915
Wen Ho Lee; United States v., 909
West; United States v., 147
Westerbrook; United States v., 297
Westfield Ins. Co. v. Harris, 257
Westmoreland; United States v., 562
Weston-Smith v. Cooley Dickinson Hosp., Inc., 470
Wheeler v. John Deere Co., 280
Whitaker; United States v., 202
White v. Arn, 761
White v. Illinois, 580, 594
White; United States v., 569
Whitmore; United States v., 363, 364
Whitted v. General Motors Corp., 208
Wholaver; Commonwealth v., 624
Whorton v. Bockting, 593
Wichita Land & Cattle Co. v. American Fed. Bank, F.S.B., 809
Wiehe v. Kissick Constr. Co., 736
Wilcox; United States v., 488
Wilkinson v. Carnival Cruise Lines, 472–473
Williams v. Long, 204
Williams v. Utica Coll., 709
Williams v. Virgin Islands, 506
Williams; United States v. (447 F.2d 1285), 688
Williams; United States v. (583 F.2d 1194), 654
Williams; United States v. (238 F.3d 871), 255
Williamson v. United States, 562
Willingham v. Crooke, 508
Wilson; United States v. (344 F.2d 1208), 362
Wilson; United States v. (985 F.2d 348), 362, 374
Wilson; United States v. (2010 WL 3023035), 508
Winkfield v. American Cont'l Ins. Co., 737
Winship, In re, 748, 751, 754, 755, 757, 758, 761, 762, 763, 764, 765, 767, 768, 769
Witness Before the Special Grand Jury 2000-2, In re, 835
Witnesses Before the Special Mar. 1980 Grand Jury Appeal of U.S., In re, 836
Wolak v. Spucci, 320
Wolfle v. United States, 859
Wood, In re Estate of, 738
Wood v. Bartholomew, 665
Wood v. State, 615
Woodruff; United States v., 807
Woolworth Corp. Sec. Class Action Litig., In re, 832
WorldCom, Inc. Sec. Litig., In re, 520, 524
Worthen; Utah v., 885
Wright v. Tatham, 437, 442
Wright v. Willamette Indus., Inc., 708, 709
Wright; United States v. (932 F.2d 868), 196
Wright; United States v. (363 F.3d 237), 574

Wright v. Willamette Indus., Inc., 708, 709
Wyatt v. United States, 869
Wynn v. State, 257

Yahweh; United States v., 151, 193
Yanez v. Minnesota, 620
Yasmin; United States v., 218
Yildiz; United States v., 475
Yoder Co., In re, 737
York; United States v., 255, 257
Young; United States v. (470 U.S. 1), 103
Young; United States v. (223 F.3d 905), 348

Young; United States v. (248 F.3d 260), 386
Zackowitz; People v., 241, 252
Zackson; United States v., 252
Zenith Radio Corp. v. Matsushita Elec. Indus.
    Co., 685
Zenni; United States v., 439
Zeus Enters., Inc. v. Alphin Aircraft, Inc., 538
Ziegler v. Department of Fire, 872
Zolin; United States v., 838
Zuchowicz v. United States, 709
Zuckerbraun v. General Dynamics
    Corp., 908
Zuniga, In re, 797

Table of Authorities

Principal authorities are in italics.

Abarbanel, In Light of *Crawford v. Washington* and the Difficult Nature of Domestic Violence Prosecutions, Maryland Should Adopt Legislation Making Admissible Prior Acts of Domestic Violence in Domestic Violence Prosecutions, 39 U. Balt. L. Rev. 467 (2010), 624

Abrams, Addressing the Tension between the Clergy-Communicant Privilege and the Duty to Report Child Abuse in State Statutes, 44 B.C. L. Rev. 1127 (2003), 895

Aiken, Sexual Character Evidence in Civil Actions: Refining the Propensity Rule, 1997 Wis. L. Rev. 1221, 311, 314

Allen, *Clark v. Arizona*: Much (Confused) Ado About Nothing, 4 Ohio St. J. Crim. L. 135 (2006), 764

_____, The Evolution of the Hearsay Rule to a Rule of Admission, 76 Minn. L. Rev. 797 (1992), 627

_____, Expertise and the *Daubert* Decision, 84 J. Crim. L. & Criminology 1157 (1994), 668

_____, Forward: *Montana v. Egelhoff*—Reflections on the Limits of Legislative Imagination and Judicial Authority, 87 J. Crim. L. & Criminology 633 (1997), 764

_____, More on Constitutional Process-of-Proof Problems, 94 Harv. L. Rev. 1795 (1981), 766

_____, The Myth of Conditional Relevancy, 25 Loy. L.A. L. Rev. 871 (1992), 231, 232

_____, Presumptions, Inferences and Burden of Proof in Federal Civil Actions—An Anatomy of Unnecessary Ambiguity and a Proposal for Reform, 76 Nw. U. L. Rev. 892 (1982), 746

_____, Rationality, Algorithms, and Juridical Proof: A Preliminary Analysis, 1 Int'l J. Evidence & Proof 253 (1997), 170

_____, Structuring Jury Decisionmaking in Criminal Cases: A Unified Constitutional Approach to Evidentiary Devices, 94 Harv. L. Rev. 321 (1980), 767, 769

Allen & DeGrazia, The Constitutional Requirement of Proof Beyond Reasonable Doubt in Criminal Cases: A Comment Upon Incipient Chaos in Lower Courts, 20 Am. Crim. L. Rev. 1 (1982), 768

Allen & Hazelwood, Preserving the Confidentiality of Internal Corporate Investigations, 12 J. Corp. L. 355 (1987), 906

Allen & Laudan, Deadly Dilemmas, 41 Tex. Tech. L. Rev. 65 (2008), 751

_____, The Devastating Impact of Prior Crimes Evidence and Other Myths of the Criminal Justice Process, 101 J. Crim. L. & Criminology 493 (2011), 378

Allen & Nafisi, *Daubert* and Its Discontents, 76 Brook. L. Rev. 131 (2010), 667

Allen & Pardo, The Problematic Value of Mathematical Models of Evidence, 36 J. Legal Stud. 107 (2007), 170

Allen et al., A Positive Theory of the Attorney-Client Privilege and the Work Product Doctrine, 19 J. Legal Stud. 359 (1990), 840, 855, 856

Allen et al., The German Advantage in Civil Procedure: A Plea for More Details and Fewer Generalities in Comparative Scholarship, 82 Nw. U. L. Rev. 705 (1988), 80

American Psychiatric Association's Statement on the Insanity Defense (1982), 696

Anderson & Twining, Analysis of Evidence (1991), 127

Andrews, The Admissibility of Other-Crimes Evidence in Acquaintance-Rape Prosecutions, 17 S. Ill. U. L.J. 341 (1993), 311, 312, 313

Annotation, Admissibility, in Negligence Action, of Absence of Other Accidents or Injuries, 10 A.L.R.5th 371 (1993), 281

Ayala & Martyn, To Tell or Not To Tell? An Analysis of Testimonial Privileges: The Parent-Child and Reporter's Privileges, 9 St. John's J. Legal Comment. 163 (1993), 899

Ball, The Moment of Truth: Probability Theory and Standards of Proof, 14 Vand. L. Rev. 807 (1961), 170

_____, The Myth of Conditional Relevancy, 14 Ga. L. Rev. 435 (1980), 125, 231

Beale, Prior Similar Acts in Prosecutions for Rape and Child Sex Abuse, 4 Crim. L.F. 307 (1993), 311

Beecher-Monas, The Heuristics of Intellectual Due Process: A Primer for Triers of Science, 75 N.Y.U. L. Rev. 1563 (2000), 709

_____, A Ray of Light for Judges Blinded by Science: Triers of Science and Intellectual Due Process, 33 Ga. L. Rev. 1047 (1999), 668

Bell, Decision Theory and Due Process: A Critique of the Supreme Court's Lawmaking for Burdens of Proof, 78 J. Crim. L. & Criminology 557 (1987), 724

Binder, D.A. & Bergman, P., Fact Investigation (1984), 126

Bingham, C. & Gansler, L.L., Class Action: The Story of Lois Jenson and the Landmark Case That Changed Sexual Harassment Law (2002), 323

Black et al., Science and the Law in the Wake of *Daubert*: A New Search for Scientific Knowledge, 72 Tex. L. Rev. 715 (1994), 668

Blakely, Article IV: Relevancy and Its Limits, 30 Hous. L. Rev. 281 (1993), 149

Brownmiller, S., Against Our Will: Men, Women and Rape (1976), 321

Bryden & Lengnick, Rape in the Criminal Justice System, 87 J. Crim. L. & Criminology 1194 (1997), 313, 322

Bryden & Park, "Other Crimes" Evidence in Sex Offense Cases, 78 Minn. L. Rev. 529 (1992), 310–311, 312

Byrom, The Use of the Excited Utterance Hearsay Exception in the Prosecution of Domestic Violence Cases After *Crawford v. Washington*, 23 Rev. Litig. 209 (2005), 624

Callen, Foreword to the First Virtual Forum: Wallace Stevens, Blackbirds and the Hearsay Rule, 16 Miss. Col. L. Rev. 1 (1995), 628

_____, Hearsay and Informal Reasoning, 47 Vand. L. Rev. 43 (1994), 442

_____, Notes on a Grand Illusion: Some Limits on the Use of Bayesian Theory in Evidence Law, 57 Ind. L.J. 1 (1982), 170

_____, Rationality and Relevance: Conditional Relevancy and Constrained Resources, 2003 Mich. St. L. Rev. 1243, 232

Cammack, Using the Doctrine of Chances to Prove Actus Reus in Child Abuse and Acquaintance Rape: *People v. Ewoldt* Reconsidered, 29 U.C. Davis L. Rev. 355 (1996), 255

Campagnolo, The Conflict Between State Press Shield Laws and Federal Criminal Proceedings: The Rule 501 Blues, 38 Gonz. L. Rev. 445 (2002/03), 903

Carodine, "The Mis-Characterization of the Negro": A Race Critique of the Prior Conviction Impeachment Rule, 84 Ind. L.J. 521 (2009), 378

Carraway, Violence Against Women of Color, 43 Stan. L. Rev. 1301 (1991), 313, 322

Case Comment, Evidence: The Clinton Administration's Battle to Gain Evidentiary Privilege for Secret Service Agents—Another Tainted Legacy?, 51 Fla. L. Rev. 743 (1999), 911

Chayes, The Role of the Judge in Public Law Litigation, 89 Harv. L. Rev. 1281 (1976), 110

Cheng & Yoon, Does *Frye* or *Daubert* Matter? A Study of Scientific Admissibility Standards, 91 Va. L. Rev. 471 (2005), 667

Cofer, Comment, Parent-Child Privilege: Constitutional Right or Specious Analogy?, 3 U. Puget Sound L. Rev. 177 (1979), 898

Cohen, J.L., Freedom of Proof, in Facts in Law (Twining ed., 1983), 121

_____, The Probable and the Provable (1977), 170

Comment, 78 Tul. L. Rev. 911 (2004), 502

Comment, Academic Researchers and the First Amendment: Constitutional Protection for Their Confidential Sources?, 14 San Diego L. Rev. 876 (1977), 904

Comment, Parent-Child Privilege: Constitutional Right or Specious Analogy?, 3 U. Puget Sound L. Rev. 177 (1979), 898

Comment, The Psychotherapist-Client Testimonial Privilege: Defining the Professional Involved, 34 Emory L.J. 777 (1985), 897

Comment, The Undoing of *Old Chief*: Harmless Error and Felon-in-Possession-of-Firearms Cases, 48 Kan. L. Rev. 431 (2000), 167

Comment, Whether Federal Rule of Evidence 803(3) Should Be Amended to Exclude Statements Offered to Prove the Subsequent Conduct of a Nondeclarant: Guidance from Louisiana, 78 Tul. L. Rev. 911 (2004), 502

Committee on Identifying the Needs of the Forensic Sciences Community, National Research Council, Strengthening Forensic Science in the United States (National Acads. Press 2009), 702, 706, 711

Committee on Scientific Assessment of Bullet Lead Elemental Composition Comparison, National Research Council, Forensic Analysis: Weighing Bullet Lead Evidence (2004), 714

Committee to Review the Scientific Evidence on the Polygraph, National Research Council, The Polygraph and Lie Detection (National Acads. Press 2003), 666

Cordray, Evidence Rule 806 and the Problem of Impeaching the Nontestifying Declarant, 56 Ohio St. L.J. 495 (1995), 484

Crenshaw, Mapping the Margins: Intersectionality, Identity Politics, and Violence Against Women of Color, 43 Stan. L. Rev. 1241 (1991), 313, 322

Crews, The Memory Wars (1997), 700

Crowley, Case Comment, Evidence: The Clinton Administration's Battle to Gain Evidentiary Privilege for Secret Service Agents—Another Tainted Legacy?, 51 Fla. L. Rev. 743 (1999), 911

Curtis, Comment, Academic Researchers and the First Amendment: Constitutional Protection for Their Confidential Sources?, 14 San Diego L. Rev. 876 (1977), 904

Cush & Delahunty, The Influence of Limiting Instructions on Processing and Judgments of Emotionally Evocative Evidence, 13 Psychiatry Psychol. & L. 110 (2006), 150

Cutler & Penrod, Mistaken Identifications: The Eyewitness, Psychology, and the Law (1995), 459

Damaska, M., The Death of Legal Torture, 87 Yale L.J. 860 (1978), 121

_____, Evidence Law Adrift (1997), 80

_____, Evidentiary Barriers to Conviction and Two Models of Criminal Procedure, 121 U. Pa. L. Rev. 506 (1973), 80

_____, The Faces of Justice and State Authority (1986), 80

Davis, K.C., Administrative Law Treatise (1958), 775

_____, Judicial Notice, 1969 Law & Soc. Order 513 (1969), 783

Davis, K.C. & Pierce, K., Jr., Administrative Law Treatise (3d ed. 1994), 787

Deason, Predictable Mediation Confidentiality in the U.S. Federal System 17 Ohio St. J. on Disp. Resol. 239 (2002), 901

DeCoux, Textual Limits on the Residual Exception to the Hearsay Rule: The "Near Miss" Debate and Beyond, 35 S.U. L. Rev. 99 (2007), 577

Devall, Jr., Comment, Whether Federal Rule of Evidence 803(3) Should Be Amended to Exclude Statements Offered to Prove the Subsequent Conduct of a Nondeclarant: Guidance from Louisiana, 78 Tul. L. Rev. 911 (2004), 502

Developments in the Law, Confronting the New Challenges of Scientific Evidence, 108 Harv. L. Rev. 1481 (1995), 668

Developments in the Law—Privileged Communications, 98 Harv. L. Rev. 1450 (1985), 794, 837, 859, 891, 899, 901

Devenport, Penrod, & Cutler, Eyewitness Identification Evidence: Evaluating Commonsense Evaluations, 3 Psychol. Pub. Pol'y & L. 338 (1997), 651

Diamond, Beyond Fantasy and Nightmare: A Portrait of the Jury, 54 Buff. L. Rev. 717 (2006), 139

Diamond & Vidmar, Jury Ruminations on Forbidden Topics, 87 Va. L. Rev. 1857 (2001), 340

Doob & Kirshenbaum, Some Empirical Evidence on the Effect of Sec. 12 of the Canada Evidence Act Upon the Accused, 15 Crim. L.Q. 88 (1972-1973), 378

Dubbleday, Comment, The Psychotherapist-Client Testimonial Privilege: Defining the Professional Involved, 34 Emory L.J. 777 (1985), 897

Ellsworth, Are 12 Heads Better Than 1?, 38 Law Quadrangle Notes 56 (1995), 114

The Evolving Role of Statistical Assessments as Evidence in the Courts (Report of the Panel on Statistical Assessments as Evidence in the Courts) (Fienberg ed., 1989), 147

Finkelstein & Levin, Compositional Analysis of Bullet Lead As Forensic Evidence, 13 J.L. & Pol'y 119 (2005), 714

Finman, Implied Assertions as Hearsay: Some Criticisms of the Uniform Rules of Evidence, 14 Stan. L. Rev. 682 (1962), 432

Flint, Child Sexual Abuse Accommodation Syndrome: Admissibility Requirements, 23 Am. J. Crim. L. 171 (1995), 707

Fox, *Crawford* at Its Limits: Hearsay and Forfeiture in Child Abuse Cases, 46 Am. Crim. L. Rev. 1245 (2009), 624

Fradella et al., The Impact of *Daubert* on the Admissibility of Behavioral Science Testimony, 30 Pepp. L. Rev. 403 (2003), 707

Fried, Too High a Price for Truth: The Exception to the Attorney-Client Privilege for Contemplated Crimes and Frauds, 64 N.C. L. Rev. 443 (1986), 833, 838

Friedman, Conditional Probative Value: Neoclassicism Without Myth, 93 Mich. L. Rev. 439 (1994), 231, 232

_____, A History of American Law (1973), 796

_____, Route Analysis of Credibility and Hearsay, 96 Yale L.J. 667 (1987), 131

Galanek, The Impact of the *Zolin* Decision on the Crime-Fraud Exception to the Attorney-Client Privilege, 24 Ga. L. Rev. 1115 (1990), 838

Gardner, The State Secret Privilege Invoked in Civil Litigation: A Proposal for Statutory Relief, 29 Wake Forest L. Rev. 567 (1994), 909

Garland & Schmitz, Of Judges and Juries: A Proposed Revision of Federal Rule of Evidence 104, 23 U.C. Davis L. Rev. 77 (1989), 227

Gee, Eyewitness Testimony and Cross-Racial Identification, 35 New Eng. L. Rev. 835 (2001), 651

Gianelli, Admissibility of Scientific Evidence, 28 Okla. City U. L. Rev. 1 (2003), 651

Gish, The Self-Critical Analysis Privilege and Environmental Audit Reports, 25 Envtl. L. 73 (1995), 907

Gowdy, Note, Should the Federal Government Have an Attorney-Client Privilege?, 51 Fla. L. Rev. 695 (1999), 835

Graham, K.W., Jr., There'll Always Be an England: The Instrumental Ideology of Evidence, 85 Mich. L. Rev. 1204 (1987), 140

Graham, M.H., Handbook of Federal Evidence (5th ed. 2001), 442

_____, "Stickperson Hearsay": A Simplified Approach to Understanding the Rule Against Hearsay, 1982 U. Ill. L. Rev. 887 (1982), 444

Green, Deceit and Classification of Crimes: Federal Rule of Evidence 609(a)(2) and the Origins of Crimen Falsi, 90 J. Crim. L. & Criminology 1087 (2000), 374

Greenwald et al., Testimonial Privileges (Trial Practice Series, 3d ed. 2005), 891, 894, 895

Groscup et al., The Effects of *Daubert* on the Admissibility of Expert Testimony in State and Federal Criminal Cases, 8 Psychol. Pub. Pol'y & L. 339 (2002), 667

Gross, Expert Evidence, 1991 Wis. L. Rev. 1113, 647

Groth et al., Undetected Recidivism Among Rapists and Child Molesters, 28 Crime & Delinq. 450 (1982), 312

Hansen, Panel to Examine Implant Evidence: Unusual Move by Two New York Federal Judges Could Be Copied Elsewhere, 82 A.B.A. J. 34 (June 1996), 701

Harding, Waiver: A Comprehensive Analysis of a Consequence of Inadvertently Producing Documents Protected by the Attorney-Client Privilege, 42 Cath. U. L. Rev. 465 (1993), 809

Harris, The Dangerous Patient Exception to the Psychotherapist-Patient Privilege: The *Tarasoff* Duty and the *Jaffee* Footnote, 74 Wash. L. Rev. 33 (1999), 889

Harrison, Reconceptualizing the Expert Witness: Social Cost, Current Controls and Proposed Responses, 18 Yale J. on Reg. 253 (2001), 667

Hart & McNaughton, Evidence and Inference in the Law, 87 Daedalus 40 (Fall 1958), 169

Hearings on Proposed Rules of Evidence Before the Special Subcommittee on Reform of Federal Criminal Laws of the House Committee on the Judiciary, 93d Cong., 1st Sess. 524 (1973), 823

Horney & Spohn, Rape Law Reform and Instrumental Change in Six Urban Jurisdictions, 25 Law & Soc. Rev. 117 (1991), 312

Hunter, Gender in Evidence, Masculine Norms vs. Feminist Reforms, 19 Harv. Women's L.J. 127 (1996), 140

Hurst, The Growth of American Law: The Lawmakers (1940), 732

Hussain, Reviving Hope for Domestic Violence Prosecutions: *Giles v. California*, 46 Am. Crim. L. Rev. 1301 (2009), 624

Hutchins & Slesinger, Some Observations on the Law of Evidence: Spontaneous Exclamations, 28 Colum. L. Rev. 432 (1928), 489

_____, Improving Judicial Gatekeeping: Technical Advisors and Scientific Evidence, 110 Harv. L. Rev. 941 (1997), 668

Imwinkelreid, E., Evidentiary Foundations (7th ed. 2008), 186, 195, 197

_____, The Meaning of "Facts or Data" in Federal Rule of Evidence 703: The Significance of the Supreme Court's Decision to Rely on Federal Rule 702 in *Daubert v. Merrell Dow Pharmaceuticals, Inc.*, 54 Md. L. Rev. 352 (1995), 668

_____, The Rivalry Between Truth and Privilege: The Weakness of the Supreme Court's Reasoning in *Jaffee v. Redmond*, 518 U.S. 1 (1996), 49 Hastings L.J. 969 (1998), 883

_____, A Small Contribution to the Debate Over the Proposed Legislation Abolishing the Character Evidence Prohibition in Sex Offense Prosecutions, 44 Syracuse L. Rev. 1125 (1993), 306

_____, The Use of Evidence of an Accused's Uncharged Misconduct to Prove Mens Rea: The Doctrines that Threaten to Engulf the Character Evidence Prohibition, 130 Mil. L. Rev. 41 (1990), 255, 257

Imwinkelreid & Tobin, Comparative Bullet Lead Analysis (CBLA) Evidence: Valid Inference or Ipse Dixit?, 28 Okla. City U. L. Rev. 43 (2003), 714

James, F., Jr., Burdens of Proof, 47 Va. L. Rev. 51 (1961), 722, 726

James et al., Civil Procedure (5th ed. 2001), 181

James, G.F., Relevancy, Probability and the Law, 29 Cal. L. Rev. 689 (1941), 135

Jefferson, The Statutory Development of the Parent-Child Privilege: Congress Responds to Kenneth Starr's Tactics, 16 Ga. St. U. L. Rev. 429 (1999), 899

Jensen, Litigating the Crossroads Between *Sweet Home* and *Daubert*, 24 V. L. Rev. 169 (2000), 667

Johnson, *Fausek v. White:* The Sixth Circuit Garners Support for a Good Cause Exception to the Attorney-Client Privilege, 18 Dayton L. Rev. 313 (1993), 800

Joseph, G.P. & Saltzburg, S.A., Evidence in America: The Federal Rules in the States (1987), 798

Joseph, A Simplified Approach to Computer-Generated Evidence and Animations, 43 N.Y.L. Sch. L. Rev. 875 (1999-2000), 194

Kagehiro & Stanton, Legal v. Quantified Definitions of Standards of Proof, 9 Law & Hum. Behav. 159 (1985), 725

Kahan, The Economics—Conventional, Behavioral, and Political—of "Subsequent Remedial Measures" Evidence, 110 Colum. L. Rev. 1616 (2010), 332–333, 344

Kalven, H., Jr., & Zeisel, H., The American Jury (1966), 321–322, 378

Kaplan, Decision Theory and the Factfinding Process, 20 Stan. L. Rev. 1065 (1968), 170, 172

_____, Of Mabrus and Zorgs—An Essay in Honor of David Louisell, 66 Cal. L. Rev. 987 (1978), 227

Kaplan & Cogan, The Case Against Recognition of a General Academic Privilege, 60 U. Det. J. Urb. L. 205 (1983), 904

Karp, Evidence of Propensity and Probability in Sex Offense Cases and Other Cases, 70 Chi.-Kent L. Rev. 15 (1995), 308

Kassirer & Cecil, Inconsistency in Evidentiary Standards for Medical Testimony, 288 JAMA 1382 (2002), 666

Kaye, Naked Statistical Evidence, 89 Yale L.J. 601 (1980), 170

_____, Rounding Up the Usual Suspects: A Legal and Logical Analysis of DNA Trawling Cases, 87 N.C. L. Rev. 425 (2009), 147, 706

Kedigh, Spoliation: To the Careless Go the Spoils, 67 UMKC L. Rev. 597 (1999), 153

Kinports, Evidence Engendered, 1991 U. Ill. L. Rev. 413, 140

Koehler, Fingerprint Error Rates and Proficiency Tests: What They Are and Why They Matter, 59 Hastings L.J. 1077 (2008), 712, 714

Koons & Grant, Compositional Variation in Bullet Lead Manufacture, 47 J. Foren. Sci. 950 (2002), 714

Krafka, C., et al., Judge and Attorney Experiences, Practices, and Concerns Regarding Expert Testimony in Federal Civil Trials, Federal Judicial Center (2002), 648

Kramer, Note, Rule by Myth: The Social and Legal Dynamics Governing Alcohol-Related Acquaintance Rapes, 47 Stan. L. Rev. 115 (1994), 313

Kuhns, The Propensity to Misunderstand the Character of Specific Acts Evidence, 66 Iowa L. Rev. 777 (1981), 266

Ladd, Techniques and Theory of Character Testimony, 24 Iowa L. Rev. 498 (1939), 295

LaFree, G.D., Rape and Criminal Justice: The Social Construction of Sexual Assault (1989), 312–313, 322

Lander & Budowle, DNA Fingerprinting Dispute Laid to Rest, 371 Nature 735 (1994), 653

Langbein, J., The German Advantage in Civil Procedure, 52 U. Chi. L. Rev. 823 (1985), 80

_____, Torture and the Law of Proof: Europe and England in the Ancien Régime (1977), 121

Laudan, Truth, Error, and Criminal Law: An Essay in Legal Epistemology 31 (2006), 751

Lauderdale, A New Trend in the Law of Privilege: The Federal Settlement Privilege and the Proper Use of Federal Rule of Evidence 501 for the Recognition of New Privileges, 35 U. Mem. L. Rev. 255 (2005), 901

Leippe, The Case for Expert Testimony About Eyewitness Memory, 1 Psychol. Pub. Pol'y & L. 909 (1995), 651

Lempert, Modeling Relevance, 75 Mich. L. Rev. 1021 (1977), 170

Lempert, R.O. & Saltzburg, S.A., A Modern Approach to Evidence (1977), 412

Lempert, R.O. et al., A Modern Approach to Evidence (3d ed. 2000), 466

Leonard, Appellate Review of Evidentiary Rulings, 70 N.C. L. Rev. 1155 (1992), 364

_____, The New Wigmore (2002), 330

_____, Selected Rules of Limited Admissibility, The New Wigmore (2002), 344

_____, The Use of Character to Prove Conduct: Rationality and Catharsis in Evidence Law, 58 U. Colo. L. Rev. 1 (1987), 240

Lieberman & Arndt, Understanding the Limits of Limiting Instructions, 6 Psychol. Pub. Pol'y & L. 677 (2000), 150

Lilly, G.C., An Introduction to the Law of Evidence (3d ed. 1996), 738

Lininger, Prosecuting Batterers After *Crawford*, 91 Va. Law Review 747 (2005), 624

Loftus, E., Eyewitness Testimony (1996), 651

Lueck & Arenz, Federal Rule of Evidence 502(d) and Compelled Quick Peek Productions, 10 Sedona Conf. J. 229 (2009), 813

Lushing, Faces Without Features: The Surface Validity of Criminal Inference, 72 J. Crim. L. & Criminology 82 (1981), 768

Maguire & Epstein, Preliminary Questions of Fact in Determining the Admissibility of Evidence, 40 Harv. L. Rev. 392 (1927), 226

Marcus, The Perils of Privilege: Waiver and the Litigator, 84 Mich. L. Rev. 1605 (1986), 809

Marino & Marino, The Scientific Basis of Causality in Toxic Tort Cases, 21 Dayton L. Rev. 1 (Fall 1995), 708

McCormick, The Borderland of Hearsay, 39 Yale L.J. 489 (1930), 432

_____, Charges on Presumptions and Burdens of Proof, 5 N.C. L. Rev. 291 (1972), 733

McCormick on Evidence (Broun ed., 6th ed. 2006), 375, 402, 465, 514, 525, 554, 556, 733, 742

McCormick on Evidence (Strong ed., 5th ed. 1999), 92, 278, 654, 836, 860

McMillin, *University of Pennsylvania v. E.E.O.C.* and *Dixon v. Rutgers*: Two Supreme Courts Speak on the Academic Freedom Privilege, 42 Rutgers L. Rev. 1089 (1990), 905

McMunigal & Sharpe, Reforming Extrinsic Impeachment, 33 Conn. L. Rev. 363 (2001), 362

McNaughton, Burden of Production of Evidence: A Function of a Burden of Persuasion, 68 Harv. L. Rev. 1382 (1955), 719

McNeely-Johnson, Comment, *United States v. Nixon*, Twenty Years After: The Good, the Bad and the Ugly—An Exploration of Executive Privilege, 14 N. Ill. U. L. Rev. 251 (1993), 910

Mendez, Essay: The Law of Evidence and the Search for Stable Personality, 45 Emory L.J. 221 (1996), 240

Milich, Hearsay Antinomies: The Case for Abolishing the Rule and Starting Over, 71 Or. L. Rev. 723 (1992), 625, 628

_____, Re-Examining Hearsay Under the Federal Rules: Some Method for the Madness, 39 Kan. L. Rev. 893 (1991), 442, 445

Mnookin, The Validity of Latent Fingerprint Identification: Confessions of a Fingerprinting Moderate, 7(2) Law Probability & Risk 127 (2008), 714

Modern Scientific Evidence: The Law and Science of Expert Testimony (Faigman et al. eds., 2002 & Supp. 2003), 666

Mogck, Are We There Yet? Refining the Test for Expert Testimony Through *Daubert*, *Kumho Tire* and Proposed Federal Rule of Evidence 702, 33 Conn. L. Rev. 303 (2000), 667–668

Morgan, Hearsay Dangers and the Application of the Hearsay Concept, 62 Harv. L. Rev. 177 (1948), 417, 432

Mosteller, *Crawford v. Washington:* Encouraging and Ensuring the Confrontation of Witnesses, 39 U.. Richmond L. Rev. 511 (2005), 624

Mueller, The Federal Psychotherapist-Patient Privilege After *Jaffee:* Truth and Other Values in a Therapeutic Age, 49 Hastings L.J. 945 (1998), 884

Mueller, C.B. & Kirkpatrick, L.C., Evidence (2d ed. 1999), 232, 423
_____, Federal Evidence (2d ed. 1994), 332

Muldering, Wharton, & Cecil, Tobacco Cases May Be Only the Tip of the Iceberg for Assaults on Privilege, 67 Def. Couns. J. 16 (2000), 833

Murphy, Spin Control and the High-Profile Client—Should the Attorney-Client Privilege Extend to Communications with Public Relations Consultants?, 55 Syracuse L. Rev. 545 (2005), 806

Nance, Conditional Relevance Reinterpreted, 70 B.U. L. Rev. 447 (1990), 231
_____, Forward: Do We Really Want to Know the Defendant?, 70 Chi.-Kent L. Rev. 3 (1994), 308

National Research Council, Committee on Identifying the Needs of the Forensic Sciences Community, Strengthening Forensic Science in the United States (National Acads. Press 2009), 702, 706, 711
_____, Committee on Scientific Assessment of Bullet Lead Elemental Composition Comparison, Forensic Analysis: Weighing Bullet Lead Evidence (2004), 714
_____, Committee to Review the Scientific Evidence on the Polygraph, The Polygraph and Lie Detection (National Acads. Press 2003), 666

Navigating Uncertainty: Gatekeeping in the Absence of Hard Science, 113 Harv. L. Rev. 1467 (2000), 668

Nelkin, The Limits of the Privilege: The Developing Scope of Federal Psychotherapist-Patient Privilege Law, 20 Rev. Litig. 1 (2000), 886

Nesson, Rationality, Presumptions, and Judicial Comment: A Response to Professor Allen, 94 Harv. L. Rev. 1574 (1981), 766

Neufeld, The (Near) Irrelevance of *Daubert* to Criminal Justice: And Some Suggestions for Reform, 95 Am. J. Pub. Health S107 (Supp. I 2005), 704

North, *University of Pennsylvania v. E.E.O.C.:* The Denial of an Academic Freedom Privilege, 18 Pepp. L. Rev. 213 (1990), 905

Note, Did Your Eyes Deceive You? Expert Psychological Testimony on the Unreliability of Eyewitness Identification, 29 Stan. L. Rev. 969 (1977), 489

Note, Evidence—Privileged Communications—The Attorney-Client Privilege in the Corporate Setting: A Suggested Approach, 69 Mich. L. Rev. 360 (1970), 823

Note, Government Secrets, Fair Trials, and the Classified Information Procedures Act, 98 Yale L.J. 427 (1988), 909

Note, Improving Judicial Gatekeeping: Technical Advisors and Scientific Evidence, 110 Harv. L. Rev. 941 (1997), 668

Note, Navigating Uncertainty: Gatekeeping in the Absence of Hard Science, 113 Harv. L. Rev. 1467 (2000), 668

Note, Overriding the Psychologist-Patient Privilege in Child Custody Disputes: Are Anyone's Best Interest Being Served?, 68 UMKC L. Rev. 169 (1999), 888

Note, Parent-Child Loyalty and Testimonial Privilege, 100 Harv. L. Rev. 910 (1987), 899

Note, Rule by Myth: The Social and Legal Dynamics Governing Alcohol-Related Acquaintance Rapes, 47 Stan. L. Rev. 115 (1994), 313

Note, Should the Federal Government Have an Attorney-Client Privilege?, 51 Fla. L. Rev. 695 (1999), 835

Noyes, Federal Rule of Evidence 502: Stirring the State Law of Privilege and Professional Responsibility with a Federal Stick, 66 Wash. & Lee L. Rev. 673 (2009), 814

Ogden, C.K. & I.A. Richards, The Meaning of Meaning (1927), 412

Orenstein, No Bad Men!: A Feminist Analysis of Character Evidence in Rape Trials, 49 Hastings L.J. 663 (1998), 313, 322

Orloff & Stedinger, A Framework for Evaluating the Preponderance-of-the-Evidence Standard, 131 U. Pa. L. Rev. 1159 (1983), 730

Pardo, Pleadings, Proof, and Judgment: A Unified Theory of Civil Litigation, 51 B.C. L. Rev. 1451 (2010), 722

_____, Second-Order Proof Rules, 61 Fla. L. Rev. 1083 (2009), 725

_____, Testimony, 82 Tul. L. Rev. 119 (2007), 442

Park, Character at the Crossroads, 49 Hastings L.J. 717 (1998), 312

_____, "I Didn't Tell Them Anything About You": Implied Assertions as Hearsay Under the Federal Rules of Evidence, 74 Minn. L. Rev. 783 (1990), 439, 442, 444

_____, McCormick on Evidence and the Concept of Hearsay: A Critical Analysis Followed by Suggestions to Law Teachers, 65 Minn. L. Rev. 423 (1981), 438

_____, A Subject Matter Approach to Hearsay Reform, 86 Mich. L. Rev. 51 (1987), 628, 629

Pennington & Hastie, A Cognitive Theory of Juror Decision Making: The Story Model, 13 Cardozo L. Rev. 519 (1991), 139, 167, 170

_____, Juror Decision-Making Models: The Generalization Gap, 89 Psychol. Bull. 246 (1981), 115

Penrod & Heuer, Tweaking Commonsense: Assessing Aids to Jury Decision Making, 3 Psychol. Pub. Pol'y & L. 259 (1997), 113

Perspectives on the Proposed Federal Rules of Evidence 413-415, 22 Fordham Urb. L.J. 265 (1995), 306

Pettys, The Emotional Juror, 76 Fordham L. Rev. 1609 (2007), 140

Pineau, Date Rape: A Feminist Analysis, 8 Law & Phil. 217 (1989), 313, 322

Plausen, Dead Man's Privilege, Vince Foster and the Demise of Legal Ethics, 68 Fordham L. Rev. 807 (1999), 800

Pudelski, The Constitutional Fate of Mandatory Reporting Statutes and the Clergy-Penitent Privilege in a Post-Smith World, 98 Nw. U. L. Rev. 703 (2004), 895

Raeder, Commentary: A Response to Professor Swift, 76 Minn. L. Rev. 507 (1992), 577

Randich et al., A Metallurgical Review of the Interpretation of Bullet Lead Compositional Analysis, 127 Foren. Sci. Int'l 174 (2000), 714

Raskin et al., The Scientific Status of Research on Polygraph Techniques: The Case for Polygraph Tests 19-2.0, in 1 Modern Science Evidence: The Law and Science of Expert Testimony (Faigman et al. eds., 2002 & Supp. 2003), 666

Regan, Spousal Privilege and the Meanings of Marriage, 81 Va. L. Rev. 2045 (1995), 868

Reisinger, Court-Appointed Expert Panels: A Comparison of Two Models, 32 Ind. L. Rev. 225 (1998), 700

Rice, Attorney-Client Privilege in the U.S., Cause to Overcome Privilege—Limitations on Applicability of *Garner*—Must the Action Be Derivative for *Garner* Rule to Apply?, ACPRIV-FED §8:20 (2010), 800

Risinger, Navigating Expert Reliability: Are Criminal Standards of Certainty Being Left on the Dock?, 64 Alb. L. Rev. 99 (2000), 666, 710

_____, Preliminary Thoughts on a Functional Taxonomy of Expertise for the Post-*Kumho* World, 31 Seton Hall L. Rev. 508 (2000), 653

Risinger et al., Exorcism of Ignorance as a Proxy for Rational Knowledge: The Lessons of Handwriting Identification "Expertise," 137 U. Pa. L. Rev. 731 (1988), 710

Roberts, Rape, Violence, and Women's Autonomy, 69 Chi.-Kent L. Rev. 359 (1993), 313, 322

Robins, Evidence at the Electronic Frontier: Introducing E-Mail at Trial in Commercial Litigation, 29 Rutgers Computer & Tech. L.J. 219 (2003), 203

Rosenthal, *State of New Jersey v. Margaret Kelly Michaels*: An Overview, 1 Psychol. Pub. Pol'y & L. 246 (1995), 707

Ross, Does Diversity in Legal Scholarship Make a Difference?: A Look at the Laws of Rape, 100 Dick. L. Rev. 795 (1966), 322

Rozell, Symposium, Executive Privilege and the Clinton Presidency, 8 Wm. & Mary Bill Rts. J. 541 (2000), 910

St. Peter-Griffith, Abusing the Privilege: The Crime-Fraud Exception to Rule 501 of the Federal Rules of Evidence, 48 U. Miami L. Rev. 259 (1993), 838

Saks & Kidd, Human Information Processing and Adjudication: Trial by Heuristics, 15 Law & Soc'y Rev. 123 (1980-1981), 139

Saltzburg, Standards of Proof and Preliminary Questions of Fact, 27 Stan. L. Rev. 271 (1975), 227

Saltzburg, S.A. & Martin, M.M., Federal Rules of Evidence Manual (5th ed. 1990), 892

Saltzburg, S.A., Martin, M.M. & Capra, D.J., Federal Rules of Evidence Manual (7th ed. 1998), 222, 441, 553, 774, 787

Sanders et al., Legal Perceptions of Science and Expert Knowledge, 8 Psychol. Pub. Pol'y & L. 139 (2002), 667

Sanders, J., Bendectin on Trial: A Study of Mass Tort Litigation (1998), 708

Scallen, Constitutional Dimensions of Hearsay Reform: Toward a Three-Dimensional Confrontation Clause, 76 Minn. L. Rev. 623 (1992), 629

Schaffner, Reconciling Attorney-Client Privilege with the Rules of Professional Conduct, 81 Ill. B.J. 410 (1993), 821

Schauer, On the Supposed Jury Dependence of Evidence Law, 155 U. Pa. L. Rev. 165 (2006), 140

Scheutzow & Gillis, Confidentiality and Privilege of Peer Review Information: More Imagined Than Real, 7 J.L. & Health 169 (1992/1993), 905

Schwartz, A Foundation Theory of Evidence, 100 Geo. L. Rev. ___ (2011), 232

Seaman, Triangular Testimonial Hearsay: The Constitutional Boundaries of Expert Opinion Testimony, 96 Geo. L.J. 827 (2008), 691

Seigel, A Pragmatic Critique of Modern Evidence Scholarship, 88 Nw. U. L. Rev. 995 (1994), 140

_____, Rationalizing Hearsay: A Proposal for a Best Evidence Hearsay Rule, 72 B.U. L. Rev. 893 (1992), 625, 628

Seymore, Isn't It a Crime: Feminist Perspectives on Spousal Immunity and Spousal Violence, 90 Nw. L. Rev. 1032 (1996), 867, 869

Simon, A Third View of the Black Box: Cognitive Coherence in Legal Decision Making, 71 U. Chi. L. Rev. 511 (2004), 139

Simon & Mahan, Quantifying Burdens of Proof, 5 Law & Soc'y Rev. 319 (1971), 725

Sklansky, Hearsay's Last Hurrah, 2009 Sup. Ct. Rev. 1 (2010), 624

Slobogin, Doubts About Daubert: Psychiatric Anecdata as a Case Study, 57 Wash. & Lee L. Rev. 919 (2000), 707

Strier, The Road to Reform: Judges on Juries and Attorneys, 30 Loy. L.A. L. Rev. 1249 (1997), 113

Swift, Abolishing the Hearsay Rule, 75 Cal. L. Rev. 495 (1987), 627

_____, A Foundation Fact Approach to Hearsay, 75 Cal. L. Rev. 1339 (1987), 628

Symposium, At the Daubert Gate: Managing and Measuring Expertise in an Age of Science, Specialization, and Speculation, 57 Wash. & Lee L. Rev. 661 (2000), 668

Symposium, Executive Privilege and the Clinton Presidency, 8 Wm. & Mary Bill Rts. J. 541 (2000), 910

Symposium, Forensic Science for the 21st Century, 50 Jurimetrics 1 (2009), 706

Symposium on Hearsay and Implied Assertions: How Would (or Should) the Supreme Court Decide the Kearley Case?, 16 Miss. Col. L. Rev. 1 (1995), 442

Symposium, Perspectives on the Proposed Federal Rules of Evidence 413-415, 22 Fordham Urb. L.J. 265 (1995), 306

Tamanaha, A Critical Review of the Classified Information Procedures Act, 13 Am. J. Crim. L. 227 (1986), 909

Thayer, J.B., A Preliminary Treatise on Evidence at Common Law (1898), 122, 407, 737

Tiersma, Reforming the Language of Jury Instructions, 22 Hofstra L. Rev. 37 (1993), 150

Tobin, Comparative Bullet Lead Analysis: A Case Study in Flawed Forensics, 28 Champion 12 (July 2004), 714

Tobin & Duerfeldt, How Probative Is Comparative Bullet Lead Analysis?, 17 Crim. Just. 26 (2002), 714

Torrey, When Will We Be Believed? Rape Myths and the Idea of a Fair Trial in Rape Prosecutions, 24 U.C. Davis L. Rev. 1013 (1991), 321, 322

Trautman, Logical or Legal Relevancy—A Conflict in Theory, 5 Vand. L. Rev. 385 (1952), 135

Tribe, Triangulating Hearsay, 87 Harv. L. Rev. 957 (1974), 412

Turner, Judicial Notice and Federal Rule of Evidence 201—A Rule Ready for Change, 45 U. Pitt. L. Rev. 181 (1983), 783

Tversky & Kahneman, Judgment Under Uncertainty: Heuristics and Biases, 185 Science 1124 (1974), 139

Twining & Stein, Evidence and Proof, The International Library of Essays in Law and Legal Theory (1992), 170

Vidmar & Hans, American Juries: The Verdict (2007), 139

Volokh, n Guilty Men, 146 U. Pa. L. Rev. 173 (1997), 751

Ward, C.A., Attitudes Toward Rape: Feminist and Social Psychological Perspectives (1995), 321

Warren, She's Gotta Have It Now: A Qualified Rape Crisis Counselor-Victim Privilege, 17 Cardozo L. Rev. 141 (1995), 897

Weinstein, The Probative Force of Hearsay, 46 Iowa L. Rev. 331 (1961), 626

Weinstein, J.B. & Berger, M.A., Weinstein's Evidence (1982), 654

_____, Weinstein's Federal Evidence (McLaughlin ed., 2d ed. 1997), 798, 799, 803, 808, 823, 914

_____, Weinstein's Federal Evidence (McLaughlin ed., 2d ed. rev. 2001), 127, 135

_____, Weinstein's Federal Evidence (McLaughlin ed., 2d ed. rev. 2002), 452

_____, Weinstein's Federal Evidence (McLaughlin ed., 2d ed. rev. 2003), 441–442

_____, Weinstein's Federal Evidence (McLaughlin ed., 2d ed. rev. 2005), 309

Wellborn, Demeanor, 76 Cornell L. Rev. 1075 (1991), 413

Wells & Motley, Reinforcing the Myth of the Crazed Rapist: A Feminist Critique of Recent Rape Legislation, 81 B.U. L. Rev. 127 (2001), 311, 313

Westen, The Supreme Court's Bout with Insanity: *Clark v. Arizona*, 4 Ohio St. J. Crim. L. 143 (2006), 764

Whitaker, The Priest-Penitent Privilege: Its Constitutionality and Doctrine, 13 Regent U. L. Rev. 145 (2000-2001), 891

Wigmore, J.H., Code of Evidence (3d ed. 1942), 145

_____, Evidence (1905), 854

_____, Evidence (Chadbourn ed, 1970), 97, 394, 396, 400

_____, Evidence (Chadbourn ed, 1978), 694

_____, Evidence (McNaughton ed, 1961), 794

_____, Evidence (Tillers ed, 1983), 135

_____, Evidence in Trials at Common Law (3d ed. 1940), 121, 135

_____, Evidence in Trials at Common Law (Chadbourn ed., 1974), 413

_____, Evidence in Trials at Common Law (Tillers rev. 1983), 272

_____, A Treatise on the System of Evidence in Trials at Common Law 1697 (1904), 92

Woocher, Note, Did Your Eyes Deceive You? Expert Psychological Testimony on the Unreliability of Eyewitness Identification, 29 Stan. L. Rev. 969 (1977), 489

Wright, C., Jr., Instructions to the Jury: Summary Without Comment, 1954 Wash. U. L.Q. 177, 731

_____, The Invasion of the Jury: Temperature of the War, 27 Temple L.Q. 137 (1953), 731

Wright & Gold, Federal Practice and Procedure: Evidence (2000), 208

Wright, C.A. & Graham, K.W., Jr., Federal Practice and Procedure (1980), 316

_____, Federal Practice and Procedure (1990), 143, 784

_____, Federal Practice and Procedure (Supp. 2001), 306, 313, 316, 796

_____, Federal Practice and Procedure: Evidence (1977), 796

Zacharias, Harmonizing Privilege and Confidentiality, 41 S. Tex. L. Rev. 69 (1999), 821

Index

A

Abuse of discretion, 157–159
Academic researcher's privilege, 903–904
Accomplices, corroboration requirement for statements inculpating, 562
Adjudicative facts, judicial notice
  defined, 774–775
  types of facts subject to judicial notice, 774
Admissibility. *See specific topic concerned*
Admissions by parties. *See* Party admissions, hearsay exemption
Adoptive admissions, hearsay exemption, 469–470
  preliminary fact-finding, 469
  rationale, 469–470
  silence, by, 470
Adversary system, 80
  hearsay, regulation premised on excesses of adversary system, 628
  natural reasoning, 109–119
  reconsideration, 109–111
Adverse witnesses, direct examination of, 96–97
Advocates. *See* Attorneys
Affirmative defenses, burden of persuasion, 755–762
  after *Patterson*, 757–762
  elements test, 755–756
  political compromise test, 756
  Powell two-part test, 757
  proportionality test, 756–757
Agents, hearsay exemption for admissions. *See* Party admissions, hearsay exemption
Amnesia, burden of persuasion in civil cases, 728–729
Ancient documents, 202–203
Animations, authentication of exhibits by, 194–195
Appellate review, preservation of error for
  FRE 103, 100
  elaboration, 106–109

interpretation and illustration, 101
general rule, 100
making record for, 107–108
  appeal of evidentiary rulings, 108
  standards of review, 108–109
Arrests
  examination of character witnesses regarding, 299
  impeachment of witness by questions about arrests, charges, and findings, 363
  hearsay, 432
Assertive conduct. *See* Hearsay
Attorney-client privilege, 804–856
  Bentham-Kaplow-Shavell theory, 847–848
  "common interest" cases, 807, 815
  communications
    attorney or representative, with, 805–807
    legal services, for purposes of, 807
  contingent claim theory, 842–846
  corporate clients, 822–834
    investigations of wrongdoing, 832–834
    Upjohn case, 823–831
  disclosure of communication or information protected by, 808–822
  duty of confidentiality, 818–820
  elements, 804–822
  exceptions, 836–839
    breach of duty, 836
    crime or fraud, communications in furtherance of, 833, 837–838
    document attested by attorney, 836
    fee information, 836–837
    identity of client, 836–837
  FRE 502
    aspects of, 811–813
    concerns raised by, 813–821
    confidentiality of relationship between attorney and client, potential damage to, 815

confidentiality order governing disclosure, effect of, 812–813
constitutionality of application to state proceedings, 814
controlling effect of FRE 502, 813
cost of discovery and, 814–815
court order governing disclosure, controlling effect of, 812–813
"data dumps," effect of, 814–815
document review still required, 813–814
general rule, 809–810
inadvertent disclosure, 811–812
inconsistent state and federal laws, 812
interpretation, 810–811
jeopardizing effect on attorney-client privilege as potential, 815
judge-initiated unilateral order, 815
limitations of, 811, 813–814
misleading disclosure, unfair to adversary, 811
party agreement, controlling effect of, 813
precautions taken to rectify error, 811–812
purposes of, 810
reasonable steps to prevent disclosure, 811–812, 816
review of documents still required, 813–814
scope of waiver, 811
selective disclosure, unfair to adversary, 811
state proceeding, disclosure made in, 812, 813, 814
subject matter waiver, 811, 815
subsequent state and federal proceedings, 811, 812, 813, 816
when inadvertent disclosure waives protection, 811–812
government clients, 834–835
holder of, 805, 815
inadvertent disclosure of confidential material, 808–810, 811–812. *See also* FRE 502, *this heading*
joint clients, 807, 815
"joint defense" cases, 807, 815
Model Rules of Professional Conduct, under, 819–820, 820–821
Morgan theory, 846
proposed Rule 503, 804–805
reflection on, 839–853
rights-based theories, 849
scope, 808
waiver of, 808–810, 832
    FRE 502, effect of. *See* FRE 502, *this heading*
    limitations on, 808–810. *See also* FRE 502, *this heading*
    protection against. *See* FRE 502, *this heading*
Wigmore theory, 848
work product doctrine, 808–822, 831, 850–853
Attorneys
attorney-client privilege. *See* Attorney-client privilege
role of, 81
work product doctrine, 808–822, 831, 850–853
Authentication, 182–209
ancient documents, 202–203
animations, by, 194–195
chain of custody, 188–191
computer-generated and recorded evidence, 194–195

demonstrative exhibits, 192–193
    assisting trier of fact, 193
    FRE 403 balancing test, applicability, 193
electronic writings and data, 203–204
FRE 901, 182
    elaboration, 187–206
    flexibility of, 206
    interpretation and illustration, 183–187
general rule, 182
in-court demonstrations and experiments, by, 193–194
judicial determination of sufficiency of evidence to support finding, 185–186
laying foundation, 186–187
production of sufficient evidence to support finding, 184–185
readily identifiable characteristic for identification, 188
real evidence, 187–192
reconstructions of events, by, 194–195
recordings, 196–201
    FRE 403 balancing test, applicability, 198
    percipient witnesses, 196–197
    "silent" witnesses, 197–198
    voice identification, 199
reenactments, by, 194–195
self-authentication, 206–209
    FRE 902, 206–207
    general rule, 206–207
    interpretation and illustration, 207–209
simulations to establish, 194–195
sufficient evidence to support finding, 183–185
voice identification, 199
what exhibit is claimed to be, 183
written documents, 201–206
    ancient documents, 202–203
    contents, 201–202
    electronic writings, 203–204
    signatures, 201

B

Bad acts evidence. *See* Specific acts evidence
Bayes' Theorem, 170–172
Behavioral sciences, expert witnesses, 706–707
Bench trials, 81
Best evidence rule, 210–223
defamation actions, 216
definitions, 210
duplicates, 210
FRE 1001, 210
FRE 1002, 210
    elaboration, 216–218
    interpretation and illustration, 211–212
FRE 1003, 210
    interpretation and illustration, 212
FRE 1004, 210
    interpretation and illustration, 212–213
FRE 1005, 211
FRE 1006, 211
    elaboration, 218–221
    interpretation and illustration, 213–214
FRE 1007, 211
FRE 1008, 221
    interpretation and illustration, 221–223
general rule, 210

inscriptions on objects as not writings, 218
other evidence of contents, 210
public records, 211
role of court and jury, 221
Seiler case, 214–216
summaries, 211, 218–221
   analytic summaries, 219
   illustrative aids, 219
   voluminous documents underlying summaries, 218–219
testimony, 211
underlying policies, 214–216
writing offered to prove its own content, 216–218
   content as fact of independent legal significance, 217
   event, writing used to prove, 217–218
   facts about writing are not "content," 218
   inscriptions on objects, 218
written admissions, 211
Bias and prejudice
   character evidence
   distinguished, 395–396
   prohibition on use of to prove conduct on particular occasion, 241–242
   child molestation evidence, 311
   conviction of crime, impeachment of witnesses by, 376
      balancing tests, 372
   extrinsic evidence, 395
   impeachment of witnesses by. *See* Impeachment of witnesses
   probative value, 144–146
   sexual assault evidence, 311
   specific acts evidence
      prohibition on use of to prove conduct on particular occasion, 241–242
      relevant acts with no character inference, admissibility, 248–249
   stereotypes, 128
Bifurcated trials, 89
Bullet lead analysis, 714–715
Burden of persuasion
   affirmative defenses in criminal cases, 755–762
      after *Patterson*, 757–762
      elements test, 755–756
      political compromise test, 756
      Powell two-part test, 757
      proportionality test, 756–757
   allocation in civil cases, 726–728, 729–730
   amnesia, 728–729
   burden of production, relationship with, 719–721
   business records, exclusion for untrustworthiness, 523
   civil cases, 722–730
   clear and convincing evidence standard in civil cases, 718, 724–725
   criminal cases, 748–765
   decision rules that manage uncertainty, 722–723
   explicit shifts in criminal cases, 751–764
   "extreme emotional distress" defense in criminal cases, 752–753
   "heat of passion" defense in criminal cases, 751–752
   higher burdens in civil cases, 724–725
   judicial summary and comment on evidence, relationship with, 733

jury instructions, 88
manslaughter, 754
mitigating factors in criminal cases, 755
Mullaney case, 751–752
Patterson case, 752–754
   affirmative defenses after, 757–762
preponderance of evidence standard in civil cases, 718, 723–724, 725, 729
presumptions, 735
reasonable doubt, proof beyond in criminal cases, 748–751
   defined, 749–750
   Due Process, 749, 754–756
   jury instructions, 750–751
relative nature of in civil cases, 725–726
role in civil cases, 722–723
uncertainty, management of, 722–723
Winship rule, 748–751
   application in other contexts, 762–764
Burden of production
   allocation in civil cases, 722
   burden of persuasion, relationship with, 719–721
   civil cases, 718–722
   criminal cases, 764–765
   procedural mechanisms for enforcement in civil cases, 721–722
   rationale, 718–719
   role in civil cases, 718–719
Burden of proof
   burden of persuasion. *See* Burden of persuasion
   burden of production. *See* Burden of production
Business records, hearsay exception. *See* Records of regularly conducted activity, hearsay exception

C

Character evidence, 235–326. *See also* Reputation evidence
   arrests, examination of character witnesses regarding, 299
   child molestation evidence. *See* Child molestation evidence
   cross-examination of character witnesses. *See* Cross-examination
   defined, 236
   essential element of claim or defense, character as, 302–306
      defamation actions, 304–305
      general rule, 303–304
      exceptions to prohibition on use of to prove conduct on particular occasion, 242, 284–302
      civil cases, 290
      conduct of victim, attacks on, 286
      defendant "opening the door" to character evidence, 285
      pertinence requirement, 286–287
      prosecution response, 285–286
      rationale, 290
      relevance of character evidence, 287–290
      witnesses, character of, 287
   FRE 404, 238
      elaboration, 240–244
      exceptions to prohibition on use of to prove conduct on particular occasion, 284–291

interpretation and illustration, 238–240
    methods of proving, 291–292, 293–302
FRE 405
    elaboration, 303–305
    interpretation and illustration, 303
    methods of proving, 291–292, 293–302
general rule, 238
habit evidence. *See* Habit evidence
impeachment of witnesses by. *See* Impeachment
    of witnesses
inherent weakness of, 300
limitations on use, 300–301
methods of proving, 238, 293–302
    opinion evidence, probative value, 294–295
    opinion evidence, reputation evidence distin-
        guished, 295–296
    reputation evidence, probative value,
        294–295
    specific acts, prohibition on use, 293–294
past sexual behavior evidence. *See* Past sexual
    behavior evidence
potential unfairness, 300–301
prohibition on use of to prove conduct on
    particular occasion, 238–244
    "bad person" prejudice, 241–242
    diversion from main issues, 241
    general rule, 238
    low probative value, 240–241
    prejudice, 241–242
    rationale, 240–242
    weakness of propensity inference, 240
reflection on, 258–267
relevancy, 235–237
    exceptions to prohibition on use of to prove
        conduct on particular occasion, 287–290
    routine practice evidence. *See* Routine practice
        evidence
sexual assault evidence. *See* Sexual assault
    evidence
similar happenings evidence. *See* Similar happen-
    ings evidence
specific acts evidence
    mental states not in dispute, problem when,
        253–255
    prohibition on use of to prove character,
        293–294
    relevance to cross-examination of character
        witnesses, 296–297
Child abuse
    hearsay and Confrontation Clause, 622
Child molestation evidence, 306–315
    character evidence, 307–308, 310–311
    federal litigation, significance to, 313–314
    FRE 403 balancing test, applicability, 308,
        310–311
    FRE 413 to 415, 307
        elaboration, 310–314
        interpretation and illustration, 307–310
    general rules, 307
    other Federal Rules of Evidence, 308–309
    preliminary fact-finding, 309
    probative value, 311–313
    rationale, 311–313
    recidivism, 312
    unfair prejudice, 311

Circumstantial evidence distinguished from direct
    evidence, 129–130
Civil cases
    burden of persuasion. *See* Burden of persuasion
    burden of production. *See* Burden of production
    hearsay
        need for, 627–628
        notice-based admission, proposal for, 628
    judicial notice
        mini-directed verdicts, 778–779
        verdicts, to preserve, 779–780
Clear and convincing evidence standard, 718,
    724–725
Clergy-communicant privilege, 890–896
    exceptions, 894–895
    expectation of confidentiality, 893–894
    holders, 892–893
    nature of communications, 893
    rationale, 891
    scope, 891–895
Closing arguments, 87–88
    sample case, 65–75
Co-conspirators, hearsay exemption for, 475–480
Communications privileges. *See* Privileges
Competency of witnesses, 176–181
    FRE 601, 176
        elaboration, 177–179
        interpretation and illustration, 176–177
    FRE 602, 179
        interpretation and illustration, 179–181
    general rule, 176
    mental competency, 177–179
    personal knowledge requirement, 179–180
    sufficient evidence to support finding, 180–181
Compromise, admissibility of offers, 335–340
    criminal cases, 337–338
    "disputed claim" requirement, 337
    exclusionary mandate, 335–336
    FRE 403 balancing test, applicability, 335–336
    FRE 408, 335
        interpretation and illustration, 335–339
    general rule, 335
    negotiations, conduct or statements made during,
        336–337
    party's own offer, 338
    permissible uses of, 335–336
    reflections on, 344
    third persons, by, 338–339
Computer documents, and hearsay exception, 527–528
Computer-generated and recorded evidence, authen-
    tication, 194–195
Conclusive presumptions, 735–737
Conditional admissibility, 227–234
    application to conditional facts, 231
    FRE 104
        elaboration, 229–231
        interpretation and illustration, 228–229
Conditional relevancy, 227–234
    application to conditional facts, 231
    FRE 104, elaboration, 229–231
    "sufficiency" standard, 229–231
Confidential information. *See* Privileges
Confrontation Clause
    hearsay, 579–624
        child abuse, 622, 624

child witnesses, 622, 624
Crawford case, 581–594
domestic violence, 622, 624
dying declarations, 621
exceptions, 621–624
exemptions and exceptions, 448
firmly rooted exceptions, 581
"forfeiture by wrongdoing," 621–624
non-firmly rooted exceptions, 581
non-testimonial statements, 619
Roberts case, 580–581
privileges, 803
testimonial statements
declarant testifying, 619–620
defined, 594–618
government forensic reports, 611–618
medical interviews and examinations, 610–611
police questioning, during, 594–610
primary purpose test, 595–610
prior opportunity for cross-examination, 620–621
satisfying confrontation right, 619–621
unavailability, 620
Confusion of issues, probative value, 146
Constitutional rights
Confrontation Clause. *See* Confrontation Clause
Due Process, proof beyond reasonable doubt in criminal cases, 749, 754–756, 757
Fifth Amendment
impeachment of witnesses by character evidence, waiver of Fifth Amendment rights, 361
party admissions, Constitutional concerns with, 466
hearsay exemption for prior statements of identification, Constitutional concerns with, 459
self-incrimination, Constitutional concerns with party admissions, 466
Contingent claim theory, attorney-client privilege, 842–846
Contradiction, impeachment of witnesses by. *See* Impeachment of witnesses
Convictions
impeachment of witnesses by. *See* Impeachment of witnesses
judgments of previous convictions, hearsay exception. *See* Judgments of previous convictions, hearsay exception
probative value of prior felonies, 167
Corporate clients
attorney-client privilege, 822–834
investigations of wrongdoing, 832–834
Corroboration
residual hearsay exception, independent corroboration, 574–575
statements against interest exception, required for, 560–562
statements inculpating accomplices, 562
Counsel. *See* Attorneys
attorney-client privilege. *See* Attorney-client privilege
Court-appointed experts, 699–701
FRE 706, 699
interpretation and illustration, 699–701
general rule, 699
Criminal cases
burden of persuasion. *See* Burden of persuasion

burden of production, 764–765
guilty pleas, admissibility of withdrawal. *See* Withdrawn pleas, admissibility
hearsay, different treatment of, 629
judicial notice, 779, 780–782
no contest pleas, admissibility of withdrawal. *See* Withdrawn pleas, admissibility
offers of compromise, 337–338
"other sexual behavior," admissibility, 320–321
plea discussions, admissibility of statements made during. *See* Withdrawn pleas, admissibility
presumptions, 767–770
reasonable doubt standard. *See* Burden of persuasion
"sexual predisposition," admissibility, 320–321
Cross-examination
character witnesses, 296–300
acts, arrests, and convictions, 299
form of questions, 299–300
likely knowledge of specific act, 297–298
prejudicial impact of specific acts inquiries, 297
reasonable belief that act occurred, 298–299
relationship between character and specific acts inquiries, 297
relevance of specific acts inquiries, 296–297
expert witnesses, 682–684
FRE 611
elaboration, 94–96
interpretation of, 92–93
goals, 95
hearsay exemptions, declarants subject to cross-examination, 449–452
denial of prior statement, 450
inability to remember prior statement, 450
inability to remember underlying events, 450–451
personal knowledge requirement, 452
preliminary fact-finding, 449–452
statement, examination concerning, 450
testimony by declarant, 449
impeachment of witnesses by specific instances of conduct, 365
leading questions. *See* Leading questions
prior inconsistent statements. *See* Prior inconsistent statements, hearsay exemption
recross-examination
FRE 611, 93
sample case, 30–31
rehabilitation by, 389–391
sample case, 15–19, 24–25, 29–30, 34–35, 43–47, 49–50, 55–57, 60–61
scope, 92–93
strategy, 95
techniques, 95–96
Culpability
liability insurance. *See* Liability insurance, inadmissibility to prove negligence
offers of compromise. *See* Compromise, admissibility of offers
payment of medical expenses. *See* Medical expenses, admissibility of payment
subsequent remedial measures. *See* Subsequent remedial measures, admissibility
Cumulative evidence, probative value, 147–148

D

Declarants. *See* Hearsay
Declarations against interest. *See* Statements against interest, hearsay exception
Defamation actions
  best evidence rule, 216
  character as essential element of claim or defense, 304–305
Deliberative process privilege, 912–915
Demonstrative evidence, probative value, 151–152
Demonstrative exhibits, authentication, 192–193
  assisting trier of fact, 193
  FRE 403 balancing test, applicability, 193
Directed verdicts, 85, 86
Direct evidence distinguished from circumstantial evidence, 129–130
Direct examination
  adverse witnesses, 96–97
  FRE 611
    elaboration, 93–94
    interpretation and illustration, 91–93
  hostile witnesses, 96–97
  redirect examination
    FRE 611, 93
    sample case, 19–20, 30, 50–51, 57–58
  sample case, 8–15, 20–24, 25–29, 32–34, 35–37, 41–43, 47–49, 51–55
Discretion of court. *See* Judicial discretion
Dismissal motions, 85
  sample case, 37–38
DNA testing, expert witnesses, 706
Domestic violence, hearsay and Confrontation Clause, 622, 624
Drinking
  habit evidence, 272–273
  lay opinion, 634
Due Process, proof beyond reasonable doubt in criminal cases, 749, 754–756, 757
Duplicates, best evidence rule, 210
Dying declarations, hearsay exception, 555–557
  Confrontation Clause, 621
  FRE 804, 555
    interpretation and illustration, 555–557
  general rule, 555
  preliminary fact-finding, 555–556
  rationale, 559

E

Electronic data
  authentication, 203–204
  business records exception, 527–528
  inadvertent disclosure of protected materials, 808–810
  records of regularly conducted activity, 527–528
Employees, hearsay exemption for. *See* Party admissions, hearsay exemption
Examination of witnesses, 90–100
  breadth of court's power, 91–92
  cross-examination. *See* Cross-examination
  direct examination. *See* Direct examination
  FRE 611, 91
    elaboration, 93–97
    interpretation and illustration, 91–93
    leading questions. *See* Leading questions
    recross-examination. *See* Recross-examination
    redirect examination. *See* Redirect examination
Exceptions to hearsay rule. *See specific exception concerned*
Excited utterances, hearsay exception, 487–495
  categorical approach, 489–493
    categories determining admissibility, 489–490
    judicial interpretation, 490–492
    preliminary fact-finding, 492–493
    proof of personal knowledge, 493
  FRE 803, 487
    elaboration, 489–494
    interpretation and illustration, 487–489
  general rule, 487
  preliminary fact-finding, 487–488
    categorical approach, 492–493
  rationale, 488–489
Exclusionary rule, 168–169
Executive privilege, 907–915
Exhibits
  authentication. *See* Authentication
  defined, 182
Expert witnesses, 646–715
  basis of opinion testimony, 684–691
    general rule, 684
    otherwise inadmissible evidence, 686–691
  behavioral sciences, 706–707
  bullet lead, compositional analysis of, 714–715
  cases in which used, 647–648
  conflicts between, 648
  court-appointed experts, 699–701
    FRE 706, 699
    general rule, 699
  cross-examination, 682–684
  disclosure of facts underlying opinion, 682–684
    general rule, 682
  DNA testing, 706
  fingerprint identification, 711–714
  FRE 403 balancing test, applicability, 652–653
  FRE 702, 649–650
    elaboration, 653–676
    interpretation and illustration, 650–653
  FRE 703, 684
    elaboration, 686–691
    interpretation and illustration, 684–686
  FRE 705, 682
    interpretation and illustration, 683–684
  frequency of use, 647
  general rule, 649–650
  handwriting identification, 710–711
  helping trier of fact, 650–651
  law enforcement investigative tools, 710–715
    bullet lead, compositional analysis of, 714–715
    fingerprint identification, 711–714
    handwriting identification, 710–711
  learned treatises, use of, 686
  litigation incentives, 652–653
  patients' statements as basis of expert opinion, 509
  psychological sciences, 706–707
  qualification, 651–652
  scientific, technical, or other specialized knowledge. *See also* Scientific evidence and expert witnesses
    Daubert case, 655–668, 677–682

Frye case, 653–655
general rule, 649–650
Kumho Tire case, 668–672
specialties, 647
summary witnesses, 653
syndrome evidence, 706–707
testimonial experience, 648
toxic tort causation, 707–709
translations, 677
treatises, use of, 686
ultimate issue, opinion on, 693–699
FRE 704, 693
general rule, 693
"Extreme emotional distress" defense, burden of
persuasion, 752–753
Extrinsic evidence
impeachment of witnesses by. *See* Impeachment
of witnesses
prejudice, 395

F

Fact-finding
judicial. *See* Judicial fact-finding
juries. *See* Juries
preliminary. *See* Preliminary fact-finding
Family history, hearsay exception for. *See* Personal
or family history, hearsay exception for statements of
Federal Rules of Evidence (FRE). *See also specific
topic concerned*
rationale, 111–113
Fifth Amendment
impeachment of witnesses by character evidence,
waiver of rights, 361
party admissions, constitutional concerns with, 466
Fingerprint identification, 711–714
Firsthand knowledge rule, 418
Forensic science
behavioral sciences, 706–707
bullet lead, compositional analysis of, 714–715
controversies in, 701–715
DNA testing, 706
fingerprint identification, 711–714
government forensic reports, Confrontation Clause
and, 611–618
handwriting identification, 710–711
law enforcement investigative tools, 709–715
psychological sciences, 706–707
toxic tort causation, 707–709
"Forfeiture by wrongdoing," 566–571
acquiescence in wrongdoing, 569–570
Confrontation Clause and, 621–624
content of statement, 568–569
declarant as witness, 567
FRE 403 balancing test, applicability, 570
FRE 804, 566
general rule, 566
hearing requirement, 570–571
intent to procure unavailability of declarant, 568
preliminary fact-finding, 567–569
procuring unavailability of declarant, 567–568
rationale, 569
Former testimony, hearsay exception, 547–555
FRE 804, 547

elaboration, 550–554
interpretation and illustration, 547–549
general rule, 547
identity of parties, 550–551
method of introducing, 553–554
not party to original action, offered against,
551–552
objections, 554
"offered on same issue" requirement, 549
opportunity to develop testimony, 550
no opportunity, 549
same party or predecessor in interest, 548
similar motive, 548–549
"trial, hearing or lawful deposition," 547
predecessors in interest
defined, 552
opportunity to develop testimony, 548
preliminary fact-finding, 547–549
rationale, 549
similar motive
lack of, due to difference in procedural context,
552–553
opportunity to develop testimony, 548–549
Foundation for proof
authentication. *See* Authentication
best evidence rule. *See* Best evidence rule
competency. *See* Competency of witnesses
conditional admissibility. *See* Conditional
admissibility
conditional relevancy. *See* Conditional
relevancy
judicial fact-finding. *See* Judicial fact-finding
witnesses; Competency of witnesses
Fraud exception to attorney-client privilege, 833,
837–838

G

Government clients and attorney-client privilege,
834–835
Government informant's privilege, 901–902
Government privileges, 907–915
Guilty pleas, admissibility of withdrawal. *See*
Withdrawn pleas, admissibility

H

Habit evidence, 267–276
character distinguished, 269–270
application of distinction, 272–273
drinking, 272–273
strategy, 271–272
defined, 237
FRE 406, 267
elaboration, 271–276
interpretation and illustration, 268–271
general rule, 267
importance, 268–269
judicial fact-finding, 270–271
methods of proving, 269
organizational behavior, 273–274
rationale, 271
similar happenings distinguished, 278–279
Handwriting identification, 710–711
Harmless error, 109, 167, 169

Hearsay, 407–629
    abolition, proposal for, 627
    accomplices, corroboration requirement for state-
        ments inculpating, 562
    adoptive admissions exemption, 469–470
        preliminary fact-finding, 469
        rationale, 469–470
        silence, by, 470
    agents, exemption for admissions. See Party admis-
        sions, hearsay exemption
    arrests, 432
    assertive vs. nonassertive conduct, 429–434
        ambiguity, danger of, 431
        difficulty of application of intent test, 430–431
        disguised assertions, 431–432
        exclusion of nonassertive conduct, 430–431
        intent test, difficulty of application, 430–431
        lack of hearsay dangers, 429–430
        necessity, 430
        nonverbal conduct, 427–428
        policy arguments regarding admission of
            nonassertive conduct, 431
    business records exception. See Business records,
        hearsay exception
    civil cases
        need for, 627–628
        notice-based admission, proposal for, 628
    co-conspirators, exemption for admissions. See
        Party admissions, hearsay exemption
    Confrontation Clause. See Confrontation Clause
    criminal cases, different treatment in, 629
    criticisms of rule, 625–629
    cross-examination, witnesses subject to. See
        Cross-examination
    declarants, witnesses distinguished, 412–414
    defined, 408
    dying declarations exception. See Dying declara-
        tions, hearsay exception
    employees, exemption for admissions. See Party
        admissions, hearsay exemption
    exceptions. See also specific exception concerned
        approach to admissibility under, 445–448
        categorical approach, 446
        Confrontation Clause, 448
        foundational requirements, 446–447
        multiple exemptions and exceptions, 447–448
        process of admission, 446
        rationale, 445–446
    excesses of adversary system, regulation premised
        on, 628
    excited utterances exception. See Excited utter-
        ances, hearsay exception
    exemptions, 448–482. See also specific exemption
        concerned
        approach to admissibility under, 445–448
        categorical approach, 446
        Confrontation Clause, 448
        cross-examination, witnesses subject to. See
            Cross-examination
        foundational requirements, 446–447
        FRE 801, 448–449
        multiple exemptions and exceptions,
            447–448
        process of admission, 446
        rationale, 445–446, 452

    family history, exception for statements of. See
        Personal or family history, hearsay exception
        for statements of
    firsthand knowledge rule, 418
    "forfeiture by wrongdoing." See "Forfeiture by
        wrongdoing"
    former testimony exception. See Former testimony,
        hearsay exception
    FRE 801, 408
        assertive vs. nonassertive conduct, 429–433
        elaboration, 416–419
        intent test, 439–441
        interpretation and illustration, 408–415
        nonhearsay statements, 419–426
        nonverbal conduct, 426–429
        revision, proposal for, 444–445
    FRE 802, 408
        elaboration, 416–419
        interpretation and illustration, 408–415
    general rule, 408
        identification, exemption for prior statements of.
            See Identification, hearsay exemption for prior
            statements of
        impeachment of witnesses by conviction of
            crime, 377–378
    implications, 416–419
    intent test, 438–445
        burden of proof, 441
        common law approach, continued adherence
            to, 441–442
        difficulties in application of, 430–431,
            439–441
        factual uncertainty, 440–441
        judicial creation of, 439
        literal approach, rejection, 438–441
        nonverbal conduct, 428–429
        sincerity risk, identifying, 439–442
        unstated beliefs, intent to assert, 439–440
        what kind of intent, 440
    interest, exception for statements against. See
        Statements against interest, hearsay exception
    judgments of previous convictions exception. See
        Judgments of previous convictions, hearsay
        exception
    judicial discretion, proposal for, 626
    lay opinion, 418
    learned treatises, 486
    medical diagnosis or treatment, exception for
        statements made for. See Medical diagnosis
        or treatment, hearsay exception for statements
        made for
    multiple hearsay. See Multiple hearsay
    nonhearsay statements, 419–426
        effect on listener, 421–422
        identifying nonhearsay uses, 423
        legally operative facts, 422–423
        statements relevant for both hearsay and non-
            hearsay uses, 424
        uses of, 420–424
    nonverbal conduct, 426–429
        assertive conduct, 427–428
        intent test, 428–429
        nonassertive conduct, 428
        relevancy, 426–427
    out-of-court statements, testimony about, 417

party admissions exemption. *See* Party admissions, hearsay exemption
past recollections recorded exception. *See* Past recollections recorded, hearsay exception
personal or family history, exception for statements of. *See* Personal or family history, hearsay exception for statements of
present recollections refreshed, 515–517
    FRE 612, 516–517
present sense impressions exception. *See* Present sense impressions, hearsay exception
prior consistent statements exemption. *See* Prior consistent statements, hearsay exemption
prior inconsistent statements exemption. *See* Prior inconsistent statements, hearsay exemption
public records and reports exception. *See* Public records and reports, hearsay exception
rationale, 625
reflection on, 444–445, 625–629
reformulation of policy, proposal for, 627–629
relevancy, 409–412
reliability, criticism of, as rationale, 625–626
residual exception. *See* Residual hearsay exception
servants, exemption for admissions. *See* Party admissions, hearsay exemption
statements against interest exception. *See* Statements against interest, hearsay exception
state-of-mind declarations exception. *See* State-of-mind declarations, hearsay exception
testimonial qualities of declarant, 409–412
truth that statement is offered to prove, 416–417
unavailability of declarant
    caused by proponent, 546
    exceptions not requiring, 483–542. *See also specific exception concerned*
    exceptions requiring, 543–571. *See also specific exception concerned*
    FRE 803, 484–486
    FRE 804, 543–544
    grounds for finding, 544–547
    other exceptions, 539
    preference for former testimony or deposition, 545
    preliminary fact-finding, 544–545
    reasonable means to procure attendance, 545–546
unstated beliefs, 434–438
    common law approach, 437–438, 441–442
    intent test, 439–441
    literal approach, 437, 438–442
    relevancy and, 435–436
    witnesses, declarants distinguished, 412–414
"Heat of passion" defense, burden of persuasion, 751–752
Hostile witnesses, direct examination of, 96–97
Hostile work environment cases, past sexual behavior evidence, 319–320
Hypothetical questions, 509, 683

I

Identification, hearsay exemption for prior statements of, 456–462
    Constitutional concerns, 459
    FRE 801, 448–449

interpretation and illustration, 456–459
general rule, 448–449
made after perceiving person, 457–458
person, identification of, 458
preliminary fact-finding, 456–458
rationale, 458–459
someone declarant perceived earlier, 457–458
Identification of exhibits. *See* Authentication
Impeachment of witnesses, 351–405
bias, by, 394–398
    character evidence distinguished, 395–396
    extrinsic evidence, 395
    relevance, 394
    Wigmore on, 394
bolstering credibility, 356
character evidence, by, 357–382
    arrests, charges, and judicial or administrative findings, questions about, 363
    bias distinguished, 395–396
    cross-examination, 365
    extrinsic evidence, prohibition against use, 361, 361–362
    Fifth Amendment waiver, 361
    FRE 403 balancing test, applicability, 363–364
    FRE 608, 357
    FRE 609, 370
    good-faith requirement, 364–365
    limited scope of inquiry, 361, 362–363
    opinion evidence of untruthfulness, 358–360
    questions about arrests, charges, and findings, 363
    reputation evidence of untruthfulness, 358–360
    specific acts of witnesses being testified about, questioning about, 366
    specific acts of witnesses themselves, questioning about, 361–365
    truthfulness, showing good character for, 358–359, 365
    untruthfulness, meaning of, 362–363
contradiction, by, 361, 400–404
    extrinsic evidence, 401
    "no extrinsic evidence to impeach on a collateral matter" doctrine, 401–403
    relevance, 400
    Wigmore on, 400
conviction of crime, by, 370–382
    balancing tests, 371–373
    criminal defendants, reverse balancing test for, 372, 374–375
    "dishonest act or false statement" convictions, automatic admissibility, 373–374
    extrinsic evidence, 376
    factual details of conviction, 372–373, 376–377
    hearsay evidence, 377–378
    misdemeanor convictions, by, 542
    other witnesses, 372
    practical considerations, 378–380
    prejudice, 376
    probative value, 371
    rationale, 375–376
    relationship between FRE 609(a) and 608(b), 377
    unfair prejudice, 371–372
extrinsic evidence, 355–356
    bias, of, 395

contradiction, of, 401
conviction of crime, of, 376
mental or sensory incapacity, of, 398–399
prior statements of witness, of, 385–386
impeachment evidence
substantive evidence distinguished, 354–355
types of, 353–354
inconsistent statements, 405
inferential process, 351–355
testimonial inferences, 351–353
learned treatises, by, 389
mental or sensory incapacity, by, 398–400
bar to testimony, 399
extrinsic evidence, 398–399
relevance, 398
misdemeanor convictions, by, 542
"no extrinsic evidence to impeach on a collateral
matter" doctrine
directly relevant evidence, 402
evidence impeaching apart from contradiction,
402
logically undermining witness's story, 402
test for "collateralness," 402–403
what is not collateral, 401–402
perjury and, 405
prior statements of witness, by, 382–393
collateral matters, inconsistent statements about,
387–388
consistent statements in other contexts, 390–391
elaboration of impeachment with prior inconsistent statements, 385–389
examination of witnesses, 383–385
experts, statements in treatises, 389
extrinsic evidence, 385–386, 391
FRE 613, 383
interpretation and illustration, 383–385
loss of memory and inconsistency, 387
prior consistent statements, 389–391
prior inconsistent statements, 385–389
probative value, 386–388
putting inconsistent statements in context, 390
rehabilitation, admissibility for, 389–391
risk of improper substantive use, 386
truth, admissibility for, 389
reflection on, 404–405
truthfulness defined, 357
Inconsistent statements, impeachment of witnesses,
405
In-court demonstrations and experiments, authentication by, 193–194
Inferences
impeachment of witnesses, testimonial inferences,
351–353
privileges, drawing adverse inferences from, 802–803
probative value, strength of underlying inferences,
142
subsequent remedial measures, inference of negligence or culpability, 328
Insanity defense, 806–807
Instructions to jury. See Jury instructions
Insurance, inadmissibility to prove negligence. See
Liability insurance, inadmissibility to prove
negligence
Intent
hearsay, intent test. See Hearsay

specific acts evidence, problems in proving,
252–255
exclusion, argument for, 254
Old Chief case, 254–255
where intent not disputed, 253–255
Interest, statements against. See Statements against
interest, hearsay exception
Intoxication
habit evidence, 272–273
lay opinion, 634
Investigative reports, hearsay exception, 532–533
factual findings in reports, 532–533
Irrebuttable presumptions, 735–737

J

JNOV, 85, 90
Journalist's privilege, 902–903
Judges
background knowledge, judicial notice of, 784
role of, 81
Judgments notwithstanding the verdict (JNOV), 85,
90
Judgments of previous convictions, hearsay exception, 541–542
FRE 803, 541
interpretation and illustration, 541–542
general rule, 541
impeachment by misdemeanor convictions, 542
preliminary fact-finding, 541–542
rationale, 542
Judicial discretion
abuse of discretion, 157–159
hearsay, proposal regarding, 626
lay opinion, 640–642
probative value
appellate review, 157–168
reflection on, 168–169
Judicial fact-finding, 223–227
admissibility, 224
burden of persuasion, 225
FRE 104, 224
interpretation and illustration, 224–225
general rule, 224
habit evidence, 270–271
process of decision, 226–227
standard of proof, 225
Judicial notice, 773–791
adjudicative facts
defined, 774–775
types of facts subject to judicial notice, 774
background knowledge, use
judge, knowledge of, 784
jury, knowledge of, 783–784
civil cases
mini-directed verdicts, 778–779
verdicts, to preserve, 779–780
common knowledge, cognizance of, without
judicial notice, 783–786
judge, general background knowledge of, 784
jury, general background knowledge of, 783–784
criminal cases
binding notice, 780
judicial comments, 779
verdicts, to preserve, 780

decision-making, as part of, 782–791
    FRE 201, 773–774
        elaboration, 776–778
        interpretation and illustration, 774–775, 778–782
        scope, 774–775
    general rule, 773–774
    judicial comments, 779
    legislative facts, cognizance, 786–788
    mini-directed verdicts, 778–779
    sources of information, 777–778
    standards, 776–777
    state of knowledge required, 775
    substantive law, cognizance, 788
    Thirtyacre case, 776–777
    timing, 779–780
Judicial summary and comment on evidence,
        730–734, 766–767
    accuracy, 734
    advantages, 731–732
    burden of persuasion, relationship with, 733
    civil cases, 730–734
    criminal cases, 766–767
    criteria for evaluating, 732
    disadvantages, 731–732
    proposed Rule, 730
    standardized comments, 733
Juries
    background knowledge, judicial notice, 783–784
    deliberations, 88–89
    instructions. *See* Jury instructions
    natural reasoning and behavior of fact finders,
        116–119
    past recollections recorded, reading to jury, 513
    peremptory challenges, 83
    probative value and danger of misleading jury,
        146–147
    role of, 80–81
    selection, 82–83
    venire, 82
    voir dire, 82–83
Jury instructions
    burden of persuasion, 88
    preliminary jury instructions, 83
    reasonable doubt, proof beyond, 750–751
    sample case, 3–5, 61–65, 75

K

Knowledge
    business records exception, personal knowledge
        requirement, 519–520
    competency of witnesses, personal knowledge
        requirement, 179–180
    cross-examination
        character witnesses, likely knowledge of specific
            act, 297–298
        hearsay exemptions, personal knowledge
            requirement, 452
    excited utterances exception, proof of personal
        knowledge, 493
    hearsay, firsthand knowledge rule, 418
    judges, judicial notice of background knowledge
        of, 784
    juries, judicial notice of background knowledge of,
        783–784

lay opinion not based on scientific, technical or
        other specialized knowledge, 638–640
    party admissions exemption, personal knowledge
        requirement
        agents, servants and employees, 474
        party's own statement, 465
    past recollections recorded exception
        accurate reflection of witness's knowledge,
            512–513
        personal knowledge, statement made with,
            511–512
    personal or family history exception, personal
        knowledge requirement, 563
    present sense impressions exception, proof of
        personal knowledge, 493
    probability of fact of consequence determined
        from knowledge and experience, 126
    statements against interest exception, ascertaining
        declarant's knowledge, 559

L

Law enforcement personnel
    investigative tools, expert witnesses, 710–715
        bullet lead, compositional analysis of, 714–715
        fingerprint identification, 711–714
        handwriting identification, 710–711
    public records and reports exception, 534–537
        prosecutorial function, 535
        relationship with other exceptions, 536–537
        routine and regular activities, 535–536
Lay opinion, 633–646
    fact vs. opinion, 634–635
    FRE 701, 633
        elaboration, 640–642
        interpretation and illustration, 633–640
    general rule, 633
    hearsay, 418
    helpful to clear understanding of testimony or
        determination of fact in issue, 636–638
    intoxication, 634
    judicial discretion, 640–642
    not based on scientific, technical or other special-
        ized knowledge, 638–640
    party admissions
        agents, servants and employees, 474
        party's own statement, 465
    rationally based on perception of witness, 635–636
Leading questions, 97–100
    defined, 98–99
    FRE 611
        elaboration, 98–100
        interpretation and illustration, 97–98
    tactical considerations, 99–100
Learned treatises
    expert witnesses using, 686
    hearsay, 486
    impeachment or rehabilitation of witnesses by, 389
Liability
    offers of compromise, admissibility. *See*
        Compromise, admissibility of offers
    payment of medical expenses, admissibility. *See*
        Medical expenses, admissibility of payment
    subsequent remedial measures, admissibility. *See*
        Subsequent remedial measures, admissibility

Liability insurance, inadmissibility to prove negligence, 340–341
    exclusionary mandate, 340–341
    FRE 411, 340
        interpretation and illustration, 340–341
    general rule, 340
    permissible uses of evidence, 341
    reflections on, 344
Libel actions
    best evidence rule, 217
    character as essential element of claim or defense, 304–305
Limited admissibility. *See* Jury instructions

M

Mandatory rebuttable presumptions. *See* Presumptions
Manslaughter, burden of persuasion, 754
Marital privileges, 856–870
    communications privilege, 857–862
        "communication," defined, 859–860
        confidentiality, 859
        elements, 857
        exceptions, 860–861
        holder, 857
        rationale, 857–860
        scope, 857
    testimonial privilege, 862–870
        elements, 862–868
        exceptions, 868–869
    valid marriage requirement, 857–859
Materiality. *See* Relevancy
Medical diagnosis or treatment, hearsay exception for statements made for, 505–510
    diagnostic evaluations for litigation, 508–509
    FRE 803, 505
        elaboration, 509
        interpretation and illustration, 505–509
    general rule, 505
    patients' statements as basis of expert opinion, 509
    pertinence requirement, 507–508
    preliminary fact-finding, 506
    proof of medical purpose, 508
    rationale, 506–507
Medical expenses, admissibility of payment, 339–340
    admissibility of statements made in conjunction with, 339
    exclusionary mandate, 339
    FRE 409, 339
        interpretation and illustration, 339–340
    general rule, 339
    permissible uses of evidence, 339–340
    reflections on, 344
    "similar" expenses, what constitutes, 340
Mental incapacity, impeachment of witnesses by, 398–400
    bar to testimony, 399
    extrinsic evidence, 398–399
    relevance, 398
Mini-directed verdicts, judicial notice, 778–779
Misleading jury, probative value, 146–147
Model Rules of Professional Conduct, attorney-client privilege under, 819–820, 820–821

Molestation evidence. *See* Child molestation evidence
Motions
    dismissal motions, 85
        sample case, 37–38
    in limine, 82
    post-trial motions, 89–90
    pretrial motions, 82
Motive, specific acts evidence used to prove, 246
Multiple hearsay
    business records exception, 525–527
        sources of information with no business duty, 525–526
        use of multiple exemptions and exceptions, 526–527
    past recollections recorded exception, 514–515
    public records and reports exception, 537–539
        administrative findings, 538–539
        admissibility of otherwise inadmissible sources, 538
        admissibility of report itself, 537–538

N

Natural reasoning
    adversary system, 109–119
    behavior of fact finders, 116–119
    trials, 113–116
Negligence
    liability insurance, inadmissibility to prove. *See* Liability insurance, inadmissibility to prove negligence
    offers of compromise, admissibility. *See* Compromise, admissibility of offers
    payment of medical expenses, admissibility. *See* Medical expenses, admissibility of payment
    subsequent remedial measures, admissibility. *See* Subsequent remedial measures, admissibility
Negotiations, privilege for communications made in, 899–901
New trials, 90
No contest pleas, admissibility of withdrawal. *See* Withdrawn pleas, admissibility
Nonassertive conduct. *See* Hearsay
Nonhearsay statements. *See* Hearsay
Nonverbal conduct. *See* Hearsay
Notice
    judicial notice. *See* Judicial notice
    past sexual behavior evidence, notice requirement, 321
    residual hearsay exception, 576–577

O

Objections, 100–109
    admissibility of answer, 101–103
    "cheat sheet," 118
    former testimony, admissibility, 554
    FRE 103, 100
        elaboration, 101–106
        interpretation and illustration, 101
    general rule, 100
    improper form of question, 101–103
    stating, 105–106
    tactical considerations, 106

timing, 103–104
types of, 101–103
Offers of compromise, admissibility. *See*
    Compromise, admissibility of offers
Offers of proof, 101
Opening statements
    sample case, 5–7, 39–40
Opinion testimony. *See also* Expert witnesses; Lay
        opinion
    basis of testimony, 684–691
        general rule, 684
    otherwise inadmissible evidence, 686–691
Opportunity, specific acts evidence used to prove,
    246
Other crimes. *See* Specific acts evidence
Out-of-court statements, testimony about, 417

P

Parent-child privilege, 897–899
Party admissions, hearsay exemption, 462–482
    adoptive admissions, 469–470
        preliminary fact-finding, 469
        rationale, 469–470
        silence, by, 470
    agents, servants and employees, 471–475
        attorneys, 471–472
        government employees, 474–475
        lay opinion, 474
        matter within scope of agent's employment,
            statement regarding, 472–473
        personal knowledge, 474
        preliminary fact-finding, 471–473
        rationale, 473–474
        specially authorized statements, 472
    Bruton case, 468
    co-conspirators, 475–480
        additional evidence requirement, 478–479
        Bourjaily case, 478
        during course of conspiracy, 476
        in furtherance of conspiracy, 477
        preliminary fact-finding, 475–477
        process for admission, 479–480
        proof of co-membership, 476
        rationale, 477
    FRE 801, 463
        adoptive admissions, 469–470
        agents, servants and employees, 471–475
        co-conspirators, 475–477, 477–480
        elaboration, 465–468
        party's own statement, 463–465
    general rule, 463
    multiparty cases, 468
    party's own statement, 463–465
        individual capacity, 464
        lay opinion, 465
        personal knowledge, 465
        preliminary fact-finding, 463–464
        representative capacity, 464
    preliminary fact-finding
        adoptive admissions, 469
        agents, servants and employees, 471–473
        co-conspirators, 475–477
        identity of declarant, 467–468
        party's own statement, 463–464

rationale, 465–467
    fairness, 466–467
    Fifth Amendment concerns, 466
    moral responsibility for own statements,
        466–467
    opportunity to explain, 466
    statements against interest distinguished, 559
Past recollections recorded, hearsay exception,
    510–518
    accurate reflection of witness's knowledge,
        512–513
    contents of statement, 511
    failed memory requirement, 511
    FRE 803, 510
        elaboration, 513–517
        interpretation and illustration, 510–513
    fresh memory, statement made with, 511–512
    general rule, 510
    multiple declarants, created by, 513–514
    multiple hearsay, 514–515
    personal knowledge, statement made with,
        511–512
    preliminary fact-finding, 511–513
    present recollections refreshed, 515–517
        FRE 612, 516–517
    rationale, 513
    record read to jury, 513
Past sexual behavior evidence, 315–326
    applicability in other contexts, 319
    defendant's right to testify, 323
    discovery, 323–324
    FRE 412, 316
        elaboration, 321–324
        interpretation and illustration, 316–321
        scope, 318–321
    general rule, 316
    hostile work environment cases, 319–320
    notice requirement, 321
    "other sexual behavior"
        approaches to exclusion, 322–323
        civil cases, admissibility in, 320
        construed, 318
        criminal cases, admissibility in, 320–321
        particular occasion, behavior on, 318–319
    rape shield laws, 323
    rationale for exclusion, 321–322
    relevance, 317
    "sexual predisposition"
        approaches to exclusion, 322–323
        civil cases, admissibility in, 320
        construed, 318
        criminal cases, admissibility in, 320–321
    underlying propensity theory, 317–318
Payment of medical expenses, admissibility. *See*
        Medical expenses, admissibility of payment
Peer review privilege, 904–905
Peremptory challenges, 83
Perjury and impeachment of witnesses, 405
Permissive presumptions, 741–742
Personal knowledge. *See* Knowledge
Personal or family history, hearsay exception for state-
        ments of, 563–566
    FRE 804, 563
    general rule, 563
    personal history, 563

personal knowledge, 563
preliminary fact-finding, 563
rationale, 564
relations and intimate associates, statements of, 563
Photographs, probative value, 151–152, 162, 167
Physician-patient privilege, 871–872
Plan, specific acts evidence used to prove, 246
Pleas, admissibility of withdrawal. *See* Withdrawn pleas, admissibility
Post-evidence matters, 86–87
Post-trial motions, 89–90
Prejudice. *See* Bias and prejudice
Preliminary fact-finding
  business records, 518–522
  child molestation evidence, 309
  dying declarations, 555–557
  excited utterances, 487–488
    categorical approach, 492–493
  "forfeiture by wrongdoing," 567–569
  former testimony, 547–549
  identification, prior statements of, 456–458
  judgments of previous convictions, 541–542
  medical diagnosis or treatment, statements made for, 506
  party admissions
    adoptive admissions, 469–470
    agents, servants and employees, 471–473
    co-conspirators, 475–477
    identity of declarant, 467–468
    party's own statement, 463–464
  personal or family history, statements of, 563
  present sense impressions, 486–487
    categorical approach, 492–493
  prior consistent statements, 454–456
  prior inconsistent statements, 452–453
  public records and reports, 531–533
  regularly conducted activity, records of, 518–522
  residual hearsay exception, 572–573
  sexual assault evidence, 309
  specific acts, 247–248
  statements against interest, 558–559
  state-of-mind declarations, 496–497
  unavailability of declarant, 544–545
Preliminary jury instructions, 83
Preparation, specific acts evidence used to prove, 246
Preponderance of evidence standard, 718, 723–724, 725, 729
Presentation of evidence
  order of presentation, 84–85
Present recollections refreshed, 515–517
  FRE 612, 516–517
Present sense impressions, hearsay exception, 486–487
  categorical approach, 489–493
    categories determining admissibility, 489–490
    judicial interpretation, 490–492
    preliminary fact-finding, 492–493
    proof of personal knowledge, 493
  FRE 803, 486
  elaboration, 489–494
  interpretation and illustration, 486–487
    general rule, 486
  preliminary fact-finding, 486–487
    categorical approach, 492–493
  rationale, 487

Preservation of error for appellate review. *See* Appellate review, preservation of error for
Presidential communications privilege, 909–911
Presumptions, 734–747, 767–770
  burden of persuasion, 735
  civil cases, 734–747
  complexity, 742–746
  conclusive presumptions, 735–737
  criminal cases, 767–770
  defined, 734
  FRE 301, 746
    "federal statute" exception, 746–747
    other means of allocating burdens of production and persuasion, relationship with, 747
  irrebuttable presumptions, 735–737
  mandatory rebuttable presumptions, 737–742
    decision-making, 740–741
    mandatory persuasion burden presumptions, 739–740
    mandatory production burden presumptions, 737–739
    permissive presumptions, 741–742
    "weak" presumptions, 741–742
  Winship rule, 767–770
Pretrial motions, 82
Prior arrests, examination of character witnesses regarding, 299
Prior consistent statements, hearsay exemption, 454–456
  FRE 801, 448–449
    statements outside scope of, 456
  general rule, 448–449
  improper influence or motive, charge of, 454–455
    rebutting, 455–456
  preliminary fact-finding, 454–456
  rationale, 456
  recent fabrication, charge of, 454–455
    express charge, 454–455
    implied charge, 454–455
    rebutting, 455–456
Prior identification. *See* Identification, hearsay exemption for prior statements of
Prior inconsistent statements, hearsay exemption, 452–454
  evasion, inconsistency due to, 453
  FRE 801, 448–449, 452
    interpretation and illustration, 452–454
    statements outside scope of, 454
  general rule, 448–449, 452
  at hearing, 453
  inconsistency, 452–453
  under penalty of perjury, 453
  preliminary fact-finding, 452–453
  at proceeding, 453
  rationale, 453–454
  at trial, 453
Prior statements, impeachment of witnesses by. *See* Impeachment of witnesses
Privileges, 793–917
  academic researcher's privilege, 903–904
  attorney-client privilege. *See* Attorney-client privilege
  clergy-communicant privilege. *See* Clergy-communicant privilege
  Confrontation Clause, 803

current status of law, 796–798
deliberative process privilege, 912–915
drawing adverse inferences from, 802–803
exceptions, 802
executive privilege, 907–915
FRE 501, 796
general rule, 796
general structure, 798–803
government informant's privilege, 901–902
government privileges, 907–915
historical background, 796–798
holders, 798
invocation, 798–800
journalist's privilege, 902–903
limits, 801
    Constitutional limitations, 803
marital privileges. *See* Marital privileges
official information privilege, 912–915
outside sources of information, protecting, 901–904
parent-child privilege, 897–899
peer review privilege, 904–905
physician-patient privilege, 871–872
Presidential communications privilege, 909–911
professional-client privileges, 896–897
psychotherapist-patient privilege. *See*
    Psychotherapist-patient privilege
scholar's privilege, 903–904
scope, 801
self-evaluative privilege, 906–907
settlement negotiations, communications made in,
    899–901
state secrets privilege, 907–909
unique operation of privilege rules, 794–795
waiver, 801–802
White House counsel, 800
Probative value, 140–169
    authentication of exhibits
        demonstrative evidence, 192–193
        recordings, 198
    balancing test, 140–148
    Bayes' Theorem, 170–172
    certainty of starting point, 142–143
    child molestation evidence, 308, 310–311
    confusion of issues, danger of, 146
    cumulative evidence, danger of, 147–148
    defined, 141
    demonstrative evidence, 151–152
    expert witnesses, 652–653
    "forfeiture by wrongdoing," 570
    FRE 403, 140
        dangers of, 144–148
        elaboration, 157–168
        interpretation and illustration, 141–157
    general rule, 140
    Hitt case, 159–162
    impeachment of witnesses
        specific instances of conduct, 365
    judicial discretion
        appellate review, 157–168
        reflection on, 168–169
    misleading jury, danger of, 146–147
    need, 143–144
    offers of compromise, 335–336
    Old Chief case, 162–166
    photographs, 151–152, 162, 167

prior felonies, 167
probability, 170–174
sexual assault evidence, 308, 310–311
similar happenings evidence, 280
spoliation of evidence, 153–154
statistics, 170–174
strength of underlying inferences, 142
subsequent remedial measures, 332
substantially outweighed by dangers of FRE 403,
    148–151
    defined, 148–149
    limiting instructions, effect of, 149–151
undue delay, danger of, 147–148
unfair prejudice, danger of, 144–146
victims' statements, 152–153
waste of time, danger of, 147–148
Professional-client privileges, 896–897
Propensity evidence, 265–266
    defined, 236
    past sexual behavior evidence, underlying propen-
        sity theory, 317–318
    reflection on, 258–267
Psychological sciences, expert witnesses, 706–707
Psychotherapist-patient privilege, 872–890
    exceptions, 886–889
        compelled disclosures, 887–888
        Constitutional limitations on, 886–887
        crime-fraud exception, 889
        dangerous patients, 888–889
    holders, 884–885
    Jaffee case, 872–883
    nature of communications, 885
    scope, 884–886
    waiver, 885–886
Public records and reports, hearsay exception, 531–539
    activities of office, 531–532
    duty, matters reported pursuant to, 532
    FRE 803, 531
        elaboration, 534–539
        interpretation and illustration, 531–534
    general rule, 531
    investigative reports, 532–533
    law enforcement personnel, 534–537
        prosecutorial function, 535
        relationship with other exceptions, 536–537
        routine and regular activities, 535–536
    multiple hearsay, 537–539
        administrative findings, 538–539
        admissibility of otherwise inadmissible sources,
            538
    preliminary fact-finding, 531–533
    rationale, 534
    untrustworthiness, exclusion for, 533

Q

Qualification as expert witnesses, 651–652

R

Rape
    rape shield laws, 323. *See also* Past sexual behavior
        evidence
Real evidence, authentication, 187–192
Reasonable doubt standard. *See* Burden of persuasion

Rebuttal examination, sample case, 58–60
Reconstructions of events, authentication of exhibits
    by, 194–195
Recordings, authentication of. *See* Authentication
Records of regularly conducted activity, hearsay
    exception, 518–531
  business duty, made pursuant to, 520–521
  computer documents, 527–528
  custodians, 521–522
  diagnoses, 524–525
  electronic data, 527–528
  FRE 803, 518
    elaboration, 522–528
    interpretation and illustration, 518–522
    scope of 803(6)(B), breadth of, 519
  general rule, 518
  multiple hearsay, 525–527
    sources of information with no business duty,
        525–526
    use of multiple exemptions and exceptions,
        526–527
  near contemporaneity requirement, 519–520
  opinions, 524–525
  personal knowledge requirement, 519–520
  preliminary fact-finding, 518–522
  qualified witnesses, 521–522
  rationale, 522
  untrustworthiness, exclusion for, 523–524
    burden of persuasion, 523
    circumstances indicating, 523–524
  website documents, 527–528
  what constitutes record of regularly conducted
      activity, 519
Recross-examination
  FRE 611, 93
  sample case, 30–31
Redirect examination
  FRE 611, 93
  sample case, 19–20, 30, 50–51, 57–58
Reenactments, authentication of exhibits by, 194–195
Refreshing memory, 515–517
  FRE 612, 516–517
Regularly conducted activities, records of. *See*
        Records of regularly conducted activity,
        hearsay exception
Rehabilitation of witnesses. *See* Impeachment of
        witnesses
Relevancy, 121–140
  analysis of, 132–134
  background information, 130–131
  chain of reasoning, 134
  character evidence, 235–237
    exceptions to prohibition on use of to prove
        conduct on particular occasion, 287–290
  circumstantial vs. direct evidence, 129–130
  conditional relevancy. *See* Conditional relevancy
  defined, 122
  direct vs. circumstantial evidence, 129–130
  FRE 401, 122
    elaboration, 131–140
    interpretation and illustration, 122–131
  FRE 402, 122
    elaboration, 131–140
    interpretation and illustration, 122–131
  general rule, 122

hearsay, 409–412
  impeachment of witnesses
    bias, by, 394
    contradiction, by, 400
    mental or sensory incapacity, by, 398–399
  materiality, 123–125
  nonverbal conduct to prove belief, 426–427
  offer for proof of fact of consequence, 123–125
  past sexual behavior evidence, 317
  probability of fact of consequence, 125–129
    admissibility, policy favoring, 128–129
    "any tendency" standard, 125
    inferential reasoning, generalized knowledge
        used in, 126
    knowledge and experience, inferential reasoning
        based on generalizations from, 126
    limits on generalizations, 127–128
    reasonable generalizations, 126–128
  reflections on
    concept of relevancy, 169–174
    requirement of relevancy, 138–140
  specific relevant acts with no character inference,
      admissibility. *See* Specific acts evidence
  sufficiency distinguished, 131
  Thayer on, 121–122
  unstated beliefs, 435–436
  Wigmore on, 121, 135
Remedial measures, admissibility. *See* Subsequent
        remedial measures, admissibility
Reputation evidence
  impeachment of witness, and reputation evidence
      of untruthfulness, 358–360
  opinion evidence distinguished, 295–296
  probative value, 294–295
Res gestae, 252
Residual hearsay exception, 572–579
  circumstantial guarantees of trustworthiness,
      573–575
  equivalency, 575
  FRE 807, 572
    elaboration, 577
    interpretation and illustration, 572–577
  general rule, 572
  how much hearsay admitted, 577
  independent corroboration, 574–575
  material fact, offered to prove, 575
  more probative than other available evidence,
      575–576
  "near miss," 575
  notice, 576–577
  preliminary fact-finding, 572–573
  serving general purposes of justice, 576
  testimonial qualities, reliability, 573–574
Rights-based theories, attorney-client privilege, 849
Routine practice evidence, 267–276
  FRE 406, 267
    elaboration, 271–276
    interpretation and illustration, 268–271
  general rule, 267
  importance, 268–269
  methods of proving, 269
  organizational behavior, 273–274
  rationale, 271
Rules of Evidence. *See also specific topic concerned*
  rationale, 111–113

S

Scientific evidence and expert witnesses, 701–715
    adversary model, 680–681
    behavioral sciences, 706–707
    bullet lead analysis, 714–715
    Daubert case, 655–668, 677–682
    deference model, 680
    DNA testing, 706
    fingerprint identification, 711–714
    Frye case, 653–655
    handwriting identification, 710–711
    Kumho Tire case, 668–672
    law enforcement investigative tools, 709–715
        bullet lead analysis, 714–715
        fingerprint identification, 711–714
        handwriting identification, 710–711
    normal educational approach, 680
    psychological sciences, 706–707
    toxic tort causation, 707–709
Self-authentication, 206–210
    FRE 902, 206–207
        interpretation and illustration, 207–209
    general rule, 206–207
Self-evaluative privilege, 906–907
Self-incrimination and party admissions, 466
Sensory incapacity, impeachment of witnesses by, 398–400
    bar to testimony, 399
    extrinsic evidence, 398–399
    relevance, 398
Servants, hearsay exemption for. *See* Party admissions, hearsay exemption
Settlements
    negotiations, privilege for communications made in, 899–901
    offers of compromise admissibility. *See* Compromise, admissibility of offers
Sex offenses
    child molestation evidence. *See* Child molestation evidence
    past sexual behavior evidence. *See* Past sexual behavior evidence
    sexual assault evidence. *See* Sexual assault evidence
Sexual assault evidence, 306–315
    character evidence, 307–308, 310–311
    federal litigation, significance to, 313–314
    FRE 403 balancing test, applicability, 308, 310–311
    FRE 413 to 415, 307
        elaboration, 310–314
        interpretation and illustration, 307–310
    general rules, 307
    "offense of sexual assault" construed, 309
    other Federal Rules of Evidence, 308–309
    preliminary fact-finding, 309
    probative value, 311–313
    rationale, 311–313
    recidivism, 312
    unfair prejudice, 311
    "without consent" construed, 309–310
Signatures, 201
Similar happenings evidence, 276–284
    approach to admissibility of, 279–280

character distinguished, 278–279
characteristics of objects, 277
FRE 403 balancing test, applicability, 280
habit distinguished, 278–279
institutional policy or practice use of to prove, 281
lack of Federal Rules governing, 277–278
nonhappenings, evidence of, 281
organizational liability, 277
organizational propensity, 277
Simulations, authentication of exhibits by, 194–195
Slander actions
    best evidence rule, 217
    character as essential element of claim or defense, 304–305
Specific acts evidence, 235–326
    analytical process for offering past specific acts evidence, 244–245, 258–264, 265
    approaches to admissibility, 265–266
    character, prohibition on use of to prove, 293–294
    child molestation evidence. *See* Child molestation evidence
    cross-examination of character witnesses. *See* Cross-examination
    defined, 236–237
    distinction between prohibited and permissible evidence, 265–266
    exceptions to prohibition to prove conduct on particular occasion, 242
    FRE 404, 238, 244
        prohibition on use of to prove conduct on particular occasion, 238–244
        relevant acts with no character inference, admissibility, 244–258
    general rule, 238
    habit evidence. *See* Habit evidence
    motive, to prove, 246
    opportunity, to prove, 246
    past sexual behavior evidence. *See* Past sexual behavior evidence
    plan, to prove, 246
    preparation, to prove, 246
    prohibition on use of to prove conduct on particular occasion, 238–244
        "bad person" prejudice, 241–242
        diversion from main issues, 241
        general rule, 238
        low probative value, 240–241
        prejudice, 241–242
        rationale, 240–242
        weakness of propensity inference, 240
    reflection on, 258–267
    relevant acts with no character inference, admissibility, 244–258
        anticoincidence theory, 255–257
        exclusion, argument for, 254
        general rule, 244
        identity, evidence showing, 247
        intent, problems in proving, 252–253
        knowledge, problems in proving, 252–253
        modus operandi and character inference, 257
        narrative of proponent's case, evidence completing, 246
        Old Chief case, 254–255
        permissible uses, 245–247
        prejudice, 248–249

preliminary fact-finding, 247–248
  probative value, 248–249
  relevant states of mind, evidence showing,
      246–247
  res gestae problem, 252
  where intent not disputed, 253–255
  routine practice evidence. *See* Routine practice
      evidence
  sexual assault evidence. *See* Sexual assault
      evidence
  similar happenings evidence. *See* Similar happen-
      ings evidence
Spoliation of evidence, 153–154
Spousal privileges. *See* Marital privileges
Statements against interest, hearsay exception, 557–562
  ascertaining declarant's knowledge, 559
  content against interest, 558
  corroboration requirement, 560–562
    statements inculpating accomplices, 561–562
  FRE 804, 559
    elaboration, 559–562
    interpretation and illustration, 557–559
  general rule, 559
  mixed motive statements, 560
  party admission distinguished, 559
  preliminary fact-finding, 558–559
  rationale, 559
    doubts regarding, 559–560
  statements inculpating accomplices, 561–562
    corroboration requirement, 562
  statements made with no motive to lie, 560
State-of-mind declarations, hearsay exception,
      496–505
  circumstantial statements, 498
  direct statements, 498
  evidence used to prove facts, 500
  FRE 803, 496
    elaboration, 498–505
    interpretation and illustration, 496–498
  future conduct, 499–500, 501–502
  future state of mind, 498–499
  general rule, 496
  Hillmon case, 500–503
  past state of mind, 498–499
  preliminary fact-finding, 496–497
  rationale, 497–498
State secrets privilege, 907–909
Statistics, probative value, 170–174
Stereotypes, 128
Stipulations, 167–168
Subsequent remedial measures, admissibility,
      328–335
  activities deemed to be, 328–330
  discouraging desirable conduct, policy against, 333
  effectiveness of, 330
  exclusionary mandate, 328–330
  FRE 403 balancing test, applicability, 332–333
  FRE 407, 328
    elaboration, 332–335
    interpretation and illustration, 328–332
  general rule, 328
  "if disputed" requirement, 331
  inference of negligence or culpability, 328
  intent to make conditions safer, no requirement
      of, 330

  low probative value, 332
  motive for making change, irrelevance of, 330
  permissible uses of evidence, 331
  prior to plaintiff's injury, 330
  punishing desirable conduct, policy against, 333
  rationale for general rule of exclusion, 332–333
  reflections on, 344
  third persons, by, 333
  timing, 330
Substantive rules of law. *See* Presumptions
Sufficiency
  authentication of exhibits, 183–185
  relevancy distinguished, 131
Summaries, best evidence rule, 211, 218–221
  analytic summaries, 219
  illustrative aids, 219
  voluminous documents underlying summaries,
      218–219
Summary expert witnesses, 653
Summing up and comment by judge. *See* Judicial
      summary and comment on evidence
Syndrome evidence, expert witnesses, 706–707

T

Testimonial privilege. *See* Marital privileges
Testimony. *See specific topic concerned*
Toxic tort causation, expert witnesses, 707–709
Transcript of sample case, 2–76
Translations, expert witnesses, 677
Treatises
  expert witnesses, 686
  hearsay, 486
  impeachment or rehabilitation of witnesses by, 389
Trials
  bench trials, 81
  bifurcated trials, 89
  burden of persuasion, 88
  burden of production, 85–86
  closing arguments, 87–88
  jury deliberations, 88–89
  jury instructions, 88
  jury selection, 82–83
  natural reasoning, 113–116
  new trials, 90
  opening statements, 83–84
  post-evidence matters, 86–87
  post-trial motions, 89–90
  preliminary jury instructions, 83
  presentation of evidence, 84–86
    order of presentation, 84–85
  pretrial motions, 82
  roles of trial participants, 80–81
  sample transcript, 2–76
  structure, 82–90
  trifurcated trials, 89
  verdicts, 88–89
Trifurcated trials, 89

U

Ultimate issue, expert opinion on, 693–699
  FRE 704, 693
    interpretation and illustration, 693–697
  general rule, 693

Unavailability of declarant. *See* Hearsay
Underlying propensity theory and past sexual behavior evidence, 317–318
Undue delay and probative value, 147–148
Unstated beliefs. *See* Hearsay
Untrustworthiness
 business records, exclusion, 523–524
  burden of persuasion, 523
 circumstances indicating, 523–524
 public records and reports, exclusion of, 533

V

Verdicts
 directed verdicts, 85
 judgments notwithstanding the verdict, 85, 90
 judicial notice to preserve
  civil cases, 779–780
  criminal cases, 780
Victims' statements, probative value, 152–153
Violent Crime Control and Enforcement Act of 1994, 306
Voice identification, 199
Voir dire, 82–83

W

Waiver
 of attorney-client privilege, 808–822
 of Fifth Amendment rights for impeachment of witnesses by character evidence, 361
 of privileges, 801–802
 of psychotherapist-patient privilege, 885–886
 subject matter waiver, 809, 811
 of withdrawn pleas, admissibility under FRE 410, 347–348
 of work product protection, 808–822
Waste of time, probative value, 147–148
"Weak" presumptions, 741–742
Website documents, and hearsay exception, 527–528
White House counsel privilege, 800
Wigmore, John Henry
 attorney-client privilege, 848
 impeachment of witnesses
  bias, by, 394
  contradiction, by, 400
 relevancy, 121, 135
Winship rule
 burden of persuasion in criminal cases, 748–751
  application in other contexts, 762–764
 presumptions, 767–770
Withdrawn pleas, admissibility, 344–349
 FRE 410, 344–345
  exceptions, 347
  interpretation and illustration, 345–348
  scope, 346–347
  waiver, 347–348
 general rule, 344–345
 guilty pleas, 345
 no contest pleas, 345
 nolo contendere pleas, 345
 statements made in conjunction with pleas, 345–346

Witnesses
 adverse witnesses. *See* Adverse witnesses
 character. *See* Character evidence
 competency. *See* Competency of witnesses
 confrontation of witnesses. *See* Confrontation Clause
 cross-examination. *See* Cross-examination
 examination. *See* Examination of witnesses
 expert. *See* Expert witnesses
 hearsay. *See* Hearsay
 hostile witnesses. *See* Hostile witnesses
 impeachment. *See* Impeachment of witnesses
 lay opinion. *See* Lay opinion
 rehabilitation of. *See* Impeachment of witnesses
Work product doctrine, 818–820, 831, 850–853
 disclosure of information protected by, 808–822.
  See also FRE 502, *this heading*
 Easterbrook theory, 853
 FRE 502
  aspects of, 811–813
  concerns raised by, 813–821
  confidentiality of attorney-client relationship, potential damage to, 815
  confidentiality order governing disclosure, effect of, 812–813
  constitutionality of application to state proceedings, 814
  controlling effect of FRE 502, 813
  cost of discovery and, 814–815
  court order on disclosure, controlling effect of, 812–813
  "data dumps," effect of, 814–815
  document review still required, 813–814
  general rule, 809–810
  inadvertent disclosure, 811–812
  inconsistent state and federal laws, 812
  interpretation, 810–811
  judge-initiated unilateral order, 815
  limitations of, 811, 813–814
  misleading disclosure, unfair to adversary, 811
  party agreement, controlling effect of, 813
  precautions taken to rectify error, 811–812
  purposes of, 810
  reasonable steps to prevent disclosure, 811–812, 816
  review of documents still required, 813–814
  scope of waiver, 811
  selective disclosure, unfair to adversary, 811
  state proceeding, disclosure made in, 812, 813, 814
  subject matter waiver, 811, 815
  subsequent state and federal proceedings, 811, 812, 813, 816
 inadvertent disclosure of protected work product. *See* FRE 502, *this heading*
 joint production theory, 851–853
 waiver of protection, 808–822. *See also* FRE 502, *this heading*
Writings
 authentication. *See* Authentication
 best evidence rule. *See* Best evidence rule
 inscriptions on objects as not writings, 218
 signatures, 201